Lecture Notes in Computer Science 14069

Founding Editors

Gerhard Goos
Juris Hartmanis

Editorial Board Members

The series Lecture Notes in Computer Science (LNCS), including its subseries Lecture Notes in Artificial Intelligence (LNAI) and Lecture Notes in Bioinformatics (LNBI), has established itself as a medium for the publication of new developments in computer science and information technology research, teaching, and education.

LNCS enjoys close cooperation with the computer science R & D community, the series counts many renowned academics among its volume editors and paper authors, and collaborates with prestigious societies. Its mission is to serve this international community by providing an invaluable service, mainly focused on the publication of conference and workshop proceedings and postproceedings. LNCS commenced publication in 1973.

Sebastia Massanet · Susana Montes ·
Daniel Ruiz-Aguilera ·
Manuel González-Hidalgo
Editors

Fuzzy Logic and Technology, and Aggregation Operators

13th Conference of the European Society for Fuzzy Logic and
Technology, EUSFLAT 2023, and 12th International Summer School
on Aggregation Operators, AGOP 2023
Palma de Mallorca, Spain, September 4–8, 2023
Proceedings

Springer

Editors
Sebastia Massanet ⓘ
University of the Balearic Islands
Palma, Spain

Susana Montes ⓘ
University of Oviedo
Gijón, Spain

Daniel Ruiz-Aguilera ⓘ
University of the Balearic Islands
Palma, Spain

Manuel González-Hidalgo ⓘ
University of the Balearic Islands
Palma, Spain

ISSN 0302-9743   ISSN 1611-3349 (electronic)
Lecture Notes in Computer Science
ISBN 978-3-031-39964-0   ISBN 978-3-031-39965-7 (eBook)
https://doi.org/10.1007/978-3-031-39965-7

This Springer imprint is published by the registered company Springer Nature Switzerland AG
The registered company address is: Gewerbestrasse 11, 6330 Cham, Switzerland

Preface

Almost 24 years ago, the 1999 EUSFLAT-ESTYLF Joint Conference was held in Palma. This conference, which took place from September 22 to 25, 1999, was organized by the University of the Balearic Islands and the European Society for Fuzzy Logic and Technology (EUSFLAT) and it was the first edition of the conferences of this society, after its foundation that same year. After the success of the first edition, this conference has been organized every two years in many European towns. Namely, Leicester (United Kingdom), Zittau (Germany), Barcelona and Gijon (Spain), Ostrava and Prague (Czech Republic), Lisbon (Portugal), Aix-Les-Bains (France), Milano (Italy), Warsaw (Poland) and Bratislava (Slovak Republic) have been the venue for subsequent editions. Now, on the eve of the 25th anniversary, it is time for the EUSFLAT conference to return to its origins, back to its roots.

The world has changed a lot since 1999. However, some facts remain stable. The aim of the conference, in line with the mission of the EUSFLAT Society, is to bring together theoreticians and practitioners working on fuzzy logic, fuzzy systems, soft computing, and related areas and to provide for them a platform for the exchange of ideas, discussing newest trends and networking. During these years and due to the successful development of fuzzy logic and the corresponding technology, interest in fuzzy logic has been growing steadily, and the EUSFLAT conference has been the main European conference in this scientific field. However, despite being a predominantly European conference, many researchers from other continents attend the EUSFLAT conferences edition after edition, recognizing that they constitute a reference point every two years for important advances in the lines of research associated with this field. In the specific case of the Balearic Islands, it should be noted that since the late 1980s intense research in fuzzy logic has been developed within the framework of the research group led by Gaspar Mayor and Joan Torrens, who are now happily retired. The new generation took the baton and the responsibility of organizing this edition of the EUSFLAT conference.

This 2023 edition of the EUSFLAT conference was co-located for the second time with two traditional events, namely with AGOP 2023 - International Summer School on Aggregation Operators; and with FQAS 2023 - International Conference on Flexible Query Answering Systems. We would like to express our thanks to the management of these events for sharing the vision of the joint multiconference. Special mention should be given to the AGOP summer school, with which these proceedings are shared. The AGOP summer school is organized biannually by the AGOP working group of EUSFLAT, reaching this year its 12th edition after its birth in 2001 in Oviedo (Spain). This event focuses on aggregation functions, a family of operators which have numerous applications, including, but not limited to, data fusion, statistics, image processing and decision making.

Therefore, this volume constitutes the proceedings of the 13th Conference of the European Society for Fuzzy Logic and Technology (EUSFLAT) and the 12th International Summer School on Aggregation Operators (AGOP). The papers included in the proceedings volume have been subject to a thorough review process by at least two highly qualified peer reviewers, by using a single-blind process. The volume contains very attractive and up-to-date topics in fuzzy logic and related fields, which will result in significant interest of the international research communities active in the covered areas. Special gratitude is due to the extremely relevant role of the organizers of the special sessions. Thanks to their vision and hard work, we have been able to collect many papers on focused topics which we are sure will result, during the conference, in very interesting presentations and stimulating discussions at the sessions. It should be noted that for EUSFLAT and AGOP 2023, 71 full papers and 90 abstracts (161 submissions in total) were submitted from which 61 full papers have been accepted.

Finally, we would like to express our gratitude to all chairs and the organizing team for making these conferences possible. We believe that we will experience an excellent and unforgettable conference. We hope that you enjoyed it and that it brought home many new fruitful ideas for your research, and also that you enjoyed this beautiful island, Mallorca, the largest island in the Balearic Islands, set in the Mediterranean Sea, with its great beaches, amazing atmosphere and cultural richness.

September 2023

Sebastia Massanet
Susana Montes
Daniel Ruiz-Aguilera
Manuel González-Hidalgo

Organization

EUSFLAT 2023 and AGOP 2023 were organized by the research group in Soft Computing, Image Processing and Aggregation (SCOPIA), from the Department of Mathematics and Computer Science of the University of the Balearic Islands (UIB), in cooperation with the EUSFLAT (European Society for Fuzzy Logic and Technology).

General Chairs

Sebastia Massanet   Universitat de les Illes Balears, Spain
Susana Montes   Universidad de Oviedo, Spain
Daniel Ruiz-Aguilera   Universitat de les Illes Balears, Spain

Organizing Chair

Manuel González-Hidalgo   Universitat de les Illes Balears, Spain

EUSFLAT Programme Chairs

Humberto Bustince   Universidad Pública de Navarra - UPNA, Spain
Vladik Kreinovich   University of Texas at El Paso, USA

Publication Chairs

Luis Martínez Lopez   Universidad de Jaén, Spain
Juan Vicente Riera   Universitat de les Illes Balears, Spain

Publicity Chairs

Przemyslaw Grzegorzewski   Warsaw University of Technology, Poland
Balasubramaniam Jayaram   Indian Institute of Technology Hyderabad, India
Manuel Ojeda Aciego   Universidad de Málaga, USA
Gabriella Pasi   Università degli Studi di Milano-Bicocca, Italy

Special Sessions Chairs

Michal Baczyński	University of Silesia in Katowice, Poland
Luis Magdalena	Universidad Politécnica de Madrid, Spain
Peter Sussner	University of Campinas, Brazil

Grants and Awards Chairs

Christophe Marsala	Université Pierre et Marie Curie, France
Javier Montero	Universidad Complutense de Madrid, Spain
Eulalia Szmidt	Polish Academy of Sciences, Poland

Organizing Committee

Isabel Aguiló	Universitat de les Illes Balears, Spain
Pedro Bibiloni	Universitat de les Illes Balears, Spain
Raquel Fernandez-Peralta	Universitat de les Illes Balears, Spain
Manuel González-Hidalgo	Universitat de les Illes Balears, Spain
Sebastia Massanet	Universitat de les Illes Balears, Spain
Arnau Mir	Universitat de les Illes Balears, Spain
Marc Munar	Universitat de les Illes Balears, Spain
Juan Vicente Riera	Universitat de les Illes Balears, Spain
Daniel Ruiz-Aguilera	Universitat de les Illes Balears, Spain
Lidia Talavera	Universitat de les Illes Balears, Spain
Llorenç Valverde	Universitat de les Illes Balears, Spain

SS1: Interval uncertainty. Organizers

Martine Ceberio	University of Texas at El Paso, USA
Vladik Kreinovich	University of Texas at El Paso, USA

SS2: Information fusion techniques based on aggregation functions, preaggregation functions and their generalizations. Organizers

Humberto Bustince	Universidad Pública de Navarra - UPNA, Spain
Graçaliz Pereira Dimuro	Universidade Federal do Rio Grande, Brazil
Javier Fernández	Universidad Pública de Navarra - UPNA, Spain
Tiago da Cruz Asmus	Universidade Federal do Rio Grande, Brazil

SS3: Evaluative linguistic expressions, generalized quantifiers and applications. Organizers

Vilém Novák	University of Ostrava, Czech Republic
Petra Murinová	University of Ostrava, Czech Republic
Stefania Boffa	University of Milano-Bicocca, Italy

SS4: Neural networks under uncertainty and imperfect information. Organizers

Humberto Bustince	Universidad Pública de Navarra - UPNA, Spain
Javier Fernández	Universidad Pública de Navarra - UPNA, Spain
Iosu Rodríguez-Martínez	Universidad Pública de Navarra - UPNA, Spain
Mikel Ferrero-Jaurrieta	Universidad Pública de Navarra - UPNA, Spain
Jonata Wieczynski	Universidad Pública de Navarra - UPNA, Spain

SS5: Imprecision modeling and management in XAI systems. Organizers

Ciro Castiello	Università degli Studi di Bari Aldo Moro, Italy
Marie-Jeanne Lesot	Sorbonne Université, France
Corrado Mencar	Università degli Studi di Bari Aldo Moro, Italy

SS6: Recent trends in mathematical fuzzy logics. Organizers

Stefano Aguzzoli	Università degli Studi di Milano, Italy
Brunella Gerla	Università dell'Insubria, Italy

SS7: Fuzzy graph-based models: theory and application. Organizers

Stefan Stanimirović	University of Niš, Serbia
Ivana Micić	University of Niš, Serbia

SS8: New frontiers of computational intelligence for pervasive healthcare systems. Organizers

Gabriella Casalino	University of Bari Aldo Moro, Italy
Giovanna Castellano	University of Bari Aldo Moro, Italy
Uzay Kaymak	Eindhoven University of Technology, The Netherlands
Gianluca Zaza	University of Bari Aldo Moro, Italy

SS9: Fuzzy implication functions. Organizers

Michal Baczyński	University of Silesia in Katowice, Poland
Balasubramaniam Jayaram	Indian Institute of Technology Hyderabad, India
Sebastia Massanet	Universitat de les Illes Balears, Spain

SS10: New challenges and ideas in statistical inference and data analysis. Organizers

Przemyslaw Grzegorzewski	Warsaw University of Technology, Poland
Katarzyna Kaczmarek-Majer	Polish Academy of Sciences, Poland

SS12: Representing and managing uncertainty: different scenarios, different tools. Organizers

Davide Ciucci	University of Milano-Bicocca, Italy
Chris Cornelis	Ghent University, Belgium
Jesús Medina	University of Cádiz, Spain
Dominik Slezak	University of Warsaw, Poland

Program Committee

Aguiló, Isabel	Universitat de les Illes Balears, Spain
Akbarzadeh-T., M.-R.	Ferdowsi University of Mashhad, Iran
Acampora, Giovanni	Università degli Studi di Napoli Federico II, Italy
Aguzzoli, Stefano	University of Milan, Italy
Aliev, Rafik Aziz	Azerbaijan State Oil and Industry University, Azerbaijan

Allahviranloo, Tofigh	İstinye University, Turkey
Alonso, Jose Maria	Universidad de Santiago de Compostela, Spain
Asmus, Tiago da Cruz	Universidade Federal do Rio Grande, Brazil
Baczyński, Michal	University of Silesia in Katowice, Poland
Batyrshin, Ildar	Instituto Politécnico Nacional, Mexico
Bloch, Isabelle	Sorbonne Université, CNRS, France
Bobillo, Fernando	Universidad de Zaragoza, Spain
Boffa, Stefania	University of Milano-Bicocca, Italy
Borisov, Vadim V.	Moscow Power Engineering Institute, Russia
Bouchon-Meunier, Bernadette	Sorbonne Université, France
Burczyński, Tadeusz S.	Polish Academy of Sciences, Poland
Burda, Michal	University of Ostrava, Czech Republic
Bustince, Humberto	Universidad Pública de Navarra, Spain
Cabrera, Inmaculada	Universidad de Málaga, Spain
Calvo, Tomasa	Universidad de Alcalá, Spain
Carlsson, Christer	Institute for Advanced Management Systems Research, Finland
Carvalho, Joao Paulo	Universidade de Lisboa, Portugal
Casalino, Gabriella	Università degli studi di Bari Aldo Moro, Italy
Castellano, Giovanna	Università degli studi di Bari Aldo Moro, Italy
Castiello, Ciro	Università degli studi di Bari Aldo Moro, Italy
Castillo, Oscar	Tijuana Institute of Technology, Mexico
Ceberio, Martine	University of Texas at El Paso, USA
Chalco-Cano, Yurilev	Universidad de Tarapacá, Chile
Chountas, Panagiotis	University of Westminster, UK
Ciucci, Davide	University of Milano-Bicocca, Italy
Collan, Mikael	Lappeenranta-Lahti University of Technology, Finland
Cordero, Pablo	Universidad de Málaga, Spain
Cordón, Oscar	Universidad de Granada, Spain
Cornelis, Chris	Ghent University, Belgium
D'Aniello, Giuseppe	University of Salerno, Italy
Dankova, Martina	University of Ostrava, Czech Republic
De Baets, Bernard	Ghent University, Belgium
De Tré, Guy	Ghent University, Belgium
Di Nola, Antonio	Università degli Studi di Salerno, Italy
Diaz, Irene	Universidad de Oviedo, Spain
Dick, Scott	University of Alberta, Canada
Dimuro, Graçaliz	Universidade Federal do Rio Grande, Brazil
Dubois, Didier	Centre National de la Recherche Scientifique, France
Durante, Fabrizio	Università del Salento, Italy

Konecny, Jan	Palacký University Olomouc, Czech Republic
Kreinovich, Vladik	University of Texas at El Paso, USA
Kupka, Jiří	University of Ostrava, Czech Republic
Lesot, Marie-Jeanne	Sorbonne Université, France
Li, Jun	Communication University of china, China
Liu, Xinwang	Southeast University, China
López-Molina, Carlos	Universidad Pública de Navarra, Spain
Lughofer, Edwin	Johannes Kepler University Linz, Austria
Magdalena Layos, Luis	Universidad Politécnica de Madrid, Spain
Marcelloni, Francesco	University of Pisa, Italy
Marsala, Christophe	Université Pierre et Marie Curie, France
Martín-Bautista, María José	Universidad de Granada, Spain
Martínez, Luis	Universidad de Jaén, Spain
Massanet, Sebastia	Universitat de les Illes Balears, Spain
Medina, Jesús	Universidad de Cádiz, Spain
Mencar, Corrado	University of Bari Aldo Moro, Italy
Mendel, Jerry	University of Southern California, USA
Mesiar, Radko	Slovak University of Technology, Slovakia
Mesiarová-Zemánková, A.	University of Ostrava, Slovakia
Michalíková, Alžbeta	Matej Bel University, Slovakia
Micić, Ivana	University of Niš, Serbia
Mir-Torres, Arnau	Universitat de les Illes Balears, Spain
Mnasri, Zied	Université de Tunis-El Manar, Tunisia
Močkoř, Jiří	University of Ostrava, Czech Republic
Montero, Javier	Universidad Complutense de Madrid, Spain
Montes, Susana	Universidad de Oviedo, Spain
Murinová, Petra	University of Ostrava, Czech Republic
Navara, Mirko	Czech Technical University, Czech Republic
Nguyen, Phuong	Thang Long University, Vietnan
Noguera, Carles	University of Siena, Italy
Novák, Vilém	University of Ostrava, Czech Republic
Nurmi, Hannu	University of Turku, Finland
Ojeda-Aciego, Manuel	Universidad de Málaga, Spain
Olivas, José Angel	Universidad de Castilla-La Mancha, Spain
Pérez-Fernández, Raúl	Universidad de Oviedo, Spain
Perfilieva, Irina	University of Ostrava, Czech Republic
Petrík, Milan	Czech University of Life Sciences Prague, Czech Republic
Pivert, Oliver	University of Rennes, France
Portmann, Edy	University of Fribourg, Switzerland
Prade, Henri	Centre national de la recherche scientifique, France

Reformat, Marek	University of Alberta, Canada
Riera-Clapés Juan Vicente	Universitat de les Illes Balears, Spain
Rodríguez-Martínez, Iosu	Universidad Pública de Navarra, Spain
Romero, Francisco P.	Universidad de Castilla-La Mancha, Spain
Rovetta, Stefano	University of Genoa, Italy
Ruiz-Aguilera, Daniel	Universitat de les Illes Balears, Spain
Ruiz, María Dolores	Universidad de Granada, Spain
Sadeghian, Alireza	Toronto Metropolitan University, Canada
Sanchez, Daniel	Universidade Estadual de Campinas, Brazil
Seising, Rudolf	Deutsches Museum, Germany
Serrano-Guerrero, Jesús	Universidad de Castilla-La Mancha, Spain
Seselja, Branimir	University of Novi Sad, Serbia
Sessa, Salvatore	Università degli Studi di Napoli Federico II, Italy
Skowron, Andrzej	University of Warsaw, Poland
Slezak, Dominik	University of Warsaw, Poland
Sostak, Alexandre	University of Latvia, Latvia
Sousa, João Miguel da Costa	Universidade de Lisboa, Portugal
Stanimirović, Stefan	University of Niš, Serbia
Stefanini, Luciano	Urbino University, Italy
Štěpnička, Martin	University of Ostrava, Czech Republic
Straccia, Umberto	Istituto di Scienza e di Tecnologie dell'Informazione, Italy
Stupňanová, Andrea	Slovak University of Technology, Slovakia
Sussner, Peter	Universidade Estadual de Campinas, Brazil
Szmidt, Eulalia	Polish Academy of Sciences, Poland
Tabacchi, Marco Elio	Universita degli Studi di Palermo, Italy
Takáč, Zdenko	Slovak University of Technology, Slovakia
Torra, Vicenç	Umeå University, Sweden
Tsai, Ching-Chih	National Chung Hsing University, Taiwan
Tulupyev, Alexander	Saint Petersburg State University, Russia
Verdegay, José Luis	Universidad de Granada, Spain
Vetterlein, Thomas	Johannes Kepler University Linz, Austria
Wang, Lipo	Nanyang Technological University, Singapore
Watada, Junzo	Waseda University, Japan
Wieczynski, Jonata	Universidad Pública de Navarra, Spain
Wilbik, Anna	Maastricht University, The Netherlands
Yarushkina, Nadejda	Ulyanovsk State Technical University, Russia
Ying, Hao	Wayne State University, USA
Yoon, Jin Hee	Sejong University, South Korea
Zadrożny, Sławomir	Systems Research Institute, Poland
Zaza, Gianluca	Università degli studi di Bari Aldo Moro, Italy

Additional Reviewers

Akhtar, Jamil
Alijani, Zahra
Ben Souissi, Souhir
Bianchi, Matteo
Boeckling, Toon
Cao, Nhung
Cruz, Anderson
Csato, Laszlo
De Miguel, Laura
Dyba, Martin
Fechner, Włodzimierz
Felix, Rudolf
Fernández Sánchez, Juan
Fernandez-Peralta, Raquel
Fiala, Karel
Flaminio, Tommaso
Franco, Carlos
Fumanal Idocin, Javier
Guarino, Alfonso
Hongjun, Zhou
Kmita, Kamil
Kumar Gupta, Vikash
Labroche, Nicolas
Lapenta, Serafina
Linh, Nguyen
Lobo, David
Madrid, Nicolas
Mandal, Sayantan
Milosevic, Pavle

Miś, Katarzyna
Munar, Marc
Murinova, Petruska
Nanavati, Kavit
Paiva, Rui
Paseka, Jan
Pazienza, Andrea
Peralta, Daniel
Picerno, Pietro
Pocs, Jozef
Poledica, Ana
Pra Baldi, Michele
Rao Vemuri, Nageswara
Rijcken, Emil
Rodríguez, Iosu
Romaniuk, Maciej
Rubio-Manzano, Clemente
Santoro, Domenico
Santos, Helida
Scaringi, Raffaele
Schicchi, Daniele
Siudem, Grzegorz
Spolaor, Simone
Tepavcevic, Andreja
Torrens, Adrià
Ubeda, Manuel
Vittaut, Jean-Noël
Yu, Peng
Żogała-Siudem, Barbara

Sponsoring Institutions

EUSFLAT (European Society for Fuzzy Logic and Technology)
Vicerectorat de Política Científica i Investigació, UIB
Department of Mathematics and Computer Science, UIB
Palma Town Council
Conselleria de Fons Europeus, Universitat i Cultura, Balearic Islands Government
MCIN (Ministry of Science and Innovation), Project PID2020-113870GB-I00

Contents

SPECIAL SESSION 3: Evaluative Linguistic Expressions, Generalized Quantifiers and Applications

SPECIAL SESSION 4: Neural Networks under Uncertainty and Imperfect Information

SPECIAL SESSION 5: Imprecision Modeling and Management in XAI Systems

SPECIAL SESSION 6: Recent Trends in Mathematical Fuzzy Logics

**SPECIAL SESSION 7: Fuzzy Graph-Based Models: Theory and
Application**

SPECIAL SESSION 8: New frontiers of Computational Intelligence for Pervasive Healthcare Systems

SPECIAL SESSION 9: Fuzzy Implication Functions

SPECIAL SESSION 10: New Challenges and Ideas in Statistical Inference and Data Analysis

EUSFLAT General Track

The Inevitability of Vagueness in Fuzzy Logic

Marco Elio Tabacchi[1,2](✉) (iD)

[1] Dipartimento di Matematica e Informatica, Università degli Studi di Palermo,
Palermo, Italy
marcoelio.tabacchi@unipa.it
[2] Istituto Nazionale di Ricerche Demopolis, Palermo, Italy

Abstract. Fuzzy Logic, in its fuzzy control incarnation, can be as well
seen as an answer to the belated question on how can an algorithm take
in account the subtle variations in a complex system – be it the simple
and paradigmatic thermostat, the description of a traffic jam or the inner
workings of a spaceship. Contrary to the best whodunit, the answer is
given at the very start, and the history of the following years of fuzziness
is a long demonstration of how, thanks to its explanatory power, a simple
idea can be implemented in countless devices, and become the manifest
for a technological society in which the logic discourse is based more on
the human approach and on embracing the permanent state of flux and
uncertainty that is the human experience than on the futile search for
absolute truths and endless precision. If the control answer is somehow
a given, so many other answers that concern foundations of Fuzzy Logic
still beget proper questions. In this paper some of such foundational
questions pertaining vagueness, its role in the definition of fuzziness and
its many incarnations are set in their historical perspective, and some of
the dots outlining the path from a rigid search for truth typical of the
end of the nineteenth century to the more nuanced approach that has
swept the twentieth century are connected.

Keywords: Vagueness · Fuzzy Logic

1 Jean van Heijenoort and the Inevitability of Vagueness

The approach of Gottlob Frege to the 'vagaries of vagueness' [10], in the recount
of Jan van Heijenoort [13], has been already discussed in [9]: vagueness can
wreak havoc on logic, and has to be avoided at all costs. Frege is in good company, as Russell and Quine are apparently guilty as well of such reductionist
stance, despite Quine attributing a different ontological status to his universe
of discourse and Russell limiting the bivalent approach to an idealised image of
the world – the «imagined celestial world» in which a perfect logic should be
applicable. Both Russell and Quine seem in this view not that concerned with
real applications – embodied, realisable – but more interested in keeping the
score with a fast changing world. Frege's position is somehow justified by the

S. Massanet et al. (Eds.): EUSFLAT 2023/AGOP 2023, LNCS 14069, pp. 3–13, 2023.
https://doi.org/10.1007/978-3-031-39965-7_1

historical period in which he was active, an aftertaste of positivism and a hint of constructivism [1] and a general attitude toward sharply delimited concepts and final definitions. van Heijenoort summarises the evident connection between the three approaches as follows [13]:

> Russell's artificial construction of a bivalent world by imagination is closer to Quine's free creation of an ontology-oriented language than to Frege's objective realism. But the three of them, Frege, Russell, Quine, agree on one point, namely that ordinary language has to be supplanted by a bivalent regimented discourse if logic is to function properly.

This focal point, i.e. the necessity of a synthesis that eliminates (or at least reduces at a minimum) vagueness from the linguistic discourse in order to obtain once again, as in Aristoteles' times, a logic that 'works', appears more mandatory for Frege: «Thus nowhere do we have firm ground under our feet. Without final definitions, no final theorems. One would not come out of imperfection and vacillation» [13]); something that is done by trade and automatically, but without respect for the true nature of things for Russell: «none of the raw material of the world has smooth logical properties, but whatever appears to have such properties is constructed artificially in order to have them» [13]; and as a mechanical construction of commonsense reasoning at the pure mercy of communication from Quine: «Implicitly the learner of [a concept by ostension] is working inductively toward a general law of English verbal behavior, though a law that he will never try to state; he is working up to where he can in general judge when an English speaker would assent...» [12]. All three were able to see how vagueness is pervasive in natural language, but at the same time they fail to take this consideration a step further, and include the vagaries of vagueness into the logical discourse (the very job that fuzziness and other non-classical logics will be set to fulfill in the years to come), preferring instead to imagine that in order to have a perfect logic in search of a perfect truth, logic and common language can be divorced; it is of marginal importance if this is due to some sort of what van Heijenoort calls objective realism (i.e. some truth that exists beyond language and whose mirror in language is but a corruption of the original, sharp idea), to the necessity of an ontological approach that is to be applied only for some particular purposes, or to the construction of an imagined world of perfectly bivalent concepts.

The closing of van Heijenoort can be read as a sort of testament (also due to this essay being among the last he wrote) [13]:

> Frege's disregard of vagueness and other vagaries was, in a way, inevitable. But his logical laws have been formulated more than hundred years ago, and it is now perhaps time to look at the vagaries.

True to the time, in 1985 Fuzzy Logic and its applications to control have been around for more than twenty years, and while the formalised idea of Computing with Words [20] was still years in conceiving, the vagaries of language were already one of the primary foci of investigation in fuzziness and beyond. In order to find something that can really be called a precursor of the idea of meddling with vagaries, a step back in time has to be done: more precisely to the short period between 1937 and 1939.

2   Max Black and the Ineluctability of Vagueness

Among all the precursors to Fuzzy Logic and the work of Lotfi A. Zadeh, a special place is surely occupied by the analytical philosopher Max Black, and his well known paper on vagueness [2]; the two shared a curious coincidences in upbringing – both men born in Baku, and both moved to the States in the forties, albeit Zadeh was educated mainly in Iran and Black in England. But the strongest connection between the two, not explicitly mentioned in Zadeh's work but noted by historians of Fuzzy Logic (see e.g. [3, 10]) has to do with the desire to tackle a constructive approach to the problem of vagueness in science: Black states [2, p.429] that:

> [T]he purpose of the constructive part of the paper [is] to indicate in outline an appropriate symbolism for vagueness by means of which deviations from a standard can be absorbed by a re-interpretation of the same standards in such a way that the laws of logic in their usual absolutistic interpretation appear as a point of departure for more elaborate laws of which they now appear as special or limiting cases. The method yields a process by which deviations, when recognized as such, can be absorbed into the form. [...] [W]ith the provision of an adequate symbolism the need is removed for regarding vagueness as a defect.

There is a direct parallel with the proposal of Zadeh [16] regarding classes that are not directly relatable to the strict mathematical definition, such as the «class of all real numbers which are much greater than 1», «the class of beautiful women» or «the class of tall men»:

> The purpose of this note is to explore in a preliminary way some of the basic properties and implications of a concept which may be of use in dealing with "classes" of the type cited above. [...] [This] notion provides a convenient point of departure for the construction of a conceptual framework which parallels in many respects the framework used in the case of ordinary sets, but is more general than the latter and, potentially, may prove to have a much wider scope of applicability.

The notion is that of a Fuzzy Set (in its first incarnation), and while the two approaches come from a different background – Black more from a linguistic point of view, Zadeh with control systems in mind, the essential problem of vagueness is posed in a strikingly similar way.

2.1   Defining Vagueness

Zadeh starts with the general problem of attributing special object to general classes, with a prudential admission that vagueness can sometimes creep in the standard definition of a class: «More often than not, the classes of objects encountered in the real physical world do not have precisely defined criteria of membership»; but then put the accent on the idea that vaguely defined classes are especially so when containing attributes that render them vague (tall, beautiful, much greater), which lends well to further the idea of a Fuzzy Set and its mathematical definition. Implicit in Zadeh's approach is the idea of measurement of class membership, and in his view of vagueness, Fuzzy sets «provide a natural way of dealing with problems in which the source of imprecision is the absence of sharply defined criteria of class membership rather than the presence of random variables».

Black, due to his background as a philosopher of language as well as of science, invests on the search of a symbolism for the «vagueness or lack of precision of a language», while at the same time recognising that vagueness is a part (and not a defective one) of each scientific endeavour. In pointing to the search of extreme precision that is the staple of mathematics, Black focus on how this creates a sort of translation problem in experimental sciences, where mathematical precision is quite useful to describe and summarise a phenomenon, but at the same time limits this description to an idealised model, that rarely if ever corresponds to the true reality of human experience [2, p. 428]:

> While the mathematician constructs a theory in terms of "perfect" objects, the experimental scientist observes objects of which the properties demanded by the theory are and can, in the very nature of measurement, be only approximately true.
> [...] There remains a gap between scientific theory and its application, which ought to be, but is not, bridged.

As a contribution to the construction of this bridge, Black proposes the aforementioned construction of the outline of an appropriate symbolism for vagueness, which would dispel the myth that vagueness by itself is a defect to be eradicated, and not part of the richness of human experience, in sciences and language alike: «vagueness is a feature of scientific as of other discourse». In carrying out this operation there is a non explicit but strong desire to free logic from the constraint of mathematics. The prevalent paradigm of the time was dictating that logic is a sort of languagey version of mathematics, using the same devices and appealing to the same devotion of precision, as van Heijenoort has observed in Frege, Russell and Quine. In this context logic is condemned to follow mathematics in being an abstraction of reality, something Black does not subscribe. Logic should be instead regarded more as an applicative science, with uncertainty built in and the realisation of objects and predicates a continuous process prone to revision. This method should not abandon mathematics tout court: "at every stage the mathematics we already employ will provide the material for the increasing accuracy of the next stage", but there is no fixed point to which this process is anchored or targeted. This is another strong similarity with Zadeh's position, which was trying to escape from the research of an exasperate precision which was typical to the control science of the time, in this shaped by the advancements in computer science proper of the fifties and sixties – something for which Zadeh himself had coined a specific term [11, 21]:

> In moving in the countertraditional direction, we are sacrificing precision to achieve significant advantages down the line. This important feature of fuzzy logic is referred to as "the fuzzy logic gambit".

The gambit entices to trade off precision for a better power of representation of vague concepts, and an actionable solution to the problem of control. To "bridge the gap", Black goes another way, offering the outline of something that can be described as a pyramidal solution to the problem of tackling vagueness, an idea quite advanced at the time, that would have been more at home with the development of computer science in the eighties. Black has a clear view of the fact that vagueness is a feature that has different levels of implementation, and that while this is a specific trait, it is generally found in all instances, not only in language. The non-linguistic example he makes is that of an «impressionist painting of a London street in a fog» that while not vague when considered as a visual impression (and, more subtly hinted but not directly expressed, when compared to the avant-garde movements already established at the time), is vague when compared to the exact measurements that could be used to represent the scene in question as measured by what we call today a digital scanning. Different levels of detail – by extending Black's example – can be considered: a cubist painting of the scene, an impressionist painting of a scene, a photograph, a digital scanning using multispectral reflectografy, a complete description of the physical system generating the scene in a 3D rendering, particle by particle. Each of these provides different levels of detail (and as such of vagueness), and by choosing one over the other a trade off, not that different from the Fuzzy Logic gambit, is made: in increasing precision and decreasing vagueness, some of the relationships between concepts, language and scientific reality are lost. Black hopes to offer a model to take this into account, without sacrificing the possibility to represent inherent vagueness but at the same time with no renounce to precision when deemed necessary. In his words [2, p. 429–430] (Cursive added by the author):

> While the vague symbol has a part to play in language *(and elsewhere)* which cannot be equally well performed by more accurate symbols from another level, transition to levels of higher accuracy can always in principle be made.

2.2   What Exactly Is Vagueness?

Another strong point of contact between Zadeh and Black is the search for a less vague definition of what vagueness is – an ironic necessity pointed out by both authors. After having discussed vagueness as a general concept that intercepts both hard and soft sciences, Black concentrates his attention on the meaning of vagueness when applied to linguistics. According to him, in that field, vagueness is strictly related with the use of symbols to describe objects, and how the building of this relationship is not just an one-to-one affair. From an object's perspective, a symbol can often be applicable or not applicable to it with certainty, but it is possible that such application is impossible to determine. In this instance, Black chooses to term the set of objects for which an application to the symbol (or its negation) is not certain as «the fringe». This is a choice of words that resonates in what was then a yet to be defined fuzziness: a fringe is a border, but of uncertain confines[1].

Black understands quite well that this «crude» definition, while helping in imbuing vagueness with more precision, still lacks the rigor that is necessary to measure vagueness. In the more technical part of the paper, he aims at introducing a way to replace the vague concept of fringe with a «statistical analysis of the frequency of deviation from strict uniformity by the "users" of a vague symbol». Resorting to opinion gathering and statistics to model vague concepts will have more than an echo in later Zadeh's proposals, where in order to determine linguistic quantifiers a recourse is made to collecting a body of evidence about them [19].

But before the technicalities, comes the disambiguation: in order to build a system that can describe vagueness in a measurable manner, using the concept of the *fringe*, and extending it by subsequent frequentistic analysis using human response as a data source, it is paramount to define exactly what vagueness is, and even more important what it is not. Two concepts that are often mistaken for vagueness, which is an intrinsic property of the world, are singled out: generality and ambiguity. The distinction is defined accordingly [2, p. 430]:

> [Generality] is constituted by the application of a symbol to a multiplicity of objects in the field of reference, [ambiguity] by the association of a finite number of alternative meanings having the same phonetic form. [...] vagueness is a feature of the boundary of its extension, and is not constituted by the extension itself.

While the distinction between generality and ambiguity may seem quite forced, this allows Black to explicitly counter Russell's argument that [8]:

> Vagueness in our knowledge is, I believe, merely a particular case of a general law of physics, namely that law that what may be called the appearances of a thing at different places are less and less differentiated as we get further away from the thing. When I speak of "appearances" I am speaking of something purely physical – the sort of thing, in fact, that, if it is visual, can be photographed. From a close-up photograph it is possible to infer a photograph of the same object at a distance, while the contrary inference is much more precarious. That is to say, there is a one-many

---

[1] As an example, the definition of a fringe of a city center is often just in the eyes of a building's owner: the author has been personally offered a rent in what was defined "a fringe" of the center, and the fastest train to the "real" center was in the best cases a 45 min trip.

relation between distant and close-up appearances. Therefore the distance appearance, regarded as a representation of the close-up appearance, is vague according to our definition. I think all vagueness in language and thought is essentially analogous to this vagueness which may exist in a photograph.

At the same time, to go back to van Heijenoort's examination, the same vagueness is a one-to-many kind of relationship critique is also applicable to Frege's stance on vagueness, and at least partially, and in retrospect, to some of the arguments that Quine will propose forty years later.

In [16], Zadeh is much less preoccupied with the definition or disambiguation of vagueness. As his aim is to present an extension of Set Theory that can include vagueness in working order, he singles out a definition of vagueness, without even mentioning the word, in relationship with sets: «More often than not, the classes of objects encountered in the real physical world do not have precisely defined criteria of membership. [...] Yet, the fact remains that such imprecisely defined "classes" play an important role in human thinking, particularly in the domains of pattern recognition, communication of information, and abstraction». This has a sharp counterpart in Black. He discusses the definition of the concept of a chair[2], its multiple realisations and the fact that [2, p. 432]:

> «One can imagine an exhibition in some unlikely museum of applied logic of a series of "chairs" differing in quality by least noticeable amounts. At one end of a long line, containing perhaps thousands of exhibits, might be a Chippendale chair: at the other, a small nondescript lump of wood. Any "normal" observer inspecting the series finds extreme difficulty in drawing the line between chair and not-chair. Indeed the demand to perform this operation is felt to be inappropriate in principle: chair is not the kind of word which admits of this sharp distinction.»

The concept of membership and its ill definition for some objects is expressed in a strikingly similar way to Zadeh: «in speaking of the vagueness of the word chair, attention is directed only to the fact that objects can be presented whose membership of the class of chairs is incurably "uncertain" or "doubtful"», the difference being in the choice of terms: "imprecise" and "ambiguous" for Zadeh, "vague" and "uncertain" for Black.

Even the graphical idea of how to represent vagueness bears resemblances between Black and Zadeh. And that despite the differences in how the graph is constructed: the meaning of axes; the process employed to build the curve, that in Black is by polling while in Zadeh is given as an example – Zadeh will turn his attention on to how to build fuzzy sets later on (Fig. 1).

2.3   Vagueness and Human Intelligence

Soon after Zadeh will develop a keen interest in the application of Fuzzy Sets to what he chose to call "humanistic problems", in his three-parter for Information

---

[2] There is a strange fixation with furniture in the history of fuzziness: probably the most egregious example, with his chair-that-transforms-into-stairs, is Bart Kosko [5].

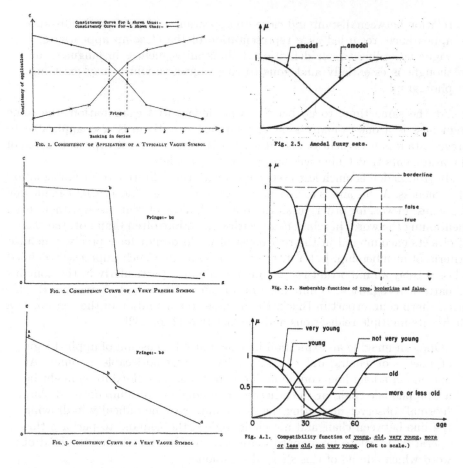

Fig. 1. Black's Consistency Profile of a symbol (left column, from [2, pp. 443–445]), and Zadeh's Fuzzy Concepts (right column, from [15]).

Science [17,18,22], and especially in [14] (preceded by a memorandum dated August 1971, but explicitly introduced as a the notes from a presentation at a "Man and Computer" conference in Bordeaux, June 1970) and [15] (preceded by a research note of the same title published internally in 1974), where the term "imprecise" is used already in the title. If vagueness is (also) a problem of language, language can be used to at least partially solve it.

Already in [14], just less than five years after the publication of [16], the aim of Zadeh moves from a better control system to a much more ambitious plan: tackling human reasoning using Fuzzy Logic. Zadeh introduces the concept of Fuzzy Language, and describes its relevance to human intelligence, and in another common thread with Black, to human language. Vagueness, once again termed as uncertainty and imprecision by Zadeh, is a central feature of the proclaimed superiority of Fuzziness in dealing with human reasoning and language [14, p. 1]:

It is suggested that the theory of fuzzy languages may have the potential of providing better models for natural languages than is possible within the framework of the classical theory of formal languages. [...] There is indeed a very basic difference between human and machine intelligence which may well prove to be a very difficult obstacle in the path of designing machines that can outperform humans in the realm of cognitive processes involving concept formation, abstraction, pattern recognition, and decision-making under uncertainty. The difference in question lies in the ability of the human brain – an ability which present day digital computers do not possess – to think and reason in imprecise, non-quantitative, terms.

Zadeh ascribes this to the relationship between complexity and precision, again remarking how the more the real world is the centre of discourse, the more vagueness comes into play: «complexity and precision bear an inverse relation to one another in the sense that, as the complexity of a problem increases, the possibility of analyzing it in precise terms diminishes. Thus it is a truism that the class of problems which are susceptible of exact solution is much smaller than that which can be solved approximately».

Many of the examples presented in the paper (autonomous parking, summarising of texts) are only been satisfactorily automatised in the present times, and this just because a vast amount of information is now at our disposal. No real advancement is currently been made on «the ability of a human brain, weighing only a few hundred grams, to manipulate complicated fuzzy concepts and act on multidimensional fuzzy sensory inputs endows it with a capability to solve rather easily a wide variety of problems. [...] the capacity of a human brain to manipulate fuzzy concepts and non-quantitative sensory inputs may well be one of its most important assets». The main takeaway notions is the fact that many problems can be solved efficiently only if a level of approximation in the result is accepted, and the idea that human reasoning thrives on this is still valid today as it was then. More than the successes of AI, this explains its failures, and highlights the fact that without «syntax or semantics or both are fuzzy in nature», as in Zadeh's proposal of a Fuzzy Language, an important part of the discourse is missing.

3   Carl G. Hempel: The Gradation of Vagueness

The debate on vagueness, language and logic will continue in the following years, mainly using the Philosophy of Science journal as its outlet[3]. Notable in this

---

[3] In reality the debate will go on and on, and on, slowing only during the second world war. Notable more recent examples with a direct reference to the work of Black and Hempel are [6, 7]. While interesting in their own right, most of the more contemporary debate from the field of language seem to ignore the advancement made by Fuzzy Logic (and other non classical logics) in the field of dealing with vagueness. It is not known if this is due to a sort of bubble effect, to sheer lack of knowledge or to any other, more esoteric explanation.

sense is an article by Carl G. Hempel [4], a direct answer to [2] in which a number of issues in Black's method for measuring vagueness using the judgement from a panel. While technicalities are out of scope in the present context, the conclusion is anyway of interest here, as it is another of the forebears of fuzziness ideas of later [4, pp. 179–180]:

> Vagueness is a gradable relation of strictly semiotic character; it involves, besides the vague term and its subject matter, also the users of the language in question. Vagueness is ineradicably connected with all terms, logical as well as descriptive, of any interpreted language. [...] The occurrence of symbols with a high degree vagueness may suggest a modification in the logical structure of the conceptual apparatus of science, namely the transition from non-gradable to gradable concepts; this procedure is in fact frequently carried out, and it contributes very essentially to diminution of vagueness in scientific language.

As Black does, Hempel recognises that vagueness is intrinsic in language, and that no amount of Fregean strong will or Russelian resorting to an idealised plane can leave it out from a logic of language. It is then time to find a permanent solution to the problem of including vagueness in the discourse, and this solution is gradation. It will just take another seventeen years to find a concrete, applicable model that will admit vagueness to the realm of hard sciences.

References

1. Bachmann, F.: Frege als konstruktiver Logizist. Das Problem der Begründung,Börger (1975)
2. Black, M.: Vagueness: an exercise in logical analysis. Philosophy Sci. 4(4), 427–455 (1937)
3. Bradley, J., Seising, R.: The gap between scientific theory and application: Black and Zadeh - vagueness and fuzzy sets. In: NAFIPS 2006–2006 Annual Meeting of the North American Fuzzy Information Processing Society, pp. 408–413 (2006). https://doi.org/10.1109/NAFIPS.2006.365444
4. Hempel, C.G.: Vagueness and logic. Philosophy Sci. 6(2), 163–180 (1939)
5. Kosko, B., Toms, M.: Fuzzy Thinking: The New Science of Fuzzy Logic, vol. 288. Hyperion, New York (1993)
6. Rolf, B.: Black and Hempel on vagueness. Zeitschrift für allgemeine Wissenschaftstheorie/J. Gen. Philosophy Sci. 332–346 (1980)
7. Rolf, B.: A theory of vagueness. J. Philos. Logic, 315–325 (1980)
8. Russell, B.: Vagueness. Australas. J. Psychol. Philosophy 1(2), 84–92 (1923)
9. Tabacchi, M.E.: Focusing Fuzzy Logic, Naturalia, vol. 6. UniPa Press (2021)
10. Tabacchi, M.E., Termini, S.: Varieties of vagueness, fuzziness and a few foundational (and ontological) questions. In: Proceedings of the 7th Conference of the European Society for Fuzzy Logic and Technology, pp. 578–583. Atlantis Press (2011)
11. Tabacchi, M.E., Termini, S.: The fuzzy logic gambit as a paradigm of Lotfi's proposals. In: Fullér, R., Giove, S., Masulli, F. (eds.) WILF 2018. LNCS (LNAI), vol. 11291, pp. 231–235. Springer, Cham (2019). https://doi.org/10.1007/978-3-030-12544-8_18

12. Van Heijenoort, J.: Ostension and vagueness. In: Selected Essays, pp. 71–74. Bibliopolis (1979)
13. Van Heijenoort, J.: Frege and vagueness. In: Selected Essays, pp. 85–98. Bibliopolis (1986)
14. Zadeh, L.: Fuzzy languages and their relation to human and machine intelligence. In: Man and Computer, pp. 130–165. Karger Publishers (1972)
15. Zadeh, L.: A fuzzy-algorithmic approach to the definition of complex or imprecise concepts. Int. J. Man-Mach. Stud. **8**(3), 249–291 (1976). https://doi.org/10.1016/S0020-7373(76)80001-6
16. Zadeh, L.A.: Fuzzy sets. Inf. Control **8**(3), 338–353 (1965)
17. Zadeh, L.A.: The concept of a linguistic variable and its application to approximate reasoning-III. Inf. Sci. **9**(1), 43–80 (1975)
18. Zadeh, L.A.: The concept of a linguistic variable and its application to approximate reasoning-II. Inf. Sci. **8**(4), 301–357 (1975)
19. Zadeh, L.A.: Fuzzy sets and information granularity. Fuzzy sets, fuzzy logic, and fuzzy systems: selected papers, pp. 433–448 (1979)
20. Zadeh, L.A.: Fuzzy logic= computing with words. Comput. Words Inf./Intell. Syst. 1: Found., 3–23 (1999)
21. Zadeh, L.A.: Is there a need for fuzzy logic? Inf. Sci. **178**(13), 2751–2779 (2008)
22. Zadeh, L.A.: The concept of a linguistic variable and its application to approximate reasoning-I. Inf. Sci. **8**(3), 199–249 (1975)

A Fuzzy Cognitive Map Learning Approach for Coronary Artery Disease Diagnosis in Nuclear Medicine

Anna Feleki[1], Ioannis D. Apostolopoulos[1] , Konstantinos Papageorgiou[1],
Elpiniki I. Papageorgiou[1] , Dimitris J. Apostolopoulos[2],
and Nikolaos I. Papandrianos[1(✉)]

[1] Department of Energy Systems, University of Thessaly, Gaiopolis Campus, 41500 Larissa,
Greece
{elpinikipapageorgiou,npapandrianos}@uth.gr
[2] Department of Nuclear Medicine, School of Medicine, University General Hospital of Patras,
University of Patras, 265-00 Patras, Greece

Abstract. Coronary artery disease (CAD) is the primary cause of death and
chronic disability among cardiovascular conditions worldwide. Its diagnosis is
challenging and cost-effective. In this research work, Fuzzy Cognitive Maps
with Particle Swarm Optimization (FCM-PSO) were used for CAD classification (healthy and diseased). In particular, a new DeepFCM framework, which
integrates image and clinical data of the patients is proposed. In this context, we
employed the FCM-PSO method enhanced by experts' knowledge, along with
an efficient attention Convolutional Neural Network, to improve diagnosis. The
proposed method is evaluated using 571 participants and achieved $77.95 \pm 5.58\%$
accuracy, 0.22 ± 0.05 loss, $76.98 \pm 8.27\%$ sensitivity, $77.39 \pm 7.13\%$ specificity, and $73.97 \pm 0.09\%$ precision, implementing a 10-fold cross-validation process. The results extracted from the proposed model demonstrate the model's
efficiency and outperform traditional machine learning algorithms. An essential
asset of the proposed DeepFCM framework is the explainability, as it offers nuclear
physicians' meaningful causal relationships between clinical factors regarding the
diagnosis.

Keywords: Fuzzy Cognitive Maps · Particle Swarm Optimization ·
Classification · Coronary artery disease

1 Introduction

Obstructive Coronary Artery Disease (CAD) is the most frequent type of cardiovascular
disease [1–3], and it occurs when at least one of the coronary arteries is blocked, which
leads to the reduction of blood inserted into the myocardium, causing stenosis. CAD is a
life-threatening disease. It requires early appropriate diagnosis and treatment to improve
a patient's condition and deflect death. Consequently, it is crucial to detect the existence
of stenosis and the danger of its advancement [4–7].

S. Massanet et al. (Eds.): EUSFLAT 2023/AGOP 2023, LNCS 14069, pp. 14–25, 2023.
https://doi.org/10.1007/978-3-031-39965-7_2

With respect to the previous studies regarding Fuzzy Cognitive Map (FCM) implementation for medical data classification, the following research studies have been analyzed. Papageorgiou et al. [8] developed an FCM model for brain tumor characterization utilizing the Activation Hebbian Algorithm. The proposed model defines the degree of tumor abnormality, with only qualitative data and experts' knowledge as input. The model achieved 90.26% and 93.22% accuracy for brain tumors of low-grade and high-grade, accordingly. Nasiriyan-Rad et al. [9] presented a new method for grading Celiac disease (CD) with the combination of FCM and Support Vector Machine (SVM), with Particle Swarm Optimization (PSO) for enhancing the results. The performance of the proposed model was compared against the fuzzy rule-based Bayesian Networks (BN), and the FCM-SVM model performed better with accuracy of 87%, 86%, and 84% for each of the three possible CD grades. Papageorgiou et al. [10] introduced a new approach for FCM learning, utilizing ensemble-based learning approaches, along with non-linear Hebbian learning (NHL) for autism classification. The proposed model outperformed with 89.41% accuracy, in contrast to FCM models that support their training procedure only on Hebbian-based learning algorithms and extracted 79.62% accuracy. The proposed model demonstrates remarkably improved performance with the utilization of ensemble techniques. Papageorgiou et al. [11] presented FCMs for the diagnosis of thyroid, combining linguistic values acquired from experts, and fuzzy rules obtained from historical data. The dataset consists of 215 samples. The developed model achieved 89.80% accuracy. Carvajal et al. [12] aimed to develop a General Type-2 (GT2) Fuzzy Logic (FL) model for blood pressure level classification and optimize the general type-2 membership functions parameters with the usage of Ant Lion Optimizer, which is a metaheuristic algorithm. The dataset included 4240 patients, and the holdout method is applied. The GT2 FL classifier outperformed with an average of 99% accuracy for all experiments, in contrast to interval-type-2 and type-1 fuzzy classifiers. Guzman et al. in [13] aimed to develop a type-2 fuzzy system for the classification of blood pressure level based on knowledge of an expert. The model attained 99.408% classification rate with a type-2 fuzzy system utilizing triangular membership functions, whereas the type-1 classifier in previous study reached 98%. Miramontes et al. [14] aimed to modify Bird Swarm algorithm (BSA), with utilizing dynamic parameter adaptation based on type-1 fuzzy systems to obtain the nocturnal blood pressure profile. The model utilized both Gaussian and trapezoidal membership functions and they performed remarkably. The proposed model exceeded the original approach and achieved 97% classification accuracy. Hoyos et al. [15] proposed a clinical decision-support system based on Fuzzy Cognitive Maps architecture to classify patients that suffer from dengue. The developed model outperformed compared to other machine learning approaches, and attained 89.4% accuracy, while providing analysis of factors and explainability of decision of results.

The contribution of this research is the development of a DeepFCM model utilizing Particle Swarm as an optimization technique for the provision of an automatic classification tool that diagnoses CAD non-invasively and is based on both image and clinical risk factors. The classification problem is two-class, and it is devoted to the presence of CAD. The added value of this research is the proposal of an explainable tool that provides interpretability, which is an important factor in sensitive areas like healthcare, compared to machine learning approaches, which are known as "black boxes". The

DeepFCM provides an analysis of relationships among features, where we can detect signs of CAD before the clinical diagnosis and recommend precautionary treatment to avoid complications and mortality [15]. The results demonstrate that our model offers high consistency and robustness, denoting that it can be adjusted in the nuclear medicine domain and assist in decision-making, as far as CAD diagnosis is concerned.

2 Material and Methods

2.1 CAD Dataset

The dataset of this study was obtained from the Clinical Sector of the Department of Nuclear Medicine of the University Hospital of Patras from 16/2/2018 to 28/02/2022. Dataset acquisition is authorized by the ethical committee of the University Hospital of Patras. All patients were given authorization for their results to be obtained anonymously. The performed methods agree with the Declaration of Helsinki.

The corresponding dataset consists of 571 instances, where 248 cases are classified as CAD-diseased and 323 as normal. The dataset consists of 79.68% male participants and 20.32% female. The age ranges from 32 to 90 years.

The participants underwent gated-SPECT-MPI (Single Photon Computed Tomography- Myocardial Perfusion Imaging) and Invasive Coronary Angiography (ICA) after 60 days of the MPI procedure. The result of this process shapes a patient's status regarding the CAD diagnosis and the result is utilized as ground truth in our study.

The available dataset contains information about the patient's status. The features used as input by the FCM classification model, after binary normalization are twenty-two: (1) Sex, (2) Age, (3) BMI, (4) known CAD, (5) previous AMI, (6) previous PCI, (7) previous CABG, (8) previous STROKE, (9) Diabetes, (10) Smoking, (11) Hypertension, (12) Dyslipidemia, (13) Peripheral Angiopathy, (14) Chronic Kidney Disease, (15) Family History of CAD, (16) Asymptomatic, (17) Atypical Symptoms, (18) Angina-like, (19) Dyspnea on Exertion, (20) Incident of precordial pain, (21) ECG, and (22) Preliminary Expert Diagnosis.

Tomographic reconstruction of raw image data was carried out on a dedicated work-station (Xeleris 3, GE Healthcare) by the OSEM (ordered subsets-expectation maximization) algorithm, using two iterations and ten subsets. After reconstruction, a low-pass filter (Butterworth, with power ten and a cut-off value of 0.40 for stress and 0.45 for rest images) was applied. Apart from 3-plane tomographic slices (in short, vertically long, and horizontal long axes), polar maps were created automatically by the software. The polar map is an image that summarizes the results of the 3-D tomographic slices into a single 2-D circular presentation. Polar maps were extracted from the workstation in DICOM (Digital Imaging and Communications in Medicine) format for further processing.

2.2 Methodology of the Proposed Framework DeepFCM

Our proposed DeepFCM model consists of the combination of CNN (Convolutional Neural Network) and FCM-PSO methodology. CNN is responsible for handling the image data and supplying the FCM-PSO model with its prediction. The DeepFCM model integrates the clinical data and the CNN's output and facilitates the final diagnosis (see Fig. 1). The fundamental concepts of the FCM are discussed in Sect. 2.2.1. The design and learning of FCM-PSO are described in Sects. 2.2.2 and 2.2.3. The CNN predictions are analyzed in Sect. 2.2.4 and the proposed DeepFCM model is discussed in Sect. 2.2.5.

2.2.1 Fuzzy Cognitive Maps

FCMs were introduced by Kosko [16] in 1986 and they are an advanced version of cognitive maps. The FCM architecture is similar to an Artificial Neural Network, since it mimics the human process of making decisions [7, 8]. FCM utilizes all the accessible knowledge and translates it into the form of concepts and interconnections between them. Concepts represent the characteristics/states of the examined system whereas interconnections denote the weighted-directed cause-effect relationships of the concepts, Interconnections values are in the spectrum of $[-1, 1]$. Whether an interconnection has a positive or negative or zero value depends on the kind of connection [8, 9].

The construction of an FCM involves the definition of concepts and the equation of calculating the future values of concepts according to historical data. The fundamental equation for computing FCM concepts is Eq. (1). To normalize the predicted values of concepts into a specific range, a transfer function is used. Generally, the sigmoid or the trivalent function is preferred.

$$A_i^{(K+1)} = f\left(A_i^{(K)} + \sum_{i,j}^{N} w_{ij} A_j^{(K)}\right) \qquad (1)$$

where, $A_i^{(K+1)}$ is the value of the concept iteration $(k + 1)$ and $A_j^{(K)}$ is the concept at the iteration (k) and f is the sigmoid function.

The strength of FCMs in general is that they consider the last state of each concept to calculate the future value. Regarding FCM learning, it is based on the construction of a weight matrix, which contains all the relationships between the concepts, utilizing unsupervised techniques with Hebbian adaptation, supervised with the inclusion of evolutionary algorithms and gradient methods. Well-known methods of FCM learning using historical data are RCGA and PSO.

2.2.2 Design of FCM Model Using Experts' Knowledge

The FCM-PSO model consists of 22 concepts, which are clinical features, with one output regarding CAD presence. All concepts have a value of 0 or 1, except for the age and BMI, where their values are normalized and rescaled into the spectrum of [0,1]. The nuclear experts of the study assigned linguistic values (represented by fuzzy sets) on the interconnections between inputs and output concepts. Table 1 gathers the fuzzy relationships among some of the most influential concepts to the output. In particular, the following fuzzy sets were defined: Very Weak (VW), Weak (W), Medium (M), Strong (S), and Very Strong (VS). For each linguistic value, we assigned a specific range of values as it is reported in the literature [17], to perform FCM learning considering the respective ranges. For the fuzzy sets Very Weak (VW) and Weak (W) we determined the ranges to be [0–0.3] and [0.15–0.5] accordingly. Also, for Medium (M), for Strong (S) and Very Strong (VS) we assigned the values to be randomly selected from the ranges [0.35–0.65], [0.5–0.85] and [0.7–1] accordingly. Concerning the negative linguistic values, we adjusted the provided values according to the positive ones. For the rest of the relationships, where no experts' knowledge is provided, they take random values within the range [−1, 1].

Table 1. Presentation of the suggested weights between meaningful input-input concepts and input-output concepts obtained from nuclear experts.

Relationships	Suggested Weight	Relationships	Suggested Weight
Sex>>Output	M	Dyslipidemia>>Output	M
AGE>>ECG	W	Angiopathy>>Output	M
BMI>>Output	W	Chronic Kidney Disease>>Output	W
Known CAD>>Output	S	Family History of CAD>>Output	W
Previous AMI>>Output	VW	Asymptomatic>>Output	-S
Previous PCI>>Output	W	Atypical symptoms>>ECG	M
Previous CABG>>Output	W	Atypical Symptoms>>Output	VS
Previous Stroke>>Output	M	Angina Like>>Output	S
Diabetes>>Output	S	Dyspnea on exertion>>Output	M
Smoking>>Output	M	Incident of precordial pain>>Output	M
Hypertension>>Output	M	Expert_Diagnosis_Binary>>Output	VS

2.2.3   Learning FCM with Particle Swarm Optimization

The initialization of weight matrices is based on the linguistic values provided by experts, which are in fuzzy format. Concerning the fuzziness contained in the suggested values, the learning of FCM should be adjusted accordingly, since FCM's performance is dependent on the calculation of the weight matrix. Instead of taking the suggested weights for granted, which would result in a static FCM, we considered assigning the FCM some freedom to learn around the suggested values and fit to the data. For this reason, we implemented FCM learning with the PSO approach.

Particle Swarm Optimization (PSO) [18] is an optimization methodology that was introduced in 1995 [9] and has a similar approach to evolutionary algorithms. PSO is a population-based methodology, and applies random initialization, among the interactions of population members, and uses a small number of parameters [9, 14]. In general,

PSO is utilized for the optimization of the objective function [14]. Regarding FCM learning, PSO is applied for the adjustment and calculation of relationships among the concepts. The estimation of the weight matrix, which consists of the relationships among all concepts is a crucial step and determines FCM's performance. The ideal conditions of the produced weight matrix are to be in a steady state, representative of the corresponding dataset and able to generate minimal error. Applying PSO to FCM learning improves FCM's performance and intensifies FCM's ability to classify correctly.

2.2.4 Attention-Based VGG-19

To make use of the Polar Map images, we trained an attention-based VGG19 network that facilitates CAD diagnosis based solely on Polar Maps.

Regarding the attention-based VGG-19 network, this modified version includes attention blocks and branch-diverging (BD) paths to improve the feature extraction capabilities of VGG-19. The attention blocks aim to focus on important image regions during feature extraction by multiplying the features with a weight mask that highlights regions of interest. This is achieved by creating a small CNN that takes the features as input and outputs a mask that is then used to weigh the original features. The BD paths, on the other hand, aim to capture more diverse features by creating multiple branches that diverge from the main CNN path and then recombine the features later in the network. This helps the model learn more complex patterns and improves its generalization capabilities. Finally, the model is trained to classify images into different categories using the categorical cross-entropy loss function and the Adam optimizer.

2.2.5 DeepFCM

The conception of a DeepFCM lies in the need to handle both clinical and image data, as illustrated in Fig. 1. Initially, we developed the attention-based VGG-19 model to process the Polar Maps and predict the class of each instance based solely on the images. Secondly, we pre-processed the clinical data, performing normalization. Thirdly, we developed an FCM for handling both the clinical data and the attention-based VGG-19 prediction. Nuclear experts have provided suggested linguistic values for most of the interconnections of input-output concepts, where we utilized them for the initialization of weight matrices. With the application of PSO methodology, the best weight matrix includes variations, of the provided suggested linguistic values, that correlate to our dataset, in order to globally minimize the error function, among the predicted and actual values of concepts. Afterward, a 10-fold cross-validation approach is applied for the assurance of stability and generability of DeepFCM results. With the predicted Deep-FCM values from the final weight matrix, the metrics are calculated, which define the model's performance.

By combining both imaging and clinical data, the proposed model DeepFCM provides a comprehensive and integrated approach to diagnosis, potentially improving accuracy and reducing the need for invasive tests.

DeepFCM is an explainable method providing interpretability, clarification, and transparency of results to reduce the complexity and scalability of other methods.

In Fig. 1, we demonstrate the total process of our proposed methodological framework. The developed DeepFCM model is provided on GitHub [https://github.com/Ann aFeleki/FCM-PSO-learning].

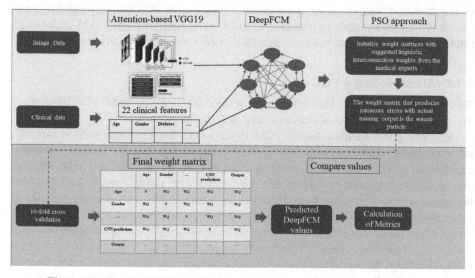

Fig. 1. Proposed methodological framework of our proposed model DeepFCM.

3 Results

In the following section, we demonstrate the most representative results of the conducted experiments where 10-fold cross-validation is applied.

The proposed model is executed on a desktop with AMD Ryzen 7 5800H with Radeon Graphics with 16 GB RAM, and NVIDIA Ge-Force RTX 3060 GPU. As regards the development of the model and the libraries, Python v3.9.13 was employed, along with TensorFlow v2.9.3 and Keras v2.9.0.

To conclude the proposed architecture, various experiments were performed, and a comparison has been applied with traditional machine learning algorithms to evaluate each model's metrics.

For model evaluation and performance testing, the metrics that were selected are accuracy, loss, sensitivity, specificity, and precision. Accuracy refers to the ratio of total number of instances classified correctly by the total number of instances [19]. Loss is the calculated error of predicted and actual values. A small loss is desirable denoting a minor deviation [5]. Sensitivity and specificity represent the percentage of true positives and true negatives, respectively. Precision indicates the ratio of the number of true positives to the total number of positive predictions [5].

We followed the inspection of the equilibrium point's exact position, where the FCM presents a steady state by experimenting with different epochs. The epochs tested are in the range of 15 to 120. The results regarding accuracy and loss for the examined number of epochs are depicted in Fig. 2. It is observed that the best value for the epochs and the equilibrium point for the proposed FCM is 35, which is achieved in the position of the highest accuracy and the lowest loss.

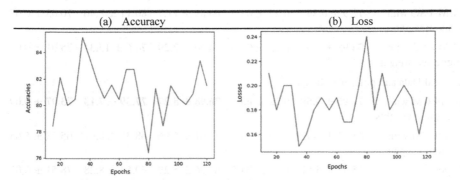

Fig. 2. Performance of proposed model with different epochs, regarding (a) Accuracy (b) Loss

The values of the performance metrics of the proposed DeepFCM model are illustrated in Table 2. The spectrum of the initial interconnections of concepts with the output for DeepFCM was based on the suggested linguistic values provided by experts. It has to be mentioned that for CNN predictions, that is utilized as added input in proposed DeepFCM model, the nuclear experts assigned a Strong relationship with the output. For comparison reasons, the previous experiment was repeated, with randomly produced relationships between input and output concepts, within the range [−1, 1]. Furthermore, we experimented with FCM-PSO with the suggested linguistic values and with random values for the initialization of the weight matrix as well. Additionally, for a further in-depth evaluation of the proposed model, a comparative analysis has been made with robust machine learning algorithms such as Bayes, Random Forest, Decision Tree, and Neural Network in their default specifications. Regarding Neural network architecture, we experimented with different network configurations, for example, the number of nodes, number of layers, optimization algorithms, and activation functions. The optimal parameters of the final model were 3 three hidden layers with 16-32-64 nodes in each layer, with 16 batch size, Adam optimizer, and sigmoid activation function. The reason we developed machine learning algorithms for our dataset is to compare the metrics of methodologies that have demonstrated efficient performance on structure data.

Comparing the results provided in Table 2, we conclude that the proposed DeepFCM model utilizing the weights suggested by experts outperforms the DeepFCM with random values and also the FCM-PSO approaches that did not contain the CNN predictions from the VGG-19 model and the machine learning methodologies as well. In this case, the proposed DeepFCM model exceeded in terms of efficiency when utilizing historical data and additional knowledge from experts.

Table 2. Comparison of results of DeepFCM model with FCM-PSO and with traditional machine learning algorithms

Models	Accuracy	Loss	Sensitivity	Specificity	Precision
Clinical Data					
FCM-PSO with random weights	72.9 ± 6.39	0.27 ± 0.06	64.89 ± 11.7	80.11 ± 8.96	70.05 ± 0.07
FCM-PSO with suggested weights	74.98 ± 5.95	0.25 ± 0.06	74.96 ± 7.29	74.6 ± 15.34	75.01 ± 0.04
Clinical Data and polar map Images					
DeepFCM with suggested weights	**77.95 ± 5.58**	**0.22 ± 0.05**	**76.98 ± 8.27**	**77.39 ± 7.13**	**73.97 ± 0.09**
DeepFCM with random weights	65.91 ± 4.42	0.36 ± 0.04	71.01 ± 5.96	68.36 ± 9.97	65.63 ± 5.65
Bayes	75.45 ± 5.57	0.24 ± 0.05	81.26 ± 5.29	69.54 ± 8.28	78.51 ± 0.07
Random Forest	78.87 ± 3.42	0.22 ± 0.03	74.26 ± 5.46	83.37 ± 5.48	76.43 ± 0.05
Decision Tree	74.13 ± 4.23	0.26 ± 0.04	72.34 ± 6.14	75.82 ± 6.14	73.43 ± 0.05
Neural Network	78.57 ± 5.49	0.28 ± 0.02	78.08 ± 6.7	79.28 ± 6.16	73.5 ± 0.09

In Table 3, we gather the range of values for every relationship between input and output concepts, that were i) suggested by nuclear experts, ii) produced from the Deep-FCM learning approach with suggested linguistic values by the experts. The first column demonstrates the suggested weights from experts for the connection of every input concept with the output, except for some Nan values. Nan values demonstrate the interconnections' values that were randomly selected from the spectrum $[-1, 1]$. The second column presents the produced weights for the interconnection between input and output concepts from the DeepFCM learning model, whose initial values are provided from the suggested ranges displayed in the first column.

The weights produced from the DeepFCM model utilizing experts' values of weights are close to the values suggested by experts and do not present large deviations, in contrast to those interconnections randomly initialized as Nan, in which large deviations were observed.

4   Discussion

We proposed a DeepFCM model for CAD diagnosis. It achieves high accuracy and also exceeds traditional machine learning algorithms. Moreover, it utilizes historical data and experts' opinions, with CNN predictions extracted from trained VGG-19. Concerning the results, DeepFCM is a transparent and explainable tool, since it produces interconnections between every input concept and the output CAD concept, which is a great advantage, in comparison to Random Forest, Bayes, Decision Tree, and Neural Networks that do not provide interpretability of conclusion of results [5].

Table 3. Presentation of extracted ranges for the relationship between input concepts and output produced from the DeepFCM model.

Suggested interconnections	Weights from experts	Produced weights by DeepFCM
Sex>>Output	[0.35–0.65]	[0.49 ± 0.09]
Age>>Output	Nan	[−0.35 ± 0.39]
BMI>>Output	[0.15–0.5]	[0.3 ± 0.11]
known CAD>>Output	[0.5–0.85]	[0.66 ± 0.07]
previous AMI>>Output	[0–0.3]	[0.16 ± 0.08]
previous PCI>>Output	[0.15–0.5]	[0.32 ± 0.12]
previous CABG>>Output	[0.15–0.5]	[0.29 ± 0.09]
previous STROKE>>Output	[0.35–0.65]	[0.47 ± 0.1]
Diabetes>>Output	[0.5–0.85]	[0.69 ± 0.11]
Smoking>>Output	[0.35–0.65]	[0.49 ± 0.07]
Hypertension>>Output	[0.35–0.65]	[0.48 ± 0.1]
Dyslipidemia>>Output	[0.35–0.65]	[0.51 ± 0.1]
Angiopathy>>Output	[0.35–0.65]	[0.48 ± 0.06]
Chronic Kidney Disease>>Output	[0.15–0.5]	[0.38 ± 0.14]
Family History of CAD>>Output	[0.15–0,5]	[0.34 ± 0.06]
Asymptomatic>>Output	[−0.85−−0.5]	[−0.66 ± 0.07]
Atypical symptoms>>Output	[0.7–1]	[0.83 ± 0.08]
Angina like>>Output	[0.5–0.85]	[0.67 ± 0.06]
Dyspnea on exertion>>Output	[0.5–0.85]	[0.6 ± 0.08]
Incident of precordial pain>>Output	[0.35–0.65]	[0.56 ± 0.8]
ECG>>Output	Nan	[−0.16 ± 0.57]
Expert_Diagnosis_Binary>>Output	[0.7–1]	[0.89 ± 0.07]
CNN predictions>>Output	[0.5–0.85]	[0.7 ± 0.15]

We experimented with different learning methods to determine the optimal for our study that achieves generability as well. We developed DeepFCM with random values and FCM-PSO with suggested values and with random values for the initial values of interconnections. DeepFCM with suggested values from experts performed better results among all the experiments. It is demonstrated that the doctor-in-the-loop approach yields better results and makes the system more informative and explainable. In addition, the integration of a CNN for offering an extra input to our system benefits the model, because it leverages the feature extraction capabilities of the CNNs in CAD screening.

The developed code can be implemented to produce results effortlessly providing nuclear experts with an autonomous decision-making tool for patients' health, regarding CAD diagnosis.

5   Conclusions

In this research study, the DeepFCM model achieved remarkable results, providing an integral tool that can assist decisions in nuclear medicine. In future work, the authors intend to implement state equations for FCM learning and obtain nuclear experts' opinions that entail certain conditions regarding patient characteristics. Furthermore, we plan to extend our work by improving FCM's performance with random values for initial interconnections. Last but not least, we intend to insert into our proposed model DeepFCM image data and perform image classification with the application of FCMs, along with clinical data and CNN predictions and develop a robust hybrid method.

Acknowledgments. The research project was supported by the Hellenic Foundation for Research and Innovation (H.F.R.I.) under the "2nd Call for H.F.R.I. Research Projects to support Faculty Members & Researchers" (Project Number: 3656).

References

1. McCullough, P.A.: Coronary artery disease. Clin. J. Am. Soc. Nephrol. **2**, 611 (2007). https://doi.org/10.2215/CJN.03871106
2. Papandrianos, N., Papageorgiou, E.: Automatic diagnosis of coronary artery disease in SPECT myocardial perfusion imaging employing deep learning. Appl. Sci. **11**, 6362 (2021). https://doi.org/10.3390/app11146362
3. Apostolopoulos, I.D., Papathanasiou, N.D., Spyridonidis, T., Apostolopoulos, D.J.: Automatic characterization of myocardial perfusion imaging polar maps employing deep learning and data augmentation. Hell. J. Nucl. Med. **23**, 125–132 (2020). https://doi.org/10.1967/s002449912101
4. Zreik, M., et al.: Deep learning analysis of the myocardium in coronary CT angiography for identification of patients with functionally significant coronary artery stenosis. Med. Image Anal. **44**, 72–85 (2018). https://doi.org/10.1016/j.media.2017.11.008
5. Papandrianos, N.I., Apostolopoulos, I.D., Feleki, A., Apostolopoulos, D.J., Papageorgiou, E.I.: Deep learning exploration for SPECT MPI polar map images classification in coronary artery disease. Ann. Nucl. Med. **36**, 823–833 (2022). https://doi.org/10.1007/s12149-022-01762-4
6. Papandrianos, N.I., Feleki, A., Moustakidis, S., Papageorgiou, E.I., Apostolopoulos, I.D., Apostolopoulos, D.J.: An explainable classification method of SPECT myocardial perfusion images in nuclear cardiology using deep learning and grad-CAM. Appl. Sci. **12**, 7592 (2022). https://doi.org/10.3390/app12157592
7. Apostolopoulos, I.D., Groumpos, P.P.: Non - invasive modelling methodology for the diagnosis of coronary artery disease using fuzzy cognitive maps. Comput. Methods Biomech. Biomed. Eng. **23**, 879–887 (2020). https://doi.org/10.1080/10255842.2020.1768534
8. Papageorgiou, E.I., et al.: Brain tumor characterization using the soft computing technique of fuzzy cognitive maps. Appl. Soft Comput. **8**, 820–828 (2008). https://doi.org/10.1016/j.asoc.2007.06.006

9. Nasiriyan-Rad, H., Amirkhani, A., Naimi, A., Mohammadi, K.: Learning fuzzy cognitive map with PSO algorithm for grading celiac disease. In: 2016 23rd Iranian Conference on Biomedical Engineering and 2016 1st International Iranian Conference on Biomedical Engineering (ICBME), pp. 341–346 (2016). https://doi.org/10.1109/ICBME.2016.7890984

10. Papageorgiou, E.I., Kannappan, A.: Fuzzy cognitive map ensemble learning paradigm to solve classification problems: application to autism identification. Appl. Soft Comput. **12**, 3798–3809 (2012). https://doi.org/10.1016/j.asoc.2012.03.064

11. Papageorgiou, E.I., Papandrianos, N.I., Apostolopoulos, D.J., Vassilakos, P.J.: Fuzzy Cognitive Map based decision support system for thyroid diagnosis management. In: 2008 IEEE International Conference on Fuzzy Systems (IEEE World Congress on Computational Intelligence), pp. 1204–1211 (2008). https://doi.org/10.1109/FUZZY.2008.4630524

12. Carvajal, O., Melin, P., Miramontes, I., Prado-Arechiga, G.: Optimal design of a general type-2 fuzzy classifier for the pulse level and its hardware implementation. Eng. Appl. Artif. Intell. **97**, 104069 (2021). https://doi.org/10.1016/j.engappai.2020.104069

13. Guzmán, J.C., Miramontes, I., Melin, P., Prado-Arechiga, G.: Optimal genetic design of type-1 and interval type-2 fuzzy systems for blood pressure level classification. Axioms **8**, 8 (2019). https://doi.org/10.3390/axioms8010008

14. Miramontes, I., Melin, P.: Interval type-2 fuzzy approach for dynamic parameter adaptation in the bird swarm algorithm for the optimization of fuzzy medical classifier. Axioms **11**, 485 (2022). https://doi.org/10.3390/axioms11090485

15. Hoyos, W., Aguilar, J., Toro, M.: A clinical decision-support system for dengue based on fuzzy cognitive maps. Health Care Manag. Sci. **25**, 666–681 (2022). https://doi.org/10.1007/s10729-022-09611-6

16. Kosko, B.: Fuzzy cognitive maps. Int. J. Man-Mach. Stud. **24**, 65–75 (1986). https://doi.org/10.1016/S0020-7373(86)80040-2

17. Sovatzidi, G., Vasilakakis, M.D., Iakovidis, D.K.: IF^3: an interpretable feature fusion framework for lesion risk assessment based on auto-constructed fuzzy cognitive maps. In: Ali, S., van der Sommen, F., Papież, B.W., van Eijnatten, M., Jin, Y., Kolenbrander, I. (eds.) CaPTion 2022. LNCS, vol. 13581, pp. 77–86. Springer, Cham (2022). https://doi.org/10.1007/978-3-031-17979-2_8

18. Wang, D., Tan, D., Liu, L.: Particle swarm optimization algorithm: an overview. Soft. Comput. **22**(2), 387–408 (2017). https://doi.org/10.1007/s00500-016-2474-6

19. Raja, J.B., Pandian, S.C.: PSO-FCM based data mining model to predict diabetic disease. Comput. Methods Programs Biomed. **196**, 105659 (2020). https://doi.org/10.1016/j.cmpb.2020.105659

Discussing Uninorms on Bounded Lattices Using Closure and Interior Operators

Gül Deniz Çaylı[✉][iD]

Department of Mathematics, Faculty of Science, Karadeniz Technical University,
61080 Trabzon, Turkey
guldeniz.cayli@ktu.edu.tr

Abstract. Uninorms on bounded lattices have recently become a significant area of study. In the present study, we describe two new approaches for creating uninorms on bounded lattices, where some necessary and sufficient conditions are required. These structures use a t-conorm and an interior operator or a t-norm and a closure operator on a bounded lattice. The newly introduced classes of uninorms and the differences between them and already existing classes of uninorms are also illustrated on several examples.

Keywords: Bounded lattice · Construction method · Closure operator · Interior operator · Uninorm

1 Introduction

Triangular norms (t-norms, for short) and triangular conorms (t-conorms, for short) were first developed in the context of probabilistic metric spaces by Menger [30] in 1942 and Schweizer and Sklar [35] in 1961, respectively. In fuzzy set theory and fuzzy logic, t-norms and t-conorms operate effectively as natural extensions of logical connectives, i.e., conjunction and disjunction, respectively. As a result, these operators have been widely applied in many fields of research, including fuzzy set theory, fuzzy logic, fuzzy systems modeling, decision-making, probabilistic metric spaces, approximate reasoning, and information aggregation [3,20,25,28].

Yager and Rybalov [37] presented uninorms on the unit interval $[0,1]$ as aggregation functions concurrently generalizing t-norms and t-conorms in 1996, and Fodor et al. [23] investigated them thoroughly in 1997. Since then, they have been extensively involved in a wide range of research fields, including neural networks, fuzzy system modeling, decision-making, fuzzy mathematical morphology, fuzzy logic, and others [4,31,36,38]. Uninorms enable their neutral element to be anywhere in the unit interval rather than at point 1 (as in t-norms) or point 0 (as in t-conorms). There are various studies about uninorms (e.g., [15–17,19]).

Because bounded lattices are more general structures than the unit interval, generalizing binary aggregation operators from the unit interval to bounded lattices becomes an attractive issue. Karaçal and Mesiar [27] in 2015 modified the notion of uninorms from the real unit interval to bounded lattices. They also

S. Massanet et al. (Eds.): EUSFLAT 2023/AGOP 2023, LNCS 14069, pp. 26–38, 2023.
https://doi.org/10.1007/978-3-031-39965-7_3

discovered the smallest and greatest uninorms on bounded lattices. Recently, these operators on bounded lattices have received considerable interest, and numerous building approaches have been provided in the literature. Bodjanova and Kalina [6] introduced the structure of uninorms based on both t-norms and t-conorms on bounded lattices. Subsequently, Çaylı et al. [12] provided two construction methods for internal and locally internal uninorms on bounded lattices using only one of the t-norm and the t-conorm. Furthermore, Çaylı [9] investigated the classes of idempotent uninorms on bounded lattices. Dan et al. [13], and Dan and Hu [14] presented further characterizations of uninorms on bounded lattices. Other corresponding constructions of uninorms on bounded lattices can also be found in (e.g., $[1, 2, 7, 8, 10, 24, 26, 33, 39]$).

In a general topology, letting the set $K \neq \emptyset$ and $\wp(K)$ be the set of all subsets of K, if a map $int : \wp(K) \to \wp(K)$ (resp. $cl : \wp(K) \to \wp(K)$) is idempotent, isotone and contractive (resp. expansive), then it is said to be an interior (resp. closure) operator on $\wp(K)$. Both these maps can be applied for generating topologies on K [21]. In particular, from the set of all interior (closure) operators on $\wp(K)$ to one of all topologies on K, a one-to-one correspondence exists. That is to say that the interior (closure) operator on $\wp(K)$ can be generated by any topology on K. Notably, interior (closure) operators on a lattice $(\wp(K), \subseteq)$ can be described when the set intersection and union are meet and join, respectively. Thence, the interior (resp. closure) operator on $\wp(K)$ to a lattice L was generalized by Everett [22], where the condition $int(K) = K$ (resp. $cl(\emptyset) = \emptyset$) is removed.

Ouyang and Zhang [32] enhanced the generation methods for uninorms employing closure and interior operators on bounded lattices. They include those presented in [27] as a particular instance inside their constructions. In this situation, one may wonder if the interior and closure operators provide new classes of uninorms on bounded lattices. This thought inspires us to characterize two new classes of uninorms on bounded lattices in the present work using closure and interior operators. Characterization investigations are crucial working areas because they provide the uninorms on bounded lattices with the appropriate structures. To be more precise, we first introduce a new technique to get uninorms on a bounded lattice L with the neutral element $e \in L \backslash \{0_L, 1_L\}$, via a t-norm on $[0_L, e]^2$ and a closure operator defined on L. Then, by virtue of a t-conorm on $[e, 1_L]^2$ and an interior operator defined on L, we describe a dual construction of uninorms on L. In addition, we explore the relationship between our constructions and those introduced in [8, 11, 39]. We also show that the construction means in the present paper differ from the ones in [8, 11, 32, 39].

The remainder of this paper is structured as follows: In Sect. 2, we present some fundamental definitions and characteristics of uninorms on bounded lattices. In Sect. 3, we enhance two generation ways for uninorms on a bounded lattice L with the neutral element $e \in L \backslash \{0_L, 1_L\}$, where some necessary and sufficient conditions are required. These ways use an interior operator on L and a t-conorm on $[e, 1_L]^2$ or a closure operator on L and a t-norm on $[0_L, e]^2$. We also provide some illustrative examples to highlight the differences between our approaches and those already in use. Some of our discussion findings are mentioned in the concluding section.

2 Preliminaries

In this section, we recall some basic concepts and results related to bounded lattices (for more information, see, e.g., [5]) and uninorms on them.

A poset $(L, \leqslant)$ is a nonempty set L equipped with an order relation $\leqslant$ (i.e., a reflexive, antisymmetric and transitive binary relation). For $a, b \in L$, the notation $a < b$ means that $a \leqslant b$ and $a \neq b$. The notation $a \parallel b$ implies that a and b are incomparable, i.e., neither $a \leqslant b$ nor $b < a$. I_a denotes the set of all elements incomparable with a, i.e., $I_a = \{u \in L : u \parallel a\}$. An element a of a subset P of L is called a smallest (resp. greatest) element of P if $x \geqslant a$ (resp. $x \leqslant a$) for all $x \in P$. L is called bounded if it has a greatest (also known as top) element and a smallest (also known as bottom) element.

A lattice $(L, \leqslant)$ is a poset such that any two elements a and b have a greatest lower bound (called meet or infimum), denoted by $a \wedge b$, as well as a smallest upper bound (called join or supremum), denoted by $a \vee b$. In this paper, unless otherwise stated, L denotes a bounded lattice $(L, \leqslant, \wedge, \vee)$ with a top element 1_L and a bottom element 0_L.

For $a, b \in L$ with $a \leqslant b$, the subinterval $[a, b]$ of L is defined such that

$$[a, b] = \{u \in L : a \leqslant u \leqslant b\}.$$

The subintervals $[a, b[$, $]a, b]$, and $]a, b[$ of L can be defined similarly. $([a, b], \leqslant , \wedge, \vee)$ is a bounded lattice with the top element b and the bottom element a.

Definition 1 ([12,27]). *A function $U : L \times L \to L$ is said to be a uninorm if, for any $a, b, c \in L$, the following conditions are fulfilled:*

 (i) $U(b, a) = U(a, b)$ (commutativity);
 (ii) If $b \leqslant a$, then $U(b, c) \leqslant U(a, c)$ (increasingness);
(iii) $U(b, U(a, c)) = U(U(b, a), c)$ (associativity);
 (iv) There is an element $e \in L$, called a neutral element, such that $U(b, e) = b$.

In particular, a uninorm U is a t-norm T (resp. t-conorm S) if $e = 1_L$ (resp. $e = 0_L$) (for more information about t-norms and t-conorms, see, e.g., [29,34]).

Example 1. (i) The largest t-norm is $T^{\wedge}$ on $[a, b]^2$ defined such that $T^{\wedge}(x, y) = x \wedge y$ for all $x, y \in [a, b]$, while the smallest one T^W on $[a, b]^2$ takes the value of $x \wedge y$ if $b \in \{x, y\}$ and a otherwise. Thus, we obtain that $T^W \leqslant T \leqslant T^{\wedge}$ for any t-norm T on $[a, b]^2$.

(ii) The smallest t-conorm is $S^{\vee}$ on $[a, b]^2$ defined such that $S^{\vee}(x, y) = x \vee y$ for all $x, y \in [a, b]$, while the largest one S^W on $[a, b]^2$ takes the value of $x \vee y$ if $a \in \{x, y\}$ and b otherwise. Thus, we obtain that $S^{\vee} \leqslant S \leqslant S^W$ for any t-conorm S on $[a, b]^2$.

Definition 2 ([18,22]). *A function $cl : L \to L$ is said to be a closure operator if, for any $a, b \in L$, the following conditions are fulfilled:*

 (i) Expansion: $b \leqslant cl(b)$.

(ii) Preservation of join: $cl(a \vee b) = cl(a) \vee cl(b)$.
(iii) Idempotence: $cl\,(cl(b)) = cl(b)$.

By (i), the case (iii) equals to $cl\,(cl(b)) \leqslant cl(b)$. Additionally, (ii) implies (ii)$'$: $cl(a) \leqslant cl(b)$ if $a \leqslant b$. Birkhoff [5] defines a closure operator by (i), (ii)$'$ and (iii).

Definition 3 ([18,22]). *A function* $int : L \to L$ *is said to be an interior operator if, for any* $a,b \in L$, *the following conditions are fulfilled:*

(i) Contraction: $int(b) \leqslant b$.
(ii) Preservation of meet: $int(a \wedge b) = int(a) \wedge int(b)$.
(iii) Idempotence: $int\,(int(b)) = int(b)$.

By (i), the case (iii) equals to $int(b) \leqslant int\,(int(b))$. Additionally, (ii) implies (ii)$'$: $int(a) \leqslant int(b)$ if $a \leqslant b$. Birkhoff [5] defines an interior operator by (i), (ii)$'$ and (iii).

3   Construction Approaches for Uninorms

In this section, we introduce in Theorem 1 a novel method for getting the family of uninorms $U_{(T,cl)}$ on a bounded lattice L with a neutral element $e \in L\backslash\{0_L, 1_L\}$. The uninorm $U_{(T,cl)}$ is derived from a t-norm T on $[0_L, e]^2$ and a closure operator cl on L. In addition, we propose in Theorem 2 a different method to obtain the family of uninorms $U_{(S,int)}$ on L with a neutral element $e \in L\backslash\{0_L, 1_L\}$. This construction is based on the existence of a t-conorm S on $[e, 1_L]^2$ and an interior operator int on L.

Theorem 1. *Let* $e \in L\backslash\{0_L, 1_L\}$, $T : [0_L, e]^2 \to [0_L, e]$ *be a t-norm and* $cl : L \to L$ *be a closure operator. The function* $U_{(T,cl)} : L \times L \to L$, *given by the formula (1), is a uninorm on* L *with a neutral element* e *iff* $cl\,(x) \vee cl\,(y) \in I_e \cup \{1_L\}$ *and* $x > z$ *for all* $x, y \in I_e$, $z \in [0_L, e[$.

$$U_{(T,cl)}\,(a,b) = \begin{cases} T\,(a,b) & if\ (a,b) \in [0_L, e]^2, \\ 1_L & if\ (a,b) \in]e, 1_L]^2, \\ cl\,(a) \vee cl\,(b) & if\ (a,b) \in]e, 1_L] \times I_e \cup I_e \times]e, 1_L] \cup I_e \times I_e, \\ a & if\ (a,b) \in (I_e \cup [e, 1_L]) \times \{e\}, \\ b & if\ (a,b) \in \{e\} \times (I_e \cup [e, 1_L]), \\ a \wedge b & otherwise. \end{cases} \quad (1)$$

Remark 1. The uninorm $U_{(T,cl)} : L \times L \to L$ in Theorem 1 can be also defined by

$$U_{(T,cl)}\,(a,b) = \begin{cases} T\,(a,b) & if\ (a,b) \in [0_L, e]^2, \\ 1_L & if\ (a,b) \in]e, 1_L]^2, \\ a & \begin{aligned} if\ (a,b) &\in [0_L, e[\times I_e \cup [0_L, e[\times [e, 1_L] \\ &\cup (I_e \cup [e, 1_L]) \times \{e\}, \end{aligned} \\ b & \begin{aligned} if\ (a,b) &\in I_e \times [0_L, e[\cup [e, 1_L] \times [0_L, e[\\ &\cup \{e\} \times (I_e \cup [e, 1_L]), \end{aligned} \\ cl\,(a) \vee cl\,(b) & if\ (a,b) \in I_e \times]e, 1_L] \cup]e, 1_L] \times I_e \cup I_e \times I_e. \end{cases}$$

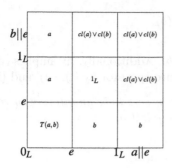

Fig. 1. Uninorm $U_{(T,cl)}$ on L

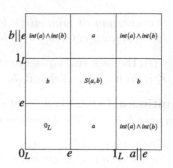

Fig. 2. Uninorm $U_{(S,int)}$ on L

Remark 2. The structure of the uninorm $U_{(T,cl)} : L \times L \to L$ is illustrated in Fig. 1.

If we take in Theorem 1 the t-norm $T : [0_L, e]^2 \to [0_L, e]$ stated by $T = T^\wedge$, we define the corresponding uninorm as the following structure:

Corollary 1. *Let* $e \in L \backslash \{0_L, 1_L\}$ *and* $cl : L \to L$ *be a closure operator. The function* $U_{(cl)} : L \times L \to L$, *given by the formula (2), is a uninorm on L with a neutral element e iff $cl(x) \vee cl(y) \in I_e \cup \{1_L\}$ and $x > z$ for all $x, y \in I_e$, $z \in [0_L, e[$.*

$$
U_{(cl)}(a,b) = \begin{cases}
1_L & if \ (a,b) \in]e, 1_L]^2, \\
cl(a) \vee cl(b) & if \ (a,b) \in]e, 1_L] \times I_e \cup I_e \times]e, 1_L] \cup I_e \times I_e, \\
a & if \ (a,b) \in (I_e \cup [e, 1_L]) \times \{e\}, \\
b & if \ (a,b) \in \{e\} \times (I_e \cup [e, 1_L]), \\
a \wedge b & otherwise.
\end{cases} \tag{2}
$$

If we allow in Theorem 1 the element $e \in L \backslash \{0_L, 1_L\}$ to be an atom, we define the corresponding uninorm as the following structure:

Corollary 2. *Let* $e \in L \backslash \{0_L, 1_L\}$ *be an atom and* $cl : L \to L$ *be a closure operator. The function* $U_{(e,cl)} : L \times L \to L$, *given by the formula (3), is a uninorm on L with a neutral element e iff $cl(x) \vee cl(y) \in I_e \cup \{1_L\}$ for all $x, y \in I_e$.*

$$
U_{(e,cl)}(a,b) = \begin{cases}
1_L & if \ (a,b) \in]e, 1_L]^2, \\
cl(a) \vee cl(b) & if \ (a,b) \in]e, 1_L] \times I_e \cup I_e \times]e, 1_L] \cup I_e \times I_e, \\
a & if \ (a,b) \in (I_e \cup [e, 1_L]) \times \{e\}, \\
b & if \ (a,b) \in \{e\} \times (I_e \cup [e, 1_L]), \\
0_L & otherwise.
\end{cases} \tag{3}
$$

Remark 3. Let $e \in L \backslash \{0_L, 1_L\}$, $S : [e, 1_L]^2 \to [e, 1_L]$ be a t-conorm and $cl : L \to L$ be a closure operator. We introduce in Theorem 1 a new construction approach for uninorms on bounded lattices. To be more precise, (i) If $(a,b) \in$ $]e, 1_L]^2 \cup]e, 1_L] \times I_e \cup I_e \times]e, 1_L] \cup I_e^2$, the method in [8, Theorem 8] puts for $U(a,b)$

the value of $S(a \vee e, b \vee e)$. On the other hand, in our construction $U_{(T,cl)}(a,b) = 1_L$ for $(a,b) \in]e, 1_L]^2$ and $U_{(T,cl)}(a,b) = cl\,(a) \vee cl\,(b)$ for $(a,b) \in]e, 1_L] \times I_e \cup I_e \times]e, 1_L] \cup I_e^2$. However, both constructions coincide in the remaining domains;

(ii) If $(a,b) \in]e, 1_L]^2$, the method in [11, Theorem 3.1] puts for $U(a,b)$ the value of $cl\,(a) \vee cl\,(b)$ while our construction puts for $U_{(T,cl)}(a,b)$ the value 1_L. However, both constructions coincide in the remaining domains;

(iii) If $(a,b) \in]e, 1_L]^2$ (resp. $(a,b) \in]e, 1_L] \times I_e \cup I_e \times]e, 1_L]$), the method in [11, Theorem 3.4] puts for $U(a,b)$ the value of $S(a,b)$ (resp. $a \vee b$) while our construction puts for $U_{(T,cl)}(a,b)$ the value 1_L (resp. $cl\,(a) \vee cl\,(b)$). However, both constructions coincide in the remaining domains;

(iv) If $(a,b) \in]e, 1_L] \times I_e \cup I_e \times]e, 1_L]$, the method in [39, Proposition 3.5] puts for $U(a,b)$ the value 1_L while our construction puts for $U_{(T,cl)}(a,b)$ the value of $cl\,(a) \vee cl\,(b)$. However, both constructions coincide in the remaining domains.

Remark 4. Let $e \in L \backslash \{0_L, 1_L\}$. Then we have the following statements:

(1) If the closure operator $cl : L \to L$ is defined by $cl(x) = 1_L$ for all $x \in L$,

(1-i) the uninorm $U_{(T,cl)}$ in Theorem 1 coincides with the uninorms in [11, Theorem 3.1] and [39, Proposition 3.5];

(1-ii) the uninorm $U_{(T,cl)}$ in Theorem 1 coincides with the uninorm in [8, Theorem 8], where e is a coatom;

(1-iii) the uninorm $U_{(T,cl)}$ in Theorem 1 coincides with the uninorms in [8, Theorem 8] and [39, Proposition 3.6], where the t-conorm $S : [e, 1_L]^2 \to [e, 1_L]$ is $S = S^W$;

(1-iv) the uninorm $U_{(T,cl)}$ in Theorem 1 coincides with the uninorm in [11, Theorem 3.4], where $y \parallel z$ for all $y \in [e, 1_L[$, $z \in I_e$, and the t-conorm $S : [e, 1_L]^2 \to [e, 1_L]$ is $S = S^W$.

(2) If the closure operator $cl : L \to L$ is defined by $cl(x) = x$ for all $x \in L$, the uninorm $U_{(T,cl)}$ in Theorem 1 coincides with the uninorm in [11, Theorem 3.4], where the t-conorm $S : [e, 1_L]^2 \to [e, 1_L]$ is $S = S^W$.

(3) If e is a coatom, the uninorm $U_{(T,cl)}$ in Theorem 1 coincides with the uninorms in [11, Theorems 3.1 and 3.4] and [39, Propositions 3.5 and 3.6].

We should point out that in [39, Proposition 3.6] it is enough to select S^W as a t-conorm on $[e, 1_L]^2$ and the construction in Theorem 1 is obtained. However, the construction in Theorem 1 can be used also in the case when the condition $f \parallel g$ for all $f \in I_e$ and $g \in [e, 1[$ is not satisfied.

Notice that the uninorm constructed by the method in Theorem 1 does not have to coincide with those introduced in [8, Theorem 8], [11, Theorems 3.1 and 3.4], and [39, Propositions 3.5 and 3.6]. In the following examples, we demonstrate this observation.

Example 2. Consider the lattice L_1 characterized by Hasse diagram in Fig. 3. Identify the closure operator $cl : L_1 \to L_1$ by $cl(0_{L_1}) = 0_{L_1}$, $cl\,(e) = e$, $cl\,(n) = cl\,(m) = m$, $cl\,(p) = cl\,(q) = q$ and $cl(1_{L_1}) = 1_{L_1}$. By virtue of the structure determined in Theorem 1, the uninorm $U^1_{(T,cl)} : L_1 \times L_1 \to L_1$ is presented in Table 1.

Table 1. Uninorm $U^1_{(T,cl)}$ on L_1

$U^1_{(T,cl)}$	0_{L_1}	e	n	m	p	q	1_{L_1}
0_{L_1}	0_{L_1}	0_{L_1}	0_{L_1}	0_{L_1}	0_{L_1}	0_{L_1}	0_{L_1}
e	0_{L_1}	e	n	m	p	q	1_{L_1}
n	0_{L_1}	n	m	m	1_{L_1}	1_{L_1}	1_{L_1}
m	0_{L_1}	m	m	m	1_{L_1}	1_{L_1}	1_{L_1}
p	0_{L_1}	p	1_{L_1}	1_{L_1}	1_{L_1}	1_{L_1}	1_{L_1}
q	0_{L_1}	q	1_{L_1}	1_{L_1}	1_{L_1}	1_{L_1}	1_{L_1}
1_{L_1}	0_{L_1}	1_{L_1}	1_{L_1}	1_{L_1}	1_{L_1}	1_{L_1}	1_{L_1}

Table 2. Uninorm U^1 on L_1

U^1	0_{L_1}	e	n	m	p	q	1_{L_1}
0_{L_1}	0_{L_1}	0_{L_1}	0_{L_1}	0_{L_1}	0_{L_1}	0_{L_1}	0_{L_1}
e	0_{L_1}	e	n	m	p	q	1_{L_1}
n	0_{L_1}	n	1_{L_1}	1_{L_1}	1_{L_1}	1_{L_1}	1_{L_1}
m	0_{L_1}	m	1_{L_1}	1_{L_1}	1_{L_1}	1_{L_1}	1_{L_1}
p	0_{L_1}	p	1_{L_1}	1_{L_1}	p	q	1_{L_1}
q	0_{L_1}	q	1_{L_1}	1_{L_1}	q	q	1_{L_1}
1_{L_1}	0_{L_1}	1_{L_1}	1_{L_1}	1_{L_1}	1_{L_1}	1_{L_1}	1_{L_1}

Table 3. Uninorm U^2 on L_1

U^2	0_{L_1}	e	n	m	p	q	1_{L_1}
0_{L_1}	0_{L_1}	0_{L_1}	0_{L_1}	0_{L_1}	0_{L_1}	0_{L_1}	0_{L_1}
e	0_{L_1}	e	n	m	p	q	1_{L_1}
n	0_{L_1}	n	m	m	1_{L_1}	1_{L_1}	1_{L_1}
m	0_{L_1}	m	m	m	1_{L_1}	1_{L_1}	1_{L_1}
p	0_{L_1}	p	1_{L_1}	1_{L_1}	p	q	1_{L_1}
q	0_{L_1}	q	1_{L_1}	1_{L_1}	q	q	1_{L_1}
1_{L_1}	0_{L_1}	1_{L_1}	1_{L_1}	1_{L_1}	1_{L_1}	1_{L_1}	1_{L_1}

Table 4. Uninorm U^3 on L_1

U^3	0_{L_1}	e	n	m	p	q	1_{L_1}
0_{L_1}	0_{L_1}	0_{L_1}	0_{L_1}	0_{L_1}	0_{L_1}	0_{L_1}	0_{L_1}
e	0_{L_1}	e	n	m	p	q	1_{L_1}
n	0_{L_1}	n	m	m	1_{L_1}	1_{L_1}	1_{L_1}
m	0_{L_1}	m	m	m	1_{L_1}	1_{L_1}	1_{L_1}
p	0_{L_1}	p	1_{L_1}	1_{L_1}	q	q	1_{L_1}
q	0_{L_1}	q	1_{L_1}	1_{L_1}	q	q	1_{L_1}
1_{L_1}	0_{L_1}	1_{L_1}	1_{L_1}	1_{L_1}	1_{L_1}	1_{L_1}	1_{L_1}

If we utilize the construction means in [8, Theorem 8] and [39, Proposition 3.6], respectively, the uninorms U^1, $U^2 : L_1 \times L_1 \to L_1$ are presented in Tables 2 and 3, respectively, where the t-conorm $S : [e, 1_{L_1}]^2 \to [e, 1_{L_1}]$ is $S = S^\vee$. By virtue of the method in [11, Theorem 3.1], the uninorm $U^3 : L_1 \times L_1 \to L_1$ is presented in Table 4. Then we have the following facts:

(i) the uninorm $U^1_{(T,cl)}$ satisfies that $U^1_{(T,cl)}(n,m) = m$ and $U^1_{(T,cl)}(p,q) = 1_{L_1}$;
(ii) the uninorm U^1 satisfies that $U^1(n,m) = 1_{L_1}$;
(iii) the uninorms U^2 and U^3 satisfy that $U^2(p,q) = U^3(p,q) = q$.

Hence, $U^1_{(T,cl)}$ differs from the uninorms U^1, U^2 and U^3 on L_1.

Example 3. Consider the lattice L_2 characterized by Hasse diagram in Fig. 4. Identify the closure operator $cl : L_2 \to L_2$ by $cl(0_{L_2}) = 0_{L_2}$, $cl(e) = cl(m) = cl(n) = cl(n) = s$, $cl(k) = k$ and $cl(1_{L_2}) = 1_{L_2}$. By virtue of the structure determined in Theorem 1, the uninorm $U^2_{(T,cl)} : L_2 \times L_2 \to L_2$ is presented in Table 5.

If we utilize the construction means in [11, Theorem 3.4] and [39, Proposition 3.5], respectively, the uninorms U^4, $U^5 : L_2 \times L_2 \to L_2$ are presented in Tables 6 and 7, respectively, where the t-conorm $S : [e, 1_{L_2}]^2 \to [e, 1_{L_2}]$ is $S = S^\vee$. Then we get the following facts:

Table 5. Uninorm $U^2_{(T,cl)}$ on L_2

$U^2_{(T,cl)}$	0_{L_2}	e	k	m	n	s	1_{L_2}
0_{L_2}	0_{L_2}	0_{L_2}	0_{L_2}	0_{L_2}	0_{L_2}	0_{L_2}	0_{L_2}
e	0_{L_2}	e	k	m	n	s	1_{L_2}
k	0_{L_2}	k	k	s	s	s	1_{L_2}
m	0_{L_2}	m	s	1_{L_2}	1_{L_2}	1_{L_2}	1_{L_2}
n	0_{L_2}	n	s	1_{L_2}	1_{L_2}	1_{L_2}	1_{L_2}
s	0_{L_2}	s	s	1_{L_2}	1_{L_2}	1_{L_2}	1_{L_2}
1_{L_2}	0_{L_2}	1_{L_2}	1_{L_2}	1_{L_2}	1_{L_2}	1_{L_2}	1_{L_2}

Table 6. Uninorm U^4 on L_2

U^4	0_{L_2}	e	k	m	n	s	1_{L_2}
0_{L_2}	0_{L_2}	0_{L_2}	0_{L_2}	0_{L_2}	0_{L_2}	0_{L_2}	0_{L_2}
e	0_{L_2}	e	k	m	n	s	1_{L_2}
k	0_{L_2}	k	k	m	n	s	1_{L_2}
m	0_{L_2}	m	m	m	n	s	1_{L_2}
n	0_{L_2}	n	n	n	n	s	1_{L_2}
s	0_{L_2}	s	s	s	s	s	1_{L_2}
1_{L_2}	0_{L_2}	1_{L_2}	1_{L_2}	1_{L_2}	1_{L_2}	1_{L_2}	1_{L_2}

(i) the uninorm $U^2_{(T,cl)}$ satisfies that $U^2_{(T,cl)}(k,n) = s$;

(ii) the uninorms U^4 and U^5 satisfy that $U^4(k,n) = n$ and $U^5(k,n) = 1_{L_2}$.

Hence, $U^2_{(T,cl)}$ differs from the uninorms U^4 and U^5 on L_2.

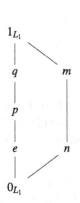

Fig. 3. The lattice L_1

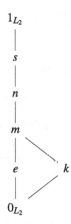

Fig. 4. The lattice L_2

Remark 5. The formula (1) in Theorem 1 clearly shows that the uninorm $U_{(T,cl)}$ coincides with the t-conorm S^W on $[e, 1_L]^2$. If we change the construction method in Theorem 1 in such a way that it will differ only on $[e, 1_L]^2$ where we will take some t-conorm S then this t-conorm cannot be arbitrary. In order to obtain the associativity and increasingness of $U_{(T,cl)}$, this t-conorm satisfies the following conditions:

(i) $S(a, cl(b \vee c)) = cl(S(a,b) \vee c)$ for $a, b \in [e, 1]$ and $c \in I_e$;

(ii) $S(a, cl(b \vee c)) = S(cl(a \vee b), c)$ for $b \in I_e$ and $a, c \in [e, 1]$;

Table 7. Uninorm U^5 on L_2

U^5	0_{L_2}	e	k	m	n	s	1_{L_2}
0_{L_2}	0_{L_2}	0_{L_2}	0_{L_2}	0_{L_2}	0_{L_2}	0_{L_2}	0_{L_2}
e	0_{L_2}	e	k	m	n	s	1_{L_2}
k	0_{L_2}	k	k	1_{L_2}	1_{L_2}	1_{L_2}	1_{L_2}
m	0_{L_2}	m	1_{L_2}	1_{L_2}	1_{L_2}	1_{L_2}	1_{L_2}
n	0_{L_2}	n	1_{L_2}	1_{L_2}	1_{L_2}	1_{L_2}	1_{L_2}
s	0_{L_2}	s	1_{L_2}	1_{L_2}	1_{L_2}	1_{L_2}	1_{L_2}
1_{L_2}	0_{L_2}	1_{L_2}	1_{L_2}	1_{L_2}	1_{L_2}	1_{L_2}	1_{L_2}

Table 8. T-conorm S' on $[e, 1_{L_2}]^2$

S'	e	m	n	s	1_{L_2}
e	e	m	n	s	1_{L_2}
m	m	n	n	1_{L_2}	1_{L_2}
n	n	n	n	1_{L_2}	1_{L_2}
s	s	1_{L_2}	1_{L_2}	1_{L_2}	1_{L_2}
1_{L_2}	1_{L_2}	1_{L_2}	1_{L_2}	1_{L_2}	1_{L_2}

(iii) $S(b,c) \geq cl(a \vee c)$ for $a \in I_e$ and $b, c \in [e, 1]$ such that $b \geq a$.

To exemplify this assertion, for the lattice L_2 in Fig. 4, the closure operator $cl : L_2 \to L_2$ is defined as in Example 3. Presume that the uninorm $U_{(T,cl)} \mid [e, 1_{L_2}]^2$ is the t-conorm $S' : [e, 1_{L_2}]^2 \to [e, 1_{L_2}]$ represented in Table 8 .

If we use the building technique in Theorem 1, then we get that

$$U_{(T,cl)}\left(U_{(T,cl)}(n,m),k\right) = U_{(T,cl)}\left(S'(n,m),k\right) = U_{(T,cl)}(n,k) = cl(n) \vee cl(k) = s,$$

and

$$U_{(T,cl)}\left(n, U_{(T,cl)}(m,k)\right) = U_{(T,cl)}(n, cl(m) \vee cl(k)) = U_{(T,cl)}(n,s) = S'(n,s) = 1_{L_2}.$$

It contradicts the associativity property of $U_{(T,cl)}$.

We suggest in Theorem 2 a dual construction method for uninorms on bounded lattices. Namely, based on a t-conorm S on $[e, 1_L]^2$ and an interior operator int on L, we define the family of uninorm $U_{(S,int)}$ on L with a neutral element $e \in L \backslash \{0_L, 1_L\}$.

Theorem 2. Let $e \in L \backslash \{0_L, 1_L\}$, $S : [e, 1_L]^2 \to [e, 1_L]$ be a t-conorm and $int : L \to L$ be an interior operator. The function $U_{(S,int)} : L \times L \to L$, given by the formula (4), is a uninorm on L with a neutral element e iff $int(x) \wedge int(y) \in I_e \cup \{0_L\}$ and $x < z$ for all $x, y \in I_e$, $z \in]e, 1_L]$.

$$U_{(S,int)}(a,b) = \begin{cases} S(a,b) & if \ (a,b) \in [e, 1_L]^2, \\ 0_L & if \ (a,b) \in [0_L, e[^2, \\ int(a) \wedge int(b) & if \ (a,b) \in I_e \times [0_L, e[\cup [0_L, e[\times I_e \cup I_e \times I_e, \\ a & if \ (a,b) \in (I_e \cup [0_L, e]) \times \{e\}, \\ b & if \ (a,b) \in \{e\} \times (I_e \cup [0_L, e]), \\ a \vee b & otherwise. \end{cases} \tag{4}$$

Remark 6. The uninorm $U_{(S,int)} : L \times L \to L$ in Theorem 2 can be also defined by

$$U_{(S,int)}(a,b) = \begin{cases} S(a,b) & if\ (a,b) \in [e,1_L]^2, \\ 0_L & if\ (a,b) \in [0_L,e[^2, \\ a & if\ (a,b) \in]e,1_L] \times I_e \cup]e,1_L] \times [0_L,e] \\ & \quad \cup (I_e \cup [0_L,e]) \times \{e\}, \\ b & if\ (a,b) \in I_e \times]e,1_L] \cup [0_L,e] \times]e,1_L] \\ & \quad \cup \{e\} \times (I_e \cup [0_L,e]), \\ int(a) \wedge int(b) & if\ (a,b) \in I_e \times [0_L,e[\cup [0_L,e[\times I_e \cup I_e \times I_e. \end{cases}$$

Remark 7. The structure of the uninorm $U_{(S,int)} : L \times L \to L$ is illustrated in Fig. 2.

If we take in Theorem 2 the t-conorm $S : [e,1_L]^2 \to [e,1_L]$ given by $S = S^\vee$, we define the corresponding uninorm as the following structure:

Corollary 3. *Let $e \in L\backslash\{0_L,1_L\}$ and $int : L \to L$ be an interior operator. The function $U_{(int)} : L \times L \to L$, given by the formula (5), is a uninorm on L with a neutral element e iff $int(x) \wedge int(y) \in I_e \cup \{0_L\}$ and $x < z$ for all $x,y \in I_e$, $z \in]e,1_L]$.*

$$U_{(int)}(a,b) = \begin{cases} 0_L & if\ (a,b) \in [0_L,e[^2, \\ int(a) \wedge int(b) & if\ (a,b) \in I_e \times [0_L,e[\cup [0_L,e[\times I_e \cup I_e \times I_e, \\ a & if\ (a,b) \in (I_e \cup [0_L,e]) \times \{e\}, \\ b & if\ (a,b) \in \{e\} \times (I_e \cup [0_L,e]), \\ a \vee b & otherwise. \end{cases} \quad (5)$$

If we allow in Theorem 2 the element $e \in L\backslash\{0_L,1_L\}$ to be a coatom, we define the corresponding uninorm as the following structure:

Corollary 4. *Let $e \in L\backslash\{0_L,1_L\}$ be a coatom and $int : L \to L$ be an interior operator. The function $U_{(e,int)} : L \times L \to L$, given by the formula (6), is a uninorm on L with a neutral element e iff $int(x) \wedge int(y) \in I_e \cup \{0_L\}$ for all $x,y \in I_e$.*

$$U_{(e,int)}(a,b) = \begin{cases} 0_L & if\ (a,b) \in [0_L,e[^2, \\ int(a) \wedge int(b) & if\ (a,b) \in I_e \times [0_L,e[\cup [0_L,e[\times I_e \cup I_e \times I_e, \\ a & if\ (a,b) \in (I_e \cup [0_L,e]) \times \{e\}, \\ b & if\ (a,b) \in \{e\} \times (I_e \cup [0_L,e]), \\ 1_L & otherwise. \end{cases} \quad (6)$$

Similarly to Examples 2 and 3, we can show that the uninorm obtained via the approach in Theorem 2 does not have to coincide with the ones introduced by [8, Theorem 11], [11, Theorems 3.10 and 3.12], and [39, Corollaries 4.2 and 4.4].

Remark 8. Let $e \in L\backslash\{0_L,1_L\}$, $cl : L \to L$ be a closure operator, and $int : L \to L$ be an interior operator. Uninorms obtained by the methods in Theorems 1 and 2 do not have to coincide with those introduced by [32, Theorems 4.1 and 5.1]. Namely, for any $x \in I_e$

36   G. D. Çaylı

(i) the uninorm $U_{(T,cl)}$ in Theorem 1 satisfies that $U_{(T,cl)}(0_L, 1_L) = 0_L$ and $U_{(T,cl)}(1_L, x) = 1_L$;
(ii) the uninorm $U_{(S,int)}$ in Theorem 2 satisfies that $U_{(S,int)}(0_L, 1_L) = 1_L$ and $U_{(S,int)}(0_L, x) = 0_L$;
(iii) the uninorm U in [32, Theorem 4.1] satisfies that $U(0_L, 1_L) = 1_L$ and $U(0_L, x) = x$;
(iv) the uninorm U in [32, Theorem 5.1] satisfies that $U(0_L, 1_L) = 0_L$ and $U(1_L, x) = x$.

Remark 9. The formula (4) in Theorem 2 clearly shows that the uninorm $U_{(S,int)}$ coincides with the t-norm T^W on $[0_L, e]^2$. If we change the construction method in Theorem 2 in such a way that it will differ only on $[0_L, e]^2$ where we will take some t-norm T then this t-norm cannot be arbitrary. In order to obtain the associativity and increasingness of $U_{(S,int)}$, this t-norm satisfies the following conditions:

(i) $T(a, int(b \wedge c)) = int(T(a, b) \wedge c)$ for $a, b \in [0, e]$ and $c \in I_e$;
(ii) $T(a, int(b \wedge c)) = T(int(a \wedge b), c)$ for $b \in I_e$ and $a, c \in [0, e]$;
(iii) $T(a, c) \leq int(b \wedge c)$ for $b \in I_e$ and $a, c \in [0, e]$ such that $a \leq b$.

To exemplify this assertion, take into consideration the lattice $L_3 = \{0_{L_3}, p, q, e, 1_{L_3}\}$ being $0_{L_3} < p < e < 1_{L_3}$, $p < q < 1_{L_3}$, $q \| e$. Identify the interior operator $int : L_3 \to L_3$ by $int(0_{L_3}) = int(p) = int(q) = 0_{L_3}$, $int(e) = e$ and $int(1_{L_3}) = 1_{L_3}$. Presume that the uninorm $U_{(S,int)} \mid [0_{L_3}, e]^2$ is the t-norm $T^\wedge : [0_{L_3}, e]^2 \to [0_{L_3}, e]$. If we apply the generation tool in Theorem 2, we get that

$$U_{(S,int)}(p, p) = T^\wedge(p, p) = p > 0_{L_3} = int(p) \wedge int(q) = U_{(S,int)}(p, q),$$

for $p < q$. It contradicts the increasingness property of $U_{(S,int)}$.

4 Conclusion

This paper characterized two novel classes of uninorms on bounded lattices via the closure and interior operators. We presented two techniques for getting uninorms on a bounded lattice L with a neutral element $e \in L\setminus\{0_L, 1_L\}$, where some necessary and sufficient conditions are required. It should be pointed out that our techniques exploit a t-norm on $[0_L, e]^2$ and a closure operator on L or a t-conorm on $[e, 1_L]^2$ and an interior operator on L. Furthermore, we added some corresponding examples in order to show that our tools do not have to coincide with the existing ones in [8,11,32,39].

References

1. Aşıcı, E., Mesiar, R.: On the construction of uninorms on bounded lattices. Fuzzy Sets Syst. **408**, 65–85 (2021)

2. Aşıcı, E., Mesiar, R.: On generating uninorms on some special classes of bounded lattices. Fuzzy Sets Syst. **439**, 102–125 (2022)
3. Beliakov, G., Pradera, A., Calvo, T.: Aggregation Functions: A Guide for Practitioners. Springer, Berlin (2007). https://doi.org/10.1007/978-3-540-73721-6
4. Benítez, J.M., Castro, J.L., Requena, I.: Are artificial neural networks black boxes? IEEE Trans. Neural Netw. **8**, 1156–1163 (1997)
5. Birkhoff, G.: Lattice Theory. American Mathematical Society Colloquium Publishers, Providence (1967)
6. Bodjanova, S., Kalina, M.: Uninorms on bounded lattices – recent development. In: Kacprzyk, J., Szmidt, E., Zadrożny, S., Atanassov, K.T., Krawczak, M. (eds.) IWIFSGN/EUSFLAT -2017. AISC, vol. 641, pp. 224–234. Springer, Cham (2018). https://doi.org/10.1007/978-3-319-66830-7_21
7. Bodjanova, S., Kalina, M.: Uninorms on bounded lattices with given underlying operations. In: Halaš, R., et al. (eds.) AGOP 2019, AISC, vol. 981, pp. 183–194. Springer, Cham (2019). https://doi.org/10.1007/978-3-030-19494-9_17
8. Çaylı, G.D.: Alternative approaches for generating uninorms on bounded lattices. Inf. Sci. **488**, 111–139 (2019)
9. Çaylı, G.D.: New methods to construct uninorms on bounded lattices. Int. J. Approx. Reason. **115**, 254–264 (2019)
10. Çaylı, G.D.: Uninorms on bounded lattices with the underlying t-norms and t-conorms. Fuzzy Sets Syst. **395**, 107–129 (2020)
11. Çaylı, G.D.: New construction approaches of uninorms on bounded lattices. Int. J. Gen Syst **50**, 139–158 (2021)
12. Çaylı, G.D., Karaçal, F., Mesiar, R.: On internal and locally internal uninorms on bounded lattices. Int. J. Gen Syst **48**, 235–259 (2019)
13. Dan, Y., Hu, B.Q., Qiao, J.: New constructions of uninorms on bounded lattices. Int. J. Approx. Reason. **110**, 185–209 (2019)
14. Dan, Y., Hu, B.Q.: A new structure for uninorms on bounded lattices. Fuzzy Sets Syst. **386**, 77–94 (2020)
15. De Baets, B.: Idempotent uninorms. Eur. J. Oper. Res. **118**, 631–642 (1999)
16. De Baets, B., Fodor, J., Ruiz-Aguilera, D., Torrens, J.: Idempotent uninorms on finite ordinal scales. Int. J. Uncertain. Fuzziness Knowl. Based Syst. **17**, 1–14 (2009)
17. Drewniak, J., Drygaś, P.: On a class of uninorms. Int. J. Uncertain. Fuzziness Knowl. Based Syst. **10**, 5–10 (2002)
18. Drossos, C.A., Navara, M.: Generalized t-conorms and closure operators. In: Proceedings of the EUFIT 1996, Aachen, pp. 22–26 (1996)
19. Drygaś, P., Rak, E.: Distributivity equation in the class of 2-uninorms. Fuzzy Sets Syst. **291**, 82–97 (2016)
20. Dubois, D., Prade, H.: Fundamentals of Fuzzy Sets. Kluwer Academic Publisher, Boston (2000)
21. Engelking, R.: General Topology. Heldermann Verlag, Berlin (1989)
22. Everett, C.J.: Closure operators, Galois theory in lattices. Trans. Am. Math. Soc. **55**, 514–525 (1944)
23. Fodor, J., Yager, R.R., Rybalov, A.: Structure of uninorms. Int. J. Uncertain. Fuzziness Knowl. Based Syst. **5**, 411–427 (1997)
24. He, P., Wang, X.P.: Constructing uninorms on bounded lattices by using additive generators. Int. J. Approx. Reason. **136**, 1–13 (2021)
25. Homenda, W., Jastrzebska, A., Pedrycz, W.: Multicriteria decision making inspired by human cognitive processes. Appl. Math. Comput. **290**, 392–411 (2016)

26. Hua, X.J., Ji, W.: Uninorms on bounded lattices constructed by t-norms and t-subconorms. Fuzzy Sets Syst. **427**, 109–131 (2022)

27. Karaçal, F., Mesiar, R.: Uninorms on bounded lattices. Fuzzy Sets Syst. **261**, 33–43 (2015)

28. Klement, E.P., Mesiar, R., Pap, E.: Triangular Norms. Kluwer Academic Publishers, Dordrecht (2000)

29. Medina, J.: Characterizing when an ordinal sum of t-norms is a t-norm on bounded lattices. Fuzzy Sets Syst. **202**, 75–88 (2012)

30. Menger, K.: Statistical metrics. PNAS USA **8**, 535–537 (1942)

31. Metcalfe, G., Montagna, F.: Substructural fuzzy logics. J. Symb. Log. **72**, 834–864 (2007)

32. Ouyang, Y., Zhang, H.P.: Constructing uninorms via closure operators on a bounded lattice. Fuzzy Sets Syst. **395**, 93–106 (2020)

33. Sun, X.R., Liu, H.W.: Further characterization of uninorms on bounded lattices. Fuzzy Sets Syst. **427**, 96–108 (2022)

34. Saminger, S.: On ordinal sums of triangular norms on bounded lattices. Fuzzy Sets Syts. **157**, 1403–1416 (2006)

35. Schweizer, B., Sklar, A.: Probabilistic Metric Spaces. Elsevier North-Holland, New York (1983)

36. Yager, R.R.: Aggregation operators and fuzzy systems modelling. Fuzzy Sets Syst. **67**, 129–145 (1994)

37. Yager, R.R., Rybalov, A.: Uninorm aggregation operators. Fuzzy Sets Syst. **80**, 111–120 (1996)

38. Yager, R.R.: Uninorms in fuzzy systems modelling. Fuzzy Sets Syst. **122**, 167–175 (2001)

39. Zhao, B., Wu, T.: Some further results about uninorms on bounded lattices. Int. J. Approx. Reason. **130**, 22–49 (2021)

Norms and Discrete Choquet Integrals Induced by Submodular Fuzzy Measures: A Discussion

Agnès Rico[1][(✉)], Marie-Jeanne Lesot[2], and Christophe Marsala[2]

[1] Univ. Lyon 1, Lyon, France
agnes.rico@univ-lyon1.fr
[2] Sorbonne Université CNRS, LIP6, Paris, France
{Marie-Jeanne.Lesot,Christophe.Marsala}@lip6.fr

Abstract. The Choquet integral is a powerful tool in multi-criteria decision making and decision under uncertainty. This paper studies the use of its discrete form for the definition of norms, in the general case beyond the often considered case of Ordered Weighted Averages. It proposes a discussion of the characterisation based on Metric Inducing Fuzzy Measures (MIFM) introduced by Bolton et al., 2008, questioning its results. It then describes a characterisation for the discrete case that relates to the notion of properties holding almost everywhere derived from the null sets associated to a fuzzy measure. It discusses in particular the case of Choquet integrals induced by possibility measures.

Keywords: Discrete Choquet integral · Distance · Norm · Submodularity · Null sets · Possibility measures

1 Introduction

The Choquet integral is a powerful tool in multi-criteria decision making and decision under uncertainty [5]: it has a high expressive power, through its parameter, namely the fuzzy measure it relies on. Depending on the definition of the latter, it can model many different types of aggregation operators, among which weighted sums and Ordered Weighted Averages (OWA) to name a few.

This paper proposes to study the use of its discrete form for the definition of distances: when applied to data described by a set of features, distances can be seen as the aggregation of the comparisons computed for each feature. For instance the Minkowski distances are defined as, possibly weighted, power means, where the individual feature comparison is defined as the absolute value of the difference in case of numerical features.

This paper examines the possibility to use the generic aggregation operators offered by the discrete Choquet integral. It studies conditions a fuzzy measure must satisfy so that the Choquet integral it induces satisfies the required properties of a norm. As detailed in Sect. 2, this question has mainly be studied

© The Author(s), under exclusive license to Springer Nature Switzerland AG 2023
S. Massanet et al. (Eds.): EUSFLAT 2023/AGOP 2023, LNCS 14069, pp. 39–51, 2023.
https://doi.org/10.1007/978-3-031-39965-7_4

for OWA or in the continuous case. This paper first proposes, in Sect. 3, a discussion of the characterisation proposed in [1] based on Metric Inducing Fuzzy Measures (MIFM). Section 4 then describes a characterisation that expresses, in the discrete case, conditions related to the notion of properties holding *almost everywhere* derived from the null sets associated to a fuzzy measure [7]. It discusses in particular the case of Choquet integrals induced by possibility measures. Section 5 concludes the paper and discusses directions for future works.

2   Background and Related Works

This section presents the background and formal definitions of the main concepts used throughout the paper, norms, distances and Choquet integrals, before summarizing some existing works studying connections between them.

2.1   Norms and Distances

Formally, for elements taken from a domain $\mathcal{X}$, a norm is a function $s : \mathcal{X} \rightarrow \mathbb{R}$ that satisfies the following properties for any $x, y \in \mathcal{X}$:

- $s(x) \geq 0$ (non-negativity)
- $s(x) = 0$ if and only if $x = 0$ (separability)
- $s(kx) = |k|s(x)$ for all $k \in \mathbb{R}$ (homogeneity)
- $s(x + y) \leq s(x) + s(y)$ (triangular inequality)

The non-negativity property can actually be deduced from the other ones, but it is most often stated explicitly in the list of properties.

A norm s induces a distance d, defined by $d(x, y) = s(x - y)$, which is non-negative, separable, commutative and satisfies the triangular inequality.

This paper focuses on the classical case of numerical vectors of dimension n, i.e. it considers $\mathcal{X} = \mathbb{R}^n$.

2.2   Fuzzy Measures and Discrete Choquet Integrals

The discrete Choquet integral (see e.g. [5] for a survey of its definition, variants and applications) is an aggregation function commonly used in multicriteria decision making. Given a finite set of n criteria $\mathcal{N} = \{1, \cdots, n\}$, and an alternative described by its evaluation over these criteria, $x = (x_1, \cdots, x_n)$, it calculates a global evaluation aggregating all the x_i values. The latter is a generalisation of the weighted sum that allows to take into account interactions between the criteria, through the use of a so-called fuzzy measure.

This section first reminds the formal definition of these fuzzy measures. It then provides the two main, equivalent, definitions of the discrete Choquet integrals and some specific cases of interest.

Fuzzy Measures. The definition of a Choquet integral relies on the specification of a fuzzy measure, also named capacity: this function associates, to any group of criteria $A \subseteq \mathcal{N}$, a numerical value that can be viewed as the weight or the importance given to these criteria. Formally

Definition 1. *A fuzzy measure (or capacity) is a set function $\mu : 2^{\mathcal{N}} \rightarrow [0,1]$ such that*

- *$\mu(\emptyset) = 0$ and $\mu(\mathcal{N}) = 1$ (boundary conditions)*
- *if $A \subseteq B$ then $\mu(A) \leq \mu(B)$ (monotonicity)*

Specific properties of interest for a fuzzy measure μ include:

- *additivity* iff $\forall A, B \subseteq \mathcal{N}$, $\mu(A \cup B) + \mu(A \cap B) = \mu(A) + \mu(B)$
- *submodularity* iff $\forall A, B \subseteq \mathcal{N}$, $\mu(A \cup B) + \mu(A \cap B) \leq \mu(A) + \mu(B)$.
- *subadditivity* iff $\forall A, B \subseteq \mathcal{N}$ such that $A \cap B = \emptyset$, $\mu(A \cup B) \leq \mu(A) + \mu(B)$

Note that a submodular fuzzy measure is subadditive.

Another property of interest, used in examples in this paper, is the symmetry one, that is satisfied when the capacity only depends on the cardinality of the subsets it applies to: μ is *symmetric* iff $\forall A, B \subseteq \mathcal{N}$, $|A| = |B| \Rightarrow \mu(A) = \mu(B)$.

A specific case of fuzzy measure corresponds to *possibility measures* [3]: they are defined as set functions $\Pi : 2^{\mathcal{N}} \rightarrow [0,1]$ such that $\Pi(\emptyset) = 0$, $\Pi(\mathcal{N}) = 1$ and $\Pi(A \cup B) = \max(\Pi(A), \Pi(B))$.

Discrete Choquet Integrals. Given a fuzzy measure indicating the weight of any subset of criteria and an alternative x, the Choquet integral [5] aggregates the evaluation of the individual criteria in x as follows

Definition 2. *The discrete Choquet integral of $x = (x_1, \cdots, x_n) \in \mathbb{R}^n$ with respect to a fuzzy measure μ is defined as*

$$C_\mu(x) = \sum_{i=1}^{n} \left(x_{\lceil i \rceil} - x_{\lceil i-1 \rceil} \right) \mu(A_{\lceil i \rceil}) \tag{1}$$

$$= \sum_{i=1}^{n} x_{\lceil i \rceil} \left(\mu(A_{\lceil i \rceil}) - \mu(A_{\lceil i+1 \rceil}) \right) \tag{2}$$

where

- *$\lceil . \rceil$ is a permutation on $\mathcal{N}$ that sorts x in increasing order: $x_{\lceil 1 \rceil} \leq \cdots \leq x_{\lceil n \rceil}$*
- *$A_{\lceil i \rceil} = \{\lceil i \rceil, \cdots, \lceil n \rceil\}$*
- *$x_{\lceil 0 \rceil} = 0$ and $A_{\lceil n+1 \rceil} = \emptyset$.*

The above definition is the usual presentation of the Choquet integral. An equivalent definition based on sorting x in decreasing order can be considered as well, as proposed in [1]. As this paper proposes, in Sect. 3, a discussion of the results presented in the latter paper, we consider both notations: $C_\mu(x)$ can equivalently be defined as

$$C_\mu(x) = \sum_{i=1}^{n} x_{\lfloor i \rfloor} \left(\mu(B_{\lfloor i \rfloor}) - \mu(B_{\lfloor i-1 \rfloor}) \right) \tag{3}$$

where

- $\lfloor . \rfloor$ is a decreasing permutation: $x_{\lfloor 1 \rfloor} \geq x_{\lfloor 2 \rfloor} \geq \cdots \geq x_{\lfloor n \rfloor}$
- $B_{\lfloor i \rfloor} = \{\lfloor 1 \rfloor, \cdots, \lfloor i \rfloor\}$ and
- $B_{\lfloor 0 \rfloor} = \emptyset$

It is useful to introduce the following notations: for any permutation σ on $\mathcal{N}$, $\forall i \in \mathcal{N}$,

$$w_{\sigma(i)} = \mu(B_{\sigma(i)}) - \mu(B_{\sigma(i-1)}) \tag{4}$$

with $B_{\sigma(i)} = \{\sigma(1), \cdots, \sigma(i)\}$ and $B_{\sigma(0)} = \emptyset$. Indeed, Eq. (3) can then be written $C_\mu(x) = \sum_{i=1}^{n} x_{\lfloor i \rfloor} w_{\lfloor i \rfloor}$.

Special Cases. Depending on the properties of the chosen fuzzy measure μ, specific cases of the Choquet integrals are induced, possibly with simplified expressions. In particular, in the case where μ is an additive measure, the Choquet integral takes the simplified form of a weighted sum: $C_\mu(x) = \sum_{i=1}^{n} \mu(\{i\}) x_i$. This follows from the fact that both the $A_{\lceil i \rceil}$ and the $B_{\lfloor i \rfloor}$ satisfy an inclusion property: for any i, $A_{\lceil i+1 \rceil} \subseteq A_{\lceil i \rceil}$ and $B_{\lfloor i \rfloor} \subseteq B_{\lfloor i+1 \rfloor}$.

A specific class of Choquet integrals implements the Ordered Weighted Average operator [8], defined as

Definition 3. *Let* $(w_1, \cdots, w_n) \in [0,1]^n$ *such that* $\sum_{i=1}^{n} w_i = 1$. *The* Ordered Weighted Average *(OWA$_w$) is the aggregation operator defined by, for any* $(x_1, \cdots, x_n) \in \mathbb{R}^n$

$$OWA_w(x_1, \cdots, x_n) = \sum_{i=1}^{n} w_i x_{\lceil i \rceil} \tag{5}$$

The following relation holds between OWA and Choquet integral [4]:

Proposition 1 (from [4]). *A discrete Choquet integral with respect to* μ *is an OWA if and only if* μ *is symmetric, i.e. the fuzzy measure only depends on the set cardinality.*

More precisely, it is then the OWA$_w$ *whose weights are defined as* $w_i = \mu(A_{n-i+1}) - \mu(A_{n-i})$ *where* A_i *denotes any subset with cardinality equal to* i.

This weight definition is an instanciation of Eq. (4) for the considered particular case of fuzzy measures.

A specific case of interest among the OWA, as detailed in Sect. 3, are the ones that satisfy an ordering constraints on the weights, called *buoyancy* [8]:

Definition 4. *The OWA$_w$ satisfies the* buyoancy *property iff*

$$w_1 \leq \cdots \leq w_n \tag{6}$$

2.3   Related Works

Within the framework recalled in the previous sections, the question is then to exploit a discrete Choquet integral to define a norm: given two data points a and b described by n features, an alternative is defined by their individual feature comparisons, $\forall i \in \{1, \ldots, n\}$, $x_i = cmp(a_i, b_i)$, e.g. for numerical features, $x_i = |a_i - b_i|$. An alternative to be assessed is thus denoted $x = (x_1, \cdots, x_n) \in \mathbb{R}^{+n}$. Indeed, the individual comparison are assumed to be non-negative values. The question is then to define a Choquet integral C_μ such that $s(x) = C_\mu(x_1, \ldots, x_n)$ defines a norm, i.e. satisfies the properties recalled in Sect. 2.1.

This section summarises results that have been established in previous works regarding this issue, except for [1], discussed in details in the next section.

Submodularity and Triangular Inequality. A first theorem establishes sufficient conditions for a Choquet integral to satisfy the triangular inequality [2]:

Proposition 2 (from   [2]). *If the fuzzy measure μ is submodular, then the Choquet integral it induces satisfies the triangular inequality: for any x, y*

$$C_\mu(x + y) \le C_\mu(x) + C_\mu(y)$$

It is easy to check that this is a necessary and sufficient condition. Indeed, let us consider a fuzzy measure μ such that for any x, y, $C_\mu(x + y) \le C_\mu(x) + C_\mu(y)$ and two sets $A, B \subseteq \mathcal{N}$. The characteristic functions $1_{A \cup B}$ and $1_{A \cap B}$ are comonotonic with a sum equals to $1_A + 1_B$. It then holds that $\mu(A \cup B) + \mu(A \cap B) = C_\mu(1_{A \cup B} + 1_{A \cap B})$ since Choquet integral is comonotonic additive. Hence $\mu(A \cup B) + \mu(A \cap B) = C_\mu(1_A + 1_B) \le C_\mu(1_A) + C_\mu(1_B) = \mu(A) + \mu(B)$ by hypothesis.

Proposition 2 can be generalised to Hölder inequalities, as shown in [7] for continuous Choquet integrals.

Relations Between OWA and Norms. Most results about the relations between Choquet integrals and norms consider the case of OWA. It has first been established by Yager [9] that OWA possessing the buoyancy property are norms:

Theorem 3 (from   [9]). *Given $(w_1, \ldots, w_n) \in [0, 1]^n$, the function $s : \mathbb{R}^{+n} \to \mathbb{R}^+$ defined by $s(x) = \sum_{i=1}^n w_i x_{\lfloor i \rfloor}$ is a norm if and only if $\forall i$, $w_i \ge w_{i+1}$.*

Note that the w_i ordering is here reversed as compared to Eq. (6) because the OWA is written in [9] with the $\lfloor . \rfloor$ ordering instead of the $\lceil . \rceil$ one.

Due to the relationship between Choquet integrals and OWA, this theorem allows us to deduce the following corollary:

Corollary 4. *A discrete Choquet integral defined by a symmetric measure is a norm if and only if for all i, $\mu(A_{n-i+1}) - \mu(A_{n-i}) \le \mu(A_{n-i}) - \mu(A_{n-i-1})$ where A_i represents any set of cardinality i.*

Proof. Under the condition that μ is symmetric, C_μ induces an OWA according to Proposition 1 whose weights satisfy the buoyancy property according to the considered hypothesis. Theorem 3 then gives the result.   □

The relation between OWA and norms is studied in more details by [9], who examines the relations between the order of Minkowski distances and the distribution of the OWA weights satisfying the buoyancy property.

General Case. Beyond the specific property of the triangular and Hölder inequalities and the specific case of OWA, studies have been conducted for continuous Choquet integrals [7], generalising the discrete sum definition (as given in Eq. (2)). The conditions under which they define norms over measurable functions are established, allowing the author to define distances for fuzzy sets defined over compact subsets of $\mathbb{R}^n$. One of the established theorems states that the Choquet integral induced by a submodular fuzzy measure that is continuous from below defines a norm on the quotient of the set of measurable functions by the equivalence relation $\sim$ a.e., based on the notion of *almost everywhere* (see the reminder of its definition in Sect. 4.3).

In this paper, in Sect. 4, we consider the case of discrete Choquet integrals, which leads to a specific characterisation of the latter case, and we study its expression in the particular case of possibility measures. Before, we discuss in Sect. 3 the equivalence proposed in a similar framework in [1].

3   A Discussion on MIFM and Induced Choquet Integrals

This section proposes a discussion of the characterisation proposed by Bolton et al. [1] of discrete Choquet integrals defining norms, which relies on the specific class of capacities called MIFM. The definition of the latter are first reminded, before presenting and questioning some results proposed in this paper.

3.1   Reminder: MIFM Induced Choquet Integrals

A specific class of specific Choquet integrals has been proposed in [1], based on a generalisation of the OWA buoyancy property (see Definition 4) to fuzzy measures using the weight definition reminded in Eq. (4) and the notation introduced in Sect. 2, where, for any permutation σ on $\mathcal{N}$, $B_{\sigma(i)} = \{\sigma(1), \ldots, \sigma(i)\}$:

Definition 5. *A fuzzy measure μ on $\mathcal{N}$ is a* Metric Inducing Fuzzy Measure *(MIFM) if for any permutation σ on $\mathcal{N}$, for all $j \in \mathcal{N} \setminus \{n\}$, $w_{\sigma(j)} \geq w_{\sigma(j+1)}$ where $w_{\sigma(j)}$ is defined as in Eq. (4), i.e. $w_{\sigma(j)} = \mu(B_{\sigma(j)}) - \mu(B_{\sigma(j-1)})$ with the convention $B_{\sigma(0)} = \emptyset$.*

This property is equivalent to the buoyancy imposed on OWA (see Eq. 6), up to the choice of the considered (increasing vs decreasing) ordering of the x values.

To make it friendlier, we propose to illustrate this definition, first for a universe of size 2, then for a universe of size 3.

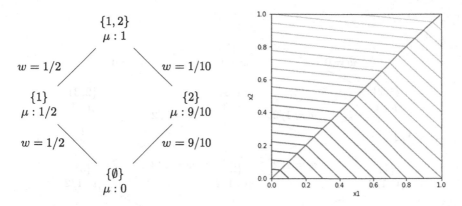

Fig. 1. (Left) Example of a MIFM for a universe containing two values, $\mathcal{N} = \{1,2\}$, (right) level lines of Choquet integral it induces (see analytical expression in Example 1).

Example 1. *Let us consider $\mathcal{N} = \{1,2\}$ and the capacity measure μ represented graphically on the left part of Fig. 1. This graph represents the lattice of the universe subsets, gives for each of them their associated capacity value, as well as the induced w values.*

μ is a MIFM: on $\mathcal{N}$, only two permutations can be considered: (i) σ equals to the identity ($\sigma(1) = 1$, $\sigma(2) = 2$, that leads to $B_{\sigma(0)} = \emptyset$, $B_{\sigma(1)} = \{1\}$, $B_{\sigma(2)} = \{1,2\}$), which corresponds to the left path in the graph shown on the figure, and (ii) τ that corresponds to the right path on the graph ($\tau(1) = 2$, $\tau(2) = 1$). On each path, the w indeed satisfy a non-increasing ordering property.

The right part of the graph shows the level lines of the Choquet integral induced when applying the definition given in Eq. (3): analytically, $C_\mu(x) = \frac{1}{2}(x_1 + x_2)$ if $x_1 \geq x_2$, and $C_\mu(x) = \frac{1}{10}(9x_2 + x_1)$ otherwise. This Choquet integral also illustrates the fact that it offers the possibility to define more expressive aggregation operators than weighted (or ordered weighted) average, introducing different behaviours on subregions of the domain.

The next example considers a more complex case, illustrating the richness of the MIFM framework.

Example 2. *Let us consider $\mathcal{N} = \{1,2,3\}$ and the symmetric fuzzy measure graphically represented in Fig. 2 and analytically defined by*

$$\mu(A) = \begin{cases} \frac{1}{2} \ if \ |A| = 1 \\ 1 \ if \ |A| = 2 \\ 1 \ if \ A = \{1,2,3\}. \end{cases}$$

As it is symmetric, the capacity values are constant level-wise on the graph, where each level is associated with a fixed cardinality and, as pointed out in Proposition 1, the induced w values are also constant level-wise (i.e. are independent of the permutation, and the path followed in the graph). In addition, for this

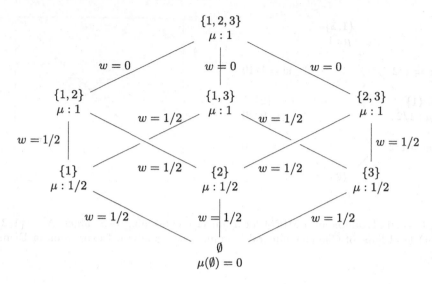

Fig. 2. Graphical representation of the fuzzy measure introduced in Example 2.

example, w is defined as $w_1 = \frac{1}{2} \geq w_2 = 1 - \frac{1}{2} = \frac{1}{2} \geq w_3 = 1 - 1 = 0$. It thus satisfies the buoyancy property, or equivalently in terms of fuzzy measures, the MIFM definition. μ is submodular, and thus also subadditive, as can be shown by exhaustive examination of subsets of $\mathcal{N}$.

As a consequence, the induced Choquet integral has the following analytical definition: $C_\mu(x) = x_{\lceil 1 \rceil} w_1 + x_{\lceil 2 \rceil} w_2 + x_{\lceil 3 \rceil} w_3 = \frac{1}{2} x_{\lceil 1 \rceil} + \frac{1}{2} x_{\lceil 2 \rceil}$.

3.2   Discussing the Relations Between MIFM and Norms

Based on the notion of MIFM, the following relation between the specific class of Choquet integrals and norms is established in [1]

Proposition 5 (from [1]). *The Choquet integral with respect to a measure μ is a norm if and only if μ is a MIFM.*

The proofs provided in [1] are complex and we argue a counterexample can be proposed to the assertion that the MIFM is a necessary condition. Indeed, let us consider the fuzzy measure Π^* graphically defined in Fig. 3 on $\mathcal{N} = \{1, 2, 3\}$ that possesses by construction the property of being a possibility measure: $\Pi^*(A)$ is defined as $\max_{i \in A} \pi_i$ for the possibility distribution π defined by the μ values associated to the singletons, i.e. at the first level of the graph. As such, it is a norm, as can be proved applying Corollary 9 established in the next section.

Yet this capacity does not satisfy the properties of a MIFM, as shown for instance when considering the permutation σ such that $\sigma(1) = 3$, $\sigma(2) = 2$, $\sigma(3) = 1$, i.e. the B path $\emptyset$, $\{3\}$, $\{2, 3\}$, $\{1, 2, 3\}$: on this path, the w values do not satisfy the required monotonicity constraint.

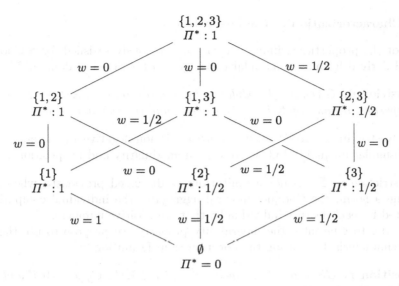

Fig. 3. Graphical representation of the possibility measure Π^* that is not a MIFM.

3.3   Discussing the Relations Between MIFM and Submodularity

In [1], it is mentioned that MIFM are mathematically equivalent to the class of submodular fuzzy measures, although this claim is not proved. We question this assertion as, by transitivity with Proposition 5 the same paper establishes, it would imply Choquet integrals induced by submodular fuzzy measures are norms.

Now this property does not hold: submodularity guarantees the triangular inequality is satisfied (see Proposition 2), but it does not guarantee the separability property is, as can be shown by the following counter-example:

Example 3. *Consider* $\mathcal{N} = \{1, 2, 3\}$ *and the possibility fuzzy measure* Π *derived from* $1 = \pi_1 \geq \pi_2 = \frac{1}{2} \geq \pi_3 = 0$. *It holds that* $C_\Pi(x) = \frac{1}{2}x_1 + \frac{1}{2}x_2$. *As a consequence,* $C_\Pi(x) = 0$ *iff* $x_1 = x_2 = 0$. *Therefore,* $C_\Pi((0, 0, 1)) = 0$, *which violates the separability property:* C_Π *is not a norm.*

However, as any possibility measure, Π *is submodular (see e.g. proof of Corollary 9 in Sect. 4.1).*

4   Discrete Choquet Integrals and Norms: A Discussion

This section discusses a necessary and sufficient characterisation that can be established in the discrete case and the characterisation it induces in the case of Choquet integrals induced by possibility measures. However, in the general case, the separability property does not hold in general and requires to consider the notion of "almost everywhere" related to that of null sets.

4.1 Characterization of the Discrete Case

Three of the properties defining a norm are obviously satisfied for a Choquet integral derived from a submodular capacity and restricted to domain $\mathbb{R}^+$:

Proposition 6. *Given a submodular μ fuzzy measure, $C_\mu : \mathbb{R}^{+n} \to \mathbb{R}$ satisfies the properties of non-negativity, homogeneity and triangular inequality.*

Proof. Restricting C_μ to $\mathbb{R}^+$ allows to prove it is non-negative and homogeneous. The triangular inequality follows from μ submodularity and Proposition 2. $\square$

The restriction to $\mathbb{R}^+$ is not a limitation: as discussed previously, when used to define a norm, the Choquet integral aggregates the individual comparisons computed for each feature individually, that are positive numbers.

In order to guarantee the separability property, we propose to use the following characterisation, using the notation as in Definition 2:

Proposition 7. *Given μ a fuzzy measure and $x \in \mathbb{R}^{+n}$, $C_\mu(x) = 0$ if and only if $\{i|x_{\lceil i\rceil} \neq 0\} \subseteq \{i|\mu(A_{\lceil i\rceil}) = \mu(A_{\lceil i+1\rceil})\}$.*

Proof. From the Choquet integral definition written as in Eq. (2), $C_\mu(x) = \sum_{i=1}^n x_{\lceil i\rceil}[\mu(A_{\lceil i\rceil}) - \mu(A_{\lceil i+1\rceil})]$, it follows that when $x \in \mathbb{R}^{+n}$, $C_\mu(x) = 0$ if and only if, for all i, $x_{\lceil i\rceil}[\mu(A_{\lceil i\rceil}) - \mu(A_{\lceil i+1\rceil})] = 0$,
i.e. either $x_{\lceil i\rceil} = 0$ or $\mu(A_{\lceil i\rceil}) - \mu(A_{\lceil i+1\rceil}) = 0$. This condition is equivalent to $\{i|x_{\lceil i\rceil} \neq 0\} \subseteq \{i|\mu(A_{\lceil i\rceil}) = \mu(A_{\lceil i+1\rceil})\}$. $\square$

Note that, according to the proof presented above, if for all σ, $\mu(A_{\sigma(i)}) > \mu(A_{\sigma(i+1)})$ then $\{i|\mu(A_{\sigma(i)}) = \mu(A_{\sigma(i+1)})\} = \emptyset$ and $C_\mu(x) = 0$ if and only if $x = 0$.

4.2 Case of Possibility Measure Induced Choquet Integral

In the case where the considered capacity is a possibility measure, the characterisation established in the previous section takes a simple form:

Proposition 8. *If Π is a possibility measure such that, for all i, $\pi(\{i\}) \neq 0$ then $C_\Pi(x) = 0$ if and only if $x = 0$.*

Proof. The Choquet integral with respect to a possibility measure possesses an expression depending only on the permutation corresponding to order on the values of π. Let us denote $\pi_i = \pi(\{i\})$ and σ the permutation on $\mathcal{N}$ that sorts the π_i in decreasing order, i.e. such that $1 = \pi_{\sigma(1)} \geq \cdots \geq \pi_{\sigma(n)} > \pi_{\sigma(n+1)} = 0$. The Choquet integral of x with respect to Π can be computed as $C_\Pi(x) = \sum_{i=1}^n (\pi_{\sigma(i)} - \pi_{\sigma(i+1)}) \max_{j=1}^i x_{\sigma(j)}$.
Under the considered hypothesis, $\pi_i \neq 0$ for all $i \in \mathcal{N}$, $\pi_{\sigma(n)} - \pi_{\sigma(n+1)} = \pi_{\sigma(n)} \neq 0$ so $C_\Pi(x) = 0$ implies $\max_{i=1}^n x_{\sigma(i)} = 0$, i.e., for $x \in \mathbb{R}^+$, $x = 0$. $\square$

Example 4. *Let us consider the possibility measure presented in Fig. 3. We have* $1 = \pi_1 > \pi_2 = \pi_3 = \frac{1}{2}$ *and for all* x, $C_\Pi(x) = (\pi_1 - \pi_2)x_1 + (\pi_2 - \pi_3)\max(x_1, x_2) + (\pi_3 - \pi_4)\max(x_1, x_2, x_3) = \frac{1}{2}x_1 + \frac{1}{2}\max(x_1, x_2, x_3)$.

So $C_\Pi(x) = 0$ *if and only if* $x = 0$.

Corollary 9. *If* Π *is a possibility measure such that* $\pi(\{i\}) \neq 0$ *for all* i, *then* C_Π *is a norm on* $\mathbb{R}^{+n}$.

Proof. Let us first prove that Π is a submodular fuzzy measure. Let $A, B \subseteq \mathcal{N}$. Π monotonicity implies $\Pi(A \cap B) \leq \Pi(A)$ and $\Pi(A \cap B) \leq \Pi(B)$ and thus $\Pi(A \cap B) \leq \min(\Pi(A), \pi(B))$. In addition, as it is a possibility measure, $\Pi(A \cup B) = \max(\Pi(A), \pi(B))$. As a consequence, $\Pi(A \cup B) + \Pi(A \cap B) \leq \max(\Pi(A), \Pi(B)) + \min(\Pi(A), \Pi(B)) = \Pi(A) + \Pi(B)$.

Proposition 6 can thus be applied and implies that the Choquet integral induced by Π satisfies the properties of non-negativity, homogeneity and triangular inequality. Separability follows from Proposition 8. □

4.3 General Case

In the general case, beyond possibility measures, the separability property does not hold in general (see Sect. 3.3) and requires to consider the notion of null sets, as also shown for the continuous case in [7]. This section first reminds the definition of null sets and properties holding almost everywhere.

Reminder on Null Sets. Given a universe $\mathcal{N}$ and a fuzzy measure μ, null sets [6] are subsets of $\mathcal{N}$ that act as neutral elements with respect to μ:

Definition 6. *A null set with respect to a fuzzy measure* μ *is a set* $N \subseteq \mathcal{N}$ *such that* $\forall A \subseteq \mathcal{N}, \mu(A \cup N) = \mu(A)$.

It is easy to check that the empty set is a null set, so there always exists at least one null set with respect to any fuzzy measure μ.

As established in [6], if μ is subadditive, then a set N is a null set with respect to μ if and only if $\mu(N) = 0$. Note that if μ is submodular then μ is subadditive and the same result holds. As a consequence, in the following, to prove that a candidate set is a null set, we show that its measure is equal to 0.

The notion of null sets is used to define the concept of "almost everywhere", with abbreviation *a.e* [2,6]: a logical proposition $P(x)$ is said to hold "almost everywhere" if it holds everywhere except on subsets with measure 0. Formally, $P(x)$ *a.e* holds if there exists a null set N such that $P(x)$ is true for all $x \in N^c$ where N^c is the complement of N. Note that a true proposition $P(x)$ is also true *a.e.* since the empty set is a null set.

Use for the Separability Property. Using the notion of null sets, the separability property can be established almost everywhere:

Proposition 10. *Given μ a submodular fuzzy measure and $x \in \mathbb{R}^{+n}$, $C_\mu(x) = 0$ if and only if $x = 0$ a.e.*

Proof. Let x be such that $C_\mu(x) = 0$. To show that $x = 0$ a.e, let us show that the candidate set $N = \{i | x_i \neq 0\}$ is a null set with respect to μ, i.e. $\mu(\{i | x_i \neq 0\}) = 0$ (indeed, $x = 0$ holds on N^c). Then $C_\mu(x) = \sum_{i=1}^n [x_{\sigma(i)} - x_{\sigma(i-1)}]\mu(A_{\sigma(i)}) = 0$ is equivalent to the fact that, for all i, it holds that $[x_{\sigma(i)} - x_{\sigma(i-1)}]\mu(A_{\sigma(i)}) = 0$. Let us denote the first coordinate different from 0 by $x_{\sigma(p)}$, $x = (0, \cdots, 0, x_{\sigma(p)}, \cdots, x_{\sigma(n)})$. We must have $x_{\sigma(p)}\mu(A_{\sigma(p)}) = 0$ where $A_{\sigma(p)} = \{i | x_i \neq 0\}$. Thus $\mu(\{i | x_i \neq 0\}) = 0$.

Reciprocally, if $x = 0$ a.e, without loss of generality, $x = (0, \ldots, 0, x_q, \ldots x_n)$ and $\{q, \ldots, n\}$ and its subsets are null sets. Then $C_\mu(x) = 0$, as all terms in the sum are 0, either because of the $x_{\sigma(i)}$ difference or because of $\mu(A_{\sigma(i)}) = 0$.   □

In the above proposition, $\{i | x_i \neq 0\}$ may be a null set different from the empty set, as illustrated in Example 3. However, the latter can now be analysed in terms of null sets:

Example 5. *Consider again Example 3, where Π is the possibility measure induced by $1 = \pi_1 \geq \pi_2 = \frac{1}{2} \geq \pi_3 = 0$ and $C_\pi(x) = \frac{1}{2}x_1 + \frac{1}{2}x_2$.*

$C_\Pi(x) = 0$ iff $x_1 = x_2 = 0$. However, $\pi_3 = 0$ and Π is a submodular measure so $\{3\} = \{1, 2\}^c$ is a null set. C_Π is a norm a.e.

5   Conclusion

In the context of establishing relations between discrete Choquet integrals and norms, this paper proposed a discussion questioning the properties of the Metric Inducing Fuzzy Measure, illustrating by a specific possibility measure that the separability property is not guaranteed by the generalisation of the buoyancy property. In the special case of possibility measures, it proposes a necessary and sufficient condition under which the induced Choquet integral is a norm. In the general case, the characterisation leads to a separability property that holds almost everywhere, but not in general. As a direction for future works, establishing the properties allowing to achieve a general result still remains an open question.

References

1. Bolton, J., Gader, P., Wilson, J.N.: Discrete Choquet integral as a distance metric. IEEE Trans. Fuzzy Syst. **16**(4), 1107–1110 (2008)
2. Denneberg, D.: Non-additive Measure and Integral. Kluwer Academic Publishers, Dordrecht (1994)
3. Dubois, D., Prade, H.: Possibility theory and its applications: where do we stand? In: Kacprzyk, J., Pedrycz, W. (eds.) Springer Handbook of Computational Intelligence, pp. 31–60. Springer, Heidelberg (2015). https://doi.org/10.1007/978-3-662-43505-2_3

4. Fodor, J., Roubens, M.: Characterization of weighted maximum and some related operations. Inf. Sci. **84**(3), 173–180 (1995)
5. Grabisch, M., Labreuche, C.: A decade of application of the Choquet and Sugeno integrals in multi-criteria decision aid. Ann. Oper. Res. **175**(1), 247–290 (2010)
6. Murofushi, T., Sugeno, M.: A theory of fuzzy measures: representations, the Choquet integral, and null sets. J. Math. Anal. Appl. **159**(2), 532–549 (1991)
7. Narukawa, Y.: Distances defined by Choquet integral. In: Proceedings of the IEEE International Conference on Fuzzy Systems, pp. 511–516 (2007)
8. Yager, R.R.: Families of OWA operators. Fuzzy Syst. Syst. **59**, 125–148 (1993)
9. Yager, R.R.: Norms induced from OWA operators. IEEE Trans. Fuzzy Syst. **18**(1), 57–66 (2010)

Some Existence Results for Fuzzy Differential Equations with a Metric-Basic Derivative of Type (ii)

Mina Shahidi[1][✉] [ID], Rosana Rodríguez-López[2] [ID], and Estevão Esmi[1] [ID]

[1] Department of Mathematics, Statistic and Scientific Computing, Unicamp, Campinas, Brazil
shahidi@ime.unicamp.br
[2] CITMAga, Departamento de Estatística, Análise Matemática e Optimización, Facultade de Matemáticas; Universidade de Santiago de Compostela, 15782 Santiago de Compostela, Spain
rosana.rodriguez.lopez@usc.es

Abstract. In this paper, we investigate sufficient conditions for the existence of a solution for a dynamical system based on a metric structure (G, u_N). Moreover, a slight variation in the assumptions allows to apply it for fuzzy functions. So, we study the existence of the solution to fuzzy differential equations under the concept of metric differentiability.

Keywords: Fuzzy differential equations · Metric dynamical systems · Metric derivative

1 Introduction

The study of fuzzy differential equations forms an appropriate context for the mathematical modeling of real world subjects in which uncertainty or vagueness pervades. There are several different approaches to studying fuzzy differential equations [3,6,7,9]. However, the meaning of a fuzzy differential equation powerfully depends on picking the concept of fuzzy derivative [2]. Therefore, there are some popular approaches to define the derivative of fuzzy functions and to examine fuzzy differential equations, for instance, Hukuhara derivative, gH-derivative, etc., see [1,4,5]. In most of the mentioned derivatives for fuzzy functions, we need to guarantee the existence of the corresponding differences. To overcome this shortcoming, a derivative is proposed for fuzzy functions that is based on the Hausdorff distance between the fuzzy numbers called metric derivative. Metric differentiability has its origins in [9] and has been extended and studied, for instance, in [8,10].

Dynamical systems from the metric perspective have their origin in the work by Panasyuk [12] who considered approximation or quasi-differential equations in the framework of a locally compact metric space. Later, Panasyuk expanded the Euler polygonal method to show the existence of solution for the equations of approximation, but the results attained were restricted to the locally compact metric space. Also, in [13], the existence of solution to ordinary differential equations with function f continuous is analyzed. However, for arbitrary spaces which are not locally compact, further results were needed. To overcome the above mentioned shortcomings, Nieto and Rodríguez-López renamed the framework presented by Panasyuk as Metric Dynamical Systems (MDS, for short) and proved several results considering the properties of the solution to MDS. In particular, in [11], they developed Euler Polygonal Method to prove the existence of solution for general MDS including equations with a nonlinear differential. From this approach, the existence of solution to fuzzy differential equations under (i)-D-derivative can be derived. Regarding the ideas presented in [11], we consider a slightly different notion of MDS (G, u_N) which is a kind of backward operator, and we prove the uniqueness and existence of solution under appropriate hypotheses. This result allows to derive, as a consequence, some results for fuzzy differential equations under a type (ii) metric derivative.

The paper is organized as follows. In Sect. 2, we recall some basic concepts and results that will be used in the rest of the paper. In Sect. 3, we study the metric dynamical system. In particular, we examined the existence of the solution of fuzzy differential equations under the concept of metric derivative.

2 Preliminaries

In this section, we recall some definitions and present the notation which will be used throughout the paper, see for example [1,5]. A fuzzy subset of $\mathbb{R}^n$ is a map $v : \mathbb{R}^n \to [0,1]$, where $v(t)$ is the degree of membership of $t \in \mathbb{R}^n$ to the fuzzy set v. For each $\alpha \in (0,1]$, the α-cut is defined by $[v]_\alpha = \{t \in \mathbb{R}^n | v(t) \geq \alpha\}$. The support of v, denoted by $[v]_0$, is the closure of the union of all its α-cuts with $\alpha \in (0,1]$. The set of normal, fuzzy convex, upper semicontinuous and compact support fuzzy sets is called the space of fuzzy numbers and it is marked by $\mathbb{R}^n_{\mathcal{F}}$. The addition in $\mathbb{R}^n_{\mathcal{F}}$ is given levelwise by

$$[v + w]_\alpha = [v]_\alpha + [w]_\alpha, \quad \alpha \in [0,1], \quad v, w \in \mathbb{R}^n_{\mathcal{F}},$$

and, for $c \in \mathbb{R}$, the scalar multiplication is given by

$$[cv]_\alpha = c[v]_\alpha, \quad v \in \mathbb{R}^n_{\mathcal{F}}.$$

The distance between elements of $\mathbb{R}^n_{\mathcal{F}}$ is defined by the supremum of the Hausdorff distance between the cuts as

$$D(v, w) = \sup_{\alpha \in [0,1]} d_H([v]_\alpha, [w]_\alpha) \quad v, w \in \mathbb{R}^n_{\mathcal{F}}.$$

It is worth mentioning that the metric space $(\mathbb{R}^n_{\mathcal{F}}, D)$ is complete.

Theorem 1. [5] *Let $u, v, w, z \in \mathbb{R}^n_{\mathcal{F}}$ and $\lambda, \mu \in \mathbb{R}$, we have*

1. $D(v + z, w + z) = D(v, w)$,

2. $D(\mu v, \mu w) = |\mu| D(v, w)$,
3. $D(u + v, w + z) \le D(u, w) + D(v, z)$,
4. $D(\lambda w, \mu w) = |\lambda - \mu| D(w, \tilde{0}), \lambda \mu > 0$, as $\tilde{0} = \chi_{\{0\}}$.

Theorem 2. [1]

(i) For any $\mu, \lambda \in \mathbb{R}$ with $\mu, \lambda \ge 0$ or $\mu, \lambda \le 0$ and any $v \in \mathbb{R}_{\mathcal{F}}^n$, we get $(\mu + \lambda)v = \mu v + \lambda v$. For general $\mu, \lambda \in \mathbb{R}$, the mentioned property does not hold.

(ii) For any $\lambda \in \mathbb{R}$ and any $v, w \in \mathbb{R}_{\mathcal{F}}^n$, we have $\lambda(v + w) = \lambda v + \lambda w$.

(iii) For any $\lambda, \mu \in \mathbb{R}$ and any $v \in \mathbb{R}_{\mathcal{F}}^n$, we have $\lambda(\mu v) = (\lambda \mu)v$.

Definition 1. [8] Let $v : I \subseteq \mathbb{R} \to \mathbb{R}_{\mathcal{F}}^n$ be named (ii)-D-differentiable at $t \in I$ if there is $v'(t) \in \mathbb{R}_{\mathcal{F}}^n$ such that

$$\lim_{h \to 0^-} \frac{1}{h} D(v(t), v(t - h) + h v'(t)) = \lim_{h \to 0^-} \frac{1}{h} D(v(t + h), v(t) + h v'(t)) = 0.$$

3   Existence of a Solution in $[0, t_N]$

To clarify the concept of this type of MDS, we consider the differential equation in $\mathbb{R}$ below:

$$v'(t) = \begin{cases} g(t, v(t)), & t \in [0, t_N], \\ v(t_N) = v_N, \end{cases} \tag{1}$$

where $g : [0, t_N] \times \mathbb{R} \to \mathbb{R}$ and $v_N \in \mathbb{R}$.

Definition 2. Let $v : [0, t_N] \to \mathbb{R}$ be a solution to problem (1) if $v(t_N) = v_N$ and, for every $t \in [0, t_N]$,

$$\lim_{h \to 0} \frac{v(t - h) - v(t)}{-h} = g(t, v(t)).$$

This implies that

$$\liminf_{h \to 0^+} \frac{v(t - h) - v(t) + h g(t, v(t))}{h} = 0, t \in [0, t_N].$$

It is equivalent to

$$\liminf_{h \to 0^+} \frac{1}{h} d(v(t - h), G(t, h, u)) = 0, t \in [0, t_N], \tag{2}$$

when $d(a, b) = |a - b|$ and

$$G(t, h, v) = v - h g(t, v). \tag{3}$$

Definition 3. Let (Y, d) be a metric space and $G : [0, t_N] \times [0, \infty) \times Y \to Y$. A function $v : [0, t_N] \to Y$ is a solution to the MDS given by G with the final data $v_N \in Y$, if $v(t_N) = v_N$, and condition (2) holds in $[0, t_N]$.

In the sequel, for this type of MDS, we achieve solutions satisfying (2) changing the lim inf by the lim.

Example 1. For the differential equation (1) and considering G given by (3), we have that, if v is a solution to (1), then v is a solution for the MDS given by G with the final condition v_N.

Example 2. Consider the fuzzy differential equation below

$$v'(t) = \begin{cases} g(t, v(t)), & t \in [0, t_N], \\ v(t_N) = v_N \in \mathbb{R}_{\mathcal{F}}^n, \end{cases}$$

where $g : [0, t_N] \times \mathbb{R}_{\mathcal{F}}^n \to \mathbb{R}_{\mathcal{F}}^n$, and $v : [0, t_N] \to \mathbb{R}_{\mathcal{F}}^n$ is differentiable in the sense of Definition 1. Therefore, the function G is considered as follows:

$$G(t, h, v) = v - hg(t, v),$$

for $h > 0$.

Analogously to the results in [11] for the concept of Metric Dynamical Systems considered in Definition 1.1 [11], we search for sufficient conditions for the existence of a unique solution in the interval $I = [0, t_N]$.

Let $G : I \times [0, \epsilon_0] \times Y \to Y$ such that the following properties hold:

– **Condition 1.** $G(t, 0, y) = y$, for every $t \in I, y \in Y$.
– **Condition 2.** $(t - h, \tilde{h}, G(t, h, y)) \in U$ for $(t, h, y) \in U, \tilde{h} \geq 0, t - h \leq t_N$.
– **Condition 3.** There is a constant $L > 0$ so that

$$d(G(t, h, y), G(t, h, z)) \leq e^{Lh} d(y, z),$$

for any $(t, h, y), (t, h, z) \in U$.
– **Condition 4.** There exists $\mathcal{B} : \mathbb{R}^+ \to \mathbb{R}^+$ non-decreasing with $\lim_{h \to 0^+} \mathcal{B}(h) = 0$ such that

$$d(G(t - h, \tilde{h}, G(t, h, y)), G(t, h + \tilde{h}, y)) \leq \mathcal{B}(h)(e^{L\tilde{h}} - 1).$$

Let $\mathcal{P}$ be a partition of I, with step $|\mathcal{P}|$. For a partition $\mathcal{P}$, we define

$$(X_{\mathcal{P}})_{t_N}^{\tau} y_N = \begin{cases} G(t_N, t_N - \tau, y_N), & \mathcal{P} \cap (\tau, t_N) = \emptyset, \\ G(a_l, a_l - \tau, (X_{\mathcal{P}})_{t_N}^{a_l} y_N), & a_l = \min \mathcal{P} \cap (\tau, t_N), \end{cases} \tag{4}$$

for $y_N \in U_{t_N}$ and $\tau \in I$. Therefore, functions $X_{\mathcal{P}}$ are a development of the switching quasi-flows for equations in metric spaces.

Lemma 1. *Let $\mathcal{P}$ be a partition of $[t_0, t_N]$, then we have*

i $(X_{\mathcal{P}})_{a_j}^{\tau} (X_{\mathcal{P}})_{t_N}^{a_j} y_N = (X_{\mathcal{P}})_{t_N}^{\tau} y_N$.
ii $d((X_{\mathcal{P}})_{t_N}^{\tau} y_N, (X_{\mathcal{P}})_{t_N}^{\tau} \bar{y}_N) \leq e^{L(t_N - \tau)} d(y_N, \bar{y}_N), \quad \forall y_N, \bar{y}_N \in U_{t_N}, \tau \in I.$
iii $d((X_{\mathcal{P}})_{t_N}^{\tau} y_N, G(t_N, t_N - \tau, y_N)) \leq \mathcal{B}(t_N - \tau)(e^{L(t_N - \tau)} - 1), \quad \forall y_N \in U_{t_N}, \tau \in I.$

iv $d((X_{\mathcal{P}})_{t_N}^{\tau} z_N, G(t_N, t_N - \tau, y_N)) \leq d(y_N, z_N)e^{L(t_N - \tau)} + \mathcal{B}(t_N - \tau)(e^{L(t_N - \tau)} - 1)$, $\forall y_N, z_N \in U_{t_N}, \tau \in I$.

Proof. The proof of (*i*) is an immediate consequence of (4). To prove (*ii*), let $\mathcal{P}$ be a partition by the set $\{c_0, c_1, \ldots, c_n = t_N\}$. If $\tau = t_N$, then we have

$$d((X_{\mathcal{P}})_{t_N}^{t_N} y_N, (X_{\mathcal{P}})_{t_N}^{t_N} \bar{y}_N) = e^{L(t_N - t_N)} d(y_N, \bar{y}_N).$$

Let $\tau < t_N$. If $\mathcal{P} \cap (\tau, t_N) = \emptyset$, then $\tau \in [c_{n-1}, t_N]$ and

$$d((X_{\mathcal{P}})_{t_N}^{\tau} y_N, (X_{\mathcal{P}})_{t_N}^{\tau} \bar{y}_N) = d(G(t_N, t_N - \tau, y_N), G(t_N, t_N - \tau, \bar{y}_N))$$
$$\leq e^{L(t_N - \tau)} d(y_N, \bar{y}_N).$$

By induction, we assume that (*ii*) is valid in $[c_{k+1}, t_N]$. If $\tau \in [c_k, c_{k+1})$, then we get

$$d((X_{\mathcal{P}})_{t_N}^{\tau} y_N, (X_{\mathcal{P}})_{t_N}^{\tau} \bar{y}_N)$$
$$= d(G(c_{k+1}, c_{k+1} - \tau, (X_{\mathcal{P}})_{t_N}^{c_{k+1}} y_N), G(c_{k+1}, c_{k+1} - \tau, (X_{\mathcal{P}})_{t_N}^{c_{k+1}} \bar{y}_N))$$
$$= e^{L(c_{k+1} - \tau)} d((X_{\mathcal{P}})_{t_N}^{c_{k+1}} y_N, (X_{\mathcal{P}})_{t_N}^{c_{k+1}} \bar{y}_N)$$
$$\leq e^{L(t_N - c_{k+1})} e^{L(c_{k+1} - \tau)} d(y_N, \bar{y}_N)$$
$$\leq e^{L(t_N - \tau)} d(y_N, \bar{y}_N),$$

which is desired result. To prove (*iii*), regarding the same partition as (*ii*) and $\tau \in [c_{n-1}, t_N]$, we get

$$d((X_{\mathcal{P}})_{t_N}^{\tau} y_N, G(t_N, t_N - \tau, y_N)) = d(G(t_N, t_N - \tau, y_N), G(t_N, t_N - \tau, y_N)) = 0.$$

Let $\tau \in [c_{n-2}, c_{n-1}]$, by Condition 4, we have

$$d((X_{\mathcal{P}})_{t_N}^{\tau} y_N, G(t_N, t_N - \tau, y_N))$$
$$= d(G(c_{n-1}, c_{n-1} - \tau, G(t_N, t_N - c_{n-1}, y_N)), G(t_N, t_N - \tau, y_N))$$
$$\leq \mathcal{B}(t_N - c_{n-1})(e^{L(c_{n-1} - \tau)} - 1)$$
$$\leq \mathcal{B}(t_N - \tau)(e^{L(t_N - \tau)} - 1).$$

By induction, we assume that (*iii*) is valid in $[c_{k+1}, t_N]$. Let $\tau \in [c_k, c_{k+1})$, then by Conditions 3,4 and the triangle inequality, we get

$$d((X_{\mathcal{P}})_{t_N}^{\tau} y_N, G(t_N, t_N - \tau, y_N))$$
$$= d(G(c_{k+1}, c_{k+1} - \tau, (X_{\mathcal{P}})_{t_N}^{c_{k+1}} y_N), G(t_N, t_N - \tau, y_N))$$
$$\leq d(G(c_{k+1}, c_{k+1} - \tau, (X_{\mathcal{P}})_{t_N}^{c_{k+1}} y_N),$$
$$G(c_{k+1}, c_{k+1} - \tau, G(t_N, t_N - c_{k+1}, G(t_N, t_N - c_{k+1}, y_N)))$$
$$+ d(G(c_{k+1}, c_{k+1} - \tau, G(t_N, t_N - c_{k+1}, G(t_N, t_N - c_{k+1}, y_N)), G(t_N, t_N - \tau, y_N))$$
$$\leq \mathcal{B}(t_N - c_{k+1})(e^{L(t_N - \tau)} - 1)$$
$$\leq \mathcal{B}(t_N - \tau)(e^{L(t_N - \tau)} - 1).$$

To prove (iv), by (ii) and (iii), we have

$$
\begin{aligned}
&d((X_{\mathcal{P}})^{\tau}_{t_N} z_N, G(t_N, t_N - \tau, y_N)) \\
&\leq d((X_{\mathcal{P}})^{\tau}_{t_N} z_N, (X_{\mathcal{P}})^{\tau}_{t_N} y_N) + d((X_{\mathcal{P}})^{\tau}_{t_N} y_N, G(t_N, t_N - \tau, y_N)) \\
&\leq d(y_N, z_N) e^{L(t_N - \tau)} + \mathcal{B}(t_N - \tau)(e^{L(t_N - \tau)} - 1).
\end{aligned}
$$

Lemma 2. *Let the partitions be comparable, that is, $\mathcal{P} \prec \widetilde{\mathcal{P}}$, then we have*

$$
d((X_{\mathcal{P}})^{\tau}_{t_N} y_N, (X_{\widetilde{\mathcal{P}}})^{\tau}_{t_N} y_N) \leq \mathcal{B}(|\mathcal{P}|)(e^{L(t_N - \tau)} - 1), \quad \forall y_N \in U_{t_N}, \tau \in I. \tag{5}
$$

Proof. We suppose that $\widetilde{\mathcal{P}}$ is given by the points $\{c_0, c_1, \ldots, c_n = t_N\}$. If $\tau \in [c_{n-1}, t_N]$, then we have

$$
d((X_{\mathcal{P}})^{\tau}_{t_N} y_N, (X_{\widetilde{\mathcal{P}}})^{\tau}_{l_N} y_N) = d(G(t_N, t_N - \tau, y_N), G(t_N, t_N - \tau, x_N)) = 0.
$$

If $\tau \in [c_{n-2}, c_{n-1}]$, we proceed in two steps:
Step1a. Let $c_{n-1} \in \mathcal{P}$. In this case, we obtain that

$$
\begin{aligned}
&d((X_{\mathcal{P}})^{\tau}_{t_N} y_N, (X_{\widetilde{\mathcal{P}}})^{\tau}_{t_N} y_N) \\
&= d(G(c_{n-1}, c_{n-1} - \tau, (X_{\mathcal{P}})^{c_{n-1}}_{t_N} y_N), G(c_{n-1}, c_{n-1} - \tau, (X_{\widetilde{\mathcal{P}}})^{c_{n-1}}_{t_N} y_N)) \\
&= d(G(c_{n-1}, c_{n-1} - \tau, G(t_N, t_N - c_{n-1}, y_N)), G(c_{n-1}, c_{n-1} - \tau, G(t_N, t_N - c_{n-1}, x_N))) \\
&= 0.
\end{aligned}
$$

Step2a. Let $c_{n-1} \notin \mathcal{P}$. Therefore, by Lemma 1, we have

$$
\begin{aligned}
d((X_{\mathcal{P}})^{\tau}_{t_N} y_N, (X_{\widetilde{\mathcal{P}}})^{\tau}_{t_N} y_N) &= d(G(t_N, t_N - \tau, y_N), (X_{\widetilde{\mathcal{P}}})^{\tau}_{l_N} y_N) \\
&\leq \mathcal{B}(t_N - \tau)(e^{L(t_N - \tau)} - 1) \\
&\leq \mathcal{B}(|\mathcal{P}|)(e^{L(t_N - \tau)} - 1),
\end{aligned}
$$

where $\mathcal{B}$ is nondecreasing, the relation $t_N - \tau \leq t_N - c_{n-1} \leq |\mathcal{P}|$. Besides, we assume that (5) is correct for $\tau \in [c_{k+1}, t_N]$ and we prove that (5) is valid for $\tau \in (c_k, c_{k+1}]$. Again, we proceed in two steps:
Step1b. If $\mathcal{P} \cap (\tau, t_N) = \emptyset$, then by Lemma 1, we have

$$
\begin{aligned}
d((X_{\mathcal{P}})^{\tau}_{t_N} y_N, (X_{\widetilde{\mathcal{P}}})^{\tau}_{t_N} y_N) &= d(G(t_N, t_N - \tau, y_N), (X_{\widetilde{\mathcal{P}}})^{\tau}_{t_N} y_N) \\
&\leq \mathcal{B}(t_N - \tau)(e^{L(t_N - \tau)} - 1) \\
&\leq \mathcal{B}(|\mathcal{P}|)(e^{L(t_N - \tau)} - 1).
\end{aligned}
$$

Step2b. Let $\min \mathcal{P} \cap (\tau, t_N) = c_j$ such that $\tau - c_j \leq |\mathcal{P}|$. Hence, we obtain that

$$
\begin{aligned}
d((X_{\mathcal{P}})^{\tau}_{t_N} y_N, (X_{\widetilde{\mathcal{P}}})^{\tau}_{t_N} y_N) &= d(G(c_j, c_j - \tau, (X_{\mathcal{P}})^{c_j}_{t_N} y_N), (X_{\widetilde{\mathcal{P}}})^{c_j}_{t_N} (X_{\widetilde{\mathcal{P}}})^{\tau}_{c_j} y_N) \\
&\leq d((X_{\mathcal{P}})^{c_j}_{t_N} y_N, (X_{\widetilde{\mathcal{P}}})^{c_j}_{t_N} y_N) e^{L(c_j - \tau)} \\
&\quad + \mathcal{B}(c_j - \tau)(e^{L(c_j - \tau)} - 1) \\
&\leq \mathcal{B}(|\mathcal{P}|)(e^{L(t_N - \tau)} - 1).
\end{aligned}
$$

Lemma 3. *Let $\mathcal{P}$ and $\widetilde{\mathcal{P}}$ be the non comparable partitions, then*

$$d((X_{\mathcal{P}})_{t_N}^{\tau} y_N, (X_{\widetilde{\mathcal{P}}})_{t_N}^{\tau} y_N) \le (\mathcal{B}(|\mathcal{P}|) + \mathcal{B}(|\widetilde{\mathcal{P}}|))(e^{L(t_N - \tau)} - 1)$$
$$\le 2\mathcal{B}(\max\{|\mathcal{P}|, |\widetilde{\mathcal{P}}|\})(e^{L(t_N - \tau)} - 1).$$

Proof. It is an immediate consequence of Lemma 2 regarding $\mathcal{P} \cup \widetilde{\mathcal{P}}$ as a partition.

Theorem 3. *Let the metric space Y be complete. Suppose that G satisfies Conditions 1–4 and is continuous in the second variable h. Then, there is a solution $\phi(t) = f_{t_N}^t y_N$ of the Metric Dynamical System (G, t_N, y_N) on I and*

$$d((X_{\mathcal{P}})_{t_N}^t y_N, f_{t_N}^t y_N) \le \mathcal{B}(|\mathcal{P}|)(e^{L(t_N - t)} - 1). \tag{6}$$

Proof. By Lemma 3 and the Cauchy Criterion, the function $(X_{\mathcal{P}})_{t_N}^t y_N$ converges uniformly on I to a function $\phi(t) = f_{t_N}^t y_N$ as $|\mathcal{P}| \to 0$. Moreover, taking the limit as $|\widetilde{\mathcal{P}}| \to 0$ in (5) with t instead of τ gives (6). Now, we need to show that ϕ is a solution of the final value problem metric dynamical system (G, t_N, x_N). The function ϕ satisfies the last condition. Indeed, $(X_{\mathcal{P}})_{t_N}^{t_N} y_N = G(t_N, t_N - t_N, y_N) = y_N$ and, passing the limit as $|\mathcal{P}| \to 0$, we deduce $\phi(t_N) = y_N$.

Let $t, t - h \in I$ be given and let $\mathcal{P}$ be a partition that includes the points $t, t - h$ and satisfies $\mathcal{P} \cap (t - h, t) = \emptyset$ as well as $|\mathcal{P}| = h$. Then, by (6), respectively y_N, t, t_N instead of $\phi, t - h, t$, we obtain

$$\frac{d(\phi(t - h), G(t, h, \phi(t)))}{h} \le \mathcal{B}(h) \frac{e^{Lh} - 1}{h},$$

as $h \to 0^+$, we deduce that ϕ is a solution of the MDS (G, t_N, y_N) on I.

Corollary 1. *Let $v_N \in \mathbb{R}_{\mathcal{F}}^n$ and $\bar{N}(v_m, r) = \{u \in \mathbb{R}_{\mathcal{F}}^n : D(u, v_m) \le r\}$. Also, let $g : I \times \bar{N}(v_m, r) \to \mathbb{R}_{\mathcal{F}}^n$ be continuous, L-lipschitzian in the second variable and such that $D(G(t, v), \tilde{0}) \le M$. Then, the MDS (G, t_N, v_N) given by $G(t, h, v) = v - hg(t, v)$ has a solution ϕ such that $\phi(t_N) = v_N$.*

Proof. It is easy to find the set U satisfying Condition 2, so we just show that the remaining Conditions hold. Indeed, we have
Condition 1. $G(t, 0, v) = v$, for any $t \in I, v \in \mathbb{R}_{\mathcal{F}}^n$.
Condition 3. By Theorem 1, we gain

$$D(G(t, h, u), G(t, h, v)) = D(u - hg(t, u), v - hg(t, v))$$
$$= D(u, v) + hD(g(t, u), g(t, v))$$
$$\le D(u, v) + LhD(u, v)$$
$$\le e^{Lh} D(u, v).$$

Condition 4. According to Theorems 1, 2, we have

$$D(G(t - h, \tilde{h}, G(t, h, u)), G(t, h + \tilde{h}, u))$$
$$= D(G(t, h, u) - \tilde{h}g(t - h, G(t, h, u)), u - (h + \tilde{h})g(t, u))$$
$$= D(u - hg(t, u(t)) - \tilde{h}g(t - h, G(t, h, u)), u - hg(t, x) - \tilde{h}g(t, u))$$
$$= \tilde{h}D(g(t - h, G(t, h, u)), g(t, u))$$
$$\leq \tilde{h}\left(D(g(t - h, G(t, h, u)), g(t - h, u)) + D(g(t - h, u), g(t, u))\right)$$
$$\leq \tilde{h}(LhM + \rho(h))$$
$$= L\tilde{h}\left(hM + \frac{\rho(h)}{L}\right)$$
$$\leq \mathcal{B}(h)(e^{L\tilde{h}} - 1),$$

where $\rho(h) = \sup\{D(g(l, x), g(\tilde{l}, x)) : l, \tilde{l} \in I, |l - \tilde{l}| \leq h\}$. Therefore, by Theorem 3, the requested result is obtained.

Corollary 2. *Let $g : I \times \mathbb{R}^n_{\mathcal{F}} \to \mathbb{R}^n_{\mathcal{F}}$ be continuous, L-lipschitzian in the second variable and $D(g(t, v), \tilde{0}) \leq M$. The fuzzy differential equation*

$$v'(t) = g(t, v(t)), v(t_N) = v_N,$$

has a solution when the derivative v' is considered in the sense of (ii)-D-differentiability.

Proof. It is a direct consequence of Theorem 3 and Corollary 1.

Acknowledgments. This article was partially supported by Fapesp under grants no. 2022/00196-1 and 2020/09838-0 and by CNPq under grant no. 313313/2020-2.

References

1. Bede, B.: Mathematics of Fuzzy Sets and Fuzzy Logic. Springer, Berlin (2013). https://doi.org/10.1007/978-3-642-35221-8
2. Buckley, J.J., Feuring, T.: Fuzzy differential equations. Fuzzy Sets Syst. **110**, 43–54 (2000)
3. Chalco-Cano, Y., Román-Flores, H.: Comparation between some approaches to solve fuzzy differential equations. Fuzzy Sets Syst. **160**, 1517–1527 (2009)
4. Chalco-Cano, Y., Rodríguez-López, R., Jiménez-Gamero, M.D.: Characterizations of generalized differentiable fuzzy functions. Fuzzy Sets Syst. **295**, 37–56 (2016)
5. Diamond, P., Kloeden, P.: Metric Spaces of Fuzzy Sets. World Scientific, Singapore (1994)
6. Hüllermeier, E.: An approach to modelling and simulation of uncertain dynamical systems. Int. J. Uncertainty Fuzziness Knowl.-Based Syst. **5**, 117–137 (1997)
7. Kaleva, O.: Fuzzy differential equations. Fuzzy Sets Syst. **24**, 301–317 (1987)
8. Khastan, A., Rodríguez-López, R., Shahidi, M.: New metric-based derivatives for fuzzy functions and properties. Fuzzy Sets Syst. **436**, 32–54 (2021)

9. Lakshmikantham, V., Nieto, J.J.: Differential equations in metric spaces: an introduction and an application to fuzzy differential equations. Dyn. Continuous Discrete Impulsive Syst. **10**, 991–1000 (2003)

10. Lupulescu, V., O'Regan, D.: A new derivative concept for set-valued and fuzzy-valued functions. Differential and integral calculus in quasilinear metric spaces. Fuzzy Sets Syst. **404**, 75–110 (2021)

11. Nieto, J.J., Rodríguez-López, R.: Euler polygonal method for metric dynamical systems. Inf. Sci. **177**, 4256–4270 (2007)

12. Panasyuk, A.I.: Quasidifferential equations in metric spaces. Differ. Equ. **21**, 914–921 (1985)

13. Pederson, S., Sambandham, M.: Numerical solution to hybrid fuzzy systems. Math. Comput. Model. **45**, 1133–1144 (2006)

Elements of Relational Power Set Theories for Semiring-Valued Fuzzy Structures

Jiří Močkoř$^{(\boxtimes)}$ (iD)

Institute for Research and Applications of Fuzzy Modeling,University of Ostrava, 30. dubna 22, 701 03 Ostrava 1, Czech Republic
Jiri.Mockor@osu.cz
http://irafm.osu.cz/

Abstract. Semiring-valued fuzzy sets represent fuzzy objects with new value set structures, which make it possible to unify part of new and frequently used fuzzy structures. The theory of semiring-valued fuzzy sets uses some basic tools of category theory and can be applied directly to these new fuzzy structures. For this reason, the development of this theory appears to be useful not only for the theory of semiring-valued fuzzy sets but also for the theory of new fuzzy structures. In this paper, we will therefore develop another part of this theory, namely, we define two basic types of relational power set theory for these structures and examine the basic relationships between these theories.

Keywords: power set theory · dual pair of semirings · monads · monadic relations · new fuzzy sets

1 Introduction

Semiring-valued fuzzy sets [11,12] represent fuzzy structures with specific sets of values. This structure is represented by a pair $(\mathcal{R}, \mathcal{R}^*)$ of dual commutative idempotent semirings defined on the same underlying set, with an involutive isomorphism between them. This construction makes it possible to use a single set of formulas to define most of the dual concepts that occur in classical fuzzy set theory, such as upper and lower approximations using fuzzy relations, upper and lower F-transformations of fuzzy sets, extensional and dual extensional fuzzy sets, closure and interior operators for fuzzy sets, and many others.

From the point of view of ordered structures, this value structure represents an intermediate stage between complete residuated lattices on the one hand and complete MV-algebras on the other. The primary motivation for the introduction of this structure was the effort to unify the theory of some new MV-valued

This work was partly supported from ERDF/ESF project CZ.02.1.01/0.0/0.0/17-049/0008414.

fuzzy structures, such as intuitionistic fuzzy sets [2,3], fuzzy soft sets [1,9] or neutrosophic fuzzy sets [8,18] and their mutual combinations such as intuitionistic fuzzy soft sets [14]. Although these new structures in a set X are traditionally called L-fuzzy sets, where L is a given MV-algebra, they are not, in fact, the classical mapping $X \to L$. A typical example is L-fuzzy soft set with the set of criteria K in a set X, which are mappings $X \to M(L, K)$, where $M(L, K)$ is the new value structure. All these structures can be transformed to $(\mathcal{R}, \mathcal{R}^*)$-valued fuzzy sets for specific dual pair of semirings [12].

In previous papers [11,12], we dealt with the construction of some parts of the theory of $(\mathcal{R}, \mathcal{R}^*)$-fuzzy sets, such as F-transform theory or rough theory for $(\mathcal{R}, \mathcal{R}^*)$-fuzzy sets. In this paper, we continue to build an analogy of classical fuzzy sets theory for $(\mathcal{R}, \mathcal{R}^*)$-fuzzy sets. We will focus on another frequently used area of fuzzy sets, namely the theory of power set structures with relational morphism. The power set structures for L-fuzzy sets represent one of the most frequently used constructions in the theory of fuzzy sets. The foundations of this theory were published by Zadeh [17], who first defined the extension of a mapping between two sets to a mapping between the respective power sets. This procedure, called Zadeh's extension principle, is still used in various variants in a wide range of applications and theories of fuzzy sets. Since then, a number of works have been published dealing with this issue and its generalization, such as [4–6,13,15,16].

For $(\mathcal{R}, \mathcal{R}^*)$-fuzzy sets (as well as for classic fuzzy sets), there are two basic types of power set structure, namely the classical set of all $(\mathcal{R}, \mathcal{R}^*)$-fuzzy sets defined in sets and the set of all $(\mathcal{R}, \mathcal{R}^*)$-fuzzy sets defined in sets with $(\mathcal{R}, \mathcal{R}^*)$-valued similarity relations. Moreover, due to the existence of two dual monads defined by the pair $(\mathcal{R}, \mathcal{R}^*)$, each of these power set structures exists in two variants. In this contribution, we describe the basic definitions and properties of these variants of power set structures.

2   Preliminaries

In this section, we repeat several basic definitions and facts that are important for the reader to understand the next parts of the paper.

Definition 1 ([12]). *Let $\mathcal{R} = (R, +, \times, 0, 1)$ and $\mathcal{R}^* = (R, +^*, \times^*, 0^*, 1^*)$ be complete idempotent commutative semirings with the same underlying set R, where $0, 1, 0^*, 1^*$ are also elements of R. The pair $(\mathcal{R}, \mathcal{R}^*)$ is called the dual pair of semirings if there exists a mapping $\neg : R \to R$ and the following axioms hold:*

1. *$\neg : \mathcal{R} \to \mathcal{R}^*$ is the involutive isomorphism of the semirings,*
2. *$\forall a \in R, S \subseteq R$ $a \times^* (\sum_{b \in S} b) = \sum_{b \in S} (a \times^* b)$,*
3. *$\forall a \in R, S \subseteq R$ $a + (\sum^*_{b \in S} b) = \sum^*_{b \in S} (a + b)$, where $\sum^*$ is the complete operation $+^*$ in $\mathcal{R}^*$,*
4. *$\forall a, b \in R,$ $a + b = a \Leftrightarrow a +^* b = b$.*

From this definition, the following simple lemma follows directly.

Lemma 1 ([12]). *Let $(\mathcal{R}, \mathcal{R}^*)$ be a dual pair of semirings and let the relations $\leq$ and $\leq^*$ be defined by*

$$x, y \in R, \quad x \leq y \Leftrightarrow x + y = y, \quad x \leq^* y \Leftrightarrow x +^* y = y.$$

Then $\mathcal{R}$ and $\mathcal{R}^*$ are isomorphic complete lattice-ordered semirings, where, for arbitrary $S \subseteq R$, $\sup S = \sum_{x \in S} x$, $\inf S = \sum_{x \in S}^* x$ in $(R, \leq)$, $\sup S = \sum_{x \in S}^* x$, $\inf S = \sum_{x \in S} x$ in $(R, \leq^*)$.

For an arbitrarily dual pair of semirings $(\mathcal{R}, \mathcal{R}^*)$ we can introduce the notion of $(\mathcal{R}, \mathcal{R}^*)$-fuzzy sets.

Definition 2 ([12]). *Let $(\mathcal{R}, \mathcal{R}^*)$ be a dual pair of semirings.*

1. *A mapping $s : X \to R$ is called a $(\mathcal{R}, \mathcal{R}^*)$-fuzzy set in a set X.*
2. *Operations with $(\mathcal{R}, \mathcal{R}^*)$-fuzzy sets are defined by*
   (a) *The intersection $s \sqcap t$ is defined by $(s \sqcap t)(x) = s(x) +^* t(x)$, $x \in X$,*
   (b) *The union $s \sqcup t$ is defined by $(s \sqcup t)(x) = s(x) + t(x)$, $x \in X$,*
   (c) *Complement $\neg s$ is defined by $(\neg s)(x) = \neg(s(x))$,*
   (d) *The external multiplication $\star$ by elements of R is defined by*
      $(a \star s)(x) = a \times s(x)$,
   (e) *The order relation $\leq$ between s, t is defined by $s \leq t \Leftrightarrow (\forall x \in X) s(x) \leq t(x)$ where $\leq$ is the order relation defined in Lemma 1.*

It is clear that, for these operations, we can define their dual versions. For example, we can set $\neg(s \sqcap^* t) = \neg s \sqcap \neg t$, $\neg(a \star^* s) = \neg a \star \neg s$.

For our purposes, we use basic properties of monads in the category **Set** of sets and mapping. For more properties of monads, see [7].

Definition 3. *The structure $\mathbf{T} = (T, \lozenge, \eta)$ is a monad in the category **Set**, if*

1. *$T : \mathbf{Set} \to \mathbf{Set}$ is mapping of objects,*
2. *η is a system of mappings $\{\eta_X : X \to T(X) | X \in \mathbf{Set}\}$,*
3. *For each pair of mappings $f : X \to T(Y)$, $g : Y \to T(Z)$, there exists a composition (called a Kleisli composition) $g \lozenge f : X \to T(Z)$, which is associative,*
4. *For every mapping $f : X \to T(Y)$, $\eta_Y \lozenge f = f$ and $f \lozenge \eta_X = f$ hold,*
5. *$\lozenge$ is compatible with the composition of mappings, that is, for mappings $f : X \to Y$, $g : Y \to T(Z)$, we have $g \lozenge (\eta_Y . f) = g . f$,*

For arbitrary dual pairs of semirings $(\mathcal{R}, \mathcal{R}^*)$ we can define a pair of basic monads describing the basis of the dual power set structures of all $(\mathcal{R}, \mathcal{R}^*)$-fuzzy sets.

Proposition 1 [12]. *Let $\mathcal{R}$ be a complete commutative idempotent semiring and let the structure $\mathbf{T}_\mathcal{R} = (T_\mathcal{R}, \lozenge, \eta)$ be defined by*

1. *The mapping $T(=T_\mathcal{R}) : \mathbf{Set} \to \mathbf{Set}$ of objects is defined by $T(X) = R^X$,*

2. *For the mappings* $f:X \to T(Y)$ *and* $g:Y \to T(Z)$ *their composition* $g \Diamond f:X \to T(Z)$
   is defined for $x \in X, z \in Z$ *by*

$$(g \Diamond f)(x)(z) = \sum_{y \in Y} f(x)(y) \times g(y)(z).$$

3. η_X *is the mapping* $X \to T(X)$ *defined by*

$$\eta_X(x)(y) = \begin{cases} 1_R, & x = y, \\ 0_R, & x \neq y, \end{cases}.$$

Then $\mathbf{T}_{\mathcal{R}}$ *is the monad in category* **Set**.

Remark 1. For arbitrary complete commutative idempotent semiring $\mathcal{R}$, by $\Diamond$ we denote the composition operation of Proposition 1.

It is clear that for a dual pair of semirings, there exist two monads $\mathbf{T}_{\mathcal{R}}$ and $\mathbf{T}_{\mathcal{R}^*}$, respectively, namely the monads $(T, \Diamond, \eta)$ and $(T, \Diamond^*, \eta^*)$, defined by operations from $\mathcal{R}$ and $\mathcal{R}^*$, respectively.

We need the notion of a monadic relation, which was introduced by Manes [10]. This notion generalizes the notion of a classical fuzzy relation, including the composition of monadic relations, and generalizes the classical composition of fuzzy relations.

Definition 4. *Let* $\mathcal{R}$ *be a complete commutative idempotent semiring and* X, Y *be sets. A (monadic)* $\mathcal{R}$*-relation* Q *from* X *to* Y *(denoted* $Q: X \rightsquigarrow Y$*) is a mapping* $Q: X \to T(Y)$*. If* $Q: X \rightsquigarrow Y$ *and* $S: Y \rightsquigarrow Z$ *are* $\mathcal{R}$*-relations, their composition is the* $\mathcal{R}$*-relation* $S \Diamond Q: X \rightsquigarrow Z$*. A* $\mathcal{R}$*-relation* $Q: X \rightsquigarrow X$ *is called a* $\mathcal{R}$*-similarity relation if*

1. *It is reflexive, that is,* $\eta_X \leq Q$,
2. *it is transitive, that is,* $Q \Diamond Q \leq Q$,
3. *it is symmetric, that is,* $Q(x)(y) = Q(y)(x)$, *for arbitrary* $x, y \in X$.

Remark 2. From this definition it follows that for a dual pair of semirings $(\mathcal{R}, \mathcal{R}^*)$ we can consider two types of relations, namely $\mathcal{R}$-relation and $\mathcal{R}^*$-relation. These two types are, in fact, identical, as follows from their definitions. Therefore, we can use the common name $(\mathcal{R}, \mathcal{R}^*)$-relations for both types of relation, or only relations, if the dual pair $(\mathcal{R}, \mathcal{R}^*)$ is obvious. On the other hand, if we consider the compositions of these relations, we need to distinguish between the types of composition, that is, $\Diamond$ and $\Diamond^*$, respectively. Therefore, we also need to distinguish between $\mathcal{R}$-similarity relations and $\mathcal{R}^*$-similarity relations.

If $(\mathcal{R}, \mathcal{R}^*)$ is a dual pair of semirings, we can construct two relational versions of the classical category **Set**, where instead of mappings as morphisms, the $\mathcal{R}$ or $\mathcal{R}^*$-relations are used, respectively, with the compositions of these morphisms defined by $\Diamond$ or $\Diamond^*$, respectively. These categories will be denoted **Set**$_{\mathcal{R}}$ and **Set**$_{\mathcal{R}^*}$, respectively, and called the *Kleisli categories* of monads $\mathbf{T}_{\mathcal{R}}$ and $\mathbf{T}_{\mathcal{R}^*}$, respectively.

3   Relational Power Set Theories in Kleisli Categories $\mathbf{Set}_\mathcal{R}$ and $\mathbf{Set}_{\mathcal{R}^*}$

The notion of a power set theory in the category **Set** of sets was introduced by Rodabaugh [15]. In the following definition we introduce a generalized version of this notion, called relational power set theory, where instead of the category **Set** we use the Kleisli categories $\mathbf{Set}_\mathcal{R}$ and $\mathbf{Set}_{\mathcal{R}^*}$, respectively.

Definition 5. *Let $\mathcal{R}$ be a complete commutative idempotent semiring and let $CSLAT$ be the category of complete $\bigvee$-semilattices with homomorphisms of semilattices as morphisms. The structure $(P, \rightarrow, \mu)$ is called a $\mathcal{R}$-relational* **power set theory** *in the Kleisli category $\mathbf{Set}_\mathcal{R}$ if*

1. *$P : \mathbf{Set}_\mathcal{R} \rightarrow CSLAT$ is a mapping of objects.*
2. *For each morphism $f : X \rightsquigarrow Y$ in the category $\mathbf{Set}_\mathcal{R}$ there exists a morphism $f^\rightarrow : P(X) \rightarrow P(Y)$ in $CSLAT$,*
3. *For each object $X \in \mathbf{Set}_\mathcal{R}$, μ_X is a mapping $\mu_X : X \rightarrow P(X)$ in the category* **Set***,*
4. *For each morphism $f : X \rightsquigarrow Y$ in $\mathbf{Set}_\mathcal{R}$,*

$$f^\rightarrow . \mu_X = \mu_Y \lozenge f, \tag{1}$$

holds.

An important example of $\mathcal{R}$-relational power set theory in $\mathbf{Set}_\mathcal{R}$ is described by the following proposition.

Proposition 2. *Let $\mathcal{R}$ be a complete commutative idempotent semiring, and let $\mathbf{T}_\mathcal{R} = (T_\mathcal{R}, \lozenge, \eta)$ be the corresponding monad of Proposition 1. The structure $(T_\mathcal{R}, \rightarrow, \eta)$ is the $\mathcal{R}$-relational power set theory in category $\mathbf{Set}_\mathcal{R}$, where for arbitrary $\mathcal{R}$-relation $f : X \rightsquigarrow Y$, the mapping $f^\rightarrow_\mathcal{R} : R^X \rightarrow R^Y$ is defined by*

$$f^\rightarrow_\mathcal{R} = f \lozenge 1_{R^X}.$$

Moreover, $T_\mathcal{R} : \mathbf{Set}_\mathcal{R} \rightarrow \mathbf{Set}$ is a functor such that for $f : X \rightsquigarrow Y$, $T_\mathcal{R}(f) = f^\rightarrow_\mathcal{R}$.

Proof. The proof is only a simple verification that identity (1) holds for both structures. It follows directly from the properties of the compositions $\lozenge$ and $\lozenge^*$. ∎

It is obvious that for dual pairs of semirings $(\mathcal{R}, \mathcal{R}^*)$ we can also define the notion of the $\mathcal{R}^*$-relational power set theory $(T_{\mathcal{R}^*}, \leftarrow, \eta^*)$ in $\mathbf{Set}_{\mathcal{R}^*}$, where we use the composition $\lozenge^*$ instead of $\lozenge$. Because objects of the Kleisli categories $\mathbf{Set}_\mathcal{R}$ and $\mathbf{Set}_{\mathcal{R}^*}$ are identical, the mappings $T_\mathcal{R}$ and $T_{\mathcal{R}^*}$ are identical.

To compare different theory of relational power sets, we introduce the notion of a morphism between theory of relational power sets in the Kleisli category $\mathbf{Set}_\mathcal{R}$.

Definition 6. *Let $\mathcal{R}$ and $\mathcal{S}$ be complete commutative idempotent semirings and let $(P, \to, \mu)$ and $(V, \leftarrow, \rho)$, respectively, be $\mathcal{R}$ and $\mathcal{S}$-relational power set theories in $\mathbf{Set}_{\mathcal{R}}$. Then $\alpha : (P, \to, \mu) \to (V, \leftarrow, \rho)$ is a morphism of these relational power set theories, if*

1. *$\alpha = \{\alpha_X : X \in \mathbf{Set}\}$, where α_X is a morphism $P(X) \to V(X)$ in the category CSLAT.*
2. *For an arbitrary morphism $f : X \rightsquigarrow Y$ in $\mathbf{Set}_{\mathcal{R}}$ the following diagrams commute.*

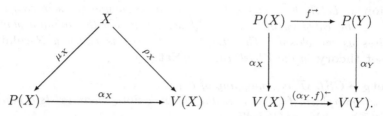

The basic example of a morphism between relational power set theories in Kleisli categories is presented below. We use the following notation. If $\Phi : \mathcal{R} \to \mathcal{S}$ is a semiring homomorphism, for an arbitrary set X the mapping $\alpha_X : R^X \to S^X$ is defined by $(\alpha_X(s))(x) = \Phi(s(x))$, where $s \in R^X, x \in X$.

Proposition 3. *Let $\mathcal{R}$ and $\mathcal{S}$ be complete commutative idempotent semirings and let $(T_{\mathcal{R}}, \Diamond_{\mathcal{R}}, \eta_{\mathcal{R}})$ and $(T_{\mathcal{S}}, \Diamond_{\mathcal{S}}, \eta)$ be the corresponding monads, respectively. If $\Phi : \mathcal{R} \twoheadrightarrow \mathcal{S}$ is a semiring epimorphism, then*

$$\alpha = \{\alpha_X : X \in \mathbf{Set}\} : (T_{\mathcal{R}}, \to, \eta_{\mathcal{R}}) \to (T_{\mathcal{S}}, \leftarrow, \eta_{\mathcal{S}}),$$

is a morphism of these relational power set theories.

Proof. We show that for arbitrary $X \in \mathbf{Set}$, $\eta_{\mathcal{S}, X} = \alpha_X . \eta_{\mathcal{R}, X}$. In fact, since α is a semiring homomorphism, for arbitrary $x, x' \in X$ we obtain

$$\alpha . \eta_{\mathcal{R}, X}(x)(x') = \begin{cases} 1_S, & \eta_{\mathcal{R}, X}(x)(x') = 1_R, \\ 0_S, & \eta_{\mathcal{R}, X}(x)(x') = 0_R \end{cases} = \eta_{\mathcal{S}, X}(x)(x').$$

Further, we prove that for arbitrary $\mathcal{R}$-relation $f : X \rightsquigarrow Y$, the identity $\alpha_Y . f^{\to} = (\alpha_X . f)^{\leftarrow} . \alpha_X$ holds. We have

$$\alpha_Y . f^{\to} = \alpha_Y . (f \Diamond_{\mathcal{R}} 1_{R^X}) = (\alpha_Y . f) \Diamond_{\mathcal{S}} (\alpha_X . 1_{R^X}) = (\alpha_Y . f) \Diamond_{\mathcal{S}} (1_{S^X} . \alpha_X) =$$
$$(\alpha_Y . f \Diamond_{\mathcal{S}} 1_{S^X}) . \alpha_X = (\alpha_Y . f)^{\leftarrow} . \alpha_X.$$

Therefore, α is a morphism of relational power set theories. ∎

Corollary 1. *Let $(\mathcal{R}, \mathcal{R}^*)$ be a dual pair of semirings.*

1. *The relational power set theories $(T_{\mathcal{R}}, \to, \eta)$ and $(T_{\mathcal{R}^*}, \leftarrow, \eta^*)$, respectively, presented in Proposition 2 for semirings $\mathcal{R}$ and $\mathcal{R}^*$, respectively, are isomorphic.*

2. *The following diagram of functors commutes, where the functor Δ is such that $\Delta(X) = X, \Delta(f) = \neg f$, where $\neg f$ is defined point-wise.*

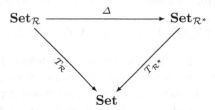

Proof. Because $\neg : \mathcal{R} \to \mathcal{R}^*$ is a semiring isomorphism, the first part follows directly from Proposition 3. In that case, for an arbitrarily $f : X \rightsquigarrow Y$, the following equality holds.

$$f_{\mathcal{R}^*}^{\leftarrow} = (\neg f)_{\mathcal{R}}^{\rightarrow} = (\neg f) \lozenge^* 1_{R^X}. \tag{2}$$

$\blacksquare$

For a dual pair of semirings, we show some relationships between operators $\rightarrow$ and $\leftarrow$. According to Remark 1, instead of $\mathcal{R}$ or $\mathcal{R}^*$-relations, we can speak of $(\mathcal{R}, \mathcal{R}^*)$-relations.

Lemma 2. *Let $(\mathcal{R}, \mathcal{R}^*)$ be the dual pair of semirings and let $f : X \rightsquigarrow Y$ be a $(\mathcal{R}, \mathcal{R}^*)$-relation. Let $a \in \mathcal{R}$ and $s, t, s_i \in \mathcal{R}^X$, $i \in I$.*

1. $f^{\rightarrow}(\bigsqcup_{i \in I} s_i) = \bigsqcup_{i \in I} f^{\rightarrow}(s_i), \ f^{\leftarrow}(\bigsqcap_{i \in I} s_i) = \bigsqcap_{i \in I} f^{\leftarrow}(s_i)$,
2. $f^{\rightarrow}(a \star s) = a \star f^{\rightarrow}(s), \ f^{\leftarrow}(a \star^* s) = a \star^* f^{\leftarrow}(s)$,
3. $s \le t \leftarrow f^{\leftarrow}(s) \le f^{\leftarrow}(t), f^{\rightarrow}(s) \le f^{\rightarrow}(t)$,
4. $f^{\leftarrow}(s) = \neg f^{\rightarrow}(\neg s), \ f^{\rightarrow}(s) = \neg f^{\leftarrow}(\neg s)$.
5. *If $f : X \rightsquigarrow X$ is reflexive, $f^{\leftarrow}(s) \le s \le f^{\rightarrow}(s)$.*
6. *Let $g : X \rightsquigarrow Y$ and $f : Y \rightsquigarrow Z$ be $(\mathcal{R}, \mathcal{R}^*)$-relations. We have*

$$f^{\rightarrow}.g^{\rightarrow} = (f \lozenge g)^{\rightarrow}, \quad f^{\leftarrow}.g^{\leftarrow} = (f \lozenge g)^{\leftarrow}.$$

4 Relational Power Set Theorie in Categories $\mathbf{Set}(\mathcal{R})$ and $\mathbf{Set}(\mathcal{R}^*)$

As we mentioned in the Introduction, the other objects for which we can define the theory of $\mathcal{R}$-relational power sets are sets with $\mathcal{R}$-relations. In order to build such a theory, instead of the Kleisli category $\mathbf{Set}_{\mathcal{R}}$, we need another category with these objects, where the morphisms should be suitable $\mathcal{R}$-relations.

Definition 7. *Let $\mathcal{R}$ be a complete commutative idempotent semiring. The category $\mathbf{Set}(\mathcal{R})$ of sets with $\mathcal{R}$-similarity relations is defined by*

1. *The objects are pairs (X, Q), where X is a set and $Q : X \rightsquigarrow X$ is a $\mathcal{R}$-similarity relation.*

2. *Morphisms* $f : (X, Q) \rightsquigarrow (Y, S)$ *are* $\mathcal{R}$-*relations* $f : X \rightsquigarrow Y$ *such that* $f \Diamond Q = f$, $S \Diamond f = f$.
3. *The composition of the morphisms* $f : (X, Q) \rightsquigarrow (Y, S)$ *and* $g : (Y, S) \rightsquigarrow (Z, V)$ *is defined by* $g \Diamond f$.
4. *For arbitrary object* (X, Q), $1_{(X,Q)} = Q : (X, Q) \rightsquigarrow (X, Q)$.

If $(\mathcal{R}, \mathcal{R}^*)$ is a dual pair of semirings, we can also define the category $\mathbf{Set}(\mathcal{R}^*)$ of sets with $\mathcal{R}^*$-similarity relations, where instead of $\Diamond$ we use $\Diamond^*$.

Analogously, as we introduced the $\mathcal{R}$-relational power set theory in the Kleisli category $\mathbf{Set}_{\mathcal{R}}$, we can introduce the $\mathcal{R}$-relational power set theory in the category $\mathbf{Set}(\mathcal{R})$.

Definition 8. *Let* $\mathcal{R}$ *be a complete commutative idempotent semiring. Structure* $(F, \uparrow, \tau)$ *is called a* $\mathcal{R}$-**relational power set theory** *in the category* $\mathbf{Set}(\mathcal{R})$ *if*

1. $F : \mathbf{Set}(\mathcal{R}) \rightarrow CSLAT$ *is a mapping of objects.*
2. *For each morphism* $f : (X, Q) \rightsquigarrow (Y, S)$ *in the category* $\mathbf{Set}(\mathcal{R})$ *there exists a morphism* $f^{\uparrow} : F(X, Q) \rightarrow F(Y, S)$ *in* $CSLAT$,
3. *For each object* $(X, Q) \in \mathbf{Set}(\mathcal{R})$, $\tau_{(X,Q)}$ *is a mapping* $X \rightarrow F(X, Q)$ *in the category* $\mathbf{Set}$,
4. *For each morphism* $f : (X, Q) \rightsquigarrow (Y, S)$ *in* $\mathbf{Set}(\mathcal{R})$,

$$f^{\uparrow} . \tau_{(X,Q)} = \tau_{(Y,S)} \Diamond f.$$

An example of $\mathcal{R}$-relational power set theory in $\mathbf{Set}(\mathcal{R})$ is described by the following proposition.

Proposition 4. *Let* $\mathcal{R}$ *be a complete commutative idempotent semiring. The structure* $(F_{\mathcal{R}}, \Uparrow, \sigma)$ *is the* $\mathcal{R}$-*relational power set theory in the category* $\mathbf{Set}(\mathcal{R})$, *where*

1. *For an arbitrary object* $(X, Q) \in \mathbf{Set}(\mathcal{R})$,

$$F_{\mathcal{R}}(X, Q) = \{ s \in R^X : Q_{\mathcal{R}}^{\rightarrow}(s) = (Q \Diamond 1_{R^X})(s) \leq s \},$$

2. *For arbitrary morphism* $f : (X, Q) \rightsquigarrow (Y, S)$ *in the category* $\mathbf{Set}(\mathcal{R})$, *the morphism* $f_{\mathcal{R}}^{\Uparrow} : F_{\mathcal{R}}(X, Q) \rightarrow F_{\mathcal{R}}(Y, S)$ *in the category* $CSLAT$ *is defined by*

$$f_{\mathcal{R}}^{\Uparrow} = S \Diamond f \Diamond 1_{R^X} (= f \Diamond 1_{R^X}).$$

3. *For arbitrary object* (X, Q), *the mapping* $\sigma : X \rightarrow F_{\mathcal{R}}(X, Q)$ *is defined by* $\sigma_{(X,Q)} = Q$.

Moreover, $F_{\mathcal{R}} : \mathbf{Set}(\mathcal{R}) \rightarrow \mathbf{Set}$ *is the functor such that* $F_{\mathcal{R}}(f) = f_{\mathcal{R}}^{\Uparrow}$.

Proof (sketch). First, we show that for arbitrarily $s \in F_{\mathcal{R}}(X, Q)$ we have $F_{\mathcal{R}}(f)(s) \in F_{\mathcal{R}}(Y, S)$. In fact, we have

$$(S \lozenge 1_{R^Y})(F_{\mathcal{R}}(f)(s)) = (S \lozenge 1_{R^Y})(S \lozenge f \lozenge 1_{R^X})(s) = S \lozenge 1_{R^Y}.(S \lozenge f \lozenge 1_{R^X})(s) =$$
$$(S \lozenge S \lozenge f \lozenge 1_{R^X})(s) \le (S \lozenge f \lozenge 1_{R^X})(s) = F_{\mathcal{R}}(f)(s),$$

Furthermore, we have

$$F_{\mathcal{R}}(Q) = Q \lozenge Q \lozenge 1_{R^X} = Q \lozenge 1_{R^X}, \quad s \le (Q \lozenge 1_{R^X})(s) \le s,$$

and it follows that $(Q \lozenge 1_{R^X})(s) = s$. Therefore, $F_{\mathcal{R}}(1_{(X,Q)}) = (Q \lozenge 1_{R^X}) = 1_{F_{\mathcal{R}}(X,Q)}$.
Finally, let $f : (X, Q) \rightsquigarrow (Y, S)$ and $g : (Y, S) \rightsquigarrow (Z, W)$ be morphisms in $\mathbf{Set}(\mathcal{R})$.
Therefore, $f \lozenge Q = f = S \lozenge f$ and $g \lozenge S = g = W \lozenge g$ and we obtain the following.

$$F_{\mathcal{R}}(g).F_{\mathcal{R}}(f) = (W \lozenge g \lozenge 1_{R^Y}).(S \lozenge f \lozenge 1_{R^X}) = W \lozenge g \lozenge S \lozenge f \lozenge 1_{R^X} =$$
$$W \lozenge g \lozenge f \lozenge 1_{R^X} = F_{\mathcal{R}}(g \lozenge f),$$

as follows from identity rule $W \lozenge W = W$ and composition rules for $\lozenge$. Therefore, $F_{\mathcal{R}}$ is the functor. ∎

If $(\mathcal{R}, \mathcal{R}^*)$ is a dual pair of semirings, we can also define the $\mathcal{R}^*$-relational power set theory in the category $\mathbf{Set}(\mathcal{R})$.

Proposition 5. *Let $(\mathcal{R}, \mathcal{R}^*)$ be a dual pair of semirings and let the structure $(F_{\mathcal{R}^*}, \Downarrow, \sigma^*)$ be defined formally in the same way as the structure $(F_{\mathcal{R}}, \Uparrow, \sigma)$, where $\lozenge^*$ is used instead of $\lozenge$. Then $(F_{\mathcal{R}}, \Downarrow, \sigma)$ is the $\mathcal{R}^*$-relational power set theory in $\mathbf{Set}(\mathcal{R}^*)$ and $F_{\mathcal{R}} : \mathbf{Set}(\mathcal{R}^*) \to \mathbf{Set}$ is a functor such that $F_{\mathcal{R}^*}(f) = f^{\Downarrow}$.*

The **proof** can be done analogously to Proposition 4 and will be omitted. ∎

For $\mathcal{R}$-relational power set theories in the category $\mathbf{Set}(\mathcal{R})$ we can also define the notion of a morphism between these theories.

Definition 9. *Let $\mathcal{R}$ and $\mathcal{S}$ be complete commutative idempotent semirings and let $(P, \Uparrow, \mu)$ and $(V, \Uparrow, \rho)$, respectively, be $\mathcal{R}$ and $\mathcal{S}$-relational power set theories in the category $\mathbf{Set}(\mathcal{R})$. Then $\alpha : (P, \Uparrow, \mu) \to (V, \Uparrow, \rho)$ is a morphism of relational power set theories in $\mathbf{Set}(\mathcal{R})$, if*

1. $\alpha = \{\alpha_{(X,Q)} : (X,Q) \in \mathbf{Set}(\mathcal{R})\}$, where $\alpha_{(X,Q)} : P(X,Q) \to V(X,Q)$ is a morphism in the category $CSLAT$.

2. For arbitrary morphism $f : (X, Q) \rightsquigarrow (Y, S)$ in $\mathbf{Set}(\mathcal{R})$, the following diagrams commute.

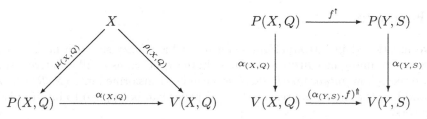

The basic example of a morphism between relational power set theories in the category $\mathbf{Set}(\mathcal{R})$ is presented below. We use the same notation Φ, α_X as in previous Section.

Proposition 6. *Let $\mathcal{R}$ and $\mathcal{S}$ be complete commutative idempotent semirings and let $(F_{\mathcal{R}}, \Uparrow_{\mathcal{R}}, \sigma_{\mathcal{R}})$ and $(F_{\mathcal{S}}, \Uparrow_{\mathcal{S}}, \sigma_{\mathcal{S}})$, respectively, be the corresponding relational power set theorie in the category $\mathbf{Set}(\mathcal{R})$, defined in Proposition 4. If $\Phi : \mathcal{R} \twoheadrightarrow \mathcal{S}$ is a semiring epimorphism, then*

$$\alpha = \{\alpha_X : X \in \mathbf{Set}\} : (F_{\mathcal{R}}, \Uparrow_{\mathcal{R}}, \sigma_{\mathcal{R}}) \to (F_{\mathcal{S}}, \Uparrow_{\mathcal{S}}, \sigma_{\mathcal{S}}),$$

is a morphism of these relational power set theories.

Corollary 2. *Let $(\mathcal{R}, \mathcal{R}^*)$ be a dual pair of semirings.*

1. *The relational power set theories $(F_{\mathcal{R}}, \Uparrow, \sigma)$ and $(F_{\mathcal{R}^*}, \Downarrow, \sigma^*)$, respectively, presented in Proposition 5 are isomorphic.*
2. *There exists the natural isomorphism $\Psi : F_{\mathcal{R}} \to F_{\mathcal{R}^*}.\Omega$, where the functor $\Omega : \mathbf{Set}(\mathcal{R}) \to \mathbf{Set}(\mathcal{R}^*)$ is such that $\Omega(X, Q) = (X, \neg Q)$, $\Omega(f) = \neg f$.*

Proof (Sketch). For arbitrary $(X, Q) \in \mathbf{Set}(\mathcal{R})$ the mapping

$$\Psi_{(X,Q)} : F_{\mathcal{R}}(X, Q) \to F_{\mathcal{R}^*}.\Omega(X, Q) = F_{\mathcal{R}^*}(X, \neg Q)$$

is defined by $\Psi_{(X,Q)}(s) = \neg s$, where $s \in F_{\mathcal{R}}(X, Q)$. For illustration only, we prove that Ψ is a natural transformation. That is, for an arbitrary morphism $f : (X, Q) \rightsquigarrow (Y, S)$ in $\mathbf{Set}(\mathcal{R})$, the following diagram commutes.

$$
\begin{array}{ccc}
F_{\mathcal{R}}(X, Q) & \xrightarrow{\Psi_{(X,Q)}} & F_{\mathcal{R}^*}.\Omega(X, Q) \\
\Big\downarrow {\scriptstyle f_{\mathcal{R}}^{\Uparrow}} & & \Big\downarrow {\scriptstyle (\Omega(f))_{\mathcal{R}^*}^{\Downarrow}} \\
F_{\mathcal{R}}(Y, S) & \xrightarrow{\Psi_{(Y,S)}} & F_{\mathcal{R}^*}.\Omega(Y, S).
\end{array}
$$

Using Propositions 4 and 5, for an arbitrary $s \in F_{\mathcal{R}}(X, Q)$ we obtain

$$(\Omega(f))_{\mathcal{R}^*}^{\Downarrow}.\Psi_{(X,Q)}(s) = (\neg f)_{\mathcal{R}^*}^{\Downarrow}(\neg s) = (\neg f \lozenge^* 1_{R^X})(\neg s) = (\neg f \lozenge^* \neg 1_{R^X})(s) =$$

$$\neg (f \lozenge 1_{R^X})(s) = \neg f_{\mathcal{R}}^{\Uparrow}(s) = \Psi_{Y,S)}.f_{\mathcal{R}}^{\Uparrow}(s).$$

Therefore, Ψ is a natural transformation.   ∎

5   Example

As we mentioned in Introduction, semirings-valued fuzzy sets can be universal value sets for many new fuzzy structures. In this section, as an illustrative example, we recall how *intuitionistic fuzzy sets* can be transformed into $(\mathcal{R}, \mathcal{R}^*)$-fuzzy sets and how the methods presented in the paper can be applied to intuitionistic fuzzy sets.

Let $(L, \vee, \wedge, \otimes, \oplus, \neg, 0_L, 1_L)$ be a complete MV-algebra. In [11] we showed that L-intuitionistic fuzzy sets can be transformed into $(\mathcal{R}, \mathcal{R}^*)$-fuzzy sets, where $R = \{(\alpha, \beta) \in L^2 : \neg \alpha \geq \beta\}$, and

1. $(\alpha, \beta) + (\alpha_1, \beta_1) := (\alpha \vee \alpha_1, \beta \wedge \beta_1)$,
2. $(\alpha, \beta) \times (\alpha_1, \beta_1) := (\alpha \otimes \alpha_1, \beta \oplus \beta_1)$,
3. $0_R = (0, 1)$, $1_R = (1, 0)$,
4. $(\alpha, \beta) +^* (\alpha_1, \beta_1) := (\alpha \wedge \alpha_1, \beta \vee \beta_1)$,
5. $(\alpha, \beta) \times^* (\alpha_1, \beta_1) := (\alpha \oplus \alpha_1, \beta \otimes \beta_1)$,
6. $0_R^* = (1, 0)$, $1_R^* = (0, 1)$,
7. $\neg R \to R$ is defined by $\neg(\alpha, \beta) = (\beta, \alpha)$.
8. From the definition of ordering in R it follows that $(\alpha, \beta) \leq (\alpha', \beta') \Leftrightarrow (\alpha \leq \alpha', \beta \geq \beta')$.

Then the algebraic structure of L-intuitionistic fuzzy sets is isomorphic to the algebraic structure of (R, R^*)-fuzzy sets. We present an example of the (R, R^*)-similarity relation $Q : X \rightsquigarrow X$ and show what elements of R-relational power set $F_R(X, Q)$ (that is, *intuitionistic fuzzy sets extensional with respect to Q*) from Proposition 4 look like.

Example 1. Let ϕ_1, ϕ_2 be arbitrary (standard) L-valued fuzzy relations $X \times X \to L$, such that

1. ϕ_1 is a L-valued similarity relation in X,
2. $\phi_2 = \neg \psi$, where ψ is a L-valued similarity relation in X,
3. $\neg\phi_1(x, y) \leq \phi_2(x, y)$, for arbitrary $x, y \in X$.

Let the example of the R-relation $Q : X \rightsquigarrow X$ be defined by

$$x, y \in X, \quad Q(x)(y) = (\phi_1(x, y), \phi_2(x, y)) \in R.$$

Then, Q is the R-similarity relation, that is, $Q \Diamond Q \leq Q$, Q is symmetric and $Q \geq \eta_X$. In fact, we have

$$Q \Diamond Q(x)(y) = \sum_{t \in X} Q(x)(t) \times Q(t)(y) = \sum_{t \in X} (\phi_1(x, t), \phi_2(x, t)) \times (\phi_1(t, y), \phi_2(t, y)) =$$

$$\sum_{t \in X} (\phi_1(x, t) \otimes \phi_1(t, y), \phi_2(x, t) \oplus \phi_2(t, y)) =$$

$$\left(\bigvee_{t \in X} \phi_1(x, t) \otimes \phi_1(t, y), \bigwedge_{t \in X} \phi_2(x, t) \oplus \phi_2(t, y) \right).$$

Since ϕ_1 is a L-similarity relation, we have $\bigvee_{t \in X} \phi_1(x, t) \otimes \phi_1(t, y) \leq \phi_1(x, y)$. In addition, we have the following.

$$\bigwedge_{t \in X} \phi_2(x, t) \oplus \phi_2(t, y) = \bigwedge_{t \in X} \neg(\neg\phi_2(x, t) \otimes \neg\phi_2(t, y)) =$$

$$\neg \bigvee_{t \in X} \psi(x, t) \otimes \psi(t, y) \geq \neg\psi(x, y) = \phi_2(x, y).$$

Therefore, $Q \Diamond Q \leq Q$ is true. Because ϕ_1, ϕ_2 are symmetric and reflexive L-fuzzy relations, Q also symmetric and $Q \geq \eta_X$. Therefore, Q is the R-similarity relation.

Now, let $s : X \to \mathcal{R}$ be an intuitionistic fuzzy set (that is, $(\mathcal{R}, \mathcal{R}^*)$-fuzzy set), where $s(x) = (s_1(x), s_2(x)) \in \mathcal{R}$. Then s is extensional to Q if $s \in F_{\mathcal{R}}(X, Q)$, that is, $(Q \lozenge 1_{R^X})(s) \le s$ and we should have

$$(Q \lozenge 1_{R^X})(s) = \sum_{t \in X} s(t) \times Q(t)(x) =$$

$$\left(\bigvee_{t \in X} s_1(t) \otimes \phi_1(t, x), \bigwedge_{t \in X} s_2(t) \oplus \phi_2(t, x) \right) \le (s_1(x), s_2(x)).$$

Therefore, $s = (s_1, s_2)$ is an element of the power set $F_{\mathcal{R}}(X, Q)$ if and only if s_1 is extensional with respect to ϕ_1 and $\neg s_2$ is extensional with respect to $\psi = \neg \phi_2$.

6   Conclusions

In the paper, we dealt with the issue of building another part of the theory of semiring-valued fuzzy sets and its applications to new fuzzy sets. We focus on theories of power set structures in two basic categories whose objects are semiring-valued fuzzy sets. The first category $\mathbf{Set}_{\mathcal{R}}$ was an analogy of the classical category of sets, but with $\mathcal{R}$-relations as morphisms. The other category $\mathbf{Set}(\mathcal{R})$ was a generalization of the category $\mathbf{Set}_{\mathcal{R}}$, where objects are pairs of sets with $\mathcal{R}$-similarity relations. The advantage of using semiring-valued fuzzy sets is, among other things, that this value structure enables the direct use of monad theory methods for the construction of pairs of concepts that are interconnected. In this way, for example, for semiring-valued fuzzy sets, two variants of power set structures describing two variants of extensional fuzzy sets can be defined and the relationships between these variants can be examined. In further research, we will focus on the application of the obtained theoretical results in new fuzzy structures, such as neutrosophic, fuzzy soft sets or their mutual combinations.

References

1. Ali, M.I.: A note on soft sets, rough soft sets and fuzzy soft sets. Appl. Soft Comput. **11**(4), 3329–3332 (2011)
2. Atanassov, K.T.: Intuitionistic fuzzy sets. Fuzzy Sets Syst. **20**(1), 87–96 (1986)
3. Atanassov, K.T.: Intuitionistic fuzzy relations. In: Antonov, L. (ed.) III International School "Automation and Scientific Instrumentation," pp. 56–57. Varna (1984)
4. Brink, C., Britz, K., Melton, A.: A note on fuzzy power relations. Fuzzy Sets Syst. **54**(1), 115–117 (1993)
5. Demirci, M.: Partially ordered fuzzy power set monads on the category of L-sets and their associated categories of topological space objects. Fuzzy Sets Syst. **460**, 1–32 (2023)
6. Georgescu, G.: Fuzzy power structures. Arch. Math. Logic **47**, 233–261 (2008)
7. Höhle, U.: Partially ordered monads, In: Many valued topology and its applications, Kluwer Academic Publishers, Boston, Dordrecht, London (2001)
8. James, J., Mathew, S.C.: Lattice valued neutrosophis sets. J. Math. Comput. Sci. **11**, 4695–4710 (2021)

9. Maji, P.K., et al.: Fuzzy soft-sets. J. Fuzzy Math. **9**(3), 589–602 (2001)
10. Manes, E.G.: Algebraic Theories. Springer, Berlin (1976). https://doi.org/10.1007/978-1-4612-9860-1
11. Močkoř, J.: Semiring-valued Fuzzy Sets and F-transform. Mathematics **9**(23), 3107 (2021)
12. Močkoř, J., Hurtik, P., Hýnar, D.: Rough semirings-valued fuzzy sets. Mathematics **10**(2274), 1–31 (2022)
13. Močkoř, J.: Powerset theory of fuzzy soft sets. Int. J. Fuzzy Logic Intell. Syst. **20**(4), 298–315 (2020)
14. Naim, C., Serkan, K.: Intuitionistic fuzzy soft set theory and its decision making. J. Intell. Fuzzy Syst. **24**(4), 829–836 (2013)
15. Rodabaugh, S.E.: Power set operator foundation for poslat fuzzy set theories and topologies. In: Höhle, U., Rodabaugh, S.E. (eds.) Mathematics of Fuzzy Sets: Logic, Topology and Measure Theory, The Handbook of Fuzzy Sets Series. Kluwer Academic Publishers, vol. 3, pp. 91–116. Boston, Dordrecht (1999)
16. Kim, Y.C., Ko, J.M.: Fuzzy preorders on fuzzy power structures. Math. Aeterna **2**(9), 815–825 (2012)
17. Zadeh, L.A.: Fuzzy sets. Inf. Control **8**, 338–353 (1965)
18. Zhang, X., Bo, C., Smarandache, F., Dai, J.: New inclusion relation of neutrosophic sets with applications and related lattice structure. Int. J. Mach. Learn. Cybern. **9**, 1753–1763 (2018)

Partial Fuzzy Relational Equations and the Dragonfly Operations – What Happens If...?

Nhung Cao[(✉)] and Martin Štěpnička

CE IT4I – IRAFM, University of Ostrava, 701 03 Ostrava, Czech Republic
{nhung.cao,martin.stepnicka}@osu.cz
http://ifm.osu.cz

Abstract. The article focuses on a problem that naturally comes to an interest by joining two classical topics, namely the solvability of systems of fuzzy relational equations, and the partiality as a tool for modeling undefined values. As the first topic basically formally investigates the correctness of fuzzy rule-based systems by the investigation of the preservation of modus ponens, the other one allows dealing in an elegant algebraic way with distinct undefined values, in the particular case of the Dragonfly algebra, the focus is on missing values, their connection is straightforward. Indeed, dealing with missing values is rather omnipresent, and distinct expert rule-based systems are not immune to it so, such an investigation is highly desirable. What is not so straightforward are the results ensuring the solvability of such systems, i.e., the existence of safe models of the rules. Some previous results have been published and they relied on restrictions on the algebraic level. This article brings a new insight and investigates, what happens if we refuse to accept such a restriction. The answer is interesting as restricting the choice of the algebra does not seem to be critical but it imposes some restrictions on the sides of the consequents. Luckily, these restrictions are not so critical and restrictive from the application point of view.

Keywords: Fuzzy relational equations · Partial Fuzzy Set Theory · Dragonfly Algebra

1 Introduction and Preliminaries

1.1 Introduction

Systems of fuzzy relational equations [15, 16, 25] can be viewed as a mathematical formalization of the preservation of the modus ponens property by a fuzzy inference system. Let the antecedent and consequent fuzzy sets be given. If the derived system is not solvable, i.e., if there is no fuzzy relation that would solve the given system, the incorrectness is inherent in the antecedents and consequents and there is no way how to build a fuzzy relation modeling the given fuzzy rule base that would not harm the preservation of modus ponens.

© The Author(s), under exclusive license to Springer Nature Switzerland AG 2023
S. Massanet et al. (Eds.): EUSFLAT 2023/AGOP 2023, LNCS 14069, pp. 74–85, 2023.
https://doi.org/10.1007/978-3-031-39965-7_7

This rather clear and fundamental area is widely explored by numerous researchers and referring to all the relevant sources is by far beyond the extent of the single article, however, whenever we move to the area of partial fuzzy set theory [3,4] the situation significantly changes. Partial fuzzy set theory, as a counterpart of partial fuzzy logic [20], allows considering elements of universes that do not have defined membership degrees to partial fuzzy set. Partial fuzzy logic is technically only an appropriate multiple-valued extension of partial 3-valued logics [13] that belong to classical topics being under investigation already since 1920. And indeed, if we consider partial fuzzy sets entering the investigation of the preservation of the modus ponens, the situation gets more complicated and much less investigated. Anyhow, even here we may point the interest of readers to the first results, namely to [8,10,11].

This particular contribution stems mainly from [9] and continues in the directions that were set up there. The object of the investigation is again a direct system of partial fuzzy relational equations and its solvability. The chosen algebra of the operations for the considered partial fuzzy set theory is the Dragonfly algebra [27]. The mainly studied model also stems from implicative fuzzy rules and also uses the external assertion operation. *The investigated question is, what happens if we drop the assumption on the underlying algebra with the multiplication that has no zero divisors, which was essential for the results provided in* [9].

1.2 System of Fuzzy Relational Equations

Recall the standard form of the system of fuzzy relational equations

$$A_i \circ R = B_i, \, i = 1, \ldots, m \tag{1}$$

which considers the direct products (also sup-T composition) denoted by $\circ$. Fuzzy sets $A_i \in \mathcal{F}(X)$ and $B_i \in \mathcal{F}(Y)$ are respectively given antecedent and consequent fuzzy sets, and fuzzy relation $R \in \mathcal{F}(X \times Y)$ is unknown.

In other words, antecedents A_i, consequents B_i, and consequently a fuzzy rule base are given, while a fuzzy relation $R \in \mathcal{F}(X \times Y)$ that solves the above-given system is a safe model [21] of the given fuzzy rule base. The use of the words comes from the fact that it is safe w.r.t. the preservation of modus ponens and we know that it guarantees that the inference, i.e., the mechanism of reasoning, is not harming basic logical prerequisites of correct functioning.

Let us recall the widely known fact that system (1) is solvable if and only if the implicative model $\hat{R}(x, y) = \bigwedge_{i=1}^{m}(A_i(x) \rightarrow B_i(y))$ is its solution. Consequently, fuzzy relation $\hat{R}$ is the primary choice for modeling the fuzzy rule bases whenever we consider the composition rule of inference modeled by $\circ$, if $\hat{R}$ does not work, nothing works.

2 Dragonfly Operations and Properties

2.1 Dragonfly Algebra

As mentioned in the Introduction, partial fuzzy sets allow not only membership degrees from the unit interval $[0, 1]$ but some elements of the universe may have undefined membership degrees. In its logical counterpart, it means we may consider propositions that are not only evaluated by truth degrees, but for some propositions, we may have undefined truth degrees. The need for such an extension stem from natural cases of distinct nature and we only refer to relevant sources [1,7,13,14].

As most of the algebras, let us mention, e.g., Bochvar, Sobocński, McCarthy, or Kleene, referred rather to other motivations for undefinedness than modeling missing or unknown values, the authors of [27] designed specific Dragonfly algebra that was designed in order to deal with the missing or unknown values. One could easily object that there are other natural approaches for modeling the unknown values, e.g., the possibility theory, and it is needed to state that this is true, however, the curse of dimensionality makes some of them hardly usable for a bit more complicated problems and so, the algebraic approach may be viewed as an approximation that is, nevertheless, easy to use and leads to meaningful results. Let us note that all the algebraic operations are implemented in the *lfl* R-package [5,6] which makes their use very straightforward.

Let us start from an underlying residuated lattice $\langle [0, 1], \wedge, \vee, \otimes, \rightarrow, 0, 1 \rangle$ that provides operations for "standard" (fully defined, non-partial) fuzzy sets. As in all previous studies, let us use the $\star$ as a denotation of the undefined value and let $[0, 1]^\star = [0, 1] \cup \{\star\}$. Then the operations of the Dragonfly algebra operating on the support $[0, 1]^\star$ are recalled in Table 1 and of course, if both values $a, b \in [0, 1]$, the Dragonfly operations comply with the operations from the underlying residuated lattice, i.e., $a \otimes_D b = a \otimes b$, for instance. It is important to mention that the new structure of the Dragonfly algebra $\langle [0, 1]^\star, \wedge_D, \vee_D, \otimes_D, \rightarrow_D, 0, 1 \rangle$ is no more a residuated lattice [12].

Table 1. Dragonfly algebra operations for $a, b \in (0, 1]$.

$(\otimes_D, \wedge_D)$			$(\vee_D)$			$(\rightarrow_D)$		
a	$\star$	$\star$	a	$\star$	a	a	$\star$	$\star$
$\star$	b	$\star$	$\star$	b	b	$\star$	b	b
$\star$	$\star$	$\star$	$\star$	$\star$	$\star$	$\star$	$\star$	1
$\star$	0	0	$\star$	0	$\star$	0	$\star$	1
0	$\star$	0	0	$\star$	$\star$	$\star$	0	$\star$

Note, that the Dragonfly operations employ the so-called lower bound strategy, i.e., they lead to a value that can be "at least" guaranteed even without knowing what is the real value that is currently not known to us and modeled by

$\star$. Indeed, $a \wedge_D \star = \star$ as we cannot guarantee anything about the conjunction of a and an unknown value. On the other hand $a \vee_D \star = a$ because no matter how small the value would replace $\star$ later on, we can be sure that the result would be still greater or equal to a.

This principle leads to two ordering relations on $[0,1]^\star$. The first one that is default and identical to, e.g., ordering on the Kleene algebra, considers $\star$ to be incomparable to any value $a \in (0,1)$ and allows to compare $\star$ only with values 0 and 1 as follows: $0 \leq \star \leq 1$. From the "lattice-like" operations $\wedge_D$ and $\vee_D$, however, we can define a lattice-like ordering (denoted by $\leq_\ell$) as follows: $0 \leq_\ell \star \leq_\ell a$ for any $a \in (0,1]$. This ordering naturally stems from the following facts: $a \wedge_D \star = \star$ and $a \vee_D \star = a$. As stated above, both relations $\leq$ as well as $\leq_\ell$ are partial orders and so, the pairs of facts $a \leq b$ and $a \geq b$ as well as $a \leq_\ell b$ and $a \geq_\ell b$ lead to the same conclusion that $a = b$. Note, that for values $a, b \in [0,1]$, both orderings coincide. Technically, this puts Dragonfly algebra in a comfortable position among other partial algebras and allows us to prove required equalities using an alternative ordering whenever one of them does not lead to the positive end.

Finally, let us also recall the external operation of *assertion* [7,18,24] that can enrich any algebra for partial fuzzy set theory and that has been shown useful in [9]. It is worth mentioning that this assertion is also included in the investigation [2]. In particular, one may find that it meets the conditions defined for the so-called intensifying hedge, one of the unary functions used to extend the solvability results of standard fuzzy relational equations. The achieved results were developed for the complete residuated lattices as the structure of truth degrees [2].

Definition 1. The operation $\downarrow: [0,1]^\star \rightarrow [0,1]^\star$ that is defined by $\downarrow a = 0$ if $a = \star$ and $\downarrow a = a$ otherwise is called *assertion*.

2.2 Auxiliary Properties

First, we present several auxiliary properties that will be needed later on.

Lemma 1. [11] *For any* $a, b, c \in [0,1]^\star$:

$$a \wedge_D b \leq_\ell a, \quad a \wedge_D b \leq_\ell b.$$

Lemma 2. *For any* $a, b \in [0,1]$ *and* $c \in [0,1]^\star$:

$$a \leq b \Rightarrow a \otimes_D c \leq_\ell b \otimes_D c, \tag{2}$$

$$a \leq b \Rightarrow c \rightarrow_D a \leq_\ell c \rightarrow_D b. \tag{3}$$

Sketch of the Proof: Property (2) is taken from [11]. Consider the case of $c = \star$. Then $\star \rightarrow_D a \leq_\ell \star \rightarrow_D b$ holds trivially for any $a \leq b$ in $[0,1]$ which proves (3). $\square$

Lemma 3. *For any* $a, b \in [0,1]^\star$ *and* $c \in [0,1]$:

$$a \otimes_D b \leq_\ell c \Rightarrow b \leq_\ell (\downarrow a) \rightarrow c. \tag{4}$$

Sketch of the Proof: The proof is done by checking all combinatorial possibilities of the replacement of a, b by $\star$ in the left inequality of (4). $\qquad\square$

Lemma 4. [9,11] *For any $a, b, c \in [0, 1]^\star$:*

$$a \leq_\ell b, \ a \leq_\ell c \ \Leftrightarrow \ a \leq_\ell b \wedge_D c, \tag{5}$$
$$a \leq_\ell c, \ b \leq_\ell c \ \Leftrightarrow \ a \vee_D b \leq_\ell c. \tag{6}$$

Lemma 5. *For any $a, c \in [0, 1]^\star$ and $b \in [0, 1]$:*

$$a \leq_\ell b \ \Rightarrow \ (\downarrow c) \to_D a \leq_\ell (\downarrow c) \to_D b.$$

Sketch of the Proof: The case of $c = \star$ is trivial. Let $a = \star$ and $b > 0$. Then $\star \leq_\ell b$ is preserved and $(\downarrow c) \to_D a = \star$ on the left-hand side, which is smaller or equal to $(\downarrow c) \to_D b$. $\qquad\square$

Lemma 6. *For any $a, b \in [0, 1]^\star$:*

$$b \leq_\ell (\downarrow a) \to_D (a \otimes_D b).$$

Sketch of the Proof: The case of $a \in \{0, \star\}$ trivially leads to the preservation of the inequality as the right-hand side is equal to 1. Let $a \notin \{0, \star\}$ and let $b = \star$. Then we get $\star \leq_\ell a \to_D (a \otimes_D \star) = a \to_D \star = \star$. $\qquad\square$

3 System with the Direct Product

Let $\mathcal{F}^\star(U) = \{A \mid A : U \to [0, 1]^\star\}$ denote the set of all partially defined fuzzy sets on a universe U. In this section, we consider the following system of partial fuzzy relational equations employing the partial Dragonfly operations and using the direct product $\circ$:

$$A_i \circ_D R = B_i, \quad i = 1, \ldots, m \tag{7}$$

where partially defined $A_i \in \mathcal{F}^\star(X)$ and fully defined $B_i \in \mathcal{F}(Y)$ be given, and $R \in \mathcal{F}^\star(X \times Y)$ is an unknown partial fuzzy relation we seek.

This particular setting differs from the very general setting investigated in [11] by imposing the consequents to be fully defined. Though at the first sight, it might be viewed as restrictive, however, it mimics a rather natural situation when the outputs (decisions, states, classes, control actions) are always known, however, on the input, we can meet undefined (mostly missing, unobserved) values. For example, in the expert classification of dragonfly species, which was the motivating application for the development of the Dragonfly algebras [27], one can often miss whether the flying dragonfly had some red dots on its body or not. Thus, such a feature x_k is missing in the input vector $x = (x_1, \ldots, x_k, \ldots, x_K)$ and we have an undefined value $A(x_k) = \star$ that leads to the input fuzzy set $A(x) = (A(x_1), \ldots, \star, \ldots, A(x_K))$.

3.1 Solvability Issues

Mimicking the default solution $\hat{R}$ for the standard systems of fuzzy relational equations led the authors of [9] to deal with $\hat{R}_{\downarrow} \in \mathcal{F}^{\star}(X \times Y)$ given by $\hat{R}_{\downarrow}(x,y) = \bigwedge_{Di=1}^{m} (\downarrow A_i(x) \to_{D} B_i(y))$ as the candidate for the solution to the system of partial fuzzy relational equations. As the problem that we study assumes the consequents to be fully defined, we may replace operation $\to_{D}$ by $\to$ and operation $\wedge_{D}$ by $\wedge$, and we get $\hat{R}_{\downarrow} \in \mathcal{F}(X \times Y)$ given by:

$$\hat{R}_{\downarrow}(x,y) = \bigwedge_{i=1}^{m} (\downarrow A_i(x) \to B_i(y)). \tag{8}$$

The searched solution or its candidate for the studied systems is naturally the implicative model in which, we simply replace missing values with values 0 as the previous study [9] showed us that this strategy may lead to satisfactory results.

As the lattice-like ordering will play an essential role in the latter parts of our investigation, we also introduce the following lattice-like inclusion denotation:

$$A_1 \subseteq_{\ell} A_2 \quad \text{if} \quad A_1(u) \leq_{\ell} A_2(u), \quad \text{for all } u \in U.$$

Theorem 1. *Let $B_i(y) > 0$ for any $y \in Y$. Then for each $i \in \{1, \ldots, m\}$:*

$$A_i \circ_{D} \hat{R}_{\downarrow} \subseteq_{\ell} B_i. \tag{9}$$

Proof. Taking into account the unlimited support of B_i due to which $\star \leq_{\ell} B_i(y)$, and the fact that $\hat{R}_{\downarrow}(x,y) \neq \star$, it suffices to use Lemma 1, Lemma 2, and the property $a \otimes (a \to b) \leq b$ valid for $a, b \in [0,1]$, as follows

$$(A_i \circ_{D} \hat{R}_{\downarrow})(y) = \bigvee_{x \in X}^{D} \left(A_i(x) \otimes_{D} \bigwedge_{j=1}^{m} (\downarrow A_j(x) \to B_j(y)) \right)$$

$$\leq_{\ell} \bigvee_{x \in X}^{D} A_i(x) \otimes_{D} (\downarrow A_i(x) \to B_i(y))$$

$$\leq_{\ell} \bigvee_{x \in X : A_i(x)=0} (A_i(x) \otimes (\downarrow A_i(x) \to B_i(y)))$$

$$\vee_{D} \bigvee_{x \in X : A_i(x)=\star}^{D} (A_i(x) \otimes_{D} (\downarrow A_i(x) \to B_i(y)))$$

$$\vee_{D} \bigvee_{x \in X : A_i(x) \notin \{0,\star\}} (A_i(x) \otimes (\downarrow A_i(x) \to B_i(y)))$$

$$= 0 \vee_{D} \star \vee_{D} \bigvee_{x \in X : A_i(x) \notin \{0,\star\}} (A_i(x) \otimes (A_i(x) \to B_i(y)))$$

$$\leq B_i(y).$$

As $\leq$ and $\leq_{\ell}$ coincide for the fully defined fuzzy sets, and as $y \in Y$ has been chosen arbitrarily, we get the proof of (9). $\qquad\square$

Theorem 2. *Let system (7) be solvable, and let $B_i(y) > 0$ for any $y \in Y$. Then, for each $i \in \{1, \ldots, m\}$:*

$$A_i \circ_D \hat{R}_\downarrow \supseteq_\ell B_i. \tag{10}$$

Proof. Let $R \in \mathcal{F}^\star(X \times Y)$ be a solution of system (7). Notice that if there was an x such that $B_i(y) <_\ell A_i(x) \otimes R(x, y)$ then by the definition of $\vee_D$ we would get $B_i(y) <_\ell (A_i \circ_D R)(y)$. Therefore, $A_i(x) \otimes_D R(x, y) \leq_\ell B_i(y)$ for all $x \in X$, and with help of Lemma 3 and Lemma 4, the following sequence of the inequalities can be derived

$$A_i(x) \otimes_D R(x, y) \leq_\ell B_i(y), \quad i = 1, \ldots, m, \ y \in Y$$
$$R(x, y) \leq_{\ell\downarrow} A_i(x) \to B_i(y), \quad i = 1, \ldots, m, \ y \in Y$$
$$R(x, y) \leq_\ell \bigwedge_{i=1}^m (\downarrow A_i(x) \to B_i(y)), \quad y \in Y$$

and hence, $R \subseteq_\ell \hat{R}_\downarrow$. Furthermore, as R is a solution of the system, i.e.,

$$\bigvee_{x \in X}^D (A_i(x) \otimes_D R(x, y)) = B_i(y) > 0,$$

there has to exist an $x' \in X$ such that $A_i(x') \neq \star$ and $R(x', y) \neq \star$, and for which $A_i(x') \otimes R(x', y) > 0$. And because $R(x, y) \leq_\ell \hat{R}_\downarrow(x, y)$ holds for any pair (x, y), it has to hold also for the above-given value x' and we get $A_i(x') \otimes R(x', y) \leq_\ell A_i(x') \otimes \hat{R}_\downarrow(x', y)$ and $A_i(x') \otimes \hat{R}_\downarrow(x', y) > 0$. Using the definition of operation $\vee_D$, this fact leads to the following inequality

$$\bigvee_{x \in X}^D (A_i(x) \otimes_D R(x, y)) \leq_\ell \bigvee_{x \in X}^D \left(A_i(x) \otimes_D \hat{R}_\downarrow(x, y) \right),$$

which means that $A_i \circ_D R \subseteq_\ell A_i \circ_D \hat{R}_\downarrow$. Thus, $B_i = A_i \circ_D R \subseteq_\ell A_i \circ_D \hat{R}_\downarrow$. $\square$

Theorem 3. *Let $B_i(y) > 0$ for any $y \in Y$. System (7) is solvable if and only if $\hat{R}_\downarrow$ is its solution. Moreover, $\hat{R}_\downarrow$ is the greatest solution of the system w.r.t. to ordering $\leq_\ell$.*

Sketch of the Proof: A direct consequence of Theorem 1 and Theorem 2. $\square$

For the sake of achieving the inclusion (10) and consequently the *solvability criterion* formulated in Theorem 3, we restricted our focus to consequents B_i that have unlimited supports, i.e., $B_i(y) > 0$ for all $y \in Y$. Such a restriction might be viewed as a too high price for dropping the restriction imposed on the underlying algebra however if we do dare to step out of conservative settings often mirrored in triangles, we learn that it does not limit us from the application point of view. Indeed, e.g. the Gaussian-shaped fuzzy sets were often experimentally confirmed as useful. And also on a theoretical level, such or any other fuzzy sets with unlimited supports were proved to ensure distinct desirable properties, e.g. the preservation of the continuity of the resulting function produced by a fuzzy rule-based system [26]. They have been also discussed in [11] as meaningful consequents with a positive impact.

3.2   Beyond the Solvability – Approximate Solutions

For the cases of the non-existence of a solution to a given system of fuzzy relational equations, distinct authors proposed so-called approximate solutions, see [22,23]. This direction has been followed also for the partial fuzzy relational equations in [9] and we again adopt the approach as it has been confirmed as inspiring and beneficial.

So, let us assume that there exists no solution of system (7). Model $\hat{R}_\downarrow$ is formulated in a form that mimics the implicative model $\hat{R}$. Moreover, it has been proven [17,22] that when system (1) is not solvable then $\hat{R}$ is its greatest approximate solution in a suitable space of approximate solutions called "space of lower approximate solutions". Such a space contains fuzzy relation $R \in \mathcal{F}(X \times Y)$ such that $A_i \circ R \subseteq B_i$. The question is whether an analogous result is preserved for the case of partial fuzzy relational equations, i.e., when system (7) is not solvable. So, we concentrate on the question of whether $\hat{R}_\downarrow$ is an approximate solution and whether it is the biggest one among the others. Under some additional assumptions, we get the positive answer. Due to the positive impact of consequents with unlimited supports on the results in the previous section, we keep this assumption also in this section.

First of all, let us refer to relevant previous works [19,22,28] and introduce the definition of an approximate solution of system (7).

Definition 2. A partial fuzzy relation $R' \in \mathcal{F}^\star(X \times Y)$ is called an *approximate solution* of system (7) if it satisfies for $i = 1, \ldots, m$ the following:

(i) the inferred output $B'_i = A_i \circ_\mathrm{D} R'$ is fully defined ($B'_i \in \mathcal{F}(Y)$), it meets $B'_i \subseteq_\ell B_i$, and it has an unlimited support ($B'_i(y) > 0, \forall y \in Y$);
(ii) the inferred output is *maximal*, i.e., for any $R'' \in \mathcal{F}^\star(X \times Y)$ and for any $B''_i \in \mathcal{F}(Y)$ such that $B''_i = A_i \circ_\mathrm{D} R''$ and $B'_i \subseteq_\ell B''_i \subseteq_\ell B_i$, it holds that $B''_i = B'_i$.

Definition 2 states that R' is an approximate solution of system (7) if it generates an output B'_i that is the maximal lower approximation of the required output B_i and it has no limited support similarly as B_i. Model R' can be also viewed as an exact solution to the modified system of partial fuzzy relational equations with A_i and B'_i. As the system associated with A_i and B'_i may have several solutions, system (7) may have several approximate solutions as well.

Theorem 4. *Assume that system (7) is not solvable and moreover, assume that $(A_i \circ_\mathrm{D} \hat{R}_\downarrow)(y) \notin \{0, \star\}$ for any $y \in Y$. Then $\hat{R}_\downarrow$ is an approximate solution of system (7), and it is the biggest one compared to the other approximate solutions of the system, with respect to ordering $\leq_\ell$.*

Sketch of the Proof: Let $B'_i = A_i \circ_\mathrm{D} \hat{R}_\downarrow$. Based on the assumption that $(A_i \circ_\mathrm{D} \hat{R}_\downarrow)(y) \notin \{0, \star\}$ for all $y \in Y$, $B'_i \in \mathcal{F}(Y)$ and $B'_i(y) > 0 \ \forall y \in Y$. Theorem 1 shows that $A_i \circ_\mathrm{D} \hat{R}_\downarrow \subseteq_\ell B_i$ and so, $B'_i \subseteq_\ell B_i$. Thus, condition (i) in Definition 2 is satisfied. Now, let there exist R'' and B''_i such that $A_i \circ_\mathrm{D} R'' = B''_i$

and $B_i' \subseteq_\ell B_i'' \subseteq_\ell B_i$. Clearly, $B_i'' \in \mathcal{F}(Y)$ and $B_i''(y) > 0$ for any $y \in Y$, and $R'' \subseteq_\ell \hat{R}_\downarrow''$, where

$$\hat{R}_\downarrow''(x,y) = \bigwedge_{i=1}^{m} (\downarrow A_i(x) \to B_i''(y)).$$

By Lemma 5 and by $B_i' \subseteq_\ell B_i'' \subseteq_\ell B_i$, we get for any x and y

$$(\downarrow A_i)(x) \to_\mathrm{D} B_i'(y) \leq_\ell (\downarrow A_i)(x) \to_\mathrm{D} B_i''(y) \leq_\ell (\downarrow A_i)(x) \to_\mathrm{D} B_i(y),$$

which leads to

$$\bigwedge_{i=1}^{m} (\downarrow A_i(x) \to_\mathrm{D} B_i'(y)) \leq_\ell \hat{R}_\downarrow''(x,y) \leq_\ell \hat{R}_\downarrow(x,y). \tag{11}$$

With help of Lemma 5 and then Lemma 6, we obtain:

$$\bigwedge_{i=1}^{m} (\downarrow A_i(x) \to_\mathrm{D} B_i'(y)) = \bigwedge_{i=1}^{m} \left(\downarrow A_i(x) \to_\mathrm{D} \left(\bigvee_{x' \in X}{}^{\mathrm{D}} A_i(x') \otimes_\mathrm{D} \hat{R}_\downarrow(x',y) \right) \right)$$

$$\geq_\ell \bigwedge_{i=1}^{m} \left(\downarrow A_i(x) \to_\mathrm{D} \left(A_i(x) \otimes_\mathrm{D} \hat{R}_\downarrow(x,y) \right) \right)$$

$$\geq_\ell \hat{R}_\downarrow(x,y).$$

Thus, the inequalities in (11) turn to equalities. Then,

$$B_i''(y) = (A_i \circ_\mathrm{D} \hat{R}_\downarrow'')(y) = (A_i \circ_\mathrm{D} \hat{R}_\downarrow)(y) = B_i'(y).$$

Hence, condition (ii) from Definition 2 is met and $\hat{R}_\downarrow$ is an approximate solution of system (7).

Let $\bar{R}$ be another approximate solution of the system, i.e., $\bar{B}_i = A_i \circ_\mathrm{D} \bar{R}$ is another maximal lower approximation of B_i, that is $\bar{B}_i \subseteq_\ell B_i$. Then necessarily $\bar{R} \subseteq_\ell \hat{R}_\downarrow$ where

$$\bar{R}_\downarrow(x,y) = \bigwedge_{i=1}^{m} (\downarrow A_i(x) \to \bar{B}_i(y)).$$

And as for any pair $(x,y) \in X \times Y$ the following inequality

$$\downarrow A_i(x) \to \bar{B}_i(y) \leq_\ell \downarrow A_i(x) \to B_i(y)$$

holds, we obtain $\bar{R} \subseteq_\ell \bar{R}_\downarrow \subseteq_\ell \hat{R}_\downarrow$.   □

In order to estimate the quality or accuracy of the approximate solution, the so-called approximation index was defined in [9].

Definition 3. [9] Let R' be an approximate solution of system (7). The *approximation index* of R' denoted by $\varphi(\tilde{R})$ is defined as follows

$$\varphi(R') = \bigwedge_{\substack{i=1 \\ \text{D}}}^{m} \bigwedge_{\substack{y \in Y \\ \text{D}}} \left((A_i \circ_{\text{D}} R')(y) \leftrightarrow_{\text{D}} B_i(y) \right). \qquad (12)$$

Definition 4. R' is said to be *the optimal approximate solution of system* (7) if for any approximate solution R'' it holds that $\varphi(R'') \leq_\ell \varphi(R')$.

Lemma 7 below conveys the information that the greatest approximate solution $\hat{R}_\downarrow$ is also the optimal approximate solution.

Lemma 7. *Let system (7) be not solvable and let* $(A_i \circ_{\text{D}} \hat{R}_\downarrow)(y) \notin \{0, \star\}$ *for any* $y \in Y$. *Then* $\hat{R}_\downarrow$ *is the optimal approximate solution of system (7).*

Sketch of the Proof: For an approximate solution R' of system (7) it holds that $R' \subseteq_\ell \hat{R}_\downarrow$. As $(A_i \circ_{\text{D}} R')(y) \notin \{0, \star\}$, we can verify that $A_i \circ_{\text{D}} R' \subseteq_\ell A_i \circ_{\text{D}} \hat{R}_\downarrow$ and so, we get $\varphi(R') \leq_\ell \varphi(\hat{R}_\downarrow)$.

$\square$

The condition $(A_i \circ_{\text{D}} \hat{R}_\downarrow)(y) \notin \{0, \star\}$ assumed in Theorem 4 for any $y \in Y$ guarantees the existence of an approximate solution whenever the exact solution does not exist. The following theorem shows, that without such an assumption, there does not exist any approximate solution.

Theorem 5. *Let system (7) be not solvable. Moreover, let there exists an* $y' \in Y$ *and* $i' \in \{1, \ldots, m\}$ *such that* $(A_{i'} \circ_{\text{D}} \hat{R}_\downarrow)(y') \in \{0, \star\}$. *Then there exists no approximate solution of system (7).*

Sketch of the Proof: Let $R \in \mathcal{F}^\star(X \times Y)$ be such that $A_i \circ_{\text{D}} R \subseteq_\ell B_i$. Following the proof of Theorem 2, we get $R \subseteq_\ell \hat{R}_\downarrow$. The fact that $(A_{i'} \circ_{\text{D}} \hat{R}_\downarrow)(y') \in \{0, \star\}$ implies that $A_{i'}(x) \otimes_{\text{D}} \hat{R}_\downarrow(x, y') \in \{0, \star\}$ for all $x \in X$, and consequently also $A_{i'}(x) \otimes_{\text{D}} R(x, y') \in \{0, \star\}$ for all $x \in X$. Hence, $(A_{i'} \circ_{\text{D}} R)(y') \in \{0, \star\}$. Consequently, R cannot be a solution of any system $A_i \circ_{\text{D}} R' = B'_i$ in which $B'_i \subseteq_\ell B_i$ and $B'_i(y) \notin \{0, \star\}$ for any $y \in Y$ and condition (i) in Definition 2 is not satisfied.

$\square$

Theorems 4 and 5 directly lead to Corollary 1 formulated below.

Corollary 1. *Let system (7) be not solvable. Then system (7) has an approximate solution if and only if for any* $y \in Y$ *and for any* $i \in \{1, \ldots, m\}$ *we have* $(A_i \circ_{\text{D}} \hat{R}_\downarrow)(y) \notin \{0, \star\}$.

4   Conclusion

We have revisited the problem of systems of partial fuzzy relational equations, which was firstly addressed for the Dragonfly algebras in [9] and then elaborated in the general setting in [11]. This contribution also addresses the case of the Dragonfly algebra and compared to [9] tries to answer the question of what happens if the essential assumption on the underlying algebra without zero divisors is dropped. The answer is positive and interesting, it leads to another setting that relaxes this algebraic condition but to assuming fully defined consequents, moreover, with unlimited supports. As long as the first assumption changes the semantics of the studied problem (which does not mean it makes it less interesting), the second is purely technical (yet still acceptable for most of the applications). Apart from the exact solvability, we have addressed also the approximate solution for the systems that are not solvable. Interestingly, the implicative model $\hat{R}_\downarrow$ that is the primary candidate for the exact solution is also the optimal approximate solution whenever an exact solution is not feasible. It only confirms its importance.

References

1. Avron, A., Konikowska, B.: Proof systems for reasoning about computation errors. Stud. Logica. **91**(2), 273–293 (2009)
2. Bartl, E., Belohlavek, R., Vychodil, V.: Bivalent and other solutions of fuzzy relational equations via linguistic hedges. Fuzzy Sets Syst. **187**(1), 103–112 (2012)
3. Běhounek, L., Daňková, M.: Variable-domain fuzzy sets - Part I: Representation. Fuzzy Sets Syst. **38**, 1–18 (2020)
4. Běhounek, L., Daňková, M.: Variable-domain fuzzy sets - Part II: Apparatus. Fuzzy Sets Syst. **38**, 19–43 (2020)
5. Burda, M.: Linguistic fuzzy logic in R. In: Proceedings of the IEEE International Conference on Fuzzy Systems, Istanbul, Turkey (2015)
6. Burda, M., Štěpnička, M.: lfl: an R package for linguistic fuzzy logic. Fuzzy Sets Syst. **431**, 1–38 (2022). Logic and Related Topics
7. Běhounek, L., Dvořák, A.: Fuzzy relational modalities admitting truth-valueless propositions. Fuzzy Sets Syst. **388**, 38–55 (2020)
8. Cao, N.: Solvability of fuzzy relational equations employing undefined values. In: The 11th Conference of the European Society for Fuzzy Logic and Technology (EUSFLAT 2019), pp. 227–234. Atlantis Press (2019)
9. Cao, N., Štěpnička, M.: Fuzzy relational equations employing dragonfly operations. In: 2019 11th International Conference on Knowledge and Systems Engineering (KSE), pp. 1–6. IEEE (2019)
10. Cao, N., Štěpnička, M.: Sufficient solvability conditions for systems of partial fuzzy relational equations. In: Lesot, M.-J., et al. (eds.) IPMU 2020. CCIS, vol. 1237, pp. 93–106. Springer, Cham (2020). https://doi.org/10.1007/978-3-030-50146-4_8
11. Cao, N., Štěpnička, M.: On solvability of systems of partial fuzzy relational equations. Fuzzy Sets Syst. **450**, 87–117 (2022)
12. Cao, N., Štěpnička, M.: Preservation of properties of residuated algebraic structure by structures for the partial fuzzy set theory. Int. J. Approximate Reasoning **154**, 1–26 (2023)

13. Ciucci, D., Dubois, D.: A map of dependencies among three-valued logics. Inf. Sci. **250**, 162–177 (2013)
14. d'Allonnes, A.R., Lesot, M.J.: If I don't know, should I infer? Reasoning around ignorance in a many-valued framework. In: Joint 17th World Congress of International Fuzzy Systems Association and 9th International Conference on Soft Computing and Intelligent Systems, IFSA-SCIS 2017, Otsu, Japan, 27–30 June 2017, pp. 1–6. IEEE (2017)
15. De Baets, B.: Analytical solution methods for fuzzy relational equations. In: Dubois, D., Prade, H. (eds.) The Handbook of Fuzzy Set Series, vol. 1, pp. 291–340. Academic Kluwer Publication, Boston (2000)
16. Di Nola, A., Sessa, S., Pedrycz, W., Sanchez, E.: Fuzzy Relation Equations and Their Applications to Knowledge Engineering. Kluwer, Boston (1989)
17. Gottwald, S.: Fuzzy control and fuzzy relation equations. A unified view as interpolation problem. In: IEEE Annual Meeting of the Fuzzy Information, Processing NAFIPS 2004, vol. 1, pp. 270–275. IEEE (2004)
18. Karpenko, A., Tomova, N.: Bochvar's three-valued logic and literal paralogics: their lattice and functional equivalence. Logic Log. Philos. **26**(2), 207–235 (2016)
19. Klir, G.J., Yuan, B.: Approximate solutions of systems of fuzzy relation equations. In: Proceedings of 1994 IEEE 3rd International Fuzzy Systems Conference, pp. 1452–1457. IEEE (1994)
20. Novák, V.: Fuzzy type theory with partial functions. Iran. J. Fuzzy Syst. **16**(2), 1–16 (2019)
21. Perfilieva, I., Lehmke, S.: Correct models of fuzzy if-then rules are continuous. Fuzzy Sets Syst. **157**, 3188–3197 (2006)
22. Perfilieva, I.: Fuzzy function as an approximate solution to a system of fuzzy relation equations. Fuzzy Sets Syst. **147**(3), 363–383 (2004)
23. Perfilieva, I., Gottwald, S.: Solvability and approximate solvability of fuzzy relation equations. Int. J. Gen. Syst. **32**(4), 361–372 (2003)
24. Prior, A.N.: Three-valued logic and future contingents. Philos. Q. 317–326 (1953)
25. Sanchez, E.: Resolution of composite fuzzy relation equations. Inf. Control **30**, 38–48 (1976)
26. Štěpnička, M., Bodenhofer, U., Daňková, M., Novák, V.: Continuity issues of the implicational interpretation of fuzzy rules. Fuzzy Sets Syst. **161**, 1959–1972 (2010)
27. Štěpnička, M., Cao, N., Běhounek, L., Burda, M., Dolný, A.: Missing values and dragonfly operations in fuzzy relational compositions. Int. J. Approximate Reasoning **113**, 149–170 (2019)
28. Wangming, W.: Fuzzy reasoning and fuzzy relational equations. Fuzzy Sets Syst. **20**(1), 67–78 (1986)

Conceptuality Degree of Oriented Crisply Generated Fuzzy Preconcepts

Alexander Šostak[1,2(✉)], Māris Krastiņš[2], and Ingrīda Uļjane[1,2]

[1] Institute of Mathematics and CS, University of Latvia, Riga 1459, Latvia
{ingrida.uljane,aleksandrs.sostaks}@lu.lv
[2] Department of Mathematics, University of Latvia, Riga 1004, Latvia
aleksandrs.sostaks@lumii.lv, mk18032@edu.lu.lv

Abstract. A serious obstacle for the use of fuzzy concept analysis in practical issues is the problem of matching between sets of objects and properties in fuzzy environment. To overcome this problem several modified versions of fuzzy concept analysis were developed. In this paper we combine Bělohlávek's crisply generated fuzzy concept approach and gradation of fuzzy preconcepts initiated in our previous papers and lay the basics of the theory of graded crisply generated oriented fuzzy preconcepts. We illustrate our ideas by two practical examples related to zoology and astronomy.

Keywords: Formal fuzzy concept analysis · crisply generated fuzzy concept · object oriented fuzzy concept · gradation of fuzzy preconcept lattice

1 Introduction

Formal concept analysis initiated by R. Wille and B. Ganter [6,21] in 80-ties of the previous century at present is one of fast developing areas of theoretical mathematics, having numerous applications in different areas of applied sciences. At present one can distinguish three branches of what could be united under the name of a formal concept analysis: the first is the "classical" formal concept analysis whose fundamentals were laid by R. Wille and B. Ganter, the second is so called property-oriented concept analysis introduced by I. Düntch and G. Gediga [5] in the process of carrying out the research in the field of model logic, and the last one, the object-oriented concept analysis introduced by Y.Y. Yao [22], as the dual one to the property-oriented approach. The starting framework for all of them is a formal context, that is a triple (X, Y, R) where X is a set, whose elements are interpreted as some abstract objects, Y is a set, whose elements are interpreted as some abstract properties and $R \subseteq X \times Y$ is a relation where the entry xRy is interpreted as "an element x has property y". The goal of

The first named author acknowledges partial financial support by the COST association CA17124 (Digital forensics evidence analysis via intelligent systems).

each version of concept analysis is to distinguish pairs (A, B) where sets $A \subseteq X$ of objects and sets $B \subseteq Y$ of properties are mutually connected by the relation R. The difference between them is the interpretation of what does the statement "are mutually connected by the relation R" actually mean.

All three branches of concept analysis started their "life" in crisp framework. However, later on mathematicians as well as specialists working in applications showed interest in possible fuzzification of concept analysis. Specifically, to develop the counterpart of each one of the three versions of concept analysis for the case of a formal fuzzy context, that is a triple (X, Y, R) where X and Y are still sets of objects and properties respectively, $R : X \times Y \to L$ is a fuzzy relation and $A : X \to L$, $B : Y \to L$ are fuzzy sets of objects and attributes respectively. The goal of the formal fuzzy analysis is again to distinguish pairs (A, B) of fuzzy objects and properties that are mutually connected by the fuzzy relation R. Indeed, theoretically very sound fuzzy versions of context analysis were soon created: the "classical" fuzzy formal analysis (i.e. in the spirits of Wille-Ganter) was introduced by R. Bělohlávek [2], fuzzy versions of property-oriented and object-oriented fuzzy analysis, as far as we know, first appeared in the paper [4]. However, as different from crisp concept analysis which has numerous applications in various areas of applied science, the *direct* practical use of fuzzy versions of concept analysis ir rather problematic. Actually we know examples of only fragmentary applications of fuzzy concept analysis in practice. The reason for this is that the precise matching between sets of objects and sets of properties in fuzzy environment is nearly impossible. Specifically, even if the set of objects $A \subseteq X$ and the set of properties $B \subseteq Y$ are crisp and only $R : X \times Y \to L$ is fuzzy, then the pair (A, B) cannot make a concept in any of the concept analysis versions except of some trivial cases. To overcome this problem different modifications of concept analysis were proposed. For example, multi-adjoint concept lattices [11], interval pattern structures [7], proto-fuzzy concepts [10], crisply generated fuzzy concepts [3,15] were introduced on the lines of Wille-Ganter fuzzy concepts, multi-adjoint concept lattices on the lines of object-oriented and property-oriented fuzzy concepts were considered in [13,14]. In [1] the authors attract the use of a structural element in the spirit of mathematical morphology in the process of applying property-oriented concept lattices in signal processing. In our papers [18,20] we introduced the so called graded approach to fuzzy concept analysis where, instead of fuzzy concept lattices, more flexible, graded fuzzy preconcept lattices were laid in the basis of the research.

Our preliminary goal when writing this paper was to propose crisply-generated object- and property-oriented versions of fuzzy concept analysis, basing on the ideas developed in [3] for the case of Wille-Ganter fuzzy concept analysis. However soon it became clear that such a direct transform of the ideas, which work well in Wille-Ganter's case, are not appropriate in other two versions of fuzzy concept analysis. As a successful possible way around this problem we suggested the combination of the two ideas: to start with the idea of crisply generated fuzzy concept, but afterwards to "soften" its expected solution by assigning to it the degree, i.e. some value in the lattice L estimating the "conceptual quality" of the obtained concept.

The paper is structured as follows. In the next, second section we recall basic notions used in this work. A short Sect. 3 is devoted to what we call the fuzzy preconcept lattice of a formal fuzzy context. Fuzzy preconcept lattices *implicitly* appear in all works in the area of fuzzy concept analysis, but in our paper they will play the framework of the study on the whole. The fourth section is the central in the paper. Here we introduce the notion of a crisply generated (object) oriented fuzzy preconcept and study its basic properties. (The restricted conditions on the scope of this work forced us to limit ourselves to one of the "oriented" approaches.) In the fifth section two examples of applications of our theory are presented, one of them concerns classification of zoological species and the second deals with the analysis of solar activity. In the last, Conclusion section we sketch some directions where we foresee the prospects for further work on the basis of this article.

2 Preliminaries

Lattices, Quantales and Residuated Lattices. In our paper $L = (L, \leq, \wedge, \vee)$ denotes a complete lattice, that is a lattice in which joins $\bigvee M$ and meets $\bigwedge M$ of all subsets $M \subseteq L$ exist. In particular $0 \in L$ and $1 \in L$ are the bottom and the top elements of L respectively. A complete lattice L is called join-distributive if $a \wedge \left(\bigvee_{i \in I} b_i \right) = \bigvee_{i \in I} (a \wedge b_i)$ for every $a \in L$ and every $\{b_i \mid i \in I\} \subseteq L$. Dually, a complete lattice L is called meet-distributive if $a \vee \left(\bigwedge_{i \in I} b_i \right) = \bigwedge_{i \in I} (a \vee b_i)$. A complete lattice is called bi-distributive if it is join- and meet-distributive. Let L be a complete lattice and $* : L \times L \to L$ be a binary associative monotone operation. The tuple $(L, \leq, \wedge, \vee, *)$ is called *a quantale* [17] if $*$ distributes over arbitrary joins: $a * \left(\bigvee_{i \in I} b_i \right) = \bigvee_{i \in I} (a * b_i), \left(\bigvee_{i \in I} b_i \right) * a = \bigvee_{i \in I} (b_i * a) \quad \forall a \in L, \{b_i \mid i \in I\} \subseteq L$. A quantale is integral if the top element acts as the unit, i.e. $1 * a = a$. A quantale is commutative, if $a * b = b * a$ for all $a, b \in L$. In what follows by *a quantale* we mean *a commutative integral quantale*.

In a quantale a further binary operation $\mapsto: L \times L \to L$, the residuum, can be introduced as associated with operation $*$ of the quantale $(L, \leq, \wedge, \vee, *)$ via the Galois connection, that is $a * b \leq c \Longleftrightarrow a \leq b \mapsto c$ for all $a, b, c \in L$.

Fuzzy Sets and Fuzzy Relations. The concept of a fuzzy set was introduced by L.A. Zadeh [23] and then extended to a more general concept of an L-fuzzy set by J.A. Goguen [9] where L is a complete lattice, in particular a quantale. Given a set X its L-fuzzy subset is a mapping $A : X \to L$. The lattice and the quantale structure of L is extended point-wise to the L-exponent of X, that is to the set L^X of all L-fuzzy subsets of X. An L-fuzzy relation between two sets X and Y is an L-fuzzy subset of the product $X \times Y$, that is a mapping $R : X \times Y \to L$, see, e.g. [24]. An L-fuzzy relation R is called left connected if $\bigwedge_{y \in Y} \bigvee_{x \in X} R(x, y) = 1$. An L-fuzzy relation R is called right connected if $\bigwedge_{x \in X} \bigvee_{y \in Y} R(x, y) = 1$. An L-fuzzy relation $R : X \times Y \to L$ is called connected if it is both left and right connected. Since in the paper L is a fixed lattice or quantale, we omit the prefix L and speak just of fuzzy sets and fuzzy relations.

Measure of Inclusion of L-Fuzzy Sets. The gradation of a preconcept lattice presented below is based on the fuzzy inclusion between fuzzy sets.

Definition 1. *By setting $A \hookrightarrow B = \bigwedge_{x \in X}(A(x) \mapsto B(x))$ for all $A, B \in L^X$, we obtain a mapping $\hookrightarrow: L^X \times L^X \to L$. We call $A \hookrightarrow B$ by the measure of inclusion of a fuzzy set A into the fuzzy set B. Let $A \hookleftarrow B =_{def} B \hookrightarrow A$. We denote $A \cong B =_{def} (A \hookrightarrow B) \wedge (B \hookrightarrow A)$ and view it as the degree of equality of fuzzy sets A and B.*

Proposition 1. Properties of the mapping $\hookrightarrow: L^X \times L^X \to L$, see, e.g. [8]:

(1) $(\bigvee_i A_i) \hookrightarrow B = \bigwedge_i (A_i \hookrightarrow B)$ *for all $\{A_i \mid i \in I\} \subseteq L^X$ and for all $B \in L^X$;*

(2) $A \hookrightarrow (\bigwedge_i B_i) = \bigwedge_i (A \hookrightarrow B_i)$ *for all $A \in L^X$, and for all $\{B_i \mid i \in I\} \subseteq L^X$;*

(3) $A \hookrightarrow B = 1$ *whenever $A \leq B$;*

(4) $1_X \hookrightarrow A = \bigwedge_x A(x)$ *for all $A \in L^X$;*

(5) $(A \hookrightarrow B) * (B \hookrightarrow C) \leq (A \hookrightarrow C)$ *for all $A, B, C \in L^X$;*

(6) $(\bigwedge_i A_i) \hookrightarrow (\bigwedge_i B_i) \geq \bigwedge_i (A_i \hookrightarrow B_i)$ *for all $\{A_i : i \in I\}$, $\{B_i : i \in I\} \subseteq L^X$;*

(7) $(\bigvee_i A_i) \hookrightarrow (\bigvee_i B_i) \geq \bigwedge_i (A_i \hookrightarrow B_i)$ *for all $\{A_i : i \in I\}$, $\{B_i : i \in I\} \subseteq L^X$.*

3   Fuzzy Preconcepts and Fuzzy Preconcept Lattices

Let L be a complete lattice (in particular, a quantale). Further, let X, Y be sets and $R : X \times Y \to L$ be a fuzzy relation. Following terminology accepted in the theory of (fuzzy) concept lattices, see, e.g. [2,21,22] we refer to the tuple (X, Y, R) as a fuzzy context.

Definition 2. *Given a fuzzy context (X, Y, R), a pair $P = (A, B) \in L^X \times L^Y$ is called a fuzzy preconcept.*

On the set $\mathbb{P} = L^X \times L^Y$ of all fuzzy preconcepts a partial order $\preceq$ is introduced as follows. Given $P_1 = (A_1, B_1)$ and $P_2 = (A_2, B_2)$, we set $P_1 \preceq P_2$ if and only if $A_1 \leq A_2$ and $B_1 \geq B_2$. Let $(\mathbb{P}, \preceq)$ be the set $L^X \times L^Y$ endowed with this partial order. Further, given a family of fuzzy preconcepts $\{P_i = (A_i, B_i) : i \in I\} \subseteq L^X \times L^Y$, we define its join (supremum) by $\veebar_{i \in I} P_i = (\bigvee_{i \in I} A_i, \bigwedge_{i \in I} B_i)$ and its meet (infimum) as $\barwedge_{i \in I} P_i = (\bigwedge_{i \in I} A_i, \bigvee_{i \in I} B_i)$.

Theorem 1. *(see, e.g. [19]) $\mathbb{P}$ is a complete lattice. Besides, if L is a infinitely bi-distributive lattice, then $(\mathbb{P}, \preceq, \barwedge, \veebar)$ is also a infinitely bi-distributive lattice.*

Let $\mathbb{P}_0$ denotes the subset of $\mathbb{P}$ formed by crisp pairs of sets $(A, B) \in 2^X \times 2^Y$. It is easy to see that $\mathbb{P}_0$ is a complete sublattice of $\mathbb{P}$ and in case L is infinitely bi-distributive the same is lattice $\mathbb{P}_0$.

4   Operators $R^\square : L^X \to L^Y, R^\blacklozenge : L^Y \to L^X$ and Crisply Generated $\blacklozenge^\square$-Preconcept Join Semilattice

4.1   Operators $R^\square : L^X \to L^Y$ and $R^\blacklozenge : L^Y \to L^X$

Let $R : X \times Y \to L$ be a fuzzy relation. Interpreting the set X as the domain and the set Y as the codomain of the fuzzy relation R gives rise to the induced forward and backward powerset operators. However, as different from the case of a function $f : X \to Y$ where there is only one categorically justified version for the image $f^{\to} : 2^X \to 2^Y$ and the preimage $f^{\leftarrow} : 2^Y \to 2^X$ powerset operators (see, e.g. [16]), in case of a fuzzy relation R there are two "natural" definitions for image and preimage powerset operators which we call upper and lower forward and backward powerset operators. Such operators can be found in the works of different authors under various names. Since our goal is to use them as the base of concept analysis, we introduce them in a form appropriate for this framework.

Definition 3. *Let (X, Y, R) be a formal fuzzy context.*
($\Box$) *$R^{\Box}$ denotes the lower forward operator $R^{\Rightarrow} : L^X \to L^Y$. That is, given $A \in L^X$ and $y \in Y$, let $R^{\Box}(A)(y) =_{def} A^{\Box}(y) = \bigwedge_{x \in X}(R(x, y) \mapsto A(x))$.*
($\blacklozenge$) *$R^{\blacklozenge}$ denotes the upper backward operator $R^{\leftarrow} : L^Y \to L^X$. That is, given $B \in L^Y$ and $x \in X$, let $R^{\blacklozenge}(B)(x) =_{def} B^{\blacklozenge}(x) = \bigvee_{y \in Y}(R(x, y) * B(y))$.*

The proof of the following two propositions is easy and can be found in, e.g. [22] (in the crisp case) and in [19](in fuzzy case):

Proposition 2. *Let X, Y be sets and $R : X \times Y \to L$ a fuzzy relation. Then*

(1) $A_1, A_2 \in L^X, A_1 \leq A_2 \implies A_1^{\Box} \leq A_2^{\Box}$;
(2) $B_1, B_2 \in L^Y, B_1 \leq B_2 \implies B_1^{\blacklozenge} \leq B_2^{\blacklozenge}$.

Proposition 3. *Let $\{A_i \mid i \in I\} \subseteq L^X$ and $\{B_i \mid i \in I\} \subseteq L^Y$. Then:*

(1) $\left(\bigwedge_{i \in I} A_i\right)^{\Box} = \bigwedge_{i \in I} A_i^{\Box}$;   (2) $\left(\bigvee_{i \in I} B_i\right)^{\blacklozenge} = \bigvee_{i \in I} B_i^{\blacklozenge}$.

Proposition 4. (see, e.g. [19])

(1) $R^{\Box}(1_X) = 1_Y$ *If R is left connected, then $R^{\Box}(a_X) = a_Y$ for every $a \in L$.*
(2) $R^{\blacklozenge}(1_Y) = 1_X$ *If R is right connected, then $R^{\blacklozenge}(b_Y) = b_X$ for every $b \in L$.*

Theorem 2. (see, e.g. [4]). *Operators $R^{\blacklozenge} : L^Y \to L^Y$ and $R^{\Box} : L^X \to L^Y$ form an isotone Galois connection (i.e. form an adjoint pair $(R^{\blacklozenge}, R^{\Box})$), that is $B^{\blacklozenge} \leq A \iff B \leq A^{\Box}$ for any $A \in L^X, B \in L^Y$.*

4.2 Crisply Generated $^{\blacklozenge\Box}$-Preconcept Join Semilattice

Let (X, Y, R) be a formal fuzzy context. For each $(A, B) \in \mathbb{P}_0$ let $(A, B)^{\blacklozenge\Box} =_{def} (B^{\blacklozenge}, A^{\Box})$. Obviously $(A, B)^{\blacklozenge\Box}$ is a fuzzy preconcept. We say that $(A, B)^{\blacklozenge\Box}$ is the ob-oriented fuzzy preconcepts induced by the crisp preconcept (A, B). Further, let $\mathbb{P}^{\blacklozenge\Box} = \{(A, B)^{\blacklozenge\Box} : (A, B) \in \mathbb{P}_0\}$ be the family of all ob-oriented fuzzy preconcept induced by crisp preconcepts (A, B). Thus we obtain an operator $^{\blacklozenge\Box} : \mathbb{P}_0 \to \mathbb{P}^{\blacklozenge\Box}$ assigning to a crisp preconcept (A, B) the fuzzy preconcept $(A, B)^{\blacklozenge\Box}$. Since operators $R^{\blacklozenge} : L^Y \to L^X$ and $R^{\Box} : L^X \to L^Y$ are isotone, we conclude that operator $\mathcal{E}^{\blacklozenge\Box} : \mathbb{P}_0 \to \mathbb{P}^{\blacklozenge\Box}$ is isotone, too.

Proposition 5. *Operator $\mathcal{E}^{\blacklozenge\Box} : \mathbb{P}_0 \to \mathbb{P}^{\blacklozenge\Box}$ is isotone: $(A, B) \preceq (C, D) \implies (A, B)^{\blacklozenge\Box} \preceq (C, D)^{\blacklozenge\Box}$ for all $(A, B), (C, D) \in \mathbb{P}_0$.*

Theorem 3. $\mathbb{P}^{\blacklozenge\square}$ *is a complete join semilattice of fuzzy preconcept lattice* $\mathbb{P}$.

Proof Let $\{(A_i, B_i) : i \in I\} \subseteq \mathbb{P}_0$ be a family of crisp preconcepts and $\{(A_i, B_i)^{\blacklozenge\square} : i \in I\} \subseteq \mathbb{P}^{\blacklozenge\square} \subseteq \mathbb{P}$. We have to prove that $\bigvee_{i\in I}(A_i, B_i)^{\blacklozenge\square} \subseteq \mathbb{P}^{\blacklozenge\square}$. Referring to Proposition 3 and Theorem 1 we prove this as follows:

$$\underline{\vee}_{i\in I}(A_i, B_i)^{\blacklozenge\square} \quad = \quad \underline{\vee}_{i\in I}(B_i^{\blacklozenge}, A_i^{\square}) \quad = \quad (\bigvee_{i\in I}B_i^{\blacklozenge}, \bigwedge_{i\in I}A_i^{\square}) \quad =$$
$$(\bigvee_{i\in I}B_i)^{\blacklozenge}, (\bigwedge_{i\in I}A_i)^{\square}).$$

We complete the proof noticing that $(\bigwedge_{i\in I}A_i), (\bigvee_{i\in I}B_i)) \in \mathbb{P}_0$ and that
$$((\bigwedge_{i\in I}A_i), (\bigvee_{i\in I}B_i))^{\blacklozenge\square} = \underline{\vee}_{i\in I}(A_i, B_i)^{\blacklozenge\square}.$$

4.3 Degree of Conceptuality of $^{\blacklozenge\square}$-Preconcepts

In the previous subsection we constructed an embedding of the lattice $\mathbb{P}_0$ into the lattice $\mathbb{P}$ obtaining in the result a join subsemilattice $\mathbb{P}^{\blacklozenge\square}$. In this way we assigned to each crisp preconcept (A, B) a fuzzy preconcept $(A, B)^{\blacklozenge\square}$. In this section we evaluate how well this procedure reflects the conceptuality for each specific original crisp preconcept (A, B). Namely, we measure the degree of coordinance between (A, B) and its image $(A, B)^{\blacklozenge\square}$ by setting $\mathcal{D}_{ob} : (A, B) = (A \cong B^{\blacklozenge}) \wedge (B \cong A^{\square})$. Varying pairs (A, B) over $\mathbb{P}_0$ we obtain operator $\mathcal{D}_{ob} : \mathbb{P}_0 \to \mathbb{P}^{\blacklozenge\square} \subseteq \mathbb{P}$. Recalling that $(A \cong B^{\blacklozenge}) = (A \hookrightarrow B^{\blacklozenge}) \wedge (A \hookleftarrow B^{\blacklozenge})$ and $(A^{\square} \cong B) = (A^{\square} \hookrightarrow B) \wedge (A^{\square} \hookleftarrow B^{\blacklozenge})$ we consider separately operators $\mathcal{D}^1_{ob}(A, B) = A^{\square} \hookrightarrow B$, $\mathcal{D}^2_{ob}(A, B) = A^{\square} \hookleftarrow B$, $\mathcal{D}^3_{ob}(A, B) = A \hookrightarrow B^{\blacklozenge}$, $\mathcal{D}^4_{ob}(A, B) = A \hookleftarrow B^{\blacklozenge}$. Obviously, $\mathcal{D}_{ob}(A, B) = \mathcal{D}^1_{ob}(A, B) \wedge \mathcal{D}^2_{ob}(A, B) \wedge \mathcal{D}^3_{ob}(A, B) \wedge \mathcal{D}^4_{ob}(A, B)$.

4.4 Operators $\mathcal{D}^1_{ob}, \mathcal{D}^2_{ob}, \mathcal{D}^3_{ob}, \mathcal{D}^4_{ob} : \mathbb{P}_0 \to L$

In this section we characterize operators $\mathcal{D}^1_{ob}, \mathcal{D}^2_{ob}, \mathcal{D}^3_{ob}, \mathcal{D}^4_{ob} : \mathbb{P}_0 \to L$ separately. Let a formal fuzzy context (X, Y, R) be given and let $(A, B) \in \mathbb{P}(X, Y, R)$. Since we start with a crisp preconcept (A, B) for the description of these operators it will be convenient to use notations $A^c = X \setminus A$ and $B^c = Y \setminus B$. Unfortunately strict limitations on the scope of this submission did not allow us to give the proofs of the corresponding statements.

Proposition 6. $\mathcal{D}^1_{ob}(A, B) = \bigwedge_{y\in B^c} \bigvee_{x\in A^c}((R(x, y) \mapsto 0) \mapsto 0)$.

Notice that if L is a Girard monoid, then $(a \mapsto 0) \mapsto 0 = a$ for any $a \in L$, i.e. implication $\mapsto$ satisfies the double negation law. Hence from the previous Proposition we get:

Corollary 1. *If* L *is a Girard-monoid, in particular, an MV-algebra, then* $\mathcal{D}^1_{ob}(A, B) = \bigwedge_{y\in B^c} \bigvee_{x\in A^c} R(x, y)$.

Theorem 4. *Properties of operator* $\mathrm{D}^1_{ob} : \mathbb{P}(X, Y, R) \to L$.

1. *Operator* $\mathcal{D}^1_{ob} : \mathbb{P}(X, Y, R,) \to L$ *is upper semicontinuous, that is*
   $$\mathcal{D}^1_{ob}\left(\bigwedge_{i\in I}(A_i, B_i)\right) \geq \bigwedge_{i\in I}\mathcal{D}^1_{ob}(A_i, B_i) \ \forall\{(A_i, B_i) : \ i \in I\} \subseteq \mathbb{P}(X, Y, R).$$

2. $\mathcal{D}^1_{ob}(A, 1_Y) = 1$ for every $A \subseteq X$. If R is left connected, then $\mathcal{D}^1_{ob}(0_X, B) = 1$ for every $B \subseteq Y$.

Proposition 7. $\mathcal{D}^2_{ob}(A, B) = \bigwedge_{y \in B} \bigwedge_{x \in A^c} (R(x, y) \mapsto 0)$.

Theorem 5. Properties of operator $\mathcal{D}^2_{ob} : \mathbb{P}(X, Y, R) \to L$.

1. Operator $\mathcal{D}^2_{ob} : \mathbb{P}(X, Y, R) \to L$ is lower semi-continuous, that is
$$\mathcal{D}^2_{ob}\left(\bigvee_{i \in I}(A_i, B_i)\right) \geq \bigwedge_{i \in I} \mathcal{D}^2_{ob}(A_i, B_i) \; \forall \{(A_i, B_i) : \; i \in I\} \subseteq \mathbb{P}(X, Y, R).$$
2. $\mathcal{D}^2_{ob}(A, 0_Y) = 1$ for every $A \subseteq X$ and $\mathcal{D}^2_{ob}(1_X, B) = 1$ for every $B \subseteq Y$.

Proposition 8. $\mathcal{D}^3_{ob}(A, B) = \bigwedge_{x \in A^c} \bigvee_{y \in B} (R(x, y))$.

Theorem 6. Properties of operator $\mathcal{D}^3_{ob} : \mathbb{P}(X, Y, R) \to L$.

1. Operator $\mathcal{D}^3_{ob} : \mathbb{P}(X, Y, R) \to L$ is upper semi-continuous, that is
$$\mathcal{D}^3_{ob}\left(\bigwedge_{i \in I}(A_i, B_i)\right) \geq \bigwedge_{i \in I} \mathcal{D}^3_{ob}(A_i, B_i) \; \forall \{(A_i, B_i) : \; \in I\} \subseteq \mathbb{P}(X, Y, R,).$$
2. $\mathcal{D}^3_{ob}(0_X, B) = 1$ for every $B \subseteq Y$. If R is right connected, then $\mathcal{D}^3_{ob}(A, 1_Y) = 1$ for every $A \subseteq X$.

Proposition 9. $\mathcal{D}^4_{ob}(A, B) = \bigwedge_{x \in A} \left(\bigvee_{y \in B} (R(x, y) \mapsto 0)\right)$.

Theorem 7. Properties of operator $\mathcal{D}^4_{ob} : \mathbb{P}(X, Y, R) \to L$.

1. Operator $\mathcal{D}^4_{ob} : \mathbb{P}(X, Y, R) \to L$ is lower semi-continuous, that is
$$\mathcal{D}^4_{ob}\left(\bigvee_{i \in I}(A_i, B_i)\right) \geq \bigwedge_{i \in I} \mathcal{D}^4_{ob}(A_i, B_i) \; \forall \{(A_i, B_i) : \; i \in I\} \subseteq \mathbb{P}(X, Y, R, L).$$
2. $\mathcal{D}^4_{ob}(A, 0_Y) = 1$ for every $A \subseteq X$ and $\mathcal{D}^4_{ob}(1_X, B) = 1$ for every $B \subseteq Y$.

Remark 1. The simplest case to study the properties of a preconcept $(A, B)^{\blacklozenge\square}$ on the lines of our work, is the case when the set of objects A coincides with the domain X and the set of properties B coincides with the codomain Y of the fuzzy relation R. In this case the formulas for calculation operators $\mathcal{D}^1$, $\mathcal{D}^2$, $\mathcal{D}^3$ and $\mathcal{D}^4$ obtained above formulas can be essentially simplified. Namely, notice first that in this case $A^\square = B$ (in particular, this means that $A^\square$ is a crisp set) and $B^\blacklozenge(x) = \bigvee_{y \in B} R(x, y)$. Therefore $\mathcal{D}^1(A, B) = A^\square \hookrightarrow B = 1$, $\mathcal{D}^2(A, B) = A^\square \hookleftarrow B = 1$ and $\mathcal{D}^4(A, B) = B^\blacklozenge \hookrightarrow A = 1$. In turn $\mathcal{D}^3(A, B) = 1 \mapsto \bigvee_{x \in A, y \in B} R(x, y)$. Therefore: $\mathcal{D}(A, B) = 1 \mapsto \bigvee_{x \in A, y \in B} R(x, y)$. In particular, $D(A, B) = \bigvee_{x \in A, y \in B} R(x, y)$ for product and Łukasiewiucz t-norms and for the Kleene-Dines implicator.

5   Examples

In this section we explain the meaning of the values expressed by operators $\mathcal{D}^i(A, B)$ on specific examples. In the first subsection these examples relate to classification of zoological species, in the second subsection the analysis of solar activity will be touched.

5.1 Examples Related to Zoology

Let the set of objects $X = \{x_1, x_2, x_3, x_4, x_5, x_6, x_7, x_8, x_9, x_{10}, x_{11}\}$ consist of animals: x_1 is an albatross, x_2 is a swift, x_3 is a sparrow x_4 is an owl, x_5 is a flying fox, x_6 is a pelican, x_7 is an penguin, x_8 is an ostrich x_9 is a kiwi bird, x_{10} is a fox x_{11} is a bear. The set of properties $Y = \{y_1, y_2\}$: y_1 an animal has wings, y_2 the animal has fur. The relation $R : X \times Y \to L$ where $L = ([0, 1], \leq, \wedge, \vee, *, \mapsto)$ is defined and interpreted as follows:

$R(x_1, y_1) = 1$. Wings allow albatross to fly long distances over the oceans.

$R(x_2, y_1) = 0.9$. Wings allow swift to fly for hours, but usually it does not fly for far distances.

$R(x_3, y_1) = 0.7$. Wings allow sparrow to fly constantly for short distances.

$R(x_4, y_1) = 0.6$. Wings allow owl to fly short distance (e.g. hunting for food).

$R(x_5, y_1) = 0.6$. Wings allow flying fox to fly for short distance (e.g. hunting for food).

$R(x_6, y_1) = 0.5$. Wings are used by pelican to create a lift, to steer and navigate in the air and fly very short distances.

$R(x_7, y_1) = 0.3$. Penguin does not use wings for flying, but it is important for penguin, for example, to paddle through the water like a boat.

$R(x_8, y_1) = 0.2$. Ostrich does not use wings for flying, but it use them to balance when running, especially when suddenly changing direction.

$R(x_9, y_1) = 0.1$. Kiwi has very short wings covered by feathers. It does not use them, at least in the process of moving.

$R(x_{10}, y_1) = 0, R(x_{11}, y_1) = 0$. Foxes and bears do not have wings $R(x_i, y_2) = 0$ for $i = 1, 2, 3, 6, 7$. Animals do not have neither fur nor even dense feather cover. $R(x_i, y_2) = 0.3$ for $i = 4, 8, 9$. Animals have dense feather cover looking like a fur. $R(x_i, y_2) = 0.8$ for $i = 5, 10$. Animals have rather dense fur cover. $R(x_i, y_2) = 1$ for $i = 11$. Animals have very dense fur cover.

Remark 2. The above information is based on materials found in the popular literature and in Internet, see, e.g. https://faunafacts.com. The specific values assigned to each relation are ours and just chosen for interpretation. Of course, professional zoologist will argue about our choice. However, we hope that this interpretation will help to illustrate the ideas and results presented in this paper.

5.1.1 The Basic Example

As the basic example we consider the case $X = A$, $B = Y$ and $R : X \times Y \to L$ defined as above. In this case we can use formulas obtained in Remark 1. Hence $\mathcal{D}^1(A, B) = \mathcal{D}^2(A, B) = \mathcal{D}^4(A, B) = 1$, $\mathcal{D}^3(A, B) = \bigwedge_{x \in A}(A(x) \hookrightarrow B^\blacklozenge(x))$ and $\mathcal{D}(A, B) = \mathcal{D}^3(A, B)$. We calculate it as follows: $B^\blacklozenge(x) = \bigvee_{y \in B} R(x, y) * B(y)$:
$B^\blacklozenge(x_1) = 1$, $B^\blacklozenge(x_2) = 0.9$, $B^\blacklozenge(x_3) = 0.7$, $B^\blacklozenge(x_4) = 0.6$, $B^\blacklozenge(x_5) = 0.8$, $B^\blacklozenge(x_6) = 0.5$, $B^\blacklozenge(x_7) = 0.3$, $B^\blacklozenge(x_8) = 0.3$, $B^\blacklozenge(x_9) = 0.3$, $B^\blacklozenge(x_{10}) = 0.8$, $B^\blacklozenge(x_{11}) = 1$. In the result we have $\mathcal{D}^3(A, B) = A \hookrightarrow B^\blacklozenge = \bigwedge_i (1 \mapsto B^\blacklozenge(x_i)) = 1 \mapsto \bigwedge_i B^\blacklozenge(x_i) = 1 \mapsto 0.3$. In particular, in case when $*$ is Łukasiewicz t-norm or the product t-norm $\mathcal{D}^3(A, B) = \bigwedge_i B^\blacklozenge(x_i) = 0.3$. Hence also $\mathcal{D}(A, B) = 0.3$.

5.1.2   Comments and Variation of the Example

– Such rather high value 0,3 of contentment may seem to be unexpected for a group of so different animals. However, this is obtained because we based the evaluation of the group taking into account very different properties: say wings (wonderful for the albatross and for the swift) and fur (perfect suiting for the bear and for the fox).
– On the other hand if we will change orientation in the parameter y_2, namely to assign higher value for animals $WITHOUT$ thick fur and lower for animals with a fur, then the estimation $\mathcal{D}(A, B)$ will look differently: for the case of the Łukasiwicz and the Product t-norm we will get $\mathcal{D}^3(A, B) = 0$ (thank that the fluffy bear cub has no wings!) and this seems much better corresponding to our intuition.
– Now we extend the first example by including one more parameter $y_3 =$ EGGS in B with the following interpretation: $R(x_i, y_3) = 1$ if an animal x_i lays eggs and $R(x_i, y_3) = 0$ otherwise. Then our table will drastically change giving
$B^\blacklozenge(x_i) = 1$ for $i = 1, 2, 3, 4, 5, 7, 8, 9$ and leaving the same $B^\blacklozenge(x_6) = 0.5$, $B^\blacklozenge(x_{10}) = 0.8$, and $B^\blacklozenge(x_{11}) = 1$.
In this case for the Łukasiewicz t-norm and for the product t-norm we get $\mathcal{D}^3(A, B) = 0.5$. And this result possibly in the best way corresponds to our intuition looking at the animals $x \in A$ as some group of animals "centered" around the group $BIRDS$.
– We modify basic example by taking $A = \{x_2, x_3, x_4, x_5, x_6, x_7, x_8, x_9, x_{10}\} \subset X$ that is we exclude from the sample A the most "outstanding"animals: albatross with "best wings" and bear with "best fur." Since we did not change B the set $B^\blacklozenge$ does not depend on A, we get $\mathcal{D}^4(A, B) = 1$ and $\mathcal{D}^3(A, B) = 0.7$ in case of the Łukasiewicz and product t-norm. In turn

$$A^\square(y_1) = \bigwedge_i (R(x_i, y_1) \mapsto A(x_i)) = \bigvee_{i \neq 1, 11} R(x_i, y_1) = 0.9;$$

$$A^\square(y_2) = \bigwedge_i (R(x_i, y_2) \mapsto A(x_i)) = \bigvee_{i \neq 1, 11} R(x_i, y_1) = 0.8.$$

In the result we have $\mathcal{D}^1(A, B) = \bigwedge_{y_i} A^\square(y_i) \mapsto B(y_i) = 1$ and $\mathcal{D}^2(A, B) = \bigwedge_{y_i} (B(y_i) \mapsto A^\square(y_i)) = 1 \mapsto \bigvee_{i \neq 1, 11} R(x_i, y_1) = 1 \mapsto 0.9 \vee 0.8 = 1 \mapsto 0.9$ and hence in case of Łukasiewicz or product t-norm $\mathcal{D}^2(A, B) = 0.9$. Hence in the result $\mathcal{D}(A, B) = 0.9$.

5.2   Example of the Assessment of Solar Activity

For the purposes of practical application of fuzzy preconcepts we also propose an example with analysis of solar activity with focus on sunspots as the most evident and also spectacular structures providing visible information about changes in the solar activity. While sunspots are neither something rare nor unique and can be observed even during the solar minimum (more details regarding solar activity and sunspots can be found on, e.g. www.swpc.noaa.gov/phenomena/

sunspotssolar-cycle), we will focus on larger sunspots with more sophisticated magnetic fields capable to produce weaker or stronger and geoeffective solar flares.

We assume that the set of objects X contains all sunspots visible on the sun on a given date. We consider the subset $A = \{x_1, x_2, x_3, x_4, x_5\} \subset X$ containing five sunspots with more sophisticated magnetic fields and capable to produce significant solar flares. We define the set of properties $Y = \{y_1, y_2\}$ as follows: y_1 the sunspot has more or less sophisticated magnetic field, y_2 the sunspot can produce the solar flare. Relation $R : X \times Y \to [0, 1]$.

$R(x_1, y_1) = 0.9$ means that the 1st sunspot has very sophisticated magnetic field.

$R(x_2, y_1) = 0.7$ means that the 2nd sunspot has sophisticated magnetic field.

$R(x_3, y_1) = 0.5$ means that the 3rd sunspot has rather sophisticated magnetic field.

$R(x_4, y_1) = 0.4$ means that the 4th sunspot has less sophisticated magnetic field.

$R(x_5, y_1) = 0.2$ means that the 5th sunspot has rather simple magnetic field.

$R(x_1, y_2) = 0.6$ means that the 1st sunspot is rather capable to produce the solar flares.

$R(x_2, y_2) = 0.8$ means that the 2nd sunspot is very capable to produce the solar flares.

$R(x_3, y_2) = 0.5$ means that the 3rd sunspot is capable to produce the solar flares.

$R(x_4, y_2) = 0.3$ means that the 4th sunspot is less capable to produce the solar flares.

$R(x_5, y_2) = 0.6$ means that the 5th sunspot is rather capable to produce the solar flares.

Based on the formulas obtained in Remark 1 $\mathcal{D}^1(A, B) = \mathcal{D}^2(A, B) = \mathcal{D}^4(A, B) = 1$ and $\mathcal{D}^3(A, B) = \bigwedge_{x \in A}(A(x) \hookrightarrow B^\blacklozenge(x))$ and $\mathcal{D}(A, B) = \mathcal{D}^3(A, B)$. We calculate the following values of $B^\blacklozenge(x) = \bigvee_{y \in B} R(x, y) * B(y)$: $B^\blacklozenge(x_1) = 0.9$, $B^\blacklozenge(x_2) = 0.8$, $B^\blacklozenge(x_3) = 0.5$, $B^\blacklozenge(x_4) = 0.4$, $B^\blacklozenge(x_5) = 0.6$. We obtain that $\mathcal{D}^3(A, B) = A \hookrightarrow B^\blacklozenge = \bigwedge_i(1 \mapsto B^\blacklozenge(x_i)) = 1 \mapsto \bigwedge_i B^\blacklozenge(x_i) = 1 \mapsto 0.4$. In particular, in case $*$ is Lukasiewicz t-norm or product t-norm $\mathcal{D}^3(A, B) = \bigwedge_i B^\blacklozenge(x_i) = 0.4$. Hence also $\mathcal{D}(A, B) = 0.4$.

Such result means that the possibility of not producing geoeffective flares by any of these five sunspots is 0.4 which is a kind of medium possibility with slightly higher chance (0.6) that such flares can be produced.

Now we extend the example adding parameter y_3 in B containing the additional condition which is very important for triggering the Northern Lights in case of any geoeffective solar flares: $R(x_1, y_3)$, $R(x_5, y_3) = 1$ meaning that the 1st and the 5th sunspots directly face the Earth, $R(x_3, y_3)$, $R(x_4, y_3) = 0.5$ meaning that the 3rd and the 4th sunspot partly face the Earth and $R(x_2, y_3) = 0.1$ meaning that the 2nd sunspot does not face the Earth and is visible close to the sun's limb. Taking into account this condition we obtain that $\mathcal{D}^1(A, B) =$

$\mathcal{D}^2(A,B) = \mathcal{D}^4(A,B) = 1$ and $\mathcal{D}^3(A,B) = A \hookrightarrow B^{\blacklozenge} = \bigwedge_i (1 \mapsto B^{\blacklozenge}(x_i)) = 1 \mapsto \bigwedge_i B^{\blacklozenge}(x_i) = 1 \mapsto 0.1$. In case $*$ is Lukasiewicz t-norm or product t-norm $\mathcal{D}^3(A,B) = \bigwedge_i B^{\blacklozenge}(x_i) = 0.1$. Hence also $\mathcal{D}(A,B) = 0.1$.

It means that the possibility of not producing geoeffective flares by any of these five sunspots has decreased to 0.1 which is low possibility, and it means that there is a very high chance (0.9) of geoeffective flares.

At the end we should admit that sunspots are often changing. This includes further increase or decrease in sophistication of magnetic fields, their stability and position on the solar disk. Therefore this example could be further enhanced taking into account all these dynamic changes and comparing the data for different dates.

6   Conclusion

In the paper we proposed an alternative approach to the study of some issues of formal fuzzy concept analysis. Of the three known to us versions of concept analysis: "classical", object-oriented and property-oriented, we stick here to the framework of the object oriented version. Having as the original motivation Bělohlávek's crisply based fuzzy concept analysis (on the lines of Wille-Ganter concept analysis) and noticing that the direct transform of Bělohlávek's ideas to object-oriented context does not make sense we decided to combine Bělohlávek's ideas with our graded approach to fuzzy concept analysis. In the result we introduced the conceptuality degree of a crisp (object-oriented) preconcept, developed the basics of the corresponding theory and illustrated the possible applications of our theory by examples related to zoology and astronomy.

Concerning our future plans for the work initiated in this paper, as the first and the most challenging one we foresee its applications in different practical problems. As the most appropriate for the use of tools presented here we assume problems of classification, specifically classification of biological issues, classification of languages, and in the study of matters related to astronomy, some of which could be of high practical value. Of course such kind of applications can be developed only in tight cooperation with specialists in the related areas of science.

On the other hand, we have perspectives for the work in this directions for us, as mathematicians. Namely, we have important challenges for the study of crisply generates fuzzy concepts in case of a more general lattice L (instead of $[0,1]$) as for the codomain of the fuzzy relation. Note that for the applications of our theory in real world problems the assumption that all values are numbers in the interval is absolutely inadequate. In this paper for animal classification we used the assumption that their properties used for classification are comparable. Such an assumption served well for us to illustrate the idea of application of our method for classification, but of course it is not viable in any practical scientific research. Thus we view a deeper investigation of crisply generated ob-oriented fuzzy preconcepts in case of general quantales as the most important theoretical problem to be studied in order to attract to our research scientists beyond pure mathematics.

References

1. Alcalde, C., Burusco, A., Díaz, J.C., Fuentes-González, R., Medina-Moreno, J.: Fuzzy property-oriented concept lattices in morphological image and signal processing. In: Rojas, I., Joya, G., Cabestany, J. (eds.) IWANN 2013. LNCS, vol. 7903, pp. 246–253. Springer, Heidelberg (2013). https://doi.org/10.1007/978-3-642-38682-4_28
2. Bělohlávek, R.: Concept lattices and order in fuzzy logic. Ann. Pure Appl. Logic **128**, 277–298 (2004)
3. Bělohlávek, R., Sklenář, V., Zacpal, J.: Crisply generated fuzzy concepts. In: Ganter, B., Godin, R. (eds.) ICFCA 2005. LNCS (LNAI), vol. 3403, pp. 269–284. Springer, Heidelberg (2005). https://doi.org/10.1007/978-3-540-32262-7_19
4. Lai, H.-L., Zhang, D.: Concept lattices of fuzzy context: formal concept analysis vs. rough set theory. Int. J. Approximate Reasoning **50**(5), 695–707 (2009)
5. Düntsch, I., Gediga, G.: Approximation operators in qualitative data analysis. In: de Swart, H., Orłowska, E., Schmidt, G., Roubens, M. (eds.) Theory and Applications of Relational Structures as Knowledge Instruments. LNCS, vol. 2929, pp. 214–230. Springer, Heidelberg (2003). https://doi.org/10.1007/978-3-540-24615-2_10
6. Ganter, B., Wille, R.: Formal Concept Analysis: Mathematical Foundations. Springer, Berlin (1999)
7. Ganter, B., Kuznetsov, S.O.: Pattern structures and their projections. In: Delugach, H.S., Stumme, G. (eds.) ICCS-ConceptStruct 2001. LNCS (LNAI), vol. 2120, pp. 129–142. Springer, Heidelberg (2001). https://doi.org/10.1007/3-540-44583-8_10
8. Han, S.-E., Šostak, A.: On the measure of M-rough approximation of L-fuzzy sets. Soft. Comput. **22**, 3843–3853 (2018)
9. Goguen, J.A.: L-fuzzy sets. J. Math. Anal. Appl. **18**(1), 145–174 (1967)
10. Krídlo, O., Krajči, S.: Proto-fuzzy concepts, their retrieval and usage. In: CLA 2008, pp. 83–95. Palacký University, Olomouc (2008)
11. Medina, J., Ojeda-Aciego, M., Ruiz-Calviño, J.: Formal concept analysis via multi-adjoint concept lattices. Fuzzy Sets Syst. **160**(2), 130 144 (2009)
12. Medina, J.: Relating attribute reduction in formal, object-oriented and property-oriented concept lattices. Comput. Math. Appl. **64**(6), 1992–2002 (2012)
13. Medina, J.: Towards multi-adjoint property-oriented concept lattices. In: Yu, J., Greco, S., Lingras, P., Wang, G., Skowron, A. (eds.) RSKT 2010. LNCS (LNAI), vol. 6401, pp. 159–166. Springer, Heidelberg (2010). https://doi.org/10.1007/978-3-642-16248-0_26
14. Medina, J.: Multi-adjoint property-oriented and object-oriented concept lattices. Inf. Sci. **190**, 95–106 (2012)
15. Pankratieva, V.V., Kuznetsov, S.O.: Relations between proto-fuzzy concepts, crisply generated fuzzy concepts, and interval pattern structures. Fund. Inform. **115**(4), 50–59 (2010)
16. Rodabaugh, S.E.: Powerset operator foundations for poslat fuzzy set theories and topologies. In: Höhle, U., Rodabaugh, S.E. (eds.) Mathematics of Fuzzy Sets. FSHS, vol. 3, pp. 91–116. Springer, Boston (1999). https://doi.org/10.1007/978-1-4615-5079-2_3
17. Rosenthal, K.I.: Quantales and Their Applications. Pitman Research Notes in Mathematics, vol. 234. Longman Scientific and Technical (1990)

18. Šostak, A., Krastiņš, M., Uļjane I.: Graded concept lattices in fuzzy rough set theory. In: CEUR Workshop Proceedings, CLA 2022, vol. 3308, pp. 19–33 (2022)
19. Šostak, A., Uļjane, I.: Fuzzy relations: the fundament for fuzzy rough approximation, fuzzy concept analysis and fuzzy mathematical morphology. In: Cornejo, M.E., Harmati, I.Á., Kóczy, L.T., Medina-Moreno, J. (eds.) Computational Intelligence and Mathematics for Tackling Complex Problems 4. SCI, vol. 1040, pp. 25–35. Springer, Cham (2023). https://doi.org/10.1007/978-3-031-07707-4_4
20. Šostak, A., Uļjane, I., Krastiņš, M.: Gradations of fuzzy preconcept lattices. Axioms **10**(1:41) (2021)
21. Wille, R.: Concept lattices and conceptual knowledge systems. Comput. Math. Appl. **23**(6–9), 493–515 (1992)
22. Yao, Y.: Concept lattices in rough set theory. In: Proceedings of 2004 Annual Meeting of the North American Fuzzy Information Processing Society (NAFIPS 2004), pp. 796–801 (2004)
23. Zadeh, L.A.: Fuzzy sets. Inf. Control **8**, 338–353 (1965)
24. Zadeh, L.A.: Similarity relations and fuzzy orderings. Inf. Sci. **3**(2), 177–200 (1971)

IFS-IBA Logical Aggregation with Frank t-norms

Pavle Milošević$^{(\boxtimes)}$ ⓘ, Ivana Dragović ⓘ, Milica Zukanović ⓘ, Ana Poledica ⓘ, and Bratislav Petrović ⓘ

Faculty of Organizational Sciences, University of Belgrade, Jove Ilića 154, 11000 Belgrade, Serbia
{pavle.milosevic,ivana.dragovic,milica.zukanovic,ana.poledica, bratislav.petrovic}@fon.bg.ac.rs

Abstract. In this paper, we present a novel aggregation method for intuitionistic fuzzy sets (IFS) based on interpolative Boolean algebra (IBA) and logical aggregation (LA). The approach is founded on IFS-IBA calculus, an approach that maintains intuitionistic presumptions when dealing with IFS. The main contribution of IFS-IBA approach is the explicit inclusion of attribute correlation and automated choice of aggregation operator. That is accomplished by introducing parametric Frank t-norm in IFS-IBA calculus and by defining a clear relation between correlation and Frank t-norm parameter. Frank t-norm is chosen since it has the same mathematical properties as a generalized product in IFS-IBA framework. Furthermore, the proposed IFS-IBA LA approach incorporates guidelines for factor normalization, I-fuzzification, logical expression modeling and aggregation. The main applicative benefits of the proposed IFS-IBA LA approach are illustrated in the example of ranking gifted students.

Keywords: IFS-IBA · aggregation · intuitionistic fuzzy sets · interpolative Boolean algebra · Frank t-norm

1 Introduction

Modeling and decision making in situations with plenty of vague, incomplete and imprecise information is a very challenging problem. Still, many fuzzy logic-based tools and approaches may facilitate that process. Many of them are based on intuitionistic fuzzy sets (IFS) [1], the theory that takes into account information about set membership, non-membership and uncertainty as separate variable.

On the other hand, attribute aggregation since it is the core of various ranking or decision algorithms. The recent effort of many scholars, regarding the aggregation of IFS information initiated a new area of IFS theory [27]. Some aggregation operators, e.g. triangular IF weighted averaging operator (TIFWA) [12] and IF order weighted operator (IFOWA) [31], have significant theoretical and applicative importance. Still, work on various aggregations of IFS is in progress.

Supported by organization x.

S. Massanet et al. (Eds.): EUSFLAT 2023/AGOP 2023, LNCS 14069, pp. 99–111, 2023.
https://doi.org/10.1007/978-3-031-39965-7_9

In this paper, we introduce a novel approach to the aggregation of IF values based on interpolative Boolean algebra (IBA) [23] and logical aggregation (LA) [24]. In fact, we aim to transfer all benefits of LA for dealing with IFS via IFS-IBA approach [21]. In that way, the aggregation procedure of IFS is transparent, easy to implement and based on assumptions of intuitionism. The proposed IFS-IBA LA approach is a complete aggregation procedure that contains guidelines for factor normalization, I-fuzzification, automated operator selection, logical expression modeling and finally aggregation of factors. From the technical point of view, the main contributions of this paper are introducing Frank t-norm as a parametric realization of IFS-IBA operations and relying on correlation for operator selection. Frank t-norm is chosen as an adequate operator since it produces values in the same interval and has the same mathematical properties as a generalized product operator in IFS-IBA framework. The aggregation procedure is illustrated in the example regarding gifted student ranking.

This paper is organized as follows. In Sect. 2, a brief overview of IFS, IBA, and IFS-IBA is presented. Section 3 reflects on the correlation measuring between IFS. In Sect. 4, we provide a brief theoretical overview of parametric t-norms. Special attention is devoted to Frank t-norm and its usage for dealing with generalized fuzzy sets. The background and main steps of the proposed IFS-IBA logical aggregation approach are elaborated in Sect. 5. An illustrative example regarding gifted students ranking is provided in Sect. 6. Finally, the main conclusions and potential directions of future work are listed in Sect. 7.

2   IFS-IBA Approach

In this section we first reflect on the essentials of IFS and IBA, and further we give a brief overview of IFS-IBA approach.

2.1   Intuitionistic Fuzzy Sets

Intuitionistic fuzzy set theory is introduced by Atanassov in [1]. Unlike traditional fuzzy sets, IFS consider non-membership degree beside standard membership degree. Therefore, IFSs are able to include more information in the modeling process and to handle a certain level of uncertainty in the data. As a generalization of the traditional fuzzy sets, IFS A infinite set X is defined as follows [1]:

$$A = \{\langle x, \mu_A(x), \nu_A(x)\rangle | x \in X\} \tag{1}$$

where $\mu_A(x) : X \to [0,1]$ and $\nu_A(x) : X \to [0,1]$ are membership and non-membership degrees with condition $0 \le \mu_A(x) + \nu_A(x) \le 1$ for every $x \in X$.

Only in the case when $\nu_A(x) = 1 - \mu_A(x)$, IFS become a traditional fuzzy set. Otherwise, IFS implies the hesitancy degree which shows the existence of a certain level of uncertainty of the element x to IFS A [1]:

$$\pi_A(x) = 1 - (\mu_A(x) + \nu_A(x)) \tag{2}$$

Basic operations and relations over two IFSs A and B are originally defined by Atanassov [1]:

$$A \cap B = \langle \min(\mu_A, \mu_B), \max(\nu_A, \nu_B) \rangle \tag{3}$$

$$A \cup B = \langle \max(\mu_A, \mu_B), \min(\nu_A, \nu_B) \rangle \tag{4}$$

$$N(A) = \langle \nu_A, \mu_A \rangle \tag{5}$$

From Eqs. (3)–(5), it can be concluded that dual fuzzy operations, t-norm and s-norm are applied over membership and non-membership degrees simultaneously when it comes to IF intersection and union. Besides standard IFS operations corresponding to minimum/maximum, many operators are introduced in the literature, e.g. operations $\cdot$ and $+$ modeled on algebraic product and probabilistic sum, IFS t-norm [5], order relations, modal operations of necessity and possibility [1], and many others [28] etc.

2.2   Interpolative Boolean Algebra

Interpolative Boolean algebra represents a consistent real-valued realization of a finite Boolean algebra [23]. It is "interpolative" as a consequence of its semantics based on a generalized Boolean polynomial (GBP). Its "consistency" comes from the fact that all the laws of Boolean algebra are preserved. It is "real-valued" realization because the elements can take any value from the unit interval [0,1], so it can be applied to fuzzy logic and sets [23], as well as fuzzy relations [25].

IBA is a multi-valued logic that preserves all Boolean laws, including the laws of contradiction and excluded middle [23]. This is achieved by introducing two levels: symbolic and value level, i.e. by separating the value of an attribute from its structure.

On **the symbolic level**, a logical expression is transformed into a corresponding generalized Boolean polynomial (GBP) according to the following transformation rules [24]:

$$(\beta(a_1, \ldots, a_n) \wedge \gamma(a_1, \ldots, a_n))^\otimes = \beta(a_1, \ldots, a_n) \otimes \gamma(a_1, \ldots, a_n) \tag{6}$$

$$\begin{aligned}(\beta(a_1, \ldots, a_n) \vee \gamma(a_1, \ldots, a_n))^\otimes = \beta(a_1, \ldots, a_n) + \gamma(a_1, \ldots, a_n) \\ -\beta(a_1, \ldots, a_n) \otimes \gamma(a_1, \ldots, a_n)\end{aligned} \tag{7}$$

$$(\neg\beta(a_1, \ldots, a_n))^\otimes = 1 - \beta(a_1, \ldots, a_n) \tag{8}$$

where $\beta(a_1, \ldots, a_n)$ and $\gamma(a_1, \ldots, a_n)$ are complex elements of Boolean algebra, i.e. all logical functions over attributes $a_i, i = 1, \ldots, n$.

For the primary attributes $a_1, \ldots, a_n$ the following applies:

$$(a_i \wedge a_j)^\otimes = \begin{cases} a_i \otimes a_j, i \neq j \\ a_i, i = j \end{cases} \tag{9}$$

$$(a_i \vee a_j)^\otimes = a_i + a_j - a_i \otimes a_j \tag{10}$$

$$(\neg a_i)^{\otimes} = 1 - a_i \tag{11}$$

The generalized Boolean polynomial (GBP) is a polynomial whose variables are elements of the Boolean algebra and the operators are standard $+$, standard $-$, and generalized product $\otimes$ (GP) [24]. GP can be any function that is a subclass of the conventional t-norm satisfying the non-negativity axiom. The choice of the appropriate t-norm for GP depends on the nature of the primary attributes and/or on their correlation. Standard minimum, algebraic product, and Lukasiewicz t-norm are the most common choices.

Only once the final structure of a logical function is determined, we can move to **the value level** and introduce the values of the primary attributes. Each element of Boolean algebra is valued using a generalized Boolean polynomial.

One of the most important applications of IBA is logical aggregation [24], a consistent and transparent procedure for aggregating factors. LA consists of two steps: data normalization and aggregation of attributes into a resulting value.

2.3   Essentials of IFS-IBA

IBA-based calculus for IFS is presented in [21], and further developed in [18,20]. The resulting IFS-IBA approach employs IFS in the original form and IBA-based logical operations with several adaptations. This approach is developed as a potential answers to the terminological debate regarding the name of IFS theory [6]. In other words, the main idea behind IFS-IBA was to develop an approach that is in line with the intuitionistic nature of IFS, i.e. the law of contradiction and the double negation rule are valid in this approach. That is accomplished by introducing IBA-based operations of conjunction and disjunction and choosing an appropriate existing IFS negation [2].

$$(A \wedge B)^{\otimes} = \langle \mu_A \otimes \mu_B, \nu_A + \nu_B - \nu_A \otimes \nu_B \rangle \tag{12}$$

$$(A \vee B)^{\otimes} = \langle \mu_A + \mu_B - \mu_A \otimes \mu_B, \nu_A \otimes \nu_B \rangle \tag{13}$$

$$(\neg A)^{\otimes} = \langle \nu_A, 1 - \nu_A \rangle \tag{14}$$

Logical expressions with IFSs are structurally transformed into GBP using the IBA transformation rules given in Eqs. (6)–(11) and an additional rule, specific to IFS:

$$\mu_A \otimes \nu_A = 0 \tag{15}$$

Therefore, in IFS-IBA, IFS holds the idea of intuition and IBA provides suitable algebra. Also, the conventional IF calculus is obtained as the special case of IFS-IBA approach, when the minimum is used as GP.

This approach was a basis for proposing IFS-IBA similarity/dissimilarity measure [20], later employed as a part of pattern recognition, clustering, and classification algorithms. Also, on the path of IFS-IBA, LBIFS-IBA is proposed, as an approach that is focused on Boolean properties [18]. However, there have been no attempts to use IFS-IBA for factor aggregation, ranking or decision making so far.

3 Correlation of IFS

Correlation is an important measure that expresses the linear relationship between elements of two sets. Since comparing fuzzy sets is an essential task, the idea of the correlation coefficient of the IFSs in finite space is first introduced in [8]. A standard/traditional correlation between the intuitionistic fuzzy set A and B is defined as:

$$C(A, B) = \sum_{i=1}^{n} [\mu_A(x_i) \cdot \mu_B(x_i) + \nu_A(x_i) \cdot \nu_B(x_i)] \tag{16}$$

and the correlation coefficient of A and B as:

$$\rho(A, B) = \frac{C(A, B)}{(C(A, A))^{1/2} \cdot (C(B, B))^{1/2}} \tag{17}$$

Based on the paper [8], Yu proposed concept of the correlation of the IFSs in the infinite space where $C(A, B)$ was given as [32]:

$$C(A, B) = \frac{1}{b-a} \int_a^b (\mu_A(x) \cdot \mu_B(x) + \nu_A(x) \cdot \nu_B(x)) dx \tag{18}$$

In [10], it has proposed another correlation coefficient of IFSs based on Hung's statistical point of view [9]. The main idea was to find out whether the sets are negatively or positively related; hence this method calculates the correlation coefficient of IFSs A and B by means of centroid.

Xu considers the situation in which the correlation coefficient of any two IFSs equal 1 if and only if these two are the same [30]. Based on that, a new method for calculating the correlation coefficient of IFSs A and B is developed.

The majority of correlation coefficients are based on membership and non-membership degrees of IFS. Yet, Zeng and Li extended further these methods by including the third parameter, the hesitancy degree [33]:

$$C(A, B) = \frac{1}{n} \sum_{i=1}^{n} [\mu_A(x_i) \cdot \mu_B(x_i) + \nu_A(x_i) \cdot \nu_B(x_i) + \pi_A(x_i) \cdot \pi_B(x_i)] \tag{19}$$

Liu and others [17] gave another correlation coefficient in which they extend the interval of value of the correlation coefficient into $[-1,1]$ and treat the membership degree and non-membership degree separately. Also, they aimed to include deviations of IF values in the calculation.

4 Parametric t-norms

The notion of t-norms was first introduced in the context of probabilistic metric spaces, but they found wide application in fuzzy set theory. A fuzzy t-norm is a binary operation on the unit interval that must fulfill at least conditions of monotonicity, commutativity and associativity. Furthermore, if it satisfies the conditions of continuity, subidempotency and strict monotonicity we can say that t-norm is the strict Archimedean t-norm. More information and formal definitions of t-norms can be found in [13].

In order to construct Archimedean t-norms we need to define properties of unary functions i.e. generators. A decreasing generator is a continuous and strictly decreasing function f from [0,1] to R such that $f(1) = 0$ [15]. The pseudo-inverse of a decreasing generator f, denoted by $f^{(-1)}$ is a function from R to [0,1] given by [15]:

$$f^{(-1)}(a) = \begin{cases} 1, \text{for } a \in (-\infty, 0) \\ f^{(-1)}(a), \text{for } a \in [0, f(0)] \\ 0, \text{for } a \in (f(0), \infty) \end{cases} \tag{20}$$

A decreasing generator f and its pseudo-inverse $f^{(-1)}$ satisfy $f^{(-1)}(f(a)) = a$ for any $a \in [0, 1]$ [15]:

$$f^{(-1)}(f(a)) = \begin{cases} 0, \text{for } a \in (-\infty, 0) \\ a, \text{for } a \in [0, f(0)] \\ f(0), \text{for } a \in (f(0), \infty) \end{cases} \tag{21}$$

One of the possible extensions of classical t-norms is parameterized t-norms, e.g. Hamacher's t-norm, Yager's t-norm, Weber-Sugeno t-norm, Schweizer-Sklar t-norm, etc. Each of them uses aggregation operators that include parameters so the aggregation process is more flexible.

4.1 Frank t-norm

Franks t-norm is based on the class of decreasing generators

$$f_s(a) = -\ln \frac{s^a - 1}{s - 1} \text{ for } s > 0, s \neq 1 \tag{22}$$

Deduced from the equation above, it can be established

$$f_{Frank}(a, b) = \begin{cases} T_{min}(a, b), \text{if } s = 0 \\ T_{prod}(a, b), \text{if } s = 1 \\ T_{Luk}(a, b), \text{if } s = +\infty \\ \log_s(1 + \frac{(s^a - 1)(s^b - 1)}{s - 1}), \text{otherwise} \end{cases} \tag{23}$$

Operators based on (parametric) t-norms are extended to the conventional fuzzy logic in order to make the reasoning and decision-making process more flexible. In [14], authors explore different approaches to fuzzy logic based on Frank t-norms. In [4], authors investigate some classes of t-norms that provide natural extensions of Lukasiewicz, product, Frank, Schweizer-Sklar and Yager t-norms which can be generated. Also, Frank t-norm has been already introduced in IBA [16].

Many research aims to improve further generalization of the concept of fuzzy sets. In [26], authors have developed operators based on Frank t-norm for picture fuzzy sets and proposed a series of new aggregation operators. In [29], authors have studied potential applications of Archimedean t-conorm and t-norm under IF environment and proposed some other operations on IFS, while [11] proposed IF similarity measures based on Frank t-norms family.

5   IFS-IBA Logical Aggregation

In this section, we introduce logical aggregation for dealing with IFSs based on IFS-IBA approach. IFS-IBA LA can be used for the aggregation of IFSs based on requirements formulated as logical conditions. Further, logical relations are treated according to IFS-IBA transformation rules, i.e. they are mapped to GBPs. Further, GP is automatically selected based on the correlation between attributes, and expression is easily calculated.

Formally, IFS-IBA LA is based on IBA frame with Frank t-norm as a realization of GP. This operator is considered as an appropriate choice since Frank t-norm can model cases between Lukasiewicz t-norm and minimum t-norm, the same as GP. By choosing parametric t-norm instead of some non-parametric norms that can model several borderline cases properly, we have tried to facilitate and automate aggregation process and enhance the generality of the approach. In this procedure, we rely on the correlation of IFS explicitly in the aggregation process in order to automate the selection of GP. In more detail, we aim to estimate the value of parameter p of Frank t-norm based on correlations of IFSs to be aggregated.

IFS-IBA LA procedure consists of these 6 steps:

I-fuzzification: Most problems are not intuitionistic by nature. Therefore, it is usual to transform the initial set of attributes $\omega = \{a_1, a_2, \ldots, a_n\}$ into an IFS attribute set $I = \{A_1, A_2, \ldots, A_m\}$. This procedure may be conducted using a chosen function $A_i = f^{if-g}(a_i)$, e.g. intuitionistic fuzzy generator [3], which can transform every element of ω into a corresponding element of I, i.e. $n = m$. On the other hand, I-fuzzification may be realized using several standard aggregation operators $A_i = f^{if-ag}(a_i, \ldots, a_j)$, if some elements of ω are of same/similar nature, i.e. $n > m$. The example regarding I-fuzzification using aggregation operators is given in Sect. 6. The prerequisite for both I-fuzzification procedures is that attributes $\omega = \{a_1, a_2, \ldots, a_n\}$ are normalized.

IFS Correlation: In cases when a dataset consists of more than a few instances, it is possible to determine correlation between attributes. Any IFS correlation coefficient $r_{kl} = \rho(A_k, A_l)$ that produces values on $[-1, 1]$ interval is appropriate in the context of IFS-IBA LA approach. For the sake of simplicity, the coefficient given in Eqs. (16) and (17) will be used further in this research.

Frank t-norm Parameter Estimation: Since the Frank t-norm is a parametric one, it is necessary to assess the value of its parameter p for each pair of attributes. In this approach, we aim to map values of p based on values of IFS correlation. This can be performed using a suitable function $p_{kl} = f^{p-est}(r_k l)$ that maps values from $[-1,1]$ to $[0,\infty]$. In fact, any function f^{p-est} that satisfies the following conditions can be used for this purpose:

- f^{p-est} is monotonically decreasing function, i.e. for $r_{kl} \leq r_{mn}$ it stands that $f^{p-est}(r_{kl}) \geq f^{p-est}(r_{mn})$;
- If $r_{kl} = 0$ then $f^{p-est}(0) = 1$;
- If $r_{kl} \in [-1, 0]$ then $f^{p-est}(r_{kl}) = p_{kl} \in [1, \infty]$;
- If $r_{kl} \in [0, 1]$ then $f^{p-est}(r_{kl}) = p_{kl} \in [0, 1]$.

IFS-IBA Symbolic Level-Structural Transformation: Before the structural transformation, in some cases, it is necessary to translate verbal model/request to logical expression. After the expression is obtained, the structural transformation based on IFS-IBA rules is conducted, i.e. the logical expression is mapped into the corresponding GPB based on Eqs. (6)–(11), and (15).

IFS-IBA Valued Level Expression Calculation: Finally, on IFS-IBA valued level, GP is realized using Frank t-norms with estimated values of parameter p, and the expression value is calculated similarly as in classical LA.

I-defuzzification/IF Comparison Method: Finally, the resulting IF value may be transformed to a crisp value in order to ease comparison and interpretation. Although the simplest I-defuzzification considers using only membership part of IF value, there are various methods in the literature [22]. On the other hand, IF values may be compared using IF order relation [7].

The final result highly depends on the choice of functions for I-fuzzification, IFS correlation, Frank t-norm parameter estimation and I-defuzzification/IF comparison method. This makes the proposed approach to be a universal one and easily adapted for a specific purpose. In other words, this allows a decision maker certain freedom and the possibility to implement his expert knowledge in the decision-making process. However, the predefined, default functions, suitable for not-so-experienced users are given in Sect. 6.

The main advantage of the IFS-IBA LA approach compared with standard/simple aggregation operators, e.g. mean, max/min, weighted sum, is the fact that it enables the inclusion of logical relations between attributes and thus the possibility of compensability of one attribute to others. Also, the statistical dependencies are also comprised in the aggregation process through the values of parameter p. Finally, it is common to combine the LA approach with weighted sum in order to create pseudo-LA functions. This is also possible for IFS-IBA LA, as presented in Sect. 6. The main limitation of this approach is complexity, especially when dealing with a large number of input attributes.

6 Application to Gifted Student Ranking

In this section, we aim to employ the proposed IFS-IBA LA approach for gifted student ranking. In fact, we will consider one simple demonstrative example of ranking 10 gifted elementary school students. The ranking should be performed based on the assessment made by three independent evaluators: a teacher, a student's parent, and a student's peer. Each evaluator assesses 9 skills of a student: logical-mathematical, linguistic/verbal, spatial, musical, bodily-kinesthetic, intrapersonal, interpersonal, naturalistic and philosophical/spiritual. The ranking criterion is that the grades given by a teacher are equally important as the aggregated grade of a parent and a peer.

I-fuzzification: First, all attributes are normalized using min-max normalization. Further, an aggregation operator is used for I-fuzzification, since a vast number of input attributes, i.e. 3 evaluators e^1, e^2, e^3 assess 9 skills $a_1^i, \ldots, a_9^i, i = 1, 2, 3$ of a student. Namely, after I-fuzzification each student will be represented with 3 IF values, one for each evaluator using following functions:

$$A^i = \langle \mu^i, \nu^i \rangle, \mu^i = \min(a_1^i, \ldots, a_9^i), \nu^i = \max(a_1^i, \ldots, a_9^i) \quad (24)$$

IFS Correlation: The next step in IFS-IBA LA approach is a calculation of IF correlation coefficients. In this case, coefficients for each pair of attributes are very high, suggesting a strong positive correlation among attributes.

Frank t-norm Parameter Estimation: In this case, we have used piece-wise linear function to estimate values of parameter p:

$$p_{kl} = \begin{cases} \infty, \text{if } r_{kl} = -1 \\ 1 - q \cdot r_{kl}, \text{if } r_{kl} = (-1, 0) \\ 1, \text{if } r_{kl} = 0 \\ 1 - r_{kl}, \text{if } r_{kl} = (0, 1] \end{cases} \quad (25)$$

The value of coefficient q should be estimated by an expert from the interval $[1, \infty)$. In this particular case, the value is set to $q = 100$.

In other words, Frank t-norm-based realization of GP between attributes k and l is depending on the correlation coefficient in the following manner:

$$\otimes_{kl} = \begin{cases} T_{Luk}(a_k, a_l), \text{if } r_{kl} = -1 \\ \log_{(1-q \cdot r_{kl})} = (1 + \frac{((1-q \cdot r_{kl})^{a_k}-1) \cdot ((1-q \cdot r_{kl})^{a_l}-1)}{q \cdot r_{kl}-1}) \text{if } r_{kl} = (-1, 0) \\ T_{prod}(a_k, a_l), \text{if } r_{kl} = 0 \\ \log_{(1-r_{kl})} = (1 + \frac{((1-r_{kl})^{a_k}-1) \cdot ((1-r_{kl})^{a_l}-1)}{r_{kl}-1}) \text{if } r_{kl} = (0, 1) \\ T_{min}(a_k, a_l), \text{if } r_{kl} = 1 \end{cases} \quad (26)$$

This is in line with GP definition in IBA-framework, as well as practical guidelines for choosing the appropriate norm for GP given in [19].

IFS-IBA Symbolic Level-Structural Transformation: The verbal model for gifted student ranking is formulated as following: "The student is considered as a successful in two cases: if a student is graded well by both parents and peers; if a student is graded well by the teacher. These expressions have the same importance. Thus, the final pseudo-logical expression for aggregation is following:

$$agg^{IFS-IBA-LA} = 0.5 \cdot (IF^{parent} \wedge IF^{peer}) + 0.5 \cdot IF^{teacher} \qquad (27)$$

After IFS-IBA transformation, we can obtain the following GBP.

$$agg^{IFS-IBA-LA} = 0.5 \cdot (IF^{parent} \otimes IF^{peer}) + 0.5 \cdot IF^{teacher} \qquad (28)$$

IFS-IBA Valued Level-Expression Calculation: According to calculated IF corre-lation coefficient, a suitable realization of Frank t-norm is chosen, and IF aggregation scores for each student are calculated.

I-defuzzification/IF Comparison Method: For the sake of simplicity, membership of the final IF scores is used as a base for final student ranking.

Final scores and ranking obtained using the IFS-IBA approach is given in Table 1. Also, students are ranked with different IFS aggregation operator, e.g. simple weighted sum, with the same I-fuzzification and I-defuzzification methods:

$$agg^{WS} = 0.25 \cdot IF^{parent} + 0.25 \cdot IF^{peer} + 0.5 \cdot IF^{teacher} \qquad (29)$$

Table 1. Ranking results of gifted students.

Student	Score (IFS-IBA LA)	Rank (IFS-IBA LA)	Score (weighted sum)	Rank (weighted sum)
S1	0.375	6	0.470	7
S2	0.367	7	0.473	6
S3	0.298	10	0.400	10
S4	0.312	9	0.423	9
S5	0.406	4	0.517	5
S6	0.317	8	0.447	8
S7	0.564	1	0.680	1
S8	0.509	2	0.623	2
S9	0.393	5	0.523	4
S10	0.463	3	0.577	3

The final results suggest that the same three students (S7, S8 and S10) are ranked as the best ones by both methods. However, the ranking of the next four students differs since the usage of $\wedge$ operator. In other words, the IFS-IBA LA function punishes students with poor assessments given by a peer or a parent.

7   Conclusion

The aggregation of IFS values is still a hot topic for both researchers and practitioners. It is mandatory that novel methods in this field include logical and statistical dependencies of input attributes as well as possible compensation effects. The proposed IFS-IBA LA procedure is in line with current trends i.e. we have introduced all benefits of standard LA into aggregation of IF values. Technically, this is accomplished by introducing parametric Frank t-norm as a realization of GP in IFS-IBA frame. Frank t-norm parameter estimation is performed based on input correlation allowing automated operator selection. Finally, the procedure is formalized as a list of consecutive steps with a suggestion of default parameter settings. Still, the end-user has the option to include domain knowledge and possible affinities in the aggregation process by altering normalization, I-fuzzification and parameter estimation functions, as well as a criterion function formalized as a logical expression. The proposed approach is illustrated on the problem of ranking gifted students. However, the example is limited in terms of the number of instances and deeper understanding of a problem. Thus, one of the routes of future research will be collecting a larger dataset and introducing more expert knowledge in the ranking process.

Acknowledgements. This study was supported by University of Belgrade - Faculty of Organizational Sciences.

References

1. Atanassov, K.: Intuitionistic fuzzy sets. Fuzzy Sets Syst. **20**, 87–96 (1986)
2. Atanassov, K.: On the intuitionistic fuzzy implications and negations. In: Cornelis, C., Deschrijver, G., Nachtegael, M., Schockaert, S., Shi, Y. (eds.) 35 Years of Fuzzy Set Theory. Studies in Fuzziness and Soft Computing, vol. 261, pp. 19–38. Springer, Heidelberg (2010). https://doi.org/10.1007/978-3-642-16629-7_2
3. Bustince, H., Kacprzyk, J., Mohedano, V.: Intuitionistic fuzzy generators application to intuitionistic fuzzy complementation. Fuzzy Sets Syst. **114**(3), 485–504 (2000)
4. Deschrijver, G.: Generalized arithmetic operators and their relationship to t-norms in interval-valued fuzzy set theory. Fuzzy Sets Syst. **160**(21), 3080–3102 (2009)
5. Deschrijver, G., Cornelis, C., Kerre, E.E.: On the representation of intuitionistic fuzzy t-norms and t-conorms. IEEE Trans. Fuzzy Syst. **12**(1), 45–61 (2004)
6. Dubois, D., Gottwald, S., Hajek, P., Kacprzyk, J., Prade, H.: Terminological difficulties in fuzzy set theory - The case of intuitionistic fuzzy sets. Fuzzy Sets Syst. **156**(3), 485–491 (2005)
7. Feng, F., Liang, M., Fujita, H., Yager, R.R., Liu, X.: Lexicographic orders of intuitionistic fuzzy values and their relationships. Mathematics **7**(2), 166 (2019)
8. Gerstenkorn, T., Manko, J.: Correlation of intuitionistic fuzzy sets. Fuzzy Sets Syst. **44**(1), 39–43 (1991)
9. Hung, W.L.: Using statistical viewpoint in developing correlation of intuitionistic fuzzy sets. Int. J. Uncertainty Fuzziness Knowl.-Based Syst. **9**(04), 509–516 (2001)
10. Hung, W.L., Wu, J.W.: Correlation of intuitionistic fuzzy sets by centroid method. Inf. Sci. **144**(1–4), 219–225 (2002)

11. Iancu, I.: Intuitionistic fuzzy similarity measures based on frank t-norms family. Pattern Recognit. Lett. **42**, 128–136 (2014)
12. Kahraman, C., Onar, S.C., Cebi, S., Oztaysi, B.: Extension of information axiom from ordinary to intuitionistic fuzzy sets: an application to search algorithm selection. Comput. Ind. Eng. **105**, 348–361 (2017)
13. Klement, E.P., Mesiar, R., Pap, E.: Triangular norms. Springer, Heidelberg (2013). https://doi.org/10.1007/978-94-015-9540-7
14. Klement, E.P., Navara, M.: Propositional fuzzy logics based on frank t-norms: a comparison. In: Dubois, D., Prade, H., Klement, E.P. (eds.) Fuzzy Sets, Logics and Reasoning about Knowledge. Applied Logic Series, vol. 15, pp. 17–38. Springer, Heidelberg (1999). https://doi.org/10.1007/978-94-017-1652-9_3
15. Klir, G., Yuan, B.: Fuzzy Sets and Fuzzy Logic. Prentice Hall, New Jersey (1995)
16. Kovačević, D., Sekulić, P., Rakićević, A.: Consistent interpolative fuzzy logic and investement decision-making. In: First Annual Conference of Young Serbian Economists, pp. 21–24. National Bank of Serbia, Belgrade (2011)
17. Liu, B., Shen, Y., Mu, L., Chen, X., Chen, L.: A new correlation measure of the intuitionistic fuzzy sets. J. Intell. Fuzzy Syst. **30**(2), 1019–1028 (2016)
18. Milošević, P., Petrović, B., Dragović, I.: A novel approach to generalized intuitionistic fuzzy sets based on interpolative Boolean algebra. Mathematics **9**(17), 2115 (2021)
19. Milošević, P., Nešić, I., Poledica, A., Radojević, D., Petrović, B.: Logic-based aggregation methods for ranking student applicants. Yugoslav J. Oper. Res. **27**(4), 461–477 (2017)
20. Milošević, P., Petrović, B., Jeremić, V.: IFS-IBA similarity measure in machine learning algorithms. Expert Syst. Appl. **89**, 296–305 (2017)
21. Milošević, P., Poledica, A., Rakićević, A., Petrović, B., Radojević, D.: Introducing interpolative boolean algebra into intuitionistic fuzzy sets. In: 2015 Conference of the International Fuzzy Systems Association and the European Society for Fuzzy Logic and Technology, pp. 1389–1394. Atlantis Press, Amsterdam (2015)
22. Radhika, C., Parvathi, R.: Defuzzification of intuitionistic fuzzy sets. Notes Intuitionistic Fuzzy Sets **22**(5), 19–26 (2016)
23. Radojević, D.: Interpolative realization of Boolean algebra as a consistent frame for gradation and/or fuzziness. In: Kacprzyk, J. (ed.) Forging New Frontiers: Fuzzy Pioneers II. Studies in Fuzziness and Soft Computing, vol. 218. Springer, Berlin (2008). https://doi.org/10.1007/978-3-540-73185-6_13
24. Radojevic, D.: Logical aggregation based on interpolative Boolean algebra. Mathware Soft Comput. **15**(1), 125–141 (2008)
25. Radojević, D.: Interpolative relations and interpolative preference structures. Yugoslav J. Oper. Res. **15**(2) (2005)
26. Seikh, M.R., Mandal, U.: Some picture fuzzy aggregation operators based on frank t-norm and t-conorm: application to MADM process. Informatica **45**(3), 447–461 (2021)
27. Senapati, T., Chen, G., Mesiar, R., Yager, R.R.: Intuitionistic fuzzy geometric aggregation operators in the framework of Aczel-Alsina triangular norms and their application to multiple attribute decision making. Expert Syst. Appl. **212**, 118832 (2023)
28. Tan, C., Chen, X.: Intuitionistic fuzzy Choquet integral operator for multi-criteria decision making. Expert Syst. Appl. **37**(1), 149–157 (2010)
29. Xia, M., Xu, Z., Zhu, B.: Some issues on intuitionistic fuzzy aggregation operators based on Archimedean t-conorm and t-norm. Knowl.-Based Syst. **31**, 78–88 (2012)

30. Xu, Z.: On correlation measures of intuitionistic fuzzy sets. In: Corchado, E., Yin, H., Botti, V., Fyfe, C. (eds.) IDEAL 2006. LNCS, vol. 4224, pp. 16–24. Springer, Heidelberg (2006). https://doi.org/10.1007/11875581_2
31. Yager, R.R.: OWA aggregation of intuitionistic fuzzy sets. Int. J. Gener. Syst. **38**(6), 617–641 (2009)
32. Yu, C.: Correlation of fuzzy numbers. Fuzzy Sets Syst. **55**(3), 303–307 (1993)
33. Zeng, W., Li, H.: Correlation coefficient of intuitionistic fuzzy sets. J. Ind. Eng. Int. **3**, 33–40 (2007)

Fuzzy Equivalence Relations for Solving a Multiple Objective Linear Programming Problem*

Olga Grigorenko(✉) and Mārtiņš Zemlītis

Institute of Mathematics and Computer Science, University of Latvia, Raina bulv.
29, Riga 1459, Latvia
ol.grigorenko@gmail.com
https://www.lumii.lv/

Abstract. We are developing an approach that is an alternative to the
Zimmermann approach to solving a multiple objective linear programming problem. We use fuzzy equivalence relations to solve the problem,
where fuzzy sets are used in the Zimmermann approach. We will prove
the effectiveness of the new approach, illustrate and compare the use of
different approaches with illustrative examples.

Keywords: Multiple objective linear programming · Fuzzy
equivalence relation · Aggregation

1   Introduction

Since the definition of fuzzy sets by L. A. Zadeh in 1965 [6], the interest of many
researchers has been focused on the study of classical mathematical concepts and
theories in the context of fuzzy sets. At the same time, fuzzy sets and related
structures began to be used to solve some real-world problems and to be involved
in related mathematical algorithms.

In this paper we propose to use fuzzy relations for solving multiple objective
linear programming (MOLP) problems. Multiple objective linear programming
problems algorithms are important tools for solving real-life optimization problems such as production planning, logistics, environment management, finance
risk planning etc. Multiple objective linear programming problem is a problem
when we solve linear programming problem with several or many objective functions which should be optimized at the same time. Thus the fuzzy approach here
helps to overcome the conflict of multiple objective functions which have their
optimal solutions in different points.

---

* This Work Is Supported by European Regional Development Fund Within the Post-
Doc Latvia Project Nr.1.1.1.2/16/I/001, Under Agreement Nr.1.1.1.2/VIAA/
4/20/707 "Fuzzy Relations and Fuzzy Metrics for Customer Behavior Modeling
and Analysis"

S. Massanet et al. (Eds.): EUSFLAT 2023/AGOP 2023, LNCS 14069, pp. 112–123, 2023.
https://doi.org/10.1007/978-3-031-39965-7_10

The idea for our investigation came from the fuzzy approach proposed by Zimmermann in ([7]) where the membership functions (or fuzzy sets) are involved to prescribe how far the concrete point from the feasible solution set is from the solution of an individual problem for each function which should be optimized. Thus for each function, which should be optimized, the membership function value for a concrete point is the belongness degree to the set which contains the individual solution/solutions. Then these fuzzy sets are aggregated by using an aggregation function and the obtained fuzzy set is optimized in the initial feasible region. We should remark, that in Zimmermann approach all the fuzzy sets are linear functions (or partially linear).

In our paper we propose to use fuzzy relations ([1,5]) instead of the membership functions used by Zimmermann and further developed by other authors. The idea of using fuzzy relations is motivated by the fact that we want to find a solution which is equal to all individual solutions. It is clear that generally it is impossible to find equivalence relation to solve this problem but fuzzy equivalence relation can help us. Here, the transitivity of fuzzy equivalence relation helps us obtain a Pareto optimal solution, which, in fact, distinguishes our approach from Zimmermann's. Fuzzy equivalence approach (FEA) provides a more general framework for handling multiple objectives. Specifically, when using the Łukasiewicz t-norm, FEA generalizes the Zimmermann approach. Additionally, we demonstrate that working with fuzzy equivalence relations enables us to defuzzify the solution approach and work with crisp metrics, which simplifies calculations.

The paper is structured in the following way: Sect. 2 contains some known facts about t-norms and fuzzy equivalence relations important for the further understanding of the material; we propose the Zimmermann approach with illustrative examples in Sect. 3; we propose the solution approach with fuzzy equivalence relations and observe the numerical example in Sect. 4; and we conclude our paper by Sect. 5.

2   Preliminaries

2.1   Triangular Norms

We start with the definition of a t-norm which plays the crucial role for the definition of transitivity for fuzzy relations:

Definition 1. *[2] A triangular norm (t-norm for short) is a binary operation T on the unit interval $[0,1]$, i.e. a function $T : [0,1]^2 \to [0,1]$ such that for all $a, b, c \in [0,1]$ the following four axioms are satisfied:*

- *$T(a,b) = T(b,a)$ (commutativity);*
- *$T(a,T(b,c)) = T(T(a,b),c)$ (associativity);*
- *$T(a,b) \le T(a,c)$ whenever $b \le c$ (monotonicity);*
- *$T(a,1) = a$ (a boundary condition).*

Some of often used t-norms are mentioned below:

- $T_M(a, b) = \min(a, b)$ the minimum t-norm;
- $T_P(a, b) = a \cdot b$ the product t-norm;
- $T_L(a, b) = \max(a + b - 1, 0)$ the Łukasiewicz t-norm;
- $T_H(a, b) = \begin{cases} \frac{a \cdot b}{a + b - a \cdot b} & \text{if } a^2 + b^2 \neq 0 \\ 0 & \text{otherwise} \end{cases}$ the Hamacher t-norm.

Definition 2. *[2] A t-norm T is called Archimedean if and only if, for all pairs $(a, b) \in (0, 1)^2$, there is $n \in \mathbb{N}$ such that $T(\underbrace{a, a, ..., a}_{n \text{ times}}) < b$.*

Product and Łukasiewicz t-norms are Archimedean while minimum t-norm is not.

We proceed recalling an important tool for the construction and study of t-norms involving only one-argument real function (additive generator) and addition. Later we use the same tool for constructing fuzzy equivalence.

Definition 3. *[2] An additive generator $g : [0, 1] \to [0, \infty]$ of a t-norm T is a strictly decreasing function which is also right-semicontinuous at 0 and satisfies $g(1) = 0$ such that for all $(a, b) \in [0, 1]^2$ we have*

$$g(a) + g(b) \in Ran(g) \cup [g(0), \infty],$$

$$T(a, b) = g^{(-1)}(g(a) + g(b)).$$

where $Ran(g)$ is the range of g.

Note that, if a t-norm T has an additive generator g, then it is uniquely determined up to a non-zero positive constant. Each t-norm with an additive generator is Archimedean.

2.2 Fuzzy Equivalence Relations

We continue with an overview of basic definitions and results on fuzzy equivalence relations. Definition of a fuzzy equivalence relation was first introduced by L.A. Zadeh in 1971 ([5]) under the name of fuzzy similarity relation.

Definition 4. *(see e.g. [1]) A fuzzy binary relation E on a set S is called a fuzzy equivalence relation with respect to a t-norm T (or T-equivalence), if and only if the following three axioms are fulfilled for all $a, b, c \in S$:*

1. *$E(a, a) = 1$ reflexivity;*
2. *$E(a, b) = E(b, a)$ symmetry;*
3. *$T(E(a, b), E(b, c)) \leq E(a, c)$ T-transitivity.*

The following result establishes principles of construction of fuzzy equivalence relations using pseudo-metrics.

Theorem 1. *[1] Let T be a continuous Archimedean t-norm with an additive generator g. For any pseudo-metric d, the mapping*

$$E_d(a,b) = g^{(-1)}(\min(d(a,b), g(0)))$$

is a T-equivalence.

Example 1. Let us consider the set of real numbers $S = \mathbb{R}$ and the metric $d(a,b) = |a - b|$ on it. Taking into account that $g_L(x) = 1 - x$ is an additive generator of T_L (Łukasiewicz t-norm) and $g_P(x) = -\ln(x)$ is an additive generator of T_P (product t-norm), we obtain fuzzy equivalence relations:

$$E_L(a,b) = \max(1 - |a - b|, 0);$$

$$E_P(a,b) = e^{-|a-b|}.$$

To fuse the information about the all objective functions we will use aggregation functions:

Definition 5. *[3] An aggregation function is a mapping $A : [0,1]^k \longrightarrow [0,1]$ which fulfills the following properties:*

- *$A(x^1, ..., x^k) \leq A(y^1, ..., y^k)$ whenever $x^i \leq y^i$ for all $i \in \{1, ..., k\}$ (monotonicity);*
- *$A(0, ..., 0) = 0$ and $A(1, ..., 1) = 1$ (boundary conditions).*

Namely, we need to fuse equivalence relations that is why we need the following theorem and example. Since in our approach we are constructing fuzzy equivalence relations from pseudo-metrics (which is quite natural) we focus only in Archimedean t-norms.

Theorem 2. *[4] Let $A : [0,1]^k \rightarrow [0,1]$ be an aggregation function, T be a continuous Archimedean t-norm with an additive generator $g : [0,1] \rightarrow [0,c]$ such that $g(0) = c$ and $c \in (0, \infty]$, and E_i for all $i \in \{1, ..., k\}$ are fuzzy equivalence relations (with respect to the t-norm T). Then*

$$E(x,y) = A(E_1(x,y), ..., E_k(x,y))$$

is also a T-equivalence relation if and only if $\mathbf{H} : [0,c]^k \rightarrow [0,c]$ constructed as

$$\mathbf{H}(a_1, \ldots, a_k) = g\left(A(g^{-1}(a_1), \ldots, g^{-1}(a_k))\right).$$

is a subadditive function on $[0,c]$, where $a_i \in [0,c], i \in \{1, \ldots, k\}$.

Example 2. Consider some weights $p_1, ..., p_k \in [0,1]$ such that $\sum_{i=1}^{k} p_i = 1$. If

$$\mathbf{H}(a_1, \ldots, a_k) = \min\left(c, \sum_{i=1}^{k} p_i a_i\right),$$ which is a subadditive function, then

$$A(a_1, \ldots, a_k) = g^{(-1)}\left(\min(g(0), \sum_{i=1}^{k} p_i \cdot g(a_i))\right)$$

preserves T-equivalences. We will use this construction to aggregate fuzzy equivalences in the further examples.

3   Zimmermann Approach for MOLP Problem

A mathematical model of multiple objective linear programming (MOLP) problem can be represented as follows:

$$\text{Maximize } Z = (z_1(x), ..., z_k(x))$$

$$\text{subject to } \sum_{j=1}^{n} a_{ij}x_j \leq b_i, \ i = 1, ..., m, \tag{1}$$

where $x \in \mathbb{R}^n$, Z is a vector of objectives or objective functions $z_l = \sum_{j=1}^{n} c_{lj}x_j$ (linear functions) where $l = 1, .., k$. That is we must find a vector $x^{opt} = (x_1^{opt}, ..., x_n^{opt})$ which maximizes k objective functions of n variables, and with m constraints. Let D denote a feasible region of the problem (1), which is the set of all possible points x that satisfy the conditions $\sum_{j=1}^{n} a_{ij}x_j \leq b_i$, $i = 1, ..., m$. For the sake of brevity further we denote vectors $(x_1, ..., x_n)$ as x $(x = (x_1, ..., x_n))$.

When solving problem (1), if trivial cases are not taken into account, all objective functions cannot reach their optimums at the same points under given constraints, since objective functions usually conflict with each other. Thus, the Pareto optimal solution (or efficient solution) and the optimal compromise solution will be introduced to explain what solutions we are going to obtain by solving problem (1):

Definition 6. *[7] Point x^{po} from the feasible region D is called Pareto optimal solution for the problem (1) if and only if there does not exist another $x \in D$ such that $z_l(x^{po}) \leq z_l(x)$ for all $l = 1, ..., k$ and $z_j(x^{po}) \neq z_j(x)$ for at least one j.*

That is, if x^{po} is a Pareto optimal solution, then it is impossible to find such x for which at least for one objective the value is greater than for x^{po} and for all other objectives the values are not less than for x.

Definition 7. *[7] The optimal compromise solution to the multiple objective linear programming problem is the solution $x \in D$, which the decision maker prefers to all other solutions, taking into account all the criteria. The optimal compromise solution will simply be referred to as the optimal solution.*

It is generally accepted that the optimal solution must be Pareto optimal. In what follows, the decision maker choice between all Pareto optimal solution, taking into account the criteria, proceeds from the original real problem to be solved using the MOLP algorithm. On the other hand, the choice of algorithm affects the choice of optimal solutions from all Pareto optimal ones.

The fuzzy approach to solving the MOLP problem proposed by Zimmermann [7] provided an efficient way to measure the degree of satisfaction of maximization of all objectives for points from the feasible region. The idea is to identify the membership functions prescribing the fuzzy goals (solutions of individual problem) for the objective functions z_i, $i = 1, .., k$. The following linear function is an example of a membership function, which is commonly used by other authors in MOLP and will be used in our work:

$$\mu_i(x) = \begin{cases} 0, & \text{if } z_i(x) < z_i^{min} \\ \dfrac{z_i(x) - z_i^{min}}{z_i^{max} - z_i^{min}}, & z_i^{min} \leq z_i(x) \leq z_i^{max} \\ 1, & z_i(x) > z_i^{max} \end{cases} ,$$

where z_i^{max} is the solution of individual problem

Maximize z_i, s.t. $\displaystyle\sum_{j=1}^{n} a_{ij}x_j \leq b_i$, $i = 1, ..., m$

and z_i^{min} is the solution of individual problem

Minimize z_i, s.t. $\displaystyle\sum_{j=1}^{n} a_{ij}x_j \leq b_i$, $i = 1, ..., m$.

Usually the membership functions μ_i are linear functions and it is argued by the "facilitation computation for obtaining solutions". Further in the "classical" fuzzy approach membership functions μ_i are aggregated. The main subject which is discussed in the large part of papers is the choice of an aggregation function. Thus the problem (1) reduces to the following problem:

$$\text{Maximize } A(\mu_1(x), ..., \mu_k(x))$$
$$\text{subject to } \sum_{j=1}^{n} a_{ij}x_j \leq b_i, \ i = 1, ..., m, \tag{2}$$

where A is an aggregation function.

Theorem 3. *If x is unique solution for problem (2) then it is a Pareto optimal solution for problem (1).*

Proof. Proof from the opposite. It is assumed that there exists a point $y \in D$ such that,

$$\begin{cases} z_j(x) < z_j(y) \\ z_l(x) \leq z_l(y) \ \forall l = 1, ..., k. \end{cases}$$

It follows that $\mu_j(x) < \mu_j(y)$ and $\mu_l(x) \leq \mu_l(y) \ \forall l = 1, ..., k$; this follows from the definition of membership functions μ_l. Then, from the monotonicity of an aggregation function it follows that

$$A(\mu_1(x), ..., \mu_k(x)) \leq A(\mu_1(y), ..., \mu_k(y)).$$

However, given that x is the solution of the problem (2), which means that

$$A(\mu_1(x), ..., \mu_k(x)) = A(\mu_1(y), ..., \mu_k(y)).$$

Now a contradiction arises with the unity of the solution of the problem (2). By this the theorem is proven.

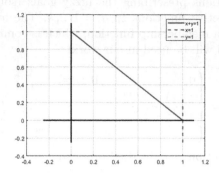

Fig. 1. Feasible region for the problem (3); dotted lines indicate level lines for individual solutions

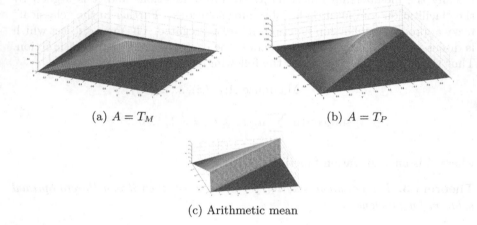

(a) $A = T_M$ (b) $A = T_P$

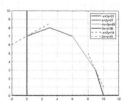

(c) Arithmetic mean

Fig. 2. $A(\mu_1(x), ..., \mu_k(x))$, where in a) $A = T_M$; b) $A = T_P$; c) A is the arithmetic mean.

Fig. 3. Feasible region for the problem (4); dotted lines indicate level lines for individual solutions

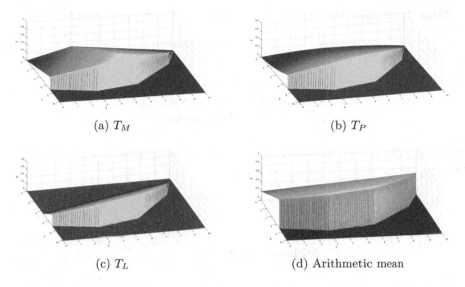

(a) T_M

(b) T_P

(c) T_L

(d) Arithmetic mean

Fig. 4. $A(\mu_1(x), ..., \mu_k(x))$, where in a) $A = T_M$; b) $A = T_P$; c) $A = T_L$; d) A is the arithmetic mean.

We illustrate all approaches with two example:

1. Triangular example:

$$\text{Maximize } Z = (z_1(x), z_2(x)),$$
$$\text{where } z_1 = x_1, \; z_2 = x_2$$
$$\text{subject to } x_1 + x_2 \leq 1, \tag{3}$$
$$x_1, x_2 \geq 0$$

For this problem we visualize the feasible region D in Fig. 1.

The Fig. 2 demonstrates the function $A(\mu_1(x), ..., \mu_k(x))$ for different aggregation functions.

Table 1 shows optimal solutions for the triangular example using different aggregation functions:

2. Zimmermann example

$$\text{Maximize } Z = (z_1(x), z_2(x)),$$
$$\text{where } z_1(x) = -x_1 + 2x_2, \; z_2(x) = 2x_1 + x_2$$
$$\text{subject to } -x_1 + 3x_2 \leq 21$$
$$x_1 + 3x_2 \leq 27 \tag{4}$$
$$4x_1 + 3x_2 \leq 45$$
$$3x_1 + x_2 \leq 30$$
$$x_1, x_2 \geq 0$$

Table 1. Solutions for triangular example using different aggregation functions.

A	Opt. solution
T_P	(0.5 ; 0.5)
T_M	(0.5 ; 0.5)
Arithmetic mean	line $x_1 + x_2 = 1$
T_L	No solution

Table 2. Solutions for the Zimmermann's example using different aggregation functions.

A	Opt. solution
T_M	(4.96 ; 7.35)
T_P	(5.7 ; 7.01)
Arithmetic mean	(6 ; 7)
T_L	(6 ; 7)

For this problem we visualize the feasible region D in Fig. 2. The Fig. 4 demonstrates the function $A(\mu_1(x), ..., \mu_k(x))$ for different aggregation functions. Table 2 shows optimal solutions for the Zimmermann example using different aggregation functions.

Triangular example is a quite simple example, but seems important to us since we would like to see how different approaches will work with the example where the affect of each of two objective functions is identical and the feasible region is symmetrical about individual solutions.

Zimmermann example was involved in [7] and since then many authors use it to compare results.

4   Fuzzy Equivalence Relations Approach

In this section we realize the approach of using fuzzy equivalence relations to show the degree of equivalence of the point from the feasible region and individual solution. First we build the following pseudo-metrics on the set D:

$$d_i(x, y) = \frac{|z_i(x) - z_i(y)|}{z_i^{max} - z_i^{min}}.$$

Thus defined d_i are indeed pseudo-metrics and applying the Theorem 1 we can build a T-equivalence relation:

$$E_i(x, y) = g^{(-1)}(\min(\frac{|z_i(x) - z_i(y)|}{z_i^{max} - z_i^{min}}, g(0))), \tag{5}$$

where g is an additive generator of a continuous Archimedean t-norm T.

Hence we should first choose a t-norm which plays a role of a generalized conjunction and further construct T-equivalences using a correspondent additive generator g.

$$E_i(x,y) = 1 - \frac{|z_i(x) - z_i(y)|}{z_i^{max} - z_i^{min}}$$

are fuzzy T_L-equivalence relations.

$$E_i(x,y) = e^{-\frac{|z_i(x) - z_i(y)|}{z_i^{max} - z_i^{min}}}$$

are fuzzy T_P-equivalence relations.

Then we aggregate the equivalence relations and solve the following problem:

$$\text{Maximize } A(E_1(x_1^{max}, y), ..., E_k(x_k^{max}, y)).$$

The approach for different t-norms we illustrate for

Triangular example (Fig. 5):

In the both cases the solutions are points of the line $x_1 + x_2 = 1$ where $0 \le x_1 \le 1$.

Zimmermann example (Fig. 6):

In the both cases the solution is $x = (6, 7)$.

Theorem 4. *If there exists a unique solution to problem:*

$$\text{Maximize } A(E_1(x_1^{max}, y), ..., E_k(x_k^{max}, y))$$

then it is a Pareto optimal MOLP problem's solution for the problem (1).

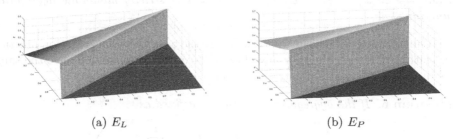

(a) E_L (b) E_P

Fig. 5. $A(E_1(x_1^{max}, y), ..., E_k(x_k^{max}, y))$ for different fuzzy equivalence relations

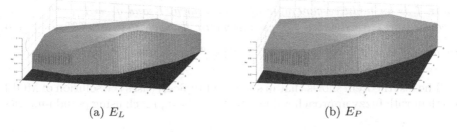

(a) E_L (b) E_P

Fig. 6. $A(E_1(x_1^{max}, y), ..., E_k(x_k^{max}, y))$ for different fuzzy equivalence relations

Proof. Let y be the unique solution to problem:

$$\text{Maximize } A(E_1(x_1^{max}, y), ..., E_k(x_k^{max}, y)).$$

Let denote $A(E_1(x_1^{max}, y), ..., E_k(x_k^{max}, y))$ by $A(x^{max}, y)$. Let prove the theorem by contradiction: suppose there is another point x, that is Pareto optimal. That means, $\forall i = 1, ..., k\, z_i(y) \leq z_i(x)$ and there exists at least one j such that $z_j(y) < z_j(x)$.

Now lets look at fuzzy equivalences: $E_i(x_i^{max}, y) =$

$$= g^{(-1)}\left(\min\left(g(0), d_i(x_i^{max}, y) \right) \right) = g^{(-1)}\left(\min\left(g(0), \frac{|z_i(x_i^{max}) - z_i(y)|}{z_i^{max} - z_i^{min}} \right) \right)$$

Because of $z_j(y) < z_j(x)$ and $z_i(y) \leq z_i(x)\, \forall i = 1, ..., k$ we have $d_j(x_j^{max}, y) > d_j(x_j^{max}, x)$ and $d_i(x_i^{max}, y) \geq d_i(x_i^{max}, x)\, \forall i = 1, ..., k$. Thus $E_i(x_i^{max}, y) \leq E_i(x_i^{max}, x)$, which means $A(x^{max}, y) \leq A(x^{max}, x)$ which is a contradiction to y being a unique solution.

It is easy to see from the prove of the above theorem that the following theorem fulfill for non-unique solutions.

Theorem 5. *The solution to the problem:*

$$\text{Maximize } A(E_1(x_1^{max}, y), ..., E_k(x_k^{max}, y))$$

is Pareto optimal MOLP problem's solution for the problem (1) if $z_j(y) < z_j(x) \implies E_i(x_i^{max}, y) < E_j(x_j^{max}, x)$ and A is strictly monotone aggregation function.

The next theorem shows that if we chose the base for the aggregation function an arithmetic mean, then for any class of T-equivalences we will have the same result (solution), which illustrate the above examples.

Theorem 6. *If the aggregation function is defined as*

$$A(a_1, ... a_k) = f^{(-1)}\left(\min\left(f(0), \sum_{i=1}^{k} p_i f(a_i) \right) \right)$$

where f is an additive-generator of some t-norm T and $a_i = E_i(x^{max}, y)$ are T-equivalences constructed for pseudo-metric d_i such that $d_i(x^{max}, y) \leq f(0)$ for all $y \in D$ and $\sum_{i=1}^{n} p_i = 1$ then $\max_{y} A(x^{max}, y) = \min_{y} \sum_{i=1}^{k} p_i d_i(x^{max}, y)$.

The last theorem shows that in some (but typical) cases the solution of MOLP problem with fuzzy approach reduces to the crisp approach using pseudo-metrics.

5   Conclusion

In the paper we proposed a solution approach for multiple objective linear programming problem where we have used fuzzy equivalence relations prescribing the degree of equivalence of a point from the feasible region and individual solutions. Fuzzy equivalence relations were aggregated to get the degree to which a point from the feasible region is equal to *all* individual solutions.

We see the potential for the future research in generalizing approach to fuzzy order relations since it will help to overcome the non-uniqueness for the solutions which compensate one another. For example we believe that with fuzzy order relations we will overcome the non-uniqueness for the triangular example.

References

1. De Baets, B., Mesiar, R.: Pseudo-metrics and T-quivalences. J. Fuzzy Math. **5**, 471–481 (1997)
2. Klement, E.P., Mesiar, R., Pap, E.: Triangular Norms. Kluwer Acad. Publ, Dodrecht (2000)
3. Grabisch, M., Marichal, J.-L., Mesiar, R., Pap, E.: Aggregation Functions (Encyclopedia of Mathematics and its Applications). Cambridge University Press, Cambridge, UK (2009)
4. Saminger, S., Mesiar, R., Bodenhofer, U.: Domination of aggregation operators and preservation of transitivity. Int. J. Uncertainty Fuzziness Knowl.-Based Syst. **10**(Suppl01), 11–35 (2002)
5. Zadeh, L.A.: Similarity relations and fuzzy orderings. Inf. Sci. **3**, 177–200 (1971)
6. Zadeh, L.A.: Fuzzy Sets. Inf. Control **1**, 338–353 (1965)
7. Zimmermann, H.-J.: Fuzzy programming and linear programming with several objective functions. Fuzzy Sets Syst. **1**, 45–55 (1978)

Applied Large-Scale Group Decision Making Using Systemic Consensus and Fuzzy Method of Comparative Linguistic Expressions

Benjamin Emmenegger[1]([✉]) [ID], Georgiana Bigea[2] [ID], and Edy Portmann[1] [ID]

[1] Human-IST Institute, University of Fribourg, 90 Bd de Perolles, 1700 Fribourg, Switzerland
{benjamin.emmenegger,edy.portmann}@unifr.ch
[2] Conflict Studies Center, Babeş Bolyai University, 71 General Traian Moşoiu St., 400132 Cluj-Napoca, Romania
georgiana.bigea@unifr.ch

Abstract. The complexity of democratic public decision-making has augmented with the surge of volumes of information. One response is using digital tools in decision-making processes to enable more flexibility than the conventional yes or no responses. We proposed a solution for a large-scale democratic decision-making process using soft computing and fuzzy logic, based on systemic consensus and action design research. Our integrative fuzzy decision-making process was designed to allow the consideration of all the arguments, the deliberation of all the alternatives, and the assessment of each alternative using comparative linguistic expressions. The method was used to resolve a conflict-generating traffic problem in Geuensee, a municipality in the Swiss canton of Luzern. The citizens voted on two dimensions of resistance and support about each of the proposed alternatives. The results were computed using fuzzy membership functions and a fuzzy logic table, evaluated with different computational variants. The output was a ranking of the best options, as assessed by the decision-makers. We found that this method for smart participation of citizens was accepted and generated involvement, leading to an effective outcome for the decision-makers. In the last section, we discuss evaluation and ethical considerations.

Keywords: participative decision making · fuzzy voting · fuzzy logic · comparative linguistic expressions · smart governance · cognitive cities

1 Introduction

Democracies rely on the majority rule, a system of decision-making where the largest group decides the outcome, while as the less numerous groups must succumb to the majority's decision. This generates the inevitable winners - losers paradigm, which impacts all levels of our democratic mentality. Thus, whenever a controversial matter

Supplementary Information The online version contains supplementary material available at https://doi.org/10.1007/978-3-031-39965-7_11.

S. Massanet et al. (Eds.): EUSFLAT 2023/AGOP 2023, LNCS 14069, pp. 124–136, 2023.
https://doi.org/10.1007/978-3-031-39965-7_11

arises, most effort is allocated to gathering the majority by convincing as many people as possible of one point of view or the other. The resulting power struggles utilize a lot of resources and often shift the conversation from the main concern. [10, 25] To prevent the manipulation of decision-makers with emotional or rhetorical methods, evidence-based decision-making has been increasingly promoted in formal settings, in which a set of objective criteria is used and weighed, based on impact or relevance. In some decision-making methods, the focus is on maximizing consensus by discussing and voting in successive rounds. [1, 7].

Also, citizens want and are expected to participate more than ever in thinking, deciding, and implementing decisions in societies. Finger and Portmann [5] have argued that the smart city – performing city-relevant duties by using ICT – must not only focus on resource management and sustainability as it is often expected, but also on the needs of the individual, which are often overlooked [19, 20]. The same applies to regions, where value can be created by bringing citizens into the decision-making process. [14].

In the following, we will present our framework and case study of Unterdorf St. in the canton of Luzern, Switzerland, where a real-life community traffic problem was resolved, and subsequent conflict was mediated, by using systemic consensus principles. We developed and applied a transdisciplinary [22] framework for large scale group decision-making (LS-GDM) using fuzzy methods, to perform comparative linguistic expressions on two scales of resistance and support about the 13 alternatives, resulting into a ranking of to be pursued in descending order of priority.

Section 2 briefly reviews the concepts of decision-making, large scale group decision-making (LS-GDM), systemic consensus, fuzzy decision-making, and comparative linguistic expressions (CLEs). Section 3 presents our framework for LS-GDM, using systemic consensus, CLEs and fuzzy logic. Section 4 introduces the case study of Underdorfstrasse, a real LS-GDM, to demonstrate the functionality of the proposed process. In Sect. 5, conclusions, ethical considerations, and reflections are presented.

2 Preliminary Definitions

2.1 Literature Review

Large-scale group decision-making [11] using fuzzy methods [26] has been researched extensively, [11] by using CLEs, trapezoidal membership functions, [7, 9] and computing with words. [13] Some of these studies also present consensus reaching processes, related to LS-GDM, often involving multi-criteria decision-making. [1, 7, 8] Public decisions are a special case of LS-GDM, for which Torres van Grinsven, Hudec, Portmann and D'Onofrio [21] proposed a paradigm of flexible voting using fuzzy sets to enable more participation [19, 20] and human-computer interaction. [2].

Most of the literature on decision-making processes using fuzzy sets [1] involves experts and focuses on arguments, criteria, weighting [7, 12] and the study of hesitance [27] while as in our case study we chose the approach of including all the affected individuals in the decision-making process and deciding only about the alternatives in a single round of voting, without any other formal criteria than the self-evaluated levels of resistance and support. [6, 22].

The main difference from other fuzzy models such as fuzzy TOPSIS or AHP is that the decision reflects the support and resistance of the citizens about the alternatives, and not their assessment of criteria, as no objective criteria are used. [7, 8, 12] The decision-makers learned all the information and the arguments collected in favor and against, discussed about them, considered all the alternatives, and voted using fuzzy sliders over the course of one single in-person event. We chose to use ordinary fuzzy sets although recent extensions of them exist, in order to make the process of decision-making very simple, explainable, and understandable by all people, since the model was used for a public, democratic decision.

Thus, the framework proposed herein is built using a 7-step decision-making process (Table 4, Appendix), ethical system design [4, 16], and action design research (ADR) [18, 24]. The latter is a computer science research paradigm, known as "knowledge through making" [10, 19, 24] Despite being criticized on its rigor and relevance, we considered it most suitable for our participative fuzzy voting case, and we relied on continuous evaluation [3] and feedback collection to ensure its validity. [15] Lastly, in choosing to include transdisciplinarity, we strived for a "generative processes of harvesting, capitalizing, and leveraging multiple expertise" [6, p. 116] by including all the stakeholders and considering their life experience as "expertise".

2.2 Group Decision-Making Methods

When a group of individuals are presented with a choice of one or more alternatives to a problem, or of means to reach a desired goal, there is a case of group decision-making (GDM). The main difference between GDM and LS-GDM, is the size of the group. [7, 11].

Consensus Reaching Process

In consensus reaching processes (CRP), the decision is the most optimal proposal that the participants support unanimously. CRP is usually characterized by the following steps: (1) gathering preferences, (2) computing agreement level, (3) consensus control, and (4) feedback generation [7], repeated as many times as necessary, until the maximum level of consensus is reached. Between repetitions, experts or representatives have guided discussions, with the goal of maximising consensus [1]. When consensus or the highest level of agreement is reached, the CRP ends.

Systemic Consensus

One alternative to classic consensus is the Systemic Consensus Principle (SCP). It does not require full consensus, but only to strive to obtain the minimum dissensus, by assessing resistance to all possible alternatives and prioritizing those with the lowest levels. The result indicates where the highest union of interests lies, in relation to each of the possibilities. [10, 25].

2.3 Fuzzy Decision-Making

In 1965 Lotfi Zadeh introduced a human computational decision-making approach that allows for more flexibility than crisp voting and enables consensus-driven processes.

[26] In contrast with 1 and 0 crisp calculation, the assignment of intermediate values represents human reasoning more precisely, because inherent hesitancy, uncertainty, and irrationality of human thinking processes can be integrated [19].

Comparative Linguistic Expressions (CLEs) and Membership Functions
Comparative linguistic expressions (CLEs) are used in fuzzy systems to implement fuzzy membership functions along a rating scale. Any two consecutive CLEs may overlap in their membership level. They enable fuzzy decision-making by using words and statuses to express the opinion about an alternative.

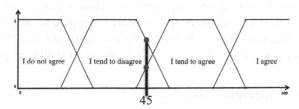

Fig. 1. Trapezoidal membership functions for agreement

Figure 1 shows all possible memberships by using four CLEs from "I do not agree" to "I agree". At any point, a maximum of two of the CLE statuses will have a membership-value above 0.

On the x-axis of Fig. 1, the chosen rating scale value 0.45 leads to a membership of the CLE "I tend to disagree" with a value of 0.6 and a membership of the CLE "I tend to agree" with a value of 0.4. The other two CLEs have a membership-value of 0.

Fuzzy Logic
Fuzzy logic is a concept in fuzzy decision-making which refers to the fact that states are linked logically and not exclusively mathematically to each other [20]. This approach opens various possibilities for dynamic decision-making. All possible combinations are to be listed in a logic table and a final state for each combination is to be defined. The logical operators AND, OR, as well as others can be used. Fuzzy logic allows for making logical connections and enables statements and weightings.

In this chapter we briefly introduced the concepts of LS-GSM, CRP, SCP, fuzzy voting, CLEs, and fuzzy logic. In the next chapter, our framework for integrative fuzzy decision-making will be introduced.

3   Framework of an Integrative Fuzzy Decision-Making Process (I-FDM)

3.1   I-FDM Framework of the Decision-Making Process

Based on the concepts in the preliminary part, we developed a fuzzy decision-making process, which integrates all affected individuals as equal impact decision-makers $D = \{d_1, \ldots d_n\}$, regardless of their specific expertise or lack thereof. The I-FDM process follows the following steps of decision-making (Fig. 2):

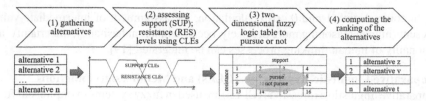

Fig. 2. The I-FDM process

After gathering the alternatives, we assess support and resistance levels by using CLE-sliders computed with membership functions. Then, we create a matrix of fuzzy logic rules, of how the CLE membership-values are computed to output statuses, indicating whether an alternative should be pursued or not. In the last step, through applying the fuzzy logic rules, a ranking of the alternatives by output statuses is generated.

3.2 Comparative Linguistic Expressions (CLEs)

In our framework, $S = \{s_1, s_2, s_3, s_4\}$ is the set of CLEs of support and $R = \{r_1, r_2, r_3, r_4\}$ is the set of CLEs for resistance. They are both represented through four statuses, as seen in Fig. 3. The following CLEs were considered the most suitable for the public decision-making process, and used for the two-slider assessment:

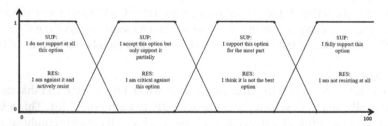

Fig. 3. Fuzzy membership function of S

The fuzzy envelopes, $envF(S)$ and $envF(R)$ are defined as a trapezoidal fuzzy membership function of support $S(a, b, c, d)$ and resistance $R(e, f, g, h)$ where $(a, b, \ldots h) \rightarrow [0, 1]$ and representing CLEs membership-degrees such that:

$$envF(S) = S(a, b, c, d) \tag{1}$$

$$envF(R) = R(e, f, g, h) \tag{2}$$

Since the single CLEs are not sharply divided, a trapezoidal membership-function of each CLE is used. Thus, we enabled a wide range on each CLE of a membership-degree of 1.00, as also shown in similar applications [1].

Computing Fuzzy Envelopes

Every decision-maker d_i assesses all alternatives $ALT_j = \{a_1, a_2 \ldots a_n\}$, evaluating each of them by using the two sliders. These assessments $T_i = \{t_i^{jS}, t_i^{jR}\}$ per ALT_j are modelled by their fuzzy envelope (1) $t_i^{jS} = \text{envF(S)}$ and (2) $t_i^{jR} = \text{envF(R)}$; where i is the unique number of the decision-maker and j represents the unique number of each alternative to be assessed.

The arithmetic average of all ALT^{jR} and ALT^{jS} were computed. In the cases where A_j was very widely distributed, we considered the value to be not as significant as needed for a resilient result.

3.3 Two-Dimensional Fuzzy Logic Table

When all decision-makers (D) have committed their opinion for each alternative through the two sliders, a two-dimensional assessment dataset $T = \{T_i, \ldots T_n\}$ results. This dataset is used for the defuzzification and fuzzy logic evaluation [1].

Table 1 shows the fuzzy logic rules in a matrix of how the assessments of support and resistance (T) are calculated into output statuses (O) by a logical conjunction. The output statuses are the CLEs $O = (o_1, o_2, o_3) \rightarrow$

{rather not pursue; pursue critical; pursue clearly}. All 16 rules are shown in the 4 × 4 matrix in Table 1.

$$\text{E.g., If } t_j^S \text{ is } s_1 \text{ AND } t_j^R \text{ is } r_1, \text{ then result } = o_1 \text{ (rather not pursue)}. \qquad (3)$$

Through this logic table, individually weighing the statuses is possible. The weighing rules were agreed upon at the beginning of the decision-making process.

The AND operation based on the rule table is computed as a MIN function ($O = (S \cap R)$). Each output status (o_1, o_2, o_3) is computed by a logical disjunction function ($o_1^{TOTAL} = o_1^A \cup o_1^B \cup \cdots \cup o_1^N$), OR operator or MAX function.

3.4 The Ranking of the Alternatives

The output of the I-FDM is a list of alternatives, compiled by using the disjunction value per output status. These alternatives are to be examined in detail, and, if possible, implemented. If the implementation is not possible, the next highest-ranking alternative will be checked.

The comparative order of the CLE sets, the formation of the alternatives, and the highest output membership-values, define the subordination. For example, the alternative ALT_j with the highest value of $o_1 = \{\text{pursue clearly}\}$ will be at the top of the ranking.

In this chapter, the I-FDM framework was introduced, comprising of four steps: (1) gathering alternatives, (2) computing SUP and RES using CLEs and fuzzy envelopes, (4) using a fuzzy logic table to compute outputs based on SUP and RES, and (4) the final output, as a ranking of alternatives. In the following chapter, the case study of Unterdorf St. will be introduced.

Table 1. Two-dimensional fuzzy logic rule in a matrix

		Support CLEs S (s_1, s_2, s_3, s_4)			
		I do not support at all this alternative	I accept this alternative but only support it partially	I support this alternative for the most part	I fully support this alternative
Resistance CLEs (r_1, r_2, r_3, r_4)	I am against it and resist active	rather not pursue	rather not pursue	rather not pursue	pursue, critical
	I am critical against this alternative	rather not pursue	rather not pursue	pursue, critical	pursue, critical
	I think it is not the best alternative	rather not pursue	rather not pursue	pursue, critical	pursue, critical
	I am not resisting at all	pursue, critical	pursue clearly	pursue clearly	pursue clearly

4   Case Study

We applied the I-FDM framework to solve a long withstanding conflict around Unterdorf St. in Geuensee, Luzern, Switzerland, where between March 2022 and December 2022 we implemented a participative process combining crowdsourcing alternatives and arguments, voting workshops, and UX-designed digital tools for fuzzy voting, to decide which of the alternative solutions should be pursued further.

4.1   Methodology

Based on the action design research methodology, we have developed a process of fuzzy decision-making, striving for systemic consensus with the use of two dimensions of resistance and support, which were then computed using a two-dimensional matrix for obtaining a ranking of the top options favored by the decision-makers (Fig. 4).

An important part of the methodology was the continuous evaluation, by means of collecting feedbacks in each production cycle: by assessing process steps, artifacts and the app through the decision-makers and other people. The collection and processing of arguments and alternatives was also reflected upon, optimized, and jointly decided by those involved in the process.

Problem Formulation

The community of around 2000 people living in Geuensee, in the canton of Luzern, Switzerland, was dissatisfied with the traffic to and from an industrial area, passing through the residential street Unterdorf St., causing noise and safety risks. Previously

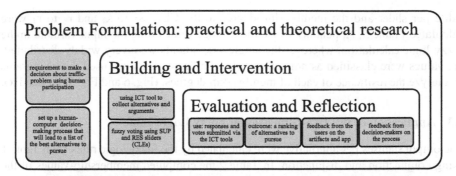

Fig. 4. Applied action design research in the process of decision-making

proposed solutions have further escalated the conflict. The decision-making process started with 9 alternatives, to which 4 others were added during the process [17].

Building and Intervention
UX experts were involved for developing a dedicated, digital web-based platform, complying with all the values and requirements of the I-FDM process. In November 2022, two voting workshops have been organized, at which the decision-makers were informed about the problem, presented with the final 13 proposed alternatives as well as with the arguments collected in earlier stages. Finally, the decision-makers $D = \{d_1, ..., d_{88}\}$ voted on the alternatives $ALT_j = \{a_1, a_2, ..., a_{13}\}$ using two CLE sliders of resistance and support.

CLE Sliders
Figure 5 shows the display screen for one of the alternatives to be assessed. There is a slider, where the CLEs describe resistance-levels. They use text-feedback only, with different transparency levels, highlighted with a blue line on the upper slider, representing the membership level to the CLEs. In Fig. 5 the CLE "I am critical against this alternative" is chosen by a membership-degree of 80%, whereas the CLE "I think it is not the best alternative" is chosen by 20%. No numerical values of the assessment were shown on the screen.

CLE Sliders

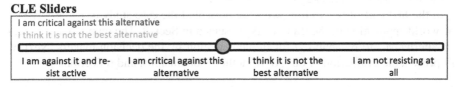

Fig. 5. Fuzzy sliders with membership functions, using transparency feedback of CLEs

4.2 Data Processing of CLE Membership-Values

A number of 2288 data entries were submitted on the 13 alternatives (ALT) by 88 decision-makers (D), during the two voting workshops. For each alternative, the average value per slider and the membership-degree to the CLEs s_1 to s_4 and r_1 to r_4 were calculated (Table 5, Appendix). Since the average values were the input variable in the fuzzy logic calculation, wherever the single assessments were very widely distributed, the values were classified as not sufficiently significant. Thus, we used the histograms to analyze the resilience of each of membership-degrees. (Fig. 6 and Fig. 7, Appendix).

4.3 Application of the Two-Dimensional Fuzzy Logic Table

The output statuses per alternative were calculated by the fuzzy logic rules from Table 1 using conjunction and disjunction. In Table 2 the computed membership-values of the output statuses are shown (Table 6, Appendix).

Table 2. Membership-degrees of output statuses of first 7 alternatives (only values > 0)

Alternative	Output statuses as CLEs			Rank
	Pursue clearly	Pursue critical	Rather not pursue	
3 Towards Sursee	0.167	0.833		1
8 Relocation		1.000		2
13 Repurposing		0.833	0.167	3
10 Combination time		0.750	0.250	4
7 Slow traffic		0.500	0.500	5
1 Schäracher St		0.500	0.500	6
9 No action		0.167	0.750	7

Only one alternative "3 Towards Sursee" reaches the output status "pursue clearly", with a membership-degree of 0.167. This option will therefore be the top priority on the ranking, followed by a descending list of the membership-degrees in the second CLE output status "pursue critical". The second priority will be "8 Relocation", followed by "13 Repurposing", and so on, and so forth. Only the alternatives that are above option 9 "No action", are to be checked in detail (Table 2).

In the first part of the section, we have presented the case study of Unterdorf St., a real-world application of the framework presented in Sect. 2. The output was a ranking of 6 alternatives to be analysed for implementation by the decision-makers. Next, we will present the evaluation of our ADR method, conclusions, and reflections.

4.4 Evaluation

Dujmovic [3] defines evaluation as a process of assessing whether an object meets the requirements of the users and/or stakeholders. Considering this perspective, we have used the following evaluation guidelines (Table 3).

Table 3. Outcome of the evaluation of the I-FDM

Use of Tools and Artifacts	We received a total of around 500 arguments on the 13 alternatives. Also, a total of 2288 CLE assessments were submitted by the 88 participants
Outcome: The Ranking	Through the I-FDM process, we have generated and delivered a 6-item ranking of the most favored alternatives to be pursued by the decision-makers
Feedback from Users on the Tools: Surveying the Decision-makers	A quantitative survey was applied to the voters about the digital platform built for the occasion. The feedback was positive: 97% answered that the decision-making tool was helpful for the assessment
User Experience	An interesting UX observation potentially indicating that decision-making participants liked and deliberatively made use of the possibility to choose in-between membership-degrees (Fig. 5), was that almost all of decision-makers (93%) chose one or more answers where two CLEs were shown at the same time, adding up to 32% of the 2288 assessments
Feedback on the Process	The result was accepted by the representatives of the decision-makers and used for further verification. We employed qualitative methods of directly speaking with them, as well as the quantitative method of the survey. The result was that 88% of the participants said that they would use this method again

5 Conclusion

In this paper an integrative fuzzy decision-making framework has been presented, as it was applied with good results in the real-life case study of Unterdorf St. Being integrative and transdisciplinary, the model included all concerned parties as decision-makers, rather than only experts. The method combined measuring support, which is conventionally assessed in consensus-reaching processes (CRPs), with measuring resistance, thus striving for systemic consensus. The voting cycles were not repeated.

The results were computed with trapezoidal functions into fuzzy envelopes. A ranking was generated by applying fuzzy logic rules, allowing to weight the resistance as considered in the SCP. The 6-item list was handed to the decision-makers, for further verification and implementation, in descending order of priority.

In the evaluation section, we showed that the voting platform used the UX element of transparency-opacity of the status description, i.e., the transition from one CLE status to the other, to communicate to the user the ability to choose concomitant status memberships on each one of the CLE sliders. This feature was used by most of the users, for around a third of the assessments.

The feedback collected through surveys and qualitative assessments was overall positive, in terms of using the digital tools and other artifacts, of the result relative to the initial goal, and of using this decision-making method again.

Ethical System and Process Design
Our application of the I-FDM framework and consequent tools and artifacts produced, follows the paradigm of value-based IT design and ethical system design [16] by actively involving the stakeholders in all the phases of the system design. We wanted to make sure that the values of confidentiality, integrity, availability of data, authenticity, accuracy, are embedded into our integrative FDM framework.

Some examples are that the decision makers had access to the entire process and to intermediary results and were informed about how the data will be handled. Also, the problem statement was made clear, known to all, as well as the decisions that were taken and assumptions that were made in the beginning. The stage of gathering the alternatives was handled with particular care and transparency.

Our transdisciplinary integrative approach allowed all the stakeholders to participate, according to their own knowledge and competencies, and obtained a democratically legitimate result. Sufficient time was given for each step, allowing participants to understand and to find time to attend. Lastly, we tried to set the right expectations for the result. We also recommended that in deciding about the implementation, short-term as well as long-term perspectives would be carefully considered.

Reflection
The results of this process can be extrapolated in two main directions. Firstly, the I-FDM is suitable and effective in real-life case studies of urban planning, community conflict resolution, and others. The people that contributed throughout and participated in the voting, validated this method by giving their attendance and positive feedback. For the design science method, a key future takeaway is continuing the evaluation from multiple perspectives, as well as maintaining constant contact with real-world cases. The lack of excessive theorization of the research method helped to design a lean process, that put the users at its core. More analysis can be done of the data, by using different computational methods.

Acknowledgements. The authors are grateful to the people involved in the Unterdorf St. project. Further thanks go to Mathias Schmid, Dominik Huber, Maurizio Hofstetter and the two HSLU teams (Fabio Stecher, Daniele Muheim, Nicole Zimmermann and Corinne Spoering) coordinated by Emmenegger, B., HSLU.
    Appendix: accessible on www.emmenegger.human-ist.ch.

References

1. Akkuzu, G., Aziz, B., Adda, M.: A fuzzy modeling approach for group decision making in social networks. In: Abramowicz, W., Corchuelo, R. (eds.) BIS 2019. LNBIP, vol. 354, pp. 74–85. Springer, Cham (2019). https://doi.org/10.1007/978-3-030-20482-2_7

2. Bigham, J.P., Bernstein, M.S., Adar, E.: Human-computer interaction and collective intelligence. In: Malone, T., Bernstein, T. (eds.) Handbook of Collective Intelligence, MIT Press (2015).

3. Dujmovic, J.: Soft Computing Evaluation Logic: The LSP Decision Method and Its Applications. Wiley-IEEE Computer Society Press (2018)

4. Drucker, P.F.: The effective decision. In: Decision Making and Problem Solving. Harvard Business Review (1967)

5. Finger, M., Portmann, E.: What are cognitive cities? In: Finger M, Portmann E (eds.) Towards Cognitive Cities. SSDC, vol. 63, pp. 1–11. Springer, Heidelberg (2016). https://doi.org/10.1007/978-3-319-33798-2_1

6. Klein, J.T.: Evaluation of interdisciplinary and transdisciplinary research: a literature review. Am. J. Prev. Med. **35**(2, Supplement), 116–223 (2008). https://doi.org/10.1016/j.amepre.2008.05.010

7. Labella, A., Rodríguez, R., Martinez, L.: An Adaptive Consensus Reaching Process Dealing with Comparative Linguistic Expressions in Large-scale Group Decision Making, p. 171. (2019). https://doi.org/10.2991/eusflat-19.2019.26

8. Liao, H., Wang, J., Tang, M., et al.: An overview of interval analysis techniques and their fuzzy extensions in multi-criteria decision-making: what's going on and what's next? Int. J. Fuzzy Syst. (2023). https://doi.org/10.1007/s40815-022-01448-z

9. Liu, F., Mendel, J.M.: Encoding words into interval type-2 fuzzy sets using an interval approach. IEEE Trans. Fuzzy Syst. **16**(6), 1503–1521 (2008)

10. Maiwald, J.: Smart Decision-Making. Systemic Consensing for Managers, 2nd revised. A-BiS Gesellschaft für Unternehmensentwicklung mbH. Holzkirchen Germany (2018)

11. Martınez, L., Ruan, D., Herrera, F., Herrera-Viedma, E., Wang, P.: Linguistic decision making: tools and applications, Inf. Sci. **179**(14 spec), 2297–2298 (2009)

12. Masdari, M., Khezri, H.: Service selection using fuzzy multi-criteria decision making: a comprehensive review. J. Ambient Intell. Humaniz. Comput. **12**(2), 2803–2834 (2020). https://doi.org/10.1007/s12652-020-02441-w

13. Mendel, J., et al.: What computing with words means to me. Discussion forum. IEEE Comput. Intell. Mag. **5**(1), 20–26 (2010)

14. Mendez, C., Pegan, A., Triga, V.: Creating public value in regional policy. Bringing citizens back in. Public Manag. Rev. (2022). https://doi.org/10.1080/14719037.2022.2126880

15. Mommsen, D., Portmann, E.: Gestaltungs- und praxisorientierte Promotionsarbeiten im Spannungsfeld zwischen Anwendung und Forschung. In: Portmann, E. (ed.) Wirtschaftsinformatik in Theorie und Praxis, pp. 11–34. Springer, Wiesbaden (2017). https://doi.org/10.1007/978-3-658-17613-6_2

16. Negulescu, O.H.: Using a decision-making process model in strategic management. Rev. Gen. Manag. **19**(1), 111–123 (2014)

17. Projekt Unterdorfstrasse. https://www.unterdorfstr.ch. Accessed 20 Jan 2023

18. Spiekermann, S.: Ethical IT Innovation: A Value-Based System Design Approach, p. 13, 172 (2015). https://doi.org/10.1201/b19060

19. Tabacchi, M.E., Portmann, E., Seising, R., Habenstein, A.: Designing cognitive cities. In: Portmann, E., Tabacchi, M.E., Seising, R., Habenstein, A. (eds.) Designing Cognitive Cities. SSDC, vol. 176, pp. 3–27. Springer, Cham (2019). https://doi.org/10.1007/978-3-030-00317-3_1

20. Teràn Tamayo, L.F., Meier, A., Pedrycz, W., Portmann (eds.): SmartParticipation. A Fuzzy-Based Recommender System for Political Community-Building. Fuzzy Management Methods, pp. 33–35. Springer, Heidelberg (2014). https://doi.org/10.1007/978-3-319-06551-9

21. Torres van Grinsven, V., Hudec, M., Portmann, E., D´Onofrio, S.: A Flexible Voting Approach for Supporting more Accurate Decisions (2021). https://doi.org/10.13140/RG.2.2.31872. 10248
22. Toš, I.: interdisciplinarity and transdisciplinarity – problems and guidelines. Coll. Antropol. **45**(1), 67–73 (2021). https://doi.org/10.5671/CA.45.1.8
23. UMass Dartmouth Media Resources. https://www.umassd.edu/media/umassdartmouth/fycm/ decision_making_process.pdf. Accessed 20 Jan 2023
24. Vaishnavi, V., Kuechler, W.: Design Science Research in Information Systems, January 20, 2004 (Updated in 2017 and 2019 by Vaishnavi, V. and Stacey, P.) (2004)
25. Visotschnig, E., Visotschnig, V.: Einführung in das SK-Prinzip. Institut für systemisches konsensieren. International (2016)
26. Zadeh, L.A.: Fuzzy sets. Inf. Control **8**(3), 338–353 (1965). https://doi.org/10.1016/S0019-9958(65)90241-X
27. Zapletal, F., Hudec, M., Švaňa, M., et al.:Three-level model for opinion aggregation under hesitance. Soft Comput. (2023). https://doi.org/10.1007/s00500-023-07853-2

Machine Learning and Fuzzy Measures: A Real Approach to Individual Classification

Inmaculada Gutiérrez[1]([✉]) [ID], Daniel Santos[1] [ID], Javier Castro[1] [ID],
Julio Alberto Hernández-Gonzalo[2], Daniel Gómez[1] [ID], and Rosa Espínola[1] [ID]

[1] Facultad de Estudios Estadísticos, Universidad Complutense de Madrid,
Madrid, Spain
{inmaguti,dasant05}@ucm.es, {jcastroc,dagomez,rosaev}@estad.ucm.es
[2] IES Rivera de Castilla, Consejería de Educación de Castilla y León,
Valladolid, Spain
jahernandezgon@educa.jcyl.es

Abstract. In the field of machine learning, a crucial task is understanding the relative importance of the different input features in a predictive model. There is an approach in the literature whose aim is to analyze the predictive capacity of some features with respect to others. Can we explain a feature of the input space with others? Can we quantify this capacity? We propose a practical approach for analyzing the importance of features in a model and the explanatory capacity of some features over others. It is based on the adaptation of existing definitions from the literature that use the Shapley value and fuzzy measures. Our new approach aims to facilitate the understanding and application of these concepts by starting from a simple idea and considering well known methods. The main objective of this work is to provide a useful and practical approach for analyzing feature importance in real world cases.

Keywords: Fuzzy Measures · Machine Learning · Features Importance · Explainable Artificial Intelligence

1 Introduction

The goal of this work is inspired by the idea that the interpretability of a machine learning model is closely related to the knowledge about the predictive capacity of the features involved [1]. In [8] it was introduced a new methodology to analyse and consider the whole available information of the known features. Based on fuzzy measures, it avoids the problem of overfitting caused by continuous features. Its goal is to predict the value of an unidentified feature knowing a set of them. That method was inspired by those of Štrumbelj et al. [11–13], who used the Shapley value [9] of a cooperative game to analyze the measurement

Supported by the Government of Spain, Grant Plan Nacional de I+D+i, PID2020-116884GB-I00, PID2021-122905NB-C21.

S. Massanet et al. (Eds.): EUSFLAT 2023/AGOP 2023, LNCS 14069, pp. 137–148, 2023.
https://doi.org/10.1007/978-3-031-39965-7_12

of the importance of the features in a machine learning model. This solution concept is used in the field of eXplainable Artificial Intelligence (XAI) to assess the importance of features in a machine learning model and to measure the predictive ability of some features over others [3]. It has gained popularity due to their flexibility and appealing axiomatization of fairness [7].

In this field, two extreme approaches are specially interesting. The method in [11] assigns a random value to the unknown feature. On the opposite, [13], fixed a specific instance to be predicted, only considers instances in which the value of the unknown feature matches with the fixed. The method in [8] is an intermediate solution between [11] and [13], which mixes random values with the consideration of exact values. That mix is supported by the use of fuzzy measures [10], monotonic set functions useful to make decisions, find good methods and logical operators for connectives and implications, represent and analyze vagueness [2].

Our goal now is a practical application of [8]. With that method as starting point, in this paper we develop an step by step methodology which details how to proceed in any case to calculate the predictive capacity measure which quantifies the predictive capacity of some features over others, apart from the predictions obtained in any scenario. To do so, and in order to establish a realistic and easy-to-implement proposal, we base on the idea of generating simple predictive models. We include a illustrative example to explain the process in detail, and a comparison with other measures in the literature.

The paper is organized as follows. The foundational concepts necessary for a comprehensive understanding of this paper are established in Sect. 2. Sect. 3 explains step by step the characterization of the new explanation method and the relative predictive fuzzy measure. Section 4 is about an application of the model and its interpretation. We finish in Sect. 5 with some final remarks.

2   Preliminaries

In this work we suggest a real approach to the measurement of the predictive ability of the features of a machine learning model. Now we introduce the theoretical models which set the starting point of the proposed application. Specifically, we show the methods [8,11,13], used to measure the importance of features in a machine learning model using the Shapley value in a cooperative game [9] with characteristic function w, $Sh_i(w)$. This solution concept has been adapted to the field of fuzzy measures [10], on whose basis we develop this paper.

On the following it is assumed that the set of players or individuals, N, refers to the input features in a machine learning model, $N = \{v_1, \ldots, v_n\}$. $\mathcal{A}$ denote the set of instances, and for $S \subseteq N$, the Cartesian product of singles instances in S is $\mathcal{A}_S = A'_1 \times A'_2 \times \ldots A'_n$, being $A'_i = \{v_i\}$, if $i \in S$, and $A'_i = \{\epsilon\}$ otherwise, being ϵ a pre-defined value that represents a missing data [12].

Finally, we present three importance measures. Given a database $\mathcal{D}$ and a specific instance x, to measure the predictive ability of the unknown features, φ^1 [11] assigns them a random value; φ^2 [13] only considers the instances in which unknown features exactly match with x, and φ^3 [8] is an intermediate solution.

Definition 1 (Explanation method for an instance φ^1 [11]). *Let $\mathcal{D}$ denote a database with n features $N = \{v_1, \ldots, v_n\}$ and a set $\mathcal{A}$ of m instances, being $x = (x_1, \ldots, x_n) \in \mathcal{A}$. Let f denote a predictive model. The importance of the feature v_j in the instance x is defined as the Shapley value for a characteristic function $\Delta^1(S)$, defined $\forall S \subseteq N$.*

$$\varphi_j^1(x) = \sum_{S \subseteq N \setminus \{v_j\}} \frac{(n - s - 1)! s!}{n!} \left(\Delta^1(S \cup \{v_j\}) - \Delta^1(S) \right) \tag{1}$$

where $s = |S|$; $\Delta^1(S) = \dfrac{1}{|\mathcal{A}_{N \setminus S}|} \displaystyle\sum_{y \in \mathcal{A}_{N \setminus S}} f\left(\tau\left(x, y, S\right)\right) - \dfrac{1}{|\mathcal{A}_N|} \displaystyle\sum_{y \in \mathcal{A}_N} f(y)$

$$\tau\left(x, y, S\right) = (z_1, z_2, \ldots, z_n), \quad \text{being } z_\ell = \begin{cases} x_\ell & \text{if } v_\ell \in S \\ y_\ell & \text{if } v_\ell \notin S \end{cases}$$

Definition 2 (Explanation method for an instance φ^2 [13]). *Let $\mathcal{D}$ denote a database with n features $N = \{v_1, \ldots, v_n\}$ and a set $\mathcal{A}$ of m instances, being $x = (x_1, \ldots, x_n) \in \mathcal{A}$. Let f denote a predictive model. The importance of the feature v_j in the instance x is defined as the Shapley value for a characteristic function $\Delta^2(S)$, defined $\forall S \subseteq N$.*

$$\varphi_j^2(x) = \sum_{S \subseteq N \setminus \{v_j\}} \frac{(n - s - 1)! s!}{n!} \left(\Delta^2(S \cup \{v_j\}) - \Delta^2(S) \right) \tag{2}$$

where $s = |S|$; $\Delta^2(S) = \dfrac{1}{|\mathcal{B}_S|} \displaystyle\sum_{y \in \mathcal{B}_S} f(y) - \dfrac{1}{|\mathcal{B}_\emptyset|} \displaystyle\sum_{y \in \mathcal{B}_\emptyset} f(y)$

being $\quad \mathcal{B}_S = \{y \in D : x_\ell = y_\ell, \forall v_\ell \in S\}$

Finally, to define φ^3, it is needed the concept of predictive fuzzy measure.

Definition 3 (Predictive fuzzy measure [8]). *Let $\mathcal{D}$ denote a database with n features $N = \{v_1, \ldots, v_n\}$ and a set $\mathcal{A}$ of m instances. Given $v_j \in N$, $\forall S \subseteq N$, $\mu_j(S)$ is defined as the predictive ability in $\mathcal{D}$, regardless randomness, of the features in S over v_j.*

$$\mu_j(S) = \frac{Error_j(\emptyset) - Error_j(S)}{Error_j(\emptyset)} \tag{3}$$

where $Error_j(\emptyset)$ and $Error_j(S)$ denote a measure of the error obtained when v_j is predicted randomly or with the features in S, respectively.

Definition 4 (Explanation method for an instance using fuzzy measures φ^3[8]). *Let $\mathcal{D}$ denote a database with n features $N = \{v_1, \ldots, v_n\}$ and a set $\mathcal{A}$ of m instances. For every $v_j \in N$ and for every $\mu_j(S)$ predictive fuzzy*

measure of the features in $S \subseteq N$ over feature v_j, being f a predictive model and
$x = (x_1, \ldots, x_n) \in \mathcal{A}$, *the importance of the feature v_j in the instance x is defined*
as the Shapley value for a characteristic function $\Delta^3(S)$, defined $\forall S \subseteq N$.

$$\varphi_j^3(x) = \sum_{S \subseteq N \setminus \{v_j\}} \frac{(n-s-1)!s!}{n!} \left(\Delta^3(S \cup \{v_j\}) - \Delta^3(S) \right) \tag{4}$$

where $s = |S|$; $\Delta^3(S, x) = \dfrac{1}{|\mathcal{A}_{N \setminus S}|} \sum_{y \in \mathcal{A}_{N \setminus S}} f(\tau(x, y', S)) - \dfrac{1}{|\mathcal{A}_N|} \sum_{y \in \mathcal{A}_N} f(\tau(x, y', \emptyset))$

$$\tau(x, y', S) = (z_1, \ldots, z_n), \quad \text{being} \quad z_\ell = \begin{cases} x_\ell & \text{if } v_\ell \in S \\ y'_\ell & \text{if } v_\ell \notin S \end{cases}$$

being y'_ℓ an estimation of the $\ell - th$ feature, v_ℓ, when knowing the features in
S, *with which an explainability percentage of $\mu_j(S)$ is guaranteed.*

3   Mathematical Model

Our goal is the proposal of a specific characterization of μ_j and φ_j^3, which allows
the calculation in real problems. To do so, we have to specify the mathematical
models for which the prediction errors are calculated for every type of feature
$v_j \in N$ (i.e. we have to specify the calculation of the predictive fuzzy measure
μ_j), and the way to obtain y' in order to guarantee the conditions of μ_j.

3.1   On the Calculation of the Predictive Fuzzy Measure

Our proposal considers simple mathematical models of prediction. Otherwise,
the calculation of μ_j would be really complex. Specifically, given a database $\mathcal{D}$
with a set N of n input features and a set $\mathcal{A}$ of m instances, and being y the
variable to be predicted, our methodology to calculate μ_j is:

(1) Organize the input features into a set of categorical features N^c; ordinal
features N^o, and numeric features N^n, where $N = N^c \cup N^o \cup N^n$, and
$N^i \cap N^j = \emptyset$, $\forall i \neq j \in \{n, o, c\}$.
(2) Preprocessing of the features depending on their nature.
　($2a$) Each categorical feature $c \in N^c$ is decomposed into dummy variables, d^c.
　　　Common methods can be used, as long as the representativeness among
　　　other criteria are guaranteed; i.e., the number of instances in which each
　　　category is observed should not be negligible, otherwise the feature has
　　　to be debugged beforehand. For example, given the categorical feature
　　　$c = \{F, M\}$, the dummy related with the category F has the values
　　　$d^c.F = 1$ if $c = F$; $d^c.F = 0$, otherwise.
　($2b$) Each ordinal feature $o \in N^o$ is decomposed into cumulative dummy
　　　variables, d^o, but not with common methods: for each specific category
　　　of the ordinal feature, the corresponding dummy variable has the value
　　　1 for each value below or equal to the analyzed category, and the value

0 otherwise. Obviously, a dummy is not needed for the last or higher category, it would trivially have all values as 1. For example, given the ordinal feature $o = (Low, Medium, High)$, the dummy related with the category $Medium$ has the values $d^o.Medium = 1$, if $o = Low$ or $Medium$; and $d^o.Medium = 0$, if $o = High$.

(2c) No preprocessing is needed for numeric features.

(3) For every categorical feature $c \in N^c$:

(3a) For every subset $S \subseteq N\backslash\{c\}$ of feasible features to predict c, we have to calculate the best logistic model (logit) to predict d^c [4].

(3b) We aggregate the predictions made by each predictive model, obtained in (3a), into a single prediction for the original categorical feature. This aggregation is done, in each instance, taking into account the proportionality obtained in the predictions of the different models. To calculate MSE_c (mean square deviation to measure the average of the squares of the errors), we consider the probability of not hitting the real value of the analyzed feature c when knowing S:

$$MSE_c(S) = \frac{1}{m} \sum_{k=1}^{m} \left(1 - P\left(\widehat{c}_k = c_k\right)\right)^2 \tag{5}$$

where $P\left(\widehat{c}_k = c_k\right)$ is the probability of the estimated value of the analyzed feature c in the instance k, $\widehat{c}_k$, fixes the real value of o in k, c_k. Regarding $c = \{F, M\}$, if the best logistic model about $d^c.F$ provides the probability 0.55, and the best logistic model about $d^c.M$ provides the probability 0.65 in a specific instance k, the aggregation is done in k as $\left(\frac{0.55}{0.55+0.65}, \frac{0.65}{0.55+0.65}\right) = \left(\frac{0.55}{1.2}, \frac{0.65}{1.2}\right)$. If $c_k = F$, the summand of $MSE_c(S)$ related to instance k is $\left(1 - \frac{0.55}{1.2}\right)^2$.

(3c) For these variables, the calculation of $\mu_c(S)$ is done considering the percent error in classification when the available information is the subset $S \subseteq N\backslash\{c\}$ or when it is the $\emptyset$. Then, the predictive fuzzy measure μ_c for a categorical feature c and a subset of features S is calculated as:

$$\mu_c(S) = \frac{MSE_c(\emptyset) - MSE_c(S)}{MSE_c(\emptyset)} \tag{6}$$

(4) For every ordinal feature $o \in N^o$:

(4a) For every subset $S \subseteq N\backslash\{o\}$ of feasible features to predict o, we have to calculate the best logistic model (logit) to predict d^o [4].

(4b) We aggregate the predictions made by each predictive model, obtained in (4a), into a single prediction for the original ordinal feature. This aggregation is done, in each instance, by taking into account the proportionality obtained in the predictions of the different models and by combining some dummy variables based on their definitions, which were obtained from ordinal features. To calculate MSE_o, we consider the probability of not hitting the real value of o when knowing S:

$$MSE_o(S) = \frac{1}{m} \sum_{k=1}^{m} (1 - P(\widehat{o}_k = o_k))^2 \tag{7}$$

where $P(\widehat{o}_k = o_k)$ is the probability of the estimated value of the analyzed feature o in the instance k, $\widehat{o}_k$, fixes the real value of o in k, o_k. Regarding $o = (Low, Medium, High)$, if the best logistic model about $d^o.Low$ provides probability 0.5 and the best logistic model about $d^o.Medium$ provides probability 0.7 in a specific instance k, the aggregation is done in k as $(0.5, 0.7 - 0.5, 1 - 0.7) = (0.5, 0.2, 0.3)$. If $o_k = Medium$, the element of $MSE_o(S)$ regarding instance k is $(1 - 0.2)^2$.

(4c) For these variables, the calculation of $\mu_o(S)$ is done considering the percent error in classification when the available information is the subset $S \subseteq N \backslash \{o\}$ or it is the $\emptyset$. Then, the predictive fuzzy measure μ_o for an ordinal feature o and a subset of features S is calculated as:

$$\mu_o(S) = \frac{MSE_o(\emptyset) - MSE_o(S)}{MSE_o(\emptyset)} \tag{8}$$

(5) For every numeric feature $n \in N^n$:

(5a) For every subset $S \subseteq N \backslash \{n\}$ of feasible features to predict n, we have to calculate the best generalized linear model (GLM) to predict n [6].

(5b) We calculate the means squared error (MSE) for every model obtained in (5a) to predict n when knowing S.

$$MSE_n(S) = \frac{1}{m} \sum_{k=1}^{m} (\widehat{n}_k - n_k)^2 \tag{9}$$

being $\widehat{n}_k$ and n_k the estimated and the real value of n in the instance k.

(5c) We define the $\mu_n(S)$ of those features as

$$\mu_n(S) = \frac{MSE_n(\emptyset) - MSE_n(S)}{MSE_n(\emptyset)} \tag{10}$$

(6) We have to recalculate μ to make it meet the condition of superadditivity.

$$\mu_j(S) = \max_{R \subseteq S} \mu_j(R) \tag{11}$$

Let us note that this readjustment is not common, as, in general, models do not get worse when the number of variables increases.

3.2 On the Calculation of the Estimation y'

To specific a particular application of the measure φ, we also have to explain the calculation of y'. As mentioned in Definition 4, given a set of features $S \subseteq N$, the value y'_ℓ is an estimation of the $\ell - th$ feature, v_ℓ, when knowing the features of a subset S. Our proposal is as follows:

1) If v_ℓ is categorical, the value assigned to y'_ℓ is a draw between the different categories of the features, by considering the probabilities defined in ($3b$).
2) If v_ℓ is ordinal, the value assigned to y'_ℓ is a draw between the different tidy categories of the features, considering the probabilities defined in ($4b$).
3) If v_ℓ is numeric, the value assigned to y'_ℓ is the prediction given by the best GLM obtained in the point ($5a$) of previous section

4   An Application and Interpretation of the Method

4.1   Definition of the Problem

We have to explicitly characterize the database and the predictive model.
⋆ Definition of the database:

- $\mathcal{D} = \{N, \mathcal{A}\}$
- $N = \{v_1, v_2, v_3\}$, where v_1 is categorical, v_2 is ordinal, and v_3 is numeric: $v_1 = \{c^1, c^2\}$; $v_2 = \{o^1, o^2, o^3\}$; v_3 is generated as a random variable $\beta(x, y)$ whose parameters depends on the combination of the values of v_1 and v_2 (see Fig. 1). The possible combinations of v_1 and v_2 are $\{c^1 - o^1;\ c^1 - o^2;\ c^1 - o^3; c^2 - o^1;\ c^2 - o^2;\ c^2 - o^3\}$. On the following we consider this order, and we state $c^1 - o^1$ as *Case 1*; $c^1 - o^2$ as *Case 2*, and so on.
- The output variable, y, is dichotomous. We establish a relation of y with the explainable variables: we calculate an auxiliary value, $aux = 0.2 * v_1.c^2 + 0.15 * v_2.o^2 + 0.3 * v_2.o^3 + v_3 + 1.5 * U(0, 1)$, and then $y = 1$, if $aux > 1.5$; $y = 0$ otherwise. This relation is showed in red color in Fig. 1.
- Each one of the 6 cases is generated 25 times, so $|\mathcal{A}| = 6 * 25 = 150$ instances.

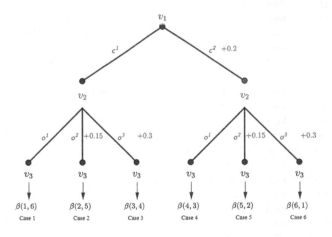

Fig. 1. Generation of the 150 instances of $\mathcal{D}$ and y.

⋆ Predictive model definition: considering the auxiliary value $aux2 = 0.2 * v_1.c^2 + 0.15 * v_2.o^2 + 0.3 * v_2.o^3 + v_3$, the mode used to predict y is:

$$f = \begin{cases} 1, & \text{if } aux2 > 1.5 \\ 0, & \text{if } aux2 < 0 \\ \frac{aux2}{1.5}, & \text{otherwise} \end{cases}$$

4.2 Comparison of φ^3 with Other Methods

We finish this section with the interpretation of the model and its comparison with other proposals, particularly, φ^1 and φ^2 [11,13]. In Table 1 we show all the calculations and elements mentioned in the enumeration proposed in Sect. 3.1, needed to calculate φ^3 for the case detailed in Sect. 4.1. The coefficients β_i in the columns refer to the parameters of each predictive model (logit or GLM); specifically, β_0 refers to intercept. To show a simple view outline we finish the table with the calculation of the MSE; we do not explicitly show the value of the predictive fuzzy measure as it is trivial with the available information.

Note that the MSE is defined for the features and not for a specific category of them. Nevertheless, in Table 1 we show a value of MSE for every feature just to have a cohesive presentation of the content. For this reason, the error of predicting $d^{v_1}.c^1$ by knowing v_3 matches with the error of predicting $d^{v_1}.c^1$ by knowing v_3, and it actually refers to $MSE_{v_1}(\{v_3\})$.

Table 1. Summary of the steps $(3a)$, $(4a)$, $(5a)$, $(3b)$, $(4b)$, $(5b)$.

id	var. indep	S	method	β_0	β_1 $(v_1.c^1)$	β_2 $(v_1.c^2)$	β_3 $(v_2.o^1)$	β_4 $(v_2.o^2)$	β_5 (v_3)	MSE
1	$d^{v_1}.c^1$	∅	logit	0						0.25
2	$d^{v_1}.c^1$	$\{v_2\}$	logit	0			0	0		0.25
3	$d^{v_1}.c^1$	$\{v_3\}$	logit	4.8					−9.8	0.099
4	$d^{v_1}.c^1$	$\{v_2, v_3\}$	logit	9.94			−5.44	−2.67	−14.6	0.058
5	$d^{v_1}.c^2$	∅	logit	0						0.25
6	$d^{v_1}.c^2$	$\{v_2\}$	logit	0			0	0		0.25
7	$d^{v_1}.c^2$	$\{v_3\}$	logit	−4.8					9.8	0.099
8	$d^{v_1}.c^2$	$\{v_2, v_3\}$	logit	−9.94			5.44	2.67	14.6	0.058
9	$d^{v_2}.o^1$	∅	logit	−0.69						0.44
10	$d^{v_2}.o^1$	$\{v_1\}$	logit	−0.69	0	0				0.44
11	$d^{v_2}.o^1$	$\{v_3\}$	logit	0.59					−2.8	0.39
12	$d^{v_2}.o^1$	$\{v_1, v_3\}$	logit	5.1	−3.96	0			−8.2	0.31
13	$d^{v_2}.o^2$	∅	logit	0.69						0.44
14	$d^{v_2}.o^2$	$\{v_1\}$	logit	0.69	0	0				0.44
15	$d^{v_2}.o^2$	$\{v_3\}$	logit	2.07					−2.56	0.39
16	$d^{v_2}.o^2$	$\{v_1, v_3\}$	logit	7.94	−4.52	0			−9.05	0.31
17	v_3	∅	GLM	0.5						0.093
18	v_3	$\{v_1\}$	GLM	0.27	0	0.047				0.038
19	v_3	$\{v_2\}$	GLM	0.65			−0.3	−0.14		0.078
20	v_3	$\{v_1, v_2\}$	GLM	0.42	0	0.047	−0.3	−0.14		0.023

Table 2. Instances analyzed: Min., Max., Median of v_3 for each case.

		$v_1.c^1$	$v_1.c^2$	$v_2.o^1$	$v_2.o^2$	$v_2.o^3$	v_3
Min.(v_3)	Case 1	1	0	1	0	0	0.00259
	Case 2	1	0	0	1	0	0.06073
	Case 3	1	0	0	0	1	0.12488
	Case 4	0	1	1	0	0	0.16851
	Case 5	0	1	0	1	0	0.35727
	Case 6	0	1	0	0	1	0.77265
Max.(v_3)	Case 1	1	0	1	0	0	0.60353
	Case 2	1	0	0	1	0	0.61575
	Case 3	1	0	0	0	1	0.57236
	Case 4	0	1	1	0	0	0.87779
	Case 5	0	1	0	1	0	0.97143
	Case 6	0	1	0	0	1	0.99753
Median.(v_3)	Case 1	1	0	1	0	0	0.09972
	Case 2	1	0	0	1	0	0.27631
	Case 3	1	0	0	0	1	0.36674
	Case 4	0	1	1	0	0	0.57562
	Case 5	0	1	0	1	0	0.75059
	Case 6	0	1	0	0	1	0.92766

Let us not that there is a Shapley value for each instance (125) and for each measure, (φ^1, φ^2, φ^3). Then, instead of comparing every value, we consider some representative scenarios. Specifically, we compare the values of the three measures φ^1, φ^2 and φ^3 for the minimum, maximum and median value of v_3, for every scenario *Case 1 - Case 6*, i.e. for 18 different instances (see Table 2).

A good method based on the Shapley value should have internal consistency, that is, if different information is known in different scenarios, the value obtained in each scenario should also be different (unless the additional information is absolutely irrelevant or redundant). This idea is fulfilled with φ^1 and φ^3, but not with φ^2: in Tables 3, 4, 5 it can be seen that $\Delta^2(\{v_3\}) = \Delta^2(\{v_1, v_3\}) = \Delta^2(\{v_2, v_3\})$, i.e., it does not affect at all to know v_1 or v_2 if v_3 is already known. This problem is not casual; it will always happen when a numerical variable is known, as already shown in [8].

Comparing φ^1 and φ^3, either one is applied depending on which of the two provides values that are most similar to the real values. Clearly, φ^1 approximates reality less than φ^3 by not taking into account the correlation between features v_1 and v_2 with v_3. For example, when we know that $v_1 = c^1$ and $v_2 = o^1$, it is very unlikely for the prediction to be 1, given that this will only happen when the sum of a random number from a $\beta(1, 6)$ plus a random number from a uniform multiplied by 1.5 exceeds the value 1.5 (if we do the calculations, that probability is approximately 0.001; as the estimation in the absence of information is 0.5 due to symmetry, the 'good' value of $\Delta^1(\{v_1, v_2\})$ and $\Delta^1(\{v_1, v_2\})$ should be

$0.001 - 0.5 = -0.499$), which is very far from the value -0.16667 obtained with Δ^1 and much closer to the value -0.42703 obtained with Δ^3 (it is the same for the minimum, the maximum or the median of v_3). Other example is when $v_1 = c^2$ and $v_2 = o^3$; the 'good' value of Δ^1 and Δ^3 should be $0.85809 - 0.5 = 0.35809$, being $\Delta^1(\{v_1, v_2\}) = 0.16667$ and $\Delta^3(\{v_1, v_2\}) = 0.42145$.

Therefore, we can affirm that the method proposed, φ^3, presents obvious advantages over the proposals φ^1 and φ^3 [11,13] and it is desirable to carry out a thorough comparison to decide in which situations each of them are better or if one of them prevails over the others in most situations.

Table 3. Calculation of Δ^1, Δ^2 and Δ^3. Minimum of v_3.

Min. v_3	Case	$\{v_1\}$	$\{v_2\}$	$\{v_3\}$	$\{v_1,v_2\}$	$\{v_1,v_3\}$	$\{v_2,v_3\}$	$\{v_1,v_2,v_3\}$	Sh_{v_1}	Sh_{v_2}	Sh_{v_3}
Δ^1	Case 1	-0.06667	-0.1	-0.33173	-0.16667	-0.39839	-0.43173	-0.49839	-0.06667	-0.1	-0.33173
	Case 2	-0.06667	0	-0.29297	-0.06667	-0.35964	-0.29297	-0.35964	-0.06667	0	-0.29297
	Case 3	-0.06667	0.1	-0.25020	0.03333	-0.31686	-0.15020	-0.21686	-0.06667	0.1	-0.25020
	Case 4	0.06667	-0.1	-0.22112	-0.03333	-0.15445	-0.32112	-0.25445	0.06667	-0.1	-0.22112
	Case 5	0.06667	0	-0.09527	0.06667	-0.02861	-0.09527	-0.02861	0.06667	0	-0.09527
	Case 6	0.06667	0.1	0.18164	0.16667	0.24831	0.28164	0.34831	0.06667	0.1	0.18164
Δ^2	Case 1	-0.22330	-0.20373	-0.49839	-0.41091	-0.49839	-0.49839	-0.49839	-0.10896	-0.09918	-0.29025
	Case 2	-0.22330	0.00558	-0.35964	-0.21038	-0.35964	-0.35964	-0.35964	-0.11043	0.00401	-0.25323
	Case 3	-0.22330	0.19815	-0.21686	-0.04861	-0.21686	-0.21686	-0.21686	-0.11556	0.09516	-0.19647
	Case 4	0.22330	-0.20373	-0.25445	0.00344	-0.25445	-0.25445	-0.25445	0.10896	-0.10455	-0.25886
	Case 5	0.22330	0.00558	-0.02861	0.22154	-0.02861	-0.02861	-0.02861	0.11043	0.00157	-0.14060
	Case 6	0.22330	0.19815	0.34831	0.44491	0.34831	0.34831	0.34831	0.11556	0.10298	0.12977
Δ^3	Case 1	-0.22330	-0.20373	-0.45012	-0.42703	-0.47055	-0.49688	-0.49839	-0.11556	-0.11894	-0.26389
	Case 2	-0.22330	0.00558	-0.40512	-0.21771	-0.41982	-0.35941	-0.35964	-0.11417	0.03047	-0.27594
	Case 3	-0.22330	0.19815	-0.35436	-0.02515	-0.36059	-0.21682	-0.21686	-0.11270	0.16990	-0.27407
	Case 4	0.22330	-0.20373	-0.31893	0.01957	-0.25191	-0.37250	-0.25445	0.16217	-0.11164	-0.30498
	Case 5	0.22330	0.00558	-0.14925	0.22888	-0.11746	-0.14676	-0.02861	0.15633	0.03282	-0.21776
	Case 6	0.22330	0.19815	0.27100	0.42145	0.25381	0.32062	0.34831	0.11801	0.13885	0.09145

Table 4. Calculation of Δ^1, Δ^2 and Δ^3. Maximum of v_3.

Max. v_3	Case	$\{v_1\}$	$\{v_2\}$	$\{v_3\}$	$\{v_1,v_2\}$	$\{v_1,v_3\}$	$\{v_2,v_3\}$	$\{v_1,v_2,v_3\}$	Sh_{v_1}	Sh_{v_2}	Sh_{v_3}
Δ^1	Case 1	-0.06667	-0.1	0.06890	-0.16667	0.00223	-0.03110	-0.09777	-0.06667	-0.1	0.06890
	Case 2	-0.06667	0	0.07705	-0.06667	0.01038	0.07705	0.01038	-0.06667	0	0.07705
	Case 3	-0.06667	0.1	0.04812	0.03333	-0.01855	0.14812	0.08145	-0.06667	0.1	0.04812
	Case 4	0.06667	-0.1	0.25174	-0.03333	0.31840	0.15174	0.21840	0.06667	-0.1	0.25174
	Case 5	0.06667	0	0.31416	0.06667	0.38083	0.31416	0.38083	0.06667	0	0.31416
	Case 6	0.06667	0.1	0.33157	0.16667	0.39823	0.43157	0.49823	0.06667	0.1	0.33157
Δ^2	Case 1	-0.22330	-0.20373	-0.09777	-0.41091	-0.09777	-0.09777	-0.09777	-0.10896	-0.09918	0.11037
	Case 2	-0.22330	0.00558	0.01038	-0.21038	0.01038	0.01038	0.01038	-0.11043	0.00401	0.11679
	Case 3	-0.22330	0.19815	0.08145	-0.04861	0.08145	0.08145	0.08145	-0.11556	0.09516	0.10185
	Case 4	0.22330	-0.20373	0.21840	0.00344	0.21840	0.21840	0.21840	0.10896	-0.10455	0.21400
	Case 5	0.22330	0.00558	0.38083	0.22154	0.38083	0.38083	0.38083	0.11043	0.00157	0.26884
	Case 6	0.22330	0.19815	0.49823	0.44491	0.49823	0.49823	0.49823	0.11556	0.10298	0.27969
Δ^3	Case 1	-0.22330	-0.20373	0.11484	-0.42703	0.08859	0.03380	-0.09777	-0.15988	-0.17749	0.23960
	Case 2	-0.22330	0.00558	0.12724	-0.21771	0.09801	0.12350	0.01038	-0.15423	-0.02704	0.19165
	Case 3	-0.22330	0.19815	0.08240	-0.02515	0.06400	0.10412	0.08145	-0.12227	0.10851	0.09521
	Case 4	0.22330	-0.20373	0.35653	0.01957	0.35766	0.21837	0.21840	0.11185	-0.17131	0.27787
	Case 5	0.22330	0.00558	0.42930	0.22888	0.44561	0.38070	0.38083	0.11441	-0.02690	0.29332
	Case 6	0.22330	0.19815	0.44923	0.42145	0.46870	0.49694	0.49823	0.11533	0.11687	0.26604

Table 5. Calculation of Δ^1, Δ^2 and Δ^3. Median of v_3.

Median v_3	Case	$\{v_1\}$	$\{v_2\}$	$\{v_3\}$	$\{v_1,v_2\}$	$\{v_1,v_3\}$	$\{v_2,v_3\}$	$\{v_1,v_2,v_3\}$	Sh_{v_1}	Sh_{v_2}	Sh_{v_3}
Δ^1	Case 1	−0.06667	−0.1	−0.26698	−0.16667	−0.33364	−0.36698	−0.43364	−0.06667	−0.1	−0.26698
	Case 2	−0.06667	0	−0.14925	−0.06667	−0.21591	−0.14925	−0.21591	−0.06667	0	−0.14925
	Case 3	−0.06667	0.1	−0.08896	0.03333	−0.15562	0.01104	−0.05562	−0.06667	0.1	−0.08896
	Case 4	0.06667	−0.1	0.05029	−0.03333	0.11696	−0.04971	0.01696	0.06667	−0.1	0.05029
	Case 5	0.06667	0	0.16694	0.06667	0.23360	0.16694	0.23360	0.06667	0	0.16694
	Case 6	0.06667	0.1	0.28499	0.16667	0.35166	0.38499	0.45166	0.06667	0.1	0.28499
Δ^2	Case 1	−0.22330	−0.20373	−0.43364	−0.41091	−0.43364	−0.43364	−0.43364	−0.10896	−0.09918	−0.22550
	Case 2	−0.22330	0.00558	−0.21591	−0.21038	−0.21591	−0.21591	−0.21591	−0.11043	0.00401	−0.10950
	Case 3	−0.22330	0.19815	−0.05562	−0.04861	−0.05562	−0.05562	−0.05562	−0.11556	0.09516	−0.03523
	Case 4	0.22330	−0.20373	0.01696	0.00344	0.01696	0.01696	0.01696	0.10896	−0.10455	0.01255
	Case 5	0.22330	0.00558	0.23360	0.22154	0.23360	0.23360	0.23360	0.11043	0.00157	0.12161
	Case 6	0.22330	0.19815	0.45166	0.44491	0.45166	0.45166	0.45166	0.11556	0.10298	0.23311
Δ^3	Case 1	−0.22330	−0.20373	−0.37444	−0.42703	−0.38419	−0.42761	−0.43364	−0.11529	−0.12721	−0.19115
	Case 2	−0.22330	0.00558	−0.22626	−0.21771	−0.21190	−0.21086	−0.21591	−0.11094	0.00402	−0.10899
	Case 3	−0.22330	0.19815	−0.13972	−0.02515	−0.12152	−0.05428	−0.05562	−0.10906	0.13528	−0.08184
	Case 4	0.22330	−0.20373	0.08585	0.01957	0.06372	0.01431	0.01696	0.10884	−0.12938	0.03749
	Case 5	0.22330	0.00558	0.25223	0.22888	0.23195	0.23036	0.23360	0.10935	−0.00030	0.12456
	Case 6	0.22330	0.19815	0.39557	0.42145	0.40539	0.44812	0.45166	0.11446	0.12325	0.21394

5   Conclusions and Further Research

In the field of machine learning, it is important to analyze the importance of features in a model. There are several approaches to this problem in the literature, including the analysis of the predictive capacity of some features about others [11–13]. In previous works, authors adapted existing definitions of feature importance based on the Shapley value [9] to a fuzzy measure context, which allows the consideration of the concepts of vagueness and capacity [5,8]. Our goal now is to propose a practical application of these measures that is useful for real-world cases, rather than being limited to a theoretical perspective. Our method is based on a simple idea and is designed to be easy to understand and apply, using well-known methods as a foundation.

The starting point of this paper is the proposal in [8] about the measurement of the predictive ability of features in a machine learning model. Inspired by previous works that used the Shapley value of a cooperative game to evaluate the predictive ability of a set of features over an unknown one, the authors proposed a solution based on the use of fuzzy measures, which allow them to represent the power of the elements of a machine learning model in a realistic way. They theoretically defined an intermediate solution that combines elements from two previous works and mixes the consideration of random values with the specification of exact values.

In this paper, we build upon a previously defined theoretical idea and focus on developing a realistic and practical application of it. We provide detailed implementation and execution instructions for applying the idea in a real-world setting. Our idea is based on the calculation of simple predictive models after a proper preprocessing of the features itself. We also include an illustrative example to explain step by step how to apply our methodology. As it can be seen in Sect. 4, a simple idea and process converge to a very interesting and helpful result.

Although it is a preliminary application, an evaluation based on benchmark is our next step, with the obtained results we can say that φ^3 improves in some aspects over other models from the literature. This new measure considers the interaction between any type of variables, something that the other definitions did not take into account. We are currently working in the development of a general model, able to consider any database with any set of features (in terms of type and amount). From our humble opinion, we think this methodology will be an added value step when analyzing complex machine learning models.

References

1. Alonso Moral, J., Castiello, C., Magdalena, L., Mencar, C.: Explainable Fuzzy Systems, Studies in Computational Intelligence, vol. 970. Springer, Cham (2021). https://doi.org/10.1007/978-3-030-71098-9
2. Beliakov, G., Gómez, D., James, S., Montero, J., Rodríguez, J.: Approaches to learning strictly-stable weights for data with missing values. Fuzzy Sets Syst. **325**, 97–113 (2017). https://doi.org/10.1016/j.fss.2017.02.003
3. Chu, C., Chan, D.: Feature selection using approximated high-order interaction components of the shapley value for boosted tree classifier. IEEE Access **8**, 112742–112750 (2020)
4. Cramer, J.: The origins of logistic regression, vol. 119. Tinbergen Institute (2002)
5. Gutiérrez, I., Santos, D., Castro, J., Gómez, D., Espínola, R., Guevara, J.: On measuring features importance in machine learning models in a two-dimensional representation scenario. In: 2022 IEEE International Conference on Fuzzy Systems (FUZZ-IEEE), pp. 1–9 (2022)
6. Nelder, J., Wedderburn, R.: Generalized linear model. J. R. Stat. Soc. Series A **135**(3), 370–384 (1972)
7. Okhrati, R., Lipani, A.: A multilinear sampling algorithm to estimate shapley values. Artif. Intell. 298 (2021)
8. Santos, D., Gutiérrez, I., Castro, J., Gómez, D., Guevara, J., Espínola, R.: Explanation of machine learning classification models with fuzzy measures: an approach to individual classification. In: Kahraman, C., Tolga, A.C., Cevik Onar, S., Cebi, S., Oztaysi, B., Sari, I.U. (eds.) INFUS 2022. LNNS, vol. 505, pp. 62–69. Springer, Cham (2022). https://doi.org/10.1007/978-3-031-09176-6_7
9. Shapley, L.: A value for $n-$person games. Ann. Math. Stud. **2**, 307–317 (1953)
10. Sugeno, M.: Fuzzy measures and fuzzy integrals: a survey. Fuzzy Automata Decis. Process **78** (1977)
11. Štrumbelj, E., Kononenko, I.: An efficient explanation of individual classifications using game theory. J. Mach. Learn. Res. **1**, 1–18 (2010)
12. Štrumbelj, E., Kononenko, I., Robnik Šikonja, M.: Explaining instance classifications with interactions of subsets of feature values. Data Knowl. Eng. **68**(10), 886–904 (2009)
13. Štrumbelj, E., Kononenko, I., Robnik Šikonja, M.: Explaining prediction models and individual predictions with feature contributions. Knowl. Inf. Syst. **41**(4), 647–665 (2014)

Exploring the Automatic Selection of Aggregation Methods in Group Recommendation

Raciel Yera[iD], Rosa M. Rodríguez[iD], and Luis Martínez[✉][iD]

Computer Science Department, University of Jaén, Jaén, Spain
martin@ujaen.es

Abstract. A recommender system is a software tool designed to support users to filter out useless options within a multitude of choices and provide them with the best possible ones. Group recommender systems have emerged as an important trend in recommendation since they recommend social items that are enjoyed by more than one individual, such as TV programs and travel packages, that are typically consumed in groups. Although algorithm selection in recommender systems is a research problem covered to some extent by the research community in which individuals' information is aggregated, this contribution is focused on the automatic selection of the most appropriate aggregation function in group recommendation. Specifically, a general framework that identifies group characteristics to be matched with the most appropriate aggregation function is presented. This approach is implemented by using a fuzzy decision tree classifier, in a content-based group recommendation approach. The development of an experimental protocol illustrates the advantage of the new proposal in relation to its corresponding baselines.

Keywords: group recommendation · fuzzy decision tree · preference aggregation

1 Introduction

The use of Recommender systems (RSs) is essential in online environments that concentrate on suggesting to users the items that most closely align with their preferences and requirements, given the overload of possible options in the product search space. Due to their functional principles, RSs have been extensively applied across a wide range of domains, including electronic commerce, e-learning, e-health, and e-tourism [14,20].

RSs have traditionally been employed to suggest items to individual users. Nonetheless, in recent times, different types of items, known as social items, that are often consumed by groups have emerged within recommendation contexts. Examples of such items include movies and tourist routes [7]. Recommending this kind of item entails an additional effort compared to individual recommendations, as preferences must be managed at both the individual and group level.

© The Author(s), under exclusive license to Springer Nature Switzerland AG 2023
S. Massanet et al. (Eds.): EUSFLAT 2023/AGOP 2023, LNCS 14069, pp. 149–160, 2023.
https://doi.org/10.1007/978-3-031-39965-7_13

This necessity has sparked the growth of Group Recommender Systems (GRSs) [7] as a separate research branch in the field of RSs.

Primarily, GRSs concentrate on processing the data linked to the members of a group. Such processing can be achieved by utilizing recommendation aggregation [8], where individual recommendations are initially calculated for each group member, and then combined via a recommendation aggregation method. Alternatively, a preference aggregation approach can also be employed [8], wherein a pseudo-user is generated that globally represents the group's preferences, and this pseudo-user profile is employed to compute the group recommendation. In both paradigms, aggregation is crucial in the recommendation process. Several authors such as De Pessemier et al. [8] have then incorporated different aggregation schemes such as Average (Avg), Least Misery (LM) or Most Pleasure (MP).

The current contribution concerns the automatic selection of the aggregation methods in group recommendation. The automatic selection of the most appropriate recommendation algorithm considering the nature of the data has been explored with some extent by the research community [6,17]. However, unlike to these research works focused on algorithm selection, our current contribution is focused on the selection of a suitable aggregator for the recommendation method. In addition, in contrast to the previous approaches centered on individuals, it is focused on group recommendation. Finally, we explore the use of fuzzy classification trees for managing the uncertainty associated to this scenario [21].

In this way, the current contribution aims at providing the following novelties:

- Developing a global methodology for performing an automatic selection of the aggregation function in group recommendation, based on the nature of the underlying group.
- The development of a working scenario for the application of the global methodology in a content-based group recommendation scenario.
- The execution of a experimental protocol for evaluating the impact of the proposed methodology in the working scenario.

The paper is structured as follows. Section 2 presents a background with an overview of the knowledge related to the proposal presentation, including group recommender systems, and automatic algorithm selection in recommender systems. Section 3 presents a general framework for automatic selection of aggregation functions in GRS. Section 4 illustrates a specific implementation of such framework, considering a fuzzy decision tree classifier and a content-based group recommendation approach. Section 5 evaluates such implementation, comparing it with associated baselines. Section 6 concludes the paper.

2   Preliminaries

The necessary background is provided here for the proposal discussion, focused on group recommendation and algorithm selection in RS.

2.1 Group Recommender Systems

RSs are AI-based systems used to provide users with the information that best fit their preferences and needs in overloaded search spaces [1]. The more spread taxonomy for identifying recommender systems, groups them into three main categories: 1) content-based recommender systems, 2) collaborative filtering-based recommender systems, and 3) hybrid recommender systems.

Herein, GRSs [8] have appeared as an emerging paradigm for scenarios in which recommended items are usually enjoyed by groups of users. Movies, touristic routes, or TV programs, are key examples of such kind of scenarios [14].

To perform item recommendations in such contexts by the content-based [16] or the collaborative filtering paradigm [8], the literature has identified two main recommendation techniques:

- *Rating aggregation:* The rating aggregation approach is based on the creation of a pseudo-user profile that represents the group's preferences [7,8]. This profile then receives the recommendation, using individual recommendation algorithms, as if it were a typical individual profile.
  To construct pseudo-user profiles, several aggregation strategies are commonly used, as described in [8]. Three of the most frequently used strategies include: 1) Average, which involves building the pseudo-user profile based on the average rating given by each member of the group for the corresponding item; 2) Least Misery, which involves building the pseudo-user profile based on the lowest rating given by any member of the group for the corresponding item; and 3) Most Pleasure, which involves building the pseudo-user profile based on the highest rating given by any member of the group for the corresponding item. These aggregation strategies are used to combine the ratings provided by individual members of the group to form a single profile that represents the group's preferences.
- *Recommendation aggregation:* This approach aggregates individual recommendations of each member of the group, to obtain the group's recommendation [8].
  In this scenario, the final stage of aggregation is based on the individual predictions made for each member of the group. There are three commonly used aggregation schemes for this purpose, as described in [8]. The first scheme is the Average approach, which involves calculating the group's prediction for a particular item as the average of the predicted ratings made by each individual user in the group for the same item. The second scheme is Least Misery, which determines the group's rating as the minimum of the predicted ratings made by each individual user. The third scheme is Most Pleasure, which determines the group's rating as the maximum of the predicted ratings made by each individual user. It is important to note that while these aggregation schemes are similar to the rating aggregation scheme, they have a different meaning in this context.

The current research work is focused on proposing a framework for facilitating the automatic selection of the aggregation measures, taking as base the content-based group recommender system approach (CB-GRS) [16]. In this way, while the previous works focused on content-based group recommendation [13,16] incorporate the aggregation approaches based on a pre-defined viewpoint, the aim of our proposal is the automatic identification of the most appropriate aggregation approach tailored to the current group features.

2.2   Automatic Algorithm Selection in Recommender Systems

The automatic selection of the most suitable recommendation algorithm, based on the nature of the data, has been explored by the research community to some extent.

In an initial study, *the problem of selecting the most appropriate Collaborative Filtering (CF)* algorithm was explored by representing the data as a graph rather than a rating matrix [12]. The study derived metafeatures that are dependent on the graph to choose among nearest neighbor (NN) algorithms. Additionally, the selection process utilized a rules-based model that leveraged domain-specific knowledge.

Subsequent studies investigated the rating matrix by utilizing statistical and/or information-theoretical metafeatures to choose between nearest neighbor (NN) and matrix factorization (MF) algorithms [2]. In these studies, the task was approached as a regression problem, with the objective of improving the Root Mean Square Error (RMSE) performance.

A different technique, which involved a decision tree regression model, was later proposed to address the problem [9]. This method examined the connection between user ratings and neighborhood data, as well as the anticipated error in the recommendations provided by a nearest neighbor (NN) algorithm. Unlike previous approaches, this method concentrated on characterizing metafeatures for individual users instead of the entire dataset.

Furthermore, Cunha et al. [6] conducted an empirical study on algorithm selection for collaborative filtering, considering statistical features of the RS dataset and their impact on the performance of different CF approaches. More recently, Polatidis et al. [17] proposed a methodology for recommender system algorithm selection using a machine learning classifier, which indicated that tree-based approaches such as Decision Tree and Random Forest perform well and provide accurate and precise results.

Unlike previous works, our proposal focuses on selecting a specific aggregation operator of the recommendation method, rather than the algorithm as a whole. Moreover, it is focused on group recommendation, rather than individual recommendation as in previous studies.

3   A General Framework for Automatic Selection of the Aggregation Measure

A methodology for performing the automatic selection of the aggregation functions in group recommendation is presented here. Figure 1 depicts this method-

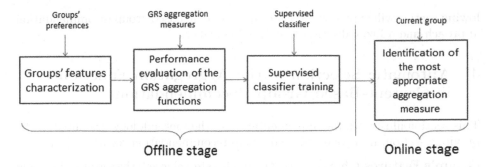

Fig. 1. General methodology for automatic selection of the aggregation function in GRS.

ology, which is composed of offline and online stages, and comprises the following steps:

1. **Group's features characterization:** It is focused on exploring groups' preferences values for extracting features that could be relevant for characterizing groups. Such features could be directly obtained from such values (e.g. rating averages, amount of ratings, the higher rating value), or depending of intermediate calculation such as the groups' member correlation values.

2. **Performance evaluation of the GRS aggregation functions:** It explores the performance of a selected GRS method, for each specific group and considering different aggregation functions. Here, the goal is to identify for each mentioned group, the aggregation function that performs best. As mentioned in Sect. 2, some of the aggregation measures usually considered in GRS are Average, Least Misery, and Most pleasure [8]. Here it is important to point out that in the next future it will be explored further power means and OWA operators at this stage [5]; however it is necessary to characterize better their behavior in the GRS context, before their use a part of an automatic selection strategy.

3. **Supervised classifier training:** It trains a supervised classifier for linking the features identified at Step 1, with the best aggregation functions identified at Step 2. This approach assummes the hypothesis that the performance of each aggregation function depends on the value of some group's features. Even though, these three stages have a low computational cost, they can be also executed in an offline phase, previously to the real-time recommendation generation process.

4. **Identification of the most appropriate aggregation function:** This step represents the online phase of the procedure. It is focused on the use of the classifier trained in the previous step, for identifying the most appropriate aggregation function that will be used for the active group, in the recommendation generation process.

The presented methodology can be implemented in different GRS and supervised classifiers scenarios, exploiting the benefits at each specific case. The following section will explore it, considering a content-based group recommendation approach and a fuzzy decision tree-based classifier.

4   Automatic Selection of the Aggregation Function in Content-Based Group Recommendation

This section illustrates the implementation of the methodology presented in the previous section, in a content-based group recommendation scenarios [16]

Group's Features Characterization: This step characterizes groups by using features with a clear semantic meaning, to facilitate the understanding of the classification procedure that will be used in the following steps.

The following group features are used:

- The minimum Pearson's correlation coefficient value between any pair of group members (M) (Eq. 1).

$$M(G) = min \ \ corr(u,v), \ \forall u,v \in G \tag{1}$$

- The amount of ratings linked to the group (A) (Eq. 2). $|R_u|$ is the number of preferences of user u.

$$A(G) = \sum_{u \in G} |R_u| \tag{2}$$

- The amount of items that have been co-evaluated by all the current group users (C) (Eq. 3).

$$C(G) = |I_c|, \ where \ I_c = \{i \ : \ \forall_{u \in G} r_{ui} \in R\} \tag{3}$$

- The rating average of the group (AV), formalized through Eqs. 4–5.

$$AV(G) = \frac{\sum_{r_{ui} \in R} r_{ui}}{|R|} \tag{4}$$

$$R = \cup_{u \in G} R_u \tag{5}$$

The selection of these features is based on previous work that raises the relevance of such information in the GRS context [4,8].

In the next step of the procedure, it will be assumed that the features are normalized into the interval [0, 1].

Performance Evaluation of the GRS Aggregation Functions: This step will use the hybrid CB-GRS approach recently presented by Pérez-Almaguer et al. [16], and that comprises the following components, not detailed here due to space reasons:

1. A content-based item and user profiling stage, facilitating the use of the approach in cold-start scenarios.

2. The use of a weighting scheme for calculating the user-item matching values.
3. The addition of a virtual user profile to the group for boosting clear tendencies across the member's preferences.
4. The possibility of using the average or minimum aggregation, for aggregating the individual predicted preferences into the group preferences.

This method is executed over the groups considered across the whole process, using both the average and minimum aggregation approaches (Step 4). Taking into account a performance metric (in this case Precision [10]), the aggregation approach that performed best is stored for each group, using it as the class in the next supervised classifier building.

Supervised Classifier Training. Here we introduce the procedure to build the fuzzy decision tree, using the group features identified before.

Here the group G is represented by a membership value to the fuzzy set D, which is initially 1 for all the groups. In this context, G is identified through the corresponding values of the four attributes considered previously ($A_i \in \{M, A, C, AV\}$), as well as the value of the corresponding class ($C_k \in \{Average, Minimum\}$). D^{C_k} is a fuzzy subset of D, being $\mu_{D^{C_k}}(G) = \mu_D(G)$ whether G class is C_k, and $\mu_{D^{C_k}}(G) = 0$ in other case. $|D^{C_k}|$ is the cardinality of the fuzzy set D^{C_k}. [19].

For sake of simplicity, the numerical attribute A_i is featured by using three triangular fuzzy sets *low*, *medium*, and *high* (Fig. 2). Table 1 illustrates the group profiling process according to this viewpoint.

Table 1. Group profiling using the fuzzy sets *low*, *medium*, and *high*.

g_1	$(\mu_{M,low}(g_1), \mu_{M,medium}(g_1), \mu_{M,high}(g_1), \mu_{A,low}(g_1), \mu_{A,medium}(g_1), \mu_{A,high}(g_1),$
	$\mu_{C,low}(g_1), \mu_{C,medium}(g_1), \mu_{C,high}(g_1), \mu_{AV,low}(g_1), \mu_{AV,medium}(g_1), \mu_{AV,high}(g_1))$
g_2	$(\mu_{M,low}(g_2), \mu_{M,medium}(g_2), \mu_{M,high}(g_2), \mu_{A,low}(g_2), \mu_{A,medium}(g_2), \mu_{A,high}(g_2),$
	$\mu_{C,low}(g_2), \mu_{C,medium}(g_2), \mu_{C,high}(g_2), \mu_{AV,low}(g_2), \mu_{AV,medium}(g_2), \mu_{AV,high}(g_2))$
...	

The approach for the fuzzy decision tree induction comprises then the subsequent steps:

1. Construct a root node, as a fuzzy set D having the groups with 1 as membership value.
2. If a candidate node t with a fuzzy set of data D verifies that $\frac{|D^{C_k}|}{|D|} \geq \theta_r$, being $C_k \in \{Average, Minimum\}$; or $|D| \leq \theta_n$; or that all the features have been already analyzed, then the current node is a leaf, and its weight for each C_k is $|D^{C_k}|$. θ_r and θ_n are thresholds which values are empirically determined.
3. Otherwise, the new decision node is constructed as follows, by selecting the attribute that maximizes the information gain $G(A_i, D)$. Therefore, for each attribute $A_i \in \{M, A, C, AV\}$ not considered before, calculate the information

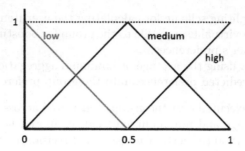

Fig. 2. Membership functions

gain $G(A_i, D)$ (Eqs. 6–9) and select the attribute A_{max} that maximizes it: $G(A_i, D) = I(D) - E(A_i, D)$ where,

$$I(D) = -\sum_{k=1}^{n}(p_k * log_2 p_k) \tag{6}$$

$$E(A_i, D) = \sum_{j=1}^{m}(p_{ij} * I(D_{A_i,j})) \tag{7}$$

$$p_k = \frac{|D^{C_k}|}{|D|} \tag{8}$$

$$p_{ij} = \frac{|D_{A_i,j}|}{\sum_{l=1}^{m}|D_{A_i,l}|} \tag{9}$$

Here $I(D)$ at Eq. (6) is the total entropy of certain dataset D, while $E(A_i, D)$ at Eq. (7) is the fuzzy classification entropy of the attribute A_i. p_k is the relative frequency of the class C_k in the dataset, and p_{ij} is the relative frequency of all objects within the branch associated to the corresponding linguistic label j and attribute A_i, into each class. $D_{A_i,j}$ is the fuzzy subset which membership is represented by the linguistic term $j \in \{low, medium, high\}$ linked to the group attribute $A_i \in \{M, A, C, AV\}$.

4. Once A_{max} is chosen, **the current D is divided into three fuzzy subsets** $D_{A_{max},low}, D_{A_{max},medium}$, **and** $D_{A_{max},high}$, each subset for each linguistic label that characterizes such attribute. The membership value of each group g to $D_{A_{max},j}$ ($j \in \{low, medium, high\}$), is then the product of the membership value of g to D, and the value $\mu_{A_{max},j}(g)$ associated to A_{max} in D.

5. Generate new nodes t_1, t_2, t_3 for fuzzy subsets $D_{A_{max},low}, D_{A_{max},medium}$, and $D_{A_{max},high}$, labelling with each corresponding linguistic term $j \in \{low, medium, high\}$, to each edge that connect them with D.

6. For each fuzzy subset $D_{A_{max},low}, D_{A_{max},medium}, D_{A_{max},high}$, repeat recursively this algorithm from step 2.

This induced fuzzy decision tree is used in the online phase of the proposal, for identifying the best aggregation function associated to a specific group.

Identification of the Most Appropriate Aggregation Function: The induced fuzzy decision tree is used for building classification rules, associated to each branch, with the format:

$$Rule\ R = \quad If\ A_{i1}\ is\ j1\ and\ ...\ and\ If\ A_{in}\ is\ jn\ then\ Class = C_k\ with\ weight\ W_k \tag{10}$$

Here $A_{i1} \in \{M, A, C, AV\}$, $j1 \in \{low, medium, high\}$, and $C_k \in \{Average, Minimum\}$. The rule weight W_k is the sum of the membership of all objects of class k, at the associated leaf.

For a group g, the classification is performed as:

1. Matching degree: The following equation obtains the activation degree of the left part of the rule, for the current group:

$$\mu_R(g) = T(\mu_{A_{i1,j1}}(g), \mu_{A_{i2,j2}}(g), ..., \mu_{A_{in,jn}}(g)) \tag{11}$$

where $\mu_{A_{i,j}}(g)$ is the membership degree of the value of the $A_i \in \{M, A, C, AV\}$ attribute for group g with the fuzzy set associated to the same attribute A_i and the linguistic term $j \in \{low, medium, high\}$. T is a T-norm [15].

2. Association degree: The association degree of g with each rule R, considering the class k is calculated as:

$$b_{Rk}(g) = T(\mu_R(g), W_k) \tag{12}$$

T is a T-norm [15].

3. Confidence degree: At last, the confidence degree of each class, for a specific group g, is reached through the aggregation of the association degrees linked to all the analyzed rules. This final calculation is used through the use of a T-conorm T^* [15]:.

$$conf_k(g) = T^*(b_{1k}(g), b_{2k}(g), b_{3k}(g), ..., b_{Rk}(g)) \tag{13}$$

The classification process assigns then to the group g, the class k that obtains the higher association degree.

5 Experiments

This section is focused on the evaluation of the approach discussed previously.

5.1 Experimental Protocol

This evaluation will use the following databases, previously employed in related works [16]:

- **Movielens 100K,** with 943 users, 1682 movies, and 100000 preferences in the interval $[1, 5]$ [11].

- **HetRec,** containing heterogeneous information, with 2213 users, 10197 movies, and 855K+ ratings. The ratings are also in the range $[1, 5]$ [3].

This evaluation process will be guided by the Precision metric (Eq. 14), frequently used in the RS evaluation [13]. For sake of space other evaluation criteria were not included here, but will be considered in the future research.

$$Precision = \frac{|recommended\ items \cap preferred\ items|}{|recommended\ items|} \quad (14)$$

Here it is used a preference threshold $r_{ui} \geq 4$, that is a usual criteria for this parameter [18].

We use the subsequent stages for performing the evaluation [4, 10]:

1. Train and test sets are created following the random procedure commonly used in previous works [4, 10].
2. We build user groups of different sizes, and the groups creation process is executed considering users with common preferences.
3. The method presented across the current paper is developed, for choosing the suitable aggregation scheme for each group.
4. For each group, we apply the CB-GRS approach proposed by Pérez-Almaguer et al. [16], using the selected aggregation function in each case.
5. The top n recommendation performance is measured with the Precision, by matching the recommendation output with the preferences in the test set. At last, the average precision is calculated for all the groups.

5.2 Results

Using the previous protocol, the proposal is evaluated with $\theta_r = 0.9$ and $\theta_n = 0.01$ as parameters. This means that the fuzzy decision tree induction is stopped if the relative frequency of a certain class exceeds 0.9, or if the current node cardinality is less than 0.01. The used group size were 4 (Movielens) and 3 (HetRec), and several sizes of the recommendation sets were considered (see Table 2).

This evaluation considers as baseline the hybrid proposal presented at [16], considering both Average and the Minimum approaches (avg and min, in Table 2), which are the state-of-art existing approaches that will be compared with the current proposal. In the context of the experimental steps presented in the previous section, Step 3 is omitted for the baseline evaluation. This step introduces the execution of the procedure discussed across this paper (dyn, in Table 2).

The results demonstrate that for both datasets, the proposal effectively identifies the optimal aggregation scheme to be used in a hybrid CB-GRS. This is evidenced by its significant outperformance of two baselines that consistently employ average and minimum aggregation.

Table 2. Performance of the proposal, in relation to previous works. Precision metric.

Dataset	top N	1	2	3	4	5	10
Movielens	avg (baseline)	0.5787	**0.5844**	0.5788	0.5684	0.5740	0.5681
Movielens	min (baseline)	0.5813	0.5725	0.5829	0.5841	0.5845	0.5754
Movielens	dyn	**0.6025**	0.5806	**0.5879**	**0.5844**	**0.5855**	**0.5760**
HetRec	avg (baseline)	0.5050	0.5075	0.5039	0.5000	0.5013	0.4957
HetRec	min (baseline)	0.5700	**0.5483**	0.5417	0.5358	0.5297	0.5080
HetRec	dyn	**0.5817**	**0.5483**	**0.5422**	**0.5363**	**0.5299**	**0.5083**

6   Conclusions

The automatic selection of the aggregation functions in GRS presented in this contribution has been initially implemented over the content-based group recommendation context, but it can also be applied to other group recommender systems. It aims to provide an automatic building of the recommendation system, which can lead to an improvement in recommendation accuracy. It is worthy to mention that most of the proposed approach can be executed offline, facilitating its deployment in recommender context with a high volume of information.

Our future work includes the exploration of new features as well as feature extraction algorithms to enrich the group profiling process. In addition, other classifiers such as deep learning-based, will be studied for the selection of the suitable aggregation approach.

Acknowledgements. This research is supported by the Research Project *ProyExcel_00257*, linked to the Andalucía Excellence Research Program. R.Yera is also supported by the Grants for the Re-qualification of the Spanish University System for 2021–2023 in the María Zambrano modality (UJAR10MZ).

References

1. Adomavicius, G., Tuzhilin, A.: Toward the next generation of recommender systems: a survey of the state-of-the-art and possible extensions. IEEE Trans. Knowl. Data Eng. **17**(6), 734–749 (2005)
2. Adomavicius, G., Zhang, J.: Impact of data characteristics on recommender systems performance. ACM Trans. Manage. Inf. Syst. (TMIS) **3**(1), 1–17 (2012)
3. Cantador, I., Brusilovsky, P., Kuflik, T.: Second workshop on information heterogeneity and fusion in recommender systems (HetRec 2011). In: Proceedings of the 5th ACM Conference on Recommender systems, RecSys 2011, ACM, New York, NY, USA (2011)
4. Castro, J., Yera, R., Martínez, L.: An empirical study of natural noise management in group recommendation systems. Decis. Support Syst. **94**, 1–11 (2017)

5. Chen, Z.S., Yang, L.L., Rodríguez, R.M., Xiong, S.H., Chin, K.S., Martínez, L.: Power-average-operator-based hybrid multiattribute online product recommendation model for consumer decision-making. Int. J. Intell. Syst. **36**(6), 2572–2617 (2021)
6. Cunha, T., Soares, C., de Carvalho, A.C.: Metalearning and recommender systems: a literature review and empirical study on the algorithm selection problem for collaborative filtering. Inf. Sci. **423**, 128–144 (2018)
7. Dara, S., Chowdary, C.R., Kumar, C.: A survey on group recommender systems. J. Intell. Inf. Syst. **54**(2), 271–295 (2020)
8. De Pessemier, T., Dooms, S., Martens, L.: Comparison of group recommendation algorithms. Multimed. Tools Appl. **72**, 2497–2541 (2014)
9. Griffith, J., O'Riordan, C., Sorensen, H.: Investigations into user rating information and predictive accuracy in a collaborative filtering domain. In: Proceedings of the 27th Annual ACM Symposium on Applied Computing, pp. 937–942 (2012)
10. Gunawardana, A., Shani, G.: A survey of accuracy evaluation metrics of recommendation tasks. J. Mach. Learn. Res. **10**, 2935–2962 (2009)
11. Harper, F.M., Konstan, J.A.: The Movielens datasets: history and context. ACM Trans. Interact. Intell. Syst. **5**(4), 19:1-19:19 (2015)
12. Huang, Z., Zeng, D.D.: Why does collaborative filtering work? transaction-based recommendation model validation and selection by analyzing bipartite random graphs. INFORMS J. Comput. **23**(1), 138–152 (2011)
13. Kaššák, O., Kompan, M., Bieliková, M.: Personalized hybrid recommendation for group of users: top-n multimedia recommender. Inf. Process. Manage. **52**(3), 459–477 (2016)
14. Lu, J., Wu, D., Mao, M., Wang, W., Zhang, G.: Recommender system application developments: a survey. Decis. Support Syst. **74**, 12–32 (2015)
15. Pedrycz, W.: Fuzzy Control and Fuzzy Systems. Research Studies Press Ltd. (1993)
16. Pérez-Almaguer, Y., Yera, R., Alzahrani, A.A., Martínez, L.: Content-based group recommender systems: a general taxonomy and further improvements. Expert Syst. Appl. **184**, 115444 (2021)
17. Polatidis, N., Kapetanakis, S., Pimenidis, E.: Recommender systems algorithm selection using machine learning. In: Iliadis, L., Macintyre, J., Jayne, C., Pimenidis, E. (eds.) EANN 2021. PINNS, vol. 3, pp. 477–487. Springer, Cham (2021). https://doi.org/10.1007/978-3-030-80568-5_39
18. Ricci, F., Rokach, L., Shapira, B.: Recommender systems: introduction and challenges. In: Ricci, F., Rokach, L., Shapira, B. (eds.) Recommender Systems Handbook, pp. 1–34. Springer, Boston, MA (2015). https://doi.org/10.1007/978-1-4899-7637-6_1
19. Umanol, M., et al.: Fuzzy decision trees by fuzzy ID3 algorithm and its application to diagnosis systems. In: Proceedings of 1994 IEEE 3rd International Fuzzy Systems Conference, pp. 2113–2118. IEEE (1994)
20. Yera, R., Alzahrani, A.A., Martinez, L.: Exploring post-hoc agnostic models for explainable cooking recipe recommendations. Knowl.-Based Syst. **251**, 109216 (2022)
21. Yera, R., Martinez, L.: Fuzzy tools in recommender systems: a survey. Int. J. Comput. Intell. Syst. **10**(1), 776 (2017)

Splitting Rules for Monotone Fuzzy Decision Trees

Christophe Marsala[1]([✉]) and Davide Petturiti[2]

[1] LIP6, Sorbonne Université CNRS, Paris, France
christophe.marsala@lip6.fr
[2] Dip. Economia, Università degli Studi di Perugia, Perugia, Italy
davide.petturiti@unipg.it

Abstract. This paper considers the problem of building monotone fuzzy decision trees when the attributes and the labeling function are in the form of partitions (in Ruspini's sense) of totally ordered labels. We define a fuzzy version of Shannon and Gini rank discrimination measures, based on a definition of fuzzy dominance, to be used in the splitting phase of a fuzzy decision tree inductive construction algorithm. These extensions generalize the rank discrimination measures introduced in previous work. Afterwards, we introduce a new algorithm to build a fuzzy decision tree enforcing monotonicity and we present an experimental analysis on an artificial data set.

Keywords: Monotone fuzzy decision tree · Fuzzy rank discrimination measure · Totally ordered fuzzy partitions

1 Introduction

Starting from the seminal paper [1], monotone classification has attracted increasing attention (see, e.g., [2,3,7,18]) due to its capacity of modeling semantic concepts like preference, priority and importance. In turn, the possibility of incorporating linguistic or vague information, has naturally led to fuzzy monotone classification (see, e.g., [19,22,23]).

In this paper, we focus on fuzzy decision trees [11,17,24] in which we aim at enforcing monotonicity, relying on a set of training examples. We consider a learning problem where the data set consists of a finite number of objects described by m attributes a_j's, each referring to a totally ordered set of fuzzy labels $(X_j, \leq)$, together with a labeling function λ that refers to a totally ordered set of fuzzy classes $(C, \leq)$. We further assume that each attribute and the labeling function are fuzzy partitions in Ruspini's sense [20]. Then, our goal is to build a fuzzy decision tree $\mathcal{T}$ which encodes a labeling function $\lambda' : X_1 \times \cdots \times X_m \to C$, that maps every m-tuple of attribute fuzzy labels to a fuzzy class and further satisfies monotonicity, that is

$$(x_1, \ldots, x_m) \leq (y_1, \ldots, y_m) \implies \lambda'(x_1, \ldots, x_m) \leq \lambda'(y_1, \ldots, y_m), \quad (1)$$

S. Massanet et al. (Eds.): EUSFLAT 2023/AGOP 2023, LNCS 14069, pp. 161–173, 2023.
https://doi.org/10.1007/978-3-031-39965-7_14

where $(x_1, \ldots, x_m) \leq (y_1, \ldots, y_m)$ stands for $x_j \leq y_j$, for $j = 1, \ldots, m$.

In general, enforcing global monotonicity requires a pre-processing of the input data sets, so as to remove possible inconsistencies. Here, we face the problem by adopting a greedy approach: at each step of the building process we choose the attribute a_j "enforcing the most" a local form of monotonicity. This approach has been already exploited in previous work [12] in case of crisp data and relies on the introduction of *rank discrimination measures* (see also [8,9]) that are inspired by classical Shannon and Gini measures. In this paper, we introduce fuzzy versions of measures introduced in [12], by relaying on a suitable additive fuzzy preference structure without incomparability [4,5,21], used to model fuzzy dominant sets. We also propose an algorithm to build a monotone fuzzy decision tree by relying on the introduced *fuzzy rank discrimination measures* and we perform its analysis on an artificial data set.

The paper is structured as follows. In Sect. 2, we define Shannon and Gini fuzzy rank discrimination measures. Section 3 presents a greedy construction algorithm parameterized by the introduced fuzzy rank discrimination measures and shows an experimental analysis on an artificial data set. Finally, Sect. 4 gathers conclusions and future perspectives.

2   Fuzzy Rank Discrimination Measures

In this section, after a recall on the background, fuzzy rank discrimination measures are presented. First of all, let us introduce the following notations:

- $\Omega = \{\omega_1, \ldots, \omega_n\}$, a finite set of **objects**;
- $\mathcal{A} = \{a_1, \ldots, a_m\}$, a finite set of **fuzzy attributes with totally ordered range of fuzzy labels**, where a_j refers to the set of labels $X_j = \{x_{j_1}, \ldots, x_{j_{t_j}}\}$ and $(X_j, \leq_{X_j})$ is totally ordered;
- λ, a **fuzzy labelling function** referring to the set of **fuzzy classes** $C = \{c_1, \ldots, c_k\}$ with $(C, \leq_C)$ totally ordered.

To avoid cumbersome notation, in what follows we suppress the subscript X_j and C from the total orders $\leq_{X_j}$ and $\leq_C$, relying on the context to clarify which relation we are referring to.

The case of crisp a_j and λ has been considered in [12]: in this case, a_j and λ correspond to (crisp) partitions of Ω:

$$a_j = \{\{a_j = x_{j_s}\} = \{\omega_h \in \Omega \ : \ a_j(\omega_h) = x_{j_s}\} \mid x_{j_s} \in X_j\}$$
$$= \{\chi_{\{a_j = x_{j_s}\}} : \Omega \to \{0,1\} \mid x_{j_s} \in X_j\},$$
$$\lambda = \{\{\lambda = c_q\} = \{\omega_h \in \Omega \ : \ \lambda(\omega_h) = c_q\} \mid c_q \in C\}$$
$$= \{\chi_{\{\lambda = c_q\}} : \Omega \to \{0,1\} \mid c_q \in C\},$$

thus, they induce a (crisp) total preorder on Ω due to $(X_j, \leq)$ and $(C, \leq)$:

$$R_{a_j}(\omega_i, \omega_h) = \begin{cases} 1 \text{ if } a_j(\omega_i) \leq a_j(\omega_h), \\ 0 \text{ otherwise.} \end{cases} \qquad R_\lambda(\omega_i, \omega_h) = \begin{cases} 1 \text{ if } \lambda(\omega_i) \leq \lambda(\omega_h), \\ 0 \text{ otherwise.} \end{cases}$$

The **dominant sets** of ω_i generated by a_j or λ have characteristic functions

$$\chi_{[\omega_i]^{\leq}_{a_j}}(\cdot) = R_{a_j}(\omega_i, \cdot) \qquad \chi_{[\omega_i]^{\leq}_\lambda}(\cdot) = R_\lambda(\omega_i, \cdot).$$

Therefore, $\mathcal{A} \cup \{\lambda\}$ can be regarded as a collection of (crisp) partitions. Moreover, R_{a_j} and R_λ form the preference structures $(P_{a_j}, I_{a_j}, R_{a_j})$ and $(P_\lambda, I_\lambda, R_\lambda)$, where P_{a_j}, P_λ are strict preference relations, I_{a_j}, I_λ are indifference relations, and R_{a_j}, R_λ are weak preference relations.

In this paper, for the fuzzy case, we assume that both a_j and λ are fuzzy partitions (in the Ruspini's sense [20]) of Ω:

$$a_j = \left\{ \mu_{\{a_j = x_{j_s}\}} : \Omega \to [0,1] \;\middle|\; x_{j_s} \in X_j, \sum_{x_{j_s} \in X_j} \mu_{\{a_j = x_{j_s}\}}(\omega_i) = 1, \omega_i \in \Omega \right\},$$

$$\lambda = \left\{ \mu_{\{\lambda = c_q\}} : \Omega \to [0,1] \;\middle|\; c_q \in C, \sum_{c_q \in C} \mu_{\{\lambda = c_q\}}(\omega_i) = 1, \omega_i \in \Omega \right\}.$$

Therefore, in the fuzzy case, $\mathcal{A} \cup \{\lambda\}$ can be regarded as a collection of Ruspini's fuzzy partitions.

Example 1. Let $\Omega = \{\omega_1, \omega_2, \omega_3\}$ be three cars evaluated according to the fuzzy attributes and labeling function below, where orders express preferences:

- $a_1 = $ comfort with $X_1 = \{$low, medium, high$\}$ ordered as low $<$ medium $<$ high,
- $a_2 = $ price with $X_2 = \{$cheap, expensive$\}$ ordered as expensive $<$ cheap,
- $\lambda = $ appreciation with $C = \{$low, high$\}$ ordered as low $<$ high.

Ω	comfort			price		appreciation	
	low	medium	high	cheap	expensive	low	high
ω_1	0.3	0.1	0.6	0.6	0.4	0.7	0.3
ω_2	0.8	0.1	0.1	0.3	0.7	0.1	0.9
ω_3	0.2	0.2	0.6	0.7	0.3	0.2	0.8

◆

The totally ordered sets $(X_j, \leq)$ and $(C, \leq)$ induce a total order on the fuzzy labels $\{a_j = x_{j_s}\}$ and $\{\lambda = c_q\}$ that we wish to "transport" somehow to Ω: the best would be to obtain a fuzzy total T-preorder on Ω, where T is a t-norm [10]. In other terms, we search for a fuzzy counterpart of the relations R_{a_j} and R_λ defined in the non-fuzzy (crisp) case. At this aim we recall the definition of fuzzy total T-preorder given in [6].

Definition 1. *A function* $R : \Omega \times \Omega \to [0,1]$ *is a* **fuzzy total T-preorder** *for a t-norm T if it satisfies:*

(1) **(strong completeness)** $\max\{R(\omega_i, \omega_h), R(\omega_h, \omega_i)\} = 1$, *for all* $\omega_i, \omega_h \in \Omega$;
(2) **(T-transitivity)** $R(\omega_i, \omega_h) \geq T(R(\omega_i, \omega_l), R(\omega_l, \omega_h))$, *for all* $\omega_i, \omega_l, \omega_h \in \Omega$.

A fuzzy preference structure is generally a weaker notion than a fuzzy total T-preorder. To have "common properties" analogous to the crisp case, a φ-transformation of the Łukasiewicz t-norm T_L (whose dual t-conorm is S_L) must be used. Below we report the definition of additive fuzzy preference structure with no incomparability [5] (see also [4,21]), where $\cap_L$ and $\cup_L$ refer to T_L and S_L, the superscript t denotes the transpose relation and co the complement.

Definition 2. *A triple (P, I, R) of functions on Ω ranging in $[0, 1]$ are an **additive fuzzy preference structure with no incomparability** if:*

(1) P is irreflexive and I is reflexive;
(2) P is T_L-asymmetric and I is symmetric;
(3) $P \cap_L I = \emptyset$;
(4) $co(P \cup_L I) = P^t$;
(5) $R = P \cup_L I$, i.e., $R(\omega_i, \omega_h) = S_L(P(\omega_i, \omega_h), I(\omega_i, \omega_h)) = P(\omega_i, \omega_h) + I(\omega_i, \omega_h)$.

Inspired to fuzzy preference structures built in the comparison of independent random variables (see [13–15]), we can provide the following probabilistic interpretation of our setup. For a fixed $a_j \in \mathcal{A}$, for each $\omega_i \in \Omega$, we set

$$p_{i,s}^j = \mu_{\{a_j = x_{j_s}\}}(\omega_i), \quad s = 1, \ldots, t_j$$

then we have

$$\begin{array}{c|cccc} a_j(\omega_i) & x_{j_1} & x_{j_2} & \cdots & x_{t_j} \\ \hline p_{i,s}^j & p_{i,1}^j & p_{i,2}^j & \cdots & p_{i,t_j}^j \end{array} \qquad \begin{cases} p_{i,s}^j \geq 0, & s = 1, \ldots, t_j, \\ \displaystyle\sum_{s=1}^{t_j} p_{i,s}^j = 1. \end{cases}$$

The evaluation $a_j(\omega_i)$ can be interpreted as a discrete random variable with assigned probability distribution.

Assumption 1. *Since objects in Ω are assumed not to influence each other, then $\{a_j(\omega_1), \ldots, a_j(\omega_n)\}$ can be considered as stochastically independent random variables.*

The above probabilistic interpretation allows us to refer to a fuzzy stochastic preference [5]:

Fuzzy strict stochastic preference relation:

$$\tilde{P}_{a_j}(\omega_i, \omega_h) = \max\{\text{Prob}(a_j(\omega_i) < a_j(\omega_h)) - \text{Prob}(a_j(\omega_i) > a_j(\omega_h)), 0\},$$

Fuzzy stochastic indifference relation:

$$\tilde{I}_{a_j}(\omega_i, \omega_h) = 1 - |\text{Prob}(a_j(\omega_i) < a_j(\omega_h)) - \text{Prob}(a_j(\omega_i) > a_j(\omega_h))|,$$

Fuzzy weak stochastic preference relation:

$$\tilde{R}_{a_j}(\omega_i, \omega_h) = S_L(\tilde{P}_{a_j}(\omega_i, \omega_h), \tilde{I}_{a_j}(\omega_i, \omega_h)) = \tilde{P}_{a_j}(\omega_i, \omega_h) + \tilde{I}_{a_j}(\omega_i, \omega_h),$$

where

$$\mathrm{Prob}(a_j(\omega_i) < a_j(\omega_h)) = \begin{cases} \sum_{s<q} p^j_{i,s} p^j_{h,q} & i \neq h, \\ 0 & i = h, \end{cases}$$

$$\mathrm{Prob}(a_j(\omega_i) > a_j(\omega_h)) = \begin{cases} \sum_{s>q} p^j_{i,s} p^j_{h,q} & i \neq h, \\ 0 & i = h. \end{cases}$$

We now consider the properties of $(\tilde{P}_{a_j}, \tilde{I}_{a_j}, \tilde{R}_{a_j})$. The triple $(\tilde{P}_{a_j}, \tilde{I}_{a_j}, \tilde{R}_{a_j})$ is an **additive fuzzy preference structure with no incomparability** satisfying the following properties

- **(generalization)** if a_j is a crisp partition then $\tilde{R}_{a_j} = R_{a_j}$,
- **(reflexivity)** $\tilde{R}_{a_j}(\omega_i, \omega_i) = 1$, for all $\omega_i \in \Omega$,
- **(strong completeness)** $\max\{\tilde{R}_{a_j}(\omega_i, \omega_h), \tilde{R}_{a_j}(\omega_h, \omega_i)\} = 1$ for all $\omega_i, \omega_h \in \Omega$.

Therefore, we can define the **fuzzy dominant set generated by** a_j as

$$\mu_{\widetilde{[\omega_i]\lesssim_{a_j}}}(\cdot) = \tilde{R}_{a_j}(\omega_i, \cdot). \tag{2}$$

A natural question concerns the T-transitivity of $\tilde{R}_{a_j}$. The following example shows that generally $\tilde{R}_{a_j}$ is not guaranteed to be T-transitive for a t-norm T, even though it may be the case.

Example 2. Take $\mathcal{A} = \{a_1, a_2\}$ with $X_1 = X_2 = \{1, 2, 3\}$ with the natural order of numbers, and $\Omega = \{\omega_1, \omega_2, \omega_3, \omega_4\}$.

	$\{a_1 = 1\}$	$\{a_1 = 2\}$	$\{a_1 = 3\}$
ω_1	0.3	0.5	0.2
ω_2	0.2	0.4	0.4
ω_3	0.1	0.8	0.1
ω_4	0.7	0.2	0.1

$\tilde{R}_{a_1}$	ω_1	ω_2	ω_3	ω_4
ω_1	1	1	1	0.61
ω_2	0.78	1	0.82	0.46
ω_3	0.91	1	1	0.46
ω_4	1	1	1	1

It follows that $\tilde{R}_{a_1}$ is not T_L-transitive and so it is not T-transitive for any Frank t-norm T (see [10]):

$$0.46 = \tilde{R}_{a_1}(\omega_3, \omega_4) < T_L(\tilde{R}_{a_1}(\omega_3, \omega_1), \tilde{R}_{a_1}(\omega_1, \omega_4))$$
$$= \max\{0.91 + 0.61 - 1, 0\} = 0.52.$$

	$\{a_2 = 1\}$	$\{a_2 = 2\}$	$\{a_2 = 3\}$
ω_1	0.3	0.3	0.4
ω_2	0.3	0.3	0.4
ω_3	0.4	0.3	0.3
ω_4	0.4	0.3	0.3

$\tilde{R}_{a_2}$	ω_1	ω_2	ω_3	ω_4
ω_1	1	1	0.87	0.87
ω_2	1	1	0.87	0.87
ω_3	1	1	1	1
ω_4	1	1	1	1

On the other hand, we get that $\tilde{R}_{a_2}$ is T_M-transitive and so it is T-transitive for any t-norm T.   ◆

Analogously, we can define the **fuzzy dominant set generated by** λ as

$$\mu_{\widetilde{[\omega_i]_\lambda^\leq}}(\cdot) = \tilde{R}_\lambda(\omega_i, \cdot). \tag{3}$$

The previous discussion allows us to fuzzify the rank discrimination measures H_S^* and H_G^* introduced in [12] (see also [8,9]). To this purpose:

- we fix the Łukasiewicz De Morgan triple $(T_L, S_L, 1 - x)$ for uniformity, to compute fuzzy set-theoretic operations;
- we use the sigma-count to compute fuzzy cardinalities.

Definition 3. *Given a_j and λ we define*

Fuzzy rank Shannon discrimination measure:

$$\tilde{H}_S^*(\lambda|a_j) = \sum_{i=1}^{|\Omega|} \frac{1}{|\Omega|} \left[-\log_2 \left(\frac{|\widetilde{[\omega_i]_\lambda^\leq \cap_L [\omega_i]_{a_j}^\leq}|}{|\widetilde{[\omega_i]_{a_j}^\leq}|} \right) \right],$$

Fuzzy rank Gini discrimination measure:

$$\tilde{H}_G^*(\lambda|a_j) = \sum_{i=1}^{|\Omega|} \frac{1}{|\Omega|} \left[1 - \left(\frac{|\widetilde{[\omega_i]_\lambda^\leq \cap_L [\omega_i]_{a_j}^\leq}|}{|\widetilde{[\omega_i]_{a_j}^\leq}|} \right) \right].$$

The following example shows the computation of measures $\tilde{H}_S^*$ and $\tilde{H}_G^*$.

Example 3. Let $\mathcal{A} = \{a_1\}$ with $X_1 = \{1, 2, 3\}$ and $C = \{1, 2\}$ with the usual order of numbers and consider the following evaluations

	$\{a_1 = 1\}$	$\{a_1 = 2\}$	$\{a_1 = 3\}$	$\{\lambda = 1\}$	$\{\lambda = 2\}$
ω_1	0.7	0.3	0	0.5	0.5
ω_2	0.5	0.1	0.4	0.2	0.8
ω_3	0.8	0.1	0.1	0.1	0.9
ω_4	0.6	0.3	0.1	1	0

$\tilde{R}_{a_1}$	ω_1	ω_2	ω_3	ω_4
ω_1	1	1	0.93	1
ω_2	0.68	1	0.67	0.79
ω_3	1	1	1	1
ω_4	0.87	1	0.82	1

$\tilde{R}_\lambda$	ω_1	ω_2	ω_3	ω_4
ω_1	1	1	1	0.5
ω_2	0.7	1	1	0.2
ω_3	0.6	0.9	1	0.1
ω_4	1	1	1	1

Both $\tilde{R}_{a_1}$ and $\tilde{R}_\lambda$ are T_L-transitive and it holds that

$$\tilde{H}_S^*(\lambda|a_1) = 0.3582 \quad \tilde{H}_G^*(\lambda|a_1) = 0.2060.$$

◆

3 Enforcing Monotonicity in Decision Tree Construction

In order to evaluate the introduced fuzzy rank discrimination measures, we propose the following algorithm for building a fuzzy decision tree, in which monotonicity between attributes and class labels is enforced in a greedy way. The algorithm is parameterized by the choice of $\tilde{H}^* \in \{\tilde{H}_S^*, \tilde{H}_G^*\}$. Since we deal with a recursive algorithm, we keep notation simple by referring to Ω and $\mathcal{A}$ as those available at the current stage of recursion.

Starting from the original Ω and $\mathcal{A}$, that are assumed not to be empty, the algorithm proceeds recursively, until a leaf is created with a label in C. If we are in a stage of the recursion with set of objects Ω and set of attributes $\mathcal{A}$, we first check if a leaf can be created. The creation of a leaf is justified when a sufficient degree of uniformity on the class label is observed in the current Ω. To choose the label in C, we compute the local threshold for class labels

$$\alpha^C = \max_{c_q \in C} \sum_{\omega \in \Omega} \frac{1}{|\Omega|} \mu_{\{\lambda = c_q\}}(\omega), \qquad (4)$$

which corresponds to the highest average membership value to a class label, of objects in the current Ω.

Next, for each $c_q \in C$, we compute the percentage of objects in Ω whose membership is greater than or equal to α^C as

$$f^{c_q} = \frac{|\{\omega \in \Omega : \mu_{\{\lambda = c_q\}}(\omega) \geq \alpha^C\}|}{|\Omega|}. \qquad (5)$$

We avoid over-fitting by creating a leaf in case there is at least one class label c_q such that $f^{c_q} > \rho$, where ρ is a fixed hyper-parameter chosen from the beginning of the procedure. We choose the class label c_q with maximum percentage f^{c_q}. Possible ties are broken by choosing the greatest class label, according to the total order of C. If no leaf is created in the current stage, then we need to split the current Ω by choosing an element of the current $\mathcal{A}$. For that, we proceed by computing $\tilde{H}^*(\lambda|a)$, for all $a \in \mathcal{A}$, and by solving

$$a^* = \arg\min_{a \in \mathcal{A}} \tilde{H}^*(\lambda|a), \qquad (6)$$

where ties are broken choosing randomly. Once the splitting attribute a^* has been chosen, a branch is created for every element of the corresponding set of labels X^*. Moreover, the following splitting threshold is computed

$$\alpha^{a^*} = \max_{x \in X^*} \sum_{\omega \in \Omega} \frac{1}{|\Omega|} \mu_{\{a^* = x\}}(\omega), \qquad (7)$$

which, again, corresponds to the highest average membership value to an attribute label, of objects in the current Ω.

Next, for every $x \in X^*$, we form the set

$$\Omega^x = \{\omega \in \Omega : \mu_{\{a^* = x\}}(\omega) \geq \alpha^{a^*}\}, \qquad (8)$$

and repeat the procedure recursively on Ω^x and $\mathcal{A}\backslash\{a^*\}$. We point out that for different $x, x' \in X^*$ it may happen $\Omega^x \cap \Omega^{x'} \neq \emptyset$.

We notice that the overlapping of splitting sets can affect labeling when $|\mathcal{A}| = 1$ and the creation of a leaf at current stage is not optimal. Indeed, in this case the only choice for the splitting attribute is the unique element a^* of $\mathcal{A}$, so, the computation of (6) can be skipped. Therefore, a leaf is directly created for each value of X^* and labeling is carried out, again maximizing the f^{c_q}'s. Nevertheless, this could lead to some non-monotonicities due to objects appearing in more than one splitting set. Hence, once the labeling of leaves is over, a possible relabeling is applied to enforce monotonicity in the generated leaves, by changing those leaves with lower value of f^{c_q} first. If the generated sub-tree has leaves with all equal labels, then it is replaced by a single leaf with the same label.

Algorithm 1 reports the pseudo-code of the procedure described above.

Algorithm 1. Construction of a fuzzy decision tree enforcing monotonicity

---

  ▷ *input:* $\mathcal{A}, \lambda, \Omega$, data set
  ▷ *input:* ρ, over-fitting hyper-parameter
  ▷ *output:* $\mathcal{T}$, tree of fuzzy labels

Compute the threshold α^C as in (4)
Compute f^{c_q} as in (5), for all $c_q \in C$
if there is $c_q \in C$ such that $f^{c_q} \geq \rho$ **then**
    Create a leaf in $\mathcal{T}$ choosing $c_q \in C$ with maximum f^{c_q}, possibly breaking ties
else if $|\mathcal{A}| = 1$ **then**
    for x in X^* **do**
        Create a leaf in $\mathcal{T}$ for the branch x
        Compute Ω^x as in (8)
        Choose $c_q \in C$ with maximum f^{c_q} in Ω^x, possibly breaking ties
    end for
    if there are non-monotone leaves **then** relabel those with lower f^{c_q} first
    if all leaves have the same label **then** replace the sub-tree with a single leaf
else
    Determine the splitting attribute a^* as in (6), possibly breaking ties
    for x in X^* **do**
        Compute Ω^x as in (8)
        Call **Algorithm 1** on $\mathcal{A}\backslash\{a^*\}, \lambda, \Omega^x$, and ρ
    end for
end if

We test Algorithm 1 by considering an artificial data set described by attributes in the set $\mathcal{A} = \{a_1, a_2, a_3\}$ and a labeling function λ. We assume that the a_j's and λ range in the interval $[0, 10]$ and each is fuzzyfied using the set of ordered labels $X_j = C = \{\texttt{low}, \texttt{medium}, \texttt{high}\}$ that correspond to the fuzzy partition (in Ruspini's sense) reported in Fig. 1.

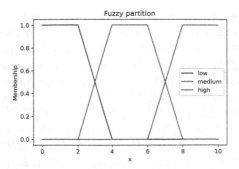

Fig. 1. Fuzzy partition {low, medium, high}.

We derive the description of $n = 1000$ objects by generating three independent random variables $A_j \sim \mathbf{Unif}([0, 10])$ and setting $\Lambda = \max\left\{A_1, \frac{A_2^2}{10}, \frac{A_3^3}{100}\right\}$, so as to range in $[0, 10]$ as well. Next, the realizations of each A_j and Λ are fuzzyfied according to the fuzzy partition reported in Fig. 1, so each object $\omega_i \in \Omega$ gives rise to a collection of probability distributions on the label set $X_j = C$. Table 1 shows the fuzzy partitions (2 decimal rounding) of Ω for the first 3 objects. We further fix the over-fitting parameter to $\rho = 70\%$.

Table 1. Fuzzy partitions for the first three objects.

	a_1			a_2			a_3			λ		
Ω	low	medium	high	low	medium	high	low	medium	high	low	medium	high
ω_1	0	0.82	0.18	0.65	0.35	0	1	0	0	0	0.82	0.18
ω_2	1	0	0	0	0	1	0	0	1	0	0.69	0.31
ω_3	0	0.97	0.03	0	0.35	0.65	0	1	0	0	0.97	0.03
$\vdots$	$\vdots$			$\vdots$			$\vdots$			$\vdots$		

Below, we show the explicit execution of Algorithm 1 on the generated data set. To keep track of the evolution in the recursion, we add a subscript index starting at 0 to all quantities, related to the current level in the tree.

Therefore, we initially set $\Omega_0 := \Omega$ and $\mathcal{A}_0 := \mathcal{A}$, where $|\Omega_0| = 1000$. The terminal condition is not met since $f_0^{\text{low}} = 0.1600$, $f_0^{\text{medium}} = 0.4660$, $f_0^{\text{high}} = 0.4310$. Moreover, being $|\mathcal{A}_0| > 1$, since $H_S^*(\lambda|a_1) = 0.2475$, $H_S^*(\lambda|a_2) = 0.4547$, $H_S^*(\lambda|a_3) = 0.6274$, and $H_G^*(\lambda|a_1) = 0.1427$, $H_G^*(\lambda|a_2) = 0.2419$, $H_G^*(\lambda|a_3) = 0.3131$, both measures agree in selecting a_1 for splitting. Now, the set of objects Ω_0 is split in three subsets corresponding to labels in X_1. The sets Ω_1^{low}, Ω_1^{medium} and Ω_1^{high} are not disjoint since $|\Omega_1^{\text{low}} \cap \Omega_1^{\text{medium}}| = 42$, $|\Omega_1^{\text{low}} \cap \Omega_1^{\text{high}}| = 0$, $|\Omega_1^{\text{medium}} \cap \Omega_1^{\text{high}}| = 42$.

We focus on Ω_1^{low} with $\mathcal{A}_1^{\text{low}} := \{a_2, a_3\}$, where $|\Omega_1^{\text{low}}| = 322$. The terminal condition is not met since $f_1^{\text{low}} = 0.4814$, $f_1^{\text{medium}} = 0.4006$, $f_1^{\text{high}} = 0.1615$. Moreover, being $|\mathcal{A}_1^{\text{low}}| > 1$, since $H_S^*(\lambda|a_2) = 0.3001$, $H_S^*(\lambda|a_3) = 0.7780$, and $H_G^*(\lambda|a_2) = 0.1691$, $H_G^*(\lambda|a_3) = 0.3194$, both measures agree in selecting a_2 for splitting. Now, the set of objects Ω_1^{low} is split in three subsets corresponding to labels in X_2. The sets $\Omega_2^{\text{low,low}}$, $\Omega_2^{\text{low,medium}}$ and $\Omega_2^{\text{low,high}}$ are not disjoint since $|\Omega_2^{\text{low,low}} \cap \Omega_2^{\text{low,medium}}| = 10$, $|\Omega_2^{\text{low,low}} \cap \Omega_2^{\text{low,high}}| = 0$, $|\Omega_2^{\text{low,medium}} \cap \Omega_2^{\text{low,high}}| = 12$.

We focus on Ω_1^{medium} with $\mathcal{A}_1^{\text{medium}} := \{a_2, a_3\}$, where $|\Omega_1^{\text{medium}}| = 440$. The terminal condition is not met since $f_1^{\text{low}} = 0$, $f_1^{\text{medium}} = 0.5955$, $f_1^{\text{high}} = 0.1227$. Moreover, being $|\mathcal{A}_1^{\text{medium}}| > 1$, since $H_S^*(\lambda|a_2) = 0.2505$, $H_S^*(\lambda|a_3) = 0.4605$, and $H_G^*(\lambda|a_2) = 0.1432$, $H_G^*(\lambda|a_3) = 0.2092$, both measures agree in selecting a_2 for splitting. Now, the set of objects Ω_1^{medium} is split in three subsets corresponding to labels in X_2. The sets $\Omega_2^{\text{medium,low}}$, $\Omega_2^{\text{medium,medium}}$ and $\Omega_2^{\text{medium,high}}$ are not disjoint as $|\Omega_2^{\text{medium,low}} \cap \Omega_2^{\text{medium,medium}}| = 14$, $|\Omega_2^{\text{medium,low}} \cap \Omega_2^{\text{medium,high}}| = 0$, $|\Omega_2^{\text{medium,medium}} \cap \Omega_2^{\text{medium,high}}| = 18$.

We focus on Ω_1^{high} with $\mathcal{A}_1^{\text{high}} := \{a_2, a_3\}$, where $|\Omega_1^{\text{high}}| = 322$. The terminal condition is met since $f_1^{\text{low}} = 0$, $f_1^{\text{medium}} = 0$, $f_1^{\text{high}} = 0.7546$. Thus, since $f_1^{\text{high}} \geq \rho$, a leaf with label $\lambda = \text{high}$ is created.

We focus on $\Omega_2^{\text{low,low}}$ with $\mathcal{A}_2^{\text{low,low}} := \{a_3\}$, where $|\Omega_2^{\text{low,low}}| = 93$. The terminal condition is met since $f_2^{\text{low}} = 0.7097$, $f_2^{\text{medium}} = 0$, $f_2^{\text{high}} = 0$. Thus, since $f_2^{\text{low}} \geq \rho$, a leaf with label $\lambda = \text{low}$ is created.

We focus on $\Omega_2^{\text{low,medium}}$ with $\mathcal{A}_2^{\text{low,medium}} := \{a_3\}$, where $|\Omega_2^{\text{low,medium}}| = 140$. The terminal condition is not met since $f_2^{\text{low}} = 0.5071$, $f_2^{\text{medium}} = 0.4285$, $f_2^{\text{high}} = 0$. The splitting is made on a_3 and the sets $\Omega_3^{\text{low,medium,low}}$, $\Omega_3^{\text{low,medium,medium}}$, $\Omega_3^{\text{low,medium,high}}$ give rise to three leaves labelled, respectively, as $\lambda = \text{medium}$, $\lambda = \text{low}$, $\lambda = \text{medium}$. Thus, we relabel leaves by setting, respectively, $\lambda = \text{low}$, $\lambda = \text{low}$, $\lambda = \text{medium}$: the first label is indeed that with lower value of f^{c_q}.

We focus on $\Omega_2^{\text{low,high}}$ with $\mathcal{A}_2^{\text{low,high}} := \{a_3\}$, where $|\Omega_2^{\text{low,high}}| = 111$. The terminal condition is not met since $f_2^{\text{low}} = 0$, $f_2^{\text{medium}} = 0.5405$, $f_2^{\text{high}} = 0.4595$. The splitting is made on a_3 and the sets $\Omega_3^{\text{low,high,low}}$, $\Omega_3^{\text{low,high,medium}}$, $\Omega_3^{\text{low,high,high}}$ give rise to three leaves labelled, respectively, as $\lambda = \text{high}$, $\lambda = \text{medium}$, $\lambda = \text{medium}$. Thus, we relabel leaves by setting, respectively, $\lambda = \text{medium}$, $\lambda = \text{medium}$, $\lambda = \text{medium}$: the first label is indeed that with lower value of f^{c_q}. Therefore, we replace the built sub-tree with a single leaf labelled as $\lambda = \text{medium}$.

We focus on $\Omega_2^{\text{medium,low}}$ with $\mathcal{A}_2^{\text{medium,low}} := \{a_3\}$, where $|\Omega_2^{\text{medium,low}}| = 138$. The terminal condition is not met since $f_2^{\text{low}} = 0$, $f_2^{\text{medium}} = 0.6087$, $f_2^{\text{high}} = 0$. The splitting is made on a_3 and the sets $\Omega_3^{\text{medium,low,low}}$, $\Omega_3^{\text{medium,low,medium}}$, $\Omega_3^{\text{medium,low,high}}$ give rise to three leaves all labeled as $\lambda = \text{medium}$. Therefore, we replace the built sub-tree with a single leaf labelled as $\lambda = \text{medium}$.

We focus on $\Omega_2^{\text{medium,medium}}$ with $\mathcal{A}_2^{\text{medium,medium}} := \{a_3\}$, where $|\Omega_2^{\text{medium,medium}}| = 186$. The terminal condition is not met since $f_2^{\text{low}} = 0$, $f_2^{\text{medium}} = 0.6290$, $f_2^{\text{high}} = 0$. The splitting is made on a_3 and the sets $\Omega_3^{\text{medium,medium,low}}$, $\Omega_3^{\text{medium,medium,medium}}$, $\Omega_3^{\text{medium,medium,high}}$ give rise to three leaves all labeled as $\lambda = \text{medium}$. Therefore, we replace the built sub-tree with a single leaf labelled as $\lambda = \text{medium}$.

We focus on $\Omega_2^{\texttt{medium,high}}$ with $\mathcal{A}_2^{\texttt{medium,high}} := \{a_3\}$, where $|\Omega_2^{\texttt{medium,high}}| = 148$. The terminal condition is not met since $f_2^{\texttt{low}} = 0$, $f_2^{\texttt{medium}} = 0.4595$, $f_2^{\texttt{high}} = 0.4865$. The splitting is made on a_3 and the sets $\Omega_3^{\texttt{medium,high,low}}$, $\Omega_3^{\texttt{medium,high,medium}}$, $\Omega_3^{\texttt{medium,high,high}}$ give rise to three leaves labeled, respectively, as $\lambda = \texttt{medium}$, $\lambda = \texttt{high}$, $\lambda = \texttt{high}$.

Figure 2 shows the monotone fuzzy decision tree $\mathcal{T}$ obtained by applying Algorithm 1, where low, medium, and high, are abbreviated as l, m, and h, respectively. A direct inspection shows that the λ' encoded in $\mathcal{T}$ satisfies (1).

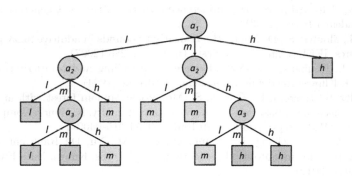

Fig. 2. Monotone fuzzy decision tree.

4 Conclusion

In this paper we consider the problem of building a fuzzy decision tree by enforcing monotonicity of the class label with respect to attributes labels, both assumed to range in totally ordered sets of labels. We propose two fuzzy versions of rank discrimination measures that generalize those proposed in [12], together with an associated construction algorithm. Due to space limitations we provided an experimental analysis on an artificial data set. A first line of future research consists in developing a hierarchical construction model of a general fuzzy rank discrimination measure in analogy with [12], and a systematic analysis of their analytical properties. Finally, we also plan to perform a deeper experimental analysis on real data: at this aim we point out the necessity of a suitable fuzzy non-monotonicity index, obtained, for instance, generalizing that in [16].

Acknowledgements. Davide Petturiti is member of the GNAMPA-INdAM research group. This research was carried out during Davide Petturiti's research stay at LIP6, Sorbonne Université.

References

1. Ben-David, A., Sterling, L., Pao, Y.: Learning and classification of monotonic ordinal concepts. Comput. Intell. **5**(1), 45–49 (1989)
2. Cano, J.R., García, S.: Training set selection for monotonic ordinal classification. Data Knowl. Eng. **112**, 94–105 (2017)
3. Cano, J.R., Gutiérrez, P., Krawczyk, B., Woźniak, M., García, S.: Monotonic classification: an overview on algorithms, performance measures and data sets. Neurocomputing **341**, 168–182 (2019)
4. De Baets, B., Fodor, J.: Principles of Fuzzy Preference Modelling and Decision Making, chap. Additive fuzzy preference structures: the next generation, pp. 15–25. Academia Press (2003)
5. Díaz, S., Montes, S., De Baets, B.: Transitivity bounds in additive fuzzy preference structures. IEEE Trans. Fuzzy Syst. **15**(2), 275–286 (2007)
6. Fodor, J., Roubens, M.: Fuzzy Preference Modelling and Multicriteria Decision Support. Kluwer Academic Publishers, Dordrecht (1994)
7. González, S., Herrera, F., García, S.: Monotonic random forest with an ensemble pruning mechanism based on the degree of monotonicity. N. Gener. Comput. **33**(4), 367–388 (2015). https://doi.org/10.1007/s00354-015-0402-4
8. Hu, Q., Che, X., Zhang, L., Zhang, D., Guo, M., Yu, D.: Rank entropy based decision trees for monotonic classification. IEEE Trans. Knowl. Data Eng. **24**(11), 2052–2064 (2012)
9. Hu, Q., Guo, M., Yu, D., Liu, J.: Information entropy for ordinal classification. Sci. China Inf. Sci. **53**, 1188–1200 (2010)
10. Klement, E., Mesiar, R., Pap, E.: Triangular Norms, Trends in Logic, vol. 8. Kluwer Academic Publishers, Dordrecht (2000)
11. Marsala, C., Bouchon-Meunier, B.: An adaptable system to construct fuzzy decision trees. In: Proceedings of the NAFIPS 1999, pp. 223–227. New York, USA (1999)
12. Marsala, C., Petturiti, D.: Rank discrimination measures for enforcing monotonicity in decision tree induction. Inf. Sci. **291**, 143–171 (2015)
13. Martinetti, D., Montes, I., Díaz, S., Montes, S.: A study on the transitivity of probabilistic and fuzzy relations. Fuzzy Sets Syst. **184**(1), 156–170 (2011)
14. Martinetti, D., Montes, S., Díaz, S., De Baets, B.: On a correspondence between probabilistic and fuzzy choice functions. Fuzzy Optim. Decis. Making **17**(3), 247–264 (2018)
15. Martinetti, D., Montes, S., Díaz, S., De Baets, B.: On the correspondence between reciprocal relations and strongly complete fuzzy relations. Fuzzy Sets Syst. **322**, 19–34 (2017)
16. Milstein, I., Ben-David, A., Potharst, R.: Generating noisy ordinal monotone datasets. Artif. Intell. Res. **3**(1), 30–37 (2014)
17. Olaru, C., Wehenkel, L.: A complete fuzzy decision tree technique. Fuzzy Sets Syst. **138**(2), 221–254 (2003)
18. Pei, S., Hu, Q.: Partially monotonic decision trees. Inf. Sci. **424**, 104–117 (2018)
19. Qian, Y., Xu, H., Liang, J., Liu, B., Wang, J.: Fusing monotonic decision trees. IEEE Trans. Knowl. Data Eng. **27**(10), 2717–2728 (2015)
20. Ruspini, E.: A new approach to clustering. Inf. Control **15**(1), 22–32 (1969)
21. Van de Walle, B., De Baets, B., Kerre, E.: Characterizable fuzzy preference structures. Ann. Oper. Res. **80**, 105–136 (1998)

22. Wang, J., Qian, Y., Li, F., Liang, J., Ding, W.: Fusing fuzzy monotonic decision trees. IEEE Trans. Fuzzy Syst. **28**(5), 887–900 (2020)
23. Wang, X., Zhai, J., Chen, J., Wang, X.: Ordinal decision trees based on fuzzy rank entropy. In: 2015 International Conference on Wavelet Analysis and Pattern Recognition (ICWAPR), pp. 208–213 (2015)
24. Yuan, Y., Shaw, M.: Induction of fuzzy decision trees. Fuzzy Sets Syst. **69**, 125–139 (1995)

Root Cause Analysis with Fuzzy Cognitive Maps and Correlation Coefficient

Theodoros Tziolas[1], Konstantinos Papageorgiou[1], Theodosios Theodosiou[1] (ID),
Aikaterini Rapti[1], Theofilos Mastos[2], Angelos Papadopoulos[2],
and Elpiniki Papageorgiou[1](✉) (ID)

[1] Department of Energy Systems, University of Thessaly, Gaiopolis Campus, 41500 Larissa,
Greece
elpinikipapageorgiou@uth.gr
[2] KLEEMANN HELLAS S.A., Kilkis Industrial Area, 61100 Kilkis, Greece

Abstract. Production line calibration is a critical industrial task that requires thoroughly planned actions. Even tiny deviations from the optimal settings can cause dramatic deficiencies. Automated Root Cause Analysis can be employed to suggest the actions that result in faulty states, and therefore, to resolve situations and prevent recurrence. This work presents a methodology for Root Cause Analysis focused on the calibration process of a valve block in an elevator system. The causalities (weighted interconnections) between oil flow control (actions) and system velocity (output) are estimated using Pearson Correlation. The produced weight matrix is evaluated by exploiting expert knowledge. An FCM model for Root Cause Analysis is developed to study the system behavior and explore the root causes of deficiencies. The proposed approach eliminates the need for labeled root causes. Results support the efficiency of the proposed FCM model for correcting the sub-optimal configurations; the proposed approach seems to work even when the calibration actions are unknown.

Keywords: Root Cause Analysis · Fuzzy Cognitive Maps · Correlation Coefficient · Elevator Industry

1 Introduction

The customization of products in manufacturing requires frequent adjustments in the production line. This process is usually performed manually and, therefore, prone to errors. Optimal configurations are mostly obtained on a try-and-error basis, which consumes valuable production time. Defects and operational deficiencies are usually associated with possible causes of a sub-optimal calibration phase and therefore corrective actions are pursued to eliminate defective products.

In the hydraulic elevator industry [1] the hydraulic power unit is a highly customized product and one of the most critical components for smooth operation. The elements of the hydraulic unit such as the pump, the valve systems, the control systems, etc., need to be modified based on the needs of the elevator installation. Several studies have

S. Massanet et al. (Eds.): EUSFLAT 2023/AGOP 2023, LNCS 14069, pp. 174–184, 2023.
https://doi.org/10.1007/978-3-031-39965-7_15

emerged regarding the control systems of the pump operation [2–4], that address cabin speed control. Moreover, anomaly detection methods have been proposed to identify deficiencies in the operation [5]. However, less attention has been given to the valve block configuration. Ineffective valve block configurations lead to inefficient oil flow control and therefore to operational deficiencies. The velocity of the elevator is affected by the corresponding oil flow adjusting bolts on the valve block. These valve bolts directly affect the velocity profile, including acceleration/deceleration phase, cruising velocity and breaking speed. Optimal velocity profiles have been determined by manufacturers to maximize passenger safety and convenience, as well as gear protection. Deviations from the optimal velocity profile are considered as operational deficiencies. An example of an optimal and a sub-optimal velocity profile is shown in Fig. 1. These curves represent the journey of an elevator cabin between two floors. Considering a normal lifting operation (Fig. 1a), the elevator initially accelerates until it reaches a predefined cruising velocity (0.4 m/s); before it reaches the desired floor, it decelerates to a lower speed, and eventually stops smoothly. In a deficient configuration (Fig. 1b), the velocity profile is quite different in terms of duration for the acceleration, cruising and deceleration/braking phases.

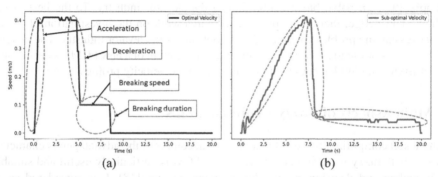

Fig. 1. Comparison between the velocity profiles for a calibrated (left) and deficient (right) elevator system. Dotted lines designate the characteristics of the velocity profile (acceleration, deceleration, breaking).

Identifying the causes of calibration deficiencies is a rather complex task that involves manual adjustments on the valve block, based on try-and-error procedures, which requires significant production time. Thus, the accurate and fast identification of the causes that result in the sub-optimal calibration of the valve block is of major importance for quality products and efficient production. This procedure is also known as Root Cause Analysis (RCA).

RCA is widely used in various industrial sectors including information technology, healthcare and manufacturing [6–8]. In essence, it aims to answer the question of why something is happening, or what is the cause of an observable effect. Several manually performed frameworks exist for RCA based on expert knowledge [9, 10]. However, these procedures pose limitations regarding the availability of knowledge, the required time for thorough analysis, and the under-exploitation of the available data from production processes. Artificial Intelligence (AI)-based RCA methods were engaged to tackle such limitations [11]. AI-based methods employ large databases to perform automated data-driven RCA. Nevertheless, new challenges have arisen with the machine learning and deep learning methods. So far, several works have addressed the data-driven RCA as a classification problem [12–14] and the most applicable classifier for their task was identified. However, these methods require massive data, as well as labeled root causes for supervised learning, which are hard to obtain in a real industrial environment. In this direction, it has been proposed to combine expert knowledge with data-driven tools towards the development of enhanced RCA techniques [15].

Fuzzy Cognitive Maps (FCMs) [16] are able to represent expert knowledge and cope with data learning, showing promising results in various domains [17]. Concentrating on FCM capabilities, an exploitation of their application in hydraulic elevator industry and the hidden causes of uncalibrated valve blocks is performed herein. FCMs are recruited in this work to mitigate the data-driven problems of the RCA as a transparent model, to address the complexity and provide decisions in a way similar to human thinking. The proposed methodology exploits FCM abilities to perform RCA in the valve block calibration where the root causes are unlabeled and unknown.

The main contribution of this research is the design of an efficient FCM model to apply RCA on valve block calibration in the elevator industry. To the best of the authors' knowledge, there is no previous research work on the investigation of FCMs for addressing the problem of determining root causes in elevator industry. The novelty of this work is oriented toward the design and development of a new FCM model capable of identifying the hidden causes of deficiencies in the velocity profiles.

2 Main Aspects of Fuzzy Cognitive Maps

Being a soft computing, powerful technique that combines the advantageous characteristics of both fuzzy logic and neural networks, FCM is particularly useful and suitable for modeling and decision-making for complex systems [18]. It is considered as an extension to Cognitive Maps (CM), introduced by Axelrod in 1976 to graphically represent the cognitive state of a system in the decision-making process. Proposed by Kosko [16], FCMs introduced fuzziness to Cognitive Maps applying fuzzy descriptions (fuzzy binaries) to the connections in order to demonstrate causal influences on the relations between concepts. From a structural point of view, FCMs can be graphically represented as a fuzzy digraph, which has the ability to explain the behavior of complex systems by integrating causal reasoning derived from the perception of expert knowledge. The system is defined as a collection of concepts, interconnected to each other with connections in the form of directed edges, reflecting the cause-effect relationships between the concepts [18].

Essentially, FCMs consist of two main components: the nodes and the edges. A node, which is commonly termed as a concept, defines a variable, a factor, a state or an attribute of the examined system; an edge reflects the causal relationship between two concepts. An FCM is comprised by a set of nodes $C = \{C_i : i = 1, 2, \ldots, N\}$ where N denotes the number of variables of this network. The overall state of the FCM can be described by the state vector $A = \{A_i : i = 1, 2, \ldots, N\}$ where the component A_i. is the degree of presence (termed as activation level) of the concept C_i in the system at a particular time.

Similarly, the degree of causal relationship (association) between two concepts C_i, C_j can be expressed with a weight $w_{i,j} \in [-1, 1]$. Equation (1) displays the computation formula [21] for the activation level A_i of each concept C_i at time $t + 1$ in terms of the respective values at the previous timestep t and the weighted interconnection w_{ji} for concept C_j towards C_i. An activation function f is employed to keep the activation levels within the desired interval; the hyperbolic tangent is employed to constrain A_i in $[-1, 1]$, while other implementations prefer the sigmoid function to constrain A_i in $[0, 1]$.

$$A_i(t+1) = f \left[A_i(t) + \sum_{\substack{j=1 \\ j \neq i}}^{N} A_j(t) \cdot w_{ji} \right] \tag{1}$$

3 Methodology

3.1 Dataset Acquisition

Experiments were performed to study the influence of each individual bolt adjustment on the velocity profile; combinations of bolt adjustments were also considered. For a system with M bolts and S possible states for each bolt, the total number of combinations to be tested is M^S. In the system under investigation, three bolts were considered and termed as {M6, M9, M8} following the manufacturer's notation. Three different states were considered for each bolt: 'Left' indicates counter-clockwise rotation by 180^0, 'Right' indicates clockwise rotation by 180^0, and 'Null' implies no rotation. Thus, $M^S = 3^3 = 27$ configurations were investigated.

The system was first calibrated by an expert. This defined the initial state of the system as well as the 'Null' rotation for each bolt. Then, the valve block configuration was systematically distorted by applying rotations {Left, Right, Null} to individual bolts, as well as combinations of them. For each distorted configuration, the elevator was allowed to travel a predefined route. Each velocity profile was then evaluated by an expert. Six profiles indicated deficient operation, whereas the remaining twenty-one were considered as optimal (within acceptable limits). Figure 2 presents some indicative velocity profiles as acquired from the experimental testing. The velocity profiles are presented as pairs (blue/cyan curves), indicating opposite bolt rotations, to assess how the direction of the rotation affected the operation. For instance, the bottom left graph in Fig. 2 depicts the effect of Left/Right rotation of bolt M6 while M9 and M8 remain at Null position. Individual experiments were designated by a unique identifier in the form 180xx, as shown in the graphs.

3.2 Processing

As illustrated in Fig. 2, the distortions on bolt configuration strongly affected the acceleration duration, the deceleration duration, the breaking speed (velocity tail) and the breaking duration. These characteristics were extracted and further exploited for the proposed FCM methodology. For the feature extraction, the time instants at which the slope of the velocity changes direction were pursued. The curves were denoised prior to the derivative calculation using a simple moving average filter with zero-padding. In addition, a future time step was acquired in the line slope calculation instead of a consecutive one, to avoid noisy estimations from sudden fluctuations in velocity. Then, the estimated times were used to isolate and extract the changes in velocity and their duration. Finally, the extracted features of each experiment were associated with the corresponding bolt rotations to produce the dataset. For the sake of consistency with the rotations of opposite directions, the derived dataset was normalized in [−1, 1].

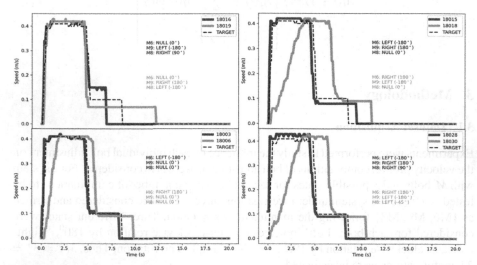

Fig. 2. Indicative velocity profiles as acquired from experimental testing. The black dashed curve is the response of the system, as calibrated by an expert. The effect of bolt rotations are depicted by blue/cyan curves. (Color figure online)

3.3   Pearson Correlation and Fuzzy Cognitive Maps

The widely used descriptive statistic Pearson Correlation Coefficient was employed to discover linear correlations between the actions performed on the bolts and the velocity characteristics. Pearson Correlation describes the strength and direction of the linear relationship between two quantitative variables in the range of [−1, 1]. However, it poses limitations and requires a systematic examination of data [19] for statistical analysis. In this work, the feature extraction procedure, that was focused on the time domain and the average speed values, ensured that the correlation was calculated in noise-free data.

The calculated linear correlation matrix between actions and velocity characteristics was fuzzified to be further evaluated by the limited available expert knowledge and by studying curves, like the ones presented in Fig. 2. In other words, the crisp values of the correlation matrix were transformed into fuzzy linguistic variables that were interpreted during the experiments to verify the causality of the output of Pearson Correlation; thus, not focusing on the accuracy but on the consideration of what proportion of the variability in the independent variable (velocity characteristic) can be justified by the dependent (bolt rotation) variable. An example of such a matrix is depicted in Fig. 3.

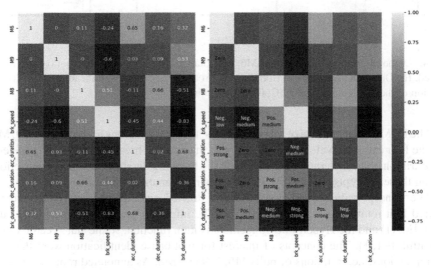

Fig. 3. The Pearson Correlation matrix and the corresponding fuzzified correlation matrix, to express correlation between the rotational actions (M6, M9, M8) and the velocity characteristics (breaking speed, acceleration duration, deceleration duration, breaking duration).

Based on these matrices, the strong influence of the actions on the velocity was verified. However, there are more complex cases where indirect influence was discovered. An example is illustrated in Fig. 4. In the first pair of curves, the Right rotation of M6 (cyan curve) increased the acceleration duration; in the second pair of curves, M8 adjustments had no effect on the acceleration duration; in the third pair of curves, the combination of the Right rotation for M6 and the Left for the M8 (cyan curve) resulted in dramatic increase for the duration of the acceleration phase.

This concludes that the rotation of M6 had indeed a considerable influence on the acceleration duration; however, when it was combined with a rotation of M8, this influence was further enhanced. The matrix in Fig. 3 shows that linear correlation of M8 with the acceleration duration is −0.11, which doesn't indicate a Root Cause for the suboptimal operation. This is confirmed in Fig. 4b, where rotation of M8 has no significant impact. In Sect. 4, Case 18023 demonstrates that rotation of M8 may affect the breaking duration and the breaking speed under certain conditions, and a more sophisticated way is needed for studying such a system. Thus, the Pearson matrix was exploited with Fuzzy Cognitive Maps (FCMs) as a weight matrix to study the non-linear behavior of the system [20].

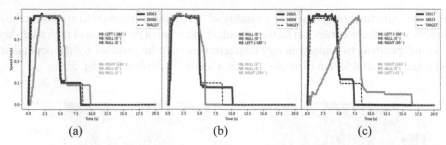

Fig. 4. Demonstration of the effects of M6, M8 rotation on the velocity profile. (a) Only M6 is rotated. (b) Only M8 is rotated. (c) Both bolts are rotated resulting in significant increase for the duration of the acceleration phase. (Color figure online)

The FCM model consists of seven concepts: the three rotations for bolts M6, M9, M8, and the four extracted velocity characteristics, namely the breaking speed, the acceleration duration, the deceleration duration, and the breaking duration. The interconnections among these concepts are initially assigned using Pearson Correlation.

The concept values correspond to the extracted velocity characteristics and the applied bolt rotations of each experiment. The inference process was performed utilizing Eq. (1) and the Hyperbolic Tangent activation function, so the state vector values lie within $[-1, 1]$. The concepts of interest for root cause identification were the calibration actions, i.e., rotations of bolts M6, M9 and M8. As annotated root causes were unavailable, the state differences for these concepts between the FCM state convergence for optimal and sub-optimal calibrations were further studied to identify causalities. In simple terms, the FCM was expected to arrive in a fixed-point state, in which the activation level for the concepts M6, M9 and M8 would differ as compared to the initial concept values for optimal and sub-optimal calibrations. According to Eq. (2), in case an activation state Mi, $i \in \{6, 8, 9\}$ lies in a different area than the activation state of the optimal calibration, then this activation state is considered as a root cause:

$$A_{Mi}^{optimal}(T) \neq A_{Mi}^{suboptimal}(T), \text{ with } A_{Mi} = \begin{cases} -1, & A_{Mi} < 0 \\ 1, & A_{Mi} \geq 0 \end{cases} \quad (2)$$

where T the time of the fixed-point state (equilibrium point). To further verify the root cause identification, a "what-if" scenario was pursued in which the alteration of values in the M diverged concepts, and the effects on the velocity profiles were examined. These are presented in the following.

4   Results and Discussion

The FCM models were developed with TensorFlow in Python 3.10 to benefit from GPU-accelerated operations. The RCA experiments were conducted assuming two scenarios: 1) with bolt rotations (M6, M9, M8 $\in [-1, 1]$), and 2) without any bolt rotation, i.e., all assumed Null. These scenarios exploit the identification of FCM causal relationships and further verify the ability of the proposed FCM model to discover the root-cause. Initially, to acquire the desired activation state of Eq. (2), the FCM convergence response was assessed for a specific target curve (Case 18002) which was calibrated by an expert. The inference process of this curve is shown in Fig. 5. It merges so that when the FCM considers the optimal velocity characteristics as inputs, all bolt rotations convergence to −1.

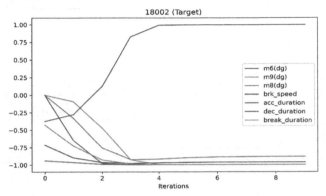

Fig. 5. The inference process of the target curve. The concepts of interest (M6, M9, M8) converged in values close to −1.

Subsequently, the values of the sub-optimal bolt configurations were considered to study the convergence of the FCM. The deficient velocity profile of Case 18008 was examined and presented as an example (Fig. 6). In this Case, only M8 was rotated, and resulted in breaking failure. Since only one distortion was enforced, the root cause was easy to identify. The FCM inference results for both scenarios of rotations (with rotation and without rotation of M8) are presented in Fig. 6. It is observed that the M8 rotation converged in an activation state ($A_{M8} = 1$) different than the optimal one in both scenarios. Thus, compared to the velocity profile of the calibrated elevator, in which all concepts converged to −1, the new FCM response can provide a decision concerning the state of the valve block system with respect to the M8 rotation, and suggest that M8 is the root cause of the deficient system. Then, by rotating M8 Left, M8 was returned to the Null position, the system got re-calibrated (black dashed curve).

A more complex example was studied in Case 18032. In this Case, the combined bolt rotations completely distorted the velocity profile, and the root cause was harder to identify. Working in the same manner, the FCM inference process for the two scenarios (with rotations and without rotations) is presented in Fig. 7. As concluded by the FCM inference, the model had M6 and M9 states activated in high values ($A_{M6} = A_{M9} = 1$) which is different than the expected value for a calibrated system ($A_{M6} = A_{M9} = -1$). Therefore, the FCM suggested that the distortion of this system was caused by the high rotation values for M6 and M9, whereas the M8 rotation had practically no effect. As a result, the Left rotation of M6 and M9 (i.e., bringing them back to the Null position) would produce optimal performance.

To further support this, Case 18005 was also examined (Fig. 7). In this Case, Null rotation was set for M6 and M9, and Left rotation for M8. The velocity profile suggests that the Left rotation of M8 had no significant effect on the velocity profile and was characterized as optimal by the expert. Therefore, it can be stated that the FCM correctly identified the root cause of deficiency, i.e., the combination of M6 and M9 rotations distorted the velocity profile in Case 18032.

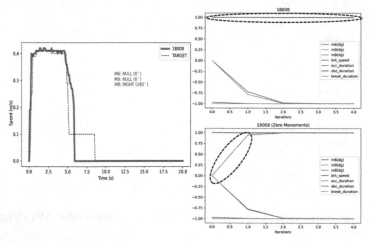

Fig. 6. Left: RCA for Case 18008 (red color). Top right: The FCM inference equilibrium point is shown when the M8 rotation is known (M8 starts at 1). Bottom right: The inference equilibrium point for unknown rotations (all Mi start at 0). (Color figure online)

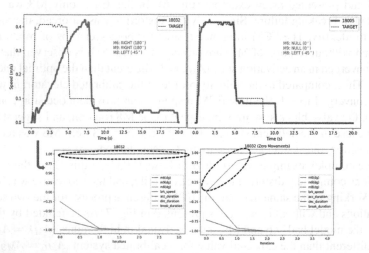

Fig. 7. RCA of the sub-optimal Case 18032 (red color). Compared to the target curve (black dashed curve), this curve had both M6 and M9 rotated Right by 180°, and M8 Left by 45°. Both scenarios accomplished through FCM inference (known rotations bottom left, unknown rotations bottom right) resulted in different activation states for the M6, and M9 values. If M6 and M9 had been rotated Left by 180° in the 18032 experiment, the optimal curve with ID 18005 (green curve) would have been produced.

The same RCA process was applied to the remaining deficient operations of the dataset, as well as to additional simulated experiments, so as to assess the potential of the methodology and further understand the causalities of the system. The FCM exhibited strong capabilities in identifying the root causes based on the underlying causalities. Interestingly, it was observed that for the investigated valve block, M6 and M9 tended to activate together, while M8 was acted as an individual root cause. Regarding the required inference steps, the FCM inference process in the examined hardware configuration required less than 10 ms for an average number of 10 FCM iterations, which is a promising performance of the FCM inference.

5 Summary

In this work, a data-driven Root Cause Analysis methodology is proposed, employing Fuzzy Cognitive Maps to capture the causality between actions and resulting deficient performance of an elevator valve block system. The weights of the FCM were estimated with Pearson Correlation and further validated with the limited existing expert knowledge. The novelty of this approach is that it does not require supervised learning with annotated root causes which can be hard to acquire. The proposed methodology can be used in a semi-unsupervised way to capture causes of sub-optimal performance based only on inputs of optimal calibration. The dataset employed for the development the methodology, was produced in a real industrial environment by manually distorting the bolt configuration of a valve block system.

Although promising, the proposed methodology exhibits a couple of limitations. These are related to 1) data scarcity and 2) the weight matrix, and open the way for further development. Data scarcity directs that the methodology should be applied in more deficient operations and additional datasets to further assess the performance of the proposed methodology. The weight matrix should be further examined with the inclusion of more samples; this practically comes from limitations of Pearson Correlation. Taking from these limitations, future work will focus on 1) the application of a more comprehensive dataset, which could address the limitations of Pearson Correlation, and 2) the exploration of additional techniques for causality calculation. Furthermore, the methodology will be extended to not only estimate the root cause, but also suggest corrective actions.

Acknowledgement. This work has been supported by EU Project OPTIMAI (H2020-NMBP-TR-IND-2020-singlestage, Topic: DT-FOF-11-2020, GA 958264). The authors acknowledge this support.

References

1. Inglis, J.: Hydraulic lifts. In: Elevator Technology 6 Proceedings of Elevcon 1995, p. 153 (1995)
2. Kumar, R., Dwivedi, P.K., Praveen Reddy, D., Das, A.S.: Design and implementation of hydraulic motor based elevator system. In: 2014 IEEE 6th India International Conference on Power Electronics (IICPE), pp. 1–6 (2014). https://doi.org/10.1109/IICPE.2014.7115821

3. Xu, X., Wang, Q.: Speed control of hydraulic elevator by using PID controller and self-tuning fuzzy PID controller. In: 2017 32nd Youth Academic Annual Conference of Chinese Association of Automation (YAC), pp. 812–817 (2017). https://doi.org/10.1109/YAC.2017.7967521

4. Murthy, A.S., Taylor, D.G.: Control of a hydraulic elevator with a variable-speed pump. In: IECON 2018 - 44th Annual Conference of the IEEE Industrial Electronics Society, pp. 2245–2250 (2018). https://doi.org/10.1109/IECON.2018.8591577

5. Tziolas, T., Papageorgiou, K., Theodosiou, T., Papageorgiou, E., Mastos, T., Papadopoulos, A.: Autoencoders for anomaly detection in an industrial multivariate time series dataset. Eng. Proc. 18 (2022). https://doi.org/10.3390/engproc2022018023

6. Solé, M., Muntés-Mulero, V., Rana, A.I., Estrada, G.: Survey on models and techniques for root-cause analysis. arXiv preprint arXiv:1701.08546 (2017)

7. Martin-Delgado, J., Martínez-García, A., Aranaz, J.M., Valencia-Martín, J.L., Mira, J.J.: How much of root cause analysis translates into improved patient safety: a systematic review. Med. Princ. Pract. 29, 524–531 (2020)

8. e Oliveira, E., Miguéis, V.L., Borges, J.L.: Automatic root cause analysis in manufacturing: an overview & conceptualization. J. Intell. Manuf. 1–18 (2022)

9. Jayswal, A., Li, X., Zanwar, A., Lou, H.H., Huang, Y.: A sustainability root cause analysis methodology and its application. Comput. Chem. Eng. 35, 2786–2798 (2011)

10. Abdelrahman, O., Keikhosrokiani, P.: Assembly line anomaly detection and root cause analysis using machine learning. IEEE Access 8, 189661–189672 (2020). https://doi.org/10.1109/ACCESS.2020.3029826

11. Papageorgiou, K., et al.: A systematic review on machine learning methods for root cause analysis towards zero-defect manufacturing (2022)

12. Wu, H., Zhao, J.: Deep convolutional neural network model based chemical process fault diagnosis. Comput. Chem. Eng. 115, 185–197 (2018)

13. Lokrantz, A., Gustavsson, E., Jirstrand, M.: Root cause analysis of failures and quality deviations in manufacturing using machine learning. Proc. CIRP 72, 1057–1062 (2018). https://doi.org/10.1016/j.procir.2018.03.229

14. Huang, D.J., Li, H.: A machine learning guided investigation of quality repeatability in metal laser powder bed fusion additive manufacturing. Mater. Des. 203, 109606 (2021). https://doi.org/10.1016/j.matdes.2021.109606

15. Steenwinckel, B., et al.: FLAGS: a methodology for adaptive anomaly detection and root cause analysis on sensor data streams by fusing expert knowledge with machine learning. Future Gener. Comput. Syst. 116, 30–48 (2021). https://doi.org/10.1016/j.future.2020.10.015

16. Kosko, B.: Fuzzy cognitive maps. Int. J. Man Mach. Stud. 24, 65–75 (1986)

17. Papageorgiou, E.I., Salmeron, J.L.: A review of fuzzy cognitive maps research during the last decade. IEEE Trans. Fuzzy Syst. 21, 66–79 (2013). https://doi.org/10.1109/TFUZZ.2012.2201727

18. Kosko, B.: Neural Networks and Fuzzy Systems: A Dynamical Systems Approach to Machine Intelligence. Prentice-Hall Inc., USA (1992)

19. Armstrong, R.A.: Should Pearson's correlation coefficient be avoided? Ophthalmic Physiol. Opt. 39, 316–327 (2019)

20. Papageorgiou, E.I., Salmeron, J.L.: Methods and algorithms for fuzzy cognitive map-based modeling. In: Papageorgiou, E. (eds.) Fuzzy Cognitive Maps for Applied Sciences and Engineering. ISRL, vol. 54, pp. 1–28. Springer, Heidelberg (2013). https://doi.org/10.1007/978-3-642-39739-4_1

21. Stylios, C.D., Groumpos, P.P., et al.: Mathematical formulation of fuzzy cognitive maps. In: Proceedings of the 7th Mediterranean Conference on Control and Automation, pp. 2251–2261. Mediterranean Control Association Nicosia, Cyprus (1999)

A Multi-criteria Group Decision-Making Method in Changeable Scenarios Based on Self-adjustment of Weights Using Reciprocal Preference Relations

José Ramón Trillo[✉] [ID], Sergio Alonso [ID], Ignacio Javier Pérez [ID],
Enrique Herrera-Viedma [ID], Juan Antonio Morente-Molinera [ID],
and Francisco Javier Cabrerizo [ID]

Andalusian Research Institute of Data Science and Computational Intelligence
(DASCI), University of Granada, 18071 Granada, Spain
{jrtrillo,zerjioi}@ugr.es,
{ijperez,viedma,jamoren,cabrerizo}@decsai.ugr.es

Abstract. Group Decision-Making is a process in which experts have to choose one or more options from a finite set of alternatives. Group Decision-Making methods were developed to assist in this type of event, but often information is lost in the alternatives analysis since not all the alternatives fulfil criteria in the same way. Moreover, in these methods, once the debate is over, it is not usually possible to reopen the decision process. Finally, the third problem that can occur in this type of method is that the experts are forced to provide preferences even though they know nothing about them, which makes the provided information incorrect. To solve these problems, we develop a novel Multi-Criteria Group Decision-Making method that allows experts to modify the reciprocal preference relation ratings whenever they wish and gives them the option of not providing a preference value if they do not know anything about it, that is, it works with incomplete reciprocal preference relations. Furthermore, the weight of each criterion is self-adjusted according to the assessments that have been made at that moment, which means that each criterion will have a different weight, thus obtaining a more versatile Group Decision-Making method that is adaptable to the different situations that may arise during a decision process.

Keywords: Multi-criteria Group Decision-Making · Changeable Scenarios · Reciprocal Preference Relations · Self-Adjustment

1 Introduction

Group Decision-Making (GDM) is a process that occurs when a set of experts need to rank a finite set of alternatives [6,11]. GDM methods have evolved and nowadays it is a standard line of research [4,23]. These methods have different

© The Author(s), under exclusive license to Springer Nature Switzerland AG 2023
S. Massanet et al. (Eds.): EUSFLAT 2023/AGOP 2023, LNCS 14069, pp. 185–196, 2023.
https://doi.org/10.1007/978-3-031-39965-7_16

ways of representing information, such as the representation of linguistic labels [1] or numerical sets [18,20]. Nevertheless, they force the experts to evaluate the alternatives by taking into account all their characteristics at once, preventing them from evaluating each alternative in detail. Moreover, they cannot modify their opinions when the process has started and must provide preferences for all the alternatives. These three problems, together with the fact that the weights of the criteria are usually equal, differentiating the experts, make it necessary to look for a method that solves these problems, making these methods more realistic and adaptable to the needs of the experts.

In this paper, we propose a novel GDM method that solves the problems mentioned above. This system implements a Multi-Criteria GDM framework with open debate allowing the experts to evaluate the criteria of the alternatives. Furthermore, they can modify their opinions whenever they wish, without having to state all their preferences at the end of the debate. Moreover, they have the possibility that if they consider not providing a specific preference value, they can skip it, as this method allows the use of incomplete reciprocal preference relations. Finally, this method, using the number of ratings, creates the weights for each criterion self-adjusting in such a way that, although the weight of the experts is the same, the weight of each criterion is modified at each moment.

This article containing the novel method is organized as follows. In Sect. 2, you can see the basic concepts related to Group Decision-Making problems. In Sect. 3, our method is explained in detail. In Sect. 4, an illustrative example is shown, to have a better understanding of the model explained in the previous section. In Sect. 5, we proceed to discuss the advantages of this model and compare it with other methods in the current literature. At last, in Sect. 6, the conclusions of the model are obtained.

2   Preliminaries

In this section, we are going to develop the basic concepts related to the GDM method. The main objective of these problems is to help a finite group of experts choose between a set of alternatives based on the information they generate [12,21]. To be able to state these methods, initially, two necessary sets have to be defined, the set of experts and the set of alternatives, $E = \{e_1, \ldots, e_k\}$ and $X = \{x_1, \ldots, x_L\}$ respectively, where $k \in \mathbb{N}$ refers to the number of experts and $L \in \mathbb{N}$ to the number of alternatives [3,14].

Once the two sets have been defined, it is necessary to define how the experts will propose their preferences. However, there are different ways of presenting the information, such as assessing each alternative separately [2]. In this article, we have opted for the use of reciprocal preference relations, through the use of numerical sets [7]. This option has been chosen because by using reciprocal preference relations it is possible to visualise the comparison of one alternative over another. Consequently, it is possible to define the reciprocal preference relations as matrices of dimension $L \times L$ that have the main diagonal empty and, in addition, as in this article the experts can choose which comparisons to make, there may be elements of the matrix other than the diagonal that is also empty [25]. These matrices, denoted as γ_t^z $z = 1 \ldots, k; t = 1, \ldots, m$, where $m \in \mathbb{N}$ is the number of criteria, is defined as $\gamma_t^z = (\beta_{t_{X_s,X_i}}^z; s \neq i = 1, \ldots, L)$, where $\beta_{t_{X_s,X_i}}^z$ is the comparison between choice x_s over choice x_i. Each element of the matrix is created by using the operator $\mu_s : X \times X \to [0,1]$. Consequently, each element of the reciprocal preference relation is equal to $\beta_{t_{X_s,X_i}}^z = \mu_t^z(X_s, X_i); X_s, X_i \in X$ [24].

With the definition of the basic concepts, it is possible to define the parts of a GDM method:

- Providing the preferences and opinions: in this first part, the experts show their opinions and ideas by talking to each other and discussing. Then, once this first part is finished, using the numerical set provided, they add to the system, thus obtaining the reciprocal preference relations of each expert.
- Consensus Analysis: in this part, we are going to verify if the information of the experts, who use the method to choose the alternative, is similar enough to affirm that there is a consensus among them. For this purpose, a consensus threshold is defined, denoted as $\alpha \in [0,1]$, which must be exceeded by the consensus value $cns \in [0,1]$ [13]. If this does not occur, a feedback process is carried out, so that the experts seek to reach an agreement. To prevent this process from being cyclical, a maximum number of rounds, $\omega \in \mathbb{N}$, is set at the beginning of the process [10].
- Aggregation of information: when the consensus threshold has been exceeded, it is necessary to aggregate the information to have only one reciprocal preference relation, this reciprocal preference relation is called the collective reciprocal preference relation. To build the matrix, which has the same dimension as the experts' reciprocal preference relations, it is possible to use aggregation operators such as the ordered weighted average (OWA) operator [16] or the weighted average (WA) operator [8], the latter being the one chosen for our method.
- Getting the ranking of alternatives: in this last part, a ranking of alternatives is performed, which allows the experts to know their favourite alternatives. To obtain such a ranking, it is necessary to use the collective reciprocal preference relation and apply an operator. There is a wide variety of operators, such as the Quantifier-Guided Degree of Dominance (QGDD) operator [5] or the VlseKriterijumska Optimizacija I Kompromisno Resenje (VIKOR) operator [22]. For this article, we have opted to use the former.

The number of methods that can currently be seen to solve a GDM problem has increased. In [9], a method is found that uses a fuzzy dithered environment for the solution of a specific problem. In [3], a Multi-Granular GDM method is developed that seeks to increase consensus among experts through recommendations. Finally, in [19], a Multi-Granular GDM method is created that seeks to adapt to different situations to be more generalist.

3   MCGDM Method in Changeable Scenarios Based on Self-adjustment of Weight

In this section, the GDM method is developed which consists of the following parts (see Fig. 1):

- **Debate and provide the preferences:** in this first part, the experts discuss the options. For this purpose, they discuss and contribute their ideas and opinions. Once the debate is over, they give the preferences they want. Nevertheless, they can change them at any time.

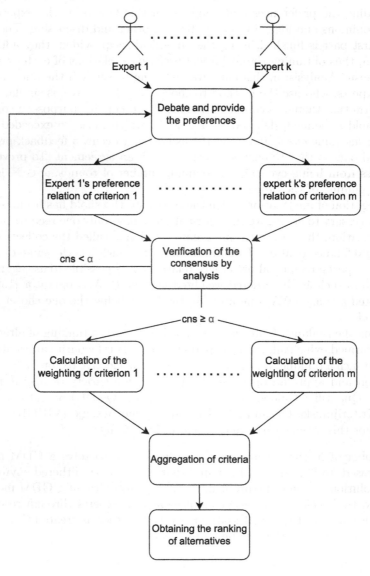

Fig. 1. Scheme of the proposed method

- **Verification of the consensus by analysis:** in this second part, it is verified that the relationship preferences of each expert are sufficiently similar to
  affirm that the decision taken by the experts is consensual. For this purpose,
  a consensus threshold is set that must be exceeded. In case this threshold is
  not exceeded, a feedback process takes place.
- **Computation of the weights of the criteria:** once the consensus among
  the experts for each criterion has been overcome, the reciprocal preference
  relations of each expert are aggregated to obtain a single reciprocal preference
  relation for each criterion and the weight of each criterion relative to the
  others is calculated.
- **Aggregation of criteria:** with the weights calculated and the criteria of
  all the experts aggregated, obtaining single reciprocal preference relation per
  criterion, are aggregated to obtain a single reciprocal preference relation,
  called the collective reciprocal preference relation.
- **Obtaining the ranking of alternatives:** With the collective reciprocal
  preference relation, the ranking of alternatives is computed, which determines
  which alternative(s) are preferred by the experts.

3.1   Debate and Provide the Preferences

In this first part, the experts will discuss the alternatives, presenting their ideas
and preferences. Once the discussion is finished, the experts can state their preferences for each criterion, which will require the use of the definitions in Sect. 2.
Once the experts have stated their preferences, they can modify them and discuss them at any other point in the process. Consequently, what you get is what
is known as an open debate. Moreover, the experts can make any comparisons
they want on any of the criteria.

3.2   Verification of the Consensus by Analysis

With the reciprocal preference relations obtained, this optional part, the consensus analysis, is carried out. The main objective of this part is to verify that the
differences between the experts are not so significant as to carry out a feedback
process. To be able to affirm that there is a consensus among the experts, a consensus threshold is established, denoted as $\alpha \in [0,1]$. This value together with a
limited number of rounds that aims to prevent the feedback process from cycling
denoted as $\omega \in \mathbb{N}$ and that for this process will have a value of $\omega = 5$, is set
at the beginning of the process. In this case, being a Multi-Criteria model, the
consensus value to be exceeded by the threshold, denoted as $cns \in [0,1]$, is computed as the arithmetic mean of the consensus values of each critter. Initially,
the consensus value for each criterion, denoted as $cns_t \in [0,1]$; $t = 1, \ldots, m$ is
computed as follows:

$$cns_t = 1 - \frac{2 \cdot \sum_{z=1}^{k-1} \sum_{y=1;y>z}^{k} \sqrt{\frac{\sum_{s=1}^{L} \sum_{i=1;s\neq i}^{L} (\beta_{t_{X_s,X_i}}^z - \beta_{t_{X_s,X_i}}^y)^2}{L \cdot L - L}}}{(k-1) \cdot k}$$

If one of the valuations does not exist, then the valuation is not performed and the value of L in this equation would be one less than its original value. Once the consensus has been calculated for each criterion, the arithmetic mean is calculated to obtain the consensus value.

$$cns = \frac{\sum_{t=1}^{m} cons_t}{m}$$

3.3   Computation of the Weights of the Criteria

Once the consensus value is higher than its respective consensus, it is necessary to aggregate the results for each criterion. For this purpose, two factors have to be taken into account: the first is that all experts have the same weight and the second is that the ratings of each criterion have to be calculated separately because the experts are free to decide which options they want to evaluate and which they do not. Consequently, on the one hand, the number of ratings of a criterion for two specific alternatives is defined as $values_{t_{X_s,X_i}}$. On the other hand, we define the reciprocal preference relation of a criterion as $\gamma_t = (\Theta_t^{si}; s \neq i; s, i = 1, \dots, L); t = 1, \dots, m$. Where the element of this matrix is defined as follows:

$$\Theta_t^{si} = \frac{\sum_{z=1;\beta_{t_{X_s,X_i}}^z \neq \varnothing}^{k} \beta_{t_{X_s,X_i}}^z}{values_{t_{X_s,X_i}}}$$

Having obtained the reciprocal preference relations for each criterion, we proceed to calculate the weight associated with each criterion, denoted as $w_t; t = 1, \dots, m$ as follows:

$$w_t = \frac{\sum_{s=1}^{L} \sum_{i=1;i\neq s}^{L} values_{t_{X_s,X_i}}}{\sum_{t=1}^{m} \sum_{s=1}^{L} \sum_{i=1;i\neq s}^{L} values_{t_{X_s,X_i}}}$$

With the weights calculated and the reciprocal preference relations for each criterion unified, the collective reciprocal preference relation is computed.

3.4 Aggregation of Criteria

Once we have a reciprocal preference relation for each criterion and its associated weight, we proceed to aggregate the criteria to obtain a single reciprocal preference relation, called the collective reciprocal preference relation and defined as $\Gamma = (\delta^{si}; \ s \neq i = 1, \ldots, L)$. This matrix has the same characteristics as the reciprocal preference relations of each expert, it has dimension $L \times L$ and the main diagonal is empty. To aggregate the criteria, an aggregation operator has to be used, in this case, the WA operator has been chosen because the weights of each criterion and its reciprocal preference relations have been calculated. Consequently, each element of the matrix is defined as:

$$\delta^{si} = \sum_{t=1}^{m} \Theta_t^{si} * w_t$$

With this matrix, it is possible to calculate the ranking of alternatives for the next section.

3.5 Obtaining the Ranking of Alternatives

In this last part of the method, the collective reciprocal preference relation, Γ, is used to determine the ranking of alternatives and therefore determine the experts' favourite option(s). For this purpose, the Quantifier-Guided Degree of Dominance (QGDD) operator is used. This operator allows us to know the degree of dominance that an alternative $X_s; s - 1, \ldots, L$ has over the rest. The QGDD operator is obtained as follows:

$$QGDD_s = \frac{\displaystyle\sum_{i=1;i\neq s}^{L} \delta^{si}}{L-1}$$

In the case that a δ^{si} does not exist the value of L will be one minus the original one. Once the values have been obtained using the average operator, as the collective reciprocal preference relation is an additive matrix it is obtained that Trillo's theorem [17] can be applied to verify that the process carried out does not have any problems. Once the theorem is verified, we proceed to obtain the maximum of the values provided by the QGDD operator, as follows:

$$X_{QGDD} = \{X_s \in X \mid QGDD_s = \max_{X_i \in X} QGDD_i\}$$

This maximum determines the experts' favourite option, thus obtaining a ranking of alternatives ordered in decreasing order according to the values provided by the QGDD operator.

4   Illustrative Example

In this section, we are going to develop an illustrative example that allows us to observe the usefulness of the method developed in Sect. 3. In this example, a set of experts, denoted as $E = \{e_1, e_2, e_3\}$ want to invest money to improve their constructions. For this, they have two criteria, the efficiency and the cost of the investment, and a set of improvements denoted as $X = \{X_1, X_2, X_3, X_4\}$, where X_1 is to install solar panels, X_2 is to improve the insulation of the windows, X_3 is to install cold insulating floors and X_4 is the investment in electric boilers. The experts begin to discuss and when they have decided that they can state their preferences, they state the preferences of the first criterion.

$$\gamma_1^1 = \begin{pmatrix} - & 0.8 & 0.7 & 0.8 \\ 0.2 & - & - & 0.5 \\ 0.3 & - & - & 0.6 \\ 0.2 & 0.5 & 0.4 & - \end{pmatrix} \quad \gamma_1^2 = \begin{pmatrix} - & 0.7 & 0.9 & 0.7 \\ 0.3 & - & 0.6 & 0.5 \\ 0.1 & 0.4 & - & 0.4 \\ 0.3 & 0.5 & 0.6 & - \end{pmatrix} \quad \gamma_1^3 = \begin{pmatrix} - & 0.7 & 0.7 & 0.7 \\ 0.3 & - & 0.5 & 0.6 \\ 0.3 & 0.5 & - & - \\ 0.3 & 0.4 & - & - \end{pmatrix}$$

Once they have stated their preferences for the first criterion, they state their preferences for the second criterion:

$$\gamma_2^1 = \begin{pmatrix} - & 0.8 & 0.7 & 0.6 \\ 0.2 & - & 0.7 & 0.7 \\ 0.3 & 0.3 & - & 0.5 \\ 0.4 & 0.3 & 0.5 & - \end{pmatrix} \quad \gamma_2^2 = \begin{pmatrix} - & 0.8 & 0.6 & 0.8 \\ 0.2 & - & 0.7 & 0.5 \\ 0.4 & 0.3 & - & 0.3 \\ 0.2 & 0.5 & 0.7 & - \end{pmatrix} \quad \gamma_2^3 = \begin{pmatrix} - & 0.6 & 0.6 & 0.6 \\ 0.4 & - & 0.5 & 0.5 \\ 0.4 & 0.5 & - & 0.5 \\ 0.4 & 0.5 & 0.5 & - \end{pmatrix}$$

At this point, the expert e_2 decides that he wants to change his preferences of the first criterion because he does not consider that the values provided are the correct ones. Consequently, the following reciprocal preference relation is obtained:

$$\gamma_1^2 = \begin{pmatrix} - & 0.7 & 0.9 & 0.7 \\ 0.3 & - & 0.6 & - \\ 0.1 & 0.4 & - & 0.4 \\ 0.3 & - & 0.6 & - \end{pmatrix}$$

With this new reciprocal preference relationship, the consensus among experts is verified. For this purpose, a threshold of consensus is set at $\alpha = 0.9$. As the consensus value, $cns = 0.9551$ then it can be stated that there is a consensus among the experts and the reciprocal preference relations of each criterion and their associated weights can be obtained. The reciprocal preference relations of each criterion are:

$$\gamma_1 = \begin{pmatrix} - & 0.73 & 0.77 & 0.73 \\ 0.27 & - & 0.55 & 0.55 \\ 0.23 & 0.45 & - & 0.50 \\ 0.27 & 0.45 & 0.50 & - \end{pmatrix} \quad \gamma_2 = \begin{pmatrix} - & 0.73 & 0.63 & 0.67 \\ 0.27 & - & 0.63 & 0.57 \\ 0.37 & 0.37 & - & 0.43 \\ 0.33 & 0.43 & 0.57 & - \end{pmatrix}$$

Before the modification of the expert e_2 the weight of each criterion was $w_1 = 0.4706$ and $w_2 = 0.5294$. Nonetheless, with the modification of the expert, the weights are self-adjusted obtaining that the weights are $w_1 = 0.4545$ and $w_2 = 0.5455$. Consequently, the collective reciprocal preference relation is equal to the:

$$\Gamma = \begin{pmatrix} - & 0.73 & 0.69 & 0.70 \\ 0.27 & - & 0.60 & 0.56 \\ 0.31 & 0.40 & - & 0.47 \\ 0.30 & 0.44 & 0.54 & - \end{pmatrix}$$

The QGDD is applied to this matrix, which will provide the values for the ranking of alternatives (see Table 1):

Table 1. QGDD values

	X_1	X_2	X_3	X_4
QGDD	0.7080	0.4737	0.3914	0.4268

With the collective reciprocal preference relation and Table 1, we can apply Trillo's theorem [17] to verify that the whole procedure is correct. As the theorem is verified, it can be stated that the procedure is correct and by obtaining the maximum of Table 1 it can be seen that the preferred option by the experts is the alternative X_1 which is the placement of solar panels.

5 Discussion

This section will show the advantages of this method at a general level and compare it with other processes in the current literature. This Multi-Criteria GDM method enhances the knowledge of the experts in one criterion against other criteria they do not know about. Moreover, it allows the experts not to have the obligation to compare all the alternatives with each other, if they do not know them, obtaining the valuations in which the experts have more knowledge. Furthermore, this new system has other advantages to be discussed:

- Modification of reciprocal preference relations when the experts desired: this method has an open debate, which means that when the debate is finished the experts do not have to give their preferences at that moment or they can give and modify them whenever they wish before the end of the process. This is an advantage because in case there is an error by an expert or if there is a simple change of opinion, he/she can make it if he/she wishes.
- Experts can answer as they wish: experts do not have to know how to make all comparisons, e.g. an expert does not have to know that one alternative is more expensive than the other. Nonetheless, in this method, they are given the option of not being able to answer if they do not want to or do not know the answer. In this way, the comments made by experts are because they can make the comparison as they have the necessary knowledge to do so.

This method has advantages when compared to other GDM methods. In [19], the criteria have no associated weight and it is up to the experts to decide between them who is more important. Nevertheless, in our method, the weights of each criterion are associated according to the experts' assessments. Moreover, while in [19] the experts have to make all the comparisons even if they do not know them, in this method they can make the comparisons they want. Additionally, in [15], a GDM method is presented that seeks to reach a consensus among experts. Nonetheless, in our method, apart from seeking consensus among the experts, they can assess the alternatives in detail, unlike [15] which are assessed in a general way. Furthermore, our method gives the option of modifying the preferences when the experts wish to do so without the need to have limited space to provide their information.

6   Conclusions

In this paper, a Multi-Criteria GDM method with open debate has been created that allows experts not to compare all the options if they do not want to perform the comparison. Moreover, with the number of ratings made by the experts, it is possible to adjust each criterion's weight, obtaining a higher weight for that criterion with a higher number of ratings. Nevertheless, in case the experts' comments are modified, the system self-adjusts their weights.

The developed system is a GDM method that makes the number of experts limited, as future work we can see the possibility of creating an LSGDM system that allows an application in a social network, making it adaptable to more realistic situations.

Lastly, this new system gives importance to the number of ratings that are made of a criterion and therefore, more weight is given to the criteria that the experts are most familiar with. Therefore, the assessments made by the experts on the criteria they know are more important than the criteria where they cannot or do not want to decide.

Acknowledgments. This work was supported by the project PID2019-103880RB-I00 funded by MCIN/AEI/10.13039/501100011033, by FEDER/Junta de Andalucía-Consejería de Transformación Económica, Industria, Conocimiento y Universidades/Proyecto B-TIC-590-UGR20, and by the Andalusian Government through the project P20_00673.

References

1. Atanassov, K.T., Atanassov, K.T.: Intuitionistic Fuzzy Sets. Springer, Heidelberg (1999)
2. Büyüközkan, G., Güleryüz, S.: A new GDM based AHP framework with linguistic interval fuzzy preference relations for renewable energy planning. J. Intell. Fuzzy Syst. **27**(6), 3181–3195 (2014)

3. Cabrerizo, F.J., Trillo, J.R., Alonso, S., Morente-Molinera, J.A.: Adaptive multi-criteria group decision-making model based on consistency and consensus with intuitionistic reciprocal preference relations: a case study in energy storage technology selection. J. Smart Environ. Green Comput. **2**(2), 58–75 (2022)
4. Cabrerizo, F.J., Trillo, J.R., Morente-Molinera, J.A., Alonso, S., Herrera-Viedma, E.: A granular consensus model based on intuitionistic reciprocal preference relations and minimum adjustment for multi-criteria group decision making. In: 19th World Congress of the International Fuzzy Systems Association (IFSA), 12th Conference of the European Society for Fuzzy Logic and Technology (EUSFLAT), and 11th International Summer School on Aggregation Operators (AGOP), pp. 298–305. Atlantis Press (2021)
5. Chiclana, F., Herrera, F., Herrera-Viedma, E.: Integrating multiplicative preference relations in a multipurpose decision-making model based on fuzzy preference relations. Fuzzy Sets Syst. **122**(2), 277–291 (2001)
6. Choudhury, A., Shankar, R., Tiwari, M.: Consensus-based intelligent group decision-making model for the selection of advanced technology. Decis. Support Syst. **42**(3), 1776–1799 (2006)
7. Dong, Y., Herrera-Viedma, E.: Consistency-driven automatic methodology to set interval numerical scales of 2-tuple linguistic term sets and its use in the linguistic gdm with preference relation. IEEE Trans. Cybern. **45**(4), 780–792 (2014)
8. Fullér, R., Majlender, P.: On obtaining minimal variability OWA operator weights. Fuzzy Sets Syst. **136**(2), 203–215 (2003)
9. Hu, Y., Pang, Z.: A novel similarity-based multi-attribute group decision-making method in a probabilistic hesitant fuzzy environment. IEEE Access **10**, 110410–110425 (2022)
10. Jiang, Y., Xu, Z., Yu, X.: Compatibility measures and consensus models for group decision making with intuitionistic multiplicative preference relations. Appl. Soft Comput. **13**(4), 2075–2086 (2013)
11. Liu, P., Naz, S., Akram, M., Muzammal, M.: Group decision-making analysis based on linguistic q-rung orthopair fuzzy generalized point weighted aggregation operators. Int. J. Mach. Learn. Cybern. 1–24 (2022)
12. Liu, S., He, X., Chan, F.T., Wang, Z.: An extended multi-criteria group decision-making method with psychological factors and bidirectional influence relation for emergency medical supplier selection. Expert Syst. Appl. **202**, 117414 (2022)
13. Meng, F., Chen, S.M., Fu, L.: Group decision making based on consistency and consensus analysis of dual multiplicative linguistic preference relations. Inf. Sci. **572**, 590–610 (2021)
14. Morente-Molinera, J.A., Cabrerizo, F., Trillo, J., Pérez, I., Herrera-Viedma, E.: Managing group decision making criteria values using fuzzy ontologies. Procedia Comput. Sci. **199**, 166–173 (2022)
15. Morente-Molinera, J.A., Kou, G., Samuylov, K., Ureña, R., Herrera-Viedma, E.: Carrying out consensual group decision making processes under social networks using sentiment analysis over comparative expressions. Knowl.-Based Syst. **165**, 335–345 (2019)
16. Torra, V.: The weighted OWA operator. Int. J. Intell. Syst. **12**(2), 153–166 (1997)
17. Trillo, J.R., Cabrerizo, F.J., Chiclana, F., Martínez, M.Á., Mata, F., Herrera-Viedma, E.: Theorem verification of the quantifier-guided dominance degree with the mean operator for additive preference relations. Mathematics **10**(12), 2035 (2022)

18. Trillo, J.R., Cabrerizo, F.J., Morente-Molinera, J.A., Herrera-Viedma, E., Zadrożny, S., Kacprzyk, J.: Large-scale group decision-making method based on trust clustering among experts. In: 2022 IEEE 11th International Conference on Intelligent Systems (IS), pp. 1–8. IEEE (2022)
19. Trillo, J.R., Herrera-Viedma, E., Cabrerizo, F.J., Morente-Molinera, J.A.: A multi-criteria group decision making procedure based on a multi-granular linguistic approach for changeable scenarios. In: Fujita, H., Selamat, A., Lin, J.C.-W., Ali, M. (eds.) IEA/AIE 2021, Part II. LNCS (LNAI), vol. 12799, pp. 284–295. Springer, Cham (2021). https://doi.org/10.1007/978-3-030-79463-7_24
20. Trillo, J.R., Herrera-Viedma, E., Morente-Molinera, J.A., Cabrerizo, F.J.: A large scale group decision making system based on sentiment analysis cluster. Inf. Fusion **91**, 633–643 (2023)
21. Trillo, J.R., Pérez, I.J., Herrera-Viedma, E., Morente-Molinera, J.A., Cabrerizo, F.J.: Multi-granular large scale group decision-making method with a new consensus measure based on clustering of alternatives in modifiable scenarios. In: Fujita, H., Fournier-Viger, P., Ali, M., Wang, Y. (eds.) IEA/AIE 2022. LNCS, vol. 13343, pp. 747–758. Springer, Cham (2022). https://doi.org/10.1007/978-3-031-08530-7_63
22. Yazdani, M., Graeml, F.R.: VIKOR and its applications: a state-of-the-art survey. Int. J. Strategic Decis. Sci. (IJSDS) **5**(2), 56–83 (2014)
23. Zhang, H., Wei, G., Chen, X.: SF-GRA method based on cumulative prospect theory for multiple attribute group decision making and its application to emergency supplies supplier selection. Eng. Appl. Artif. Intell. **110**, 104679 (2022)
24. Zhang, Q., Huang, T., Tang, X., Xu, K., Pedrycz, W.: A linguistic information granulation model and its penalty function-based co-evolutionary PSO solution approach for supporting GDM with distributed linguistic preference relations. Inf. Fusion **77**, 118–132 (2022)
25. Zhang, Y., Xu, Z., Liao, H.: A consensus process for group decision making with probabilistic linguistic preference relations. Inf. Sci. **414**, 260–275 (2017)

Towards Imprecise Scores in Multi-criteria Decision Making with Ranked Weights

Pavel Novoa-Hernández$^{(\boxtimes)}$, Boris Pérez-Cañedo , David A. Pelta ,
and José Luis Verdegay

Grupo de Investigación sobre Modelos de Decisión y Optimización, Departamento de
Ciencias de la Computación e Inteligencia Artificial, Universidad de Granada, 18014
Granada, Spain
{pavelnovoa,inv.bpcanedo,dpelta,verdegay}@ugr.es

Abstract. There is a vast number of contributions in the literature
dealing with problems for which they *explicitly* consider the imprecision
in the inputs while keeping the output in crisp terms. Moreover, as the
complexity in the representation of imprecision increases (for example,
from triangular fuzzy numbers to type-2 fuzzy sets), a higher effort is
required from the user to determine the input information. This situation
is quite clear in the context of multicriteria decision making problems.
Here we focus on these problems under three premises: 1) the input
information is known to be of a fuzzy (imprecise) type but such fuzziness
is not represented explicitly, 2) the relative importance of the criteria is
given as ranked weights and 3) there exist an infinite number of potential
weights (under the ranked weights conditions) definitions thus leading
to an infinite number of potential scores that an alternative can achieve.
Under these premises, it has perfect sense to assign the alternatives an
imprecise score. The aim of this contribution is to propose how to model
and calculate such imprecise scores as intervals first, and as triangular
fuzzy numbers secondly. Using an illustrative example, the outputs are
displayed and compared. Several discussions regarding the usefulness of
more complex proposals are raised.

Keywords: multi-criteria decision making · fuzzy scores · fuzzy
numbers · intervals · imprecision · ranking

1 Introduction

Multi-criteria decision making (MCDM) [15] is becoming increasingly relevant
in today's complex and dynamic decision-making environment. With the rise of
big data, the availability of multiple and conflicting information sources, and the
need to make decisions considering multiple aspects, MCDM provides a structured approach for considering various criteria and making informed choices.
MCDM techniques are used in various fields such as finance, engineering, health
care, environmental science and others to support decisions under uncertainty

© The Author(s), under exclusive license to Springer Nature Switzerland AG 2023
S. Massanet et al. (Eds.): EUSFLAT 2023/AGOP 2023, LNCS 14069, pp. 197–207, 2023.
https://doi.org/10.1007/978-3-031-39965-7_17

and ambiguity. Its use is growing as organizations strive to make decisions that are not only technically sound but also socially, economically, and environmentally responsible.

Our interest here is in MCDM problems containing a set of m alternatives together with their overall performance on a set of n criteria. We assume that a decision maker (DM) provides:

- *Input 1:* An evaluation matrix $E_{m \times n} = \{e_{ij}\}$, where e_{ij} is the evaluation provided to alternative i at criterion j.
- *Input 2:* A preference order of criteria $C = \{c_1, \ldots, c_n\}$, from which a rank for the corresponding weights is derived: $w_{\pi(1)} \geq w_{\pi(2)} \cdots \geq w_{\pi(n)}$, where $\pi : \mathbb{N} \to \mathbb{N}$ is an index permutation function. Additionally, weights are constrained to $w_1 + \ldots + w_n = 1$ and $w_j \geq 0$ $(\forall j = 1, \ldots, n)$.

Let's assume the global score of each alternative i is computed using a weighted sum model:

$$z_i(w) = w^T e_i \tag{1}$$

where $z_i : \mathbb{R}^n \to \mathbb{R}$ is the scoring function for alternative i at a given realization of the vector of weights $w = (w_1, \ldots, w_n)$.

Under these basic premises, two critical aspects arise.

The first one is the representation of the e_{ij}. The simplest approach is to assume $e_{ij} \in \mathbb{R}$. But, if we consider that such values are given as "around e_{ij}", then fuzzy numbers [5] would be suitable tools to model such kind of imprecision, thus leading to fuzzy multi-criteria decision making problems [7,11]. The body of literature on potential representations of imprecision is huge. A good example is the review in [14] where adaptations of the TOPSIS method are considered for different types of imprecisions.

In the last years, a wide number of extensions of fuzzy sets have been proposed (rough, hesitant, Pythagorean, Fermatean, etc.). However, in the context of MCDM problems those extensions lead to a paradoxical situation: the DM must provide an increasing number of *precise values* to define a single imprecise e_{ij} value.

The second critical aspect is the weights determination, which is far from trivial. One alternative is to resort to specific formulae to calculate "ranked weights" as in [1]. Another alternative is to derive the weights from an AHP process and then, some MCDM method, (like TOPSIS), is applied to rank the alternatives [8].

In the MCDM setting we describe, it should be noted that there exist an infinite number of realizations of weights' vectors satisfying the conditions indicated previously and, therefore, it makes perfect sense to assume that the score of an alternative cannot be defined as a single value. In fact, there is a *set of potential scores that an alternative can achieve* (one element for each vector w satisfying the three constraints defined in *Input 2*).

The representation of the imprecision in the input has been extensively explored in the past. But, as far as we know, the way an imprecise score can be computed has been little studied.

In turn, we consider that the output obtained after manipulation of imprecise information of fuzzy type (either considering it implicitly or explicitly) should be also imprecise. Consequently, we should not expect to provide a score like "3.234" for an alternative. It would make more sense to say something like "the score is in the interval [a, b]" or simply, "the solution score is high". While the first approach would involve approaching the problem from an interval perspective [3], the second would do so from a linguistic labeling perspective [4,9]. In the present paper we will focus on the first approach.

Considering the above motivations, the objectives of this contribution are: 1) to propose a model for such imprecise scores in two forms: as intervals and as triangular fuzzy numbers; 2) to provide efficient ways to compute their corresponding parameters. Both ideas are illustrated by means of a simple example.

The remainder of this paper is organized as follows. In Sect. 2 we establish some definitions that we will use in our proposals, which are presented in Sect. 3. An illustrative example is developed in Sect. 4, while Sect. 5 is devoted to the discussion and conclusions of the results obtained.

2 Preliminaries

In this section we recall some basic concepts that will be used later. The emphasis is on weight approximation methods, which will help us to calculate the core of the fuzzy numbers we use for defining the alternative scores.

2.1 Approximate Weighting Methods

There are several approaches in the literature to deal with the uncertainty of decision scenarios where weights are not explicitly defined [10]. In the following, we will consider the ones we use in our proposal; the interested reader is referred to [2] for further information.

One of the most widespread weight approximation approaches in the context of ranked weights is the *rank-order centroid* (ROC) [1]. According to this method, each weight w_j is obtained as:

$$w_j = \frac{1}{n} \sum_{k=j}^{n} \frac{1}{k} \quad \forall j = 1, \ldots, n \tag{2}$$

Other two common methods are the *rank-sum* (RS) weights and *rank reciprocal* (RR) weights, which were proposed in [6] and [16], respectively. Specifically, the RS weights w_j are computed as follows:

$$w_j = \frac{n+1-j}{\sum_{k=1}^{n} k} = \frac{2(n+1-j)}{n(n+1)} \quad \forall j = 1, \ldots, n \tag{3}$$

In the case of RR, weights are obtained as:

$$w_j = \frac{1/j}{\sum_{k=1}^{n} 1/k} \quad \forall j = 1, \ldots, n \tag{4}$$

3   Towards Imprecise Scores

From now on we consider that the input values have a fuzzy type (not probabilistic, nor linguistic...) but we will not model such fuzziness in an explicit way. So, initially $e_{ij} \in \mathbb{R}$, thus reducing the effort required from the DM to define the matrix of alternatives. The score of each alternative i is calculated as shown in Eq. 1 and the ranked weights are given. Now we describe below our proposal for modelling imprecise scores.

3.1   Imprecise Scores as Intervals

As we previously stated, there exist an infinite number of realizations of the w vector, thus leading to an infinite number of potential scores that an alternative can achieve. Two specific scores values are relevant: the minimum and the maximum. If we can calculate such values, then an interval for the alternative can be readily obtained.

Following [17] and the references therein, it is possible to calculate such bounds solving the two following linear programming problems for every alternative. Formally, let P_w be the region of admissible weights induced by the constraints defined in *Input 2* (Sect. 1) and $I_i = [l_i, u_i]$ the interval of scores for the solution i. Then l_i (respectively u_i) is obtained by minimizing (resp. maximizing) for w the following linear programming problem: $\{z_i = w^T e_i \ : \ w \in P_w\}$.

Due to some properties of this model, obtaining the solution is simple. The constraints over the weights (*Input 2*) induce a convex region of admissible weights in the form of a $n - 1$ dimensional polyhedron P_w of n vertices [12]. As is well known, both the minimum and maximum of a linear problem (if they exist) occur at a vertex of the feasible region. Here, every vertex is a particular configuration of the weights, so we just need to evaluate the alternative i in every vertex and keep the max/min scores found.

As shown in [12], those vertices (weights configurations) can be arranged in a $n \times n$ matrix V with the following structure:

$$V = \begin{pmatrix} 1 & 0 & 0 & \dots & 0 \\ \frac{1}{2} & \frac{1}{2} & 0 & \dots & 0 \\ \vdots & \vdots & \vdots & \ddots & \vdots \\ \frac{1}{n} & \frac{1}{n} & \frac{1}{n} & \dots & \frac{1}{n} \end{pmatrix} \tag{5}$$

where each row v_i is a vertex (extreme point) of P_w. As the reader may notice, the first row indicate that all the weight is given to the more important criteria. The second row divides the weight between the two more relevant criteria and so on. The last row assigns the same weight to all the criteria.

So, using this strategy we can calculate an alternative's imprecise score as an interval containing the range of the potential scores that can be achieved.

Table 1. Variants to obtain the core (b) of the fuzzy number corresponding to the score of the solutions.

Variant	Core value b is defined as
IC	the midpoint of the interval
EW	the score calculated with equals weights
ROC	the score calculated with weights as in Eq. 2
RS	the score calculated with weights as in Eq. 3
RR	the score calculated with weights as in Eq. 4
MWS	the mean of the scores calculated from the previous weights

3.2 Imprecise Scores as Triangular Fuzzy Numbers

Let's call $\tilde{z}_i$ the fuzzy score of an alternative i. For the sake of simplicity and as a first approach, we represent $\tilde{z}_i$ as a triangular fuzzy number, which just require three values (a, b, c) for its definition.

Given an alternative i, the results of the previous section allowed to obtain an interval $I_i = [l_i, u_i]$ so we propose to define the support of $\tilde{z}_i$ as $S_{\tilde{z}_i} = \{z : l_i < z < u_i\}$.

Now, the problem is how to calculate the core value b. One approach that immediately arise is to take b as the value corresponding to the center of the interval, thus leading to a symmetrical triangular fuzzy number. However, such approach completely ignores the inner distribution of the scores for a given set of weights. Additionally, the score corresponding to this center of the interval would not necessarily have the same weight associated with it for each solution of the problem.

So, as an initial approach we propose to calculate the value of b from a set of *relevant* scores. By relevant we mean those scores that are obtained from weights that are representative within the set of admissible weights, that is, according to the set of constraints for weights defined in *Input 2* (Sect. 1). Here we would be including those from the extreme points of matrix in Eq. 5, and those computed from methods defined in Sect. 2.1. Although each weight configuration would give us a specific value of b, it is also possible to obtain b from an aggregation of these individual scores.

Table 1 summarizes a set of variants to calculate the b parameter. When *EW, ROC, RS, RR* are stated, the meaning is that those weights are used to calculate the corresponding scores. For sake of comparison, we have also included the variant based on the center of the interval (*IC*).

4 An Illustrative Example

Now, we present an example to illustrate our proposal and promote further analyses. We consider a decision problem with ten solutions and five criteria.

Without loss of generality, we will assume that the weights associated with these criteria have the following order: $w_1 \geq w_2 \geq w_3 \geq w_4 \geq w_5$. Besides, the entries in the evaluation matrix are defined on a scale from 0 to 10. Consequently, the score of each solution is also be defined in that range.

Firstly, the results using intervals for scores are presented. Secondly, those related with fuzzy scores.

4.1   Scores as Intervals

Figure 1-a) shows the intervals of scores obtained for each solution. Some useful information can be easily obtained. Consider solutions $S3$, $S4$. As their corresponding intervals do not overlap, then it is impossible that $S4$ obtains a higher crisp score than $S3$ under the given order of the weights.

For solution $S9$, there is a specific set of weights that allows to achieve the highest score over all the solutions. It is also interesting to note the variability in the lengths of the intervals. While (depending on the specific weights) $S1$ can obtain a score between 0.0 to 5.7, or $S9$ between 5.0 to 10, the range of potential scores for $S4$ is quite short.

In order to gain some insights in the inner distribution of the potential scores within the intervals, Fig. 1-b) displays the scores associated with the extreme weights. In this case, it can be seen how the corresponding scores do not show any clear pattern.

In fact, the lower and upper bounds of each interval are obtained from different extreme weight vectors. For example, consider solution $S1$, in which its lower bound is due to the score obtained in the weights $(1, 0, 0, 0, 0)$. In contrast, solutions such as $S4$ or $S8$, $S9$, owe their lower bound to the vector of weights $(0.2, 0.2, 0.2, 0.2, 0.2)$, corresponding to the case where all criteria have the same importance. Notice that this particular configuration, called Equal Weights (EW) allowed to obtain the maximum score for $S3$.

Similarly, Fig. 1-c) shows the distribution of scores associated with other weight vectors: those obtained by applying the approximation methods defined in Sect. 2. We include EW again in this plot for comparison purposes. Note that the approximate weights ROC, RS and RR are distributed to inner zones of the intervals. Again, no clear pattern arises. Looking at solution $S1$ we observe a quite wide interval. However, most of the calculated scores are between 3.0 and 6.0 (considering both plots). For solution $S7$, a similar situation appears: most of the scores are grouped closer to the upper than to the lower bound. For $S9$ the situation is exactly the opposite.

4.2   Scores as Fuzzy Numbers

Now, we will further elaborate on the proposal to model the score intervals as triangular fuzzy numbers. As mentioned above, the main question here lies in how to define the core of this number (parameter b). We explore here the options described in Table 1.

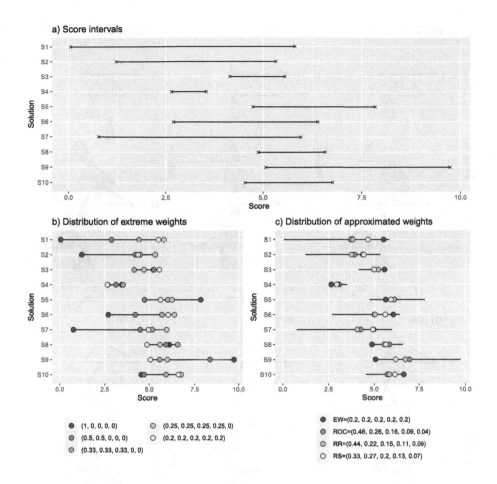

Fig. 1. Distribution of extreme weights (a) and approximated weights (b) along the solution score interval.

Figure 2 displays the fuzzy scores of every alternative for the different ways of assigning the b value. At first sight, the option in Fig. 2-a), where the core is the centre of the interval, looks more "interpretable" than the other approaches, i.e., in the sense of a fuzzy number representing the concept of *around the value x*.

Among the other approaches, most of the differences appeared when compared with the equal weights approach (Fig. 2-b)), where the core is closer to the bounds of the support.

Differences among ROC, RR, RS, and MWS are hard to detect so one may ask if having more complex ways to assign the b parameter provides any benefit. One way to answer such question is the following: sort the alternatives and check how similar the corresponding rankings are. In turn, this implies defining a way to compare fuzzy numbers and here, the literature is enormous (see [18,19]).

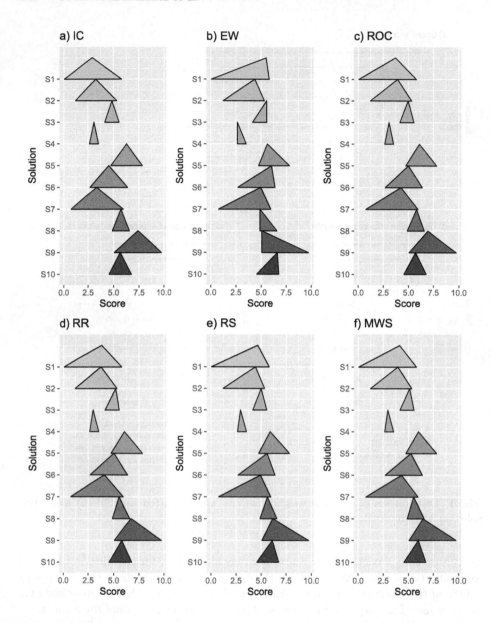

Fig. 2. Fuzzy scores for every alternative under different definitions of the core value.

Nevertheless, we set the question as follows: given the current dataset, and the Yager's $Y2$ index [18] for comparison of fuzzy numbers, how similar the different rankings of the alternatives (one for each plot in Fig. 2) are?

To quantify this level of coincidence we relied on two measures: the Kendall's tau correlation coefficient and the matching rate of the top 5 solutions. Figure 3

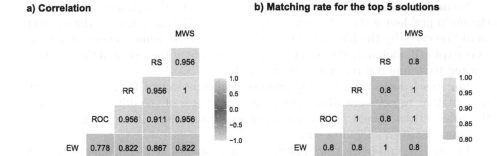

Fig. 3. Kendall's correlation coefficient (a) and matching rate for the top 5 solution (b).

displays the results. Overall, there is indeed a strong correlation between the variants (Fig. 3a). The rankings derived from *RR* and *MWS* are the same. The more dissimilar rankings are those produced by *IC* and *EW*. It is interesting to note here that the correlation between MWS and IC is very high. Regarding the matching rate, it can be seen from Fig. 3b) that the variants exhibit high levels of agreement in the top 5 alternatives.

5 Discussion and Conclusion

In this work, we focused in MCDM problems with three features: 1) we know that the input information has a fuzzy (imprecise) type but we do not represent such fuzziness explicitly, 2) the relative importance of the criteria is given as ranked weights and 3) there exist an infinite number of potential weights (under the ranked weights condition) thus leading to an infinite number of potential scores that an alternative can achieve.

Under these assumptions, it makes a lot of sense to assign the alternatives an imprecise score. We proposed first to model such scores as intervals, and secondly, as triangular fuzzy numbers.

In general, there are a vast number of contributions in the literature that *explicitly* considers the imprecision in the inputs while keeping the output in crisp terms (crisp scores). This proposal explores a different way to deal with imprecise information.

Although generalizations should be taken with caution due to the small experimentation performed, some preliminary conclusions can be outlined.

Firstly, the use of intervals to model imprecise scores is simple to understand and easy to calculate. However, it provides no information regarding the inner distribution of the scores within the intervals.

Secondly, when considering the imprecise scores as triangular fuzzy numbers, the main problem is the determination of the kernel of the set, since the support would be given by the interval of possible scores. In this sense, several proposals were explored, including the trivial one (e.g., the core as the center of the interval) leading to symmetric triangular fuzzy numbers.

Since each decision-maker may propose a different way of defining the core, we suggest that to get some ideas about the advantages of the different proposals, the alternatives should be ranked using any comparison index, and then the rankings obtained should be analyzed.

In our case, and in the third place, the main conclusion of such analysis is that the ranking produced when the core of the fuzzy number is calculated using the basic approach (IC) shows a high level of agreement with the one provided using the MWS approach (which considers, at least partially, the inner distribution of the scores within the interval).

In our opinion, this is unexpected. Even in the simple example we showed, it was rather clear that the scores are not evenly distributed along the intervals. Of course, other distributions can be observed if different sets of weights are sampled, but this is a topic that deserves further research.

Also, and as future research, we plan to replicate these results over a wide set of multi-criteria decision making problems to further understand the role of considering imprecision scores.

In any case and following the line against the *artificial complexification* of the problems being solved posed in [13], we discourage further exploration of other (more complex) representations of fuzzy scores or exploring different ways of sorting fuzzy numbers.

Acknowledgments. Authors acknowledge support from projects PID2020-112754GB-I00, MCIN/AEI /10.13039/501100011033 and FEDER/Junta de Andalucía - Consejería de Transformación Económica, Industria, Conocimiento y Universidades/Proyecto (2020B-TIC-640-UGR20).

References

1. Barron, F.H., Barrett, B.E.: Decision quality using ranked attribute weights. Manage. Sci. **42**(11), 1515–1523 (1996). https://doi.org/10.1287/mnsc.42.11.1515
2. Butler, J., Jia, J., Dyer, J.: Simulation techniques for the sensitivity analysis of multi-criteria decision models. Eur. J. Oper. Res. **103**(3), 531–546 (1997). https://doi.org/10.1016/S0377-2217(96)00307-4
3. Chinnakum, W., Ramos, L.B., Iyiola, O., Kreinovich, V.: Decision making under interval uncertainty: toward (somewhat) more convincing justifications for Hurwicz optimism-pessimism approach. Asian J. Econ. Bank. **5**(1), 32–45 (2021). https://doi.org/10.1108/ajeb-07-2020-0029
4. Delgado, M., Verdegay, J.L., Vila, M.A.: Linguistic decision-making models. Int. J. Intell. Syst. **7**(5), 479–492 (1992). https://doi.org/10.1002/int.4550070507
5. Dubois, D., Prade, H.: Operations on fuzzy numbers. Int. J. Syst. Sci. **9**(6), 613–626 (1978). https://doi.org/10.1080/00207727808941724

6. Einhorn, H.J., McCoach, W.: A simple multiattribute utility procedure for evaluation. In: Zionts, S. (ed.) Multiple Criteria Problem Solving. LNE, vol. 155, pp. 87–115. Springer, Heidelberg (1978). https://doi.org/10.1007/978-3-642-46368-6_6

7. Guo, S., Zhao, H.: Fuzzy best-worst multi-criteria decision-making method and its applications. Knowl.-Based Syst. **121**, 23–31 (2017). https://doi.org/10.1016/j.knosys.2017.01.010

8. Hanine, M., Boutkhoum, O., Tikniouine, A., Agouti, T.: Application of an integrated multi-criteria decision making AHP-TOPSIS methodology for ETL software selection. SpringerPlus **5**(1), 1–17 (2016). https://doi.org/10.1186/s40064-016-1888-z

9. Herrera, F., Herrera-Viedma, E., Verdegay, J.: A model of consensus in group decision making under linguistic assessments. Fuzzy Sets Syst. **78**(1), 73–87 (1996). https://doi.org/10.1016/0165-0114(95)00107-7

10. Liu, D., Li, T., Liang, D.: An integrated approach towards modeling ranked weights. Comput. Industr. Eng. **147**, 106629 (2020). https://doi.org/10.1016/j.cie.2020.106629

11. Liu, H.W., Wang, G.J.: Multi-criteria decision-making methods based on intuitionistic fuzzy sets. Eur. J. Oper. Res. **179**(1), 220–233 (2007). https://doi.org/10.1016/j.ejor.2006.04.009

12. Mármol, A.M., Puerto, J., Fernández, F.R.: The use of partial information on weights in multicriteria decision problems. J. Multi-Criteria Decis. Anal. **7**(6), 322–329 (1998). https://doi.org/10.1002/(SICI)1099-1360(199811)7:6<322::AID-MCDA203>3.0.CO;2-4

13. Pelta, D.A., Lamata, M.T., Verdegay, J.L., Cruz, C., Salas, A.: Against artificial complexification: crisp vs. fuzzy information in the TOPSIS method. In: Joint Proceedings of the 19th World Congress of the International Fuzzy Systems Association (IFSA), the 12th Conference of the European Society for Fuzzy Logic and Technology (EUSFLAT), and the 11th International Summer School on Aggregation Operators (AGOP). Atlantis Press (2021). https://doi.org/10.2991/asum.k.210827.046

14. Salih, M.M., Zaidan, B., Zaidan, A., Ahmed, M.A.: Survey on fuzzy TOPSIS state-of-the-art between 2007 and 2017. Comput. Oper. Res. **104**, 207–227 (2019). https://doi.org/10.1016/j.cor.2018.12.019

15. Stewart, T.J.: Multicriteria decision analysis. In: Lovric, M. (ed.) International Encyclopedia of Statistical Science, pp. 872–875. Springer, Heidelberg (2011). https://doi.org/10.1007/978-3-642-04898-2_384

16. Stillwell, W.G., Seaver, D.A., Edwards, W.: A comparison of weight approximation techniques in multiattribute utility decision making. Organ. Behav. Hum. Perform. **28**(1), 62–77 (1981). https://doi.org/10.1016/0030-5073(81)90015-5

17. Torres, M., Pelta, D.A., Lamata, M.T., Yager, R.R.: An approach to identify solutions of interest from multi and many-objective optimization problems. Neural Comput. Appl. **33**(7), 2471–2481 (2021). https://doi.org/10.1007/s00521-020-05140-x

18. Wang, X., Kerre, E.E.: Reasonable properties for the ordering of fuzzy quantities (I). Fuzzy Sets Syst. **118**(3), 375–385 (2001). https://doi.org/10.1016/s0165-0114(99)00062-7

19. Wang, X., Kerre, E.E.: Reasonable properties for the ordering of fuzzy quantities (II). Fuzzy Sets Syst. **118**(3), 387–405 (2001). https://doi.org/10.1016/S0165-0114(99)00063-9

A Multitask Deep Learning Approach for Staples and Wound Segmentation in Abdominal Post-surgical Images

Gabriel Moyà-Alcover[2,3] , Miquel Miró-Nicolau[2,3] , Marc Munar[1,4] ,
and Manuel González-Hidalgo[1,3,4(✉)]

[1] Soft Computing, Image Processing and Aggregation (SCOPIA) Research Group,
Department of Mathematics and Computer Science,
University of the Balearic Islands, Palma, Spain
`marc.munar@uib.es`
[2] Computer Graphics and Vision and AI (UGIVIA) Research Group,
Department of Mathematics and Computer Science,
University of the Balearic Islands, Palma, Spain
[3] Laboratory of Artificial Intelligence Applications (LAIA@UIB),
University of the Balearic Islands, Palma, Spain
`{gabriel.moya,manuel.gonzalez}@uib.es, miquel.miro@uib.cat`
[4] Health Research Institute of the Balearic Islands (IdISBa), Palma, Spain

Abstract. Deep learning techniques provide a powerful and versatile tool in different areas, such as object segmentation in medical images. In this paper, we propose a network based on the U-Net architecture to perform the segmentation of wounds and staples in abdominal surgery images. Moreover, since both tasks are highly interdependent, we propose a multitask architecture that allows to simultaneously obtain, in the same network evaluation, the masks with the staples and wound location of the image. When performing this multitasking, it is necessary to formulate a global loss function that linearly combines the losses of both partial tasks. This is why the study also involves the GradNorm algorithm to determine which weight is associated to each loss function during each training step. The main conclusion of the study is that multitask segmentation offers superior performance compared to segmenting by separate tasks.

Keywords: Medical images · Abdominal surgery images · Deep learning · Multitask learning · Segmentation

1 Introduction

Postoperative follow-ups are essential in ensuring the successful recovery of a patient after a surgery and preventing potential complications. While the importance of these revisions cannot be overstated, advancements in telemedicine and eHealth have made it possible for some of these evaluations to be conducted remotely. This offers numerous benefits, including reducing the need for physical

S. Massanet et al. (Eds.): EUSFLAT 2023/AGOP 2023, LNCS 14069, pp. 208–219, 2023.
https://doi.org/10.1007/978-3-031-39965-7_18

travel, which enhances the patient's quality of life, and overcoming geographical barriers. It is in this context that many studies on telemedicine and eHealth have appeared, for instance [2,10,11,15,20]. In turn, the emergence of telemedicine and eHealth has spurred the development of advanced techniques in the automatic analysis of medical images in different areas. For example, using non-deep learning techniques, in [8] the authors proposed the use of a 3D reconstruction algorithm to determine the area of wounds of various types from an image. Furthermore, in [5,6] the authors described a method for detecting complications in images of abdominal surgery using staples as suture method through the application of mathematical morphology based on fuzzy sets. With the location of the staples, which are typically situated near the wound, the method classifies the pixels based on chromatic information. This allows the identification of regions classified as red, as redness is commonly considered a sign of infection. On the other side of the coin, using deep learning techniques, studies such as [18] have been conducted for dermal lesion segmentation, [4,9,19] for pressure ulcer tracking, and [16] for corneal ulcer segmentation. Further advancements have been made through the use of multitasking techniques in the deep learning approaches, which not only perform segmentation, but also classify the complication into several categories. Examples of such studies are [1,17] in dermatology, and [12,13] for segmentation, severity classification, and time tracking of ulcers.

Having established the context of our work, this paper builds upon the previous studies about automatic analysis of images of abdominal surgery conducted in [5,6], without losing sight of the progress already made by the research community in other fields of medical image analysis. Our objective is to address the wound and staples segmentation through the application of deep learning methods. Furthermore, as well as other studies present in the literature, we aim to examine the interdependence of these two tasks by proposing a multitask approach that can perform simultaneous wound and staples segmentation on postoperative wound images. Namely, we propose a deep learning multitasking approach that leverages the widely recognised U-Net architecture, which was originally designed for biomedical image segmentation. Our approach involves a modification of the U-Net architecture by incorporating a second decoding branch, as depicted in Fig. 1. This modification provides a common feature extractor for two tasks: wound segmentation and staples segmentation, taking advantage of the idea that many of the features that are beneficial for one task are also useful for the other, while maintaining the independence of the two segmentations. To accommodate the change in the architecture, the network loss function must consist of two terms, which we balanced using the GradNorm algorithm.

The paper is organized as follows. In Sect. 2, we present the methodology in our study, including the description of the dataset, the neural network architecture of our approach, and the metrics used in the evaluation process. In Sect. 3, we outline the experimental framework used. Then, in Sect. 4, we present and analyse the results obtained in our study. Finally, in Sect. 5, the paper concludes with a summary of the findings and proposals for future work.

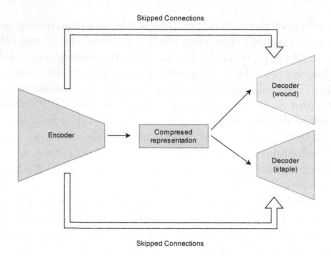

Fig. 1. Simplified diagram of the proposed network.

2 Methodology

In this section, we outline the methodology and the experimental framework for the study. First, in Sect. 2.1, we describe the dataset that will feed the experimentation. Then, in Sect. 2.2, we explain the metrics that will be used to evaluate performance. In Sects. 2.3, and 2.4, we delve into the neural network architectures that will be considered and the weight balancing algorithm, respectively.

2.1 Dataset

The image dataset we utilized in this investigation was provided by the physicians of the Department of Surgery at the University Hospital Son Espases (HUSE) situated in Palma, Spain. In total, 394 images were acquired using the cameras of patients' smartphones, without any control of the lighting or environmental conditions. The objective of that study was to assess the presence of any complications in post-surgical wounds through an automatic analysis integrated within the Redscar mobile application. All the images in the dataset depict post-operative wounds closed using staples as suture method.

To perform this study, we generated binary masks to accurately highlight the location of the wounds and staples. These masks were created by marking in white the pixels that correspond to the objects of interest, and also they underwent validation by medical specialists to ensure their precision and accuracy. Furthermore, to enhance visualisation, the masks were superimposed on the original images, allowing for a quick and clear assessment of the segmentation results. Figure 2 shows a sample image from the dataset, along with the two binary masks that depict the position of the staples and the wound, and two colour masks that highlight the location of the objects of interest within the image.

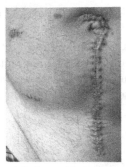  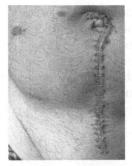

| (a) Original image. | (b) Binary image with the position of the staples. | (c) Binary mask with the position of the staples drawn over the original image. |

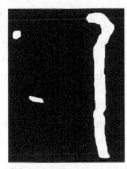 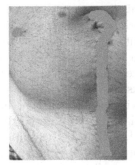

| (d) Binary image with the position of the wound. | (e) Binary mask with the position of the wound drawn over the original image. |

Fig. 2. Example of an image from the dataset and the two ground truth masks we used to perform the wound and staples segmentation tasks.

Finally, to ensure consistency across all experiments, the original images of the dataset, which varied in size, were resized to a size of 512×512. We also divided the dataset into training and test sets, which comprised 275 and 119 images, respectively. These sets remained constant throughout the study.

2.2 Metrics

To assess the efficacy of our method on the Redscar dataset and allow for future comparisons, we adopted a set of evaluation metrics that are specific to the task at hand. These metrics are based on the confusion matrix, which comprises the following basic statistics: true positive (TP), true negative (TN), false positive (FP), and false negative (FN). In the context of deep learning, the output is typically continuous. Therefore, it is necessary to define positive and negative samples. In our case, we define a pixel as positive if its value is greater than 0.5 and negative otherwise.

For both, the wound and staples segmentation tasks, we employed the Intersection over Union (IoU) metric, also known as Jaccard's index. This metric calculates the extent of overlap between the predicted and ground-truth segmentations and is widely used in the evaluation of image segmentation techniques. It is calculated from the confusion matrix as follows:

$$IoU = \frac{TP}{TP + FP + FN}. \tag{1}$$

2.3   Neural Network

The U-Net architecture, introduced by Ronnenberger et al. [14], is a Fully Convolutional Network (FCN) tailored for the purpose of segmenting biomedical images. In this instance, we based our solution using the conventional version of the network, with the integration of a batch normalization layer following every convolution in the contracting section. Batch normalization standardizes the inputs to a layer for each mini-batch, having the effect of stabilizing the learning process and reducing the number of training epochs required to train deep networks.

Dealing with a problem that involves multiple tasks requires a specialized strategy. Initially, we attempted to solve the problem by adding more channels at the network output, but this approach did not lead to successful segmentation of two disjoint classes. Recognizing the need for a different approach, we decided to modify the traditional U-Net architecture. We then attempted to solve the problem using a two-step algorithm, involving two consecutive segmentations with U-Net. Unfortunately, the results were not satisfactory. Finally, we proposed to solve this problem by using two reconstruction branches, since we are dealing with a problem that is solved by two distinct tasks that we assume share characteristics. In this way, we can have a part of the network that is specific to each task. In Fig. 3 we can see the details of the network architecture.

Loss Function. We defined our training loss function as

$$L = \sigma \cdot L_{\text{wound}} + \lambda \cdot L_{\text{staples}}, \tag{2}$$

where L_{wound} and L_{staples} are the conventional Dice loss, and σ and λ are two weighting coefficients that were initially set to 1. The Dice loss is defined as $D(\boldsymbol{p}, \boldsymbol{q}) = 1 - D_{\text{loss}}(\boldsymbol{p}, \boldsymbol{q})$, where $D_{\text{loss}}(\boldsymbol{p}, \boldsymbol{q})$ is defined as

$$D_{\text{loss}}(\boldsymbol{p}, \boldsymbol{q}) = \frac{2 \sum_{x,y} (\boldsymbol{p}_{x,y} \cdot \boldsymbol{q}_{x,y})}{\sum_{x,y} \boldsymbol{p}_{x,y}^2 + \sum_{x,y} \boldsymbol{q}_{x,y}^2}. \tag{3}$$

In this expression, $\boldsymbol{p}_{x,y}$ and $\boldsymbol{q}_{x,y}$ refer to the value of pixel located at (x, y) in the predicted soft mask $\boldsymbol{p}$ and the ground truth mask $\boldsymbol{q}$. The soft mask range for $\boldsymbol{p}$ is between 0 and 1, while $\boldsymbol{q}$ is a binary mask that can only take on the values of 0 or 1. Despite this difference between the two masks, there is no issue

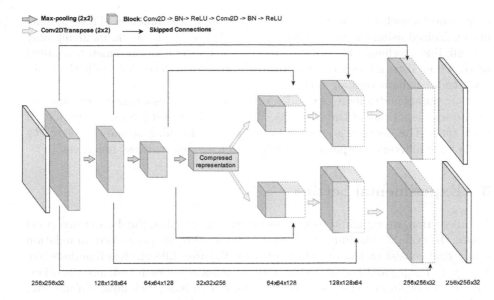

Fig. 3. The proposed network has a Coder-Decoder shape with two decoding branches, one for each of the two tasks. The encoder extracts high-level features from the input data, which are then used by the two independent decoders to produce their respective outputs. The network diagram shows the layers and connections involved in the process, with shared and unique layers for each task in the decoding branches.

since the loss function utilized can handle both discrete and continuous values in the same expression.

2.4 Adaptive Balancing Tasks: GradNorm

Multitask networks pose a significant challenge in training due to the need to balance different objectives. This arises from the requirement to converge to a shared solution that accounts for all tasks, rather than optimizing only one of them. The difficulty can be addressed by using the weights of the loss function to balance the tasks.

In multitask networks, loss functions are typically defined as the linear combination of individual task-specific loss functions. In our approach, as discussed previously, we have defined the loss functions as a weighted sum, see Eq. (2). This composite loss function involves two weights, σ and λ, which were initially set to the same value to indicate equal importance. However, as each task complexity can vary, one of the tasks (in our case, segmenting the wound) can dominate the training process, leading to unbalanced results.

To tackle the issue at hand, we propose leveraging the GradNorm algorithm introduced by Chen et al. [3]. This adaptive method addresses the loss rate imbalance problem by adjusting the weights of the neural network at each training step. Specifically, the algorithm introduces an additional set of learnable parameters, one for each task, which act as weights in the loss function. These weights are optimized using the same learning algorithm as the network, incurring only a negligible overhead. The method requires only one hyperparameter, denoted as α, which determines the strength of the restoring force that pulls the tasks back to a common training rate.

One notable advantage of GradNorm is that it ensures a convex combination of the loss functions of the subtasks, thereby guaranteeing optimal training of each task. This feature is critical for multi-task learning scenarios where the tasks have different complexity, thereby also have different loss functions.

3   Experimental Setting

In this section, we explain the experiments we performed on the dataset described above. To evaluate the impact of learning both tasks, we performed an ablation study that consist on training the network with three different loss functions (see Eq. 2): L, L_{wound} and L_{staples} to evaluate the influence of each task into the other. Finally, we evaluated the use of the well-known training technique, GradNorm, to balance the importance of each task. The aim of the experiments is to assess the feasibility and effectiveness of extracting shared features to perform the two tasks or, alternatively, to determine if different learning approaches are more effective.

3.1   Training Details

We experimented with two main configurations for our training: one utilising GradNorm and one without. We want to minimise the differences between the two configurations as much as possible to make a fair comparison between them.

To train our network, on the one hand we utilised 120 epochs. The configuration without GradNorm utilized Adam optimizer [7] with a learning rate of $1 \cdot 10^{-3}$ and a weight decay of $1 \cdot 10^{-4}$. Our training mini-batch was constructed using a total of 10 images. On the other hand, the configuration with GradNorm used the Adam optimizer for both the network and layer weights, with a learning rate of $1 \cdot 10^{-3}$ and $5 \cdot 10^{-3}$, respectively. We used 2 images per mini-batch due to the increase in parameters produced by the GradNorm algorithm, and the limitations of our hardware. We set α to 0.006.

4   Results and Discussion

In this section, we present the results of our experiments, including an analysis of the mean Intersection over Union (IoU) and standard deviation (STD) for the wound and staple segmentation tasks across all images, which are gathered in Table 1. In addition, we provide visual results of the segmentation output for the image presented in Fig. 2. Finally, we conclude the section with a discussion of the main findings and their implications.

Table 1. Experimentation results: In the first column, the experiment performed is indicated. In the second and third columns, the average IoU and standard deviation for performing wound segmentation and the staples segmentation tasks among all images, respectively, are given.

Experiment	IoU of wound segm.	IoU of staples segm.
Wound	0.670 ± 0.185	-
Staples	-	0.459 ± 0.184
Wound and staples	$\mathbf{0.714 \pm 0.186}$	0.474 ± 0.174
GradNorm (Wound and staples)	$\mathbf{0.711 \pm 0.206}$	$\mathbf{0.488 \pm 0.171}$

From the results shown in Table 1, we can see that in terms of the IoU measure, performing one single task, which is indicated in the first and second rows, provides worse performance than the multitasking approach, which is indicated in the third and fourth rows. Therefore, we can conclude that the two tasks are complementary and also that these two tasks share some features, as we obtain better IoU.

Figure 4 illustrates the outcomes obtained using the GradNorm algorithm and both tasks. Figure 4c displays the contrast between the ground truth and the predicted mask for the staple positions. False positives (FP) are depicted by the white regions, false negatives (FN) by the black regions, and true positives (TP) by the gray regions. The proposed methods demonstrate a tendency to over-segment the objects, leading to an increase in size in comparison to the ground truth.

These visual results are compatible with the metrics shown in Table 1. The low IoU values obtained for all methods in the tasks of segmenting the staples can be attributed to the generation of coarse segmentation. Due to the small size of the object to be segmented, even minor differences can have a significant impact on the final result. In Fig. 5 we can see a challenging configuration in our dataset, since most wounds are found to be vertically oriented. Correctly segmenting this type of images shows us the generalisation capability of our network. In Fig. 6 we can observe how the two tasks are closely related: in the area where the network has not been able to correctly segment the wound, it has not been able to find any staples.

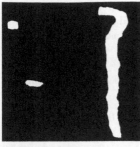 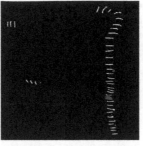 

(a) Predicted binary mask of the wound from the original image.

(b) Predicted binary mask of the staples from the original image.

(c) Difference between the predicted mask of the staples and the ground truth mask of the staples.

Fig. 4. Example of the results obtained with the proposed model using GradNorm on the original image depicted in Fig. 2.

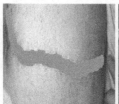  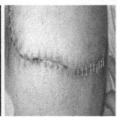 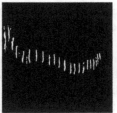

(a) Ground truth of the wound.

(b) Predicted binary mask of the wound.

(c) Ground truth of the staples.

(d) Predicted binary mask of the staples.

Fig. 5. Example of the results obtained with the proposed model using GradNorm on an image with an horizontal wound.

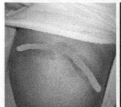  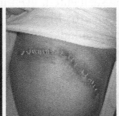 

(a) Ground truth of the wound.

(b) Predicted binary mask of the wound.

(c) Ground truth of the staples.

(d) Predicted binary mask of the staples.

Fig. 6. Example of the results obtained with the proposed model using GradNorm on a difficult image. In this sample, we can see how the two tasks are closely related, in the area where the network has not been able to correctly segment the wound, it has not been able to find any staples.

5   Conclusions and Future Work

The application of deep learning techniques in medical image processing has emerged as a potent tool to improve healthcare professionals' decision-making. In this study, we undertook a novel investigation into the potential of deep learning algorithms for wound and staple segmentation in abdominal surgery images. Specifically, we proposed a multitask deep learning approach to segment wounds and staples from medical images, and modified the well-known U-Net network architecture by incorporating a second decoding branch. This modification provided a common feature extractor for both tasks while maintaining the independence of the two segmentations. To accommodate the change in architecture, the loss function of the network was constructed using a linear combination of the loss of each partial task, whose weights we balanced using the GradNorm algorithm. To enable future work and for scientific progress, we published in a GitHub repository the weights obtained after training the models and the code definition of the two models we used in this research (https://github.com/miquelmn/multitask-wounds).

Based on the results obtained from our experimental setup, we can conclude that the multitask approach outperforms the single task approach. This suggests that the two segmentation tasks share common features, and that they can mutually benefit from each other.

As future work, we have identified two key areas for improvement. Firstly, we need to address the size diversity within our dataset, which presents objects of varying sizes. Convolutional networks, by definition, are not size invariant, which can lead to suboptimal results as observed in our provided images. We plan to incorporate to the model a pyramid of features maps, used extensively in the literature, to overcome this challenge. Secondly, our dataset includes a third task, which involves classifying wounds into two categories: infected or non-infected. In our future work, we aim to integrate this additional task into our neural network to enhance its overall performance.

Acknowledgements. This work was partially supported by the R+D+i Project PID2020-113870GB-I00-"Desarrollo de herramientas de Soft Computing para la Ayuda al Diagnóstico Clínico y a la Gestión de Emergencias (HESOCODICE)", funded by MCIN/AEI/10.13039/501100011033/. Project PID2019-104829RA-I00 "EXPLainable Artificial INtelligence systems for health and well-beING (EXPLAINING)" funded by MCIN/AEI/10.13039/501100011033.

Miquel Miró-Nicolau benefited from the fellowship FPI/035/2020 from Govern de les Illes Balears.

References

1. Alenezi, F., Armghan, A., Polat, K.: A novel multi-task learning network based on melanoma segmentation and classification with skin lesion images. Diagnostics **13**(2), 262 (2023)

2. Chen, Y.W., Hsu, J.T., Hung, C.C., Wu, J.M., Lai, F., Kuo, S.Y.: Surgical wounds assessment system for self-care. IEEE Trans. Syst. Man Cybern. Syst. **50**(12), 5076–5091 (2020)
3. Chen, Z., Badrinarayanan, V., Lee, C.Y., Rabinovich, A.: Gradnorm: Gradient normalization for adaptive loss balancing in deep multitask networks. In: International Conference on Machine Learning, pp. 794–803. PMLR (2018)
4. Chino, D.Y., Scabora, L.C., Cazzolato, M.T., Jorge, A.E., Traina, C., Jr., Traina, A.J.: Segmenting skin ulcers and measuring the wound area using deep convolutional networks. Comput. Methods Programs Biomed. **191**, 105376 (2020)
5. González-Hidalgo, M., et al.: Detection and automatic deletion of staples in images of wound of abdominal surgery for m-health applications. In: Tavares, J.M.R.S., Natal Jorge, R.M. (eds.) VipIMAGE 2019. LNCVB, vol. 34, pp. 219–229. Springer, Cham (2019). https://doi.org/10.1007/978-3-030-32040-9_23
6. González-Hidalgo, M., Munar, M., Bibiloni, P., Moyà-Alcover, G., Craus-Miguel, A., Segura-Sampedro, J.J.: Detection of infected wounds in abdominal surgery images using fuzzy logic and fuzzy sets. In: 2019 International Conference on Wireless and Mobile Computing, Networking and Communications (WiMob), pp. 99–106 (2019)
7. Kingma, D.P., Ba, J.: Adam: a method for stochastic optimization. In: Bengio, Y., LeCun, Y. (eds.) 3rd International Conference on Learning Representations, ICLR 2015, San Diego, CA, USA, May 7–9, 2015, Conference Track Proceedings (2015)
8. Liu, C., Fan, X., Guo, Z., Mo, Z., Chang, E.I.C., Xu, Y.: Wound area measurement with 3D transformation and smartphone images. BMC Bioinform. **20**(1), 724 (2019)
9. Mahbod, A., Schaefer, G., Ecker, R., Ellinger, I.: Automatic foot ulcer segmentation using an ensemble of convolutional neural networks. In: 26th International Conference on Pattern Recognition (ICPR), pp. 4358–4364. IEEE Computer Society, Los Alamitos, CA, USA (2022)
10. Martínez-Ramos, C., Cerdán, M.T., López, R.S.: Mobile phone-based telemedicine system for the home follow-up of patients undergoing ambulatory surgery. Telemed. e-Health **15**(6), 531–537 (2009)
11. Ng, H.J.H., Huang, D., Rajaratnam, V.: Diagnosing surgical site infections using telemedicine: a systematic review. Surgeon **20**(4), e78–e85 (2022)
12. Oliveira, B., et al.: A multi-task convolutional neural network for classification and segmentation of chronic venous disorders. Sci. Rep. **13**(1), 761 (2023)
13. Oota, S.R., Rowtula, V., Mohammed, S., Galitz, J., Liu, M., Gupta, M.: Healtech - a system for predicting patient hospitalization risk and wound progression in old patients. In: IEEE Winter Conference on Applications of Computer Vision (WACV), pp. 2462–2471 (2021)
14. Ronneberger, O., Fischer, P., Brox, T.: U-Net: convolutional networks for biomedical image segmentation. In: Navab, N., Hornegger, J., Wells, W.M., Frangi, A.F. (eds.) MICCAI 2015. LNCS, vol. 9351, pp. 234–241. Springer, Cham (2015). https://doi.org/10.1007/978-3-319-24574-4_28
15. Segura-Sampedro, J.J., Rivero-Belenchón, I., et al.: Feasibility and safety of surgical wound remote follow-up by smart phone in appendectomy: a pilot study. Ann. Med. Surg. **21**, 58–62 (2017)
16. Sun, Q., Deng, L., Liu, J., Huang, H., Yuan, J., Tang, X.: Patch-based deep convolutional neural network for corneal ulcer area segmentation. In: Cardoso, M.J., et al. (eds.) FIFI/OMIA -2017. LNCS, vol. 10554, pp. 101–108. Springer, Cham (2017). https://doi.org/10.1007/978-3-319-67561-9_11

17. Talavera-Martínez, L., Bibiloni, P., González-Hidalgo, M.: A multitasking learning framework for dermoscopic image analysis. In: Tavares, J.M.R.S., Papa, J.P., González Hidalgo, M. (eds.) CIARP 2021. LNCS, vol. 12702, pp. 34–44. Springer, Cham (2021). https://doi.org/10.1007/978-3-030-93420-0_4
18. Talavera-Martínez, L., Bibiloni, P., Giacaman, A., Taberner, R., Del Pozo Hernando, L.J., González-Hidalgo, M.: A novel approach for skin lesion symmetry classification with a deep learning model. Comput. Biol. Med. **145**, 105450 (2022)
19. Wang, C., Anisuzzaman, D.M., Williamson, V., Dhar, M.K., Rostami, B., Niezgoda, J., Gopalakrishnan, S., Yu, Z.: Fully automatic wound segmentation with deep convolutional neural networks. Sci. Rep. **10**(1), 21897 (2020)
20. Wu, J.M., Tsai, C.J., Ho, T.W., Lai, F., Tai, H.C., Lin, M.T.: A unified framework for automatic detection of wound infection with artificial intelligence. Appl. Sci. **10**(15), 5353 (2020)

FIDOC: A New Combination of Fuzzy Impulse Noise Detection and Open-Close Filtering

Peter Sussner[1]([✉])[iD] and Manuel González-Hidalgo[2,3][iD]

[1] Department of Applied Mathematics, IMECC, University of Campinas,
Campinas, SP, Brazil
`sussner@unicamp.br`
[2] SCOPIA Research Group, University of the Balearic Islands, Palma, Spain
`manuel.gonzalez@uib.es`
[3] Health Research Institute of the Balearic Islands (IdISBa), 07010 Palma, Spain

Abstract. Image noise can be viewed as unwanted disturbances in a digital image that should be removed or reduced before further processing and analysis. Impulsive noise, also known as impulse noise, is a very disruptive type of noise, characterized by abrupt variations in brightness in a subset of the image pixels. Impulsive noise commonly occurs during image acquisition and transmission. To mitigate its effects, various impulsive noise reduction methods have been proposed by the image processing community. In contrast to classical filters such as the median filter, most current impulsive noise reduction techniques implement a two-step approach that consists of a noise detection phase to identify noisy pixels and a filtering phase to reduce the amount of noise in the presumably corrupted pixels.

The approach presented in this paper is also along this line. To be more precise, we draw on the principles of two state-of-the-art impulsive noise reduction methods, namely the *adaptive fuzzy transform based image filter* (ATIF) and the *improved fuzzy mathematical morphology open-close filter* (i-FMMOCS), in order to propose a new method for general impulsive noise reduction.

Keywords: Image noise · Impulsive noise · Fuzzy image processing · Noise detector · Fuzzy image filter

1 Introduction

There are a number of different ways in which fuzzy logic can be applied to digital image processing. One possible option is to represent a grayscale digital image as a function from a universe X to (a finite subset of) the unit interval,

Supported in part by CNPq under grant no. 315638/2020-6 ("Lattice Computing with an Emphasis on L-Fuzzy Systems and Mathematical Morphology") and FAPESP under grant no. 2020/09838-0 (Brazilian Institute of Data Science) as well as the Grant PID2020-113870GB-I00-"Desarrollo de herramientas de Soft Computing para la Ayuda al Diagnóstico Clínico y a la Gestión de Emergencias (HESOCODICE)", funded by MCIN/AEI/10.13039/501100011033/.

S. Massanet et al. (Eds.): EUSFLAT 2023/AGOP 2023, LNCS 14069, pp. 220–231, 2023.
https://doi.org/10.1007/978-3-031-39965-7_19

identifying these images with fuzzy sets. This way, one may use operators of fuzzy logic such as (discrete) t-norms and implications as a tool for processing grayscale images. Another option is to use fuzzy sets as a model for coping with vagueness, imprecision, ambiguity, and uncertainty that frequently arise in image processing, analysis, and understanding. In both scenarios, one may additionally resort to fuzzy logic in order to extract valuable information regarding features of an image [1]. Fuzzy logic may for instance be used to determine if a given pixel should be considered corrupted or not. To this end, one often takes information regarding the pixels with neighboring locations into account. This strategy was in particular applied in the impulse noise detection phases of Schulte et al.'s fuzzy impulse noise detection and reduction method (FIDRM) [2], Schuster's and Sussner's adaptive image filter based on the fuzzy transform (ATIF) [3], and Yueksel's and Bastuerk's type-2 fuzzy logic filtering to reduce noise in color images [4]. Many other impulse noise reduction methods such as weighted couple sparse representation of Chen et al. [5], unified impulse noise removal using a reference sequence-to-sequence similarity detector [6], and the adaptive window-based filter for high-density impulse noise suppression [7] also execute a noise detection phase before proceeding with the filtering phase. This comment applies in particular to the improved fuzzy mathematical morphology open-close filter (i-FMMOCS) of González-Hidalgo et al. [8] that was specifically designed to first detect and then remove salt-and-pepper noise in grayscale images.

Interestingly, the ATIF and i-FMMOCS methods share a common framework in image algebra [9]. To be more precise, their filtering phases can be described in terms of (compositions of direct and inverse) linear and lattice fuzzy transforms [10,11]. The latter can be viewed as special cases of image-template products in the mathematical theory of image algebra [12]. A number of comparative experimental results in applications of the ATIF and i-FMMOCS methods [3,8] to salt-and-pepper noise reduction indicate a superior performance of the ATIF for low and medium and the i-FMMOCS for high noise levels [9].

Unfortunately, similar comparative experiments cannot be performed for the purpose of impulse noise reduction because, due to its noise detection phase that is only concerned with salt-and-pepper noise, the current version of i-FMMOCS filter is not suitable for general impulse noise. However, its filtering phase is, in principle, applicable to any type of impulsive noise and should entail excellent results. Therefore, we propose to combine the noise detector phase of the ATIF, which is essentially identical to the one of Schulte et al.'s fuzzy impulse noise detection and reduction method (FIDRM) [2], with the filtering phase of the i-FMMOCS so as to obtain a new filter, called *fuzzy impulse noise detection based open-close filter* (FIDOC). Our paper is organized as follows:

In Sects. 2 and 3, we briefly review the ATIF of the i-FMMOCS models including the necessary mathematical backgrounds. In Sect. 4, we introduce our proposed combination of the noise detector phase of the ATIF with the filtering phase of the i-FMMOCS. The next section presents some simulations in which we compare the performance of the ATIF and the combination of the ATIF/FIDRM noise detector and the i-FMMOCS filtering stage, using both flat and non-flat structuring elements. We finish the paper with some concluding remarks.

2 A Brief Review of the Adaptive Image Filter Based on the Fuzzy Transform (ATIF)

The focus of this paper is on impulsive noise reduction for grayscale images. Recall that a grayscale digital image is given by a function G from an $M \times N$ array X to a finite value set such as $\{0, 1, \ldots, 255\}$. For the purposes of this paper, the values of G are normalized so as to reside in the interval $[0, 1]$. This way, G can be identified with a fuzzy set over the universe X. A pixel is given by its location (i, j) and its value $G(i, j)$, where i and j range respectively from 1 to M and 1 to N. Let us recall the well-known random-valued impulse noise (RVIN) model. Using the symbols $G(i, j)$ and $O(i, j)$ to denote, respectively, the brightness values of the noisy and the original gray-scale images, we have

$$G(i,j) = \begin{cases} O(i,j) \text{ with probability } 1 - p, \\ \eta(i,j) \text{ with probability } p, \end{cases} \tag{1}$$

where $\eta(i, j)$ is an uniformly generated brightness value and $p \in [0, 1]$ a probability of occurrence of impulsive noise. Figure 1 depicts a grayscale image that is corrupted by 50% impulse noise. As mentioned above, the ATIF model consists of two stages, namely a noise detection followed by a filtering stage.

Fig. 1. Left: Original image; Center: Corrupted image containing 50% impulse noise; Right: Locations of detected noisy pixels in white.

2.1 The Noise Detection Stage

Given any pixel $((i, j), G(i, j))$, where $(i, j) \in \{1, \ldots, M\} \times \{1, \ldots, N\}$, the goal of the noise detection stage is to decide whether this pixel should be considered corrupted or not. To this end, the ATIF noise detector takes eight directional gradients into account. The eight directions in question are determined by the Moore neighborhood of the pixel location (i, j), visualized in Fig. 1. It goes almost without saying that the acronyms $NW, N, \ldots, SE$ stand for northwest, north, ..., and southeast, respectively.

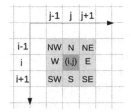

Fig. 2. Moore neighborhood of the pixel location (i, j).

According to Schulte et al. [2], the *directional gradient value* at (i, j) in direction $D \in \{NW, N, \ldots, SE\}$, denoted $\nabla_D G(i, j)$, is given by a difference $G(i, j) - G(i + k, j + l)$ for some $k, l \in \{-1, 0, 1\}$. For example, (k, l) equals $(0, 1)$ for $D = E$ as the reader can easily check by taking a brief glance at Fig. 2.

Note that a high absolute value of $\nabla_D G(i, j)$ may indicate either a corruption by impulsive noise or an edge. To distinguish between corrupted and edge pixels, the ATIF noise detector also considers the so called related gradient values of $\nabla_D G(i, j)$, denoted $\nabla'_D G(i, j)$ and $\nabla''_D G(i, j)$, for each location (i, j). If $\nabla_D G(i, j) = G(i + k, j + l) - G(i, j)$ for $k, l \in \{-1, 0, 1\}$, then $\nabla'_D G(i, j) = \nabla_D G(i + k, j - l)$ and $\nabla''_D G(i, j) = \nabla_D G(i - k, j + l)$. Based on this information, the ATIF noise detector evaluates the possibility that the pixel at location (i, j) is an "impulse noise pixel in direction D" (cf. Schulte et al.) in terms of the degree of truth of a fuzzy proposition IMP_D. The latter involves fuzzy sets "big positive" (BIG_POS), "big negative" (BIG_NEG), SMALL, and LARGE (for simplicity, we write $A(x)$ instead of $\mu_A(x)$ for any $A \in \mathcal{F}(X)$, where $\mathcal{F}(X)$ stands for the class of fuzzy sets over the universe X).

Considering an arbitrary but fixed location (i, j) and modeling the logical connectives AND and OR respectively using the minimum t-norm and maximum t-conorm, denoted $\wedge$ and $\vee$, respectively, $IMP_D(i, j)$ is given by

$$[\text{LARGE}(|\nabla_D|) \wedge \text{SMALL}(|\nabla'_D|] \vee [\text{LARGE}(|\nabla_D|) \wedge \text{SMALL}(|\nabla''_D|]$$
$$\vee [\text{BIG\_POS}(|\nabla_D|) \wedge \text{BIG\_NEG}(|\nabla'_D|) \wedge \text{BIG\_NEG}(|\nabla''_D|]$$
$$\vee [\text{BIG\_NEG}(|\nabla_D|) \wedge \text{BIG\_POS}(|\nabla'_D|) \wedge \text{BIG\_POS}(|\nabla''_D|].$$

The final decision depends on the outcome of the following decision rule: If most of the eight values $IMP_D(i, j)$, where $D \in \{NW, N, \ldots, SE\}$, are large, i.e., $\geq \theta$, then the pixel at (i, j) is flagged as noisy.

Apart from the parameter $\theta \in [0, 1]$, the ATIF noise detector depends on the specification of $a', a \in [-1, 0]$ and $b, b', c, c' \in [0, 1]$ used to design trapezoidal fuzzy sets BIG_NEG, BIG_POS, SMALL, and LARGE. In this paper, we adopted the same parameters as in [3]. On the right-hand side of Fig. 1, the locations of the detected noisy pixels are depicted in white.

2.2   The Filtering Stage

The filtering stage of the ATIF relies heavily on the linear fuzzy transform (FT) introduced by Perfilieva [10]. Like classical transforms such as the Fourier and wavelet transforms [12], the FT consists of a direct and an inverse transform, denoted respectively $\bar{\mathcal{F}}$ and $\bar{\mathbf{f}}$ in this paper.

Given a corrupted grayscale image G, the noise detection stage results in a set of locations of detected noisy pixels that we denote using the symbol $\mathcal{D}$. Then the ATIF executes the following steps in its filtering stage:

1. Application of a so called variably sized median filter, denoted μ, to every $(i, j) \in \mathcal{D}$, that is:
   (a) Compute the median of the values in the 3×3 window centered at (i, j). The symbol $\mu_3(i, j)$ stands for the resulting median value.
   (b) If $\mu_3(i, j) = G(p', q')$ for some (p', q') in the 3×3 window centered at (i, j) such that $(p', q') \notin \mathcal{D}$, then $\mu(G)(i, j) = \mu_3(i, j)$. Otherwise, increase the window size until a median value is found which equals the value of a presumably noiseless pixel in the current window.
2. Application of a coarse-grained direct fuzzy transform $\bar{\mathcal{F}}$ [10] to g given by

$$g(i, j) = \begin{cases} G(i, j), & \text{if } (i, j) \notin \mathcal{D} \\ \mu(G)(i, j), & \text{otherwise.} \end{cases} \tag{2}$$

3. Application of the inverse fuzzy transform $\bar{\mathbf{f}}$ to $\bar{\mathcal{F}}(g)$;
4. Substitution of the pixels marked as noisy with the ones produced by the fuzzy transform, yielding an image R such that

$$R(i, j) = \begin{cases} G(i, j), & \text{if } (i, j) \notin \mathcal{D} \\ (\bar{\mathbf{f}} \circ \bar{\mathcal{F}})(g)(i, j), & \text{otherwise.} \end{cases} \tag{3}$$

Generally speaking, the ATIF method was shown to produce excellent results in terms of the peak-signal-to-noise ratio (PSNR) and the structural similarity index in comparison with other competitive impulse noise reduction methods [3,5].

3   The Filtering Stage of the I-FMMOCS

Let us briefly review the improved fuzzy mathematical morphology open-close filter (i-FMMOCS) [8]. This filter employs operators of fuzzy mathematical morphology [13,14] that are defined in terms of fuzzy connectives such as t-norms and implications [15,16]. In the following, T denotes a t-norm, and I a fuzzy implication.

The improved fuzzy mathematical morphology open-close filter (i-FMMOCS) is based on the so called "uncorrupted" fuzzy dilation and erosion operators. Consider an arbitrary image $G : X \to [0, 1]$. Let $\mathcal{D} \subseteq X$ be the set of locations of pixels that, according to some noise detection method, are deemed to be corrupted. Thus, $\mathcal{U} = X \setminus \mathcal{D}$ consists of the locations of pixels that are considered uncorrupted. Let S be a fuzzy structuring element (SE) which is nothing else than an image from a subset X_S of X to $[0,1]$. If X_S is an $N \times N$ array centered at $(0,0)$, then S is said to be of size $N \times N$.

Definition 1 ([8]). *For every* $\mathbf{y} = (i_{\mathbf{y}}, j_{\mathbf{y}}) \in X$, *the values of the* uncorrupted fuzzy dilation $D_T^*(G, S)$ *and the* uncorrupted fuzzy erosion $E_I^*(G, S)$ *of G by S at $\mathbf{y}$ are respectively given by*

$$
\begin{aligned}
D_T^*(G, S)(\mathbf{y}) &= \sup_{\mathbf{x} \in \mathcal{U}_{\mathbf{y}}} T(S(\mathbf{x} - \mathbf{y}), G(\mathbf{x})), \\
E_I^*(G, S)(\mathbf{y}) &= \inf_{\mathbf{x} \in \mathcal{U}_{\mathbf{y}}} I(S(\mathbf{x} - \mathbf{y}), G(\mathbf{x})),
\end{aligned}
\tag{4}
$$

where $\mathcal{U}_{\mathbf{y}} = \mathcal{U} \cap \{\mathbf{x} \in X \mid \mathbf{x} - \mathbf{y} \in X_S\}$.

Definition 1 gives rise to the uncorrupted fuzzy opening and closing of a grayscale image G by an SE S whose reflection $\overline{S} : -X_S \to [0,1]$ is defined by $\overline{S}(\mathbf{x}) = S(-\mathbf{x})$. Here, $-X_S = \{(-i, -j) \mid (i,j) \in X_S\}$.

Definition 2 ([8]). *For every* $\mathbf{y} = (i_{\mathbf{y}}, j_{\mathbf{y}}) \in X$, *the values of the* uncorrupted fuzzy closing $C_{T,I}^*(G, S)$ *and the* uncorrupted fuzzy opening $O_{T,I}^*(G, S)$ *of the image G by the SE S at $\mathbf{y}$ are given by*

$$
\begin{aligned}
C_{T,I}^*(G, S)(\mathbf{y}) &= E_I(D_T^*(G, S), \overline{S})(\mathbf{y}), \\
O_{T,I}^*(G, S)(\mathbf{y}) &= D_T(E_I^*(G, S), \overline{S})(\mathbf{y}).
\end{aligned}
\tag{5}
$$

Let us list the steps of the filtering stage of the improved fuzzy mathematical morphology filter for each pixel (i,j) of the corrupted image G. Given set $\mathcal{D}$ pixel locations that correspond to corrupted pixels according to a noise detection method, the following steps are executed:

1. Determine the minimum value $N \in \{3, 5, \ldots\}$ for which there exists an element of $\mathcal{U} = X \setminus \mathcal{D}$ in an $N \times N$ window centered at position (i,j).
2. Following Definition 2, compute the arithmetic mean of the uncorrupted fuzzy closing and the uncorrupted fuzzy opening using a structuring element of size $N \times N$, i.e., compute

$$
F'(i,j) = \frac{C_{T,I}^*(G, S)(i,j) + O_{T,I}^*(G, S)(i,j)}{2},
$$

3. Return the filtered pixel $F(i,j)$ given by

$$
F(i,j) = \begin{cases} G(i,j), & \text{if } (i,j) \in \mathcal{U}, \\ F'(i,j), & \text{if } (i,j) \in \mathcal{D}. \end{cases}
$$

4   Reduction of General Impulsive Noise Using a New Combination of Noise Detection and Impulse Noise Filtering

Just like general impulsive noise, salt-and-pepper noise is also characterized by Eq. 1. However, $\eta(i,j)$ is not uniformly distributed in the value set but equal to its minimum or maximum value. Thus, for grayscale images whose values are normalized in the range $[0,1]$, we have $\eta(i,j) \in \{0,1\}$.

Both the ATIF and the i-FMMOCS are suited to remove salt-and-pepper noise from images while preserving image details. Figure 3 taken from [9] presents a visual comparison of the results. A visual inspection shows that the i-FMMOCS yields a better result than the ATIF in Fig. 3. More generally, Sussner and Schuster observed in a number of simulations that the ATIF outperformed the i-FMMOCS in applications to images corrupted by 30 and 50% salt-and-pepper noise. The contrary occurred for images corrupted by 80% salt-and-pepper noise.

Fig. 3. *From left to right, top to bottom,* detailed views of the original 'boats' image, a corrupted version containing 70% *salt and pepper* noise, and reconstructions generated by the AFT-IF, and by the i-FMMOCS.

Note that the i-FMMOCS was designed for salt-and-pepper noise reduction and is unsuited for removing general impulsive noise but this fact is only due to its noise detection phase. Therefore, our proposal for high-density impulsive noise reduction consists of the following two phases:

1. ATIF/FIDRM noise detection;
2. i-FMMOCS filtering.

As mentioned before, we refer to this combined method as the *fuzzy impulse noise detection based open-close filter* (FIDOC). Of course, it is questionable if this combination outperforms - as expected - the ATIF when it comes to high-density impulsive noise reduction. The following section presents some experimental results.

Table 1. PSNR, SSIM and NMSE for the three filters considered for the 'peppers' image at different noise densities.

Noise	PSNR			SSIM			NMSE		
	FIDOC-fl	FIDOC-nfl	ATIF	FIDOC-fl	FIDOC-nfl	ATIF	FIDOC-fl	FIDOC-nfl	ATIF
10	33.8395	33.8402	*34.5464*	0.9212	0.9173	*0.9251*	*0.0095*	*0.0095*	0.0181
20	*32.0821*	32.0146	31.8850	0.9057	0.9052	*0.9087*	*0.0179*	0.0180	0.0288
30	31.2367	31.3100	*31.3128*	0.8922	0.8920	*0.8950*	0.0205	*0.0192*	0.0299
40	30.4018	*30.4213*	30.3259	*0.8768*	0.8766	0.8741	*0.0197*	*0.0197*	0.0312
50	29.4635	*29.5033*	29.3979	0.8552	*0.8554*	0.8418	0.0181	*0.0180*	0.0292
60	28.1919	*28.2233*	28.0495	*0.8264*	*0.8264*	0.7984	*0.0191*	0.0197	0.0331
70	26.3920	*26.4668*	26.1541	0.7704	*0.7719*	*0.7213*	0.0257	*0.0250*	0.0381
80	24.4972	*24.6157*	24.4490	0.6932	*0.6973*	0.6458	0.0333	*0.0329*	0.0476
90	22.1173	22.2556	*22.4982*	0.5765	*0.5837*	0.5516	0.0497	*0.0494*	0.0631

5   Experimental Results

In this section, we evaluate the performances of the proposed FIDOC method and the ATIF in the task of filtering images that are corrupted by impulsive noise. To this end, we performed simulations using four well know images, namely 'Barbara', 'boats', 'Lena', and 'peppers', with the probability of impulsive noise varying from 10% to 90% with increments of 10%. In addition to a visual comparison of the filtered images obtained by the algorithms, the restoration performances are quantitatively measured in terms of three widely used performance measures, namely peak signal-to-noise ratio (PSNR), structural similarity index (SSIM), and normalized mean square error (NMSE).

The definition of the i-FMMOCS filter depends on the following parameters: A t-norm and its residual implication, as well as the structuring elements for Step 2 of the i-FMMOCS filter. In this work, we employed the minimum t-norm T_M and its residual implication I_{GD}, i.e., the same operators that were previously used in [8]. With regards to the structuring elements, we only considered isotropic shapes. The sizes of the structuring elements are determined by Step 2 of the algorithm anyway. Motivated by the work of González-Hidalgo et al., we took flat structuring elements into account but in this paper we also conducted experiments using normalized isotropic structuring elements with a Gaussian decay from the origin, and a value of 1 at the center. In previous simulations [8], the i-FMMOCS filter exhibited a better performance when used in conjunction with flat structuring elements. The FIDOC using flat and non-flat SEs are respectively referred to using the acronyms "FIDOC-fl" and "FIDOC-nfl".

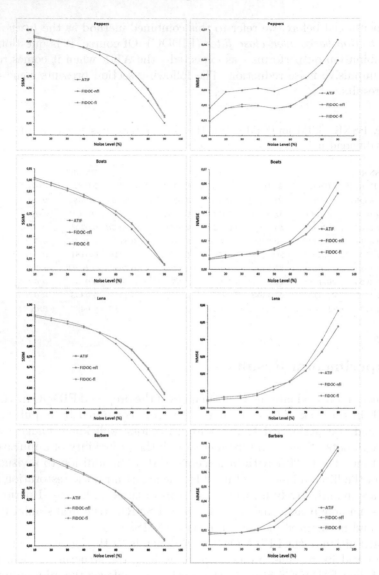

Fig. 4. SSIM and NMSE values produced by the ATIF, the FIDOC-nfl, and the FIDOC-fl in applications to images that contain 10 to 90% impulsive noise.

Table 1 presents the PSNR, SSIM, and NMSE values resulting from applications of the FIDOC-fl, FIDOC-nfl, and ATIF methods to the 'peppers' image corrupted by impulsive noise with densities ranging from 10 to 90%. Generally speaking, the FIDOC-nfl method slightly outperformed both the FIDOC-fl and the ATIF. This fact is especially noticeable for noise densities over 50%. Similar observations can be made with respect to the other three images under consideration. Figure 4 displays the evolution of the SSIM and NMSE values obtained

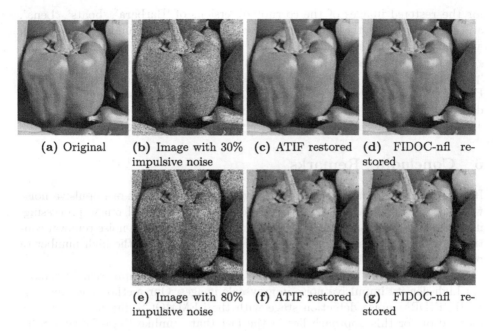

(a) Original   (b) Image with 30% impulsive noise   (c) ATIF restored   (d) FIDOC-nfl restored

(e) Image with 80% impulsive noise   (f) ATIF restored   (g) FIDOC-nfl restored

Fig. 5. Top row from left to right: Detailed views of the original 'peppers' image, a corrupted version containing 30% impulsive noise, and the ATIF and FIDOC-nfl filtered images; Bottom row from left to right: A corrupted version containing 80% impulsive noise, and the ATIF and FIDOC-nfl filtered images.

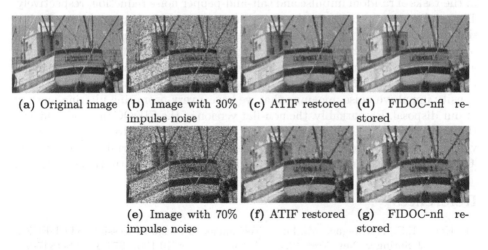

(a) Original image   (b) Image with 30% impulse noise   (c) ATIF restored   (d) FIDOC-nfl restored

(e) Image with 70% impulse noise   (f) ATIF restored   (g) FIDOC-nfl restored

Fig. 6. Top row from left to right: Detailed views of the original 'boats' image, a corrupted version containing 30% impulsive noise, and the ATIF and FIDOC-nfl filtered images; Bottom row from left to right: A corrupted version containing 70% impulsive noise, and the ATIF and FIDOC-nfl filtered images.

for the restored images of the corrupted versions of 'Barbara', 'boats', 'Lena', and 'peppers'. Since the PSNR curves for the three methods under consideration are almost indistinguishable, we decided to omit them.

Figures 5 and 6 show the restoration results for corrupted versions of the 'peppers' and 'boats' images, respectively. A visual inspection reveals that the FIDOC-nfl method suppresses most of the impulsive noise while preserving details and edges. The benefits of the FIDOC-nfl in comparison to the ATIF are especially noticeable for the relatively high noise densities of 70 and 80%.

6   Concluding Remarks

It is of utmost importance to drastically reduce the amount of impulsive noise while preserving image details before executing higher level image processing, image analysis, or computer vision tasks. Therefore, impulse noise removal continues to be a very active area of research as indicated by the high number of recent publications [17–19] and websites on this topic.

In this paper, we introduced the FIDOC method, a new approach for removing high-density impulsive noise in grayscale images. Our method combines the ATIF/FIDRM noise detection stage with the i-FMMOCS filtering stage. The motivation for this approach lies in the fact that – unlike the i-FMMOCS filtering stage – the noise detector of the i-FMMOCS, that was designed as a salt-and-pepper image noise reduction method, is not meant to be applied to images corrupted by general impulsive noise.

Recall that the ATIF and the i-FMMOCS have exhibited excellent performances [8,11] in comparison to a number of highly competitive filtering methods in the tasks of random impulse and salt-and-pepper noise reduction, respectively. The preliminary experimental results presented in this paper (due to limitations in the number of pages, additional experiments including comparisons with other state-of-the-art algorithms have to be postponed) indicate that the new algorithm slightly outperforms its predecessors – both visually and in terms of PSNR, SSIM and NMSE values – in applications to images corrupted by high density impulsive noise, meaning that we have a very promising filtering method at our disposal. Remarkably, the non-flat version of the FIDOC method achieved the best performance in our simulations which may be due to the fact that the values of the pixels corrupted by impulsive noise are uniformly distributed in [0, 1]. However, further research is necessary in order to confirm this hypothesis.

References

1. Kerre, E.E., Nachtegael, M.: Fuzzy Techniques in Image Processing. STUDFUZZ, vol. 52. Springer, New York (2000). https://doi.org/10.1007/978-3-7908-1847-5
2. Schulte, S., Nachtegael, M., De Witte, V., Van der Weken, D., Kerre, E.E.: A fuzzy impulse noise detection and reduction method. IEEE Trans. Image Process. **15**(5), 1153–1162 (2006)
3. Schuster, T., Sussner, P.: An adaptive image filter based on the fuzzy transform for impulse noise reduction. Soft. Comput. **21**(13), 3659–3672 (2017)

4. Yüksel, M.E., Bastürk, A.: Application of type 2 fuzzy logic filtering to reduce noise in color images. IEEE Comput. Intell. Mag. **7**(3), 25–36 (2012)
5. Chen, C.L.P., Liu, L., Chen, L., Tang, Y.Y., Zhou, Y.: Weighted couple sparse representation with classified regularization for impulse noise removal. IEEE Trans. Image Process. **24**(11), 4014–4026 (2015)
6. Panetta, K., Bao, L., Agaian, S.: A new unified impulse noise removal algorithm using a new reference sequence-to-sequence similarity detector. IEEE Access **6**, 37225–37236 (2018)
7. Rani, S., Chabbra, Y., Malik, K.: Adaptive window-based filter for high-density impulse noise suppression. Measur. Sens. **24**, 100455 (2022)
8. Gonzalez-Hidalgo, M., Massanet, S., Mir, A., Ruiz-Aguilera, D.: Improving salt and pepper noise removal using a fuzzy mathematical morphology-based filter. Appl. Soft Comput. **63**, 167–180 (2018)
9. Sussner, P., Schuster, T.: Linear versus lattice fuzzy transforms: image algebra representation, observations, and results in image denoising. In: 2018 IEEE International Conference on Fuzzy Systems (FUZZ-IEEE), pp. 1–8 (2018)
10. Perfilieva, I.: Fuzzy transforms: theory and applications. Fuzzy Sets Syst. **157**, 993–1023 (2006)
11. Sussner, P.: Lattice fuzzy transforms from the perspective of mathematical morphology. Fuzzy Sets Syst. **288**, 115–128 (2016)
12. Ritter, G.X., Wilson, J.N.: Handbook of Computer Vision Algorithms in Image Algebra, 2nd edn. CRC Press, Boca Raton (2001)
13. Bloch, I., Maitre, H.: Fuzzy mathematical morphologies: a comparative study. Pattern Recogn. **28**(9), 1341–1387 (1995)
14. De Baets, B.: Fuzzy morphology: a logical approach. In: Ayyub, B.M., Gupta, M.M. (eds.) Uncertainty Analysis in Engineering and Science: Fuzzy Logic, Statistics, and Neural Network Approach, pp. 53–67. Kluwer Academic Publishers, Norwell (1997)
15. Baczyński, M., Jayaram, B.: Fuzzy Implications. STUDFUZZ, vol. 231. Springer, Heidelberg (2008). https://doi.org/10.1007/978-3-540-69082-5
16. Klement, E.P., Mesiar, R., Pap, E.: Triangular Norms. Kluwer Academic Publishers, London (2000)
17. Bindal, N., Ghumaan, R.S., Sohi, P.J.S., Sharma, N., Joshi, H., Garg, B.: A systematic review of state-of-the-art noise removal techniques in digital images. Multimed. Tools Appl. **81**(22), 31529–31552 (2022)
18. Yin, M., Adam, T., Paramesran, R., Hassan, M.F.: An ℓ0-overlapping group sparse total variation for impulse noise image restoration. Signal Process.: Image Commun. **102**, 116620 (2022)
19. Orazaev, A., Lyakhov, P., Baboshina, V., Kalita, D.: Neural network system for recognizing images affected by random-valued impulse noise. Appl. Sci. **13**(3) (2023)

Fuzzy Fingerprinting Large Pre-trained Models

Rui Ribeiro[1,2]([✉])[iD], Patrícia Pereira[1,2][iD], Luísa Coheur[1,2][iD],
Helena Moniz[1,3][iD], and Joao P. Carvalho[1,2][iD]

[1] INESC-ID, Lisbon, Portugal
{helena.moniz,joao.carvalho}@inesc-id.pt
[2] Instituto Superior Técnico, Universidade de Lisboa, Lisbon, Portugal
{rui.m.ribeiro,patriciaspereira,luisa.coheur}@tecnico.ulisboa.pt
[3] Faculdade de Letras, Universidade de Lisboa, Lisbon, Portugal

Abstract. Large pre-trained models like BERT and RoBERTa have gained massive popularity as they have surpassed previous state-of-the-art models in various Natural Language Processing (NLP) tasks. Nevertheless, interpreting their behavior is still an ongoing challenge as these models are composed of millions of parameters. The introduction of the Fuzzy Fingerprint (FFP) framework provided a straightforward classification technique able to deliver result interpretations, however, this method was outperformed by these large pre-trained models. In this work, we introduce a novel method that combines the simplicity of the FFPs with the ability to detect complex patterns of large pre-trained models, in order to build a more interpretable classification framework. Furthermore, we show that it is feasible to obtain unique FFPs for each label that enable the examination of incorrect classifications. We evaluate our new method on four text classification benchmark datasets and show that it is possible to gain interpretability without any noticeable loss in performance.

Keywords: Fuzzy Fingerprints · Pre-Trained Language Models · Text Classification

1 Introduction

The emergence of large pre-trained language models has contributed to major advances in various NLP tasks. Particularly, in text classification tasks such as sentiment analysis, topic classification, and emotion classification, these new models have achieved state-of-the-art results by fine-tuning with a few samples

Supported by Fundação para a Ciência e a Tecnologia (FCT), through Portuguese national funds Ref. UIDB/50021/2020, Agência Nacional de Inovação (ANI), through the projects CMU-PT MAIA Ref. 045909, Plano de Recuperação e Resiliência (PRR) Center for Responsible AI C645008882-00000055, and the COST Action Multi3Generation Ref. CA18231.

S. Massanet et al. (Eds.): EUSFLAT 2023/AGOP 2023, LNCS 14069, pp. 232–243, 2023.
https://doi.org/10.1007/978-3-031-39965-7_20

from the target dataset [10,12,13]. However, interpreting the prediction outputs is notoriously difficult as they contain millions of parameters with complex internal patterns.

Homem and Carvalho (2011) [2,3] introduced the Fuzzy Fingerprint (FFP) framework[1] for identifying users based on a minimal set of features that describe their behaviors. These features are obtained from the idiosyncratic habits of the users, for instance, the most frequent words utilized, the frequency someone calls their contacts, the most accessed web pages, etc. Furthermore, the frequency of the gathered features can be measured in order to construct individual fingerprints, which can then be exploited for identifying and distinguishing between a set of possible candidate users.

The principle of FFPs has been adapted to the classification setting [2,3,7]. The authors obtained the FFP of the test sample and compared it to the FFPs from each label of the dataset using fuzzy-inspired similarity functions. Although achieving competing results against other classification methods, especially when the number of classes increased considerably, this method was later outperformed by large pre-trained language models such as BERT [4] and RoBERTa [6]. Nevertheless, FFPs have the advantage of being simpler and more interpretable than these models, as it is possible to diagnose the classification errors by comparing the FFP obtained against the FFPs from the classes.

In this paper, we propose to merge large deep learning models with the Fuzzy Fingerprint framework and combine the robustness of pre-trained models and the interpretability of FFPs. Moreover, we introduce a method that exploits the hidden representations learned from large pre-trained models such as BERT or RoBERTa to build compact fingerprints that uniquely identify each label from the datasets. In the first stage, we follow the common procedure and fine-tune a large pre-trained model in the target datasets; after that, we obtain the fingerprint for each class using the samples from the training data; finally, to classify, we compare the fingerprint from the test sample with the fingerprint of each label using a fuzzy similarity function. We evaluate our models in the sentiment analysis, topic classification, and ontology classification tasks, where the results obtained demonstrate a promising research direction of the proposed framework.

2   Background and Related Work

2.1   Pre-trained Models

Since the introduction of the Transformers framework [11], a deep neural network encoder-decoder architecture, most of the previous state-of-the-art models were surpassed in various NLP tasks. A very popular large pre-trained model is BERT [4], a multi-layer bidirectional Transformer encoder trained to perform language modeling and next-sentence prediction. This model was trained on English Wikipedia and the BooksCorpus during a computationally expensive

---

[1] FFP should not be confused with the identically named work by Stein et al. [9].

process, where it learns deep contextual embeddings, i.e., vectors representing the semantics of each word or sequence of words. In a lesser expensive operation, BERT can be fine-tuned to fulfill other tasks using a much smaller data size. Currently, most NLP works resort to these pre-trained language models [1,5,8]. For instance, to fine-tune BERT for a downstream text classification task, a classification module, usually a fully connected Neural Network (NN), is attached to the last layer of the language model. Due to the bidirectional setting of BERT, a typical approach is to add a special classification token ([CLS]) at the beginning of the input sequence and use the final hidden state of the [CLS] token as the contextual representation of the whole input. This vector is then passed through the classification module to output a probability for each label in the dataset.

RoBERTa [6], a successor to BERT, contains the same architecture as BERT but leverages a different pre-training scheme. Furthermore, it is pre-trained with more data and for a longer period of time than BERT. It also uses larger mini-batches and a larger learning rate and discards BERT's task of next-sentence prediction. RoBERTa has outperformed BERT in various tasks using the same amount of data.

In this work, we use fine-tuned BERT and RoBERTa as the basis for our classification model: sentences are fed as inputs to the language model and we use the final hidden state of the [CLS] classification token to create the FFPs.

2.2   Fuzzy Fingerprints

Fingerprint identification is a well-known and widely documented technique in forensic sciences. In computer science, a fingerprint is a procedure that maps an arbitrarily large data item (such as a computer file, or author set of texts) to a much more compact information block (a fingerprint) that uniquely identifies the original data for all practical purposes, just as human fingerprints uniquely identify people for practical purposes.

In order to serve classification, a fingerprint must be able to capture the identity of a given class. In other words, the probability of a collision, i.e., two classes yielding the same fingerprint, must be small. Typically, FFPs are built based on feature frequency. For example, for text classification purposes, we consider a set of texts associated with a given class to build the class fingerprint and can use the frequency of each word in each text to build the fingerprint for that class.

The set of Fuzzy Fingerprints of all classes is known as the fingerprint library. Given a fingerprint library and an instance to be classified, for example, a text, we obtain the text fingerprint using a process similar to the one used to create the fingerprint of each class, and then find the class that has the most similar fingerprint.

Fuzzy Fingerprint Creation and Fuzzy Fingerprint Libraries. The training set is divided by the different classes and is processed to compute the top-k feature list for each class. Consider F_j as the set of events of class j (simplistic example: the set of all words for all texts belonging to class j). The result consists of a list of k pairs $\{v_i, n_i\}$, $1 < i \leq k$, where v_i is the i-th most frequent feature and n_i the corresponding count (simplistic example: an ordered k-sized list containing the most frequent distinct words). The next step consists in fuzzifying each top-k list in order to obtain the class fingerprint: a membership value is assigned to each feature in the set based only on the order in the list (the rank). For instance, when the features are the word frequencies, the rank is considered instead of the frequency due to empirical experiments that show that the order of the frequency seems more relevant than the actual frequency value [2]. The more frequent features will have a higher membership value.

The fingerprint (Φ), which is based on the top-k list, consists of a size-k fuzzy vector where each position i contains an element v_i and a membership value μ_i representing the fuzzified value of v_i's rank (the membership of the rank). A class j will be represented by its fingerprint $\Phi_j = \Phi(F_j)$. Formally, the fingerprint $\Phi_j = \{(v_{ji}, \mu_{ji}) \mid i = 1 \ldots k_j\}$ has length k_j, with $S_j = \{v_{ji} \mid i = 1 \ldots k_j\}$ representing the set of v's in Φ_j. The set of all class fingerprints will constitute the fingerprint library.

Fuzzy Fingerprint Detection. In order to find the class of an unknown instance, for example, a text T, we start by computing the size-k fingerprint of T, Φ_T. Then we compare the fingerprint of T with the fingerprints Φ_j of all classes present in the fingerprint library. The unknown text is classified as j if it has the most similar fingerprint to Φ_j. The fingerprint comparison, $\text{sim}(\Phi_T, \Phi_j)$, is calculated using

$$\text{sim}(\Phi_T, \Phi_j) = \sum_{v \in S_T \cup S_j} \frac{\min(\mu_v(\Phi_T), \mu_v(\Phi_j))}{k}, \tag{1}$$

where $\mu_v(\Phi_x)$ is the membership value associated with the rank of element v in fingerprint x. This function is based on the fuzzy AND. We use the minimum or Gödel t-norm in accordance with [2], but other t-norms could also be used.

3 Fuzzy Fingerprinting Large Pre-trained Models

3.1 Fine-Tuning BERT and RoBERTa

In the first stage, we need to obtain a model capable of outputting representations for the target dataset. For that, we adopt the common procedure for fine-tuning a large pre-trained encoder ($\mathcal{M}^E$) such as BERT or RoBERTa in the text classification datasets.

Consider one sentence $x = \{\,\texttt{[CLS]}, w_1, ..., w_n\}$ composed of n words and the [CLS] token. First, we utilize the encoder $\mathcal{M}^E$ to obtain a hidden representation h with size N from the input sentence x. Then, we include a softmax classifier on top of $\mathcal{M}^E$ to obtain the probability distribution over the set of possible classes. Formally, we obtain the probability of label y with:

$$h = \mathcal{M}^E(x), \quad p(y|x) = \text{softmax}(Wh), \tag{2}$$

where W is the learnable parameter matrix from the classification layer. We fine-tune $\mathcal{M}^E$ and learn W parameters by maximizing the log probability of the correct label.

3.2 Fuzzy Fingerprint Creation from Pre-trained Models

Since the output from the model (the final hidden state of the [CLS] classification token) is a real-valued vector with size N, where each element's value does not have a known meaning, it is simply not possible to create an FFP based on feature frequencies (as described in Sect. 2.2). In order to address this issue, we propose to use the intensity of the activation of each element from $\mathcal{M}^E$ output as a proxy for feature frequency.

The process to create a class fingerprint can be therefore succinctly described as "ranking the activation of the $\mathcal{M}^E$ outputs through the training set (of that class)". After fine-tuning $\mathcal{M}^E$ for the task and considering an output size of N from $\mathcal{M}^E$, the procedure is described as follows:

1. The training data is used to create Fuzzy Fingerprints for each class;
2. The fingerprint for each class begins as a N-sized vector of pairs, where each pair in the vector is composed of an index (corresponding to a hidden unit from $\mathcal{M}^E$ out of the possible N units) and a value initialized to 0;
3. The fine-tuned $\mathcal{M}^E$ is fed with all the training examples of a given class (one by one);
4. For each example, the hidden vector h from Eq. 2 is added to the fingerprint of the corresponding class. Hence, after all the training examples (of a given class) are fed into $\mathcal{M}^E$, the fingerprint of the class consists of a vector where each position contains an index of a hidden unit and the accumulated value of the $\mathcal{M}^E$ for that hidden unit;
5. Order the fingerprint vector by the accumulated value (in descending order);
6. Remove the element containing the accumulated values from the pairs (only the rank matters). As a result, we have, for each class, a vector of dimension N, containing the indexes of the most activated $\mathcal{M}^E$ hidden outputs for that class, i.e., the $\mathcal{M}^E$ outputs are ranked by activation on the training set;
7. The final FFP is obtained by fuzzifying the top-k sized vector according to a function inspired by the Pareto Rule, where roughly 80% of the membership value is assigned to the first 20% positions of the ranking:

$$
\mu_i = \begin{cases} 1 - \frac{0.8 \times i}{0.2k}, & i < 0.2k \\ -\frac{0.2 \times i}{0.8k} + 0.25, & 0.2k < i < k \end{cases} \tag{3}
$$

in which i is the position of an element in the sorted vector and k is the fingerprint size;
8. Instead of the whole N outputs, the fingerprint only considers the top-k $\mathcal{M}^E$ outputs for classification purposes, i.e., only the top-k elements will have a membership value higher than zero, and exactly zero for the remaining. For simplicity, we refer to this representation as a fingerprint of size k.

In sum, the FFP of a pre-trained language model is a Fuzzy Set in the discrete universe of the N outputs from $\mathcal{M}^E$, where each one has associated a membership value, and only the top-k elements have a membership greater than zero. For practical purposes, the set is ordered by the membership function of its elements (in descending order).

3.3   Classification Using Fuzzy Fingerprints

After obtaining the fingerprints for all classes (the Fingerprint Library), the classification of a sample can be performed. Given an instance I to be classified:

1. Pass I through $\mathcal{M}^E$;
2. Create the fingerprint of I using the same procedure used to create the fingerprint of a class (i.e. rank the activation of the output vector, select the top-k elements and fuzzify the resulting vector (calculate the membership values with Eq. 3);
3. Check the similarity of the fingerprint of I against the fingerprint of each class using the Fuzzy similarity function from Eq. 1, and select the class with the highest similarity.

In Fig. 1, we provide an illustration of the complete structure of the framework. For simplification purposes, we omit the membership values and only present the hidden units ranked by activation.

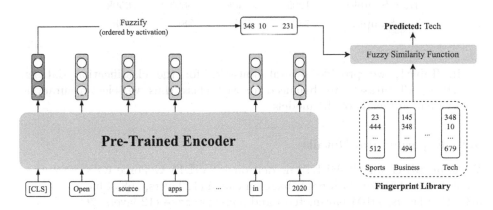

Fig. 1. Illustration of the classification using FFPs.

4   Experiments

4.1   Datasets

We evaluate our models on four text classification benchmark datasets [14]:

- AG News: a topic classification dataset composed of a collection of news articles that have been gathered from more than 2000 news sources by Come-ToMyHead in more than 1 year of activity. ComeToMyHead is an academic news search engine that has been running since July 2004.
- DBPedia: an ontology classification dataset composed of 14 non-overlapping classes from DBpedia 2014, a project that focuses on the extraction of structured content from the Wikipedia project.
- Yelp-2 and Yelp-5: two sentiment classification datasets extracted from the Yelp platform, from the Yelp Dataset Challenge 2015 data. The Yelp-5 contains five sentiment labels ranging from 1 (Very Bad) to 5 (Very Good) while Yelp-2 considers only two classes (positive or negative).

Table 1. Statistics of the text classification datasets.

	AG News	DBPedia	Yelp-2	Yelp-5
Classification Task	Topic	Ontology	Sentiment	Sentiment
Num. Classes	4	14	2	5
Train Samples	120k	560k	560k	650k
Test Samples	7.6k	70k	38k	50k

In Table 1, we provide several statistics for the classification datasets described. All datasets are balanced for each class, thus we select accuracy as the evaluation metric of the models.

4.2   Experimental Details

We train BERT and RoBERTa models on 1 NVIDIA GeForce RTX 3080 using a batch size of 16 for both `bert-base-uncased` (12 layers, 768 of hidden size, 12 attention heads, 110M parameters) and `roberta-base` (12 layers, 768 of hidden size, 12 attention heads, 125M parameters). Models are trained to minimize the cross entropy using Adam optimizer with a learning rate of $2e^-5$. We train the models for all datasets for 35k steps in the training corpus. All experiments are implemented using the HuggingFace[2] and PyTorch[3] libraries.

FFPs were implemented in Python using our own code. We experiment with different k values for the fingerprints, varying between 1 and 768 (the maximum hidden size of the models).

---

[2] https://huggingface.co/.
[3] https://pytorch.org/.

4.3   Results and Discussion

We present the obtained results in the four classification datasets and compare our results with fine-tuned BERT and RoBERTa models.

The accuracy of fine-tuned BERT and RoBERTa models is presented in Table 2. We can observe that RoBERTa predominantly achieves the highest score. The most challenging corpus for the models is Yelp-5, where the difference between the best score with the other datasets is higher. This is plausible as the dataset is composed of five sentiment labels, ranging from 1 (Very Bad) to 5 (Very Good), and, as we will investigate next, the models fail to distinguish the labels that are closest to each other.

Fuzzy Fingerprints. In order to understand the influence of the fingerprint size, we experiment the FFP framework for different k ranging from 1 to 768 (the maximum output size of BERT and RoBERTa from our experiments).

In Figs. 2 and 3, we plot the accuracy scores obtained by varying the size of the FFPs. We only plot for k lower than 100, since for higher k the scores stabilize and fluctuate minimally. We can observe that in all datasets, the accuracy converges with the results obtained from the best fine-tuned model. In the datasets with higher accuracy obtained from BERT and RoBERTa (DBPedia and Yelp-2), the FFP models reach similar results using small k values. For instance,

Table 2. Accuracy (%) for fine-tuned BERT and RoBERTa.

Models	AG News	DBPedia	Yelp-2	Yelp-5
BERT	94.78	**99.33**	97.40	69.00
RoBERTa	**95.24**	99.27	**97.45**	**69.52**

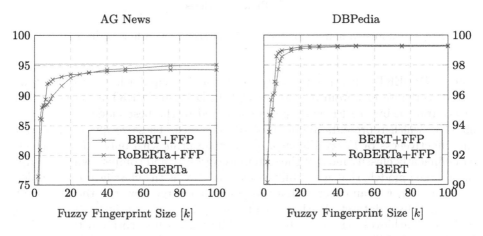

Fig. 2. Accuracy (%) for Fuzzy Fingerprint size up to $k = 100$. We also plot the best model in the dataset from Table 2. Left: AG News. Right: DBPedia.

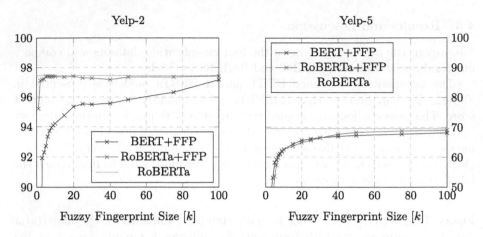

Fig. 3. Accuracy (%) for Fuzzy Fingerprint size up to $k = 100$. We also plot the best model in the dataset from Table 2. Left: Yelp-2. Right: Yelp-5.

	1	2	3	4	5
1	7216 82%	2538 22%	210 2%	17 0%	19 0%
2	1324 15%	6234 53%	1849 17%	581 5%	12 0%
3	112 1%	1736 15%	6574 62%	1479 14%	99 1%
4	50 1%	146 1%	1767 17%	6128 58%	1909 23%
5	64 1%	1041 9%	196 2%	2416 23%	6283 75%

Correct Class (vertical axis) — Predicted Class (horizontal axis)

Fig. 4. Confusion matrix for the Yelp-5 dataset using a fingerprint $k = 20$.

using a RoBERTa fingerprint of only 2 elements in Yelp-2 achieves 97.11% compared to the 97.45% from the best model. In DBPedia, BERT achieves 98.81% in accuracy using a FFP with size 8 compared to the best model that reaches 99.33%, which represents about 0.5% of difference. These results demonstrate the effectiveness of Fuzzy Fingerprints: a fingerprint with only a few elements can efficiently classify most of the examples correctly and compete with the large pre-trained models that use a fully connected NN as the classification module.

Moreover, we can observe that the models converge slower in the most challenging Yelp-5 dataset. With a small fingerprint size, for instance, $k = 10$, RoBERTa achieves a score of 62.50%, while with a fingerprint with $k = 100$, it achieves 69.04%, a more ambitious result against the best model that scores 69.52%. As explained before, this is expected due to the nature of the Yelp-5 cor-

Table 3. Fuzzy Fingerprints ($k = 20$) of the 5 sentiment classes from Yelp-5. For readability purposes, the RoBERTa outputs are ordered by descending membership. Color represents values that share exactly 2 fingerprints and in bold share 3 or more class fingerprints.

FFP$_1$ = {(**588**, 1), (**453**, 0.8), (77, 0.6), (**664**, 0.4), (409, 0.2), (553, 0.1875), (202, 0.175), (397, 0.1625), (254, 0.15), (**647**, 0.1375), (493, 0.125), (**240**, 0.1125), (19, 0.1), (103, 0.0875), (206, 0.075), (573, 0.0625), (61, 0.05), (21, 0.0375), (79, 0.025), (344, 0.0125)}

FFP$_2$ = {(**588**, 1), (**453**, 0.8), (77, 0.6), (248, 0.4), (409, 0.2), (61, 0.1875), (662, 0.175), (**647**, 0.1625), (553, 0.15), (504, 0.1375), (521, 0.125), (573, 0.1125), (**664**, 0.1), (560, 0.0875), (163, 0.075), (611, 0.05), (565, 0.0375), (156, 0.025), (765, 0.0125)}

FFP$_3$ = {(**588**, 1), (**453**, 0.8), (611, 0.6), (561, 0.4), (**131**, 0.2), (629, 0.1875), (259, 0.175), (248, 0.1625), (109, 0.15), (107, 0.1375), (**240**, 0.125), (34, 0.1125), (380, 0.1), (621, 0.0875), (121, 0.075), (449, 0.0625), (229, 0.05), (653, 0.0375), (765, 0.025), (155, 0.0125)}

FFP$_4$ = {(**588**, 1), (**453**, 0.8), (**664**, 0.6), (4, 0.4), (103, 0.2), (265, 0.1875), (531, 0.175), (**240**, 0.1625), (190, 0.15), (629, 0.1375), (**131**, 0.125), (255, 0.1125), (550, 0.1), (102, 0.0875), (580, 0.075), (523, 0.0625), (380, 0.05), (609, 0.0375), (408, 0.025), (432, 0.0125)}

FFP$_5$ = {(**588**, 1), (**453**, 0.8), (4, 0.6), (523, 0.4), (**647**, 0.2), (476, 0.1875), (455, 0.175), (473, 0.1625), (311, 0.15), (**664**, 0.1375), (564, 0.125), (359, 0.1125), (113, 0.1), (255, 0.0875), (78, 0.075), (259, 0.0625), (503, 0.05), (550, 0.0375), (504, 0.025), (**131**, 0.0125)}

pus: the fingerprint size needs to be larger to reasonably represent the differences in representations from the reviews.

In Fig. 4, we report the confusion matrix obtained for a Fuzzy Fingerprint RoBERTa with $k = 20$. This confirms our hypothesis about the difficulty of Yelp-5: the majority of the incorrect predictions are the labels adjacent to the correct label; additionally, in the extreme labels (1 and 5), the model is more capable of identifying the correct labels, whereas it fails more frequently in the central labels.

Fuzzy Fingerprint Analysis. We dissect the FFPs obtained from our framework in order to understand the influence of the fingerprints and their components in the final classification of the examples.

In Table 3, we present the fingerprints for the 5 sentiment classes present in the Yelp-5 corpus, highlighting in color the values that are shared by exactly 2 labels. We observe that the fingerprints that share the most values are the ones that are closest to each other, for instance, class 1 (Very Bad) shares the most number of values with class 2 (Bad), while class 3 (Neutral) shares with class 2 (Bad) and class 4 (Good), etc. When we analyze the values shared by 3 or more, we see that these values may induce some errors in the classification. For instance, if we look again at the confusion matrix from Fig. 4, when the correct class is 5, the model predicted 9% of the times the label 2. This could be induced by the values shared between the fingerprints from classes 5 and 2: the value 647 appears in the 5th position in class 5 and appears in the 8th position in class 2. Additionally, the values 504 and 664 are shared between the two classes and may also influence the decision of the model.

To further understand the influence of the shared components, in Table 4, we present an example incorrectly predicted by our model along with the respective

Table 4. Example of an incorrect classification for Yelp-5 dataset. For readability purposes, the RoBERTa outputs are ordered by descending membership.

Class 5 FFP (Correct Class):	**FFP Similarity Score: 0.3375**

$FFP_5 = \{(588, 1), (453, 0.8), (4, 0.6), (523, 0.4), (647, 0.2), (476, 0.1875), (455, 0.175),$
$(473, 0.1625), (311, 0.15), (664, 0.1375), (564, 0.125), (359, 0.1125), (113, 0.1), (255,$
$0.0875), (78, 0.075), (259, 0.0625), (503, 0.05), (550, 0.0375), (504, 0.025), (131, 0.0125)\}$

Class 2 FFP (Predicted Class):	**FFP Similarity Score: 0.4875**

$FFP_2 = \{(588, 1), (453, 0.8), (77, 0.6), (248, 0.4), (409, 0.2), (61, 0.1875), (662, 0.175),$
$(647, 0.1625), (553, 0.15), (504, 0.1375), (521, 0.125), (573, 0.1125), (664, 0.1), (560,$
$0.0875), (490, 0.075), (163, 0.0625), (611, 0.05), (565, 0.0375), (156, 0.025), (765, 0.0125)\}$

Sample FFP:

$FFP_s = \{(564, 1), (252, 0.8), (376, 0.1875), 0.6), (573, 0.4), (662, 0.2), (286, , 0.175), (441,$
$0.1625), (113, 0.15), (223, 0.1375), (561, 0.125), (497, 0.1125), (363, 0.1), (469, 0.0875),$
$(511, 0.075), (248, , 0.0625), (647, 0.05), (453, 0.0375), (229, 0.025), (8, (163, 0.0125)\}$

Sample Text:

I have been getting my hair cut here for 15 years. Marjorie is amazing and priceless. I am as picky about my hairstylist as I am my dentist or doctor. I travel extensively for work and get compliments no matter where I travel. Wouldn't go anywhere else!

fingerprint. We can observe that the sample FFP contains more elements in common with class 2 than class 5, although the top value from the sample FFP (564) belongs to class 5. Moreover, the sample contains 2 elements that are shared between both classes (647 and 453), where 647 appears in a higher position in class 5 than class 2. However, as described in Eq. 1, the fuzzy similarity score considers the minimum (lowest ranking) from both fingerprints, which delivers a lower score. These results suggest further research in the FFP ranking directly obtained from the large pre-trained models.

5   Conclusions and Future Work

In this work, we introduced a new technique that combines the interpretability and compact characteristics of the Fuzzy Fingerprint framework with the robustness of the large pre-trained models. We defined the approach that leverages the FFPs from these models and evaluated our method on four text classification datasets. The results showed that with a small FFP size, the models can generalize and compete with the results from fine-tuned models. Furthermore, we give an example of how it is possible to interpret classification errors by checking the FFP of the classes and the incorrectly classified instances. In future work, we would like to extend the use of FFPs to other NLP tasks and investigate unexplored optimizations for the FFPs acquired from pre-trained models.

References

1. Ghosal, D., Majumder, N., Gelbukh, A., Mihalcea, R., Poria, S.: Cosmic: commonsense knowledge for emotion identification in conversations. arXiv preprint arXiv:2010.02795 (2020)

2. Homem, N., Carvalho, J.P.: Authorship identification and author fuzzy "finger-prints". In: 2011 Annual Meeting of the North American Fuzzy Information Processing Society, pp. 1–6. IEEE (2011)
3. Homem, N., Carvalho, J.P.: Web user identification with fuzzy fingerprints. In: 2011 IEEE International Conference on Fuzzy Systems (FUZZ-IEEE 2011), pp. 2622–2629. IEEE (2011)
4. Kenton, J.D.M.W.C., Toutanova, L.K.: BERT: pre-training of deep bidirectional transformers for language understanding. In: Proceedings of NAACL-HLT, pp. 4171–4186 (2019)
5. Li, J., Lin, Z., Fu, P., Wang, W.: Past, present, and future: conversational emotion recognition through structural modeling of psychological knowledge. In: Findings of the Association for Computational Linguistics: EMNLP 2021, pp. 1204–1214 (2021)
6. Liu, Y., et al.: RoBERTa: a robustly optimized BERT pretraining approach (2019). http://arxiv.org/abs/1907.11692
7. Rosa, H., Batista, F., Carvalho, J.P.: Twitter topic fuzzy fingerprints. In: 2014 IEEE International Conference on Fuzzy Systems (FUZZ-IEEE), pp. 776–783. IEEE (2014)
8. Shen, W., Chen, J., Quan, X., Xie, Z.: DialogXL: all-in-one XLNet for multi-party conversation emotion recognition. arXiv preprint arXiv:2012.08695 (2020)
9. Stein, B.: Fuzzy-fingerprints for text-based information retrieval. In: Proceedings of the 5th International Conference on Knowledge Management (I-KNOW 2005), Graz, Journal of Universal Computer Science, pp. 572–579. Citeseer (2005)
10. Sun, C., Qiu, X., Xu, Y., Huang, X.: How to fine-tune BERT for text classification? In: Sun, M., Huang, X., Ji, H., Liu, Z., Liu, Y. (eds.) CCL 2019. LNCS (LNAI), vol. 11856, pp. 194–206. Springer, Cham (2019). https://doi.org/10.1007/978-3-030-32381-3_16
11. Vaswani, A., et al.: Attention is all you need. arXiv preprint arXiv:1706.03762 (2017)
12. Xie, Q., Dai, Z., Hovy, E., Luong, T., Le, Q.: Unsupervised data augmentation for consistency training. In: Advances in Neural Information Processing Systems, vol. 33, pp. 6256 6268 (2020)
13. Yang, Z., Dai, Z., Yang, Y., Carbonell, J., Salakhutdinov, R.R., Le, Q.V.: XLNet: generalized autoregressive pretraining for language understanding. In: Advances in Neural Information Processing Systems, vol. 32 (2019)
14. Zhang, X., Zhao, J., LeCun, Y.: Character-level convolutional networks for text classification. In: Advances in Neural Information Processing Systems, vol. 28 (2015)

AGOP General Track

Aggregation Using Penalty and Moderate Deviation Functions

Jana Špirková[1]([✉]) [iD] and Juliana Beganová[2] [iD]

[1] Faculty of Economics, Matej Bel University in Banská Bystrica, Tajovského 10,
975 90 Banská Bystrica, Slovakia
jana.spirkova@umb.sk
[2] Faculty of Civil Engineering, Slovak University of Technology in Bratislava,
Radlinského 2766/11, 810 05 Bratislava, Slovakia
juliana.beganova@stuba.sk

Abstract. This paper discusses the connection between the local penalty function and the moderate deviation function in the construction of aggregation functions. The basic idea is related to the fact that finding the minimum of a local penalty function and finding the roots of its derivative leads to the corresponding moderate deviation function. It is not always possible to obtain a local penalty function by integrating the moderate deviation function. In addition, the paper introduces the extension of the theory of the construction of aggregation functions using the construction of global moderate deviation functions by different moderate deviation functions, respectively, penalty functions using different local penalty functions, and weighting functions, which are functional values of individual inputs.

Keywords: Aggregation function · Local penalty function · Moderate deviation function · Weights · Weighting functions

1 Introduction

The construction of specific averages using the so-called deviation function was introduced by Daróczy more than 50 years ago [5]. These means are based on the deviation between two real values and can be used to merge a set of input values into one aggregated output value. The main goal of these functions is to obtain an output value that represents the entire set of input values as accurately as possible. However, Daróczy's means do not always remain monotonic, so they are generally not aggregation functions. We should mention, for example, the so-called mixture functions, whose sufficient monotonicity conditions can be found in [10,14].

Therefore, the authors in [6,7], have introduced the so-called moderate deviation function, which ensures that functions based on moderate deviation functions satisfy all properties of aggregation functions. Currently, research offers various constructions of aggregation functions, which are based on the use of moderate deviation functions [1,6,7,12].

The work of Jana Špirková has been supported by the Slovak Scientific Grant Agency VEGA no. 1/0150/21.

Another option for the construction of aggregation functions is to determine them as the minimum of the so-called penalty functions. Yager in [16] has attempted to present the initial ideas related to the use of a penalty function to help the aggregation processes. Later, Yager and Rybalov in [17] extended the initial idea of penalty-based aggregation. However, the existence of a minimum was not yet guaranteed in their approach. The theory of the construction of aggregation functions using penalty functions was further improved and developed in [2–4] and [13].

The basic idea of our contribution is to determine which aggregation functions can be generated by the penalty function and, at the same time, by the moderate deviation function. Another question is whether we can construct aggregation functions using the penalty function, which cannot be constructed using the moderate deviation function, or vice versa.

The paper is organized as follows. Section 2 – Preliminaries gives basic definitions related to the moderate deviation function and the local penalty function. Section 3 – Moderate deviation-based and penalty-based aggregation points to the mutual relationship between the moderate deviation function and the local penalty function when determining the aggregate value or the fused value of the inputs. Section 4 – Generalization of the global moderate deviation function and penalty function in a certain way expands the theory regarding the interconnection of the mentioned functions, their weights, or weight functions. Section 5 – Conclusion discusses possible open problems in the theory of the construction of aggregation functions using both mentioned functions.

2   Preliminaries

We denote by $\mathbf{I} = [a, b] \subset \bar{\mathbf{R}} = \mathbf{R} \cup \{-\infty, \infty\}$ a closed interval. Thus, $\mathbf{I}^n = \{\mathbf{x} = (x_1, \ldots, x_n) \mid x_i \in \mathbf{I}, i = 1, \ldots, n\}$ is the set of all vectors $\mathbf{x}$ whose components are in the interval $\mathbf{I}$. Taking into account $\mathbf{x}, \mathbf{y} \in \mathbf{I}^n$, $\mathbf{x} = (x_1, \ldots, x_n)$, $\mathbf{y} = (y_1, \ldots, y_n)$, we say that $\mathbf{x} \leq \mathbf{y}$ if and only if $x_i \leq y_i$ for each $i = 1, \ldots, n$.

2.1   Moderate Deviation Function

In this section, we present the basic definitions that will lead us to the construction of aggregation functions using moderate deviation functions. The functions generated in this way are idempotent symmetric aggregation functions.

Definition 1. ([1,12]) *Consider a mapping $\mathcal{D} : \mathbf{I}^2 \to \bar{\mathbf{R}}$, which fulfills*

(i) for every $x \in \mathbf{I}$, $\mathcal{D}(x, \cdot) : \mathbf{I} \to \bar{\mathbf{R}}$ is increasing (not necessarily strictly);
(ii) for every $y \in \mathbf{I}$, $\mathcal{D}(\cdot, y) : \mathbf{I} \to \bar{\mathbf{R}}$ is decreasing (not necessarily strictly);
(iii) $\mathcal{D}(x, y) = 0$ if and only if $x = y$, $x \in \mathbf{I}$, $y \in \mathbf{I}$.

Then $\mathcal{D}$ is called a moderate deviation function. The set of all moderate deviation functions is denoted as $\mathbf{D}$.

Definition 2. [12] *Consider a moderate deviation function $\mathcal{D} \in \mathbf{D}$ and $n \in \mathbf{N}$. Then the function $\mathcal{G}^{\mathcal{D}} : \mathbf{I}^n \times \mathbf{I} \to \bar{\mathbf{R}}$ given by*

$$\mathcal{G}^{\mathcal{D}}(\mathbf{x}, y) = \sum_{i=1}^{n} \mathcal{D}(x_i, y) \tag{1}$$

is called a global moderate deviation function.

Definition 3. [12] *Consider a moderate deviation function $\mathcal{D} \in \mathbf{D}$ and $n \in \mathbf{N}$. Then the mapping $U^{\mathcal{D}} : \mathbf{I}^n \to \mathbf{I}$ given by*

$$U^{\mathcal{D}}(\mathbf{x}) = \frac{1}{2} \left(\sup \left\{ y \in \mathbf{I} \middle| \sum_{i=1}^{n} \mathcal{D}(x_i, y) < 0 \right\} \right.$$
$$\left. + \inf \left\{ y \in \mathbf{I} \middle| \sum_{i=1}^{n} \mathcal{D}(x_i, y) > 0 \right\} \right) \tag{2}$$

is called a $\mathcal{D}$-mean, with standard conventions $\sup\{y \in [a,b] | y \in \emptyset\} = a$ and $\inf\{y \in [a,b] | y \in \emptyset\} = b$.

Theorem 1. [12] *Let $\mathcal{D} \in \mathbf{D}$. Then the $\mathcal{D}$-mean $U^{\mathcal{D}} : \mathbf{I}^n \to \mathbf{I}$ is an idempotent symmetric aggregation function.*

Remark 1. We also consider the convention $\sup\{y \in [a,b] | y \in \emptyset\} = a$ and $\inf\{y \in [a,b] | y \in \emptyset\} = b$ in other definitions.

2.2   Local Penalty Function

As we mentioned in the introduction, several authors tried to define the penalty function and subsequently the penalty-based aggregation functions as precisely as possible. For the purposes of our paper, we present the definitions of the most recent articles [2,3].

Definition 4. (e.g. [2,3]) *The function $LP : \mathbf{I}^2 \to \bar{\mathbf{R}}^+; \mathbf{I} \subseteq \bar{\mathbf{R}}$ is said to be a local penalty function if, for any $x_i, x_j, y \in \bar{\mathbf{R}}$ and $i, j = 1, \dots, n$, it satisfies:*

(i) $LP(x_i, y) = 0$ if and only if $x_i = y$;
(ii) $LP(x_i, y) \geq LP(x_j, y)$ if $|x_i - y| \geq |x_j - y|$.

Definition 5. (e.g. [2,3]) *Let $LP : \mathbf{I}^2 \to \bar{\mathbf{R}}^+$ be a local penalty function. A penalty function $P : \mathbf{I}^{n+1} \to \bar{\mathbf{R}}^+$ is defined for any $\mathbf{x} \in \mathbf{I}^n$ and $y \in \mathbf{I}$ as*

$$P(\mathbf{x}, y) = \sum_{i=1}^{n} LP(x_i, y), \tag{3}$$

where $y \in \mathbf{I}$ is called the fused value of $\mathbf{x} \in \mathbf{I}^n$.

The best fused value of the elements in $\mathbf{x}$ is the value y^* that minimizes the penalty function P

$$y^* = f_P(x_1, \ldots, x_n).$$

Definition 6. (e.g. [2,3]) *The best fused value of* $\mathbf{x}$ *is obtained as the value* y^* *such that*

$$P(\mathbf{x}, y^*) = \arg\min_y P(\mathbf{x}, y), \tag{4}$$

where y^* *is the unique minimizer or* y^* *is the set of minimizers that is the interval* $]a, b[\subset \mathbf{I}$ *(*$[a, b]$*) then* $y^* = \frac{a+b}{2}$*, and* y^* *is called a penalty based function.*

2.3 Faithful Local Penalty Function

In order for the solution of the best fused value to be exactly one value, Calvo et al. in [4] defined the so-called faithful local penalty function as follows:

Definition 7. (e.g. [3,4]) *The function* $LP : \mathbf{I}^2 \to \bar{\mathbf{R}}^+$ *given by*

$$LP(x, y) = K\left(f(x), f(y)\right), \tag{5}$$

where $f : \mathbf{I} \to \bar{\mathbf{R}}$ *is some continuous strictly monotone function and* K *is a penalty function on* $\bar{\mathbf{R}}$ *convex in each component, called a faithful penalty function.*

Definition 8. (e.g. [3,4]) *Let* $K : \bar{\mathbf{R}} \to \bar{\mathbf{R}}^+$ *be a convex function with a unique minimum* $K(0) = 0$ *and let* $f : \mathbf{I} \to \bar{\mathbf{R}}$ *be a strictly monotone continuous function. Then the function* $LP : \mathbf{I}^2 \to \bar{\mathbf{R}}^+$ *given by* $LP(x, y) = K\left(f(x) - f(y)\right)$ *is called a dissimilarity function (on* $\mathbf{I}$*).*

Definition 9. (e.g. [3,4]) *Let* $LP : \mathbf{I}^2 \to \bar{\mathbf{R}}^+$ *be a faithful local penalty function. A function* $f_P : \bigcup_{n \in \mathbf{N}} \mathbf{I}^n \to \mathbf{I}$ *defined for all* $\mathbf{x} \in \mathbf{I}^n$ *and* $n \in \mathbf{N}$*, by*

$$f_{P(\mathbf{x})} = \frac{1}{2}\left(\sup\left\{u \in \mathbf{I} \middle| \forall v \in \mathbf{I} : P(\mathbf{x}, u) \le P(\mathbf{x}, v)\right\}\right.$$
$$\left. + \inf\left\{u \in \mathbf{I} \middle| \forall v \in \mathbf{I} : P(\mathbf{x}, u) \le P(\mathbf{x}, v)\right\}\right) \tag{6}$$

is called a penalty-based function.

2.4 Weighted Penalty Function

If we consider that each observation has its own weight, then we can define a weighted penalty function. We can assume both constant weights and weights as weighting functions. For more information, see [3,15].

Definition 10. ([3])   *Let $LP : \mathbf{I}^2 \to \bar{\mathbf{R}}^+$ be a local penalty function. Then a weighted penalty function $wP : \mathbf{I}^{n+1} \to \bar{\mathbf{R}}^+$ is defined for any $\mathbf{x} \in \mathbf{I}^n$ and $y \in \mathbf{I}$ as follows:*

$$wP(\mathbf{x}, y) = \sum_{i=1}^{n} w_i \cdot LP(x_i, y) \tag{7}$$

where $w_i \geq 0$ are the weights associated with the observations x_i; $i = 1, \ldots, n$. The vector $\mathbf{w} = (w_1, \ldots, w_n)$ is called a weighting vector.

Weighted penalty function - with weighting functions

Definition 11. (e.g. [15])   *Let $LP : \mathbf{I}^2 \to \bar{\mathbf{R}}^+$ be a local penalty function. Then a mixture penalty function $gP : \mathbf{I}^{n+1} \to \bar{\mathbf{R}}^+$ is defined for any $\mathbf{x} \in \mathbf{I}^n$ and $y \in \mathbf{I}$ as follows:*

$$gP(\mathbf{x}, y) = \sum_{i=1}^{n} g_i(x_i) \cdot LP(x_i, y), \tag{8}$$

where $g_i : \mathbf{I} \to]0, \infty[$ are continuous weighting functions associated with the input values x_i, $i = 1, 2, \ldots, n$.

3   Moderate Deviation-Based and Penalty-Based Aggregations

In this section, we offer a summary of the aggregation functions that can be generated using both the moderate deviation function and the penalty function. In some cases, in which weights are applied to the respective deviations, the monotonicity of functions constructed in this way may be violated. In that case, we are talking about the so-called fusion functions. However, under certain sufficient conditions, functions constructed in this way can be aggregation functions.

3.1   Mean as a Penalty and Deviation-Based Function

Table 1 gives an overview of the aggregation functions that are generated by the penalty function or the moderate deviation function. In some cases, conventions are defined so that functions meet the required properties. The basic idea is related to the fact that finding the minimum of the local penalty function and finding the roots of its derivative leads to the corresponding moderate deviation function. In some cases, certain conventions are necessary to obtain correct moderate deviation functions by derivation. However, by integrating the moderate deviation function, we do not get the local penalty function.

Table 1 gives an overview of some aggregation functions that can be constructed using a moderate deviation function and a local penalty function, too.

Remark 2. In the case of the geometric mean, we consider the convention $\log 0 - \log 0 = 0$, and in the case of the harmonic mean $\frac{1}{0} - \frac{1}{0} = 0$.

252   J. Špirková and J. Beganová

Table 1. Deviation-based and penalty-based aggregation functions

Aggregation function	Moderate deviation function	Local penalty function
AM arithmetic mean	$\mathcal{D}(x,y) = y - x$	$LP(x,y) = (x-y)^2$
QAM quasi-arithmetic mean	$\mathcal{D}(x,y) = f(y) - f(x)$	$LP(x,y) = (f(x) - f(y))^2$
GM geometric mean	$\mathcal{D}(x,y) = \log y - \log x$	$LP(x,y) = (\log x - \log y)^2$
HM harmonic mean	$\mathcal{D}(x,y) = \frac{1}{x} - \frac{1}{y}$	$LP(x,y) = \left(\frac{1}{y} - \frac{1}{x}\right)^2$

Example 1. Let us consider a local penalty function in the form

$$LP(x,y) = \left(x^{2k+1} - y^{2k+1}\right)^{2k} \tag{9}$$

for $k \in Z^+$. By deriving this penalty function, we get a moderate deviation function

$$LP'_y(x,y) = 2k \cdot (2k+1) \cdot y^{2k} \cdot \left(y^{2k+1} - x^{2k+1}\right)^{2k-1}. \tag{10}$$

It is obvious that the determination of the minimum penalty function actually represents the search for the roots of the moderate deviation function.

Example 2. Let us look at the situation on the construction of the geometric mean. The first derivative of the penalty function is as follows

$$P'_y(\mathbf{x},y) = \frac{2}{y} \cdot \sum_{i=1}^{n}(\log y - \log x_i).$$

In general, for positive $\phi(y)$, we obtain the global moderate deviation function in the form $\phi(y) \cdot \sum_{i=1}^{n} \mathcal{D}(x_i,y)$, from which we obtain the geometric mean.

Example 3. By integrating the moderate deviation function

$$\mathcal{D}(x,y) = m^y - m^x; \tag{11}$$

$m > 1$, we do not obtain a local penalty function.

Based on Definitions 10 and 11, we can use the local penalty functions and the moderate deviation functions of Table 1 to generate the corresponding weighted averages. However, in the case of the local penalty function and moderate deviation function, which are generated using continuous weighting functions, the respective averages satisfy the properties of aggregation functions only under certain conditions (Table 2). These conditions can be found, for example, in [8, 9, 11, 14, 15].

Table 2. Deviation-based and penalty-based aggregation functions

Aggregation function under certain conditions	Moderate deviation function	Local penalty function
mixture function M_g	$\mathcal{D}(x,y) = g(x) \cdot (y - x)$ g weighting function	$LP(x,y) = g(x) \cdot (x - y)^2$
quasimixture function M_g^f	$\mathcal{D}(x,y) = g(x) \cdot \big(f(y) - f(x)\big)$ f is strictly increasing continuous	$LP(x,y) = g(x) \cdot \big(f(x) - f(y)\big)^2$

3.2 Median and Other Quantiles

Until now, we only considered moderate deviation functions, which were continuous and strictly monotone by Definition 1. We now want to turn our attention to functions that are neither strictly monotonic nor continuous.

If we look at the function $LP(x,y) = |x - y|$, it is obvious that to obtain a moderate deviation function it is necessary to introduce a convention.

$$LP'_y(x,y) = \begin{cases} 1 & \text{for } x < y \\ \text{convention } 0 & \text{for } x = y \\ -1 & \text{for } x > y. \end{cases}$$

Therefore, we obtain the corresponding moderate deviation function.

$$\mathcal{D}(x,y) = \text{sign}(y - x) = \begin{cases} 1 & \text{for } x < y \\ 0 & \text{for } x = y \\ -1 & \text{for } x > y \end{cases}$$

For any $\mathbf{I} = [a,b] \subset \bar{\mathbf{R}}$ let

$$\mathcal{D}(x,y) = \begin{cases} 1, & y > x, \\ 0, & y = x, \\ -c_{i,n}, & y < x. \end{cases} \tag{12}$$

According to [4] we can take $c_{i,n} = \frac{i - \frac{1}{2}}{n - i + \frac{1}{2}}$, $c_{i,n} \in [0, \infty]$, $n \in \mathbf{N}$. Then $\mathcal{D}$-mean w.r.t. Definition 3 is the ith-order statistics and represents $\alpha \cdot 100\%$ quantil operator, where $\alpha = \frac{c_{i,n}}{1 + c_{i,n}}$.

The similarity of the moderate deviation function (12) with the faithful penalty function can be seen in [4]. However, the faithful penalty function does not meet the monotonicity conditions based on Definition 1, so its derivative according to y already meets them.

The authors in [11] discuss in detail the so-called mixture functions with applied local penalty function in the form $LP(x,y) = g(x) \cdot |x - y|$. At the same time, they establish sufficient conditions under which they fulfill all the properties of aggregation functions. The corresponding moderate deviation function is then supplemented with a convention that is written in Table 3.

Table 3. Deviation-based and penalty-based aggregation functions

Aggregation function under certain conditions	Moderate deviation function	Local penalty function
Median		
Upper Median	$\mathcal{D}(x,y) = \begin{cases} g(x) & \text{for } y > x \\ \text{convention } 0 & \text{for } x = y \\ -g(x) & \text{for } y < x \end{cases}$	$LP(x,y) = g(x) \cdot |x - y|$
Lower Median	g weighting function	

It is obvious that individual deviations can have different weights; therefore, aggregations or fusions, respectively, can be extended by introducing appropriate weights. Weighted moderate deviation functions and weighted penalty functions have already been investigated in various papers, for example, in [12,13,15], but we formally introduce the corresponding definitions so that we can subsequently extend the theory with the constructions of the so-called weighted global moderate deviation functions and the mixture global moderate deviation functions.

Definition 12. (e.g. [6,7]) *Consider a moderate deviation function* $\mathcal{D} \in \mathbf{D}$ *and* $n \in \mathbf{N}$. *Then a weighted global moderate deviation function* $w\mathcal{G}^{\mathcal{D}} : \mathbf{I}^{n+1} \to \bar{\mathbf{R}}$ *is defined for any* $\mathbf{x} \in \mathbf{I}^n$ *and* $y \in \mathbf{I}$ *as follows:*

$$w\mathcal{G}^{\mathcal{D}}(\mathbf{x}, y) = \sum_{i=1}^{n} w_i \cdot \mathcal{D}(x_i, y) \qquad (13)$$

where $w_i \geq 0$ *are the weights associated with the observations* x_i; $i = 1, \ldots, n$. *The vector* $\mathbf{w} = (w_1, \ldots, w_n)$ *is called the weighting vector.*

Definition 13. (e.g. [6,7]) *Consider a moderate deviation function* $\mathcal{D} \in \mathbf{D}$, $n \in \mathbf{N}$ *and the weighting vector* $\mathbf{w} = (w_1, \ldots, w_n)$. *Then the mapping* $wU^{\mathcal{D}} : \mathbf{I}^n \to \mathbf{I}$ *given by*

$$wU^{\mathcal{D}}(\mathbf{x}) = \frac{1}{2} \left(\sup \left\{ y \in \mathbf{I} \Big| \sum_{i=1}^{n} w_i \cdot \mathcal{D}(x_i, y) < 0 \right\} \right.$$
$$\left. + \inf \left\{ y \in \mathbf{I} \Big| \sum_{i=1}^{n} w_i \cdot \mathcal{D}(x_i, y) > 0 \right\} \right) \qquad (14)$$

is called a weighted $\mathcal{D}$*-mean.*

Weighted deviation functions have already been mentioned, for example, in [12], but we now present concrete definitions using weighting functions on the basis of which we would like to extend the theory of the construction of aggregation functions.

Definition 14. *Consider a moderate deviation function $\mathcal{D} \in \mathbf{D}$ and $n \in \mathbf{N}$. Then a mixture global moderate deviation function $g\mathcal{G}^{\mathcal{D}} : \mathbf{I}^{n+1} \to \bar{\mathbf{R}}$ is defined for any $\mathbf{x} \in \mathbf{I}^n$ and $y \in \mathbf{I}$ as follows:*

$$g\mathcal{G}^{\mathcal{D}}(\mathbf{x}, y) = \sum_{i=1}^{n} g_i(x_i) \cdot \mathcal{D}(x_i, y), \tag{15}$$

where the vector $\mathbf{g} = (g_1, \ldots, g_n)$ is called the weighting vector, where $g_i : \mathbf{I} \to]0, \infty[$ are continuous weighting functions associated with the input values x_i, $i = 1, 2, \ldots, n$.

Definition 15. *Consider a moderate deviation function $\mathcal{D} \in \mathbf{D}$, $n \in \mathbf{N}$ and the weighting vector $\mathbf{g} = (g_1, \ldots, g_n)$. Then the mapping $gU^{\mathcal{D}} : \mathbf{I}^n \to \mathbf{I}$ given by*

$$gU^{\mathcal{D}}(\mathbf{x}) = \frac{1}{2} \left(\sup \left\{ y \in \mathbf{I} \,\Big|\, \sum_{i=1}^{n} g_i(x_i) \cdot \mathcal{D}(x_i, y) < 0 \right\} \right.$$

$$\left. + \inf \left\{ y \in \mathbf{I} \,\Big|\, \sum_{i=1}^{n} g_i(x_i) \cdot \mathcal{D}(x_i, y) > 0 \right\} \right) \tag{16}$$

is called a mixture $\mathcal{D}$-mean.

However, in order for the fused functions that are constructed using thinning definitions to be aggregation functions, they must satisfy certain conditions. Several sufficient conditions are known, which can be found, e.g., in [11,14,15]. For example, a mixture $\mathcal{D}$-mean (or a generalized mixture function) $M_{\mathbf{g}} : \mathbf{I}^n \to \mathbf{I}$ given by

$$M_{\mathbf{g}}(x_1, \ldots, x_n) = \frac{\sum\limits_{i=1}^{n} g_i(x_i) \cdot x_i}{\sum\limits_{i=1}^{n} g_i(x_i)}, \tag{17}$$

Construction by $\mathcal{D}(x, y) = y - x$ on the interval $\mathbf{I} = [a, b]$, with increasing (no necessity strictly), piecewise differentiable weighting functions $\mathbf{g} : \mathbf{I} \to [0, \infty[$, based on Definition 15 is monotone increasing if weighting functions satisfy at least one of the following conditions: $g_i(x) \geq g_i'(x) \cdot (b-a)$ or $g_i(x) \geq g_i'(x) \cdot (b-x)$ or for a fixed n, $n > 1$, $\frac{g_i^2(x)}{\sum\limits_{j \neq i} g_j(b)} + g_i(x) \geq g_i'(x) \cdot (b - x)$.

4 Generalization of the Global Moderate Deviation Function and Penalty Function

Let us think about a situation where we would use different moderate deviation functions for different inputs, or corresponding penalty functions for them, and, moreover, the different inputs would have different weights. Therefore, we first define the so-called generalized global moderate function and also the generalized penalty function.

Definition 16. *Consider moderate deviation functions $\mathcal{D}_i \in \mathbf{D}$; $i = 1, \ldots, n$ and $n \in \mathbf{N}$. Then a generalized weighted global moderate deviation function $Gw\mathcal{G}^{\mathcal{D}} : \mathbf{I}^{n+1} \to \bar{\mathbf{R}}$ is defined for any $\mathbf{x} \in \mathbf{I}^n$ and $y \in \mathbf{I}$ as follows:*

$$Gw\mathcal{G}^{\mathcal{D}}(\mathbf{x}, y) = \sum_{i=1}^{n} w_i \cdot \mathcal{D}_i(x_i, y), \tag{18}$$

where $w_i \geq 0$ are the weights associated with the observations x_i.
The vector $\mathbf{w} = (w_1, \ldots, w_n)$ is called a weighting vector.

Definition 17. *Consider moderate deviation functions $\mathcal{D}_i \in \mathbf{D}$; $i = 1, \ldots, n$, $n \in \mathbf{N}$ and the weighting vector $\mathbf{w} = (w_1, \ldots, w_n)$. Then the mapping $GwU^{\mathcal{D}} : \mathbf{I}^n \to \mathbf{I}$ given by*

$$GwU^{\mathcal{D}}(\mathbf{x}) = \frac{1}{2} \left(\sup \left\{ y \in \mathbf{I} \middle| \sum_{i=1}^{n} w_i \cdot \mathcal{D}_i(x_i, y) < 0 \right\} \right.$$
$$\left. + \inf \left\{ y \in \mathbf{I} \middle| \sum_{i=1}^{n} w_i \cdot \mathcal{D}_i(x_i, y) > 0 \right\} \right) \tag{19}$$

is called a generalized weighted $\mathcal{D}$-mean.

Definition 18. *Let $LP_i : \mathbf{I}^2 \to \bar{\mathbf{R}}^+$; $i = 1, \ldots, n$, be local penalty functions. Then a generalized weighted penalty function $GwP : \mathbf{I}^{n+1} \to \bar{\mathbf{R}}^+$ is defined for any $\mathbf{x} \in \mathbf{I}^n$ and $y \in \mathbf{I}$ as follows:*

$$GwP(\mathbf{x}, y) = \sum_{i=1}^{n} w_i \cdot LP_i(x_i, y), \tag{20}$$

where $w_i \geq 0$ are the weights associated to the observations x_i.
The vector $\mathbf{w} = (w_1, \ldots, w_n)$ is called a weighting vector.

Definition 19. *Consider local penalty functions $LP_i : \mathbf{I}^2 \to \bar{\mathbf{R}}^+$; $i = 1, 2, \ldots, n$, $n \in \mathbf{N}$ and the weighting vector $\mathbf{w} = (w_1, \ldots, w_n)$. Then the mapping $Gwf_{P(\mathbf{x})} : \mathbf{I}^n \to \mathbf{I}$ defined for all $\mathbf{x} \in \mathbf{I}^n$, by*

$$Gwf_{P(\mathbf{x})} = \frac{1}{2} \left(\sup \left\{ u \in \mathbf{I} \middle| \forall v \in \mathbf{I} : GwP(\mathbf{x}, u) \leq GwP(\mathbf{x}, v) \right\} \right.$$
$$\left. + \inf \left\{ u \in \mathbf{I} \middle| \forall v \in \mathbf{I} : GwP(\mathbf{x}, u) \leq GwP(\mathbf{x}, v) \right\} \right) \tag{21}$$

is called a generalized weighted penalty-based function.

Definition 20. *Consider moderate deviation functions $\mathcal{D}_i \in \mathbf{D}$; $i = 1, 2, \ldots, n$ and $n \in \mathbf{N}$. Then a generalized mixture global moderate deviation function $Gg\mathcal{G}^{\mathcal{D}} : \mathbf{I}^{n+1} \to \bar{\mathbf{R}}$ is defined for any $\mathbf{x} \in \mathbf{I}^n$ and $y \in \mathbf{I}$ as follows:*

$$Gg\mathcal{G}^{\mathcal{D}}(\mathbf{x}, y) = \sum_{i=1}^{n} g_i(x_i) \cdot \mathcal{D}_i(x_i, y), \tag{22}$$

where $g_i : \mathbf{I} \to]0, \infty[$ are continuous weighting functions associated with input values x_i. The vector $\mathbf{g} = (g_1, \ldots, g_n)$ is called a weighting vector.

Definition 21. *Consider moderate deviation functions* $\mathcal{D}_i \in \mathbf{D}$; $i = 1, 2, \ldots, n$, $n \in \mathbf{N}$ *and a weighting vector* $\mathbf{g} = (g_1, \ldots, g_n)$. *Then the mapping* $GgU^{\mathcal{D}} : \mathbf{I}^n \to \mathbf{I}$ *given by*

$$GgU^{\mathcal{D}}(\mathbf{x}) = \frac{1}{2} \left(\sup \left\{ y \in \mathbf{I} \Big| \sum_{i=1}^{n} g_i(x_i) \cdot \mathcal{D}_i(x_i, y) < 0 \right\} \right.$$
$$\left. + \inf \left\{ y \in \mathbf{I} \Big| \sum_{i=1}^{n} g_i(x_i) \cdot \mathcal{D}_i(x_i, y) > 0 \right\} \right) \tag{23}$$

is called a generalized mixture $\mathcal{D}$-mean.

Example 4 points out that introducing weights into the fusion of input values when using penalty functions and their corresponding moderate deviation functions may not give the same result.

Example 4. Consider the input values $(0.6, 0.2)$, the corresponding weighting vector $\mathbf{w} = (1/3, 2/3)$ and the moderate deviations functions $\mathcal{D}_1(x, y) = y - x$, $\mathcal{D}_2(x, y) = \log y - \log x$. Based on Definition 16 we get

$$Gw\mathcal{G}^{\mathcal{D}}(\mathbf{x}, y) = \frac{1}{3}(y - 0.6) + \frac{2}{3}(\log y - \log 0.2).$$

Then the mapping given by (19) acquires value $GwU^{\mathcal{D}}(0.6, 0.2) = 0.239503$. But if we use a generalized weighted penalty function to aggregate the inputs $GwP(\mathbf{x}, y) = \frac{1}{3}(0.6 - y)^2 + \frac{2}{3}(\log 0.2 - \log y)^2$ and $GwP'_y = \frac{2}{3}(y - 0.6) + \frac{4}{3y}(\log y - \log 0.2) = 0$, the result is $Gwf_{P(0.6, 0.2)} = 0.208328$.

5   Conclusion

In the paper, we point out the mutual connection between the local penalty function and the moderate deviation function in the construction of aggregation functions. We introduced the so-called generalized weighted/mixture penalty functions and generalized weighted/mixture global moderate deviation functions, where we assumed the application of different functions and different constant weights for individual inputs or where the weights represent the functional values of individual inputs, respectively. We still have open problems. Our goal is to determine aggregation functions that can be constructed using the penalty function, but not using the moderate deviation function and vice versa. Our next goal is to determine the conditions under which our generalized functions would be aggregation functions.

References

1. Altalhi, A.H., Forcén, J.I., Pagola, M., Barrenechea, E., Bustince, H., Takáč, Z.: Moderate deviation and restricted equivalence functions for measuring similarity between data. Inf. Sci. **2**(5), 19–29 (2019). https://doi.org/10.1016/j.ins.2019.05.078

2. Calvo, T., Beliakov, G.: Aggregation functions based on penalties. Fuzzy Sets Syst. **161**(10), 1420–1436 (2010). https://doi.org/10.1016/j.fss.2009.05.012
3. Bustince, H., Beliakov, G., Pereira Dimuro, G., Bedregal, B., Mesiar, R.: On the definition of penalty functions in data aggregation. Fuzzy Sets Syst. **323**, 1–18 (2017). https://doi.org/10.1016/j.fss.2016.09.011
4. Calvo, T., Mesiar, R., Yager, R.R.: Quantitative weights and aggregation. IEEE Trans. Fuzzy Syst. **12**(1), 62–69 (2004). https://doi.org/10.1109/TFUZZ.2003.822679
5. Daróczy, Z.: Über eine Klasse von Mittelwerten. Publ. Math. Debrecen **19**, 211–217 (1972)
6. Decký, M., Mesiar, R., Stupňanová, A.: Deviation-based aggregation functions. Fuzzy Sets Syst. **332**, 29–36 (2018). https://doi.org/10.1016/j.fss.2017.03.016
7. Decký, M., Mesiar, R., Stupňanová, A.: Aggregation functions based on deviations. In: Medina, J., et al. (eds.) IPMU 2018. CCIS, vol. 853, pp. 151–159. Springer, Cham (2018). https://doi.org/10.1007/978-3-319-91473-2_13
8. Grabisch, M., Marichal, J.L., Mesiar, R., Pap, E.: Aggregation Functions. Cambridge University Press, Cambridge (2009)
9. Marques Pereira, R.A., Pasi, G.: On non-monotonic aggregation: mixture operators. In: Proceedings of the 4th Meeting of the EURO Working Group on Fuzzy Sets (EUROFUSE 1999) and 2nd International Conference on Soft and Intelligent Computing (SIC 1999), Budapest, Hungary, pp. 513–517 (1999)
10. Mesiar, R., Špirková, J.: Weighted means and weighting functions. Kybernetika **42**(2), 151–160 (2006). https://dml.cz/handle/10338.dmlcz/135706
11. Mesiar, R., Špirková, J., Vavríková, L.: Weighted aggregation operators based on minimization. Inf. Sci. **17**(4), 1133–1140 (2008). https://doi.org/10.1016/j.ins.2007.09.023
12. Stupňanová, A., Smrek, P.: Generalized deviation functions and construction of aggregation functions. In: Proceedings of the 11th Conference of the European Society for Fuzzy Logic and Technology (EUSFLAT 2019), pp. 96–100. Atlantis Studies in Uncertainty Modelling (2019). https://doi.org/10.2991/eusflat-19.2019.15
13. Stupňanová, A.: Weighted penalty-based aggregation. In: Harmati, I.Á., Kóczy, L.T., Medina, J., Ramírez-Poussa, E. (eds.) Computational Intelligence and Mathematics for Tackling Complex Problems 3. SCI, vol. 959, pp. 47–56. Springer, Cham (2022). https://doi.org/10.1007/978-3-030-74970-5_7
14. Špirková, J., Beliakov, G., Bustince, H., Fernandez, J.: Mixture functions and their monotonicity. Inf. Sci. **481**, 520–549 (2019). https://doi.org/10.1016/j.ins.2018.12.090
15. Špirková, J., Král', P.: Mixture functions based on deviation and dissimilarity functions. In: Halaš, R., Gagolewski, M., Mesiar, R. (eds.) AGOP 2019. AISC, vol. 981, pp. 255–266. Springer, Cham (2019). https://doi.org/10.1007/978-3-030-19494-9_24
16. Yager, R.R.: Toward a general theory of information aggregation. Inf. Sci. **68**(3), 191–206 (1993). https://doi.org/10.1016/0020-0255(93)90104-T
17. Yager, R.R., Rybalov, A.: Understanding the median as a fusion operator. Int. J. Gen. Syst. **26**(3), 239–263 (1997). https://doi.org/10.1080/03081079708945181

An Interval-Valued Multi-attribute Decision Making Based on Combined QUALIFLEX-EAST Methodology

Debasmita Banerjee[1], Debashree Guha[2(✉)], Debjani Chakraborty[3], and Fateme Kouchakinejad[4]

[1] Department of Mathematics, Indian Institute of Technology, Patna, Bihta 801103, India
debasmitabanerjee12@gmail.com
[2] School of Medical Science and Technology, Indian Institute of Technology, Kharagpur, Kharagpur 721302, India
debashree_smst@smst.iitkgp.ac.in
[3] Department of Mathematics, Indian Institute of Technology, Kharagpur, Kharagpur 721302, India
[4] Department of Statistics, Faculty of Mathematics and Computer Science, Shahid Bahonar University of Kerman, Kerman, Iran

Abstract. In the traditional QUALIFLEX method to choose the best ranking order among m alternatives, all $m!$ permutations of the ranking order of alternatives are considered; however, that is not required always. Besides, the number of permutations increases drastically with an increase in the number of alternatives. To avoid such significant computational intricacy, in this paper we tried to generate only the possible preference orders of alternatives from the decision matrix by implementing the EAST method premised on the graph-theoretic approach. To facilitate this, the proposed decision-making framework considers the transformation of the decision matrix into a pair-wise comparison matrix where the uncertainty is modeled by interval-valued fuzzy sets. The consistency analysis is performed by modeling the interaction between the lower and upper parts of the preference matrix. Further, to evaluate the aggregated value in order to obtain the optimal ranking, we use discrete Choquet integral which can capture some degree of inter-dependence among the attribute set. Finally, the concordance/discordance index analysis is done to choose the best alternative.

Keywords: Multi-attribute decision making · QUALIFLEX method · EAST method

1 Introduction

The main characteristic of the outranking method is comparing all feasible alternatives in pair and then exploiting it in an appropriate way for obtaining a final ranking of alternatives. The aim of constructing one or several (crisp, fuzzy, or

S. Massanet et al. (Eds.): EUSFLAT 2023/AGOP 2023, LNCS 14069, pp. 259–270, 2023.
https://doi.org/10.1007/978-3-031-39965-7_22

embedded) outranking relation(s) is to compare each pair of actions in a comprehensive way with the idea that for an outranking relation to be validated a sufficient majority of attributes should be in favor of the required statement. A binary outranking relation refers to the assertion "at least as good as" where between two actions in any of these situations; preference, indifference, or incomparability can occur. For example, any couple of actions (a, b), "a outranks b" means action a is preferable to action b. A survey of these outranking methods is presented elaborately in [1]. Among the outranking methods, QUALIFLEX (i.e., QUALItative FLEXible multiple criteria method) is very well known where general idea of outranking is globally implemented and has been applied to many real-life problems in different environments. QUALIFLEX was first developed as a generalization of Jacquet-Lagreze's permutation method based on the evaluation of all possible rankings of alternatives under consideration [2]. Further several significant achievements have been made by many researchers [3–7].

Due to the less complexity and high applicability, the QUALIFLEX method in decision-making fields has been thoroughly studied in previous years. Although the extant frameworks used in QUALIFLEX till now present some drawbacks. First, this method evaluates all possible rankings or permutations of alternatives, subsequently for each couple of alternatives of the said permutations concordance and discordance index and comprehensive rank of them are computed. In this process, it is worth noting that the number of permutations increases drastically with an increase in the number of alternatives. Although, to choose the best ranking order it is not required to always consider all permutations of the ranking order of alternatives. Second, in real-life problems, different types of interrelationships exist among the attributes. However, the traditional QUALIFLEX framework does not consider any type of dependency relationship among the attributes. To obtain the aggregated value classical weighted arithmetic mean is used [3,5] which is incompetent to capture interaction among the attribute set. To handle such a situation, following [4], we can implement a nonadditive aggregation operator, known as Choque integral. Furthermore, fuzziness exists in such evaluation information. Therefore, a new decision-making framework, which can overcome the aforementioned deficiencies, is necessary.

With these observations, this study aims to develop a novel decision-making framework based on the QUALIFLEX and EAST methods where we can decrease the computational complexity by computing only the possible permutations of alternatives, as well as to give an acceptable and satisfactory ranking method. This new approach also belongs to the class of outranking methods where the outranking relation can be interpreted as a simple crisp relation and makes it easier to solve problems with less computational complexity. Moreover, we take into account the fuzziness of the expert's opinions modeled by interval-valued fuzzy with respect to capturing dependence among the attributes during the evaluation of alternatives, a suitable aggregation method is used.

The paper is set out as follows: Sect. 2 describes some basic concepts of interval-valued fuzzy sets. Section 3 presents a transformation function for utility values and multiplicative preference relations, with a detailed consistency analysis. Section 4 proposes a combined QUALIFLEX-EAST method to rank alternatives. Finally, some conclusions and future works are presented in Sect. 5.

2   Preliminaries

2.1   Interval-Valued Fuzzy Set

Definition 1. [8] *An IVFS $\tilde{\mathbb{A}}$, on the universe $\mathbf{U} \neq \phi$, is a set such that, $\tilde{\mathbb{A}} = \{(u, \mathbb{A}(u) = [a^-_{\mathbb{A}(u)}, a^+_{\mathbb{A}(u)}]) \mid u \in \mathbf{U}\}$, where the function $\mathbb{A} : \mathbf{U} \to \mathbb{L}([0,1])$ is called the membership function.*

For a singleton space $\mathbf{U} = \{u\}$, the class of all IVFS(s) is isomorphic to that of $(\mathbb{L}, \preceq)$-fuzzy sets. Hence, an IVFS is a specific kind of $\mathbb{L}$-fuzzy set, in the sense that, for every $u \subset U, [a^-_{\mathbb{A}(u)}, a^+_{\mathbb{A}(u)}] \in (\mathbb{L}, \preceq)$. Thus, the lattice $(\mathbb{L}, \preceq)$ gives us an elegant and compact environment in which we can perform the computations with IVFS(s). For this reason, we use the names "interval-valued fuzzy set" and "$(\mathbb{L}, \preceq)$-fuzzy set" synonymously. Hereinafter, we shall call the object $\bar{a} = [a^-, a^+]$ as interval-valued representation of the data.

Next the most relevant for our purposes are logical connectives like conjunction and disjunction, which are modeled by t-norm and t-conorm.

Definition 2. [9] *A t-norm (or, t-conorm) is a function $T(or, S) : [0,1] \times [0,1] \to [0,1]$ such that it is symmetric, associative, non decreasing in each argument and $T(x,1) = x$ (or, $S(x,0) = x$), $\forall\, x \in [0,1]$. A strict t-norm (or, strict t-conorm) is represented by its additive generator g (or, h) $: [0,1] \to [0,\infty]$, which is a decreasing function (or, increasing function), such that $T(x,y) = g^{-1}(g(x) + g(y))$ (or, $S(x,y) = h^{-1}(h(x) + h(y)))$.*

If S is a strict t-conorm dual to a strict t-norm T, i.e. $S(x,y) = 1 - T(1 - x, 1 - y)$ and T has an additive generator g, then h given by $h(x) = g(1 - x)$ is an additive generator of S. Then using concept of strict t-conorm and strict t-norm with their respective additive generators, one can define interval arithmetic operational laws as follows:

Definition 3. *Let $\bar{a} = [a^-, a^+]$ and $\bar{b} = [b^-, b^+]$ be the two intervals from $\mathbb{L}([0,1])$. Then,*

(I) $\bar{a} \oplus \bar{b} = [S(a^-, b^-), S(a^+, b^+)] = [h^{-1}(h(a^-) + h(b^-)), h^{-1}(h(a^+) + h(b^+))]$
(II) $\bar{a} \otimes \bar{b} = [T(a^-, b^-), T(a^+, b^+)] = [g^{-1}(g(a^-) + g(b^-)), g^{-1}(g(a^+) + g(b^+))]$
(III) $\alpha \bar{a} = [h^{-1}(\alpha h(a^-)), h^{-1}(\alpha h(a^+))]$, for any $\alpha \geq 0$
(IV) $\bar{a}^\alpha = [g^{-1}(\alpha g(a^-)), g^{-1}(\alpha g(a^+))]$, for any $\alpha \geq 0$.

In this contribution, to prove all the relevant theorems, properties of the proposed operators and to preserve the individual multiplicative preference structure into collective decision in a convenient manner, we will use strict t-norm $T_p(x,y) = xy$ generated by $h(t) = -\log(1-t)$ and we will use $S(x,y) = min\{1, x + y\}$ (which is not a strict t-conorm) generated by additive generator identity $h(t) = t$. Thus, here our used t-norm is conditionally distributive over S-norm. It is also needed to be mentioned that we will not unnecessarily restrict the domain and range of these functions and we consider $\mathbb{L}$ as the set $\mathbb{L}([a,b])$, i.e., the set of all closed subintervals of some arbitrary interval $[a,b] \subset \mathbb{R}^+ = [0, \infty]$ i.e., $\mathbb{L}([a,b]) = \{[a^-, a^+] | a \leq a^- \leq a^+ \leq b\}$. With the above notations and interpretations, the interval arithmetic operational laws can be defined as follows:

Definition 4. *Let* $\bar{a} = [a^-, a^+]$ *and* $\bar{b} = [b^-, b^+]$ *be the two intervals from* $\mathbb{L}([a,b])$. *Then,*

(i) *Addition:* $\bar{a} \oplus \bar{b} = [a^- + b^-, a^+ + b^+]$
(ii) *Subtraction:* $\bar{a} - \bar{b} = [a^- - b^+, a^+ - b^-]$
(iii) *Multiplication:* $\bar{a} \otimes \bar{b} = [a^- b^-, a^+ b^+]$
(iv) *Division:* $\bar{a}/\bar{b} = [a^-/b^+, a^+/b^-]$ *where* $b^-, b^+ > 0$
(v) *Scalar multiplication:* $\alpha \bar{a} = [\alpha a^-, \alpha a^+]$, *for any* $\alpha \geq 0$
(vi) *Exponential:* $\bar{a}^\alpha = [a^{-\alpha}, a^{+\alpha}]$, *for any* $\alpha \geq 0$.

Remark 1. The division is derived from multiplication by means of Galois connection.

As in this proposal we are dealing with the set of intervals from $\mathbb{L}([a,b])$, thus it is clear that to each interval $[a^-, a^+]$ from $\mathbb{L}([a,b])$ we can assign uniquely a point $(a^-, a^+) \in \mathbb{R}^2$ and the intervals can be ordered by using the usual partial order in $\mathbb{R}^2$. Thus the intervals can be ordered in the following way $[a^-, a^+] \leq_2 [b^-, b^+] \Leftrightarrow a^- \leq b^- \wedge a^+ \leq b^+$ [8].

3   Interval Valued Multiplicative Preference Relation

Definition 5. [10] *Consider a set of alternatives* $\{X_1, X_2, ..., X_m\}$. *Preferences are given on the basis of a positive ratio scale* $U = \{\bar{u}_i : i = 1, 2, ..., m\}$, $\bar{u}_i \in \mathbb{L}([0,1])$. *These interval values* $\bar{u}_i$ *for each alternative* X_i *are called utility values.*

Another way of expressing opinions is based on pairwise comparison where the experts affix some degree of credibility of preference of any alternative over another. Consider that decision maker provides the ratio of preference intensity for an alternative X_i to that of X_j by the value $\bar{\zeta}_{ij}$; $i, j = 1, 2, ...m$. It estimates that alternative X_i is $\bar{\zeta}_{ij}$ times better than alternative X_j.

Definition 6. [11] *An interval judgment matrix* $M = (\bar{\zeta}_{ij})_{m \times m} = ([\zeta_{ij}^-, \zeta_{ij}^+])_{m \times m}$ *where,* ζ_{ij}^- *and* ζ_{ij}^+ *are non negative real numbers and* $\zeta_{ij}^- \leq \zeta_{ij}^+$, *is said to be a interval valued multiplicative preference relation, if the elements of* M *satisfy* $\bar{\zeta}_{ij} = 1/\bar{\zeta}_{ji}$, $\zeta_{ii}^- = \zeta_{ii}^+ = 1$, $1/S \leq \zeta_{ij}^- \leq \zeta_{ij}^+ \leq S$, $\forall\, i, j = 1, 2, ..., m$ *where,* $\bar{\zeta}_{ij}$ *represents a multiplicative preference degree of alternative* X_i *over* X_j *and* $[1/S, S]$ *be a multiplicative ratio scale with neutral value of 1.*

In Definition (6), we are taking the condition of interval valued multiplicative preference relation as, $\bar{\zeta}_{ij} = 1/\bar{\zeta}_{ji}$ which implies $\zeta_{ij}^- = 1/\zeta_{ji}^+$ and $\zeta_{ij}^+ = 1/\zeta_{ji}^-$. From interval arithmetic operational laws (Definition 4) one knows, $\bar{\zeta}_{ij} = 1/\bar{\zeta}_{ji} \nLeftrightarrow \bar{\zeta}_{ij} \otimes \bar{\zeta}_{ji} = 1$. Thus for an interval valued matrix $M = (\bar{\zeta}_{ij})_{m \times m}$ we often have $\bar{\zeta}_{ij} \otimes \bar{\zeta}_{ji} \neq 1$, but to satisfy the multiplicative preference relation M has to satisfy reciprocity law $\bar{\zeta}_{ij} = 1/\bar{\zeta}_{ji}$.

3.1 Saaty's Definition of Consistency for Multiplicative Preference Relation and Its Extension with Interval Data

Definition of consistency for multiplicative preference matrix was first proposed in [12]. According to Saaty, preference matrix M is said to be a consistent multiplicative preference relation if the preference relation satisfies transitivity property i.e., if elements of the preference matrix M satisfy,

$$\bar{\zeta}_{ij} = \bar{\zeta}_{ik} \otimes \bar{\zeta}_{kj}, \forall\ i, j, k = 1, 2, ..., m. \tag{1}$$

Since we are here dealing with interval-valued preference matrix, according to [13] an interval multiplicative reciprocal matrix $M = (\bar{\zeta}_{ij})_{m \times m} = ([\zeta_{ij}^-, \zeta_{ij}^+])_{m \times m}$ is said to be consistent if the two multiplicative reciprocal matrices $M^L = (\zeta_{ij}^L)_{m \times m}$ and $M^U = (\zeta_{ij}^U)_{m \times m}$ are consistent where,

$$\zeta_{ij}^L = \begin{cases} \zeta_{ij}^+ & \text{if } i < j \\ 1 & \text{if } i = j \\ \zeta_{ij}^- & \text{if } i > j \end{cases} \qquad\qquad \zeta_{ij}^U = \begin{cases} \zeta_{ij}^- & \text{if } i < j \\ 1 & \text{if } i = j \\ \zeta_{ij}^+ & \text{if } i > j \end{cases}$$

In [11,14], some drawbacks of Liu's definition of consistency were illustrated using examples. They also suggested a new definition for consistency of interval multiplicative preference matrix as follows:

Definition 7. [14] *An interval valued preference matrix* $M = (\bar{\zeta}_{ij})_{m \times m}$ *is called consistent if*

$$\zeta_{ij}^- \zeta_{ij}^+ = \zeta_{ik}^- \zeta_{ik}^+ \zeta_{kj}^- \zeta_{kj}^+ \ \forall\ i, j, k = 1, 2, ..., m \tag{2}$$

The concept behind this definition was not clearly discussed there in [14]. With an aim to give more clarity, We analyze the Definition 7 as given below.

Remark 2. Basically, the interval arithmetic-based transitivity equation of the interval-valued preference matrix M is defined by taking into account the interaction between both the lower and upper parts of the preference matrix. First, the consistency condition of the lower and upper part of the interval-valued preference matrix can be obtained based on Eq. (1) as follows.

$$\zeta_{ij}^- = \zeta_{ik}^- \zeta_{kj}^-, \ \zeta_{ij}^+ = \zeta_{ik}^+ \zeta_{kj}^+. \tag{3}$$

Now the interaction between the lower and upper parts of the interval multiplicative preference matrix can be modeled by using the t-norm. The effectiveness of the product t-norm operator inspires us and we use it to define the condition of consistency for the interval-valued preference matrix. Thus Eq. (3) leads us to the Definition 7. Here instead of taking into account the consistency of two separated matrices, i.e., lower and upper matrices, we calculate the consistency for the whole interval multiplicative reciprocal matrix. Thus by this new consistency formula, we can avoid the loss of information that may arise by considering the upper and lower boundaries of the interval data.

Remark 3. If lower and upper matrices constructed from the interval multiplicative preference matrix according to the concept of Liu et al. [13] is consistent then the original matrix will be definitely consistent by (2). Further, there may be some cases where the original multiplicative preference matrix is consistent, however, the two separated matrices are not consistent.

In the following section, we analyze the functions to transform interval-based utility values into multiplicative preference relations to facilitate our decision-making process.

3.2 Transformation Between Utility Value and Multiplicative Preference Relation

In the context of interval-valued data, a multiplicative preference relation from a set of utility values can be obtained by using the following transformation function $f : L([0,1]) \times L([0,1]) \rightarrow L([a,b])$ such that, $\bar{\zeta}_{ij} = f(\bar{u}_i, \bar{u}_j)$ where f satisfies the following properties,

P1. Transformation function should satisfy multiplicative reciprocity condition i.e., $f(\bar{u}_i, \bar{u}_j) = \frac{1}{f(\bar{u}_j, \bar{u}_i)}$.
P2. When the alternatives satisfy some attributes with the same intensity, the transformation function will take the value unity i.e., $f(\bar{u}_i, \bar{u}_i) = [1,1]$.
P3. Decision maker will give a higher preference value to the alternative with a higher utility value than the other with respect to some other alternative i.e., if $\bar{u}_i \leq \bar{u}_j$ then it implies, $f(\bar{u}_i, \bar{u}_s) \leq f(\bar{u}_j, \bar{u}_s)$ where $s \in \{1, 2, ..., n\}$.

If we assign some specific form of h, the multiplicative preference relation can be evaluated by using a special type of transformation function. For example, $\bar{\zeta}_{ij} = f(\bar{u}_i, \bar{u}_i) = \left(\frac{\bar{u}_i}{\bar{u}_j}\right)^c$ where, $c > 0$. Taking $c = 1$ and using interval value operational law (iv) we get the simplest function to obtain the ratio of preference intensity for alternative X_i to that of X_j (where $i \neq j$ and $i, j = 1, 2, ..., m$) on the basis of some specific attribute as,

$$\bar{\zeta}_{ij} = \frac{\bar{u}_i}{\bar{u}_j} = \frac{[u_i^-, u_i^+]}{[u_j^-, u_j^+]} = \left[\frac{u_i^-}{u_j^+}, \frac{u_i^+}{u_j^-}\right]. \tag{4}$$

Remark 4. Interval preference relation derived from utility values using Eq. (4) is multiplicative reciprocal and consistent.

The fact that this special transformation function (Eq. 4) will also preserve the preference relation i.e., alternatives with high utility value will be definitely preferable to the decision maker than the other.

Remark 5. We have $\bar{u}_i \leq_2 \bar{u}_j$ for all $i, j \in \{1, 2, ..., m\}$ then, using the ordering principle of interval data we obtain, $u_i^- \leq u_j^- \wedge u_i^+ \leq u_j^+$.

Now for any $s \in \{1, 2, ..., n\}$ we get, $\frac{u_i^-}{u_i^+} \leq \frac{u_j^-}{u_s^+} \wedge \frac{u_i^+}{u_s^-} \leq \frac{u_j^+}{u_s^-}$.Which implies,

$$\left[\frac{u_i^-}{u_s^+}, \frac{u_i^+}{u_s^-}\right] \leq_2 \left[\frac{u_j^-}{u_s^+}, \frac{u_j^+}{u_s^-}\right] \Rightarrow f(\bar{u}_i, \bar{u}_s) \leq_2 f(\bar{u}_j, \bar{u}_s) \Rightarrow \bar{\zeta}_{is} \leq_2 \bar{\zeta}_{js}.$$

Thus the transformation functions do not disturb the ranking among the alternatives established by different representation structures.

Following the discussions provided in the previous sections, we will now develop our decision-making mechanism.

4 The New Ranking Mechanism Combining QUALIFLEX and EAST

4.1 Construction of Pairwise Comparison Matrix for Each Attribute Based on the Decision Matrix

Consider a decision-making scenario where the decision maker provides his/her opinion for m alternatives $X_1, X_2, ..., X_m$ based on n attributes $C_1, C_2, ..., C_n$ in the form of interval number $\bar{A}_{ik} = [A_{ik}^-, A_{ik}^+] \in \mathbb{L}([0, 1])$ for i^{th} alternative with respect to k^{th} attribute. The decision maker's opinion can be summarized in the following decision matrix:

$$D = \begin{array}{c} \\ X_1 \\ X_2 \\ \vdots \\ X_m \end{array} \begin{array}{c} C_1 \quad C_2 \quad \cdots \quad C_n \\ \begin{pmatrix} \bar{A}_{11} & \bar{A}_{12} & \cdots & \bar{A}_{1n} \\ \bar{A}_{21} & \bar{A}_{22} & \cdots & \bar{A}_{2n} \\ \vdots & \vdots & \cdots & \vdots \\ \bar{A}_{m1} & \bar{A}_{m2} & \cdots & \bar{A}_{mn} \end{pmatrix} \end{array}.$$

In a decision-making problem, benefit attributes and cost attributes may occur simultaneously. In order to unify all attribute values, decision-makers need to normalize the decision matrix. Suppose among n attributes $\{C_1, C_2, ..., C_n\}$, C_k is the cost attribute then the evaluation value $\bar{A}_{ik}$ of alternative X_i with respect to attribute C_k should be normalised as, $N(\bar{A}_{ik}) = 1 - \bar{A}_{ik} = 1 - [A_{ik}^-, A_{ik}^+] = [1 - A_{ik}^+, 1 - A_{ik}^-]$. Now let $\bar{A}_{ij}^k$ denotes the preference value of alternative X_i over X_j for one particular attribute C_k, where $k = 1, 2, ..., n$. Then, the multiplicative preference relation $\bar{A}_{ij}^k$ can be evaluated by using the special type of transformation function in the line of Eq. (4) as,

$$\bar{A}_{ij}^k = [A_{ij}^{k-}, A_{ij}^{k+}] = \begin{cases} [1, 1] & \text{if } i = j \\ \left(\frac{\bar{A}_{ik}}{\bar{A}_{jk}}\right)^c & \text{otherwise} \end{cases} \tag{5}$$

where, $c > 0$. For the sake of simplicity, consider $c = 1$ and we get the ratio of preference intensity for alternative X_i to that of X_j with respect to attribute C_k (where $i \neq j$ and $i, j = 1, 2, ..., m$) as , $\frac{\bar{A}_{ik}}{\bar{A}_{jk}} = \frac{[A_{ik}^-, A_{ik}^+]}{[A_{jk}^-, A_{jk}^+]} = \left[\frac{A_{ik}^-}{A_{jk}^+}, \frac{A_{ik}^+}{A_{jk}^-}\right]$. The preference values with respect to attribute C_k can be summarized into the interval decision matrix $D_{C_k} = (\bar{A}_{ij}^k)_{m \times m}$.

Remark 6. For k-th attribute the interval matrix D_{C_k}, derived from the decision matrix D using Eq. (5) is multiplicative reciprocal and consistent.

4.2   Construction of the Aggregated Matrix After Accumulation of the Preference Matrix over All Attributes

Now in order to aggregate individual judgments into collective judgments with respect to all attributes, we use the interval-valued geometric mean operator (IV-GM). This evaluation is represented in matrix format as,

$$
M = \begin{matrix} & \begin{matrix} X_1 & X_2 & \cdots & X_m \end{matrix} \\ \begin{matrix} X_1 \\ X_2 \\ \vdots \\ X_m \end{matrix} & \begin{pmatrix} \bar{\varrho}_{11} & \bar{\varrho}_{12} & \cdots & \bar{\varrho}_{1m} \\ \bar{\varrho}_{21} & \bar{\varrho}_{22} & \cdots & \bar{\varrho}_{2m} \\ \vdots & \vdots & \cdots & \vdots \\ \bar{\varrho}_{m1} & \bar{\varrho}_{m2} & \cdots & \bar{\varrho}_{mm} \end{pmatrix} \end{matrix}.
$$

$$
\bar{\varrho}_{ij} = IV - GM(\bar{A}_{ij}^1, \bar{A}_{ij}^2, ..., \bar{A}_{ij}^n) = \left[\prod_{k=1}^{n} \left(\bar{A}_{ij}^{k^+} \right), \prod_{k=1}^{n} \left(A_{ij}^{k^-} \right) \right] = [\varrho_{ij}^-, \varrho_{ij}^+].
$$

Remark 7. As every interval matrix $D_{C_k} = (\bar{A}_{ij}^k)_{m \times m}$ satisfies multiplicative reciprocity and consistency conditions so, $\bar{A}_{ij}^k = \frac{1}{\bar{A}_{ji}^k}, \forall \ k = 1, 2, ..., n$. i.e., $A_{ij}^{k^-} = \frac{1}{A_{ij}^{k^+}}$ and $A_{ij}^{k^+} = \frac{1}{A_{ij}^{k^-}}, \forall \ k = 1, 2, ..., n$. Now, we get $\bar{\varrho}_{ij} = IV - GM(\bar{A}_{ij}^1, \bar{A}_{ij}^2, ..., \bar{A}_{ij}^n) = [\varrho_{ij}^-, \varrho_{ij}^+] = \frac{1}{[\frac{1}{\varrho_{ij}^+}, \frac{1}{\varrho_{ij}^-}]} = \frac{1}{[\varrho_{ji}^-, \varrho_{ji}^+]} = \frac{1}{\bar{\varrho}_{ji}}$. Similarly, we get $\varrho_{il}^- \varrho_{il}^+ \varrho_{lj}^- \varrho_{lj}^+ = \varrho_{ij}^- \varrho_{ij}^+$.

Thus, the aggregated preference matrix $M = (\bar{\varrho}_{ij})_{m \times m}$ constructed above is multiplicative reciprocal and consistent if all interval matrix $D_{C_k} = (\bar{A}_{ij}^k)_{m \times m}$ for k-th attribute, $k = 1, 2, ..., n$, are multiplicative reciprocal and consistent.

Thus utilizing the IV-GM operator, aggregated preference matrix M can be generated over all attributes from the decision matrix D.

4.3   Enumerating only Possible Preference Orders from Aggregated Preference Matrix Using Graph Theoretic Approach

Now before selecting the best ranking order, our aim is to generate only the possible preference orders from aggregated preference matrix M by using a graph theoretic approach. For this purpose, we take the set of m alternatives as vertices of a complete directed graph $G = (X, J)$ and edges connecting them as preference degrees between each pair of alternatives where J represents the weighted edges. Then we can generate a forest $\Gamma = \{S_1, S_2, ..., S_\eta\}$ containing η number of spanning trees where each tree presents an independent judgment. Back in 1889,

Cayley developed the well-known formula $\eta = m^{(m-2)}$ for the number of spanning trees in the complete graph with m vertices. If we draw all those spanning trees in a figure then this displays every possible combination of minimum edges connecting all those m vertices together. Each spanning tree S_l, $l = 1, 2, ..., \eta$ represents a set of $(m-1)$ independent judgments. For more details see [5].

From each independent judgment, the weight vector of the alternatives $W = (W_1, W_2, ..., W_m)$, where $W_i > 0$, can be calculated by using some weight computation method for interval data using a fuzzy linear programming problem. Several methods have been proposed for weight computation of interval data in the literature [11,15]. However, in this study, we focus on the weight computation method given in [15] based on the linear membership function due to their simplicity and usefulness in practical applications.

As our aggregated preference matrix M is perfectly consistent in its judgments, thus weight vector $W = (W_1, W_2, ..., W_m)$, where $W_i > 0$ of the set of m alternatives $\{X_1, X_2, ..., X_m\}$ can be calculated by using the formulas, $\bar{\varrho}_{ij} = \frac{W_i}{W_j}$, $\sum W_i = 1$. As, preference of an alternative X_i over X_j is represented as an interval $\bar{\varrho}_{ij} = [\varrho_{ij}^-, \varrho_{ij}^+]$ where ϱ_{ij}^- and ϱ_{ij}^+ are respectively the lower and upper bounds. So, in that context weight vector satisfies the constraint: $\varrho_{ij}^- \leq \frac{W_i}{W_j} \leq \varrho_{ij}^+$.

By transforming this double-side inequality into a set of two single side-inequalities we obtain,

$$W_i + \varrho_{ij}^- W_j \leq 0, \ W_i - \varrho_{ij}^+ W_j \leq 0.$$

Evidently, the decision maker would prefer a solution around the middle of the interval $\bar{\varrho}_{ij}$ denoted by m_{ij}. This implies that the DM's degree of satisfaction with the solution ratio should be represented as a monotonous continuous function, gradually increasing towards the interval mid-point which gives us a convex membership function for this interval:

$$\mu_{ij}(W_i, W_j) = \begin{cases} 1 - \frac{-W_i + \varrho_{ij}^- W_j}{d_{ij}}, & \text{if } \frac{W_i}{W_j} \leq m_{ij} \\ 1 - \frac{W_i - \varrho_{ij}^+ W_j}{d_{ij}}, & \text{otherwise.} \end{cases} \tag{6}$$

where d_{ij} is the tolerance parameter for the considered interval. Without loss of generality, one can assume that the tolerance parameters for the lower and upper bounds are equal. Finally, the corresponding optimization problem can be represented by the following fuzzy linear programming problem:

$$\begin{cases} Max \ (\lambda) \\ Subject \ to, \\ d_{ij}\lambda - W_i + \varrho_{ij}^- W_j \leq d_{ij}. \\ d_{ij}\lambda + W_i - \varrho_{ij}^+ W_j \leq d_{ij}. \\ i = 1, 2, ..., n, \ J = 1, 2, ..., n-1, \ j > i. \\ \sum W_i = 1. \\ W_i > 0, \ i = 1, 2, ..., n. \end{cases} \tag{7}$$

From the optimal value of λ one can measure the consistency of the DM's judgments. So it is called a consistency index. As in our decision model the aggregated preference matrix M is perfectly consistent, thus the constraint of the weight vector is purely satisfied, and in that case, the value of the membership function given by Eq. (6) is equal or greater than one. Thus in our model we will get from Eq. (7) $\lambda \geq 1$.

From each spanning tree, depending on η by solving Eq. (7), different weight vectors are generated and subsequently, we can rank alternatives in all possible ways. So by this process, we obtain at most η different preference orderings of alternatives.

4.4 Computation of Concordance/Discordance Index for Every Possible Preference Ordering

Suppose from the aggregated preference matrix, $P = \{P_1, P_2, ..., P_\eta\}$ be the set of all possible rankings of alternatives obtained using Sect. 4.3. Let $P_l = (..., X_\rho, ..., X_\beta, ...)$ denote the l-th ranking order of alternatives where, $l = 1, 2, ..., \eta$ and in P_l, alternative X_ρ is ranked higher than or equal to X_β.

To compute the value of concordance/discordance index denoted as, $I_k^l(X_\rho, X_\beta)$, for each pair of alternatives (X_ρ, X_β) in the preference ranking P_l with respect to the attribute C_k we use the following,

$$I_k^l(X_\rho, X_\beta) = d(\bar{A}_{\rho k}, \bar{0}) - d(\bar{A}_{\beta k}, \bar{0}). \tag{8}$$

where we can calculate the distance of the interval $\bar{A}_{\rho k} = [A_{\rho k}^-, A_{\rho k}^+]$ from $\bar{0} = [0, 0]$, using the formula : $d(\bar{A}_{\rho k}, \bar{0}) = (mid\ \bar{A}_{\rho k} - mid\ \bar{0})^2 + (spr\ \bar{A}_{\rho k} - spr\ \bar{0})^2$ with $mid\ \bar{A}_{\rho k} = \frac{(A_{\rho k}^- + A_{\rho k}^+)}{2}$ as the center of the interval and the spread of $\bar{A}_{\rho k}$ as $spr\ \bar{A}_{\rho k} = \frac{(A_{\rho k}^+ - A_{\rho k}^-)}{2}$ which is half of the length of an interval $\bar{A}_{\rho k}$.

If $I_k^l(X_\rho, X_\beta) > 0, I_k^l(X_\rho, X_\beta) = 0, I_k^l(X_\rho, X_\beta) < 0$, then it is said to be concordance, ex-aequo, discordance index respectively.

Next, to determine the weighted concordance/discordance index for each pair of alternative (X_ρ, X_β) in P_l on the ground that, there exists dependence structure among the set of attributes, here we employ discrete Choquet integral. In [4], the Choquet integral has been applied in the hierarchical QUALIFLEX method to capture the dependence relationships among the main criteria. With the same spirit, in line of the idea of discrete Choquet integral suppose $I_{(k)}^l(X_\rho, X_\beta)$ denotes the k-th smallest element in the set $\{I_1^l(X_\rho, X_\beta),\ I_2^l(X_\rho, X_\beta),\ ...,\ I_n^l(X_\rho, X_\beta)\}$. Let, $\mu(C_{(k)})$ denote the degree of importance of the combination of sub-set of attributes $C_{(k)} = \{C_k, C_{k+1}, ..., C_n\}$. Thus, $\mu(C_{(1)}) = 1$ and $\mu(C_{(n+1)}) = 0$. Therefore, weighted concordance/discordance index $I^l(X_\rho, X_\beta)$ for each pair of (X_ρ, X_β) in P_l can be defined as follows,

$$I^l(X_\rho, X_\beta) = \sum_{k=1}^{n} I_{(k)}^l(X_\rho, X_\beta).[\mu(\mathcal{C}_{(k)}) - \mu(\mathcal{C}_{(k+1)})]$$

$$= \sum_{k=1}^{n} \left(d(\bar{A}_{\rho(k)}, \bar{A}_{\beta(k)}) \right).[\mu(\mathcal{C}_{(k)}) - \mu(\mathcal{C}_{(k+1)})]. \tag{9}$$

The value of the degree of importance of the combination of a subset of attributes can be obtained by using some fuzzy integration procedure based on λ-measure or by analytical hierarchy process or directly from the decision-makers. Then, derive the comprehensive concordance/discordance index I^l for each P_l using formula:

$$I^l = \sum_{X_\rho, X_\beta \in X} \sum_{k=1}^{n} I_{(k)}^l(X_\rho, X_\beta).[\mu(\mathcal{C}_{(k)}) - \mu(\mathcal{C}_{(k+1)})]$$

$$= \sum_{X_\rho, X_\beta \in X} \sum_{k=1}^{n} \left(d(\bar{A}_{\rho(k)}, \bar{A}_{\beta(k)}) \right).[\mu(\mathcal{C}_{(k)}) - \mu(\mathcal{C}_{(k+1)})]. \tag{10}$$

The highest value of the comprehensive concordance/discordance index indicates a better ranking of the alternatives.

A structural comparison of the proposed method with the existing QUAL-IFLEX methodologies is presented in Table 1.

Table 1. Comparison with different extended QUALIFLEX methodologies

Methods	Environment	Combined with method	Conco./disco	Dependence index
Zhang et al. [4]	IVPFS	–	Closeness index	Yes
Li and Wang [3]	PHFE	–	Hausdorff distance	No
Ji et al. [6]	SVTNS	TODIM	Distance measure	No
Liang et al. [7]	LNN	VIKOR	Hamming distance	No
Proposed method	IVFS	EAST	Distance measure with mid and spread	Yes

5   Conclusion

The contributions of this proposal are as follows. First, instead of considering all $m!$ permutations of alternatives the proposed framework employs the graph theoretic approach to find only the possible preference of alternatives, and subsequent concordance-discordance analysis is done. Second, the proposed decision-making framework employs discrete Choquet integral to model the dependence relationship among the attribute set. Third, the transformation function is analyzed to relate utility values and multiplicative preference relation within the interval value context. In the future, we can extend this new outranking method to a linguistic decision framework where due to lack of knowledge decision makers will not be able to express their preferences precisely in exact quantitative form.

References

1. Figueira, J., Greco, S., Ehrgott, M.: Multiple Criteria Decision Analysis: State of the Art Surveys, vol. 78. Springer, Heidelberg (2005). https://doi.org/10.1007/b100605
2. Paelinck, J.H.: Qualiflex: a flexible multiple-criteria method. Econ. Lett. **1**(3), 193–197 (1978)
3. Li, J., Wang, J.: An extended QUALIFLEX method under probability hesitant fuzzy environment for selecting green suppliers. Int. J. Fuzzy Syst. **19**(6), 1866–1879 (2017)
4. Zhang, X.: Multicriteria Pythagorean fuzzy decision analysis: a hierarchical QUAL-IFLEX approach with the closeness index-based ranking methods. Inf. Sci. **330**, 104–124 (2016)
5. Banerjee, D., Guha, D., Kouchakinejad, F.: Ranking alternatives using QUAL-IFLEX method by computing all spanning trees from pairwise judgements. In: Bansal, J.C., Das, K.N., Nagar, A., Deep, K., Ojha, A.K. (eds.) Soft Computing for Problem Solving. AISC, vol. 816, pp. 235–247. Springer, Singapore (2019). https://doi.org/10.1007/978-981-13-1592-3_18
6. Ji, P., Zhang, H., Wang, J.: Fuzzy decision-making framework for treatment selection based on the combined QUALIFLEX-TODIM method. Int. J. Syst. Sci. **48**(14), 3072–3086 (2017)
7. Wz, L., Gy, Z., Cs, H.: Performance assessment of circular economy for phosphorus chemical firms based on VIKOR-QUALIFLEX method. J. Clean. Prod. **196**, 1365–1378 (2018)
8. Bustince, H., Fernández, J., Kolesárová, A., Mesiar, R.: Generation of linear orders for intervals by means of aggregation functions. Fuzzy Sets Syst. **220**, 69–77 (2013)
9. Klement, E.P., Mesiar, R., Pap, E.: Triangular Norms, vol. 8. Springer, Heidelberg (2013). https://doi.org/10.1007/978-94-015-9540-7
10. Chiclana, F., Herrera, F., Herrera-Viedma, E.: Integrating multiplicative preference relations in a multipurpose decision-making model based on fuzzy preference relations. Fuzzy Sets Syst. **122**(2), 277–291 (2001)
11. Li, K.W., Wang, Z.J., Tong, X.: Acceptability analysis and priority weight elicitation for interval multiplicative comparison matrices. Eur. J. Oper. Res. **250**(2), 628–638 (2016)
12. Saaty, T.L.: What is the analytic hierarchy process? In: Mitra, G., Greenberg, H.J., Lootsma, F.A., Rijkaert, M.J., Zimmermann, H.J. (eds.) Mathematical Models for Decision Support. NATO ASI Series, vol. 48, pp. 109–121. Springer, Heidelberg (1988). https://doi.org/10.1007/978-3-642-83555-1_5
13. Liu, F.: Acceptable consistency analysis of interval reciprocal comparison matrices. Fuzzy Sets Syst. **160**(18), 2686–2700 (2009)
14. Wang, Z.J.: A note on "A goal programming model for incomplete interval multiplicative preference relations and its application in group decision-making". Eur. J. Oper. Res. **247**(3), 867–871 (2015)
15. Mikhailov, L.: A fuzzy approach to deriving priorities from interval pairwise comparison judgements. Eur. J. Oper. Res. **159**(3), 687–704 (2004)

On an Edge Detector Based on Ordinal Sums of Conjunctive and Disjunctive Aggregation Functions

Marc Munar[1,2](✉)[ID], Miroslav Hudec[3,4][ID], Sebastia Massanet[1,2][ID], Erika Mináriková[3][ID], and Daniel Ruiz-Aguilera[1,2][ID]

[1] Soft Computing, Image Processing and Aggregation (SCOPIA) Research Group, Department of Mathematics and Computer Science, University of the Balearic Islands, Palma, Spain
{marc.munar,s.massanet,daniel.ruiz}@uib.es

[2] Health Research Institute of the Balearic Islands (IdISBa), Palma, Spain

[3] Faculty of Economic Informatics, University of Economics in Bratislava, Bratislava, Slovakia
{miroslav.hudec,erika.minarikova}@euba.sk

[4] Faculty of Economics, VSB - Technical University of Ostrava, Ostrava, Czech Republic
miroslav.hudec@vsb.cz

Abstract. Aggregation functions have been used in the last decade in several edge detectors with notable success. Recently, a new family of aggregation functions defined as ordinal sums of conjunctive and disjunctive aggregation functions have been introduced with good results in classification problems. Due to this performance, in this paper, this family is considered in the aggregation step of the edge detection algorithm based on uninorms. This new edge detector is compared with other classical edge detectors concluding that this class of ordinal sums is a feasible family to be used for edge detection.

Keywords: Edge detection · Aggregation functions · Ordinal sums · Uninorms · Canny

1 Introduction

Edge detection has been one of the most studied topics in image processing in the last decades [15]. Being a low-level operation, its performance is important for the final results of high-level operations such as segmentation, pattern recognition or other computer vision techniques. Due to this reason, a plethora of edge detection algorithms have been introduced by considering very different theories and techniques. Namely, we can highlight the classical algorithms based on convolution masks such as Sobel, Prewitt or Canny edge detectors (see [16]) or the new techniques based on fuzzy sets and their extensions (see [1,3]), which take into account the fact that edges are an intuitive concept. In fact, almost every mathematical theory has been considered for this task.

S. Massanet et al. (Eds.): EUSFLAT 2023/AGOP 2023, LNCS 14069, pp. 271–282, 2023.
https://doi.org/10.1007/978-3-031-39965-7_23

Within the context of edge detectors based on fuzzy logic, aggregation functions play a significant role in many of them. These operators are crucial to define the fuzzy morphological gradient in any edge detector based on the fuzzy mathematical morphology. In [9], the performance of the standard fuzzy morphological gradient is studied depending on the choice of t-norm and fuzzy implication function considered in the definition of the fuzzy dilation and fuzzy erosion, respectively. In [6] and [7], basic fuzzy morphological operators (and consequently, the fuzzy morphological gradient) are generalized by considering more general aggregation functions instead of the usual minimum and maximum. On the other hand, other edge detectors which are not based on the fuzzy mathematical morphology have been also proposed. For instance, in [8] a novel edge detection algorithm is proposed that considers uninorms to aggregate the directional gradients. All these edge detectors obtain competitive results with respect to the classical algorithms based on convolution masks both from the quantitative and qualitative points of view.

In this paper, a novel edge detector will be proposed by modifying the edge detector based on uninorms presented in [8]. Although uninorms have proved their potential for edge detection purposes, some of their properties such as the associativity and the neutral element are quite restrictive and they do not have a clear meaning in this context. For this reason, in this paper, we will investigate the performance of an edge detector that considers the novel class of ordinal sums of a conjunctive and disjunctive aggregation functions (instead of the uninorms) to perform the aggregation of the directional gradients in the edge detector proposed in [8]. This class of aggregation functions was proposed in [12] (and improved in [11]) for classification problems with classes Yes, No and Maybe containing a tendency to the classes Yes and No. Since edge detection can be understood as a classification problem where a pixel must be classified as edge or non-edge, it is worth studying their performance in edge detection.

The structure of the paper is as follows. First, in Sect. 2, some preliminaries on aggregation functions are recalled. Then, in Sect. 3, the edge detector presented in [8] is fully described in order to present, after that, the proposed modification. Finally, Sects. 4 and 5 introduce the experimental setup for the comparison experiments and the analysis of the results. The paper ends with some conclusions and future work.

2   Preliminaries

In order to make this paper as self-contained as possible, the fundamental concepts that will be used throughout the study are presented below. Let us start with the basic concepts of fuzzy conjunction and disjunction.

Definition 1. *A fuzzy conjunction (fuzzy disjunction) is a binary operation* $C : [0,1]^2 \to [0,1]$ *($D : [0,1]^2 \to [0,1]$) such that it is increasing in each argument and satisfies the boundary conditions* $C(0,1) = C(1,0) = 0$ *and* $C(1,1) = 1$ *($D(0,1) = D(1,0) = 1$ and $D(0,0) = 0$).*

As a particular case of fuzzy conjunction, we recall the concept of a t-norm.

Definition 2 ([13]). *A* t-norm *is a fuzzy conjunction* $T : [0,1]^2 \to [0,1]$ *such that it is commutative, associative and has 1 as neutral element.*

By modifying only the neutral element, the concept of t-conorm (a particular case of fuzzy disjunction) can be derived from the axioms of t-norm; specifically, a t-conorm is a fuzzy disjunction $S : [0,1]^2 \to [0,1]$ that is commutative, associative and has 0 as neutral element. In fact, the interrelated nature of the definitions of both families enables the transformation of a t-norm into a t-conorm, and vice versa, through the notion of duality: $S(x,y) = 1 - T(1-x, 1-y)$, for all $x, y \in [0,1]$, is the dual t-conorm of the t-norm T.

In this paper, we will consider members of the family of Schweizer-Sklar t-norms and t-conorms, given, respectively, by:

$$T_\mu^{SS}(x,y) = \begin{cases} T_M(x,y), & \text{if } \mu = -\infty, \\ T_P(x,y), & \text{if } \mu = 0, \\ T_D(x,y), & \text{if } \mu = +\infty, \\ (\max\{0, x^\mu + y^\mu - 1\})^{\frac{1}{\mu}}, & \text{if } \mu \in]-\infty, 0[\cup]0, +\infty[. \end{cases} \quad (1)$$

$$S_\mu^{SS}(x,y) = \begin{cases} S_M(x,y), & \text{if } \mu = -\infty, \\ S_P(x,y), & \text{if } \mu = 0, \\ S_D(x,y), & \text{if } \mu = +\infty, \\ 1 - (\max\{0, (1-x)^\mu + (1-y)^\mu - 1\})^{\frac{1}{\mu}}, & \text{if } \mu \in]-\infty, 0[\cup]0, +\infty[. \end{cases} \quad (2)$$

where T_M, T_P and T_D denote the t-norms minimum, product and drastic, respectively, and S_M, S_P and S_D denote their corresponding dual t-conorms, respectively (see [13] for further details).

We will now focus on the family of uninorms.

Definition 3 ([4,14]). *A* uninorm *is a binary operation* $U : [0,1]^2 \to [0,1]$ *such that it is commutative, associative, increasing in both arguments and has* $e \in [0,1]$ *as the neutral element.*

From its definition, it is straightforward to conclude that when $e = 0$, the uninorm is a t-conorm, whereas when $e = 1$, it is a t-norm. Otherwise, when $0 < e < 1$, the uninorm is referred to as proper. Among the proper uninorms, their structure is completely known: In the subregion $[0,e]^2$, a uninorm U behaves as a t-norm, represented by T_U; in the subregion $[e,1]^2$, it behaves as a t-conorm, denoted by S_U. In the remaining area, denoted with C_e and referred to as the compensation space, they satisfy $\min\{x,y\} \leq U(x,y) \leq \max\{x,y\}$, for all $(x,y) \in C_e = ([0,e[\times]e,1])\cup(]e,1]\times[0,e[)$. Specifically, when $U(x,y) = \min\{x,y\}$ or $U(x,y) = \max\{x,y\}$, for all $(x,y) \in C_e$, two classes of uninorms are obtained. We will denote these two classes by $U = \langle T, e, S\rangle_{\min}$ and $U = \langle T, e, S\rangle_{\max}$, respectively. For more information on uninorms and the different existing families, we recommend the reader to consult [14].

3 From the Edge Detector Based on Uninorms to a New One Based on Ordinal Sums

In this section, the new edge detector based on ordinal sums of conjunctive and disjunctive aggregation functions will be presented. First of all, in Sect. 3.1, we will recall the key features of the edge detector based on uninorms (see [8]). After that, in Sect. 3.2, we will introduce the new edge detector, focusing on the differences with respect to the one based on uninorms.

3.1 Edge Detection Using Uninorms

The method outlined in [8] considers as input a grey-scale image, modeled as a mapping $I : \mathcal{D}_I \subset \mathbb{Z}^2 \to [0,1]$, where $\mathcal{D}_I$ represents the domain of the image. The initial step of the method involves the computation of the basic directional gradients of the image. Given a coordinate $(i,j) \in \mathcal{D}_I$ and its 3×3 neighborhood, the algorithm computes the following three directional gradients in the horizontal direction, given by

$$y^l_{i-1,i+1} = |I(i-1,l) - I(i+1,l)|, \tag{3}$$

for all $l \in \{j-1, j, j+1\}$, and the following three directional gradients in the vertical direction, given by

$$x^k_{i-1,i+1} = |I(k, j-1) - I(k, j+1)|, \tag{4}$$

for all $k \in \{i-1, i, i+1\}$. These six basic directional gradients are aggregated in order to obtain two general gradients for each coordinate. Each of these general gradients is defined as the aggregation of the three directional gradients of the corresponding direction by a uninorm $U = \langle T, e, S \rangle$. Specifically, for the vertical direction, the vertical gradient at point (i,j) is defined as

$$\nabla_y(i,j) = U(x^{i-1}_{i-1,i+1}, x^i_{i-1,i+1}, x^{i+1}_{i-1,i+1}), \tag{5}$$

while the horizontal gradient at the point (i,j) is defined as

$$\nabla_x(i,j) = U(y^{j-1}_{i-1,i+1}, y^j_{i-1,i+1}, y^{j+1}_{i-1,i+1}). \tag{6}$$

Remark 1. In Eqs. (5) and (6), the aggregation of three elements is performed using a uninorm U, which is a binary operator. However, due to the associativity and commutativity of U, the order in which the aggregation is performed is inconsequential, as these properties ensure that the output is independent of the order in which the elements are aggregated.

Remark 2. Given the construction of the gradients in Eqs. (3) and (4), it is possible that some of the coordinates $(i-1, l)$, $(i+1, l)$, $(k, j-1)$, or $(k, j+1)$ may fall outside the domain $\mathcal{D}_I$ for some $k \in \{i-1, i, i+1\}$ or $l \in \{j-1, j, j+1\}$. To overcome this, the following convention is applied: if (i,j) is located on the boundary of $\mathcal{D}_I$, then $\nabla_y(i,j) = 0$ and $\nabla_x(i,j) = 0$; otherwise, it is evaluated using the corresponding expression.

Finally, in order to combine the two gradients, the authors propose to compute the magnitude of $\nabla_x(i,j)$ and $\nabla_y(i,j)$ by the expression

$$M(i,j) = \sqrt{\nabla_x(i,j)^2 + \nabla_y(i,j)^2}. \tag{7}$$

The computed value of $M(i,j)$ can be greater than 1. To ensure the values fall within $[0,1]$, a normalization process is applied. The resulting fuzzy edge image contains, for each coordinate (i,j), the membership value of this coordinate to the edge set. However, in order to compare the performance of several edge detection algorithms, Canny's restrictions establish that the edges must be binary and of one-pixel width. Therefore, after obtaining the fuzzy edge image, the final binary edge image is obtained through the application of a Non-Maxima Suppression technique, followed by a hysteresis thresholding operation (see [8] for the details).

3.2 Towards Edge Detection Using Commutative Aggregation Functions

The approach outlined in Sect. 3.1 primarily depends on the choice of the uninorm U, considered for the aggregation of directional gradients. The idea behind the use of uninorms for this specific task was explained in [8]. Namely, if the values of the basic directional gradients are high (belonging to the interval $[e,1]$ where e is the neutral element of the uninorm), the respective directional general gradient is computed by using the underlying t-conorm S_U of the uninorm U and since $S_U \geq \max$, these values are boosted as an indicator of a presence of a remarkable edge point. On the other hand, if the values of the basic directional gradients are low (belonging to the interval $[0,e]$), the respective directional general gradient is computed by using the underlying t-norm T_U and since $T_U \leq \min$, these values are reduced taking into account that this coordinate seems not to be an edge point.

Although this idea is interesting, uninorms present two features which are not completely adequate for the edge detection task:

- The neutral element of the uninorm does not provide any positive outcome for this task and it makes no sense that a particular value of gradient is neglected in favour of the other when the aggregation is performed.
- The uninorms that provide the best results in [8] are the ones belonging to the families $U = \langle T, e, S \rangle_{\min}$ and $U = \langle T, e, S \rangle_{\max}$. Note that these uninorms behave as the minimum or the maximum in C_e. In that region of the unit square, the aggregation is performed between a high gradient value and a small one. Therefore, there is a lack of sufficient information to definitively determine if the values of the basic directional gradients correspond with an edge or a non-edge. Consequently, the use of conjunctive or disjunctive uninorms that in C_e behave as the minimum or the maximum should be revised. Indeed, it would be more adequate for edge detection purposes that the output in this case would be a truly averaging value between both inputs and not exactly one of inputs as the minimum and the maximum provide.

Moreover, the associativity reduces greatly the number of possible operators to be considered. For all these reasons, the main goal of this paper is to consider more general aggregation functions without neutral element such that in the compensation region behave as a truly averaging function.

One class of aggregation functions that satisfy the above requirements is the class of ordinal sums of conjunctive and disjunctive aggregation functions that was considered in [12] and [11]. Their expression is, when adopting the convex combination of geometric and dual geometric mean, given by

$$
A_{C,D,e,\lambda}(x,y) = \begin{cases} eC\left(\frac{x}{e}, \frac{y}{e}\right), & \text{if } (x,y) \in [0,e]^2, \\ e + (1-e) \cdot D\left(\frac{x-e}{1-e}, \frac{y-e}{1-e}\right), & \text{if } (x,y) \in [e,1]^2, \\ \frac{\lambda}{e}xy + (1-\lambda)\left(1 - \frac{1}{1-e} \cdot (1-x)(1-y)\right), & \text{otherwise,} \end{cases}
$$
(8)

where C is a commutative conjunction and D is a commutative disjunction. We will denote this function simply by $A = \langle C, D, e, \lambda \rangle$. The parameter e will play a role similar to the neutral element of the uninorm being interpreted as follows: if the values belong to the square $[e,1]^2$, the aggregation is performed using the underlying disjunction since the coordinate is considered as a potential edge. If the values belong to $[0,e]^2$, the underlying conjunction is applied, indicating that the coordinate does not seem an edge. In the case of values belonging to the region $([0,e[\times]e,1]) \cup (]e,1] \times [0,e[)$, an scaled averaging aggregation function generated from the geometric mean and its dual is used (see [11] for details). In this case, the weight given to each function is adjusted by the parameter λ.

It is important to note several features of this family. First of all, e is not a neutral element. Secondly, the aggregation function $A = \langle C, D, e, \lambda \rangle$ may not be associative, even if C and D are a t-norm and a t-conorm, respectively.

By using aggregation functions of this family, we propose a modification of the edge detector recalled in Sect. 3.1. Concretely, the overall framework will be retained, except for the evaluation of Eqs. (5) and (6) which will be performed using the aggregation functions $A_{C,D,e,\lambda}$. Note that since these aggregation functions are not associative, a criterion must be established to evaluate the gradient $\nabla_x(i,j)$ in a consistent manner. The proposed solution is to order $x^{i-1}_{i-1,i+1}, x^i_{i-1,i+1}, x^{i+1}_{i-1,i+1}$ in increasing order[1], and then aggregate them pairwise from the smallest to the largest. Analogously, we apply this process to evaluate $\nabla_y(i,j)$.

4   Experimental Setup

To evaluate both the original method and the proposed modification along with other edge detectors, a case study is conducted. In Sect. 4.1, the images used in the study are presented. The metrics for performance evaluation are outlined in Sect. 4.2, and the different combinations of parameters for each method are described in Sect. 4.3. All experiments have been run on an Intel Core i7-10750H processor with 32 GB of RAM.

---

[1] The performance of the edge detector is similar if a decreasing order is applied.

4.1   Image Dataset

The image set used in the study consists of 50 images from the public dataset provided by the University of South Florida [2]. Each sample includes both the original image and an image with edge specifications, that will be considered the ground truth image, i.e., the image that contains the true edges. Figure 1 depicts some images with their respective ground truths. Black pixels in the ground truth indicate edges, grey pixels represent regions that should not be considered for performance evaluation[2], and white pixels represent non-edge pixels.

4.2   Evaluation Metrics

To evaluate the effectiveness of edge detection, three widely used measures in the literature will be considered.

- The ρ-coefficient [10], defined as

$$\rho = \frac{E_{\text{TP}}}{E_{\text{TP}} + E_{\text{FN}} + E_{\text{FP}}}, \tag{9}$$

where E_{TP} indicates the number of correctly detected edges, E_{FN} indicates the number of non-detected edges that should have been detected, and E_{FP} indicates the number of detected edges that should not have been detected.
- The F-measure or F-score, defined as the harmonic mean of precision and recall. Its final expression is given by

$$F = \frac{2 \cdot E_{\text{TP}}}{2 \cdot E_{\text{TP}} + E_{\text{FN}} + E_{\text{FP}}}. \tag{10}$$

- The Pratt's figure of merit [16]. This metric provides a measure of the goodness of edge detection while taking into account small deviations in the location of the detected edge. The expression of this measure is

$$\text{FoM} = \frac{1}{\max\{E_I, E_{\text{TP}} + E_{\text{FP}}\}} \sum_{i=1}^{E_{\text{TP}}+E_{\text{FP}}} \frac{1}{1 + \alpha \cdot d(e_i)^2}, \tag{11}$$

where E_I is the number of ideal edges (those pixels in the ground truth that are edges), α is a scaling constant (experimentally-set by Pratt to $\alpha = \frac{1}{9}$) and $d(e_i)$ is the distance of the edge e_i detected by the method to the nearest edge of the ground truth.

Although the expressions of the measures depend on the values of the confusion matrix, as outlined in [10], it is recommended to adopt a more flexible approach when determining TP, TN, FP, and FN. This is because the detected edge may not exactly match the position of the edge in the ground truth, but it is still considered a correct detection if an edge is present in a 5×5 neighbourhood centred on the same coordinates in the ground truth. All measures have values in $[0, 1]$, with higher values indicating higher performance in edge detection.

---

[2] These regions contain mostly textures and an edge detector should not be penalized whatever result it obtains.

4.3 Parameter Tuning

In order to thoroughly examine the behaviour of the method, we have tried several combinations of parameters. With respect to the edge detector based on ordinal sums introduced in Sect. 3.2, we have considered as conjunction the Schweizer-Sklar t-norms parametrized by μ, and as disjunction the dual of the considered t-norm (with the same parameter μ). The considered combinations are:

- As neutral element of the aggregation function, $e \in \{0, 0.02, 0.04, \ldots, 0.2\} \cup \{0.01\}$.
- As weight-control, $\lambda \in \{0, 0.25, 0.5, 0.75, 1\}$.
- As t-norm selection, $\mu \in \{-15, -14, \ldots, -1, 0\}$.

Thus, a total of 960 configurations have been performed. With respect to the original method based on uninorms, we have considered the following configurations:

- As uninorm selection, the families of $U = \langle T, e, S \rangle_{\min}$ and $U = \langle T, e, S \rangle_{\max}$ with T_{nM}, T_P or T_L, the nilpotent minumum, the product or the Łukasiewicz t-norms, respectively, as underlying t-norms and their duals, as underlying t-conorms.
- As neutral element of the uninorm, $e \in \{0.02, 0.04, 0.06, 0.08\}$.

Thus, 24 configurations have been considered. Finally, in order to compare with classical methods, we have implemented the edge detectors of Canny (with $\sigma \in \{0.5, 1, 1.5, 2, 2.5\}$), Sobel, Roberts and Prewitt (see [5] for more information about these methods). In total, 992 different edge detectors have been tested.

5 Analysis of the Results

Each configuration has been applied to the 50 images and the three considered measures have been computed for each result. Thus, Table 1 ranks, for each measure, the five top configurations in decreasing order of the average of the measure values obtained by the configuration. As shown, the edge detector with configuration $U = \langle T_P, 0.02, S_P \rangle_{\min}$ obtains the first position according to ρ-coefficient and F-measure, while Canny edge detector with $\sigma = 1$ hold the top position according to FoM. Several configurations of the proposed edge detector based on ordinal sums are listed in the ranking. Specifically, 3 in the top 5 of both ρ-coefficient and FoM and 4 in the top 5 of F-measure. Only four edge detectors appear in the top 5 for more than one measure. Namely, Canny edge detector with $\sigma = 1$, the uninorm-based method with $U = \langle T_P, 0.02, S_P \rangle_{\min}$ and the ordinal sum-based methods with $A = \langle T_{-2}^{SS}, S_{-2}^{SS}, 0.02, 1 \rangle$ and $A = \langle T_0^{SS}, S_0^{SS}, 0.02, 1 \rangle$ show a consistent performance. In Fig. 1, we have depicted the results of these edge detectors for several images.

Now, in order to determine which method has statistically a better performance, we have conducted a Wilcoxon signed-rank test to each metric to assess whether there are significant differences between the 4 prominent edge detectors outlined above. After conducting the tests with each metric, the same conclusion is reached. The results of the tests indicate that there is no significant evidence to support the claim that one method outperforms the others, concluding that they perform similarly for each measure. Thus, it can be concluded that the edge detectors with $U = \langle T_\text{P}, 0.02, S_\text{P} \rangle_\text{min}$, $A = \langle T_0^\text{SS}, S_0^\text{SS}, 0.02, 1 \rangle$, Canny with $\sigma = 1$ and $A = \langle T_{-2}^\text{SS}, S_{-2}^\text{SS}, 0.02, 1 \rangle$ exhibit similar performance across all measures.

Table 1. Summary of the top five configurations for each metric, including the mean and standard deviation computed for all images. Those configurations that ranked in the top five for another metric are highlighted.

Ranking	ρ-coefficient	F-measure	Pratt's FoM
1	$U = \langle T_\text{P}, 0.02, S_\text{P} \rangle_\text{min}$ 0.7509 ± 0.1264	$U = \langle T_\text{P}, 0.02, S_\text{P} \rangle_\text{min}$ 0.8507 ± 0.1002	Canny, $\sigma = 1$ 0.7839 ± 0.1956
2	$A = \langle T_0^\text{SS}, S_0^\text{SS}, 0.02, 1 \rangle$ 0.7505 ± 0.1255	$A = \langle T_0^\text{SS}, S_0^\text{SS}, 0.02, 1 \rangle$ 0.8504 ± 0.1022	Canny, $\sigma = 1.5$ 0.7718 ± 0.1270
3	Canny, $\sigma = 1$ 0.7503 ± 0.1929	$A = \langle T_0^\text{SS}, S_0^\text{SS}, 0.02, 0.75 \rangle$ 0.8499 ± 0.1022	$A = \langle T_0^\text{SS}, S_0^\text{SS}, 0.01, 0 \rangle$ 0.7676 ± 0.1287
4	$A = \langle T_{-2}^\text{SS}, S_{-2}^\text{SS}, 0.02, 1 \rangle$ 0.7502 ± 0.1277	$A = \langle T_{-2}^\text{SS}, S_{-2}^\text{SS}, 0.02, 1 \rangle$ 0.8498 ± 0.1058	$A = \langle T_0^\text{SS}, S_0^\text{SS}, 0.01, 1 \rangle$ 0.7672 ± 0.1304
5	$A = \langle T_{-1}^\text{SS}, S_{-1}^\text{SS}, 0.02, 1 \rangle$ 0.7498 ± 0.1275	$A = \langle T_{-1}^\text{SS}, S_{-1}^\text{SS}, 0.02, 1 \rangle$ 0.8497 ± 0.1049	$A = \langle T_0^\text{SS}, S_0^\text{SS}, 0.01, 0.75 \rangle$ 0.7670 ± 0.1307

Finally, we have computed, for each image and measure, the rankings of the four prominent edge detectors. These results are summarized in Table 2. Specifically, it shows, for each edge detector and measure, the number of images in which the method achieved the first position, the average ranking of the method across all images and edge detectors, and the average ranking of the method considering only the 4 prominent edge detectors. As observed, both the ρ-coefficient and the F-measure produce the same rankings in all cases. The edge detector $U = \langle T_\text{P}, 0.02, S_\text{P} \rangle_\text{min}$ achieves the best mean absolute ranking for both the ρ-coefficient and the F-measure. However, when considering the FoM, the configuration $A = \langle T_{-2}^\text{SS}, S_{-2}^\text{SS}, 0.02, 1 \rangle$ has the best mean absolute ranking, followed by $A = \langle T_0^\text{SS}, S_0^\text{SS}, 0.02, 1 \rangle$. Regarding the relative rankings, according to ρ-coefficient and F-measure, Canny edge detector has the best mean relative ranking, although it also has the highest standard deviation, indicating that it is the least stable of the four methods. Both configurations $A = \langle T_{-2}^\text{SS}, S_{-2}^\text{SS}, 0.02, 1 \rangle$ and $U = \langle T_\text{P}, 0.02, S_\text{P} \rangle_\text{min}$ stand on the second best mean relative ranking, but it is $A = \langle T_{-2}^\text{SS}, S_{-2}^\text{SS}, 0.02, 1 \rangle$ that has the lower standard deviation of the two and, in fact, has the lowest standard deviation among all configurations.

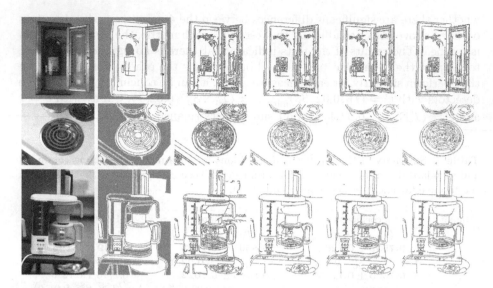

Fig. 1. Example of some images of the dataset, their ground truths and the results of some edge detectors. In order of appearance, from left to right, Canny with $\sigma = 1$, the uninorm-based method with $U = \langle T_{\mathrm{P}}, 0.02, S_{\mathrm{P}} \rangle_{\min}$, the ordinal sum-based method with $A = \langle T_{-2}^{\mathrm{SS}}, S_{-2}^{\mathrm{SS}}, 0.02, 1 \rangle$ and the ordinal sum-based method with $A = \langle T_0^{\mathrm{SS}}, S_0^{\mathrm{SS}}, 0.02, 1 \rangle$.

Table 2. Ranking of the selected methods for each metric. The second column indicates the number of images for which the configuration was ranked first. The third column indicates the mean and standard deviation of the ranking of that method among all the considered configurations. The fourth column indicates the mean and standard deviation of the ranking of the experiment when considering only the four selected configurations.

Method and metric		First positions	Abs. ranking	Rel. ranking
$U = \langle T_{\mathrm{P}}, 0.02, S_{\mathrm{P}} \rangle_{\min}$	ρ-coef.	11	119.8 ± 227.81	2.54 ± 1.14
	F-meas.	11	119.8 ± 227.81	2.54 ± 1.14
	FoM	5	112.48 ± 209.42	2.82 ± 1.02
$A = \langle T_0^{\mathrm{SS}}, S_0^{\mathrm{SS}}, 0.02, 1 \rangle$	ρ-coef.	0	154.32 ± 271.6	2.78 ± 0.61
	F-meas.	0	154.32 ± 271.6	2.78 ± 0.61
	FoM	2	110.6 ± 222.7	2.74 ± 0.69
$A = \langle T_{-2}^{\mathrm{SS}}, S_{-2}^{\mathrm{SS}}, 0.02, 1 \rangle$	ρ-coef.	9	147.2 ± 274.87	2.54 ± 1.05
	F-meas.	9	147.2 ± 274.87	2.54 ± 1.05
	FoM	9	93.8 ± 221.1	2.5 ± 1.07
Canny, $\sigma = 1$	ρ-coef.	30	306.26 ± 437.12	2.14 ± 1.44
	F-meas.	30	306.26 ± 437.12	2.14 ± 1.44
	FoM	34	253.08 ± 403.8	1.94 ± 1.39

6 Conclusions and Future Work

In this paper, a modification of the edge detector based on uninorms presented in [8] has been proposed by means of changing the uninorms by ordinal sums of conjunctive and disjunctive aggregation functions of the class introduced in [11]. The new edge detector has been compared with the one based on uninorms and some classical edge detectors through a series of experiments by considering three well-known performance measures in edge detection.

The comparison experiments lead to several conclusions. First of all, four edge detectors highlight among the 960 considered, namely, Canny with $\sigma = 1$, the uninorm-based method with $U = \langle T_P, 0.02, S_P \rangle_{\min}$, the ordinal sum-based method with $A = \langle T_{-2}^{SS}, S_{-2}^{SS}, 0.02, 1 \rangle$ and the ordinal sum-based method with $A = \langle T_0^{SS}, S_0^{SS}, 0.02, 1 \rangle$. Secondly, although a Wilcoxon signed-rank test ensures that none of these edge detectors performs significantly better than the others, they present different behavior according to the measures. While Canny edge detector obtains the best results for a high number of images, it is more unstable than the ordinal sum-based methods whose performance is more stable across images. Finally, it seems that (i) the product t-norm and its dual t-conorm present the best performance since they are considered in the best configurations of both the uninorm-based method and the ordinal sum-based method ($T_0^{SS} = T_P$) and (ii) $e = 0.02$, which is associated to gradient values of $255 \cdot 0.02 \approx 5$, is the best value to delimit the borders between the different regions (non-edge, edge, compensation) of the ordinal sum.

As future work, we would like to study which features of an image determine the performance of each of these edge detectors. Moreover, it would be interesting to propose an adaptive edge detector that applies, for each pixel, different aggregation functions according to some criteria.

Acknowledgements. This work was partially supported by the R+D+i Project PID2020-113870GB-I00-"Desarrollo de herramientas de Soft Computing para la Ayuda al Diagnóstico Clínico y a la Gestión de Emergencias (HESOCODICE)", funded by MCIN/AEI/10.13039/501100011033/, the KEGA No. 025EU-4/2021 by the Ministry of Education, Science, Research and Sport of the Slovak Republic, and SGS SP2023/078 by the Ministry of Education, Youth and Sports of the Czech Republic.

References

1. Barrenechea, E., Bustince, H., De Baets, B., Lopez-Molina, C.: Construction of interval-valued fuzzy relations with application to the generation of fuzzy edge images. IEEE Trans. Fuzzy Syst. **19**(5), 819–830 (2011)
2. Bowyer, K., Kranenburg, C., Dougherty, S.: Edge detector evaluation using empirical ROC curves. In: Proceedings of the 1999 IEEE Computer Society Conference on Computer Vision and Pattern Recognition, vol. 1, pp. 354–359 (1999)
3. Bustince, H., Barrenechea, E., Pagola, M., Fernandez, J.: Interval-valued fuzzy sets constructed from matrices: application to edge detection. Fuzzy Sets Syst. **160**(13), 1819–1840 (2009)

4. Fodor, J., Yager, R., Rybalov, A.: Structure of uninorms. Int. J. Uncertainty Fuzziness Knowl.-Based Syst. **5**, 411–428 (1997)
5. Gonzalez, R.C., Woods, R.E.: Digital Image Processing, 3rd edn. Prentice-Hall Inc., Hoboken (2006)
6. González-Hidalgo, M., Massanet, S., Mir, A., Ruiz-Aguilera, D.: On the generalization of the fuzzy morphological operators for edge detection. In: Alonso, J.M., et al. (eds.) 2015 Conference of the International Fuzzy Systems Association and the European Society for Fuzzy Logic and Technology (IFSA-EUSFLAT 2015). Atlantis Press (2015)
7. González-Hidalgo, M., Massanet, S., Mir, A., Ruiz-Aguilera, D.: On the generalization of the uninorm morphological gradient. In: Rojas, I., Joya, G., Catala, A. (eds.) IWANN 2015. LNCS, vol. 9095, pp. 436–449. Springer, Cham (2015). https://doi.org/10.1007/978-3-319-19222-2_37
8. González-Hidalgo, M., Massanet, S., Mir, A., Ruiz-Aguilera, D.: A new edge detector based on uninorms. In: Laurent, A., Strauss, O., Bouchon-Meunier, B., Yager, R.R. (eds.) IPMU 2014. CCIS, vol. 443, pp. 184–193. Springer, Cham (2014). https://doi.org/10.1007/978-3-319-08855-6_19
9. González-Hidalgo, M., Massanet, S., Mir, A., Ruiz-Aguilera, D.: On the choice of the pair conjunction-implication into the fuzzy morphological edge detector. IEEE Trans. Fuzzy Syst. **23**(4), 872–884 (2015)
10. Grigorescu, C., Petkov, N., Westenberg, M.: Contour detection based on nonclassical receptive field inhibition. IEEE Trans. Image Process. **12**(7), 729–739 (2003)
11. Hudec, M., Mináriková, E., Mesiar, R.: Aggregation functions in flexible classification by ordinal sums. In: Ciucci, D., et al. (eds.) IPMU 2022. CCIS, vol. 1601, pp. 372–383. Springer, Cham (2022). https://doi.org/10.1007/978-3-031-08971-8_31
12. Hudec, M., Mináriková, E., Mesiar, R., Saranti, A., Holzinger, A.: Classification by ordinal sums of conjunctive and disjunctive functions for explainable AI and interpretable machine learning solutions. Knowl.-Based Syst. **220**, 106916 (2021)
13. Klement, E.P., Mesiar, R., Pap, E.: Triangular Norms. TREN, Springer, Dordrecht (2000). https://doi.org/10.1007/978-94-015-9540-7
14. Mas, M., Massanet, S., Ruiz-Aguilera, D., Torrens, J.: A survey on the existing classes of uninorms. J. Intell. Fuzzy Syst. **29**, 1021–1037 (2015)
15. Papari, G., Petkov, N.: Edge and line oriented contour detection: state of the art. Image Vis. Comput. **29**(2–3), 79–103 (2011)
16. Pratt, W.K.: Digital Image Processing: PIKS Scientific Inside. Wiley, Hoboken (2007)

SPECIAL SESSION 1: Interval Uncertainty

Why Fractional Fuzzy

Mehran Mazandarani[1]🆔, Olga Kosheleva[2]🆔, and Vladik Kreinovich[2(✉)]🆔

[1] Department of Mechatronics and Control Engineering, Shenzhen University, Shenzhen, China
memazandarani@szu.edu.cn
[2] University of Texas at El Paso, El Paso, TX, USA
{olgak,vladik}@utep.edu

Abstract. In many practical situation, control experts can only formulate their experience by using imprecise ("fuzzy") words from natural language. To incorporate this knowledge in automatic controllers, Lotfi Zadeh came up with a methodology that translates the informal expert statements into a precise control strategy. This methodology – and its following modifications – is known as fuzzy control. Fuzzy control often leads to a reasonable control – and we can get an even better control result by tuning the resulting control strategy on the actual system. There are many parameters that can be changed during tuning, so tuning usually is rather time-consuming. Recently, it was empirically shown that in many cases, quite good results can be attained by using a special 1-parametric tuning procedure called fractional fuzzy inference – we get up to 40% improvements just by selecting the proper value of a single parameter. In this paper, we provide a theoretical explanation of why fractional fuzzy inference works so well.

Keywords: Fuzzy control · Fractional fuzzy inference · Tuning

1 Formulation of the Problem

Need for Expert Knowledge in Control. In some cases – e.g., in controlling a spaceship – we know the exact equations describing the spaceship's trajectory, we know how exactly the spaceship will react to different controls. In such cases, selection of a proper control becomes a mathematical problem.

However, there are also many control situations when an exact model is not known. Such situations are typical in many areas, e.g., in chemical engineering, in

This work was supported in part by the project of the Guoqiang Research Institute of Tsinghua University (No. 2020GQG1001), by the National Science Foundation grants 1623190 (A Model of Change for Preparing a New Generation for Professional Practice in Computer Science), HRD-1834620 and HRD-2034030 (CAHSI Includes), and by the AT&T Fellowship in Information Technology. It was also supported by the program of the development of the Scientific-Educational Mathematical Center of Volga Federal District No. 075-02-2020-1478, and by a grant from the Hungarian National Research, Development and Innovation Office (NRDI).

S. Massanet et al. (Eds.): EUSFLAT 2023/AGOP 2023, LNCS 14069, pp. 285–296, 2023.
https://doi.org/10.1007/978-3-031-39965-7_24

medicine, etc. In many such situations, the control is implemented by experts. The problem is that experts differ in their experience, and there are usually very few top experts, not enough to cover all possible control applications. It is therefore desirable to incorporate the knowledge of top experts into an automatic system that would help others share the benefit of the top expert's knowledge.

Need for Fuzzy Techniques. Most experts are willing to share their expertise: most of them actually teach students and others. The problem is that they cannot formulate their knowledge in precise numerical terms. This makes perfect sense; e.g., in the US, the vast majority of people can drive, but hardly anyone can answer a question that would naturally arise in automatic control: if you are on a freeway at 100 km/hr, and the car 10 m in front of you slows down to 95 km/hr, with how many kiloNewtons of force and for how many milliseconds should you press the brake pedal? A natural answer that most driver will give is "press a little bit, for a short time". Such answers – expressed by using imprecise ("fuzzy") words from natural language – are rather typical.

So, to incorporate expert knowledge into a precise control strategy, we need to translate such imprecise statements into precise terms. Techniques for such a translation – pioneered by Lofti Zadeh – are known as *fuzzy techniques*, see, e.g., [1,4,7–9,12].

Need for Tuning. In many practical situations, fuzzy techniques provide a reasonable control strategy. However, the resulting control – based on approximate imprecise expert rules – is usually not optimal. To improve the quality of the resulting control, it is necessary to apply it to a real-life system and to "tune it" – i.e., to modify the control strategy based on the results of this application.

Fractional Fuzzy Techniques are Surprisingly Successful. A control strategy is a function that assigns, to each possible state of the system, an appropriate value(s) of the control. To uniquely determine a function, we need to describe infinitely many numerical values – e.g., the values of this function at all rational inputs. Not surprisingly, most currently used tuning methods tune the values of a large number of parameters – parameters of the corresponding membership functions, etc. (see detailed explanation in the following text). Because we need to determine the values of many different parameters, tuning usually requires a significant amount of computation time.

Interestingly, recently a new tuning technique has been developed – called *fractional fuzzy* technique – that allows to drastically improve the quality of the resulting control by tuning the value of only one parameter; see, e.g., [5,6]. For example, for the inverted pendulum, this simple 1-parametric tuning leads to a 40% improvement in control quality.

Remaining Challenge and What We Do in this Paper. While fractional fuzzy technique has been empirically successful, there has been no convincing theoretical explanation for its success. In this paper, we provide such an explanation.

The structure of this paper is as follows. To make our explanations clear, in Sect. 2, we briefly recall how fuzzy techniques work. In Sect. 3, we describe our main idea – the use of natural invariance, and we show that invariance requirement indeed leads to a few-parametric family that includes fractional fuzzy techniques as a particular case. In Sect. 4, we show that techniques from this family are actually optimal – in some reasonable sense.

2   Fuzzy Control Techniques: A Brief Reminder

How Experts Present Their Knowledge. We want to describe, for each state x – characterized by the values $x_1, \ldots, x_n$ of the corresponding parameters – the appropriate value of the control y. We want to extract such a strategy from the expert statements, and these statements are usually formulated by if-then rules:

if $x_1, \ldots, x_n$ have certain property, then some restrictions are placed on y.

By definition, fuzzy techniques transform expert knowledge into a precise control strategy. So, to describe fuzzy techniques, it is important to recall how experts present their knowledge. This knowledge is usually represented by if-then rules. The most typical situation is when both the conditions and the conclusions of the rules are described by imprecise natural language terms, i.e., when all the rules have the form

if x_1 is A_1 and ... and x_n is A_n, then y is B,

where A_i and B are the corresponding terms. For example, we can have a rule

if x_1 is small positive, then y is small negative.

In some cases, experts have a more detailed approximate description of the conclusion, i.e., use rules of the following type

if x_1 is A_1 and ... and x_n is A_n, then y is approximately equal to $f(x_1, \ldots, x_n)$,

for some function $f(x_1, \ldots, x_n)$.

What Needs to be Done to Transform this Knowledge into a Precise Control Strategy. The expert rules are formed by using imprecise natural-language terms by applying logical connectives like "and" and "if-then". Thus, to transform the experts' if-then rules into a precise control strategy, we need:

– first, to describe natural-language terms like "small" in precise terms, and
– second, to describe how logical connectives – that are usually applied to precise statements – can be applied to the resulting imprecise statements.

Let us describe these two stages one by one.

How to Describe Natural-Language Terms Like "Small" in Precise Terms. In the original fuzzy technique, to describe an imprecise property A, we assign, to each real number x, the degree (from the interval $[0, 1]$) to which the value x has this property – for example, to which x is small. Here:

- the degree 1 means that we are absolutely sure that x has this property,
- the degree 0 means that we are absolutely sure that x does not have this property, and
- values between 0 and 1 correspond to intermediate degrees of belief.

For most properties, as the input x increases, the degree first (non-strictly) increases, then (non-strictly) decreases. Such properties are known as *fuzzy numbers*.

Where do we get these degrees from? For some values x, we can ask the expert to provide such degrees by marking a number on the scale from 0 to 1. However, there are infinitely many real numbers, and we can only ask finitely many questions. Thus, in practice, we ask the expert about several values, and then use some extrapolation/interpolation techniques to estimate the other degrees. The resulting function assigning a degree $d(x)$ to each real number x is called a *membership function*, or, alternatively, a *fuzzy set*.

For example:

- if we know that the degree $d(x)$ is equal to 0 for $x = x_-$, to 1 for $x = m$, and to 0 for $x = x_+$, for some $x_- < m < x_+$, then linear interpolation leads to a so-called *triangular* membership function;
- if $d(x_-) = d(x_+) = 0$ and $d(m_-) = d(m_+) = 1$ for some $x_- < m_- < m_+ < x_+$, then linear interpolation leads to a so-called *trapezoid* membership function.

For continuous fuzzy numbers, and for each degree $\alpha > 0$, the set of all the values x for which $\mu(x) \geq \alpha$ is an interval. This interval is known as an α-*cut* of the original fuzzy set. Alpha-cuts are nested: if $\alpha < \alpha'$, then the α-cut corresponding to α' is a subset of the α-cut corresponding to α. Once we know all α-cuts $\mathbf{x}(\alpha)$, we can uniquely reconstruct the original membership function as $d(x) = \sup\{\alpha : x \in \mathbf{x}(\alpha)\}$. Thus, the nested family of α-cuts provides an alternative representation of the fuzzy set. This representation is useful in many applications – since it often makes computations easier.

How to Describe Logical Connectives and What to Do After that. In situations when each statement is either true or false, the truth value of each composite statement like $A \& B$ is uniquely determined by the truth values of the component statements A and B. In our case, we only have degrees of confidence in statements A and B, and this information does not uniquely determine the expert's degree of confidence in $A \& B$.

In the ideal world, we should ask the expert about all such computations. However, in practice, there are too many such combinations, and it is not possible to ask the expect about all of them. It is therefore necessary to be able to estimate the degree of confidence in a combination like $A \& B$ based only on the available information, i.e., only on the experts' degrees of certainty a and b in the statements A and B. The function that assigns, to each pair of numbers a and b, the corresponding degree is called an *"and"-operation*, or, for historical reasons, a *t-norm*. We will denote the value of the t-norm by $f_\&(a, b)$.

Similarly, if all we know are the degrees of confidence a and b in statements A and B, then our estimate for the degree of confidence in a statement $A \vee B$ will be denoted by $f_\vee(a, b)$, and our estimate for the degree of confidence in an implication $A \to B$ will be denoted by $f_\to(a, b)$.

How can we use these operations? For the general case, when we have rules with imprecise conclusions

$$\text{if } x_1 \text{ is } A_{k1} \text{ and } \ldots \text{ and } x_n \text{ is } A_{kn}, \text{ then } y \text{ is } B_k,$$

for $k = 1, \ldots, K$, there are two approaches: logical and Mamdani.

In the logical approach, we estimate the degree of belief $d_k(x_1, \ldots, x_n, y)$ that the k-th rule is satisfied as

$$d_k(x_1, \ldots, x_n, y) = f_\to(f_\&(A_{k1}(x_1), \ldots, A_{kn}(x_n)), B_k(y)),$$

and then compute the degree of belief $d(x_1, \ldots, x_n, y)$ that y is a reasonable control for given data x_i as

$$d(x_1, \ldots, x_n, y) = f_\&(d_1(x_1, \ldots, x_n, y), \ldots, d_K(x_1, \ldots, x_n, y)).$$

In the Mamdani approach, we take into account that y is reasonable if one of the rules is applicable, i.e., if for one of the rules, all conditions are satisfied, and the conclusion is satisfied too. In this case, the degree of belief $d_k(x_1, \ldots, x_n, y)$ that the k-th rule is satisfied is equal to

$$d_k(x_1, \ldots, x_n, y) = f_\&(A_{k1}(x_1), \ldots, A_{kn}(x_n), B_k(y)),$$

and the degree of belief $d(x_1, \ldots, x_n, y)$ that y is a reasonable control for given data x_i is equal to

$$d(x_1, \ldots, x_n, y) = f_\vee(d_1(x_1, \ldots, x_n, y), \ldots, d_K(x_1, \ldots, x_n, y)).$$

In both cases, for each input $x_1, \ldots, x_n$, we get a membership function $m(y) \stackrel{\text{def}}{=} d(x_1, \ldots, x_n, y)$ that describes to what extent different values y are possible. For automatic control, we need to select a single control value $\overline{y}$. The procedure of transforming a (fuzzy) membership function into a single value is known as *defuzzification*. One of the most widely used defuzzification methods is *centroid defuzzification*, where

$$\overline{y} = \frac{\int y \cdot m(y)\, dy}{\int m(y)\, dy}.$$

In situations when we know an exact description of the conclusion, i.e., when we have rules of the type

$$\text{if } x_1 \text{ is } A_{k1} \text{ and } \ldots \text{ and } x_n \text{ is } A_{kn}, \text{ then } y \text{ is approximately equal to}$$
$$f_k(x_1, \ldots, x_n),$$

we first compute the degree $d_k(x_1, \ldots, x_n)$ to which the conditions of each rule are satisfied:

$$d_k(x_1, \ldots, x_n) = f_\&(A_{k1}(x_1), \ldots, A_{kn}(x_n)),$$

and then generate the following control value:

$$\overline{y} = \frac{\sum_{k=1}^{K} d_k(x_1, \ldots, x_n) \cdot f_k(x_1, \ldots, x_n)}{\sum_{k=1}^{K} d_k(x_1, \ldots, x_n)}.$$

Need for Tuning. In the above description, we only took into account the expert's imprecise knowledge. To get a more adequate control, we need to test it on a real-life system, and make adjustments if needed. This real-system-based procedure is known as *tuning*.

3   Fractional Fuzzy Techniques: Motivations, Description, Successes, and Remaining Challenge

Motivations: Need for Faster Tuning Techniques. In general, there are many parameters to tune: e.g., the parameters describing all the membership functions $A_{ki}(x_i)$ and $B_k(y)$. Such tuning takes a lot of computation time. To speed up computations, it is therefore desirable to come up with tuning methods that require only a small number of parameters.

Fractional Fuzzy Techniques: Description. Recently, a new few-parametric tuning method was proposed; see, e.g., [5,6]. There are, three versions of this method:

- In the first version, we select a real number $\beta_+ > 0$, and we replace each α-cut interval $[\underline{x}, \overline{x}]$ with a new interval $[\underline{x}, \underline{x} + \beta_+ \cdot (\overline{x} - \underline{x})]$.
- In the second version, we select a real number $\beta_- < 1$, and we replace each α-cut interval $[\underline{x}, \overline{x}]$ with a new interval $[\underline{x} + \beta_- \cdot (\overline{x} - \underline{x}), \overline{x}]$.
- In the combined third version, we select two numbers $\beta_- \leq \beta_+$, and we replace each α-cut interval $[\underline{x}, \overline{x}]$ with a new interval

$$[\underline{x} + \beta_- \cdot (\overline{x} - \underline{x}), \underline{x} + \beta_+ \cdot (\overline{x} - \underline{x})].$$

In each version of this method, we replace each α-cut with its fraction; thus, this method is known as *fractional fuzzy* technique.

Fractional Fuzzy Techniques: Successes. Practical applications show that these techniques work very well. For example, for the inverted pendulum, each of the first two versions – corresponding to 1-parametric tuning – leads to a 40% improvement in control quality [5,6].

Fractional Fuzzy Techniques: Remaining Challenge, and What We Do in this Paper. A natural question is: how can we explain this empirical success? In this paper, we explain why this method is so successful.

4   Our Main Idea and How it Explains the Empirical Success of Fractional Fuzzy Techniques

Experts Are Not Perfect. Suppose that the best estimate of the corresponding quantity is $\tilde{x}$, and the actual uncertainty – that can be derived from what we know – is $\pm\Delta$, meaning that the actual value of the quantity x is somewhere in the interval $[\tilde{x} - \Delta, \tilde{x} + \Delta]$. This is what an ideal expert should return.

Actual experts are not perfect, they produce intervals $[x_0 - \delta, x_0 + \delta]$ which are, in general, different from the ideal interval:

- an expert may overestimate the value of the quantity x, by producing a larger value $x_0 > \tilde{x}$;
- an expert may underestimate this value, by producing $x_0 < \tilde{x}$;
- an expert may overestimate the inaccuracy, by producing a value $\delta > \Delta$;
- an expert may underestimate the inaccuracy, by producing a value $\delta < \Delta$.

In all these cases, the interval $[x_0 - \delta, x_0 + \delta]$ produced by an expert is different from the desired interval $[\tilde{x} - \Delta, \tilde{x} + \Delta]$.

So, to make a control more adequate, a natural idea is to take this into account and to transform the expert's interval back into the desired interval. For this purpose, we need to come up with a transformation T that transforms intervals into intervals.

Natural Properties of the Transformation T. Both inputs and outputs of the transformation T are intervals of values of a physical quantity, i.e., intervals for which both endpoints are values of this quantity. We would like to deal with the actual values, but in practice, we can only deal with numerical values, and numerical values depend on what unit we choose for this quantity and what starting point we choose.

If we select a measuring unit which is λ times smaller than the original one, then all the numerical values are multiplied by λ: $x \mapsto \lambda \cdot x$. For example, if we replace meters with centimeters, then 1.7 m becomes $1.7 \cdot 100 = 170$ cm.

If we select a new starting point which is x_0 units smaller than the original one, then this value x_0 is added to all the numerical values: $x \mapsto x + x_0$. For example, if we replace Celsius scale for temperature to Kelvin, then we need to add 273 to all the numerical values.

The choices of a measuring unit and of a starting point are often arbitrary, coming from a reasonably arbitrary agreement. It is therefore reasonable to require that the desired transformation T lead to the same interval of real values. So, we arrive at the following definitions.

Definition 1. *We say that the mapping T from intervals to intervals is* scale-invariant *if for every interval $[a, b]$ and for every real number $\lambda > 0$, the equality $[c, d] = T([a, b])$ implies that $[c', d'] = T([a', b'])$, where we denoted $a' = \lambda \cdot a$, $b' = \lambda \cdot b$, $c' = \lambda \cdot c$, and $d' = \lambda \cdot d$.*

Definition 2. *We say that the mapping T from intervals to intervals is* shift-invariant *if for every interval $[a, b]$ and for every real number x_0, the equality*

$[c, d] = T([a, b])$ *implies that* $[c', d'] = T([a', b'])$, *where we denoted* $a' = a + x_0$, $b' = b + x_0$, $c' = c + x_0$, *and* $d' = d + x_0$.

Comment. Similar invariance conditions were used in [2] to explain another empirically successful interval transformations [3,10,11]. However, these papers only dealt with overestimation or underestimation of uncertainty. Our analysis analyzes a more general situation, where the estimate itself can also be biased.

Proposition 1. *A mapping* T *is scale- and shift-invariant if and only if it has the form*

$$T([a, b]) = [a + \beta_- \cdot (b - a), a + \beta_+ \cdot (b - a)]$$

for some $\beta_- \leq \beta_+$.

Comment.

- For $\beta_- = 0$, we get the first version of the fractional fuzzy techniques.
- For $\beta_+ = 1$, we get the second version of the fractional fuzzy techniques.
- In general, we get the third (combined) version of these techniques.

Thus, indeed, this proposition provides an explanation for fractional fuzzy techniques.

Proof. Let us denote the endpoint of the interval $T([0, 1])$ by, correspondingly, β_- and β_+, i.e., $T([0, 1]) = [\beta_-, \beta_+]$. Let us show that for every interval $[a, b]$, the result $T([a, b])$ of applying this transformation has the desired form.

Indeed, due to scale-invariance for $\lambda = b - a$, we have

$$T([0, b - a]) = [\beta_- \cdot (b - a), \beta_+ \cdot (b - a)].$$

Now, due to shift-invariance with $x_0 = a$, we get the desired formula

$$T([a, b]) = [a + \beta_- \cdot (b - a), a + \beta_+ \cdot (b - a)].$$

The proposition is proven.

5   Fractional Fuzzy Techniques are Optimal – In Some Reasonable Sense

What Do We Mean by Optimal. Usually, when people talk about optimality, they assume that there is some numerical criterion, and the optimal alternative is the one that has the largest (or the smallest) value of this criterion. For example:

- an optimal path may be the shortest path,
- an optimal investment portfolio is the one with the largest expected gain, etc.

However, this is not the most general description of optimality. For example, if we have two alternative investment portfolios with the same expected gain, it is reasonable to select the one with the smallest expected deviation from this gain, etc. Thus, the optimality criterion can be more complicated than simply comparing numerical values.

In general, what we want from an optimality criterion is that it should allow us, at least for some pairs of alternatives a, a' to decide:

- whether a is better than a' (we will denote it by $a' < a$)
- or a' is better than a ($a < a'$),
- or a and a' are of the same quality to the user (we will denote it by $a \sim a'$).

Of course, there should be natural transitivity requirements: e.g., if a is better than a' and a' is better than a'', then a should be better than a''.

As we have mentioned in the beginning of the previous paragraph, if we have several alternatives which are optimal with respect to some optimality criterion, this means that this criterion is not final: we can use this non-uniqueness to optimize something else. So, when the criterion is final, there is exactly one alternative that is optimal with respect to this criterion. Thus, we arrive at the following definitions.

Definition 3. *By an* optimality criterion *on a set A, we mean a pair $(<, \sim)$ of binary relations on this set that satisfy the following properties:*

- *if $a < b$ and $b < c$, then $a < c$;*
- *if $a < b$ and $b \sim c$, then $a < c$;*
- *if $a \sim b$ and $b < c$, then $a < c$;*
- *if $a \sim b$ and $b \sim c$, then $a \sim c$;*
- *if $a < b$ then $a \not\sim b$;*
- *if $a \sim b$, then $b \sim a$;*
- *always $a \sim a$.*

Definition 4. *We say that an alternative a is* optimal *with respect to an optimality criterion $(<, \sim)$ if for every $b \in A$, we have either $b < a$ or $b \sim a$.*

Definition 5. *We say that an optimality criterion $(<, \sim)$ is* final *if there is exactly one alternative that is optimal with respect to this criterion.*

The Optimality Criterion Should be Invariant. In our case, alternatives are transformation functions. It is reasonable to require that if one transformation is better than another one, then it will still be better if we use a different measuring unit or a different starting point. Let us describe this in precise terms.

Suppose that we have an interval $[a, b]$ expressed in the original units. If we use a new measuring unit which is λ times smaller, then the interval becomes $\lambda \cdot [a, b] \stackrel{\text{def}}{=} [\lambda \cdot a, \lambda \cdot b]$. If we apply a transformation T to this new interval, we get the interval $T([\lambda \cdot a, \lambda \cdot b])$. This interval is in the new units; in the original units, it will have the form $\lambda^{-1} \cdot T([\lambda \cdot a, \lambda \cdot b])$. This is equivalent to using a transformation T_λ for which

$$T_\lambda([a, b]) = \lambda^{-1} \cdot T([\lambda \cdot a, \lambda \cdot b]). \tag{1}$$

In these terms, invariance means that:

- if $T < T'$, then we should have $T_\lambda < T'_\lambda$, and
- if $T \sim T'$, then we should have $T_\lambda \sim T'_\lambda$.

Similarly, suppose that we have an interval $[a, b]$ corresponding to the original starting point. If we use a new starting point which is x_0 units smaller, then the interval becomes $[a, b] + x_0 \overset{\text{def}}{=} [a + x_0, b + x_0]$. If we apply a transformation T to this new interval, we get the interval $T([a + x_0, b + x_0])$. The endpoints of this interval correspond to the new starting point; with respect to the original starting point, it will have the form $T([a + x_0, b + x_0]) - x_0$. This is equivalent to using a transformation $T_{(x_0)}$ for which

$$T_{(x_0)}([a, b]) = T([a + x_0, b + x_0]) - x_0. \tag{2}$$

In these terms, invariance means that:

- if $T < T'$, then we should have $T_{(x_0)} < T'_{(x_0)}$, and
- if $T \sim T'$, then we should have $T_{(x_0)} \sim T'_{(x_0)}$.

Definition 6. *We say that an optimality criterion on the set of all interval-to-interval transformation is* scale-invariant *if for every two transformations T and T' and for every real number $\lambda > 0$,*

- *$T < T'$ implies $T_\lambda < T'_\lambda$ and*
- *$T \sim T'$ implies $T_\lambda \sim T'_\lambda$,*

where T_λ and T'_λ are described by the formula (1).

Definition 7. *We say that an optimality criterion on the set of all interval-to-interval transformations is* shift-invariant *if for every two transformation T and T' and for every real number x_0,*

- *$T < T'$ implies $T_{(x_0)} < T'_{(x_0)}$ and*
- *$T \sim T'$ implies $T_{(x_0)} \sim T'_{(x_0)}$,*

where $T_{(x_0)}$ and $T'_{(x_0)}$ are described by the formula (2).

Proposition 2. *For every scale-invariant, shift-invariant, and final optimality criterion, the optimal transformation has the form*

$$t([a, b]) = [a + \beta_- \cdot (b - a), a + \beta_+ \cdot (b - a)]$$

for some $\beta_- \leq \beta_+$.

Comment. The optimal transformation has exactly the form used in fractional fuzzy techniques. Thus, this result provides a theoretical explanation for the empirical fact that these techniques work well in many control situations.

Proof. Let $(<, \sim)$ be scale-invariant, shift-invariant, and final optimality criterion, and let t be optimal with respect to this criterion.

Let us prove that t is scale-invariant, i.e., that for all λ, we have $t_\lambda = t$. Indeed, since t is optimal, for every T, we have $T < t$ or $T \sim t$. In particular, this is true for $T_{\lambda^{-1}}$, i.e., we have $T_{\lambda^{-1}} < t$ or $T_{\lambda^{-1}} \sim t$. Due to the fact that the optimality criterion is scale-invariant, we conclude that for every T, we have either $T < t_\lambda$ or $T \sim t_\lambda$. By definition of optimality, this means that the transformation t_λ is optimal. However, t is also optimal, and we assumed that the optimality criterion is final, i.e., that there is only one optimal alternative. Thus, $t_\lambda = t$.

Similarly, we can prove that the transformation t is shift-invariant. Thus, by Proposition 1, the transformation t has the desired form.

6   Conclusions

In many areas of human activity, there are people who are very good in the corresponding tasks: top medical doctors excel in diagnosing and treating diseases, top pilots excel in piloting planes, etc. It is desirable to incorporate their expertise into automated systems that would help others make similarly effective decisions – or even make these decision by themselves, without the need for a human controller. These top folks are usually willing to share their knowledge and their skills, but the problem is that they often formulate a significant part of their skills not in precise numerical terms, but by using imprecise ("fuzzy") words from natural language, like "small". To transform such knowledge into numerical computer-understandable form, Lotfi Zadeh invented fuzzy techniques. In these techniques, we first translate expert knowledge into numerical terms, and then tune the resulting control so as to make it as effective as possible.

This procedure has led to many successful applications. However, in many cases, achieving this success required a lot of time and efforts: indeed, there are usually many parameters to tune, and, as a result, tuning is often very time-consuming. To speed up the tuning process, it is desirable to come up with effective few-parametric tuning procedures. In this paper, we analyze one such procedure – known as fractional fuzzy techniques – in which we replace each α-cut interval with its (appropriately defined) fraction. This procedure turned out to be very effective – e.g., it improves the quality of decisions by up to 40% in the case of the reverse pendulum problem.

A natural question is: how to explain this empirical success? In this paper, we provide a theoretical explanation for this success: namely, we show that the corresponding few-parametric family of tunings is, in some reasonable sense, optimal.

Acknowledgements. The authors are greatly thankful to all the participants of the 2022 IEEE International Conference on Systems, Man, and Cybernetics (Prague, Czech Republic, October 9–12, 2022) for valuable discussions, and to the anonymous referees for useful suggestions.

References

1. Belohlavek, R., Dauben, J.W., Klir, G.J.: Fuzzy Logic and Mathematics: A Historical Perspective. Oxford University Press, New York (2017)
2. Berrout Ramos, L.A., Kreinovich, V., Autchariyapanitkul, K.: Correcting interval-valued expert estimates: empirical formulas explained. In: Thach, N.N., Kreinovich, V., Ha, D.T., Trung, N.D. (eds.) Financial Econometrics: Bayesian Analysis, Quantum Uncertainty, and Related Topics, pp. 1–7. Springer, Cham (2022). https://doi.org/10.1007/978-3-030-98689-6_1
3. Gajdos, T., Vergnaud, J.-C.: Decisions with conflicting and imprecise information. Soc. Choice Welfare **41**, 427–452 (2013)
4. Klir, G., Yuan, B.: Fuzzy Sets and Fuzzy Logic. Prentice Hall, Upper Saddle River (1995)
5. Mazandarani, M., Xiu, L.: Fractional fuzzy inference system: the new generation of fuzzy inference systems. IEEE Access **8**, 126066–126082 (2020)
6. Mazandarani, M., Xiu, L.: Interval type-2 fractional fuzzy inference systems: towards an evolution in fuzzy inference systems. Expert Syst. Appl. **189**, 115947 (2022)
7. Mendel, J.M.: Uncertain Rule-Based Fuzzy Systems: Introduction and New Directions. Springer, Cham (2017)
8. Nguyen, H.T., Walker, C.L., Walker, E.A.: A First Course in Fuzzy Logic. Chapman and Hall/CRC, Boca Raton (2019)
9. Novák, V., Perfilieva, I., Močkoř, J.: Mathematical Principles of Fuzzy Logic. Kluwer, Boston (1999)
10. Smithson, M.: Conflict and ambiguity: preliminary models and empirical tests. In: Proceedings of the Eighth International Symposium on Imprecise Probability: Theories and Applications, ISIPTA 2013, Compiegne, France, 2–5 July 2013, pp. 303–310 (2013)
11. Smithson, M.: Probability judgments under ambiguity and conflict. Front. Psychol. **6**, Paper 674 (2015)
12. Zadeh, L.A.: Fuzzy sets. Inf. Control **8**, 338–353 (1965)

Interval-Valued and Set-Valued Extensions of Discrete Fuzzy Logics, Belnap Logic, and Color Optical Computing

Victor L. Timchenko[1], Yury P. Kondratenko[2,3], and Vladik Kreinovich[4(✉)] ⓘ

[1] Admiral Makarov National University of Shipbuilding, Mykolaiv, Ukraine
vl.timchenko58@gmail.com
[2] Petro Mohyla Black Sea National University, Mykolaiv 54003, Ukraine
yuriy.kondratenko@chmnu.edu.ua, y_kondrat2002@yahoo.com
[3] Institute of Artificial Intelligence Problems of MES and NAS of Ukraine,
Kyiv 01001, Ukraine
[4] University of Texas at El Paso, El Paso, TX 79968, USA
vladik@utep.edu

Abstract. It has been recently shown that in some applications, e.g., in ship navigation near a harbor, it is convenient to use combinations of basic colors – red, green, and blue – to represent different fuzzy degrees. In this paper, we provide a natural explanation for the efficiency of this empirical fact: namely, we show: (1) that it is reasonable to consider discrete fuzzy logics, (2) that it is reasonable to consider their interval-valued and set-valued extensions, and (3) that a set-valued extension of the 3-valued logic is naturally equivalent to the use of color combinations.

Keywords: Fuzzy logic · Set-valued extension · Interval-valued extension · Color optical computing

1 Formulation of the Problem

Color Optical Computing Representation of Fuzzy Degrees. It has been recently shown that in some practical applications of fuzzy logic – e.g., in ship navigation near a harbor – it is convenient to represent different fuzzy degrees by colors, namely, by combinations of the three pure basic colors: red, green, and blue; see, e.g., [10–13]. To be more precise, these papers use $2^3 = 8$ combinations of pure colors, where each of the three basic colors is either present or not present:

- *black* corresponding to no colors at all,
- *white* corresponding to the presence of all three basic colors,
- three pure colors corresponding to the case when only one of the three basic colors is present, and
- three combinations of two basic colors.

S. Massanet et al. (Eds.): EUSFLAT 2023/AGOP 2023, LNCS 14069, pp. 297–303, 2023.
https://doi.org/10.1007/978-3-031-39965-7_25

Question. This empirical success prompts a natural question: why is this representation efficient?

What We Do in This Paper. In this paper, we explain the empirical success of color optical computing representation by showing how the main ideas behind fuzzy logic naturally lead to this representation. Namely, we show:

- that it is reasonable to consider discrete fuzzy logics,
- that it is reasonable to consider interval-valued and set-valued extensions of these logics, and
- that a set-valued extension of the 3-valued logic is naturally equivalent to the use of combinations of pure colors.

We also show that the set-valued extensions of discrete fuzzy logics are related to the formalism of Belnap's logic, that allows parts of the knowledge base to be inconsistent.

2   Why Interval-Valued and Set-Valued Extensions of Discrete Fuzzy Logics

Fuzzy Degrees: A Brief Reminder. One of the main ideas behind fuzzy logic is to assign, to each imprecise natural-language statement such as "John is tall", a degree describing to what extent this statement is true – e.g., to what extent John is tall; see, e.g., [3–5, 8, 9, 14].

Need for Discrete Fuzzy Logic. In the original fuzzy logic, these degrees were represented by numbers from the interval $[0, 1]$. From the mathematical viewpoint, this interval contains infinitely many numbers. When the numbers are significantly different, they represent different degrees of certainty. However, when the two numbers are very close, we cannot distinguish the corresponding degrees: e.g., hardly anyone can distinguish between degrees 0.80 and 0.81.

In general, according to psychological experiments, we can meaningfully distinguish at most 7 ± 2 different degrees: some of us can only distinguish $7 - 2 = 5$ different degrees, some can distinguish $7 + 2 = 9$ different degrees; see, e.g., [6, 7]. In other words, in practice, we use, in effect, a discrete set of fuzzy degrees.

Fuzzy Degrees Come with Uncertainty. In the ideal case, we have a single perfect expert who selects a single degree – and experts are perfect in the sense that other experts would assign the exact same degree. In practice, the situation is more complicated.

- First, an expert can be unsure what exact degree to assign. At best, the expert can provide a lower bound a and an upper bound b for this degree – just like when estimating the height of a person entering the room, the expert will not produce an exact value but rather a range of values. In this case, possible degrees form an *interval* $[a, b] \stackrel{\text{def}}{=} \{x : a \leq x \leq b\}$.
- Second, even if an expert produces an exact degree, other experts may produce different degrees. In this case, to describe uncertainty, it is reasonable to list all these degrees, i.e., to produce the *set* of experts' estimates. This extension of fuzzy logic is known as *hesitant* fuzzy logic.

In the following text, we will analyze such interval-valued and set-valued versions of the simplest discrete fuzzy logics, and we will show that this analysis indeed naturally leads to color optical computing.

Comment. Following this line of reasoning, it is also possible to have several experts producing intervals. This option may be worth exploring.

3 Interval-Valued and Set-Valued Extensions of 2-Valued Logic

Why 2-Valued Logic. In general, a discrete fuzzy logic is a finite subset of the interval $[0, 1]$ that contains both 0 ("false") and 1 ("true"). From this viewpoint, the simplest case is when this subset contains only 0 and 1, i.e., when we have a usual 2-valued logic.

Interval-Values Extension of 2-Valued Logic. In a logic consisting of two elements $0 < 1$, there are exactly three possible intervals:

- two degenerate intervals $[0, 0] = \{0\}$ and $[1, 1] = \{1\}$ consisting of a single original value, and
- a non-degenerate interval $[0, 1] = \{0, 1\}$ containing both values.

The general interpretation of interval-valued extensions – that was described in the previous section – provides the following explanation for the new truth value $[0, 1]$: this truth value corresponds to the case when we do not know whether the statement is true or false – i.e., corresponds to uncertainty. Thus, we get a usual 3-valued logic with three possible truth values: true, false, and uncertain. These values can be naturally described as 1, 0, and an intermediate value 0.5.

Set-Valued Extension of 2-Valued Logic. In a 2-valued logic with the set of truth values $\{0, 1\}$, there are four subsets:

- two 1-elements subsets $\{0\}$ and $\{1\}$;
- the original set $\{0, 1\}$, and
- the empty set $\emptyset$.

The general interpretation of set-valued extensions – that was described in the previous section – provides the following interpretation of these four subsets:

- the set $\{0\}$ means that all experts agree that the statement is false;
- the set $\{1\}$ means that all experts agree that the statement is true;
- the set $\{0, 1\}$ means that some experts believe that the statement is true, while some other experts believe that the statement is false;
- finally, the empty set means that no experts have any opinion about this statement.

Here, both the set $\{0, 1\}$ and the empty set correspond to uncertainty, but there is a difference between the two cases:

– the empty set means, in effect, that we know nothing about the statement;
– in contrast, the set $\{0, 1\}$ means, in effect, that we have some arguments in favor of the given statement, and some arguments against this statement.

How is This Related to Interval-Valued Fuzzy Techniques. The need to distinguish between these two types of uncertainty is often emphasized as the need to go from the traditional fuzzy logic to its interval-valued version. Indeed, in the traditional fuzzy logic, the same value 0.5 can mean two different things:

– it can mean that we know nothing about the given statement, and
– it can also mean that we have as many arguments in favor of this statement as against it.

In the interval-valued case:

– the first situation – when we know nothing, the statement can be false or true – is naturally described by the interval $[0, 1]$ containing all possible truth values, while
– for the second situation, a value 0.5 – corresponding to the degenerate (1-point) interval $[0.5, 0.5]$ seems to be a better match.

How is This Related to Belnap Logic. The above four truth values have been analyzed in a non-fuzzy context, under the name of Belnap logic [1,2]. In this context, instead of expert opinions about the truth of a statement, we consider the actual validity of this statement. In this interpretation, the set $\{0, 1\}$ corresponds to inconsistency – when our knowledge base mistakenly contains both the information that this statement is true and the information that this same statement is false.

The need to consider this logic was caused by the fact that in the usual 2-valued logic, once we have a single contradiction, we can conclude that all statements are true – and that all statements are false. So, if we use the usual logic, one wrong statement added to the database – e.g., that the train leaves at 1 pm and that this same train leaves at 1.01 pm – would make the whole knowledge base useless.

4   Interval-Valued and Set-Valued Extensions of 3-Valued Logic and Their Relation to Color Optical Computing

3-Valued Logic. After the simplest 2-valued logic, the next simplest is 3-valued logic, when we add, to the usual 0 ("false") and 1 ("true"), and additional intermediate degree corresponding to uncertainty. For simplicity, let us denote this degree by 0.5.

Interval-Valued Extension of 3-Valued Logic. For this logic, with 3 truth values $0 < 0.5 < 1$, there are six possible intervals:

– the degenerate interval $[0, 0] = \{0\}$ meaning that the expert believes that the given statement is false;

- the degenerate interval $[1,1] = \{1\}$ meaning that the expert believes that the given statement is true;
- the degenerate interval $[0.5, 0.5] = \{0.5\}$ meaning that the expert is uncertain;
- the interval $[0, 0.5] = \{0, 0.5\}$ meaning the expert is uncertain but is leaning towards "false";
- the interval $[0.5, 1] = \{0.5, 1\}$ meaning the expert is uncertain but is leaning towards "true"; and
- the interval $[0, 1] = \{0, 0.5, 1\}$ meaning that the expert is uncertain, but has some arguments in favor and against the given statement.

Comment. In the 2-valued case, the interval extension did not allow us to distinguish between two different situations:

- not having any information about a statement and
- having arguments for and argument against the statement.

To distinguish between these two cases, we had to consider set-valued extension of the 2-valued logic.

Interesting, in the 3-valued case, already the interval extension enables us to distinguish between these two situations.

Set-Valued Extension of 3-Valued Logic. In the set-valued extension of the 3-valued logic, in addition to the six sets corresponding to interval-valued extension of this logic, we have two more sets:

- the empty set $\emptyset$ corresponding to situations in which no expert has any opinion, and
- the set $\{0, 1\}$ corresponding to the polarized case when some experts strongly believe that the given statement is true while others as strongly believe that this statement is false – case typical in politics.

Set-Valued Extension of 3-Valued Logic Naturally Leads to Color Optical Computing. In color optical computing, we start with three basic colors read (R), green (G), and blue (B) whose position on the spectrum is described as $R < G < B$, and we consider combinations of some of these colors, i.e., all subsets of the set $\{R, G, B\}$:

- we can have three pure colors corresponding to three 1-element sets $\{R\}$, $\{G\}$, and $\{B\}$;
- we can have white – a combination of all three basic colors – corresponding to the set $\{R, G, B\}$;
- we can have black – where there are no colors at all – corresponding to the empty set; and
- we can also have combinations of two of three colors.

These $2^3 = 8$ combinations are in natural 1-to-1 correspondence with eight subsets that form the set-valued extension of the 3-valued logic. This provides a natural explanation of the color optical interpretation of fuzzy logic.

5   Conclusions

In the classical logic, every statement is either true or false. In a computer, "true" is usually represented by 1, and "false" by 0. In many practical situations, we are unsure whether the statement is true or false. To describe different degrees of confidence in a statement, Lotfi Zadeh proposed to use real numbers between 0 and 1. From the purely mathematical viewpoint, there are infinitely many real numbers between 0 and 1. However, we humans can only meaningfully distinguish between a small number of different degrees of confidence. Thus, to make the description of degrees of confidence more adequate, it makes sense to restrict ourselves to finite (discrete) subsets of the interval $[0, 1]$.

To make this description even more adequate, it is desirable to also take into account that sometimes, experts are unsure which of the possible degrees better describe their degree of confidence. To cover such situations, we need to consider subsets of the set of possible degrees – i.e., set-valued extensions of discrete fuzzy logics. An important particular case is an interval-valued extension, when we only consider intervals – the set of all the degrees between two bounds.

It turns out that these extension ideas naturally lead to several known effective techniques – and thus, provide an explanation for their effectiveness. Namely:

- the set-theoretic extension of the 2-valued logic naturally leads to the known technique of Belnap's logic, technique that enables us to allow knowledge bases with inconsistencies, and
- the set-theoretic extension of the 3-valued discrete fuzzy logic naturally leads to color optical computing – an empirically successful way of representing and processing fuzzy degrees by different colors.

Acknowledgment. The authors are greatly thankful the anonymous referees for valuable suggestions.

References

1. Belnap, N.: How computers should think. In: Ryle, G. (ed.) Contemporary Aspects of Philosophy, pp. 30–56. Oriel Press, London (1975)
2. Belnap, N.: A useful four-valued logic. In: Dunn, J.M., Epstein, G. (eds.) Modern Uses of Multiple-Valued Logic. Episteme, vol. 2, pp. 5–37. Springer, Dordrecht (1977). https://doi.org/10.1007/978-94-010-1161-7_2
3. Belohlavek, R., Dauben, J.W., Klir, G.J.: Fuzzy Logic and Mathematics: A Historical Perspective. Oxford University Press, New York (2017)
4. Klir, G., Yuan, B.: Fuzzy Sets and Fuzzy Logic. Prentice Hall, Upper Saddle River (1995)
5. Mendel, J.M.: Uncertain Rule-Based Fuzzy Systems: Introduction and New Directions. Springer, Cham (2017). https://doi.org/10.1007/978-3-319-51370-6
6. Miller, G.A.: The magical number seven plus or minus two: some limits on our capacity for processing information. Psychol. Rev. **63**(2), 81–97 (1956)
7. Reed, S.K.: Cognition: Theories and Application. SAGE Publications, Thousand Oaks (2022)

8. Nguyen, H.T., Walker, C.L., Walker, E.A.: A First Course in Fuzzy Logic. Chapman and Hall/CRC, Boca Raton (2019)
9. Novák, V., Perfilieva, I., Močkoř, J.: Mathematical Principles of Fuzzy Logic. Kluwer, Boston, Dordrecht (1999)
10. Timchenko, V., Kondratenko, Y., Kreinovich, V.: Efficient optical approach to fuzzy data processing based on colors and light filter. Int. J. Prob. Control Inform. **52**(4), 89–105 (2022)
11. Timchenko, V., Kondratenko, Y., Kreinovich, V.: Decision support system for the safety of ship navigation based on optical color logic gates. In: Proceedings of the IX International Conference "Information Technology and Implementation" IT&I-2022, Kyiv, Ukraine, 30 November - 2 December, 2022 (2022)
12. Timchenko, V., Kondratenko, Y., Kreinovich, V.: Implementation of optical logic gates based on color filters. In: Proceedings of the he 6th International Conference on Computer Science, Engineering and Education Applications ICCSEEA2023, Warsaw, Poland, 17–19 March, 2023 (2023)
13. Timchenko, V.L., Kondratenko, Y.P., Kreinovich, V.: Why Color Optical Computing? In: Phuong, N.H., Kreinovich, V. (eds.) Deep Learning and Other Soft Computing Techniques. Studies in Computational Intelligence, vol. 1097, pp. 227–233. Springer, Cham (2023). https://doi.org/10.1007/978-3-031-29447-1_20
14. Zadeh, L.A.: Fuzzy sets. Inf. Control **8**, 338–353 (1965)

SPECIAL SESSION 2: Information Fusion Techniques Based on Aggregation Functions, Preaggregation Functions and Their Generalizations

Measuring the Distance Between Machine Learning Models Using F-Space

Mariam Taha[✉] and Vicenç Torra

Department of Computing Science, Umeå University, 901 87 Umeå, Sweden
{mariamt,vtorra}@cs.umu.se

Abstract. Probabilistic metric spaces are a natural generalization of metric spaces in which the function that computes the distance outputs a distribution on the real numbers rather than a single number. Such a function is called a distribution function. In this paper, we construct a distance for linear regression models using one type of probabilistic metric space called F-space. F-spaces use fuzzy measures to evaluate a set of elements under certain conditions. By using F-spaces to build a metric on machine learning models, we permit to represent more complex interactions of the databases that generate these models.

Keywords: Fuzzy Measures · Probabilistic Metric Space · Machine Learning

1 Introduction

Probabilistic metric spaces [1] are a natural generalization of metric spaces in which the function that computes the distance outputs a distribution on the real numbers rather than a single number. Such a function is called a distribution function. Constructing a probabilistic metric space (PMS) is not a straightforward process. There are different methods in the literature that aim to construct these spaces. Among them we find the E-spaces [2,3], where the probabilistic metric space is defined in terms of sets of functions and a probability space. These functions map from a probability space into a metric space. Another construction are the F-spaces, which generalize E-spaces by replacing the probability space with a measure space. Hence, the distribution functions are defined in terms of non-additive measures. We have introduced these F-spaces in a previous work [4].

In this paper, our interest lies in measuring the distance between machine learning models taking into account the set of databases that generate these models. We call such sets generators. The distance between models is defined in terms of distribution functions, and the probabilistic metric space is constructed in terms of a F-space. Since we consider models that can be defined in terms

This study was partially funded by the Wallenberg AI, Autonomous Systems and Software Program (WASP) funded by the Knut and Alice Wallenberg Foundation.

of their generators, the distribution functions are based on these generators and their distances. By using fuzzy measures and F-spaces to construct models distances, it would be possible to model the interactions of the databases in the spaces. Such interactions can be interpreted in terms of coverage of a set of databases or any other properties on the databases. The study of probabilistic metric spaces and their relevance to the problem of model selection were previously studied in [12] where it was linked to data privacy, and in [5] where the authors developed these spaces taking into account transitions that occur among the database and modeled it using Markov chains and transition matrices.

This paper is structured as follows. In Sect. 2 we introduce the definitions that are needed later in the paper. In particular, we review some concepts related to fuzzy measures and their properties. In Sect. 3, we introduce probabilistic metric spaces and F-spaces along with some results and toy examples. In Sect. 4 we illustrate our results. Section 5 concludes the paper with some conclusions and research directions.

2   Fuzzy Measures

Fuzzy measures were first introduced by Sugeno [6]. They are also called capacities, nonadditive measures, and monotone measures. Fuzzy measures are considered as a generalization of classical measures [7–10].

Definition 1. *Let $(\Omega, \mathcal{A})$ be a measurable space. A set function μ defined on $\mathcal{A}$ is called a non-additive measure if an only if*

- $0 \leq \mu(A) \leq \infty$ *for any $A \in \mathcal{A}$;*
- $\mu(\emptyset) = 0$;
- *If $A_1 \subseteq A_2 \subseteq \mathcal{A}$ then*

$$\mu(A_1) \leq \mu(A_2)$$

If in addition $\mu(A) = 1$, then the fuzzy measure is said to be a normalized space. We consider finite sets Ω, and for simplicity we assume $\mathcal{A} = 2^{\Omega}$.

Definition 2. *Let μ be a non-additive measure on the measurable space $(X, \mathcal{A})$. Then,*

- μ *is additive if $\mu(A \cup B) = \mu(A) + \mu(B)$ when $A \cap B = \emptyset$;*
- μ *is superadditive if $\mu(A \cup B) \geq \mu(A) + \mu(B)$ when $A \cap B = \emptyset$;*
- μ *is subadditive if $\mu(A \cup B) \leq \mu(A) + \mu(B)$ when $A \cap B = \emptyset$;*
- μ *is submodular if $\mu(A) + \mu(B) \geq \mu(A \cup B) + \mu(A \cap B)$;*
- μ *is supermodular if $\mu(A) + \mu(B) \leq \mu(A \cup B) + \mu(A \cap B)$;*
- μ *is symmetric if for finite X, when $|A| = |B|$, then $\mu(A) = \mu(B)$.*

A supermodular measure implies superadditivy, while a submodular measure implies subadditivity. When additive fuzzy measures are normalized, they are probability measures. In this paper we will use two families of fuzzy measures in our experiments, Sugeno λ-measures and the non-additive measure μ_{A_0}. Their definitions are as follows.

Definition 3. *Let Ω be a finite set and let $\lambda > -1$. A Sugeno λ-measure is a function $\mu : 2^{\Omega} \to [0,1]$ such that*

- $\mu(\Omega) = 1$
- *if $A, B \subseteq \mathbf{X}$ with $A \cap B = \emptyset$ then*
  $\mu(A \cup B) = \mu(A) + \mu(B) + \lambda\mu(A)\mu(B)$

For Sugeno λ-measures, as a convention, the measure of the singletons $\omega_i \in \Omega$ is called a density and it is noted by $v(\omega_i)$. In this case, as the measure is normalized when $\Omega = \{\omega_1, \omega_2, ..., \omega_n\}$, λ should satisfy the following:

$$\lambda + 1 = \prod_{i=1}^{n} 1 + \lambda v(\omega_i). \tag{1}$$

Once the densities are known, the above polynomial can be used to uniquely determine the value of λ. Then given the densities and λ, the fuzzy measure $\mu(A)$ is defined as:

$$\mu(A) = \begin{cases} v(x_i), & A = x_i \\ \frac{1}{\lambda} \prod_{x_i \in A} (1 + \lambda v(x_i)) - 1), & |A| \neq 1 \quad \& \quad \lambda \neq 0 \\ \sum_{x_i \in A} v(x_i), & \lambda = 0 \quad \& \quad |A| \neq 1 \end{cases}$$

For Sugeno λ-measures, when $\lambda > 0$, μ is supermodular. Whereas, when $\lambda > 0$, μ is submodular.

Definition 4. *Let A_0 be a subset of Ω, then the set function defined by $\mu_{A_0}(A) = 1$ if and only if $A_0 \subseteq A$, is a non-additive measure.*

3   Probabilistic Metric Space

In this section, we review some concepts related to probabilistic metric spaces and their properties. Following this, we introduce E-space and F-spaces.

Definition 5. *Let $d : S \times S \to \mathbb{R}^+$, then d is called a metric on S if the following properties hold for $a, b, c \in S$:*

- $d(a, b) \geq 0$ *with equality if and only if $a = b$ (positive property),*
- $d(a, b) = d(b, a)$ *(symmetry property), and*
- $d(a, b) \leq d(a, c) + d(c, b)$ *(triangle inequality property).*

Definition 6. *[11] The pair (S, d) is called a metric space when d is a metric on the set S. Where $d : S \times S \to \mathbb{R}^+$ plays the role of distance on the set S. Here, we understand $\mathbb{R}^+ = [0, \infty)$ and $\overline{\mathbb{R}^+} = [0, \infty]$.*

When the distance does not satisfy the symmetry condition, we say that (S, d) is a quasimetric space; and when the distance does not satisfy the triangle inequality, we say that (S, d) is a semimetric space. Probabilistic metric spaces are a generalization of metric spaces in which the distance function is replaced by a distribution distance function.

Definition 7. [1] *A distance distribution function F is a nondecreasing function defined on $\mathbb{R}^+$ that satisfies (i) $F(0) = 0$; (ii) $F(\infty) = 1$, and (iii) that is left continuous on $(0, \infty)$.*

Therefore, $F(x)$ can be interpreted as the probability that the distance is less than or equal to x. The set of all distance distribution functions is denoted as Δ^+, while the distance distribution function that represents a classical distance is denoted by ϵ_a and is defined as below.

Definition 8. [1] *For any a in $\mathbb{R}^+$, we define $\epsilon_a \in \Delta^+$ by*

$$\epsilon_a(x) = \begin{cases} 0, & 0 \leq x \leq a \\ 1, & a < x \leq \infty \end{cases}$$

Next, we introduce the concepts of t-norms and triangle functions in order to construct a probabilistic metric space.

Definition 9. [13] *A function $\top : [0,1] \times [0,1] \to [0,1]$ is a t-norm if and only if it satisfies the following properties:*

- $\top(x,y) = \top(y,x)$ *(symmetry or commutativity)*
- $\top(\top(x,y),z) = \top(x,\top(y,z))$ *(associativity)*
- $\top(x,y) \leq \top(x',y')$ *if $x \leq x'$ and $y \leq y'$ (monotonicity)*
- $\top(x,1) = x$ *for all x (neutral element 1)*

One example of t-norm is the minimum function $T(x,y) = min(x,y)$ which is denoted by $\wedge$, i.e $T(x,y) = \wedge(x,y)$. Another t-norm is the bounded difference $W(x,y)$ defined as $T(x,y) = max(0, x+y-1)$.

Definition 10. [1] *A Triangle function T is a binary operation on Δ^+ that for any $F, G, H, K \in \Delta^+$, it satisfies the following:*

- $T(F, \epsilon_0) = F$
- $T(F,G) = T(G,F)$
- $T(F,G) \leq T(H,K)$ *whenever $F \leq H, G \leq K$*
- $T(T(F,G),H) = T(F,T(G,H))$

For a t-norm $\top$, we have that the function $\tau_\top(F,G)(x) = \top(F(x),G(x))$ is a triangle function. Next, we introduce probabilistic metric spaces along with their properties.

Definition 11. [1] *Let $(S, \mathcal{F}, \tau)$ be a triple where S is a nonempty set, $\mathcal{F}$ is a function from $S \times S$ into Δ^+, and τ is a triangle function; then $(S, \mathcal{F}, \tau)$ is a probabilistic metric space (PM space) if the following conditions are satisfied for all p, q, and r in S:*

- $\mathcal{F}(p,p) = \epsilon_0$
- $\mathcal{F}(p,q) \neq \epsilon_0$ *if $p \neq q$*
- $\mathcal{F}(p,q) = \mathcal{F}(q,p)$
- $\mathcal{F}(p,r) \geq \tau(\mathcal{F}(p,q), \mathcal{F}(q,r))$.

For simplicity we will use F_{pq} instead of $\mathcal{F}(p, q)$ and denote the value of the latter at x as $F_{pq}(x)$. Special names are given when some of the above conditions fail. A probabilistic metric space that doesn't satisfy the second condition is called a probabilistic pseudometric space. If the space doesn't satisfy triangle inequality it is called a probabilistic semimetric space, while it is a probabilistic quasi metric space if the symmetry property is invalid.

F-spaces are one family of probabilistic metric spaces. They permit to compute the distance between functions that map from a measurable space to a metric space, where the distance distribution function is defined in terms of measuring those elements that are at most at distance x.

Definition 12. [4] *Let $(\Omega, \mathcal{A})$ be a measurable space, and let μ be a non-additive measure on $(\Omega, \mathcal{A})$. Let (M, d) be a metric space, let S be a set of functions from Ω into M and let $\mathcal{F}$ be a mapping from $S \times S$ into Δ^+. Then, $(S, \mathcal{F})$ is an F-space with base $(\Omega, \mathcal{A}, \mu)$ and target (M, d) if*

  - *For all p, q in S and all x in $\mathbb{R}^+$ the set*

$$\{\omega \in \Omega | d(p(\omega), q(\omega)) < x\}$$

   belongs to $\mathcal{A}$.
  - *For all p, q in S, $\mathcal{F}(p, q) = F_{pq}$ with*

$$F_{pq}(x) = \mu(\{\omega \in \Omega | d(p(\omega), q(\omega)) < x\}). \tag{2}$$

Definition 13. [2,3] *When the measure μ is additive, Definition 12 corresponds to E-spaces.*

Lemma 1. [2,3] *Let $(S, \mathcal{F})$ be an F-space with base $(\Omega, \mathcal{A}, \mu)$ and target (M, d). Then if μ is additive, it is an E-space .*

If F satisfies the first three properties in Definition 11, then $(S, \mathcal{F})$ is a canonical F-space.

The following theorems have been proven in [4], which describe the type of probabilistic metric space when a specific fuzzy measure is used

Theorem 1. [4] *Let $(\Omega, \mathcal{A})$ be a measurable space, let μ be a non-additive measure on $(\Omega, \mathcal{A})$ and $(S, \mathcal{F})$ be an F-space with base $(\Omega, \mathcal{A}, \mu)$.*

   Then, if μ is a supermodular non-additive measure on $(\Omega, \mathcal{A})$, it follows that $(S, \mathcal{F})$ is a probabilistic pseudometric space under bounded difference τ_W.

Theorem 2. [4] *Let $(S, \mathcal{F})$ be an F-space. Let μ_{A_0} be a non-additive measure defined on $(\Omega, \mathcal{A})$ for a given set $A_0 \subseteq \mathcal{A}$. Then $(S, \mathcal{F})$ is a probabilistic pseudometric space under $\tau_{\min}$.*

Next, we give an example to show how to construct an F-space.

Example 1. Let $\Omega := \{\omega_1, \omega_2, \omega_3\}$, and $\mathcal{A} := 2^{\Omega}$. Then $(\Omega, \mathcal{A})$ is a measurable space. Let $M := [0, \infty)$ and let $d(a, b) := |a - b|$ for $a, b \in M$. Then, (M, d) is a metric space. Define the functions $p, q, r : \Omega \to M$ as given in Table 1. Then, let $S = \{p, q, r\}$ and define for $p_1, p_2 \in S$ the following functions: $H_{p_1 p_2}(x) := \{\omega | \ |p_1(\omega) - p_2(\omega)| < x\}$ for $0 \le x$. Then we have the sets H_{pq} as given in Table 2.

Now let us define a Sugeno λ-measure on $(\Omega, \mathcal{A})$ using Eq. 1 from Definition 3, and solve the equation for $\lambda = 0.4$. Under the assumption that all the densities are equal, we get $v(\omega_i) = 0.296722$. Therefore we construct the functions F as described in Table 3.

Table 1. Functions p, q, and r from $\Omega := \{\omega_1, \omega_2, \omega_3\}$ into M for Example 1.

	ω_1	ω_2	ω_3
p	1	0	0
q	0	0	1
r	0	1	1

Table 2. Functions H_{p_1, p_2} for $p_1, p_2 \in S$ for Example 1.

	$x = 0$	$0 < x \le 1$	$x > 1$
H_{pq}	$\emptyset$	$\{\omega_2\}$	Ω
H_{pr}	$\emptyset$	$\emptyset$	Ω
H_{qr}	$\emptyset$	$\{\omega_1, \omega_3\}$	Ω

Table 3. Functions F_{p_1, p_2} for $p_1, p_2 \in S$ for Example 1.

	$x = 0$	$0 < x \le 1$	$x > 1$
F_{pq}	0	0.296722	1
F_{pr}	0	0	1
F_{qr}	0	0.628662	1

If we choose the t-norm $\tau = W$, then $(S, \mathcal{F}, \tau)$ is a canonical space under W as we can see that all inequalities hold in Definition 11.

4   Metrics for Machine Learning Models

In Machine Learning, data are continuously generated, hence models need to be updated to reflect any new insights from the underlying data. However, it has been shown [15] that an adversary can get access to sensitive information by exploiting changes in the models themselves. One of the privacy models that overcome this issue is Integral Privacy [16]. Its goal is that model transformations caused by the training data should not leak any information on the training data. It recommends selecting a machine learning model which can be generated by sufficiently large and diverse datasets. Such models are called recurrent models and can be used to implement Integral privacy. Then, it may also happen that even when two models are different they may be generated from similar data.

The similarity of models in terms of the data that generated them is relevant for model selection. Between two such models we would prefer the one that is more privacy-preserving. From an integral privacy perspective that would be the one with more generators. Similarly, the same applies to the algorithms that produce the models. As we have discussed in [12], probabilistic metric spaces can be useful to define metrics for machine learning models, and thus helps in this process.

In a previous work [5] we considered a simpler approach to construct PMS, where we proposed the use of Markov chains, together with transition matrices to represent, respectively, sequences of changes in databases and the probability of changes of databases to define model similarities. In this paper, we are considering probabilities and fuzzy measures in the space of databases, in order to define metrics on the models.

In this paper, we show how this can be applied to real machine learning models. We consider simple machine learning models such as Linear Regression models. Our goal is to construct distances between such models taking into account the interaction of their generators. We run the experiments on the dataset *Salary_Data* which describes the salaries of employees and their years of experience. Figure 1 illustrates the scatter plot of this dataset [14]. In this experiment, the space $(\Omega, \mathcal{A})$ corresponds to the space of possible databases and $\mathcal{A} := 2^{\Omega}$. Then, P and μ are probabilities and fuzzy measures, respectively, on this space. In order to build the model space, we define the set S as the set of three different linear regression algorithms p, q, and r defined as follows:

- Linear Regression as (p)
- Huber Regression as (q)
- Ridge Regression as (r)

Therefore, given our approximated database space $(\Omega, \mathcal{A})$ together with the set S, we construct the target space (M, d) such that for any $p \in S$, $p(DB)$ is the trained model we obtain after applying one of the linear regression algorithm p on the database DB. Since the problem is a simple linear regression, each model can be characterized by its slope β and y-intercept α. We choose d here to be the Euclidean distance. Hence $(M, d) = (\mathbb{R}^2, d)$ where $d = \sqrt{(\alpha_1 - \alpha_2)^2 + (\beta_1 - \beta_2)^2}, (\alpha_i, \beta_i) \in \mathbb{R}^2$.

Finally, we identify $\mathcal{F}$ as a mapping from $S \times S$ into Δ^+.

Following this setup, we illustrate our experiments to construct the space $(S, \mathcal{F})$ with respect to different measures and t-norms. Since it is impossible to cover the full database space, we used the subsampling method to sample 1000 datasets in order to approximate the full space $(\Omega, \mathcal{A})$ [17]. We ran the

Fig. 1. Scatter Plot of *Salary_Data* dataset

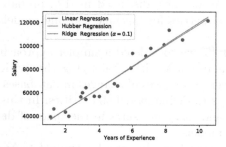

Fig. 2. Three regression models of *Salary_Data* dataset.

experiments under Python and Sklearn library, and the value of the penalty term α in Ridge regression algorithm is chosen to be 0.1 (see Fig. 2).

We will consider in the next sections two different cases. First, an additive measure. That is, a probability. This will permit us to obtain results that correspond to an E-space. Then, we consider fuzzy measures, to obtain a proper F-space. These measures permit us to represent a characteristic or property of the space of databases. In our example, we will represent interactions between databases which are all either positive or negative (as complementarity or redundancy). We finish the section discussing the meaning of measures in this setting.

4.1   Case 1: Additive Measure

In this experiment, the database space is a probability space $(\Omega, \mathcal{A}, P)$ where P is the additive measure defined by $P(DB) = 1/1000$ for any database (DB) in the space. The model space is built as we described above. Figure 3 shows the histograms of the distances among the three functions.

Now let us define the function $H_{p_1 p_2}$ as follows: for any $p_1, p_2 \in S$ and for $x \geq 0$,

$$H_{p_1, p_2}(x) = \{DB| \quad |p_1(DB) - p_2(DB)| < x\}.$$

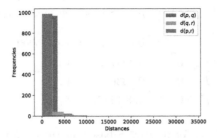

Fig. 3. Histogram of the three different distances.

Let us define the function $l(H)$ as the number of elements in H (i.e., the cardinality of the set). This function $l(H)$ is given in Table 4. We will define the probability P using $l(H)$ and dividing by the total number of the generated databases (i.e. 1000). This is detailed below.

Table 4. Functions $l(H_{p_1 p_2})(x)$ for $p_1, p_2 \in S$.

	$x = 0$	$0 < x \le 500$	$x < 35000$
$l(H_{pq})$	0	475	1000
$l(H_{qr})$	0	484	1000
$l(H_{pr})$	0	968	1000

Now, using Eq. 2 and since P is additive, $F_{pq}(x) = \frac{l(H_{pq}(x))}{1000}$. Functions $\mathcal{F}$ are given in Table 5. Since $\mathcal{F}$ satisfies the first three properties in Definition 11, then $(S, \mathcal{F})$ is a canonical F-space.

Table 5. Functions F_{p_1, p_2} for $p_1, p_2 \in S$ based on additive measure P

	$x = 0$	$0 < x \le 500$	$x < 35000$
F_{pq}	0	0.475	1
F_{qr}	0	0.484	1
F_{pr}	0	0.968	1

4.2   Case 2: Fuzzy Measures

In the following experiments, we use two different fuzzy measures. We start with a Sugeno λ-measure (μ) followed by the fuzzy measure μ_{A_0}. We use Sugeno λ-measures because they are easy to define and flexible enough to represent both subadditive and superadditive cases. That is, negative and positive interactions.

Table 6. Functions F_{p_1, p_2} for $p_1, p_2 \in S$ based on Sugeno λ-measure ($\lambda = 0.5$)

	$x = 0$	$0 < x \leq 500$	$x < 35000$
F_{pq}	0	0.424786	1
F_{qr}	0	0.43365	1
F_{pr}	0	0.961327	1

Table 7. Functions F_{p_1, p_2} for $p_1, p_2 \in S$ based on Sugeno λ-measure ($\lambda = -0.96$)

	$x = 0$	$0 < x \leq 500$	$x < 35000$
F_{pq}	0	0.815875	1
F_{qr}	0	0.822323	1
F_{pr}	0	0.995479	1

Sugeno λ-Measure. In this experiment, we use Sugeno λ-measure from Definition 3 to build the database space $(\Omega, \mathcal{A}, \mu)$. The construction of the databases space, the Model Space M, and the set S is similar to the previous example.

For simplicity, all the singleton measures are assumed to be equal. I.e. $v(x_i) = k$, for all $x_i \in X$. Therefore, solving Eq. 1 for k yields:

$$k = \frac{1}{\lambda}(\exp(\frac{1}{n}\ln(1+\lambda)) - 1) \tag{3}$$

Suppose $\lambda = 0.5$, we use Eq. 3 to compute the values of the measure for the singletons. The functions F are derived for Table 4, and the results are given in Table 6. Since the measure here is supermodular, the results are aligned with Theorem 1, in which the space (S, F, τ) is a probabilistic pseudo metric space under bounded difference τ_W. Figure 4(a) demonstrates the correctness of the triangular inequality of Definition 11. That is, in our case $\mathcal{F}(p, q) \geq \tau(\mathcal{F}(p, r), \mathcal{F}(q, r))$ as the blue line is larger than the orange one. Observe that in most of the domain both distributions are the same.

The same steps are now repeated but with submodular measures. I.e., when $\lambda < 0$ and also tested with respect to the t-norm τ_W. While some measures resulted in probabilistic pseudo metric spaces, some measures yield probabilistic semimetric spaces (i.e., triangle inequality does not hold). An example of the latter case is when $\lambda = -0.96$. The results for this case are given by Table 7 and Fig. 4(b). As we can see, in this case:

$$\mathcal{F}(p, q) \geq \tau(\mathcal{F}(p, r), \mathcal{F}(q, r))$$
$$0.815 \geq \tau(0.822323, 0.995479)$$
$$0.815 \geq max(0, 0.822323 + 0.995479 - 1) = 0.817.$$

Since 0.815 is not greater than 0.817, thus the inequality does not hold.

Fuzzy Measure μ_{A_0}. Our last experiment is based on the fuzzy measure μ_{A_0}, which is introduced in Definition 4. Let us define A_0 as the set $H_{pq}(x)$ for any

x in the range $0 < x \leq 500$, then in this example the other two sets H_{pr} and H_{qr} are incomparable with respect to inclusion of $H_{pq}(x)$ i.e.: $H_{pr} \not\subseteq H_{pq}$ and $H_{qr} \not\subseteq H_{pq}$. The functions F are given in Table 8. It is clear that the space $(S, \mathcal{F})$ is a probabilistic pseudo metric space under $\tau_{\min}$. Therefore, this result is aligned with Theorem 2.

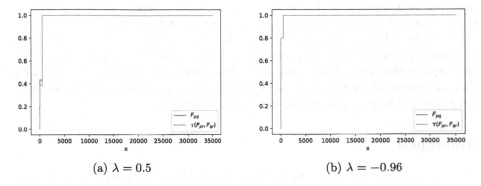

(a) $\lambda = 0.5$ (b) $\lambda = -0.96$

Fig. 4. Testing the triangle inequality with t-norm τ_W for $\lambda = 0.5$ and $\lambda = -0.96$ in Case 2. We observe that the inequality holds when the $\lambda = 0.5$, and does not hold when $\lambda = -0.96$.

Table 8. Functions F_{p_1,p_2} for $p_1, p_2 \in S$ based fuzzy measure μ_{A_0}

	$x = 0$	$0 < x \leq 500$	$x < 35000$
F_{pq}	0	1	1
F_{pr}	0	0	1
F_{qr}	0	0	1

4.3   The Interpretation of the Fuzzy Measures

Fuzzy measures are set functions that use the monotonicity property instead of additivity. Therefore, naturally, we would have that the larger the set of databases, the larger the coverage. In our experiment, all the fuzzy measures are defined on the space of the databases, where we considered either each database has the same relevance with the probability $P(DB) = 1/1000$ (i.e. the measure is additive), or all have the same interaction under the Sugeno λ-measure. Whereas, in the fuzzy measure μ_{A_0}, the value of the measure is computed with respect to the inclusion relationship of a reference set. Therefore the measure is either zero or one. Fuzzy measures can alternatively be defined using the Choquet integral or Sugeno integral, to define measures that represent the coverage with a characteristic of the database itself [18].

5   Conclusions

In this paper, we have constructed a probabilistic metric space to evaluate the distance between machine learning models built from databases. The probabilistic metric space is based on fuzzy measures and F-space in which the distance distribution function is computed based on functions that map from the database space to the model space. In our case, these functions were represented by different Linear Regression algorithms. Our experiment is based on different measures, both additives and non-additives. In future work, we consider studying additional properties of these probabilistic metric spaces, as well as considering their application in real-size databases. Also, since our experiments are based only on deterministic functions, we would like to expand the study on random functions and hence consider non-deterministic models.

References

1. Schweizer, B., Sklar, A.: Probabilistic Metric Spaces. Elsevier-North-Holland (1983)
2. Sherwood, H.: On E-spaces and their relation to other classes of probabilistic metric spaces. J. London Math. Soc. **44**, 441–448 (1969)
3. Stevens, S.S.: Metrically generated probabilistic metric spaces. Fund. Math. **61**, 259–269 (1968)
4. Narukawa, Y., Taha, M., Torra, V.: On the definition of probabilistic metric spaces by means of fuzzy measures. Fuzzy Sets Syst. **465**, 108528 (2023). https://doi.org/10.1016/j.fss.2023.108528
5. Torra, V., Taha, M., Navarro-Arribas, G.: The space of models in machine learning: using Markov chains to model transitions. Prog. Artif. Intell. **10**(3), 321–332 (2021)
6. Sugeno, M.: Theory of fuzzy integrals and its applications. Ph.D. thesis, Tokyo Institute of Technology (1974)
7. Torra, V., Narukawa, Y., Sugeno, M.: Non-additive Measure-Theory and Applications. Studies in Fuzziness and Soft Computing, vol. 310. Springer, Berlin (2014). https://doi.org/10.1007/978-3-319-03155-2
8. Denneberg, D.: Non-additive Measure and Integral. Kluwer Academic (1994)
9. Wang, Z., Klir, G.J.: Generalized Measure Theory. Springer, Cham (2009). https://doi.org/10.1007/978-0-387-76852-6
10. Torra, V., Narukawa, Y.: Modeling Decisions: Information Fusion and Aggregation Operators. Springer, Heidelberg (2007). https://doi.org/10.1007/978-3-540-68791-7
11. Searcóid, M.O.: Metric Spaces. Springer, Heidelberg (2007). https://doi.org/10.1007/1-84628-244-6
12. Torra, V., Navarro-Arribas, G.: Probabilistic metric spaces for privacy by design machine learning algorithms: modeling database changes. In: Garcia-Alfaro, J., Herrera-Joancomartí, J., Livraga, G., Rios, R. (eds.) DPM/CBT 2018. LNCS, vol. 11025, pp. 422–430. Springer, Cham (2018). https://doi.org/10.1007/978-3-030-00305-0_30
13. Klement, E.P., Mesiar, R., Pap, E.: Triangular Norms. Kluwer Academic Publisher (2000)

14. Salary data. https://www.kaggle.com/datasets/karthickveerakumar/salary-data-simple-linear-regression. Accessed 30 Apr 2022
15. Salem, A., Bhattacharya, A., Backes, M., Fritz, M., Zhang, Y.: Updates leak: data set inference and reconstruction attacks in online learning. In: Proceedings of the 29th USENIX Security Symposium, pp. 1291–1308 (2019)
16. Torra, V., Navarro-Arribas, G.: Integral privacy. In: Foresti, S., Persiano, G. (eds.) CANS 2016. LNCS, vol. 10052, pp. 661–669. Springer, Cham (2016). https://doi.org/10.1007/978-3-319-48965-0_44
17. Senavirathne, N., Torra, V.: Integrally private model selection for decision trees. Comput. Secur. **83**, 167–181 (2019)
18. Zhang, X., Wang, J., Zhan, J., Dai, J.: Fuzzy measures and choquet integrals based on fuzzy covering rough sets. IEEE Trans. Fuzzy Syst. **30**(7), 2360–2374 (2022). https://doi.org/10.1109/TFUZZ.2021.3081916

On the Relationship Between Multidistances and n-Distances Revisited

Tomasa Calvo Sánchez[1] and Pilar Fuster-Parra[2,3]($\boxtimes$)

[1] Department of Computer Science, Universidad de Alcalá, 28871 Alcalá de Henares, Madrid, Spain
tomasa.calvo@uah.es
[2] Department of Mathematics and Computer Sciences, Universitat Illes Balears, 07122 Palma de Mallorca, Balears, Spain
pilar.fuster@uib.es
[3] Institut d' Investigació Sanitária Illes Balears (IdISBa), Hospital Universitari Son Espases, 07120 Palma, Illes Balears, Spain

Abstract. Extensions of the concept of distance include the known multidistances and n-distances, which are related in this paper. In particular, a characterization of those multidistances that can also be an n-distance is given in terms of known properties of multidistances. A necessary condition for a multidistance to be an n-distance is presented. Properties of n-distances in order to be a multidistance is also considered. Some exemples are also presented.

Keywords: Distance · Metric Space · Multidistance · n-distance

1 Introduction

The concept of distance has been extended to more of two elements in order to measure to what extent these elements are expanded, measuring how different or separated are the coordinates [3,4]. These extensions include the wellknown n-distances [2,5–7] and multidistances [1,8–10], which may be appropriate to define dispersion measures in data analysis and/or statistics. Given an n-tuple $(x_1, \ldots, x_n) \in X^n$, n-distances and multidistances may be used to measure the similarity among its elements. Both, n-distances [5–7] and multidistances [8–10] are given as functions of n variables and include a natural generalization of the triangle inequality to a higher dimensional setting. However, multidistances have an indefinite number of arguments, contrary to n-distances that have a fixed number of arguments. Furthermore, an n-distance can be defined without referring to any ordinary distance.

We are interested in determining those properties that allow obtaining multidistances from n-distances and reciprocally. In this context, in the works of Kiss et al. [5–7] it is showed that some n-distances can not be used to define multidistances [5–7]. For instance, the area of the smallest circle enclosing n points in $\mathbb{R}^2$ can not be used to define a multidistance (because the triangle inequality does not hold when $n = 2$). And the authors give a characterization about how multidistances can be defined from a special type of n-distances as it is showed in the following Proposition 1.

Proposition 1 ([7]). *Let $(d^n)_{n \geq 2}$ be a sequence, where $d^n : X^n \to \mathbb{R}_+$ is a standard n-distance on X satisfying*

$$d^n(x_n, z_n, \ldots, z_n) \leq d^2(x_n, z_n), \quad n \geq 2, \quad x_n, z_n \in X.$$

Then $(D_n)_{n \geq 2}$ defined by $D_n = d^n$ for all $n \geq 2$ is a multidistance on X.

On other hand, some n-distances can not be obtained from multidistances as it is possible to see in [6,7]. Their authors establish the following result (see Proposition 2) characterizing those multidistances that can also be n-distances.

Proposition 2 ([7]). *Let the sequence $(D_n)_{n \geq 1}$ be a multidistance on X and let $n \geq 3$ be an integer. If $(D_n)_{n \geq 1}$ satisfies:*

(i) $D_n(x_1, \ldots, x_{n-1}, x_n) \geq D_n(x_1, \ldots, x_{n-1}, x_1)$ for any $x_1, \ldots, x_n \in X$,
(ii) $D_2(x, z) \leq D_n(x, z, \ldots, z)$ for all $x, z \in X$,

then $d^n = D_n$ is an n-distance.

Property (i) in Proposition 2 is also referred as "non-increasing under identification of variables" [7].

In this work we evaluate to what extend these properties give a complete characterization. The paper is organized as follows, Sect. 2 presents the necessary notions to follow this work. Section 3 studies properties that characterize multidistances that can be n-distances, and a necessary condition for a multidistance in order to be an n-distance is given. Section 4 shows that the characterization of n-distances to be a multidistance is always achieved by any multidistance. And finally, in Sect. 5 some conclusions are given.

2 Preliminaries

An overview of the necessary background on this topic is given. Let us start remembering the concept of metric space.

Definition 1. *A metric space is a pair (X, d), where X is a non-empty set and d is a function $d : X^2 \to \mathbb{R}_+$ (where $\mathbb{R}_+$ denotes $[0, +\infty)$) satisfying the following conditions:*

(i) $d(x_1, x_2) = 0$ if and only if $x_1 = x_2$ (identity),
(ii) $d(x_1, x_2) = d(x_2, x_1)$ (symmetry),
(iii) $d(x_1, x_2) \leq d(x_1, z) + d(z, x_2)$ for all $x_1, x_2, z \in X$ (triangle inequality).

Function d is called a distance or metric on X.

In [1,8] the concept of multidistance was introduced as a measure that determines how long are more than two points. A multidistance is defined on an n-dimensional ordered list of elements by means of an axiomatic procedure.

Definition 2. *Let X be a nonempty set. A sequence of functions $(D_n)_{n\geq 1}$, with $D_n : X^n \to \mathbb{R}_+$ is said to be a* multidistance *when the following properties hold:*

(i) *For any $n \in \mathbb{N}$ and $(x_1,\ldots,x_n) \in X^n$, $D_n(x_1,\ldots,x_n) = 0$ if and only if $x_1 = \ldots = x_n$. In particular, $D_1(x) = 0$ holds for every $x \in X$;*

(ii) *For all $n \in \mathbb{N}$ and $(x_1,\ldots,x_n) \in X^n$, it holds that $D_n(x_1,\ldots,x_n) = D_n(x_{\pi(1)},\ldots,x_{\pi(n)})$ for any permutation π of de set $1,\ldots,n$;*

(iii) *For any $n \in \mathbb{N}$, $n \geq 2$, and $(x_1,\ldots,x_n,y) \in X^{n+1}$ it holds that $D_n(x_1,\ldots,x_n) \leq D_2(x_1,y) + \ldots + D_2(x_n,y)$.*

Observe that if $(D_n)_{n\geq 1}$ is a multidistance on X, then the restriction of $(D_n)_{n\geq 1}$ to X^2, $D_{|X_2} = D_2$, is an ordinary distance on X. On other hand, any ordinary distance d on X can be extended in order to obtain a multidistance. For instance, we can define for any $n \in \mathbb{N}$ and $(x_1,\ldots,x_n) \in X^n$ a function D_n^M in this way:
$$D_n^M(x_1,\ldots,x_n) = \max\{d(x_i,x_j), \ i < j\}.$$
Properties of mutidistances have been studied in [1,9], let us remember the notions of regular, replication invariance, and stable multidistance.

Definition 3. *A multidistance $(D_n)_{n\geq 1}$ is said to be* regular *if*
$$D_{n+1}(x_1,\ldots,x_n,y) \geq D_n(x_1,\ldots,x_n)$$
for all $(x_1,\ldots,x_n) \in \bigcup_{n\geq 1} X^n$, $y \in X$.

In a regular multidistance, the multidistance of a list cannot decrease when adding a new element.

Definition 4. *A multidistance $(D_n)_{n\geq 1}$ is* stable *if*
$$D_n(x_1,\ldots,x_n) = D_{n+1}(x_1,\ldots,x_n,x_i).$$
for all $x_1,\ldots,x_n \in X$ and for all x_i in the list $(x_1,\ldots,x_n)$.

According to the last definition, the repetition of one element of the list in a stable multidistance is superfluous.

Other generalizations of the concept of distance have been investigated by several authors [4]. This is the case of the concept of n-distance, which is introduced in [5–7] as a generalization on n elements of the classical notion of distance.

Definition 5. *Let $n \geq 2$ be an integer. Given a non-empty set X, (X,d^n) is an* n-metric space *if d^n is a function $d^n : X^n \to \mathbb{R}_+$ satisfying the following conditions:*

(i) *$d^n(x_1,\ldots,x_n) = 0$ if and only if $x_1 = \ldots = x_n$,*

(ii) *$d^n(x_1,\ldots,x_n) = d^n(x_{\pi(1)},\ldots,x_{\pi(n)})$ for any permutation π of $1,\ldots,n$,*

(iii) *$d^n(x_1,\ldots,x_n) \leq \sum_{i=1}^n d^n(x_1,\ldots,x_n)_{x_i=z}$ for all $x_1,\ldots,x_n, z \in X$.*

Then, the function d^n is called an n-distance.

Where condition (iii) in Definition 5 is referred to as the simplex inequality [4] (triangle inequality if $n = 2$). When $n = 2$ the concept of 2-distance on a non empty set is the same that the concept of distance on a non empty set.

3   From Multidistances to n-Distances

In Proposition 2 in [7] the n-distances that can be obtained from multidistances are characterized through two properties:

(i) $D_n(x_1, \ldots, x_{n-1}, x_n) \geq D_n(x_1, \ldots, x_{n-1}, x_1)$ for any $x_1, \ldots, x_n \in X$,
(ii) $D_2(x, z) \leq D_n(x, z, \ldots, z)$ for all $x, z \in X$.

It seems natural to wonder to what extend these properties give a complete characterization. However, there are n-distances that can be derived from multidistances and at least do not verified some property of the mentioned Proposition 2 [7] as the following example shows.

Example 1. The sum based λ-multidistance $(D_{n,\lambda})_{n \geq 1}$ is defined by

$$\begin{cases} D_{1,\lambda}(x_1) = 0 \\ D_{n,\lambda}(x_1, \ldots, x_n) = \lambda(n) \sum_{i<j} d(x_i, x_j). \end{cases}$$

and it is a multidistance if and only if:

(i) $\lambda(2) = 1$,
(ii) $0 < \lambda(n) \leq 1/(n-1) \quad n \geq 3$.

Now, let us consider a sum based λ-multidistance, that verifies:

(i) $\lambda(2) = 1$,
(ii) $0 < \lambda(n) < 1/(n-1) \quad n \geq 3$.

which is also a multidistance. However, it does not verifies property (ii) of Proposition 2 [7] when

(i) $\lambda(2) = 1$,
(ii) $0 < \lambda(n) < 1/(n-1)$.

because

$$D_{n,\lambda}(x_1, x_2, \ldots, x_2) = \lambda(n)(n-1)D_2(x_1, x_2)$$

$$< \tfrac{1}{n-1}(n-1)D_{2,\lambda}(x_1, x_2)$$

$$= D_{2,\lambda}(x_1, x_2).$$

Now, considering $d^n = D_{n,\lambda}$ is easy to see that it is an n-distance based on $\lambda(n)$ where $(D_{n,\lambda})_{n \geq 1}$ is a sum-based multidistance. Properties (i) and (ii) of Definition 5 follow directly, and property (iii):

$$\sum_{i=1}^{n} d^n(x_1,\ldots,x_n)_{x_i=z} = \sum_{i=1}^{n} D_{n,\lambda}(x_1,\ldots,x_n)_{x_i=z} \quad =$$

$$D_{n,\lambda}(z,\ldots,x_n) + D_{n,\lambda}(x_1,z,\ldots,x_n) + \ldots + D_{n,\lambda}(x_1,\ldots,z) \quad =$$

$$D_{n,\lambda}(y_1^1,\ldots,y_n^1) + D_{n,\lambda}(y_1^2,\ldots,y_n^2) + \ldots + D_{n,\lambda}(y_1^n,\ldots,y_n^n) \quad =$$

$$\lambda(n)\sum_{i<j} d(y_i^1,y_j^1) + \lambda(n)\sum_{i<j} d(y_i^2,y_j^2) + \ldots + \lambda(n)\sum_{i<j} d(y_i^n,y_j^n) \geq$$

$$\lambda(n)\sum_{i<j} d(x_i,x_j) = D_{n,\lambda}(x_1,\ldots,x_n) = d^n(x_1,\ldots,x_n)$$

where $(y_1^1,y_2^1,\ldots,y_n^1) = (z,x_2,\ldots,x_n)$, $(y_1^2,y_2^2,\ldots,y_n^2) = (x_1,z,\ldots,x_n)$, $\ldots$, $(y_1^n,y_2^n,\ldots,y_n^n) = (x_1,x_2,\ldots,z)$.

In the following, we characterize those multidistances that can also be n-distances in a more precise way.

Proposition 3. *Let the sequence $(D_n)_{n\geq 1}$ be a multidistance on X and let $n \geq 3$ be an integer. If $(D_n)_{n\geq 1}$ satisfies:*

(i) $D_n(x_1,\ldots,x_{n-1},x_n) \geq D_n(x_1,\ldots,x_{n-1},x_1)$ for any $x_1,\ldots,x_n \in X$,
(ii) $D_2(x,z) \leq D_n(x,z,\ldots,z)$ for all $x,z \in X$,

then D_n is a regular multidistance.

Proof. Assume by reduction to the absurd that $(D_n)_{n\geq 1}$ is not regular, i.e., $\exists\, x_1,\ldots,x_n$ such that $D_{n+1}(x_1,\ldots,x_n,y) < D_n(x_1,\ldots,x_n)$. Therefore,

$$D_n(x_1,\ldots,x_n) \quad > \quad D_{n+1}(x_1,\ldots,x_n,y)$$

$$\geq^{(i)} D_{n+1}(x_1,\ldots,x_n,x_1)$$

$$\vdots \qquad \vdots$$

$$\geq^{(i)} D_{n+1}(x_1,x_1\ldots,x_1,x_2)$$

$$\geq^{(ii)} D_2(x_1,x_2)$$

but, as $(D_n)_{n\geq 1}$ is a multidistance, we have,

$$D_n(x_1,\ldots,x_n) \leq D_2(x_1,y) + D_2(x_2,y) + \ldots + D_2(x_n,y)$$

with $(x_1,\ldots,x_n,y) \in X^{n+1}$ in particular for $y = x_2$, and therefore we achieve a contradiction.

□

The following result shows that for regular multidistances is possible to achieve property (ii) of Proposition 3.

Proposition 4. *Let the sequence* $(D_n)_{n\geq 1}$ *be a regular multidistance on* X *then* $D_2(x, z) \leq D_n(x, z, \ldots, z)$ *for all* $x, z \in X$.

Proof. As $(D_n)_{n\geq 1}$ is a regular multidistance,

$$D_n(x, z, \ldots, z) \geq D_{n-1}(x, z \ldots, z) \geq \ldots \geq D_2(x, z).$$

$\square$

However property (i) of Proposition 3 is not always verified for a regular multidistance.

Example 2. Let us consider a multidistance based on an OWA operator, where $w = \{w_n / n \geq 2\}$ is a family of OWA operators, and w_n is of $\binom{n}{2}$ dimension with weights $w_1^{\binom{n}{2}}, \ldots, w_{\binom{n}{2}}^{\binom{n}{2}}$ which are applied to the $\binom{n}{2}$ distances of elements from the list taken from two to two in a decreasing way, i.e.,

$$D_n^w(x_1, \ldots, x_n) = \begin{cases} 0 & if \ n = 1 \\ w_n(d(x_1, x_2), \ldots, d(x_{n-1}, x_n)) & if \ n \geq 2, \end{cases}$$

for all list $(x_1, \ldots, x_n) \in X^n$.
D_n^w is a multidistance if and only if

$$w_1^{\binom{n}{2}} + \ldots + w_{\binom{n}{2}}^{\binom{n}{2}} > 0 \quad \forall n \geq 3.$$

Considering the OWA operator of weights $(\frac{1}{2}, \frac{1}{2}, 0, 0, \ldots, 0)$ with $n \geq 2$ is a regular multidistance which is also an n-distance; D_w consists of the half sum of the two biggest ordinary distances between two elements of the list. Let us consider three points $a, b, c \in X$ such that $d(a, b) < d(a, c) < d(b, c)$, then

$$D_3^w(a, b, c) = \frac{d(a, c) + d(b, c)}{2}$$

$$D_3^w(b, b, c) = \frac{d(b, c) + d(b, c)}{2}$$

therefore, $D_3^w(a, b, c) < D_3^w(b, b, c)$, and property (i) of Proposition 3 is not satisfied.

The requirement to achieve property (i) of Proposition 3 for regular multidistances is given in the following proposition.

Proposition 5. *Let the sequence* $(D_n)_{n\geq 1}$ *be a regular and stable multidistance on* X, *then* $(D_n)_{n\geq 1}$ *verifies*

$$D_n(x_1, \ldots, x_{n-1}, x_n) \geq D_n(x_1, \ldots, x_{n-1}, x_1)$$

for any $x_1, \ldots, x_n \in X$.

Proof. Let $x_1, \ldots, x_n \in X$, then,

$$D_n(x_1, \ldots, x_{n-1}, x_n) \geq_{(regularity)} D_{n-1}(x_1, \ldots, x_{n-1})$$

$$=_{(stability)} D_n(x_1, \ldots, x_{n-1}, x_1).$$

$\square$

The next result yields a necessary condition to ensure when a multidistance can be regarded as an n-distance in terms of regular multidistances.

Proposition 6. *Let $(D_n)_{n \geq 1}$ be a regular multidistance on a non-empty set X, then $d^n = D_n$ with $n \geq 2$ is an n-distance on X.*

Proof. Properties (i) and (ii) of an n-distance is derived directly from properties (i) and (ii) of multidistances. Property (iii) can be obtained because of regularity of D,

$$\sum_{i=1}^n d^n(x_1, \ldots, x_n)_{x_i=z} = \sum_{i=1}^n D_n(x_1, \ldots, x_n)_{x_i=z} \geq$$

$$D_2(x_1, z) + D_2(x_2, z) + \ldots + D_2(x_n, z) \qquad \geq$$

$$D_n(x_1, \ldots, x_n) = d^n(x_1, \ldots, x_n)$$

$\square$

The reciprocal of Proposition 6 is not necessarily true as it is shown in the following examples. Observe that the sum based λ-multidistance of Example 1 is not regular.

Proposition 7. *The sum based λ-multidistance $(D_{n,\lambda})_{n \geq 1}$ is regular if and only if $\lambda(n) = \frac{1}{n-1}$ for all $n \geq 2$.*

Proof. Let us suppose $(D_{n,\lambda})_{n \geq 1}$ is regular, then taking $(\underbrace{x, \ldots, x}_{n-1}, y)$

$$D_{n,\lambda}(x, \ldots, x, y) = \lambda(n)(n-1)D_2(x, y)$$

$$\geq D_{2,\lambda}(x, y),$$

where the last inequality is due to regularity. So, $\lambda(n) \geq \frac{1}{n-1}$ and therefore $\lambda(n) = \frac{1}{n-1}$.

Let now see that the multidistance is regular. the condition of regularity is

$$D_{n,\lambda}(x_1, \ldots, x_n) \leq D_{n+1,\lambda}(x_1, \ldots, x_n, y)$$

$$\frac{1}{n-1}\sum_{i<j} d(x_i, x_j) \leq \frac{1}{n}(\sum_{i<j} d(x_i, x_j) + \sum_{i=1}^n d(x_i, y)), \quad \forall y \in X,$$

therefore,

$$\sum_{i<j} d(x_i, x_j) \leq (n-1)(\sum_{i=1}^{n} d(x_i, y)),$$

which is satisfied, as the triangular inequality shows

$$\sum_{i<j} d(x_i, x_j) \leq (\sum_{i<j} d(x_i, y) + d(x_j, y)),$$

$$= (n-1)(\sum_{i=1}^{n} d(x_i, y)).$$

Example 3. The λ-multidistance of Fermat $(D_{n,F}^{\lambda})_{n\geq 1}$ is only regular when $\lambda(n) = 1$, so considering:

$$D_{n,F}^{\lambda}(x_1, \ldots, x_n) = \lambda(n) \min_{y \in X} \sum d(x_i, y) = \lambda(n) D_{n,F}(x_1, \ldots, x_n)$$

where $\lambda(n) \in (0,1)$ and $D_{n,F}$ denotes de multidistance of Fermat. Then, as $D_{n,F}$ is regular, it is also an n-distance (by Proposition 6) and verifies:

$$D_{n,F}(x_1, \ldots, x_n) \qquad \leq \sum D_{n,F}(x_1, \ldots, x_n)_{x_i = y}$$

$$\lambda(n) D_{n,F}(x_1, \ldots, x_n) \leq \lambda(n) \sum D_{n,F}(x_1, \ldots, x_n)_{x_i = y}$$

$$D_{n,F}^{\lambda}(x_1, \ldots, x_n) \qquad \leq \sum D_{n,F}^{\lambda}(x_1, \ldots, x_n)_{x_i = y}$$

therefore, $D_{n,F}^{\lambda}$ is an n-distance.

Example 4. The λ-multidistance of Fermat $(D_{n,F}^{\lambda})_{n\geq 1}$ defined in $(\mathbb{P}, d_k)$ where $\mathbb{P}$ is a set of preferences, and a preference $P \in \mathbb{P}$ is represented by a matrix (a_{ij}), in this framework d_k is de Kemeny distance defined by

$$d_k(P, P') = \sum_{i<j} |a_{ij} - a'_{ij}| \qquad \forall\ P\ and\ P' \in \mathbb{P}$$

it can be proved that $D_{n,F}^{\lambda}$ is not regular for $\lambda(n) = \frac{4}{n^2}$ as it is contractive, however as $D_{n,F}$ is regular, it is also an n-distance (by Proposition 6) and verifies:

$$D_{n,F}(x_1, \ldots, x_n) \qquad \leq \sum D_{n,F}(x_1, \ldots, x_n)_{x_i = y}$$

$$\frac{4}{n^2} D_{n,F}(x_1, \ldots, x_n) \leq \frac{4}{n^2} \sum D_{n,F}(x_1, \ldots, x_n)_{x_i = y}$$

$$D_{n,F}^{\lambda}(x_1, \ldots, x_n) \qquad \leq \sum D_{n,F}^{\lambda}(x_1, \ldots, x_n)_{x_i = y}$$

therefore, $D_{n,F}^{\lambda}$ is an n-distance.

4 From n-Distances to Multidistances

In the Proposition 1 of [7] the multidistances can be obtained from n-distances whenever the property

$$d^n(x_n, z_n, \ldots, z_n) \leq d^2(x_n, z_n), \quad n \geq 2, \quad x_n, z_n \in X$$

holds. In this case, this property is always satisfy by any multidistance.

The following example shows that the arithmetic mean based n-distance can be a multidistance whenever its binary version is doubled [6].

Example 5. Let us consider the sequence $(d^n)_{n \geq 2}$. The arithmetic mean based n-distance $(X = \mathbb{R})$

$$d^n(x_1, \ldots, x_n) = \frac{1}{n} \sum_{i=1}^{n} x_i - \min\{x_1, \ldots, x_n\}.$$

For any $n \geq 3$, $d^n(x_n, z_n \ldots, z_n) \leq d^2(x_n, z_n)$ if and only if $z_n \leq x_n$. And replacing d^2 by the map $(d^2)' : \mathbb{R}^2 \to \mathbb{R}_+$ defined by

$$(d^2)'(x, z) = d^n(x, z \ldots, z) + d^n(z, x \ldots, x) = 2d^2(x, z),$$

then, $d^n(x_n, z_n \ldots, z_n) \leq d^2(x_n, z_n)$ for all $n \geq 2$, and $x_n, z_n \in \mathbb{R}$, and the sequence $(d^n)_{n \geq 2}$ is a multidistance $(D_n)_{n \geq 2}$.

5 Conclusions

We have study multidistances and n-distances as an extension of the concept of distance. Furthermore, we were interested in determining how the charaterization given by Kiss et al. [5–7] to obtain n-distances from multidistances and reciprocally was a complete characterization. A characterization of multidistances in terms of their properties was presented. Moreover, a necessary condition for a multidistance to be an n-distance is given.

References

1. Aguiló, I., Martín, J., Mayor, G., Suñer, J., Valero, O.: Smallest enclosing ball multidistance. Commun. Inf. Syst. **12**(3), 185–194 (2012)
2. Calvo Sánchez, T., Fuster-Parra, P.: On the aggregation of n-distances. In: Ciucci, D., et al. (eds.) IPMU 2022. Communications in Computer and Information Science, vol. 1601, pp. 47–59. Springer, Cham (2022). https://doi.org/10.1007/978-3-031-08971-8_5
3. Campion, M.J., et al.: Multidistances and inequlity measures on abstract sets: an axiomatic approach. Fuzzy Set Syst. **437**, 53–68 (2022). https://doi.org/10.1016/j.fss.2021.05.010
4. Deza, M.M., Deza, E.: Encyclopedia of Distances. Springer, Heidelberg (2016). https://doi.org/10.1007/978-3-662-52844-0

5. Kiss, G., Marichal, J.L., Teheux, B.: An extension of the concept of distance as functions of several variables. In: Proceedings of the 36th Linz Seminar on Fuzzy Set Theory (LINZ 2016), Linz, Austria, pp. 53–56 (2016)
6. Kiss, G., Marichal, J.L., Teheux, B.: A generalization of the concept of distance based on the simplex inequality. Beitr. Algebra Geom. **59**, 247–266 (2018). https://doi.org/10.1007/s13366-018-0379-5
7. Kiss, G., Marichal, J.L.: On the best constants associated with n-distances. Acta Math. Hung. **161**, 341–365 (2020). https://doi.org/10.1007/s10474-020-01023-8
8. Martín, J., Mayor, G.: Multi-argument distances. Fuzzy Set Syst. **167**, 92–100 (2010). https://doi.org/10.1016/j.fss.2010.10.018
9. J. Martín, G. Mayor, Some Properties of Multi-argument Distances and Fermat Multidistance. In: Hüllermeier E., Kruse R., Hoffmann F. (eds) Information Processing and Management of Uncertainty in Knowledge-Based Systems. Theory and Methods. IPMU 2010. Communications in Computer and Information Science, vol 80. Springer, Berlin, Heidelberg. https://doi.org/10.1007/978-3-642-14055-6$_$74
10. Molinari, F.: About a new family of multidistances. Fuzzy Set Syst. **195**, 118–122 (2012). https://doi.org/10.1016/j.fss.2011.10.014

Fuzzy Integrals for Edge Detection

C. Marco-Detchart[1]([✉]) [iD], G. Lucca[3] [iD], G. Dimuro[3] [iD], T. Asmus[6] [iD],
C. Lopez-Molina[4,5] [iD], E. Borges[3] [iD], J. A. Rincon[1,2] [iD], V. Julian[1,2] [iD],
and H. Bustince[4,5] [iD]

[1] Valencian Research Inst. Artificial Intelligence,
Univ. Politècnica de València, Valencia, Spain
{cedmarde,vjulian}@upv.es, jrincon@dsic.upv.es
[2] Valencian Graduate School and Research Network of Artificial Intelligence,
Universitat Politècnica de València, Valencia, Spain
[3] Centro de Ciências Computacionais, Univ. Federal do Rio Grande,
Porto Alegre, Brazil
{giancarlo.lucca,gracalizdimuro,eduardoborges}@furg.br
[4] Dept. Estadistica, Informa. y Matem., Univ. Publica de Navarra, Pamplona, Spain
{carlos.lopez,bustince}@unavarra.es
[5] Navarrabiomed, Hospital Univ. de Navarra (HUN), IdiSNA, Pamplona, Spain
[6] Instituto de Matemática, Estadística e Física, Univ. Federal do Rio Grande,
Porto Alegre, Brazil
tiagoasmus@furg.br

Abstract. In this work, we compare different families of fuzzy integrals in the context of feature aggregation for edge detection. We analyze the behaviour of the Sugeno and Choquet integral and some of its generalizations. In addition, we study the influence of the fuzzy measure over the extracted image features. For testing purposes, we follow the Bezdek Breakdown Structure for edge detection and compare the different fuzzy integrals with some classical feature aggregation methods in the literature. The results of these experiments are analyzed and discussed in detail, providing insights into the strengths and weaknesses of each approach. The overall conclusion is that the configuration of the fuzzy measure does have a paramount effect on the results by the Sugeno integral, but also that satisfactory results can be obtained by sensibly tuning such parameter. The obtained results provide valuable guidance in choosing the appropriate family of fuzzy integrals and settings for specific applications. Overall, the proposed method shows promising results for edge detection and could be applied to other image-processing tasks.

Keywords: Fuzzy integrals · Choquet integral · Sugeno integral · Feature extraction · Edge detection

1 Introduction

Fuzzy integrals [29] are becoming one of the most relevant tools for information fusion in the Fuzzy Set Theory, providing a framework for modelling and

S. Massanet et al. (Eds.): EUSFLAT 2023/AGOP 2023, LNCS 14069, pp. 330–341, 2023.
https://doi.org/10.1007/978-3-031-39965-7_28

analysing uncertainty and imprecision. These integrals are based on the concept of fuzzy sets [35], which allow the representation of uncertainty by assigning values in the form of membership degrees to elements of a set. Fuzzy integrals provide a way to combine the information contained in multiple fuzzy sets and to model decision-making processes under uncertainty.

There is an extensive range of applications and research areas where fuzzy integrals have been applied, such as Brain-Computer Interface [34], Energy [23], Decision support [20], Medical image [36], Classification [33], sequential image/text classification [8], Multi-criteria [31] and Group Decision Making [32].

A widely used example of fuzzy integrals is the fuzzy transform [25], a powerful tool used in data and image processing that enables the analysis of imprecise and uncertain data. Fuzzy transforms are used, in the context of image processing, to remove noise over data [24,27], improve image quality and extract features [26]. In terms of image or signal processing, by transforming an image into the fuzzy domain, it becomes possible to analyze and manipulate its data in terms of fuzzy sets. This allows for more sophisticated processing, including the ability to perform image operations that are not possible in the traditional pixel-based domain and even define operations at a linguistic level.

Among the vast armamentarium of fuzzy integrals, this work focuses on two of them: the Sugeno integral [29] and the Choquet integral [5]. Both integrals have been used to aggregate information in many studies and have been generalized to cope up with different types of information. See [6,9,21] for a detailed review on the historical and contemporary use of these integrals.

Nowadays, one of the most studied problems in the field of computer vision is related to edge detection [17]. The difficulty of this task arises from the inherent capture process and even from the edge definition itself, as there is no exact definition of what an edge is. Besides that, in a general way, an edge can be considered a significant enough intensity variation between neighbour regions or pixels [30]. But even with this simple definition, some essential aspects are not considered, such as textures or *hallucinated boundaries* [17], where no edges should be detected or do not appear with a clear intensity. It is necessary to point out that this problem is also related to the type of considered image. That is, if the colours are presented respectively in grayscale or coloured. In the first case, the pixels present values between [0, 255], while in the second one, these values appear for each RGB channel. While the idea of *intensity change* can be indistinctly applied to both grayscale (monochannel) and colour (multichannel) imagery, only the former can be straightforwardly based on partial derivatives; In the latter, the derivatives would form a Jacobian matrix at each pixel, causing severe interpretation problems.

Recently, we introduced an approach to edge feature aggregation based on the Choquet integral and its generalizations [15]. This study, considered grey-scaled images, demonstrated that the usage of fuzzy integrals and their generalizations is an interesting approach to deal with this topic.

This study aims to analyze the performance of the Sugeno and Choquet integrals when dealing with edge detection problems and study the influence of the selected fuzzy measure. Precisely, we consider these functions to aggregate the values related to the neighbour of a specific pixel. Additionally, we provide an exclusive analysis (in terms of detecting edges in coloured images), taking into account the best generalizations achieved in [15]. We remark that the main aim of this work is not to evaluate if the performance of the fuzzy integrals is better to the literature approaches but to study the effects of the fuzzy measures over the different fuzzy integrals family and show if they are suitable for using them in colour edge detection.

This paper is organized as follows. In Sect. 2, the preliminaries concepts are shown. Section 3 presents the adopted methodology. Section 4 point out the achieved results, and the conclusions are drawn at the end.

2   Preliminaries

This section provides the main theoretical concepts related to the paper. First we present the concepts of fuzzy measure, Choquet and Sugeno integrals. After that, the concepts related to the evaluation of the proposal are shown.

2.1   Fuzzy Measure, Choquet and Sugeno Integral

Here, we present the definitions of the considered fuzzy measure and fuzzy integrals. Additionally, any function $F : [0,1]^n \rightarrow [0,1]$ is called a fusion function [3].

Definition 1. [22] *A function* $m : 2^N \rightarrow [0,1]$ *is a* fuzzy measure *if, for all* $X, Y \subseteq N = \{1, \ldots, n\}$, *the following properties hold: (i) if* $X \subseteq Y$, *then* $m(X) \leq m(Y)$; *(ii)* $m(\emptyset) = 0$ *and* $m(N) = 1$.

Definition 2. [5] *The discrete Choquet integral, related with the fuzzy measure* m, *is the function* $\mathfrak{C}_m : [0,1]^n \rightarrow [0,1]$, *defined, for all* $x \in [0,1]^n$, *by* $\mathfrak{C}_m(x) = \sum_{i=1}^n \left(x_{(i)} - x_{(i-1)} \right) \cdot m \left(A_{(i)} \right)$, *where* $(x_{(1)}, \ldots, x_{(n)})$ *is an increasing permutation of* x, $x_{(0)} = 0$ *and* $A_{(i)} = \{(i), \ldots, (n)\}$ *is the subset of indices of* $n - i + 1$ *largest components of* x.

Definition 3. [14] *The following properties of a bivariate fusion function* $F : [0,1]^2 \rightarrow [0,1]$ *are important: (LAE) (left 0-absorbent element)* $\forall y \in [0,1] :$ $F(0,y) = 0$; *(RNE) Right Neutral Element:* $\forall x \in [0,1] : F(x,1) = x$; *(LC) Left Conjunctive:* $\forall x, y \in [0,1] : F(x,y) \leq x$.

An important concept on the context of fusion functions is the following:

Definition 4. [14] *A fusion function* $A : [0,1]^n \rightarrow [0,1]$ *is said to be an* n-ary r-*pre-aggregation function, for some* $r \in \mathbb{R}^n, r \neq 0$, *if the following conditions hold: (A1) A is* r-*increasing, that is, for all* $x \in [0,1]^n$ *and* $c > 0$ *such that* $x + cr \in [0,1]^n : A(x + cr) \geq A(x)$; *(A2) A satisfies the boundary conditions:* $A(0) = 0$ *and* $A(1) = 0$.

Table 1. C_F-integrals that obtained best results in [15]

C_F-integral	Base Function F	Class of F [14]
$\mathfrak{C}_m^{C_F}$	$C_F(x,y) = xy + x^2y(1-x)(1-y)$	copula
$\mathfrak{C}_m^{O_B}$	$O_B(x,y) = \min\{x\sqrt{y}, y\sqrt{x}\}$	overlap function
$\mathfrak{C}_m^{F_{BPC}}$	$F_{BPC}(x,y) = xy^2$	aggregation function
$\mathfrak{C}_m^{\text{Hamacher}}$	$T_{HP}(x,y) = \begin{cases} 0 & \text{if } x = y = 0 \\ \dfrac{xy}{x+y-xy} & \text{otherwise} \end{cases}$	t-norm

Definition 5. [14] *Let $F : [0,1]^2 \to [0,1]$ be a bivariate fusion function and $\mathfrak{m}$ be a fuzzy measure. The Choquet-like integral based on F with respect to $\mathfrak{m}$, called C_F-integral, is the function $\mathfrak{C}_m^F : [0,1]^n \to [0,1]$, defined, for all $\mathbf{x} \in [0,1]^n$, by*

$$\mathfrak{C}_m^F(\mathbf{x}) = \min\left\{1, \sum_{i=1}^n F\left(x_{(i)} - x_{(i-1)}, \mathfrak{m}\left(A_{(i)}\right)\right)\right\}, \tag{1}$$

where (i) is a permutation on 2^N such that $x_{(i-1)} \le x_{(i)}$ for all $i = 1, \ldots, n$, with $x_{(0)} = 0$ and $A_{(i)} = \{(1), \ldots, (i)\}$.

Theorem 1. [14] *For any fuzzy measure m: (i) if F satisfies (LAE-RNE), then $\mathfrak{C}_m^F$ is a 1-pre-aggregation function; (ii) if F satisfies (LAE) and is an $(1,0)$-pre-aggregation function, then $\mathfrak{C}_m^F$ is a 1-pre-aggregation function; (iii) Moreover, if F also satisfies (LC), then $\mathfrak{C}_m^F$ is idempotent and averaging.*

In this study, we have selected the C_F-integrals that presented the best results in [15], which are defined by the functions F shown in Table 1, whose particular properties were studied previously in [14].

Definition 6. [29] *The discrete Sugeno integral is defined with respect to a fuzzy measure $\mathfrak{m}$ by:*

$$Su_\mathfrak{m}(\boldsymbol{x}) = \bigvee_{i=1}^n \left(x_{(i)} \wedge \mathfrak{m}(A_{(i)})\right)$$

where (i) is a permutation on 2^N such that $x_{(i-1)} \le x_{(i)}$ for all $i = 1, \ldots, n$, with $x_{(0)} = 0$ and $A_{(i)} = \{(1), \ldots, (i)\}$.

Sugeno and Choquet integrals share the same averaging and idempotency characteristics [10]. The only C_F-integral of Table 1 that is non-averaging (also non-idempotent) is $\mathfrak{C}_m^{O_B}$ [15].

2.2 Evaluation of the Proposal

We consider images to be functions $D : R \times C \mapsto L$, with $R = \{1, ..., r\}$ and $C = \{1, ..., c\}$, representing the set of rows and columns, and L representing the set of tones of the image. The set L defines the type of image in question. For binary images, $L = \{0, 1\}$, whereas $L = \{0, ..., 255\}$ for gray-scale image pixels. In the case of colour images, L is the Cartesian product of the tonal palettes at each of the colour stimuli (e.g. $L = \{0, ..., 255\}^3$ for RGB images). Assuming some given D, $\mathbb{I}_L$ represents the set of all images with a certain tonal palette L. In this work, we consider real-valued colour images, $i.e$ images in $\mathbb{I}_{[0,1]^3}$.

To detect whether our solution is correct, a confusion matrix is built following Martin *et al.* approach [16], where True Positive (TP), True Negative (TN), False Positive (FP) and False Negative (FN) are extracted. Then, to quantify the results the following well-known Precision (PREC), Recall (REC) and F_α measures are considered:

$$\text{PREC} = \frac{\text{TP}}{\text{TP} + \text{FP}}, \quad \text{REC} = \frac{\text{TP}}{\text{TP} + \text{FN}}, \quad F_\alpha = \frac{\text{PREC} \cdot \text{REC}}{\alpha \cdot \text{PREC} + (1 - \alpha) \cdot \text{REC}}.$$

We select the most-used descriptor, which is the $F_{0.5}$ measure [12, 16].

3   Methodology

In this section, we provide the methodology followed in the experiments, along with a brief explanation of the dataset and the configuration of the hyperparameter used.

3.1   Dataset

To put to the test the selected fuzzy functions, experiments have been performed on the Berkeley Segmentation Dataset (BSDS500) [1], composed of three different partitions, *train*, *test* and *val*. For the sake of the experiment, we stick to the *test* partition where 200 images can be found. Each of the images of the dataset comes with 4 to 9 ground-truth images defined by experts (Fig. 1).

As ground-truth images are binary images where each pixel defines the presence of an edge or not, the performance of each method is evaluated as a binary classification problem. The evaluation strategy consists of comparing the obtained binary edges with those of the ground truth by using the standard procedure from Estrada and Jepson [7]. For this comparison to be fair and sound, a certain tolerance must be taken into account. This tolerance is needed so that some of the detected edges are counted as true positives, even if a slight displacement exists. For the experiments conducted in this study, we set a spatial tolerance of 2.5 % of the length of the diagonal of the image.

3.2   Experimental Framework

The experiments in this study have been done following the Bezdek Breakdown Structure (BBS) framework [2], that specifies edge detection as a 4-step task: (i) *Conditioning* (Application of a Gaussian filter), (ii) *Feature extraction*, (iii)

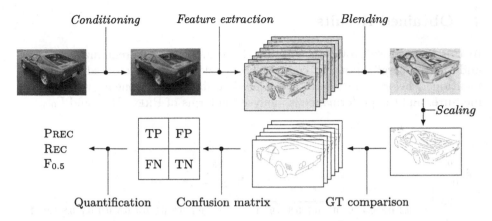

Fig. 1. Schematic representation of the BBS followed in this article, along with the performance evaluation process.

Blending (Obtention of a thinned image) and (iv) *Scaling* (Binarization of the thinned image). The schema of this approach is detailed in Fig. 1.

The *Conditioning* phase is done by applying a Gaussian filter with $\sigma = 2$, in order to remain the closest to the original Canny proposal and to have a simpler and fast setup. Then for *Feature extraction*, either one of the fuzzy integrals or a literature method is used to fuse intensity variations between pixels. Once the feature images are generated, non-maxima suppression [4] is applied for the *Blending* phase, and finally, the thinned image is binarized with hysteresis [19] in the *Scaling* phase.

As it can be seen from the schema in Fig. 1, the second and third steps are related to the application of the two considered fuzzy integrals. To do so, a 3×3 sliding window is used where the intensity variation between the central pixel and its neighbours is computed and then ordered increasingly. Then the fuzzy integrals are applied using as fuzzy measure the power measure, $PM = \left(\frac{|A|}{n}\right)^{q}$, considering a q exponent varying from 0.1 to 1.

The main objective of this work is to compare the different results obtained by the selected variants of fuzzy integrals and study the influence of the fuzzy measure over each of them. As an additional experiment, to analyse the behaviour of fuzzy integrals in colour edge detection, we compare their performance to those obtained with some well-known classical methods of the literature:

- The Canny method [4] with $\sigma_C = 2.25$ as a usual value in [13,18].
- The Gravitational Edge Detection (GED) method [11] with two configurations:
  - Probabilistic sum (G_{S_P}).
  - Maximum (G_{S_M}).
- Sobel filtering [28].

4   Obtained Results

In this section, we provide the obtained results of the different fuzzy integrals and their generalizations to cope with edge detection in coloured images. As mentioned before, the results are related to different exponents with a fuzzy measure, and the performance is analysed in terms of PREC, REC and $F_{0.5}$.

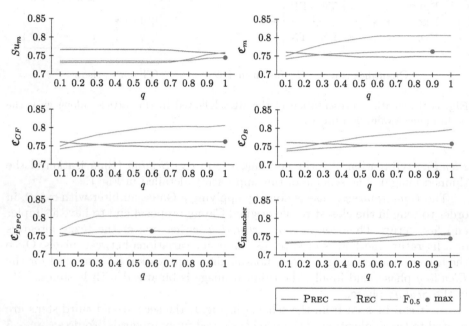

Fig. 2. Results obtained in terms of PREC, REC and $F_{0.5}$ with the different Fuzzy Integrals compared to the classical methods in the literature.

The results are shown graphically in Fig. 2, where the different fuzzy measures are related to the performance measures. If we observe the graph obtained by the Sugeno integral, we can see that the parameter q used does affects the detection with higher values. In this sense, the performance values remain globally unaltered upon $q = 0.7$ and being the best performer when computed with $q = 1$. If we observe the Choquet integral family, we can also depict a similar behaviour with a performance increase while q is increased, except for the particular case of $\mathfrak{C}_{F_{BPC}}$ which obtains its best performance with $q = 0.6$.

We can state that both Choqued-based integrals family and Sugeno integral are suited for edge detection and that the best choice for q is to have a higher value. Moreover, in contrast to the classical methods to whom we compare, all the tested fuzzy integrals obtain better performance, except for the Sobel filtering method, which obtains the same performance as $\mathfrak{C}_{F_{BPC}}$, as it can be seen in Table 2.

In terms of visual results, we can observe in Fig. 3 that the Sugeno integral and the Choquet integral and its generalizations obtain very similar features and edges, varying only in some edges belonging to the ground texture of the image and some od the object external limits. The $\mathfrak{C}_{\text{Hamacher}}$ depicts more non-suitable edges, thus obtaining lower performance. The Sobel filtering approach is among the selected literature methods the best performer, being similar to the fuzzy integrals approaches.

An important aspect to consider is the computational complexity of the different fuzzy measures. The Choquet integral and its generalizations are computationally more complex than the Sugeno integral, which can be a limitation for some applications. However, the improved performance obtained with the Choquet integral family may outweigh the increased computational complexity in certain cases.

In summary, the experiments demonstrate that fuzzy integrals are a compelling option for edge detection, delivering comparable outcomes to well-established methods such as the Sugeno filtering or the Canny method. However, it is essential to carefully consider the parameter values and computational complexity of the different fuzzy integral families before selecting the appropriate approach for a particular application. Furthermore, it is worth noting that the performance of the different methods may vary depending on the type and quality of the input image, and the specific requirements of the application. As a result, the choice of method should be based on a thorough analysis of the application's specific requirements and the input data's characteristics.

Another aspect to consider is the trade-off between accuracy and computational efficiency. In many applications, the computational resources available are limited, and it may be necessary to balance the need for accuracy with the need for processing speed. Fuzzy integrals offer a flexible approach that allows the trade-off between accuracy and computational efficiency to be optimized, making it possible to deliver reliable results while meeting the computational constraints of the application.

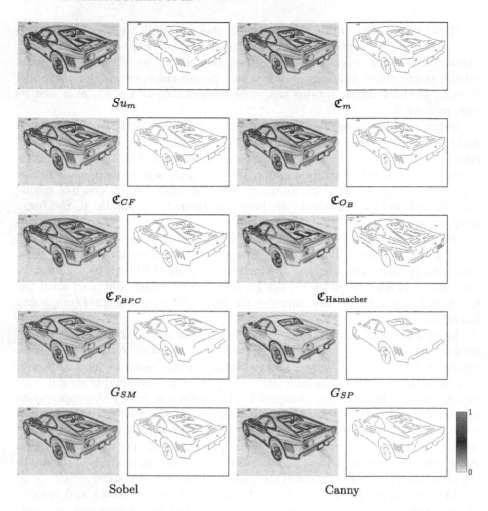

Su_m $\mathfrak{C}_m$

$\mathfrak{C}_{CF}$ $\mathfrak{C}_{O_B}$

$\mathfrak{C}_{F_{BPC}}$ $\mathfrak{C}_{Hamacher}$

G_{SM} G_{SP}

Sobel   Canny

Fig. 3. Image features and final edges extracted from original image 29030 of the BSDS test set with the different approaches tested.

Table 2. Comparison of the different fuzzy functions selected, along with the gravitational, Sobel filtering and the Canny method approaches in terms of PREC, REC and $F_{0.5}$.

Method	PREC	REC	$F_{0.5}$
Su_m^1	.756	.759	.745
$\mathfrak{C}_m^{0.9}$	.749	.807	.763
$\mathfrak{C}_{CF}^1$	.748	.807	.763
$\mathfrak{C}_{O_B}^1$	.748	.798	.759
$\mathfrak{C}_{F_{BPC}}^{0.6}$	.747	**.809**	**.764**
$\mathfrak{C}_{\text{Hamacher}}^1$	.757	.761	.746
G_{S_M}	745	.772	.743
G_{S_P}	.740	.790	.749
Sobel	.748	**.809**	**.764**
Canny	**.760**	.785	.760

5   Conclusions and Future Works

In this work, we have considered the Sugeno and Choquet integrals and some of their generalizations to study their behaviour in the context of colour edge detection. The experimental results demonstrated a trend that the fuzzy measure affects the fuzzy integrals, specially with higher q values and that the methods achieved satisfactory results to cope with the problem. We provide a deeper understanding of the behaviour of different fuzzy integral families in the context of feature aggregation for edge detection and can help to improve the performance of edge detection algorithms.

The experiments done in this work highlight the potential use of fuzzy integral for edge detection, providing a flexible and robust approach that can deliver accurate results while accommodating the specific requirements of a given application. Further research is needed to fully explore the potential of fuzzy integrals and to develop new methods that can deliver even better results.

One of the possible future research lines considered is to study a broader range of fuzzy measures in the context of using the Sugeno integral for feature aggregation in edge detection. Another line of research is testing the experimental framework we have used in this study with other generalizations of the Choquet integral. While we have focused on the Sugeno and Choquet integrals in this work, other variations of the Choquet integral have been proposed in the literature. These generalizations have been found to be effective in other contexts, such as classification and decision-making. It would be interesting to see if they can also be applied to edge detection with similar success. This could include the study of the generalized $C_{F_1 F_2}$-integrals as well as the d-XC integrals.

Acknowlegements. This work was partially supported with grant PID2021-123673OB-C31 funded by MCIN/AEI/ 10.13039/501100011033 and by "ERDF A way of making Europe", Consellería d'Innovació, Universitats, Ciencia i Societat Digital from Comunitat Valenciana (APOSTD/2021/227) through the European Social Fund (Investing In Your Future), grant from the Research Services of Universitat Politècnica de València (PAID-PD-22), FAPERGS/Brazil (Proc. 19/2551-0001279-9, 19/2551-0001660) and CNPq/Brazil (301618/2019-4, 305805/2021-5, Edital 07/2022), Programa de Apoio á Fixação de Jovens Doutores no Brasil (23/2551-0000126-8).

References

1. Arbelaez, P., Maire, M., Fowlkes, C., Malik, J.: Contour detection and hierarchical image segmentation. IEEE Trans. Pattern Anal. Mach. Intell. **33**(5), 898–916 (2011)
2. Bezdek, J., Chandrasekhar, R., Attikouzel, Y.: A geometric approach to edge detection. IEEE Trans. Fuzzy Syst. **6**(1), 52–75 (1998)
3. Bustince, H., Fernandez, J., Kolesárová, A., Mesiar, R.: Directional monotonicity of fusion functions. Eur. J. Oper. Res. **244**, 300–308 (2015)
4. Canny, J.F.: A computational approach to edge detection. IEEE Trans. Pattern Anal. Mach. Intell. **8**(6), 679–698 (1986)
5. Choquet, G.: Theory of capacities. Annales de l'Institut Fourier **5**, 131–295 (1953–1954)
6. Dimuro, G.P., et al.: The state-of-art of the generalizations of the Choquet integral: from aggregation and pre-aggregation to ordered directionally monotone functions. Inf. Fusion **57**, 27–43 (2020)
7. Estrada, F.J., Jepson, A.D.: Benchmarking image segmentation algorithms. Int. J. Comput. Vis. **85**(2), 167–181 (2009)
8. Ferrero-Jaurrieta, M., et al.: VCI-LSTM: Vector Choquet integral-based long short-term memory. IEEE Trans. Fuzzy Syst. 1–14 (2022)
9. Fumanal-Idocin, J., et al.: A generalization of the Sugeno integral to aggregate interval-valued data: an application to brain computer interface and social network analysis. Fuzzy Sets Syst. **451**, 320–341 (2022)
10. Grabisch, M., Marichal, J., Mesiar, R., Pap, E.: Aggregation Functions. Cambridge University Press, Cambridge (2009)
11. Lopez-Molina, C., Bustince, H., Fernandez, J., Couto, P., De Baets, B.: A gravitational approach to edge detection based on triangular norms. Pattern Recogn. **43**(11), 3730–3741 (2010)
12. Lopez-Molina, C., De Baets, B., Bustince, H.: Quantitative error measures for edge detection. Pattern Recogn. **46**(4), 1125–1139 (2013)
13. Lopez-Molina, C., De Baets, B., Bustince, H.: A framework for edge detection based on relief functions. Inf. Sci. **278**, 127–140 (2014)
14. Lucca, G., Sanz, J.A., Dimuro, G.P., Bedregal, B., Bustince, H., Mesiar, R.: CF-integrals: a new family of pre-aggregation functions with application to fuzzy rule-based classification systems. Inf. Sci. **435**, 94–110 (2018)
15. Marco-Detchart, C., Lucca, G., Lopez-Molina, C., De Miguel, L., Pereira Dimuro, G., Bustince, H.: Neuro-inspired edge feature fusion using Choquet integrals. Inf. Sci. **581**, 740–754 (2021)
16. Martin, D.R., Fowlkes, C.C., Malik, J.: Learning to detect natural image boundaries using local brightness, color, and texture cues. IEEE Trans. Pattern Anal. Mach. Intell. **26**(5), 530–549 (2004)
17. Martin, D.R.: An empirical approach to grouping and segmentation. University of California, Berkeley (2002)

18. Medina-Carnicer, R., Madrid-Cuevas, F.J., Carmona-Poyato, A., Muñoz-Salinas, R.: On candidates selection for hysteresis thresholds in edge detection. Pattern Recogn. **42**(7), 1284–1296 (2009)
19. Medina-Carnicer, R., Muñoz-Salinas, R., Yeguas-Bolivar, E., Diaz-Mas, L.: A novel method to look for the hysteresis thresholds for the Canny edge detector. Pattern Recogn. **44**(6), 1201–1211 (2011)
20. Mesiar, R.: Fuzzy integrals as a tool for multicriteria decision support. In: Melo-Pinto, P., Couto, P., Serôdio, C., Fodor, J., De Baets, B. (eds.) Eurofuse 2011, pp. 9–15. Springer, Heidelberg (2012). https://doi.org/10.1007/978-3-642-24001-0_3
21. Murofushi, T., Sugeno, M.: Fuzzy T-conorm integral with respect to fuzzy measures: generalization of Sugeno integral and Choquet integral. Fuzzy Sets Syst. **42**(1), 57–71 (1991)
22. Murofushi, T., Sugeno, M., Machida, M.: Non-monotonic fuzzy measures and the Choquet integral. Fuzzy Sets Syst. **64**(1), 73–86 (1994)
23. Naidu, B.R., Saini, K.K., Bajpai, P., Chakraborty, C.: A novel framework for resilient overhead power distribution networks. Int. J. Electr. Power Energy Syst. **147**, 108839 (2023)
24. Novák, V., Perfilieva, I., Holčapek, M., Kreinovich, V.: Filtering out high frequencies in time series using F-transform. Inf. Sci. **274**, 192–209 (2014)
25. Perfilieva, I.: Fuzzy transforms: theory and applications. Fuzzy Sets Syst. **157**(8), 993–1023 (2006)
26. Perfilieva, I., Hurtik, P.: The F-transform preprocessing for JPEG strong compression of high-resolution images. Inf. Sci. **550**, 221–238 (2021)
27. Perfilieva, I., Valášek, R.: Fuzzy transforms in removing noise. In: Reusch, B. (ed.) Computational Intelligence, Theory and Applications. Advances in Soft Computing, vol. 33, pp. 221–230. Springer, Heidelberg (2005). https://doi.org/10.1007/3-540-31182-3_19
28. Sobel, I., Feldman, G., et al.: A 3×3 isotropic gradient operator for image processing. A talk at the Stanford Artificial Project, pp. 271–272 (1968)
29. Sugeno, M.: Theory of fuzzy integrals and its applications. Ph.D. thesis, Tokyo Institute of Technology, Tokyo (1974)
30. Suresh, K., Srinivasa Rao, P.: Various image segmentation algorithms: a survey. Smart Innov. Syst. Technol. **105**, 233–239 (2019)
31. Wieczynski, J., et al.: d-XC integrals: on the generalization of the expanded form of the Choquet integral by restricted dissimilarity functions and their applications. IEEE Trans. Fuzzy Syst. **30**(12), 5376–5389 (2022)
32. Wieczynski, J., Lucca, G., Borges, E., Dimuro, G., Lourenzutti, R., Bustince, H.: Application and comparison of CC-integrals in business group decision making. In: Filipe, J., Śmiałek, M., Brodsky, A., Hammoudi, S. (eds.) Enterprise Information Systems, pp. 129–148. Springer, Cham (2022). https://doi.org/10.1007/978-3-031-08965-7_7
33. Wieczynski, J., et al.: dc_F-integrals: generalizing C_F-integrals by means of restricted dissimilarity functions. IEEE Trans. Fuzzy Syst. **31**(1), 160–173 (2023)
34. Wu, S.L., et al.: Fuzzy integral with particle swarm optimization for a motor-imagery-based brain-computer interface. IEEE Trans. Fuzzy Syst. **25**(1), 21–28 (2017)
35. Zadeh, L.A.: Fuzzy sets. Inf. Control **8**(3), 338–353 (1965)
36. Zhang, R., et al.: RFI-GAN: a reference-guided fuzzy integral network for ultrasound image augmentation. Inf. Sci. **623**, 709–728 (2023)

Transformation Techniques for Interval-Valued Intuitionistic Fuzzy Sets: Applications to Aggregation and Decision Making

José Carlos R. Alcantud[1]([✉])[iD] and Gustavo Santos-García[2,3][iD]

[1] BORDA Research Group and Multidisciplinary Institute of Enterprise (IME), University of Salamanca, Salamanca, Spain
jcr@usal.es
[2] FADoSS Research Unit, Universidad Complutense de Madrid, Madrid, Spain
[3] Multidisciplinary Institute of Enterprise (IME), University of Salamanca, Salamanca, Spain
santos@usal.es
http://diarium.usal.es/jcr, http://diarium.usal.es/santos

Abstract. This article investigates the use of two operational transformation techniques –that represent one interval-valued intuitionistic fuzzy number by two intuitionistic fuzzy numbers in a constructive manner– for the smooth aggregation of interval-valued intuitionistic fuzzy numbers, and for multi-attribute decision making in this framewok. Decisions and prioritizations are made by comparison laws involving the concepts of score and accuracy of an interval-valued intuitionistic fuzzy number. We show how these figures can be derived from the corresponding proxies for the intuitionistic fuzzy numbers that represent it. A comparative study concludes this investigation.

Keywords: interval-valued intuitionistic fuzzy set · Intuitionistic fuzzy set · Score · Aggregation · Decision making

1 Introduction

This work concerns the interval-valued intuitionistic fuzzy set (IVIFS) model [2]. Any IVIFS evaluates every alternative of a set by means of an interval-valued intuitionistic fuzzy number (IVIFN). In turn, an IVIFN shares characteristics of both intuitionistic fuzzy numbers (IFN) [3,11] and interval-valued fuzzy numbers [9,13].

Alcantud is grateful to the Junta de Castilla y León and the European Regional Development Fund (Grant CLU-2019-03) for the financial support to the Research Unit of Excellence "Economic Management for Sustainability" (GECOS). The research of Santos-García was funded by the project ProCode-UCM (PID2019-108528RB-C22) from the Spanish Ministerio de Ciencia e Innovación.

S. Massanet et al. (Eds.): EUSFLAT 2023/AGOP 2023, LNCS 14069, pp. 342–353, 2023.
https://doi.org/10.1007/978-3-031-39965-7_29

Not surprisingly, the research about IVIFSs closely resembles the intuitionistic fuzzy set (IFS) case. In addition to the study of arithmetic operations and algebraic manipulations, a number of works contributed to the field with their inspection of other topics. For example, scores and accuracies were defined that produced comparison laws [12,14]. Also aggregation operators, or decision-making methodologies, in the framework of IVIFSs were considered by other authors. In fact, aggregation operators and comparison laws have taken part in many decision making (DM) strategies [7,16,19]. This includes the case of multi-attribute decision making (MADM).

It is noteworthy that in order to define aggregation operators for either IFSs or IVIFSs, one simply needs to be able to aggregate their constituent IFNs and IVIFNs. Two fundamental methodologies can be identified. One uses operational laws for IFNs, respectively, IVIFNs, to produce aggregation operators for IFNs and IFSs, respectively, IVIFNs and IVIFSs. Another methodology makes use of aggregation operators on crisp numbers. Nevertheless, often the intricacy of the IVIFS model generates long formulas, the intuitive interpretation of which is lost.

This work investigates the utilization of two operational transformation techniques –that represent one IVIFN by two related IFNs in a constructive manner– for the smooth aggregation of IVIFNs, and for MADM in this framewok. These transformation techniques were recently introduced in [1]. One focus will be the derivation of scores and accuracies of IVIFNs from the scores and accuracies of the two IFNs that characterize them. With both tools –transformation techniques and scores/accuracies– it is possible to put forward respective flexible MADM methodologies in the framework of IVIFSs –one for each transformation technique. We just need to use an aggregation operator on IFNs to aggregate the IFNs that characterize the IVIFNs that define each IVIFS, according to the corresponding transformation, and then use a comparison law (for example, one that is based on scores and accuracies) to prioritize the alternatives characterized by the IVIFSs. We argue that in fact, if the aggregation operator and comparison law for IFNs remain fixed, both methodologies are equivalent. Finally, this common methodology will be compared with existing solutions.

The rest of this article is organized as follows. We recall some necessary concepts and results in Sect. 2. In particular, we state the two transformation theorems for IVIFNs and their intuitive background. Visual representations illustrate the main ideas and the two theorems. Section 3 contains our results. Some conclusions end this work in Sect. 4.

2 Preliminary Concepts

In this article X will be a fixed set of alternatives, and $D[0, 1]$ will be the set of all closed intervals that are included in $\mathcal{I} = [0, 1]$.

By an *orthopair* we mean a pair $(\mu, \nu) \in \mathcal{I} \times \mathcal{I}$, thus $0 \leqslant \mu, \nu \leqslant 1$. This orthopair is an intuitionistic fuzzy number (also, IFN) when $\mu + \nu \leqslant 1$ [20]. Henceforth $\mathbb{A}$ will denote the set of all IFNs.

Definition 1. Suppose that (μ_1, ν_1), (μ_2, ν_2) are orthopairs. Then we define the following two orthopairs:

$$(\mu_1, \nu_1) \vee (\mu_2, \nu_2) = (\max\{\mu_1, \mu_2\}, \max\{\nu_1, \nu_2\}), \text{ and}$$
$$(\mu_1, \nu_1) \wedge (\mu_2, \nu_2) = (\min\{\mu_1, \mu_2\}, \min\{\nu_1, \nu_2\}).$$

We shall also need the following two partial orders $\preccurlyeq$ and $\leqslant_L$ on the set of all orthopairs: suppose that (μ_1, ν_1), (μ_2, ν_2) are orthopairs, then we declare

$$(\mu_1, \nu_1) \preccurlyeq (\mu_2, \nu_2) \text{ if and only if } \mu_1 \leqslant \mu_2 \text{ and } \nu_2 \leqslant \nu_1 \text{ [3], and}$$
$$(\mu_1, \nu_1) \leqslant_L (\mu_2, \nu_2) \text{ if and only if } \mu_1 \leqslant \mu_2 \text{ and } \nu_1 \leqslant \nu_2 \text{ [5].}$$

The IFNs $\mathbf{1} = (1, 0)$ and $\mathbf{0} = (0, 1)$ are, respectively, the top and bottom elements of the partial order $\preccurlyeq$.

The partial order $\leqslant_L$ defined on $\mathcal{I} \times \mathcal{I}$ can be generalized to a partial order on $\mathcal{I} \times \overset{n}{\ldots} \times \mathcal{I}$ in the following manner: if $(a_1, \ldots, a_n), (b_1, \ldots, b_n) \in \mathcal{I} \times \overset{n}{\ldots} \times \mathcal{I}$, then the notation $(a_1, \ldots, a_n) \leqslant_L (b_1, \ldots, b_n)$ is equivalent to $a_i \leqslant b_i$ for each i.

2.1   Intuitionistic Fuzzy Sets: Concepts and operations

The concept of interval-valued intuitionistic fuzzy set was initiated by K. Atanassov. For this reason, many authors use the term Atanassov's intuitionistic fuzzy sets.

Definition 2 (Atanassov [3]). An *intuitionistic fuzzy set* (also, IFS) A over X is $A = \{\langle x, (\mu_A(x), \nu_A(x)) \rangle \mid x \in X\}$, with the condition that for each $x \in X$ $(\mu_A(x), \nu_A(x))$ is an IFN.

The set of all IFSs over X will be denoted by $\mathrm{IFS}(X)$.

On occasions the intuitionistic fuzzy set A is abbreviated as $A = \langle \mu_A, \nu_A \rangle$.

It is assumed that $\mu_A, \nu_A : X \to [0, 1]$ represent the membership degree (MD) and non-membership degree (NMD) of each element $x \in X$ to the intuitionistic fuzzy set A.

The concepts defined for orthopairs (hence, for IFNs) in Definition 1 can be applied to IFSs too. Consider the case of the two partial orders defined there. To extend them, let $A = \langle \mu_A, \nu_A \rangle$ and $B = \langle \mu_B, \nu_B \rangle$ be two IFSs. Then the notation $A \leqslant_L B$, respectively, $A \preccurlyeq B$, means $(\mu_A(x), \nu_A(x)) \leqslant_L (\mu_B(x), \nu_B(x))$, respectively, $(\mu_A(x), \nu_A(x)) \preccurlyeq (\mu_B(x), \nu_B(x))$, for every $x \in X$. Of course, the IFSs $A \wedge B$ and $A \vee B$ can be given with the corresponding pointwise definitions. Importantly, *it is not guaranteed* that $A \vee B$ produces an IFS when A and B are IFSs (see Fig. 1 below). We can only assure that $A \vee B$ produces an orthopair fuzzy set (associating an orthopair with each $x \in X$).

Some algebraic concepts have been extended to IFSs and IFNs:

Definition 3   [3]. *The union and intersection of* $A = \langle \mu_A, \nu_A \rangle$ *and* $B = \langle \mu_B, \nu_B \rangle$, *two IFSs, are, respectively,*

$$A \cup B = \{\langle x, (\max\{\mu_A(x), \mu_B(x)\}, \min\{\nu_A(x), \nu_B(x)\}) \rangle \mid x \in X\} \tag{1}$$

$$A \cap B = \{\langle x, (\min\{\mu_A(x), \mu_B(x)\}, \max\{\nu_A(x), \nu_B(x)\})\rangle \mid x \in X\} \qquad (2)$$

Subsethood is defined by:

$$A \subseteq B \Leftrightarrow (\mu_A(x), \nu_A(x)) \preceq (\mu_B(x), \nu_B(x)) \text{ for all } x \in X. \qquad (3)$$

The concepts of union and intersection of IFSs induce union and intersection of IFNs. Both operators produce respective IFNs as follows: let (μ_1, ν_1), (μ_2, ν_2) be IFNs, then

$$(\mu_1, \nu_1) \cup (\mu_2, \nu_2) = (\max\{\mu_1, \mu_2\}, \min\{\nu_1, \nu_2\}), \qquad (4)$$

$$(\mu_1, \nu_1) \cap (\mu_2, \nu_2) = (\min\{\mu_1, \mu_2\}, \max\{\nu_1, \nu_2\}). \qquad (5)$$

Figure 1 illustrates concepts defined in this section. We consider two cases. When (μ_1, ν_1), (μ_2, ν_2) are IFNs, we can observe that $I_1 \vee I_2$ may not produce an IFN.

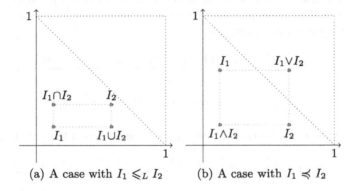

(a) A case with $I_1 \leqslant_L I_2$ (b) A case with $I_1 \preceq I_2$

Fig. 1. Visual representation of Definition 1 and Eqs. (4) and (5). Both I_1 and I_2 are IFNs in the two figures.

Remark 1. Suppose that I_1 and I_2 are IFNs. Then one has:
$I_1 \leqslant_L I_2 \Leftrightarrow I_1 \vee I_2 = I_2 \Leftrightarrow I_1 \wedge I_2 = I_1$, and also
$I_1 \preceq I_2 \Leftrightarrow I_1 \cup I_2 = I_2 \Leftrightarrow I_1 \cap I_2 = I_1$.

In order to compare IFNs by their performance, standard rules use their scores and accuracies since [20, Definition 1]. The score of $J = (\mu, \nu)$, an IFN, was defined in [8] as $S(J) = \mu - \nu$. Higher scores are preferable, however ties appear often. A tie-breaking rule in the case of equal scores uses the respective accuracies of the IFNs. The accuracy of J was defined in [10] as $H(J) = \mu + \nu$.

To mention but one antecedent of transformation techniques in the framework of IFSs, we recall that Atanassov and Gargov [2] defined a bijection between $IFS(X)$ and the set of all interval-valued fuzzy sets [13]. Both this bijection and its inverse mapping are defined by explicit expressions. We shall not use them in this article.

2.2 Interval-Valued Intuitionistic Fuzzy Sets: Concepts and Results

The concept of interval-valued intuitionistic fuzzy set was initiated by Atanassov and Gargov:

Definition 4 (Atanassov and Gargov [2]**).** An *interval-valued intuitionistic fuzzy set* (IVIFS) A over X is $A = \{\langle x, (\mu^A(x), \nu^A(x))\rangle \mid x \in X\}$, with the condition that for each $x \in X$, $\mu^A(x) = [\mu_L^A(x), \mu_M^A(x)] \in D[0,1]$, $\nu^A(x) = [\nu_L^A(x), \nu_M^A(x)] \in D[0,1]$ and $\mu_M^A(x) + \nu_M^A(x) \leqslant 1$.

The set of all IVIFSs over X will be denoted by IVIFS(X).

Any pair $([\mu, \mu'], [\nu, \nu']) \in D[0,1] \times D[0,1]$ such that $\mu' + \nu' \leqslant 1$ is an interval-valued intuitionistic fuzzy number (also, IVIFN) [19]. Equivalently, an IVIFN is a pair $P = ([\mu, \mu'], [\nu, \nu']) \in D[0,1] \times D[0,1]$ with the property that (μ', ν') is an IFN. Its score is $s(P) = \frac{1}{2}(\mu - \nu + \mu' - \nu')$, and $h(P) = \frac{1}{2}(\mu + \mu' + \nu + \nu')$ is its accuracy [19]. As in the case if IFNs, IVIFNs with higher scores are preferable, and accuracy is used to break ties between IVIFNs with equal score.

Other scores that attempt to improve the performance of the definition above include the next formulas from [14]:

$$s_{wc1}(P) = \frac{\mu + \mu' + \sqrt{\mu'\nu'}(1 - \mu - \nu) + \sqrt{\mu\nu}(1 - \mu' - \nu')}{2}, \text{ and}$$

$$s_{wc2}(P) = \frac{(\mu + \mu')(\mu + \nu) - (\nu + \nu')(\mu' + \nu')}{2}.$$

Alternative expressions for the accuracy have been proposed too [12], remarkably,

$$m(P) = \mu + \nu - 1 + \frac{1}{2}(\nu + \nu') = \frac{\mu - (1 - \mu - \nu) + \mu' - (1 - \mu' - \nu')}{2}, \text{ and}$$

$$l(P) = \frac{\mu + \mu' - \nu'(1 - \mu') - \nu(1 - \mu)}{2}.$$

The basic set-theoretic operations (subsethood, union, and intersection), plus arithmetic manipulations (sum and multiplication) were extended to IVIFSs [2,4]. With their help, and other operational laws (such as Einstein's sum and product [16]) novel averaging operators were produced that rely on renewed arithmetic operations on IVIFSs. The Einstein operational laws were also used to the purpose of aggregation for multi-attribute decision-making in both [17] and [15].

Now we proceed to recall two structural theorems proven in [1]. Both are concerned with related transformation techniques that allow us to study IVIFN by means of pairs of suitable IFNs. Their respective intuitive foundations are represented by corresponding figures below in this section.

First Bijection. To state the first transformation theorem, we need to define a subset $\mathcal{O}_1 \subseteq \text{IFS}(X) \times \text{IFS}(X)$ as follows:

$$\mathcal{O}_1 = \{(A_1, A_2) \mid A_1 \preccurlyeq A_2, A_1 \vee A_2 \in \text{IFS}(X)\}. \tag{6}$$

Now we are ready to define the following f_1 : IVIFS(X) $\longrightarrow$ $\mathcal{O}_1$. Let $A = \{\langle x, (\mu^A(x), \nu^A(x))\rangle \,|\, x \in X\} \in$ IVIFS(X) such that for each $x \in X$, we write $\mu^A(x) = [\mu_L^A(x), \mu_M^A(x)]$, $\nu^A(x) = [\nu_L^A(x), \nu_M^A(x)]$. Then $f_1(A) = (I_1^A, I_2^A)$ is given by the formulas:

$$I_1^A(x) = (\mu_L^A(x), \nu_M^A(x)), \ I_2^A(x) = (\mu_M^A(x), \nu_L^A(x)) \tag{7}$$

for each $x \in X$. In addition, consider the mapping $(f_1)^{-1}$: $\mathcal{O}_1 \longrightarrow$ IVIFS(X) defined as follows. For any $(I_1, I_2) \in \mathcal{O}_1$ such that $I_i = \{\langle x, (\mu_i(x), \nu_i(x))\rangle \,|\, x \in X\}$, $i = 1, 2$, consider

$$A_{(I_1, I_2)} = \{\langle x, ([\mu_1(x), \mu_2(x)], [\nu_2(x), \nu_1(x)])\rangle \,|\, x \in X\} \tag{8}$$

and let $(f_1)^{-1}(I_1, I_2) = A_{(I_1, I_2)}$.

Theorem 1 [1]. *The mapping f_1 : IVIFS(X) $\longrightarrow$ $\mathcal{O}_1$ is a bijection, and its inverse mapping is $(f_1)^{-1}$: $\mathcal{O}_1 \longrightarrow$ IVIFS(X).*

Second Bijection. To state the second transformation theorem, we need to define another subset $\mathcal{O}_2 \subseteq$ IFS$(X) \times$ IFS(X) as follows:

$$\mathcal{O}_2 = \{(A_1, A_2) \in \text{IFS}(X)^2 \,|\, A_1 \leqslant_L A_2\}. \tag{9}$$

Now we are ready to define the following f_2 : IVIFS(X) $\longrightarrow$ $\mathcal{O}_2$. Consider $A = \{\langle x, (\mu^A(x), \nu^A(x))\rangle \,|\, x \in X\} \in$ IVIFS(X) such that for each $x \in X$, we write $\mu^A(x) = [\mu_L^A(x), \mu_M^A(x)]$, $\nu^A(x) = [\nu_L^A(x), \nu_M^A(x)]$. Then $f_2(A) = (J_1^A, J_2^A)$ is given by the formulas:

$$J_1^A(x) = (\mu_L^A(x), \nu_L^A(x)), \ J_2^A(x) = (\mu_M^A(x), \nu_M^A(x)) \tag{10}$$

for each $x \in X$. In addition, consider the mapping $(f_2)^{-1}$: $\mathcal{O}_2 \longrightarrow$ IVIFS(X) defined as follows. For any $(I_1, I_2) \in \mathcal{O}_2$ such that $I_i = \{\langle x, (\mu_i(x), \nu_i(x))\rangle \,|\, x \in X\}$, $i = 1, 2$, consider

$$A^{(I_1, I_2)} = \{\langle x, ([\mu_1(x), \mu_2(x)], [\nu_1(x), \nu_2(x)])\rangle \,|\, x \in X\} \tag{11}$$

and let $(f_2)^{-1}(I_1, I_2) = A^{(I_1, I_2)}$.

Theorem 2 [1]. *The mapping f_2 : IVIFS(X) $\longrightarrow$ $\mathcal{O}_1$ is a bijection, and its inverse mapping is $(f_2)^{-1}$: $\mathcal{O}_1 \longrightarrow$ IVIFS(X).*

The intuitive performance of Theorems 1 and 2 is illustrated in Fig. 2.

3   Results

Note that the transformations f_1 and f_2 stated in Theorems 1 and 2 operate on IVIFSs. By considering their constituent IVIFNs, they also induce respective transformations that associate each IVIFN with respective pairs of IFNs. To reduce notational burden, we denote those transformations of IVIFNs by the same names, i.e., f_1 and f_2. And we shall refer to these reduced specifications for IVIFNs in this section.

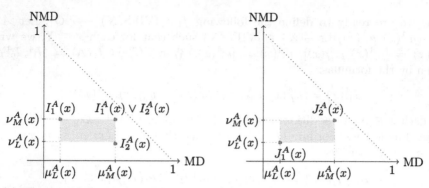

(a) Elements defining f_1 in Theorem 1 (b) Elements defining f_2 in Theorem 2

Fig. 2. Visual representation of the transformations f_1 and f_2 stated in Theorems 1 and 2.

3.1 Scores and Accuracies

We proceed to prove that the transformations f_1 and f_2 enable us to compute the standard scores, respectively, accuracies, for IVIFNs if we know the scores, respectively, accuracies, of their associated IFNs. We do this in the next result:

Proposition 1. Let $P = ([\mu, \mu'], [\nu, \nu'])$ be an IVIFN. For $i = 1, 2$, let $f_i(P) = (I_1^i, I_2^i)$, so that all $I_1^1, I_2^1, I_1^2, I_2^2$ are IFNs. Then

$$s(P) = \frac{1}{2}(S(I_1^1) + S(I_2^1)) = \frac{1}{2}(S(I_1^2) + S(I_2^2)) \tag{12}$$

and

$$h(P) = \frac{1}{2}(H(I_1^1) + H(I_2^1)) = \frac{1}{2}(H(I_1^2) + H(I_2^2)). \tag{13}$$

Proof. By definition, $f_1(P) = (I_1^1, I_2^1)$ means $I_1^1 = (\mu, \nu')$ and $I_2^1 = (\mu', \nu)$, whereas $f_2(P) = (I_1^2, I_2^2)$ means $I_1^2 = (\mu, \nu)$ and $I_2^2 = (\mu', \nu')$. Proofs follow from direct computations. Notice that we can prove the equalities

$$s(P) = \frac{1}{2}(\mu - \nu + \mu' - \nu') = \frac{1}{2}(S(I_1^1) + S(I_2^1)) = \frac{1}{2}(S(I_1^2) + S(I_2^2))$$

because $S(I_1^1) = \mu - \nu'$, $S(I_2^1) = \mu' - \nu$, $S(I_1^2) = \mu - \nu$, $S(I_2^2) = \mu' - \nu'$. Similarly, the equalities

$$h(P) = \frac{1}{2}(\mu + \mu' + \nu + \nu') = \frac{1}{2}(H(I_1^1) + H(I_2^1)) = \frac{1}{2}(H(I_1^2) + H(I_2^2))$$

follow from $H(I_1^1) = \mu + \nu'$, $H(I_2^1) = \mu' + \nu$, $H(I_1^2) = \mu + \nu$, $H(I_2^2) = \mu' + \nu'$.

Both f_1 and f_2 associate one IVIFN with two IFNs. Proposition 1 proves that in each case, the score/accuracy of the IVIFN can be computed as the arithmetic average of the scores/accuracies of the two IFNs that are linked to them.

3.2   Aggregation

The main purpose of [1] was to use the theoretical advancements proven by Theorems 1 and 2 in order to design flexible strategies for the aggregation of IVIFSs. This achievement was then applied to group decision making with the help of scores. In this section we complement the information given in [1].

The strategy that was developed in [1] is summarized by Algorithm 1. As said above, here we concentrate in IVIFNs, but [1] worked in the framework of IVIFSs. So Algorithm 1 has been modified accordingly.

Algorithm 1. A flexible procedure for aggregation of IVIFNs. Alternatively: a flexible procedure that encapsulates one IVIFS in one IVIFN.

Input: A finite list of IVIFNs (or alternatively: one IVIFS, characterized by one IVIFN associated with each alternative).

  Elective element: a suitable aggregation operator for IFNs.

  1: Apply bijection f_2 (defined in Theorem 2) to the IVIFNs.

  With each IVIFN in the list we get a pair of IFNs.

  2: Use an to aggregation operator to transform this list of pairs into one pair of IFNs that satisfies the required structural property.

  We apply aggregation separately to the first component of the pairs, and then to their second components.

  3: Apply f_2^{-1} to this aggregate pair of IFNs.

Output: Aggregate IVIFN of the original list of IVIFNs (or alternatively: one IVIFN that encapsulates the information in the IVIFS).

The Effect of Replacing the Representation Theorem. Although [1] did not consider the algorithm that uses the other representation theorem (i.e., f_1 at step 1 and then f_1^{-1} at step 3), below we state that the reason is that both algorithms are the same:

Proposition 2. *If we replace f_2 with f_1 in Algorithm 1, then the aggregate output does not change.*

A formal proof of this proposition is long and tedious, but straightforward. Hence we omit it here.

3.3   Multi-attribute Decision Making Using Representation Theorems

Once an IVIFS is associated with an IVIFN (e.g., with the utilization of Algorithm 1 or any other methodology), it is possible to use the scores and accuracies of IVIFNs defined in Sect. 2.2 to rank the IVIFSs [1]. The next section explains this issue and compares the results with existing methodologies.

MADM: A Comparative Analysis. Another exercise that was missing in [1] is a comparative analysis with respect to existing aggregation methodologies. We do this in this section. We shall use data from a case study described in [19]. To simplify matters, consider the three IVIFSs described in Table 1. They are from [19, Section 4], although that article studies ten IVIFSs.

Table 1. Three projects and their characteristics.

	B_1	B_2	B_3
A_1	$([0.5, 0.6], [0.2, 0.3])$	$([0.3, 0.4], [0.4, 0.6])$	$([0.4, 0.5], [0.3, 0.5])$
A_9	$([0.2, 0.4], [0.4, 0.5])$	$([0.6, 0.7], [0.2, 0.3])$	$([0.5, 0.6], [0.2, 0.3])$
A_{10}	$([0.5, 0.7], [0.1, 0.3])$	$([0.6, 0.7], [0.1, 0.3])$	$([0.4, 0.5], [0.2, 0.5])$

In Table 1, each project A_i is characterized by its performance in terms of three attributes, namely, B_1, B_2 and B_3. Then [19] suggest that the overall performance of each A_i can be faithfully described by the aggregate IVIFNs of their corresponding IVIFNs. Once these IVIFNs are computed, the projects are ranked from highest to lowest score of the aggregate IVIFNs that summarize them. We supplement their exercise with the calculation of scores by s_{wc1} and s_{wc2}.

We shall compare the results obtained with this methodology, and with the flexible Algorithm 1 (or its counterpart with f_1). We shall refer to two examples of aggregation operators on IFNs. Both use a weighting vector $v = (v_1, \ldots, v_n)$, which therefore satisfies $v_1 + \ldots + v_n = 1$ and $v_i \in \mathcal{I}$ for all $i = 1, \ldots, n$ [6, Def. 2.5]. Now when $I_i = (\mu_i, \nu_i)$ are IFNs , $i = 1, \ldots, n$:

- IWAM$_v(I_1, \ldots, I_n) = (\sum_{i=1}^n v_i \mu_i, \sum_{i=1}^n v_i \nu_i)$ [5, Eq. (13)] defines the intuitionistic fuzzy weighted arithmetic mean associated with v.
- IFWG$_v(I_1, \ldots, I_n) = (\prod_{i=1}^n \mu_i^{v_i}, 1 - \prod_{i=1}^n (1 - \nu_i)^{v_i})$ [20, Definition 2] defines the intuitionistic fuzzy weighted geometric mean associated with v.

It is timely to explain that a version of IFWG$_v$ has been defined that incorporates the foundations of the OWA operator, and it was named IFOWG$_v$. And also, that many other aggregation operators on IFNs have been proposed in the literature.

In our comparison, we shall use the vector of weights $v = (0.5, 0.3, 0.2)$ that formed part of the aggregation methodology of [19]. And we shall compare the results obtained by [19] and by the application of Algorithm 1 with IWAM$_v$ and IFWG$_v$. In each case, we work with three score rankings that correspond to the formulas given in Sect. 2.2. Tables 2 and 3 summarize the elements that motivate our subsequent discussion. Notice that we do not need to compute accuracies, since ties do not appear in the score-based comparisons.

We can observe that the choice of the decision making mechanism is not innocuous. Indeed, the prioritization recommended by each methodology varies:

Table 2. Aggregate IFNs and scores of the projects in Table 1.

	Method in [19]	Algorithm 1 (IWAM$_v$)	Algorithm 1 (IFWG$_v$)
A_1	([0.3941, 0.4990], [0.2852, 0.4380])	([0.42, 0.52], [0.28, 0.43])	([0.4102, 0.5123], [0.2855, 0.4467])
A_9	([0.3964, 0.5635], [0.2751, 0.3748])	([0.38, 0.53], [0.3, 0.4])	([0.3340, 0.5131], [0.3072, 0.4084])
A_{10}	([0.5237, 0.6560], [0.1218, 0.3440])	([0.51, 0.66], [0.12, 0.34])	([0.5051, 0.6544], [0.1210, 0.3456])

Table 3. Three scores for the projects in Table 1.

	Method in [19]			Algorithm 1 (IWAM$_v$)			Algorithm 1 (IFWG$_v$)		
	s	s_{wc1}	s_{wc2}	s	s_{wc1}	s_{wc2}	s	s_{wc1}	s_{wc2}
A_1	0.0850	0.5321	−0.0355	0.115	0.5495	−0.0083	0.0952	0.5410	−0.0302
A_9	0.1550	0.5656	0.0174	0.105	0.5405	−0.0161	0.06575	0.5182	−0.0581
A_{10}	0.3570	0.6741	0.1478	0.355	0.6726	0.1386	0.34645	0.6687	0.1297

- If we use [19], the recommendation is $A_{10} \succ A_9 \succ A_1$ regardless of score selection.
- If we use Algorithm 1 (either with IWAM$_v$ or with IFWG$_v$), the recommendation becomes $A_{10} \succ A_1 \succ A_9$ regardless of score selection.

Hence the decision between A_1 and A_9 is different. The recommendations by Algorithm 1 coincide in declaring $A_1 \succ A_9$, however the procedure in [19] consistently declares $A_9 \succ A_1$.

4   Concluding Remarks

This work has shown that the operational transformation techniques rendered in [1] deserve further attention. We have not yet exploited the full capabilities of Algorithm 1, because other aggregation operators can be used and their performance compared with the cases studied so far.

In addition, it is possible to pose the problem of relating the alternative scores s_{wc1} and s_{wc2}, and accuracies m and l, defined in Sect. 2.2 with our transformations. Proposition 1 is our source of inspiration. And a similar exercise can be done for the membership uncertainty index and hesitation uncertainty index of an IVIFV defined in [18] to guarantee the anti-symmetry of ranking method.

We expect to return to these issues in the future.

References

1. Alcantud, J.C.R., Santos-García, G.: Aggregation of interval valued intuitionistic fuzzy sets based on transformation techniques. In: 2023 IEEE International Conference on Fuzzy Systems (FUZZ-IEEE) (2023)
2. Atanassov, K., Gargov, G.: Interval valued intuitionistic fuzzy sets. Fuzzy Sets Syst. **31**(3), 343–349 (1989). https://doi.org/10.1016/0165-0114(89)90205-4, https://www.sciencedirect.com/science/article/pii/0165011489902054

3. Atanassov, K.T.: Intuitionistic fuzzy sets. Fuzzy Sets Syst. **20**, 87–96 (1986)
4. Atanassov, K.T.: New operations defined over the intuitionistic fuzzy sets. Fuzzy Sets Syst. **61**(2), 137–142 (1994). https://doi.org/10.1016/0165-0114(94)90229-1, https://www.sciencedirect.com/science/article/pii/0165011494902291
5. Beliakov, G., Bustince, H., Goswami, D., Mukherjee, U., Pal, N.: On averaging operators for Atanassov's intuitionistic fuzzy sets. Inf. Sci. **181**(6), 1116–1124 (2011). https://doi.org/10.1016/j.ins.2010.11.024, https://www.sciencedirect.com/science/article/pii/S0020025510005694
6. Beliakov, G., Pradera, A., Calvo, T.: Aggregation Functions: A Guide for Practitioners, Studies in Fuzziness and Soft Computing, vol. 221. Springer, Berlin, Heidelberg (2007). https://doi.org/10.1007/978-3-540-73721-6, http://dblp.uni-trier.de/db/series/sfsc/index.html
7. Chen, S.M., Cheng, S.H., Tsai, W.H.: Multiple attribute group decision making based on interval-valued intuitionistic fuzzy aggregation operators and transformation techniques of interval-valued intuitionistic fuzzy values. Inf. Sci. **367–368**, 418–442 (2016). https://doi.org/10.1016/j.ins.2016.05.041, https://www.sciencedirect.com/science/article/pii/S0020025516303802
8. Chen, S.M., Tan, J.M.: Handling multicriteria fuzzy decision-making problems based on vague set theory. Fuzzy Sets Syst. **67**(2), 163–172 (1994). https://doi.org/10.1016/0165-0114(94)90084-1, https://www.sciencedirect.com/science/article/pii/0165011494900841
9. Deng, J., Zhan, J., Herrera-Viedma, E., Herrera, F.: Regret theory-based three-way decision method on incomplete multi-scale decision information systems with interval fuzzy numbers. IEEE Trans Fuzzy Syst. 1–15 (2022). https://doi.org/10.1109/TFUZZ.2022.3193453
10. Hong, D.H., Choi, C.H.: Multicriteria fuzzy decision-making problems based on vague set theory. Fuzzy Sets Syst. **114**(1), 103–113 (2000). https://doi.org/10.1016/S0165-0114(98)00271-1, https://www.sciencedirect.com/science/article/pii/S0165011498002711
11. Huang, X., Zhan, J., Xu, Z., Fujita, H.: A prospect-regret theory-based three-way decision model with intuitionistic fuzzy numbers under incomplete multi-scale decision information systems. Expert Syst. Appl. **214**, 119144 (2023). https://doi.org/10.1016/j.eswa.2022.119144, https://www.sciencedirect.com/science/article/pii/S0957417422021625
12. Lakshmana Gomathi Nayagam, V., Muralikrishnan, S., Sivaraman, G.: Multicriteria decision-making method based on interval-valued intuitionistic fuzzy sets. Expert Syst. Appl. **38**(3), 1464–1467 (2011). https://doi.org/10.1016/j.eswa.2010.07.055, https://www.sciencedirect.com/science/article/pii/S0957417410006834
13. Sambuc, R.: Functions Φ-floues, application à l'aide au diagnostic en pathologie thyroïdienne. Ph.D. thesis, Université de Marseille (1975)
14. Wang, C.Y., Chen, S.M.: A new multiple attribute decision making method based on linear programming methodology and novel score function and novel accuracy function of interval-valued intuitionistic fuzzy values. Inf. Sci. **438**, 145–155 (2018). https://doi.org/10.1016/j.ins.2018.01.036, https://www.sciencedirect.com/science/article/pii/S0020025518300483
15. Wang, Q., Sun, H.: Interval-valued intuitionistic fuzzy Einstein geometric Choquet integral operator and its application to multiattribute group decision-making. Math. Probl. Eng. **2018**, 9364987 (2018). https://doi.org/10.1155/2018/9364987, https://doi.org/10.1155/2018/9364987

16. Wang, W., Liu, X.: Interval-valued intuitionistic fuzzy hybrid weighted averaging operator based on Einstein operation and its application to decision making. J. Intell. Fuzzy Syst. **25**(2), 279–290 (2013). https://doi.org/10.3233/IFS-120635
17. Wang, W., Liu, X.: The multi-attribute decision making method based on interval-valued intuitionistic fuzzy Einstein hybrid weighted geometric operator. Comput. Math. Appl. **66**(10), 1845–1856 (2013). https://doi.org/10.1016/j.camwa.2013.07.020, https://www.sciencedirect.com/science/article/pii/S0898122113004641
18. Wang, Z., Li, K.W., Wang, W.: An approach to multiattribute decision making with interval-valued intuitionistic fuzzy assessments and incomplete weights. Inf. Sci. **179**(17), 3026–3040 (2009). https://doi.org/10.1016/j.ins.2009.05.001, https://www.sciencedirect.com/science/article/pii/S0020025509002102
19. Xu, Z., Chen, J.: On geometric aggregation over interval-valued intuitionistic fuzzy information. In: Fourth International Conference on Fuzzy Systems and Knowledge Discovery (FSKD 2007), vol. 2, pp. 466–471 (2007). https://doi.org/10.1109/FSKD.2007.427
20. Xu, Z., Yager, R.R.: Some geometric aggregation operators based on intuitionistic fuzzy sets. Int. J. Gen. Syst. **35**(4), 417–433 (2006)

SPECIAL SESSION 3: Evaluative Linguistic Expressions, Generalized Quantifiers and Applications

Verifying Validity of Selected Forms of Syllogisms with Intermediate Quantifiers Using Peterson's Rules

Petra Murinová[(✉)] and Vilém Novák

Institute for Research and Applications of Fuzzy Modeling, NSC IT4Innovations,
University of Ostrava, 30. dubna 22, 701 03 Ostrava 1, Czech Republic
{petra.murinova,vilem.novak}@osu.cz

Abstract. The most reliable method for how the validity of a logical syllogism can be verified is to formalize it and show that there is either a formal proof or it is true in any model. A specific method for proving validity is to use special rules that have been used by logicians. However, we cannot be sure that they indeed verify the validity of syllogisms. The goal of this paper is to show that the rules indeed work. In his book [15], Peterson studied syllogisms with intermediate quantifiers and suggested extension of the rules also to them. In this paper, we formalize them and prove that a logical syllogism of Figure I with intermediate quantifiers is valid iff it satisfies four extended Peterson's rules.

Keywords: Intermediate quantifiers · Peterson's rules · Validity of logical syllogisms

1 Introduction

This paper continues study of logical syllogisms with intermediate quantifiers. In papers [7,8], we presented these syllogisms and proved their validity/invalidity using syntactic proofs. The main idea is based on the mathematical definition of intermediate quantifiers which belong to the class of generalized (fuzzy) quantifiers (see [4,5]). *Intermediate quantifiers*, were introduced by Peterson in [15] and formalized by Novák in [11].

In this paper we utilize the position of intermediate quantifiers in the graded Peterson's square of opposition (see [6]) and verify validity of selected forms of syllogisms with intermediate quantifiers using generalized Peterson's rules, see [12]. We prove that a logical syllogism of Figure I with intermediate quantifiers is valid iff it satisfies all the extended Peterson's rules *quality, quantity and distributivity*.

OP PIK CZ.01.1.02/0.0/0.0/17147/0020575 AI-Met4Laser: Consortium for industrial research and development of new applications of laser technologies using artificial intelligence methods (10/2020–6/2023), of the Ministry of Industry and Trade of the Czech Republic.

S. Massanet et al. (Eds.): EUSFLAT 2023/AGOP 2023, LNCS 14069, pp. 357–368, 2023.
https://doi.org/10.1007/978-3-031-39965-7_30

2   Preliminaries

2.1   The Algebraic Structure of the Truth Values

We will assume that truth values form the linearly ordered MV_Δ-algebra (see [1,14]) $\mathcal{L}_\Delta = \langle L, \vee, \wedge, \otimes, \rightarrow, 0, 1, \Delta \rangle$. A special case is the standard Łukasiewicz MV_Δ-algebra $\mathcal{L}_\Delta^{Luk}$ with $L = [0, 1]$. For a more detailed explanation of the introduction of the delta operation, we refer the reader to [3]. By a fuzzy set A we understand a function $A : N \rightarrow L$ where N is a universe. A set of all fuzzy sets is denoted by $\mathcal{F}(N)$.

Intermediate quantifiers are modeled in a special theory T^{IQ} of fuzzy type theory. Its model will be denoted by $\mathcal{N} \models T^{IQ}$. If $A_{o\alpha}$ is a formula of type $o\alpha$ then its interpretation $\mathcal{N}(A_{o\alpha})$ is a fuzzy set $A \in \mathcal{F}(N)$.

For the theory of intermediate quantifiers, we need a special operation called *cut of a fuzzy set B w.r.t. a fuzzy set Z* which is defined as follows: let M be a universum and $B, Z \subseteq M$. Then for any $u \in M$ the operation $B|Z$ "cuts" B is $B|Z(u) = B(u) = Z(u)$ if $B(u) = Z(u)$. Otherwise $(B|Z)(u) = 0$. If there is no such u then $B|Z = \emptyset$. The motivation and explanation for the introduction of this operation can be found in [9].

2.2   Evaluative Linguistic Expressions

The theory of intermediate quantifiers is based on the theory of evaluative linguistic expressions that are special natural language expressions such as *very small, about medium, roughly big, very short, more or less deep, quite roughly strong, extremely high*, etc. The formal theory T^{Ev} of their semantics and more details about their structure can be found in [10,13].

Evaluative linguistic expressions are represented in the theory T^{Ev} by formulas

$$Sm\,\nu, Me\,\nu, Bi\,\nu, Ze\nu \tag{1}$$

where ν represents a linguistic hedge. For example, $Sm\,Ve$ is a formula construing the evaluative expression "very small". We will also consider an *empty hedge* $\bar{\nu}$ that is always present in front of *small, medium* and *big* if no other hedge is given.

Recall that *very (Ve), extremely (Ex)* and *utmost (Δ)* are linguistic hedges that are modeled using special unary functions on $[0, 1]$ which are ordered as follows:

$$Ex \preceq Si \preceq Ve \preceq \bar{\nu} \preceq ML \preceq Ro \preceq QR \preceq VR \tag{2}$$

where $\bar{\nu}$ is the empty hedge.

Each evaluative expression characterizes a certain imprecisely determined position on a bounded linearly ordered scale. The scale is represented by a *context* which is an interval $[v_L, v_S] \cup [v_S, v_R]$.[1] The context is *standard* if $v_L = 0, v_S =$

---

[1] We write this interval as a union of two intervals to emphasize the role of the central point v_S which represents "typical medium".

$0.4, v_R = 1$. More details about the theory of evaluative linguistic expressions can be found in [9,10] and elsewhere.

The following inequality can be proved in the theory of evaluative expressions.

Lemma 1. *Let us consider the standard context. Then*

$$a_{not\,Sm} = \inf \text{Supp}(\neg\,Sm) < 0.5 < a_{Bi\,Ve} = \inf \text{Supp}(Bi\,Ve) \leq$$
$$a_{Bi\,Ex} = \inf \text{Supp}(Bi\,Ex) \leq \inf \text{Supp}(Bi\,\Delta) = 1.$$

In this paper, we also assume the following:

$$\inf \text{Supp}(\neg\,Sm) \oplus \inf \text{Supp}(Bi\,Ex) = 1, \tag{3}$$
$$\inf \text{Supp}(\neg\,Sm) \oplus \inf \text{Supp}(Bi\,Ve) < 1. \tag{4}$$

2.3 The Theory of Intermediate Quantifiers

Let us remind that intermediate quantifiers are modeled using special formulas of the formal theory T^{Ev} from Ł-FTTwhich express a quantification over the universe represented by a fuzzy set whose size is characterized by a measure. The reader will find a more detailed explanation of the introduction of the measure and the required axioms in [9].

Syntactic Definition of Fuzzy Intermediate Quantifiers. In [9], we formally characterized measure of a fuzzy set which characterizes its "size". A formula $\mu_{o(o\alpha)(o\alpha)} \equiv \lambda z_{o\alpha} \lambda x_{o\alpha} (R z_{o\alpha}) x_{o\alpha}$ represents a *measure on fuzzy sets* in the universe of type $\alpha \in$ *Types*. A fuzzy set is measurable if there is a measure of it. The special theory of intermediate quantifiers is denoted by T^{IQ}.

An intermediate quantifier of type $\langle 1, 1 \rangle$ is one of the following formulas:

$$(Q^{\forall}_{Ev}\, x_\alpha)(B_{o\alpha}, A_{o\alpha}) \equiv (\exists z)[(\forall x)((B|z)\, x \Rightarrow Ax) \wedge Ev((\mu B)(B|z))], \tag{5}$$
$$(Q^{\exists}_{Ev}\, x_\alpha)(B_{o\alpha}, A_{o\alpha}) \equiv (\exists z)[(\exists x)((B|z)x \wedge Ax) \wedge Ev((\mu B)(B|z))]. \tag{6}$$

where Ev is a formula representing some evaluative linguistic expression, z, x are variables and A, B are formulas where B represents a universe of quantification and it is a measurable fuzzy set. Either of the quantifiers (5) or (6) construes the sentence

$$\langle \text{Quantifier} \rangle\ B's\ \text{are}\ A \tag{7}$$

where $\langle \text{Quantifier} \rangle$ is a quantifier in a linguistic form.

Semantic Definition of Fuzzy Intermediate Quantifiers. The semantic definition of the meaning of intermediate quantifiers follows from interpretation of formulas (5) and (6).

Definition 1. *Interpretation of the measure μ is a function $R : \mathcal{F}(N) \setminus \{\emptyset\} \times \mathcal{F}(N) \to L$ fulfilling the following conditions for all $A, A' \in \mathcal{F}(N)$ and $B, B' \in \mathcal{F}(N) \setminus \{\emptyset\}$:*

(i) $R(B,B) = 1$, $R(B, B \setminus A) = \neg R(B,A)$.
(ii) If $A \nsubseteq B$ then $R(B,A) = 0$.
(iii) If $A \subseteq A'$ then $R(B,A) \leq R(B,A')$,
(iv) If $B \subseteq B'$ then $R(B',A) \leq R(B,A)$.

Definition 2. *Let N be a set, $A, B, Z \in \mathcal{F}(N)$. Put[2]*

$$F_{Ev}^{R}(B, B|Z) = Ev(R(B, B|Z)) \tag{8}$$

where Ev is a fuzzy set representing extension of some evaluative expression in the standard context $\langle 0, 0.4, 1 \rangle$ (for explanation, see [13]). Then a semantic interpretation of the intermediate quantifiers (5) and (6) are the following truth values:[3]

$$Q_{Ev}^{\forall}(B, A) = \bigvee \left\{ \bigwedge_{u \in N} ((B|Z)(u) \to A(u)) \wedge F_{Ev}^{R}(B, B|Z) \mid Z \in \mathcal{F}(N) \right\}, \tag{9}$$

$$Q_{Ev}^{\exists}(B, A) = \bigvee \left\{ \bigvee_{u \in N} ((B|Z)(u) \wedge A(u)) \wedge F_{Ev}^{R}(B, B|Z) \mid Z \in \mathcal{F}(N) \right\}. \tag{10}$$

If we replace the metavariable Ev in (5) or (6) by a formula representing a specific evaluative linguistic expression then we obtain definition of the concrete intermediate quantifier. The following are *semantic representations* of the specific intermediate quantifiers.

Definition 3.

(A) *"All B's are A":* $\bigwedge_{u \in N}(B(u) \to A(u))$,
(E) *"No B's is A":* $\bigwedge_{u \in N}(B(u) \to \neg A(u))$,
(P) *"Almost all B's are A":*
$$\bigvee_{Z \in \mathcal{F}(N)} \left(\bigwedge_{u \in N}((B|Z)(u) \to A(u)) \wedge F_{BiEx}^{R}(B, B|Z) \right),$$
(B) *"Almost all B's are not A":*
$$\bigvee_{Z \in \mathcal{F}(N)} \left(\bigwedge_{u \in N}((B|Z)(u) \to \neg A(u)) \wedge F_{BiEx}^{R}(B, B|Z) \right),$$
(T) *"Most B's are A":*
$$\bigvee_{Z \in \mathcal{F}(N)} \left(\bigwedge_{u \in N}((B|Z)(u) \to A(u)) \wedge F_{BiVe}^{R}(B, B|Z) \right),$$
(D) *"Most B's are not A":*
$$\bigvee_{Z \in \mathcal{F}(N)} \left(\bigwedge_{u \in N}((B|Z)(u) \to \neg A(u)) \wedge F_{BiVe}^{R}(B, B|Z) \right),$$
(K) *"Many B's are A":*
$$\bigvee_{Z \in \mathcal{F}(N)} \left(\bigwedge_{u \in N}((B|Z)(u) \to A(u)) \wedge F_{\neg Sm}^{R}(B, B|Z) \right),$$

---

[2] Note that (8) is a semantic interpretation of the formula $Ev((\mu B)(B|z))$ occurring in (5) and (6).
[3] Recall that the quantifiers $\forall$ and $\exists$ are in fuzzy logic interpreted by $\bigwedge$ and $\bigvee$, respectively.

(G) *"Many B's are not A":*
$$\bigvee_{Z \in \mathcal{F}(N)} \left(\bigwedge_{u \in N} ((B|Z)(u) \to \neg A(u)) \land F^R_{\neg Sm}(B, B|Z) \right),$$
(I) *"Some B's are A":* $\bigvee_{u \in N}(B(u) \land A(u))$,
(O) *"Some B's are not A":* $\bigvee_{u \in N}(B(u) \land \neg A(u))$.

3   Extended Syllogisms with Intermediate Quantifiers

A *syllogism* is a triple of formulas $\mathcal{P}_1, \mathcal{P}_2, \mathcal{C}$ of the theory T^{IQ} where $\mathcal{P}_1$ is a *major premise*, $\mathcal{P}_2$ a *minor premise* and $\mathcal{C}$ is a *conclusion*. We say that it is *valid* if $T^{IQ} \vdash \mathcal{P}_1 \& \mathcal{P}_2 \Rightarrow \mathcal{C}$. By the completeness theorem, syllogism is valid iff $\mathcal{N}(\mathcal{P}_1) \otimes \mathcal{N}(\mathcal{P}_2) \leq \mathcal{N}(\mathcal{C})$ holds in any model $\mathcal{N} \models T^{IQ}$. Validity of all syllogisms presented in [15] was proven syntactically in [7,8].

Let Q_1, Q_2, Q_3 be quantifier symbols from (5) or (6) and S, P, M be formulas[4] representing properties of elemements of type α. The formula S is a *subject*, P is a *predicate* and M is a *middle formula*. As usual, syllogisms are gathered into the following four figures:

Figure I	Figure II	Figure III	Figure IV
Q_1 M are P	Q_1 P are M	Q_1 M are P	Q_1 P are M
Q_2 S are M	Q_2 S are M	Q_2 M are S	Q_2 M are S
Q_3 S are P	Q_3 S are P	Q_3 S are P	Q_3 S are P

where the first line in each figure is the major premise $\mathcal{P}_{1,o}$, the second line is the minor premise $\mathcal{P}_{2,o}$ and the third line is the conclusion $\mathcal{C}_o$. If all $Q_1, Q_2, Q_3 \in \{\forall, \exists\}$ then the corresponding syllogism is classical.

Lemma 2. *Let $X_1, X_2, X_3 \in \{P, B, T, D, K, G\}$ be symbols (cf. Definition 3) and $M, P, S \in \mathcal{F}(M)$ be fuzzy sets representing properties. Then, in general, the inequality*
$$Q_{X_1}(M, P) \otimes Q_{X_2}(S, M) \leq Q_{X_3}(S, P) \tag{11}$$
does not hold, i.e., the corresponding syllogism of Figure I is not valid.

Proof. By a counterexample: Let us consider fuzzy sets $M, S, P \in \mathcal{F}(M)$ as follows.

Let $Z = M \cap P$ be such that $M(u) = P(u)$ for $u \in \text{Supp}(Z)$ except for some u_0 for which $M(u_0) > P(u_0)$ and assume that $Ev_1(\mu(M, M|Z)) = 1$. Then $Q_{X_1}(M, P) = 1$. Furthermore, let S be such that $\text{Supp}(S \cap M)$ is small w.r.t. M but large enough so that $Ev_2(\mu(S, S|Z')) = 1$ for a suitable Z'. Finally, let $S(u) \geq M(u) \geq P(u)$, $u \in \text{Supp}(S \cap M)$ and for at least one u_0 let $S(u_0) > M(u_0) > P(u_0)$. Then $Q_{X_2}(S, M) > Q_{X_3}(S, P)$.

---

[4] Many authors speak about *terms* instead of formulas. We call S, P, M *formulas* as is common in logic.

It follows from this lemma, that syllogisms with three non-trivial intermediate quantifiers (i.e., those different from $\forall, \exists$) cannot be valid. For example, syllogism saying that "Most(M is P) and Most(S is M) implies Most(S is P)" is not valid. Similarly for this kind of syllogism with the other non-trivial intermediate quantifiers.

4   Extended Peterson's Rules for Checking Validity of Syllogisms

In Peterson's approach, the distribution index is based on the number of intermediate quantifiers which form Peterson's square of opposition (cf. [2] and also [12]).

The distribution index in our approach is derived from the characteristic shape of the fuzzy set modeling the extension of the evaluative expression in the standard context $\langle 0, 0.4, 1 \rangle$.

Definition 4 (Distribution index). *Let* $A, B \in \mathcal{F}(M)$ *be fuzzy sets and* $Q_{Ev}^K(B, A)$, $K \in \{\forall, \exists\}$ *be an intermediate quantifier determined by the evaluative expression Ev. The distribution index* $\mathrm{DI}(X, Q_{Ev}^K(B, A))$ *(or shortly,* $\mathrm{DI}(X, Q^K))$ *of the fuzzy set* $X \in \mathcal{F}(M)$ *is:*

$$\mathrm{DI}(X, Q_{Ev}^K(B, A)) = \begin{cases} \inf \mathrm{Supp}(Ev) & \text{if } K = \forall \text{ and } X = B, \\ 0 & \text{if } K = \forall \text{ and } X = A, \\ 0 & \text{if } K = \exists \text{ and } X \in \{A, B\}, \end{cases}$$

$$\mathrm{DI}(\neg X, Q) = \neg \mathrm{DI}(X, Q).$$

Let $Q_{\mathcal{P}_1}, Q_{\mathcal{P}_2}, Q_C$ denote quantifiers occurring in the major premise, minor premise, and conclusion, respectively. Below we recall extended Peterson's rules (denoted by (ERx)) and their formalization (denoted by (fERx)) using our notation and concepts. For the detailed explanation see [12].

1. *Peterson's Rules of Distribution*
(ER1) In a valid syllogism, the sum of the distribution indices for the middle formula must exceed 5.
   (fER1) $\mathrm{DI}(X, Q_{\mathcal{P}_1}^K) \oplus \mathrm{DI}(X, Q_{\mathcal{P}_2}^L) = 1$ where $X \in \{M, \neg M\}$.
(ER2) No formula may be more nearly distributed in the conclusion than it is in the premises. Let $K, L \in \{\forall, \exists\}$.
   (fER2a) $\mathrm{DI}(X, Q_C^K) \leq \mathrm{DI}(Y, Q_{\mathcal{P}_2}^L)$ where $X, Y \in \{S, \neg S\}$,
   (fER2b) $\mathrm{DI}(X, Q_C^K) \leq \mathrm{DI}(Y, Q_{\mathcal{P}_1}^L)$ where $X, Y \in \{P, \neg P\}$.
2. *Peterson's Rules of Quality*
(ER3) At least one premise must be affirmative.
   (fER3) Let $X, Y \in \{S, P, M\}$, $X \neq Y$ and $K \in \{\forall, \exists\}$. Then at least one of the following holds: $\mathcal{P}_1 = Q_{Ev}^K(Y, X)$ or $\mathcal{P}_2 = Q_{Ev}^K(Y, X)$.
(ER4) The conclusion is negative if and only if one of the premises is negative.

(fER4) Let $X, Y \in \{S, P, M\}$, $X \neq Y$ and $K, L \in \{\forall, \exists\}$. Then

$$\mathcal{C} = Q_{Ev}^K(S, \neg P) \iff \mathcal{P} = Q_{Ev}^L(Y, \neg X)$$

where $\mathcal{P} \in \{\mathcal{P}_1, \mathcal{P}_2\}$.

3. *Peterson's Rules of Quantity*

(ER5) At least one premise must have a quantity of majority (**T** or **D**) or higher.

(fER5) $0.5 < \inf \operatorname{Supp}(Ev_{\mathcal{P}_1}) \vee \inf \operatorname{Supp}(Ev_{\mathcal{P}_2})$.

(ER6) If any premise is non-universal, then the conclusion must have a quantity that is less than or equal to that premise.

(fER6) $\inf \operatorname{Supp}(Ev_{\mathcal{C}}) \leq \inf \operatorname{Supp}(Ev_{\mathcal{P}_1}) \wedge \inf \operatorname{Supp}(Ev_{\mathcal{P}_2})$.

Recall from [12] that rules (fER1)–(fER4) are sufficient because they imply (fER5) and (fER6).

5 Checking Validity of Syllogisms by Extended Peterson's Rules

The main objective of this section is to show that Peterson's rules can be used for checking validity (or invalidity) of syllogisms with intermediate quantifiers. First, we will verify that if a given logical syllogism is valid then it satisfies extended Rules (fER1)–(fER4).

5.1 Valid Syllogisms Satisfy Extended Peterson's Rules

Lemma 3. *Syllogisms **AAA**, **AAP**, **AAT**, **AAK**, **A(*A)I** of Figure I satisfy Rules (fER1)–(fER4).*

Proof. Let us consider syllogism **AAA**. Then $\mathcal{P}_1 = Q_{Bi\,\mathbf{\Delta}}^{\forall}(M, P)$, $\mathcal{P}_2 = Q_{Bi\,\mathbf{\Delta}}^{\forall}(S, M)$, $\mathcal{C} = Q_{Bi\,\mathbf{\Delta}}^{\forall}(S, P)$ and

$$Q_{Bi\,\mathbf{\Delta}}^{\forall}(M, P) \otimes Q_{Bi\,\mathbf{\Delta}}^{\forall}(S, M) \leq Q_{Bi\,\mathbf{\Delta}}^{\forall}(S, P).$$

Then $\operatorname{DI}(M, Q_{Bi\,\mathbf{\Delta}}^{\forall}(M, P)) = 1$ and $\operatorname{DI}(M, Q_{Bi\,\mathbf{\Delta}}^{\forall}(S, M)) = 0$. Therefore, Rule (fER1) is satisfied. The same argument can be applied also to syllogisms **AAP**, **AAT**, **AAK**, **A(*A)I** of Figure-I and, hence, they also satisfy Rule (fER1).

Furthermore, $\operatorname{DI}(S, Q_{Bi\,\mathbf{\Delta}}^{\forall}(S, M)) = 1$ and $\operatorname{DI}(S, Q_{Bi\,\mathbf{\Delta}}^{\forall}(S, P)) = 1$. This means that syllogism **AAA** satisfies Rule (fER2a). The inequality

$$\operatorname{DI}(S, Q_{\neg\,Sm}^{\forall}(S, P)) \leq \operatorname{DI}(S, Q_{Bi\,Ve}^{\forall}(S, P)) \leq \operatorname{DI}(S, Q_{Bi\,Ex}^{\forall}(S, P))$$
$$\leq \operatorname{DI}(S, Q_{Bi\,\mathbf{\Delta}}^{\forall}(S, M)) = 1,$$

implies that Rule (fER2a) is satisfied by syllogisms **AAP**, **AAT**, **AAK**. Because $\operatorname{DI}(S, Q_{Bi\,\mathbf{\Delta}}^{\exists}(S, P)) = 0$ then Rule (fER2a) is satisfied by syllogism **A(*A)I**.

Let $K = \{\forall, \exists\}$. Rule (fER2b) is satisfied by all the considered syllogisms as well because $0 = \operatorname{DI}(P, Q_{Ev}^K(S, P)) \leq \operatorname{DI}(P, Q_{Ev}^{\forall}(M, P))$.

Rule (fER3) is obviously satisfied and Rule (fER4) does not apply.

Lemma 4. *Syllogisms* **APP, APT, APK, A(*P)I** *of Figure-I satisfy Rules (fER1)–(fER4).*

Proof. Let us consider syllogism **APP**. Then $\mathcal{P}_1 = Q^{\vee}_{Bi\,\Delta}(M, P)$, $\mathcal{P}_2 = Q^{\vee}_{Bi\,Ex}(S, M)$, $\mathcal{C} = Q^{\vee}_{Bi\,Ex}(S, P)$ and

$$Q^{\vee}_{Bi\,\Delta}(M, P) \otimes Q^{\vee}_{Bi\,Ex}(S, M) \leq Q^{\vee}_{Bi\,Ex}(S, P).$$

Then $\mathrm{DI}(M, Q^{\vee}_{Bi\,\Delta}(M, P)) = 1$ and $\mathrm{DI}(M, Q^{\vee}_{Bi\,Ex}(S, M)) = 0$. Therefore, Rule (fER1) is satisfied by **APP** and, consequently, also by **APT, APK, A(*P)I**.

Furthermore,

$$\inf \mathrm{Supp}(Bi\,Ex_{\mathcal{C}}) \leq \inf \mathrm{Supp}(Bi\,Ex_{\mathcal{P}_2})$$

which means that $\mathrm{DI}(S, Q^{\vee}_{Bi\,Ex}(S, P)) \leq \mathrm{DI}(S, Q^{\vee}_{Bi\,Ex}(S, M))$ and, therefore, Rule (fER2a) is satisfied.

Let $K = \{\forall, \exists\}$. Since $0 = \mathrm{DI}(P, Q^{\vee}_{Bi\,\Delta_{\mathcal{P}_1}}(M, P)) = \mathrm{DI}(P, Q^{K}_{Evc}(S, P)) = 0$ for all the evaluative expressions occurring in syllogisms **APP, APT, APK, A(*P)I**, Rule (fER2b) is also satisfied.

Rule (fER3) is obviously satisfied and (fER4) does not apply.

Similarly to above, we can verify the validity for negative logical syllogisms of Figure-I.

Theorem 1. *All 30 valid syllogisms of Figure-I satisfy Rules (fER1)–(fER4).*

Proof. It follows from Lemma 3 and Lemma 4.

5.2   Syllogisms Which Satisfy Extended Peterson's Rules are Valid

In the previous subsection we showed that if a syllogism is valid then it satisfies generalized Rules (fER1)–(fER4). In this subsection we will prove also the opposite implication.

Lemma 5. *Let us consider an arbitrary syllogism of Figure-I and assume that it satisfies Rules (fER1)–(fER4). Then it is valid.*

Proof. Possible forms of syllogisms of Figure-I are the following:

$$
\begin{array}{lllll}
& Q_{\mathcal{P}_1}(M, P) & Q_{\mathcal{P}_1}(M, \neg P) & Q_{\mathcal{P}_1}(M, \ P) & Q_{\mathcal{P}_1}(M, \neg P) \\
\text{(a):} & \dfrac{Q_{\mathcal{P}_2}(S, M)}{Q_{\mathcal{C}}\ (S\ \ P)} & \text{(b):}\ \dfrac{Q_{\mathcal{P}_2}(S,\ M)}{Q_{\mathcal{C}}\ (S\,\neg P)} & \text{(c):}\ \dfrac{Q_{\mathcal{P}_2}(S, \neg M)}{Q_{\mathcal{C}}\ (S\ \neg P)} & \text{(d):}\ \dfrac{Q_{\mathcal{P}_2}(S, \neg M)}{Q_{\mathcal{C}}\ (S\ \neg P)} & \text{(e):}
\end{array}
$$

$$
\begin{array}{lllll}
Q_{\mathcal{P}_1}(M, \neg P) & Q_{\mathcal{P}_1}(M, \neg P) & Q_{\mathcal{P}_1}(M, \ P) & Q_{\mathcal{P}_1}(M, \ P) \\
\dfrac{Q_{\mathcal{P}_2}(S,\ M)}{Q_{\mathcal{C}}\ (S\ \ P)}\ \text{(f):} & \dfrac{Q_{\mathcal{P}_2}(S, \neg M)}{Q_{\mathcal{C}}\ (S\ \ P)}\ \text{(g):} & \dfrac{Q_{\mathcal{P}_2}(S, \neg M)}{Q_{\mathcal{C}}\ (S\ \ P)}\ \text{(h):} & \dfrac{Q_{\mathcal{P}_2}(S,\ M)}{Q_{\mathcal{C}}\ (S\,\neg P)}
\end{array}
$$

It can be verified that forms (a) and (b) fulfill all Rules (fER1)-(fER4). Form (c) violates Rule (fER2b), because $\mathrm{DI}(P, \mathcal{P}_1) = 0$ and $\mathrm{DI}(P, \mathcal{C}) = 1$. So the inequality $\mathrm{DI}(P, \mathcal{C}) \leq \mathrm{DI}(P, \mathcal{P}_1)$ is not satisfied.

Forms (d) and (f) violate Rule (fER3) because at least one premise must have the form $Q_{Ev}^K(Y, X)$ where $K \in \{\forall, \exists\}$ and $Y, X \in \{S, P, M\}$, $X \neq Y$.

The form (e), (g) and (h) violate Rule (fER4). We explain in the detail the form (e). The first premise is negative which means that $\mathcal{P}_1 = Q_{Ev}^K(M, \neg P)$. The conclusion has the form $\mathcal{C} = Q_{Ev}^K(S, P)$ which violates Rule (fER4). Forms (g) and (h) do not fulfill Rule (fER4) for the same reason.

Let us examine two remaining forms:

Form (a) (affirmative): Put $\mathcal{P}_1 = Q_{\mathcal{P}_1}(M, P)$, $\mathcal{P}_2 = Q_{\mathcal{P}_2}(S, M)$ and $\mathcal{C} = Q_{\mathcal{C}}(S, P)$: Evidently, $\mathrm{DI}(M, \mathcal{P}_1) = \inf \mathrm{Supp}(Ev_{\mathcal{P}_1})$, $\mathrm{DI}(M, \mathcal{P}_2) = 0$ and because of (fER1), $\inf \mathrm{Supp}(Ev_{\mathcal{P}_1}) = 1$ i.e., by [12, Lemma 10] $Q_{\mathcal{P}_1}$ is $\forall$ and we have

$$\mathcal{P}_1 = \bigwedge_{u \in N} (M(u) \to P(u)). \tag{12}$$

Using Rule (fER2b) for the subject, the minor premise must have the form:

$$\mathcal{P}_2 = \bigvee_{Z \in \mathcal{F}(N)} \left(\bigwedge_{u \in N} ((S|Z)(u) \bowtie M(u)) \wedge F_{Ev_{\mathcal{P}_2}}^R(S, S|Z) \right) \tag{13}$$

and at the same time using Rule (fER2a) for predicate the conclusion has the following possible form:

$$\mathcal{C} = \bigvee_{Z \in \mathcal{F}(N)} \left(\bigwedge_{u \in N} ((S|Z)(u) \bowtie P(u)) \wedge F_{Ev_{\mathcal{C}}}^R(S, S|Z) \right) \tag{14}$$

where $Ev_{\mathcal{P}_2} \prec Ev_{\mathcal{C}}$ and $\bowtie \in \{\to, \wedge\}$.

Using (12), (13) and (14) we conclude that the following inequalities should hold:

$$\mathcal{P}_1 \otimes \mathcal{P}_2 = \bigwedge_{u \in N} (M(u) \to P(u)) \otimes$$

$$\bigvee_{Z \in \mathcal{F}(N)} \left(\bigvee_{u \in N} (S|Z)(u) \otimes \bigwedge_{u \in N} ((S|Z)(u) \to M(u)) \wedge F_{Ev, \mathcal{P}_2}^R(S, S|Z) \right)$$

$$\leq \bigvee_{Z \in \mathcal{F}(N)} \left(\bigwedge_{u \in N} ((S|Z)(u) \wedge P(u)) \wedge F_{Ev_{\mathcal{C}}}^R(S, S|Z) \right) = \mathcal{C} \tag{15}$$

and

$$\mathcal{P}_1 \otimes \mathcal{P}_2 = \bigwedge_{u \in N} (M(u) \to P(u)) \otimes$$

$$\bigvee_{Z \in \mathcal{F}(N)} \left(\bigwedge_{u \in N} ((S|Z)(u) \to M(u)) \wedge F_{Ev_{\mathcal{P}_2}}^R(S, S|Z) \right)$$

$$\leq \bigvee_{Z \in \mathcal{F}(N)} \left(\bigwedge_{u \in N} ((S|Z)(u) \to P(u)) \wedge F_{Ev_{\mathcal{C}}}^R(S, S|Z) \right) = \mathcal{C} \tag{16}$$

$$\mathcal{P}_1 \otimes \mathcal{P}_2 = \bigwedge_{u \in N} (M(u) \to P(u))$$

$$\otimes \bigvee_{Z \in \mathcal{F}(N)} \left(\bigwedge_{u \in N} ((S|Z)(u) \wedge M(u)) \wedge F_{Ev_{\mathcal{P}_2}}^R (S, S|Z) \right)$$

$$\leq \bigvee_{Z \in \mathcal{F}(N)} \left(\bigwedge_{u \in N} ((S|Z)(u) \wedge P(u)) \wedge F_{Ev_{\mathcal{C}}}^R (S, S|Z) \right) = \mathcal{C} \quad (17)$$

where $Ev_{\mathcal{P}_2} \prec Ev_{\mathcal{C}}$. It can be verified using the properties of MV-algebra that both inequalities (15), (16) and (17) hold true (cf. [12]). In case (15) this inequality holds true provided that the term with the existential import (presupposition) is added. This term is in (15) marked by square brackets.

By setting concrete evaluative linguistic expressions we obtain several valid forms of positive syllogisms of Figure-I. If in (15) we put $Ev_{\mathcal{P}_2} = Ev_{\mathcal{C}} := Bi\,\Delta$ then we obtain classical syllogism **A(*A)I-I**. If in (17) we put $Ev_{\mathcal{P}_2} = Ev_{\mathcal{C}} := Bi\,\Delta$ then we obtain classical syllogism **AII-I**.

Furthermore, if in (16) we put $Ev_{\mathcal{P}_2} = Ev_{\mathcal{C}} := Bi\,\Delta$ we obtain classical syllogism **AAA-I**. If in (15) we put $Ev_{\mathcal{P}_2} = Ev_{\mathcal{C}} := Bi\,Ex, Bi\,Ve, \neg\,Sm$ then we obtain syllogisms **APP-I, ATT-I, AKK-I**, respectively.

At the same time, $\mathrm{DI}(S, \mathcal{C}) = \inf \mathrm{Supp}(Ev_{\mathcal{C}})$ and $\mathrm{DI}(S, \mathcal{P}_2) = \inf \mathrm{Supp}(Ev_{\mathcal{P}_2})$. Rule (fER2a) says that

$$\inf \mathrm{Supp}(Ev_{\mathcal{C}}) \leq \inf \mathrm{Supp}(Ev_{\mathcal{P}_2}), \quad (18)$$

which means from their position in **5**-graded square of opposition that $Q_{\mathcal{P}_2}^K$ is equal to or super-altern of $Q_{\mathcal{C}}^K$ where $K = \{\forall, \exists\}$. From it follows

$$Q_{\mathcal{P}_2}^K(S, P) \leq Q_{\mathcal{C}}^K(S, P) \quad (19)$$

which yields valid syllogisms **AAP-I, AAT-I, AAK-I**.

We continue with syllogisms with intermediate quantifiers in the minor premise and in the conclusion. From the previous construction we know that the first premise is universal. From (18) and (19) follow valid syllogisms **ATK-I, APT-I, APK-I**. By putting concrete evaluative linguistic expressions in (15) we obtain valid syllogisms **A(*P)I-I, A(*T)I-I, A(*K)I-I**.

Form (b) (negative): Put $\mathcal{P}_1 = Q_{\mathcal{P}_1}(M, \neg P)$, $\mathcal{P}_2 = Q_{\mathcal{P}_2}(S, M)$ and $\mathcal{C} = Q_{\mathcal{C}}(S, \neg P)$. The proof is analogous to Figure-I (a).

We conclude that if an arbitrary syllogism of Figure-I fulfills all the extended Peterson's rules then it belongs among 30 valid syllogisms.

Theorem 2. *If an arbitrary syllogism with intermediate quantifiers of Figures-I satisfies Rules (fER1)–(fER4) then it is valid.*

Proof. This is a consequence of Lemma 5 and others lemmas which can be proved analogously.

Joining Theorems 1 and 2 we obtain the following corollary.

Corollary 1. *A syllogism of Figures-I with intermediate quantifiers is valid iff it satisfies Rules (fER1)–(fER4).*

6   Example of Peterson's Logical Syllogism

In this section we will demonstrate application of Peterson's rules. For this purpose, we will consider the following syllogism of Figure-I:

PTT-I

Almost all M are P

Most S are M
***
Most S are P

This syllogism is invalid. We will demonstrate its invalidity on Venn's diagram.

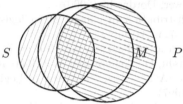

We can observe that the fuzzy set P is denoted by ▨ and the fuzzy set S is denoted by ▤ . Furthermore, we can observe that if Almost all M are in P and also Most S are in M then the resulting part, which is created by overlapping both colors, does not represent a part Most S are P. The syllogism is invalid.

Verification of the invalidity of the above syllogism using extended Peterson's rules is the following:

Rule (fER1): $DI(M, \mathcal{P}_1) = \text{Inf Supp}(Ex\,Bi_{\mathcal{P}_1}) > 0.5$ and $DI(M, \mathcal{P}_2) = 0$. So the Rule (fER1) is not satisfied.
Rule (fER2a): Furthermore, $DI(S, \mathcal{P}_2) = \text{inf Supp}(Bi\,Ve_{\mathcal{P}_2}) > 0.5$ and $DI(S, \mathcal{C}) = \text{inf Supp}(Bi\,Ve_{\mathcal{P}_2})$ which means that $DI(S, \mathcal{C}) \leq DI(S, \mathcal{P}_2)$. So Rule (fER2a) is satisfied.
Rule (fER2b): $DI(P, \mathcal{P}_1) = 0$ and $DI(P, \mathcal{C}) = 0$. So $DI(P, \mathcal{C}) \leq DI(P, \mathcal{P}_1)$ and Rule (fER2b) is satisfied.
Rule (fER3): it is trivially fulfilled.
Rule (fER4): it is trivially fulfilled.

*We can observe that the syllogism **PTT-I** is not valid because the Rule (fER1) is not satisfied. However, if we replace the quantifier "Almost all" with the universal quantifier "All" in the major premise, then Rule (fER1) will be fulfilled and the syllogism becomes valid. The reason for changing the quantifier in the first figure is based on the position of the middle formula in the antecedent because then* $DI(M, \mathcal{P}_1) = 1$.

7   Conclusion

In this article we returned to the extended Peterson's rules for checking validity of logical syllogisms. We proved that every syllogism of Figure-I with the intermediate quantifiers "all, almost all, most, many, some" is valid if and only if it satisfies Peterson's extended rules. A detailed elaboration of this theorem for all figures will appear in a journal.

Further work will be focused on extension of the rules to syllogisms with other kinds of intermediate quantifiers, namely "a few, several, a little". Furthermore, we will try to generalize the rules to syllogisms with arbitrary intermediate quantifiers.

References

1. Cignoli, R.L.O., D'Ottaviano, I.M.L., Mundici, D.: Algebraic Foundations of Many-valued Reasoning. Kluwer, Dordrecht (2000)
2. Gainor, J.: What is distribution in categorical syllogisms (2011). https://www.youtube.com/watch?v=7_Y-Bxr4apQ
3. Hájek, P.: Metamathematics of Fuzzy Logic. Kluwer, Dordrecht (1998)
4. Keenan, E.L., Westerståhl, D.: Generalized quantifiers in linguistics and logic. In: Benthem, J.V., Meulen, A.T. (eds.), Handbook of Logic and Language, Elsevier Ch. 15, pp. 837–893 (1997)
5. Mostowski, A.: On a generalization of quantifiers. Fundam. Math. **44**, 12–36 (1957)
6. Murinová, P.: Graded structures of opposition in fuzzy natural logic. Log. Univers. **265**, 495–522 (2020)
7. Murinová, P., Novák, V.: A formal theory of generalized intermediate syllogisms. Fuzzy Sets Syst. **186**, 47–80 (2013)
8. Murinová, P., Novák, V.: The structure of generalized intermediate syllogisms. Fuzzy Sets Syst. **247**, 18–37 (2014)
9. Murinová, P., Novák, V.: The theory of intermediate quantifiers in fuzzy natural logic revisited and the model of "many." Fuzzy Sets Syst. **388**, 56–89 (2020)
10. Novák, V.: A comprehensive theory of trichotomous evaluative linguistic expressions. Fuzzy Sets Syst. **159**(22), 2939–2969 (2008)
11. Novák, V.: A formal theory of intermediate quantifiers. Fuzzy Sets Syst. **159**(10), 1229–1246 (2008)
12. Novák, V., Murinová, P., Ferbas, P.: Formal analysis of Peterson's rules for checking validity of syllogisms with intermediate quantifiers. Int. J. Approx. Reason. **150**, 122–138 (2022)
13. Novák, V., Perfilieva, I., Dvořák, A.: Insight into Fuzzy Modeling. Wiley & Sons, Hoboken, New Jersey (2016)
14. Novák, V., Perfilieva, I., Močkoř, J.: Mathematical Principles of Fuzzy Logic. Kluwer, Boston (1999)
15. Peterson, P.: Intermediate Quantifiers. Logic, linguistics, and Aristotelian semantics. Ashgate, Aldershot (2000)

From Graded Aristotle's Hexagon to Graded Peterson's Hexagon of Opposition in Fuzzy Natural Logic

Petra Murinová[1(✉)] and Stefania Boffa[2]

[1] Institute for Research and Applications of Fuzzy Modeling, NSC IT4Innovations, University of Ostrava, 30. dubna 22, 701 03 Ostrava 1, Czech Republic
petra.murinova@osu.cz
[2] Universitá degli Studi di Milano-Bicocca, DISCo, Viale Sarca 336, 20126 Milan, Italy
stefania.boffa@unimib.it

Abstract. In this publication we will first focus on the construction of the graded Aristotle's hexagon in fuzzy natural logic (see [8]). The main goal will be to mathematically formulate a new definition of the contradictory property. In past publications, this definition was based on delta operation, which gave very unnatural results. We will show that the contradictory property can behave more naturally. In the end, we will present another extension possibility in the form of a graded Peterson hexagon with fuzzy intermediate quantifiers.

Keywords: Graded Aristotle's hexagon of opposition · Fuzzy intermediate quantifiers · Graded Peterson's hexagon of opposition · Fuzzy natural logic

1 Introduction

This publication will focus on the construction of the graded Aristotle's and Peterson's hexagons of opposition in fuzzy natural logic as an extension of graded Aristotle's square of opposition. The Aristotle's square of opposition ([20]) was studied in many publications. Note that the Aristotle's square of opposition is fulfilled with *presupposition* only. The reader can find further details about the necessity of presupposition in [9]. In [15,19]), the authors draw a crucial distinction between the "classical" Aristotelian square of opposition and the "modern" duality one based on the concepts of inner and outer negation. Another extension using intermediate quantifiers, which in terms of meaning are just among the classic quantifiers, was developed first by Thompson by adding the

OP PIK CZ.01.1.02/0.0/0.0/17147/0020575 AI-Met4Laser: Consortium for industrial research and development of new applications of laser technologies using artificial intelligence methods (10/2020–6/2023), of the Ministry of Industry and Trade of the Czech Republic.

S. Massanet et al. (Eds.): EUSFLAT 2023/AGOP 2023, LNCS 14069, pp. 369–380, 2023.
https://doi.org/10.1007/978-3-031-39965-7_31

intermediate quantifiers "Almost all" and "Many" (see [18]). The final form was later proposed by Peterson (see [16]), who introduced and philosophically explained the position of the basic five intermediate quantifiers ("All", "Almost all", "Most", "Many" and "Some") in the square. Graded version of both squares was syntactically and also semantically analyzed in [9].

Béziau in [3] suggested to extend square of opposition into a hexagon. This technically means to add two new formulas **U** and **Y** that are defined as disjunction of the two top corners of the square and conjunction of the two bottom corners:

$$\mathbf{U} = \mathbf{A} \vee \mathbf{E} : \text{All or No } B \text{ are } A \tag{1}$$

$$\mathbf{Y} = \mathbf{I} \wedge \mathbf{O} : \text{Some but Not All } B \text{ are } A. \tag{2}$$

We obtain Aristotelian hexagon as follows[1]:

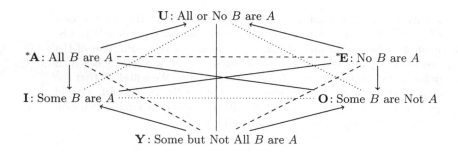

In [17], we can find differences between the Aristotelian hexagon and the Duality hexagon. A more complex 3D generalization of the hexagon was proposed by in ([6,14]). Polygons of opposition with quantifier-based operators in fuzzy formal concept analysis were studied in [4].

Another motivation of this publication is the introduction of new forms of fuzzy intermediate quantifiers based on the graded Peterson's square of opposition and to construct graded Peterson's hexagon of opposition. The new construction leads us to the idea of using natural language to describe new properties.

A few people are vaccinated against COVID 19 and a few people are not vaccinated against COVID 19

---

[1] The diagonal lines represent contradictories, the formulas **A** and **E** are contraries, **A** and **E** entail **U**, while **Y** entails both formulas **I** as well as **O**. It is interesting to see that the logical hexagon obtains three Aristotle's squares of opposition, namely, **AEIO**, **AYOU** and **EYUI**.

2 Preliminaries

2.1 Formal Definition of fuzzy Intermediate Quantifiers

In this paper, we will work with the fuzzy type theory (the higher-order fuzzy logic) and the theory of evaluative linguistic expressions. All the details can be found in the papers [9]. Recall that the basic syntactical objects of L-FTT are classical, namely the concepts of type and formula (cf. [1]).

The semantics is defined using the concept of general model in which the type o of truth values is assigned a linearly ordered MV_Δ-algebra which is an MV-algebra extended by the delta operation (see [5,13]). In this paper we will consider only models whose algebra of truth values forms the standard Łukasiewicz MV_Δ-algebra

$$\mathcal{L} = \langle [0,1], \vee, \wedge, \otimes, \rightarrow, 0, 1, \Delta \rangle. \tag{3}$$

The following special formulas are important in our theory:

$$\Upsilon_{oo} \equiv \lambda z_o \cdot \neg\Delta(\neg z_o), \qquad \text{(nonzero truth value)}$$

$$\hat{\Upsilon}_{oo} \equiv \lambda z_o \cdot \neg\Delta(z_o \vee \neg z_o). \qquad \text{(general truth value)}$$

Thus, $\mathcal{M}(\Upsilon(A_o)) = 1$ iff $\mathcal{M}(A_o) > 0$, and $\mathcal{M}(\hat{\Upsilon}(A_o)) = 1$ iff $\mathcal{M}(A_o) \in (0,1)$ holds in any model $\mathcal{M}$.

The main change is the introduction of the so-called cut of a fuzzy set. We define the special operation "cut of a fuzzy set" for given fuzzy sets $y, z \in$ Form$_{o\alpha}$: $y|z \equiv \lambda x_\alpha \cdot zx \& \Delta(\Upsilon(zx) \Rightarrow (yx \equiv zx))$.

Lemma 1 [9]. *Let $\mathcal{M}$ be a model and p an assignment such that $B = \mathcal{M}_p(y) \subseteq M_\alpha, Z = \mathcal{M}_p(z) \subseteq M_\alpha$. Then for any $m \in M_\alpha$*

$$\mathcal{M}_p(y|z)(m) = (B|Z)(m) = \begin{cases} B(m), & \text{if } B(m) = Z(m), \\ 0 & \text{otherwise.} \end{cases}$$

As we can see in the Lemma 1 by this operation we pick elements from B exactly in their degree of membership or we do not pick them at all.

The following completeness theorem will be often used below.

Theorem 1 ([10]).

(a) A theory T is consistent iff it has a general model $\mathcal{M}$.
(b) For every theory T and a formula A_o, $T \vdash A_o$ iff $T \models A_o$.

2.2 Theories of Evaluative Linguistic Expressions

The main constituent of FNL is the theory of evaluative linguistic expressions. These are special natural language expressions such as *small, medium, big, very short, more or less deep, quite roughly strong, extremely high*, etc. A formal theory of their semantics was introduced in [11].

The evaluative linguistic expression is represented in the theory T^{Ev} by one of the following formulas:

$$Sm\,\nu, Me\,\nu, Bi\,\nu, \nu \tag{4}$$

where ν is a hedge. For example, $Sm\,Ve$ is a formula construing the evaluative expression "very small".

2.3   Fuzzy Intermediate Quantifiers

Definition 1 (Fuzzy intermediate quantifiers, [9]). *Let Ev be a formula representing an evaluative expression, x be variables and A, B, z be formulas. Let μ be a fuzzy measure. Then either of the following formulas construes the sentence "Quantifier B's are A".*

$$(Q_{Ev}^{\forall}\,x)(B, A) \equiv (\exists z)[(\forall x)((B|z)\,x \Rightarrow Ax) \wedge Ev((\mu B)(B|z))), \tag{5}$$

$$(Q_{Ev}^{\exists}\,x)(B, A) \equiv (\exists z)[(\exists x)((B|z)x \wedge Ax) \wedge Ev((\mu B)(B|z)). \tag{6}$$

If we put instead of Ev concrete evaluative linguistic expressions we obtain the following fuzzy intermediate quantifiers:

$$\textbf{A: All } B\text{'s are } A := (Q_{Bi\Delta}^{\forall}x)(B, A),$$

$$\textbf{E: No } B\text{'s are } A := (Q_{Bi\Delta}^{\forall}x)(B, \neg A),$$

$$\textbf{P: Almost all } B\text{'s are } A := (Q_{Bi\,Ex}^{\forall}x)(B, A)$$

$$\textbf{B: Almost all } B\text{'s are not } A := (Q_{Bi\,Ex}^{\forall}x)(B, \neg A)$$

$$\textbf{T: Most } B\text{'s are } A := (Q_{Bi\,Ve}^{\forall}x)(B, A)$$

$$\textbf{D: Most } B\text{'s are not } A := (Q_{Bi\,Ve}^{\forall}x)(B, \neg A)$$

$$\textbf{K: Many } B\text{'s are } A := (Q_{\neg\,Sm}^{\forall}x)(B, A)$$

$$\textbf{G: Many } B\text{'s are not } A := (Q_{\neg\,Sm}^{\forall}x)(B, \neg A)$$

$$\textbf{F: A few (A little) } B\text{'s are } A := (Q_{Sm\,Si}^{\forall}x)(B, A)$$

$$\textbf{V: A few (A little) } B\text{'s are not } A := (Q_{Sm\,Si}^{\forall}x)(B, \neg A)$$

$$\textbf{S: Several } B\text{'s are } A := (Q_{Sm\,Ve}^{\forall}x)(B, A)$$

$$\textbf{Z: Several } B\text{'s are not } A := (Q_{Sm\,Ve}^{\forall}x)(B, \neg A)$$

$$\textbf{I: Some } B\text{'s are } A := (Q_{Bi\Delta}^{\exists}x)(B, A),$$

$$\textbf{O: Some } B\text{'s are not } A := (Q_{Bi\Delta}^{\exists}x)(B, \neg A).$$

In the following Theorem we will describe monotonic behavior of fuzzy intermediate quantifiers.

Theorem 2 [12]. *Let $\boldsymbol{A}, \ldots, \boldsymbol{O}$ are intermediate quantifiers. Then the following set of implications is provable in T^{IQ} (theory of intermediate quantifiers):*

1. $T^{IQ} \vdash \boldsymbol{A} \Rightarrow \boldsymbol{P}, T^{IQ} \vdash \boldsymbol{P} \Rightarrow \boldsymbol{T}, T^{IQ} \vdash \boldsymbol{T} \Rightarrow \boldsymbol{K},$
   $T^{IQ} \vdash \boldsymbol{K} \Rightarrow \boldsymbol{F}, T^{IQ} \vdash \boldsymbol{F} \Rightarrow \boldsymbol{S}, T^{IQ} \vdash \boldsymbol{S} \Rightarrow \boldsymbol{I}.$
2. $T^{IQ} \vdash \boldsymbol{E} \Rightarrow \boldsymbol{B}, T^{IQ} \vdash \boldsymbol{B} \Rightarrow \boldsymbol{D}, T^{IQ} \vdash \boldsymbol{D} \Rightarrow \boldsymbol{G},$
   $T^{IQ} \vdash \boldsymbol{G} \Rightarrow \boldsymbol{V}, T^{IQ} \vdash \boldsymbol{V} \Rightarrow \boldsymbol{Z}, T^{IQ} \vdash \boldsymbol{Z} \Rightarrow \boldsymbol{O}.$

By ***A, *E, *P, *B, *T, *D, *K, *G, *I, *O** we denote fuzzy intermediate quantifiers with presupposition (for precise definition see [9]).

3   From Graded Aristotle's Square to Graded Aristotle's Hexagon

Before the actual construction of the graded Aristotle's hexagon of opposition, let us first recall the basic formulas that form the graded Aristotle's square of opposition. At this point, we will not recall and discuss in detail the necessity of presupposition. We refer the reader to the publication [9].

The graded Aristotle's square of opposition in Ł-FTT works with the following four formulas with presupposition:

*A :All B are A	$(\forall x)(Bx \Rightarrow Ax)\,\&\,(\exists x)Bx,$	(7)
E :No B are A	$(\forall x)(Bx \Rightarrow \neg Ax),$	(8)
I :Some B are A	$(\exists x)(Bx \wedge Ax),$	(9)
*O :Some B are not A	$(\exists x)(Bx \wedge \neg Ax)\,\nabla\,\neg(\exists x)Bx.$	(10)

We follow the classical approach of Béziau approach, who in [2,3] suggested to extend a square of opposition into the hexagon of opposition. This technically means to add two new generalized formulas **U** and **Y** that are defined as the **strong** disjunction of the two top corners of the square and the **strong** conjunction of the two bottom corners:

We define the new general formulas as follows:

$$\boldsymbol{U} := \boldsymbol{A} \,\nabla\, \boldsymbol{E} \quad \text{All or No } B \text{ are } A. \tag{11}$$

$$\boldsymbol{Y} := \boldsymbol{I}\,\&\,\boldsymbol{O} \quad \text{Some but Not All } B \text{ are } A. \tag{12}$$

3.1   Generalized Definition that Form Graded Structures

In this subsection we will focus on the mathematical formulation of the definitions that form the graded Aristotle square, graded Peterson square as well as their extension to hexagons of opposition.

Let us recall at this point that the first result of this publication is the presentation of a modified definition of the contradictory property, which in previous publications was designed using the delta logical operation (see [7]). We first recall the original definition of the contradictory property with a concrete example of the graded Aristotle's hexagon and explain to the reader the motivation of the new definition which will be introduced below. Other definitions of other properties used in example below can be found in Definition 3.

Definition 2. *Let T be a consistent theory of Ł-FTT, $\mathcal{M} \models T$ be its model.*

- P_1 *and* P_2 *are* contradictories *in the model* $\mathcal{M}$ *if*
  - $\mathcal{M}(\Delta P_1) \otimes \mathcal{M}(\Delta P_2)) = \mathcal{M}(\bot)$
  - $\mathcal{M}(\Delta P_1) \oplus \mathcal{M}(\Delta P_2)) = \mathcal{M}(\top)$

They are contraries *in the theory* T *if*
$T \vdash \neg(\Delta P_1 \,\&\, \Delta P_2)$ *and* $T \vdash \Delta P_1 \,\nabla\, \Delta P_2$. *By completeness, this is equivalent to semantic definition above for every model* $\mathcal{M} \models T$.

Example 1. Let us consider a model $\mathcal{M} \models T^{\text{IQ}}$ such that $\mathcal{M}(\mathbf{A}) = a > 0$ (e.g., $a = 0.2$). Since $\mathbf{A}, \mathbf{E}$ are contraries, we have $\mathcal{M}(\mathbf{E}) = e \leq 1 - a$. We know that $\mathcal{M}(\Delta \mathbf{A}) = 0$ and so $\mathcal{M}(\Delta \mathbf{O}) = 1$ because $\mathcal{M}(\Delta \mathbf{A}) \otimes \mathcal{M}(\Delta \mathbf{O}) = 0$ and $\mathcal{M}(\Delta \mathbf{A}) \oplus \mathcal{M}(\Delta \mathbf{O}) = 1$ which means that $\mathbf{A}$ and $\mathbf{O}$ are contradictories. The same is fulfilled for $\mathbf{U}$ and $\mathbf{Y}$ Consequently, $\mathbf{O}$ is subaltern of $\mathbf{E}$.

The $\mathbf{I}$ is subaltern of $\mathbf{A}$ and thus $\mathcal{M}(\mathbf{I}) = i \geq 0.2$. However, $\mathbf{I}$ is contradictory with $\mathbf{E}$ and so $\mathcal{M}(\mathbf{I}) = i = 1$. Finally, $\mathbf{I}$ is sub-contrary with $\mathbf{O}$ because $\mathcal{M}(\mathbf{O} \,\nabla\, \mathbf{I}) = 1$ and $\mathbf{I}$ is subaltern of $\mathbf{A}$. These results are summarized in the following scheme (Fig. 1):

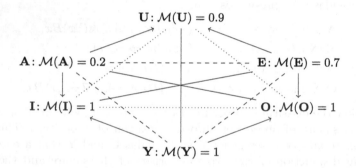

Fig. 1. Graded Aristotle's hexagon of opposition

From the example we can observe that the quantifiers U *and* Y *are contradictory and yet they can be true to quite a large degree, which is unnatural.*

Below we present an overview of all mathematical definitions forming graded structures of opposition, including a modified definition of the contradictory property.

Definition 3. *Let T be a consistent theory of Ł-FTT, $\mathcal{M} \models T$ be its model and $P_1, P_2 \in \text{Form}_o$ be closed formulas of type o.*

- P_1 *and* P_2 *are* contraries *in the model* $\mathcal{M}$ *if*

$$\mathcal{M}(P_1) \otimes \mathcal{M}(P_2) = 0. \qquad (13)$$

They are contraries *in the theory* T *if* $T \vdash \neg(P_1 \,\&\, P_2)$. *By completeness, this is equivalent to (13) for every model* $\mathcal{M} \models T$.

– P_1 and P_2 are sub-contraries in the model $\mathcal{M}$ if

$$\mathcal{M}(P_1) \oplus \mathcal{M}(P_2) = 1. \tag{14}$$

They are sub-contraries in the theory T if $T \vdash (P_1 \nabla P_2)$. By completeness, this is equivalent to (14) for every model $\mathcal{M} \models T$.

– P_1 and P_2 are contradictories in the model $\mathcal{M}$ if both

$$\mathcal{M}(P_1) \otimes \mathcal{M}(P_2) = 0 \text{ as well as } \mathcal{M}(P_1) \oplus \mathcal{M}(P_2) = 1. \tag{15}$$

They are contradictories in the theory T if both $T \vdash P_1 \,\&\, P_2 \equiv \perp$ as well as $T \vdash P_1 \nabla P_2$. By completeness, this means that (15) hold for every model $\mathcal{M} \models T$.

– The formula P_2 is a subaltern of P_1 and the formula P_1 is a superaltern of P_2 in the model $\mathcal{M}$ if

$$\mathcal{M}(P_1) \leq \mathcal{M}(P_2). \tag{16}$$

It is subaltern in the theory T if $T \vdash P_1 \Rightarrow P_2$. By completeness, this means that the inequality (16) holds true in every model $\mathcal{M} \models T$.

3.2   Formal Proofs of Properties with A,E,I,O

Theorem 3. The formulas *A and *E are contraries in T^{IQ}.

Proof. It follows from the following provable formula in T^{IQ}:

$$T^{IQ} \;\vdash\; (\forall x)(Bx \;\Rightarrow\; Ax) \,\&\, (\forall x)(Bx \;\Rightarrow\; \neg Ax) \;\Rightarrow\; ((\exists x)(Bx)^2 \;\Rightarrow\; \perp).$$

By the provable property $\vdash (\exists x)(Bx)^2 \equiv (\exists x)Bx \,\&\, (\exists x)Bx$ we obtain that

$$T^{IQ} \;\vdash\; (\forall x)(Bx \;\Rightarrow\; Ax) \,\&\, (\exists x)Bx \,\&\, (\forall x)(Bx \;\Rightarrow\; \neg Ax) \,\&\, (\exists x)Bx \;\Rightarrow\; \perp$$

which is equivalent to $T^{IQ} \vdash \neg(\text{*A} \,\&\, \text{*E})$.

Theorem 4. The formulas *I and *O are sub-contraries in T^{IQ}.

Proof. Analogously as in Theorem 3.

Lemma 2. The following is true:

(a) $T^{IQ} \vdash \neg(\text{*A} \,\&\, O)$, $T^{IQ} \vdash A \nabla \text{*O}$, $T^{IQ} \vdash \neg(\text{*E} \,\&\, I)$, $T^{IQ} \vdash E \nabla \text{*I}$

Proof. (a) By properties of Ł-FTT we have

$$T^{IQ} \vdash ((Bx \Rightarrow Ax) \,\&\, Bx) \Rightarrow (Bx \wedge Ax).$$

By weakening and applying of transitivity we obtain

$$T^{IQ} \vdash ((Bx \Rightarrow Ax) \,\&\, Bx) \Rightarrow Ax. \tag{17}$$

By $T^{IQ} \vdash (Bx \wedge \neg Ax) \Rightarrow \neg Ax$ and from (17) we get

$$T^{IQ} \vdash (((Bx \Rightarrow Ax) \,\&\, Bx) \,\&\, (Bx \wedge \neg Ax)) \Rightarrow \perp.$$

By quantifiers properties we obtain

$$T^{IQ} \vdash \neg(((\forall x)(Bx \Rightarrow Ax) \,\&\, (\exists x)Bx) \,\&\, (\exists x)(Bx \wedge \neg Ax)).$$

Theorem 5 (contradictories). *The following is true:*

(a) the formulas *A *and* O *are contradictories in* T^{IQ},
(b) the formulas *E *and* I *are contradictories in* T^{IQ}.

Proof It follows from Lemma (2).

3.3   Formal Proofs of Properties of A,E,Y

Theorem 6. *The following is true:*

(a) the formulas *A *and* Y *are contraries in* T^{IQ}.
(b) the formulas *E *and* Y *are contraries in* T^{IQ}.

Proof. (a) From Lemma 2(a) by the definition of negation and by weakening of &
we obtain $T^{IQ} \vdash (\text{*}\mathbf{A}\,\&\,(\mathbf{I}\,\&\,\mathbf{O})) \Rightarrow \bot$. Finally we conclude that $T^{IQ} \vdash \neg(\text{*}\mathbf{A}\,\&\,\mathbf{Y})$.

3.4   Formal Proofs of Properties of U,O,I

Theorem 7 (sub-contraries). *The following is true:*

(a) the formulas U *and* *O *are sub-contraries in* T^{IQ}.
(b) the formulas U *and* *I *are sub-contraries in* T^{IQ}.

Proof. (a) From Lemma 2(a) and by $T^{IQ} \vdash (\mathbf{A}\,\nabla\,\text{*}\mathbf{O}) \Rightarrow (\mathbf{E}\,\nabla\,(\mathbf{A}\,\nabla\,\text{*}\mathbf{O}))$ and by
associativity of ∇ we conclude that $T^{IQ} \vdash \mathbf{U}\,\nabla\,\text{*}\mathbf{O}$.

3.5   Formal Proofs of Properties of Y,U

Theorem 8. *The following is true:*

– the formulas U *and* Y *are contradictories in* T^{IQ}.

Proof. By weakening of $\wedge$ and by quantifiers properties we have

$$T^{IQ} \vdash \underbrace{(\exists x)(Bx \wedge Ax)}_{\mathbf{I}}\,\&\,\underbrace{(\exists x)(Bx \wedge \neg Ax)}_{\mathbf{O}} \Rightarrow \bot \tag{18}$$

Once more by weakening of & we obtain

$$T^{IQ} \vdash (\mathbf{A}\,\nabla\,\mathbf{E})\,\&\,(\mathbf{I}\,\&\,\mathbf{O}) \Rightarrow (\mathbf{I}\,\&\,\mathbf{O})$$

From this, applying of (18) and by transitivity we conclude that $T^{IQ} \vdash \neg(\mathbf{U}\,\&\,\mathbf{Y})$.
The second property $T^{IQ} \vdash \mathbf{U}\,\nabla\,\mathbf{Y}$ can be proved analogously.

3.6 Formal Proofs of Properties of A,E,I,O,U,Y

Lemma 3. *The following is provable:*

(a) $T^{IQ} \vdash \mathbf{A} \Rightarrow \mathbf{U}$, $T^{IQ} \vdash \mathbf{E} \Rightarrow \mathbf{U}$, $T^{IQ} \vdash \mathbf{Y} \Rightarrow \mathbf{O}$, $T^{IQ} \vdash \mathbf{Y} \Rightarrow \mathbf{I}$.

Proof. All properties follow from the following provable formulas: $T^{IQ} \vdash (Ax \,\&\, Bx) \Rightarrow Ax$ and $T^{IQ} \vdash Ax \Rightarrow (Ax \,\nabla\, Bx)$.

Theorem 9 (sub-alterns). *The following is true:*

(a) *the formula* **A** *is superaltern of* **U**, *the formula* **E** *is superaltern of* **U**,
(b) *the formula* **Y** *is superaltern of* **O**, *the formula* **Y** *is superaltern of* **I**.

Proof. It follows from Lemma 3.

Example 2. Let us consider the same model $\mathcal{M} \models T^{IQ}$ as in the previous example. We will discuss mainly the property of contradictory. The formula **A** is contradictory with **O** as well as **E** with **I**. So $\mathcal{M}(A) \otimes \mathcal{M}(O) = 0$ and $\mathcal{M}(E) \oplus \mathcal{M}(I) = 1$, The same is fulfilled for **U** with **Y**. Below we can see the concrete example (Fig. 2).

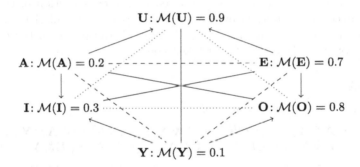

Fig. 2. Modified graded Aristotle's hexagon of opposition

From the above modified graded hexagon, we can see that the new quantifiers U and Y satisfy the contradictory property. At the same time, the new definition of the contradictory property gives more natural interpretations of the quantifiers representing graded Aristotle square and hexagon of opposition.

4   Future Direction: From Graded Peterson's Square to Graded Peterson's Hexagon

In this part of the article we outline another idea to continue studying the graded Peterson's hexagon of opposition.

We propose new forms of fuzzy intermediate quantifiers as follows:

$$\mathbf{U}_{Bi\ Ex} := \text{Almost all } B \text{ are } A \text{ or Almost all } B \text{ are not } A \qquad (19)$$

$$\mathbf{U}_{Bi\ Ve} := \text{Most } B \text{ are } A \text{ or Most } B \text{ are not } A \qquad (20)$$

$$\mathbf{Y}_{\neg\ Sm} := \text{Many } B \text{ are } A \text{ and Many } B \text{ are not } A \qquad (21)$$

$$\mathbf{Y}_{Sm\ Si} := \text{A few } B \text{ are } A \text{ and A few } B \text{ are not } A \qquad (22)$$

$$\mathbf{Y}_{Sm\ Ve} := \text{Several } B \text{ are } A \text{ and Several } B \text{ are not } A. \qquad (23)$$

Below we present an overview of all new quantifiers, which are always formed using one positive and one negative quantifier.

- $\mathbf{U}_{Bi\ Ex} := \mathbf{P}\nabla\mathbf{B}, \mathbf{U}_{Bi\ Ve} := \mathbf{T}\nabla\mathbf{D}$
- $\mathbf{Y}_{\neg\ Sm} := \mathbf{K}\,\&\,\mathbf{G}, \mathbf{Y}_{Sm\ Si} := \mathbf{F}\,\&\,\mathbf{V}, \mathbf{Y}_{Sm\ Ve} := \mathbf{S}\,\&\,\mathbf{Z}.$

New forms of fuzzy intermediate quantifiers offers the idea of working with new natural language expressions.

4.1 Selected Properties of Fuzzy Intermediate Quantifiers

In this subsection, we will focus on formally proving selected properties related to new fuzzy intermediate quantifiers. We will also mention the results that have already been proven and are closely related to the construction of the graded hexagon. Since we are limited by the number of pages, we will give an example of a graded Peterson hexagon without showing all the proofs of the individual properties for the sake of clarity for the reader.

Contraries

Lemma 4. *The following is provable:*

(a) $T^{IQ} \vdash \neg(^*\mathbf{A}\,\&\,\mathbf{Y}_{Sm\ Ve}),\ T^{IQ} \vdash \neg(^*\mathbf{A}\,\&\,\mathbf{Y}_{Sm\ Si}),\ T^{IQ} \vdash \neg(^*\mathbf{A}\,\&\,\mathbf{Y}_{\neg\ Sm})$

(d) $T^{IQ} \vdash \neg(^*\mathbf{E}\,\&\,\mathbf{Y}_{Sm\ Ve}), T^{IQ} \vdash \neg(^*\mathbf{E}\,\&\,\mathbf{Y}_{Sm\ Si}),\ T^{IQ} \vdash \neg(^*\mathbf{E}\,\&\,\mathbf{Y}_{\neg\ Sm})$

Proof. ad) (a) Using Lemma 2(a) we have that $T^{IQ} \vdash {}^*\mathbf{A}\,\&\,(\mathbf{I}\,\&\,\mathbf{O}) \Rightarrow \bot$. Then by Theorem 2 we know that $T^{IQ} \vdash \mathbf{S}\,\&\,\mathbf{Z} \Rightarrow \mathbf{I}\,\&\,\mathbf{O}$. From this we have

$$T^{IQ} \vdash {}^*\mathbf{A}\,\&\,(\mathbf{S}\,\&\,\mathbf{Z}) \Rightarrow {}^*\mathbf{A}\,\&\,(\mathbf{I}\,\&\,\mathbf{O}).$$

Finally, by the transitivity we obtain $T^{IQ} \vdash {}^*\mathbf{A}\,\&\,(\mathbf{S}\,\&\,\mathbf{Z}) \Rightarrow \bot$.

Other properties can be proved analogously.

5   Conclusion

In this paper, we build on previous results concerning graded structures of oppositions. The first main result was to propose a modified definition of the contradictory property, which already gives the expected results for the considered fuzzy intermediate quantifiers. Furthermore, we focused on the introduction of new forms of fuzzy intermediate quantifiers. Properties of the new forms of intermediate quantifiers are shown in Table 1.

Table 1. Graded Peterson's hexagon of opposition with "A few" and "Several"

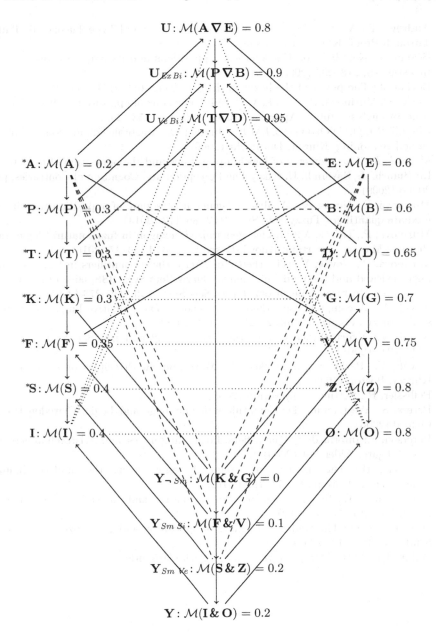

$$\text{U}: \mathcal{M}(\mathbf{A}\nabla\mathbf{E}) = 0.8$$

$$\text{U}_{Ex\,Bi}: \mathcal{M}(\mathbf{P}\nabla\mathbf{B}) = 0.9$$

$$\text{U}_{Ve\,Bi}: \mathcal{M}(\mathbf{T}\nabla\mathbf{D}) = 0.95$$

$${}^{*}\mathbf{A}: \mathcal{M}(\mathbf{A}) = 0.2 \qquad\qquad {}^{*}\mathbf{E}: \mathcal{M}(\mathbf{E}) = 0.6$$

$${}^{*}\mathbf{P}: \mathcal{M}(\mathbf{P}) = 0.3 \qquad\qquad {}^{*}\mathbf{B}: \mathcal{M}(\mathbf{B}) = 0.6$$

$${}^{*}\mathbf{T}: \mathcal{M}(\mathbf{T}) = 0.3 \qquad\qquad {}^{*}\mathbf{D}: \mathcal{M}(\mathbf{D}) = 0.65$$

$${}^{*}\mathbf{K}: \mathcal{M}(\mathbf{K}) = 0.3 \qquad\qquad {}^{*}\mathbf{G}: \mathcal{M}(\mathbf{G}) = 0.7$$

$${}^{*}\mathbf{F}: \mathcal{M}(\mathbf{F}) = 0.35 \qquad\qquad {}^{*}\mathbf{V}: \mathcal{M}(\mathbf{V}) = 0.75$$

$${}^{*}\mathbf{S}: \mathcal{M}(\mathbf{S}) = 0.4 \qquad\qquad {}^{*}\mathbf{Z}: \mathcal{M}(\mathbf{Z}) = 0.8$$

$$\mathbf{I}: \mathcal{M}(\mathbf{I}) = 0.4 \qquad\qquad \emptyset: \mathcal{M}(\mathbf{O}) = 0.8$$

$$\mathbf{Y}_{\neg\,Sm}: \mathcal{M}(\mathbf{K}\,\&\,\mathbf{G}) = 0$$

$$\mathbf{Y}_{Sm\,Si}: \mathcal{M}(\mathbf{F}\,\&\,\mathbf{V}) = 0.1$$

$$\mathbf{Y}_{Sm\,Ve}: \mathcal{M}(\mathbf{S}\,\&\,\mathbf{Z}) = 0.2$$

$$\mathbf{Y}: \mathcal{M}(\mathbf{I}\,\&\,\mathbf{O}) = 0.2$$

References

1. Andrews, P.: An Introduction to Mathematical Logic and Type Theory: To Truth Through Proof. Kluwer, Dordrecht (2002)
2. Béziau, J.: New light on the square of oppositions and its nameless corner. Log. Investig. **10**, 218–233 (2003)
3. Béziau, J.: The power of the hexagon. Log. Univers. **6**(1–2), 1–43 (2012)
4. Boffa, S., Murinová, P., Novák, V.: Graded polygons of opposition in fuzzy formal concept analysis. Int. J. Approx. Reason. **132**, 128–153 (2021)
5. Cignoli, R.L.O., D'Ottaviano, I.M.L., Mundici, D.: Algebraic Foundations of Many-valued Reasoning. Kluwer, Dordrecht (2000)
6. Moretti, A.: The geometry of logical oppositions and the opposition of logic to it. In: Bianchi, I., Savaradi, U. (eds.) The Perception and Cognition of Contraries, pp. 20–60 (2009)
7. Murinová, P., Novák, V.: Analysis of generalized square of opposition with intermediate quantifiers. Fuzzy Sets Syst. **242**, 89–113 (2014)
8. Murinová, P., Novák, V.: Graded generalized hexagon in fuzzy natural logic. Inf. Process. Manag. Uncertain. Knowl.-Based Syst. **611**, 36–47 (2016)
9. Murinová, P., Novák, V.: The theory of intermediate quantifiers in fuzzy natural logic revisited and the model of "many." Fuzzy Sets Syst. **388**, 56–89 (2020)
10. Novák, V.: On fuzzy type theory. Fuzzy Sets Syst. **149**, 235–273 (2005)
11. Novák, V.: A comprehensive theory of trichotomous evaluative linguistic expressions. Fuzzy Sets Syst. **159**(22), 2939–2969 (2008)
12. Novák, V.: A formal theory of intermediate quantifiers. Fuzzy Sets Syst. **159**(10), 1229–1246 (2008)
13. Novák, V., Perfilieva, I., Močkoř, J.: Mathematical Principles of Fuzzy Logic. Kluwer, Boston (1999)
14. Pellissier, R.: Setting n-opposition (2008)
15. Peters, S., Westerståhl, D.: Quantifiers in Language and Logic. Claredon Press, Oxford (2006)
16. Peterson, P.: Intermediate Quantifiers. Logic, Linguistics, and Aristotelian Semantics. Ashgate, Aldershot (2000)
17. Smesaert, H.: The classical aristotelian hexagon versus the modern duality hexagon. Log. Univers. **6**, 171–199 (2012)
18. Thompson, B.E.: Syllogisms using "few", "many" and "most." Notre Dame J. Form. Log. **23**, 75–84 (1982)
19. Westerståhl, D.: The traditional square of opposition and generalized quantifiers. Stud. Log. **2**, 1–18 (2008)
20. Wikipedia (2004). http://en.wikipedia.org/wiki/aristotle

Analysis of the Number of Valid Peterson's Syllogisms

Karel Fiala[1(⊠)] and Petra Murinová[2]

[1] University of Ostrava, 30. dubna 22, 701 03 Ostrava, Czech Republic
karel.fiala@osu.cz
[2] Institute for Research and Applications of Fuzzy Modeling,
NSC IT4Innovations, University of Ostrava, 30. dubna 22,
701 03 Ostrava 1, Czech Republic
petra.murinova@osu.cz

Abstract. This publication aims to continue the study of fuzzy Peterson's logical syllogisms with fuzzy intermediate quantifiers. The main idea of this article is not to formally or semantically prove the validity of syllogisms, as was the case in previous publications. The main idea is to find a mathematical formula by which we are able to derive the number of valid Peterson syllogisms based on the number of intermediate quantifiers.

Keywords: Peterson logical syllogisms · Fuzzy intermediate quantifiers · Fuzzy natural logic

1 Introduction

A syllogism is a kind of logical argument that applies deductive reasoning to arrive at a conclusion based on two propositions that are asserted or assumed to be true. Logical syllogisms were already addressed by Aristotle himself, whose work was followed up by several authors from the fields of philosophy, psychology, medicine, and other fields. In this publication, we will focus on the special forms of logical syllogisms that were first proposed by Thompson [15] and then continued by Peterson in his book [14]. Peterson devoted himself mainly to the study of the basic five intermediate quantifiers "All, Almost all, Most, Many, Some" and verified the validity of 105 logical syllogisms using Venn's diagrams. He thus followed the work of Thompson [15] and proposed 12 new non-trivial syllogisms with intermediate quantifiers in both premises.

This group of logical syllogisms belongs to the group of generalized quantifiers (see [3,5]). Another generalization came with the introduction of the concept of

Supported by OP PIK CZ.01.1.02/0.0/0.0/17147/0020575 AI-Met4Laser: Consortium for industrial research and development of new applications of laser technologies using artificial intelligence methods (10/2020–6/2023), of the Ministry of Industry and Trade of the Czech Republic.

S. Massanet et al. (Eds.): EUSFLAT 2023/AGOP 2023, LNCS 14069, pp. 381–392, 2023.
https://doi.org/10.1007/978-3-031-39965-7_32

fuzzy set, which was proposed by Zadeh already in 1965 [17]. Therefore, another group of authors [13,16] began to study fuzzy syllogisms of different types using different verification methods. Zadeh himself was already studying fuzzy intermediate quantifiers and related fuzzy logical syllogisms [18].

We followed Peterson's work in several other publications [2,6,7], where we first proposed mathematical definitions of the aforementioned quantifiers and later formally verified the validity of all 105 fuzzy logical syllogisms with fuzzy intermediate quantifiers.

As we stated above, in general, a logical syllogism assumes two premises and a conclusion derived from them. Based on the position of the middle formula, we are talking about four possible figures and assuming five quantifiers about 4000 possible forms of logical syllogisms.

In this publication, we will first discuss a mathematical formula proposed by Peterson for calculating the number of valid logical syllogisms given a known number of intermediate quantifiers. Furthermore, we will show that the proposed Peterson formula does not give the correct number of valid syllogisms in individual figures.

2 Preliminaries

2.1 The Algebraic Structure

We will assume for this work a linearly ordered MV_Δ-algebra $\mathcal{L}_\Delta = \langle L, \vee, \wedge, \otimes, \rightarrow, 0, 1, \Delta \rangle$. A special case is the standard Łukasiewicz MV_Δ-algebra $\mathcal{L}_\Delta^{Luk}$ with $L = [0,1]$, $a \otimes b = \max\{0, a+b-1\}$, $a \rightarrow b = \min\{1, 1-a+b\}$ and a unary operation $\Delta(a) = 1$ if $a = 1$ and $\Delta(a) = 0$ otherwise, $a, b \in [0,1]$ (see [1,12]). For the theory of intermediate quantifiers, we need a special operation called *cut of a fuzzy set B w.r.t. a fuzzy set Z* which is defined as follows: let M be a universum and $B, Z \subseteq M$. Then for any $u \in M$ the operation $B|Z$ "cuts" B is $B|Z(u) = B(u) = Z(u)$ if $B(u) = Z(u)$. Otherwise $(B|Z)(u) = 0$. If there is no such u then $B|Z = \emptyset$. The motivation and explanation for the introduction of this operation can be found in [8].

Let $\mathcal{M} \models T^{IQ}$ be a model of the theory T^{IQ}. If A is a formula then its interpretation $\mathcal{M}(A)$ is a fuzzy set $A \in \mathcal{F}(M)$. Precise definitions and other details of T^{IQ} can be found in [6,10].

2.2 Evaluative Linguistic Expressions

Natural language evaluation expressions are part of the mathematical definition of fuzzy intermediate quantifiers. We have already written several times about the theory of evaluative language expressions in previous publications. At this point, we will therefore only mention the necessary terms for this publication.

The theory of intermediate quantifiers is based on the theory of evaluative linguistic expressions that are expressions of natural language such as *very small, about medium, roughly big, very short, more or less deep, quite roughly strong, extremely high*, etc. The formal theory of their semantics and more details about this theory can be found in [9,11].

2.3   Mathematical Definition of Fuzzy Intermediate Quantifiers

Recall that fuzzy intermediate quantifiers are modeled by selected formulas of a special formal theory of L-FTT. These formulas express quantification over the universe represented by a fuzzy set whose size is characterized by a measure which was formally characterized in [8]. At this point, we will not present all the definitions of the theory of intermediate quantifiers (T^{IQ}) in detail. We refer the reader to previous publications.

Let us recall that an intermediate quantifier of type $\langle 1, 1 \rangle$ is one of the following formulas:

$$(Q_{Ev}^{\forall} x)(B, A) \equiv (\exists z)[(\forall x)((B|z)\, x \Rightarrow Ax) \land Ev((\mu B)(B|z))], \qquad (1)$$

$$(Q_{Ev}^{\exists} x)(B, A) \equiv (\exists z)[(\exists x)((B|z)x \land Ax) \land Ev((\mu B)(B|z))]. \qquad (2)$$

where Ev is a formula representing some evaluative linguistic expression, z, x are variables and A, B are formulas where B represents a universe of quantification where $B, B|z$ are measurable fuzzy sets. Either of the quantifiers (1) or (2) construes the sentence

$$\langle \text{Quantifier} \rangle \; B's \text{ are } A \qquad (3)$$

where $\langle \text{Quantifier} \rangle$ is a quantifier in a linguistic form.

If we put concrete evaluative linguistic expression instead of Ev, we obtain these fuzzy intermediate quantifiers:

$$\mathbf{A} : \text{All } B\text{'s are } A := (Q_{Bi\Delta}^{\forall} x)(B, A) \equiv (\forall x)(Bx \Rightarrow Ax),$$

$$\mathbf{E} : \text{No } B\text{'s are } A := (Q_{Bi\Delta}^{\forall} x)(B, \neg A) = (\forall x)(Bx \Rightarrow \neg Ax),$$

$$\mathbf{P} : \text{Almost all } B\text{'s are } A := (Q_{Bi\,Ex}^{\forall} x)(B, A)$$

$$\mathbf{B} : \text{Almost all } B\text{'s are not } A := (Q_{Bi\,Ex}^{\forall} x)(B, \neg A)$$

$$\mathbf{T} : \text{Most } B\text{'s are } A := (Q_{Bi\,Ve}^{\forall} x)(B, A)$$

$$\mathbf{D} : \text{Most } B\text{'s are not } A := (Q_{Bi\,Ve}^{\forall} x)(B, \neg A)$$

$$\mathbf{K} : \text{Many } B\text{'s are } A := (Q_{\neg\,Sm}^{\forall} x)(B, A)$$

$$\mathbf{G} : \text{Many } B\text{'s are not } A := (Q_{\neg\,Sm}^{\forall} x)(B, \neg A)$$

$$\mathbf{I} : \text{Some } B\text{'s are } A := (Q_{Bi\Delta}^{\exists} x)(B, A) \equiv (\exists x)(Bx \land Ax),$$

$$\mathbf{O} : \text{Some } B\text{'s are not } A := (Q_{Bi\Delta}^{\exists} x)(B, \neg A) \equiv (\exists x)(Bx \land \neg Ax).$$

By ***A, *E, *P, *B, *T, *D, *K, *G, *I, *O** we denote fuzzy intermediate quantifiers with presupposition (for precise definition see [8]). Quantifiers **A,P,T,K,I** are called affirmative quantifiers. Quantifiers **E,B,D,G,O** are called negative quantifiers. These fuzzy intermediate quantifiers can be ordered by monotonicity:

Theorem 1 (Monotonicity).*[10] Let $A, \ldots, O$ are fuzzy intermediate quantifiers. Then the following set of implications is provable in T^{IQ}:*

1. $T^{IQ} \vdash A \Rightarrow P, T^{IQ} \vdash P \Rightarrow T, T^{IQ} \vdash T \Rightarrow K, T^{IQ} \vdash K \Rightarrow I.$
2. $T^{IQ} \vdash E \Rightarrow B, T^{IQ} \vdash B \Rightarrow D, T^{IQ} \vdash D \Rightarrow G, T^{IQ} \vdash G \Rightarrow O.$

2.4   Formalization of Syllogisms

The *syllogism* is a triple of formulas $\mathcal{P}_1, \mathcal{P}_2, \mathcal{C}$ of the theory T^{IQ} where $\mathcal{P}_1$ is a *major premise*, $\mathcal{P}_2$ a *minor premise* and $\mathcal{C}$ is a *conclusion*. We say that it is *strongly valid*[1] if

$$T^{IQ} \vdash \mathcal{P}_1 \,\&\, \mathcal{P}_2 \Rightarrow \mathcal{C}. \tag{4}$$

By the completeness theorem, syllogism (4) is strongly valid iff

$$\mathcal{M}(\mathcal{P}_1) \otimes \mathcal{M}(\mathcal{P}_2) \leq \mathcal{M}(\mathcal{C}) \tag{5}$$

holds in any model $\mathcal{M} \models T^{IQ}$. Validity of (4) for all syllogisms presented in [14] was proven syntactically in [6,7].

Let Q_1, Q_2, Q_3 be quantifier symbols and S, P, M be formulas[2] representing properties of elements. The formula S is a *subject*, P is a *predicate* and M is a *middle formula*. As usual, syllogisms are gathered into the following four figures:

Figure-I	Figure-II	Figure-III	Figure-IV
$Q_1 \; M$ are P	$Q_1 \; P$ are M	$Q_1 \; M$ are P	$Q_1 \; P$ are M
$Q_2 \; S$ are M	$Q_2 \; S$ are M	$Q_2 \; M$ are S	$Q_2 \; M$ are S
$Q_3 \; S$ are P	$Q_3 \; S$ are P	$Q_3 \; S$ are P	$Q_3 \; S$ are P

where the first line in each figure is the major premise $\mathcal{P}_1$, the second line is the minor premise $\mathcal{P}_2$ and the third line is the conclusion $\mathcal{C}$. To write syllogisms, we use the abbreviation $\mathcal{P}_1\mathcal{P}_2\mathcal{C}$, where instead of $\mathcal{P}_1\mathcal{P}_2\mathcal{C}$ we substitute the respective fuzzy intermediate quantifiers expressed by their letter abbreviation. We distinguish between trivial and non-trivial syllogisms. Trivial syllogisms contain one or two classical quantifiers (**A, E, I, O**) in the premises. Non-trivial syllogisms do not contain classical quantifiers in the premises. In this text, we will deal with Peterson's syllogisms, they are formed by fuzzy intermediate quantifiers defined by the formula (1) or (2). We will refer to these Peterson's syllogisms as syllogisms.

---

[1] In Peterson's approach, we use the term valid syllogism. Our definition is based on strong conjunction then we use the term strongly valid syllogism.

[2] Many authors speak about *terms* instead of formulas. We call S, P, M *formulas* as is common in logic.

3   The Number of Strongly Valid Peterson's Syllogisms

In this section, we will focus on a detailed explanation of Peterson's formula (see [14]) for calculating the number of valid Peterson's syllogisms. Recall that we mean a group of logical syllogisms with intermediate quantifiers that form Peterson's square of opposition.

3.1   The Importance of the Size of the Quantifier

Below we present Peterson's formula for computing the number of valid Peterson's syllogisms with intermediate quantifiers. Let us recall that this formula is designed to calculate logical syllogisms with two premises and therefore one middle formula is assumed. This ensures that the resulting syllogisms will belong to one of the four Figures.

Proposition 1. *Let one middle formula be assumed. Let k be a number of intermediate quantifiers.[3] Then the formula as follows:*

$$6(k^2 + k)/2 + 3k, \tag{6}$$

determines the number of valid Peterson's syllogisms.

As we can see the formula (6) uses only the number of quantifiers to calculate the number of valid Peterson's syllogisms. This formula does not use the size of particular quantifiers[4]. In the following example, we will show that the size of particular quantifiers affects the number of strongly valid Peterson's syllogisms.

Below we present strongly valid syllogisms that have been proved on the basis of the old definition of fuzzy intermediate quantifiers. It should be emphasized that the strongly valid syllogisms are also held for the modified definition given in this publication. For details see [8].

Example 1. Let us have quantifiers **all, almost all, most, many, some**. We know that these syllogisms of Figure-III are strongly valid:

Theorem 2. *[7] The following syllogisms of Figure-III are strongly valid in T^{IQ}:*

$$A(*A)I \; (*P)AI \; (*T)AI \; (*K)AI \; IAI$$
$$A(*P)I \; *(PP)I \; *(TP)I \; *(KP)I$$
$$A(*T)I \; *(PT)I \; *(TT)I$$
$$A(*K)I \; *(PK)I$$
$$AII$$

---

[3] We count affirmative and negative form of the same quantifier as one quantifier. The number of quantifiers on the page 383 is $k = 5$.

[4] The size of the quantifier "Q B's are A" is determined by the proportion of B which has the property A.

Let us add quantifier Q_1 which is defined by formula (1), to these quantifiers. We assume that added quantifier Q_1 satisfies the following assumption.

Assumption 1. *1.* $T^{IQ} \vdash A \Rightarrow Q_1, T^{IQ} \vdash Q_1 \Rightarrow P, T^{IQ} \vdash P \Rightarrow T,$
$T^{IQ} \vdash T \Rightarrow K, T^{IQ} \vdash K \Rightarrow I.$

From these fuzzy intermediate quantifiers, we can obtain these strongly valid Peterson's syllogisms of Figure-III.

Theorem 3. *The following syllogisms of Figure-III are strongly valid in* T^{IQ}:

$$A(*A)I \quad (*Q_1)AI \quad (*P)AI \quad (*T)AI \quad (*K)AI \quad IAI$$
$$A(*Q_1)I \quad *(Q_1Q_1)I \quad *(PQ_1)I \quad *(TQ_1)I \quad *(KQ_1)I$$
$$A(*P)I \quad *(Q_1P)I \quad *(PP)I \quad *(TP)I \quad *(KP)I$$
$$A(*T)I \quad *(Q_1T)I \quad *(PT)I \quad *(TT)I$$
$$A(*K)I \quad *(Q_1K)I \quad *(PK)I$$
$$AII$$

Proof. From strongly valid syllogism **IAI-III** and Assumption 1 we obtain strong validity of syllogisms in the first row by transitivity. From strongly valid syllogism ***(KP)I-III** and Assumption 1 we obtain strong validity of syllogisms in the fifth column by transitivity. Similarly, we can obtain strong validity of syllogisms in the first, in the third, and in the fourth column. From strongly valid syllogism ***(PK)I-III** and Assumption 1 we obtain strong validity of syllogism ***(Q₁K)I-III** by transitivity. Then from strongly valid syllogism ***(Q₁K)I-III** and by Assumption 1 we obtain strong validity of syllogisms in the second column by transitivity.

As we can see in Theorem 3, we obtained 24 strongly valid syllogisms. Let us note that in Assumption 1 we ordered quantifiers by size, but we do not know exactly their size.

Let us add to the quantifiers **All, almost all, most, many, some** a quantifier Q_2, which is defined by formula (1). We assume that added quantifier Q_2 satisfies the following assumption.

Assumption 2. *1.* $T^{IQ} \vdash A \Rightarrow P, T^{IQ} \vdash P \Rightarrow T, T^{IQ} \vdash T \Rightarrow K,$
$T^{IQ} \vdash K \Rightarrow Q_2, T^{IQ} \vdash Q_2 \Rightarrow I.$

Let us note that now we assume a smaller quantifier than in Assumption 1.

Theorem 4. *The following syllogisms of Figure-III are strongly valid in* T^{IQ}:

$$A(*A)I \quad (*P)AI \quad (*T)AI \quad (*K)AI \quad (*Q_2)AI \quad IAI$$
$$A(*P)I \quad *(PP)I \quad *(TP)I \quad *(KP)I$$
$$A(*T)I \quad *(PT)I \quad *(TT)I$$
$$A(*K)I \quad *(PK)I$$
$$A(*Q_2)I$$
$$AII$$

Proof. From strongly valid syllogism **AII-III** and by Assumption 2 we obtain strong validity of syllogisms in the first column by transitivity. From strongly valid syllogism **IAI-III** and by Assumption 2 we prove by transitivity strongly valid syllogisms in the first row. We know that the remaining quantifiers are strongly valid from Theorem 2. We can conclude that in this case, we obtain 17 affirmative valid logical syllogisms.

In Example 1, we added one quantifier to the quantifiers **All, almost all, most, many, some**. Depending on the size of the quantifier, we got a different number of strongly valid syllogisms.

We showed that the total number of strongly valid Peterson's syllogisms is affected by the size of intermediate quantifiers. Generally for calculating the number of strongly valid syllogisms, we can not use Peterson's formula, but as we will see in the following subsections some parts of this formula can be applied.

3.2   Discussion about Non-trivial Syllogisms of Figure-III

In the previous subsection, we got a different number of strongly valid syllogisms depending on the size of the added quantifier. This difference was caused by non-trivial quantifiers which occur on Figure-III. We show an example of how generally non-trivial syllogisms of Figure-III work. For that, we will use Venn diagrams. Peterson proposed his quantifiers to a description of quantities by words of natural language. He also assigned individual intermediate quantifiers their percentage meaning. In the following example, we will deal with the quantifier "Most" which we can express as a percentage of "at least 60 %". Classical quantifier "Some" express "at least one".

Example 2. Let us assume that M consists of one hundred objects (for example one hundred people), so M=100. Let us consider syllogism **TTI-III**:

> **T**: Most M's are P
> **T**: Most M's are S
> ―――――――――――――
> **I**: Some S are P

We assume that the first premise is valid. That means that at least 60% of M's has a property P. Most M's (60% of 100 = 60) are P. We assume that the second premise is valid. That means that at least 60% of M's has a property S. Most M's (60% of 100 = 60) are S. If we put these results into Venn's diagram we obtain this result:

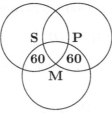

We can see that we can not have 60 M's are S and 60 different M's which are P, because we have 100 M's in total. That means that we have at least 20 of M's which are S and also P as we can see in Venn's diagram:

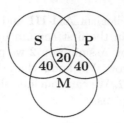

From premises we concluded that at least 20 of S's are P. This means that also at least one of S's are P which is classical quantifier "Some".

We can see that in general, for valid non-trivial Peterson's syllogisms we need the percentage sum of the premises to be higher than 100 % since it guarantees at least one of S's are P in the conclusion.

3.3   Peterson's Formula for Concrete Figure

In this subsection, we will discuss in detail how to use Peterson's formula to calculate strongly valid Peterson's syllogisms for individual figures. We will show that we can partially apply Peterson's formula for individual figures.

Peterson's formula can be split into these respective formulas for the concrete figure as follows:

Figure-I: $2(k^2 + k)/2$
Figure-II: $2(k^2 + k)/2$
Figure-III: $2(k^2 + k)/2$
Figure-IV: $3k$

3.4   Assumptions

Before we start to examine particular Figures we need to mention some assumptions for the calculation of the number of strongly valid syllogisms.

Let $Ev_1, \ldots, Ev_m$ be evaluative linguistic expressions that differ only in the hedges they contain. The hedges induce the following natural ordering (the definition can be found in [10]):

$$Ev_1 \preceq Ev_2 \preceq \cdots \preceq Ev_m . \tag{7}$$

We introduce the following general intermediate quantifiers;

$$(Q^{\vee}_{i,Ev_i} x)(B, A) := (\exists z)(((\forall x)((B|z)\, x \Rightarrow Ax)) \wedge Ev_i((\mu B)(B|z)) \tag{8}$$

for all $i = 1, \ldots, m$. If the presupposition is needed then (8) is modified as follows:

$$(^{*}Q^{\vee}_{i,Ev_i} x)(B, A) := (\exists z)[((\forall x)((B|z)\, x \Rightarrow Ax)\, \&(\exists x)zx) \wedge Ev_i((\mu B)(B|z))] \tag{9}$$

for all $i = 1, \ldots, m$.

The quantifiers in (8) or (9) are called *affirmative* and we will denote them by Q_i^a or $^*Q_i^a$, respectively, $i = 1, \ldots, m$. If the formula A is replaced by its negation $\neg A$ then we call the respective quantifiers *negative* and denote them by Q_i^n or $^*Q_i^n$, respectively. Note that all intermediate quantifiers are, according to the classification introduce in ([4]), of type $\langle 1, 1 \rangle$.

Assumption 3. *We always assume classical quantifiers A,E,I,O.*

Assumption 4. *Let* $Q_1^a, Q_2^a, \ldots, Q_m^a$ *and* $Q_1^n, Q_2^n, \ldots, Q_m^n$ *be quantifiers obtained by the formula (8).*
For these quantifiers we assume:

- *If there exists a quantifier Q_k^a then also exists quantifier Q_k^n and vice versa.*
- *These quantifiers are intermediate*
  $Q_1^a, Q_2^a, \ldots, Q_m^a, Q_1^n, Q_2^n, \ldots, Q_m^n \not\equiv A, E, I, O.$
- *We assume different quantifiers $Q_1^a \not\equiv Q_2^a \not\equiv \ldots \not\equiv Q_m^a$ and $Q_1^n \not\equiv Q_2^n \not\equiv \ldots \not\equiv Q_m^n$*

We also assume that we are able to order these quantifiers by their size as follows:

Assumption 5. $T^{IQ} \vdash A \Rightarrow Q_1^a$, $T^{IQ} \vdash Q_1^a \Rightarrow Q_2^a$, $\ldots$ $T^{IQ} \vdash Q_m^a \Rightarrow I$.

Assumption 6. $T^{IQ} \vdash A \Rightarrow Q_1^n$, $T^{IQ} \vdash Q_1^n \Rightarrow Q_2^n$, $\ldots$ $T^{IQ} \vdash Q_m^n \Rightarrow I$.

Validity of Assumption 5 and Assumption 6 was proved in [7]. The ordering of evaluative language expressions was used for this proof.

We will distinguish affirmative syllogisms which contain only affirmative quantifiers, and negative syllogisms which contain some negative quantifiers in the following text.

3.5 Figure-I

If we assume quantifiers **all, almost all, most, many, some** we get these affirmative strongly valid syllogisms:

Theorem 5 ([7]). *The following syllogisms of Figure-I are strongly valid in* T^{IQ}:

$$AAA$$
$$AAP \quad APP$$
$$AAT \quad APT \quad ATT$$
$$AAK \quad APK \quad ATK \quad AKK$$
$$A(^*A)I\ A(^*P)I\ A(^*T)I\ A(^*K)I\ AII$$

We can see that we ordered affirmative strongly valid syllogisms by monotonicity in Theorem 5. We get there a triangle. In the vertexes of this triangle are classical syllogisms (these syllogisms contain only classical quantifiers). In the diagonal of this triangle are syllogisms whose first premise is a classical quantifier A, the second premise and the conclusion consist of the same quantifier. We can see that we are weakening the conclusion in the columns. We can use this information to generalize this pattern of Figure-I.

Theorem 6. *The following syllogisms of Figure-I are strongly valid in T^{IQ}:*

$$AAA$$
$$AAQ_1^a \quad AQ_1^aQ_1^a$$
$$AAQ_2^a \quad AQ_1^a\,Q_2^a \quad AQ_2^a\,Q_2^a$$
$$\vdots \qquad \vdots \qquad \vdots \qquad \ddots$$
$$AAQ_m^a \quad AQ_1^a\,Q_m^a \quad AQ_2^a\,Q_m^a \,\cdots\, AQ_m^a\,Q_m^a$$
$$A(*A)I \; A(*Q_1^a)I \; A(*Q_2^a)I \,\cdots\, A(*Q_m^a)I \; AII$$

Proof. This was already proved in [7].

We can see that we can obtain the number of strongly valid syllogisms by the formula $(k^2 + k)/2$ in Theorem 6. We can see that we ordered generalized syllogisms by monotonicity into the triangle in Theorem 6 and we will call this triangle a general pattern of the respective Figure.

There are also negative strongly valid syllogisms of Figure-I. Their general pattern is similar to the Theorem 6 (see [7]), so the number of strongly valid syllogisms can be obtained by the same formula $(k^2 + k)/2$.

Corollary 1. *The number of strongly valid syllogisms for generalized patterns of Figure-I is given by formula $2(k^2 + k)/2$.*

3.6   Figure-II

We are able to order generalized syllogisms of Figure-II into similar generalized patterns as generalized syllogisms of Figure-I (see [7]).

Corollary 2. *The number of strongly valid syllogisms for generalized patterns of Figure-II is given by formula $2(k^2 + k)/2$.*

3.7   Figure-III

Figure-III contains both non-trivial and trivial valid syllogisms. As we can see in Example 1 the number of strongly valid syllogisms depends also on the size of the quantifiers. If we look at Example 1 more closely the difference between the number of strongly valid syllogisms is caused by non-trivial syllogisms.

We will focus on the trivial syllogisms of Figure-III. From quantifiers **all, almost all, most, many, some**, we can construct strongly valid trivial syllogisms on this figure. We can find affirmative strongly valid trivial syllogisms of Figure-III in the first row and the first column in Theorem 2.

We can generalize this case by using our assumptions.

Theorem 7. *The following syllogisms of Figure-III are strongly valid in T^{IQ}:*

$$A(*A)I \quad (*Q_1^a)AI \; (*Q_2^a)AI \ldots (*Q_m^a) \; IAI$$
$$A(*Q_1^a)I$$
$$A(*Q_2^a)I$$
$$\vdots$$
$$A*(Q_m^a)I$$
$$AII$$

Proof. Syllogisms **AII-III** and **IAI-III** are strongly valid in T^{IQ}. We obtain from strongly valid syllogism **IAI-III** and from Assumption 5 strong validity of syllogisms in the first row by transitivity. From strongly valid syllogism **AII-III** and from Assumption 5 we obtain strong validity of syllogisms in the first column by transitivity.

The formula for calculation of the number of strongly valid trivial syllogisms in Theorem 7 is $(2k-1)$. We can also find negative strongly valid trivial syllogisms of Figure-III. Their generalized pattern is similar to the pattern in Theorem 7 (see [7]) and the number of strongly valid trivial syllogism can be obtained by the same formula $2k-1$.

Corollary 3. *The number of strongly valid syllogisms for generalized patterns of Figure-III is given by formula* $2(2k-1)$.

3.8 Figure IV

We are able to order strongly valid generalized syllogisms of Figure-IV into columns according to monotonicity.

Theorem 8 ([7])**.** *The following syllogisms of Figure-IV are strongly valid in* T^{IQ}:

$$
\begin{array}{ccc}
(*A)AI & AEE & E(*A)O \\
(*Q_1^a)AI & AEQ_1^n & E(*Q_1^a)O \\
(*Q_2^a)AI & AEQ_2^n & E(*Q_2^a)O \\
\vdots & \vdots & \vdots \\
(*Q_m^a)AI & AEQ_m^n & E(*Q_m^a)O \\
IAI & A(*E)O & EIO
\end{array}
$$

Corollary 4. *The number of strongly valid syllogisms of Figure-IV in Theorem 8 is given by the formula* $3k$.

4   Conclusion and Future Work

In this article, we focused on studying Peterson's formula for computing valid Peterson's logical syllogisms. We analyzed all four figures in detail and showed that for the third figure, Peterson's formula does not work quite exactly. As we showed in this paper the number of strongly valid syllogisms is also affected by the size of quantifiers.

The size of quantifiers affects the number of strongly valid non-trivial syllogisms. If we consider only trivial syllogisms we are able to compute the number of strongly valid trivial syllogisms for generalized patterns by our assumptions and the number of quantifiers by the formula $4(k^2+k)/2+3k+2(2k-1) = 2k^2+9k-2$.

In the future, we will follow the work of this text by investigating of non-trivial syllogisms from our mathematical point of view. The idea for the future is also to program the generator of strongly valid syllogisms based on the presented generalizations.

References

1. Cignoli, R.L.O., D'Ottaviano, I.M.L., Mundici, D.: Algebraic Foundations of Many-valued Reasoning. Kluwer, Dordrecht (2000)
2. Fiala, K. Červeňová, V., Murinová, P.: On modelling of generalized Peterson's syllogisms with more premises. In: Atlantis Studies in Uncertainty Modelling 2021-09-19 Bratislava, pp. 375–382 (2021)
3. Keenan, E.L., Westerståhl, D.: Generalized quantifiers in linguistics and logic. In: Benthem, J.V., Meulen, A.T. (eds.), Handbook of Logic and Language, Elsevier Ch. 15, pp. 837–893 (1997)
4. Lindström, P.: First order predicate logic with generalized quantifiers. Theoria **32**, 186–195 (1966)
5. Mostowski, A.: On a generalization of quantifiers. Fundam. Math. **44**, 12–36 (1957)
6. Murinová, P., Novák, V.: A formal theory of generalized intermediate syllogisms. Fuzzy Sets Syst. **186**, 47–80 (2013)
7. Murinová, P., Novák, V.: The structure of generalized intermediate syllogisms. Fuzzy Sets Syst. **247**, 18–37 (2014)
8. Murinová, P., Novák, V.: The theory of intermediate quantifiers in fuzzy natural logic revisited and the model of "many." Fuzzy Sets Syst. **388**, 56–89 (2020)
9. Novák, V.: A comprehensive theory of trichotomous evaluative linguistic expressions. Fuzzy Sets Syst. **159**(22), 2939–2969 (2008)
10. Novák, V.: A formal theory of intermediate quantifiers. Fuzzy Sets Syst. **159**(10), 1229–1246 (2008)
11. Novák, V., Perfilieva, I., Dvořák, A.: Insight into Fuzzy Modeling. Wiley & Sons, Hoboken, New Jersey (2016)
12. Novák, V., Perfilieva, I., Močkoř, J.: Mathematical Principles of Fuzzy Logic. Kluwer, Boston (1999)
13. Pereira-Fariña, M., Vidal, J.C., Díaz-Hermida, F., Bugarín, A.: A fuzzy syllogistic reasoning schema for generalized quantifiers. Fuzzy Sets Syst. **234**, 79–96 (2014)
14. Peterson, P.: Intermediate Quantifiers. Logic, Linguistics, and Aristotelian Semantics. Ashgate, Aldershot (2000)
15. Thompson, B.E.: Syllogisms using "few", "many" and "most." Notre Dame J. Form. Log. **23**, 75–84 (1982)
16. Yager, R.R.: Reasoning with fuzzy quantified statements: part II. Kybernetes **15**, 111–120 (1986)
17. Zadeh, L.A.: Fuzzy sets. Inf. Control **8**, 338–353 (1965)
18. Zadeh, L.A.: A computational approach to fuzzy quantifiers in natural languages. Comput. Math. **9**, 149–184 (1983)

Logical Relations Between T-Scaling Quantifiers and Their Implications in Fuzzy Relational Concept Analysis

Stefania Boffa[1]([⊠]) [iD] and Petra Murinová[2]

[1] DISCo, Universitá degli Studi di Milano-Bicocca,
Viale Sarca 336, 20126 Milan, Italy
stefania.boffa@unimib.it
[2] Institute for Research and Applications of Fuzzy Modeling NSC IT4Innovations,
University of Ostrava, 30. dubna 22, 701 03 Ostrava 1, Czech Republic
petra.murinova@osu.cz

Abstract. T-scaling quantifiers are special fuzzy quantifiers employed to extract information from datasets in fuzzy relational concept analysis. In this article, we expand the class of t-scaling quantifiers by introducing the so-called *negative t-scaling quantifiers* and *(positive and negative) existential scaling quantifiers*. Then, we explore the logical relations of opposition between fuzzy formal contexts deriving from quantifiers of different types. Finally, we study the consequences of such relations on a special pair of operators used to construct concepts in fuzzy formal concept analysis.

Keywords: Fuzzy quantifiers · Logical relations of opposition · Formal concept analysis · Fuzzy relational concept analysis · Fuzzy Concepts

1 Introduction

T-scaling quantifiers are special fuzzy quantifiers employed to extract information from datasets in fuzzy relational concept analysis [1]. A t-scaling quantifier is a function $\mathcal{S}_t$ depending on a threshold $t \in [0,1]$ and assigning a value of $[0,1]$ to each pair of fuzzy sets of a given universe X. Its meaning can be understood with an example. Suppose that X is the set of users of a given community, and A and B are fuzzy sets of X such that let $x \in X$, $A(x)$ and $B(x)$ are respectively the degrees to which "*x is young*" and "*x likes sport*"; then $\mathcal{S}_{0.6}(A, B)$ expresses how much "*a part (being at least as big as 0.6 in the scale [0,1]) of the young users of the community like sport*". T-scaling quantifiers generalize crisp scaling quantifiers on classical sets introduced in [2] and are interpretations in a model of *intermediate quantifiers*, which are special formulas of the *formal theory of generalized intermediate quantifiers* [3,4]. Let us underline that the t-scaling quantifiers formula carries an *existential import*, also called *presupposition*, corresponding to the assumption that the universe of quantification must be non-empty.

© The Author(s), under exclusive license to Springer Nature Switzerland AG 2023
S. Massanet et al. (Eds.): EUSFLAT 2023/AGOP 2023, LNCS 14069, pp. 393–404, 2023.
https://doi.org/10.1007/978-3-031-39965-7_33

The first goal of this article is to introduce new quantifiers in fuzzy relational concept analysis: the class of *negative t-scaling quantifiers* $\{S_t^- \mid t \in [0,1]\}$ and the *(positive and negative) existential scaling quantifiers* $S_\exists$ and $S_\exists^-$. The quantifiers S_t^- with $t \in [0,1]$ and $S_\exists^-$ catch negative information in the initial dataset, i.e. information based on the absence of a certain amount of properties. According to the previous example, $S_t^-(A,B)$ with $t \in [0,1]$, $S_\exists(A,B)$, and $S_\exists^-(A,B)$ respectively represent the degrees to which "*a part (being at least as big as t in the scale* $[0,1]$*) of the young users of the community do not like sport*", "*at least a young user of the community likes sport*", and "*at least a young user of the community do not like sport*".

Fuzzy relational concept analysis (FRCA) mines information from datasets organized as *fuzzy relational context families*, which are collections of fuzzy object-attribute relations called *fuzzy formal contexts*[1] and fuzzy object-object relations [6]. This approach extends the method proposed in [2,7] by using fuzzy logic.

In this article, we focus on the simplest fuzzy relational context family **K** containing a pair of fuzzy formal contexts (X,Y,I) and (Z,W,J), and a fuzzy relation $r : X \times Z \to [0,1]$. So, starting from **K**, a quantifier S is chosen to generate a new fuzzy formal context (X,Y_J,I_S) by merging the information related to (Z,W,J) and r. After that, using one of the techniques existing in literature [8], fuzzy formal concept lattices are extracted from (Z,W,J) and $(X,Y \cup Y_J, I \cup I_S)$ to represent the information hidden in **K**, where the fuzzy formal context $(X,Y \cup Y_J, I \cup I_S)$ is obtained by integrating (X,Y,I) with (X,Y_J,I_S): the attributes of Y_J are added to those of Y together with I_S, which is applied to the pairs of $X \times Y_J$.

Let us notice that (X,Y_J,I_S) and $(X,Y_J,I_{S'})$ may not coincide when the related quantifiers S and S' are diverse. Therefore, in order to understand if and how (X,Y_J,I_S) and $(X,Y_J,I_{S'})$ are connected, the second aim of this article is to present logical relations of opposition characterizing Aristotle's square [9,10] and holding between (X,Y_J,I_S) and $(X,Y_J,I_{S'})$. In mathematical logic, the logical relations of opposition between the propositions **A** and **E** are the following: **A** and **E** are *contraries* if and only if they cannot be true together, but they both can be false; *sub-alterns* if and only if **A** implies **E**; *sub-contraries* if and only if they cannot be false together, but they both can be true; *contradictories* if and only if **A** is the negation of **E**.

There exist several approaches to derive fuzzy concepts from fuzzy formal contexts and here, we have chosen that proposed in [8]. In this case, given a fuzzy formal context (X,Y,I), fuzzy concepts are generated by using a pair of operators (F_I,G_I) depending on a threshold $T \in (0,1]^2$, where F_I transforms a fuzzy set of objects in a crisp set of attributes and dually G_I transforms a

---

[1] Let us recall that a fuzzy formal context is a triple (X,Y,I), where X is a set of objects, Y is a set of attributes, and I is a fuzzy relation between X and Y [5].

[2] In this paper, we choose the symbols t and T to indicate different and independent thresholds: t serves to define t-scaling quantifiers and T to define the operators F_I and G_I.

crisp set of attributes in a fuzzy set of objects [8]. So, the last goal of this article is to show the existence of some relations between F_{I_S} and $F_{I_{S'}}$, and G_{I_S} and $G_{I_{S'}}$, which derive from a given relation of opposition between (X, Y_J, I_S) and $(X, Y_J, I_{S'})$.

2   Preliminaries

This section describes some preliminary notions and results that we need in this article.

2.1   Mathematical Tools for Fuzzy Logic

In this paper, we consider the *standard Łukasiewicz MV-algebra*

$$\langle [0, 1], \wedge, \vee, \otimes, \rightarrow, 0, 1 \rangle$$

where $a \vee b = \max\{a, b\}$, $a \wedge b = \min\{a, b\}$, $a \otimes b = \max\{0, a + b - 1\}$, and $a \rightarrow b = \min\{1, 1 - a + b\}$ for each $a, b \in [0, 1]$.

Moreover, these additional operations are considered: for each $a, b \in [0, 1]$, $\neg a = 1 - a$ (negation) and $a \oplus b = \min\{1, a + b\}$ (strong summation).

Lemma 1. *[11]   Let* $\langle [0, 1], \wedge, \vee, \otimes, \rightarrow, 0, 1 \rangle$ *be the standard Łukasiewicz MV-algebra, then the following properties hold for all* $a, b, c, a_i, b_i \in [0, 1]$ *with* $i \in I$:

1. $a = \neg\neg a$ *(double negation law)*;
2. *if* $a = b$ *then* $\neg a = \neg b$;
3. *if* $a_i = b_i$ *for each* $i \in I$, *then* $\bigwedge_{i \in I} a_i = \bigwedge_{i \in I} b_i$;
4. $\bigwedge_{i \in I} a_i \leq a_k$ *for each* $k \in I$;
5. $a \leq a_i$ *for each* $i \in I$ *if and only if* $a \leq \bigwedge_{i \in I} a_i$;
6. *if* $a \leq b$ *then* $c \rightarrow a \leq c \rightarrow b$;
7. *if* $a_i \leq b_i$ *for each* $i \in I$ *then* $\bigwedge_{i \in I} a_i \leq \bigwedge_{i \in I} b_i$;
8. *if* $a \leq b$ *then* $a \otimes c \leq b \otimes c$;
9. *if* $a \leq b$ *then* $a \oplus c \leq b \oplus c$;
10. $a \otimes \neg a = 0$;
11. *if* $a \leq b$ *then* $\neg b \leq \neg a$;
12. $a \oplus b = \neg(\neg a \otimes \neg b)$.

In the sequel, we use the symbol $[0, 1]^X$ to denote the collection of all fuzzy sets of a universe X (i.e. the functions from X to $[0, 1]$).

The next definition lists the relations of opposition between predicates represented by fuzzy relations (by a fuzzy relation between X and Z we mean a function $X \times Z \rightarrow [0, 1]$).

Definition 1 (Relations of opposition). *Let* P_A *and* P_B *be predicates interpreted by* $A, B \in [0, 1]^{X \times Z}$.

– P_A *and* P_B *are contraries if and only if* $A(x, z) \otimes B(x, z) = 0$ *for all* $x \in X$ *and* $z \in Z$,

- P_A and P_B are sub-contraries *if and only if* $A(x,z) \oplus B(x,z) = 1$ *for all* $x \in X$ *and* $z \in Z$,
- P_B is sub-altern *of* P_A *if and only if* $A(x,z) \leq B(x,z)$ *for all* $x \in X$ *and* $z \in Z$,
- P_A and P_B are contradictories *if and only if* $A(x,z) = \neg B(x,z)$ *for all* $x \in X$ *and* $z \in Z$.

2.2 Fuzzy Formal Concept Analysis

The next definition presents a pair of fuzzy formal concept analysis operators (FFCA operators), which are employed to form fuzzy concepts in [8].

Definition 2. *Let* (X, Y, I) *be a fuzzy formal context and let* $T \in (0,1]$. *We consider* $F_I : [0,1]^X \to 2^{Y\,3}$ *and* $G : 2^Y \to [0,1]^X$ *such that given* $A \in [0,1]^X$ *and* $B \subseteq Y$,

(a)

$$F_I(A) = \left\{ y \in Y \mid \bigwedge_{x \in X} (A(x) \to I(x,y)) \geq T \right\}$$

(b)

$$G_I(B)(x) = \begin{cases} \bigwedge_{y \in B} I(x,y) & \text{if } \bigwedge_{y \in Y} I(x,y) \geq T \\ 0 & \text{otherwise} \end{cases} \quad \text{for each } x \in X.$$

$F_I(A)$ *is the set of all attributes of* Y *shared by all objects of* A *with degree at least* T *and* $G_I(B)(x)$ *represents the smallest degree to which* x *has the attributes of* B, *when it is greater than or equal to* T.

Definition 3. *Let* (X, Y, I) *be a fuzzy formal context. A pair* (A, B) *with* $A \in [0,1]^X$ *and* $B \in [0,1]^Y$ *is a* fuzzy concept *of* (X, Y, I) *if and only if* $F(A) = B$ *and* $G(B) = A$.

We denote the set of all fuzzy concepts of (X, Y, I) with $\mathcal{B}(X, Y, I)$. The collection of all fuzzy concepts extracted from (X, Y, I), is usually equipped with the following relation: $(A_1, B_1) \preceq (A_2, B_2)$ if and only if $A_1 \subseteq A_2$ (or equivalently $B_2 \supseteq B_1$). On the other hand, in this paper, we are not interested in the algebraic properties of $(\mathcal{B}(X, Y, I), \preceq)$. Finally, let us recall that the method to construct fuzzy concepts by means of (F_I, G_I) is called *One-Sided Threshold Approach*.

2.3 Fuzzy Relational Concept Analysis

This subsection recalls the definition of t-scaling quantifies and explains how these are used in fuzzy relational concept analysis.

The definition of t-scaling quantifiers is based on the following notions[4].

---

[3] The symbol 2^Y denotes the power set of Y.
[4] We write $A = \emptyset$ when $A(x) = 0$ for each $x \in X$, $A = B$ when $A(x) = B(x)$ for each $x \in X$, and $A \subseteq B$ when $A(x) \leq B(x)$ for each $x \in X$.

Definition 4. *The* cardinality *of* $A \in [0,1]^X$ *is given by* $|A| = \sum_{x \in X} A(x)$.

Definition 5. *Let* $A, B \in [0,1]^X$, *we put*

$$\mu_A(B) = \begin{cases} 1 & \text{if } A = \emptyset; \\ \frac{|B|}{|A|} & \text{if } A \neq \emptyset \text{ and } B \subseteq A; \\ 0 & \text{otherwise;} \end{cases}$$

$\mu_A(B)$ *measures "how large the size of B is w.r.t. the size of A".*

Definition 6. *Let* $A, B \in [0,1]^X$. *We put*

$$(A|B)(x) = \begin{cases} A(x) & \text{if } A(x) = B(x); \\ 0 & \text{otherwise;} \end{cases}$$

for each $x \in X$.

$A|B$ *is called* cut *of A w.r.t. B.*

Definition 7. *Let* $t \in [0,1]$, *we consider the function* $\Delta_t : [0,1] \to [0,1]$ *such that*

$$\Delta_t(a) = \begin{cases} 1 \text{ if } a \geq t; \\ 0 \text{ otherwise;} \end{cases}$$

for each $a \in [0,1]$.

Definition 8. *A* t-scaling quantifier *is a function*

$$\mathcal{S}_t : [0,1]^X \times [0,1]^X \to [0,1]^X \text{ with } t \in [0,1]$$

such that for each $A, B \in [0,1]^X$,

$$\mathcal{S}_t(A, B) = \bigvee_{Z \in [0,1]^X} \left(\left(\bigwedge_{x \in X} (A|Z)(x) \to B(x) \right) \otimes \bigvee_{x \in X} (A|Z)(x) \right) \wedge \Delta_t(\mu_A(A|Z)).$$

$\mathcal{S}_t(A, B)$ is the degree of the statement: *there exists a cut $A|Z$ of A such that "all elements of $A|Z$ belong to B", "there exists at least one element in $A|Z$", and "the size of $A|Z$ is at least as large as t (in the scale $[0,1]$) w.r.t. the size of A".*

We have proved that $\mathcal{S}_1$ is the quantifier *all* having this formula:

$$\mathcal{S}_1(A, B) = \bigwedge_{x \in X} ((A)(x) \to B(x)) \otimes \bigvee_{x \in X} A(x).$$

As a consequence, the formula of $\mathcal{S}_t(A, B)$ can be rewritten as follows:

$$\mathcal{S}_t(A, B) = \bigvee_{Z \in [0,1]^X} (\, \mathcal{S}_1(A|Z, B) \wedge \Delta_t(\mu_A(A|Z)) \,). \tag{1}$$

2.4   Extracting Concepts from a Fuzzy Relational Context Family

This subsection describes the FRCA procedure, which was introduced in [6] to mine fuzzy concepts from fuzzy multi-relational datasets[5].

We confine to the simplest fuzzy relational context family $(\mathbf{K}, \mathbf{R})$, where $\mathbf{K}$ is made of two fuzzy formal contexts (X, Y, I) and (Z, W, J), and $\mathbf{R}$ is made of a fuzzy relation $r : X \times Z \rightarrow [0, 1]$. Moreover, let $x \in X$, we use the symbol r^x to denote the fuzzy set of Z such that $r^x(z) = r(x, z)$ for each $z \in Z$.

The input of the FRCA procedure is $(\mathbf{K}, \mathbf{R})$ and the output is obtained in three fundamental steps.

1. A collection of fuzzy concepts $\mathcal{B}(Z, W, J)$ is generated by using one of the existing fuzzy FCA algorithms.
2. A new fuzzy formal context $(X, Y \cup Y_J, I \cup I_t)$ is constructed by uniting (X, Y, I) and (X, Y_J, I_t) such that $Y_J = \{y_C \mid C \in \mathcal{B}(Z, W, J)\}$[6] and

$$I_t(x, y) = S_t(r^x, E_C) \text{ for all } x \in X \text{ and } y_C = y \in Y_J, \tag{2}$$

where E_C is the extent of the concept C of $\mathcal{B}(Z, W, J)$. Therefore,

$$(I \cup I_t)(x, y) = \begin{cases} I(x, y) & \text{if } y \in Y; \\ I_t(x, y) & \text{if } y = y_C. \end{cases} \tag{3}$$

3. A collection of fuzzy concepts $\mathcal{B}(X, Y \cup Y_J, I \cup I_t)$ is extracted from $(X, Y \cup Y_J, I \cup I_t)$ adopting the same algorithm chosen in the first step.

So, $\{\mathcal{B}(X, Y \cup Y_J, I \cup I_t), \mathcal{B}(Z, W, J)\}$ is the final result generated by the FRCA procedure.

3   Relations of Opposition Between Fuzzy Formal Contexts

In this section, we provide the definition of new quantifiers in fuzzy relational concept analysis and then we study the relations of opposition between fuzzy formal contexts deriving from quantifiers of different types.

Definition 9. *A negative t-scaling quantifier is a function*

$$\mathcal{S}_t^- : [0, 1]^X \times [0, 1]^X \rightarrow [0, 1]^X \text{ with } t \in [0, 1]$$

such that for each $A, B \in [0, 1]^X$,

$$\mathcal{S}_t^-(A, B) = \bigvee_{Z \in [0,1]^X} \left(\left(\bigwedge_{x \in X} (A|Z)(x) \rightarrow \neg B(x) \right) \otimes \bigvee_{x \in X} (A|Z)(x) \right) \wedge \Delta_t(\mu_A(A|Z)). \tag{4}$$

---

[5] Recall that FRCA is the abbreviation of Fuzzy Relational Concept Analysis.
[6] Notice that a new attribute y_C is considered for each concept C of $\mathcal{B}(Z, W, J)$. See [6] for more details on the meaning of y_C.

$S_t^-(A, B)$ *is the truth degree of the statement:* there exists a cut $A|Z$ of A such that "all elements of $A|Z$ do not belong to B", "there exists at least one element in $A|Z$", and "the size of $A|Z$ is at least as large as t (in the scale [0,1]) w.r.t. the size of A".

We can observe that $S_t^-(A, B) = S_t(A, \neg B)$, for all $A \in [0,1]^X$ and $B \in [0,1]^X$.

From now on, quantifiers given by Definition 8 are called *positive t-scaling quantifiers*.

Definition 10. *The* positive existential quantifier *is a function*

$$S_\exists : [0,1]^X \times [0,1]^X \to [0,1]^X$$

such that for each $A, B \in [0,1]^X$,

$$S_\exists(A, B) = \bigvee_{x \in X} A(x) \to \bigvee_{x \in X} (A(x) \otimes B(x)).$$

$S_\exists(A, B)$ *is the degree of the statement:* "if there exists at least one element in A, then there exists at least one element in both A and B".

Definition 11. *The* negative existential quantifier *is a function*

$$S_\exists^- : [0,1]^X \times [0,1]^X \to [0,1]^X$$

such that for each $A, B \in [0,1]^X$,

$$S_\exists^-(A, B) = \bigvee_{x \in X} A(x) \to \bigvee_{x \subset X} (A(x) \otimes \neg B(x)).$$

$S_\exists^-(A, B)$ *is the degree of the statement:* "if there exists at least one element in A, then there exists at least one element in A that does not belong to B".

Analogously the to positive and negative t-scaling quantifiers, the equality $S_\exists^-(A, B) = S_\exists(A, \neg B)$ is true for all $A, B \in [0,1]^X$.

In the sequel, let $t \in [0,1]$, we use the symbols (X, Y_J, I_t^+), (X, Y_J, I_t^-), $(X, Y_J, I_\exists^+)$, and $(X, Y_J, I_\exists^-)$ to denote the fuzzy formal contexts respectively obtained from S_t, S_t^-, $S_\exists$, and $S_\exists^-$ by means of (2).

The following theorem lists some relations of opposition between fuzzy formal contexts generated by quantifiers of different types. Its proof is analogous to those of the theorems presented in [12] to prove that the so-called *fuzzy quantifier-based concept-forming operators* form polygons of opposition.

Theorem 1. *Let $s, t \in [0,1]$ such that $s \leq t$, then*

(a) I_1^+ and I_1^- are contraries;
(b) $I_\exists^+$ and $I_\exists^-$ are sub-contraries;
(c) I_s^+ is sub-altern of I_t^+;
(d) I_s^- is sub-altern of I_t^-;

(e) $I_{\exists}^+$ *is sub-altern of* I_1^+;
(f) $I_{\exists}^-$ *is sub-altern of* I_1^-;
(g) I_1^+ *and* $I_{\exists}^-$ *are contradictories;*
(h) I_1^- *and* $I_{\exists}^+$ *are contradictories.*

Example 1. Consider the fuzzy relational context family

$$(\mathbf{K} = \{(X, Y, I), (Z, W, J)\}, \mathbf{R} = \{r : X \times Z \to [0, 1]\}).$$

Then, according to Subsect. 2.4, a fuzzy formal context (X, Y_J, I^*) can be constructed choosing one of the quantifiers of $\{\mathcal{S}_t \mid t \in [0, 1]\} \cup \{\mathcal{S}_t^- \mid t \in [0, 1]\} \cup \{\mathcal{S}_{\exists} \cup \mathcal{S}_{\exists}^-\}$. Let us focus on the value assumed by I^* on $(x, y_{(A,B)})$, where $x \in X$ and (A, B) is the concept of $\mathcal{B}(Z, W, J)$ having the following extent

$$A = \{z_1, 0.2/z_2, 0.2/z_3, z_4, z_5, 0.9/z_6, z_8, 0.5/z_{10}\}.$$

If $r^x = \{z_1, z_2, 0.7/z_3, 0.6/z_4, z_6, 0.8/z_7, z_8, 0.8/z_9\}$, then we get

$$I_{0.6}^+(x, y_{(A,B)}) = 0.5, I_1^+(x, y_{(A,B)}) = 0.2, I_{\exists}^+(x, y_{(A,B)}) = 1,$$

$$I_{0.7}^-(x, y_{(A,B)}) = 0.1, I_1^-(x, y_{(A,B)}) = 0, \text{ and } I_{\exists}^+(x, y_{(A,B)}) = 0.8.$$

Therefore, it is easy to verify that $I_1^+(x, y_{(A,B)}) \otimes I_{0.7}^-(x, y_{(A,B)}) = 0.2 \otimes 0.1 = 0$ (relation of contrary); $I_1^+(x, y_{(A,B)}) \le I_{0.6}^+(x, y_{(A,B)}) \le I_{\exists}^+(x, y_{(A,B)})$ because $0.2 \le 0.5 \le 1$ and $I_1^-(x, y_{(A,B)}) \le I_{0.7}^-(x, y_{(A,B)}) \le I_{\exists}^-(x, y_{(A,B)})$ because $0 \le 0.1 \le 0.8$ (relations of sub-alternation); $I_1^+(x, y_{(A,B)}) = 0.2 = 1 - 0.8 = 1 - I_{\exists}^-(x, y_{(A,B)})$ and $I_1^-(x, y_{(A,B)}) = 0 = 1 - 0 = 1 - I_{\exists}^+(x, y_{(A,B)})$ (relations of contradictory); finally, $I_{\exists}^+(x, y_{(A,B)}) \oplus I_{\exists}^-(x, y_{(A,B)}) = 1 \oplus 0.8 = 1$ (relation of sub-contrary).

Remark 1. Let us underline that I_1^+, I_1^-, $I_{\exists}^+$, and $I_{\exists}^-$ can be viewed as the vertices of a graded square of opposition, which is given in [13].

4   Relations Between FFCA Operators

In this section, we study the consequences of the relations of opposition between fuzzy formal contexts proposed by Theorem 1 ((c)–(h)) on the operators given by Definition 2. In addition to the contexts having the form (X, Y_J, I^*) where $I^* \in \{I_t^+, I_t^- \mid t \in [0, 1]\} \cup \{I_{\exists}^+, I_{\exists}^-\}$, we also consider the contexts like $(X, Y_J, \neg I^*)$, where $\neg I^*(x, y) = 1 - I^*(x, y)$ for each $x \in X$ and $y \in Y_J$.

Proposition 1. *Let* $A \in [0, 1]^X$, *then*

(a) $F_{I_1^+}(A) = F_{\neg I_{\exists}^-}(A)$ *and* $F_{\neg I_1^+}(A) = F_{I_{\exists}^-}(A)$;
(b) $F_{I_1^-}(A) = F_{\neg I_{\exists}^+}(A)$ *and* $F_{\neg I_1^-}(A) = F_{I_{\exists}^+}(A)$.

Proof.(a) Let $y \in Y$. By Theorem 1 (g), $I_1^+(x, y)$ is equal to $\neg I_{\exists}^-(x, y)$ for each $x \in X$. Then, the thesis follows from Definition 2.
Let $y \in Y$. By Theorem 1 (g), $I_1^+(x, y)$ is equal to $\neg I_{\exists}^-(x, y)$ for each $x \in X$. By Lemma 1 (2 and 1), $\neg I_1^+(x, y) = I_{\exists}^-(x, y)$. Then, the thesis follows from Definition 2.

(b) The proof follows from Theorem 1 (h) and it is analogous to that of item (a).

Example 2. Let $(\mathbf{K} = \{(X, Y, I), (Z, W, J)\}, \mathbf{R} = \{r : X \times Z \to [0,1]\})$ be the fuzzy relational context family defined in [6] (see Example 3.14). Then, the extents of the concepts of $\mathcal{B}(Z, W, J)$ and the relation r are defined by Table 1.

Table 1. The extents of the concepts of $\mathcal{B}(Z, W, J)$ and the fuzzy relation r

	z_1	z_2
$E_{y_{C_1}}$	1	1
$E_{y_{C_2}}$	1	0.5
$E_{y_{C_3}}$	0.5	1
$E_{y_{C_4}}$	0.5	0.5
$E_{y_{C_5}}$	0	1
$E_{y_{C_6}}$	0	0.5

r	z_1	z_2
x_1	1	0.5
x_2	0	1

By (2), the fuzzy formal contexts (X, Y_J, I_1^+), (X, Y_J, I_1^-), $(X, Y_J, I_\exists^+)$, and $(X, Y_J, I_\exists^-)$ are represented by the following tables (Table 2).

Table 2. .

I_1^+	y_{C_1}	y_{C_2}	y_{C_3}	y_{C_4}	y_{C_5}	y_{C_6}
x_1	1	1	0.5	0.5	0	0
x_2	1	0.5	1	0.5	1	0.5

$I_\exists^+$	y_{C_1}	y_{C_2}	y_{C_3}	y_{C_4}	y_{C_5}	y_{C_6}
x_1	1	1	0.5	0.5	0.5	0
x_2	1	0.5	1	0.5	1	0.5

I_1^-	y_{C_1}	y_{C_2}	y_{C_3}	y_{C_4}	y_{C_5}	y_{C_6}
x_1	0	0	0.5	0.5	0.5	1
x_2	0	0.5	0	0.5	0	0.5

$I_\exists^-$	y_{C_1}	y_{C_2}	y_{C_3}	y_{C_4}	y_{C_5}	y_{C_6}
x_1	0	0	0.5	0.5	1	1
x_2	0	0.5	0	0.5	0	0.5

If $A = \{1/x_1, 0.5/x_2\}$ and $T = 0.6$, it is easy to verify that $F_{I_1^+}(A) = F_{\neg I_\exists^-}(A) = \{y_{C_1}, y_{C_2}\}$. Indeed, $\bigwedge_{x \in X}(A(x) \to I_1^+(x, y_{C_1})) = \bigwedge_{x \in X}(A(x) \to I_1^+(x, y_{C_2})) = \bigwedge_{x \in X}(A(x) \to \neg I_\exists^-(x, y_{C_1})) = \bigwedge_{x \in X}(A(x) \to \neg I_\exists^-(x, y_{C_2})) = 1$, $\bigwedge_{x \in X}(A(x) \to I_1^+(x, y_{C_3})) = \bigwedge_{x \in X}(A(x) \to I_1^+(x, y_{C_4})) = \bigwedge_{x \in X}(A(x) \to \neg I_\exists^-(x, y_{C_3})) = \bigwedge_{x \in X}(A(x) \to \neg I_\exists^-(x, y_{C_4})) = 0.5$, and $\bigwedge_{x \in X}(A(x) \to I_1^+(x, y_{C_5})) = \bigwedge_{x \in X}(A(x) \to I_1^+(x, y_{C_6})) = \bigwedge_{x \in X}(A(x) \to \neg I_\exists^-(x, y_{C_5})) = \bigwedge_{x \in X}(A(x) \to \neg I_\exists^-(x, y_{C_6})) = 0$.

Furthermore, $F_{\neg I_1^+}(A) = F_{I_\exists^-}(A) = \{y_{C_6}\}$, $F_{I_1^-}(A) = F_{\neg I_\exists^+}(A) = \{y_{C_6}\}$, and $F_{\neg I_1^-}(A) = F_{I_\exists^+}(A) = \{y_{C_1}, y_{C_2}\}$.

Proposition 2. *Let* $B \subseteq Y_J$, *then* $G_{I_1^+}(B) = G_{\neg I_\exists^-}(B)$ *and* $G_{I_1^-}(B) = G_{\neg I_\exists^+}(B)$.

Proof. Let $x \in X$. By Theorem 1 (g), we get $I_1^+(x,y) = \neg I_\exists^-(x,y)$ for each $y \in B$. Consequently, $\bigwedge_{y \in B} I_1^+(x,y) = \bigwedge_{y \in B} \neg I_\exists^-(x,y)$ from Lemma 1 (3). Finally, $G_{I_1^+}(B)(x) = G_{\neg I_\exists^-}(B)(x)$.

Analogously, the proof of $G_{I_1^-}(B) = G_{\neg I_\exists^+}(B)$ follows from Theorem 1 (h). $\blacksquare$

Example 3. Consider Example 2 and suppose that $B = \{y_{C_1}, y_{C_3}\}$. Then, we get $G_{I_1^+}(B) = G_{\neg I_\exists^-}(B) = \{x_2\}$. Indeed, $I_1^+(x_1, y_{C_1}) \wedge I_1^+(x_1, y_{C_3}) = \neg I_\exists^-(x_1, y_{C_1}) \wedge \neg I_\exists^-(x_1, y_{C_3}) = 1 \wedge 0.5 = 0.5$ that is less than T and $I_1^+(x_2, y_{C_1}) \wedge I_1^+(x_2, y_{C_3}) = \neg I_\exists^-(x_2, y_{C_1}) \wedge \neg I_\exists^-(x_2, y_{C_3}) = 1 \wedge 1 = 1$.

Furthermore, $G_{I_1^-}(B) = G_{\neg I_\exists^+}(B) = \emptyset$, namely $G_{I_1^-}(B)(x_1) = G_{I_1^-}(B)(x_2) = 0$ and $G_{\neg I_\exists^+}(B)(x_1) = G_{\neg I_\exists^+}(B)(x_2) = 0$.

Proposition 3. *Let* $s \leq t$, *let* $A \in [0,1]^X$, *and* $B \subseteq Y_J$. *Then,*

(a) $F_{I_t^+}(A) \subseteq F_{I_s^+}(A)$, $F_{I_t^-}(A) \subseteq F_{I_s^-}(A)$, $F_{I_1^+}(A) \subseteq F_{I_\exists^+}(A)$, *and* $F_{I_1^-}(A) \subseteq F_{I_\exists^-}(A)$;

(b) $G_{I_t^+}(B) \subseteq G_{I_s^+}(B)$, $G_{I_t^-}(B) \subseteq G_{I_s^-}(B)$, $G_{I_1^+}(B) \subseteq G_{I_\exists^+}(B)$, *and* $G_{I_1^-}(B) \subseteq G_{I_\exists^-}(B)$.

Proof.(a) Let $y \in F_{I_t^+}(A)$, then $\bigwedge_{x \in X}(A(x) \to I_t^+(x,y)) \geq T$. Consequently, by Lemma 1 (5), $A(x) \to I_t^+(x,y) \geq T$ for each $x \in X$. Furthermore, using Theorem 1 (c), $I_t^+(x,y) \leq I_s^+(x,y)$ for each $x \in X$. By Lemma 1 (6) $I_t^+(x,y) \leq I_s^+(x,y)$ implies that $A(x) \to I_t^+(x,y) \leq A(x) \to I_s^+(x,y)$ for each $x \in X$. Then, using 1 (5) again, $\bigwedge_{x \in X} A(x) \to I_s^+(x,y) \geq T$. Finally, $y \in F_{I_s^+}(A)$.

Analogously, the other implications respectively follow from Theorem 1 (d), (e), and (f).

(b) Let $x \in X$. If $G_{I_t^+}(B)(x) = 0$, then it is trivial that $G_{I_t^+}(B)(x) \leq G_{I_s^+}(B)(x)$. So, let us suppose that $G_{I_t^+}(B)(x) > 0$. Moreover, by Theorem 1 (c), $I_t^+(x,y) \geq I_s^+(x,y)$ for each $y \in Y_J$. Then, $\bigwedge_{y \in B} I_t^+(x,y) \geq \bigwedge_{y \in B} I_s^+(x,y)$ from Lemma 1 (7); so, $G_{I_t^+}(B)(x) \leq G_{I_s^+}(B)(x)$.

Analogously, the other implications respectively follow from Theorem 1 (d), (e), and (f). $\blacksquare$

Example 4. Consider Example 2, then $I_{0.3}^+$ and $I_{0.3}^-$ are represented by Table 3.

Thus, the inclusions of Proposition 3 hold for $A = \{1/x_1, 0.5/x_2\}$ and $B = \{y_{C_1}, y_{C_3}\}$ because $F_{I_1^+}(A) = F_{I_\exists^+}(A) = \{y_{C_1}, y_{C_2}\}$, $F_{I_{0.3}^+}(A) = \{y_{C_1}, y_{C_2}\}$, $F_{I_1^-}(A) = F_{I_\exists^-}(A) = \{y_{C_6}\}$, $F_{I_{0.3}^-}(A) = \{y_{C_2}, y_{C_6}\}$, $G_{I_1^+}(B) = G_{I_\exists^+}(B) = \{x_2\}$, $G_{I_{0.3}^+}(B) = \{x_2\}$, and $G_{I_1^-}(B) = G_{I_{0.3}^-}(B) = G_{I_\exists^-}(B) = \emptyset$.

Proposition 4. *Let* $A \in [0,1]^X$, *then* $F_{I_1^-}(A) \subseteq F_{\neg I_1^+}(A)$, $F_{I_1^+}(A) \subseteq F_{\neg I_1^-}(A)$, $F_{\neg I_\exists^+}(A) \subseteq F_{I_\exists^-}(A)$, *and* $F_{\neg I_\exists^-}(A) \subseteq F_{I_\exists^+}(A)$.

Table 3. .

$I_{0.3}^+$	y_{C_1}	y_{C_2}	y_{C_3}	y_{C_4}	y_{C_5}	y_{C_6}
x_1	1	1	0.5	0.5	0.5	0.5
x_2	1	0.5	1	0.5	1	0.5

$I_{0.3}^-$	y_{C_1}	y_{C_2}	y_{C_3}	y_{C_4}	y_{C_5}	y_{C_6}
x_1	0	1	0.5	0.5	1	1
x_2	0	0.5	0	0.5	0	0.5

Proof. The thesis clearly follows from Proposition 3(a) and Theorem 1 ((g) and (h)).

Example 5. Consider Example 2 and $A = \{x_1, 0.5/x_2\}$, then $F_{I_1^-}(A) = F_{\neg I_1^+}(A) = F_{\neg I_3^+}(A) = F_{I_3^-}(A) = \{y_{C_6}\}$ and $F_{I_1^+}(A) = F_{\neg I_1^-}(A) = F_{\neg I_3^-}(A) = F_{I_3^+}(A) = \{y_{C_1}, y_{C_2}\}$.

Proposition 5. *Let* $B \subseteq Y_J$, *then* $G_{I_1^+}(B) \subseteq G_{\neg I_1^-}(B)$, $G_{I_1^-}(B) \subseteq G_{\neg I_1^+}(B)$, $G_{\neg I_3^+}(B) \subseteq G_{I_3^-}(B)$, *and* $G_{\neg I_3^-}(B) \subseteq G_{I_3^+}(B)$.

Proof. The thesis clearly follows from Proposition 3(b) and Theorem 1 ((g) and (h)).

Example 6. Consider Example 2 and $B = \{y_{C_1}, y_{C_3}\}$, then $G_{I_1^+}(B) = G_{\neg I_1^-} = \{x_2\}$, $G_{I_1^-}(B) = G_{\neg I_1^+}(B) = \emptyset$, $G_{\neg I_3^+}(B) = G_{I_3^-}(B) = \emptyset$, and $G_{\neg I_3^-}(B) = G_{I_3^+}(B) = \{x_2\}$.

5   Conclusions and Future Directions

In this article, we have discovered some logical relations of opposition between the fuzzy formal contexts I and I^*, which are generated from two different quantifiers S and S^*. To do this, we have expanded the class of t-scaling quantifiers by defining the negative t- scaling quantifies and the (positive and negative) existential quantifiers. Furthermore, we have found out some consequences of the relations of opposition between fuzzy formal contexts by focusing on a special pair of fuzzy formal concept analysis operators. In the future, we will extend this work as follows. Firstly, given a fuzzy relational context family, we want to find $[s_1, s_2], [t_1, t_2] \subseteq [0, 1]$ so that I_t^+ and I_s^- are contraries for each $s \in [s_1, s_2]$ and $t \in [t_1, t_2]$. Similarly, we will find $[t_1^+, t_2^+], [t_1^-, t_2^-] \subseteq [0, 1]$ so that I_3^+ is sub-altern of $I_{t^+}^+$ and I_3^- is sub-altern of $I_{t^-}^-$ for each $t^+ \in [t_1^+, t_2^+]$ and $t^- \in [t_1^-, t_2^-]$. Then, we intend to construct structures of opposition (analogous to those defined in [12, 14]), which have fuzzy formal contexts as vertices. Moreover, we would like to discover the implications of the relations presented by Theorem 1 (especially by items (a) and (b)) on the operators of Definition 2 and on other pairs of FFCA operators like those defined in [5]. Eventually, we will find out connections between fuzzy concepts generated using different quantifiers. Finally, we could analyze how the thresholds t and T are related, for example, by determining under which conditions (t_1, T_1) and (t_2, T_2) produce the same collection of fuzzy concepts.

References

1. Boffa, S.: Extracting concepts from fuzzy relational context families. IEEE Trans. Fuzzy Syst. **31**(4), 1202–1213 (2023)
2. Braud, A., Dolques, X., Huchard, M., Le Ber, F.: Generalization effect of quantifiers in a classification based on relational concept analysis. Knowl.-Based Syst. **160**, 119–135 (2018)
3. Novák, V.: A formal theory of intermediate quantifiers. Fuzzy Sets Syst. **159**(10), 1229–1246 (2008)
4. Murinová, P., Novák, V.: Graded generalized hexagon in fuzzy natural logic. Inf. Process. Manag. Uncertainty Knowl.-Based Syst. **611**, 36–47 (2016)
5. Bělohlávek, R.: Fuzzy Relational Systems: Foundations and Principles, vol. 20. Springer, Heidelberg (2012)
6. Boffa, S., Murinová, P., Novák, V.: A proposal to extend relational concept analysis with fuzzy scaling quantifiers. Knowl.-Based Syst. **231**, 107452 (2021)
7. Rouane-Hacene, M., Huchard, M., Napoli, A., Valtchev, P.: Relational concept analysis: mining concept lattices from multi-relational data. Ann. Math. Artif. Intell. **67**(1), 81–108 (2013)
8. Boffa, S., De Maio, C., Di Nola, A., Fenza, G., Ferraioli, A.R., Loia, V.: Unifying fuzzy concept lattice construction methods. In: 2016 IEEE International Conference on Fuzzy Systems (FUZZ-IEEE), pp. 209–216. IEEE (2016)
9. Miclet, L., Prade, H.: Analogical proportions and square of oppositions. In: Laurent, A., Strauss, O., Bouchon-Meunier, B., Yager, R.R. (eds.) IPMU 2014. CCIS, vol. 443, pp. 324–334. Springer, Cham (2014). https://doi.org/10.1007/978-3-319-08855-6_33
10. Pellissier, R.: "Setting" n-opposition. Logica Universalis **2**(2), 235–263 (2008)
11. Novák, V., Perfilieva, I., Močkoř, J.: Mathematical Principles of Fuzzy Logic, vol. 517. Kluwer and Springer, Boston and Dordrecht (1999/2012)
12. Boffa, S., Murinová, P., Novák, V.: Graded polygons of opposition in fuzzy formal concept analysis. Int. J. Approximate Reasoning **132**, 128–153 (2021)
13. Dubois, D., Prade, H., Rico, A.: Graded cubes of opposition and possibility theory with fuzzy events. Int. J. Approximate Reasoning **84**, 168–185 (2017)
14. Boffa, S., Murinová, P., Novák, V., Ferbas, P.: Graded cubes of opposition in fuzzy formal concept analysis. Int. J. Approximate Reasoning **145**, 187–209 (2022)

An Analysis of FRCA Quantifiers

Stefania Boffa[1]($\boxtimes$)(iD) and Brunella Gerla[2]

[1] University of Milano-Bicocca, Milano, Italy
stefania.boffa@unimib.it
[2] University of Insubria, Varese, Italy

Abstract. FRCA quantifiers are significant tools to extract information from data organized as collections of fuzzy object-attribute and object-object relations. This article mainly presents some comparisons between classes of FRCA quantifiers introduced in previous works.

Keywords: Fuzzy quantifiers · Fuzzy concept lattices · Fuzzy relational concept analysis

1 Introduction

Formal Concept Analysis (FCA), introduced in [1], is a mathematical tool used to deal with relations between objects and attributes. A formal concept is a pair (A, B) made by a set of objects and a set of attributes such that all objects in A have the properties of B and all properties of B are satisfied by the objects in A. The set of all objects in a given context can be ordered by a lattice structure. When the property of an object to have an attribute is vague, it is possible to introduce *Fuzzy Formal Concept Analysis* (FFCA) [2] in which the context is a fuzzy relation.

On the other hand, *Relational Concept Analysis* (RCA) has been introduced to deal with multiple sets of attributes and objects and with relations between them [3]. Dealing with such structures the typical question could be *"how many objects of X have all attributes of W, if we know that the objects of X are in relation with the objects of Z and we also know the correspondence between the objects of Z and the attributes of W?"*. The answer was provided by using the so-called *scaling quantifiers* in the RCA process [4]. An example is represented by the relation $\mathcal{Q}_{60}$ such that given two sets A and B, $\mathcal{Q}_{60}(A, B) = 1$ if and only if *"more than 60% of elements of A belong to B"*.

In order to extend RCA to the fuzzy case, we need the definitions for fuzzy quantifiers. Indeed, *Fuzzy relational concept analysis* (FRCA) mines fuzzy concepts from a fuzzy multi-relational datasets by employing FRCA quantifiers together with the standard FFCA techniques [5,6].

FRCA quantifiers are special fuzzy quantifiers generalizing the quantifier *all*, which is already used to construct concepts in fuzzy formal concept analysis. Mathematically, a FRCA quantifier is a function assigning a value $\mathcal{S}_V(A, B)$ of the real interval $[0, 1]$ to a pair of fuzzy sets A and B so that $\mathcal{S}_V(A, B)$ expresses how much "all $A|Z$ are B", where $A|Z$ is a part of A having a certain size that is

S. Massanet et al. (Eds.): EUSFLAT 2023/AGOP 2023, LNCS 14069, pp. 405–416, 2023.
https://doi.org/10.1007/978-3-031-39965-7_34

evaluated by V. According to the formula of V, we can distinguish the following classes of FRCA quantifiers.

- *T-scaling quantifiers* are introduced in [6] by putting $V = \Delta_t$, where t is a threshold belonging to $[0, 1]$. Therefore, given $t \in [0, 1]$, $\mathcal{S}_{\Delta_t}(A, B)$ represents how much "all $A|Z$ are B", where $A|Z$ is a part of A being at least as big as t (in the scale $[0, 1]$).
- *Fuzzy scaling quantifiers* are proposed in [5] by putting $V = Bi_\nu$ such that Bi_ν is a normal and increasing function from $[0, 1]$ to $[0, 1]$ modeling an *evaluative linguistic expression* having the form $\langle hedge \rangle \langle big \rangle$, where *hedge* is an adverbial modification like *very*, *extremely*, *roughly*, and so on[1]. Therefore, if Bi_ν represents the expression Very Big, then $\mathcal{S}_{Bi_\nu}$ expresses how much "all $A|Z$ are B", where $A|Z$ is a Very Big part of A.

All FRCA quantifiers are generalizations of RCA quantifiers given in [4] and are interpretations in a model of *intermediate quantifiers*, which are special formulas of the *formal theory of intermediate generalized quantifiers* [9,10].

Let us underline that during the FRCA process, a quantifier must be selected for each fuzzy object-object relation of the initial dataset. Thus, the final concept classification depends on the choice of the quantifiers: we could obtain different fuzzy concepts by employing different quantifiers. This aspect has motivated us to investigate in this paper if and when fuzzy scaling and t-scaling quantifiers produce the same fuzzy concepts. The article is composed of two main parts: in Sect. 2 we recall the FRCA procedure and the notion of FRCA quantifiers and we exhibit an illustrative example where the initial fuzzy relations have an intuitive meaning. In Sect. 3 we find the conditions needed for a set of t-scaling quantifiers to generate the same concepts of a given fuzzy scaling quantifier.

2   Fuzzy Relational Concept Analysis

2.1   Fuzzy Formal Concept Analysis

We assume that the basic structures of truth values is the *standard Łukasiewicz MV-algebra* $\langle [0, 1], \wedge, \vee, \otimes, \rightarrow, 0, 1 \rangle$, where $a \vee b = \max\{a, b\}$, $a \wedge b = \min\{a, b\}$, $a \otimes b = \max\{0, a + b - 1\}$, and $a \rightarrow b = \min\{1, 1 - a + b\}$ for each $a, b \in [0, 1]$.

Moreover, we use the symbol $[0, 1]^X$ to denote the collection of all fuzzy sets of a universe X.

Definition 1. *A fuzzy formal context is a triple* (X, Y, I), *where X is a set of objects, Y is a set of attributes, and I is a fuzzy relation on $X \times Y$.*

Definition 2. *[2, 11] Let* (X, Y, I) *be a fuzzy formal context. If* $A \in [0, 1]^X$ *and* $B \in [0, 1]^Y$, *then* $A^{\uparrow I}(y) = \bigwedge_{x \in X}(A(x) \rightarrow I(x, y))$ *and* $B^{\downarrow I}(x) = \bigwedge_{y \in Y}(B(y) \rightarrow I(x, y))$, *for all $x \in X$ and $y \in Y$.*

---

[1] Moreingeneral,*evaluativelinguisticexpressions*areexpressionsofnaturallanguage andtheirtheoryisconstructedinaformalsystemofhigher-order fuzzylogic(fuzzytypetheory)[7,8].

$A^{\uparrow^I}(y)$ and $B^{\downarrow_I}(x)$ are the truth degrees of the statements "y is shared by all objects of A" and "x has all attributes of B", respectively.

Definition 3. Let (X,Y,I) be a fuzzy formal context, let $A \in [0,1]^X$, and let $B \in [0,1]^Y$. Then, (A,B) is a fuzzy concept of (X,Y,I) if and only if $A^{\uparrow_I} = B$ and $B^{\downarrow_I} = A$.

We denote the set of all fuzzy concepts of (X,Y,I) with $\mathcal{B}(X,Y,I)$.

$(\mathcal{B}(X,Y,I), \mathcal{R})$ is a complete fuzzy lattice called the fuzzy concept lattice of (X,Y,I), where $\mathcal{R}$ is defined by $\mathcal{R}((A_1,B_1),(A_2,B_2)) = \bigwedge_{x\in X}(A_1(x) \to A_2(x))$, for all $(A_1,B_1),(A_2,B_2) \in \mathcal{B}(X,Y,I)$ [12].

Example 1. We consider here an example taken from [12] and adapted with fuzzy values. In this example, objects are pizzas and attributes are ingredients that can be present with a certain degree. Figures 1 and 2 respectively show the fuzzy formal context representing the relation between pizzas and ingredients, and the corresponding fuzzy concept lattice, where $C_0 = (\{margherita, capricciosa, 4cheese\ veg\}, \emptyset)$, $C_1 = (\{margherita, capricciosa, 4cheese\}, \{dairy\})$, $C_2 = (\{margherita, capricciosa, veg\}, \{tomato\})$, $C_3 = (\{0.5 /capricciosa, veg\}, \{tomato, vegetables\})$, $C_4 = (\{margherita, capricciosa\}, \{tomato, dairy\})$, and $C_5 = (\{0.5/capricciosa\}, \{tomato, meat, dairy, vegetables\})$.

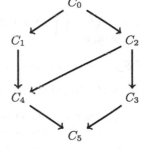

Pizzas	tomato	meat	dairy	vegetables
margherita	1	0	1	0
capricciosa	1	0.5	1	0.5
4cheese	0	0	1	0
veg	1	0	0	1

Fig. 1. Fuzzy formal context *Pizzas*   **Fig. 2.** Fuzzy concept lattice of *Pizzas*

2.2 Fuzzy Relational Concept Analysis

FRCA Quantifiers. We fix the notation for the following well-known concepts in fuzzy logic as follows: let $A, B \in [0,1]^X$ [2],

- $|A| = \sum_{x\in X} A(x)$ is the *cardinality* of A;

---

[2] We write $A = \emptyset$ when $A(x) = 0$ for each $x \in X$, $A = B$ when $A(x) = B(x)$ for each $x \in X$, and $A \subseteq B$ when $A(x) \le B(x)$ for each $x \in X$.

- $\mu_B(A)$ measures *"how large the size of A is w.r.t. the size of B"* and it is given by

$$\mu_B(A) = \begin{cases} 1 & \text{if } A = \emptyset \text{ or } A = B; \\ \frac{|A|}{|B|} & \text{if } A \neq \emptyset \text{ and } A \subseteq B; \\ 0 & \text{otherwise}; \end{cases}$$

- $A|B$ is the *cut* of A at B and it is defined, for every $x \in X$, by $(A|B)(x) = A(x)$ if $A(x) = B(x)$ while $(A|B)(x) = 0$ otherwise.
- Δ_t is a function $\Delta_t : [0,1] \to [0,1]$ such that let $k \in [0,1]$,

$$\Delta_t(k) = \begin{cases} 1 \text{ if } k \geq t; \\ 0 \text{ otherwise}. \end{cases}$$

By $Bi_\nu : [0,1] \to [0,1]$ we denote a normal and increasing function modeling a given evaluative linguistic expression with the form $\langle hedge \rangle \langle big \rangle$, where *hedge* is an adverb related to *big* modeled by ν. The formal definition can be found in [7], see Example 2 for a possible interpretation in the case *hedge = very*. We further set $\mathcal{E}$ as the set of the models of all evaluative linguistic expressions like $\langle hedge \rangle \langle big \rangle$.

Definition 4 (FRCA quantifiers). *Let $V \in \mathcal{E} \cup \{\Delta_t \mid t \in [0,1]\}$. The FRCA quantifier with respect to V is a function $\mathcal{S}_V : [0,1]^X \times [0,1]^X \to [0,1]$ defined by*

$$\mathcal{S}_V(A,B) = \bigvee_{Z \in [0,1]^X} \left(\left(\bigwedge_{x \in X} (A|Z)(x) \to B(x) \right) \otimes \bigvee_{x \in X} (A|Z)(x) \right) \wedge V(\mu_A(A|Z)).$$

$\mathcal{S}_{Bi_\nu}$ *and* $\mathcal{S}_{\Delta_t}$ *are respectively called* fuzzy scaling *and* t-scaling *quantifiers.*

We attach the following meaning to $\mathcal{S}_V(A,B)$:

- if $V = Bi_\nu$, then $\mathcal{S}_V(A,B)$ is the degree of the statement: *there exists a cut $A|Z$ of A such that "all elements of $A|Z$ belong to B", "there exists at least one element in $A|Z$", and "the size of $A|Z$ is $\langle hedge \rangle$ large w.r.t. the size of A"*;
- if $V = \Delta_t$, then $\mathcal{S}_V(A,B)$ is the degree of the statement: *there exists a cut $A|Z$ of A such that "all elements of $A|Z$ belong to B", "there exists at least one element in $A|Z$", and "the size of $A|Z$ is at least as large as t (in the scale $[0,1]$) w.r.t. the size of A"*.

Note that the expression $\bigvee_{x \in X}(A|Z)(x)$ in the definition of $\mathcal{S}_V(A,B)$ is needed to exclude the case in which the set of quantification (i.e., $A|Z$) is empty, see [5].

Remark 1. The first connection between t-scaling and fuzzy scaling quantifiers is provided in [6]: if $t \geq 50$, then there exists a fuzzy scaling quantifier $\mathcal{S}_{Bi_\nu}$ such that $\mathcal{S}_{\Delta_t} = \mathcal{S}_{Bi_\nu}$. In other words, $\{\mathcal{S}_{\Delta_t} \mid t \geq 0.5\}$ is strictly included in the class of fuzzy scaling quantifiers $\{\mathcal{S}_{Bi_\nu} \mid Bi_\nu \in \mathcal{E}\}$.

Putting $\mathcal{S}_1(A|Z,B) = \bigwedge_{x\in X}((A|Z)(x) \to B(x)) \otimes \bigvee_{x\in X}(A|Z)(x)$, we can rewrite the formula of $\mathcal{S}_V(A,B)$ as follows:

$$\mathcal{S}_V(A,B) = \bigvee_{Z\in[0,1]^X} (\mathcal{S}_1(A|Z,B) \wedge V(\mu_A(A|Z))). \tag{1}$$

Let us recall that $\mathcal{S}_1$ is the quantifiers *all* and it is equal to $\mathcal{S}_{\Delta_1}$.

According to the next theorem, $\mathcal{S}_V(A,B)$ has been computed in [6] by taking into account the following class of fuzzy sets that depend on A and B.

Definition 5. *Let* $A, B \in [0,1]^X$, *we consider* $\mathsf{K}_{(A,B)} = \{k \in [0,1] \mid A(x) \to B(x) = k$, *for some* $x \in X\}$. *Then, let* $k \in \mathsf{K}_{(A,B)}$, *we put*

$$A_k(x) = \begin{cases} A(x) & \text{if } A(x) \to B(x) \geq k; \\ 0 & \text{otherwise.} \end{cases} \quad \text{for each } x \in X.$$

In this article, we use the symbol $\mathsf{C}_{(A,B)}$ to denote the set of all cuts given by Definition 5, i.e. $\mathsf{C}_{(A,B)} = \{A_k \mid k \in \mathsf{K}_{(A,B)}\}$.

Theorem 1. *[6] Let* $Bi_\nu \in \mathcal{E}$ *and* $t \in [0,1]$. *Then, for each* $A, B \in [0,1]^X$,

(a) $\mathcal{S}_{Bi_\nu}(A,B) = \bigvee_{A_k\in\mathsf{C}_{(A,B)}} (\mathcal{S}_1(A_k,B) \wedge Bi_\nu(\mu_A(A_k)))$;

(b) $\mathcal{S}_{\Delta_t}(A,B) = \bigvee_{\{A_k\in\mathsf{C}_{(A,B)} \mid \mu_A(A_k)\geq t\}} \mathcal{S}_1(A_k,B)$.

2.3 Extracting Concepts from a Fuzzy Relational Context Family

The dataset analyzed in FRCA is called *Fuzzy Relational Context Family* (FRCF). In this paper, we focus on the simplest FRCF $(\mathbf{K},\mathbf{R})$, where $\mathbf{K}$ is made of two fuzzy formal contexts (X,Y,I) and (Z,W,J), and $\mathbf{R}$ is made of a fuzzy relation $r: X \times Z \to [0,1]$. Moreover, in the sequel, we use the symbol r^x to denote the fuzzy set of Z such that $r^x(z) = r(x,z)$ for each $z \in Z$. The input of the FRCA procedure is $(\mathbf{K},\mathbf{R})$ and the output is obtained in three fundamental steps.

1. A fuzzy concept lattice $\mathcal{B}(Z,W,J)$ is generated by using one of the existing fuzzy FCA algorithms.
2. A new fuzzy formal context $(X, Y \cup Y_J, I_V)$ is constructed starting from $\mathcal{B}(Z,W,J)$ and a selected quantifier $\mathcal{S}_V$; in particular a new attribute y_C is added for every fuzzy concept $C \in \mathcal{B}(Z,W,J)$:

$$Y_J = \{y_C \mid C \in \mathcal{B}(Z,W,J)\} \text{ and } I_V(x,y) = \begin{cases} I(x,y) & \text{if } y \in Y; \\ \mathcal{S}_V(r^x, E_C) & \text{if } y = y_C; \end{cases} \tag{2}$$

where E_C is the *extent* (i.e. the set of objects) of the concept C of $\mathcal{B}(Z,W,J)$.
3. A fuzzy concept lattice $\mathcal{B}(X, Y \cup Y_J, I_V)$ is extracted from $(X, Y \cup Y_J, I_V)$ adopting the same algorithm chosen in the first step.

So, $\{\mathcal{B}(X, Y \cup Y_J, I_V), \mathcal{B}(Z,W,J)\}$ is the final result generated by the FRCA process.

Example 2. Keeping the notation above, we extend here Example 1 denoting by Z the set of pizzas and by W the set of ingredients (see Fig. 1). We further consider the fuzzy formal context of Fig. 3 having the set X of people as set of objects and, for the sake of readability, trivial attributes forming the set Y. Moreover, Fig. 4 represents a fuzzy relation between people in X and pizzas in Z (how much a person likes a pizza).

People	ArthurID	JohnID	AliceID	JulielID
Arthur	1	0	0	0
John	0	1	0	0
Alice	0	0	1	0
Juliel	0	0	0	1

Like	margherita	capricciosa	4chees	veg
Arthur	0.5	0	1	0
John	1	0.5	0	1
Alice	0	1	0.5	0.5
Juliet	1	1	0.5	0

Fig. 3. Fuzzy formal context *People*   **Fig. 4.** Fuzzy relation *Like*

FRCA process introduces new attributes $Y_{Pizzas} = \{y_{C_0}, \ldots, y_{C_7}\}$ for people in Fig. 1, with degrees given by I_V that can be interpreted as "how much" a given person likes pizzas having the ingredients in a given concept. For example, let us consider the quantifiers $\mathcal{S}_{Bi_{Ve}}$ and $\mathcal{S}_{\Delta_{0.7}}$, where $Bi_{Ve} : [0,1] \to [0,1]$ models the linguistic expression "*very big*" and has the following formulas: let $x \in [0,1]$

$$Bi_{Ve}(x) = \begin{cases} 1, & x \in [0.915, 1]; \\ 1 - \frac{(0.915-x)^2}{0.03}, & x \in [0.79, 0.915); \\ \frac{(x-0.675)^2}{0.0276}, & x \in (0.675, 0.79); \\ 0, & x \in [0, 0.675]. \end{cases} \tag{3}$$

Since $\mathcal{S}_{Bi_{Ve}}$ in the quantifier "*most*", $I_{Bi_{Ve}}(Juliet, y_{C_2}) = \mathcal{S}_{Bi_{Ve}}(A, B) = 0.48$, where $A = \{marherita, capricciosa, 0.5/4chees\}$ expresses the degree of preference of Juliet about the pizzas and $B = \{margherita, capricciosa, veg\}$ is the set of pizzas in C_2, is the degree to which "*Juliet likes most pizzas having tomato (i.e. all ingredients of pizzas in C_2)*". Analogously, $I_{\Delta_{0.7}}(Juliet, y_{C_2}) = 1$ is the degree to which "*Juliet likes a part of pizzas in C_2 being at least as big as 0.7 (in the scale [0,1]), namely a part of the pizzas characterized to have tomato as ingredient*". Finally, it is easy to understand that the fuzzy concepts extracted from $\mathcal{B}(X, Y \cup Y_{Pizzas}, I_{Bi_{Ve}})$ and $\mathcal{B}(X, Y \cup Y_{Pizzas}, I_{\Delta_{0.7}})$ captures the preferences of people about the ingredients.

3   Comparing Fuzzy Scaling and t-Scaling Quantifiers

In this section, given $Bi_\nu \in \mathcal{E}$, we investigate the existence of $t \in [0,1]$ such that the corresponding fuzzy formal context $(X, Y \cup Y_J, I_{\Delta_t})$ coincides with $(X, Y \cup Y_J, I_{Bi_\nu})$.

We suppose that I, J, and r are $Ł_n$-relations, where n is a positive integer and the structure $\langle Ł_n, \wedge, \vee, \otimes, \to, 0, 1 \rangle$ is a Łukasiewicz chain, namely $Ł_n = \left\{ \dfrac{k}{n} \mid k \in \mathbb{Z} \text{ and } 0 \leq k \leq n \right\}$ and $\wedge, \vee, \otimes$, and $\to$ are the operations of the standard Łukasiewicz MV-algebra.

Remark 2. First of all, we can observe that, for each $t \in [0, 1]$, the relation I_{Δ_t} assumes all its values in $Ł_n$. This is because I_{Δ_t} is defined using $\wedge, \vee, \otimes$, and $\to$ (see (2) and Definition 4), and $Ł_n$ is closed under the operations of the standard Łukasiewicz MV-algebra.

Reamark 2 cannot be extended to the relations in $\{I_{Bi_\nu} \mid Bi_\nu \in \mathcal{E}\}$. Namely, let $Bi_\nu \in \mathcal{E}$, there exists a fuzzy relational context family so that "$I_{Bi_\nu}(x, y_C) \notin Ł_n$ for some $x \in X$ and $y_C \in Y_J$". This occurs when $I_{Bi_\nu}(x, y_C) = Bi_\nu(\mu_{r^x}(A))$ with $A \in C_{(r^x, E_C)}$ and $Bi_\nu(\mu_{r^x}(A)) \notin Ł_n$ (let us underline that $x \in Ł_n$ does not imply that $Bi_\nu(x) \notin Ł_n$). See Example 2, $I_{Bi_{Ve}}(Juliet, y_{C_2}) = 0.48 \notin \{0, 0.5, 1\}$.

Remark 3. Trivially, if $I_{Bi_\nu}(x, y_C) \notin Ł_n$ for some $x \in X$ and $y_C \in Y_j$, then $I_{Bi_\nu} \neq I_{\Delta_t}$ for each $t \in [0, 1]$. On the other hand, although I_{Bi_ν} assumes all its values in $Ł_n$, it could not coincide with any I_{Δ_t}. This is possible whenever "$I_{Bi_\nu}(x, y_C) = Bi_\nu(\mu_{r^x}(A))$ and $I_{Bi_\nu}(x, y_C) \neq S_1(B, E_C) \; \forall B \in C''_{(r^x, E_C)}$.

In case $I_{Bi_\nu}(x, y_C) \in Ł_n$ for each $(x, y_C) \in X \times Y_J$, it is sometimes possible to find out a set of thresholds so that their related fuzzy formal context is equal to $(X, Y \cup Y_J, I_{Bi_\nu})$. This aim is achieved by Theorem 2, which is based on the following notations.

Definition 6. *Let* $(x, y_C) \in X \times Y_J$ *such that* $I_{Bi_\nu}(x, y_C) = S_1(A, E_C)$ *with* $A \in C_{(r^x, E_C)}$, *we put*

$$\mathcal{L}_{(x, y_C)} = \{B \in C_{(r^x, E_C)} \mid S_1(B, E_C) > S_1(A, E_C) \text{ and } \mu_{r^x}(B) \leq \mu_{r^x}(A)\}.$$

Example 3. Suppose that $r^x = \{z_1, z_2, z_3, z_4\}$ and $E_C = \{0.1/z_2, 0.2/z_3, 0.3/z_4\}$. Then, by Definition 5, $C_{(r^x, E_C)} = \{r^x, A, B, D\}$, where $A = \{z_2, z_3, z_4\}$, $B = \{z_3, z_4\}$, and $D = \{z_4\}$.

According to Theorem 1 (a), if we consider Bi_{Ve} given by (3), then $S_{Bi_{Ve}}(r^x, E_C) = (S_1(r^x, E_C) \wedge Bi_{Ve}(\mu_{r^x}(r^x))) \vee (S_1(A, E_C) \wedge Bi_{Ve}(\mu_{r^x}(A))) \vee (S_1(r^x, B) \wedge Bi_{Ve}(\mu_{r^x}(B))) \vee (S_1(D, E_C) \wedge Bi_{Ve}(\mu_{r^x}(D))) = 0.1$, where let $H \in \{r^x, A, B, D\}$, the values $S_1(H, E_C)$ and $Bi_{Ve}(\mu_{r^x}(H))$ are defined by Table 1.

Therefore, we can easily verify that $I_{Bi_{Ve}}(x, y_C) = S_1(A, E_C)$ (both equal 0.1) and $\mathcal{L}_{(x, y_C)} = \{B, D\}$ (the size of B and D is smaller than the size of A, moreover $S_1(B, E_C) = 0.2$ and $S_1(B, E_C) = 0.3$ are greater than $S_1(A, E_C) = 0.1$).

Proposition 1. *Let* $(x, y_C) \in X \times Y_J$ *such that* $I_{Bi_\nu}(x, y_C) = S_1(A, E_C)$ *with* $A \in C_{(r^x, E_C)}$. *If* $\mathcal{L}_{(x, y_C)} = \emptyset$ *then* $S_1(A, E_C) \geq S_1(B, E_C)$ *for each* $B \in C_{(r^x, E_C)}$.

Proof. By Definition 6, for each $B \in C_{(r^x, E_C)}$, $S_1(B, E_C) \leq S_1(A, E_C)$ or $\mu_{r^x}(A) < \mu_{r^x}(B)$ by considering that $\mathcal{L}_{(x, y_C)} = \emptyset$. Then, $\mu_{r^x}(A) < \mu_{r^x}(B)$

Table 1. $\mathcal{S}_1(H, E_C)$ and $Bi_{Ve}(\mu_{r^x}(H))$ with $H \in \{r^x, A, B, D\}$.

H	$\mu_{r^x}(H)$	$Bi_{Ve}(\mu_{r^x}(H))$	$\mathcal{S}_1(H, E_C)$
r^x	1	1	0
A	0.75	0.2	0.1
B	0.5	0	0.2
D	0.25	0	0.3

implies that $Bi_\nu(\mu_{r^x}(A)) < Bi_\nu(\mu_{r^x}(B))$ because Bi_ν is an increasing function. Also, since $I_{Bi_\nu}(x, y_C) = \mathcal{S}_1(A, E_C)$, it must be $\mathcal{S}_1(A, E_C) \leq Bi_\nu(\mu_{r^x}(A))$ and $\mathcal{S}_1(A, E_C) \geq \mathcal{S}_1(B, E_C) \wedge Bi_\nu(\mu_{r^x}(B))$. Let us focus on the last inequality and suppose that $\mathcal{S}_1(A, E_C) \geq Bi_\nu(\mu_{r^x}(B))$. Then, the latter together with $Bi_\nu(\mu_{r^x}(B)) > Bi_\nu(\mu_{r^x}(A))$ implies that $\mathcal{S}_1(A, E_C) > Bi_\nu(\mu_{r^x}(A))$, which contradicts $\mathcal{S}_1(A, E_C) \leq Bi_\nu(\mu_{r^x}(A))$. Finally, we have $\mathcal{S}_1(B, E_C) \leq \mathcal{S}_1(A, E_C)$.

Definition 7. *Let* $(x, y_C) \in X \times Y_J$ *such that* $I_{Bi_\nu}(x, y_C) = \mathcal{S}_1(A, E_C)$ *with* $A \in C_{(r^x, E_C)}$, *we put*

$$a_{(x,y_C)} = \begin{cases} \max\{\mu_{r^x}(B) \mid B \in \mathcal{L}_{(x,y_C)}\} & \text{if } \mathcal{L}_{(x,y_C)} \neq \emptyset, \\ 0 & \text{otherwise,} \end{cases} \quad \text{and} \quad (4)$$

$$b_{(x,y_C)} = \max\{\mu_{r^x}(B) \mid B \in C_{(x,y_C)} \text{ and } \mathcal{S}_1(B, E_C) = \mathcal{S}_1(A, E_C)\}. \quad (5)$$

Example 4. If we consider Example 3, then $a_{(x,y_C)} = \max\{\mu_{r^x}(B), \mu_{r^x}(D)\} = \max\{0.5, 0.25\} = 0.5$ and $b_{(x,y_C)} = \mu_{r^x}(A) = 0.75$.

The most important result of this section is Theorem 2, which is based on the following lemma.

In the sequel, given $(x, y_C) \in X \times Y_J$ such that $I_{Bi_{Ve}}(x, y_C) = \mathcal{S}_1(A, E_C)$ with $A \in C_{(r^x, E_C)}$, we put

$$Int_{(x,y)} = \begin{cases} (a_{(x,y_C)}, b_{(x,y_C)}] & \text{if } \mathcal{L}_{(x,y_C)} \neq \emptyset, \\ [a_{(x,y_C)}, b_{(x,y_C)}] & \text{otherwise.} \end{cases} \quad (6)$$

Lemma 1. *Let* $Bi_\nu \in \mathcal{E}$ *and let* $(x, y_C) \in X \times Y_J$, *if* $I_{Bi_\nu}(x, y_C) = \mathcal{S}_1(A, E_C)$ *with* $A \in C_{(r^x, E_C)}$, *then* $I_{Bi_\nu}(x, y_C) = I_{\Delta_t}(x, y_C)$ *for each* $t \in Int_{(x,y_C)}$.

Proof. Let $t \in Int_{(x,y_C)}$, we inted to prove that $I_{\Delta_t}(x, y_C) = \mathcal{S}_1(A, E_C)$.
According to Theorem 1 (b),

$$I_{\Delta_t}(x, y_C) = \bigvee_{\{B \in C_{(r^x, E_C)} \mid \mu_{r^x}(B) \geq t\}} \mathcal{S}_1(B, E_C). \quad (7)$$

By hypothesis, $t \leq b_{(x,y_C)}$. Thus, by (5), t is less than or equal to the size of B, which is the biggest cut of $C_{(r^x, E_C)}$ satisfying $\mathcal{S}_1(B, E_C) = \mathcal{S}_1(A, E_C)$. This guarantees the existence of $B \in C_{(r^x, E_C)}$ such that $\mu_{r^x}(B) \geq t$ and $\mathcal{S}_1(B, E_C) =$

$\mathcal{S}_1(A, E_C)$. Hence, by (7), we get $\mathcal{S}_1(A, E_C) \leq I_{\Delta_t}(x, y_C)$, considering that the property "$a \leq a_1 \vee \ldots \vee a_l$ for each $a \in \{a_1, \ldots, a_l\}$" holds in the standard Łukasiewicz MV-algebra.

Now, we want to show that $I_{\Delta_t}(x, y_C) \leq \mathcal{S}_1(A, E_C)$. If $\mathcal{L}_{(x, y_C)} = \emptyset$, then $\mathcal{S}_1(B, E_C) \leq \mathcal{S}_1(A, B)$ for each $B \in \mathsf{C}_{(r^x, E_C)}$ from Proposition 1. So, suppose that $\mathcal{L}_{(x, y_C)} \neq \emptyset$, then $t \in (a_{(x, y_C)}, b_{(x, y_C)}]$ from (6). Since the property "$a_1 \vee \ldots \vee a_l \leq a$ if and only if $a_i \leq a$ for each $i \in \{1, \ldots, l\}$" holds in the standard Łukasiewicz MV-algebra, we need to verify that

$$\mathcal{S}_1(A, E_C) \geq \mathcal{S}_1(B, E_C) \text{ for each } B \in \mathsf{C}_{(r^x, E_C)} \text{ such that } \mu_{r^x}(B) \geq t.$$

We can view the set $\{B \in \mathsf{C}_{(r^x, E_C)} \mid \mu_{r^x}(B) \geq t\}$ as the union of the sets $\mathcal{A} = \{B \in \mathsf{C}_{(r^x, E_C)} \mid t \leq \mu_{r^x}(B) \leq \mu_{r^x}(A)\}$ and $\mathcal{B} = \{B \in \mathsf{C}_{(r^x, E_C)} \mid \mu_{r^x}(B) > \mu_{r^x}(A)\}$.

Let $B \in \mathcal{A}$, then $t > a_{(x, y_C)}$ and $\mu_{r^x}(B) \leq t$ imply that $\mu_{r^x}(B) > a_{(x, y_C)}$. By (4), $a_{(x, y_C)} = \mu_{r^x}(\tilde{B})$, where $\tilde{B}$ is the biggest fuzzy set in $\mathcal{L}_{(x, y_C)}$. Consequently, $B \notin \mathcal{L}_{(x, y_C)}$. Moreover, $\mu_{r^x}(B) \leq \mu_{r^x}(A)$ because we have supposed that $B \in \mathcal{A}$. Then, the last two sentences together with Definition 6 imply that the inequality $\mathcal{S}_1(B, E_C) \leq \mathcal{S}_1(A, E_C)$ holds.

Let $B \in \mathcal{B}$, then $\mu_{r^x}(B) > \mu_{r^x}(A)$. Hence, $Bi_\nu(\mu_{r^x}(B)) > Bi_\nu(\mu_{r^x}(A))$ because Bi_ν is an increasing function. Let us show that $\mathcal{S}_1(A, E_C) < \mathcal{S}_1(B, E_C)$ leads to a contradiction. To do this, we need to recall that the following property holds in the standard Łukasiewicz MV-algebra: "if $a < c$ and $b < d$ then $a \wedge b < c \wedge d$". Hence, $Bi_\nu(\mu_{r^x}(A)) < Bi_\nu(\mu_{r^x}(B))$ and $\mathcal{S}_1(A, E_C) < \mathcal{S}_1(B, E_C)$ imply that $\mathcal{S}_1(A, E_C) \wedge Bi_\nu(\mu_{r^x}(A)) < \mathcal{S}_1(B, E_C) \wedge Bi_\nu(\mu_{r^x}(B))$. Since $\mathcal{S}_1(A, E_C) \wedge Bi_\nu(\mu_{r^x}(A)) = \mathcal{S}_1(A, E_C)$, we have $\mathcal{S}_1(A, E_C) < \mathcal{S}_1(B, E_C) \wedge Bi_\nu(\mu_{r^x}(B))$, which contradicts the assumption $I_{Bi_\nu}(x, y_C) = \mathcal{S}_1(A, E_C)$. Finally, we can conclude that $\mathcal{S}_1(B, E_C) \leq \mathcal{S}_1(A, E_C)$.

Example 5. Let $(x, y_C) \in X \times Y_J$ given by Example 3. By Lemma 1, $I_{Bi_{V_e}}(x, y_C) = I_{\Delta_t}(x, y_C)$ for each $t \in (0.5, 0.75]$. For instance, choosing the values 0.4, 0.6, and 0.9, we respectively obtain $I_{0.4}(x, y_C) = \mathcal{S}_1(r^x, E_C) \vee \mathcal{S}_1(A, E_C) \vee \mathcal{S}_1(B, E_C) = 0 \vee 0.1 \vee 0.2 = 0.2 \neq I_{Bi_{V_e}}(x, y_C)$, $I_{0.6}(x, y_C) = \mathcal{S}_1(r^x, E_C) \vee \mathcal{S}_1(A, E_C) = 0.1 = I_{Bi_{V_e}}(x, y_C)$, and $I_{0.9}(x, y_C) = \mathcal{S}_1(r^x, E_C) = 0 \neq I_{Bi_{V_e}}(x, y_C)$.

Theorem 2. *Let $Bi_\nu \in \mathcal{E}$ such that for each $(x, y_C) \in X \times Y_J$ there exists $A \in \mathsf{C}_{(r^x, E_C)}$ with $I_{Bi_\nu}(x, y_C) = \mathcal{S}_1(A, E_C)$. Then, $I_{Bi_\nu} = I_{\Delta_t}$ if and only if $t \in \bigcap_{(x, y_C) \in X \times Y_J} Int_{(x, y_C)}$.*

Proof. ($\Leftarrow$). This implication follows from Lemma 1.

($\Rightarrow$). Suppose that $t \notin \bigcap_{(x, y_C) \in X \times Y_C} Int_{(x, y_C)}$. Then, there exists (x^*, y_{C^*}) such that $t \notin Int_{(x^*, y_{C^*})}$. Thus, if $\mathcal{L}_{(x^*, y_{C^*})} = 0$ then $t > b_{(x^*, y_{C^*})}$. Hence, by (5), $t > \mu_{r^{x^*}}(B)$ for each $B \in \mathsf{C}_{(r^{x^*}, E_{C^*})}$ such that $\mathcal{S}_1(A, E_{C^*}) = \mathcal{S}_1(B, E_{C^*})$. Consequently, $I_{\Delta_t}(x^*, y_{C^*}) = a_1 \vee \ldots \vee a_l$ with $a_1, \ldots, a_l \neq \mathcal{S}_1(A, E_{C^*})$. Then, $I_{\Delta_t}(x^*, y_C^*) \neq \mathcal{S}_1(A, E_{C^*})$, which implies that $I_{\Delta_t} \neq I_{Bi_\nu}$. If $\mathcal{L}_{(x^*, y_{C^*})} \neq 0$ then $t > b_{(x^*, y_{C^*})}$ or $t \leq a_{(x^*, y_{C^*})}$. The last inequality means that there exists

$B \in \mathcal{L}_{(x^*, y_{C^*})}$ such that $t \leq \mu_{r^x}(B)$. Then, $\mathcal{S}_1(B, E_C) > \mathcal{S}_1(A, E_C)$. Finally, $I_{\Delta_t} \neq I_{Bi_\nu}$.

Example 6. Let us focus on the FRCF given by Example *IV.*6 in [6], where the fuzzy relation $r : X \times Z \to [0, 1]$ and the fuzzy concepts of (Z, W, J) are defined by Table 2.

Table 2. Fuzzy relation $r : X \times Z \to [0, 1]$ and fuzzy concepts of (Z, W, J).

r^x	z_1	z_2	z_3	z_4
x_1	0.5	0.5	1	1
x_2	0.75	0	0.25	0
x_3	1	0	0.5	0.75

C_1	$(\{z_1, z_2, z_3, z_4\}, \emptyset)$
C_2	$(\{z_1, z_2, 0.75/z_3, z_4\}, \{0.25/w_1, 0.25/w_2\})$
C_3	$(\{z_1, z_2, 0.5/z_3, z_4\}, \{0.5/w_1, 0.5/w_2\})$
C_4	$(\{z_1, z_2, 0.75/z_4\}, \{w_1, 0.5/w_2\})$
C_5	$(\{0.5/z_1, z_2, z_4\}, \{0.75/w_1, w_2\})$
C_6	$(\{0.75/z_1, z_2, 0.75/z_4\}, \{w_1, 0.75/w_2\})$
C_7	$(\{0.5/z_1, z_2, 0.75/z_4\}, \{w_1, w_2\})$

We also consider $\mathsf{L}_4 = \{0, 0.25, 0.5, 0.75, 1\}$ and Bi_{Ve} given by (3). Applying Theorem 1 (a), we can check that the hypothesis of Theorem 2 is satisfied, namely "$I_{Bi_{Ve}}(x_i, y_{C_j}) = \mathcal{S}_1(r^{x_i}, E_{C_j})$ for each $(i, j) \in \{1, 2, 3\} \times \{1, \ldots, 7\}$".

In order to find the vales assumed by $I_{Bi_{Ve}}$, we use Tables 3, 4, and 5, which respectively list

- the cuts related to $C_{(M,N)}$ for each $(M, N) \in \{r^{x_1}, r^{x_2}, r^{x_3}\} \times \{C_1, \ldots, C_7\}$, where we put $A = \{0.5/z_1, 0.5/z_2, z_4\}$, $B = \{0.5/z_1, 0.5/z_2\}$, $D = \{0.75/z_1\}$, $E = \{z_1, 0.75/z_4\}$, and $F = \{0.75/z_4\}$;
- the values of $\mathcal{S}_1(M, N)$ for each $(M, N) \in \{r^{x_1}, r^{x_2}, r^{x_3}\} \times \{C_1, \ldots, C_7\}$.
- the sizes of the cuts A, B, D, E, F, and and their evaluation employing Bi_{Ve}.

For example, we get $\mathcal{S}_{Bi_{Ve}}(r^{x_i}, E_{C_j}) \wedge Bi_{Ve}(\mu_{r^{x_i}}(r^{x_i})) = \mathcal{S}_1(r^{x_i}, E_{C_j})$ for $(i, j) = (1, 1)$ and $(i, j) \in \{2, 3\} \times \{1, 2, 3\}$, $I_{Bi_{Ve}}(x, y_{C_j}) = (\mathcal{S}_1(A, E_{C_i}) \wedge Bi_{Ve}(\mu_{r^{x_1}}(A))) \vee (\mathcal{S}_1(r^{x_1}, E_{C_i}) \wedge Bi_{Ve}(\mu_{r^{x_1}}(r^{x_1}))) = \mathcal{S}_1(r^{x_1}, E_{C_j})$ for $j \in \times\{2, 3, 5, 6\}$, and so on. Moreover, according to Definition 6, $\mathcal{L}_{(x, y_C)} = C_{(r^x, E_C)} \setminus \{r^x\}$ for each $x \in \{x_1, x_2, x_3\}$ and $C \in \{C_1, \ldots, C_7\}$. By Definition 7, $b_{(x, y_C)} = 1$ because r^{x_1} has size 1. Furthermore, $a_{(x_i, y_{C_j})} = 0$ for $(i, j) = (1, 1)$, $(i, j) \in \{2, 3\} \times \{1, 2, 3\}$, and $(i, j) \in \{(2, 5), (2, 7)\}$; $a_{(x_i, y_{C_j})} = 0.67$ for $(i, j) \in \{1\} \times \{2, \ldots, 7\}$, $a_{(x_i, y_{C_j})} = 0.75$ for $(i, j) \in \{(2, 4), (2, 6)\}$; $a_{(x_i, y_{C_j})} = 0.33$ for $(i, j) = (3, 5)$; $a_{(x_i, y_{C_j})} = 0.78$ for $(i, j) \in \{(3, 4), (3, 6), (3, 7)\}$. Finally, we can conclude that $I_{Bi_{Ve}} = I_{\Delta_t}$ for each $t \in [0, 1] \cap (0.67, 1] \cap (0.75, 1] \cap (0.78, 1] \cap (0.33, 1] = (0.78, 1]$. For example, as shown by Table 6, since $0.8 \in (0.78, 1]$, $I_{\Delta_{0.8}}$ coincides with $I_{Bi_{Ve}}$. Moreover, we can view that $I_{\Delta_{0.5}} \neq I_{Bi_{Ve}}$ because $0.5 \in (0.78, 1]$.

Remark 4. It is possible that the hypothesis of Theorem 2 is verified by $I_{Bi_{Ve}}$ but it is not possible to generate the context $(X, Y_J, I_{Bi_{Ve}})$ by using a t-scaling quantifier. This occurs when the intersection of the intervals $Int_{(x, y_C)}$ with $x \in X$ and $y_C \in Y_J$ is empty.

Table 3. Cuts of r^{x_1}, r^{x_2}, and r^{x_3} according to Definition 5

(M,N)	cuts of $C_{(M,N)}$
(r^{x_1}, E_{C_1})	r^{x_1}
(r^{x_1}, E_{C_2})	A, r^{x_1}
(r^{x_1}, E_{C_3})	A, r^{x_1}
(r^{x_1}, E_{C_4})	A, B, r^{x_1}
(r^{x_1}, E_{C_5})	A, r^{x_1}
(r^{x_1}, E_{C_6})	A, r^{x_1}
(r^{x_1}, E_{C_7})	A, B, r^{x_1}

(M,N)	cuts of $C_{(M,N)}$
(r^{x_2}, E_{C_1})	r^{x_2}
(r^{x_2}, E_{C_2})	r^{x_2}
(r^{x_2}, E_{C_3})	r^{x_2}
(r^{x_2}, E_{C_4})	D, r^{x_2}
(r^{x_2}, E_{C_5})	$\emptyset, r^{x_2}$
(r^{x_2}, E_{C_6})	D, r^{x_2}
(r^{x_2}, E_{C_7})	$\emptyset, r^{x_2}$

(M,N)	cuts of $C_{(M,N)}$
(r^{x_3}, E_{C_1})	r^{x_3}
(r^{x_3}, E_{C_2})	r^{x_3}
(r^{x_3}, E_{C_3})	r^{x_3}
(r^{x_3}, E_{C_4})	E, r^{x_3}
(r^{x_3}, E_{C_5})	F, r^{x_1}
(r^{x_3}, E_{C_6})	E, F, r^{x_1}
(r^{x_3}, E_{C_7})	F, r^{x_1}

Table 4. The values of $S_1(M,N)$

$S_1(M,N)$	C_1	C_2	C_3	C_4	C_5	C_6	C_7
r^{x_1}	1	0.75	0.5	0	0	0	0
A		1	1	0.75	1	1	0.75
B				0.5			0.5
r^{x_2}	0.75	0.75	0.75	0.5	0.5	0.5	0.5
$\emptyset$					1		1
D				0.75		0.75	
r^{x_3}	1	1	1	0.5	0.5	0.5	0.5
E				1		0.75	
F					0.75	0.75	0.75

Table 5. Evaluation of the size of cuts using Bi_{Ve}

H	$\mu_{r^{x_1}}(H)$	$Bi_{Ve}(\mu_{r^{x_1}}(H))$	H	$\mu_{r^{x_2}}(H)$	$Bi_{Ve}(\mu_{r^{x_2}}(H))$	H	$\mu_{r^{x_1}}(H)$	$Bi_{Ve}(\mu_{r^{x_1}}(H))$
r^{x_1}	1	1	r^{x_2}	1	1	r^{x_3}	1	1
A	0.67	0	D	0.75	0.2	E	0.78	0.4
B	0.33	0	$\emptyset$	0	0	F	0.33	0

Table 6. $a_{(x,y_C)}$ for each $x \in \{x_1, x_2, x_2\}$ and $C \in \{C_1, \ldots, C_7\}$.

$I_{\Delta_{0.5}}$	C_1	C_2	C_3	C_4	C_5	C_6	C_7
x_1	1	1	1	0.75	1	0.75	0.75
x_2	0.75	0.75	0.75	0.75	0.5	0.75	0.5
x_3	1	1	1	1	0.5	0.75	0.5

$I_{Bi_{Ve}} = I_{\Delta_{0.8}}$	C_1	C_2	C_3	C_4	C_5	C_6	C_7
x_1	1	0.75	0.5	0	0	0	0
x_2	0.75	0.75	0.75	0.5	0.5	0.5	0.5
x_3	1	1	1	0.5	0.5	0.5	0.5

4   Future Directions

As a future project, we intend to continue in this direction by solving the following problem. Let $Bi_\nu \in \mathcal{E}$ such that I_{Bi_ν} is different from the relation generated by any t-scaling quantifiers; we can consider $t^* \in [0,1]$ so the $I_{\Delta_{t^*}}$ is the closest relation to I_{Bi_ν} (we could find t^* by using the *least squares method*: t^* is the threshold satisfying $\sum_{(x,y_C)}(I_{Bi_\nu}(x,y) - I_{\Delta_{t^*}}(x,y))^2 = \min\{\sum_{(x,y)}(I_{Bi_\nu}(x,y) - I_{\Delta_t}(x,y))^2 \mid t \in [0,1]\}$). So, it could be interesting to understand if and how the lattices $\mathcal{B}(X, Y \cup Y_J, I_{Bi_\nu})$ and $\mathcal{B}(X, Y \cup Y_J, I_{\Delta_{t^*}})$ diverge, for example with respect to their size, especially when the cardinality of $Y \cup Y_J$ increases. Note that the set $\mathcal{E}$ of linguistic expressions only considers modification through a hedge of the adjective *big*, since in this case we have a generalization of quantifiers used in [4]. Other linguistic expressions can be considered instead of Bi_ν, adapting the formula of FRCA quantifiers.

References

1. Wille, R.: Restructuring lattice theory: an approach based on hierarchies of concepts. In: Ferré, S., Rudolph, S. (eds.) ICFCA 2009. LNCS (LNAI), vol. 5548, pp. 314–339. Springer, Heidelberg (2009). https://doi.org/10.1007/978-3-642-01815-2_23

2. Bělohlávek, R.: Fuzzy Relational Systems: Foundations and Principles, vol. 20. Springer Science & Business Media, New York (2012). https://doi.org/10.1007/978-1-4615-0633-1

3. Huchard, M., Roume, C., Valtchev, P.: When concepts point at other concepts: the case of UML diagram reconstruction. In: Proceedings of the 2nd Workshop on Advances in Formal Concept Analysis for Knowledge Discovery in Databases (FCAKDD), pp. 32–43 (2002)

4. Braud, A., Dolques, X., Huchard, M., Le Ber, F.: Generalization effect of quantifiers in a classification based on relational concept analysis. Knowl.-Based Syst. **160**, 119–135 (2018)

5. Boffa, S., Murinová, P., Novák, V.: A proposal to extend relational concept analysis with fuzzy scaling quantifiers. Knowl.-Based Syst. **231**, 107452 (2021)

6. Boffa, S.: Extracting concepts from fuzzy relational context families. IEEE Trans. Fuzzy Syst. **31**(4), 1202–1213 (2023)

7. Novák, V., Perfilieva, I., Dvorak, A.: Insight into Fuzzy Modeling. John Wiley & Sons, Hoboken (2016)

8. Novák, V.: A comprehensive theory of trichotomous evaluative linguistic expressions. Fuzzy Sets Syst. **159**(22), 2939–2969 (2008)

9. Novák, V.: A formal theory of intermediate quantifiers. Fuzzy Sets Syst. **159**(10), 1229–1246 (2008)

10. Murinová, P., Novák, V.: Graded generalized hexagon in fuzzy natural logic. Inf. Process. Manag. Uncertain. Knowl.-Based Syst. **611**, 36–47 (2016)

11. Pollandt, S.: Fuzzy-Begriffe: Formale Begriffsanalyse unscharfer Daten. Springer-verlag, Berlin, Heidelberg (2013). https://doi.org/10.1007/978-3-642-60460-7

12. Bělohlávek, R.: Concept lattices and order in fuzzy logic. Ann. Pure Appl. Log. **128**(1–3), 277–298 (2004)

SPECIAL SESSION 4: Neural Networks under Uncertainty and Imperfect Information

Arbitrariness of Outward Closeness in Laplacian Dimensionality Reduction

Jiří Janeček[1]([✉])[iD] and Irina Perfilieva[2][iD]

[1] Department of Mathematics, Faculty of Science, University of Ostrava,
30. dubna 22, 701 03 Ostrava, Czech Republic
`Jiri.Janecek@osu.cz`
[2] Institute for Research and Applications of Fuzzy Modeling, University of Ostrava,
30. dubna 22, 701 03 Ostrava, Czech Republic
`Irina.Perfilieva@osu.cz`

Abstract. In this paper, we recall the dimensionality reduction technique of Laplacian eigenmaps. Its result (lower-dimensional embedding, e.g. a single real vector) depends on the initial setting of weights describing closeness on the set of all data points. Then, a weighted graph naturally emerges. We propose to split these weights in two parts: the outward closeness describes the closeness of any point to all the other points, whereas the inward closeness is given by the evaluation of all self-loops. In this contribution, we are interested in the inverse problem to the dimensionality reduction which consists in finding the weights leading to a given result. We show that under certain conditions, the outward closeness is almost arbitrary, i.e. only the inward closeness must be computed to fit the result of the Laplacian eigenmaps to the given vector.

Keywords: Laplacian eigenmaps · Closeness · Inverse problem

1 Introduction

Our long-term research, e.g. [2], is focused on dimensionality reduction (DR) based on analysis of the Laplacian matrix of a weighted graph. The DR technique of Laplacian eigenmaps (LE) was introduced in [1] and serves as the basis for this contribution. We recall that the Laplacian matrix describes the geometric structure of the data and is fully determined by the weighted adjacency matrix that characterizes the space we work with in terms of local closeness (each edge weight is a value of closeness between two data points represented by the graph vertices) – that is why we also call it the closeness matrix. The generalized eigenvectors that correspond to the smallest generalized eigenvalues of the Laplacian matrix give the result of LE as they minimize its criterion (points that are close in the input, higher-dimensional space, should be mapped close to each other).

For the purpose of this paper, we establish a new terminology: recall that closeness is any non-negative symmetric function on the set of all pairs of objects

Supported by the University of Ostrava.

(in our case, data points); we split its domain and create the notions of the outward and inward closeness. The outward closeness is defined on all pairs that consist of different objects (and hence, it describes how much close is any data point to all other points). Complementarily, the inward closeness is defined on all pairs consisting of the same object (therefore, it describes closeness of any point to itself). This self-closeness must by properly understood. As opposed to a metric space where two objects are equal if and only if their distance is zero (we emphasize that 0 is the common reference value for all pairs of objects in the metric space but there is no common reference value in the general closeness space), closeness is a local expression of alikeness, not fully comparable with other closeness values – its definition lacks the triangular inequality, and therefore, each object is considered independently when evaluating its closeness to all objects including itself. Moreover, as the geometric meaning of the inward closeness value is weaker than that of the outward closeness value, the inward closeness value can be easily changed without breaking the data structure.

The motivation of this paper is to analyse the inverse problem to the Laplacian DR (how to set all weights to initiate LE, s.t. the images of the given inputs fit the given outputs), namely to set conditions under which the result of LE is not influenced by the outward closeness weights. It would demonstrate that setting these weights needs not be too complicated, and hence by choosing a simple method, a potential mistake can be avoided. (For example, if the input data space is endowed by a metric, it can always be transformed into closeness and then used in the outward closeness setting.) Moreover, it would suggest that the inward closeness is more important than one might have thought (requiring the reflexivity of the overall closeness is indeed too restrictive and generally unsupported as shown in [3] where the preimage problem established in the fuzzy partitioned closeness space is discussed, as well as the relationship of closeness, metric and similarity). Such results would extend our research in the area of inverse problems and make it more settled.

Another motivation of this paper is the possible application of the inverse problem to DR in image fusion, e.g. in medical multi-modal registration. Consider a set of 3-D measurements of a certain object (e.g. a bone) made by different techniques or different devices. If we can force them to be mapped in an aligned way to 1-D or 2-D (consider a fixed part of the object, then the corresponding input points that are originally not comparable because, e.g., their coordinates are not all Euclidean, or each device produces different scaling in various directions, are mapped in all cases on the same lower-dimensional vectors), we can than combine (fuse) the reduced representations with no spatial transformation.

2   Laplacian Dimensionality Reduction

In this section, we recall the dimensionality reduction (DR) technique of Laplacian eigenmaps (LE) introduced in [1]. Let us have a fixed set of n objects ($n \in \mathbb{N}$):

$$X = \{x_i \,|\, i = 1, \ldots, n\},$$

indexed by the set
$$I = \{1, \ldots, n\}.$$

These objects are generally of any kind (possibly specified by a large number of attributes), or they can be simply high-dimensional vectors $x_i \in \mathbb{R}^h$. The aim of DR is to find a mapping $f \colon X \to \mathbb{R}^m$ where $m < h$ ($\forall i \in I \colon x_i \mapsto y_i \in \mathbb{R}^m$), s.t. a certain criterion is optimised. The criterion for LE is stated at the end of this section.

Definition 1 (Closeness). *Let $X = \{x_i \mid i = 1, \ldots, n\}$ be a set, $n \in \mathbb{N}$. Then, closeness on X is any non-negative, symmetric function*

$$w \colon X^2 \to \mathbb{R}$$

where $X^2 = X \times X$ is the Cartesian product of the set X with itself. The pair (X, w) is called a closeness space.

Closeness between any two objects x_i and x_j in X is given by the value $w(x_i, x_j)$ and specifies a certain alikeness between them. Closer objects have larger closeness value than the less close ones. As explained in the Introduction, this value cannot be taken absolutely as closeness is a relative, local concept that takes into account only its arguments and hence, closeness value $w(x_{i_1}, x_{i_2})$ is incomparable with $w(x_{i_3}, x_{i_4})$ whereas it is comparable with $w(x_{i_1}, x_{i_3})$.

Above, we described closeness as a general notion. From now on, we assume that the set X is connected[1] w.r.t. a given closeness w which is necessary for the usage of LE.

Let us introduce a weighted graph $G(V, E, W)$ where

$$V = X, \quad E = V^2$$

and where the adjacency matrix $W \in \mathbb{R}^{n \times n}$ is given by

$$w_{ij} = w(x_i, x_j) \quad \text{for } i, j \in I,$$

containing the weights of the edges (x_i, x_j), where $w(x_i, x_j)$ is closeness between x_i and x_j. Therefore, we call W the *closeness matrix*. The matrix W determines a connected graph[2]. Then, $G(V, E, W)$ describes not only the geometric structure of X but also the closeness space (X, w).

Following [1], we derive a diagonal matrix $D \in \mathbb{R}^{n \times n}$ with diagonal entries given by

$$d_{ii} = \sum_{j=1}^{n} w_{ij}.$$

---

[1] Connectedness of X w.r.t. w means that for all pairs of objects $x, y \in X$, there exists a number $n \in \mathbb{N}$ and objects $x_1, \ldots, x_n \in X$, s.t. all closeness values $w(x_0, x_1), w(x_1, x_2), \ldots, w(x_{n-1}, x_n)$ are positive where $x = x_0$ and $y = x_n$. In the other words, the considered closeness does not isolate any object, nor any proper subset of X, from all the other objects.

[2] This follows our assumption that X is connected w.r.t. w and it means that in the graph $G(V, E, W)$, we can find a path with positive weights between any two vertices.

As the matrix D describes degrees of all vertices, we call it the *degree matrix*. Following the connectedness of X, all degrees d_{ii} are positive.

Definition 2 (Laplacian matrix). Laplacian matrix $L \in \mathbb{R}^{n \times n}$ *of the graph* $G(V, E, W)$ *is given by*

$$L = D - W.$$

Note that both the degree matrix D as well as the closeness matrix W are symmetric, and hence the Laplacian matrix L is also symmetric. Moreover, it is positive semi-definite as for any vector $y \in \mathbb{R}^n$, it holds that

$$y^\top L y = \frac{1}{2} \sum_{i,j=1}^{n} (y_i - y_j)^2 w_{ij} \geq 0,$$

where $y = \begin{bmatrix} y_1 \\ \vdots \\ y_n \end{bmatrix}$.

The pairs of generalized eigenvectors $y \in \mathbb{R}^n$ and the corresponding generalized eigenvalues $\lambda \in \mathbb{R}_0^+$ are the solutions to the generalized eigenvalue problem

$$L y = \lambda D y. \tag{1}$$

For $m < n$, the m-dimensional representation of X given by LE (the result of DR) is determined by the generalized eigenvectors of the Laplacian matrix L corresponding to the second up to the $(m+1)$-th smallest generalized eigenvalues. From now on, we assume $m = 1$, i.e. X is mapped on a single real vector ($f \colon X \mapsto y \in \mathbb{R}^n$). On condition $y^\top D 1 = 0$, the generalized eigenvector y corresponding to the second smallest generalized eigenvalue satisfy

$$y = [y_1, \ldots, y_n]^\top = \operatorname{argmin} \sum_{i,j=1}^{n} |y_i - y_j|^2 w_{ij},$$

and therefore, it forms the non-trivial solution to DR problem provided by LE as above, there is the optimization criterion of this technique that ensures a certain locality preservation, namely w.r.t. the given closeness.

Further on, we will refer to the denotation of the set X, closeness w, matrices W, D, L and the graph $G(V, E, W)$ as they were introduced above.

3   Laplacian Decomposition

In this section, we split X^2 – the domain of closeness – to define two complementary notions, outward and inward closeness. After that, we decompose the Laplacian matrix using only the values derived from the outward closeness.

Definition 3 (Outward Closeness). *Let $X = \{x_i \mid i = 1, \ldots, n\}$ be a set, $n \in \mathbb{N}$, then the* outward closeness *on X is any non-negative, symmetric function* $w^* \colon X^2 \setminus \{(x_i, x_i) \mid i = 1, \ldots, n\} \to \mathbb{R}$.

Definition 4 (Inward Closeness). *Let $X = \{x_i \,|\, i = 1, \ldots, n\}$ be a set, $n \in \mathbb{N}$, then the* inward closeness *on X is any non-negative function $w^{**} \colon \{(x_i, x_i) \,|\, i = 1, \ldots, n\} \to \mathbb{R}$.*

Obviously, the function $w \colon X^2 \to \mathbb{R}$ defined using both aforementioned notions,

$$w(x_i, x_j) = \begin{cases} w^*(x_i, x_j) & i \neq j \\ w^{**}(x_i, x_j) & i = j, \end{cases}$$

is closeness on X.

Recall that the weighted graph $G(V, E, W)$ has n^2 edges as $V = X$, $E = X^2$ and W is the matrix of closeness on X that describes adjacency of all vertices. Assume that the edges $E = \{e_i \,|\, i = 1, \ldots, n^2\}$ are indexed as follows: $e_1 = (x_1, x_1)$, $e_2 = (x_1, x_2)$, $\ldots$, $e_n = (x_1, x_n)$, $e_{n+1} = (x_2, x_1)$, $\ldots$, $e_{n^2} = (x_n, x_n)$. From now on, we will use two functions (p and q given below) encoding the indices of all edges in $G(V, E, W)$:

Definition 5 (Edge Index Functions). *Let $i = 1, \ldots, n^2$ be an edge index of $G(V, E, W)$, then $p \colon \{1, \ldots, n^2\} \to \{0, \ldots, n - 1\}$ and $q \colon \{1, \ldots, n^2\} \to \{1, \ldots, n\}$ given by*

$$q(i) \equiv i \mod n,$$

$$p(i) = \frac{i - q(i)}{n},$$

are edge index functions of $G(V, E, W)$.

Obviously, each edge index i is then expressed in the following unique way:

$$i = p(i)n + q(i).$$

Now, we can use the edge index functions to define the ordinary weighted incidence matrix (OWIM)[3] $B \in \mathbb{R}^{n^2 \times n}$ of the weighted graph $G(V, E, W)$. The matrix B is given by $\forall i = 1, \ldots, n^2$, $j = 1, \ldots, n$:

$$b_{ij} = \begin{cases} -\sqrt{w_{p(i)+1, q(i)}} & j = p(i) + 1 \,\&\, p(i) + 1 \neq q(i) \\ \sqrt{w_{p(i)+1, q(i)}} & j = q(i) \,\&\, q(i) \neq p(i) + 1 \\ 0 & \text{otherwise} \end{cases} \qquad (2)$$

The i-th row of the matrix B encodes the i-th edge of $G(V, E, W)$ that is assigned the weight $w_{p(i)+1, q(i)}$. If we split closeness on X (weights stored in the matrix

---

[3] Ordinary weighted incidence matrix ignores self-loops but indicates all other oriented edges. Initial and ending point of each edge are denoted by non-zero entries that differ in sign that encodes the edge orientation. We follow the convention that an edge with no orientation is identified with a pair of oppositely oriented edges. If 0 denotes a self-loop, it can be seen as a sum of the two differently signed values – in fact, the beginning and ending point of any self-loop is the same vertex. In this paper, we consider this matrix to be transposed in comparison with the standard case of the graph incidence matrix.

W) in outward and inward closeness, we see that all non-zero entries of OWIM correspond to values of the outward closeness. In the other words, 0 denotes no incidence of the edge i with the vertex x_j, or a self-loop in $G(V, E, W)$. Then, obviously, OWIM contains no information about the values of the inward closeness.

Theorem 1. *The Laplacian matrix $L = D - W \in \mathbb{R}^{n \times n}$ of $G(V, E, W)$ can be expressed as $L = \frac{1}{2}B^\top B$ where the matrix B is given by (2).*

The above agrees with the fact that L is independent on the values of inward closeness w_{ii} which are purposefully neglected in our definition of B.

4   Inverse Problem

In this section, we present the idea that setting the outward closeness in the inverse problem to the Laplacian DR is almost arbitrary. As closeness is a local expression of alikeness, we assume that for all $i, j = 1, \ldots, n$, it holds that $i \neq j \Rightarrow x_i \neq x_j$, i.e. we want to avoid a meaning-violating conflict in closeness.

Moreover, we assume that the given vector $\boldsymbol{y}$ of 1-D images of X satisfies the following condition:

$$\forall i = 1, \ldots, n \colon y_i \neq 0 . \tag{3}$$

Definition 6 (Inverse Problem to the Laplacian Dimensionality Reduction). *Let $X = \{x_i \,|\, i = 1, \ldots, n\}$ be a set, $n \in \mathbb{N}$, and $\boldsymbol{y} \in \mathbb{R}^n$ be a real vector, then the inverse problem to the Laplacian dimensionality reduction is to find closeness $w \colon X^2 \to \mathbb{R}$ on X, s.t. the non-trivial solution to DR problem provided by LE coincides with $\boldsymbol{y}$.*

Based on (1), the non-trivial ($\boldsymbol{y}^\top D\mathbf{1} = 0$) solution to DR problem provided by LE satisfies

$$D^{-1}L\boldsymbol{y} = \lambda_1 \boldsymbol{y} ,$$

where λ_1 is the second smallest generalized eigenvalue of the Laplacian matrix L and, based on our assumption on graph connectedness, is positive. Hence,

$$\lambda_1 = \frac{\boldsymbol{y}^\top D^{-1}L\boldsymbol{y}}{\boldsymbol{y}^\top \boldsymbol{y}} .$$

Therefore, we can define a real function f:

$$f(\lambda, \boldsymbol{y}, D, L) = \frac{1}{\lambda} \cdot \frac{\boldsymbol{y}^\top D^{-1}L\boldsymbol{y}}{\boldsymbol{y}^\top \boldsymbol{y}} .$$

If λ and $\boldsymbol{y}$ are the generalized eigenvalue and the corresponding eigenvector of the Laplacian matrix L derived from the closeness matrix W and the corresponding degree matrix D, we have

$$f(\lambda, \boldsymbol{y}, D, L) = 1 .$$

The above can be substantially simplified: for a fixed graph (represented by a fixed closeness matrix W), the second smallest generalized eigenvalue of L is unique – let us denote the corresponding function as λ_1, $\lambda_1 \colon W \mapsto \lambda_1(W) \in \mathbb{R}^+$. The matrices D and L are also fixed and fully determined by the closeness matrix W – let us denote the corresponding matrix-valued functions as D and L, respectively, $D \colon W \mapsto D(W) \in \mathbb{R}^{n \times n}$, $L \colon W \mapsto L(W) = D(W) - W \in \mathbb{R}^{n \times n}$. Therefore, we can write

$$1 = \frac{1}{\lambda_1} \cdot \frac{\boldsymbol{y}^\top D^{-1} L \boldsymbol{y}}{\boldsymbol{y}^\top \boldsymbol{y}} = f(\lambda_1(W), \boldsymbol{y}, D(W), L(W)),$$

From the above where (W) was added to all right-hand sides to emphasize the dependence (determination) on W, it is clear that the simplification can be performed in the following way:

$$1 = f(W, \boldsymbol{y}), \tag{4}$$

the vector $\boldsymbol{y}$ is dependent on $\lambda_1(W)$ but it is not fully determined by it (any nonzero multiple of an eigenvector is the same eigenvector but a different vector).

Based on (4), we denote

$$f_{\boldsymbol{y}} = f(\cdot, \boldsymbol{y}),$$

and then, we can formulate the requirement of the inverse problem to the Laplacian dimensionality reduction as follows:

$$W \in f_{\boldsymbol{y}}^{-1}(1)[1],$$

i.e. the matrix W we are looking for is the first argument that belongs to the inverse relation given by the value of 1 where the second argument of the direct mapping $f_{\boldsymbol{y}}$ is given by $\boldsymbol{y}$.

From the above, it is clear that there are multiple matrices solving this problem. That is why we propose to set conditions that restrict the number of possibilities how to set weights entered in W and moreover, in this step, we must specify the connection between the initial data X and the weights, otherwise no connection between X and $\boldsymbol{y}$ would be taken into account.

Let us now derive some necessary properties of the solution. Following (1), for every $i = 1, \ldots, n$, we have

$$(L\boldsymbol{y})_i = (\lambda D \boldsymbol{y})_i,$$

$$\sum_{j=1}^{n} l_{ij} y_j = \lambda d_{ii} y_i, \tag{5}$$

$$y_i = \frac{\sum_{\substack{j=1 \\ j \neq i}}^{n} l_{ij} y_j}{\lambda d_{ii} - l_{ii}}. \tag{6}$$

Equation (6) expresses each lower-dimensional image as a certain linear combination of all other images. To incorporate this property, such combination must be possible, hence the denominator must be non-zero for any generalized eigenvalue, including λ_1:

$$\forall i = 1, \ldots, n: \lambda_1 \neq 1 - \frac{w_{ii}}{d_{ii}}. \tag{7}$$

Secondly, following (5), for every $i = 1, \ldots, n$, we have $\frac{L^i y}{y_i} = \lambda_1 d_{ii} > 0$ as both λ_1 and d_{ii} are positive. Note that the left-hand side does not depend on the inward closeness which motivates the following notation. Let w^* be the outward closeness on X derived from the closeness w, then the matrix $L^* \in \mathbb{R}^{n \times n}$ given by

$$i, j = 1, \ldots, n: l_{ij}^* = \begin{cases} -w^*(x_i, x_j) & i \neq j \\ \sum\limits_{\substack{j=1 \\ j \neq i}}^{n} w^*(x_i, x_j) & i = j, \end{cases} \tag{8}$$

coincides with the Laplacian matrix L given by w. Therefore, the solution must satisfy the condition

$$\forall i = 1, \ldots, n: \frac{L^{*i} y}{y_i} > 0, \tag{9}$$

where L^{*i} denotes the i-th row of the matrix L^*.

To avoid too many solutions to the inverse problem, we assume that there is an expert who suggest the values of the outward closeness and show that such approach is correct. For simplicity, we assume that $X \subset \mathbb{R}^h$, $h \geq 2$, i.e. the initial objects are high-dimensional real vectors. To prevent the expert to violate the local characterization of closeness, we restrict his choice by the condition that w^* is non-increasing w.r.t. the (Euclidean) norm, which means

$$\forall i, j, k = 1, \ldots, n: \|x_i - x_j\| < \|x_i - x_k\| \Rightarrow w^*(x_i, x_j) \geq w^*(x_i, x_k). \tag{10}$$

4.1   Arbitrariness of Outward Closeness

To solve the inverse problem to the Laplacian DR given X and y, we need to determine W, and hence to compute n^2 variables $\{w_{ij} \mid i, j = 1, \ldots, n\}$.

Let us define a vector $z \in \mathbb{R}^{n^2}$ given by

$$\forall i = 1, \ldots, n^2: z_i = \begin{cases} \sqrt{w^*_{p(i)+1,q(i)}}(y_{q(i)} - y_{p(i)+1}) & p(i) + 1 \neq q(i) \\ 0 & \text{otherwise} \end{cases}.$$

The matrix equation $By = z$ contains $n^2 - n$ variables (all w_{ij} for $i \neq j$) in n^2 equations, n of which are in the form $0 = 0$. Note that $w_{ij} = w_{ij}^*$ for $i \neq j$ is always a solution. This is the solution in the form of the outward closeness provided by en expert, s.t. it satisfies conditions (9) and (10).

To prove the correctness of this (almost arbitrary) choice, it is sufficient to show that after fixing the outward closeness, the remaining variables, namely all values of the inward closeness, can be computed.

Recall that D is the unknown degree matrix, determining it is equivalent with determining closeness. Let us solve the matrix equation $Ly = Vy$ where

$V = \lambda_1 D \in \mathbb{R}^{n \times n}$ is an auxiliary diagonal matrix containing n variables: $v_1 = \lambda_1 d_{11}, \ldots, v_n = \lambda_1 d_{nn} > 0$. All of them are positive and the solution always exists, both following (9). We get the system of n equations with n variables. We see that we can always find a small value of $\lambda_1 > 0$, s.t.

$$\forall i = 1, \ldots, n \colon d_{ii} \geq \sum_{\substack{j=1 \\ j \neq i}}^{n} w_{ij},$$

and satisfying (7). Then, we can compute the remaining values of (inward) closeness:

$$\forall i = 1, \ldots, n \colon w_{ii} = d_{ii} - \sum_{\substack{j=1 \\ j \neq i}}^{n} w_{ij}.$$

This demonstrates that the solution to the inverse problem to the Laplacian DR satisfying (3) always exists and that we can start with almost arbitrary outward closeness, following (7), (9) and (10).

5   Conclusions

In this paper, we showed that setting of outward closeness when solving the inverse problem to the Laplacian dimensionality reduction is almost arbitrary, i.e. under certain condition, for any outward closeness we can always find an inward closeness to get the same lower-dimensional representation (as given) provided by the Laplacian eigenmaps. Moreover, it demonstrates that the outward part (of closeness) itself is not essential.

The future work includes investigating how to extend the solution to the inverse problem (the found closeness) on a superset of the original set of objects considering that it was a suitable set of samples that were mapped to a lower dimension with a proper care (or high cost).

Acknowledgments. The support of the student grant SGS15/PřF-MF/2023 of the University of Ostrava is kindly announced.

References

1. Belkin, M., Niyogi, P.: Laplacian eigenmaps for dimensionality reduction and data representation. Neural Comput. **15**(6), 1373–1396 (2003)
2. Janeček, J., Perfilieva, I.: Dimensionality Reduction and Its F-Transform Representation. Atlantis Studies in Uncertainty Modelling, Atlantis Press (2019)
3. Janeček, J., Perfilieva, I.: Preimage problem inspired by the F-transform. Mathematics **10**(17), 3209 (2022)

SPECIAL SESSION 5: Imprecision Modeling and Management in XAI Systems

Fuzzy Logic Function as a Post-hoc Explanator of the Nonlinear Classifier

Martin Klimo$^{(\boxtimes)}$ and Ľubomír Králik

University of Žilina, Žilina, Slovakia
{martin.klimo,lubomir.kralik}@fri.uniza.sk

Abstract. Pattern recognition systems implemented using deep neural networks achieve better results than linear models. However, their drawback is the black box property. This property means that one with no experience utilising nonlinear systems may need help understanding the outcome of the decision. Such a solution is unacceptable to the user responsible for the final decision. He must not only believe in the decision but also understand it. Therefore, recognisers must have an architecture that allows interpreters to interpret the findings. The idea of post-hoc explainable classifiers is to design an interpretable classifier parallel to the black box classifier, giving the same decisions as the black box classifier. This paper shows that the explainable classifier completes matching classification decisions with the black box classifier on the MNIST and FashionMNIST databases if Zadeh's fuzzy logic function forms the classifier and DeconvNet importance gives the truth values. Since the other tested significance measures achieved lower performance than DeconvNet, it is the optimal transformation of the feature values to their true values as inputs to the fuzzy logic function for the databases and recogniser architecture used.

Keywords: Explainable classification · Deep neural networks · Fuzzy logic functions · Features importance · Post-hoc explanation

1 Introduction

Nonlinear pattern recognition systems implemented by Deep Neural Networks (DNN) reached superior performance compared to optimal linear systems [1]. Humans have experience in small, low-speed changes that we can easily approximate by linear behaviour. Therefore, we can explain the behaviour of systems under these conditions. Due to missing superposition properties, we cannot give accurate forecasts, even omitting other nonlinear systems properties like chaotic behaviour, many attractors or sensitivity to initial conditions [2]. This nonlinearity inside the black box does not allow us to explain how the classifier has reached its decision. Suppose the final responsibility for the consequences of the decision lies with the user of the neural network. In that case, the missing explanation will prevent the user from blindly using the reached decision. Therefore, decision explainability is essential in DNN research [3]. In this paper, we focus on the explainability of the classifier. We let the feature extractor find the best features to obtain more accurate recognition without dealing with their explanation.

S. Massanet et al. (Eds.): EUSFLAT 2023/AGOP 2023, LNCS 14069, pp. 431–442, 2023.
https://doi.org/10.1007/978-3-031-39965-7_36

There are two approaches to getting an explainable classification. Firstly (explainability by design) – restrict the classifier to self-explaining systems (e.g., fuzzy logical function). Secondly (post-hoc explanation) – leave the nonlinear classifier as a black box. Nevertheless, we have put together an explanation classifier to explain the decision of the black box classifier. We use this method in the paper to maintain a high recognition accuracy, and we utilize a fuzzy logic function as a post-hoc explainable classifier. The fuzzy logic function assumes the truth values of the logic variables at the input and generates the truth value of the logic function at the output. The primary purpose of this paper is to investigate the explainability of a black box classifier when we apply the significance of the features instead of feature values as the truth values.

Mining the importance of internal DNN variables (e.g. inputs or features) is nowadays the primary tool for explaining the decision taken [4]. However, we only consider these input variables that need support with a logical expression that will generate the same conclusion as given by the black box classifier to maintain its accuracy. More specifically, these measures of local importance are fed into a model that explains the trained classifier, which is formed by the neural network. After normalising the importance measure, we can interpret this as a measure of the statement's truth that the feature's occurrence is necessary for the resulting decision (a negated statement is that the feature must not occur for a given decision). We must avoid the influence of features that are indifferent to the outcome of the decision (a truth value of about one-half). We label such features irrelevant and do not use them as input to an explainable classifier. The problem addressed in this paper is finding the measures of the feature importance that will be the best inputs to a fuzzy logic function in the post-hoc explainable classifier role. A similar problem is addressed in the paper [5]. L1 regularised logistic regression, and Gini importance computes the feature importance measure. Random forest and LIME represent explainable classifiers.

The remainder of the text is organised as follows: Sect. 2 provides the background for the proposed solution. Section 2.1 describes analysed measures of the feature importance, and Sect. 2.2 explains the functionality of the fuzzy logic function in the role of a post-hoc explanator. Section 3 presents the obtained results, and Sect. 4 concludes the paper.

2 Background

Figure 1 gives the principal block diagram of the post-hoc explanator. At the input of the DNN, we will attach a pattern from which we will extract the features. The nonlinear classifier recognises the class of the sample. During the training, we optimise the weights of the DNN to reach maximum precision according to the available classes in the training dataset.

Methods described in Sect. 2.1 mine the feature importance measures and move them to the explainable classifier input. The fuzzy logic function will generate truth values for the pattern membership of each class. From these, to explain the decision of the black box classifier, we select the same one as determined by the nonlinear classifier. Consequently, we have a logic function that generates a decision and truth values for the input features and the resulting decision. The role of the post-hoc explainer is to mimic as closely as possible the decision-making of the black box classifier. Therefore, the paper

Explained Reasoning

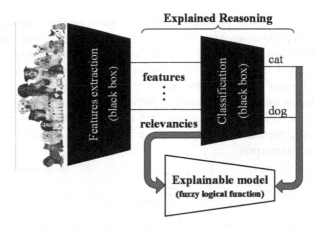

Fig. 1. The principal block diagram of the post-hoc explanator

evaluates different feature importance measures according to matching the recognised classes regardless of whether determining the categories is correct.

2.1 Feature Importance Measures

The input data must pass through the whole architecture with learned weights and, through nonlinear activation, functions to make predictions with neural networks. A single prediction involves millions of operations. Thus, humans cannot follow an accurate mapping of the input information through the network. For such a process, we would have to consider millions of complex parameters that interact with the data. For this reason, specific explanatory methods must interpret model behaviour [6].

In general, they can be broadly divided into two different types:

– Occlusion-based or Perturbation-based - methods such as LIME manipulate parts of the image to generate explanations (model-agnostic approach)
– Gradient-based - methods compute a gradient of prediction concerning input attributes.

The standard model-agnostic methods are possible to use, but methods developed explicitly for DNNs have some advantages, such as:

– DNNs learn features and concepts in their hidden layers, and hence unique methods for their interpretation are needed.
– The gradient could be used in the implementation of explainable methods, thus making the computation more efficient than model-agnostic methods.

The most important for our purpose is Gradient-based methods because they carry the information about how much a slight change in image pixel would affect the model's prediction. Explainable gradient-based methods are, therefore, a specific case of feature assignment, or more precisely, in this case, pixel assignment, since pixels, words, or tabular data can represent the features. These methods explain individual model predictions by assigning each input feature to how much it affected the prediction (negative or positive).

These approaches usually produce an output explanation that's the same size as the input image. Each pixel is assigned a value that represents how important it is for the final prediction or classification. This property can be extended into any feature vector produced by the DNN. Thus, we can create the vector containing the relevance measures that we can use later as the input to the post-hoc fuzzy explanator.

Saliency Map is the first and most straightforward method for feature importance measures [7]. This method computes the gradient of the selected neuron we want to explain concerning the individual pixels of the input image, or in general, concerning features we want to interpret:

$$\frac{\partial S}{\partial f}\bigg|_{f=a}, \tag{1}$$

where S is the selected neuron, f is the features we want to interpret, and a is the feature vector given by DNN for the given pattern. Note this method does not modify the derivation of the nonlinear ReLU function, i.e.:

$$\phi'(\cdot) = \begin{cases} 0, & f \le 0 \\ R^{l+1}, f > 0, \end{cases} \tag{2}$$

where f is the feature vector, the ReLU is applied to, R^{l+1} It is the backpropagated signal from the next deeper layer. Note that backpropagated signal is controlled just by the vector f.

The following considered method DeconvNet [8], slightly modifies the previous method. The authors originally proposed this method to create the "Deconvolutional network", which backpropagates the signal in reversed order - from the selected neuron back to the input space. This backpropagation allows only positive signals to backpropagate, showing which pixels positively influence the activation of the selected neuron. The deconvolutional network is thus built-in reverse order. Convolutional layers use transposed weights, and max-pooling layers store the locations of maxims (called "Switches"), indicating where the signal should be placed in the backpropagation process. Finally, the nonlinear ReLU function is used to discard any negative signal after using these switches. After a detailed investigation, all these steps converge to the simple and effective implementation solution when the derivation of the nonlinear ReLU function at layer l is expressed as:

$$\phi'(\cdot) = \begin{cases} R^{l+1}, R^{l+1} > 0 \\ 0, \quad R^{l+1} \le 0, \end{cases} \tag{3}$$

where R^{l+1} is the backpropagated signal.

The third method, Guided backpropagation [9], combines the abovementioned methods into a single one. The derivation rule for the nonlinear ReLU function is defined as:

$$\phi'(\cdot) = \begin{cases} R^{l+1}, R^{l+1} > 0 \wedge f > 0 \\ 0, \quad R^{l+1} \le 0 \wedge f \le 0. \end{cases} \tag{4}$$

The signal from deeper layers (closer to the selected neuron) is backpropagated through ReLU only if it is positive and values in the feature vector f obtained in the inference phase are also positive. This approach can be viewed as a strict filtering rule that keeps only the most essential signal parts.

The last considered method for feature importance measures is called Layer-Wise Relevance Propagation (LRP) [10, 11], which is a method for interpreting the decisions made by DNN by assigning relevance scores to the input features. The method propagates the relevance scores from the output layer back through the network, layer by layer, using a set of propagation rules. These rules ensure that the relevance scores are conserved, meaning that the total relevance at the output of a layer is equal to the total relevance at its input. Mathematically, relevance scores R can be defined as:

$$R_i^l = \sum_{k=1}^{B_{l+1}} R_{i \leftarrow k}^{l,l+1} = \sum_{k=1}^{B_{l+1}} \frac{a_i^l w_{i,k}^{l,l+1}}{\epsilon + \sum_{j=1}^{B_l} a_i^l w_{j,k}^{l,l+1}} R_k^{l+1}, \tag{5}$$

where $i \in \{1, \ldots, B_l\}, l \in \{1, \ldots, L-1\}$, L is the total number of layers and B is the number of neurons in *the* l-th layer. This view allows the user to understand which input features were most important in determining the network's output. Several different propagation rules can be used in LRP, and the choice of which one to use depends on the specific network architecture and task. Standard propagation rules include:

- Z^+ rule: The relevance at the output of a neuron is divided proportionally among its input neurons based on their positive activation values.
- Z^- rule: The relevance at the output of a neuron is divided proportionally among its input neurons based on their negative activation values.
- ε rule: A small positive constant epsilon is added to all the activation values before dividing the relevance. This trick is used to avoid dividing by zero.
- $\alpha - \beta$ rule: A combination of the Z^+ and Z^- rules, where the relevance is divided proportionally among the input neurons based on a combination of their positive and negative activation values.

2.2 Post-hoc Fuzzy Explanator

The paper [12] assigns a code vector to each feature vector. The first step is *min-max* linear normalisation.

$$\tilde{y}_i = \frac{y_i - y_{min}}{y_{max} - y_{min}}, \quad y_{min} = min\{y_1, \ldots, y_M\}, \quad y_{max} = max\{y_1, \ldots, y_M\},$$

where $y_i \in \mathcal{R}, i \in \{1, \ldots, M\}$ are the features importance measures, and $\tilde{y}_i \in [0, 1]$, $i \in \{1, \ldots, M\}$ are the features of truth values. The second step is mapping importance into relevance categories: $c = 0$ is a negative relevance, $c = 1$ is a positive relevance, and $c = X$ is an irrelevant feature. Rounding

$$c_i = \begin{cases} 1, & \tilde{y}_i > \frac{1}{2} + \Delta \\ X, & \frac{1}{2} - \Delta \leq \tilde{y}_i \leq \frac{1}{2} + \Delta, i \in \{1, \ldots M\}, \\ 0, & \tilde{y}_i < \frac{1}{2} - \Delta \end{cases} \tag{7}$$

(where Δ gives an irrelevance range), assigns the relevance codewords from the set

$$C_{full} = \left\{ c^j = \left(c_1^j, \ldots, c_M^j \right) \in \{0, X, 1\}^M \right\}, j = 1, \ldots, 3^M$$

to each truth vector $\tilde{y} = (\tilde{y}_1, \ldots, \tilde{y}_M) \in [0, 1]^M$. After filtering irrelevant features, we calculate a truth value of the statement that the feature is relevant (negatively or positively)

$$t(\tilde{y}_i = c_i) = \begin{cases} 1 - \tilde{y}_i, & c_i = 0 \\ \tilde{y}_i, & c_i = 1 \end{cases}, c_i \neq X, \ i \in \{1, \ldots, M\}, \tag{8}$$

and how relevant the codeword is

$$t\left(\tilde{c} = c^j \right) = \min_{\substack{i = 1, \ldots, M \\ c_i^j \neq X}} t\left(\tilde{c}_i = c_i^j \right), j = 1, \ldots, 3^M. \tag{9}$$

As one can see, we apply the Zadeh fuzzy logic. Figure 2 shows the block diagram of an explainable classifier based on the fuzzy logic function.

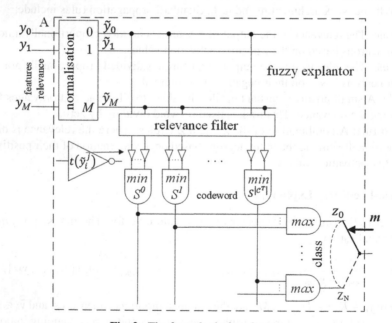

Fig. 2. The fuzzy logical explanator

The result of training is the set of codewords $C^T = \left\{ C_1^T, \ldots, C_N^T \right\} \subset C_{full}$ that occurred during the training, where the codeword $c \in C_i^T$ belongs to the class $i \in \{1, \ldots, N\}$. Let the black box forecast $\tilde{m} \in \{1, \ldots, N\}$ as a winning class and the winning class from the explainable classifier is the class $\widetilde{\widetilde{m}} \in \{1, \ldots, N\}$ associated with the codeword

$$\tilde{c} = \underset{\substack{j:c^j \in \mathcal{C}^T \\ c_i^j \neq X}}{\text{argmax}} \min_{i = 1, \ldots, M} t\left(\tilde{c}_i = c_i^j\right). \tag{10}$$

We can look at the explainable and the black box classifiers as competing systems and ask which one has higher classification accuracy. However, the main task of the explainable classifier is to explain the decisions of the black box classifier. Therefore, we will consider it a success if its classification joins the black box classifier, and the success rate is

$$p = \frac{\sum_{i=1}^n \delta\left(\widetilde{\widetilde{m}}_i = \tilde{m}_i\right)}{n}, \tag{11}$$

where $\delta\left(\widetilde{\widetilde{m}}_i = \tilde{m}_i\right) = \begin{cases} 1, & \widetilde{\widetilde{m}}_i = \tilde{m}_i \\ 0, & \widetilde{\widetilde{m}}_i \neq \tilde{m}_i \end{cases}$ And n is the number of tested samples. We evaluate in Sect. 3 several measures of the feature importance according to this measure.

To explain the decision of the black box classifier, we identify the codeword with the highest truth value within the codewords belonging to the same class $\mathcal{C}^{MT}$ within the explainer

$$\tilde{c} = \underset{\substack{j:c^j \in \mathcal{C}_{\tilde{m}}^T \\ c_i^j \neq X}}{\text{argmax}} \min_{i = 1, \ldots, M} t\left(\tilde{c}_i = c_i^j\right). \tag{12}$$

We can display this relevance codeword $\tilde{c} = (\tilde{c}_1, \tilde{c}_M)$, $\tilde{c}_i \in \{0, X, 1\}$, its truth value $t(\tilde{c}) = \min_{\substack{i = 1, \ldots, M \\ \tilde{c}_i \neq X}} t(\tilde{c}_i)$ and truth values of the codeword components $t(\tilde{c}_i)$, $\tilde{c}_i \neq X$.

Available are also features values, their importance measures $y_i \in \mathcal{R}$ or normalised importance measures $\tilde{y}_i \in [0, 1]$.

3 Results

For designed experiments, we used two different datasets on the same architecture. By doing so, we can compare other feature extraction methods and their effectiveness. The first dataset is the well-known MNIST [13] which contains Handwritten Digits images. The second one – Fashion MNIST [14], is a slightly challenging version of the Base MNIST. The images are still grey scaled, with exact resolution and quantity. However, this data consists of different clothing with more complex shapes. We trained LeNet-5 [13] architecture on these datasets, but we performed some enhancements to reach state-of-the-art accuracy on this model. The convolution part of the net was expanded, aiming at more complex features, while the classification head was denser and deeper to accommodate increased network parameters. The hyperparameters and regularisation were also included and tweaked for the best performance. Optimisations significantly helped push the accuracy of the model over 99%. Everything was assembled in the TensorFlow framework. Table 1 gives results obtained for MNIST and FashionMNIST datasets. The reported values represent the success rate according to (11). We have trained ten models with different starting seeds to get more accurate results. So, the reported values are averaged over these individual runs of training. The average black box's accuracy for MNIST and FashionMNIST is 99.61% and 92.46%, respectively.

Table 1. Rate of matching between explainable and black box classifier

Feature importance method	MNIST	FashionMNIST
Raw features	99.20%	91.83%
Saliency maps	99.47%	98.33%
DeconvNet	**100.00%**	**100.00%**
Guided Backpropagation	99.79%	99.59%
LRP	98.35%	93.38%

We compute the feature interpretation methods from chapter 2.1 and the respective metrics to compare these methods (11). Also, to conclude if the post-hoc explanatory model can match our nonlinear classifier in terms of accuracy, thus explain it. The gradient-based methods provide highly accurate results, while DeconvNet outperformed them with perfect compliance with the classifier. The LRP method with the ε rule seems to give the worst feature information but is still relevant with high accuracy. Unexpectedly, the raw normalised feature vector after feature extraction from the LeNet-5 classifier is sufficient to feed the fuzzy explanatory with the appropriate input information.

Looking at Figs. 3, 4, 5 and 6 below can achieve better intuition behind our proposed approach. Figures 3 and 4 depict the example of accurate classification of the handwritten image of 8 (shown in Fig. 3). Figures 5 and 6 depicted the example of inaccurate classification when the handwritten image of 8 was classified as the number 6. One can see that the number of Positive relevance features is relatively low compared to the number of Negative relevance features. Note that the features which do not appear in the figure have a truth value equal to zero. This value means that the test pattern must indeed not contain these features. In the presented case, we used a uniform distribution of truth values over the unit interval among positively relevant, irrelevant, and negatively relevant features: $c_i = X, \frac{1}{2} - \Delta \leq \tilde{y}_i \leq \frac{1}{2} + \Delta, \Delta = \frac{1}{6}$ (truth value above 66%). This margin can be experimented with and increasing it would reduce the number of negatively relevant features and make the decision easier to interpret. Truth values of critical features are circled in Figs. 3 a) and 5 a). Unlike interpreting image pixels, when explaining a pattern, the user loses the connection between the image and the result of its recognition. Therefore, we underline that the explanation of the classification result is only a partial result that must coexist with the explanation of the relevant features. This task can be set aside for a separate study and is not part of the paper.

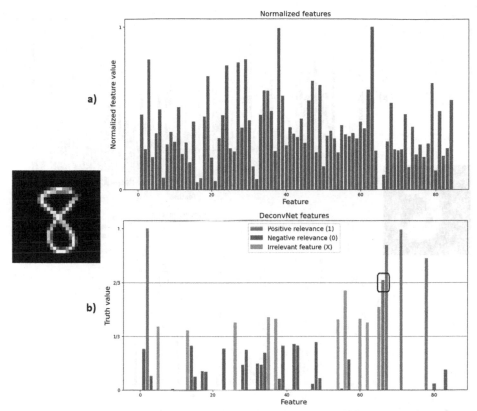

Fig. 3. a) Normalized features vector from LeNet-5 layer after feature extraction on *accurate classification*, **b)** Computed features by DeconvNet method with Positive/Negative and Irrelevant contributions

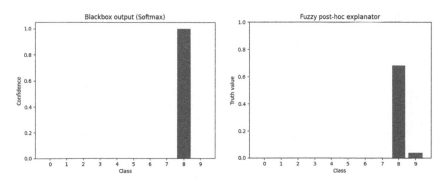

Fig. 4. Confidence score in case of *accurate classification* given by LeNet-5 classifier (on the right) and truth value given by Fuzzy post-hoc explanator (on the left) for the input image from Fig. 1.

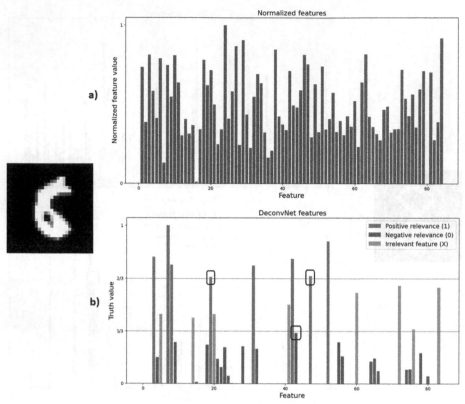

Fig. 5. **a)** Normalized features vector from LeNet-5 layer after feature extraction on data image with *wrong classification,* **b)** Computed features by DeconvNet method with Positive/Negative and Irrelevant contributions

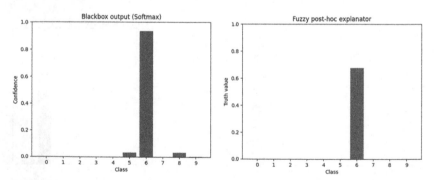

Fig. 6. Confidence score in the case of *wrong classification* given by LeNet-5 classifier (on the right) and truth value given by Fuzzy post-hoc explanator (on the left) for the input image from Fig. 1.

4   Conclusions

Pattern recognition systems implemented using deep neural networks achieve better results than linear models. However, their drawback is the black box property. This property means that one with no experience utilising nonlinear systems may need help understanding the outcome of the decision. Such a solution is unacceptable to the user responsible for the final decision. He must not only believe in the decision but also understand it. Therefore, recognisers must have an architecture that allows interpreters to interpret the findings. European culture has a two-thousand-year history of using Aristotle's logic. Consequently, we assume that a decision expressed as a logical statement will be meaningful to the user. This paper focuses on the explainability of a classification subsystem that generates a decision from the extracted features. To respect the data uncertainty, we apply Zadeh's fuzzy logic. The question is how adding an explainability condition will worsen the recognition success rate. Hence, it is not desirable to replace the black box classifier with an explainable classifier but to require the explainable classifier to explain the decision of the black box classifier. Therefore, when designing a post hoc classifier, we need it to replicate the findings of the black box classifier as closely as possible.

The inputs to the fuzzy logic function are the truth values of the features. This demand does not mean these are the feature values normalised to a unit interval, just as pixels saturation does not express their significance. Today, a palette of measures of pixel importance in an image is available, which can also be used to measure features' extent (truth value). We selected the four most widely used relevance measures for comparison with flag values: Saliency Maps, DeconvNet, Guided Backpropagation and Layer-Wise Relevance Propagation. The MNIST and FashionMNIST databases show that importance levels can be worse or better than the directly unit-interval-normalised feature values. Using the DeconvNet as the feature truth value on the fuzzy logic classifier inputs emerges as the clear winner of the above tests. In this case, the explainable classifier ultimately achieves the decisions of the black box classifier. In all instances of the test set, the best explainable decisions are those by the black box classifier. DeconvNet provides the best measure of feature importance from a scrubbing perspective. If this result is confirmed on multiple databases and recognition systems, it will imply that DeconvNet is the optimal feature importance measure.

References

1. Alzubaidi, L., et al.: Review of deep learning: concepts, CNN architectures, challenges, applications, future directions. J. Big Data **8**(1), 1–74 (2021). https://doi.org/10.1186/s40 537-021-00444-8
2. Mellodge, P.: Characteristics of Nonlinear Systems. A Practical Approach to Dynamical Systems for Engineers, pp. 215–250 (2016). https://doi.org/10.1016/B978-0-08-100202-5. 00004-8
3. Gerlings, J., Shollo, A., Constantiou, I.: Reviewing the need for explainable artificial intelligence (XAI). In: Proceedings of the Annual Hawaii International Conference on System Sciences, 2020-January, pp. 1284–1293 (2021). https://doi.org/10.24251/HICSS.2021.156
4. Aha, D.W., Darrell, T., Doherty, P., Magazzeni, D.: Explainable Artificial Intelligence (2018)

5. Saarela, M., Jauhiainen, S.: Comparison of feature importance measures as explanations for classification models. SN Appl. Sci. **3**, 1–12 (2021). https://doi.org/10.1007/S42452-021-04148-9/TABLES/4
6. Molnar, C.: Interpretable Machine Learning: A Guide for Making Black Box Models Explainable. Leanpub, Munich (2022)
7. Simonyan, K., Vedaldi, A., Zisserman, A.: Deep Inside Convolutional Networks: Visualising Image Classification Models and Saliency Maps (2013). https://doi.org/10.48550/arxiv.1312.6034
8. Zeiler, M.D., Fergus, R.: Visualizing and understanding convolutional networks. In: Fleet, D., Pajdla, T., Schiele, B., Tuytelaars, T. (eds.) ECCV 2014. LNCS, vol. 8689, pp. 818–833. Springer, Cham (2014). https://doi.org/10.1007/978-3-319-10590-1_53
9. Springenberg, J.T., Dosovitskiy, A., Brox, T., Riedmiller, M.: Striving for simplicity: the all convolutional net. In: 3rd International Conference on Learning Representations, ICLR 2015 - Workshop Track Proceedings (2014). https://doi.org/10.48550/arxiv.1412.6806
10. Kohlbrenner, M., Bauer, A., Nakajima, S., Binder, A., Samek, W., Lapuschkin, S.: Towards best practice in explaining neural network decisions with LRP. In: Proceedings of the International Joint Conference on Neural Networks (2020). https://doi.org/10.1109/IJCNN48605.2020.9206975.
11. Binder, A., Montavon, G., Lapuschkin, S., Müller, K.-R., Samek, W.: Layer-wise relevance propagation for neural networks with local renormalization layers. In: Villa, A.E.P., Masulli, P., Pons Rivero, A.J. (eds.) ICANN 2016. LNCS, vol. 9887, pp. 63–71. Springer, Cham (2016). https://doi.org/10.1007/978-3-319-44781-0_8
12. Klimo, M., Lukáč, P., Tarábek, P.: Deep neural networks classification via binary error-detecting output codes. Appl. Sci. **11** (2021). https://doi.org/10.3390/app11083563
13. LeCun, Y., Bottou, L., Bengio, Y., Haffner, P.: Gradient-based learning applied to document recognition. Proc. IEEE (1998). https://doi.org/10.1109/5.726791
14. Han, X., Kashif, R., Vollgraf, R.: Fashion-MNIST: a Novel Image Dataset for Benchmarking Machine Learning Algorithms. https://arxiv.org/pdf/1708.07747.pdf. Accessed 15 Sept 2017

A Bayesian Interpretation of Fuzzy C-Means

Corrado Mencar[(✉)][iD] and Ciro Castiello[iD]

Department of Computer Science, University of Bari Aldo Moro, Bari, Italy
{corrado.mencar,ciro.castiello}@uniba.it

Abstract. In Explainable Artificial Intelligence, the interpretation of
the decisions provided by a model is of primary importance. In this
context, we consider Fuzzy C-Means (FCM), which is a clustering algorithm that induces a model from data by assigning, to each data-point,
a degree of membership to each cluster such that the sum of memberships is one. A fuzzification parameter is also used to tune the degree
of fuzziness of clusters. The distribution of membership degrees suggests
an interpretation of membership degrees within the Probability Theory.
This paper shows that the membership degrees resulting from FCM can
be interpreted as posterior probabilities derived from a Bayesian model,
which assumes that data are generated through a specific probability
density function. The results give a clear interpretation of the membership degrees of FCM, as well as its fuzzification parameter, within a
sound theoretical framework, and shed light on possible extensions of
the algorithm.

Keywords: Fuzzy C-Means · Bayesian Model · Explainable Artificial
Intelligence · Probability Theory

1 Introduction

In the realm of Explainable Artificial Intelligence (XAI), the emphasis is on
the ability of intelligent systems in providing human-oriented explanations for
their decisions [10,13]. This goal translates into a plethora of methods, which
are aimed at designing a number of different models, commonly distinguished as
ante-hoc (or transparent) models, *post-hoc* explanatory models, or hybrid models
[1,3,5,9,16].

Within XAI, fuzzy logic plays a special role, because it enables the representation and processing of imprecise and gradual information. Indeed, imprecision
and graduality are key aspects of human-centric information processing; however, the mere adoption of fuzzy logic does not imply the guarantee of providing
human-oriented explanations, as past research on interpretable fuzzy modeling
put in evidence [2,12].

In this study, we focus on fuzzy clustering, and Fuzzy C-Means (FCM) [6,7]
in particular. By clustering, we intend a broad category of unsupervised methods that are able to group data into clusters representing some kind of structure in data, thus enabling further analysis and pattern discovery. The informal

S. Massanet et al. (Eds.): EUSFLAT 2023/AGOP 2023, LNCS 14069, pp. 443–454, 2023.
https://doi.org/10.1007/978-3-031-39965-7_37

assumption is that data points in the same clusters are similar, while data points in different clusters are dissimilar. That is the basic idea which contributes to provide meaning to the clustering process.

In most hard clustering methods, each data point belongs to one cluster only, so that different clusters partition a dataset and form a granular structure of the data domain. Possibly, these methods endow uncertainty on cluster assignment by defining a probability distribution of clusters conditioned to observed data points. Eventually, data points are assigned to the most probable cluster, or to a cluster that minimizes some loss function.

The added value of fuzzy clustering lies in a partial membership that can be assigned to data points when they are related to different clusters. Yet, this form of graduality is not understood as probability, rather it is a degree of membership which can be interpreted as a degree of similarity of a data point with respect to a cluster prototype. It is noteworthy that in classical Machine Learning the meaning of membership degrees is less relevant as long as the clustering results satisfy some measurable criteria, whereas in XAI the interpretation of membership degrees is instrumental to provide meaningful explanations.

FCM is a very popular fuzzy clustering method. Its popularity is due to its efficient algorithm, its robustness (especially when compared to its hard counterpart, i.e. k-means), as well as the requirement of few hyperparameters (namely, the number of clusters and a "fuzzification" parameter) [17]. Furthermore, FCM has been extended far and wide, with a huge corpus of literature that is beyond the scope of this paper [4,14].

Fuzzy clusters resulting from FCM form a *Ruspini partition* [15] because the sum of membership degrees of any data point to all clusters is equal to one. This poses an interpretation problem, because the resulting clusters have a non-convex shape; therefore, the membership degrees can be hardly interpreted in terms of similarity with respect to a prototype. In fact, membership degrees derived by FCM have also been interpreted as "degrees of sharing" [8], thus putting forward a concept that requires a contextualization in an appropriate theory to claim a clear meaning.

In this study, the membership degrees resulting from FCM are provided with an interpretation in the realm of Probability Theory. More specifically, we show that a membership degree can be interpreted as a posterior probability of a data point belonging to a cluster, given some assumptions that are made explicit and formalized.

The probabilistic interpretation has a number of advantages. First, the concept of "degree of sharing" is made clear because it is contextualized in a sound theory: the degree of sharing is the probability that a data point belongs to a cluster, given the assumptions. Therefore, in coherence with the Bayesian analysis, the membership degree of a data point to a cluster represents the belief that the data point belongs to the cluster, the latter being a crisp—yet unknown—subset of data.

As an additional advantage, the "fuzzification" parameter can be interpreted in probabilistic terms, since it is related to the expected value of the likelihood function, i.e., the probability that a data-point falls at a given distance from a cluster prototype. Finally, by weakening the reported assumptions, it may be possible to design extended versions of FCM by preserving the interpretation of the membership degrees.

The rest of the paper is organized as follows. The next section is devoted to the formalization of FCM. In Sect. 3 the probabilistic interpretation of the membership degrees is presented and demonstrated. Section 4 concludes the paper with a discussion and some hints for further investigation.

2   Fuzzy C-Means

Let $\mathbf{X}$ be a finite collection of N data points x_j in $\mathbb{R}^n$, to be mapped to c clusters. The objective of FCM is to derive a collection $\mathbf{V}$ of c prototypes v_i, and a partition matrix $\mathbf{U}$ such that u_{ji} is the membership degree of data point x_j to cluster i. To this pursuit, the following objective function is minimized:

$$J(\mathbf{U}, \mathbf{V}) = \sum_{i=1}^{c} \sum_{j=1}^{N} u_{ji}^m \|x_j - v_i\|_2^2 \tag{1}$$

subject to the constraints:

$$\forall x_j : \sum_{i=1}^{c} u_{ji} = 1 \tag{2}$$

$$\forall i : 0 < \sum_{j=1}^{N} u_{ji} < N \tag{3}$$

where $m > 1$ is the "fuzzification" hyperparameter.

The objective function (1) is minimized through an iterative process; at each step, the membership degrees and prototypes are derived as:

$$u_{ji} = \frac{1}{\sum_k \left(\frac{\|x_j - v_i\|_2}{\|x_j - v_k\|_2} \right)^{\frac{2}{m-1}}} \tag{4}$$

and

$$v_i = \frac{\sum_j u_{ji}^m x_j}{\sum_j u_{ji}^m} \tag{5}$$

In the case that $x_j = v_i$, then $u_{ji} = 1$; if $x_j = v_k$, with $k \neq i$, then $u_{ji} = 0$.

The iterative process stops when there is a negligible reduction of J or when a maximum number of iterations is reached.

For the sake of our discussion, we can rewrite (4) as a function of x_j, i.e.:

$$u_i(x_j) = \frac{1}{\sum_k \left(\frac{d_i}{d_k} \right)^{\frac{2}{m-1}}} \tag{6}$$

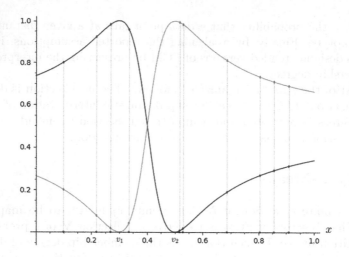

Fig. 1. Example of clustering 10 random one-dimensional data-points in two clusters with prototypes $v_1 = 0.3$ and $v_2 = 0.5$.

where $d_i = d_i(x_j) = ||x_j - v_i||_2$ for $i = 1, 2, \ldots, c$. The functional form (6) allows the computation of the membership degree of any data point in $\mathbb{R}^n$ once the optimization process is completed.

Figure 1 depicts the membership degrees of two one-dimensional clusters computed on 10 random data points and on the whole interval $[0, 1]$. Such a configuration is consistent with the results deriving from an application of the FCM algorithm. Each membership function u_i does not form a convex fuzzy set because it is not monotonically decreasing as the distance of a data point to the cluster prototype increases. This makes the interpretation of membership degrees as similarity degrees hard to accept: for example, $v_2 = 0.5$ stands as the prototype of the green cluster, but the membership degree of a data point located at $x = 0.1$ is higher than the membership degree of a data point located at $x = 0.35$ even if the latter is closer to the prototype than the former.

For such a reason, the membership degrees resulting from FCM are interpreted as "degrees of sharing", often leaving the meaning of this term to intuition. However, this interpretation might be unsatisfactory where the meaning of the outputs of a model must be clear (this is the case of the XAI context). As an example, the concept of "sharing" may be interpreted in terms of the requirement that a data point is decomposable into parts, with parts assigned to clusters in an exclusive way; yet, decomposability depends on the nature of the problem, while FCM can be always applied provided that data points have a numerical representation.

In our opinion, the quest for a general interpretation—where the sum of membership degrees finds a suitable meaning—represents a relevant research topic that may be of interest to scholars in this field. In the next Section, this interpretation is formalized within Probability Theory thanks to Bayesian analysis.

3   Bayesian Interpretation

Let X be a random data point[1] in a domain $\mathcal{X} \subset \mathbb{R}^n$. It is assumed that X occurs with a probability distribution represented by a mixture model of c clusters:

$$f_X(x|\theta) = \sum_{i=1}^{c} \Pr(C = i) f_{X|C}(x|i, \theta) \tag{7}$$

being θ the array of parameters of the model, C the random cluster, and f denoting the probability density functions (pdf) of (possibly conditioned) continuous random variables. (This approach is similar to defining a Gaussian Mixture Model, but we are not assuming a Gaussian distribution for $f_{X|C}$.) In the following, we are going to evaluate the pdf (7) on the basis of a number of assumptions.

First, we consider all the clusters to be equiprobable, i.e.,

$$\Pr(C - i) = \frac{1}{c} \tag{8}$$

It is further assumed that each cluster i corresponds to a prototype $v_i \in \mathcal{X}$, where v_i is a member of θ.

Given a cluster $C = i$, the random data point X can be represented in spherical coordinates, as a random pair (A, D) in which A is a $(n-1)$-dimensional vector of angular coordinates $A = (A_1, A_2, \ldots, A_{n-1})$ where $A_1, \ldots, A_{n-2} \in [0, \pi]$ and $A_{n-1} \in [0, 2\pi)$, while D is the random radial coordinate defined as the Euclidean distance $D = ||X - v_i||_2$. In Fig. 2 we refer to an exemplifying scenario where $n = 3$ and a cluster v are considered: an instance x of the random data point X can be represented in terms of $\alpha = (\alpha_1, \alpha_2)$ and d as instances of the random pair (A, D).

Based on the spherical representation of X, the conditional pdf $f_{X|C}$ involved in (7) can be expressed as:

$$
\begin{aligned}
f_{X|C}(x|i, \theta) &= f_{A,D|C}(\alpha, d|i, \theta) \\
&= \frac{f_{A,D,C}(\alpha, d, i|\theta)}{f_C(i|\theta)} \\
&= \frac{f_{A|D,C}(\alpha|d, i, \theta) \cdot f_{D,C}(d, i|\theta)}{f_C(i|\theta)} \\
&= \frac{f_{A|D,C}(\alpha|d, i, \theta) \cdot f_{D|C}(d|i, \theta) \cdot f_C(i|\theta)}{f_C(i|\theta)} \\
&= f_{A|D,C}(\alpha|d, i, \theta) \cdot f_{D|C}(d|i, \theta)
\end{aligned}
\tag{9}
$$

In the following, we are going to derive a suitable expression for $f_{A|D,C}$ and $f_{D|C}$, i.e. the pdfs involved in (9).

---

[1] Throughout the paper, we will denote random variables with uppercase letters, and their instances with lowercase letters, e.g. X/x, A/α, D/d, etc.

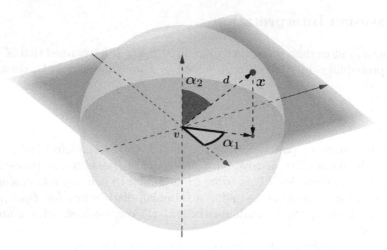

Fig. 2. A random point instance x represented in spherical coordinates inside a three-dimensional scenario.

Concerning $f_{A|D,C}$, it is assumed that all the angles A can be independently observed with the same probability evaluated inside their own range of values, irrespective of the data point's distance from the prototype, i.e., $f_{A|D,C} = f_{A|C}$. By recalling that $A_{n-1} \in [0, 2\pi)$ and $A_p \in [0, \pi]$ for $p = 1, 2, \ldots, n-2$, we obtain:[2]

$$
\begin{aligned}
f_{A|D,C}(\alpha|d, i, \theta) &= \prod_{p=1}^{n-1} f_{A_p|C}(\alpha_p|i, \theta) \\
&= f_{A_{n-1}|C}(\alpha_{n-1}|i, \theta) \cdot \prod_{p=1}^{n-2} f_{A_p|C}(\alpha_p|i, \theta) \\
&= \frac{1}{2\pi} \cdot \prod_{p=1}^{n-2} \frac{1}{\pi} = \frac{1}{2\pi} \cdot \left(\frac{1}{\pi}\right)^{n-2} \\
&= \frac{1}{2\pi^{n-1}}
\end{aligned}
\tag{10}
$$

Concerning $f_{D|C}$, some further assumptions are made. X is in a neighbourhood of v_i admitting both a lower and an upper bound. To avoid collapsing on the prototype, we assume there exists a threshold $a > 0$ such that $D \geq a$ (in practice, a can be assumed to be related to a very small value, such as 10^{-3}). The data point's distance from the prototype is also limited by an upper bound $l > a$ such that $D \leq l$ (for example, $l = 1$ can be assumed in case of L_2 normalized data).

---

[2] In the case $n = 1$, A can be either 0 or π with probability $1/2$.

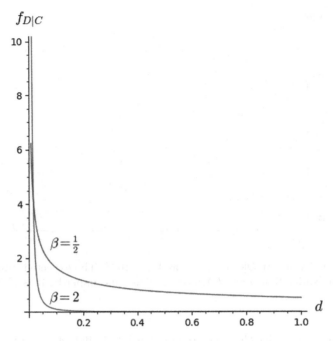

Fig. 3. Plots of the pdf $f_{D|C}$ evaluated for different values of β by setting $a = 10^{-3}$, $l = 1$: $\beta = 2$ (green line) and $\beta = 0.5$ (red line). (Color figure online)

Based on these assumptions, we define the pdf $f_{D|C}$ as:

$$f_{D|C}(d|i, \theta) = \frac{1}{K} \cdot d^{-\beta} \tag{11}$$

where $\beta > 0$. Being $f_{D|C}$ a pdf, its analytical expression must be such that its integral evaluated on the interval $[a, l]$ is equal to one. Therefore, we write:

$$
\begin{aligned}
\text{case I} \quad (\beta = 1) &: \int_a^l \frac{1}{K} \frac{1}{d'}\, dd' = \frac{1}{K} \log |d'|\Big|_a^l = \frac{1}{K}\Big(\log(l) - \log(a)\Big) \\
\text{case II} \quad (\beta \neq 1) &: \int_a^l \frac{1}{K} d'^{-\beta}\, dd' = \frac{1}{K} \frac{d'^{1-\beta}}{1-\beta}\Big|_a^l = \frac{1}{K}\left(\frac{a^{1-\beta}}{\beta - 1} - \frac{l^{1-\beta}}{\beta - 1}\right)
\end{aligned}
\tag{12}
$$

By doing so, we are able to express the value of the normalization coefficient K:

$$
K =
\begin{cases}
\log(l) - \log(a) & \text{if } \beta = 1 \\[2mm]
\dfrac{a^{1-\beta} - l^{1-\beta}}{\beta - 1} & \text{if } \beta \neq 1
\end{cases}
\tag{13}
$$

To provide an illustrative example, in Fig. 3 we plot the pdf $f_{D|C}$ for some chosen values of β, leaving the other parameters a, l fixed. Observing the shape

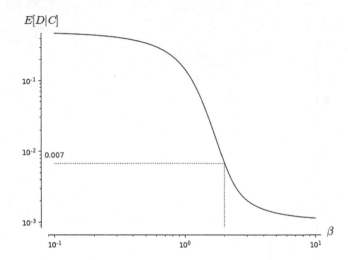

Fig. 4. Expected value of $D|C$ for $l = 1$ and $a = 10^{-3}$. The expected value for $\beta = 2$ is highlighted. Notice that a and l denote the lower and upper bounds of the expected value.

of the function, we notice that the green line is highly flattened. This means that, under certain assumptions (corresponding to the value $\beta = 2$) the probability to find data points at a greater distance from the considered prototype quickly decreases, which in turn implies that we are facing a scenario where all the data is expected to be concentrated very close to the prototype. On the other hand, if a different value of β is considered, the scenario changes accordingly. The red line in the figure (corresponding to the value $\beta = 0.5$) indicates an increased variance in the data location, with a greater probability to find points scattered far from the prototype.

As a further exploration in this direction, we can consider the expected value $E[D|C]$ (whose analytical form is rather complex and it is not reported here). A graph of $E[D|C]$ is illustrated in Fig. 4 for $l = 1$ and $a = 10^{-3}$, by varying β from 10^{-1} to 10 (the expected value for $\beta = 2$ is highlighted). Interestingly, for $\beta \gg 1$ the expected value is close to a, which presupposes that data are almost totally concentrated toward the prototype. On the other hand, for $\beta \ll 1$, the expected value becomes close to l, thus meaning that data are expected to be more scattered across the domain.

The pdf $f_{X|C}$ reported in (9), expressed as the combination of $f_{A|D,C}$ and $f_{D|C}$ is related to the probability of finding a data point given a particular cluster and its prototype, under the specified assumptions. We can exploit such a result to evaluate the probability of identifying a cluster (all of them have been initially assumed equiprobable) given a particular data point, under the same specified assumptions. Noticeably, this can be intended as the probability $\Pr(C = i | X = x, \theta)$ that a data point x belongs to a cluster i. It is possible to derive this probability by applying the Bayes' theorem to the previous results:

$$\Pr\left(C = i \mid X = x, \theta\right) = \frac{f_{X|C}\left(x \mid i, \theta\right) \cdot \Pr\left(C = i\right)}{f_X\left(x \mid \theta\right)}$$

$$= \frac{f_{A,D|C}\left(\alpha, d \mid i, \theta\right) \cdot \Pr\left(C = i\right)}{\sum_k f_{A,D|C}\left(\alpha, d \mid k, \theta\right) f_C(k)}$$

$$= \frac{\frac{1}{2\pi^{n-1}} \cdot \frac{1}{K} \cdot d_i^{-\beta} \cdot \frac{1}{c}}{\sum_k \left(\frac{1}{2\pi^{n-1}} \cdot \frac{1}{K} \cdot d_k^{-\beta} \cdot \frac{1}{c}\right)} \qquad (14)$$

$$= \frac{d_i^{-\beta}}{\sum_k d_k^{-\beta}}$$

It is now possible to relate (14) with (6), thus giving an interpretation to the membership degrees of FCM. Let

$$m = 1 + \frac{2}{\beta}$$

where it is possible to notice that $m > 1$. Then:

$$-\frac{2}{m-1} = -\beta \qquad (15)$$

therefore:

$$\Pr\left(C = i \mid X = x, \beta\right) = \frac{d_i^{-\frac{2}{m-1}}}{\sum_{k=1}^{c} d_k^{-\frac{2}{m-1}}}$$

$$= \frac{\frac{1}{d_i^{\frac{2}{m-1}}}}{\sum_{k=1}^{c} \frac{1}{d_k^{\frac{2}{m-1}}}} \qquad (16)$$

$$= \frac{1}{d_i^{\frac{2}{m-1}} \sum_{k=1}^{c} \frac{1}{d_k^{\frac{2}{m-1}}}}$$

$$\frac{1}{\sum_{k=1}^{c} \left(\frac{d_i}{d_k}\right)^{\frac{2}{m-1}}}$$

By recalling (6), we can observe that the expression of $\Pr(C = i \mid X = x, \theta)$ is analogous to the one adopted to describe the membership degrees evaluated by FCM while assigning a data point x to a cluster i. In this way, the FCM algorithm gets its own interpretation in the realm of the Probability Theory, and the "degrees of sharing" can be actually intended as probability values (under the assumptions discussed in this section).

4   Conclusive Remarks and Hints for Further Investigation

The Fuzzy C-Means algorithm is a popular clustering method whose effectiveness has been demonstrated in a wide range of applications. It has also been variously adopted in several contexts and adapted in a number of variations by scholars in the field of fuzzy modelling. However, FCM embeds a constraint which escapes a clear explanation within the framework of fuzzy logic, i.e. the sum-to-one of all the membership degrees evaluated for each data point when all clusters are considered. This constraint in turn implies some interpretation problems, since the clusters are characterized by membership degrees that can hardly be interpreted in terms of prototype similarity. Thus, despite the success of FCM, when it comes to applying it in contexts where explainability is a major concern, the aforementioned issues undermine its feasibility.

Based on the above considerations, we engaged a deeper investigation of the FCM algorithm with the aim of framing its machinery in the Probability Theory. This paper formally demonstrates that the membership degrees can be intended (under certain assumptions) as probability values, thus providing a sound interpretation of the "degrees of sharing" commonly invoked to describe the FCM results. More properly, we should talk about a-posterior probabilities of points belonging to clusters, as long as the specified assumptions stay effective. The probabilistic interpretation of membership degrees as posterior probabilities is in full compliance with Ruspini's work and provides a convincing meaning to otherwise elusive concepts.

Also, our results attribute a more precise role to one of the parameters involved in the FCM algorithm. We have pointed out that the fuzzification parameter is related to one of the terms at the basis of the pdf which describes the distribution of the data points around the prototypes associated to each cluster. In this sense, we have shown how the setting of the fuzzification parameter in FCM (a common a-priori choice made by practitioners) actually implies another (unverified) assumption concerning the dense or scattered concentration of points in the neighbourhood of the prototypes. This specific remark paves the way for further analysis. In fact, it makes sense to propose that the fuzzification parameter, rather than being chosen blindly a priori, should be derived through an investigation that appropriately takes into account the dispersion of data around the prototypes. Even, an analysis may be designed to determine several degrees of dispersion, possibly different for each cluster. Of course, there should also be room for estimating the associated costs in terms of additional computational burden.

Finally, we propose a quick comparison between the FCM and another clustering algorithm allowing for each data point a *soft* degree of assignment to each cluster, that is the soft counterpart to the classical (hard) K-means algorithm, i.e. the Soft K-means (SKM) [11]. In Fig. 5 we illustrate a one-dimensional clustering scenario involving two prototypes: $v_1 = -0.5$ and $v_2 = 0.5$. The membership functions depicted by solid lines refer to the results of the FCM, while the dashed lines represent the responsibility functions derived by the SKM algorithm. In both cases, the blue and the green clusters refer to the prototypes v_1 and v_2 respectively, and the degrees of assignment satisfy the sum-to-one requirement. Some differences can be easily observed from the analysis of the figure:

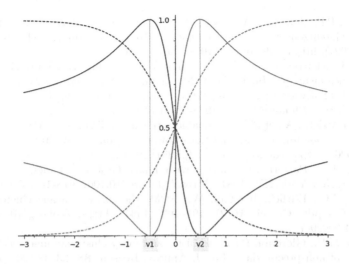

Fig. 5. A one-dimensional clustering scenario, based on two prototypes v_1, v_2, where both FCM and SKM are involved. Blue and green clusters refers to v_1 and v_2, respectively. Solid and dashed lines refer to FCM and SKM, respectively.

- the FCM algorithm organises the membership functions in such a way that the maximum probability that a data point belongs to a cluster corresponds to the prototype; instead, in the SKM case, the probability value corresponding to the prototype is less than one;
- when we consider the outermost regions of the domain (i.e. the left/right sides of the graph towards infinity, where the points furthest from the prototypes are located), we notice that SKM asymptotically tends to an extreme probability value (0 or 1); instead, FCM associates these regions to the maximum degree of uncertainty, since the membership functions asymptotically tend to the value 0.5 (or $1/c$ in the general case).

Both SKM and FCM share the same theoretical framework based on the computation of the posterior cluster probability (SKM differs from FCM only in the definition of the likelihood pfd $f_{X|C}$, which is Gaussian). As a consequence, all enhancements and methodological approaches to SKM (e.g., a Bayesian analysis of the parameters) can be, in principle, applied to FCM, thus opening the door to further extensions of the algorithm and novel theoretical insights.

References

1. Adadi, A., Berrada, M.: Peeking inside the black-box: a survey on explainable artificial intelligence (XAI). IEEE Access **6**, 52138–52160 (2018). https://doi.org/10.1109/ACCESS.2018.2870052
2. Alonso Moral, J.M., Castiello, C., Magdalena, L., Mencar, C.: Explainable Fuzzy Systems. SCI, vol. 970. Springer, Cham (2021). https://doi.org/10.1007/978-3-030-71098-9

3. Angelov, P.P., Soares, E.A., Jiang, R., Arnold, N.I., Atkinson, P.M.: Explainable artificial intelligence: an analytical review. WIREs Data Min. Knowl. Discov. **11**(5), 1–13 (2021). https://doi.org/10.1002/widm.1424

4. Arora, J., Khatter, K., Tushir, M.: Fuzzy c-means clustering strategies: a review of distance measures. In: Hoda, M.N., Chauhan, N., Quadri, S.M.K., Srivastava, P.R. (eds.) Software Engineering. AISC, vol. 731, pp. 153–162. Springer, Singapore (2019). https://doi.org/10.1007/978-981-10-8848-3_15

5. Barredo Arrieta, A., et al.: Explainable artificial intelligence (XAI): concepts, taxonomies, opportunities and challenges toward responsible AI. Inf. Fusion **58**, 82–115 (2020). https://doi.org/10.1016/j.inffus.2019.12.012

6. Bezdek, J.C.: Pattern Recognition with Fuzzy Objective Function Algorithms. Springer, New York, NY (1981). https://doi.org/10.1007/978-1-4757-0450-1

7. Bezdek, J.C., Ehrlich, R., Full, W.: FCM: the fuzzy c-means clustering algorithm. Comput. Geosci. **10**(2), 191–203 (1984). https://doi.org/10.1016/0098-3004(84)90020-7

8. Ferraro, M.B., Giordani, P.: Possibilistic and fuzzy clustering methods for robust analysis of non-precise data. Int. J. Approx. Reason. **88**, 23–38 (2017). https://doi.org/10.1016/j.ijar.2017.05.002

9. Guidotti, R., Monreale, A., Ruggieri, S., Turini, F., Giannotti, F., Pedreschi, D.: A survey of methods for explaining black box models. ACM Comput. Surv. **51**(5), 1–42 (2018). https://doi.org/10.1145/3236009

10. Gunning, D., Aha, D.W.: DARPA's explainable artificial intelligence (XAI) program. AI Mag. **40**(2), 44–58 (2019). https://doi.org/10.1609/aimag.v40i2.2850

11. MacKay, D.J.C.: Information Theory, Inference and Learning Algorithms. Cambridge University Press, Cambridge, TAS, Australia (2003)

12. Mendel, J.M., Bonissone, P.P.: Critical thinking about explainable AI (XAI) for rule-based fuzzy systems. IEEE Trans. Fuzzy Syst. **29**(12), 3579–3593 (2021). https://doi.org/10.1109/TFUZZ.2021.3079503

13. Miller, T.: Explanation in artificial intelligence: insights from the social sciences. Artif. Intell. **267**, 1–38 (2019). https://doi.org/10.1016/j.artint.2018.07.007

14. Nayak, J., Naik, B., Behera, H.S.: Fuzzy C-means (FCM) clustering algorithm: a decade review from 2000 to 2014. In: Jain, L.C., Behera, H.S., Mandal, J.K., Mohapatra, D.P. (eds.) Computational Intelligence in Data Mining - Volume 2. SIST, vol. 32, pp. 133–149. Springer, New Delhi (2015). https://doi.org/10.1007/978-81-322-2208-8_14

15. Ruspini, E.: A new approach to clustering. Inf. Control **15**(1), 22–32 (1969). https://doi.org/10.1016/S0019-9958(69)90591-9

16. Speith, T.: A review of taxonomies of explainable artificial intelligence (XAI) methods. In: 2022 ACM Conference on Fairness, Accountability, and Transparency, pp. 2239–2250. FAccT '22 (2022). https://doi.org/10.1145/3531146.3534639

17. Wu, K.L.: Analysis of parameter selections for fuzzy c-means. Pattern Recogn. **45**(1), 407–415 (2012). https://doi.org/10.1016/j.patcog.2011.07.012

The Role of Speculations for Explainable and Trustworthy Artificial Intelligence: A Use Case on Art Genre Classification

Jose Maria Alonso-Moral[1]([✉])(iD) and Vicent Costa[2](iD)

[1] Centro Singular de Investigación en Tecnoloxías Intelixentes (CiTIUS),
Universidade de Santiago de Compostela, Santiago de Compostela, Spain
josemaria.alonso.moral@usc.es
[2] Artificial Intelligence Research Institute (IIIA),
Spanish National Research Council (CSIC), Bellaterra, Spain
vicent@iiia.csic.es

Abstract. In this work, we have introduced a new way of speculative reasoning for intelligent systems. In addition, we have illustrated the utility of this way of reasoning in the context of a use case on art genre classification, where explainability and trustworthiness are a matter of major concern. Speculative reasoning is natural for humans and it turns up as a powerful tool, especially in the case of intelligent systems dealing with incomplete, vague, and imprecise information.

Keywords: Explainable AI · Logical Commonsense Reasoning · Horn Clauses · T-norm based Propositional Fuzzy Logic

1 Introduction

The research agenda in the field of Explainable and Trustworthy Artificial Intelligence (AI) addresses the challenges of adequate treatment of privacy, reliability, transparency, and interpretability of models and results associated with intelligent systems which are pervading many aspects of our Society [1].

In the context of Explainable AI, contrary-to-factual (or just counterfactual) explanation may be of crucial importance to go beyond summarizing available information about the reasoning behind the system's output and offer an insight into how alternative outcomes could be reached and appreciated by humans [13,14]. Being contrastive by nature, counterfactual explanations are claimed to increase users' trust only if they are in agreement with commonsense reasoning [12]. Accordingly, commonsense reasoning constitutes a cornerstone for counterfactual thinking [2]. In addition, abductive reasoning, complementary to the usual deductive and inductive reasoning, has already been successfully applied to time series interpretation [16].

It is worth noting that Trillas and De Soto [17] proved how combining generalized versions of the well-known Modus Ponens and Modus Tollens, it is possible

S. Massanet et al. (Eds.): EUSFLAT 2023/AGOP 2023, LNCS 14069, pp. 455–467, 2023.
https://doi.org/10.1007/978-3-031-39965-7_38

to verify or refute conjectures, what constitutes a way of advance abductive reasoning. More precisely, they first formalized the concept of conjecture in lattices. Then, they defined speculations as a specific type of conjecture in a pre-ordered set. Later, they defined a taxonomy of conjectures which includes consequences, hypotheses, and speculations.

In this work, we present an advanced speculative reasoning approach that is built on top of the logical reasoning approach previously proposed by [17] and briefly introduced in Sect. 2. A use case on art genre classification is described in Sect. 3, which also includes some illustrative examples of speculative reasoning. The manuscript ends with concluding remarks in Sect. 4.

2   Preliminaries

In Sect. 2.1, we recall the basics of the mathematical model developed by Trillas et al. for reasoning with speculations, to be used later in Sect. 3. Then, in Sect. 2.2, we define the five art genres to be taken into account later in the illustrative examples that are presented in Sect. 3.

2.1   A Formal Framework For Handling Speculations

Human reasoning, including commonsense reasoning, goes beyond deduction and abduction (understood as the seeking of consequences and hypothesis, respectively) and especially involves guessing, conjecturing, or inducing [15,20,22]. In a series of publications, Trillas et al. [18–21], developed a mathematical model, the so-called *skeleton*, to study this kind of reasoning. In this subsection, we revisit some of the main definitions and properties of this *skeleton*.

According to that model, a first and crucial step towards mathematical studying this kind of reasoning is the formalization of the so-called inferential relation, denoted by $<$. The binary $<$ relation recognizes an intellectual *movement* between linguistic terms, concepts, or statements. In this way, the expression $p < q$ abbreviates "If p, then q" (from now on, let us denote any linguistic statement using the letters $p, q, r, \ldots$). But this linguistic relation has no fixed interpretation in the language: for instance, in quantum physics, it would be $\neg p \vee (p \wedge q)$ or $q \vee (\neg p \wedge \neg q)$; in mathematics, $\neg p \vee q$; and often $p \wedge q$ in the ordinal language (observe that ordinal language does not always interpret the conjunction as the classical one). For this reason, this model conceives the inferential relation as a primitive relation, and when using $<$, its interpretation must be explicit, i.e., $<$ must be rendered in terms of connectives. Furthermore, for any p, q, the inference relation $<$ must hold the five general laws of commonsense reasoning (which can be considered as the reasoning principles which does not accept the contradiction):

1. Reflexivity: $p < p$.
2. If $p < q$, then $\neg q < \neg p$.
3. $p \wedge q < p$, and $p \wedge q < q$.

4. $p < p \lor q$, and $q < p \lor q$.
5. Modus Ponens: $p \land (p < q) < q$.

In addition, it is worth noting that due to its linguistic character, $<$ cannot always be assumed to be transitive (i.e., transitivity does not hold for any triplet of statements; local transitivity, however, is allowed).

The expression $p \not< q$ indicates that it does not hold $p < q$. Furthermore, whenever $p \not< q$ and $q \not< p$, we say that p and q are orthogonal, and this is represented by $p \diamond q$. Regarding the conclusions of one reasoning, provided that $p \not< \neg p$, the following basic definitions are considered:

- q is a *consequence* of p if $p < q$;
- h is a *hypothesis* of p whenever $h < p$, $h \not< \neg h$ (i.e., h is not self-contradictory) and $p \not< h$;
- if $p < \neg r$, we say r is a *refutation* of p;
- c is a *conjecture from* p if $p \not< \neg c$.

Regarding the negation, four types are considered:

1. *Weak negation*: $p < \neg\neg p$.
2. *Intuitionistic negation*: $\neg\neg p < p$.
3. *Strong negation*: $\neg$ is weak and intuitionistic.
4. *Wild negation*: $\neg$ is neither weak nor intuitionistic (i.e., $p \diamond \neg\neg p$).

Whenever q is a conjecture from p (i.e., $p \not< \neg q$), we say that q is a speculation from p if $p \diamond q$. In this way, since provided $p \not< \neg q$, it can be either $p < q$, or $q < p$, or $p \diamond q$, conjectures can be classified into consequences, hypotheses, and speculations. Accordingly, reasoning in the *skeleton* introduced above can be defined as the process to reach conjectures and refutations [17]. Again, transitivity is crucial to make effective and efficient reasoning. In this context, valid admissible premises are those statements that can be inferred and conjectured from themselves, no conjecture being a consequence of a premise is self-contradictory (under transitivity). Speculations can be categorized into two main types:

1. *Weak speculation*: $\neg q < p$. Notice that, the negation of a weak speculation is a hypothesis.
2. *Strong speculation*: $p \diamond \neg q$.

Finally, handling speculations implies combining properly deduction and abduction. On the one hand, deduction or forwards inference means that given p, we look for q such that $p < q$ (consequences are attained by chains of deductions). On the other hand, abduction or backward inference means that given p, the search is for some q such that $q < p$ (hypotheses are obtained by chains of abductions). Observe that reasoning from p means conjecturing from p to find out and validate a consequence/hypotheses/speculation q, or refuting p.

2.2 Art Genres

Genres are types of painting, i.e., categories of painting compositions characterized by a particular style, form, or content. A genre system divides paintings
according to depicted themes and objects. The first genre system, which we use
in this paper, was established in the 17th century by the French Academy, and it
considers five genres: history painting, portrait, genre painting, landscape, and
still life. History paintings provide a message set in a historical, religious, allegor-
ical, or mythological context[1]. Portraits are paintings whose theme is the face.
Another art genre is the genre painting, which includes those paintings concerning scenes from everyday life, presented in a generally realistic manner [4]. The
landscape is the genre of paintings whose principal theme is the representation
of a scenic view as rivers, mountains, or seascapes[2]. Still life paintings mostly
depict an arrangement of inanimate objects as their subject[3]. These objects are
typically flowers, vases, food, glasses, or books, among others. Figure 1 shows
some illustrative examples of the art genres enumerated above.

A history painting.   A portrait.   A genre painting.   A landscape.   A still life painting.

Fig. 1. Examples of paintings from the QArt-Dataset classified by art genre. All rights
under © creative commons, public license.

In this paper, we classify and reason with paintings from the QArt-Dataset [9,
10]. This dataset contains 90 images by Diego Velázquez, Johannes Vermeer,
Pierre-Auguste Renoir, Claude Monet, Vincent van Gogh, and Paul Gauguin.
All the paintings in the figures of this paper belong to this dataset.

3   Logical Deduction and Speculation Regarding Art Genres

In this section, we categorize the five main art genres briefly introduced in
previous Sect. 2.2 and present the design of an explainable art genre classifier
(see Sect. 3.1). Then, we use the model of speculations previously introduced
(in Sect. 2.1) to derive speculations on the genre of a painting (see Sect. 3.2).
Finally, we use these categorizations to evaluate the worthiness of weak speculations when reasoning on two illustrative examples with imprecise information
(see Sect. 3.3).

---

[1] http://www.visual-arts-cork.com/genres/history-painting.htm.
[2] http://www.visual-arts-cork.com/genres/landscape-painting.htm.
[3] https://mymodernmet.com/what-is-still-life-painting-definition/.

3.1   Logical Deduction for Classifying Art Genres

For categorizing the five art genres under consideration, we use the evaluated syntax of the Horn fragment of continuous t-norm based propositional fuzzy logic, which we recall next. We consider a set of propositional variables Var, the binary connectives $\&$ and $\rightarrow$, and the truth-constants are $\overline{k}$ so that k is a rational number and $k \in [0,1]$, where $[0,1] \subseteq \mathbb{R}$ and $\mathbb{R}$ denotes the set of real numbers. An *atomic evaluated formula* (φ, k) is defined as $\overline{k} \rightarrow \varphi$, where φ is an atomic formula without truth constants apart from $\overline{0}$ and $\overline{1}$. An *evaluated Horn clause* [6] has the form $(\varphi_1, k_1)\&\ldots\&(\varphi_n, k_n) \rightarrow (\varphi, s)$, where $(\varphi_1, k_1), \ldots, (\varphi_n, k_n)$ and (φ, s) are atomic evaluated formulas.

Concerning semantics, we recall that a $[0,1]$-*evaluation* e is a mapping $e : Var \rightarrow [0,1]$ and, let $*$ be a continuous t-norm, an evaluation e extends uniquely to an evaluation e^* of the set of well-formed formulas as usual (as common, for the sake of simplicity, no distinction between e and e^* is made and the notation is simplified to e in both cases). We say that a propositional variable q is *Boolean* if for any evaluation e, $e(q) \in \{0,1\}$.

To start with the categorizations, we propose 7 Boolean propositional variables (see Table 1) and 2 non-Boolean propositional variables (see Table 2). These variables are selected based on art experts' definitions of the genres presented in Sect. 2.2. Notice that, for any digital painting dp in the QArt-Dataset, we can consider an evaluation e_{dp} whose truth values are obtained from dp by answering the questions in Tables 1 and 2. For instance, let us consider the painting *The Surrender of Breda* by Velázquez ($v3$ in the QArt-Dataset and the first picture from the left in Fig. 1):

$$e_{v3}(weapons) = e_{v3}(flowers) = 1, \, e_{v3}(person) = e_{v3}(table) = 0,$$
$$e_{v3}(glasses) = e_{v3}(jewelry) = e_{v3}(buildings) = 0, \text{ and}$$
$$e_{v3}(people) = e_{v3}(trees) = 1.$$

Table 1. Boolean variables corresponding to 7 distinctive features of art genres.

Variable	yes/no question to determine the value of the variable
weapons	is there any weapon (a spear, sword, rifle, etc.) in the image?
flowers	is there any flower (or plant) in the image?
person	is there exactly one person in the image?
table	is there any table in the image?
glasses	is there any glass (or vase or basket) in the image?
jewelry	is there any jewelry in the image?
buildings	is there any building (house, hut, skyscraper, etc.) in the image?

Art genres, as explained in Sect. 2.2, are categories of paintings used since the 17th century. However, as it commonly occurs with art definitions, non-unambiguous categorizations (and exceptions) are very frequent. Genres are

Table 2. Non-boolean variables corresponding to 2 distinctive features of art genres.

Variable	Criteria to determine the truth value of the variable
people	no person appearing in the image (0), 1–2 people (0.33), 3–4 people (0.66), more than 4 people (1)
trees	no tree appearing in the image (0), 1–5 trees (0.5), more than 5 trees (1)

especially difficult to classify since they are related to cultural and social interpretations of the scenes. For instance, a painting showing an everyday scene, in
principle, should be classified as a genre painting; however, if the scene belongs to
a mythological myth, then the painting should be classified as a history painting.
Ultimately, some classifications need additional data apart from that included
in the painting for disambiguation. Thus, the proposals from art experts, even
if often enough to classify paintings into art genres, cannot serve as a very accurate classification. Considering this, we next propose five evaluated Horn clauses,
understood as expert rules, which characterize the five art genres under consideration. Let ψ_1 be an evaluated Horn clause, as follows:

$$\psi_1 = (weapons, 0.5)\&(flowers, 0.8)\&(people, 0.9) \rightarrow (history\_painting, 1)$$

We propose the formula ψ_1 as an expert rule for characterizing the genre of
history painting. ψ_1 expresses that the appearances of weapons, flowers, and
plants, and the presence of a group of people (at least four people) indicate that
the given painting might be classified as a history painting.

Analogously, we propose the evaluated Horn clauses $\psi_2, \psi_3, \psi_4, \psi_5$ corresponding to the portrait, genre painting, landscape, and still life, respectively:

$$\psi_2 = (person, 1)\&(flowers, 0.35) \rightarrow (portrait, 1)$$
$$\psi_3 = (table, 0.5)\&(glasses, 0.5)\&(jewelry, 0.25)\&(people, 0.65) \rightarrow (genre\_painting, 1)$$
$$\psi_4 = (flowers, 0.8)\&(trees, 0.75)\&(buildings, 0.8) \rightarrow (landscape, 1)$$
$$\psi_5 = (table, 0.5)\&(glasses, 1)\&(flowers, 1) \rightarrow (still\_life, 1)$$

Let us note that the parameters in the antecedents of the evaluated Horn clauses
$\psi_1, \ldots, \psi_5$ have been obtained empirically from the QArt-Dataset.

To classify paintings into art genres, we obtain the membership degrees to
the five genres in the following way. For a painting dp, its membership degree of
each genre is defined as the minimum value[4] of all truth values for computing e_{dp}
from $\psi_1, \psi_2, \ldots, \psi_5$. Therefore, the computed value depends on the semantics of
the selected logic. In this paper, we have set the Rational Pavelka Logic. For
instance, the membership degree of $v3$ to the history painting genre is:

---

[4] The interested reader can see further details about how to compute membership
degrees associated with evaluated Horn Clauses in [8].

$e_{v3}((history\_painting, 1))$ $=$ $e_{v3}((weapons, 0.5)\&(flowers, 0.8)\&(people,$
$0.9)) =$
$max\{0, e_{v3}((weapons, 0.5)) + e_{v3}((flowers, 0.8)) + e_{v3}((people, 0.9)) - 2\} =$
$max\{0, min\{1 - 0.5 + e_{v3}(weapons), 1\} + min\{1 - 0.8 + e_{v3}(flowers), 1\} +$
$min\{1 - 0.9 + e_{v3}(people), 1\} - 2\} =$
$max\{0, min\{1.5, 1\} + min\{1.2, 1\} + min\{1.1, 1\} - 2\} =$
$max\{0, 1 + 1 + 1 - 2\} = max\{0, 1\} = 1.$

The remaining membership degrees are obtained analogously, using ψ_2, ψ_3, ψ_4 and ψ_5. Finally, the paintings are classified into an art genre according to the higher membership. Following with $v3$, the painting is classified as a history painting since the membership degree corresponding to this genre obtains the highest value.

We have tested this classifier with all paintings in the QArt-Dataset and it achieved a classification rate of 61.1%. In addition, similarly to other explainable classifiers (e.g., those classifiers published by Costa et al. [5,7,8]), this logic-based approach provides users not only with a classification but also with a meaningful explanation regarding the influence of each propositional variable on the identified genre (see an example in Fig. 2).

```
v3 is a history painting.
The presence of weapons, flowers, and plants
is an evidence for this genre.
The fact that more than four people appear
in the painting reinforces the evidence in favor
of this genre.
```

Fig. 2. Classification (and related explanation) for the painting *The Surrender of Breda* by Velázquez ($v3$ in the QArt-Dataset). All rights under © creative commons, public license.

3.2 Speculating on Features Related to Art Genres

In this section, we use the formal framework presented in Sect. 2.1 to reason on the art genre of the painting *Bal du moulin de la Galette* by Pierre-Auguste Renoir ($rn2$ in the QArt-Dataset - see Fig. 3). First, in Example 1, we propose an interpretation of the inference relation $<$, commonly used in the related literature, and show how to deal with consequences and hypotheses related to the painting. Then, to improve the results obtained, we propose another interpretation of $<$ and analyze the changes (Example 2).

Fig. 3. *Bal du moulin de la Galette* by Pierre-Auguste Renoir. All rights under ©
creative commons, public license.

We will begin with establishing definitions and assumptions for both examples. We define the universe of discourse as the set $\{v1, v2, \ldots, gg15\}$ (i.e., the
paintings from the QArt-Dataset), assume transitivity, and use the propositional variables presented in Sect. 3.1. Furthermore, to make the reasoning about
each painting even richer and more natural, we add three statements, *Baroque*,
Impressionism, and *Postimpressionism*, which express a painting's belonging to
the corresponding art style. The evaluation of these three statements is done (for
each painting selected from the QArt-Dataset) regarding the values computed
by the classifier ℓ-SHE^{RPL} presented in [8], in terms of intensity of colors present
in the image. Notice that, in the rest of the manuscript, such evaluations take
values in $[0, 1]$.

Example 1. *Let us interpret the inference relation $<$ as the linear order on the
real line. It is easy to check that $<$ holds the laws of commonsense reasoning
recalled in Sect. 2.1), and the negation $\neg$ as a strong negation (i.e., $\neg p = 1 - p$).
The premise of this example is Impressionism, whose value is 0.891. Observe
that this value is obtained from the classifier ℓ-SHE^{RPL} [8], from which we also
get that Baroque is 0.855, and Postimpressionism is 0.463. Furthermore, from
the data in the painting, we obtain that flowers $=$ table $=$ glasses $=$ jewelry $=$
people $=$ trees $= 1$, and 0 for the rest of the statements.*

*It is worth noting that $\neg Impressionism = 1 - 0.891 = 0.109$. Accordingly,
Impressionism $\not< \neg Impressionism$. Therefore, Impressionism is an admissible
premise because it is not self-contradictory. It is easy to check that, in this example, the set of non-self-contradictory statements includes Baroque, Impressionism, flowers, table, glasses, jewelry, people, and trees. Regarding Postimpressionism, we recall that it is a self-contradictory statement (Postimpressionism $<
\neg Postimpressionism$ because $\neg Postimpressionism = 0.537$).*

*Concerning the refutations of Impressionism, they are those r such that
Impressionism $< \neg r$. Therefore, considering the interpretation of $\neg$ and $<$, we
find that those statements such as $r \leq 0.109$ are self-contradictory and they can
be deemed as refutations. In addition, consequences of Impressionism are flowers, table, glasses, jewelry, people, and trees. For instance, Impressionism $=
0.891 \not< \neg people = 1$ and Impressionism $= 0.891 < people = 1$.*

Regarding hypotheses, we discover that Baroque is the only hypothesis for Impressionism because Impressionism $\not<$ ¬Baroque and Baroque $<$ Impressionism.

Finally, we identified some statements which are orthogonal to Impressionism: history_painting, portraits, genre_painting, landscape, and still_life (because all of these variables satisfy Var◇Impressionism).

The hypothesis obtained in Example 1 does not seem reasonable. Indeed, it is hard to imagine how belonging to the Baroque style could be a hypothesis for belonging to Impressionism. In other words, this kind of reasoning would not be informative when explained to an end user. So, having reached these statements, we could state that the linear order, frequently used in related literature, seems more appropriate to reason on ordering real numbers than on art categorizations like genre or style. Let us, thus, propose another interpretation of $<$.

Example 2. *Let us now interpret the inferential relation as the classical conditional (i.e., $p < q$ is ¬$p \lor q$, where $\lor$ is interpreted using the maximum function). Again, we consider the strong negation and the same values for the evaluation of statements Baroque Impressionism, and Postimpressionism.*

The non-self-contradictory statements are those whose value is different from 0, that is, those in the set {flowers, table, glasses, jewelry, people, trees, Baroque, Impressionism, Postimpressionism}. In addition, since Impressionism $\neq 0$, the refutations are now weapons, person, and buildings, and any non-self-contradictory statement is a conjecture. Moreover, the consequences are flowers, table, glasses, jewelry, people, and trees.

Notice that, there is not any hypothesis of Impressionism: since Impressionism $\neq 1$, a hypothesis h of Impressionism needs to have value 0, but then $h < ¬h$. Finally, since the values of history_painting, portrait, genre_painting, landscape, and still_life are unknown, we can conclude that the speculations from Impressionism are those non-self-contradictory statements concerning the genres.

The results obtained in Example 2 suggest this interpretation of the inferential relation $<$ is more suitable for reasoning on paintings' traits related to the art genre. However, the speculations reached did not seem to be very informative. Notice that, in the two previous examples, all the traits related to genres were known, and we hypothesize that this affects the reaching of speculations. Motivated by this observation, we next propose two additional illustrative examples where speculative reasoning is more effective.

3.3   Examples of Speculative Reasoning with Imprecise Information

This section presents two illustrative examples of blurred paintings, i.e., artworks in which some data is missing (see Fig. 4). In both cases, we propose to use, together with the speculations reached, the genre categorizations presented in Sect. 3.1 to guess the genre of the painting.

The first illustrative example is a version of the painting *rn2* (see the picture on the left of Fig. 4 versus Fig. 3), where we can only visualize at least 3 people in

Fig. 4. Two blurred paintings from the QArt-Dataset.

the image, and we know that *Impressionism* is 0.891, but nothing else. In such a scenario, the expert system presented in Sect. 3.1, based on deductive reasoning, cannot yield a satisfactory result because it gets the value 0 for all the related membership degrees.

Let us see whether reasoning with speculations, consequently, is more suitable in this case. So, let us try to reach a speculation from *Impressionism*. The interpretation of $<$ and $\neg$ are the same as in Example 2. On the one hand, by forwards inference from *Impressionism* we get *Impressionism* $<$ *Impressionism* $\vee$ *people*; and, by abduction, *Impressionism* $\vee$ *people* $>$ *people*. That is, *Impressionism* $<$ *Impressionism* $\vee$ *people* $>$ *people* (analogously, *Impressionism* $>$ *Impressionism* $\wedge$ *people* $<$ *people*). Then, *Impressionism* $\diamond$ *people*. On the other hand, since at least 3 people appear in the painting, *impressionism* $\not<$ $\neg$ *people* (at most, $\neg$ *people* is 0.34). Therefore, *people* is a speculation from *Impressionism*. And similarly, *Impressionism* is orthogonal with the five statements regarding genres. However, having reached the speculation *people*, we can use the genre categorizations proposed in this paper and guess that the painting belongs to *genre_painting* or *history_painting*.

The second illustrative example is the painting on the right in Fig. 4 (i.e., *Tulip Fields at Sassenheim, Near Leiden* by Monet, $m8$ in the QArt-Dataset). Here, we start with the premise *Impressionism* = 0.961, which is a valid premise because *Impressionism* $\not<$ $\neg$*Impressionism*. In addition, by observing the image, we know that *flowers*, *plants*, and *at least one tree* appear in the painting. Hence, *trees* is, at least, 0.5, and *flowers* = 1. In this way, *flowers* is not a speculation from the premise (no matter whether the inferential relation is interpreted as the classical conditional or the linear order). However, *trees* is a weak speculation when interpreting $<$ as the linear order, and orthogonal with *Impressionism* whether $<$ is interpreted as the classical conditional. Taking into consideration the weak speculation and the genre categorizations, we could guess that the more probable genre for this painting would be the *landscape*. The fully explained classification of $m8$ is shown in Fig. 5. It is worth noting that the explanation includes the speculation reached, that is, the presence of trees.

```
m8 is a landscape.
The presence of flowers, plants, and buildings
evidences this genre. The fact that more than
five trees appear in the painting is
another evidence in favor of this genre.
```

Fig. 5. Classification and explanation of the painting *Tulip Fields at Sassenheim, Near Leiden* by Claude Monet (*m*8 in the QArt-Dataset). All rights under © creative commons, public license.

4   Concluding Remarks and Future Work

In this work, we have presented two logic-based approaches to reason on art genres and related features. First, we proposed an expert system for classifying genres based on deduction. Then, we discussed and highlighted some challenges when dealing with speculations in our application domain. Finally, we analyzed some illustrative examples, where we highlighted the strengths and weaknesses of each approach, and suggested a hybrid procedure that provides users with useful, trustworthy, and richer explanations.

As future work, we intend to improve the faithfulness and naturalness of automated explanations. We will test the classifier with a larger dataset (e.g., the dataset introduced in [3]). We will also make a comparison of the presented approach with other classification methods. In addition, it is worth noting that current attributes are manually defined as a proof of concept, but an automatic feature extraction stage, such as the usage of an object detector, is to be taken into account for the sake of scalability and generality of results. Furthermore, we will compare the produced explanations with those provided by other explainable classifiers, analyzing their rationality level [11]. In addition, we plan to enhance the implementation of the formalism described in Sect. 3.2, similarly to [15], to automatize the reach of speculations and refutations in our application domain. Finally, the main open challenge is running a human study for carefully evaluating the worthiness of speculations and guessing art genres.

Acknowledgement. This work was supported by the Spanish Ministry of Science, Innovation and Universities (grants PID2021-123152OB-C21 and TED2021-130295B-C33) and the Galician Ministry of Culture, Education, Professional Training and University (grants ED431G2019/04 and ED431C2022/19). These grants were co-funded by the European Regional Development Fund (ERDF/FEDER program). V. Costa is a Juan de la Cierva researcher (FJC2021-047274-I).

References

1. Alonso-Moral, J.M., Mencar, C., Ishibuchi, H.: Explainable and trustworthy artificial intelligence. IEEE Comput. Intell. Mag. **17**, 14–15 (2022). https://doi.org/10.1109/MCI.2021.3129953
2. Byrne, R.M.J.: Cognitive processes in counterfactual thinking about what might have been. Psychol. Learn. Motiv. **37**, 105–154 (1997)
3. Castellano, G., Digeno, V., Sansaro, G., Vessio, G.: Leveraging knowledge graphs and deep learning for automatic art analysis. Knowl.-Based Syst. **248**, 108859.1–108859.8 (2022). https://doi.org/10.1016/j.knosys.2022.108859
4. Charles, V., Carl, K.H.: Baroque Art. e-Parkstone International (1979)
5. Costa, V.: The art painting style classifier based on logic aggregators and qualitative colour descriptors (C-LAD). In: Rudolph, S., Marreiros, G. (eds.) Proceedings of the 9th European Starting AI Researchers' Symposium, co-located with the 24th European Conference on Artificial Intelligence (ECAI), Santiago Compostela, Spain. CEUR Workshop Proceedings, vol. 2655. CEUR-WS.org (2020)
6. Costa, V., Dellunde, P.: Term models of horn clauses over rational pavelka predicate logic. In: 47th IEEE International Symposium on Multiple-Valued Logic (ISMVL), Novi Sad, Serbia, pp. 112–117. IEEE Computer Society (2017)
7. Costa, V., Dellunde, P., Falomir, Z.: Style painting classifier based on horn clauses and explanations (SHE). In: Falomir, Z., Gibert, K., Plaza, E. (eds.) Artificial Intelligence Research and Development - Current Challenges, New Trends and Applications, CCIA, 21st International Conference of the Catalan Association for Artificial Intelligence. Frontiers in Artificial Intelligence and Applications, vol. 308, pp. 37–46. IOS Press (2018)
8. Costa, V., Dellunde, P., Falomir, Z.: The logical style painting classifier based on horn clauses and explanations (l-she). Log. J. IGPL **29**(1), 96–119 (2021)
9. Falomir, Z., Cabedo, L.M., Abril, L.G.: A model for colour naming and comparing based on conceptual neighbourhood. an application for comparing art compositions. Knowl. Based Syst. **81**, 1–21 (2015)
10. Falomir, Z., Cabedo, L.M., Sanz, I., Abril, L.G.: Categorizing paintings in art styles based on qualitative color descriptors, quantitative global features and machine learning (QArt-Learn). Expert Syst. Appl. **97**, 83–94 (2018)
11. Falomir, Z., Costa, V.: On the rationality of explanations in classification algorithms. In: Villaret, M., Alsinet, T., Fernández, C., Valls, A. (eds.) Artificial Intelligence Research and Development - Proceedings of the 23rd International Conference of the Catalan Association for Artificial Intelligence (CCIA). Frontiers in Artificial Intelligence and Applications, vol. 339, pp. 445–454. IOS Press (2021)
12. Mueller, E.: Commonsense Reasoning: An Event Calculus Based Approach. Elsevier Science, Amsterdam, (2014)
13. Stepin, I., Alonso-Moral, J.M., Catala, A., Pereira-Farina, M.: An empirical study on how humans appreciate automated counterfactual explanations which embrace imprecise information **618**, 379–399 (2022). https://doi.org/10.1016/j.ins.2022.10.098
14. Stepin, I., Alonso, J.M., Catalá, A., Pereira-Fariña, M.: A survey of contrastive and counterfactual explanation generation methods for explainable artificial intelligence. IEEE Access **9**, 11974–12001 (2021). https://doi.org/10.1109/ACCESS.2021.3051315
15. Tabacchi, M.E.: Logic and computational aspects of computing with speculations. Arch. Philos. Hist. Soft Comput. **1**, 3–10 (2022)

16. Teijeiro, T., Félix, P.: On the adoption of abductive reasoning for time series interpretation. Artif. Intell. **262**, 163–188 (2018)
17. Trillas, E., de Soto, A.: On the search of speculations. New Math. Nat. Comput. **18**, 9–18 (2022). https://doi.org/10.1142/S1793005722500028
18. Trillas, E.: A model for "crisp reasoning" with fuzzy sets. Int. J. Intell. Syst. **27**(10), 859–872 (2012)
19. Trillas, E.: Glimpsing at guessing. Fuzzy Sets Syst. **281**, 32–43 (2015)
20. Trillas, E.: On the Logos: A Naïve View on Ordinary Reasoning and Fuzzy Logic, Studies in Fuzziness and Soft Computing, vol. 354. Springer, Cham (2017). https://doi.org/10.1007/978-3-319-56053-3
21. Trillas, E., García-Honrado, I., Pradera, A.: Consequences and conjectures in pre-ordered sets. Inf. Sci. **180**(19), 3573–3588 (2010)
22. Trillas, E., Termini, S., Tabacchi, M.E.: Reasoning and Language at Work - A Critical Essay, Studies in Computational Intelligence, vol. 991. Springer, Cham (2022). https://doi.org/10.1007/978-3-030-86088-2

Fuzzy Sets: A Key Towards Hybrid Explainable Artificial Intelligence for Image Understanding

Isabelle Bloch$^{(\boxtimes)}$ (iD)

Sorbonne Université, CNRS, LIP6, Paris, France
isabelle.bloch@sorbonne-universite.fr

Abstract. In this paper, we propose a basis for discussing the role of fuzzy sets theory in the context of explainable artificial intelligence. We advocate that combining several frameworks in artificial intelligence, including fuzzy sets theory, adopting a hybrid point of view both for knowledge and data representation and for reasoning, offers opportunities towards explainability. This idea is instantiated on the example of image understanding, expressed as a spatial reasoning problem.

Keywords: Fuzzy Sets · Hybrid Artificial Intelligence · Explainable Artificial Intelligence (XAI) · Image Understanding · Spatial Reasoning

1 Introduction

The role and usefulness of fuzzy sets to represent imprecision at various levels of information (pertaining to both data and knowledge) and to reason on such imprecise information have been recognized for many years. This applies, among others, to the domain of image and computer vision, for various tasks ranging from low level image processing, to analysis and higher level image understanding [10,17].

As part of artificial intelligence (AI), fuzzy sets theory has a key position in the landscape of hybrid AI, with important features for explainable AI (XAI), see e.g. [19] and the references therein. While symbolic methods and statistical machine learning methods for AI have been developed rather independently for decades, with alternated predominance of one or the other along time, a trend is to merge both types of approaches. Examples include neuro-symbolic approaches (see e.g. [26,34,35,41,43]), among others. However, in this paper hybrid AI is intended in a broader sense, as the combination of several AI methods, whatever their type. These methods may belong to the domains of abstract knowledge representation and formal reasoning, based on logics, structural representations

I. Bloch—This work was partly supported by the author's chair in Artificial Intelligence (Sorbonne Université and SCAI). A part of the work was performed while the author was with LTCI, Télécom Paris, Institut Polytechnique de Paris.

(such as graphs and hypergraphs, ontologies, concept lattices...), machine learning, etc. In particular, fuzzy sets can be considered as a stand-alone framework, but can also be successfully associated with several of these methods.

Such combinations of approaches take inspiration from cognitive functions. Roughly speaking, according to Kahneman [40] who distinguished two systems for thinking, named system 1 and system 2, we may consider, from a (strongly simplified) AI point of view, modeling system 1 by deep learning and system 2 by symbolic reasoning. Developing neuro-symbolic approaches is a new trend to combine the two systems (see e.g. [41]). But again, more theories will be committed in our view of hybrid AI, in particular for image understanding.

This paper is a position paper, and its aim is not to propose new methods for hybrid AI, but rather to highlight how this way of thinking and designing AI systems offers opportunities towards explainability, in the field of XAI, and as a mean to maintain the link between knowledge and data, based on previous work by the author and her co-authors. In that domain too, the two main branches are developed quite independently, with early work (e.g. Peirce at the end of the 19th century) focusing on logical reasoning based on abduction on the one hand, versus recent methods focusing on features or data most involved in a decision on the other hand (to name but a few). In the first paradigm, knowledge is represented by symbols, in a given logic, and the reasoning power of this logic plays then a major role. Reasoning is based on axioms, theories and inference rules, leading to provable, non-refutable conclusions. In the second paradigm, where data and experience play the major role, statistical guarantees can be achieved, but conclusions are potentially refutable. Fuzzy sets can cope with both approaches, and establish links between them.

As an example, these ideas are illustrated in the field of image understanding, formulated as a spatial reasoning problem (Sect. 2). Examples of combinations of different AI methods are given both for knowledge and data representation in Sect. 3, and for reasoning in Sect. 4. These methods find concrete applications in several domains, such as medical imaging (only briefly mentioned in this paper). The question of explanations is addressed in Sect. 5. Finally a short discussion on open research directions concludes the paper (Sect. 6).

This paper is an extension of [13], and focuses on the role of fuzzy sets, and on the explainability aspects. It does not contain technical details, but those can be found in the mentioned references.

2 Image Understanding and Spatial Reasoning

Image understanding refers, at the simplest level, to the problem of recognizing an object or structure, or several objects in an image, either real, as an observation of a part of the real world, or synthetic. But this may not be sufficient, and, more generally, relations between these objects should be considered, towards a global recognition of the scene and a higher level interpretation, beyond individual objects. Furthermore, the recognition of an individual object can benefit from the recognition of others.

The question of semantics is central since it is not directly in the image, but should be inferred based on visual features. We advocate that knowledge should be involved in this process. Indeed, while purely data driven approaches have proved powerful in image and computer vision problems, with sometimes impressive results, they still require a good accessibility to numerous and annotated data, where annotations bring the semantic information. This is not always possible and induces high costs (in terms of both human interactions and computation). For instance in pediatric medical imaging, data may be scarce and present a high variability, while anatomical and medical knowledge is important, and was gathered over centuries. Knowledge and models have then an important role to play. Image understanding is then formulated as a spatial reasoning problem, combining representations of data and knowledge, pertaining to both objects and relations between objects (in particular spatial relations), and reasoning on them.

Spatial reasoning has been largely developed in symbolic AI, based mostly on logics and benefitting from the reasoning apparatus of these logics [1]. It has been much less developed for image understanding, where purely symbolic approaches are limited to account for numerical information. This again votes for hybrid approaches. Spatial reasoning evolved from purely qualitative and symbolic approaches to more and more hybrid methods, involving methods from mathematical morphology, fuzzy sets, graphs, machine learning, etc. to gain in expressivity (sometimes at the price of increased complexity). As an example, let us mention region connection calculus (RCC) that was first proposed in logical frameworks (first order, modal), and then augmented with fuzzy sets to handle imprecision, with mathematical morphology, with lattice-based reasoning, etc. [1,3,12,42,50,52,53]. The main ingredients in spatial reasoning include knowledge representation, imprecision representation and management, fusion of heterogeneous information (whether knowledge or data), reasoning and decision making. Approaches for spatial reasoning take a lot of inspiration from work in philosophy, linguistics, human perception, cognition, neuro-imaging, art, etc. (see e.g. a related discussion for the case of spatial distances in [8]).

Models for image understanding are particularly useful to represent, in a formal way, knowledge (about the domain, the scene content and in particular its structure), image information (type of acquisition, geometry, characteristics of signal and noise...), the potential imperfections of knowledge and data (imprecision, uncertainty, incompleteness...), as well as the combination of knowledge and image information. These models are then included in algorithms to guide image understanding in concrete applications. Conversely, models can be built from data, to infer knowledge, or to provide a digital twin of a patient as a 3D model, useful to plan a surgery or a therapy, as well as to explain the plan.

An important issue is the semantic gap [54], with the following question: how to link visual percepts from the images to symbolic descriptions? In AI, this is close to the notions known as the anchoring or symbol grounding problem [23,38]. Solving the semantic gap issue has bidirectional consequences: on the one hand, it allows moving from a concept to its instantiation in the image (or feature) space, as a guide during spatial reasoning. On the other hand, it is part of the explainability, since it links results inferred from the image to concepts related to prior knowledge. For instance, anatomical knowledge says that the heart is between the lungs. Since the heart might be difficult to recognize directly in a medical image (e.g. a non-enhanced computed tomography (CT) image), we may rely on its relative position with respect to the lungs (which are easier to detect in such images) to perform the task. This is an example where the recognition of an object benefits from the recognition of other objects, as mentioned at the beginning of this section. Conversely, we can explain the recognition of an image region as the heart *because* it is between the lungs (see Sect. 5).

3 Information and Knowledge Representation

Representations of spatial entities can take various forms, either in the spatial domain (region, key points, bounding box...), or abstractly, as in RCC, as formulas in a given logic. Semi-quantitative (or semi-qualitative) representations as fuzzy sets (in either domain) constitute a good midway and can accommodate both numerical and symbolic representations [59]. Representations as numbers, imprecise numbers, intervals, distributions, linguistic values can all find a unifying framework with fuzzy sets. In this framework, different types of imperfections can be easily modeled, such as imprecision on the boundaries of an object, on its location, shape or appearance, ambiguity, partial lack of information, etc. These imperfections can have varied sources, starting with the observed phenomenon, the sensors and the associated image reconstruction algorithms, and can also result from image processing steps such as filtering, registration, segmentation.

Spatial reasoning involves models of spatial entities, but also spatial relations between these entities. Here the advantages of fuzzy representations becomes even more significant. This was already stated in the 1970's [33], but formal mathematical models were developed only later. The objective is to account for the intrinsic imprecision of concepts such as "close to", "to the left of", "between", that are nevertheless perfectly understandable by humans in a given context, and to account for the imprecision of the objects (even for a conceptually well-defined relation). In our previous work, we designed mathematical models of several relations (set theoretical, topological, distances, directional relations, more complex relations such as between, along, parallel...) by combining formalisms from mathematical morphology and fuzzy sets. They are detailed in [17], Chapter 6, and in the references cited therein.

From a mathematical point of view, the common underlying structure is the one of complete lattices, that allows instantiating the definitions, with the very same formalism, in different frameworks: sets, fuzzy sets, graphs and hypergraphs, formal concept lattices, conceptual graphs, ontologies..., that can all be endowed with a lattice structure with appropriate partial orders. This becomes particularly useful when defining spatial relations based on mathematical morphology, a theory where deterministic operators are usually defined in a lattice. Our main idea was to design structuring elements, defined as fuzzy sets in the spatial domain, that provide the semantics of the spatial relation. Then applying a fuzzy morphological dilation of a reference object (whether fuzzy or not) using this structuring element provides the region of space where the considered relation is satisfied. The membership value of a point to the resulting fuzzy set is then interpreted as the degree to which the relation of this point to the reference object is satisfied. This approach applies for several classes of spatial relations: topological, distances, relative direction, and more complex ones such as along, parallel, between... (see e.g. [11,17] and the references therein). It applies to objects defined as sets or fuzzy sets in the spatial domain, but also defined more abstractly as logical formulas, vertices of a (hyper-)graph, concepts, etc.

Note that most of the frameworks mentioned above carry structural information, useful for instance to represent the spatial arrangement of objects in a scene and in an image. To take a simple example, a graph can represent this structure, where vertices correspond to objects (e.g. anatomical structures in medical images) and edges correspond to relations between objects (e.g. contrast between two structures in a given imaging modality, relative position between objects...), this graph being enhanced with the fuzzy representations of objects and their properties, and of relations. For instance, the representation of a spatial relation can be abstract, as extracted from an ontology for example, or linked to the concrete domain of an image (degree of satisfaction of the relation, region of space where the relation to some object is satisfied...), using linguistic variables, as explained next. Other structured representations of knowledge (including spatial knowledge) may rely on grammars, decision trees, relational algebras on temporal or spatial configurations, or graphical models. They can also benefit from a fuzzy modeling layer, to cope with imprecision.

The relevance of fuzzy sets for knowledge representation relies in their capability to capture linguistic as well as quantitative knowledge and information. A useful notion is the one of linguistic variable [60], where symbolic values, defined at an ontological level, have semantics defined by membership functions on a concrete domain, at the image or features level. The membership functions and their parameters can be handcrafted, according to some expert knowledge on the application domain. They can also be learned, for instance from annotated data [6]. The advantage of such representations is that linguistic characterizations may be less specific than numerical ones (and therefore need less information). Their two levels (syntactic and semantic) allow on the one hand for approximate modeling of vague concepts and reasoning on them, and on the other hand constitute an efficient way to solve the semantic gap issue (see Sect. 2) by providing semantics in concrete domains, according to each specific context. Linguistic variables, maintaining the consistency between concepts and data, play therefore an important role for explainability. Similarly the goals of an image understanding problem can be expressed in an imprecise way, and again translating vague concepts into useful representations and algorithms benefits from fuzzy modeling, in particular using linguistic variables.

4 Reasoning

Based on the previous representations, the reasoning part takes various forms, separately or in combination, again in the spirit of hybrid AI. Let us mention a few, mostly from our previous work, which led to applications in medical imaging, in particular for brain structure recognition[1]: matching between a model and an image based on graph representations [4,20,31,48]; sequential spatial reasoning mimicking the usual cognitive process where one may focus on an object that is easy to detect and to recognize, and then move progressively to more and more difficult objects by exploring the space based on the spatial relations with respect to previously recognized objects [15,22,27,32]; exploration of the whole space and reducing progressively the potential region for each object, again mimicking a type of cognitive process, for instance by expressing the task as a constraint satisfaction problem [29,47]; logical reasoning based on abduction, to find the best explanations to the observations according to the available knowledge [58]; logical reasoning driven by an ontology [39].

In all these methods, an important feature is the combination of several approaches within the framework of hybrid AI, with the aim of explainability. Abstract knowledge representation and formal reasoning (typically using logics) allow building a knowledge base representing prior information (on anatomy for the considered examples), and to reason on it. Structural representations (graphs and hypergraphs, ontologies, conceptual graphs, concept lattices...) are frameworks to convert expert knowledge on the spatial organization of objects (e.g. organs in medical imaging) into operational computational models. As mentioned in Sect. 3, converting knowledge into meaningful representations and algorithms highly benefits from fuzzy modeling, in particular using linguistic variables to fill the semantic gap. This is indeed key to explainability. These models are then associated with structural representations to enrich them. For instance fuzzy models of object features (shape, appearance) and of spatial relations can be attributes of vertices or edges of graphs, can provide the semantics of concepts in ontologies or conceptual graphs, can be considered as properties in fuzzy extensions of concept lattices, or can provide semantics of logical formulas.

Usually several pieces of knowledge are involved together in the reasoning process. The advantages of fuzzy sets rely in the variety of combination operators, offering a lot of flexibility in their choice, that can be adapted to any situation at hand, and which may deal with heterogeneous information [30,57]. A classification of these operators was proposed in [7], with respect to their behavior (in terms of conjunctive, disjunctive, compromise [30]), the possible control of this behavior, their properties and their decisiveness.

Now, considering the huge recent developments in machine learning, and in particular deep learning, a recent trend is to combine such approaches with knowledge driven methods. This can be done at several levels (see e.g. [56]): to enhance the input (e.g. by including in the input of a neural network a result

---

[1] These are only examples and similar approaches have been developed in other application domains, such as satellite imaging, video, music representations, etc.

of some image processing method as in [25]); as regularization terms in the loss function (e.g. to force the satisfaction of some relations) or to focus attention on specific patches based on geometric or topological information (e.g. vessel tree [55]); or as post-processing to improve results (e.g. [21]). Conversely, in some situations the neural networks can use implicitly spatial relations to solve a task, such as object segmentation and recognition, as soon as the concerned objects are within the receptive field [51]. Again one of the advantages of such hybrid approaches is to improve interpretability and explainability. This is particularly important in medical imaging to increase the confidence the user may have in an approach based on deep learning, and therefore to increase the adoption of such techniques.

Finally, the result of an image understanding system can be expressed in various forms (sets of (fuzzy) objects, classes, properties of objects and their relations, linguistic descriptions...), again finding in fuzzy sets a unifying representation framework. The next step is to provide explanations to these results.

5   Explanations

A first way to provide explanations is to rely on abductive reasoning. Mathematical morphology is a useful theory for abductive reasoning in various logics [2,9,16]. An example is the use of erosion or derived operators to provide explanations to observations according to a knowledge base by applying these operators to the set of models of logical formulas or to a concept lattice. For instance, from a knowledge base on anatomy, expressed in some logics, and from segmentation and recognition results, higher level interpretations of an image can be derived using such a method for abductive reasoning [5,58]. Then the image understanding problem itself is formulated as an explanatory process. The logic is endowed with a fuzzy semantics, to cope with imprecise statements in the knowledge base, such as "the lateral ventricles are dark in T1 weighted magnetic resonance images, the caudate nuclei are external to the lateral ventricles and close to them". The observation is the image and results of some segmentation and recognition procedure. Therefore there is an interpretation at two levels: at the object level first, using the approaches presented in the previous sections, involving fuzzy representations and structural models, and then globally at the scene level. The advantage of abstract formulation in a logic is that this second, higher level, interpretation can take intelligible forms, such as "this image present an enhanced tumor, which is subcortical and has a small deforming impact on the other structures".

The language in which the knowledge is expressed should be defined according to the granularity level expected for the interpretation and to whom the description is dedicated (the explainee). For instance the description of the content of a pathological brain image will depend on whether the explainee is anyone (without assuming any particular expertise), the patient, or a medical expert who wants to make a decision guided by this description and to interact with other experts.

To go further, another level of explanation is to identify which part of the knowledge base has actually be involved in the reasoning process or is relevant in the object or scene description. We mentioned above an implicit method to do so, via neural networks [51]. More explicit methods are also very relevant to provide meaningful explanations to a user. Fuzzy sets are then useful to establish a link between the results derived from the image and concepts expressed in the knowledge base, as mentioned at the end of Sect. 2. A simple example is to assess to which degree a spatial relation is satisfied between the resulting objects. Then explanations such as "this object is the left caudate nucleus because it is close to the left ventricle and to the left of it" are easy to derive. For instance, a given spatial relation between to identified objects can be computed, as a number or as a distribution, and then compared with the fuzzy model of this relation [14]. An approach based on fuzzy frequent itemset mining has also been proposed in [49]. Considering the example of structure recognition based on spatial reasoning, explanations become natural by identifying the spatial relations that actually play a role in the recognition. Furthermore, we can make use of hedges and quantifiers to know whether "most" of the relations in a given set are indeed satisfied by a result, or involved in the image understanding process.

In all what precede, fuzzy sets are at the core of:

- knowledge representation (object properties and relations between objects),
- attribute definition for graphs, hypergraphs or other computational models representing the structure (in the sense of spatial organization) of a scene,
- semantics of logics,
- semantic gap solving,
- spatial reasoning for image understanding,
- computing similarities between a model and a result,
- providing descriptions of an image in a given language,
- providing cues for explainability.

They are the main medium to travel from knowledge to data, and conversely explain results obtained from the data according to the available knowledge.

6   Discussion

To go further in the field of hybrid AI and XAI for image understanding, principles expressed and discussed more generally in AI could be instantiated in this particular domain of application, and pave the way for new research directions.

This starts with the definition of interpretability and explainability. While many definitions have been proposed, an interesting distinction is made in [28], where interpretability is defined via the composition of elements that are meaningful for humans, while explanation is strongly related to causality, and understanding is linked to unifying diversity under a commun principle (this is maybe somewhat different when interpreting an individual image as in medical imaging). In the works summarized in this paper, fuzzy sets are used to make explicit the components of knowledge and image information that are involved in a reasoning process. This is done in a semi-qualitative way, close to human understanding, and therefore directly useful to provide explanations.

Seeing explanations as causality has been widely addressed, in particular by Halpern and Pearl [36,37], and by Miller [44,45], where structural models play a major role. Links with argumentation frameworks [46] and extensions of contrastive explanations to fuzzy sets [18] have recently been proposed. Notions such as contrast and relevance are put to the fore, and would be also important to consider in image understanding. For instance, explaining why a decision was proposed by an algorithm and not another decision is a way to make explanations more convincing. A simple way to do so, based on the methods presented here, would be to compare resulting image descriptions with different models or decisions, and to identify which components in the knowledge or in the reasoning was responsible for a particular decision proposal. This would be particularly interesting in medical imaging where explanations are mostly required when the result provided by an algorithm differs from the expected one. This would deserve further investigation. The level of explanation should depend on the explainee, as mentioned before, and a deeper study of this aspect could take inspiration from the work on intelligibility in [24] (for instance based on projections on a given vocabulary). This goes with the idea of human-centered evaluation of AI systems.

It has been advocated in [43] that new research should aim at developing *a hybrid, knowledge driven, reasoning based approach, centered around cognitive models, that could provide the substrate for a richer, more robust AI than is currently possible.* This is exactly what research in image understanding based on hybrid AI is trying to do, but still at a modest level.

Finally it would be interesting to investigate more deeply to which extent hybrid AI and XAI could help answering questions related to ethics, in particular in radiology.

Acknowledgements. The author would like to thank all her co-authors, and to emphasize that the ideas summarized in this paper benefitted from many joint works with PhD candidates, post-doctoral researchers, colleagues in universities and research centers in several countries, with university hospitals, and with industrial partners.

References

1. Aiello, M., Pratt-Hartmann, I., van Benthem, J. (eds.): Handbook of Spatial Logic. Springer, Dordrecht (2007). https://doi.org/10.1007/978-1-4020-5587-4
2. Aiguier, M., Atif, J., Bloch, I., Pino Pérez, R.: Explanatory relations in arbitrary logics based on satisfaction systems, cutting and retraction. Int. J. Approximate Reasoning **102**, 1–20 (2018)
3. Aiguier, M., Bloch, I.: Logical dual concepts based on mathematical morphology in stratified institutions. J. Appl. Non-Classical Log. **29**(4), 392–429 (2019)
4. Aldea, E., Bloch, I.: Toward a better integration of spatial relations in learning with graphical models. In: Guillet, F., Ritschard, G., Zighed, D.A., Briand, H.

(eds.) Advances in Knowledge Discovery and Management. SCI, vol. 292, pp. 77–94. Springer, Heidelberg (2010). https://doi.org/10.1007/978-3-642-00580-0_5

5. Atif, J., Hudelot, C., Bloch, I.: Explanatory reasoning for image understanding using formal concept analysis and description logics. IEEE Trans. Syst. Man Cybern. Syst. 44(5), 552–570 (2014)

6. Atif, J., Hudelot, C., Fouquier, G., Bloch, I., Angelini, E.: From generic knowledge to specific reasoning for medical image interpretation using graph-based representations. In: International Joint Conference on Artificial Intelligence, IJCAI 2007, Hyderabad, India, pp. 224–229 (2007)

7. Bloch, I.: Information combination operators for data fusion: a comparative review with classification. IEEE Trans. Syst. Man Cybern. 26(1), 52–67 (1996)

8. Bloch, I.: On fuzzy spatial distances. In: Hawkes, P. (ed.) Advances in Imaging and Electron Physics, vol. 128, pp. 51–122. Elsevier, Amsterdam (2003)

9. Bloch, I.: Spatial reasoning under imprecision using fuzzy set theory, formal logics and mathematical morphology. Int. J. Approximate Reasoning 41(2), 77–95 (2006)

10. Bloch, I.: Fuzzy sets for image processing and understanding. Fuzzy Sets Syst. 281, 280–291 (2015)

11. Bloch, I.: Mathematical morphology and spatial reasoning: fuzzy and bipolar setting. TWMS J. Pure Appl. Math. 12(1), 104–125 (2021). Special Issue on Fuzzy Sets in Dealing with Imprecision and Uncertainty: Past and Future Dedicated to the Memory of Lotfi A. Zadeh

12. Bloch, I.: Modeling imprecise and bipolar algebraic and topological relations using morphological dilations. Math. Morphol. Theory Appl. 5(1), 1–20 (2021)

13. Bloch, I.: Hybrid artificial intelligence for knowledge representation and model-based medical image understanding - towards explainability. In: Baudrier, É., Naegel, B., Krähenbühl, A., Tajine, M. (eds.) DGMM 2022. LNCS, vol. 13493, pp. 17–25. Springer, Cham (2022). https://doi.org/10.1007/978-3-031-19897-7_2

14. Bloch, I., Atif, J.: Defining and computing Hausdorff distances between distributions on the real line and on the circle: link between optimal transport and morphological dilations. Math. Morphol. Theory Appl. 1(1), 79–99 (2016)

15. Bloch, I., Géraud, T., Maître, H.: Representation and fusion of heterogeneous fuzzy information in the 3D space for model-based structural recognition - application to 3D brain imaging. Artif. Intell. 148, 141–175 (2003)

16. Bloch, I., Lang, J., Pérez, R.P., Uzcátegui, C.: Morphologic for knowledge dynamics: revision, fusion, abduction. Technical report. arXiv:1802.05142, arXiv cs.AI (2018)

17. Bloch, I., Ralescu, A.: Fuzzy Sets Methods in Image Processing and Understanding: Medical Imaging Applications. Springer, Cham (2023). https://doi.org/10.1007/978-3-031-19425-2

18. Bloch, I., Lesot, M.J.: Towards a formulation of fuzzy contrastive explanations. In: IEEE International Conference on Fuzzy Systems (FUZZ-IEEE), pp. 1–8 (2022)

19. Bouchon-Meunier, B., Lesot, M.J., Marsala, C.: Lotfi A. Zadeh, the visionary in explainable artificial intelligence. TWMS J. Pure Appl. Math. 12(1), 5–13 (2021)

20. Cesar, R., Bengoetxea, E., Bloch, I., Larranaga, P.: Inexact graph matching for model-based recognition: evaluation and comparison of optimization algorithms. Pattern Recogn. 38, 2099–2113 (2005)

21. Chopin, J., Fasquel, J.B., Mouchère, H., Dahyot, R., Bloch, I.: Improving semantic segmentation with graph-based structural knowledge. In: El Yacoubi, M., Granger, E., Yuen, P.C., Pal, U., Vincent, N. (eds.) ICPRAI 2022. LNCS, vol. 13363, pp. 173–184. Springer, Cham (2022). https://doi.org/10.1007/978-3-031-09037-0_15

22. Colliot, O., Camara, O., Bloch, I.: Integration of fuzzy spatial relations in deformable models - application to brain MRI segmentation. Pattern Recogn. **39**, 1401–1414 (2006)
23. Coradeschi, S., Saffiotti, A.: Anchoring symbols to vision data by fuzzy logic. In: Hunter, A., Parsons, S. (eds.) ECSQARU 1999. LNCS (LNAI), vol. 1638, pp. 104–115. Springer, Heidelberg (1999). https://doi.org/10.1007/3-540-48747-6_10
24. Coste-Marquis, S., Marquis, P.: From explanations to intelligible explanations. In: 1st International Workshop on Explainable Logic-Based Knowledge Representation (XLoKR 2020) (2020)
25. Couteaux, V., et al.: Automatic knee meniscus tear detection and orientation classification with Mask-RCNN. Diagn. Interv. Imaging **100**, 235–242 (2019)
26. De Raedt, L., Dumancic, S., Manhaeve, R., Marra, G.: From statistical relational to neuro-symbolic artificial intelligence. In: Bessiere, C. (ed.) Twenty-Ninth International Joint Conference on Artificial Intelligence, IJCAI-2020, pp. 4943–4950 (2020)
27. Delmonte, A., Mercier, C., Pallud, J., Bloch, I., Gori, P.: White matter multi-resolution segmentation using fuzzy set theory. In: IEEE International Symposium on Biomedical Imaging (ISBI), Venice, Italy, pp. 459–462 (2019)
28. Denis, C., Varenne, F.: Interprétabilité et explicabilité de phénomènes prédits par de l'apprentissage machine. Revue Ouverte d'Intelligence Artificielle **3**, 287–310 (2022)
29. Deruyver, A., Hodé, Y.: Constraint satisfaction problem with bilevel constraint: application to interpretation of over-segmented images. Artif. Intell. **93**(1–2), 321–335 (1997)
30. Dubois, D., Prade, H.: A review of fuzzy set aggregation connectives. Inf. Sci. **36**, 85–121 (1985)
31. Fasquel, J., Delanoue, N.: A graph based image interpretation method using a priori qualitative inclusion and photometric relationships. IEEE Trans. Pattern Anal. Mach. Intell. **41**(5), 1043–1055 (2019)
32. Fouquier, G., Atif, J., Bloch, I.: Sequential model-based segmentation and recognition of image structures driven by visual features and spatial relations. Comput. Vis. Image Underst. **116**(1), 146–165 (2012)
33. Freeman, J.: The modelling of spatial relations. Comput. Graph. Image Process. **4**(2), 156–171 (1975)
34. d'Avila Garcez, A., Lamb, L.C.: Neurosymbolic AI: the 3rd wave. CoRR abs/2012.05876 (2020)
35. Garnelo, M., Shanahan, M.: Reconciling deep learning with symbolic artificial intelligence: representing objects and relations. Curr. Opin. Behav. Sci. **29**, 17–23 (2019)
36. Halpern, J.Y., Pearl, J.: Causes and explanations: a structural-model approach. Part I: causes. Br. J. Philos. Sci. **56**(4), 843–887 (2005)
37. Halpern, J.Y., Pearl, J.: Causes and explanations: a structural-model approach. Part II: explanations. Br. J. Philos. Sci. **56**(4), 889–911 (2005)
38. Harnad, S.: The symbol grounding problem. Physica **42**, 335–346 (1990)
39. Hudelot, C., Atif, J., Bloch, I.: Fuzzy spatial relation ontology for image interpretation. Fuzzy Sets Syst. **159**, 1929–1951 (2008)
40. Kahneman, D.: Thinking, Fast and Slow. Penguin, New York (2012)
41. Kautz, H.: The third AI summer: AAAI Robert S. Engelmore memorial lecture. AI Mag. **43**(1), 93–104 (2022)

42. Landini, G., Galton, A., Randell, D., Fouad, S.: Novel applications of discrete mereotopology to mathematical morphology. Sig. Process. Image Commun. **76**, 109–117 (2019)
43. Marcus, G.: The next decade in AI: four steps towards robust artificial intelligence. CoRR abs/2002.06177 (2020)
44. Miller, T.: Explanation in artificial intelligence: insights from the social sciences. Artif. Intell. **267**, 1–38 (2019)
45. Miller, T.: Contrastive explanation: a structural-model approach. Knowl. Eng. Rev. **36**, E14 (2021)
46. Munro, Y., Bloch, I., Chetouani, M., Lesot, M.J., Pelachaud, C.: Argumentation and causal models in human-machine interaction: a round trip. In: 8th International Workshop on Artificial Intelligence and Cognition, Örebro, Sweden (2022)
47. Nempont, O., Atif, J., Bloch, I.: A constraint propagation approach to structural model based image segmentation and recognition. Inf. Sci. **246**, 1–27 (2013)
48. Perchant, A., Bloch, I.: Fuzzy morphisms between graphs. Fuzzy Sets Syst. **128**(2), 149–168 (2002)
49. Pierrard, R., Poli, J.P., Hudelot, C.: Spatial relation learning for explainable image classification and annotation in critical applications. Artif. Intell. **292**, 103434 (2021)
50. Randell, D., Cui, Z., Cohn, A.: A spatial logic based on regions and connection. In: Nebel, B., Rich, C., Swartout, W. (eds.) Principles of Knowledge Representation and Reasoning, KR1992, pp. 165–176. Kaufmann, San Mateo (1992)
51. Riva, M., Gori, P., Yger, F., Bloch, I.: Is the U-Net directional-relationship aware? In: International Conference on Image Processing, Bordeaux, France, pp. 3391–3395 (2022)
52. Schockaert, S., De Cock, M., Cornelis, C., Kerre, E.E.: Fuzzy region connection calculus: representing vague topological information. Int. J. Approximate Reasoning **48**(1), 314–331 (2008)
53. Schockaert, S., De Cock, M., Kerre, E.E.: Spatial reasoning in a fuzzy region connection calculus. Artif. Intell. **173**(2), 258–298 (2009)
54. Smeulders, A., Worring, M., Santini, S., Gupta, A., Jain, R.: Content-based image retrieval at the end of the early years. IEEE Trans. Pattern Anal. Mach. Intell. **22**(12), 1349–1380 (2000)
55. Virzì, A., et al.: Segmentation of pelvic vessels in pediatric MRI using a patch-based deep learning approach. In: Melbourne, A., et al. (eds.) PIPPI/DATRA -2018. LNCS, vol. 11076, pp. 97–106. Springer, Cham (2018). https://doi.org/10.1007/978-3-030-00807-9_10
56. Xie, X., Niu, J., Liu, X., Chen, Z., Tang, S., Yu, S.: A survey on incorporating domain knowledge into deep learning for medical image analysis. Med. Image Anal. **69**, 101985 (2021)
57. Yager, R.R.: Connectives and quantifiers in fuzzy sets. Fuzzy Sets Syst. **40**, 39–75 (1991)
58. Yang, Y., Atif, J., Bloch, I.: Abductive reasoning using tableau methods for high-level image interpretation. In: Hölldobler, S., Krötzsch, M., Peñaloza, R., Rudolph, S. (eds.) KI 2015. LNCS (LNAI), vol. 9324, pp. 356–365. Springer, Cham (2015). https://doi.org/10.1007/978-3-319-24489-1_34
59. Zadeh, L.A.: Fuzzy sets. Inf. Control **8**, 338–353 (1965)
60. Zadeh, L.A.: The concept of a linguistic variable and its application to approximate reasoning. Inf. Sci. **8**, 199–249 (1975)

Contextual Boosting to Explainable SVM Classification

Marcelo Loor[1]([⊠])[iD], Ana Tapia-Rosero[2][iD], and Guy De Tré[1][iD]

[1] Department of Telecommunications and Information Processing, Ghent University,
Sint-Pietersnieuwstraat 41, 9000 Ghent, Belgium
{Marcelo.Loor,Guy.DeTre}@UGent.be
[2] Department of Electrical and Computer Engineering,
ESPOL Polytechnic University, Campus Gustavo Galindo, Guayaquil, Ecuador
atapia@espol.edu.ec

Abstract. Finding suitable mechanisms whereby rationale behind *support vector machine* (SVM) predictions can be known and understood without substantial difficulties is an ongoing challenge. Aiming to find such a mechanism, we look into the contextualization of SVM models. Hence, we propose a novel explainable SVM classifier that makes use of a parallel arrangement of contextualized SVM models for offering predictions that depend on a particular event, situation or idea. The proposed classifier allows decision makers to state in a clear manner the context of the predictions they would like to be offered. This aspect is deemed to be important since decision makers can take advantage of the improvement in the interpretability of such contextualized predictions for making more informed decisions. The improvement in interpretability is illustrated through an example in which digitized handwritten vowels are contextually identified. Another example where hand gestures are recognized by means of electromyography (EMG) signals shows how the proposed classifier can also improve the accuracy of the resulting models.

Keywords: Explainable SVM · Contextual machine learning ·
Augmented appraisal degrees · Augmented fuzzy sets

1 Introduction

The lack of transparency in predictions made by an *artificial intelligence* (AI) system can suppress its use in decision making processes where decision makers are required to justify their actions or resolutions [11]. Such opacity is usually related to the complexity of the knowledge model that is part of an AI system. Because of this, AI systems containing models that result from the original formulation of *support vector machines* (SVMs) [25] are deemed to be difficult for decision makers to understand [3,10].

To change that and, thus, foster the usability of SVM in decision making, several approaches have been proposed in the literature. One of them is the extraction of rules that make the predictions resulting from SVM models more

S. Massanet et al. (Eds.): EUSFLAT 2023/AGOP 2023, LNCS 14069, pp. 480–491, 2023.
https://doi.org/10.1007/978-3-031-39965-7_40

intelligible [2,21,27]. Therein, the set of extracted rules constituted a twin model that is expected to be less complex than the original SVM model. Another approach is the construction of simplified local models in the immediate vicinity to the evaluated object [10,24]. In this case, multiple synthetic objects are evaluated to build an interpretable model that resembles the behavior of the original SVM model in that vicinity. An alternative approach makes use of *augmented appraisal degrees* (AADs) [14] to put SVM predictions in context [16,17]. Such AADs are used during the evaluation process for recording aspects that have high influence on the results. Those aspects are then used for explaining the reasons behind one or more predictions.

Aiming to make AI systems based on SVM models easier to understand, in this paper we explore the contextualization of SVM models and propose a novel explainable SVM classifier that uses a parallel arrangement of contextualized SVM models. A general view of this classifier, named *XSVM@ctx*, is shown in Fig. 1. Notice that, while the learning process makes use of contextualized data sets to produce contextualized SVM models, the evaluation process makes use of those contextualized models to produce contextualized predictions. Notice also that decision makers can make use of a context selector to specify the context of the resulting predictions. This is an important aspect of XSVM@ctx since it allows decision makers to state the context of the predictions they would like to be offered by the system. For instance, a biologist can request XSVM@ctx to take into account a particular geographical area while trying to identify a disease in specimens collected in that area. In this aspect, XSVM@ctx differed from works like [4,5,8,23] where context is approximated considering (synthetic) contextual data located around the objects under evaluation.

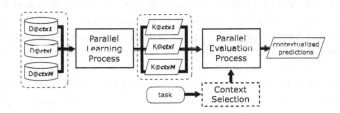

Fig. 1. A general view of an explainable SVM classifier that uses a parallel arrangement of contextualized SVM models.

Another important aspect of XSVM@ctx is that it lends itself to parallel processing. Thus, the computational costs of processing large data sets can be distributed and the size of the SVM models can be reduced. In this aspect the learning process of XSVM@ctx is more or less similar to the learning process of the boosting algorithm described in [7] where a training data set is partitioned into reduced subsets to train moderately rough classifiers. The main difference is that while in that work the training set is randomly partitioned, in our work the training set is partitioned in a way that is related to the context of the concepts under study.

As noticed, we assume that the data set can be clearly partitioned into a given number of contextual subsets that can be independently processed. This assumption can be seen as a drawback due to the potential loss of generalization in the resulting contextualized SVM models. However, we consider that a clear characterization of the context and its inclusion in the selection criteria are two decisive aspects of XSVM@ctx in the trade-off between interpretability and loss of generalization. In addition, this assumption can help us to answer the question: *can the contextualization of knowledge models yield better explainable classifiers?* which is a strong motivation for this work.

To present XSVM@ctx the paper has been structured as follows. In Sect. 2, concepts related to explainable SVM classification are presented. In Sect. 3, XSVM@ctx is described. Two illustrative examples showing the use of XSVM@ctx are presented in Sect. 4. Related work is presented in Sect. 5. The paper is concluded in Sect. 6.

2   Preliminaries

A *classifier* is usually understood as a person (or system) that evaluates one or more objects to determine (or predict) the classes those objects should belong to. While evaluations performed by a *plain classifier* are expected to be convenient for making predictions without any explanation, (contextualized) evaluations carried out by an *explainable classifier* are expected to be useful for explaining the reasons behind its predictions.

Evaluations made by plain classifiers can be represented as *membership grades* in the framework of *fuzzy set theory* [26]. For instance, given an object x and a class A, the level to which x is member of A can be denoted by a membership grade $\mu_A(x)$, which is a number in the unit interval $[0,1]$ where 0 and 1 correspond to the lowest and the highest membership levels respectively. When such an evaluation also includes the level to which the object does not belong to the class, it can be denoted by an *intuitionistic fuzzy set (IFS) element* in the *IFS framework* [1]. For example, the evaluation above can be denoted by an IFS element $\langle \mu_A(x), \nu_A(x) \rangle$, where the *nonmembership grade* $\nu_A(x)$ is also a number in $[0,1]$ but, in this case, 0 and 1 correspond to the lowest and the highest nonmembership levels respectively.

Even though evaluations made by an explainable classifier could be represented as membership grades or IFS elements, such contextualized evaluations are better represented as AADs [14]. An AAD is a generalization of a membership (or nonmembership) grade by which not only the level but also the aspects that are relevant during an evaluation can be recorded. For instance, a contextualized evaluation of the level to which x is member of A according to the knowledge K can be denoted by a membership AAD $\hat{\mu}_{A@K}(x) = \langle \mu_{A@K}(x), F_{\mu_{A@K}}(x) \rangle$, where $F_{\mu_{A@K}}(x)$ represents a collection of the aspects of x that explain the membership level $\mu_{A@K}(x)$. Analogous to plain evaluations, when a contextualized evaluation includes the level to which the object does not belong to the class, it can be denoted by an *augmented IFS element* [14]. For instance, the previous evaluation can be denoted by an augmented IFS element $\langle \hat{\mu}_{A@K}(x), \hat{\nu}_{A@K}(x) \rangle$ where in addition to the membership AAD $\hat{\mu}_{A@K}(x)$, the nonmembership AAD $\hat{\nu}_{A@K}(x) = \langle \nu_{A@K}(x), F_{\nu_{A@K}}(x) \rangle$ is included. In this case, $F_{\nu_{A@K}}(x)$ denotes a collection of the aspects of x that explain the nonmembership level $\nu_{A@K}(x)$.

An explainable SVM classifier that represents its contextualized evaluations with AADs has been presented in [17]. That classifier makes use of the *most influential support vectors* (MISVs) for putting the evaluations in context. From a semantical standpoint, a *positive MISV* is the most similar to the vector characterizing the evaluated object that favors the membership of the object in a particular class. Likewise, a *negative MISV* is the most similar vector to the vector characterizing the evaluated object that is against the membership of this object in a given class. Figure 2 shows an example of a prediction produced by XSVMC-Lib [19] where positive and negative MISVs have been used for putting the underlying evaluations in context.

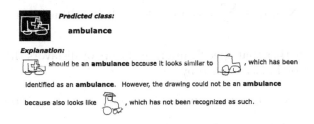

Fig. 2. Example of a contextualized prediction using MISVs.

The aforementioned explainable SVM classifier put the evaluations in context using contextless SVM models. We consider that the interpretability of the predictions made by that classifier might be benefited from the contextualization of the underlying SVM models. Hence, in the next section we present XSVM@ctx, which is an explainable SVM classifier that uses a parallel arrangement of contextualized SVM models for making predictions.

3   XSVM@ctx

As was mentioning in the introduction, we aim to foster the usability of AI systems based on SVM in decision making through the contextualization of SVM models. Such contextualization can be achieved by solving the following problem.

Let $D = \{(x_1, y_1), \cdots, (x_N, y_N)\}$ be a set of N tuples (x_i, y_i) where x_i is an object associated with a label $y_i \in \{+1, -1\}$ denoting whether or not x_i belongs to a category A. Assume that D can be partitioned in T non-empty pairwise disjoint contextual subsets $D_{@ctx_1}, \cdots, D_{@ctx_T}$ such that $D_{@ctx_1} \cup \cdots \cup D_{@ctx_T} = D$. Let $K_{A@ctx}$ be a contextual knowledge model denoting the knowledge about A acquired in context ctx. Let $h(x, ctx)$ be a function by which the label that should be assigned to object x in context ctx is predicted. Find $K_{A@ctx_1}, \cdots, K_{A@ctx_T}$ such that for each (x, y) in $D_{@ctx_t}$ the number of times $h(x, ctx_t)$ agrees with y is maximized.

As was done in [17], to solve this problem we use the *feature-influence representational model* proposed in [15] for characterizing all the objects and the knowledge models in a m-dimensional feature space $\mathcal{M}$. In $\mathcal{M}$, an object x is represented as a vector $\mathbf{x} = \sum_{j=1}^{m} \beta_j \hat{\mathbf{f}}_j$ where $\hat{\mathbf{f}}_j$ is a unit vector denoting the dimension related to a feature f_j and β_j is a value denoting the overall influence of f_j in x. The knowledge about A acquired in context ctx is represented as a line in $\mathcal{M}$ described by a pair $\langle \hat{\mathbf{u}}_{A@ctx}, t_{A@ctx} \rangle$. In this pair, $\hat{\mathbf{u}}_{A@ctx}$ is a unit vector that points to a location where the membership in A is favored, and t_A is a point in the line where the membership in A is neither favored nor disfavored. The specific influence of the x's features on the appraisal of its membership in A (in context ctx) is given by

$$\mathbf{x}_{A@ctx} = \sum_{j=1}^{m} \beta_{j_A} \hat{\mathbf{u}}_{A@ctx} = (\mathbf{x} \cdot \hat{\mathbf{u}}_{A@ctx}) \hat{\mathbf{u}}_{A@ctx}. \tag{1}$$

To determine whether that specific influence favors or disfavors the membership of x in A, a vector $\mathbf{l}_{A@ctx}$ defined by

$$\mathbf{l}_{A@ctx} = \mathbf{x}_{A@ctx} - t_{A@ctx} \hat{\mathbf{u}}_{A@ctx} = (\mathbf{x} \cdot \hat{\mathbf{u}}_{A@ctx} - t_{A@ctx}) \hat{\mathbf{u}}_{A@ctx} \tag{2}$$

is computed: if both $\mathbf{l}_{A@ctx}$ and $\hat{\mathbf{u}}_{A@ctx}$ point to the same direction, the membership in A is favored, otherwise is disfavored. The level to which that membership is favored or disfavored is given by the magnitude of $\mathbf{l}_{A@ctx}$, i.e.,

$$\|\mathbf{l}_{A@ctx}\| = \mathbf{x} \cdot \hat{\mathbf{u}}_{A@ctx} - t_{A@ctx}. \tag{3}$$

The problem of finding the optimal $K_{A@ctx} = \langle \hat{\mathbf{u}}_{A@ctx}, t_{A@ctx} \rangle$ in context ctx can be related to the problem of finding an optimal separating hyperplane $H_{A@ctx} : \mathbf{w}_{A@ctx} \cdot \mathbf{x} + b_{A@ctx} = 0$ in the original definition of SVM [25] by means of the equations [17]

$$\hat{\mathbf{u}}_{A@ctx} = \frac{\mathbf{w}_{A@ctx}}{\|\mathbf{w}_{A@ctx}\|} \tag{4}$$

and

$$t_{A@ctx} = -\frac{b_{A@ctx}}{\|\mathbf{w}_{A@ctx}\|}. \tag{5}$$

To compute the values $\mathbf{w}_{A@ctx}$ and $b_{A@ctx}$, the Euclidean distance between the hyperplanes $H_{A@ctx}^+ : \mathbf{w}_{A@ctx} \cdot \mathbf{x} + b_{A@ctx} = +1$ and $H_{A@ctx}^- : \mathbf{w}_{A@ctx} \cdot \mathbf{x} + b_{A@ctx} = -1$ given by $d(H_{A@ctx}^+, H_{A@ctx}^-) = 2/\|\mathbf{w}_{A@ctx}\|$ should be maximized subject to $|\mathbf{w}_{A@ctx} \cdot \mathbf{x} + b_{A@ctx}| \geq 1$ [6]. The results are given by

$$\mathbf{w}_{A@ctx} = \sum_{i=1}^{n} \lambda_i y_i \mathbf{x}_i \tag{6}$$

and

$$b_{A@ctx} = y_i - (\mathbf{w}_{A@ctx} \cdot \mathbf{x}_i), \tag{7}$$

where n is the number of *support vectors*, $\mathbf{x}_i$ is one of those support vectors, y_i is the label associated with object x_i represented by $\mathbf{x}_i$, λ_i is the Lagrange multiplier associated with $\mathbf{x}_i$, C is a *regularization parameter* and $0 < \lambda_i < C$ – the interested reader is referred to [17] for a detailed explanation of these results.

After finding $K_{A@ctx_t} = \langle \hat{\mathbf{u}}_{A@ctx_t}, t_{A@ctx_t} \rangle$ for each $ctx_t \in \{ctx_1, \cdots, ctx_T\}$, we can define $h(x, ctx)$ as follows – recall that $h(x, ctx)$ is a function that predicts the label of x in context ctx. Let $v(x)$ be a utility function that returns a vector $\mathbf{x}$ representing a given object x in the aforementioned m-dimensional feature space $\mathcal{M}$. Let $s(ctx)$ be another utility function that returns the most similar context to ctx in $\{ctx_1, \cdots, ctx_T\}$. Under these considerations and using (3), we define $h(x, ctx)$ as

$$h(x, ctx) = \text{sign}\left(v(x) \cdot \hat{\mathbf{u}}_{A@s(ctx)} - t_{A@s(ctx)}\right). \tag{8}$$

We can replace $\hat{\mathbf{u}}_{A@ctx}$ and $t_{A@ctx}$ in (8) by (4) and (5) respectively to obtain

$$h(x, ctx) = \text{sign}\left(\frac{v(x) \cdot \mathbf{w}_{A@s(ctx)} + b_{A@s(ctx)}}{\|\mathbf{w}_{A@s(ctx)}\|}\right). \tag{9}$$

Then, we can replace $\mathbf{w}_{A@ctx}$ by (6) and, for the sake of readability, suppress the unnecessary denominator for the sign function to obtain the following expression based on the collection of support vectors $S_{A@s(ctx)} = \{\mathbf{x}_i | i = 1, \cdots, n\}$

$$h(x, ctx) = \text{sign}\left(b_{A@s(ctx)} + \sum_{i=1}^{n} \lambda_i y_i v(x) \cdot \mathbf{x}_i\right). \tag{10}$$

Finally, we can use the *kernel trick* [6] and replace $v(x) \cdot \mathbf{x}_i$ by a *kernel function* $K(v(x), \mathbf{x}_i)$ in (10) to obtain

$$h(x, ctx) = \text{sign}\left(b_{A@s(ctx)} + \sum_{i=1}^{n} \lambda_i y_i K(v(x), \mathbf{x}_i)\right), \tag{11}$$

which is required for predicting the label of x in non-linear classification. For instance, a *polynomial kernel* of degree d given by $K(\mathbf{x}, \mathbf{x}_i) = (\mathbf{x} \cdot \mathbf{x}_i)^d$ can be used.

In analogy to what was done in [17], a contextualized evaluation of the level to which x is member of A in context ctx can be denoted by an augmented IFS element $\langle \hat{\mu}_{A@ctx}(x), \hat{\nu}_{A@ctx}(x) \rangle = \langle \langle \mu_{A@ctx}(x), F_{\mu_{A@ctx}}(x) \rangle, \langle \nu_{A@ctx}(x), F_{\nu_{A@ctx}}(x) \rangle \rangle$ (see Sect. 2). Given $\mathbf{x} = v(x)$ and the collection of support vectors $S_{A@s(ctx)} = \{\mathbf{x}_i | i = 1, \cdots, n\}$, the components $\mu_{A@ctx}(x)$ and $\nu_{A@ctx}(x)$ can be obtained by:

$$\mu_{A@ctx}(x) = \breve{\mu}_{A@ctx}(x)/\eta_{A@ctx}(x) \tag{12}$$

and

$$\nu_{A@ctx}(x) = \check{\nu}_{A@ctx}(x)/\eta_{A@ctx}(x), \tag{13}$$

where

$$\eta_{A@ctx}(x) = \max(1, \check{\mu}_{A@ctx}(x) + \check{\nu}_{A@ctx}(x)), \tag{14}$$

$$\check{\mu}_{A@ctx}(x) = \begin{cases} \frac{\sum_{i=1}^{n} \lambda_i y_i K(\mathbf{x},\mathbf{x}_i)+b}{||\mathbf{x}|| ||\sum_{i=1}^{n} \lambda_i y_i \mathbf{x}_i ||} & \text{iff}(\mathbf{x}_i \in S_{A@s(ctx)}) \\ & \wedge(\lambda_i y_i K(\mathbf{x},\mathbf{x}_i) > 0) \wedge (b > 0); \\ \frac{\sum_{i=1}^{n} \lambda_i y_i K(\mathbf{x},\mathbf{x}_i)}{||\mathbf{x}|| ||\sum_{i=1}^{n} \lambda_i y_i \mathbf{x}_i ||} & \text{iff}(\mathbf{x}_i \in S_{A@s(ctx)}) \\ & \wedge(\lambda_i y_i K(\mathbf{x},\mathbf{x}_i) > 0) \wedge (b \leq 0); \\ 0 & \text{otherwise}; \end{cases} \tag{15}$$

and

$$\check{\nu}_{A@ctx}(x) = \begin{cases} \frac{\sum_{i=1}^{n} |\lambda_i y_i K(\mathbf{x},\mathbf{x}_i)|+|b|}{||\mathbf{x}|| ||\sum_{i=1}^{n} \lambda_i y_i \mathbf{x}_i ||} & \text{iff}(\mathbf{x}_i \in S_{A@s(ctx)}) \\ & \wedge(\lambda_i y_i K(\mathbf{x},\mathbf{x}_i) < 0) \wedge (b < 0); \\ \frac{\sum_{i=1}^{n} |\lambda_i y_i K(\mathbf{x},\mathbf{x}_i)|}{||\mathbf{x}|| ||\sum_{i=1}^{n} \lambda_i y_i \mathbf{x}_i ||} & \text{iff}(\mathbf{x}_i \in S_{A@s(ctx)}) \\ & \wedge(\lambda_i y_i K(\mathbf{x},\mathbf{x}_i) > 0) \wedge (b \geq 0); \\ 0 & \text{otherwise}. \end{cases} \tag{16}$$

The collections $F_{\mu_{A@ctx}}(x)$ and $F_{\nu_{A@ctx}}(x)$ can be obtained by means of the positive MISV $\mathbf{v}_{A@ctx}^{+}$ and the negative MISV $\mathbf{v}_{A@ctx}^{-}$, which are given by

$$\mathbf{v}_{A@ctx}^{+} = \text{argmax}_{\mathbf{x}_i}\{\lambda_i y_i K(\mathbf{x},\mathbf{x}_i) : (\lambda_i y_i K(\mathbf{x},\mathbf{x}_i) > 0) \wedge (\mathbf{x}_i \in S_{A@s(ctx)})\} \tag{17}$$

and

$$\mathbf{v}_{A@ctx}^{-} = \text{argmax}_{\mathbf{x}_i}\{|\lambda_i y_i K(\mathbf{x},\mathbf{x}_i)| : (\lambda_i y_i K(\mathbf{x},\mathbf{x}_i) < 0) \wedge (\mathbf{x}_i \in S_{A@ctx})\} \tag{18}$$

respectively, where $i = 1, \cdots, n$.

Since an augmented IFS is constituted by several augmented IFS elements, the contextualized evaluations of the level to which several objects in a collection X are member of A in context ctx can be denoted by an augmented IFS $\hat{A}_{@ctx} = \{\langle \hat{\mu}_{A@ctx}(x), \hat{\nu}_{A@ctx}(x)\rangle | x \in X\}$. In this regard, we can follow a technique similar to the presented in [18] for identifying the most similar contextual models linked to A by means of contextualized evaluations. For instance, we can compute the level of similarity between $\hat{A}_{@ctx1}$ and $\hat{A}_{@ctx2}$, as well as the similarity between $\hat{A}_{@ctx1}$ and $\hat{A}_{@ctx3}$ to determine whether $K_{A@ctx1}$ is more similar to $K_{A@ctx2}$ or more similar to $K_{A@ctx3}$.

In the next section we illustrate how the interpretability of the predictions about a topic, say A, might be benefited from the contextualization of the underlying SVM model $K_{A@ctx} = \langle \hat{\mathbf{u}}_{A@ctx}, t_{A@ctx}\rangle$ computed by (4) and (5).

4   Illustrative Examples

Since SVM classification can be effective in situations where the dimension of the feature space $\mathcal{M}$ is greater than the number of samples [25], we shall use the data set depicted in Fig. 3 to explain how the interpretability of predictions can be boosted by XSVM@ctx. This data set consists of two contextualized subsets ($D_{@ctx1}$ and $D_{@ctx2}$) of 50 digitized handwritten vowels each. Every digitized vowel is made up of 784 pixels, each associated with a value representing the strength of the trace resulting after writing the vowel. Similar to the characterization of handwritten numbers made in [19], each vowel has been represented by a vector in 784-dimensional feature space, where the constituent pixels correspond to the features in that space. We use the first 5 columns of each contextualized subset as training samples to obtain a contextualized knowledge model $K_{vowel@ctx_i}$ for each vowel and each context. In this training process, a polynomial kernel of degree 5 with regularization parameter $C = 0.001$ was used.

(a) $D_{@ctx1}$ (b) $D_{@ctx2}$

Fig. 3. Contextualized datasets.

The last 5 columns of $D_{@ctx1}$ in Fig. 3a were used as test samples to predict the categories ('a', 'e', 'i', 'o' and 'u') those digitized handwritten vowels should belong to. The predictions are depicted in Fig. 4: while $data@ctx1$ represents the test samples, $pred@ctx1$ and $pred@ctx2$ represent the predictions made by the contextualized models built for $ctx1$ and $ctx2$ respectively. In such predictions, the positive MISVs have been used for the contextualization. Such MISVs (located below the predicted vowels) represent the handwritten vowels that are most similar to the test samples and, in addition, favor the membership of these samples in the predicted vowels. The shaded part in the handwritten vowels denotes disagreement with the categories in the test set.

Fig. 4. Contextualized predictions.

Notice that the MISVs of the predictions made in the same context of the test samples (i.e., the MISVs in $pred@ctx1$) represent in an appropriate way what have been important to the classifier while predicting the categories of the handwritten vowels. In contrast, the MISVs of the predictions in $pred@ctx2$, which are made in a different context, struggle while trying to find the features in the test samples that justify those predictions. Although the simplicity of this case, it illustrates how the predictions of the categories can be benefited from the contextualization of the SVM models. Notice also that while most of the predictions in $pred@ctx1$ are in agreement with the categories related to digitized vowels in the test set, more than a half of the predictions in $pred@ctx2$ are in disagreement.

To further explore such potential improvement in accuracy due to the contextualization of the SVM models, we probe XSVM@ctx with a data set of EMG signals that are used for recognizing hand gestures [13]. This data set contains 4,237,907 records with EMG data from 36 subjects that performed 7 hand gestures: 'hand at rest', 'hand clenched in a fist', 'wrist flexion', 'wrist extension', 'radial deviations', 'ulnar deviations' and 'extended palm'. Records having unmarked gestures were removed during the preprocessing step. The 8 EMG channels of the remaining 1,512,750 records were normalized using the L2 norm. Considering that the values of the 8 EMG channels depend on each of the 36 subjects, we partitioned the data set in 36 contextual subsets – reducing the number of contextual subsets is subject to further study. Half of the records in each contextual subset were randomly chosen to be part of the training set while the remaining records were used for testing. A polynomial kernel of 10 degree with a regularization parameter of 100 was used during the parallel training process of XSVM@ctx to obtain a contextualized model for each hand gesture and each context. An accuracy of 0.974 was computed after performing the evaluation process of XSVM@ctx with the test set.

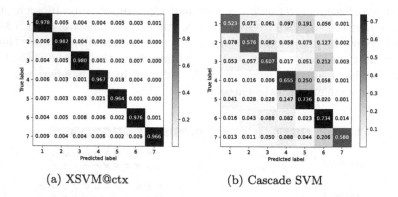

(a) XSVM@ctx   (b) Cascade SVM

Fig. 5. Hand gestures recognition - confusion matrices.

To have an idea of the improvement of the accuracy, we also train the *cascade formulation of SVM* [9] with the aforementioned kernel configuration. The computed accuracy in this case was 0.639. Such improvement is also reflected through the corresponding confusion matrices depicted in Fig. 5. Notice the positive effect of the contextualization in the unbalanced class 7 ('extended palm' gesture) – this effect on unbalanced classes is also subject to further study.

5   Related Work

A systematic literature review presented in [12] covers indexed journals in the period between 1992 and 2020 where several applications of SVM models are mentioned. For instance, image classification SVM models are applied in geosciences, biomedical imaging, molecular biology, among others. Although this literature review does not mention contextualization or explainability in a explicit form is it important to recall that the contextualization of knowledge models for a better classification are our contribution within this work.

An interesting article presented in [20] shows the importance of contextual based predictions and their potential to improve the performance of computer vision algorithms. This article follows the line of imitating the human visual system based on a convolutional neural network (CNN) and the use of a pretrained SVM classification model. Moreover this article discusses the fact that a human observer might apply different (priming and) searching strategies for a given task. Thus, when a visual input is ambiguous, predictions may help in the decision process and in maintaining a coherent interpretation of the environment. As an example, it presents the recognition of two identical objects shown in two different places (contexts).

Regarding the computational costs of processing large data sets the following approaches are available in the literature. One in which the training set is randomly partitioned [8] was mentioned in Sect. 1, but it differs with our proposal where the partitions are context based. The use of different contextual dimensions that are relevant to be analyzed for partitioning the data, e.g., temporal or spatial information, has been proposed in [22]. This proposal produces partitions that also consider the data distribution of each contextual dimension, but it has not been used with SVM models.

6   Conclusions

In this paper, we have proposed a novel explainable SVM classifier, named XSVM@ctx, that makes use of a parallel arrangement of contextualized SVM models for offering contextual predictions. XSVM@ctx uses contextualized data sets as input for building such contextualized SVM models during the training process. The resulting models are then used as inputs for making contextualized predictions during the evaluation process.

An important characteristic of XSVM@ctx is its context selector, which allows decision makers to specify the context of the predictions they would like to be offered. During the evaluation process, XSVM@ctx makes use of the model(s) having the context that is the most similar to the specified context(s) for making the predictions.

An example in which handwritten vowels are contextually identified has illustrated how the interpretability of the predictions can be improved by XSVM@ctx. An improvement in the accuracy of the resulting models has been also illustrated in an example where hand gestures are recognized through EMG signals.

Acknowledgements. This study has been supported by both the research project "Interpretable Artificial Intelligence (XAI) in Group Decision-Making" (FIEC-200-2020) from ESPOL Polytechnic University and the "Onderzoeksprogramma Artificiële Intelligentie (AI) Vlaanderen" from the Flemish Government.

References

1. Atanassov, K.T.: Intuitionistic fuzzy sets. Fuzzy Sets Syst. **20**(1), 87–96 (1986). https://doi.org/10.1016/S0165-0114(86)80034-3
2. Barakat, N.H., Bradley, A.P.: Rule extraction from support vector machines: a review. Neurocomputing **74**(1), 178–190 (2010). https://doi.org/10.1016/j.neucom.2010.02.016
3. Barredo Arrieta, A., et al.: Explainable Artificial Intelligence (XAI): concepts, taxonomies, opportunities and challenges toward responsible AI. Inf. Fusion **58**, 82–115 (2020). https://doi.org/10.1016/j.inffus.2019.12.012
4. Bovolo, F., Bruzzone, L., Marconcini, M.: A novel context-sensitive SVM for classification of remote sensing images. In: 2006 IEEE International Symposium on Geoscience and Remote Sensing, pp. 2498–2501 (2006). https://doi.org/10.1109/IGARSS.2006.646
5. Bruzzone, L., Persello, C.: A novel context-sensitive semisupervised SVM classifier robust to mislabeled training samples. IEEE Trans. Geosci. Remote Sens. **47**(7), 2142–2154 (2009). https://doi.org/10.1109/TGRS.2008.2011983
6. Burges, C.J.: A tutorial on support vector machines for pattern recognition. Data Min. Knowl. Discov. **2**(2), 121–167 (1998). https://doi.org/10.1023/A:1009715923555
7. Freund, Y., Schapire, R.E.: A decision-theoretic generalization of on-line learning and an application to boosting. J. Comput. Syst. Sci. **55**(1), 119–139 (1997). https://doi.org/10.1006/jcss.1997.1504
8. García-Gutiérrez, J., Mateos-García, D., Garcia, M., Riquelme-Santos, J.C.: An evolutionary-weighted majority voting and support vector machines applied to contextual classification of LiDAR and imagery data fusion. Neurocomputing **163**, 17–24 (2015). https://doi.org/10.1016/j.neucom.2014.08.086
9. Graf, H., Cosatto, E., Bottou, L., Dourdanovic, I., Vapnik, V.: Parallel support vector machines: the cascade SVM. In: Saul, L., Weiss, Y., Bottou, L. (eds.) Advances in Neural Information Processing Systems, vol. 17. MIT Press (2004). https://proceedings.neurips.cc/paper/2004/file/d756d3d2b9dac72449a6a6926534558a-Paper.pdf
10. Guidotti, R., Monreale, A., Giannotti, F., Pedreschi, D., Ruggieri, S., Turini, F.: Factual and counterfactual explanations for black box decision making. IEEE Intell. Syst. **34**(6), 14–23 (2019). https://doi.org/10.1109/MIS.2019.2957223
11. Kaminski, M.E.: The right to explanation, explained. Berkeley Technol. Law J. **34**, 189 (2019). https://doi.org/10.15779/Z38TD9N83H

12. Lengua, M.A.C., Quiroz, E.A.P.: A systematic literature review on support vector machines applied to classification. In: 2020 IEEE Engineering International Research Conference (EIRCON), pp. 1–4. IEEE (2020)
13. Lobov, S., Krilova, N., Kastalskiy, I., Kazantsev, V., Makarov, V.: EMG data for gestures data set - UCI machine learning repository (2019). https://archive.ics.uci.edu/ml/datasets/EMG+data+for+gestures
14. Loor, M., De Tré, G.: On the need for augmented appraisal degrees to handle experience-based evaluations. Appl. Soft Comput. **54**, 284–295 (2017). https://doi.org/10.1016/j.asoc.2017.01.009
15. Loor, M., De Tré, G.: Identifying and properly handling context in crowdsourcing. Appl. Soft Comput. **73**, 203–214 (2018). https://doi.org/10.1016/j.asoc.2018.04.062
16. Loor, M., De Tré, G.: Explaining computer predictions with augmented appraisal degrees. In: 2019 Conference of the International Fuzzy Systems Association and the European Society for Fuzzy Logic and Technology (EUSFLAT 2019). Atlantis Press (2019). https://doi.org/10.2991/eusflat-19.2019.24
17. Loor, M., De Tré, G.: Contextualizing support vector machine predictions. Int. J. Comput. Intell. Syst. **13**, 1483–1497 (2020). https://doi.org/10.2991/ijcis.d.200910.002
18. Loor, M., De Tré, G.: Handling subjective information through augmented (fuzzy) computation. Fuzzy Sets Syst. **391**, 47–71 (2020). https://doi.org/10.1016/j.fss.2019.05.007
19. Loor, M., Tapia-Rosero, A., De Tré, G.: An open-source software library for explainable support vector machine classification. In: 2022 IEEE International Conference on Fuzzy Systems (FUZZ-IEEE), pp. 1–7 (2022). https://doi.org/10.1109/FUZZ-IEEE55066.2022.9882731
20. Malowany, D., Guterman, H.: Biologically inspired visual system architecture for object recognition in autonomous systems. Algorithms **13**(7), 167 (2020)
21. Martens, D., Baesens, B., Van Gestel, T.: Decompositional rule extraction from support vector machines by active learning. IEEE Trans. Knowl. Data Eng. **21**(2), 178–191 (2009). https://doi.org/10.1109/TKDE.2008.131
22. Migliorini, S., Belussi, A., Quintarelli, E., Carra, D.: A context-based approach for partitioning big data. In: EDBT, pp. 431–434 (2020)
23. Negri, R.G., Dutra, L.V., Sant'Anna, S.J.S.: An innovative support vector machine based method for contextual image classification. ISPRS J. Photogramm. Remote. Sens. **87**, 241–248 (2014). https://doi.org/10.1016/j.isprsjprs.2013.11.004
24. Ribeiro, M.T., Singh, S., Guestrin, C.: "Why should i trust you?": Explaining the predictions of any classifier. In: Proceedings of the 22nd ACM SIGKDD International Conference on Knowledge Discovery and Data Mining, KDD 2016, pp. 1135–1144. ACM, New York (2016). https://doi.org/10.1145/2939672.2939778
25. Vapnik, V.N., Vapnik, V.: Statistical Learning Theory, vol. 1. Wiley, New York (1998)
26. Zadeh, L.: Fuzzy sets. Inf. Control **8**(3), 338–353 (1965). https://doi.org/10.1016/S0019-9958(65)90241-X
27. Zhu, P., Hu, Q.: Rule extraction from support vector machines based on consistent region covering reduction. Knowl.-Based Syst. **42**, 1–8 (2013). https://doi.org/10.1016/j.knosys.2012.12.003

SPECIAL SESSION 6: Recent Trends in Mathematical Fuzzy Logics

Ideals in the Two-Sorted Variety of Equational States

Serafina Lapenta[✉], Sebastiano Napolitano, and Luca Spada[✉]

Department of Mathematics, University of Salerno, Fisciano, Italy
{slapenta,lspada}@unisa.it, s.napolitano40@studenti.unisa.it

Abstract. We investigate the recently introduced two-sorted variety of *equational states*. We show that, similarly to MV-algebras, in equational states ideals are in bijection with two-sorted congruences. Differently from MV-algebras, not every equational state is the subdirect product of linearly ordered ones. We finally show that the variety of equational states is not generated by the linearly ordered ones.

Keywords: MV-algebra · Equational states · many-sorted algebra · Ideal

1 Introduction

An *Abelian lattice-ordered group* is an Abelian group endowed with a lattice order that is invariant under translations, i.e., $x \leq y$ implies $z + x \leq z + y$. A lattice-ordered group G is called *unital* if it possesses an element u such that for any $g \in G$ there exists $n \in \mathbb{N}$ for which u exceeds the n-fold sum $g + \cdots + g$. A *state* on a unital Abelian lattice-ordered group is a normalised, positive, group homomorphism into $\mathbb{R}$, see e.g., [5]. It has longly been recognised that unital Abelian lattice-ordered groups and their states provide an abstraction of bounded real random variables and of expected-value operators, respectively.

An important result of D. Mundici establishes an equivalence between the category of unital lattice-ordered groups (with unit-preserving lattice-group homomorphisms as morphisms) and the category of MV-algebras with their homomorphisms. Through this equivalence, states of lattice-ordered groups correspond to certain [0, 1]-valued functions on MV-algebras, which again go under the name of states [7].

Both states on lattice-ordered groups and MV-algebras can be easily generalised to take values in any unital Abelian lattice-ordered group or any MV-algebra, respectively. Therefore, one can consider the category of Abelian lattice-ordered groups with states as morphisms between them and the category of MV-algebras with their states as morphisms. In [6] the authors extend Mundici's equivalence to these two latter categories. Furthermore, the authors introduce a class of two-sorted algebras, called *equational states* and prove that it is categorically equivalent to the category of states between unital Abelian lattice-ordered

S. Massanet et al. (Eds.): EUSFLAT 2023/AGOP 2023, LNCS 14069, pp. 495–504, 2023.
https://doi.org/10.1007/978-3-031-39965-7_41

groups. As a consequence of these results, one can think of equational states as a two-sorted *equational* theory of states between lattice-ordered groups. This opens the way to a purely algebraic study of states, e.g., in [6] the authors prove the existence of *universal* states.

In this paper we continue the purely algebraic study of states by investigating properties of the two-sorted variety of equational states. In particular, in Corollary 1 we show that ideals of equational states are in bijection with two-sorted congruences. In Lemma 2 we characterise ideals generated by a (two-sorted) subset of an equational state. Furthermore, we provide examples showing that not every equational state is a subdirect product of linearly ordered equational states (see Remark 1) and that the variety of equational states is not generated by it linearly ordered members (see Example 2). We conclude the paper with a characterisation of simple and semisimple equational states (Propositions 2 and 3).

2   Preliminaries

We start by recalling some basic facts in the theory of MV-algebras. For further details we refer the reader to [1]. An *MV-algebra* is an algebra $\mathbf{A} := (A, \oplus, \neg, 0)$ such that $(A, \oplus, 0)$ is a commutative monoid; $\neg$ is an involution —i.e., $\neg\neg a = a$ for all $a \in A$— and, for any $x, y \in A$, $\neg(\neg x \oplus y) \oplus y = \neg(\neg y \oplus x) \oplus x$. New operations can be derived from $\oplus$ and $\neg$, in particular we use the following ones:

$$x \odot y := \neg(\neg x \oplus \neg y), \quad x \ominus y := x \odot \neg y, \quad x \Rightarrow y := \neg x \oplus y, \quad 1 := \neg 0.$$

Any MV-algebra has a natural lattice structure, where the order is defined by setting $x \leq y$ if and only if $x \Rightarrow y = 1$. The meet and join with respect to this order can also be defined as

$$x \wedge y := x \odot (x \Rightarrow y) \text{ and } x \vee y := \neg(\neg x \oplus y) \oplus y.$$

For any $a \in A$ and $n \in \mathbb{N}$, we write na as an abbreviation for the n-fold sum $a \oplus \ldots \oplus a$.

Let $\mathbf{A}$ be an MV-algebra. An *ideal* J of $\mathbf{A}$ is a non-empty subset of A that is downward closed and closed under $\oplus$. An ideal J is *prime* if for each $x, y \in A$ $x \ominus y \in J$ or $y \ominus x \in J$. If $T \subseteq A$, we call the intersection of all ideals containing T the *ideal generated* by T, and we denote it by J_T. A more explicit description of J_T is given by

$$J_T = \{a \in A \mid \exists n \in \mathbb{N}, \exists t_1, \ldots, t_n \in T \quad a \leq t_1 \oplus \cdots \oplus t_n\}. \tag{1}$$

It is well known that the lattice of all ideals of any MV-algebra is isomorphic to the lattice of congruences, via the correspondence that associates to any ideal J the congruence $\equiv_J$ defined by $a \equiv_J b$ if and only if $a \ominus b \in J$ and $b \ominus a \in J$ and to any congruence $\equiv$ the ideal $J := \{x \mid x \equiv 0\}$. In view of this isomorphism, we simply write $\mathbf{A}/J$ for $\mathbf{A}/\equiv_J$. The quotient algebra $\mathbf{A}/J$ is an MV-chain (i.e., a totally ordered MV-algebra) if and only if J is a prime ideal. MV-algebras have "enough" prime ideals, in the precise sense of next lemma.

Lemma 1. *Let* **A** *be an MV-algebra. For any non-zero* $a \in A$ *there exists a prime ideal* J^a *such that* $a \notin J^a$. *As a consequence, the intersection of all prime ideals of* **A** *is* $\{0\}$.

It follows that every non-trivial MV-algebra is a subdirect product of MV-chains and thus an equation is valid in all MV-algebras if and only if it is valid in all MV-chains.

We now recall some basic fact on many-sorted algebras. For further details see e.g. [8, Section 2.1 and 2.2].

Definition 1. Let S be a set. An *S-sorted set* is a family of sets $X := \{X_s \mid s \in S\}$. The elements of S are called *sorts*. If $X := \{X_s \mid s \in S\}$ and $Y := \{Y_s \mid s \in S\}$ are S-sorted sets, an *S-sorted function* from X into Y is a family of functions $\{f_s \colon X_s \to Y_s \mid s \in S\}$.

If $X := \{X_s \mid s \in S\}$ is an S-sorted set, we write $x \in X$ as a shorthand for $x \in X_s$ for some $s \in S$. Standard constructions like subsets, unions, intersections, Cartesian products, equivalence relations, and quotients straightforwardly generalise to S-sorted sets.

Definition 2. A *many-sorted signature* is a triad $\Sigma = (S, \Omega, a)$, where:

- S is a set (called the *set of sorts* of Σ);
- Ω is a set (called the *set of functions symbols* of Σ)
- a is a function $a \colon \Omega \to S^* \times S$, where S^* is the set of all finite sequences of elements of S.

Given a many-sorted signature $\Sigma = (S, \Omega, a)$, a Σ-*algebra* **A** consists of an S-sorted set A and, for any $f \in \Omega$ with $a(f) = (s_1, \ldots, s_n, s)$, an S-sorted function $f^{\mathsf{A}} \colon A_{s_1} \times \cdots \times A_{s_n} \to A_s$.

We fix $\underline{\Sigma} := (\underline{S}, \underline{\Omega}, \underline{a})$ where $\underline{S} := \{1, 2\}$, $\underline{\Omega} := \{\oplus_1, \neg_1, 0_1, \oplus_2, \neg_2, 0_2, s\}$ and $\underline{a}$ can be easily deduced from the following definition.

Definition 3 ([6, Definition 3.1]). An *equational state* is a $\underline{\Sigma}$-algebra

$$\mathsf{A} = \langle (A_1, A_2), \oplus_1^A, \neg_1^A, 0_1^A, \oplus_2^A, \neg_2^A, 0_2^A, s^A \rangle$$

such that:

1. $(A_1, \oplus_1^A, \neg_1^A, 0_1^A)$ is an MV-algebra;
2. $(A_2, \oplus_2^A, \neg_2^A, 0_2^A)$ is an MV-algebra;
3. $s^A \colon A_1 \to A_2$ is a unary operation, called *state-operation*, such that, for each $a, b \in A_1$:
   - (S1) $s^A(0_1^A) = 0_2^A$;
   - (S2) $s^A(\neg_1^A a) = \neg_2^A s^A(a)$;
   - (S3) $s^A(a \oplus_1^A b) = s^A(a) \oplus_2^A s^A(b \wedge_1^A (\neg_1^A a))$.

It will be convenient to indicate an equational state like the one in Definition 3 by $A = (\mathbf{A}_1, \mathbf{A}_2)$ and drop the superscripts for the MV-algebraic operations, when the context suffices to disambiguate. When the operations s of two equational states $A := (\mathbf{A}_1, \mathbf{A}_2)$ and $B := (\mathbf{B}_1, \mathbf{B}_2)$ need to be distinguished we write s^A and s^B. An equational state $(\mathbf{A}_1, \mathbf{A}_2)$ is called *linearly ordered* (or an *equational state-chain*) if both $\mathbf{A}_1$ and $\mathbf{A}_2$ are MV-chains. Notice that, by [6, Proposition 3.1], the unary operation s is order-preserving.

The following definitions are adaptations of the definitions in [8, Section 2.2] to the particular case of equational states.

Definition 4 Let $A := (\mathbf{A}_1, \mathbf{A}_2)$ and $B := (\mathbf{B}_1, \mathbf{B}_2)$ be two equational states. An $\underline{S}$-sorted function $h := (h_1, h_2) \colon A \to B$ is said to be a *homomorphism of equational states* (or $\underline{\Sigma}$-*homomorphism*) if $h_1 \colon \mathbf{A}_1 \to \mathbf{B}_1$ and $h_2 \colon \mathbf{A}_2 \to \mathbf{B}_2$ are homomorphisms of MV-algebras, and $h_2 \circ s^A = s^B \circ h_1$.

Definition 5 A $\underline{\Sigma}$-*congruence* $(\equiv_1, \equiv_2)$ is an $\underline{S}$-equivalence relation that is compatible with the operations of MV-algebras and the state-operation, i.e., if $x \equiv_1 y$ then $s(x) \equiv_2 s(y)$.

Definition 6 Let $A := (\mathbf{A}_1, \mathbf{A}_2)$ be an equational state and $\equiv := (\equiv_1, \equiv_2)$ a $\underline{\Sigma}$-congruence. Then the quotient algebra over $\equiv$, $Q := (\mathbf{Q}_1, \mathbf{Q}_2)$ is the equational state defined by:

- $\mathbf{Q}_i := \mathbf{A}_i / \equiv_i$ for $i \in \{1, 2\}$;
- if $a, b \in A_i$, then $[a]_{\equiv_i} \oplus [b]_{\equiv_i} := [a \oplus b]_{\equiv_i}$ and $\neg[a]_{\equiv_i} := [\neg a]_{\equiv_i}$;
- if $a \in A_1$, then $s([a]_{\equiv_1}) := [s(a)]_{\equiv_2}$.

Let $X := (X_1, X_2)$ be a fixed but arbitrary $\underline{S}$-sorted set of variables. We denote by $T_{\underline{\Sigma}}(X)_1$ the set of MV-terms over the variables in X_1 and by $T_{\underline{\Sigma}}(X)_2$ the set of terms of the form $\tau(t_1, \ldots, t_n)$, where τ is an MV-term and each t_i is either an MV-term in the variables in X_2 or one of the form $s(t)$ for $t \in T_{\underline{\Sigma}}(X)_1$. The $\underline{S}$-sorted set of $\underline{\Sigma}$-terms in X is given by $T_{\underline{\Sigma}}(X) := (T_{\underline{\Sigma}}(X)_1, T_{\underline{\Sigma}}(X)_2)$.

Definition 7 A $\underline{\Sigma}$-*equation* is a pair of terms t, t' either both belonging to $T_{\underline{\Sigma}}(X)_1$ or to $T_{\underline{\Sigma}}(X)_2$, together with an $\underline{S}$-sorted set of variables Y. We write $\forall Y.t = t'$ to indicate a $\underline{\Sigma}$-equation. A Y-*valuation* in an equational state A is simply an $\underline{S}$-function from Y into A. Any Y-valuation v extends, in a unique way, to an $\underline{S}$-homomorphism, which we still indicate with v, from $T_{\underline{\Sigma}}(Y)$ to A. An equational state A verifies a $\underline{\Sigma}$-equation $\forall Y.t = t'$ if for any Y-valuation $v \colon Y \to A$ the equality $v(t) = v(t')$ holds in A. An equation $\forall Y.t = t'$ is called *finitary* if Y is finite.

Because the class of equational states has a finite set of sorts and it is definable by a set of finitary equations, by (the many-sorted version of) Birkhoff's Variety Theorem [8, Corollary 3.14] the class of equational states is a variety of many-sorted algebras.

3   Ideals of Equational States

Definition 8 Let $A := (A_1, A_2)$ be an equational state. A $\underline{\Sigma}$-*ideal* is an $\underline{S}$-sorted subset $J := (J_1, J_2)$ of A such that, for $i \in \{1, 2\}$, J_i is an MV-ideal of A_i and $s(J_1) \subseteq J_2$.

A $\underline{\Sigma}$-ideal $J = (J_1, J_2)$ is called *proper* if $J \neq A$ and it is called *prime* if for $i \in \{1, 2\}$ and any $x, y \in A_i$, $x \ominus y \in J_i$ or $y \ominus x \in J_i$. Notice that J is prime if and only if J_1 and J_2 are both prime as ideals of MV-algebras. A routine argument shows that for any family $\{J_i\}_{i \in I}$ of $\underline{\Sigma}$-ideals of a given equational state, the intersection $\bigcap_{i \in I} J_i$ is a $\underline{\Sigma}$-ideal.

Definition 9 Let (T_1, T_2) be an $\underline{S}$-subset of an equational state A. The $\underline{\Sigma}$-*ideal generated* by (T_1, T_2), denoted by $J_{(T_1, T_2)}$, is the smallest $\underline{\Sigma}$-ideal containing (T_1, T_2).

Lemma 2 *Let (T_1, T_2) be an $\underline{S}$-subset of an equational state $A = (A_1, A_2)$. The $\underline{\Sigma}$-ideal generated by (T_1, T_2) is $(J_{T_1}, J_{s(J_{T_1}) \cup T_2})$.*

Proof Let us temporarily denote the $\underline{S}$-sorted set $(J_{T_1}, J_{s(J_{T_1}) \cup T_2})$ by J^*. Since J^* is obviously a $\underline{\Sigma}$-ideal and (T_1, T_2) is contained in J^*, one has that $J_{(T_1, T_2)} \subseteq J^*$.

For the converse inclusion, let a be an element of J^*. If $a \in J_{T_1}$, it is obviously an element in $J_{(T_1, T_2)}$. Suppose that $a \in J_{s(J_{T_1}) \cup T_2}$. Then, using (1),

$$a \leq \left(\bigoplus_{i=1}^{t} n_i s(x_i) \right) \oplus \left(\bigoplus_{j=1}^{t'} m_j y_j \right)$$

for $x_1, \dots, x_t \in J_{T_1}$, $y_1, \dots, y_{t'} \in T_2$ and $n_1, \dots, n_t, m_1, \dots, m_{t'} \in \mathbb{N}$. Notice that, for any $1 \leq i \leq t$, $s(x_i)$ belongs to $J_{(T_1, T_2)}$ by the definition of $\underline{\Sigma}$-ideals. Additionally, since $y_j \in T_2$, for any $1 \leq j \leq t'$, also $y_j \in J_{(T_1, T_2)}$. Thus, by Definition 8, we have that

$$\left(\bigoplus_{i=1}^{t} n_i s(x_i) \right) \oplus \left(\bigoplus_{j=1}^{t'} m_j y_j \right) \in J_{(T_1, T_2)}.$$

Hence $a \in J_{(T_1, T_2)}$ and $J^* \subseteq J_{(T_1, T_2)}$ as required.

Definition 10 Let $J = (J_1, J_2)$ be a $\underline{\Sigma}$-ideal of an equational state S. We define the relation $\equiv_J$ as follows: for any $x, y \in A_i$ and $i \in \{1, 2\}$,

$$x \equiv_J y \text{ if and only if } x \ominus y \in J_i \text{ and } y \ominus x \in J_i.$$

Lemma 3 *For any equational state S and any $\underline{\Sigma}$-ideal $J = (J_1, J_2)$, the relation $\equiv_J$ is a $\underline{\Sigma}$-congruence.*

Proof Symmetry, reflexivity and transitivity of $\equiv_J$, as well as compatibility with the MV-operations are immediate consequences of the fact that J_1 and J_2 are both ideals. It remains to be shown that if $a \equiv_{J_1} b$ then $s(a) \equiv_{J_2} s(b)$, the latter condition being equivalent to $s(a) \ominus s(b) \in J_2$ and $s(b) \ominus s(a) \in J_2$. We prove the first condition, the proof of the second condition is similar. Since J is a $\underline{\Sigma}$-ideal, if $a \ominus b \in J_1$ then $s(a \ominus b) \in J_2$. Moreover, for all $x, y \in A_1$

$$
\begin{aligned}
s(x \Rightarrow y) &= s(\neg x \oplus y) && \text{by definition of} \Rightarrow \\
&= s(\neg x) \oplus s(y \wedge x) && \text{by (S3)} \\
&\leq \neg s(x) \oplus s(y) && \text{by (S2) and monotonicity of } s \quad (2) \\
&= s(x) \Rightarrow s(y) && \text{by definition of} \Rightarrow .
\end{aligned}
$$

An easy calculation shows that $a \ominus b = \neg(\neg b \Rightarrow \neg a)$. Therefore:

$$
\begin{aligned}
s(a \ominus b) &= s(\neg(\neg b \Rightarrow \neg a)) \\
&= \neg s(\neg b \Rightarrow \neg a) && \text{by (S2)} \\
&\geq \neg(\neg s(b) \Rightarrow \neg s(a)) && \text{by (2) and the involutivity of} \neg \\
&= s(a) \ominus s(b).
\end{aligned}
$$

Therefore, $s(a) \ominus s(b) \leq s(a \ominus b)$. Since $s(a \ominus b) \in J_2$ and J_2 is downward closed, we conclude that $s(a) \ominus s(b) \in J_2$.

Lemma 4 *Let* A $:= (\mathbf{A}_1, \mathbf{A}_2)$ *be an equational state and* $\equiv := (\equiv_1, \equiv_2)$ *be a* $\underline{\Sigma}$-*congruence of* A. *The* $\underline{S}$-*sorted set* J $:= (J_1, J_2)$, *where* $J_i := \{x \mid x \equiv_i 0\}$ *is a* $\underline{\Sigma}$-*ideal of* A.

Proof It is clear that J_1 and J_2 are ideals of the MV-algebras $\mathbf{A}_1$ and $\mathbf{A}_2$ respectively. So, it is sufficient to show that $s(J_1) \subseteq J_2$. Let $a \in A_1$ be such that $a \in J_1$. Hence $a \equiv_1 0_{A_1}$ and consequently $s(a) \equiv_2 0_{A_2}$, because $\equiv$ is a $\underline{\Sigma}$-congruence. It follows that $s(a) \in J_2$.

The inclusion relation between S-sets induces a lattice order on both the set of $\underline{\Sigma}$-ideals and $\underline{\Sigma}$-congruences.

Corollary 1 *The correspondence that associates to any $\underline{\Sigma}$-ideal J the congruence $\equiv_J$ and to any $\underline{\Sigma}$-congruence $\equiv$ the $\underline{\Sigma}$-ideal J $= (J_1, J_2)$ with $J_i := \{x \mid x \equiv_i 0\}$ is an isomorphism between the lattice of $\underline{\Sigma}$-congruences of any equational states and its lattice of $\underline{\Sigma}$-ideals.*

Proof It is a consequence of Lemmas 3 and 4, and the correspondence between congruences and ideals in MV-algebras.

Henceforth, we write A/J for A/ $\equiv_J$.

Theorem 1 *The quotient equational state* A/J *is an equational state-chain if and only if* J *is a prime $\underline{\Sigma}$-ideal.*

Proof Let $\mathsf{A} := (\mathbf{A}_1, \mathbf{A}_2)$ be an equational state and $\mathsf{J} := (J_1, J_2)$ a $\underline{\Sigma}$-ideal. Notice that $\mathsf{A}/\mathsf{J} = (\mathbf{A}_1/J_1, \mathbf{A}_2/J_2)$. So A/J is an equational state-chain if and only if $\mathbf{A}_1/J_1$ and $\mathbf{A}_2/J_2$ are both MV-chains. This latter condition is equivalent to saying that J_1 and J_2 are both prime ideals, which in turn is true if and only if J is a prime $\underline{\Sigma}$-ideal.

Theorem 2 *Let* $\mathsf{A} := (\mathbf{A}_1, \mathbf{A}_2)$ *be an equational state, where* $\mathbf{A}_1$ *is an MV-chain. Then for any non-zero* $x \in \mathsf{A}$ *there exists a prime* $\underline{\Sigma}$-*ideal* J *such that* $x \notin \mathsf{J}$.

Proof If $x \in A_1$, then by Lemma 1 there exists a prime ideal J^x such that $x \notin J^x$. The $\underline{S}$-sorted set $\mathsf{J} = (J^x, \mathbf{A}_2)$ is a prime $\underline{\Sigma}$-ideal, and $x \notin \mathsf{J}$. Now, suppose $x \in A_2$. Again by Lemma 1, there exists an ideal J^x in $\mathbf{A}_2$ such that $x \notin J^x$. We define the following set:

$$J_1 := \overleftarrow{s}(J^x) = \{x \mid s(x) \in J^x\}.$$

Notice that J_1 is an ideal for $\mathbf{A}_1$. Indeed, if $a, b \in J_1$ then $s(a) \oplus s(b) \in J^x$. By the monotonicity of s and axiom (S3), one obtains $s(a \oplus b) \leq s(a) \oplus s(b)$, and so $s(a \oplus b) \in J^x$. Thus $a \oplus b \in J_1$. Furthermore, let $a \in J_1$ and $b \leq a$. From the last inequality we obtain $s(b) \leq s(a)$. Therefore, $s(b) \in J^x$ and $b \in J_1$. The fact that J_1 is a prime ideal follows from the fact that $\mathbf{A}_1$ is an MV-chain and any ideal is prime in MV-chains. Moreover, $s(J_1) = s(\overleftarrow{s}(J^x)) \subseteq J^x$. Thus, $\mathsf{J} = (J_1, J^x)$ is the wanted prime $\underline{\Sigma}$-ideal.

It is strictly necessary that the first sort is an MV-chain, as the following example shows.

Example 1 Let $\mathbf{L}_n$ be the n-element MV-chain on $\{\frac{i}{n-1} \mid i \in \mathbb{N} \text{ and } i \leq n-1\}$. Consider the equational state $\mathsf{S} = (\mathbf{L}_3{}^2, \mathbf{L}_5)$, where s is defined as follows:

$$s(0,0) := 0 \qquad\qquad s(1/2,0) := s(0,1/2) = 1/4$$
$$s(1,0) := s(0,1) = s(1/2,1/2) = 1/2 \qquad s(1,1/2) := s(1/2,1) = 3/4$$
$$s(1,1) := 1.$$

The prime ideals of $\mathbf{L}_3{}^2$ are $\mathbf{L}_3{}^2$ itself, $P_1 := \{(x,0) \mid x \in \{0,1/2,1\}\}$ and $P_2 := \{(0,x) \mid x \in \{0,1/2,1\}\}$. Since $\mathbf{L}_5$ is simple, its prime ideals are $\{0\}$ and $\mathbf{L}_5$ itself. Since a $\underline{\Sigma}$-ideal $\mathsf{J} = (J_1, J_2)$ must have the property $s(J_1) \subseteq J_2$, the prime $\underline{\Sigma}$-ideals of S are $(\mathbf{L}_3{}^2, \mathbf{L}_5)$, $(P_1, \mathbf{L}_5)$, and $(P_2, \mathbf{L}_5)$. Hence, all prime $\underline{\Sigma}$-ideals contain the elements $\frac{1}{4}, \frac{1}{2}, \frac{3}{4}$ and 1 of $\mathbf{L}_5$.

Recall that if $f: \mathbf{A} \rightarrow \mathbf{B}$ is a homomorphism of MV-algebras, then $\ker f$ is defined as the set of elements of $\mathbf{A}$ that are sent into 0_B by f. Similarly, if $h = (h_1, h_2): \mathsf{A} \rightarrow \mathsf{B}$ is a homomorphism of equational states, we define $\mathsf{Ker}\, h := (\ker h_1, \ker h_2)$, where the latter are the kernels of the respective MV-homomorphisms. It is easy to prove that $\mathsf{Ker}\, h$ is a $\underline{\Sigma}$-ideal.

Lemma 5 *Let $h \colon A \to B$ a Σ-homomorphism. If h is surjective then $A/\operatorname{Ker} h$ is isomorphic to B. Moreover, for any Σ-ideal J there exists a Σ-homomorphism h' such that $\operatorname{Ker} h' = J$.*

Proof The first part of the claim is a consequence of the more general results in [8, Subsection 2.3]. For the second part, let J be any Σ-ideal and consider the homomorphism $q_J \colon S \to S/J$ that assigns to each a the equivalence class $[a]_J$. It is easy to see that $\operatorname{Ker} q_J = J$.

The proof of the following lemma is a straightforward consequence of its equivalent in the context of MV-algebras.

Lemma 6 *A Σ-homomorphism h is injective if and only if $\operatorname{Ker} h = (\{0\}, \{0\})$.*

Corollary 2 *Let S be an equational state and $\{J_i \mid i \in I\}$ a family of Σ-ideals of S; call q_i the canonical homomorphism from S into S/J_i. The homomorphism $q = (\prod_{i \in I} q_i) \colon S \to \prod_{i \in I} S/J_i$, is injective if and only if $\bigcap_{i \in I} J_i = (\{0\}, \{0\})$.*

Proof It is straightforward to prove that $\operatorname{Ker} q = \bigcap_{i \in I} \operatorname{Ker} q_i = \bigcap_{i \in I} J_i$. Hence, an application of Lemma 6 concludes the proof.

Remark 1 In contrast with the case of MV-algebras, not every equational state is subdirect product of equational state-chains. (The notion of subdirect product of many-sorted algebras is a straightforward generalisation of the same notion for one-sorted algebras.) Indeed, consider the equational state in the Example 1 and suppose that there exists a family $\{S_i\}_{i \in I}$ of equational state-chains such that S is subalgebra of $\prod_{i \in I} S_i$. Using Lemma 5, one can replace each S_i with S/J_i, where J_i is a Σ-ideal and $i \in I$. The ideals J_i are prime, because S/J_i are equational state-chains, and the homomorphism q of Corollary 2 is injective. Hence $\bigcap_{i \in I} J_i = (\{(0,0)\}, \{0\})$. But this contradicts the fact that prime Σ-ideals of $\underline{S}$ have the form (P, L_5) with P a prime ideal of $L_3{}^2$.

The subdirect representation by equational state-chains holds if we add a new hypothesis.

Lemma 7 *Any equational state $A = (A_1, A_2)$, where A_1 is an MV-chain, is a subdirect product of equational state-chains.*

Proof Let $\mathcal{J}$ denote the class of all prime Σ-ideals of A. Using Theorem 2, $\bigcap_{J \in \mathcal{J}} J = (\{0_A\}, \{0_B\})$. Therefore, the function q defined in Corollary 2 is injective. Finally, A/J are all equational state-chain because all J's are prime.

Example 2 In addition to Remark 1, it should be noted that the variety of equational states is not generated by its linearly ordered members. Indeed, there are equations that fail in some equational state but are valid in all linearly ordered ones, an example is

$$s(x \wedge y) = s(x) \wedge s(y). \tag{3}$$

It is readily seen that (3) fails in the equational state of Example 1. Let now $A = (\mathbf{A}_1, \mathbf{A}_2)$ be an equational state in which $\mathbf{A}_1$ is linearly ordered and consider any pair $a, b \in A_1$. Without loss of generality assume that $a \leq b$. It follows that $s(a \wedge b) = s(a)$ and $s(a) \wedge s(b) = s(a)$ because s preserves the order. Thus A satisfies (3) and the claim is proved.

We conclude the paper with some observations on simple and semisimple equational states.

Definition 11 A proper $\underline{\Sigma}$-ideal is *maximal* if does not exist another proper $\underline{\Sigma}$-ideal J' such that $\mathsf{J} \subset \mathsf{J}'$.

Proposition 1 *Let J be a $\underline{\Sigma}$-ideal of an equational state $(\mathbf{A}_1, \mathbf{A}_2)$. Then J is maximal if and only if $\mathsf{J} = (J_m, A_2)$, where J_m is a maximal ideal of $\mathbf{A}_1$.*

Proof Clearly, any $\underline{\Sigma}$-ideal of the form $\mathsf{J} = (J_m, A_2)$, with J_m a maximal ideal of $\mathbf{A}_1$, is maximal. For the other direction, suppose that $\mathsf{J} = (J_1, J_2)$ is maximal. Notice that $J_1 \neq A_1$, otherwise $s(1) = 1 \in J_2$ and hence $J_2 = A_2$, against the fact that J is proper. Also, J_1 is maximal in $\mathbf{A}_1$, otherwise J_1 would be properly contained in a proper ideal M and $\mathsf{J} \subset (M, J_2)$. Finally, $J_2 = A_2$, otherwise (J_1, J_2) would be strictly contained in (J_1, A_2), again against the maximality of J.

Definition 12 A nontrivial equational state is called:

– *simple* if the only $\underline{\Sigma}$-ideals are $(\{0\}, \{0\})$ and itself.
– *semisimple* if the intersection of all its maximal $\underline{\Sigma}$-ideals is $(\{0\}, \{0\})$.

Proposition 2 *An equational state is simple if and only if it is of the form $(\mathbf{A}, \{0\})$, where $\mathbf{A}$ is a simple MV-algebra.*

Proof If $(\mathbf{A}_1, \{0\})$ is an equational state with $\mathbf{A}_1$ simple, then it is clear that its only $\underline{\Sigma}$-ideals are $(\{0\}, \{0\})$ and $(A_1, \{0\})$, thus it is simple.

Vice versa, suppose $A = (\mathbf{A}_1, \mathbf{A}_2)$ is a simple equational state. Since (J, A_2) is a $\underline{\Sigma}$-ideal for any ideal J, the algebra in the second sort must be the trivial. Moreover, the algebra in the first sort must have only $\{0_A\}$ and itself as ideals. Thus $\mathbf{A}_1$ is a simple MV-algebra.

Proposition 3 *An equational state is semisimple if and only if it is of the form $(\mathbf{A}, \{0\})$, where $\mathbf{A}$ is a semisimple MV-algebra.*

Proof The direction from right to left is straightforward. Suppose that $S := (\mathbf{A}, \mathbf{B})$ is semisimple. By Proposition 1 every maximal $\underline{\Sigma}$-ideal is in the form $(J, \mathbf{B})$. So the intersection of all maximal ideals of S is equal to be $\mathbf{B}$ in the second sort. Therefore, the second algebra must be the trivial one. Moreover, the first algebra is such that the intersection of its maximal ideals is $\{0\}$. So, $\mathbf{A}$ is semisimple.

As a consequence of Propositions 2 and 3, simple and semisimple equational states have a trivial state operation, i.e. the function s sends the whole domain into 0. This is in contrast with the case of SMV-algebras, introduced in [4] and further studied in [2,3]. Indeed, there are examples of simple SMV-algebras with a non-trivial internal state.

Acknowledgement. The authors are indebted with Prof. Vincenzo Marra for suggesting the Example 2. This work was supported by the PRIN2017 "Theory and applications of resource sensitive logics". S. Lapenta was also funded by the POC Innovazione e Ricerca 2014-2020, project AIM1834448-1 and the Research Grant "Un approccio algebrico alla statistica per applicazioni industriali".

References

1. Cignoli, R.L.O., D'Ottaviano, I.M.L., Mundici, D.: Algebraic Foundations of Many-Valued Reasoning. Kluwer Academic Publishers, Alphen aan den Rijn (2000)
2. Di Nola, A., Dvurečenskij, A.: State-morphism MV-algebras. Ann. Pure Appl. Logic **161**(2), 161–173 (2009)
3. Dvurečenskij, A., Kowalski, T., Montagna, F.: State morphism MV-algebras. Int. J. Approximate Reasoning **52**(8), 1215–1228 (2011)
4. Flaminio, T., Montagna, F.: MV-algebras with internal states and probabilistic fuzzy logics. Int. J. Approximate Reasoning **50**(1), 138–152 (2009)
5. Goodearl, K.: Partially Ordered Abelian Groups with Interpolation. Mathematical Surveys and Monographs, vol. 20. American Mathematical Society, Providence (1986)
6. Kroupa, T., Marra, V.: The two-sorted algebraic theory of states, and the universal states of MV-algebras. J. Pure Appl. Algebra **225**, 106771 (2021)
7. Mundici, D.: Averaging the truth-value in Łukasiewicz logic. Stud. Logica. **55**(1), 113–127 (1995)
8. Tarlecki, A.: Some nuances of many-sorted universal algebra: a review. Bull. EATCS **104**, 89–111 (2011)

Maximal Theories of Product Logic

Valeria Giustarini[1] and Sara Ugolini[2]($^{(\boxtimes)}$) (iD)

[1] DIISM, Università di Siena, Siena, Italy
valeria.giustarini@student.unisi.it
[2] Artificial Intelligence Research institute (IIIA), CSIC, Bellaterra, Barcelona, Spain
sara@iiia.csic.es

Abstract. Product logic is one of the main fuzzy logics arising from a continuous t-norm, and its equivalent algebraic semantics is the variety of product algebras. In this contribution, we study maximal filters of product algebras, and their relation with product hoops. The latter constitute the variety of 0-free subreducts of product algebras. Given any product hoop, we construct a product algebra of which the product hoop is (isomorphic to) a maximal filter. This entails that product hoops coincide exactly with the maximal filters of product algebras, seen as residuated lattices. In this sense, we characterize the equational theory of maximal filters of product algebras.

Keywords: Product logic · Maximal filters · product hoops · cancellative hoops

1 Introduction

Whenever a logic $\mathcal{L}$ has a variety V as its equivalent algebraic semantics à la Blok-Pigozzi [6], the theories of the logic $\mathcal{L}$ correspond to the congruence filters of the free algebras of V. In the same flavor, maximally consistent theories correspond to maximal congruence filters of free algebras. This contribution is about the equational theory of the maximal filters in varieties of algebras related to fuzzy logics. More precisely, we are interested in one of the most relevant axiomatic extensions of Hájek Basic Logic $\mathcal{BL}$ [14], product logic. The latter has been introduced in [15], and it is the fuzzy logic associated to the product t-norm (the binary operation of product among real numbers in the real unit interval $[0,1]$). Basic Logic is the logic of continuous t-norms [10], and product logic is, together with Łukasiewicz logic and Gödel logic, one of the fundamental fuzzy logics in Hájek's framework. Indeed, Mostert-Shields' Theorem [16] shows that a t-norm is continuous if and only if it can be built from Łukasiewicz, Gödel and product t-norms by the construction of ordinal sum.

Basic Logic and its extensions are all algebraizable, and their equivalent algebraic semantics are varieties of BL-algebras. The latter can be seen as particular bounded commutative residuated lattices, in the signature $(\cdot, \rightarrow, \wedge, \vee, 0, 1)$. Congruence filters of BL-algebras (called just *filters* in what follows) are subsets of the domain of the algebras, closed under product and upwards (with respect to the lattice order).

S. Massanet et al. (Eds.): EUSFLAT 2023/AGOP 2023, LNCS 14069, pp. 505–517, 2023.
https://doi.org/10.1007/978-3-031-39965-7_42

In this work, we will characterize the equational theory of the maximal filters of product algebras, seen as residuated lattices. It is indeed easy to see that congruence filters are actually substructures in the 0-free signature of commutative residuated lattices $(\cdot, \rightarrow, \wedge, \vee, 1)$. As a consequence, all filters (and thus in particular maximal filters) of any variety V of BL-algebras belong, in this sense, to the variety V_0 of 0-free subreducts of algebras in V.

It is then natural to ask whether the converse is true, that is, is any algebra in V_0 isomorphic to a maximal filter of some algebra in V? Notice that in general, a 0-free subreduct of a bounded commutative residuated lattice **A** is not necessarily closed upwards, thus it might not be a filter of **A**. However, the question can be answered positively if V is the variety of MV-algebras, the equivalent algebraic semantics of infinite-valued Łukasiewicz logic. In [1], the authors indeed start from a Wajsberg hoop (i.e., a 0-free subreduct of some MV-algebra), and construct an MV-algebra of which the Wajsberg hoop is a maximal filter. The same is true if V is the variety of Gödel algebras, the equivalent algebraic semantics of Gödel logic. Subreducts of Gödel algebras are called Gödel hoops, and if one adds a bottom element to any Gödel hoop **G** (extending all operations in the obvious way), this generates a Gödel algebra of which the Gödel hoop is the only maximal filter, as we will see in detail in the Preliminaries section.

We will show the analogous result for the third most relevant fuzzy logic belonging to Hájek's framework, i.e., product logic. In particular, taken any product hoop **S** (that is, a 0-free subreduct of a product algebra), we construct a product algebra of which **S** is (isomorphic to) a maximal filter.

2   Preliminaries

In this section we introduce the algebraic structures that will be object of our study. For all the unexplained notions of universal algebra we refer to [9], and for the theory of residuated lattices to [13]. A *bounded commutative integral residuated lattice* (or BCIRL) is an algebra $\mathbf{A} = (A, \cdot, \rightarrow, \wedge, \vee, 0, 1)$ of type $(2, 2, 2, 2, 0, 0)$ such that:

1. $(A, \cdot, 1)$ is a commutative monoid;
2. $(A, \wedge, \vee, 0, 1)$ is a bounded lattice with $0 \leq x \leq 1$ for all $x \in A$;
3. the residuation law holds: $x \cdot y \leq z$ iff $y \leq x \rightarrow z$.

We will often write xy for $x \cdot y$, and x^n for $x \cdot \ldots \cdot x$ (n times). Moreover, we will consider a negation operator defined as $\neg x = x \rightarrow 0$.
A *BL-algebra* is a BCIRL that further satisfies *divisibility*:

$$x \wedge y = x(x \rightarrow y) \tag{div}$$

and *prelinearity*:

$$(x \rightarrow y) \vee (y \rightarrow x) = 1. \tag{prel}$$

Satisfying the divisibility equation is equivalent to saying that the order $\leq$ induced by the lattice operations is the inverse divisibility ordering, that is,

$x \leq y$ if and only if there exists z such that $x = yz$. The prelinearity equation instead characterizes BCIRLs generated by *chains*, that is, totally ordered algebras (see [13]).

In BL-algebras, the lattice operations can actually be rewritten in terms of the monoidal operation and the implication, as:

$$x \wedge y = x(x \to y),$$
$$x \vee y = ((x \to y) \to y) \wedge ((y \to x) \to x).$$

Thus we may consider BL-algebras in the language of *bounded hoops* (see [2,7] for the theory of hoops), that is, as algebras in the signature $(\cdot, \to, 0, 1)$.

MV-algebras, the equivalent algebraic semantics of infinite-valued Łukasiewicz logic, are BL-algebras satisfying *involutivity*:

$$\neg\neg x = x; \tag{1}$$

Gödel algebras, the equivalent algebraic semantics of Gödel logic, are BL-algebras satisfying *idempotency*:

$$x^2 = x; \tag{2}$$

product algebras, the equivalent algebraic semantics of product logic, are BL-algebras satisfying the following identity:

$$\neg x \vee ((x \to (x \cdot y)) \to y) = 1. \tag{3}$$

Given a variety of BL-algebras, the class of its 0-free subreducts is a variety of *basic hoops* [2]. 0-free subreducts of MV-algebras, Gödel algebras, and product algebras constitute, respectively, the varieties of Wajsberg, Gödel, and product hoops.

With respect to their structure theory, all these algebras are very well behaved. In particular, congruences are totally determined by their 1-blocks (i.e., the set of elements in relation with 1). If **A** is a BL-algebra (or a basic hoop), the 1-block of a congruence of **A** is called a *congruence filter* (or *filter* for short). Filters corresponds to the *deductive filters* induced by the corresponding logic, which, in the algebra on formulas, are exactly deductively closed theories. It can be shown that a filter of **A** is a nonempty subset of **A** closed under multiplication and upwards. It is then easy to prove that a filter F of a BL-algebra (or a basic hoop) **A**, endowed with the inherited operations of **A**, is itself a basic hoop **F**.

Filters form an algebraic lattice isomorphic with the congruence lattice of **A** and if $X \subseteq A$ then the filter generated by X is

$$\mathrm{Fil}_{\mathbf{A}}(X) = \{a \in A : x_1 \cdot \ldots \cdot x_n \leq a, \text{ for some } n \in \mathbb{N} \text{ and } x_1, \ldots, x_n \in X\}.$$

The isomorphism between the filter lattice and the congruence lattice is given by the maps:

$$\theta \longmapsto 1/\theta$$
$$F \longmapsto \theta_F = \{(a, b) : a \to b, \ b \to a \in F\},$$

where θ is a congruence and F a filter.

We call a filter F *maximal* if it is not contained in any proper filter. Moreover, we call *radical* of an algebra $\mathbf{A}$ the intersection of its maximal filters, and we denote it as $\mathrm{Rad}(\mathbf{A})$. Finally, given a BL-algebra $\mathbf{A}$, another subset of its domain that will be relevant in what follows is the *Boolean skeleton* of $\mathbf{A}$, $\mathcal{B}(\mathbf{A})$. $\mathcal{B}(\mathbf{A})$ is the largest Boolean subalgebra of $\mathbf{A}$, and its domain is the set of its complemented elements, i.e., elements $x \in A$ such that $x \wedge \neg x = 0$, $x \vee \neg x = 1$.

2.1 Product Algebras and Product Triples

Product algebras are a variety generated by chains, since they satisfy the prelinearity equation. Product chains can be easily constructed starting with totally ordered *cancellative hoops*. The latter are the variety of basic hoops where the monoidal operation is cancellative in the usual sense. Product chains can be obtained by cancellative hoops with the following construction.

Consider a CIRL $\mathbf{A}$, that is, the 0-free subreduct of some BCIRL. We define its *lifting* to be the algebra $\mathbf{2} \oplus \mathbf{A}$, with domain $A \cup \{0\}$, and the operations extending the ones of $\mathbf{A}$ in the obvious way: for $x \in A$, $x0 = 0x = 0$, $x \rightarrow 0 = 0$, $0 \rightarrow x = 1$. See Fig. 1 for a pictorial intuition.

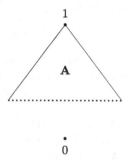

Fig. 1. The algebra $\mathbf{2} \oplus \mathbf{A}$, given any CIRL $\mathbf{A}$.

Then, product chains are all the algebras of the form $\mathbf{2} \oplus \mathbf{C}$, for $\mathbf{C}$ a totally ordered cancellative hoop [11]. Product chains are exactly the finitely subdirectly irreducible product algebras. Subdirectly irreducible product algebras are then the totally ordered algebras of the kind $\mathbf{2} \oplus \mathbf{C}$ with $\mathbf{C}$ a subdirectly irreducible cancellative hoop.

This decomposition yields a decomposition of the elements of a product algebra in a *Boolean* and a *cancellative* component, as shown in [17] (and in higher generality in [5]).

Lemma 1 [5,17]. *Let $\mathbf{P}$ be a product algebra. Then every element $x \in \mathbf{P}$ can be written as $x = \neg\neg x \cdot (x \vee \neg x)$, where $\neg\neg x \in \mathcal{B}(\mathbf{P})$ and $x \vee \neg x \in \mathrm{Rad}(\mathbf{P})$.*

Interestingly, both elements $\neg\neg x$ and $x \vee \neg x$ can be written in the 0-free language.

Lemma 2. *Let P be a product algebra. Then $\neg\neg x = (x \to x^2) \to x$ and $x \vee \neg x = x \to x^2$.*

Proof. The two identities can be easily shown to hold in chains. Indeed, let $x \in 2 \oplus C$, with C totally ordered. Suppose first $x \in C$. Thus $\neg\neg x = 1$, and $(x \to x^2) \to x = x \to x = 1$. Similarly, $x \vee \neg x = x = x \to x^2$. Suppose now $x = 0$, then $\neg\neg 0 = 0 = (0 \to 0^2) \to 0$ and $0 \vee \neg 0 = 1 = 0 \to 0^2$.

Now, if an equation holds in all the subdirectly irreducible algebras, it holds in every algebra of the variety, thus the claim follows.   □

Given the previous lemma, for any product algebra P we define for each $x \in P$:

$$b(x) = (x \to x^2) \to x, \qquad c(x) = x \to x^2. \tag{4}$$

Therefore:

Proposition 1. *Let P be a product algebra. For each $x \in P$, $x = b(x) \cdot c(x)$, or equivalently $x = b(x) \wedge c(x)$.*

The representation of the elements seems to suggest that a product algebra is identified by its Boolean skeleton and the set of its cancellative elements, but it turns out that they are not enough to identify a unique product algebra (see [17]). The algebraic category of product algebras has been indeed shown in [17] to be equivalent to a category whose objects are triples of the kind $(\mathbf{B}, \mathbf{C}, \vee_e)$, such that $\mathbf{B}$ is a Boolean algebra, $\mathbf{C}$ is a cancellative hoop such that $B \cap C = \{1\}$, and $\vee_e$ is a binary operation $\vee_e : \mathbf{B} \times \mathbf{C} \to \mathbf{C}$ intuitively representing the join operation between Boolean and cancellative elements. More precisely, for $b \in B$ and $c \in C$, let

$$h_b(x) = b \vee_e x; \qquad k_c(x) = x \vee_e c. \tag{5}$$

Then we have the following definition.

Definition 1. *A map $\vee_e : B \times C \to C$ is an external join between $\mathbf{B}$ and $\mathbf{C}$ if it satisfies the following:*

(V1) For fixed $b \in B$ and $c \in C$, h_b is an endomorphism of $\mathbf{C}$ and k_c is a lattice homomorphism from (the lattice reduct of) $\mathbf{B}$ into (the lattice reduct of) $\mathbf{C}$.
(V2) h_0 is the identity on $\mathbf{C}$, and h_1 is constantly equal to 1.
(V3) For all $b, b' \in B$ and for all $c, c' \in C$, $h_b(c) \vee h_{b'}(c') = h_{b \vee b'}(c \vee c') = h_b(h_{b'}(c \vee c'))$.
(V4) For all $b \in B$ and for all $c, c' \in C$, $(b \vee_e c) \cdot c' = (\neg b \vee_e c') \wedge (b \vee_e (c \cdot c'))$.

Given any such a triple $(\mathbf{B}, \mathbf{C}, \vee_e)$, following [17], one can obtain a product algebra of which $\mathbf{B}$ is a Boolean skeleton, and $\mathbf{C}$ is the radical. First, consider the direct product $B \times C$, and the following equivalence relation $\sim$ on $B \times C$: given $(b, c), (b', c') \in B \times C$, let

$$(b, c) \sim (b', c') \text{ if and only if } b = b' \text{ and } \neg b \vee_e c = \neg b \vee_e c'. \tag{6}$$

Let us denote the elements of an equivalence class $(b, c)/\sim$ by $[b, c]$. Then $\mathbf{B} \otimes_{\vee_e} \mathbf{C}$ is the product algebra with domain $(B \times C/\sim)$, and operations denoted by $(\otimes, \Rightarrow, \sqcap, \sqcup, [0, 1], [1, 1])$ and defined as follows:

$$[b, c] \otimes [b', c'] = [b \wedge b', c \cdot c']$$
$$[b, c] \sqcap [b', c'] = [b \wedge b', c \wedge c']$$
$$[b, c] \sqcup [b', c'] = [b \vee b', ((\neg b \vee \neg b') \vee_e (c \vee c')) \wedge ((b \vee \neg b') \vee_e c') \wedge ((\neg b \vee b') \vee_e c)]$$
$$[b, c] \Rightarrow [b', c'] = [b \to b', \neg b \vee_e (c \to c')].$$

In [17] it is shown in particular that every product algebra $\mathbf{A}$ is isomorphic to the one obtained by the triple $(\mathcal{B}(\mathbf{A}), \mathrm{Rad}(\mathbf{A}), \vee)$, where $\vee$ is the join of $\mathbf{A}$.

We observe that, given any Boolean algebra $\mathbf{B}$, and any cancellative hoop $\mathbf{C}$, it is always possible to define an external join between them. Let indeed M be a maximal filter of $\mathbf{B}$, we define $\vee_M : B \times C \to C$ as follows:

$$b \vee_M c = \begin{cases} 1 & \text{if } b \in M, \\ c & \text{otherwise.} \end{cases}$$

Lemma 3. *Let $\mathbf{B}$ be a Boolean algebra, $\mathbf{C}$ a cancellative hoop, with $B \cap C = \{1\}$. Then $\vee_M : B \times C \to C$ defined above is an external join, and $(\mathbf{B}, \mathbf{C}, \vee_M)$ is a product triple.*

Proof. Given $b \in B, c \in C$, let $h_b(x) = b \vee_M x$ and $k_c(x) = x \vee_M c$. We only need to show the properties $(V1)$–$(V4)$ in Definition 1.

For $(V1)$, fix an element $b \in B$, then it is easy to see that h_b is an endomorphism of $\mathbf{C}$. Indeed, either $b \in M$, and then h_b is the map constantly equal to 1, or $b \notin M$, and then h_b is the identity map. Let us now fix some $c \in C$, we need to prove that k_c is a lattice homomorphism from the lattice reduct of $\mathbf{B}$ to the lattice reduct of $\mathbf{C}$. That is, we need to show that $k_c(x \wedge y) = k_c(x) \wedge k_c(y)$ and $k_c(x \vee y) = k_c(x) \vee k_c(y)$. We show the case of $\wedge$. If both x, y are in M, then $x \wedge y \in M$ as well, thus $k_c(x \wedge y) = 1 = k_c(x) \wedge k_c(y)$. Otherwise, if at least one element among x and y is not in M, $x \wedge y$ is not in M (since filters are closed upwards). Thus $k_c(x \wedge y) = c = k_c(x) \wedge k_c(y)$. The case of $\vee$ can be shown analogously.

For (V2), it follows from the definition that h_0 is exactly the identity on $\mathbf{C}$, and h_1 is constantly equal to 1.

We now show (V3), that is, for all $b, b' \in B$ and $c, c' \in C$:

$$h_b(c) \vee h_{b'}(c') = h_{b \vee b'}(c \vee c') = h_b(h_{b'}(c \vee c')).$$

If one among b, b' is in M, then clearly $h_b(c) \vee h_{b'}(c') = h_{b \vee b'}(c \vee c') = h_b(h_{b'}(c \vee c')) = 1$. If instead both $b, b' \notin M$, then the three terms are all $c \vee c'$, since complement of a maximal Boolean filter is closed under join.

We are left to prove (V4), that is, for all $b \in B$ and $c, c' \in C$,

$$(b \vee_M c) \cdot c' = (\neg b \vee_M c') \wedge (b \vee_M (c \cdot c')).$$

If $b \in M$, then $(b \vee_M c) \cdot c' = 1 \cdot c'$ and $(\neg b \vee_M c') \wedge (b \vee_M (c \cdot c')) = c' \wedge 1 = c'$, and the equality holds. If $b \notin M$, then $(b \vee_M c) \cdot c' = c \cdot c'$ and $(\neg b \vee_M c') \wedge (b \vee_M (c \cdot c')) = 1 \wedge c \cdot c' = c \cdot c'$. This completes the proof. $\qquad\square$

2.2   Maximal Filters of Boolean, MV, and Gödel Algebras

We observe that, in general, a 0-free subreduct $\mathbf{A}$ of a BCIRL $\mathbf{B}$ is not necessarily closed upwards, thus it might not be a filter of $\mathbf{A}$. Even more, $\mathbf{A}$ is not necessarily a filter of the subalgebra $\mathbf{S_A}$ of $\mathbf{B}$ generated by $\mathbf{A}$. Indeed, for instance, given any element $x \in A$, its double negation will be in $\mathbf{S_A}$ and in any filter containing x, since $x \leq \neg\neg x$, but $\neg\neg x$ does not have to belong to $\mathbf{A}$ (see [3, Example 2.6] for a specific example).

In this section we will see some known constructions that start from a subreduct $\mathbf{A}$ of an algebra $\mathbf{B}$ in a variety V of BCIRLs, and obtain a new algebra $\mathbf{C}$ in V of which $\mathbf{A}$ is isomorphic to a maximal filter. In particular, we will see this for V being the variety of MV, Boolean, and Gödel algebras. It will also become apparent that these constructions cannot be used to show the analogous result for the case of product algebras.

Let us start from MV-algebras. In [1], the authors show that, given any Wajsberg hoop $\mathbf{A}$, one can construct an MV-algebra of which $\mathbf{A}$ is (isomorphic to) a maximal filter. We recall the construction since we will use it in what follows. Let $\mathbf{A}$ be a Wajsberg hoop, then its *MV-closure* is the algebra

$$\mathbf{MV(A)} = (A \times \{0, 1\}, \cdot_{mv}, \rightarrow_{mv}, 0_{mv}, 1_{mv})$$

where

$$0_{mv} = (1, 0), \qquad 1_{mv} = (1, 1)$$

and, letting $a \oplus b = (a \rightarrow ab) \rightarrow b$ for $a, b \in A$,

$$(a, i) \cdot_{mv} (b, j) \begin{cases} (a \cdot b, 1) \text{ if } i = j = 1 \\ (a \rightarrow b, 0) \text{ if } i = 1 \text{ and } j = 0 \\ (b \rightarrow a, 0) \text{ if } i = 0 \text{ and } j = 1 \\ (a \oplus b, 0) \text{ if } i = j = 0 \end{cases}$$

$$(a, i) \rightarrow_{mv} (b, j) \begin{cases} (a \rightarrow b, 1) \text{ if } i = j = 1 \\ (a \cdot b, 0) \text{ if } i = 1 \text{ and } j = 0 \\ (a \oplus b, 1) \text{ if } i = 0 \text{ and } j = 1 \\ (b \rightarrow a, 1) \text{ if } i = j = 0. \end{cases}$$

Negation is then defined as: $\neg_{mv}(x, i) = (x, 1 - i)$. We notice that $\mathbf{MV(A)}$ is the disjoint union of the sets $\{(a, 1) : a \in A\}$ and $\{\neg_{mv}(a, 1) : a \in A\}$.

We observe that the MV-closure construction is also (independently) used in [4] in order to obtain a free MV-algebra from a free Wajsberg hoop.

Now, Boolean algebras can be seen as particular MV-algebras such that $x \vee \neg x = 1$ holds. Their 0-free subreducts constitute the variety of *generalized Boolean algebras*, and they have been studied in [12]. Generalized Boolean algebras can be characterized as idempotent Wajsberg hoops, and every generalized Boolean algebra $\mathbf{G}$ is a maximal filter of some Boolean algebra $\mathbf{B}$. In particular, let us show that to construct such a Boolean algebra, one can use the MV-closure construction.

Proposition 2. *Let $\mathbf{A}$ be a generalized Boolean algebra, then its MV-closure $\mathbf{MV}(\mathbf{A})$ is a Boolean algebra.*

Proof. Let $\mathbf{A}$ be a generalized Boolean algebra, that is, an idempotent Wajsberg hoop. We can then apply the MV-closure construction recalled above and obtain an MV-algebra. Since Boolean algebras can be characterized as idempotent MV-algebras, it suffices to check that $\cdot_{mv}$ is idempotent. By definition,

$$(x,1) \cdot (x,1) = (x^2, 1) = (x,1),$$

and

$$(x,0) \cdot (x,0) = ((x \to x^2) \to x, 0) = ((x \to x) \to x, 0) = (x,0).$$

Therefore, $\mathbf{MV}(\mathbf{A})$ is a Boolean algebra. □

We observe that the MV-closure construction cannot be used (as is) in order to construct a product algebra from a product hoop, nor a Gödel algebra from a Gödel hoop, since it generates an involutive structure, and the only involutive Gödel and product algebras are Boolean algebras.

However, given a Gödel hoop $\mathbf{G}$, the lifting $\mathbf{2} \oplus \mathbf{G}$ is a Gödel algebra of which $\mathbf{G}$ is the unique maximal filter, and actually every directly indecomposable Gödel algebra has this shape (see for instance [5]).

Finally, we observe that the lifting construction cannot be used for product algebras and MV-algebras. Indeed, in general, given $\mathbf{H}$ a product hoop (or a Wajsberg hoop), $\mathbf{2} \oplus \mathbf{H}$ is not necessarily a product algebra (or an MV-algebra). Indeed, we have the following easy counterexample.

Example 1. Consider $\mathbf{2}_0$ to be the 0-free reduct of the $\mathbf{2}$ element Boolean algebra. Then $\mathbf{2}_0$ is a generalized Boolean algebra that is both a product hoop and a Wajsberg hoop. Now, $\mathbf{2} \oplus \mathbf{2}_0$ is the three-element Gödel chain, that is not a product algebra nor an MV-algebra.

3   Constructing a Product Algebra from a Product Hoop

In this section, given a product hoop $\mathbf{S}$, we construct a product algebra $\mathbf{P}(\mathbf{S})$ such that $\mathbf{S}$ is (isomorphic to) a maximal filter of $\mathbf{P}(\mathbf{S})$.

Notice that, given a product hoop $\mathbf{S}$, we have that $\mathbf{S}$ is the 0-free subreduct of some product algebra $\mathbf{A}$. Thus, the elements in $\mathbf{S}$ can be represented as in Proposition 1, $x = b(x) \wedge c(x)$. We therefore consider the following sets:

$$\mathbf{C}(\mathbf{S}) = \{c(x) : x \in S\}, \qquad \mathbf{G}(\mathbf{S}) = \{b(x) : x \in S\}. \tag{7}$$

Lemma 4. *Let S be a product hoop, and consider $C(S)$ and $G(S)$ defined as above. Then $C(S)$ is a cancellative hoop and $G(S)$ is a generalized Boolean algebra.*

Proof. We assume that S is a subreduct of a product algebra A.

First we show that $C(S)$ is a cancellative hoop. Given any $x \in S$, since $c(x) = x \to x^2$ and S is closed under the hoop operations, we get that $c(x)$ is itself an element of S. It follows that $C(S)$ is closed under all the hoop operations as well. Since $C(S)$ is a subset of the radical of A, which is a cancellative hoop, it follows that $C(S)$ is a cancellative hoop itself.

We now consider $G(S)$, and proceed with the analogous reasoning as above. Given any $x \in S$, $b(x) = (x \to x^2) \to x \in S$, thus $G(S)$ is closed under the hoop operations and is a subset of the Boolean skeleton of A, that is a Boolean algebra. Therefore, $G(S)$ is the subreduct of a Boolean algebra, that is, a generalized Boolean algebra. □

Given a product hoop S, let then $B(S) = MV(G(S))$, the MV-closure of $G(S)$. By Proposition 2, $B(S)$ is a Boolean algebra of which $G(S)$ is (isomorphic to) a maximal filter. We can then define a binary operation $\vee_S : B(S) \times C(S) \to C(S)$ as follows:

$$b \vee_S c = \begin{cases} 1 & \text{if } b \in G(S), \\ c & \text{otherwise.} \end{cases}$$

By Lemma 3, we obtain the following.

Proposition 3. *Let S be a product hoop, and $B(S)$, $C(S)$, $\vee_S$ be defined as above. Then $(B(S), C(S), \vee_S)$ is a product triple.*

Thus, we can consider the product algebra associated to the product triple $(B(S), C(S), \vee_S)$, and define:

$$P(S) = B(S) \otimes_{\vee_S} C(S). \qquad (8)$$

We are now ready to show that, given a product hoop S, we can construct a product algebra of which S is a maximal filter.

Theorem 1. *Let S be a product hoop. Then S is isomorphic to a maximal filter of $P(S)$.*

Proof. Let $x \in S$, then $x = b(x) \wedge c(x)$. Let $f : S \to P(S)$ be defined by $f(x) = [b(x), c(x)]$. It can be directly checked that f is a hoop isomorphism from S to the subset of $P(S)$ given by the elements $S(S) = \{[b, c] : b \in G(S), c \in C(S)\}$. For the reader interested in the details, since we can see S as a subreduct of a product algebra A, the fact that f is a hoop homomorphism is a consequence of [17, Theorem 6.1]. In particular from the part (b) of the proof of [17, Theorem 6.1], we get exactly that f is a hoop isomorphism from S to the elements in $S(S)$.

We now show that $\mathbf{S(S)}$ is a filter of $\mathbf{P(S)}$. Since $\mathbf{S(S)}$ is a product hoop (because $\mathbf{S}$ is), it is closed under product and it contains $[1,1]$. Suppose now $[b(x), c(x)] \in \mathbf{S(S)}$ and $[b(x), c(x)] \leq [b(y), c(y)]$, or equivalently,

$$[b(x), c(x)] \Rightarrow [b(y), c(y)] = [1,1].$$

We want to show that $[b(y), c(y)] \in \mathbf{S(S)}$. By definition of the operations,

$$[b(x), c(x)] \Rightarrow [b(y), c(y)] = [b(x) \to b(y), \neg b(x) \vee_S (c(x) \to c(y))].$$

Thus, by the definition of the equivalence relation $\sim$ in (6), $b(x) \to b(y) = 1$, or equivalently, $b(x) \leq b(y)$. Since $\mathbf{G(S)}$ is a filter of $\mathbf{B(S)}$, $b(y) \in \mathbf{G(S)}$. Moreover, again by the definition of $\sim$, we get that:

$$\neg b(x) \vee_S (c(x) \to c(y)) = 1,$$

and since $\neg b(x)$ is not in $\mathbf{G(S)}$ (given that $b(x)$ is), we get that $c(x) \to c(y) = 1$, or equivalently $c(x) \leq c(y)$. Since $\mathbf{C(S)}$ is the radical of $\mathbf{P(S)}$, it is a filter, and thus $c(y) \in \mathbf{C(S)}$. Therefore, $[b(y), c(y)] \in \mathbf{S(S)}$, and $\mathbf{S(S)}$ is a filter of $\mathbf{P(S)}$.

Now it is left to show that $\mathbf{S(S)}$ is a maximal filter, that is, it is not contained in any proper filter. Suppose that $[b(x), c(x)] \in \mathbf{P(S)}, [b(x), c(x)] \notin \mathbf{S(S)}$. Then necessarily $b(x) \notin \mathbf{G(S)}$, meaning that $\neg b(x) \in \mathbf{G(S)}$. Thus if we consider a filter F of $\mathbf{P(S)}$ which includes both $\mathbf{S(S)}$ and $[b(x), c(x)]$, the following product is also in F:

$$[b(x), c(x)] \cdot [\neg b(x), c(x)] = [b(x) \wedge \neg b(x), (c(x))^2] = [0, (c(x))^2] = [0,1].$$

That is, F is not proper since $[0,1]$ is the bottom element. We conclude that $\mathbf{S(S)}$ is a maximal filter of $\mathbf{P(S)}$, and the proof is complete. $\qquad\square$

Therefore:

Corollary 1. *Product hoops coincide with the class of maximal filters of product algebras, seen as residuated lattices with the restricted operations.*

Let us show the following particular instance of our construction.

Example 2. Let $\mathbf{S}$ be a cancellative hoop. Then $\mathbf{P(S)} \cong \mathbf{2} \oplus \mathbf{S}$. Indeed, if $\mathbf{S}$ is a cancellative hoop, $\mathbf{G(S)} = \{1\}$. As a consequence, $\mathbf{B(S)} \cong \mathbf{2}$. Moreover, $\mathbf{C(S)} = \mathbf{S}$. Then, we can see the elements of $\mathbf{P(S)}$ as either of the form $[1, c]$ or $[0, c]$, for $c \in \mathbf{S}$. By the equivalence relation $\sim$ in (6), all of the elements of the form $(0, c)$ belong to the same equivalence class, while $(1, c) \sim (1, c')$ if and only if $c = c'$. Thus, we can see the domain of $\mathbf{P(S)}$ as $\{[1, s] : s \in S\} \cup \{[0, 1]\}$. It follows from the definition of the operations that $\mathbf{P(S)}$ is isomorphic to $\mathbf{2} \oplus \mathbf{S}$.

Example 3. Let $\mathbf{S}$ be the 0-free reduct of a product algebra $\mathbf{P} = \mathbf{2} \oplus \mathbf{C}$, where $\mathbf{C}$ is a cancellative hoop. Then, $\mathbf{P(S)} \cong \mathbf{2} \times (\mathbf{2} \oplus \mathbf{C})$. Indeed, $\mathbf{G(S)} = \mathbf{2}$, which means that $\mathbf{B(S)} \cong \mathbf{4}$, the Boolean algebra with 4 elements. Moreover, $\mathbf{C(S)} = \mathbf{C}$. As a result, the elements of $\mathbf{P(S)}$ are of the form $[1, c], [0, c], [\neg 0, c]$ or $[\neg 1, c]$, for

$c \in C$. By the equivalence relation $\sim$ in (6), all the elements of the form $(\neg 0, c)$ belong to the same equivalence class, as well as the ones of the form $(\neg 1, c)$. On the other hand, $(1, c) \sim (1, c')$ if and only if $c = c'$, and $(0, c) \sim (0, c')$ if and only if $c = c'$. Thus, the domain of $\mathbf{P}(\mathbf{S})$ is given by: $\{[1, c] : c \in C\} \cup \{[0, c] : c \in C\} \cup \{[\neg 0, 1]\} \cup \{[\neg 1, 1]\}$. It can then be directly checked that $\mathbf{P}(\mathbf{S})$ is isomorphic $\mathbf{2} \times (\mathbf{2} \oplus \mathbf{C})$. If $\mathbf{C}$ is a chain, the Hasse diagram of $\mathbf{P}(\mathbf{S})$ is as in Fig. 2.

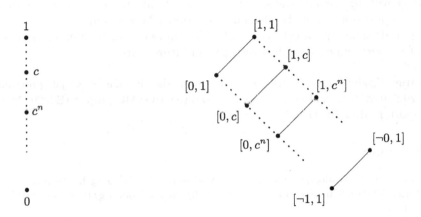

Fig. 2. On the left, $\mathbf{2} \oplus \mathbf{C}$, given a cancellative hoop chain $\mathbf{C}$. On the right, $\mathbf{P}(\mathbf{2} \oplus \mathbf{C})$.

Remark 1. An interesting observation stems from the last example. Given any BCIRL $\mathbf{A}$ in a variety V, the direct product $\mathbf{2} \times \mathbf{A}$ is in V. Moreover, the 0-free reduct of $\mathbf{A}$ is isomorphic to the maximal filter of $\mathbf{2} \times \mathbf{A}$ given by the elements $\{(1, a) : a \in A\}$. Thus, for any variety of BCIRLs V, and $\mathbf{A} \in \mathsf{V}$, the 0-free reduct of $\mathbf{A}$ belongs to the class of maximal filters. Notice that this does not mean that any 0-free *subreduct* of $\mathbf{A}$ does.

4   Conclusions

We have shown that, given a product hoop $\mathbf{S}$, we can construct a product algebra $\mathbf{P}$ such that $\mathbf{S}$ is isomorphic to a maximal filter of $\mathbf{P}$. Since every maximal filter can be seen as a product hoop, in this sense, we have characterized the equational theory of maximal filters of product algebras.

At present, we do not know if this property is shared by bounded residuated lattices in general. That is, given a variety V of BL-algebras (or, more in general, BCIRLs), does the variety V_0 of 0-free subreducts of algebras in V coincide with the class of maximal filters of algebras in V, seen as residuated lattices? We have seen that this holds for the equivalent algebraic semantics of the three most relevant extensions of Hájek Basic Logic.

In future work we plan to extend and generalize our approach to a larger class of residuated structures. In particular, we observe that the triple construction in

[17], that we have used in this work, has been extended and generalized in [5] and [8] to encompass a large class of residuated structures. In particular, this class includes several important varieties related to fuzzy logics and other nonclassical logics, among which: the variety generated by perfect MV-algebras, nilpotent minimum algebras, Stonean Heyting algebras, regular Nelson residuated lattices. We plan to study to what extent our construction can be extended to this wider setting.

Moreover, the representation of the elements of product algebras naturally gives a representation of the elements of product hoops, hinting at a triple-like representation for such algebras as well. We believe this to be another interesting line of research which we will investigate in future work.

Funding. Ugolini acknowledges support from the Ramón y Cajal programme (RyC2021-032670-I), and partial support from the MOSAIC project (H2020- MSCA-RISE-2020 Project 101007627).

References

1. Abad, M., Castaño, D., Varela, J.: MV-closures of Wajsberg hoops and applications. Algebra Univers. **64**, 213–230 (2010). https://doi.org/10.1007/s00012-010-0101-4
2. Aglianò, P., Ferreirim, I.M.A., Montagna, F.: Basic hoops: an algebraic study of continuous t-norms. Stud. Logica. **87**(1), 73–98 (2007). https://doi.org/10.1007/s11225-007-9078-1
3. Aglianò, P., Ugolini, S.: Projectivity and unification in substructural logics of generalized rotations. Int. J. Approximate Reasoning **153**, 172–192 (2023)
4. Aguzzoli, S., Bova, S.: The free n-generated BL-algebra. Ann. Pure Appl. Log. **161**, 1144–1170 (2010)
5. Aguzzoli, S., Flaminio, T., Ugolini, S.: Equivalences between subcategories of MTL-algebras via Boolean algebras and prelinear semihoops. J. Log. Comput. **27**(8), 2525–2549 (2017)
6. Blok, W.J., Pigozzi, D.: Algebrizable Logics, vol. 396. Memoirs of the American Mathematical Society, Providence (1989)
7. Blok, W.J., Ferreirim, I.M.A.: On the structure of hoops. Algebra Univers. **43**, 233–257 (2000). https://doi.org/10.1007/s000120050156
8. Busaniche, M., Marcos, M., Ugolini, S.: Representation by triples of algebras with an MV-retract. Fuzzy Sets Syst. **369**, 82–102 (2019)
9. Burris, S., Sankappanavar, H.P.: A Course in Universal Algebra. Springer, New York (1981)
10. Cignoli, R., Esteva, F., Godo, L., Torrens, A.: Basic Fuzzy Logic is the logic of continuous t-norms and their residua. Soft. Comput. **4**, 106–112 (2000). https://doi.org/10.1007/s005000000044
11. Cignoli, R., Torrens, A.: An algebraic analysis of product logic. Multiple-Valued Log. **5**, 45–65 (2000)
12. Galatos, N.: Minimal varieties of residuated lattices. Algebra Univers. **52**(2), 215–239 (2005). https://doi.org/10.1007/s00012-004-1870-4
13. Galatos, N., Jipsen, P., Kowalski, T., Ono, H.: Residuated Lattices: An Algebraic Glimpse at Substructural Logics. Studies in Logics and the Foundations of Mathematics, vol. 151. Elsevier, Amsterdam (2007)

14. Hájek, P.: Metamathematics of fuzzy logic. Trends in Logic-Studia Logica Library (4), Kluwer Academic Publisher, Dordrecht, Boston, London (1998)
15. Hájek, P., Godo, L., Esteva, F.: A complete many-valued logic with product conjunction. Arch. Math. Log. **35**, 191–208 (1996). https://doi.org/10.1007/BF01268618
16. Klement, E.P., Mesiar, R., Pap, E.: Triangular Norms. Kluwer Academic Publishers, Dordrecht (2000)
17. Montagna, F., Ugolini, S.: A categorical equivalence for product algebras. Stud. Logica. **103**(2), 345–373 (2015). https://doi.org/10.1007/s11225-014-9569-9

Free Product Hoops

Francesco Manfucci[1] and Sara Ugolini[2]([✉]) [iD]

[1] DIISM, Università di Siena, Siena, Italy
`francesco.manfucci@student.unisi.it`
[2] Artificial Intelligence Research institute (IIIA), CSIC, Bellaterra, Barcelona, Spain
`sara@iiia.csic.es`

Abstract. In this contribution we are interested in the 0-free fragment of product logic, the fuzzy logic arising from the product t-norm. This logic has the variety of product hoops as its equivalent algebraic semantics. Our main result shows a functional representation of free finitely generated product hoops, which characterizes the Lindenbaum-Tarski algebra of formulas of the corresponding logic over a finite number of variables.

Keywords: Product logic · Hoops · Functional representation

1 Introduction

Product logic has been introduced by Hájek, Godo, and Esteva in [15], and, together with Łukasiewicz and Gödel logic, is one of the main propositional fuzzy logics arising from a continuous t-norm. Indeed, Mostert-Shields' theorem [16] shows that a t-norm is continuous if and only if it can be built from Łukasiewicz, Gödel and product t-norms by the construction of ordinal sum. These three operations determine the corresponding three algebraizable propositional logics (bringing the same names as their associated t-norms), whose equivalent algebraic semantics are the varieties of MV, Gödel and product algebras respectively. In particular, each one of these varieties is generated by the algebra on the real unit interval $[0, 1]$ endowed with the operations $(\cdot, \rightarrow, 0, 1)$, where $\cdot$ is one of the t-norms and $\rightarrow$ is its residuum (see [14]). This algebra is usually called the *standard model* of the corresponding logic.

Product logic has been deeply studied in recent years. Relevant results have been obtained with respect to: categorical representation of its algebras [17] and duality [12], SMT-solvers [19], modal extensions [20], structural completeness [10]. In particular, the representations of its free finitely generated algebras in [9] and [8] have shown to be particulary fruitful. They have indeed been used, for instance, to study: unification problems [2]; the probability theory of events seen as product logic formulas [11]; invertible substitutions [3].

In this contribution we are interested in a fragment of product logic: the positive (i.e., 0-free) fragment. We show that the standard model for the fragment is the real unit interval $[0, 1]$, with operations $(\cdot, \rightarrow, 1)$, where $\cdot$ is the product

S. Massanet et al. (Eds.): EUSFLAT 2023/AGOP 2023, LNCS 14069, pp. 518–529, 2023.
https://doi.org/10.1007/978-3-031-39965-7_43

t-norm and $\to$ is its residuum. Algebraically, its equivalent algebraic semantics is given by *product hoops*, i.e., the variety of 0-free subreducts of product algebras. Our main result provides a functional representation for the finitely generated free product hoops, which we obtain as a particular subreduct of the corresponding free product algebra. The key idea is to identify those functions in the representation of free product algebras in [9] that correspond to 0-free terms of product logic. We point out that free n-generated algebras in an algebraizable logic correspond to the Lindenbaum-Tarski algebras of formulas with n variables of the logic, thus our findings are relevant from both the algebraic and logical point of view.

2   Preliminaries

We now introduce the algebras that are object of our study. For all the unexplained notions of universal algebra we refer to [5]. A *bounded commutative integral residuated lattice* (or BCIRL) is an algebra $\mathbf{A} = (A, \cdot, \to, \wedge, \vee, 0, 1)$, of type $(2, 2, 2, 2, 0, 0)$, such that:

1. $(A, \cdot, 1)$ is a commutative monoid;
2. $(A, \wedge, \vee, 0, 1)$ is a bounded lattice with $0 \leq x \leq 1$ for all $x \in A$;
3. the residuation law holds: $x \cdot y \leq z$ iff $y \leq x \to z$.

BCIRLs form a variety, often called FL_{ew} since they are the equivalent algebraic semantics of the Full Lambek Calculus with exchange and weakening (see [13]). A commutative integral residuated lattice (or CIRL) is a 0-free subreduct of a BCIRL. A *BL-algebra* is a BCIRL that further satisfies *divisibility*:

$$x \wedge y = x \cdot (x \to y) \tag{div}$$

and *prelinearity*:

$$(x \to y) \vee (y \to x) = 1. \tag{prel}$$

A *product algebra* is a BL-algebra that satisfies the following identity:

$$\neg x \vee ((x \to (x \cdot y)) \to y) = 1. \tag{1}$$

Product algebras then form a variety which we denote by P. We will often write xy for $x \cdot y$, and x^n for $x \cdot \ldots \cdot x$ (n times). Moreover, we will consider a negation operator defined as $\neg x = x \to 0$.

The double negation operator in particular plays an interesting role in product algebras. Indeed, given a product algebra $\mathbf{P}$, the set of elements $\{\neg\neg x : x \in P\}$ is the so-called *Boolean skeleton* of $\mathbf{P}$, $\mathcal{B}(\mathbf{P})$. The Boolean skeleton of a bounded residuated lattice is its maximum Boolean subalgebra, and its domain coincides with the set of complemented elements, i.e., elements x such that $x \wedge \neg x = 0, x \vee \neg x = 1$.

We point out that in product algebras (and more generally in BL-algebras), the lattice operations can actually be rewritten in terms of the monoidal operation and the implication, as:

$$x \wedge y = x(x \to y),$$
$$x \vee y = ((x \to y) \to y) \wedge ((y \to x) \to x).$$

Thus we may consider BL-algebras in the language of *bounded hoops* (see [1,4] for the theory of hoops), that is, as algebras in the signature $(\cdot, \rightarrow, 0, 1)$. Henceforth, we will use this reduced language.

In what follows, given a variety V, we write $\mathbf{F}_V(X)$ for the free algebra over X in V. Given any variety V and any set of variables $X = \{x_1, \ldots, x_n\}$, an *assignment* of X into an algebra $\mathbf{A} \in V$ is a function h mapping each variable x_i to an element of $\mathbf{A}$, say $h(x_i) = a_i \in A$, for $i = 1, \ldots, n$. Then h extends to a homomorphism (that we also call h) from the free algebra $\mathbf{F}_V(X)$ to $\mathbf{A}$. Given this notation, considering a term t over the variables X, we write $t^{\mathbf{A}}(x_1, \ldots, x_n)$ for the element $h(t)$. Moreover, given terms $t(x_1, \ldots, x_n), u(x_1, \ldots, x_n)$ over the language of V, we write $\models_{\mathbf{A}} t \approx u$ if for any assignment h of the variables $x_1, \ldots, x_n$ to elements of $\mathbf{A}$, $h(t(x_1, \ldots, x_n)) = h(u(x_1, \ldots, x_n))$ in $\mathbf{A}$. Equivalently, if $t^{\mathbf{A}}(a_1, \ldots, a_n) = u^{\mathbf{A}}(a_1, \ldots, a_n)$ for all $a_1, \ldots, a_n \in A$. We write $\models_V t \approx u$ if $\models_{\mathbf{A}} t \approx u$ for all $\mathbf{A} \in V$.

2.1   Free Product Algebras

The variety of product algebras P is generated by the standard algebra:

$$[0,1]_\mathsf{P} = ([0,1], \cdot, \rightarrow, 0, 1),$$

where $x \cdot y$ is the product of real numbers and $\rightarrow$ is Goguen's implication: if $x \leq y$ then $x \rightarrow y = 1$; otherwise if $x > y$ then $x \rightarrow y = y/x$. By standard universal algebraic arguments, this implies that the free n-generated product algebra is (isomorphic to) the subalgebra of the algebra of real-valued functions from $[0,1]^n$ to $[0,1]$, generated by the projection functions, and with operations defined pointwise by the ones of the standard algebra. From now on, we identify the free n-generated product algebra with this algebra of functions, which we denote by $\mathbf{F}_\mathsf{P}(n)$. In [9], the authors give a description of $\mathbf{F}_\mathsf{P}(n)$, for all $n \in \mathbb{N}$, that we now recall. Let us call any function belonging to a free product algebra a *product function*.

Remark 1. Any n-ary term of product logic $p(x_1, \ldots, x_n)$ is associated to a product function $\overline{p} : [0,1]^n \rightarrow [0,1]$ such that, for each $(a_1, \ldots, a_n) \in [0,1]^n$:

$$\overline{p}(a_1, \ldots, a_n) = p^{[0,1]_\mathsf{P}}(a_1, \ldots, a_n). \tag{2}$$

This relation is not one-one: in fact, to each product function of $\mathbf{F}_\mathsf{P}(n)$ corresponds a class of n-ary terms of product logic that are logically equivalent. That is, given n-ary terms p and q, $\overline{p} = \overline{q}$ (as functions over $[0,1]^n$) if and only if $\models_\mathsf{P} p \approx q$. We will use this key fact in the rest of the paper.

The key idea of the representation is that the domain of product functions can be partitioned in subsets over which product functions are either constantly equal to 0, or they are piecewise monomial functions (see [9] for details). Moreover, this partition can be obtained by considering the atoms of the Boolean skeleton of the free product algebra, and considering the areas where the atoms have value either 0 or 1.

Now, let us consider the free n-generated product algebra, $\mathbf{F}_P(n)$, and let us call its generators $\{x_1, \ldots, x_n\}$. Its Boolean skeleton $\mathcal{B}(\mathbf{F}_P(n))$ is (isomorphic to) the free Boolean algebra over the generators $\{\neg\neg x_1, \ldots, \neg\neg x_n\}$ [8]. As it is well-known, the atoms of a free Boolean algebra can be written as all the possible meets of the generators and their negations. Thus, in order to list all the possible atoms, it suffices to pick, for each generator x_i, either its negation $\neg x_i$ or its double negation $\neg\neg x_i$. To each one of these choices, it corresponds both an atom, and an area of the domain $[0,1]^n$ where the said atom has value 1. That is, the area corresponding to the indexes i where we picked the double negation $\neg\neg x_i$. Let us now encode this idea.

Definition 1. *Let $n \in \mathbb{N}$. Given $\varepsilon = (\varepsilon_1, \ldots, \varepsilon_n) \in \{1,2\}^n$, we define $|\varepsilon| = |\{i \in \{1,2\}^n : \varepsilon_i = 2\}|$, and $G_\varepsilon = \{\mathbf{x} = (x_1, \ldots, x_n) \in [0,1]^n : x_i > 0 \text{ iff } \varepsilon_i = 2\}$.*

The G_ε's give a partition of $[0,1]^n$. We have the following result.

Theorem 1 ([9]). *The free product algebra on n generators $\mathbf{F}_P(n)$ is isomorphic to the algebra of functions $f : [0,1]^n \to [0,1]$ such that for all $\varepsilon \in \{1,2\}^n$, with $|\varepsilon| = k$, the restriction of f in G_ε is either equal to the constant function 0, or it is equal to a piecewise monomial function in k variables.*

Let us call a_ε the Boolean atom corresponding to a G_ε, i.e., such that the product function $\overline{a}_\varepsilon$ is 1 over G_ε and 0 outside. Letting $\neg^1 = \neg$ and $\neg^2 = \neg\neg$, it is:

$$a_\varepsilon = \bigwedge_{i=1}^{n} \neg^{\varepsilon_i} x_i. \tag{3}$$

Given that the G_ε's give us a partition of $[0,1]^n$, given an n-ary term q, we use the Boolean atoms to see each $\overline{q}$ as a join of functions $\overline{q}_\varepsilon$ that coincide with $\overline{q}$ on G_ε. Formally, we have:

Lemma 1. *Let q be a n-ary term. If for each $\varepsilon \in \{1,2\}^n$, q_ε is a term such that $\overline{q}(\mathbf{x}) = \overline{q}_\varepsilon(\mathbf{x})$ for all $\mathbf{x} \in G_\varepsilon$, then $\models_P q \approx \bigvee(q_\varepsilon \wedge a_\varepsilon)$.*

Proof. Let $\mathbf{x} \in G_{\varepsilon'}$. Then $\overline{a}_\varepsilon(\mathbf{x}) = 0$ if $\varepsilon \neq \varepsilon'$, and $\overline{a}_\varepsilon(\mathbf{x}) = 1$ if $\varepsilon = \varepsilon'$, thus $\overline{q}_\varepsilon(\mathbf{x}) \wedge \overline{a}_\varepsilon(\mathbf{x}) = \overline{q}_\varepsilon(\mathbf{x})$ if $\varepsilon = \varepsilon'$, otherwise $\overline{q}_\varepsilon(\mathbf{x}) \wedge \overline{a}_\varepsilon(\mathbf{x}) = 0$ if $\varepsilon \neq \varepsilon'$.

Then for each ε' and $\mathbf{x} \in G_{\varepsilon'}$:

$$\bigvee(\overline{q}_\varepsilon(\mathbf{x}) \wedge \overline{a}_\varepsilon(\mathbf{x})) = \overline{q}_{\varepsilon'}(\mathbf{x}) \wedge \overline{a}_{\varepsilon'}(\mathbf{x}) = \overline{q}_{\varepsilon'}(\mathbf{x}) = \overline{q}(\mathbf{x})$$

and given that the G_ε's are a partition of $[0,1]^n$, we have (by the observation in Remark 1) that $\models_P \bigvee(q_\varepsilon \wedge a_\varepsilon) \approx q$. $\square$

An example of the previous lemma can be given by considering the one-variable term $x \to x^2$, whose function is 1 at 0 and coincides with x elsewhere; given $a_1 = \neg x$ and $a_2 = \neg\neg x$, we can rewrite $x \to x^2$ as $(a_1 \wedge 1) \vee (a_2 \wedge x)$ (see Example 1 for a picture).

3 Standard Product Hoop

Basic hoops are the variety of CIRLs satisfying divisibility and prelinearity, and they are the 0-free subreducts of BL-algebras. The 0-free subreducts of product algebras are called *product hoops*, and they are a variety of basic hoops by [1, Proposition 1.10]. In the same paper, product hoops have been axiomatized as basic hoops further satisfying:

$$(y \to z) \vee ((y \to xy) \to x) = 1. \tag{PH}$$

We denote the variety of product hoops by PH. We will now see that PH is generated by the 0-free subreduct of the standard product algebra, and that this fact is an instance of a more general observation.

Theorem 2. *Let* V *be a variety of algebras over a language* $\mathcal{L}$. *Let* $\mathcal{L}^-$ *be a sublanguage of* $\mathcal{L}$ *such that the class of subreducts of algebras in* V *over the language* $\mathcal{L}^-$ *is a variety, call it* V^-. *Then if* V *is generated by an algebra* $\mathbf{A} \in V$, V^- *is generated by the reduct of* $\mathbf{A}$ *over the language* $\mathcal{L}^-$.

Proof. Let us call $\mathbf{A}^-$ the reduct of $\mathbf{A}$ in the language $\mathcal{L}^-$. Since $\mathbf{A}^- \in V^-$, $\mathbf{A}^-$ satisfies all the equations that are valid in V^-. Vice versa, suppose that an equation $t \approx u$ in the language $\mathcal{L}^-$ over variables in a set X is not valid in V^-. That is, there exists $\mathbf{B} \in V^-$ and an assignment of the variables in X to $\mathbf{B}$ that do not validate $t \approx u$. Since $\mathbf{B}$ is a subreduct of an algebra $\mathbf{B}^+ \in V$, the same assignment shows that also $\mathbf{B}^+ \not\models t \approx u$. Therefore, since $\mathbf{A}$ generates V, $\mathbf{A} \not\models t \approx u$. Since $t \approx u$ is an equation in the language $\mathcal{L}^-$, we get that $\mathbf{A}^- \not\models t \approx u$. Thus, $\mathbf{A}^-$ and V^- have the same equational theory, which means that the variety generated by $\mathbf{A}^-$ is exactly V^-. □

As a result:

Corollary 1. *The 0-free reduct of the standard product algebra generates* PH.

We will henceforth refer to the 0-free reduct of the standard product algebra as the *standard product hoop*, $[0,1]_{\mathsf{PH}}$. Thus, it follows that the free n-generated product hoop is an algebra of real-valued functions from $[0,1]^n$ to $[0,1]$, generated by the projection functions and with operations defined pointwise by $[0,1]_{\mathsf{PH}}$. In order to give a description of the free n-generated product hoop we will make use of the following result. The proof uses standard universal algebraic arguments (for details see [18], where the result is shown in general for varieties of bounded commutative residuated lattices).

Theorem 3. *Let X be any set, then the free product hoop $\mathbf{F}_{\mathsf{PH}}(X)$ is isomorphic to the subalgebra of the 0-free reduct of the free product algebra $\mathbf{F}_{\mathsf{P}}(X)$ generated by X.*

That is, in order to describe the free n-generated product hoop, it suffices to identify the product functions corresponding to (equivalence classes of) 0-free terms. More precisely, in reference to the notation introduced in Remark 1:

Definition 2. *We call a product function $f \in \mathbf{F}_{\mathsf{P}}(n)$ positive if there is a 0-free term p of product logic in n variables such that $\overline{p} = f$.*

4   Positive Product Functions

In this section we characterize positive product functions. First, an easy observation.

Proposition 1. *Let p be a 0-free n-ary term, then $\bar{p}(\mathbf{x}) > 0$ for all $\mathbf{x} \in (0,1]^n$.*

Proof. The claim can be shown by induction on the construction of the term p. Let p be a positive term of complexity 1, then $\bar{p}$ is either equal to $\mathbf{1}$ (the function constantly equal to 1) or to a projection, thus $\bar{p}(\mathbf{x}) > 0$ for all $\mathbf{x} \in (0,1]^n$.

Now, suppose that the claim holds for terms p of complexity less than m, and let p be a positive term with complexity m. Then p is either of the form $s \cdot q$ or $s \to q$ for positive terms s, q. By inductive hypothesis, $\bar{s}(\mathbf{x}) > 0$ and $\bar{q}(\mathbf{x}) > 0$ for all $\mathbf{x} \in (0,1]^n$. It follows that $\bar{p}(\mathbf{x}) > 0$ for all $\mathbf{x} \in (0,1]^n$. $\square$

The previous proposition identifies a necessary condition for a product function to be positive. In the rest of the section we will see that this condition is also sufficient. The key idea is to use Lemma 1 to rewrite those terms p whose corresponding product function is positive over $(0,1]^n$ by means of positive terms only. In particular, we will use suitable positive terms p_ε, in such a way that $\bigvee(p_\varepsilon \wedge a_\varepsilon)$, which is equivalent to p by Lemma 1, is shown to be equivalent to a positive term. First, a preliminary result.

Proposition 2. *Let p be a n-ary term such that $\bar{p}(\mathbf{x}) = 1$ for all $\mathbf{x} \in (0,1]^n$. Then for each $\varepsilon \in \{1, 2\}^n$ there exists a positive n-ary term p_ε such that $\bar{p}(\mathbf{x}) = \bar{p}_\varepsilon(\mathbf{x})$ for all $\mathbf{x} \in G_\varepsilon$.*

Proof. Let $p(x_1, \ldots, x_n)$ be a n-ary term. If $\varepsilon = (2, \ldots, 2)$, then $G_\varepsilon = (0,1]^n$, thus by construction $p_\varepsilon = \mathbf{1}$. Now consider $\varepsilon = (\varepsilon_1, \ldots, \varepsilon_n)$ such that $\varepsilon_i = 1$ for some $i = 1, \ldots, n$; if p is a positive term take $p_\varepsilon = p$. If p is not a positive term, take p_ε constructed from p by substituting each occurrence of $\mathbf{0}$ with x_i. Such p_ε is a positive term, and if $\mathbf{x} \in G_\varepsilon$ then $\bar{p}(\mathbf{x}) = \bar{p}_\varepsilon(\mathbf{x})$, since $\bar{x}_i(\mathbf{x}) = 0$ holds for $\mathbf{x} \in G_\varepsilon$. $\square$

We now have two technical lemmas.

Lemma 2. *Let p, q be n-ary terms, then the following hold:*

(1) $\models_\mathsf{P} \neg\neg p \approx (p \to p^2) \to p$.
(2) $\models_\mathsf{P} \neg p \to q \approx \neg\neg p \vee q$.

Proof. We use again that, as pointed out in Remark 1, $\models_\mathsf{P} p \approx q$ iff $\bar{p}(\mathbf{x}) = \bar{q}(\mathbf{x})$ for all $\mathbf{x} \in [0,1]^n$. We show (1). For $\mathbf{x} \in [0,1]^n$ we distinguish the following cases:

(i) if $\bar{p}(\mathbf{x}) = 0$ then $\neg\neg\bar{p}(\mathbf{x}) = 0$ and $(0 \to 0^2) \to 0 = 0$;
(ii) if $\bar{p}(\mathbf{x}) = 1$ then $\neg\neg\bar{p}(\mathbf{x}) = 1$ and $(1 \to 1) \to 1 = 1$;
(iii) if $\bar{p}(\mathbf{x}) = y \in (0,1)$ then $\neg\neg\bar{p}(\mathbf{x}) = 1$ and $(y \to y^2) \to y = y \to y = 1$.

This proves that $\models_\mathsf{P} \neg\neg p \approx (p \to p^2) \to p$. (2) can be shown with the same technique, and follows by easy computations. $\square$

Observe that by point (1) of the previous lemma, if p is a positive term, its double negation $\neg\neg p$ is equivalent to a positive term. Thus:

Proposition 3. *Let $\bar{\varepsilon} = (2, \ldots, 2)$. Then $a_{\bar{\varepsilon}}$ is equivalent to a positive term.*

However, for all the other ε this does not hold, as a_{ε} contains at least a negation; nonetheless, we notice that $a_{\bar{\varepsilon}} \vee a_{\varepsilon}$ is always equivalent to a positive term, in fact:

Lemma 3. *Let $\bar{\varepsilon} = (2, \ldots, 2)$, then $a_{\bar{\varepsilon}} \vee a_{\varepsilon}$ is equivalent to a positive term for all $\varepsilon \in \{1, 2\}^n$.*

Proof. By definition $a_{\bar{\varepsilon}} = \bigwedge_{j=1}^{n} \neg\neg x_j$ and $a_{\varepsilon} = \bigwedge_{i=1}^{n} \neg^{\varepsilon_i} x_i$. Now

$$\overline{a}_{\bar{\varepsilon}} \vee \overline{a}_{\varepsilon} = \left(\bigwedge_{j=1}^{n} \neg\neg \overline{x}_j \right) \vee \left(\bigwedge_{i=1}^{n} \neg^{\varepsilon_i} \overline{x}_i \right) = \bigwedge_{i=1}^{n} \bigwedge_{j=1}^{n} (\neg^{\varepsilon_i} \overline{x}_i \vee \neg\neg \overline{x}_j).$$

If $\varepsilon_i = 2$, by Lemma 2 $\neg\neg x_i \vee \neg\neg x_j$ is equivalent to a positive term. If $\varepsilon_i = 1$, again by Lemma 2, we get $\neg \overline{x}_i \vee \neg\neg \overline{x}_j = \neg\neg\neg \overline{x}_i \vee \neg\neg \overline{x}_j = \neg\neg \overline{x}_i \to \neg\neg \overline{x}_j$, and $\neg\neg x_i \to \neg\neg x_j$ is equivalent to a positive term. Hence, $a_{\bar{\varepsilon}} \vee a_{\varepsilon}$ is a composition of terms equivalent to positive terms and thus is equivalent to a positive term. $\square$

We are now ready to characterize positive product functions.

Proposition 4. *A product function f in $\mathbf{F_P}(n)$ is positive if and only if $f(\mathbf{x}) > 0$ for all $\mathbf{x} \in (0, 1]^n$.*

Proof. Let $f \in \mathbf{F_P}(n)$ be positive, that is, such that $f = \overline{p}$ for some positive term p. Then by Proposition 1, if $\mathbf{x} \in (0, 1]^n$, $f(\mathbf{x}) > 0$.

For the other direction, suppose $f \in \mathbf{F_P}(n)$ is such that $f(\mathbf{x}) > 0$ for all $\mathbf{x} \in (0, 1]^n$, and consider a term p associated with f, i.e., such that $\overline{p} = f$. We show that p is equivalent to a positive term, by induction on the complexity of p. If p is a constant or a variable, p is not $\mathbf{0}$ since $\overline{\mathbf{0}}(\mathbf{x}) = 0$ for all $\mathbf{x} \in (0, 1]^n$, while $\mathbf{1}$ and all variables are 0-free terms.

For the inductive step, we assume that every term q, of complexity smaller than m, and such that $\overline{q}(\mathbf{x}) > 0$ for all $\mathbf{x} \in (0, 1]^n$, is equivalent to a positive term. We now consider p to be of complexity m, then p is either of the form $s \cdot q$ or $s \to q$ for some terms s, q of complexity less than m. Suppose first $p = s \cdot q$. Since $\overline{p}(\mathbf{x}) > 0$ for all $\mathbf{x} \in (0, 1]^n$ by hypothesis, necessarily also $\overline{s}$ and $\overline{q}$ are not 0 over $(0, 1]^n$. By inductive hypothesis, s and q are equivalent to positive terms, and thus the same holds for p.

Assume now that $p = s \to q$. Observe that it cannot be that $\overline{s}(\mathbf{x}) > 0$ and $\overline{q}(\mathbf{x}) = 0$ for all $\mathbf{x} \in (0, 1]^n$, otherwise $\overline{p}$ would be 0 over $(0, 1]^n$, a contradiction. While if $\overline{s}(\mathbf{x})$ and $\overline{q}(\mathbf{x})$ are not 0 over $(0, 1]^n$, by inductive hypothesis, s and q are equivalent to some positive terms and then so is p. It is left to check the following case: $\overline{s}(\mathbf{x}) = 0$ for all $\mathbf{x} \in (0, 1]^n$. Then for all $\mathbf{x} \in (0, 1]^n$, $\overline{s}(\mathbf{x}) \to \overline{q}(\mathbf{x}) = 1$. By Proposition 2, we have that for each $\varepsilon \in \{1, 2\}^n$, there exists a positive n-ary term p_ε such that $\overline{p}$ coincides with $\overline{p}_\varepsilon$ on G_ε. By Lemma 1, p is equivalent to $\bigvee(p_\varepsilon \wedge a_\varepsilon)$. Let $a_{\overline{\varepsilon}} = \bigwedge_{i=1}^{n} \neg\neg x_i$. Given that $\overline{p}(\mathbf{x}) = 1$ for all $\mathbf{x} \in (0,1]^n$, we have

$$\overline{p} = \overline{p} \vee \overline{a}_{\overline{\varepsilon}} = \left(\bigvee(\overline{p}_\varepsilon \wedge \overline{a}_\varepsilon)\right) \vee \overline{a}_{\overline{\varepsilon}} = \bigvee\left((\overline{p}_\varepsilon \wedge \overline{a}_\varepsilon) \vee \overline{a}_{\overline{\varepsilon}}\right) = \bigvee(\overline{p}_\varepsilon \vee \overline{a}_{\overline{\varepsilon}}) \wedge (\overline{a}_\varepsilon \vee \overline{a}_{\overline{\varepsilon}}).$$

Hence, by Lemmas 2 and 3, p is equivalent to a positive term, and the proof is complete. $\qquad\square$

5   Functional Representation of Free Product Hoops

Combining Proposition 4 and Theorem 1 we get our main result.

Theorem 4. *The free n-generated product hoop $\mathbf{F}_{\mathsf{PH}}(n)$ is isomorphic to the 0-free subreduct of the free product algebra $\mathbf{F}_{\mathsf{P}}(n)$ given by the functions f in $\mathbf{F}_{\mathsf{P}}(n)$ such that $f(\mathbf{x}) > 0$ for all $\mathbf{x} \in (0,1]^n$.*

The following lemma will yield alternative characterizations for free finitely generated product hoops. We remind the reader that $\overline{\varepsilon} = \{2, \ldots, 2\}$.

Lemma 4. *Let p be an n-ary term of product logic. Then the following are equivalent:*

(1) $\overline{p}(\mathbf{x}) > 0$ for all $\mathbf{x} \in (0,1]^n$,
(2) $\neg\neg\overline{p}(\mathbf{x}) = 1$ for all $\mathbf{x} \in (0,1]^n$,
(3) $\overline{a}_{\overline{\varepsilon}} \leq \neg\neg\overline{p}$,
(4) $\overline{p} \not\leq \neg\overline{a}_{\overline{\varepsilon}}$.

Proof. (1) $\Rightarrow$ (2). If $\overline{p}$ does not have value 0 over $(0,1]^n$, then $\neg\overline{p}$ is 0 over $(0,1]^n$, and consequently $\neg\neg\overline{p}(\mathbf{x}) = 1$ for all $\mathbf{x} \in (0,1]^n$.
(2) $\Rightarrow$ (3). If $\neg\neg\overline{p}(\mathbf{x}) = 1$ for all $\mathbf{x} \in (0,1]^n$, then $\overline{a}_\varepsilon(\mathbf{x}) = 1 \leq \neg\neg\overline{p}(\mathbf{x})$ for all $\mathbf{x} \in (0,1]^n$. Moreover, if $\mathbf{x} \notin (0,1]^n$, we have $\overline{a}_{\overline{\varepsilon}}(\mathbf{x}) = 0$, hence $\overline{a}_{\overline{\varepsilon}}(\mathbf{x}) \leq \neg\neg\overline{p}(\mathbf{x})$. Thus, $\overline{a}_{\overline{\varepsilon}} \leq \neg\neg\overline{p}$.
(3) $\Rightarrow$ (4). If $a_{\overline{\varepsilon}} \leq \neg\neg p$, then $\neg p \leq \neg a_{\overline{\varepsilon}}$. Thus, for $\mathbf{x} \in G_{\overline{\varepsilon}}$, $\neg\overline{p}(\mathbf{x}) \leq \neg\overline{a}_{\overline{\varepsilon}}(\mathbf{x}) = 0$ and $\overline{p}(\mathbf{x}) > 0$. Thus $\overline{p} \not\leq \neg\overline{a}_{\overline{\varepsilon}}$.
(4) $\Rightarrow$ (1). We prove the last implication by contraposition. Notice that $\neg\overline{a}_{\overline{\varepsilon}}(\mathbf{x})$ is equal to 0 if $\mathbf{x} \in (0,1]^n$, and it is equal to 1 otherwise. Recall that product functions are either 0 or strictly greater than 0 over any G_ε. Thus, if $\overline{p}(\mathbf{x}) = 0$ for all $\mathbf{x} \in (0,1]^n$, $\overline{p}(\mathbf{x}) \leq \neg\overline{a}_{\overline{\varepsilon}}(\mathbf{x})$ for all $\mathbf{x} \in [0,1]^n$. Hence, $\overline{p} \leq \neg\overline{a}_{\overline{\varepsilon}}$, and the proof is complete. $\qquad\square$

Notice that the last point characterizes those functions that *do not* correspond to positive terms. The characterization theorem can be rewritten as follows:

Theorem 5. *The free n-generated product hoop $\mathbf{F}_{\mathsf{PH}}(n)$ is isomorphic to the algebra of functions f in $\mathbf{F}_{\mathsf{P}}(n)$ such that one of the following equivalent conditions holds:*

1. $f(\mathbf{x}) > 0$ for all $\mathbf{x} \in (0,1]^n$;

2. $\neg\neg f(\mathbf{x}) = 1$ *for all* $\mathbf{x} \in (0, 1]^n$;
3. $\bar{a}_{\bar{\varepsilon}} \leq \neg\neg f$;
4. $f \not\leq \neg\bar{a}_{\bar{\varepsilon}}$.

Let us show an example of how we can use our characterization to analyze free product hoops.

Example 1. Let us obtain the free 1-generated product hoop $\mathbf{F}_{\mathsf{PH}}(x)$ from the free 1-generated product algebra $\mathbf{F}_{\mathsf{P}}(x)$. The latter has the elements shown in Fig. 1; from the next graphs one can see how to represent them as one-variable functions.

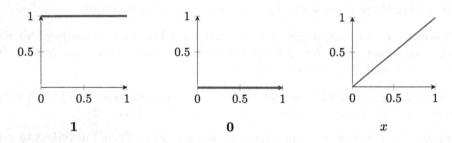

$$1 \qquad\qquad 0 \qquad\qquad x$$

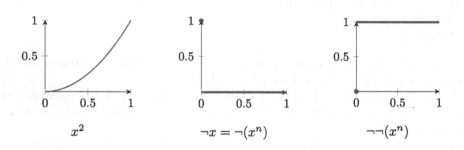

$$x^2 \qquad\qquad \neg x = \neg(x^n) \qquad\qquad \neg\neg(x^n)$$

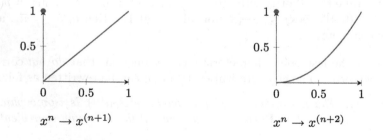

$$x^n \to x^{(n+1)} \qquad\qquad x^n \to x^{(n+2)}$$

By Theorem 4 it is then easy to see that the free 1-generated product hoop only lacks the functions associated to $\neg x$ and $\mathbf{0}$. We represent the Hasse diagram of both free algebras in Fig. 1.

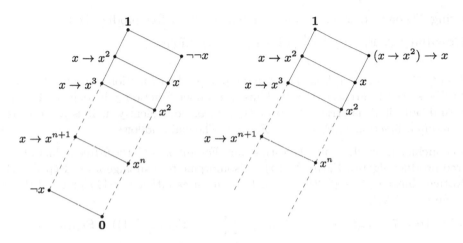

Fig. 1. On the left $\mathbf{F}_P(x)$, on the right $\mathbf{F}_{PH}(x)$.

6 Alternative Representation

We now consider the representation of free product algebras in [6]. Let CH be the variety of cancellative hoops, that is, basic hoops whose monoidal operation is cancellative in the usual sense. Cancellative hoops are generated by the algebra $((0,1], \cdot, \rightarrow, 1)$ where $\cdot, \rightarrow$ are the product t-norm and its residuum. Free cancellative hoops have a functional representation in terms of piecewise monomial functions (see [7]). Moreover, given any CIRL $\mathbf{A}$, let $\mathbf{2} \oplus \mathbf{A}$ be the algebra with domain $A \cup \{0\}$, and operations extending the ones of $\mathbf{A}$ in the obvious way: $x0 = 0x = 0, x \rightarrow 0 = 0, 0 \rightarrow x = 1$ for all $x \in A$.

Theorem 6 ([6]). *The free product algebra on n generators $\mathbf{F}_P(n)$ is isomorphic to*

$$\prod_{\varepsilon \in \{1,2\}^n} [\overline{0}, a_\varepsilon] \cong \prod_{\varepsilon \in \{1,2\}^n} \mathbf{2} \oplus \mathbf{F}_{CH}(|\varepsilon|).$$

In particular, with reference to the functional representation in [9] we have used in the previous section, the isomorphism can be defined in the following way. Given any product function $f \in \mathbf{F}_P(n)$, and any $\varepsilon \in \{1,2\}^n$, let f_ε be the restriction of f to G_ε. Then f_ε is either 0, or it is a piecewise monomial function that belongs to the free cancellative hoop with $|\varepsilon| = \{i \in \{1,2\}^n : i = 2\}$ generators.

Then, combining the description in [9] with Theorem 6, the isomorphism associates a product function $f \in \mathbf{F_P}(n)$ to

$$(f_{\varepsilon_1}, \ldots, f_{\varepsilon_{2^n}}) \in \prod_{\varepsilon \in \{1,2\}^n} \mathbf{2} \oplus \mathbf{F_{CH}}(|\varepsilon|).$$

Using Theorem 4, we can show a similar result for free product hoops.

Corollary 2. $\mathbf{F_{PH}}(n) \cong \left(\prod_{\varepsilon \neq \bar{\varepsilon}} (\mathbf{2} \oplus \mathbf{F_{CH}}(|\varepsilon|)) \right) \times \mathbf{F_{CH}}(n)$.

Proof. By Theorem 4, $\mathbf{F_{PH}}(n)$ is the hoop of product functions whose restriction to $G_{\bar{\varepsilon}}$ is strictly greater than 0. Thus, a product function f belongs to $\mathbf{F_{PH}}(n)$ if and only if $f_{\bar{\varepsilon}}$ is strictly greater than 0, or equivalently, if it is a piecewise monomial function in $\mathbf{F_{CH}}(|\bar{\varepsilon}|) = \mathbf{F_{CH}}(n)$. The claim follows. □

In conclusion, we show an interesting fact. For any $n \in \mathbb{N}$, the 0-free reduct of the free product algebra $\mathbf{F_P}(n)$, $\mathbf{F_P^0}(n)$, is isomorphic to a subalgebra of $\mathbf{F_{PH}}(n+1)$. Notice that any $\xi \in \{1,2\}^{n+1}$ can be written as either $\varepsilon \times \{1\}$ or $\varepsilon \times \{2\}$ for some $\varepsilon \in \{1,2\}^n$.

Theorem 7. $\mathbf{F_{PH}}(n+1) \cong \mathbf{F_P^0}(n) \times \prod_{\substack{\varepsilon \times \{2\} \\ \varepsilon \neq \bar{\varepsilon}}} (\mathbf{2} \oplus \mathbf{F_{CH}}(|\varepsilon| + 1)) \times \mathbf{F_{CH}}(n+1)$.

Proof. Let $\xi \in \{1,2\}^{n+1}$, then by Corollary 2 we get

$$\mathbf{F_{PH}}(n+1) \cong \prod_{\xi \neq \bar{\xi}} (\mathbf{2} \oplus \mathbf{F_{CH}}(|\xi|)) \times \mathbf{F_{CH}}(n+1).$$

Then we can rewrite every ξ as $(\varepsilon \times \{1\})$ or $(\varepsilon \times \{2\})$ for some $\varepsilon \in \{1,2\}^n$; notice that $|\varepsilon \times \{1\}| = |\varepsilon|$ and $|\varepsilon \times \{2\}| = |\varepsilon| + 1$. Thus we get:

$$\mathbf{F_{PH}}(n+1) \cong \prod_{\varepsilon \times \{1\}} (\mathbf{2} \oplus \mathbf{F_{CH}}(|\varepsilon|)) \times \prod_{\substack{\varepsilon \times \{2\} \\ \varepsilon \neq \bar{\varepsilon}}} (\mathbf{2} \oplus \mathbf{F_{CH}}(|\varepsilon| + 1)) \times \mathbf{F_{CH}}(n+1).$$

Since, by Theorem 6, $\mathbf{F_P}(n) \cong \prod_{\varepsilon} \mathbf{2} \oplus \mathbf{F_{CH}}(|\varepsilon|)$, it follows that $\mathbf{F_P^0}(n)$ is isomorphic to $\prod_{(\varepsilon \times \{1\})} \mathbf{2} \oplus \mathbf{F_{CH}}(|\varepsilon|)$. The claim follows. □

7   Conclusions

We have shown a functional representation of free finitely generated product hoops. In future work, we expect to use an analogous approach in order to describe free algebras in the variety of 0-free subreducts of the variety generated by perfect MV-algebras. Moreover, we expect to use the methods developed in [2] to study projective algebras and the unification type of the mentioned varieties of hoops.

Funding. Ugolini acknowledges support from the Ramón y Cajal programme (RyC2021-032670-I), and partial support from the MOSAIC project (H2020- MSCA-RISE-2020 Project 101007627).

References

1. Aglianò, P., Ferrerim, I.M.A., Montagna, F.: Basic hoops: an algebraic study of continuous *t*-norms. Stud. Logica. **87**(1), 73–98 (2007). https://doi.org/10.1007/s11225-007-9078-1
2. Aglianò, P., Ugolini, S.: Projectivity and unification in substructural logics of generalized rotations. Int. J. Approximate Reasoning **153**, 172–192 (2023)
3. Aguzzoli, S., Gerla, B.: Invertible substitutions in logics with algebraic semantics equivalent to Product algebras. In: 2022 IEEE International Conference on Fuzzy Systems (FUZZ-IEEE), Padua, Italy, pp. 1–8 (2022)
4. Blok, W.J., Ferreirim, I.M.A.: On the structure of hoops. Algebra Univers. **43**, 233–257 (2000). https://doi.org/10.1007/s000120050156
5. Burris, S., Sankappanavar, H.P.: A Course in Universal Algebra. Springer, New York (1981)
6. Cignoli, R., Torrens, A.: An algebraic analysis of product logic. Multiple Valued Log. **5**, 45–65 (2000)
7. Cignoli, R., Torrens, A.: Free cancellative hoops. Algebra Univers. **43**, 213–216 (2000)
8. Cignoli, R., Torrens, A.: Free algebras in varieties of Glivenko MTL-algebras satisfying the equation $2(x^2) = (2x)^2$. Stud. Logica. **83**, 157–181 (2006). https://doi.org/10.1007/s11225-006-8302-8
9. Cintula, P., Gerla, B.: Semi-normal forms and functional representation of product fuzzy logic. Fuzzy Sets Syst. **143**(1), 89–110 (2004)
10. Cintula, P., Metcalfe, G.: Structural completeness in fuzzy logic. Notre Dame J. Formal Log. **50**(2), 153–182 (2009)
11. Flaminio, T., Godo, L., Ugolini, S.: Towards a probability theory for product logic: states, integral representation and reasoning. Int. J. Approximate Reasoning **93**, 199–218 (2018)
12. Fussner, W., Ugolini, S.: A topological approach to MTL-algebras. Algebra Univers. **80**, 38 (2019). https://doi.org/10.1007/s00012-019-0612-6
13. Galatos, N., Jipsen, P., Kowalski, T., Ono, H.: Residuated Lattices: An Algebraic Glimpse at Substructural Logics. Studies in Logics and the Foundations of Mathematics, vol. 151. Elsevier, Amsterdam (2007)
14. Hájek, P.: Metamathematics of Fuzzy Logic. Trends in Logic-Studia Logica Library, no. 4. Kluwer Academic Publishers, Dordrecht, Boston, London (1998)
15. Hájek, P., Godo, L., Esteva, F.: A complete many-valued logic with product conjunction. Arch. Math. Log. **35**, 191–208 (1996). https://doi.org/10.1007/BF01268618
16. Klement, E.P., Mesiar, R., Pap, E.: Triangular Norms. Kluwer Academic Publishers, Dordrecht (2000)
17. Montagna, F., Ugolini, S.: A categorical equivalence for product algebras. Stud. Logica. **103**(2), 345–373 (2015). https://doi.org/10.1007/s11225-014-9569-9
18. Ugolini, S.: The polyhedral geometry of Wajsberg hoops. J. Log. Comput. (2023). https://doi.org/10.1093/logcom/exad007
19. Vidal, A.: MNiBLoS: a SMT-based solver for continuous t-norm based logics and some of their modal expansions. Inf. Sci. **372**, 709–730 (2016)
20. Vidal, A., Esteva, F., Godo, L.: On modal extensions of product fuzzy logic. J. Log. Comput. **27**(1), 299–336 (2017)

A Logic to Reason About f-Indices of Inclusion over Ł$_n$

Tommaso Flaminio[1]([✉]), Lluis Godo[1], Nicolás Madrid[2],
and Manuel Ojeda-Aciego[2]

[1] IIIA-CSIC, 08193 Bellaterra, Spain
{tommaso,godo}@iiia.csic.es
[2] Departamento de Matemática Aplicada, Universidad de Málaga, 29071 Málaga,
Spain
{nicmadlab,aciego}@uma.es

Abstract. In this paper we provide a sound and complete logic to formalise and reason about f-indices of inclusion. The logic is based on finite-valued Łukasiewicz logic Ł$_n$ and its S5-like modal extension S5(Ł$_n$) with additional unary operators.

1 Introduction

Inclusion is one of the most fundamental relations between sets. In previous work [10], it was shown how the degree of inclusion between two L-fuzzy sets can be represented in terms of a function that specifically determines the minimal modifications required in one L-fuzzy set to be included (in Zadeh's sense) in another.

The key idea was the notion of f-inclusion, which defines a family of crisp binary relations between L-fuzzy sets that are used as indexes of inclusion and, subsequently, we define the f-index of inclusion as the most suitable f-inclusion under certain criteria. In addition, it was shown that the f-index of inclusion satisfies versions of many common axioms usually required for measures of inclusion in the literature, namely the axiomatic approaches of Kitainik [8] and Sinha-Dougherty [14].

In [11], the f-index was shown to be definable by means of a fuzzy conjunction which is part of an adjoint pair. Moreover, it is also proven in [11] that when the underlying structure in the modus ponens inference rule is given by adjoint pairs, the f-index provides the maximum possible truth-value in the conclusion obtained by fuzzy modus ponens using any other possible adjoint pair.

In this paper, we continue the study of the logical properties of the f-index of inclusion. Specifically, we provide a first step towards a logical account of the notion of f-index of inclusion for fuzzy sets in the frame of an S5-like modal logic over the n-valued Łukasiewicz logic with truth-constants Ł$_n^c$. We take advantage of the good logical and expressive properties of this logical setting to define the logic IL$_n$ to reason about f-indexes of inclusion between n-valued propositions.

S. Massanet et al. (Eds.): EUSFLAT 2023/AGOP 2023, LNCS 14069, pp. 530–539, 2023.
https://doi.org/10.1007/978-3-031-39965-7_44

The paper is structured as follows. After this introduction, we first provide the necessary background on finite-valued Łukasiewicz logic and its S5-like modal extension S5(Ł$_n^c$), and on the f-index of inclusion of fuzzy sets. Then in Sect. 3 we define a logic IŁ$_n$ based on S5(Ł$_n^c$) with additional unary operators to formalise and reason about f-indices of inclusion. We finish with some prospects for future work.

2 Preliminaries

2.1 The Finite-Valued Łukasiewicz Logic

Consider the propositional language $\mathcal{L}$ whose set of formulas $Fm_{\mathcal{L}}$ is built from a *finite* set of propositional variables Var, the connective $\rightarrow$ (implication) and truth constants $\bar{r}$ for each $r \in \mathrm{VŁ}_n = \{0, \frac{1}{n-1}, \ldots, \frac{n-2}{n-1}, 1\}$ for some fixed natural $n \geq 2$. Further connectives are defined as follows:

$$\neg\phi := \phi \rightarrow \bar{0} \qquad\qquad \phi \wedge \psi := \phi \otimes (\phi \rightarrow \psi)$$
$$\phi \otimes \psi := \neg(\phi \rightarrow \neg\psi) \qquad\qquad \phi \oplus \psi := \neg(\neg\phi \otimes \neg\psi)$$
$$\phi \vee \psi := ((\phi \rightarrow \psi) \rightarrow \psi) \qquad\qquad \phi \equiv \psi := (\phi \rightarrow \psi) \otimes (\psi \rightarrow \phi)$$

with ϕ and ψ being arbitrary formulas.[1]

A *propositional evaluation* is a mapping $e : Var \rightarrow \mathrm{VŁ}_n$ that is extended to formulas as follows: if ϕ and ψ are formulas and $r \in \mathrm{VŁ}_n$, then

$$e(\phi \rightarrow \psi) = e(\phi) \Rightarrow e(\psi) \text{ and } e(\bar{r}) = r,$$

where $x \Rightarrow y = \min(1, 1 - x + y)$ for $x, y \in \mathrm{Ł}_n$. Note that $x \Rightarrow y = 1$ iff $x \leq y$. The set of all such evaluations will be denoted by Ω_n. Notice that, in particular, for every formula ϕ and ψ and for every $e \in \Omega_n$, we have:

$$e(\neg\phi) = 1 - e(\phi) \qquad\qquad e(\phi \wedge \psi) = \min(e(\phi), e(\psi))$$
$$e(\phi \otimes \psi) = \max(e(\phi) + e(\psi) - 1, 0) \qquad e(\phi \oplus \psi) = \min(1, e(\phi) + e(\psi))$$
$$e(\phi \vee \psi) = \max(e(\phi), e(\psi)) \qquad\qquad e(\phi \equiv \psi) = 1 - |e(\phi) - e(\psi)|.$$

A formula ϕ is said to be *satisfiable* if there exists an $e \in \Omega_n$ such that $e(\phi) = 1$. In such a case we say that e is a *model* of ϕ and e is a model of a set of formulas T if e is a model of every formula in T. A *tautology* is a formula ϕ such that $e(\phi) = 1$ for each $e \in \Omega_n$. A formula ϕ is a *semantic consequence* of a set of formulas Γ, written as $\Gamma \models \phi$, if it holds that every model of Γ is also a model of ϕ.

This logic based on the language $\mathcal{L}$, which we will denote by $\mathrm{Ł}_n^c$, has a sound and a strongly complete axiomatization, see e.g. [4] for details. In particular, the axioms of $\mathrm{Ł}_n^c$ are

---

[1] For the sake of simplicity, along this paper we will use the same symbol to denote both a logical language $\mathcal{L}$ and its corresponding set of formulas $Fm_{\mathcal{L}}$ built in the usual way. This will be done with no danger of confusion.

(Ł1) $\varphi \to (\psi \to \varphi)$,
(Ł2) $(\varphi \to \psi) \to ((\psi \to \chi) \to (\varphi \to \chi))$,
(Ł3) $((\varphi \to \overline{0}) \to (\psi \to \overline{0})) \to (\psi \to \varphi)$,
(Ł4) $((\varphi \to \psi) \to \psi) \to ((\psi \to \varphi) \to \varphi)$,
(Ł5) $(n-1)\varphi \equiv n\varphi$,
(Ł6) $(k\varphi^{k-1})^n \equiv n\varphi^k$, for each $k \in \{2, \ldots, n-2\}$ not dividing $n-1$,
(Q1) $(\overline{r_1} \to \overline{r_2}) \equiv \min\{1, 1-r_1+r_2\}$, for each $r_1, r_2 \in V\text{Ł}_n$,

and the only deduction rule is modus ponens (from ϕ and $\phi \to \psi$ infer ψ). Axioms (Ł1)-(Ł4) form an axiomatization for Łukasiewicz logic, and in axioms (Ł5) and (Ł6), $k\varphi$ is an abbreviation for $\varphi \oplus \overset{k}{\ldots} \oplus \varphi$ (k repetitions) and φ^k for $\varphi \otimes \overset{k}{\ldots} \otimes \varphi$ (k repetitions). Axiom (Q1) is a bookkeeping axiom for truth-constants. It is needed to derive how truth-constants are combined with the different connectives.

Ł_n^c is strongly complete in the following sense: if $\vdash$ denotes the notion of proof defined from the set of axioms of Ł_n^c and modus ponens, then we have that for any countable (possibly infinite) set of formulas $T \cup \{\psi\}$, it holds that $T \vdash \psi$ iff $T \models \psi$. A formula ψ that can be proven from the axioms of Ł_n^c and modus ponens is called a *theorem*; in this case we will write $\vdash \psi$.

For each formula ϕ we will denote by $\Delta\phi$ the formula ϕ^n. Since we only have n truth values this formula is Boolean. Indeed, it is easy to check that

$$e(\Delta\phi) = \begin{cases} 1, & \text{if } e(\phi) = 1 \\ 0, & \text{if } e(\phi) < 1 \end{cases}$$

Note that Δ corresponds to the well-known Baaz-Monteiro projection operator [1, 13].

Remark 1. For every formula φ of Ł_n^c and for every nonempty subset S of Ω_n we can associate a fuzzy subset f_φ of S. Precisely, $f_\varphi : S \to \text{Ł}_n$ is defined by the stipulation

$$f_\varphi : w \in S \mapsto w(\varphi) \in V\text{Ł}_n.$$

Conversely, given S and a fuzzy set $f : S \to V\text{Ł}_n$, we can define a formula φ_f of Ł_n^c such that $f = f_{\varphi_f}$. Precisely, let

$$\varphi_f := \bigwedge_{w \in S} (1_w \to \overline{f(w)})$$

where $1_w := \bigwedge_{p \in Var} \Delta(p \equiv \overline{w(p)})$ is such that f_{1_w} is the characteristic function of w in S.

This description of formulas as fuzzy sets will allow us to describe mathematical properties of fuzzy sets in the logical framework. In the present paper, we will deal with a logical treatment of the f-index of inclusion between fuzzy sets that we will recall in Subsect. 2.2.

Now, we recall the logic $S5(\text{Ł}_n^c)$ from [2], an S5-like modal extension of the logic Ł_n^c. To this end, let $\mathcal{L}_n^\square$ be the expansion of the language $\mathcal{L}_n$ of the logic Ł_n^c

by a unary modal operator $\boxdot$. An $S5(Ł_n^c)$-*interpretation* for formulas in $\mathcal{L}_n^\boxdot$ is a mapping σ determined by a pair (w, S),[2] where $w \in \Omega_n$ is a $Ł_n$-evaluation and $S \subseteq \Omega_n$ is a set of $Ł_n$-evaluations such that $w \in S$. Formally, each pair (w, S) determines the map $\sigma : \mathcal{L}_n^\boxdot \to VŁ_n$ by the following stipulations:

- if $\varphi \in \mathcal{L}_n$, $\sigma(\varphi) = w(\varphi)$
- $\sigma(\boxdot\psi) = \inf\{(w', S)(\psi) \mid w' \in S\}$; (in particular, if $\psi \in \mathcal{L}_n$, $\sigma(\boxdot\psi) = \inf\{w'(\psi) \mid w' \in S\}$)
- $\sigma(\varphi \star \psi) = \sigma(\varphi) \,\overline{\star}\, \sigma(\psi)$, for $\star$ being a connective of Łukasiewicz logic

We will denote by Σ the set of $S5(Ł_n^c)$-interpretations, i.e. $\Sigma = \{\sigma = (w, S) \in \Omega_n \times 2^{\Omega_n} \mid w \in S\}$. We say that $\sigma \in \Sigma$ is a model of a formula φ, written $\sigma \models \varphi$, when $\sigma(\varphi) = 1$.

Now, let us recall from [2] the definition of the logic $S5(Ł_n^c)$ as the modal logic over $Ł_n^c$ whose axioms and rules are:

(Łn) Axioms of $Ł_n^c$
(M1) $\boxdot(\varphi \wedge \psi) \to (\boxdot\varphi \wedge \boxdot\psi)$
(M2) $\boxdot(\overline{r} \to \varphi) \equiv (\overline{r} \to \boxdot\varphi)$
(M3) $\boxdot(\varphi \oplus \varphi) \equiv (\boxdot\varphi \oplus \boxdot\varphi)$
(K) $\boxdot(\varphi \to \psi) \to (\boxdot\varphi \to \boxdot\psi)$
(T) $\boxdot\varphi \to \varphi$
(4) $\boxdot\varphi \to \boxdot\boxdot\varphi$
(5) $\neg\boxdot\varphi \to \boxdot\neg\boxdot\varphi$

Rules: modus ponens and necessitation for $\boxdot$

The logic $S5(Ł_n^c)$ is proved in [2, Theorem 2, Proposition 2] to be strongly complete with respect to the class of structures Σ defined above.

Theorem 1. *Let $T \cup \{\varphi\}$ be a countable set of formulas in $\mathcal{L}_n^\boxdot$. Then $\Gamma \vdash \varphi$ iff for all $\sigma \in \Sigma$ such that $\sigma \models \gamma$ for all $\gamma \in \Gamma$, then $\sigma \models \varphi$.*

2.2 The f-Index of Inclusion

The f-index of inclusion represents the inclusion between fuzzy sets by means of mappings from $[0, 1]$ to $[0, 1]$. This feature is an important difference from the standard approaches [6,8,14,16], where the inclusion of one fuzzy set into another is given, in general, by a value in the unit interval $[0, 1]$. Not any mapping from $[0, 1]$ to $[0, 1]$ can be used to represent the f-index of inclusion: the set of possible assignable mappings is introduced below, together with the basic notion of f-inclusion.

Definition 1 (cf. [12]).

- *The set of indexes of inclusion, denoted by $\mathcal{F}$, consists of every monotonically increasing mapping $f \colon [0, 1] \to [0, 1]$ such that $f(x) \leq x$ for all $x \in [0, 1]$.*

---

[2] Actually, we will henceforth identify both notations σ and (w, S) to indicate this map, and we can even write $\sigma = (w, S)$.

– *Let A and B be two fuzzy sets over the same universe $\mathcal{U}$, and consider $f \in \mathcal{F}$. We say that A is f-included in B (denoted by $A \subseteq_f B$) if and only if the inequality $f(A(u)) \leq B(u)$ holds for all $u \in \mathcal{U}$.*

The suitability of the set $\mathcal{F}$ as a proper set of indexes to represent the inclusion is explained in [9,10,12]. In order to choose a convenient index among all in $\mathcal{F}$ to represent a specific inclusion between two fuzzy sets, in [12], we introduced the following definition.

Definition 2 (f-index of inclusion [12]). *Let A and B be two fuzzy sets over a same domain. The f-index of inclusion of A in B, denoted by $Inc(A, B)$, is defined as*

$$Inc(A, B) = \max\{f \in \mathcal{F} \mid A \subseteq_f B\}$$

The previous definition is correct, in the sense that it can be proved that the set $\{f \in \mathcal{F} \mid A \subseteq_f B\}$ has always a maximum for every pair of fuzzy sets A and B. An interesting interpretation of the f-index of inclusion is given by considering mappings $f \in \mathcal{F}$ as modifiers of membership degrees. Accordingly, the lesser pointwisely the mapping $f \in \mathcal{F}$ is, the greater the modification is. Therefore, taking the maximum $f \in \mathcal{F}$ such that $A \subseteq_f B$ is equivalent to consider the minimal modifications of membership degrees in A to include it into B in the Zadeh's sense. This interpretation brings the f-index of inclusion closer to the notion of truth stressers in fuzzy logic [3,5,7,15], since they modify truth degrees. This relation is used in the next section to define a unary operator in VL_n.

Lastly, we recall two interesting results of the f-index of inclusion that will be used in the next section. The first one determines an analytical structure of the f-index of inclusion.

Theorem 2 (cf. [10]). *Let A and B be two fuzzy sets over $\mathcal{U}$, then*

$$Inc(A, B)(x) = \bigwedge_{u \in \mathcal{U}} \{B(u) \wedge x \mid x \leq A(u)\},$$

for all $x \in [0, 1]$.

The second result provides some properties that support the use of the f-index of inclusion as a representation of the inclusion between fuzzy sets.

Theorem 3 (cf. [10]). *Let A, B and C be fuzzy sets over $\mathcal{U}$. The following properties hold:*

1. *(Full inclusion) $Inc(A, B) = id$ if and only if $A(u) \leq B(u)$ for all $u \in \mathcal{U}$.*
2. *(Null inclusion) $Inc(A, B) = \perp$ if and only if there is a set of elements in the universe $\{u_i\}_{i \in I} \subseteq \mathcal{U}$ such that $A(u_i) = 1$ for all $i \in I$ and $\bigwedge_{i \in I} B(u_i) = 0$.*
3. *(Pseudo transitivity) $Inc(B, C) \circ Inc(A, B) \leq Inc(A, C)$.*
4. *(Monotonicity) If $B(u) \leq C(u)$ for all $u \in \mathcal{U}$ then, $Inc(C, A) \leq Inc(B, A)$.*
5. *(Monotonicity) If $B(u) \leq C(u)$ for all $u \in \mathcal{U}$ then, $Inc(A, B) \leq Inc(A, C)$.*
6. *(Transformation Invariance) Let $T: \mathcal{U} \rightarrow \mathcal{U}$ be a bijection on $\mathcal{U}$, then $Inc(A, B) = Inc(A \circ T, B \circ T)$.*
7. *(Relationship with intersection) $Inc(A, B \cap C) = Inc(A, B) \wedge Inc(A, C)$.*
8. *(Relationship with union) $Inc(A \cup B, C) = Inc(A, C) \wedge Inc(B, C)$.*

3   A Logic to Reason About the f-Index of Inclusions over $Ł_n^c$

In this section we introduce an axiomatic extension of the finite-valued fuzzy modal logic $S5(Ł_n^c)$ with new unary operators $\Box_{\varphi,\psi}$, one for every pair of formulas φ, ψ from $\mathcal{L}_n^c$, that will provide us with a logical formalisation of the f-index of inclusion between fuzzy concepts represented as propositions in $Ł_n^c$. Recall the representation of formulas as fuzzy sets from Remark 1. In this section, by *truth-stresser* we will mean a non-decreasing function $\tau : VŁ_n \to VŁ_n$ such that $\tau(x) \le x$ for all $x \in VŁ_n$.

We start by defining the syntax and semantics of our logic, and later we axiomatise it.

3.1   Syntax and Semantics

Let $\mathcal{IL}$, where $\mathcal{I}$ stands for *inclusion*, be the expansion of the modal language $\mathcal{L}_n^\Box$ by adding to its signature a unary operator $\Box_{\varphi,\psi}$ for every pair of formulas φ, ψ from $\mathcal{L}_n$.

The semantics for $\mathcal{IL}$ is still given by pairs $\sigma = (w, S) \in \Sigma$, which now further interpret the new operators $\Box_{\varphi,\psi}$.

- If $\varphi \in \mathcal{L}_n^\Box$, then $\sigma(\varphi)$ is defined as in $S5(Ł_n^c)$ (see Sect. 2.1). Moreover, for each $\varphi \in \mathcal{L}_n^\Box$ we denote by φ_σ its corresponding fuzzy set on S defined as: $\varphi_\sigma(w') = \sigma'(\varphi)$, where $\sigma' = (w', S)$. Note that if $\varphi \in \mathcal{L}_n$ then $\sigma'(\varphi) = w'(\varphi)$ and hence the fuzzy set associated to φ is defined as in Remark 1.
- σ interprets operators $\Box_{\varphi,\psi}$ as one-place functions $\sigma(\Box_{\varphi,\psi}) : VŁ_n \to VŁ_n$ defined as

$$\sigma(\Box_{\varphi,\psi}) = \max\{\tau : VŁ_n \to VŁ_n \text{ truth-stresser} \mid \tau(\varphi_\sigma) \le \psi_\sigma\}.$$

- Finally, as customary, the interpretation by σ of a formula $(\Box_{\varphi,\psi}\chi)$ is defined as follows: $\sigma(\Box_{\varphi,\psi}\chi) = \sigma(\Box_{\varphi,\psi})(\sigma(\chi))$. In particular, if $\chi \in \mathcal{L}_n$, then $\sigma(\Box_{\varphi,\psi}\chi) = \sigma(\Box_{\varphi,\psi})(w(\chi))$.

Obviously, we can give a similar meaning to $\Box_{\varphi,\psi}$ than the one given to f-index of inclusion in the previous section. Firstly, note that the inequality $\tau(\varphi_\sigma) \le \psi_\sigma$ holds if, and only if, σ validates the implication $\varphi_\tau \to \psi$, where φ_τ is the formula defined as

$$\varphi_\tau := \bigvee_{s \in VŁ_n} \Delta(\varphi \equiv \overline{s}) \wedge \overline{\tau(s)},$$

and, as it can be easily checked, it is such that $(\varphi_\tau)_\sigma = \tau(\varphi_\sigma)$.[3] Secondly, the larger the truth stresser (as a mapping), the smaller the degree of truth stress

---

[3] Indeed, if $w(\varphi) = r_0$, then $w(\psi) = \max_r \min(w(\Delta(\varphi \equiv \overline{r}), \tau(r)) =$
$= \max(\max_{r \ne r_0} w(\Delta(\varphi \equiv \overline{r}) \wedge \overline{\tau(r)}), w(\Delta(\varphi \equiv \overline{r_0}) \wedge \overline{\tau(r_0)}) = \max(0, \min(1, \tau(r_0)) =$
$= 0 \vee \tau(r_0) = \tau(w(\varphi))$.

(semantically). For example, the identity mapping imposes no truth stress, while the mapping $\perp$ (which always takes the value 0) imposes a drastic truth stress that makes false even true statements. Therefore, $\Box_{\varphi,\psi}$ determines the minimal amount of truth stress in φ we need to make the formula $\varphi \to \psi$ valid. In other words, we can rewrite the definition of the semantics of $\Box_{\varphi,\psi}$ as

$$\sigma(\Box_{\varphi,\psi}) = \max\{\tau : \text{VŁ}_n \to \text{VŁ}_n \text{ truth-stresser} \mid \sigma \models \varphi_\tau \to \psi\}.$$

We will use the notation Σ^I to refer to the set of interpretations $(w, S) \in \Sigma$ when applied to the expanded language $\mathcal{IL}$ as prescribed above.

Two remarks are in order here:

(i) As in the case of modal formulas $\Box\varphi$, the interpretation of formulas of the type $\Box_{\varphi,\psi}$ by a pair $\sigma = (w, S)$ does not actually depend on the particular world w but only on the set S.

(ii) By Theorem 2, we have that $\sigma(\Box_{\varphi,\psi}\varphi) = \min\{w'(\psi) \mid w' \in S, w(\varphi) \leq w'(\varphi)\} \wedge w(\varphi) = \min\{\psi_\sigma(w') \mid w' \in S, \varphi_\sigma(w) \leq \varphi_\sigma(w')\} \wedge \varphi_\sigma(w)$.

3.2   The Logic IL$_n$: Axiomatic System, Soundness and Completeness

Based on the properties of the f-index of inclusion recalled in Sect. 2.2, we axiomatically define the logic IL$_n$ as an axiomatic expansion of $S5(\text{Ł}_n^c)$ as follows, where we make use of the intended semantics of the modal S5 operator $\boxdot$ as a sort of universal quantifier over the set of interpretations.

Definition 3. *Axioms and rules of IL$_n$ are those of $S5(\text{Ł}_n^c)$ plus:*

(A1) $\boxdot(\Box_{\varphi,\psi}\chi \to \chi)$
(A2) $\boxdot(\Box_{\varphi,\psi}\varphi \to \psi)$
(A3) $\Delta\boxdot(\Box_{\gamma,\delta}\varphi \to \psi) \to \boxdot(\Box_{\gamma,\delta}\chi \to \Box_{\varphi,\psi}\chi)$
(A4) $\boxdot(\Delta(\gamma \to \delta) \to (\Box_{\varphi,\psi}\gamma \to \Box_{\varphi,\psi}\delta))$
(A5) $\bigvee_{s \in V\text{Ł}_n} \boxdot(\Box_{\varphi,\psi}\bar{r} \equiv \bar{s})$, *for any* $r \in V\text{Ł}_n$
(A6) $\boxdot(\Delta(\varphi \equiv \bar{r}) \to (\overline{\tau(r)} \to \Box_{\varphi,\varphi_\tau}\varphi))$, *for any truth-stresser* τ

The above mentioned fact that the modal S5 operator $\boxdot$ behaves as a universal quantifier over the set of evaluations, shows that the above axioms force a behavior of $\Box_{\varphi,\psi}$ that reflects that of the f-indexes of inclusion functions. In particular:

– Axiom (A1) states that for all evaluations the value of $\Box_{\varphi,\psi}$ in χ takes a lower value than χ itself. This hence reflects the property that every index of inclusion function f satisfies $f(x) \leq x$.
– Axiom (A2), encodes the fact the result of applying the index of inclusion of φ in ψ to the fuzzy set given by φ is indeed included into the fuzzy set given by ψ.

- Axiom (A3) captures the maximality property of the index of inclusion; that is the function associated to $\square_{\varphi,\psi}$ is the maximal one among those that, applied to φ, give a fuzzy set included into ψ.
- Axiom (A4) is monotonicity, while axiom (A5) states that the index of inclusion of a constant function is constant as well. These two axioms are needed to prove that $\square_{\varphi,\psi}$ is indeed interpreted as a function.
- Axiom (A6) expresses a technical property of the functions like $\square_{\varphi,\psi}$ that will be used below to prove that the truth-stressers defined in this way are sufficiently many to ensure that the maximal stresser is attained within the set of functions $\square_{\varphi,\psi}$.

All these intuitive semantic interpretations of the axioms are supported by the semantics of the operators $\square_{\varphi,\psi}$ given above, which faithfully reflect in turn the properties of the f-indices of inclusion described in Sect. 2.2. Then, it is not difficult to show that the above axioms are indeed sound.

Proposition 1. $IŁ_n$ *is sound with respect to the class of structures* Σ^I.

Since $IŁ_n$ is an axiomatic expansion of $S5(Ł_n^c)$, one can reduce proofs in $IŁ_n$ to proofs in $S5(Ł_n^c)$ taking the axioms (A1)-(A6) as additional premises. In the following, $Ax(IŁ_n)$ will stand for all the instances of the additional axioms (A1)-(A6).

Lemma 1. *For any set of $IŁ_n$-formulas $T \cup \{\phi\}$, it holds that $T \vdash_{IŁ_n} \phi$ iff $T \cup \{Ax(IŁ_n)\} \vdash_{S5(Ł_n^c)} \phi$, where $\vdash_{S5(Ł_n^c)}$ stands for proof in pure $S5(Ł_n^c)$.*

Finally, we can prove that $IŁ_n$ is (sound and) complete with respect to the semantics previously defined.

Theorem 4. *For any set of $IŁ_n$-formulas, $T \cup \{\phi\}$ we have that, $T \vdash_{IŁ_n} \phi$ iff $T \models_{IŁ_n} \phi$.*

Proof. (Sketch). Assume $T \not\vdash_{IŁ_n} \phi$. By the above Lemma 1, this means that $T \cup \{Ax(IŁ_n)\} \not\vdash_{S5(Ł_n^c)} \phi$, and by completeness of $S5(Ł_n^c)$, $T \cup \{Ax(IŁ_n)\} \not\models_{S5(Ł_n^c)} \phi$. Therefore, there exists an $S5(Ł_n^c)$-interpretation $\sigma = (w, S) \in \Sigma$ such that $\sigma(T) = \sigma(Ax(IŁ_n)) = 1$ and $\sigma(\phi) < 1$. It remains to prove that in fact σ belongs to Σ^I, that is, that σ correctly interprets formulas of the kind $\square_{\varphi,\psi}\chi$ as specified in Sect. 3.1.

If $\varphi, \psi \in \mathcal{L}$ are propositional, the fact that σ evaluates to 1 all the axioms (A1)-(A6) implies a set of conditions on the evaluation by $\sigma = (w, S)$ of formulas of the kind $\square_{\varphi,\psi}\chi$. In particular, axioms (A4) and (A5) allow us to interpret each operator $\square_{\varphi,\psi}$ as a unique unary function on $VŁ_n$, and the rest of the axioms allows one to prove that such a function is indeed the f-inclusion index of φ into ψ, once they are interpreted as fuzzy sets on S. This shows that $\sigma \in \Sigma^I$, hence $T \not\models_{IŁ_n} \phi$, and the proof is completed.

4   Conclusions and Future Work

In this paper we have provided a first step towards a logical account of the notion of f-index of inclusion for fuzzy sets in the frame of an S5-like modal logic over the n-valued Łukasiewicz logic with truth-constants. We have taken advantage of the good logical and expressive properties of this logical setting to define the logic IL_n to reason about f-indexes of inclusion between n-valued propositions. Actually, our goal has been to syntactically link a particular truth-stresser, corresponding to the modality $\square_{\varphi,\psi}$, to each pair of formulas φ and ψ in order to represent "the minimal amount of truth stress in φ we need to make the formula $\varphi \to \psi$ valid", not just to consider different and arbitrary truth-stressers in a logic. The question whether we can do all this without this syntactical link between pairs of formulas φ, ψ and modalities $\square_{\varphi,\psi}$ is left for further work, although we think it can be a difficult task.

Note that equivalence classes of formulas determine the same truth-stresser by the modalities (i.e., $\varphi \equiv \varphi', \psi \equiv \psi' \vdash_{IL_n} \square_{\varphi,\psi}\chi \equiv \square_{\varphi',\psi'}\chi$), thus in fact there are only finitely-many distinct modalities, but that fact does not invalidate the use of both modalities $\square_{\varphi,\psi}$ and $\square_{\varphi',\psi'}$ in the language of the logic IL_n.

As for future work, we plan the study in depth the connection of modalities with the deduction theorem of Łukasiewicz logic or the existence of truth stressers, if any, that cannot be represented as a modality of the type $\square_{\varphi,\psi}$. We also plan to consider a more general many-valued logical setting, lifting the assumption of dealing with finitely-many truth-degrees.

Acknowledgments. Flaminio and Godo acknowledge partial support by the MOSAIC project (EU H2020-MSCA-RISE-2020 Project 101007627) and by the Spanish project PID2019-111544GB-C21/AEI/10.13039/501100011033. Madrid and Ojeda-Aciego acknowledge partial support by the project VALID (PID2022-140630NB-I00 funded by MCIN/AEI/10.13039/501100011033), and by Plan Propio de la Universidad de Málaga.

References

1. Baaz, M.: Infinite-valued Gödel logics with 0-1-projections and relativizations. Lect. Notes Logic **6**, 23–33 (1996)
2. Blondeel, M., Flaminio, T., Schockaert, S., Godo, L., Cock, M.D.: On the relationship between fuzzy autoepistemic logic and fuzzy modal logics of belief. Fuzzy Sets Syst. **276**, 74–99 (2015)
3. Ciabattoni, A., Metcalfe, G., Montagna, F.: Algebraic and proof-theoretic characterizations of truth stressers for MTL and its extensions. Fuzzy Sets Syst. **161**(3), 369–389 (2010)
4. Cignoli, R., D'Ottaviano, I.M.L., Mundici, D.: Algebraic foundations of many-valued reasoning. Trends in Logic-Studia Logica Library, vol. 7. Kluwer Academic Publishers, Dordrecht (2000)
5. Esteva, F., Godo, L., Noguera, C.: A logical approach to fuzzy truth hedges. Inf. Sci. **232**, 366–385 (2013)

6. Fan, J., Xie, W., Pei, J.: Subsethood measure: new definitions. Fuzzy Sets Syst. **106**, 201–209 (1999)
7. Hájek, P.: On very true. Fuzzy Sets Syst. **124**(3), 329–333 (2001)
8. Kitainik, L.M.: Fuzzy inclusions and fuzzy dichotomous decision procedures. In: Kacprzyk, J., Orlovski, S.A. (eds.) Optimization Models Using Fuzzy Sets and Possibility Theory. Theory and Decision Library, vol. 4, pp. 154–170. Springer, Netherlands, Dordrecht (1987). https://doi.org/10.1007/978-94-009-3869-4_11
9. Madrid, N., Ojeda-Aciego, M.: A view of f-indexes of inclusion under different axiomatic definitions of fuzzy inclusion. In: Moral, S., Pivert, O., Sánchez, D., Marín, N. (eds.) SUM 2017. LNCS (LNAI), vol. 10564, pp. 307–318. Springer, Cham (2017). https://doi.org/10.1007/978-3-319-67582-4_22
10. Madrid, N., Ojeda-Aciego, M.: Functional degrees of inclusion and similarity between L-fuzzy sets. Fuzzy Sets Syst. **390**, 1–22 (2020)
11. Madrid, N., Ojeda-Aciego, M.: The f-index of inclusion as optimal adjoint pair for fuzzy modus ponens. Fuzzy Sets Syst. **466**, 108474 (2023)
12. Madrid, N., Ojeda-Aciego, M., Perfilieva, I.: f-inclusion indexes between fuzzy sets. In: Alonso, J.M., et al. (eds.) Proceedings of IFSA-EUSFLAT 2015, AISR 89, Atlantis Press, pp. 1528–1533 (2015)
13. Monteiro, A.: Sur les algèbres de Heyting simétriques. Portugal. Math. **39**, 1–237 (1980)
14. Sinha, D., Dougherty, E.: Fuzzification of set inclusion: theory and applications. Fuzzy Sets Syst. **55**, 15–42 (1993)
15. Vychodil, V.: Truth-depressing hedges and BL-logic. Fuzzy Sets Syst. **157**(15), 2074–2090 (2006)
16. Young, V.: Fuzzy subsethood. Fuzzy Sets Syst. **77**, 371–384 (1996)

SPECIAL SESSION 7: Fuzzy Graph-Based Models: Theory and Application

Reduction Graph for Minimal Determinization of Fuzzy Automata

Aitor G. de Mendívil Grau[1]([✉])(iD), Stefan Stanimirović[2](iD),
and Federico Fariña[1](iD)

[1] Depto. Estadística, Informática y Matemáticas, Univeridad Pública de Navarra,
Campus de Arrosadía, 31006 Pamplona, Spain
{aitor.gonzalezdemendivil,fitxi}@unavarra.es
[2] Faculty of Sciences and Mathematics, University of Niš, Višegradska 33,
18000 Niš, Serbia
stefan.stanimirovic@pmf.edu.rs

Abstract. We introduce a minimal determinization procedure for fuzzy
finite automata (FfAs) with membership values in a complete residuated lattice (CRL). The method is based on the well-known determinization method via factorization of fuzzy states. However, different to other
determinization methods, we do not assume that the CRL is zero divisors
free. This fact requires modifying the functions that define the factorization to avoid the zero divisor values when creating the fuzzy states in
the determinization procedure. After generating a right-irreducible fuzzy
deterministic finite automaton (FDfA) equivalent to the original FfA by
determinization via factorization, we construct the so-called reduction
graph of this fuzzy automaton, where each arc represents the notion
that a fuzzy state is left-reducible by another fuzzy state. By making
these left-reductions, we obtain the equivalent minimal FDfA. It is worth
mentioning that an empty fuzzy state is always reducible by a nonempty
fuzzy state. This behavior, specific for a CRL with zero divisors, has also
to be taken into account when the state reduction is carried out.

Keywords: Fuzzy finite automata · minimal determinization method ·
factorization of fuzzy states · divisible complete residuated lattice ·
reduction graph

1 Introduction

It is well-known that many specific problems, such as lexical analysis and pattern
matching, are implemented using deterministic finite automata (DFAs) (cf. [11]).
On the other hand, formal languages are easier described with nondeterministic

S. Stanimirović acknowledges the support of the Science Fund of the Republic of Serbia, GRANT No. 7750185, Quantitative Automata Models: Fundamental Problems
and Applications - QUAM, and the Ministry of Education, Science and Technological
Development, Republic of Serbia, Contract No. 451-03-68/2022-14/200124.

S. Massanet et al. (Eds.): EUSFLAT 2023/AGOP 2023, LNCS 14069, pp. 543–554, 2023.
https://doi.org/10.1007/978-3-031-39965-7_45

finite automata (NFAs). However, converting an NFA into its equivalent DFA comes at an exponential computation cost (cf. [5]). This shortcoming can be compensated if this conversion outputs a minimal deterministic finite automaton. Brzozowski's double reversal determinization algorithm is one of the best-known *minimal determinization procedures* [4]. In fuzzy automata theory, designing a minimal determinization procedure is particularly challenging, mainly for two reasons. First, there are many definitions of a deterministic fuzzy automaton. Namely, the concepts of the (crisp) deterministic fuzzy automaton (cDFA, for short) and the fuzzy deterministic automaton (FDA, for short) have emerged in the recent literature, with cDFA being a particular case of the FDA. And second, the determinization for fuzzy finite automata (FfAs) is not always feasible for a given model of a deterministic fuzzy automaton.

Two minimal determinization procedures for fuzzy finite automata were developed in [13,14]. In particular, Jančić and Ćirić [13] adapted Brzozowski's method to FfAs with membership values in a complete residuated lattice (CRL). Moreover, Micić et al. [14] have proposed the method based on the *degree of language inclusion* for the same type of FfAs. Both methods output a minimal cDFA for a given FfA. However, note that the size of a minimal FDA is always less or equal to the size of any cDFA equivalent to it, because a cDFA is a particular case of an FDA [6].

Afterward, various determinization methods that output an FDA have been developed in [9,17] for FfAs over a divisible CRL. These methods use the concept of factorizations of fuzzy states. Consequently, some variants of Brzozowski's method have been developed to get minimal determinization procedures for FfAs. In particular, in [7], the author has studied the necessary and sufficient conditions to get a minimal FDA using Brzozowski's method and maximal factorizations. Furthermore, in [8], the authors have proposed a minimal determinization procedure for FfAs over the Godel structure that does not admit a maximal factorization; and more recently, in [10], the authors have generalized the method in [8] to obtain a minimal determinization procedure for FfAs over a totally ordered, divisible and zero divisor free CRL. Such CRLs include the product and the Gödel structure, but not the Łukasiewicz structure. In order to develop a minimal determinization procedure for FfAs over a CRL that includes the Łukasiewicz structure, the zero-divisor-free condition must be lifted up.

This paper introduces a minimal determinization procedure for FfAs with membership values in totally ordered and divisible CRL (without the condition zero divisor free on the lattice). The method outputs a minimal FDfA equivalent to the input FfA and it is based on determinization via factorization of fuzzy states. However, it is necessary to modify the definition of the functions which form the factorization in order to cope with the fact that the underlying CRL may have zero divisors elements (Sect. 3). The modification basically consists on assure that no zero divisor is created in a factorized fuzzy state when a zero value is in the original fuzzy state. This modification seems simple, but many properties have to be revised as a consequence of it. The proposed method uses the notion of the *Reduction Graph* to get the minimal FDfA, but in this graph the fuzzy state **0** (if it appears in the determinization) must be also reducible if the lattice admits zero divisors (Sect. 5). In Sect. 6, we illustrate the minimization procedure by an example using the standard Łukasiewicz structure.

2   Preliminaries

In this paper, we use a *complete residuated lattice* as a structure of membership values [2,3], which can be regarded as a tuple $\mathcal{L} = (L, \vee, \wedge, \otimes, \to, 0, 1)$ satisfying: (**L1**) $(L, \vee, \wedge, 0, 1)$ is a *complete lattice*; (**L2**) $(L, \otimes, 1)$ is a commutative monoid; and (**L3**) for all $x, y, z \in L$: $x \otimes y \leq z \Leftrightarrow x \leq y \to z$. Operations $\otimes$ and $\to$ form an *adjoint pair* (L3) which represent the conjunction and implication of the corresponding logical calculus. In addition, for any $x, y, z, w \in L$: (**L4**) $x \otimes y \leq x$ and $x \leq y \to x$; (**L5**) $x \to x = 1$ and $1 \to x = x$; (**L6**) $(x \to y) \otimes (z \to w) \leq (x \otimes z) \to (y \otimes w)$; (**L7**) $x \otimes (x \to y) = y$ if and only if $(\exists z)\, x \otimes z = y$; (**L8**) $(x \otimes y) \to z = x \to (y \to z) = y \to (x \to z)$; and (**L9**) $x \otimes \bigvee_{i \in K} y_i = \bigvee_{i \in K} x \otimes y_i$, for any $\{y_i\}_{i \in K} \subseteq L$.

In this paper, we assume that $\mathcal{L}$ satisfies the conditions: (**C1**) L is a *totally ordered* set w.r.t $\leq$; and (**C2**) $\mathcal{L}$ is *divisible*, i.e., for every $x, y \in L$ with $x \geq y$ there exists $z \in L$ such that $x \otimes z = y$.

The application of fuzzy sets and fuzzy relations over $\mathcal{L}$ in the Theory of Fuzzy Languages and Automata is well established in the literature [12–16]. Let Q be a finite set of states. Any mapping $S : Q \to L$, $S \in L^Q$, is called a *fuzzy state* of Q. In this paper, **0** denotes the fuzzy state in which all states have value 0. For any $x \in L$ and $S \in L^Q$, $x \otimes S$ is the fuzzy state $(x \otimes S)(q) = x \otimes S(q)$ for every $q \in Q$. Any mapping $T : Q \times Q \to L$, $T \in L^{Q \times Q}$, is called a *fuzzy transition relation* on Q. The *equality relation* E_Q, is defined as $E_Q(p, p) = 1$ for any $p \in Q$ and 0 otherwise. We use the common standard composition $\circ$ ($\bigvee - \otimes$) for fuzzy transitions and fuzzy states.

A **fuzzy finite automaton** (FfA) (over $\mathcal{L}$) is a tuple $A = (Q, \Sigma, I, T, F)$ where Q is a finite set of states, Σ is an alphabet, $I \in L^Q$ is the *initial fuzzy state*, $F \in L^Q$ is the *final fuzzy state*, and $T : \Sigma \to L^{Q \times Q}$ defines a fuzzy transition on Q for each symbol in the alphabet. In the following, ε denotes the *empty word* in Σ^*. The extension of T to $T^* : \Sigma^* \to L^{Q \times Q}$ is defined as: (i) $T^*(\varepsilon) = E_Q$; and (ii) $T^*(\alpha\sigma) = T^*(\alpha) \circ T(\sigma)$ for any $\alpha \in \Sigma^*$, $\sigma \in \Sigma$. To simplify notation, T^* is also denoted by T. By associativity, $T(\alpha\beta) = T(\alpha) \circ T(\beta)$ for any two words α, β. The *fuzzy language* recognized by A, $[A] : \Sigma^* \to L$, is defined by

$$[A](\alpha) = I \circ T(\alpha) \circ F = \bigvee_{p, q \in Q} I(p) \otimes T(\alpha)(p, q) \otimes F(q) \tag{1}$$

for any word α. The size of a FfA A, denoted by $|A|$ is the cardinal of its set of states. In addition, two FAs A and A' are *equivalent* if they recognize the same fuzzy language, i.e., $[A] = [A']$.

A **fuzzy deterministic finite automaton** (FDfA), $D = (Q^d, \Sigma, I^d, T^d, F^d)$, is a FfA such that it has a singleton initial fuzzy state $I^d = \{u/I^d(u)\}$ and each fuzzy transition $T^d(\sigma)$ is *complete* and *deterministic*. In this case, $p_\sigma =$

$q \Leftrightarrow T^d(\sigma)(p, q) > 0$ determines the function $Q^d \times \Sigma \to Q^d$, and its extension $Q^d \times \Sigma^* \to Q^d$ is defined as habitual: (i) $p_\varepsilon = p$; and (ii) $p_{\alpha\sigma} = (p_\alpha)_\sigma$ for any $\alpha \in \Sigma^*$, $\sigma \in \Sigma$. The state p_α represents the unique reachable state from p via the word α. Thus, a state $q \in Q^d$ is *accessible* if there is a word α such that $q = u_\alpha$. By using this notation, values of transitions between states are calculated as follows

$$T^d(\varepsilon)(p, p_\varepsilon) = 1; \quad T^d(\alpha\sigma)(p, p_{\alpha\sigma}) = T^d(\alpha)(p, p_\alpha) \otimes T^d(\sigma)(p_\alpha, p_{\alpha\sigma}); \text{ and} \atop T^d(\alpha)(p, q) = 0 \text{ otherwise} \tag{2}$$

with $\alpha \in \Sigma^*$, $\sigma \in \Sigma$. By (2) and (1), the fuzzy language recognized by a FDfA D is

$$[D](\alpha) = I^d(u) \otimes T^d(\alpha)(u, u_\alpha) \otimes F^d(u_\alpha) \tag{3}$$

for any word α. Given an accessible state u_α, $[D_{u_\alpha}]$ is the fuzzy language defined by $[D_{u_\alpha}](\beta) = T^d(\beta)(u_\alpha, u_{\alpha\beta}) \otimes F^d(u_{\alpha\beta})$ for any word β. Thus, it is simple to prove that, for any word α,

$$\alpha^{-1}[D] = w^d(\alpha) \otimes [D_{u_\alpha}] \text{ with } w^d(\alpha) = I^d(u) \otimes T^d(\alpha)(u, u_\alpha) \tag{4}$$

A FDfA D is *accessible* if $Q^d = \{u_\alpha | \alpha \in \Sigma^*\}$. If a FDfA D satisfies $I^d(u) = 1$ and $T^d(\sigma)$ is a crisp relation on Q, for every $\sigma \in \Sigma$, then, Eq. (3) becomes simply $[D](\alpha) = F^d(u_\alpha)$. In this case, D is called **crisp-deterministic fuzzy finite automaton** (cDFfA) in the literature [1]. Let us observe that a cDFfA is just a particular case of a FDfA.

Definition 1. *A FDfA D (over $\mathcal{L}$) is a* minimal *FDfA if $|D| \le |D'|$ for any FDfA D' equivalent to D.*

As a non-accessible FDfA can not be a minimal FDfA, then in the following definitions we will consider accessible FDfAs.

Definition 2. *An accessible FDfA D is* right-reducible *if there are two states p, $q \in Q^d$, with $p \neq q$, such that $[D_p] = [D_q]$. In this case, we say that q and p are* right-reducible.

For the next definition, we introduce the notion of the maximum value for all words that reach an accessible state $p \in Q^d$:

$$w_\vee^d(p) = \bigvee_{\{\alpha \in \Sigma^* \,|\, p = u_\alpha\}} w^d(\alpha) \tag{5}$$

The value $w_\vee^d(p)$ is well-defined because (a) L is totally ordered; (b) $\otimes$ is monotone; and (c) D is a finite automaton.

Definition 3. *An accessible FDfA D is* left-reducible *if there are two states p, $q \in Q^d$, with $[D_p] \neq [D_q]$, such that $w_\vee^d(q) \otimes [D_p] = w_\vee^d(q) \otimes [D_q]$. In this case, we say that p* left-reduces *q.*

It is simple to prove that a right or left-reducible accessible FDfA is not a minimal FDfA. It is also possible that a right and left-irreducible accessible FDfA is not a minimal FDfA. For example, let us consider that an accessible cDFfA is right-irreducible; then it is trivially left-irreducible since $w_\vee^d(p) = 1$ for every state. This fact does not prevent that there exists an equivalent FDfA whose size is lesser than the size of the irreducible cDFfA. The question of when an irreducible FDfA is a minimal FDfA is discussed in Sect. 5.

A FfA $C = (Q^c, \Sigma, I^c, T^c, F^c)$ is a **crisp co-accessible co-deterministic FfA** (CFfA) if and only if its reverse automaton $r(C)$ is a cDFfA. In this case, C has a (singleton) final fuzzy state $F^c = \{e/1\}$. If two states p and p' satisfy that $T^c(\beta)(p, e) = 1$ and $T^c(\beta)(p', e) = 1$ for the same word β then $p = p'$. This is because C is co-deterministic. Since C is complete and co-deterministic, the composition $T^c(\beta) \circ F^c = T^c(\beta) \circ \{e/1\}$ outputs a singleton crisp state $\{p/1\}$ where p is the unique state such that $T^c(\beta)(p, e) = 1$. This state is denoted by e_β. In fact, the set of states Q^c is the finite set $\{e_\beta \mid \beta \in \Sigma^*\}$ because C is co-accessible. This analysis allows us to calculate the next expression for any fuzzy state $S \in L^{Q^c}$ and word β:

$$S \circ T^c(\beta) \circ \{e/1\} = S(e_\beta) \tag{6}$$

Thus, the fuzzy language $[C]$ fulfills $[C](\beta) = I^c \circ T^c(\beta) \circ \{e/1\} = I^c(e_\beta)$ for any word β. Let us observe that the set $\{I_\alpha^c \mid \alpha \in \Sigma^*\}$, where $I_\alpha^c = I^c \circ T^c(\alpha)$, is a finite set since $T^c(\alpha)$ is a crisp relation for any word α. In addition, $[C]$ is the same fuzzy language for any CRL $\mathcal{L}_\otimes$ defined over the same support set L. The same fact happens to the fuzzy states I_α^c. In this sense, we can say that a CFfA C is independent of the CRL that is applied to compute its behavior, i.e., it only depends on the set L. The construction of a CFfA equivalent to a FfA has been discussed in [8,13,14]. We omit it here by brevity.

3   Factorization in Divisible Complete Residuated Lattices

In this section, we present factorization of fuzzy states in divisible and totally ordered complete residuated lattices $\mathcal{L}$ (dCRL in short). Different to the papers [7–10,17], we do not consider the zero divisor free condition on the lattices. As $\mathcal{L}$ is divisible, then, by (L7), $x \otimes (x \to y) = y$ for $x, y \in L$ with $x \geq y$.

Definition 4. *Let $\mathcal{L}$ be a dCRL and let Q be a non-empty finite set of states. Functions $g : L^Q \to L$ and $f : L^Q \to L^Q$ are defined for any $S \in L^Q$, $q \in Q$ as*

$$g(S) = \bigvee_{q \in Q} S(q) \text{ with } S \neq \mathbf{0}; \quad \text{and} \quad g(\mathbf{0}) = 1 \tag{7}$$

$$f(S)(q) = g(S) \to S(q) \text{ if } S(q) \neq 0, \text{ and } f(S)(q) = 0 \text{ otherwise} \tag{8}$$

The pair of functions (f, g), provided in Definition 4, satisfies the following properties for any $S \in L^Q$, $q \in Q$ and $x \in L$:

(F1) $g(S) \geq S(q)$; **(F2)** $g(S) > 0$; **(F3)** $f(S) \geq S$;
(F4) $f(S)(q) = 0 \Leftrightarrow S(q) = 0$; **(F5)** $g(S) \otimes f(S) = S$;
(F6) $g(x \otimes S) = x \otimes g(S)$ with $\forall q : S(q) \neq 0 \Rightarrow x \otimes S(q) \neq 0$;
(F7) $f(S) \leq f(x \otimes S)$ with $\forall q : S(q) \neq 0 \Rightarrow x \otimes S(q) \neq 0$;
(F8) $f(S) = f(f(S))$; and **(F9)** $S \neq \mathbf{0} \Rightarrow \exists q \in Q : f(S)(q) = 1$.

We do not provide the proofs, as they are similar to the ones conducted in [9,10,17] for analogous properties. By the property (F5), the pair (f, g) is a factorization of L^Q in the sense given in [9]. The proposed factorization does not explicitly provide zero divisors (if any in $\mathcal{L}$) due to the second condition in (8).

4   Determinization of a CFfA

The common method for determinization of a FfA A over a CRL is via the construction of the Nerode automaton $N(A)$ of A. Recall that $N(A)$ is a cDFfA equivalent to A whose finite set of states is $Q^{N(A)} = \{I_\alpha | \alpha \in \Sigma^*\}$ where $I_\alpha = I \circ T(\alpha)$ for any word α (see [12] for more details). A generalization of this construction, based on the notion of factorization of fuzzy states, was provided in [9] for FfAs over a zero divisor free CRL. However, this method of determinization can be easily extended for any dCRL.

Definition 5. *For a FfA $A = (Q, \Sigma, I, T, F)$ over a dCRL $\mathcal{L}$, the fuzzy automaton $D_{fA} = (Q^{fA}, \Sigma, I^{fA}, T^{fA}, F^{fA})$ obtained by the determinization of A via a factorization (f, g) of L^Q is defined as follows: (i) the initial fuzzy state is the singleton set $I^{fA} = \{f(I)/g(I)\}$; (ii) the set of states Q^{fA} are computed by the recurrence $R_{\alpha\sigma} = f(R_\alpha \circ T(\sigma))$ for any word α and symbol σ, where initially $R_\varepsilon = f(I)$; (iii) for each symbol σ, the fuzzy transition $T^{fA}(\sigma)$ satisfies $T^{fA}(\sigma)(R_\alpha, R_{\alpha\sigma}) = g(R_\alpha \circ T(\sigma))$ for any word α, and 0 otherwise; and (iv) the final fuzzy state F^{fA} is defined by $F^{fA}(R_\alpha) = R_\alpha \circ F$ for any word α.*

The fuzzy automaton D_{fA} provided in Definition 5 is an accessible fuzzy complete deterministic automaton equivalent to A (see further details in [9,17]). Each state $R_\alpha \in Q^{fA}$ is a fuzzy state of Q which represents the accessible state from the initial state R_ε by the word α. The following properties are derived by Definition 5 and by induction. For any $\alpha, \beta \in \Sigma^*$ and $\sigma \in \Sigma$:

(D1) $R_\alpha \circ T(\sigma) = T^{fA}(\sigma)(R_\alpha, R_{\alpha\sigma}) \otimes R_{\alpha\sigma}$; **(D2)** $I_\alpha = w^{fA}(\alpha) \otimes R_\alpha$
(D3) $[A] = [D_{fA}]$ (equivalence); and **(D4)** $[(D_{fA})_{R_\alpha}](\beta) = R_\alpha \circ T(\beta) \circ F$

Lemma 1. *Let $C = (Q^c, \Sigma, I^c, T^c, \{e/1\})$ be a CFfA with membership values in L. Given any dCRL $\mathcal{L}$ and a factorization (f, g) of L^{Q^c} then, for any fuzzy state $S \in L^{Q^c}$ and $\sigma \in \Sigma$:*

$$f(f(S) \circ T^c(\sigma)) = f(S \circ T^c(\sigma)) \tag{9}$$

Proof. For any $\sigma \in \Sigma$, the fuzzy transition relation $T^c(\sigma)$ satisfies the conditions: (i) it is a crisp transition; (ii) it is complete backward; and (iii) it is co-deterministic. Thus, for each $q \in Q$ there exists a unique state $q_\sigma \in Q$ such that $T^c(\sigma)(q_\sigma, q) = 1$ and equal 0 for the rest of states. Thus, $(f(S) \circ T^c(\sigma))(q) = f(S)(q_\sigma)$ and $(S \circ T(\sigma))(q) = S(q_\sigma)$ for any $S \in L^Q$ and $q \in Q$.

(1) First, we prove that $\forall q : (f(S) \circ T^c(\sigma))(q) \neq 0 \Rightarrow g(S) \otimes (f(S) \circ T^c(\sigma))(q) \neq 0$.
$\forall q : f(S)(q_\sigma) \neq 0 \Rightarrow S(q_\sigma) \neq 0$, this is true by (F4). As by (F5) $g(S) \otimes f(S)(q_\sigma) = S(q_\sigma)$, then, $\forall q : f(S)(q_\sigma) \neq 0 \Rightarrow g(S) \otimes f(S)(q_\sigma) \neq 0$.
By (F6), and the proven condition, the next holds:
$g(S) \otimes g(f(S) \circ T^c(\sigma)) = g(g(S) \otimes (f(S) \circ T^c(\sigma)) =$
$g((g(S) \otimes f(S)) \circ T^c(\sigma)) = g(S \circ T^c(\sigma))$ **

(2) For any $q \in Q$, and by definition (8) of $f(.)$: by (F4), $f(f(S) \circ T^c(\sigma))(q) = 0$ if $(f(S) \circ T^c(\sigma))(q) = f(S)(q_\sigma) = 0$, by (F4), $S(q_\sigma) = 0$ and $(S \circ T^c(\sigma))(q) = 0$. Then, by (8), $f(S \circ T^c(\sigma))(q) = 0$. In conclusion, $f(f(S) \circ T^c(\sigma))(q) = f(S \circ T^c(\sigma))(q) = 0$ holds.

(3) Let us consider now that $f(f(S) \circ T^c(\sigma))(q) \neq 0$, then, $f(S)(q_\sigma) \neq 0$, and by (F4), $S(q_\sigma) \neq 0$. By definition (8) $f(f(S) \circ T^c(\sigma))(q) = g(f(S) \circ T^c(\sigma)) \rightarrow (f(S) \circ T^c(\sigma))(q) = g(f(S) \circ T^c(\sigma)) \rightarrow f(S)(q_\sigma) =$, by (8) $g(f(S) \circ T^c(\sigma)) \rightarrow (g(S) \rightarrow S(q_\sigma)) =$, by (L8) $g(S) \otimes g(f(S) \circ T^c(\sigma)) \rightarrow S(q_\sigma) =$, by the proof above ** and (8), $g(S \circ T^c(\sigma)) \rightarrow (S \circ T^c(\sigma))(q) = f(S \circ T^c(\sigma))(q)$. In conclusion, $f(f(S) \circ T^c(\sigma))(q) = f(S \circ T^c(\sigma))(q) \neq 0$ holds.

Lemma 2. *Let $C = (Q^c, \Sigma, I^c, T^c, \{e/1\})$ be a CFfA with membership values in L. Given any dCRL $\mathcal{L}$, then the fuzzy automaton D_{fC}, obtained by the determinization of C via factorization (g, f) of L^{Q^c}, satisfies, for any word $\alpha \in \Sigma^*$:*

$$(a)\ f(I_\alpha^c) = R_\alpha; \quad and \quad (b)\ f(w^{fC}(\alpha) \otimes R_\alpha) = R_\alpha; \tag{10}$$

$$(c)\ I_\alpha^c \neq \mathbf{0} \Rightarrow g(I_\alpha^c) = w^{fC}(\alpha); \quad and \quad (d)\ I_\alpha^c = \mathbf{0} \Rightarrow w^{fC}(\alpha) > 0. \tag{11}$$

Proof. The proof of (10)(a) is by induction, Definition 5 and (9); (10)(b) is derived from (10)(a) and (**D2**). (11)(c) is obtained by induction, Definition 5 and (**F6**); and (11)(d) is derived from (11)(c), Definition 5(iii) and (7).

Theorem 1. *Let $C = (Q^c, \Sigma, I^c, T^c, \{e/1\})$ be a CFfA with membership values in L. Given any dCRL $\mathcal{L}$ then, the determinization of C via factorization (g, f) of L^{Q^c}, the automaton D_{fC}, is an accessible right-irreducible FDfA equivalent to C.*

Proof. The automaton D_{fC} is an accessible fuzzy complete deterministic automaton equivalent to C [9,17]. In addition, D_{fC} is a finite automaton because the set $\{I_\alpha^c | \alpha \in \Sigma^*\}$ is finite (see the ending text in Sect. 2), and by (10)(a), then the set $Q^{fC} = \{R_\alpha | \alpha \in \Sigma^*\}$ is also finite. Finally, by (**D4**) and (6), if $[(D_{fC})_{R_\alpha}] = [(D_{fA})_{R_\beta}]$ then $R_\alpha = R_\beta$. This fact concludes that D_{fC} is right-irreducible.

5 Minimality via the Reduction Graph

Let $C = (Q^c, \Sigma, I^c, T^c, \{e/1\})$ be a CFfA with membership values in L, and let $\mathcal{L}$ be any dCRL. As by Theorem 1, D_{fC} is right-irreducible then, it is possible that two states $P, S \in Q^{fC}$ may satisfy P left-reduces S. In this case, D_{fC} is not a minimal FDfA. In this section, we study how to obtain a minimal FDfA equivalent to C by using D_{fC} and the notion of *Reduction Graph* of D_{fC}. In this section, to simplify notation, we use D instead of D_{fC} when it is clear in the context of discussion.

What does 'P *left-reduces* S' mean in D? We recall that P and S are fuzzy subsets of Q^c. By Definition 3, $[D_P] \neq [D_S]$ is equivalent to $P \neq S$ because D is right-irreducible (by Theorem 1). As P and S are accessible states in D, $P = f(I^c_{\alpha^P_\vee})$ and $S = f(I^c_{\beta^S_\vee})$ (by Lemma 2, (10)(a)) where $\alpha^P_\vee \neq \beta^S_\vee$. The condition $w^D_\vee(S) \otimes [D_S] = w^D_\vee(S) \otimes [D_P]$ in Definition 3 is equivalent to

$$w^D_\vee(S) \otimes S = w^D_\vee(S) \otimes P \tag{12}$$

(by (**D4**) and (6)). Let us observe that if $P = \mathbf{0}$ in (12) implies $w^D_\vee(S) \otimes S = \mathbf{0}$ and then, (by (10)(b) in Lemma 2 and (F4)) $S = \mathbf{0}$. A contradiction with the fact that $P \neq S$. Assume that $S = \mathbf{0}$ and $P \neq \mathbf{0}$ in (12). As $w^D_\vee(S) > 0$ (by Lemma 2, (11)(d)) and $P \neq \mathbf{0}$ is the factorization $f(I^c_{\alpha^P_\vee})$, then, by (F4) and (F9), $w^D_\vee(S) \otimes P \neq \mathbf{0}$. A contradiction with the hypothesis. Thus, $P \neq S$, $P \neq \mathbf{0}$, and $S \neq \mathbf{0}$ is fulfilled.

Let us consider now that $w^D_\vee(S) = w^D_\vee(P)$ holds. Then, in (12), $f(w^D_\vee(S) \otimes S) = f(w^D_\vee(P) \otimes P)$. By Lemma 2, (10)(b), we obtain $S = P$ which is a contradiction with $P \neq S$. If we consider now that $w^D_\vee(S) > w^D_\vee(P)$, then, as $\mathcal{L}$ is divisible, $w^D_\vee(P) \otimes S = w^D_\vee(P) \otimes P$ also holds. By (10)(b), we have $S = f(w^D_\vee(S) \otimes P)$ and $P = f(w^D_\vee(P) \otimes S)$. It is simple to prove by definition of $f(.)$ (8) that $S(q) = 0$ if and only if $P(q) = 0$ for any $q \in Q^c$, i.e., $\mathrm{Supp}(S) = \mathrm{Supp}(P)$. In addition, by (F9) and definition of $g()$ (7), for any $q \in Q^c$:

$$S(q) = w^D_\vee(S) \to w^D_\vee(S) \otimes P(q) \text{ and } P(q) = w^D_\vee(P) \to w^D_\vee(P) \otimes S(q)$$

with $P(q) \neq 0$ ($S(q) \neq 0$). By (L6) and (L5), $S(q) \geq P(q)$ and $P(q) \geq S(q)$. This derives in the contradiction $P = S$. Therefore, $w^D_\vee(P) > w^D_\vee(S)$ holds.

In conclusion, for two states $P, S \in Q^{fC}$, 'P *left-reduces* S' in D is equivalent to

$$P \neq \mathbf{0}, \ S \neq \mathbf{0}, \ w^D_\vee(P) > w^D_\vee(S), \text{ and } w^D_\vee(S) \otimes S = w^D_\vee(S) \otimes P \tag{13}$$

The intuition behind P left-reduces S lies in the observation (see (12)) that every word that reaches S could alternative reach P without modifying the language recognized by D. In other words, it is possible to build a new accessible FDfA D' with lesser size than D by moving every arc ending in S in D to P in the new automaton D'. By this reduction process, S becomes an inaccessible state in D' and it can be safely removed.

The particular case of the empty state $\mathbf{0} \in Q^{fC}$ is of interest when $\mathcal{L}$ has zero divisors. In this particular case, for any state $P \in Q^{fC}$ with $P \neq \mathbf{0}$ the following trivial relation holds: $w_V^D(\mathbf{0}) \otimes \mathbf{0} = (w_V^D(\mathbf{0}) \otimes z_P) \otimes \mathbf{0} = w_V^D(\mathbf{0}) \otimes (z_P \otimes P)$ where z_p is a zero divisor for all the values in the image of P. This also means that $\mathbf{0}$ is left-reducible by any other nonempty state without changing the fuzzy language. In the following, we introduce a relation between the states of D in order to define the *Reduction Graph* of D.

Definition 6. *Let $C = (Q^c, \Sigma, I^c, T^c, \{e/1\})$ be a CFfA with membership values in L, and let $\mathcal{L}$ be any dCRL. Given the automaton D_{fC} whose set of states is Q^{fC}; then, two sates $P, S \in Q^{fC}$ satisfy the relation $P \ll S$ if and only if*

$$(a)\, P\, left\text{-}reduces\, S\, (13);\, or\, (b)\, S = \mathbf{0}, P \neq \mathbf{0}\, and\, \exists z_p > 0 : z_P \otimes P = \mathbf{0}\, (14)$$

It is not difficult to prove that $(Q^{fC}, \ll)$ is a strict partial ordered set, i.e., $\ll$ is irreflexive, asymmetric and transitive. Therefore, the *Reduction Graph* of the automaton D_{fC} is basically a directed graph whose nodes are the states in Q^{fC} and the arcs represent the relation $\ll$ between two states. We say that the Reduction Graph is *empty* when no arc is in the graph.

Theorem 2. *Let $C = (Q^c, \Sigma, I^c, T^c, \{e/1\})$ be a CFfA with membership values in L, and let $\mathcal{L}$ be any dCRL. The determinization of C via factorization (f, g) of L^{Q^c}, the automaton D_{fC}, is a minimal FDfA if and only if the Reduction Graph of D_{fC} is empty.*

This Theorem can be proven by the same technique used in [10], taken into account that $\mathcal{L}$ may have zero divisors. We omit the proof by lack of space.

6   Example

In this section, we present a simple example in order to show how the minimal determinization procedure based on the reduction graph is able to produce a minimal FDfA which recognizes a given fuzzy language. In this example, we compare the results using the Gödel structure and the Łukasiewicz structure.

Let us consider the fuzzy language $K = \{a/0.8,\ aa/0.6, aaa/0.4,\ aaaa/0.2\}$ defined over the alphabet $\Sigma = \{a\}$ with membership values in $[0, 1]$. For brevity, we start with the CFfA C with membership values in $[0, 1]$ which recognizes the fuzzy language K. This automaton is graphically represented in Fig. 1.

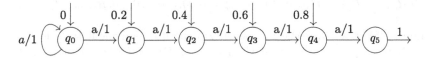

Fig. 1. The CFfA C which recognizes the fuzzy language K.

As we indicated at the end of Sect. 2, the CFfA C can be determinizable by using different divisible CRLs that share the same support set, in this example the closed interval $[0, 1]$. In particular, we shall construct the determinization of C via factorization (g, f) of $[0, 1]^{Q^c}$ over the Gödel structure which is a zero divisor free structure. Let us recall that in the Gödel structure: $x \otimes y = \min\{x, y\}$ and $x \to y = y$ if $x > y$ and 1 otherwise. By Definition 5, we obtain the following states and transitions:

$R_\varepsilon = f(I^c) = f((0, 0.2, 0.4, 0.6, 0.8, 0)) = (0, 0.2, 0.4, 0.6, 1, 0); \ g(I^c) = 0.8,$
$R_a = f(R_\varepsilon \circ T_a^c) = f((0, 0, 0.2, 0.4, 0.6, 1)) = (0, 0, 0.2, 0.4, 0.6, 1); \ g(R_\varepsilon \circ T_a^c) = 1,$
$R_{aa} = f(R_a \circ T_a^c) = f((0, 0, 0, 0.2, 0.4, 0, 6)) = (0, 0, 0, 0.2, 0.4, 1); \ g(R_a \circ T_a^c) = 0.6,$
$R_{aaa} = f(R_{aa} \circ T_a^c) = f((0, 0, 0, 0, 0.2, 0.4)) = (0, 0, 0, 0, 0.2, 1); \ g(R_{aa} \circ T_a^c) = 0.4,$
$R_{aaaa} = f(R_{aaa} \circ T_a^c) = f((0, 0, 0, 0, 0, 0.2)) = (0, 0, 0, 0, 0, 1); \ g(R_{aaa} \circ T_a^c) = 0.2,$
$\mathbf{0} = f(R_{aaaa} \circ T_a^c) = f((0, 0, 0, 0, 0, 0)) = (0, 0, 0, 0, 0, 0); \ g(R_{aaaa} \circ T_a^c) = 1.$

The automaton D_{fC} equivalent to C is shown in Fig. 2. This automaton also includes the values for each final state. It is simple to prove that the Reduction Graph of D_{fC} is empty, what indicates, by Theorem 2, that D_{fC} is the minimal FDfA over the Gödel structure which recognizes the fuzzy language K.

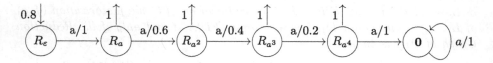

Fig. 2. The FDfA D_{fC} over the Gödel structure equivalent to C.

Now, we construct the determinization of C via factorization (g, f) of $[0, 1]^{Q^c}$ over the Łukasiewicz structure which has zero divisor elements. Let us recall that $x \otimes y = \max\{0, x + y - 1\}$ and $x \to y = 1 - x + y$ if $x > y$ and 1 otherwise. By Definition 5, we obtain the following states and transitions:

$R_\varepsilon = f(I^c) = f((0, 0.2, 0.4, 0.6, 0.8, 0)) = (0, 0.4, 0.6, 0.8, 1, 0); \ g(I^c) = 0.8,$
$R_a = f(R_\varepsilon \circ T_a^c) = f((0, 0, 0.4, 0.6, 0.8, 1)) = (0, 0, 0.4, 0.6, 0.8, 1); \ g(R_\varepsilon \circ T_a^c) = 1,$
$R_{aa} = f(R_a \circ T_a^c) = f((0, 0, 0, 0.4, 0.6, 0, 8)) = (0, 0, 0, 0.6, 0.8, 1); \ g(R_a \circ T_a^c) = 0.8,$
$R_{aaa} = f(R_{aa} \circ T_a^c) = f((0, 0, 0, 0, 0.6, 0.8)) = (0, 0, 0, 0, 0.8, 1); \ g(R_{aa} \circ T_a^c) = 0.8,$
$R_{aaaa} = f(R_{aaa}^{Lkw} \circ T_a^c) = f((0, 0, 0, 0, 0, 0.8)) = (0, 0, 0, 0, 0, 1); \ g(R_{aaa} \circ T_a^c) = 0.8,$
$\mathbf{0} = f(R_{aaaa} \circ T_a^c) = f((0, 0, 0, 0, 0, 0)) = (0, 0, 0, 0, 0, 0); \ g(R_{aaaa} \circ T_a^c) = 1.$

The FDfA D_{fC} over the Łukasiewicz structure equivalent to C is shown in Fig. 3. It is simple to prove that the reduction Graph of D_{fC} is not empty (see the table below the Fig. 3), what indicates, by Theorem 2, that D_{fC} is not a minimal FDfA over this structure.

The reduction Graph of D_{fC} is shown in the following table. The construction is done by using Definition 6 and Eq. (14) (P left-reduces S).

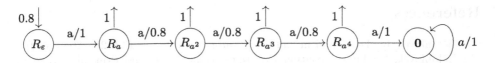

Fig. 3. The FDfA D_{fC} over the Łukasiewicz structure equivalent to C.

P	fuzzy state	$w_\vee(P)$	S	R_ε	R_a	R_{aa}	R_{aaa}	R_{aaaa}	0
R_ε	(0, 0.4, 0.6, 0.8, 1, 0)	0.8							≪
R_a	(0, 0, 0.4, 0.6, 0.8, 1)	0.8				≪	≪	≪	≪
R_{aa}	(0, 0, 0, 0.6, 0.8, 1)	0.6					≪	≪	≪
R_{aaa}	(0, 0, 0, 0, 0.8, 1)	0.4						≪	≪
R_{aaaa}	(0, 0, 0, 0, 0, 1)	0.2							≪
0	(0, 0, 0, 0, 0, 0)	0.2							

Let us observe that the state R_a left-reduces any state in $\{R_{aa}, R_{aaa}, R_{aaaa}, \mathbf{0}\}$. Each arc ending in any of these states is moved through R_a. In this case, it is not necessary to compute z_p (see Definition 6) since $\mathbf{0}$ will be not accessible in the resulting automaton. After this simple left-reduction process, all inaccessible states are removed. The final minimal FDfA is shown in Fig. 4.

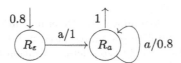

Fig. 4. Minimal FDfA over the Łukasiewicz structure equivalent to C.

7   Conclusion

In [10], the authors have introduced a minimal determinization procedure for FfAs over totally ordered, divisible, and zero divisor free CRLs. This paper generalizes this result and aims at introducing the minimal determinization procedure for the same FfAs, but without the restriction on the CRL to be zero divisor free. As the proposed method employs the concept of factorization of fuzzy states, this weakening of the conditions on the CRL requires a change in the definition of this concept. Although it sounds simple, this modification requires the revision of many properties that are covered in this paper. We provided a simple example in which the proposed method outputs the minimal FDfA, while other determinization methods fail to do so. In future work, we will explore the minimization of FfAs over a partially ordered divisible CRL.

References

1. Bělohlávek, R.: Determinism and fuzzy automata. Inf. Sci. **143**, 205–209 (2002)
2. Bělohlávek, R.: Fuzzy Relational Systems: Foundations and Principles. Kluwer, New York (2002)
3. Bělohlávek, R., Vychodil, V.: Fuzzy Equational Logic. Studies in Fuzziness and Soft Computing, Springer, Heidelberg (2005). https://doi.org/10.1007/b105121
4. Brzozowski, J.A.: Canonical regular expressions and minimal state graphs for definite events. In: Mathematical Theory of Automata. Volume 12 of MRI Symposia Series, pp. 529–561. Polytechnic Press, Polytechnic Institute of Brooklyn, N.Y. (1962)
5. van Glabbeek, R., Ploeger, B.: Five determinisation algorithms. In: Ibarra, O.H., Ravikumar, B. (eds.) CIAA 2008. LNCS, vol. 5148, pp. 161–170. Springer, Heidelberg (2008). https://doi.org/10.1007/978-3-540-70844-5_17
6. de Mendívil, J.R.G.: A generalization of Myhill-Nerode theorem for fuzzy languages. Fuzzy Sets Syst. **301**, 103–115 (2016)
7. de Mendívil, J.R.G.: Conditions for minimal fuzzy deterministic finite automata via Brzozowski's procedure. IEEE Trans. Fuzzy Syst. **26**(4), 2409–2420 (2018)
8. de Mendívil, J.R.G., Figueredo, F.F.: Canonization of max-min fuzzy automata. Fuzzy Sets Syst. **376**, 152–168 (2019)
9. de Mendívil, J.R.G., Garitagoitia, J.R.: Determinization of fuzzy automata via factorization of fuzzy states. Inf. Sci. **283**, 165–179 (2014)
10. de Mendívil Grau, A.G., Stanimirović, S., Figueredo, F.F.: Minimal determinization procedure for fuzzy automata. techRxiv (2022). Preprint. https://doi.org/10.36227/techrxiv.21770510.v1
11. Hopcroft, J.E., Motwani, R., Ullman, J.: Introduction to Automata Theory, 3rd edn. Addison-Wesley (2007)
12. Ignjatović, J., Ćirić, M., Bogdanović, S.: Determinization of fuzzy automata with membership values in complete residuated lattices. Inf. Sci. **178**, 164–180 (2008)
13. Jančić, Z., Ćirić, M.: Brzozowski type determinization for fuzzy automata. Fuzzy Sets Syst. **249**, 73–82 (2014)
14. Micić, I., Jančić, Z., Ignjatović, J., Ćirić, M.: Determinization of fuzzy automata by means of the degrees of language inclusion. IEEE Trans. Fuzzy Syst. **23**(6), 2144–2153 (2015)
15. Qiu, D.W.: Automata theory based on completed residuated lattice-valued logic (I). Sci. China Ser. F **44**(6), 419–429 (2001). https://doi.org/10.1007/BF02713945
16. Qiu, D.W.: Automata theory based on completed residuated lattice-valued logic (ii). Sci. China Ser. F **45**(6), 442–452 (2002). https://doi.org/10.1360/02yf9038
17. Stanimirović, S., Ćirić, M., Ignjatović, J.: Determinization of fuzzy automata by factorizations of fuzzy states and right invariant fuzzy quasi-orders. Inf. Sci. **469**, 79–100 (2018)

Finite Nerode Construction for Fuzzy Automata over the Product Algebra

Zorana Jančić[1]([⊠])[iD], Ivana Micić[1][iD], Stefan Stanimirović[1][iD],
Jose Ramón Gonzalez de Mendívil[2][iD], and Miroslav Ćirić[1][iD]

[1] Faculty of Science and Mathematics, University of Niš, Niš, Serbia
{zorana.jancic,ivana.micic,stefan.stanimirovic,miroslav.ciric}@pmf.edu.rs
[2] Departamento de Estadística, Informática y Matemáticas,
Universidad Pública de Navarra, 31006 Pamplona, Spain
mendivil@unavarra.es

Abstract. The Nerode's automaton of a given fuzzy automaton $\mathcal{A}$ is a crisp-deterministic fuzzy automaton obtained by determinization of $\mathcal{A}$ using the well-known accessible fuzzy subset construction. This celebrated construction of a crisp-deterministic fuzzy automaton has served as a basis for various determinization procedures for fuzzy automata. However, the drawback of this construction is that it may not be feasible when the underlying structure for fuzzy automata is the product algebra because it is not locally finite. This paper provides an alternative way to construct a Nerode-like fuzzy automaton when the input fuzzy automaton is defined over the product algebra. This construction is always finite, since the fuzzy language recognized by this fuzzy automaton has a finite domain. However, this new construction does not accept the same fuzzy language as the initial fuzzy automaton. Nonetheless, it differs only in words accepted to some very small degree, which we treat as irrelevant. Therefore, our construction is an excellent finite approximation of Nerode's automaton.

Keywords: fuzzy automata · determinization · Nerode's automaton · product algebra

1 Introduction

One of the main reasons for introducing the concept of fuzzy automata and fuzzy languages is the attempt to overcome the discrepancy between the vagueness and ambiguity of natural languages on the one hand, and the precision and exactness of formal languages on the other [14,15]. Moreover, fuzzy automata and

Z. Jančić, I. Micić, S. Stanimirović and M. Ćirić acknowledge the support of the Science Fund of the Republic of Serbia, GRANT No. 7750185, Quantitative Automata Models: Fundamental Problems and Applications - QUAM, and of the Ministry of Education, Science and Technological Development, Republic of Serbia, Contract No. 451-03-68/2022-14/200124.

S. Massanet et al. (Eds.): EUSFLAT 2023/AGOP 2023, LNCS 14069, pp. 555–566, 2023.
https://doi.org/10.1007/978-3-031-39965-7_46

fuzzy languages have a variety of applications, such as learning systems, control systems, pattern recognition, neural networks, artificial intelligence, lexical analysis, string matching, and many others (cf. [13]).

Many researchers have focused on studying various methods for determinization of fuzzy automata [1–3, 7, 11, 12]. The well-known accessible fuzzy subset construction [5] is one of the most influential determinization methods for fuzzy automata, as it serves as the basis for many other such methods [4, 8, 9, 16]. This method constructs a crisp-deterministic fuzzy automaton, called the Nerode automaton [6], which is equivalent to a given fuzzy automaton. However, if the underlying structure of truth values is not locally finite, which is the case for the product algebra, the Nerode automaton is not necessarily finite (see [5, 6] for more details).

In this paper, we propose a new procedure for constructing a crisp-deterministic fuzzy automaton whose primary goal is to overcome the above mentioned problem. Starting from a fuzzy automaton over the product algebra, this algorithm always generates a finite crisp-deterministic fuzzy automaton. Although this procedure has a termination property and results in an algorithm, the drawback is that the output fuzzy automaton does not recognize the same fuzzy language as the input fuzzy automaton. Nevertheless, the fuzzy language it recognizes is what we call here the truncating fuzzy language of the fuzzy language that the original fuzzy automaton recognizes. Consequently, these two fuzzy languages differ only in those words whose degree of acceptance by the original fuzzy language was very low. In other words, these two fuzzy languages are equivalent in all the words whose acceptance degree by the original automaton was greater than a certain value. The truncating language is an approximation to the original fuzzy language, and is defined for a certain value $\varepsilon > 0$. The smaller the value ε, the smaller the difference between the fuzzy languages. Different kind of approximation of fuzzy languages was proposed by Yang and Li in [17]. They defined fuzzy ε-approximate regular languages and minimal deterministic fuzzy automaton ε-accepting them. The main advantage of our approach is that original fuzzy language and truncating fuzzy language differ only for those words whose degree of acceptance by the given automaton is smaller than some predefined value, contrary to ε-approximate regular languages which are different form original fuzzy languages in every word.

The structure of the paper is as follows. Section 2 recalls basic definitions and properties regarding fuzzy sets, fuzzy relations and fuzzy automata over the product algebra. Section 3 introduces the notion of a truncating fuzzy language that provides an image-finite fuzzy language of any fuzzy automaton. Section 4 focuses on the Nerode-like construction of a crisp-deterministic fuzzy finite automaton that recognizes the image-finite truncating fuzzy language for a given fuzzy automaton. In the same section, we present an algorithm for constructing this crisp-deterministic fuzzy finite automaton and an illustrative example. Section 5 contains some concluding remarks.

2 Preliminaries

As a structure of truth values, we use the product algebra, which is the typle $(P, \vee, \cdot)$ consisting of the support set $P = [0, 1]$ equipped with meet and operation $\cdot$ (ordinary product operation for real numbers). Recall that the operation $\cdot$, as it is a t-norm on $[0, 1]$, satisfies the laws of commutativity, associativity and monotonicity, and has 1 as the neutral element.

For a nonempty set A, a function $f : A \to P$ is called a *fuzzy subset* of A, while a function $f : A \times A \to P$ is called a *fuzzy relation* on A. The set of all fuzzy subsets of A is denoted by P^A, while the set of all fuzzy relations on A is denoted by $P^{A \times A}$. The equality and the inclusion for fuzzy subsets (resp. fuzzy relations) are defined in the same way as the equality and the inclusion between mappings. The join ($\vee$) of the family of fuzzy subsets is defined to be coordinate-wise.

The compositions between fuzzy subsets and fuzzy relations, as well as between a fuzzy subset and a fuzzy relation, are defined in the following way: Let A, B and C be nonempty sets, $\varphi : A \times B \to P$, $\phi : B \times C \to P$ be fuzzy relations and $f, g : A \to P$ and $h : B \to P$ be fuzzy subsets, then $\varphi \circ \phi$ is a fuzzy relation between A and C, $f \circ \varphi$ and $\varphi \circ h$ are fuzzy subsets of B and A respectively, and $f \circ g$ is a value from P defined by:

$$(\varphi \circ \phi)(a, c) = \bigvee_{b \in B} \varphi(a, b) \cdot \phi(b, c),$$

$$(f \circ \varphi)(b) = \bigvee_{a \in A} f(a) \cdot \varphi(a, b),$$

$$(\varphi \circ h)(a) = \bigvee_{b \in B} \varphi(a, b) \cdot g(b),$$

$$f \circ g = \bigvee_{d \in A} f(d) \cdot g(d)$$

for every $a \in A$, $b \in B$, and $c \in C$. The fact that the composition between fuzzy subsets and fuzzy relations (resp. between a fuzzy subset and a fuzzy relation) is associative is easy to prove.

With X we denote a finite nonempty set called the alphabet, with X^* we denote the free monoid over the alphabet X, and with e we denote the empty word in X^*. A fuzzy automaton over X and P is a tuple $\mathcal{A} = (A, \sigma, \delta, \tau)$ such that: A is a nonempty set; σ is a fuzzy subset of A also known as the fuzzy set of initial states; δ is a fuzzy subset of $A \times X \times A$ over P called the fuzzy transition function, while τ is a fuzzy subset of A named the fuzzy set of terminal states.

Fuzzy transition relations are defined for every nonempty word $u \in X^* \backslash \{e\}$ by:

$$\delta_u = \delta_{x_1} \circ \cdots \circ \delta_{x_n},$$

where $u = x_1 \cdots x_n$ and for every $i \in \{1, ..., n\}$ $\delta_{x_i} : A \times A \to P$ determined by $\delta_{x_i}(a, b) = \delta(a, x_i, b)$, $(a, b) \in A \times A$. Furthermore, δ_e is also a fuzzy relation on

A given by:

$$\delta_e(a,b) = \begin{cases} 1, & a = b \\ 0, & \text{otherwise} \end{cases}, \quad a,b \in A.$$

Additionally, for every word $u \in X^*$, σ_u is defined to be a fuzzy subset of A by:

$$\sigma_u = \sigma \circ \delta_u.$$

A fuzzy language recognized by the automaton A over X and P, denoted as $[\![A]\!]$, is a fuzzy subset of X^* defined by:

$$[\![A]\!](u) = \bigvee_{a,b \in A} \sigma(a) \cdot \delta_u(a,b) \cdot \tau(b) = \sigma \circ \delta_u \circ \tau,$$

where $u \in X^*$ is an arbitrary word.

If a fuzzy automaton $\mathcal{A} = (A, \sigma, \delta, \tau)$ satisfies the following two conditions: (1) For every $x \in X$ and $a \in A$, there exists $b \in A$ such that $\delta_x(a,b) = 1$ and $\delta_x(a,c) = 0$, for every $c \in A\backslash\{b\}$, and (2) There exists $a_0 \in A$ such that $\sigma(a_0) = 1$ and $\sigma(a) = 0$ for every $a \in A\backslash\{a_0\}$, then $\mathcal{A}$ is called a crisp-deterministic fuzzy automaton, and when in addition A is finite, then $\mathcal{A}$ is called a crisp-deterministic fuzzy finite automaton (cDFfA, for short).

A fuzzy language recognized by a cDFfA $\mathcal{A}$ is given by:

$$[\![A]\!](u) = \tau(\delta_*(a_0, u)),$$

for every $u \in X^*$, where $\delta_*(a_0, u)$ is the unique state reachable from a_0 given the word u. More precisely, the range of a fuzzy language $[\![A]\!]$, with $\mathcal{A}$ being a cDFfA, is contained in the range of τ, which is finite because A is finite. Therefore, cDFfAs recognize fuzzy languages of finite range (cf. [4,5,10]).

3   Truncating Fuzzy Languages

If a fuzzy language accepts a certain word only to a very low degree, it can be assumed that this fuzzy language does not accept this word. That is, if the degree of acceptance of a particular word by a fuzzy language is very low, then the concrete value of that degree is irrelevant. Consequently, it is reasonable to observe a fuzzy language that accepts words with a degree higher than a specific value ε. It is natural to assume that the value ε is very small. In a particular case where we observe a language $[\![A]\!]$ of a fuzzy automaton $\mathcal{A} = (A, \sigma, \delta, \tau)$, it is reasonable to assume that the value ε is smaller than all non-zero values taken by the functions δ, σ and τ.

Let $\mathcal{A} = (A, \sigma, \delta, \tau)$ be a fuzzy automaton over X and P, and let $\varepsilon \in P$ be a given threshold. Then we define an ε-truncating fuzzy language of $\mathcal{A}$ as a fuzzy language $[\![A]\!]_\varepsilon : X^* \to L$ in the following way:

$$[\![A]\!]_\varepsilon(u) = \begin{cases} [\![A]\!](u), & \text{if } [\![A]\!](u) > \varepsilon, \\ 0, & \text{otherwise.} \end{cases}$$

The importance of considering the truncating fuzzy language of a fuzzy language recognized by a fuzzy automaton is that the majority of words are accepted with a very small degree due to the many multiplications for words going through a cycle in the given fuzzy automaton.

In general, a fuzzy language recognized by a fuzzy automaton over the product structure has an infinite range. In contrast, the ε-truncating fuzzy language of the fuzzy automaton always has a finite range, for any chosen threshold $\varepsilon \neq 0$. Although this result was provided by Li [10], we provide a slightly different and detailed proof with the following theorem.

Theorem 1. *The fuzzy language $[\![A]\!]_\varepsilon$ is image finite, for every fuzzy automaton $A = (A, \sigma, \delta, \tau)$ and $\varepsilon > 0$.*

Proof. We conduct the proof by estimating the upper bound for the number of different elements of the set $Im([\![A]\!]_\varepsilon)\backslash\{1\}$. Let $A = (A, \sigma, \delta, \tau)$ be a fuzzy automaton and $\varepsilon > 0$. Consider an arbitrary word $u = x_1 x_2 .. x_k \in X^*$ of length $k \in \mathbb{N}$. Then the degree to which A accepts this word is equal to:

$$[\![A]\!](u) = \bigvee_{a_1, a_2, \dots a_{n+1} \in A} \sigma(a_1) \cdot \delta_{x_1}(a_1, a_2) \cdot \delta_{x_2}(a_2, a_3) \cdot \dots \cdot \delta_{x_k}(a_k, a_{k+1}) \cdot \tau(a_{k+1}).$$

$$(1)$$

Since the underlying structure of truth values is the product structure P, there exists a path in the graph of A that goes through some states $\tilde{a}_1, \tilde{a}_2, \dots, \tilde{a}_{k+1} \in A$ in which the maximum value in (1) is reached. That means:

$$[\![A]\!](u) = \sigma(\tilde{a}_1) \cdot \delta_{x_1}(\tilde{a}_1, \tilde{a}_2) \cdot \delta_{x_2}(\tilde{a}_2, \tilde{a}_3) \cdot \dots \cdot \delta_{x_k}(\tilde{a}_k, \tilde{a}_{k+1}) \cdot \tau(\tilde{a}_{k+1}). \qquad (2)$$

Among $k + 2$ values $\sigma(\tilde{a}_1), \delta_{x_1}(\tilde{a}_1, \tilde{a}_2), \dots, \delta_{x_k}(\tilde{a}_k, \tilde{a}_{k+1})$ and $\tau(\tilde{a}_{k+1})$ from (2), some of them may be equal to 1. However, these values do not influence the calculation of the value of $[\![A]\!](u)$, because 1 is the neutral for the multiplication. Assume that there are n values ($n \leqslant k$) among the values $\sigma(\tilde{a}_1), \delta_{x_1}(\tilde{a}_1, \tilde{a}_2)$, $\dots, \delta_{x_k}(\tilde{a}_k, \tilde{a}_{k+1})$ and $\tau(\tilde{a}_{k+1})$ that are different from 1, and denote them by $c_1, c_2, \dots, c_n$ (among these values, there may be the values that are the same, but they are all different from 1). Assume that the word u is accepted by the ε-truncating fuzzy language of A. Then (2) becomes:

$$\varepsilon < [\![A]\!](u) = c_1 \cdot c_2 \cdot \dots \cdot c_n \leqslant M^n,$$

where M is the maximum value of the set $S = Im\{\sigma \cup \delta \cup \tau\}\backslash\{1\}$ consisting of all values different from 1 that functions σ, δ and τ take. Note that this maximum value M exists in the product structure and $M < 1$. Because both M and ε are values smaller than 1, the properties of the logarithmic function yield:

$$\varepsilon < M^n \quad \text{if and only if} \quad n < \log_M \varepsilon.$$

By denoting $n_0 = \lfloor \log_M \varepsilon \rfloor + 1$, we conclude that $1 > [\![A]\!](u) > \varepsilon$ if and only if the number of values different from 1 in (2) is at most n_0. In other words, in order for an arbitrary word $u \in X^*$ of a length $k \in \mathbb{N}$ to be accepted by $[\![A]\!]_\varepsilon$, it must have at most n_0 values in (2) different from 1.

Assume that some word $u \in X^*$ is accepted by $[\![\mathcal{A}]\!]_\varepsilon$ and has p values in (2) different from 1. Denote these values with $c_1, c_2, \ldots, c_p$. Each of these p values can take one value (not necessarily all different) from the set S. In order to estimate the upper bound for the cardinality of the set $Im([\![\mathcal{A}]\!]_\varepsilon)\backslash\{1\}$, we need to estimate all different values that the expression $c_1 \cdot c_2 \cdot \ldots \cdot c_p$ can take. This problem boils down to calculating how many ways we can obtain different values for the expression $c_1 \cdot c_2 \cdot \ldots \cdot c_p$. Because multiplication is commutative, this comes down to calculating all combinations of size p with repetition (in the notation $C(S)$), where each element from the combination is an element from the set S. If we denote with $m = |S|$, then the number of such combinations with repetition is equal to $\binom{p+m-1}{p}$. In the end, since p can be any natural number not greater than n_0, we come to the upper bound for $|Im([\![\mathcal{A}]\!]_\varepsilon)\backslash\{1\}|$, which is equal to:

$$|Im([\![\mathcal{A}]\!]_\varepsilon)\backslash\{1\}| \leqslant \sum_{p=1}^{n_0} \binom{p+m-1}{p}, \tag{3}$$

where $n_0 = \lfloor \log_M \varepsilon \rfloor + 1$ and $M = \max\{Im\{\sigma \cup \delta \cup \tau\}\backslash\{1\}\}$. In other words, the value $|Im([\![\mathcal{A}]\!]_\varepsilon)|$ is some number less than or equal to the number on the right-hand side of the sign $\leqslant$ in (3) plus one, i.e. it is finite.

4   Crisp-Deterministic Fuzzy Finite Automata Accepting Truncating Fuzzy Languages

According to Theorem 1, the fuzzy language $[\![\mathcal{A}]\!]_\varepsilon$ has a finite image, for every fuzzy automaton $\mathcal{A}$ and a threshold $\varepsilon \neq 0$. However, the same theorem does not indicate whether there exists a (deterministic) fuzzy finite automaton that recognizes $[\![\mathcal{A}]\!]_\varepsilon$. Recall again that a cDFfA recognizes a fuzzy language of finite image. Because $[\![\mathcal{A}]\!]_\varepsilon$ is of a finite image, we prove in this section that $[\![\mathcal{A}]\!]_\varepsilon$ is cDFfA-recognizable, and give a way to construct such cDFfA.

Let $\mathcal{A} = (A, \sigma, \delta, \tau)$ be a fuzzy finite automaton and let $\varepsilon \neq 0$ be a chosen threshold. As shown in Theorem 1, the set $Im([\![\mathcal{A}]\!]_\varepsilon)$ is finite. Denote with $G = C(S) \cup \{0, 1\}$, where $C(S)$ has the same meaning as in the proof of Theorem 1. Then, define a family of fuzzy sets $A^\varepsilon = \{\sigma_u^\varepsilon | u \in X^*\}$, where $\sigma_u^\varepsilon : A \to G$ for every $u \in X^*$, inductively by:

$$\sigma_e^\varepsilon(a) = \begin{cases} \sigma(a), & \sigma(a) > \varepsilon \\ 0, & \text{otherwise} \end{cases}, \tag{4}$$

$$\sigma_{ux}^\varepsilon(a) = \begin{cases} (\sigma_u^\varepsilon \circ \delta_x)(a), & (\sigma_u^\varepsilon \circ \delta_x)(a) > \varepsilon \\ 0, & \text{otherwise} \end{cases}, \quad \text{for every } u \in X^* \text{ and } x \in X.$$

for every $a \in A$. Given this family, define a fuzzy automaton $\mathcal{A}^\varepsilon = (A^\varepsilon, \sigma^\varepsilon, \delta^\varepsilon, \tau^\varepsilon)$, where we define functions $\sigma^\varepsilon : A \to G$, $\delta^\varepsilon : A^G \times X \to A^G$ and $\tau^\varepsilon : A^G \to G$ in the following way:

$$\sigma^\varepsilon = \sigma_e^\varepsilon,$$

$$\delta^\varepsilon(\sigma_u^\varepsilon, x) = \sigma_{ux}^\varepsilon,$$

$$\tau^\varepsilon(\sigma_u^\varepsilon) = \begin{cases} \sigma_u^\varepsilon \circ \tau, & \text{if } \sigma_u^\varepsilon \circ \tau > \varepsilon, \\ 0, & \text{otherwise.} \end{cases}$$

Then we have the following result.

Lemma 1. *For every fuzzy finite automaton $\mathcal{A} = (A, \sigma, \delta, \tau)$, the fuzzy automaton $\mathcal{A}^\varepsilon = (A^\varepsilon, \sigma^\varepsilon, \delta^\varepsilon, \tau^\varepsilon)$ is a well-defined cDFfA.*

Proof. The set of all fuzzy sets over A and G is finite, since A is a finite set by the assumption and G is a finite set by Theorem 1. Therefore, the set A^ε is clearly finite, as it is a subset of a finite set G^A. This means that $\mathcal{A}^\varepsilon$ is a finite fuzzy automaton. We prove that $\mathcal{A}^\varepsilon$ is well-defined and crisp-deterministic directly by following its definition.

Note that the elements of the set A^ε are constructed in the iterative manner. With the following result, we give an alternative way to construct these elements. Namely, we claim that each σ_u^ε can be constructed directly from σ_u, for every $u \in X^*$.

Lemma 2. *For every $u \in X^*$ and $\varepsilon \neq 0$, the following holds:*

$$\sigma_u^\varepsilon(a) = \begin{cases} \sigma_u(a), & \sigma_u(a) > \varepsilon \\ 0, & \text{otherwise} \end{cases}, \quad \text{for every } a \in A. \tag{5}$$

Proof. We prove the theorem by means of the mathematical induction. For $u = e$, the assertion follows directly from the definition. Assume that (5) holds for any $u \in X^*$. Then for every $x \in X$ we have:

$$\sigma_{ux}^\varepsilon(a) = \begin{cases} (\sigma_u^\varepsilon \circ \delta_x)(a), & (\sigma_u^\varepsilon \circ \delta_x)(a) > \varepsilon \\ 0, & \text{otherwise} \end{cases}$$

$$= \begin{cases} \bigvee_{b \in A} \sigma_u^\varepsilon(b) \cdot \delta_x(b, a), & \bigvee_{b \in A} \sigma_u^\varepsilon(b) \cdot \delta_x(b, a) > \varepsilon \\ 0, & \text{otherwise} \end{cases}$$

Denote with $c \in A$ an element such that $\bigvee_{b \in A} \sigma_u^\varepsilon(b) \cdot \delta_x(b, a) = \sigma_u^\varepsilon(c) \cdot \delta_x(c, a)$. Assume that $\sigma_u^\varepsilon(c) \cdot \delta_x(c, a) > \varepsilon$. This further yields $\sigma_u^\varepsilon(c) > \varepsilon$ and $\delta_x(c, a) > \varepsilon$. According to the induction hypothesis, we have that $\sigma_u(c) = \sigma_u^\varepsilon(c)$, which means that $\sigma_{ux}^\varepsilon(a) = \sigma_u(c) \cdot \delta_x(c, a)$.
Denote with $d \in A$ an element such that $\bigvee_{b \in A} \sigma_u(b) \cdot \delta_x(b, a) = \sigma_u(d) \cdot \delta_x(d, a)$, and such that $d \neq c$. This means that

$$\sigma_u(d) \cdot \delta_x(d, a) > \sigma_u(c) \cdot \delta_x(c, a) = \sigma_{ux}^\varepsilon(a). \tag{6}$$

According to the initial assumption, $\sigma_{ux}^{\varepsilon}(a) > \varepsilon$. This means $\sigma_u(d) \cdot \delta_x(d, a) > \varepsilon$. But in that case, we have $\sigma_u(d) > \varepsilon$ and $\delta_x(d, a) > \varepsilon$. But according to the induction hypothesis, $\sigma_u(d) = \sigma_u^{\varepsilon}(d)$. Putting this into (6), from the way we have chosen the element $c \in A$, we get:

$$\sigma_u^{\varepsilon}(d) \cdot \delta_x(d, a) > \sigma_u^{\varepsilon}(c) \cdot \delta_x(c, a) = \bigvee_{b \in A} \sigma_u^{\varepsilon}(b) \cdot \delta_x(b, a).$$

But since by the assumption $d \neq c$, we conclude that d is the element reaching the value greater than the maximum value achieved in the element c, which is a contradiction. Finally, we conclude that in this case:

$$\sigma_{ux}^{\varepsilon}(a) = \bigvee_{b \in A} \sigma_u^{\varepsilon}(b) \cdot \delta_x(b, a) = \bigvee_{b \in A} \sigma_u(b) \cdot \delta_x(b, a) = \sigma_{ux}(a).$$

In conclusion, we obtain that:

$$\sigma_{ux}^{\varepsilon}(a) = \begin{cases} \sigma_{ux}(a), & \sigma_{ux}(a) > \varepsilon \\ 0, & \text{otherwise} \end{cases}$$

which was to be proved.

Theorem 2. *Let $\mathcal{A} = (A, \sigma, \delta, \tau)$ be a fuzzy automaton and let $\varepsilon \neq 0$ be a chosen threshold. Then the fuzzy language $[\![\mathcal{A}]\!]_{\varepsilon}$ is cDFfA-recognizable.*

Proof. Lemma 1 verifies that $\mathcal{A}^{\varepsilon}$ is a cDFfA. It remains to prove that $\mathcal{A}^{\varepsilon}$ recognizes the fuzzy language $[\![\mathcal{A}]\!]_{\varepsilon}$. By definition, the fuzzy language recognized by $\mathcal{A}^{\varepsilon}$ is equal to:

$$[\![\mathcal{A}^{\varepsilon}]\!](u) = \tau^{\varepsilon}(\delta^{\varepsilon}(\sigma^{\varepsilon}, u)) = \tau^{\varepsilon}(\sigma_u^{\varepsilon}), \quad u \in X^*.$$

According to the definition of τ^{ε} and Lemma 2, for every $u \in X^*$ we have:

$$[\![\mathcal{A}^{\varepsilon}]\!](u) = \begin{cases} \sigma_u^{\varepsilon} \circ \tau, & \text{if } \sigma_u^{\varepsilon} \circ \tau > \varepsilon \\ 0, & \text{otherwise} \end{cases}$$

According to the previous theorem, we have that $\sigma_u(a) = \sigma_u^{\varepsilon}(a)$, for every $a \in A$ such that $\sigma_u^{\varepsilon}(a) \neq 0$. That means that, for some $b \in A$ for such that the value $\sigma_u^{\varepsilon} \circ \tau > \varepsilon$ reaches its maximum value, it also means that for the same $b \in A$ the value $\sigma_u \circ \tau > \varepsilon$ reaches its maximum value. In other words, it is impossible to reach a maximum value in both expressions $\sigma_u \circ \tau > \varepsilon$ and $\sigma_u^{\varepsilon} \circ \tau > \varepsilon$ in some state $c \in A$ such that $\sigma_u^{\varepsilon}(c) = 0$. Thus, we conclude that $\sigma_u^{\varepsilon} \circ \tau > \varepsilon$ implies $\sigma_u \circ \tau > \varepsilon$. This allows us to obtain:

$$[\![\mathcal{A}^{\varepsilon}]\!](u) = \begin{cases} \sigma_u \circ \tau, & \text{if } \sigma_u \circ \tau > \varepsilon \\ 0, & \text{otherwise} \end{cases} = [\![\mathcal{A}]\!]_{\varepsilon}(u).$$

which was to be proved.

Algorithm 1: Construction of $\mathcal{A}^\varepsilon = (A^\varepsilon, \sigma^\varepsilon, \delta^\varepsilon, \tau^\varepsilon)$

---

input : A fuzzy automaton $\mathcal{A} = (A, \sigma, \delta, \tau)$, a degree $\varepsilon > 0$
output: cDFfA $\mathcal{A}^\varepsilon = (A^\varepsilon, \sigma^\varepsilon, \delta^\varepsilon, \tau^\varepsilon)$

1 Initialize an empty set $\mathcal{A}^\varepsilon$ and an empty queue $\mathcal{A}^{\varepsilon*}$

2 $\sigma_e^\varepsilon(a) \leftarrow \begin{cases} \sigma(a), & \sigma(a) > \varepsilon \\ 0, & \text{otherwise} \end{cases}$, $\quad a \in A$

3 $A^\varepsilon \leftarrow A^\varepsilon \cup \{\sigma^\varepsilon\}$

4 Enqueue$(A^{\varepsilon*}, \sigma^\varepsilon)$

5 **while** $A^{\varepsilon*} \neq \emptyset$ **do**

6 $\quad$ $\mu \leftarrow$ Dequeue$(A^{\varepsilon*})$

7 $\quad$ $\tau^\varepsilon(\mu) = \mu \circ \tau$

8 $\quad$ **foreach** $x \in X$ **do**

9 $\quad\quad$ $\mu_x(a) \leftarrow \begin{cases} (\mu \circ \delta_x)(a), & (\mu \circ \delta_x)(a) > \varepsilon \\ 0, & \text{otherwise} \end{cases}$, $\quad a \in A$

10 $\quad\quad$ $\delta^\varepsilon(\mu, x) = \mu_x$

11 $\quad\quad$ **if** $\mu_x \notin A^\varepsilon$ **then**

12 $\quad\quad\quad$ $A^\varepsilon \leftarrow A^\varepsilon \cup \{\mu_x\}$

13 $\quad\quad\quad$ Enqueue$(A^{\varepsilon*}, \mu_x)$

14 $\quad\quad$ **end**

15 $\quad$ **end**

16 **end**

As a consequence, we get the following corollary, which can be regarded as a variant of Theorem 3.4 [11].

Corollary 1. *Let* $L : X^* \to P$ *be an FfA-recognizable fuzzy language, and* $\varepsilon > 0$ *be an arbitrary value. Then the fuzzy language* L_ε *is cDFfA-recognizable.*

In the following, we present an algorithm for computing the cDFfA $\mathcal{A}^\varepsilon = (A^\varepsilon, \sigma^\varepsilon, \delta^\varepsilon, \tau^\varepsilon)$ for a given fuzzy automaton $\mathcal{A}$ and a given $\varepsilon \in P$. The algorithm is based on the following principle: in each step of the algorithm, we take a state that has not been processed yet. For each letter x in X, we generate its successor and add a transition marked x from the state to its successor. If a follower represents a newly generated state (i.e., it is not equal to a previously generated state), then we add that state to the set of states of $\mathcal{A}^\varepsilon$ and the queue of unprocessed states ($A^{\varepsilon*}$). After we have created all successors of a given state, we mark this state as processed, i.e., we remove it from the queue. Initially, the queue of unprocessed states and the set of states of $\mathcal{A}^\varepsilon$ contains only one state, and this state is σ^ε defined by (4). At the same time, for each state of $\mu \in A^\varepsilon$, we compute $\tau^\varepsilon(\mu)$. The algorithm is finished when there are no more unprocessed states, i.e., when the queue $A^{\varepsilon*}$ is empty.

The following example illustrates the importance of Algorithm 1. To be specific, it demonstrates the case where the Nerode automaton recognizing a given fuzzy language is infinite, whereas the fuzzy automaton A^ε that recognizes the truncating fuzzy language is finite.

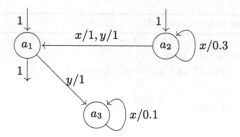

Fig. 1. A graphical representation of the fuzzy automaton from Example 1

Example 1. Consider the fuzzy automaton $\mathcal{A} = (A, \sigma, \delta, \tau)$ over the product structure, where $A = \{a_1, a_2, a_3\}$, $X = \{x, y\}$, graphically represented in Fig. 1.

In other words, we have that $\sigma = \begin{bmatrix} 1\,1\,0 \end{bmatrix}$, $\tau = \begin{bmatrix} 1\,0\,0 \end{bmatrix}^{\mathrm{T}}$, and transition functions are given by:

$$\delta_x = \begin{bmatrix} 0 & 0 & 0 \\ 1 & 0.3 & 0 \\ 0 & 0 & 0.1 \end{bmatrix}, \qquad \delta_y = \begin{bmatrix} 0\,0\,1 \\ 1\,0\,0 \\ 0\,0\,0 \end{bmatrix}.$$

The minimal crisp deterministic automaton equivalent to a given fuzzy automaton is infinite, because the fuzzy language $[\![A]\!]$ has infinite range. However, according to Theorem 2, there exists a finite cdfa recognizing ε-truncating fuzzy language for every ε. First let us compute σ_u, $u \in X^*$:

$\sigma_e = \begin{bmatrix} 1\,1\,0 \end{bmatrix}$, $\quad \sigma_y = \begin{bmatrix} 1\,0\,1 \end{bmatrix}$ $\quad \sigma_{yy} = \begin{bmatrix} 0\,0\,1 \end{bmatrix}$,

$\sigma_{x^n} = \begin{bmatrix} 0.3^{n-1}\ 0.3^n\ 0 \end{bmatrix}$, $\quad \sigma_{x^n y} = \begin{bmatrix} 0.3^n\ 0\ 0.3^{n-1} \end{bmatrix}$, $\quad n \in N$,

$\sigma_{x^n y^2} = \begin{bmatrix} 0\,0\,0.3^n \end{bmatrix}$, $\quad n \in N$,

$\sigma_{x^n y x^k} = \begin{bmatrix} 0\ 0\ 0.3^{n-1} 0.1^k \end{bmatrix}$, $\quad \sigma_{x^n y^2 x^k} = \begin{bmatrix} 0\ 0\ 0.3^n 0.1^k \end{bmatrix}$, $\quad n \in N$, $\quad k \in N$,

$\sigma_{yx^n} = \sigma_{y^2 x^n} = \begin{bmatrix} 0\ 0\ 0.1^n \end{bmatrix}$, $\quad n \in N$,

$\sigma_u = \begin{bmatrix} 0\,0\,0 \end{bmatrix}$, $\quad u \in X^* \backslash \{e, y, y^2, x^n, x^n yx^k, x^n y^2 x^k, yx^n, y^2 x^n\}, n \in N, k \in N_0$.

Then, given $\varepsilon = 0.01$ we obtain:

$\sigma_e^\varepsilon = \begin{bmatrix} 1\,1\,0 \end{bmatrix}$, $\quad \sigma_y^\varepsilon = \begin{bmatrix} 1\,0\,1 \end{bmatrix}$ $\quad \sigma_{yy}^\varepsilon = \begin{bmatrix} 0\,0\,1 \end{bmatrix}$

$\sigma_{x^n}^\varepsilon = \begin{bmatrix} 0.3^{n-1}\ 0.3^n\ 0 \end{bmatrix}$, $\quad \sigma_{x^n y}^\varepsilon = \begin{bmatrix} 0.3^n\ 0\ 0.3^{n-1} \end{bmatrix}$, $\quad n \in \{1, 2, 3\}$,

$\sigma_{x^n y^2}^\varepsilon = \begin{bmatrix} 0\ 0\ 0.3^n \end{bmatrix}$, $\quad n \in \{1, 2, 3\}$,

$\sigma_{x^4}^\varepsilon = \begin{bmatrix} 0.3^3\ 0\ 0 \end{bmatrix}$, $\quad \sigma_{x^4 y}^\varepsilon = \begin{bmatrix} 0\ 0\ 0.3^3 \end{bmatrix}$, $\quad \sigma_{xy^2 x}^\varepsilon = \begin{bmatrix} 0\ 0\ 0.03 \end{bmatrix}$,

$\sigma_{yx}^\varepsilon = \sigma_{y^2 x}^\varepsilon = \begin{bmatrix} 0\ 0\ 0.1 \end{bmatrix}$, $\quad \sigma_{x^n yx}^\varepsilon = \begin{bmatrix} 0\ 0\ 0.3^{n-1} 0.1 \end{bmatrix}$, $\quad n \in \{1, 2\}$,

$\sigma_u^\varepsilon = \begin{bmatrix} 0\,0\,0 \end{bmatrix}$,

$(u \in X^* \backslash \{e, y, y^2, x, x^2, x^3, x^4, xy, x^2 y, x^3 y, x^4 y, xy^2 x, yx, y^2 x, xyx, x^2 yx\})$.

In other words, the fuzzy automaton $\mathcal{A}^\varepsilon$ recognizing 0.01-truncating fuzzy language has 20 states.

5   Conclusion

In this paper, we propose a finite Nerode-like construction for fuzzy automata over the product algebra. The importance of the Nerode automaton is well known in the literature [4–6], and this paper provides a solution to the problem that may arise in the product algebra, namely that the Nerode automaton need not be finite. That is, our construction always leads to a finite crisp-deterministic fuzzy automaton. However, it need not recognize the same fuzzy language as the original fuzzy automaton. Nevertheless, the difference between these two fuzzy languages is only in words accepted with a very low degree, which we consider irrelevant. We would like to note that the concepts of truncating fuzzy languages and approximate construction of a crisp deterministic fuzzy automaton are new and different from the similar concepts studied in [10,17].

In this work, we used the specific properties of the product algebra. We leave the generalization of the results for fuzzy automata defined over other nonlocally finite structures to future work.

References

1. Bělohlávek, R.: Determinism and fuzzy automata. Inf. Sci. **143**, 205–209 (2002)
2. de Mendívil, J.R.G.: Conditions for minimal fuzzy deterministic finite automata via Brzozowski's procedure. IEEE Trans. Fuzzy Syst. **26**(4), 2409–2420 (2018)
3. de Mendívil, J.R.G., Figueredo, F.F.: Canonization of max-min fuzzy automata. Fuzzy Sets Syst. **376**, 152–168 (2019)
4. de Mendívil, J.R.G., Garitagoitia, J.R.: Determinization of fuzzy automata via factorization of fuzzy states. Inf. Sci. **283**, 165–179 (2014)
5. Ignjatović, J., Ćirić, M., Bogdanović, S.: Determinization of fuzzy automata with membership values in complete residuated lattices. Inf. Sci. **178**, 164–180 (2008)
6. Ignjatović, J., Ćirić, M., Bogdanović, S., Petković, T.: Myhill-Nerode type theory for fuzzy languages and automata. Fuzzy Sets Syst. **161**(9), 1288–1324 (2010)
7. Jančić, Z., Ćirić, M.: Brzozowski type determinization for fuzzy automata. Fuzzy Sets Syst. **249**, 73–82 (2014)
8. Jančić, Z., Ignjatović, J., Ćirić, M.: An improved algorithm for determinization of weighted and fuzzy automata. Inf. Sci. **181**, 1358–1368 (2011)
9. Jančić, Z., Micić, I., Ignjatović, J., Ćirić, M.: Further improvement of determinization methods for fuzzy finite automata. Fuzzy Sets Syst. **301**, 79–102 (2015)
10. Li, Y.: Approximation and robustness of fuzzy finite automata. Int. J. Approximate Reasoning **47**(2), 247–257 (2008)
11. Li, Y., Pedrycz, W.: Fuzzy finite automata and fuzzy regular expressions with membership values in lattice-ordered monoids. Fuzzy Sets Syst. **156**(1), 68–92 (2005)
12. Micić, I., Jančić, Z., Ignjatović, J., Ćirić, M.: Determinization of fuzzy automata by means of the degrees of language inclusion. IEEE Trans. Fuzzy Syst. **23**(6), 2144–2153 (2015)
13. Mordeson, J.N., Malik, D.S.: Fuzzy Automata and Languages. Chapman and Hall/CRC (2002)
14. Qiu, D.W.: Automata theory based on completed residuated lattice-valued logic (I). Sci. China Ser. F **44**(6), 419–429 (2001). https://doi.org/10.1007/BF02713945

15. Qiu, D.W.: Automata theory based on completed residuated lattice-valued logic (II). Sci. China Ser. F **45**(6), 442–452 (2002). https://doi.org/10.1360/02yf9038
16. Stanimirović, S., Ćirić, M., Ignjatović, J.: Determinization of fuzzy automata by factorizations of fuzzy states and right invariant fuzzy quasi-orders. Inf. Sci. **469**, 79–100 (2018)
17. Yang, C., Li, Y.: Fuzzy ε-approximate regular languages and minimal deterministic fuzzy automata ε-accepting them. Fuzzy Sets Syst. **420**, 72–86 (2021)

Towards New Types of Weak Bisimulations for Fuzzy Automata Using the Product T-Norm

Ivana Micić[1]([⊠]) [iD], Jelena Matejić[1] [iD], Stefan Stanimirović[1] [iD],
and Linh Anh Nguyen[2,3] [iD]

[1] Faculty of Science and Mathematics, University of Niš, Niš, Serbia
{ivana.micic,jelena.matejic,stefan.stanimirovic}@pmf.edu.rs
[2] Faculty of Mathematics, Informatics and Mechanics, University of Warsaw,
Banacha 2, 02-097 Warsaw, Poland
nguyen@mimuw.edu.pl
[3] Faculty of Information Technology, Nguyen Tat Thanh University,
Ho Chi Minh City, Vietnam

Abstract. Weak bisimulations for fuzzy automata (FAs) are a well-known generalization of bisimulations. While they preserve the language equivalence between two FAs and perform better in the state reduction of FAs, their main disadvantage is that they cannot be computed for all $(\vee, \cdot)$-FAs, where $\vee$ denotes the maximum operation and $\cdot$ is the product t-norm on the real-unit interval $[0, 1]$. The reason is that weak bisimulations are solutions to specific linear systems of fuzzy relation inequalities, and such systems can consist of infinitely many inequalities when observed under such FAs. This paper introduces new types of weak bisimulations for such FAs aiming to overcome this problem. Namely, for a chosen small value $\varepsilon > 0$, we define ε-weak bisimulations. They allow us to obtain finite systems of fuzzy relation inequalities. They preserve a new kind of approximation of language equivalence. Namely, we show that two $(\vee, \cdot)$-FAs that are ε-weak bisimilar recognize each word in degrees which are either equal or both less than or equal to ε. As ε-weak bisimulations have this property for an arbitrarily small value $\varepsilon > 0$, they model a kind of "almost-equivalence" between two FAs, as the words accepted in a degree smaller than or equal to ε can be treated as irrelevant.

Keywords: fuzzy bisimulations · fuzzy relation inequalities · product t-norm · approximation degree

I. Micić, J. Matejić and S. Stanimirović acknowledge the support of the Science Fund of the Republic of Serbia, GRANT No. 7750185, Quantitative Automata Models: Fundamental Problems and Applications - QUAM, and the Ministry of Education, Science and Technological Development, Republic of Serbia, Contract No. 451-03-68/2022-14/200124.

S. Massanet et al. (Eds.): EUSFLAT 2023/AGOP 2023, LNCS 14069, pp. 567–578, 2023.
https://doi.org/10.1007/978-3-031-39965-7_47

1   Introduction

The notion of bisimulation has an important place in the fuzzy automata literature. Intuitively, it allows us to model the equivalence of two fuzzy automata by the way they match each other's moves. In other words, bisimulation allows us to model the indistinguishability of the states of fuzzy automata. Various approaches have been taken in the study of bisimulation for fuzzy automata (see [3,4,7,12,13,15] for more details). Afterward, various fast algorithms for computing the greatest (fuzzy or crisp) bisimulation between fuzzy automata and more generalized fuzzy structures have been developed [9–11,16].

Various generalizations of bisimulations for fuzzy automata have been proposed. The so-called approximate bisimulations have appeared in a number of recent publications [8,14,17–19]. Their main disadvantage is that the multiplication operation from the underlying set of truth values must be idempotent. Another generalization has been proposed by the concept of weak bisimulation [5]. Namely, weak bisimulations are defined for fuzzy automata with membership values over any complete residuated lattice. However, they are defined as fuzzy relations that are solutions to certain systems of fuzzy relation inequalities. Such systems may have infinitely many inequalities if the underlying complete residuated lattice is not locally finite. This means that they cannot be computed in all cases when the underlying lattice is not locally finite. For example, weak bisimulations are not always computable for $(\vee, \cdot)$-fuzzy automata, where $\vee$ denotes the maximum operation and $\cdot$ is the product t-norm on the real unit interval $[0, 1]$.

This paper proposes a generalization of weak bisimulations for $(\vee, \cdot)$-fuzzy automata. We call them ε-weak bisimulations, where ε can be any small value close to zero. These ε-weak bisimulations can be computed for any $(\vee, \cdot)$-fuzzy automata and any $\varepsilon > 0$. However, they do not establish strict language equivalence between the observed fuzzy automata. More precisely, we prove that if there is a ε-weak bisimulation between two $(\vee, \cdot)$-fuzzy automata, they are ε-equivalent, in the sense that they are equivalent w.r.t. words accepted up to a degree greater than ε. However, since we choose ε to be arbitrarily small, we treat words accepted in a degree not greater than ε as irrelevant, which means that ε-weak bisimulations provide a good approximation of language equivalence between fuzzy automata. Note that the concept of ε-equivalence of fuzzy languages is new and different from other concepts of language approximation, for example, that in [6], where the degree of equivalence for every word has to be greater than ε.

This paper is structured as follows. Section 2 recalls basic notions on fuzzy subsets, fuzzy relations, fuzzy languages and fuzzy automata defined over the real-unit interval equipped with the product t-norm and the meet and join operations. Section 3 provides a finite construction of a set of fuzzy terminal states for a given fuzzy automaton. This construction is needed to define ε-weak bisimulations afterward. Section 4 explores the concepts of ε-inclusive and ε-equivalent fuzzy languages, for any $\varepsilon > 0$. In the end, Sect. 5 introduces ε-weak bisimulations, explores their properties and provides a way to compute them. An illustrative example is also given in Sect. 5. Some concluding remarks close the paper.

2   Preliminaries

2.1   Fuzzy Subsets and Fuzzy Relations

As a structure of truth values, we use the real-unit interval $I = [0,1]$ equipped with (not necessarily countable) infimum $\wedge$ and supremum $\vee$, as well as the product t-norm $\cdot : I \times I \to I$ defined as the multiplication of the reals in the usual way. The product operation $\cdot$ admits the *residuum operation* defined as:

$$x \to y = \begin{cases} 1 & \text{if } x \leqslant y, \\ y/x & \text{otherwise.} \end{cases}$$

for every $x, y \in I$. The *biresiduum operation* is naturally defined as $(x \leftrightarrow y) = (x \to y) \wedge (y \to x)$, for every $x, y \in I$.

For a nonempty set A, a function $f : A \to I$ is called a *fuzzy subset* of A. The set of all fuzzy subsets of A is denoted by I^A, with the equality and the inclusion (ordering) of fuzzy sets being defined coordinate-wise. For a family $\{f_j\}_{j \in J}$ of fuzzy subsets of A, the join (union) $\bigvee_{j \in J} f_j$ and the meet (intersection) $\bigwedge_{j \in J} f_j$ of this family is also defined coordinate-wisely (see [1,2] for more details).

For two nonempty sets A and B, a *fuzzy relation between A and B* is any mapping from $A \times B$ to I, i.e., any fuzzy subset of $A \times B$. The equality, inclusion and the join of fuzzy relations are defined as for fuzzy sets.

Let A, B and C be nonempty sets. For fuzzy relations $\varphi \in I^{A \times B}$, $\theta \in I^{B \times C}$ and fuzzy sets $\alpha \in I^A$, $\beta \in H^B$, we define *compositions* $\varphi \circ \theta \in I^{A \times C}$, $\alpha \circ \varphi \in I^B$ and $\varphi \circ \beta \in I^A$ with

$$(\varphi \circ \theta)(a, c) = \bigvee_{b \in B} \varphi(a, b) \cdot \theta(b, c),$$

$$(\alpha \circ \varphi)(b) = \bigvee_{a \in A} \alpha(a) \cdot \varphi(a, b),$$

$$(\varphi \circ \beta)(a) = \bigvee_{b \in B} \varphi(a, b) \cdot \beta(b),$$

for every $a \in A$, $b \in B$ and $c \in C$. All these compositions are associative fuzzy relations.

For given fuzzy sets $\varphi \in I^A$ and $\psi \in I^B$, the *right residual* $\varphi \backslash \psi \in I^{A \times B}$ of ψ by φ and the *left residual* $\psi / \varphi \in I^{A \times B}$ of ψ by φ, respectively, are fuzzy relations defined as follows:

$$(\varphi \backslash \psi)(a, b) = (\varphi(a) \to \psi(b)), \quad \text{for } a \in A \text{ and } b \in B;$$
$$(\psi / \varphi)(a, b) = (\psi(b) \to \varphi(a)), \quad \text{for } a \in A \text{ and } b \in B.$$

For given fuzzy sets $\varphi \in I^A$ and $\psi \in I^B$, the meet of the left residual of ψ by φ and the right residual of ψ by φ is denoted by $\varphi | \psi$ and we have:

$$(\varphi | \psi)(a, b) = (\varphi(a) \leftrightarrow \psi(b)), \quad \text{for } a \in A \text{ and } b \in B.$$

It can be shown that the right and left residuals satisfy the following two adjunction properties:

$$\varphi \circ \chi \leqslant \psi \quad \text{iff} \quad \chi \leqslant \varphi \backslash \psi, \tag{1}$$

$$\chi \circ \psi \leqslant \varphi \quad \text{iff} \quad \chi \leqslant \psi / \varphi, \tag{2}$$

where $\chi \in I^{A \times B}$ is a fuzzy relation between A and B.

2.2   Fuzzy Languages and Fuzzy Automata

With X we denote a finite nonempty set called the alphabet, with X^* we denote the free monoid over the alphabet X, and with e we denote the empty word in X^*. A $(\vee, \cdot)$-*fuzzy finite automaton*, or just a *fuzzy finite automaton (FFA)* in what follows, is a quadruple $\mathcal{A} = (A, \sigma^A, \delta^A, \tau^A)$ such that A is a finite nonempty set, called the *set of states*, $\sigma^A : A \to I$ is a fuzzy subset of A called the *fuzzy set of initial states*, $\delta^A : A \times X \times A \to I$ is a fuzzy subset of $A \times X \times A$ called the *fuzzy transition function*, and $\tau^A : A \to I$ is a fuzzy subset of A called the *fuzzy set of terminal states*. The fuzzy transition function $\delta^A : A \times X \times A \to I$ inductively induces a family $\{\delta_u^A\}_{u \in X^*}$ of fuzzy relations, where $\delta_u^A : A \times A \to I$ for each $u \in X^*$ is defined in the following way: for every $a, b \in A$ we set $\delta_e^A(a, a) = 1$ and $\delta_e^A(a, b) = 0$ for $a \neq b$, $\delta_x^A(a, b) = \delta^A(a, x, b)$, for every $a, b \in A$ and $x \in X$, and for every $u \in X^*$ and $x \in X$

$$\delta_{ux}^A = \delta_u^A \circ \delta_x^A.$$

By associativity, for any two words $u, v \in X^*$ we have $\delta_{uv}^A = \delta_u^A \circ \delta_v^A$. Also, if $u = x_1 x_2 \ldots x_n$ we have $\delta_u^A = \delta_{x_1}^A \circ \delta_{x_2}^A \circ \ldots \circ \delta_{x_n}^A$. We call $\{\delta_u^A\}_{u \in X^*}$ the *family of fuzzy transition relations* of $\mathcal{A}$. Similarly, we define a *family of fuzzy initial sets* $\{\sigma_u^A\}_{u \in X^*}$, as well as a *family of fuzzy terminal sets* $\{\tau_u^A\}_{u \in X^*}$, where $\sigma_u^A : A \to I$ and $\tau_u^A : A \to I$ are fuzzy subsets of A defined by

$$\sigma_u^A = \sigma^A \circ \delta_u^A, \quad \tau_u^A = \delta_u^A \circ \tau^A,$$

for each $u \in X^*$.

The fuzzy language recognized by a fuzzy automaton $\mathcal{A} = (A, \sigma^A, \delta^A, \tau^A)$ is a mapping $[\![\mathcal{A}]\!] : X^* \to I$ defined by

$$[\![\mathcal{A}]\!](u) = \bigvee_{a_0, \ldots, a_n \in A} \sigma^A(a_0) \cdot \delta_{x_1}^A(a_0, a_1) \cdot \ldots \cdot \delta_{x_n}^A(a_{n-1}, a_n) \cdot \tau^A(a_n), \tag{3}$$

for any $u = x_1 x_2 \ldots x_n \in X^*$ and $n \in \mathbb{N}_0$. Note that (3) can be equivalently written as $[\![\mathcal{A}]\!](u) = \sigma^A \circ \delta_u^A \circ \tau^A$, for every $u \in X^*$.

2.3   Weak Bisimulations for Fuzzy Automata

Weak simulations and weak bisimulations for fuzzy automata were introduced in [5] as a generalization of simulations and bisimulations introduced by Ćirić [3], respectively. In this subsection, we recall the definitions needed for the rest of the paper.

Let $\mathcal{A} = (A, \sigma^A, \delta^A, \tau^A)$ and $\mathcal{B} = (B, \sigma^B, \delta^B, \tau^B)$ be two fuzzy automata, and let $\varphi \in I^{A \times B}$ be a fuzzy relation between the sets of states of fuzzy automata. Then φ is a *weak forward simulation* between $\mathcal{A}$ and $\mathcal{B}$ if it satisfies the following fuzzy relation inequalities:

$$\sigma^A \leqslant \sigma^B \circ \varphi^{-1}, \tag{4}$$

$$\varphi^{-1} \circ \tau_u^A \leqslant \tau_u^B, \quad \text{for every } u \in X^*. \tag{5}$$

Furthermore, if φ is a weak forward simulation between $\mathcal{A}$ and $\mathcal{B}$, and φ^{-1} is a weak forward simulation between $\mathcal{B}$ and $\mathcal{A}$, meaning that φ satisfies (4)–(5) and:

$$\sigma^B \leqslant \sigma^A \circ \varphi, \tag{6}$$

$$\varphi \circ \tau_u^B \leqslant \tau_u^A, \quad \text{for every } u \in X^*, \tag{7}$$

then φ is a *weak forward bisimulation* between $\mathcal{A}$ and $\mathcal{B}$. Dually, one can define weak backward (bi)simulations between $\mathcal{A}$ and $\mathcal{B}$ using the family $\{\sigma_u^A\}_{u \in X^*}$ (cf. [5] for more details). In what follows, we drop the word "between $\mathcal{A}$ and $\mathcal{B}$" when fuzzy automata under consideration are clear from the context. We also call weak forward (bi)simulations simply just weak (bi)simulations.

As noted above, weak (bi)simulations [5] are a generalization of the (bi)simulations defined by Ćirić [3]. The main advantage of weak (bi)simulations (when just observing their definitions) is that weak (bi)simulations are defined as solutions to specific linear systems of fuzzy relation equations (see (4)–(7)). Consequently, they can be computed using the well-known formulae for solving linear systems (when they are solvable). On the other hand, bisimulations, as given in [3], are defined as solutions to the so-called weakly linear systems, which can be computed by the iterative procedure that may not have a termination condition.

However, a significant drawback of weak bisimulations is that any of the families $\{\tau_u^A\}_{u \in X^*}$ and $\{\tau_u^B\}_{u \in X^*}$ may be infinite. Although this is not a problem from the mathematical aspect, it means that there are situations when weak (bi)simulations cannot even be computed, as the systems (4)–(7) may consist of the infinite number of inequalities. Through the rest of the paper, we aim to provide a solution to this problem. We do this by introducing new types of weak bisimulations for fuzzy automata, which can be used in such situations. We continue exploring the properties of such bisimulations.

3   Finite Construction of Fuzzy Terminal States

Let $\mathcal{A} = (A, \sigma^A, \delta^A, \tau^A)$ be a fuzzy automaton. As noted in Subsect. 2.3, the family of fuzzy terminal states $\{\tau_u^A\}_{u \in X^*}$ can consist of infinitely many fuzzy subsets of A, meaning that a weak forward simulation between $\mathcal{A}$ and some other fuzzy automaton cannot be computed. In this section we show that, for an arbitrary small threshold $\varepsilon > 0$, we can construct a finite family $\{(\tau_u^A)^\varepsilon\}_{u \in X^*}$, which is defined below. We explore the connection between τ_u^A and $(\tau_u^A)^\varepsilon$, for every $u \in X^*$, and their connection with the fuzzy language accepted by $\mathcal{A}$.

For a fuzzy automaton $\mathcal{A} = (A, \sigma^A, \delta^A, \tau^A)$ and $\varepsilon > 0$, by $\{(\tau_u^A)^\varepsilon \mid u \in X^*\}$ we denote the family of fuzzy subsets of A where each of them is inductively defined for every $a \in A$ as follows:

$$(\tau_e^A)^\varepsilon(a) = \begin{cases} \tau^A(a) & \text{if } \tau^A(a) > \varepsilon, \\ 0 & \text{otherwise;} \end{cases} \tag{8}$$

$$(\tau_{xu}^A)^\varepsilon(a) = \begin{cases} \left(\delta_x \circ (\tau_u^A)^\varepsilon\right)(a) & \text{if } \left(\delta_x \circ (\tau_u^A)^\varepsilon\right)(a) > \varepsilon, \\ 0 & \text{otherwise.} \end{cases} \tag{9}$$

The previous definition gives an inductive way to construct all elements of the family $\{(\tau_u^A)^\varepsilon | u \in X^*\}$, for every fuzzy automaton $\mathcal{A}$ and $\varepsilon > 0$. With the following result, we give an alternative way to construct these elements. Namely, we claim that each $(\tau_u^A)^\varepsilon$ can be constructed directly from τ_u^A, for every $u \in X^*$.

Lemma 1. *Let $\mathcal{A} = (A, \sigma^A, \delta^A, \tau^A)$ be a fuzzy automaton and let $\varepsilon > 0$. For every $u \in X^*$ and $a \in A$, the following holds:*

$$(\tau_u^A)^\varepsilon(a) = \begin{cases} \tau_u^A(a) & \text{if } \tau_u^A(a) > \varepsilon, \\ 0 & \text{otherwise.} \end{cases} \tag{10}$$

Proof. We prove the statement of the lemma by induction on the length of the word $u \in X^*$. The base case $|u| = 0$ (i.e., when $u = e$) holds by the definition (8). For the induction step, assume that (10) holds for any word $u \in X^*$ such that $|u| \leqslant k$, where $k \in \mathbb{N}$. Consider a word $u' = xu$, where $u' \in X^*$, $|u| = k$ and $x \in X$, and an arbitrary $a \in A$. We need to show that

$$(\tau_{xu}^A)^\varepsilon(a) = \begin{cases} \tau_{xu}^A(a) & \text{if } \tau_{xu}^A(a) > \varepsilon, \\ 0 & \text{otherwise.} \end{cases}$$

Consider the case where $(\delta_x \circ (\tau_u^A)^\varepsilon)(a) > \varepsilon$. Denote with $c \in A$ the state from $\mathcal{A}$ in which the maximum value

$$\delta_x^A(a, c) \cdot (\tau_u^A)^\varepsilon(c) = \bigvee_{b \in A} \delta_x^A(a, b) \cdot (\tau_u^A)^\varepsilon(b) = (\delta_x^A \circ (\tau_u^A)^\varepsilon)(a)$$

is reached. Since $\delta_x^A(a, c) \cdot (\tau_u^A)^\varepsilon(c) > \varepsilon$, it follows that $(\tau_u^A)^\varepsilon(c) > \varepsilon$. Therefore, according to the induction assumption, $(\tau_u^A)^\varepsilon(c) = \tau_u^A(c)$. Consequently,

$$(\delta_x^A \circ (\tau_u^A)^\varepsilon)(a) = \delta_x^A(a, c) \cdot \tau_u^A(c) \leqslant (\delta_x^A \circ \tau_u^A)(a) = \tau_{xu}^A(a). \tag{11}$$

Assume that $\tau_{xu}^A(a) = \delta_x^A \circ \tau_u^A = \bigvee_{b \in A} \delta_x^A(a,b) \cdot \tau_u^A(b)$ is reached in $d \in A$. Then, according to (11) we have

$$\delta_x^A(a,d) \cdot \tau_u^A(d) = \tau_{xu}^A(a) \geqslant \delta_x^A \circ (\tau_u^A)^\varepsilon(a) > \varepsilon,$$

which implies $\tau_u^A(d) > \varepsilon$. By the induction assumption, it follows that $\tau_u^A(d) = (\tau_u^A)^\varepsilon(d)$, which means:

$$\left(\delta_x^A \circ (\tau_u^A)^\varepsilon\right)(a) \geqslant \delta_x^A(a,d) \cdot (\tau_u^A)^\varepsilon(d) = \delta_x^A(a,d) \cdot \tau_u^A(d) = \tau_{xu}^A(a). \tag{12}$$

From (11) and (12) we obtain $\left(\delta_x^A \circ (\tau_u^A)^\varepsilon\right)(a) = \tau_{xu}^A(a)$. Therefore, $\tau_{xu}^A(a) > \varepsilon$ and $(\tau_{xu}^A)^\varepsilon(a) = \tau_{xu}^A(a)$.

Consider the case where $(\delta_x \circ (\tau_u^A)^\varepsilon)(a) \leqslant \varepsilon$.

We need to show that $\tau_{xu}^A(a) \leqslant \varepsilon$. For a contradiction, assume that $\tau_{xu}^A(a) > \varepsilon$. But then there exists $d \in A$ such that

$$\tau_{xu}^A(a) = \bigvee_{b \in A} \delta_x^A(a,b) \cdot \tau_u^A(b) = \delta_x^A(a,d) \cdot \tau_u^A(d),$$

which implies $\tau_u^A(d) > \varepsilon$, and by the induction assumption, it follows that $\tau_u^A(d) = (\tau_u^A)^\varepsilon(d)$. So,

$$\varepsilon < \delta_x^A(a,d) \cdot \tau_u^A(d) = \delta_x^A(a,d) \cdot (\tau_u^A)^\varepsilon(d) \leqslant \left(\delta_x^A \circ (\tau_u^A)^\varepsilon\right)(a),$$

which contradicts the fact that $\left(\delta_x^A \circ (\tau_u^A)^\varepsilon\right)(a) \leqslant \varepsilon$. This completes the proof. ∎

As 0 is the smallest element of I, the following result is a direct consequence of Lemma 1.

Corollary 1. *For a fuzzy automaton* $\mathcal{A} = (A, \sigma^A, \delta^A, \tau^A)$ *and* $\varepsilon > 0$ *we have:*

$$(\tau_u^A)^c \leqslant \tau_u^A, \quad \text{for every } u \in X^*. \tag{13}$$

The following lemma is needed to prove the results of the rest of the paper.

Lemma 2. *Let* $\mathcal{A} = (A, \sigma^A, \delta^A, \tau^A)$ *be a fuzzy automaton and let* $\varepsilon > 0$. *Then the following holds:*

$$[\![\mathcal{A}]\!](u) = \sigma^A \circ (\tau_u^A)^\varepsilon, \quad \text{for every } u \in X^* \text{ such that } [\![\mathcal{A}]\!](u) > \varepsilon. \tag{14}$$

Proof. Choose an arbitrary $u \in X^*$ such that $[\![\mathcal{A}]\!](u) > \varepsilon$. Assume that the maximum value of

$$[\![\mathcal{A}]\!](u) = \bigvee_{a \in A} \sigma^A(a) \cdot \tau_u^A(a) = \sigma^A(b) \cdot \tau_u^A(b)$$

is reached in the state $b \in A$. Since $[\![\mathcal{A}]\!](u) > \varepsilon$ by the assumption, we have that $\tau_u^A(b) > \varepsilon$. According to Lemma 1, we have $(\tau_u^A)^\varepsilon(b) = \tau_u^A(b)$. So,

$$\sigma^A \circ (\tau_u^A)^\varepsilon \geqslant \sigma^A(b) \cdot (\tau_u^A)^\varepsilon(b) = \bigvee_{a \in A} \sigma^A(a) \cdot \tau_u^A(a) = [\![\mathcal{A}]\!](u).$$

Note that the other inequality follows from (13), since

$$\sigma^A \circ (\tau^A_u)^\varepsilon \leqslant \sigma^A \circ \tau^A_u = [\![A]\!](u),$$

which completes the proof.   ■

Lemma 3. *Let* $\mathcal{A} = (A, \sigma^A, \delta^A, \tau^A)$ *be a fuzzy automaton. Then the set* $\{(\tau^A_u)^\varepsilon \mid u \in X^*\}$ *is finite, for every* $\varepsilon > 0$.

Proof. Note that the product t-norm is Archimedean and continuous t-norm satisfying $a \cdot a < a$, for every $a \in (0,1)$. As proved in [6, Lemma 2.2], that means that the subalgebra G generated by all the values of τ and δ that are greater than ε is finite. But, note that every fuzzy subset $(\tau^A_u)^\varepsilon$ $(u \in X^*)$ is a mapping $A \to G$. Since G is a finite set, there can be a finite number of such mappings.   ■

4 ε-Inclusive and ε-Equivalent Fuzzy Languages

Let $\mathcal{A} = (A, \sigma^A, \delta^A, \tau^A)$ be a fuzzy automaton. As we use the product t-norm, note that the value $[\![A]\!](u)$, calculated by (3), does not increase as we increase the length of the word u. Moreover, the structure $(I, \cdot)$ is not locally finite, meaning that the value $[\![A]\!](u)$ may be different from all the values $[\![A]\!](v)$, where $|v| \leqslant |u|$. In other words, very long words may be accepted by $\mathcal{A}$ with a very small acceptance degree.

If we choose a very small degree $\varepsilon > 0$, it can be naturally assumed that the words accepted by a fuzzy automaton $\mathcal{A}$ below the chosen threshold ε are irrelevant or insignificant. Therefore, we can treat such words as not accepted by $\mathcal{A}$ (or accepted in the degree 0 instead of some degree below ε). Naturally, the value ε is chosen to be smaller than all non-zero values that functions δ^A, σ^A and τ^A take. With this in mind, we give the following three definitions.

Definition 1. *Let* $\mathcal{A} = (A, \sigma^A, \delta^A, \tau^A)$ *be a fuzzy automaton and* $\varepsilon > 0$. *Then the* ε-*fuzzy language accepted by* $\mathcal{A}$, *in the notation* $[\![A]\!]_\varepsilon$, *is defined by:*

$$[\![A]\!]_\varepsilon(u) = \begin{cases} [\![A]\!](u) & \text{if } [\![A]\!](u) > \varepsilon, \\ 0 & \text{otherwise.} \end{cases}$$

Definition 2. *Let* $\mathcal{A} = (A, \sigma^A, \delta^A, \tau^A)$ *and* $\mathcal{B} = (B, \sigma^B, \delta^B, \tau^B)$ *be fuzzy automata and* $\varepsilon > 0$. *Then:*

– *the fuzzy language* $[\![A]\!]$ *is* ε-*included in the fuzzy language* $[\![B]\!]$ *if:*

$$[\![A]\!]_\varepsilon \leqslant [\![B]\!]_\varepsilon; \tag{15}$$

– *the fuzzy language* $[\![A]\!]$ *is* ε-*equivalent to the fuzzy language* $[\![B]\!]$ *if:*

$$[\![A]\!]_\varepsilon = [\![B]\!]_\varepsilon; \tag{16}$$

– *fuzzy automata* $\mathcal{A}$ *and* $\mathcal{B}$ *are* ε-*equivalent if* $[\![A]\!]$ *is* ε-*equivalent to* $[\![B]\!]$.

5 ε-Weak Bisimulations for Fuzzy Automata

Let $\mathcal{A} = (A, \sigma^A, \delta^A, \tau^A)$ and $\mathcal{B} = (B, \sigma^B, \delta^B, \tau^B)$ be fuzzy automata and let $\varepsilon > 0$. A fuzzy relation $\varphi \in I^{A \times B}$ is an ε-weak *forward simulation* between $\mathcal{A}$ and $\mathcal{B}$ if the following inequalities are satisfied:

$$\sigma^A \leqslant \sigma^B \circ \varphi^{-1}, \tag{17}$$

$$\varphi^{-1} \circ (\tau_u^A)^\varepsilon \leqslant (\tau_u^B)^\varepsilon, \quad \text{for all } u \in X^*. \tag{18}$$

Furthermore, if φ is an ε-weak forward simulation between $\mathcal{A}$ and $\mathcal{B}$ and φ^{-1} is an ε-weak forward simulation between $\mathcal{B}$ and $\mathcal{A}$, or in other words, if φ satisfies (17), (18) and:

$$\sigma^B \leqslant \sigma^A \circ \varphi, \tag{19}$$

$$\varphi \circ (\tau_u^B)^\varepsilon \leqslant (\tau_u^A)^\varepsilon, \quad \text{for all } u \in X^*, \tag{20}$$

then φ is an ε-weak forward bisimulation between $\mathcal{A}$ and $\mathcal{B}$. In what follows, we drop the expression "between $\mathcal{A}$ and $\mathcal{B}$" when fuzzy automata $\mathcal{A}$ and $\mathcal{B}$ are clear from the context. Moreover, we call ε-weak forward (bi)simulations simply just ε-weak (bi)simulations. It is important to emphasize that, by the properties proved in Sect. 3, there are finitely many inequalities in (18) and (20). So, in the contrast to the case of classical weak (bi)simulations, here we can always check the existence of ε-weak (bi)simulations.

The following theorem provides a fundamental property of ε-weak simulations and ε-weak bisimulations.

Theorem 1. *Let* $\mathcal{A} = (A, \sigma^A, \delta^A, \tau^A)$ *and* $\mathcal{B} = (B, \sigma^B, \delta^B, \tau^B)$ *be fuzzy automata and let* $\varepsilon > 0$. *Then:*

a) *if there exists an ε-weak simulation between $\mathcal{A}$ and $\mathcal{B}$, then $[\![\mathcal{A}]\!]$ is ε-included in $[\![\mathcal{B}]\!]$, i.e., (15) holds;*
b) *if there exists an ε-weak bisimulation between $\mathcal{A}$ and $\mathcal{B}$, then $[\![\mathcal{A}]\!]$ is ε-equivalent to $[\![\mathcal{B}]\!]$, i.e., (16) holds.*

Proof. a) Let φ be an ε-weak forward bisimulation between $\mathcal{A}$ and $\mathcal{B}$, for some $\varepsilon > 0$. Choose an arbitrary word $u \in X^*$. Consider separately the following two cases:
Case 1): Assume that $[\![\mathcal{A}]\!](u) > \varepsilon$. Then, according to Lemma 2, we have that $\sigma^A \circ \tau_u^A = \sigma^A \circ (\tau_u^A)^\varepsilon$. By using the fact that φ is an ε-weak forward simulation, as well as (13), we get:

$$[\![\mathcal{A}]\!](u) = \sigma^A \circ \tau_u^A = \sigma^A \circ (\tau_u^A)^\varepsilon \leqslant \sigma^B \circ \varphi^{-1} \circ (\tau_u^A)^\varepsilon \leqslant \sigma^B \circ (\tau_u^B)^\varepsilon$$
$$\leqslant \sigma^B \circ \tau_u^B = [\![\mathcal{B}]\!](u).$$

In conclusion, we obtained that $\varepsilon < [\![\mathcal{A}]\!](u) \leqslant [\![\mathcal{B}]\!](u)$. Thus, $[\![\mathcal{A}]\!]_\varepsilon(u) \leqslant [\![\mathcal{B}]\!]_\varepsilon(u)$.
Case 2): Assume that $[\![\mathcal{A}]\!](u) \leqslant \varepsilon$. Then $[\![\mathcal{A}]\!]_\varepsilon(u) = 0 \leqslant [\![\mathcal{B}]\!]_\varepsilon(u)$. This completes the proof for part a).
b) The assertion follows immediately from the assertion a). ∎

As we can see from the definition and the previous theorem, ε-weak (bi)simulations are very important from the two points. First, in the contrast to the case of weak (bi)simulations, it is always possible to check the existence of ε-weak (bi)simulations. Second, ε-weak (bi)simulations preserve the language (equivalence) inclusion for all the words which are accepted by one automaton with reasonable degree (since we chose the value ε to be extremely small, we can assume that words are not accepted by some automaton if they are accepted with values smaller than that given value).

Example 1. Let $\mathcal{A} = (A, \sigma^A, \delta^A, \tau^A)$ and $\mathcal{B} = (B, \sigma^B, \delta^B, \tau^B)$ be fuzzy automata over the product structure and the alphabet $X = \{x\}$, where:

$$\sigma^A = \begin{bmatrix} 1 & 1 & 0 \end{bmatrix}, \quad \delta^A_x = \begin{bmatrix} 1 & 1 & 0 \\ 1 & 1 & 0 \\ 0 & 0 & \frac{1}{2} \end{bmatrix}, \quad \tau^A = \begin{bmatrix} 1 \\ 1 \\ \frac{1}{2} \end{bmatrix},$$

$$\sigma^B = \begin{bmatrix} 1 & 1 \end{bmatrix}, \quad \delta^B_x = \begin{bmatrix} 1 & 0 \\ 0 & \frac{1}{2} \end{bmatrix}, \quad \tau^B = \begin{bmatrix} 1 \\ \frac{4}{5} \end{bmatrix}.$$

The system of fuzzy relation inequalities for checking whether a given fuzzy relation $\varphi \in I^{A \times B}$ is a weak forward bisimulation between $\mathcal{A}$ and $\mathcal{B}$ is equal to:

$$\begin{bmatrix} 1 & 1 & 0 \end{bmatrix} \leqslant \begin{bmatrix} 1 & 1 \end{bmatrix} \circ \varphi^{-1}, \qquad \begin{bmatrix} 1 & 1 \end{bmatrix} \leqslant \begin{bmatrix} 1 & 1 & 0 \end{bmatrix} \circ \varphi,$$

$$\varphi^{-1} \circ \begin{bmatrix} 1 \\ 1 \\ \frac{1}{2^{n+1}} \end{bmatrix} \leqslant \begin{bmatrix} 1 \\ \frac{1}{2^n} & \frac{4}{5} \end{bmatrix}, \qquad \varphi \circ \begin{bmatrix} 1 \\ \frac{1}{2^n} & \frac{4}{5} \end{bmatrix} \leqslant \begin{bmatrix} 1 \\ 1 \\ \frac{1}{2^{n+1}} \end{bmatrix}, \qquad \text{for } n \in \mathbb{N}.$$

Note that the system consists of infinitely many inequalities. On the other hand, in the case when $\varepsilon = 0.01$, the system for determining if a fuzzy relation is an ε-weak forward bisimulation is finite, and for the case $n \geqslant 6$ previous system of inequalities transforms to:

$$\varphi^{-1} \circ \begin{bmatrix} 1 \\ 1 \\ 0 \end{bmatrix} \leqslant \begin{bmatrix} 1 \\ \frac{1}{2^6} & \frac{4}{5} \end{bmatrix}, \qquad \varphi \circ \begin{bmatrix} 1 \\ \frac{1}{2^6} & \frac{4}{5} \end{bmatrix} \leqslant \begin{bmatrix} 1 \\ 1 \\ 0 \end{bmatrix},$$

$$\varphi^{-1} \circ \begin{bmatrix} 1 \\ 1 \\ 0 \end{bmatrix} \leqslant \begin{bmatrix} 1 \\ 0 \end{bmatrix}, \qquad \varphi \circ \begin{bmatrix} 1 \\ 0 \end{bmatrix} \leqslant \begin{bmatrix} 1 \\ 1 \\ 0 \end{bmatrix}.$$

The following theorem provides a way to determine the greatest ε-weak forward (bi)simulation.

Theorem 2. *Let $\mathcal{A} = (A, \sigma^A, \delta^A, \tau^A)$ and $\mathcal{B} = (B, \sigma^B, \delta^B, \tau^B)$ be fuzzy automata, and let $\varepsilon > 0$. Then:*

a) if a fuzzy relation $\varphi = \bigwedge_{u \in X^*} (\tau_u^A)^\varepsilon \backslash (\tau_u^B)^\varepsilon$ satisfies the condition (17), then it is the greatest ε-weak forward simulation between $\mathcal{A}$ and $\mathcal{B}$;

b) if a fuzzy relation $\varphi = \bigwedge_{u \in X^*} (\tau_u^A)^\varepsilon | (\tau_u^B)^\varepsilon$ satisfies the conditions (17) and (19), then it is the greatest ε-weak forward bisimulation between $\mathcal{A}$ and $\mathcal{B}$.

Proof. We prove only the part a). A fuzzy relation $\varphi \in I^{A \times B}$ is an ε-weak forward simulation between $\mathcal{A}$ and $\mathcal{B}$ if it satisfies the conditions (17) and (18). Using the adjunction property, it can be proven that (18) is equivalent to:

$$\varphi \leqslant \bigwedge_{u \in X^*} (\tau_u^A)^\varepsilon \backslash (\tau_u^B)^\varepsilon.$$

Therefore, if $\bigwedge_{u \in X^*} (\tau_u^A)^\varepsilon \backslash (\tau_u^B)^\varepsilon$ satisfies (17), then it is the greatest ε-weak forward simulation between $\mathcal{A}$ and $\mathcal{B}$. ∎

Example 2. Consider the fuzzy automata from the previous example. Using Theorem 2, we compute the greatest ε-weak forward bisimulation, which is equivalent to:

$$\varphi = \begin{bmatrix} 1 & 0 \\ 1 & 0 \\ 0 & \frac{5}{8} \end{bmatrix}.$$

6 Conclusion

This paper introduces ε-weak bisimulations for fuzzy automata defined over the real-unit interval and the product t-norm, where $\varepsilon > 0$ is a very small value. We demonstrated that such ε-weak bisimulations are always computable, in contrast to their counterpart weak bisimulations introduced in [5]. The main result is that, if there exists an ε-weak bisimulation between two fuzzy automata, then they are ε-equivalent, in a sense that they accept each word in degrees that are either equal or both less than or equal to ε. We would like to note that this approximation of fuzzy languages is new and different from the similar concept studied in [6].

In this work, we used the specific properties of the product t-norm. We leave the generalization of the results for fuzzy automata defined over other nonlocally finite structures to future work.

References

1. Bělohlávek, R.: Fuzzy Relational Systems: Foundations and Principles. Kluwer, New York (2002)
2. Bělohlávek, R., Vychodil, V.: Fuzzy Equational Logic. Studies in Fuzziness and Soft Computing, Springer, Heidelberg (2005). https://doi.org/10.1007/b105121
3. Ćirić, M., Ignjatović, J., Damljanović, N., Bašić, M.: Bisimulations for fuzzy automata. Fuzzy Sets Syst. **186**(1), 100–139 (2012)
4. Ćirić, M., Ignjatović, J., Jančić, I., Damljanović, N.: Computation of the greatest simulations and bisimulations between fuzzy automata. Fuzzy Sets Syst. **208**, 22–42 (2012)
5. Jančić, I.: Weak bisimulations for fuzzy automata. Fuzzy Sets Syst. **249**, 49–72 (2014)
6. Li, Y.: Approximation and robustness of fuzzy finite automata. Int. J. Approximate Reasoning **47**(2), 247–257 (2008)

7. Micić, I., Jančić, Z., Stanimirović, S.: Computation of the greatest right and left invariant fuzzy quasi-orders and fuzzy equivalences. Fuzzy Sets Syst. **339**, 99–118 (2018)
8. Micić, I., Nguyen, L.A., Stanimirović, S.: Characterization and computation of approximate bisimulations for fuzzy automata. Fuzzy Sets Syst. **442**, 331–350 (2022)
9. Nguyen, L.: Computing crisp simulations for fuzzy labeled transition systems. J. Intell. Fuzzy Syst. **42**(4), 3067–3078 (2022)
10. Nguyen, L., Tran, D.: Computing crisp bisimulations for fuzzy structures. CoRR abs/2010.15671 (2020)
11. Nguyen, L., Tran, D.: Computing fuzzy bisimulations for fuzzy structures under the Gödel semantics. IEEE Trans. Fuzzy Syst. **29**(7), 1715–1724 (2021). https://doi.org/10.1109/TFUZZ.2020.2985000
12. Pan, H., Li, Y., Cao, Y., Li, P.: Nondeterministic fuzzy automata with membership values in complete residuated lattices. Int. J. Approximate Reasoning **82**, 22–38 (2017)
13. Qiao, S., Zhu, P., Feng, J.E.: Fuzzy bisimulations for nondeterministic fuzzy transition systems. IEEE Trans. Fuzzy Syst. **31**(7), 2450–2463 (2022). https://doi.org/10.1109/TFUZZ.2022.3227400
14. Stanimirović, S., Micić, I., Ćirić, M.: Approximate bisimulations for fuzzy automata over complete Heyting algebras. IEEE Trans. Fuzzy Syst. **30**, 437–447 (2022)
15. Wu, H., Chen, T., Han, T., Chen, Y.: Bisimulations for fuzzy transition systems revisited. Int. J. Approximate Reasoning **99**, 1–11 (2018)
16. Wu, H., Chen, Y., Bu, T., Deng, Y.: Algorithmic and logical characterizations of bisimulations for non-deterministic fuzzy transition systems. Fuzzy Sets Syst. **333**, 106–123 (2018)
17. Yang, C., Li, Y.: Approximate bisimulation relations for fuzzy automata. Soft Comput. **22**(14), 4535–4547 (2018). https://doi.org/10.1007/s00500-017-2913-z
18. Yang, C., Li, Y.: ϵ-bisimulation relations for fuzzy automata. IEEE Trans. Fuzzy Syst. **26**(4), 2017–2029 (2018)
19. Yang, C., Li, Y.: Approximate bisimulations and state reduction of fuzzy automata under fuzzy similarity measures. Fuzzy Sets Syst. **391**, 72–95 (2020)

On Relationships Between Approximate Bisimulations for Fuzzy Graphs and Their Approximation Degrees

Stefan Stanimirović[1]([✉])[ID], Ivana Micić[1][ID], and Linh Anh Nguyen[2,3][ID]

[1] Faculty of Science and Mathematics, University of Niš, Niš, Serbia
{stefan.stanimirovic,ivana.micic}@pmf.edu.rs
[2] Faculty of Mathematics, Informatics and Mechanics, University of Warsaw,
Banacha 2, 02-097 Warsaw, Poland
nguyen@mimuw.edu.pl
[3] Faculty of Information Technology, Nguyen Tat Thanh University,
Ho Chi Minh City, Vietnam

Abstract. Approximate bisimulations have recently gained broad attention in the fuzzy community. As they aim to fuzzify the equivalence between the observed two fuzzy systems, they are very convenient to connect two fuzzy systems that may not be strictly equivalent, but which might be regarded as "more or less" equivalent, or equivalent to some extent. This paper provides further advancement regarding approximate bisimulations. First, we define them over a general notion of a fuzzy graph that includes various specific fuzzy systems as particular cases. We study the properties of such approximate bisimulations. We investigate the connections between fuzzy graphs, approximate bisimulations, and their approximation degrees.

Keywords: Approximate bisimulations · Fuzzy graphs ·
Approximation degree

1 Introduction

Bisimulation is a well-established and extensively studied notion used to model the equivalence between various systems. Among others, bisimulations have been studied from various aspects to model the equivalence of numerous fuzzy systems. Some pioneering works include the study of bisimulations for fuzzy automata [3, 4,10], fuzzy labeled transition systems [15,20,23], fuzzy Kripke models [5,7], fuzzy social networks [8,9] and fuzzy interpretations in description logic [13,14]. Bisimulations have been studied both as crisp and fuzzy relations.

S. Stanimirović and I. Micić acknowledge the support of the Science Fund of the Republic of Serbia, GRANT No. 7750185, Quantitative Automata Models: Fundamental Problems and Applications - QUAM, and of the Ministry of Education, Science and Technological Development, Republic of Serbia, Contract No. 451-03-68/2022-14/200124.

S. Massanet et al. (Eds.): EUSFLAT 2023/AGOP 2023, LNCS 14069, pp. 579–590, 2023.
https://doi.org/10.1007/978-3-031-39965-7_48

Recently, scholars have focused on the so-called approximate bisimulations for various fuzzy systems. These approximate bisimulations generalize the notion of the bisimulation so that it can connect systems that are "more or less" equivalent, or equivalent to some degree. In other words, approximate bisimulations do not consider the equivalence of the observed systems as the crisp phenomenon (we do not say that the two systems are equivalent or not) but rather as the fuzzy phenomenon (we say that they are equivalent to some extent).

The most recent advances in the study of approximate bisimulations have been established in the setting of fuzzy automata, where they have been defined as crisp [24–26] and fuzzy relations [11,21]. In addition, the latter approach has been applied in the positional analysis of fuzzy social networks [12]. As it turns out, approximate bisimulations are not just a generalization of the concept of bisimulations. That is, not only that we can compute them in cases when there are no bisimulations between the observed fuzzy systems, but there are many properties that are characteristic only for them (see the above-referenced papers, as well as [22] for a more general setting).

This paper aims to bring further insights into approximate bisimulations and their properties, mainly concerning their approximation degrees. Our contributions are the following. First, we define approximate bisimulations (Definition 1) over the so-called *fuzzy graphs*, a general structure recently introduced in [17,19] capable of wrapping the definitions of commonly occurred fuzzy graph-based structures, including fuzzy automata, fuzzy labeled transition systems, fuzzy Kripke models, fuzzy social networks and fuzzy interpretations in description logic. Although similar, our definition of approximate bisimulations is new and different from the definition of approximate bisimulations given in other fuzzy settings (see references above). Then, we prove the conditions for the existence of the greatest approximate bisimulation in a degree at least λ in Theorem 1. In the end, three results exploring the connections between approximate bisimulations and their approximation degrees are given by Theorems 2, 3 and 4. The visual depictions of these results are provided in Figs. 1, 2 and 3.

2   Preliminaries

In this paper, we use a *Heyting algebra* as the underlying structure of truth values, which is an algebraic structure $\mathcal{H} = (H, \wedge, \vee, \rightarrow, 0, 1)$ such that $(H, \wedge, \vee, 0, 1)$ is a bounded lattice such that for all $u, v \in H$ there is the greatest element $x \in H$ such that $u \wedge x \leq v$. This element is the *relative pseudo-complement of u with respect to v*, and is denoted by $u \rightarrow v$ (see [6]). A *complete Heyting algebra* is a Heyting algebra that is a complete lattice. It can be proved (see [6, Proposition 1.5.4]) that a complete lattice $(H, \wedge, \vee)$ is a Heyting algebra if and only if the infinite distributive law holds in H, i.e. for an arbitrary index set I, $u \in H$ and $\{v_i\}_{i \in I} \subseteq H$:

$$u \wedge \left(\bigvee_{i \in I} v_i \right) = \bigvee_{i \in I} (u \wedge v_i).$$

Every Heyting algebra admits the *biimplication*, the operation on H (labeled $\leftrightarrow$) defined with $u \leftrightarrow v = (u \rightarrow v) \wedge (v \rightarrow u)$.

One of the most prominent example of a Heyting algebra is the *Gödel algebra*, in which $H = [0,1]$, $\wedge$ = min, $\vee$ = max and $u \rightarrow v = 1$ if $u \le v$ and $u \rightarrow v = v$ otherwise. Other prominent examples include the Boolean algebra, the Lindenbaum algebra of propositional intuitionistic logic, and Łukasiewicz-Moisil algebras (LM_n, for every $n \in \mathbb{N}$). Moreover, every complete residuated lattice with the idempotent multiplication is a Heyting algebra (see [1,2,22] for more details).

In what follows, let $\mathcal{H}$ be a complete Heyting algebra. A *fuzzy subset* of a set U over $\mathcal{H}$, or simply a *fuzzy subset* of U, is any mapping from U into H, with the equality and the inclusion (ordering) of fuzzy sets being defined coordinate-wise (cf. [1,2]). With H^U we denote the collection of all fuzzy subsets of U.

A *fuzzy relation* between two sets U and V is any mapping from $U \times V$ to H, i.e., any fuzzy subset of $U \times V$. Consequently, the equality and the inclusion (ordering) of fuzzy relations are defined as for fuzzy sets. The set of all fuzzy relations between U and V is denoted by $H^{U \times V}$. For a fuzzy relation $A \in H^{U \times V}$, the fuzzy relation $A^{-1} \in H^{V \times U}$ is the *inverse* of A, and is given by $A^{-1}(v, u) = A(u, v)$, for every $u \in U$ and $v \in V$.

Let U, V and W be nonempty sets. For fuzzy relations $A \in H^{U \times V}$, $B \in H^{V \times W}$ and fuzzy sets $f \in H^U$, $g \in H^V$, we define *compositions* $A \circ B \in H^{U \times W}$, $f \circ A \in H^V$ and $A \circ g \in H^U$ with

$$(A \circ B)(u, w) = \bigvee_{v \in V} A(u, v) \wedge B(v, w),$$

$$(f \circ A)(v) = \bigvee_{u \in U} f(u) \wedge A(u, v),$$

$$(A \circ g)(u) = \bigvee_{v \in V} A(u, v) \wedge g(v),$$

for every $u \in U$, $v \in V$ and $w \in W$, as well as the *composition* $f_1 \circ f_2 \in H$, for fuzzy sets $f_1, f_2 \in H^U$ with

$$f_1 \circ f_2 = \bigvee_{u \in U} f_1(u) \wedge f_2(u).$$

It can be easily verified that $\circ$ is an associative operation, regardless of the types of fuzzy sets or the fuzzy relations that take part in the composition, as long as the composition is possible. In addition, it is monotonic in both parameters. Moreover, the following properties can also be proved:

$$\left(\bigvee_{i \in I} A_i \right) \circ B = \bigvee_{i \in I} (A_i \circ B), \qquad \left(\bigvee_{i \in I} A_i \right)^{-1} = \bigvee_{i \in I} A_i^{-1}. \tag{1}$$

For two fuzzy sets $f, g \in H^U$, we define their *degree of subsethood* $f \lesssim g \in H$ as

$$f \lesssim g = \bigwedge_{u \in U} f(u) \rightarrow g(u).$$

Similarly, we define their *degree of similarity* $f \approx g \in H$ as

$$f \approx g = \bigwedge_{u \in U} f(u) \leftrightarrow g(u).$$

Intuitively, $f \lesssim g$ measures the *degree of subsethood* (or the *inclusion degree*) of the fuzzy set f in the fuzzy set g. Similarly, $f \approx g$ measures the *degree of equality* of fuzzy sets f and g, i.e., the degree to which f and g are *similar*. These notations are easily extended for fuzzy relations. The following properties that hold for every $A, B, C, D \in H^U$ are used through the rest of the paper (see [1] for more details):

$$(A \lesssim A) = 1, \quad (A \approx A) = 1, \tag{2}$$
$$(A \approx B) = (B \approx A), \tag{3}$$
$$(A \approx B) = ((A \lesssim B) \wedge (B \lesssim A)), \tag{4}$$
$$(A \lesssim B) = 1 \text{ iff } A \leq B, \tag{5}$$
$$((A \lesssim B) \wedge (B \lesssim C)) \leq (A \lesssim C), \tag{6}$$
$$((A \approx B) \wedge (B \lesssim C) \wedge (C \approx D)) \leq (A \lesssim D). \tag{7}$$

Moreover, for every $A_i, B \in H^U$, where $i \in I$, we have:

$$\left(\left(\bigvee_{i \in I} A_i \right) \lesssim B \right) = \left(\bigwedge_{i \in I} (A_i \lesssim B) \right). \tag{8}$$

Additionally, for fuzzy relations $R_1, R_2 \in H^{U \times V}$ and $P_1, P_2 \in H^{V \times W}$, we have (see also [1]):

$$((R_1 \approx R_2) \wedge (P_1 \approx P_2)) \leq ((R_1 \circ P_1) \approx (R_2 \circ P_2)). \tag{9}$$

3   Approximate Bisimulations for Fuzzy Graphs

In the sequel, let $\mathcal{H}$ be a complete Heyting algebra. A *fuzzy labeled graph*, or simply just a *fuzzy graph*, is a tuple $G = (V, E, L, \Sigma_V, \Sigma_E)$, where:

- V is a nonempty set of vertices,
- Σ_V is a set of *vertex labels*,
- Σ_E is a set of *edge labels*,
- $E : V \times \Sigma_E \times V \to H$ is the fuzzy set of labeled edges,
- $L : V \to (\Sigma_V \to H)$ is called the labeling function of vertices.

For every vertex label $p \in \Sigma_V$ we define the fuzzy subset $L_p : V \to H$ as $L_p(x) = L(p)(x)$, for every $x \in V$. Similarly, for every edge label $r \in \Sigma_E$ we define the fuzzy relation $E_r : V \times V \to H$ as $E_r(x, y) = E(x, r, y)$, for every $x, y \in V$. Intuitively, $L_p(x)$ represents the degree to which a node x has a label p, while $E_r(x, y)$ represents the degree to which there is a directed edge from

x to y labeled by r. Because the underlying structure of the truth values is a complete Heyting algebra, we allow the sets V, Σ_V and Σ_E to be infinite.

The notion of a fuzzy graph was introduced in [17,19], and includes as particular cases other well-known fuzzy graph-based notions. For example, fuzzy automata are fuzzy graphs with the set $\Sigma_V = \{i, f\}$, where L_i is called the fuzzy set of initial states, while L_f is called the fuzzy set of final states of a fuzzy automaton. Note that fuzzy automata are fuzzy graphs that can accept sequences of symbols (i.e., words) to a certain degree.

Definition 1. *Let* $G = (V, E, L, \Sigma_V, \Sigma_E)$ *and* $G' = (V', E', L', \Sigma_V, \Sigma_E)$ *be fuzzy graphs over the same signature* (Σ_V, Σ_E), *and let* $\lambda \in H$ *be a scalar from the Heyting algebra* $\mathcal{H}$. *A fuzzy relation* $R \in H^{V \times V'}$ *is called a* λ-*approximate bisimulation between* G *and* G' *if:*

$$\lambda = \bigwedge_{p \in \Sigma_V} \left((R^{-1} \circ L_p \lesssim L'_p) \wedge (R \circ L'_p \lesssim L_p) \right)$$

$$\wedge \bigwedge_{r \in \Sigma_E} \left((R^{-1} \circ E_r \lesssim E'_r \circ R^{-1}) \wedge (R \circ E'_r \lesssim E_r \circ R) \right). \tag{10}$$

When $\lambda = 1$, then approximate bisimulations, as given by Definition 1, come down to bisimulations given in [7,13,16]. Following the approach given in [11,21], one can aim to define two types of approximate simulations and four types of approximate bisimulations, where each type of approximate (bi)simulation can be defined by the specific combination of elements in (10), and to have $\approx$ instead of $\lesssim$ in some places. As the full difference between these types of approximate (bi)simulations is already explained in [11], and it is irrelevant for the current study, as all the results in this paper for one type of approximate (bi)simulation can be easily extended to other types using (4), we do not find it relevant to study all types separately. Rather, we focus on the one type of approximate bisimulation given by Definition 1. Recall again that, in the setting of fuzzy automata, approximate simulations preserve the language subsethood to the certain degree, while approximate bisimulations preserve the language similarity to the certain degree between fuzzy automata (cf. [11,21]).

It should be emphasized that, if a fuzzy relation $R \in H^{V \times V'}$ is a λ-approximate bisimulation between $G = (V, E, L, \Sigma_V, \Sigma_E)$ and $G' = (V', E', L', \Sigma_V, \Sigma_E)$, then the following holds:

$$\lambda \leq (R^{-1} \circ L_p \lesssim L'_p), \quad \text{for every } p \in \Sigma_V, \tag{11}$$

$$\lambda \leq (R \circ L'_p \lesssim L_p), \quad \text{for every } p \in \Sigma_V, \tag{12}$$

$$\lambda \leq (R^{-1} \circ E_r \lesssim E'_r \circ R^{-1}), \quad \text{for every } r \in \Sigma_E, \tag{13}$$

$$\lambda \leq (R \circ E'_r \lesssim E_r \circ R), \quad \text{for every } r \in \Sigma_E. \tag{14}$$

Note that a fuzzy relation is either a bisimulation between two fuzzy graphs or not. On the other hand, every fuzzy relation is an approximate bisimulation between two fuzzy graphs to a certain degree. The following result concerns when there exists the greatest approximate bisimulation between two fuzzy graphs for a chosen approximation degree.

Theorem 1. *Let $G = (V, E, L, \Sigma_V, \Sigma_E)$ and $G' = (V', E', L', \Sigma_V, \Sigma_E)$ be fuzzy graphs over the same signature (Σ_V, Σ_E) such that they admit at least one approximate bisimulation in a degree at least λ, for some $\lambda \in H$. Then there exists the greatest approximate bisimulation between G and G' in a degree at least λ.*

Proof. As a consequence of the assumptions of the Theorem, we get that the family $\{R_j\}_{j \in J}$ of all fuzzy relations between V and V' that satisfy (11)–(14) is nonempty. As we work with complete Heyting algebras, then there exists the join of all elements from this family, which we denote by R. Then we need to prove that R also satisfies (11)–(14). In order to prove that R satisfies (11), we use (8) and (1) to obtain that for every $p \in \Sigma_V$:

$$\lambda \leq \bigwedge_{j \in J} (R^{-1} \circ L_p \precsim L'_p) = \left(\bigvee_{j \in J} (R_j^{-1} \circ L_p) \precsim L'_p \right)$$

$$= \left(\left(\left(\bigvee_{j \in J} R_j \right)^{-1} \circ L_p \right) \precsim L'_p \right) = ((R^{-1} \circ L_p) \precsim L'_p).$$

We can prove that R satisfies (12) analogously. We now prove that R satisfies (13). By the construction of R, we have that $R_j \leq R$, for every $j \in J$, which means that $R_j^{-1} \leq R^{-1}$, and further $E'_r \circ R_j^{-1} \leq E'_r \circ R^{-1}$, for every $j \in J$ and $r \in \Sigma_E$. According to (5), we have that $1 = (E'_r \circ R_j^{-1} \precsim E'_r \circ R^{-1})$, for every $j \in J$ and $r \in \Sigma_E$, which by (6) further yields:

$$(R_j^{-1} \circ E_r \precsim E'_r \circ R_j^{-1}) = (R_j^{-1} \circ E_r \precsim E'_r \circ R_j^{-1}) \wedge (E'_r \circ R_j^{-1} \precsim E'_r \circ R^{-1})$$
$$\leq (R_j^{-1} \circ E_r \precsim E'_r \circ R^{-1})$$

As (13) holds for every R_j (in the place of R), by using the previous inequality, we get that for every $r \in \Sigma_E$:

$$\lambda \leq \left(\bigwedge_{j \in J} (R_j^{-1} \circ E_r \precsim E'_r \circ R_j^{-1}) \right) \leq \left(\bigwedge_{j \in J} (R_j^{-1} \circ E_r \precsim E'_r \circ R^{-1}) \right).$$

Now we can apply (8) and (1) to obtain that, for every $r \in \Sigma_E$,

$$\lambda \leq \left(\left(\bigvee_{j \in J} (R_j^{-1} \circ E_r) \right) \precsim E'_r \circ R^{-1} \right) = (R^{-1} \circ E_r \precsim E'_r \circ R^{-1}),$$

which means that R satisfies (13). We can prove that R satisfies (14) analogously. $\blacksquare$

As every fuzzy relation between the sets of nodes of two fuzzy graphs is an approximate bisimulation between these two fuzzy graphs to some degree, it comes naturally to ask what is the connection between different fuzzy relations and their approximation degrees. The following theorem aims at providing the answer.

Theorem 2. *Let $G = (V, E, L, \Sigma_V, \Sigma_E)$ and $G' = (V', E', L', \Sigma_V, \Sigma_E)$ be fuzzy graphs over the same signature (Σ_V, Σ_E). Furthermore, let $R, P \in H^{V \times V'}$ be two fuzzy relations such that R is a λ-approximate bisimulation and P is a μ-approximate bisimulation between G and G'. Then:*

$$(R \approx P) \leq (\lambda \leftrightarrow \mu).$$

Proof. As $R \in H^{V \times V'}$ is a λ-approximate bisimulation between G and G', it satisfies (11)–(14). Let $P \in H^{V \times V'}$ be an arbitrary fuzzy relation. We first focus on (13). Starting from this inequality, we obtain:

$$\lambda \wedge (R \approx P) \leq \left(\bigwedge_{r \in \Sigma_E} (R^{-1} \circ E_r \lesssim E'_r \circ R^{-1}) \right) \wedge (R \approx P)$$

$$= \bigwedge_{r \in \Sigma_E} \left((R^{-1} \circ E_r \lesssim E'_r \circ R^{-1}) \wedge (R^{-1} \approx P^{-1}) \right).$$

Given (2) and the fact that $(R^{-1} \approx P^{-1}) = (R^{-1} \approx P^{-1}) \wedge (R^{-1} \approx P^{-1})$, we further obtain:

$$\lambda \wedge (R \approx P) \leq \bigwedge_{r \in \Sigma_E} \left((R^{-1} \circ E_r \lesssim E'_r \circ R^{-1}) \wedge (R^{-1} \approx P^{-1}) \wedge (E_r \approx E_r) \right.$$

$$\left. \wedge (E'_r \approx E'_r) \wedge (R^{-1} \approx P^{-1}) \right).$$

But (9) further yields:

$$\lambda \wedge (R \approx P) \leq \bigwedge_{r \in \Sigma_E} \left((R^{-1} \circ E_r \lesssim E'_r \circ R^{-1}) \wedge (R^{-1} \circ E_r \approx P^{-1} \circ E_r) \right.$$

$$\left. \wedge (E'_r \circ R^{-1} \approx E'_r \circ P^{-1}) \right).$$

By (3) and (7), it follows that:

$$\lambda \wedge (R \approx P) \leq \bigwedge_{r \in \Sigma_E} (P^{-1} \circ E_r \lesssim E'_r \circ P^{-1}).$$

Thus, we have proved that P satisfies (13) for the threshold $\lambda \wedge (R \approx P)$. We can prove that P satisfies (11), (12) and (14) for the same threshold completely analogously. This further yields:

$$\lambda \wedge (R \approx P) \leq \bigwedge_{p \in \Sigma_V} \left((P^{-1} \circ L_p \lesssim L'_p) \wedge (P \circ L'_p \lesssim L_p) \right)$$

$$\wedge \bigwedge_{r \in \Sigma_E} \left((P^{-1} \circ E_r \lesssim E'_r \circ P^{-1}) \wedge (P \circ E'_r \lesssim E_r \circ P) \right) = \mu.$$

In this way, we have proved that $(R \approx P) \leq \lambda \to \mu$. Completely analogously, we prove that $(P \approx R) \leq \mu \to \lambda$. But, since (3) holds, the proof follows.   ■

Theorem 2 is visually represented in Fig. 1, and can be verbally interpreted as follows: If a fuzzy relation R is a λ-approximate bisimulation between fuzzy graphs G and G', and a fuzzy relation P is μ-approximate bisimulation between G and G', then the degree of equality of fuzzy relations R and P is not greater than the degree of equality of degrees λ and μ.

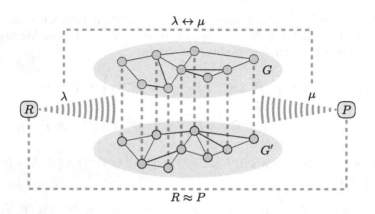

Fig. 1. A visual depiction of Theorem 2.

Theorem 2 has the following application potential. Let G and G' be two fuzzy systems that can be modelled by fuzzy graphs, and let R be some fuzzy relation between G and G', and say that it is an approximate bisimulation in a degree λ. Then, if we want to choose another fuzzy relation P as an approximate bisimulation, then it also has its approximation degree μ. But according to Theorem 2, if the chosen fuzzy relations R and P are equal to a very high degree, then their approximation degrees will also be equal.

If we interpret Theorem 2 for fuzzy graphs defined over a linearly ordered Heyting algebra, we get the following result.

Corollary 1. *Let $G = (V, E, L, \Sigma_V, \Sigma_E)$ and $G' = (V', E', L', \Sigma_V, \Sigma_E)$ be fuzzy graphs over the same signature (Σ_V, Σ_E) defined over a linearly ordered Heyting algebra $\mathcal{H}$. Furthermore, let $R \in H^{V \times V'}$ be a λ-approximate bisimulation between G and G', and let $P \in H^{V \times V'}$ be a μ-approximate bisimulation between G and G'. Then, either $\lambda = \mu$ or $(R \approx P) \leq \min\{\lambda, \mu\}$.*

This corollary follows immediately from Theorem 2. The reason is that, when the underlying Heyting algebra is linearly ordered, $(\lambda \leftrightarrow \mu)$ is equal to 1 when $\lambda = \mu$ and equal to $\min\{\lambda, \mu\}$ when $\lambda \neq \mu$.

In what follows, we measure the similarity degree of two fuzzy graphs, and find its connection with the approximation degrees of approximate bisimulations.

Definition 2. *Let* $G = (V, E, L, \Sigma_V, \Sigma_E)$ *and* $G' = (V', E', L', \Sigma_V, \Sigma_E)$ *be fuzzy graphs over the same signature* (Σ_V, Σ_E). *Then the* degree of equality *of fuzzy graphs* G *and* G' *is defined by:*

$$(G \approx G') = \left(\bigwedge_{r \in \Sigma_E} E_r \approx E'_r \right) \wedge \left(\bigwedge_{p \in \Sigma_V} L_p \approx L'_p \right). \tag{15}$$

Theorem 3. *Let* $G_1 = (V, E_1, L_1, \Sigma_V, \Sigma_E)$ *and* $G'_1 = (V', E'_1, L'_1, \Sigma_V, \Sigma_E)$ *be fuzzy graphs over the same signature* (Σ_V, Σ_E) *such that* $R \in H^{V \times V'}$ *is a* λ-*approximate bisimulation between* G_1 *and* G'_1. *Furthermore, let* $G_2 = (V, E_2, L_2, \Sigma_V, \Sigma_E)$ *and* $G'_2 = (V', E'_2, L'_2, \Sigma_V, \Sigma_E)$ *be fuzzy graphs over the same signature* (Σ_V, Σ_E) *such that* G_1 *and* G_2 *(resp.* G'_1 *and* G'_2*) share the same set of nodes.*[1] *In addition, let* R *be a* μ-*approximate bisimulation between* G_2 *and* G'_2. *Then:*

$$(G_1 \approx G_2) \wedge (G'_1 \approx G'_2) \leq (\lambda \leftrightarrow \mu).$$

Proof. Again, we firstly focus on (13). We use the fact that, for any two fuzzy graphs, their degree of equality is less than or equal to any of the two values given on the right-hand side of (15). This further gives:

$$\lambda \wedge (G_1 \approx G_2) \wedge (G'_1 \approx G'_2)$$

$$\leq \lambda \wedge \left(\bigwedge_{r \in \Sigma_E} (E_1)_r \approx (E_2)_r \right) \wedge \left(\bigwedge_{r \in \Sigma_E} (E'_1)_r \approx (E'_2)_r \right)$$

$$\leq \left(\bigwedge_{r \in \Sigma_E} (R^{-1} \circ (E_1)_r \lesssim (E'_1)_r \circ R^{-1}) \right) \wedge \left(\bigwedge_{r \in \Sigma_E} (E_1)_r \approx (E_2)_r \right)$$

$$\wedge \left(\bigwedge_{r \in \Sigma_E} (E'_1)_r \approx (E'_2)_r \right).$$

Using the same reasoning as in the proof of Theorem 2, we further obtain:

$$\lambda \wedge (G_1 \approx G_2) \wedge (G'_1 \approx G'_2)$$

$$\leq \bigwedge_{r \in \Sigma_E} [(R^{-1} \approx R^{-1}) \wedge ((E_1)_r \approx (E_2)_r) \wedge (R^{-1} \circ (E_1)_r \lesssim (E'_1)_r \circ R^{-1})$$

$$\wedge ((E'_1)_r \approx (E'_2)_r) \wedge (R^{-1} \approx R^{-1})]$$

$$\leq \bigwedge_{r \in \Sigma_E} [(R^{-1} \circ (E_1)_r \approx R^{-1} \circ (E_2)_r) \wedge (R^{-1} \circ (E_1)_r \lesssim (E'_1)_r \circ R^{-1})$$

$$\wedge ((E'_1)_r \circ R^{-1} \approx (E'_2)_r \circ R^{-1})]$$

$$\leq \bigwedge_{r \in \Sigma_E} (R^{-1} \circ (E_2)_r \lesssim (E'_2)_r \circ R^{-1}).$$

---

[1] Theoretically speaking, it is enough to assume that there is a bijection between the sets of nodes of fuzzy graphs G_1 and G_2, as well as there is also a bijection between the set of nodes of fuzzy graphs G'_1 and G'_2.

Analogously, we prove that the conditions (11), (12) and (14) hold for the degree $\lambda \wedge (G_1 \approx G_2) \wedge (G_1' \approx G_2')$ and the fuzzy relation R. Thus, $\lambda \wedge (G_1 \approx G_2) \wedge (G_1' \approx G_2') \leq \mu$. By symmetry, we have $\mu \wedge (G_1 \approx G_2) \wedge (G_1' \approx G_2') \leq \lambda$, which completes the proof. ∎

Theorem 3 is visually represented in Fig. 2, and can be verbally interpreted as follows: Assume that a fuzzy relation R is a λ-approximate bisimulation between fuzzy graphs G_1 and G_1', and there exist fuzzy graphs G_2 and G_2' such that G_1 and G_2, as well as G_1' and G_2' have the same sets of nodes. Then, if R is a μ-approximate bisimulation between G_2 and G_2', then the meet of the degree of equality of G_1 and G_2 and the degree of equality of G_1' and G_2' does not exceed the degree of equality of λ and μ).

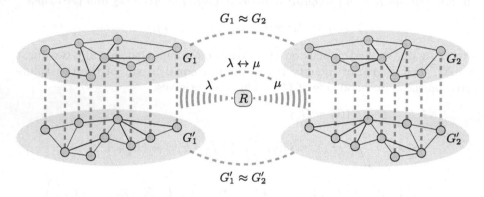

Fig. 2. A visual depiction of Theorem 3.

To sum up, we can combine Theorem 2 and Theorem 3 into a single one.

Theorem 4. *Let $G_1 = (V, E_1, L_1, \Sigma_V, \Sigma_E)$ and $G_1' = (V', E_1', L_1', \Sigma_V, \Sigma_E)$ be fuzzy graphs over the same signature (Σ_V, Σ_E) such that $R \in H^{V \times V'}$ is a λ-approximate bisimulation between G_1 and G_1'. Furthermore, let $G_2 = (V, E_2, L_2, \Sigma_V, \Sigma_E)$ and $G_2' = (V', E_2', L_2', \Sigma_V, \Sigma_E)$ be fuzzy graphs over the same signature (Σ_V, Σ_E) such that G_1 and G_2 (resp. G_1' and G_2') share the same set of nodes. Then, any fuzzy relation $P \in H^{V \times V'}$ is a μ-approximate bisimulation between G_2 and G_2' with*

$$(R \approx P) \wedge (G_1 \approx G_2) \wedge (G_1' \approx G_2') \leq (\lambda \leftrightarrow \mu).$$

Similar corollaries for Theorems 3 and 4 can be derived as we did for Theorem 2.

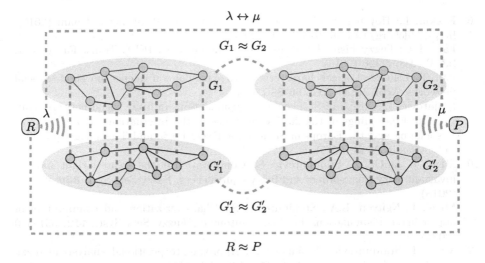

Fig. 3. A visual depiction of Theorem 4.

4 Conclusions

Approximate bisimulations between various fuzzy systems have recently emerged as an important tool that allows us to fuzzify the equivalence between the observed systems. In this paper, we have introduced the concept of approximate bisimulation between two fuzzy graphs. Note that a fuzzy graph is a general structure that includes fuzzy automata, fuzzy labeled transition systems, fuzzy Kripke models, fuzzy social networks and fuzzy interpretations in description logic as particular cases. That means that our definition is applicable in various fuzzy settings. We provide several theorems that establish the connections between the similarity degrees of fuzzy graphs, approximate bisimulations between them, and their approximation degrees. We leave for future work defining approximate bisimulations for fuzzy graphs in other ways (cf. [18] for more details) and developing algorithms for their computation.

References

1. Bělohlávek, R.: Fuzzy Relational Systems: Foundations and Principles. Kluwer, New York (2002)
2. Bělohlávek, R., Vychodil, V.: Fuzzy Equational Logic. Studies in Fuzziness and Soft Computing, Springer, Heidelberg (2005). https://doi.org/10.1007/b105121
3. Ćirić, M., Ignjatović, J., Damljanović, N., Bašić, M.: Bisimulations for fuzzy automata. Fuzzy Sets Syst. **186**(1), 100–139 (2012)
4. Ćirić, M., Ignjatović, J., Jančić, I., Damljanović, N.: Computation of the greatest simulations and bisimulations between fuzzy automata. Fuzzy Sets Syst. **208**, 22–42 (2012)
5. Eleftheriou, P., Koutras, C., Nomikos, C.: Notions of bisimulation for Heyting-valued modal languages. J. Log. Comput. **22**(2), 213–235 (2012)

6. Esakia, L.: Heyting Algebras: Duality Theory, vol. 50. Springer, Cham (2019). https://doi.org/10.1007/978-3-030-12096-2
7. Fan, T.F.: Fuzzy bisimulation for Gödel modal logic. IEEE Trans. Fuzzy Syst. **23**(6), 2387–2396 (2015)
8. Fan, T., Liau, C.: Logical characterizations of regular equivalence in weighted social networks. Artif. Intell. **214**, 66–88 (2014)
9. Ignjatović, J., Ćirić, M., Stanković, I.: Bisimulations in fuzzy social network analysis. In: Proceedings of the 2015 Conference of the International Fuzzy Systems Association and the European Society for Fuzzy Logic and Technology, pp. 404–411. Atlantis Press (2015)
10. Micić, I., Jančić, Z., Stanimirović, S.: Computation of the greatest right and left invariant fuzzy quasi-orders and fuzzy equivalences. Fuzzy Sets Syst. **339**, 99–118 (2018)
11. Micić, I., Nguyen, L.A., Stanimirović, S.: Characterization and computation of approximate bisimulations for fuzzy automata. Fuzzy Sets Syst. **442**, 331–350 (2022)
12. Micić, I., Stanimirović, S., Jančić, Z.: Approximate positional analysis of fuzzy social networks. Fuzzy Sets Syst. **454**, 149–172 (2023)
13. Nguyen, L.A., Ha, Q., Nguyen, N.T., Nguyen, T.H.K., Tran, T.: Bisimulation and bisimilarity for fuzzy description logics under the Gödel semantics. Fuzzy Sets Syst. **388**, 146–178 (2020)
14. Nguyen, L.A.: Bisimilarity in fuzzy description logics under the Zadeh semantics. IEEE Trans. Fuzzy Syst. **27**(6), 1151–1161 (2019)
15. Nguyen, L.A.: Characterizing fuzzy simulations for fuzzy labeled transition systems in fuzzy propositional dynamic logic. Int. J. Approximate Reasoning **135**, 21–37 (2021)
16. Nguyen, L.A.: Logical characterizations of fuzzy bisimulations in fuzzy modal logics over residuated lattices. Fuzzy Sets Syst. **431**, 70–93 (2022)
17. Nguyen, L.A.: Computing the fuzzy partition corresponding to the greatest fuzzy auto-bisimulation of a fuzzy graph-based structure under the Gödel semantics. Inf. Sci. **630**, 482–506 (2023)
18. Nguyen, L.A.: Fuzzy simulations and bisimulations between fuzzy automata. Int. J. Approximate Reasoning **155**, 113–131 (2023)
19. Nguyen, L.A., Tran, D.X.: Computing crisp bisimulations for fuzzy structures. CoRR abs/2010.15671 (2020). arXiv:2010.15671
20. Qiao, S., Zhu, P., Feng, J.E.: Fuzzy bisimulations for nondeterministic fuzzy transition systems. IEEE Trans. Fuzzy Syst. **31**(7), 2450–2463 (2022). https://doi.org/10.1109/TFUZZ.2022.3227400
21. Stanimirović, S., Micić, I., Ćirić, M.: Approximate bisimulations for fuzzy automata over complete Heyting algebras. IEEE Trans. Fuzzy Syst. **30**, 437–447 (2022)
22. Stanimirović, S., Micić, I.: On the solvability of weakly linear systems of fuzzy relation equations. Inf. Sci. **607**, 670–687 (2022)
23. Wu, H., Chen, Y., Bu, T., Deng, Y.: Algorithmic and logical characterizations of bisimulations for non-deterministic fuzzy transition systems. Fuzzy Sets Syst. **333**, 106–123 (2018)
24. Yang, C., Li, Y.: Approximate bisimulation relations for fuzzy automata. Soft Comput. **22**(14), 4535–4547 (2018). https://doi.org/10.1007/s00500-017-2913-z
25. Yang, C., Li, Y.: ϵ-bisimulation relations for fuzzy automata. IEEE Trans. Fuzzy Syst. **26**(4), 2017–2029 (2018)
26. Yang, C., Li, Y.: Approximate bisimulations and state reduction of fuzzy automata under fuzzy similarity measures. Fuzzy Sets Syst. **391**, 72–95 (2020)

SPECIAL SESSION 8: New frontiers of Computational Intelligence for Pervasive Healthcare Systems

An Information Extraction Study: Take in Mind the Tokenization!

Christos Theodoropoulos[1,2(✉)] and Marie-Francine Moens[1,2]

[1] KU Leuven, Oude Markt 13, 3000 Leuven, Belgium
{christos.theodoropoulos,sien.moens}@kuleuven.be
[2] Language Intelligence and Information Retrieval Lab, Celestijnenlaan 200A,
3001 Leuven, Belgium

Abstract. Current research on the advantages and trade-offs of using characters, instead of tokenized text, as input for deep learning models, has evolved substantially. New token-free models remove the traditional tokenization step; however, their efficiency remains unclear. Moreover, the effect of tokenization is relatively unexplored in sequence tagging tasks. To this end, we investigate the impact of tokenization when extracting information from documents and present a comparative study and analysis of subword-based and character-based models. Specifically, we study Information Extraction (IE) from biomedical texts. The main outcome is twofold: tokenization patterns can introduce inductive bias that results in state-of-the-art performance, and the character-based models produce promising results; thus, transitioning to token-free IE models is feasible.

Keywords: Information Extraction · Tokenization · Inductive Bias

1 Introduction

Currently, neural network models are replacing traditional Natural Language Processing (NLP) pipelines, as their ability to learn abstract and meaningful representations improves the performance. Hence, the complex and error-prone handcrafted feature engineering has been substantially reduced. However, the word-level or subword-level tokenization step remains, being carried over from the traditional era of NLP systems. Designing a custom tokenizer based on linguistic characteristics is time-consuming, expensive, and language specific and requires feature engineering and linguistic-related expertise. To alleviate these issues, data-driven approaches, such as WordPiece [35], Byte Pair Encoding [27], and SentencePiece [15], tokenize the text by splitting the strings based on frequent words and subwords (word pieces) given a corpus. Nonetheless, these algorithms struggle to handle special linguistic morphologies [5] and their impact in sequence tagging tasks, such as Named Entity Recognition (NER), is relatively unexplored. The open research discussion on the tokenization step motivates the first research question of the study:

S. Massanet et al. (Eds.): EUSFLAT 2023/AGOP 2023, LNCS 14069, pp. 593–606, 2023.
https://doi.org/10.1007/978-3-031-39965-7_49

– How does the tokenization step affect the performance in the IE task? (RQ1)

In this paper, we conduct a tokenization analysis and inductive bias study to explore the existence of potential patterns, related to the tokenization step, by solving the IE task in the biomedical domain using subword-based models. We refer to the general definition of inductive bias in AI models, as the set of assumptions that the learner uses to predict outputs of given inputs that it has not encountered [20]. We base our study on Partition Filter Network (PFN) [37], which solves the NER [10,21] and Relation Extraction (RE) [23,28] tasks jointly by modeling the interaction between the tasks and learning independent and shared representations. We choose this model because it leverages the Language Model (LM) representations by design. Hence, we can experiment with different LMs and explore their effectiveness. The main outcome of the analysis is that the tokenization patterns introduce inductive bias in the IE task. Additionally, the similarity analysis of the learned entity representations probes the existence of inductive bias. Following this key finding, we explore the capabilities of a tokenization bias-free model and answer the second research question:

– Can a transition to character-level models be carried out without significant performance degradation? (RQ2)

Recently, new character-based models [6,9,30,36] that directly process sequences of characters have been released, and transitioning to this kind of model by replacing subword-based models without losing performance has become a focus of research. Hence, we conduct a comparative study for the IE task, including subword-based and character-based models. Additionally, we present a hyphenation analysis to detect possible linguistic characteristics, by exploring patterns of subwords with a length of 4 characters, and probe the hypothesis that character-based models are more capable of capturing special text morphology.

In summary, the key contributions are as follows:

– We present an extensive analysis to investigate the effect of tokenization in the IE task for the biomedical domain and raise awareness.
– We identify the existence of inductive bias when specific tokenization patterns are detected, which leads to new state-of-the-art (SOTA) performance in the ADE dataset [11].
– We present a comparative study, including subword-based and character-based models, and draw insights supported by the hyphenation analysis.

2   Related Work

Ács et al. (2021) [1] explore the effect of subword pooling on three tasks: morphological probing, POS, and NER tagging. Zhang and Tan (2021) [38] present a comparison of different textual representations for cross-lingual information retrieval. Traditional token [26], subword [32] and character-level representations are compared for the German, French and Japanese languages. The main outcome is that leveraging the traditional token representations results in the best performance, and combining subword representations can be beneficial in some cases. In our study, we compare the pretrained representations of subword-based and character-based LMs in the IE task. In addition, we explore the performance of the different models in an end-to-end training setup.

Itzhak and Levy (2021) [12] discuss models that implicitly learn at the character level even when they are trained on the subword level. More precisely, they explore the capabilities of RoBERTa-base and Large [19], GPT2-medium [24], and AraBERT-large [3] in word spelling. The main results indicate that the embedding layer of the subword-level LMs contains considerable information about the character composition of the tokens. The study does not include character-based LMs (e.g. CharacterBERT) by design. In contrast, we compare subword-based and character-based LMs in the IE task and implicitly explore the capabilities of the models on capturing special linguistic morphology (biomedical text) by presenting a hyphenation analysis.

To the best of our knowledge, there is no related work for the first research question of our paper and the revealing of inductive bias in the IE task when tokenization patterns are present.

3   Tokenization Analysis - Datasets

In this section, we conduct a tokenization analysis for the dataset used in the study. We choose the biomedical (ADE) dataset to explore the effect of tokenization in a special domain. The ADE dataset contains entities of Drugs and Adverse Effects (AE) and has labels for the relations between them. The tokenizer of cased BERT [7] and bioclinical BERT (b-BERT) [2] is based on the WordPiece algorithm, while ALBERT [16] adopts the SentencePiece algorithm.

In Table 2, we present the effect of tokenization on the average sentence length, in terms of word pieces (subwords), for each dataset. The sentence length increases by approximately 12 tokens, up to 58%, after the tokenization in the biomedical domain. To further explore the number of word pieces per entity type, we isolate the unique entities[1]. Then, we find the unique words that are part of each entity type and tokenize the unique entities and words using the different tokenizers to notice the difference in the length and the addition of the word pieces. In Table 1 the last column represents the average tokenized word length per entity type, and the *Out* type describes the words that are not part of an entity of interest. In the ADE dataset, the length of the drug and AE entities increases substantially, and the drug entities are split into more word pieces. Particularly, a word that is part of a drug entity is split into approximately 4 word pieces, on average, when using the tokenizer of cased BERT and b-BERT. The tokenizer of ALBERT tends to split the entities of interest into fewer pieces.

---

[1] We note that the set of unique entities for the case and uncased text processing is different, which is why the initial average entity length might be different.

Table 1. Average Entity Length - ADE dataset

Tokenizer	Type	Entity	Tokenized Entity[a]	Word
cased BERT	Drug	1.37	4.78 (+248.9%)	3.92
b-BERT		1.37	4.79 (+249.6%)	3.93
ALBERT		1.42	4.37 (+207.7%)	3.38
cased BERT	AE	2.66	6 (+125.6%)	2.81
b-BERT		2.66	5.9 (+121.8%)	2.77
ALBERT		2.72	5.29 (+94.5%)	2.38
cased BERT	Out	–	–	2.11
b-BERT		–	–	2.06
ALBERT		–	–	2.09

[a] (+ × %): percentage increase

Table 2. Average Sentence Length

Tokenizer	Dataset	Sentence	Tokenized Sentence[a]
cased BERT	ADE	21.23	33.56 (+58.1%)
b-BERT			33.1 (+55.9%)
ALBERT			33.25 (+56.6%)

[a] (+ × %): percentage increase

4   Inductive Bias

In this section, we answer the first research question (RQ1). Following the observations of the tokenization analysis, we conduct a study to investigate whether tokenization patterns introduce inductive bias in the IE task.

4.1   Experimental Setup

The overall model architecture of this paper is presented in Fig. 1. The sentence is processed by an LM, followed by an aggregation step that constructs the word-level embeddings by calculating the summed and averaged representations. When the aggregation step is not used, the model operates in the subword level as the PFN module directly processes the output of the LM. The PFN module models a two-way interaction between the NER and RE tasks, as it leverages the representations of the LM and segments the neurons into two task partitions (independent representations) and one shared partition (inter-task interaction). PFN consists of a partition filter encoder, a NER unit, and a RE unit [37]. The partition filter encoder is a recurrent feature encoder that stores information in intermediate memories. In each step, the neurons of the encoder are divided into three partitions: the relation, entity, and shared partitions. Then the encoder combines these partitions for task-specific feature generation and filters out irrelevant, for each task, information [37]. The NER-specific and RE-specific features are the input of the NER and RE units respectively. In this section, we focus on the subword-based LMs (cased BERT, b-BERT, ALBERT XLL) and run experiments with and without the aggregation step to explore differences in performance. The models are trained end-to-end.

We train the PFN module[2] (Fig. 1) using the hyperparameters that are selected in the official paper of the model [37] to solve the joint IE task. The training epochs are set to 100, the batch size is 20, and the learning rate is 2e-5. We use ADAM [14] as the optimizer and keep the best model based on the

---

[2] All the experiments are executed using a GeForce RTX 3090 24GB GPU.

performance in the development set in each run. For the ADE dataset, 10-fold cross-validation[3] is applied [4,8,18], and 15%[4] of the training set is used as the development set. We use strict evaluation of the IE task [4,29]. An entity is predicted correctly if the boundaries and the type are detected. A relation is correct if the type and the two involved entities are predicted correctly. We conduct a statistical t-test (p-value ≤ 0.05) of the evaluation results to draw conclusions in a more robust manner[5]. The results of the statistical t-test are available in the Appendix section. We highlight that the inductive bias study is based on the intra-model comparison, as we focus on the effect of the aggregation step.

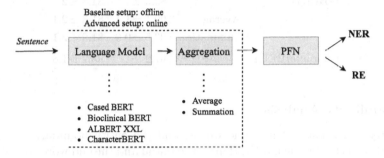

Fig. 1. Model Architecture: The input sentence passes through the language model and then the embeddings are aggregated if needed. Finally, the representations are the input of the PFN module and the final predictions for the NER and RE task are extracted.

4.2   Results - Discussion

For every model, the aggregation is beneficial as it improves the performance in both NER and RE tasks (Table 3). More precisely, the addition of summed aggregation improves the performance by 0.7%, 0.9% (NER task), and 0.3%, 0.8% (RE task) for the cased BERT-based and b-BERT-based models respectively, compared to the aggregation-free models. For the ALBERT-based model the averaged aggregation boosts the performance by 0.7% in both tasks. Coupling this finding with the tokenization analysis (Table 2), the pattern of wordpiece splitting for words of interest (Drugs and AE) acts as inductive bias when aggregation is used. The intra-model comparison reveals the existence of inductive bias since the only difference lies in the addition of the aggregation step. Even if the aggregation layer (simple summation and averaging) is not trainable, the incoming gradient (backpropagation, [25]) from the PFN module appears to be more informative for the IE task.

---

[3] We use the same split as [8].

[4] Random split with the same seed for a fair comparison.

[5] The code and trained models are publicly available in the repository of the paper for reproducibility and to facilitate further research. https://github.com/christos42/ inductive_ bias_IE.

Table 3. End-to-end training - Results

Language Model	Aggregation	NER	RE
cased BERT	–	89.2 ±1.3	80.2 ±2.6
	Average	89.7 ±1.1	80.5 ±2.3
	Summation	89.9 ±1.1	80.5 ±2
ALBERT XXL	–	90.8 ±0.9	83.2 ±2.1
	Average	**91.5 ±0.8**	**83.9 ±1.6**
	Summation	91.2 ±0.8	83 ±1.3
b-BERT	–	89.6 ±1	81.1 ±2.2
	Average	90.1 ±1.1	81.3 ±2.1
	Summation	90.5 ±0.9	81.9 ±2.1
CharacterBERT	–	91.2 ±1	83.2 ±1.8

4.3   Similarity Analysis

An entity can consist of multiple words, and the entity boundaries should be detected correctly by the model. Hence, the initial and the end words of the entity are important. An entity can be split into multiple word pieces. For example, the drug *sodium polystyrene sulfonate* (3 words) is split into *sodium p-oly-sty-rene su-lf-ona-te* (9 word pieces) when the tokenizer of BERT is used. When the aggregation step is not used, the model should detect the initial word (sodium) and the end token (su) of the entity. In the inference step, the correctly detected entity can be reconstructed with detokenization.

To more deeply investigate the inductive bias phenomenon, we conduct a cosine similarity analysis for the different entities. The hypothesis is that the detected inductive bias in the biomedical text can increase the similarity and robustness of the entity representations. We use the trained LM of each run of the inductive bias study, with and without aggregation, and extract the representations of the test set. Then, we separate the words of the entities based on the entity type and the ordering of the words (start/end words). Hence, we have two groups per entity. One contains the start words, and another contains the end words. The *Joint* group consists of both the start and end words. The average similarity of each group is calculated. As we run the experiments using 10-fold cross-validation for the ADE dataset, we average the averaged similarity scores across the different splits. The results discussion is based on the intra-model comparison.

In the ADE dataset (Table 4), generally, the averaged entity similarity is increased when aggregation is used. Hence, the detected inductive bias, which is correlated with the tokenization patterns, results in more similar entity representations. In particular, the summed representations of cased BERT and b-BERT are more or almost equally similar compared to the averaged and the aggregation-free representations for both entity types. Especially, for the *Drug* entity, the similarity increment is up to 10.5%, 3%, and 14.5% for the *Start-word*,

End-word, and *Joint* groups respectively, when aggregation is used. Accordingly, for the *Adverse-Effect* entity, the similarity increase is up to 11.5%, 4%, and 13.5%. For the ALBERT XXL language model, where the tokenization patterns are less profound (Table 2), the similarity slightly increases, when aggregation is used, in most cases. However, the increment is significantly lower than that detected with the representations of cased BERT and b-BERT.

Table 4. Similarity Analysis: Average cosine similarity scores per entity group. The total average scores across the different experimental runs are presented.

Language Model	Aggregation	Drugs			Adverse Effects		
		Start	End	Joint	Start	End	Joint
cased BERT	–	67.43	82.65	56.84	51.43	78.24	40.44
	Average	68.3	**85.73**	61.15	56.78	**82.5**	49.75
	Summation	**78.02**	84.5	**71.11**	**61.54**	81.18	**50.89**
b-BERT	–	67.76	84.51	57.06	53.86	79.92	41
	Average	68.91	**86.01**	63.3	60.84	**83.07**	53.85
	Summation	**78.12**	85.52	**70.87**	**65.23**	81.55	**54.63**
ALBERT XXL	–	65.41	**82.06**	57.23	**55.46**	77.79	44.62
	Average	65.89	81.03	57.88	55.18	**78.46**	**46.11**
	Summation	**67.53**	77.06	**59.93**	53.44	73.42	43.68

5 Comparative Study

The existence of inductive bias that is related to the initial tokenization of the text motivates the second research question (RQ2) of the paper. When tokenization patterns are present and the likelihood of splitting a word of interest (part of an entity) into multiple word pieces is higher, the addition of an aggregation step increases the performance and the robustness of the entity representations. Since the improved performance is correlated with this kind of inductive bias, a comparison with character-based models that do not include a tokenization step is important.

5.1 Baseline Setup: Frozen Embeddings

As we want to explore how feasible the transition to tokenizer-free models is, we categorize the LMs into two categories based on the way they handle the input text: subword-based and character-based models. In the comparative study, we use bioclinical BERT for the ADE dataset[6] to represent the subword-based set

---

[6] We use the Transformers library [34].

of models and we select CharacterBERT [9] as character-based representative. CharacterBERT processes the initial text at the character level and removes the tokenization step by incorporating the character-CNN module [22] to learn representations at the word level. Since we intend to evaluate the significance of tokenization, we include CharacterBERT and BERT models in the study, as their main architecture is identical and their difference lies in the tokenization step.

In the baseline setup, we want to directly evaluate the quality of the "off-the-shelf" representations of different LMs when solving the IE task. As we directly evaluate the pretrained representations, it is important to mention the corpus that was used for pretraining the different LMs. Bioclinical BERT was initialized with BioBERT (pretrained on PubMed abstracts and PMC OA[7] [17] parameters and pretrained on MIMIC III notes [13]. The medical version of CharacterBERT was retrained on MIMIC III notes and PMC OA biomedical article abstracts. Hence, the medical version of CharacterBERT and b-BERT were pretrained with almost identical data and a comparison between these groups of LMs is safe.

First, we extract the word representations of each LM of the study offline. We aggregate the subword-level embeddings (b-BERT) and construct the word-level embeddings by calculating the averaged and summed representations. CharacterBERT extracts word-level representations by design. The overall experimental setup (hyperparameter) is the same as the inductive bias study setting. The only difference is that the LM is frozen (Fig. 1).

Table 5. Baseline Setup - Results

Language Model	Aggregation	NER	RE
b-BERT	Average	85.6 ± 0.7	75.7 ± 1.7
	Summation	85.7 ± 0.7	75.1 ± 1.7
CharacterBERT	–	**87.5 ± 0.8**	**77.9 ± 1.5**

The model that leverages the representations of medical CharacterBERT performs significantly better, as it outperforms the model that uses the b-BERT representations by around 2% in both RE and NER tasks (Table 5). This finding illustrates that medical CharacterBERT is more capable of exploring and learning the special linguistic characteristics of biomedical text, as it produces more meaningful representations than b-BERT. For the subword-based LM, the two aggregation strategies result in similar performance.

5.2 Advanced Setup: End-to-End Training

In the advanced setup, we conduct experiments with end-to-end training to also fine-tune the LMs and make comparisons on the final performance. To

---

[7] PubMed   Central   Open   Access: https://www.ncbi.nlm.nih.gov/pmc/tools/openftlist/).

this end, we extend the setup of the inductive bias study and incorporate the character-based model of the comparative study. The CharacterBERT-based model achieves very competitive results and outperforms the b-BERT-based models in the advanced setup. The performance improvement is 0.7% (NER task) and 1.3% (RE task) (Table 3). This is an additional indication that Character-BERT is more capable of detecting special linguistic characteristics of medical-related text, despite the suggestion that the subword-based LMs can independently learn the essential character compositions [12].

5.3   Hyphenation Analysis

The comparative study reveals that the model that leverages CharacterBERT is very competitive in the biomedical text. Following this main observation, we conduct a hyphenation analysis to explore possible special linguistic characteristics in the biomedical domain. The hypothesis is that the CharacterBERT-based model performs very well because there is domain-specific linguistic morphology in the biomedical text. We find the unique words for each entity type and then we extract all subwords with a length of 4 characters and calculate the frequency of each subword per entity type.

Figures 2 and 3 present the 25 most frequent subwords, excluding those that are in the 50 most frequent subwords of the out-of-entity words[8], for the *Drug* and *Adverse-Effect* entities respectively. A special morphology is noticeable for both entity types. Specifically, the words that are part of the *Drug* and the *Adverse-Effect* entity have 11 (e.g. *amin, minc, midc,* etc.) and 19 (*itis, osis, emia,* etc.) subwords accordingly, with frequencies higher than 20. These findings confirm the initial hypothesis of the hyphenation analysis.

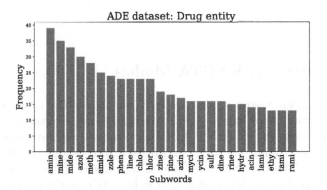

Fig. 2. Drug entity: 25 most frequent subwords with a length of 4 characters

---

[8] The unique words that are not a part of any entity type of the dataset.

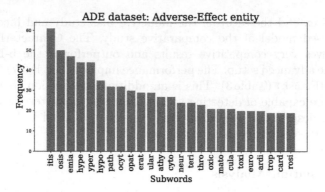

Fig. 3. Adverse-Effect entity: 25 most frequent subwords with a length of 4 characters

Table 6 presents the number of entity subwords with frequencies equal to or higher than a set of thresholds. Noticeable patterns can be detected in the biomedical domain where all of the 25 most frequent subwords for both entities (*Drug* and *Adverse-Effect*) have a higher than 10 frequency.

Table 6. Number of entity subwords with frequency higher than a specific threshold, subword length: 4 characters

Entity type	Threshold			
	≥ 40	≥ 30	≥ 20	≥ 10
Drug	0	3	11	25
Adverse-Effect	5	8	19	25

6   Comparison with SOTA Models

For comparison, we choose models that are trained on the same dataset without extra external data. In the ADE dataset, we outperform the SOTA models. More precisely, the ALBERT XLL-based model with average aggregation improves the performance by 0.7% and 0.2% in the RE and NER task respectively (Table 7). The inductive bias that is introduced by the tokenization patterns and is exploited with the aggregation layer boosts the performance.

Table 7. Comparative Results - SOTA

Dataset	Model	NER	RE
ADE	Eberts and Ulges (2020) [8]	89.3	79.2
	Theodoropoulos et al. (2021) [31]	88.3	80.0
	Wang and Lu (2020) [33]	89.7	80.1
	Zhao et al. [39]	89.4	81.1
	Yan et al. [37]	91.3	83.2
	ALBERT XXL (Avg. Aggr.), PFN	**91.5**	**83.9**

7 Conclusion

This paper identifies the existence of inductive bias in the IE task that is correlated with tokenization patterns, where the words of interest are more likely to be split into subwords. We highlight the introduction of inductive bias in the biomedical domain, supported by a similarity analysis based on entity representations. Additionally, we conduct a comparative study, including subword-based and character-based models, pointing out that the transition to token-free IE models is achievable. In future work, we intend to explore the effect of tokenization in other sequence tagging problems.

Limitations

A limitation of the paper is that the dataset is relatively small. Nevertheless, this is a common problem in the IE field, and in our case, it is beneficial in the sense that we can experiment quickly and run multiple experiments to draw conclusions. If the dataset is large, the computational power needed for the study will increase by a considerable factor. Potentially, additional language models can be incorporated into the comparative study [6,36] but retraining with identical data is needed to alleviate the influence of the different pretraining corpora. Isolating and exploring the effect of tokenization in a comparative inter-model setup is challenging because other factors, such as the different architecture of the language models, can affect the performance. We highlight that, for this reason, we incorporate BERT and CharacterBERT in the comparative study as these models have the same architecture and their only difference lies in the tokenization step.

References

1. Ács, J., Kádár, Á., Kornai, A.: Subword pooling makes a difference. In: Proceedings of the 16th Conference of the European Chapter of the Association for Computational Linguistics: Main Volume, pp. 2284–2295. Association for Computational Linguistics, Online (2021). https://doi.org/10.18653/v1/2021.eacl-main.194, https://aclanthology.org/2021.eacl-main.194

2. Alsentzer, E., et al.: Publicly available clinical BERT embeddings. In: Proceedings of the 2nd Clinical Natural Language Processing Workshop, pp. 72–78. Association for Computational Linguistics, Minneapolis (2019). https://doi.org/10.18653/v1/W19-1909, https://aclanthology.org/W19-1909

3. Antoun, W., Baly, F., Hajj, H.: AraBERT: transformer-based model for Arabic language understanding. In: Proceedings of the 4th Workshop on Open-Source Arabic Corpora and Processing Tools, with a Shared Task on Offensive Language Detection, pp. 9–15. European Language Resource Association, Marseille (2020). https://aclanthology.org/2020.osact-1.2

4. Bekoulis, G., Deleu, J., Demeester, T., Develder, C.: Joint entity recognition and relation extraction as a multi-head selection problem. Expert Syst. Appl. **114**, 34–45 (2018). https://doi.org/10.1016/j.eswa.2018.07.032

5. Clark, J.H., Garrette, D., Turc, I., Wieting, J.: CANINE: pre-training an efficient tokenization-free encoder for language representation. arXiv preprint arXiv:2103.06874 (2021)

6. Clark, J.H., Garrette, D., Turc, I., Wieting, J.: CANINE: pre-training an efficient tokenization-free encoder for language representation. Trans. Assoc. Comput. Linguist. **10**, 73–91 (2022). https://aclanthology.org/2022.tacl-1.5

7. Devlin, J., Chang, M.W., Lee, K., Toutanova, K.: BERT: pre-training of deep bidirectional transformers for language understanding. In: Proceedings of the 2019 Conference of the North American Chapter of the Association for Computational Linguistics: Human Language Technologies, Volume 1 (Long and Short Papers), pp. 4171–4186. Association for Computational Linguistics, Minneapolis (2019). https://doi.org/10.18653/v1/N19-1423, https://aclanthology.org/N19-1423

8. Eberts, M., Ulges, A.: Span-based joint entity and relation extraction with transformer pre-training. In: ECAI 2020, pp. 2006–2013. IOS Press (2020). https://doi.org/10.3233/FAIA200321

9. El Boukkouri, H., Ferret, O., Lavergne, T., Noji, H., Zweigenbaum, P., Tsujii, J.: CharacterBERT: reconciling ELMo and BERT for word-level open-vocabulary representations from characters. In: Proceedings of the 28th International Conference on Computational Linguistics, pp. 6903–6915. International Committee on Computational Linguistics, Barcelona (2020). https://doi.org/10.18653/v1/2020.coling-main.609, https://aclanthology.org/2020.coling-main.609

10. Florian, R., Pitrelli, J., Roukos, S., Zitouni, I.: Improving mention detection robustness to noisy input. In: Proceedings of the 2010 Conference on Empirical Methods in Natural Language Processing, pp. 335–345. Association for Computational Linguistics, Cambridge (2010). https://aclanthology.org/D10-1033

11. Gurulingappa, H., Rajput, A.M., Roberts, A., Fluck, J., Hofmann-Apitius, M., Toldo, L.: Development of a benchmark corpus to support the automatic extraction of drug-related adverse effects from medical case reports. J. Biomed. Inform. **45**(5), 885–892 (2012). https://doi.org/10.1016/j.jbi.2012.04.008

12. Itzhak, I., Levy, O.: Models in a spelling bee: language models implicitly learn the character composition of tokens. arXiv preprint arXiv:2108.11193 (2021)

13. Johnson, A.E., et al.: MIMIC-III, a freely accessible critical care database. Sci. Data **3**(1), 1–9 (2016). https://doi.org/10.1038/sdata.2016.35

14. Kingma, D.P., Ba, J.: Adam: a method for stochastic optimization. arXiv preprint arXiv:1412.6980 (2014)

15. Kudo, T., Richardson, J.: Sentencepiece: a simple and language independent subword tokenizer and detokenizer for neural text processing. In: Proceedings of the 2018 Conference on Empirical Methods in Natural Language Processing:

System Demonstrations, pp. 66–71. Association for Computational Linguistics, Brussels (2018). https://doi.org/10.18653/v1/D18-2012, https://aclanthology.org/D18-2012

16. Lan, Z., Chen, M., Goodman, S., Gimpel, K., Sharma, P., Soricut, R.: ALBERT: a lite BERT for self-supervised learning of language representations. arXiv preprint arXiv:1909.11942 (2019)

17. Lee, J., et al.: BioBERT: a pre-trained biomedical language representation model for biomedical text mining. Bioinform. (Oxford Engl.) **36**(4), 1234–1240 (2020). https://doi.org/10.1093/bioinformatics/btz682

18. Li, F., Zhang, M., Fu, G., Ji, D.: A neural joint model for entity and relation extraction from biomedical text. BMC Bioinform. **18**(1), 1–11 (2017). https://doi.org/10.1186/s12859-017-1609-9

19. Liu, Y., et al.: RoBERTa: a robustly optimized BERT pretraining approach. arXiv preprint arXiv:1907.11692 (2019)

20. Mitchell, T.M.: The need for biases in learning generalizations. Department of Computer Science, Laboratory for Computer Science Research, Rutgers Univ. (1980)

21. Nadeau, D., Sekine, S.: A survey of named entity recognition and classification. Lingvisticae Invest. **30**(1), 3–26 (2007). https://doi.org/10.1075/li.30.1.03nad

22. Peters, M.E., et al.: Deep contextualized word representations. In: Proceedings of the 2018 Conference of the North American Chapter of the Association for Computational Linguistics: Human Language Technologies, Volume 1 (Long Papers), pp. 2227–2237. Association for Computational Linguistics, New Orleans (2018). https://doi.org/10.18653/v1/N18-1202, https://aclanthology.org/N18-1202

23. Plank, B., Moschitti, A.: Embedding semantic similarity in tree kernels for domain adaptation of relation extraction. In: Proceedings of the 51st Annual Meeting of the Association for Computational Linguistics (Volume 1: Long Papers), pp. 1498–1507. Association for Computational Linguistics, Sofia (2013). https://aclanthology.org/P13-1147

24. Radford, A., et al.: Language models are unsupervised multitask learners. OpenAI Blog **1**(8), 9 (2019)

25. Rumelhart, D.E., Hinton, G.E., Williams, R.J.: Learning representations by back-propagating errors. Nature **323**(6088), 533–536 (1986). https://doi.org/10.1038/323533a0

26. Sasaki, S., Sun, S., Schamoni, S., Duh, K., Inui, K.: Cross-lingual learning-to-rank with shared representations. In: Proceedings of the 2018 Conference of the North American Chapter of the Association for Computational Linguistics: Human Language Technologies, Volume 2 (Short Papers), pp. 458–463. Association for Computational Linguistics, New Orleans (2018). https://doi.org/10.18653/v1/N18-2073, https://aclanthology.org/N18-2073

27. Sennrich, R., Haddow, B., Birch, A.: Neural machine translation of rare words with subword units. In: Proceedings of the 54th Annual Meeting of the Association for Computational Linguistics (Volume 1: Long Papers), pp. 1715–1725. Association for Computational Linguistics, Berlin (2016). https://doi.org/10.18653/v1/P16-1162, https://aclanthology.org/P16-1162

28. Sun, A., Grishman, R., Sekine, S.: Semi-supervised relation extraction with large-scale word clustering. In: Proceedings of the 49th Annual Meeting of the Association for Computational Linguistics: Human Language Technologies, pp. 521–529. Association for Computational Linguistics, Portland (2011). https://aclanthology.org/P11-1053

29. Taillé, B., Guigue, V., Scoutheeten, G., Gallinari, P.: Let's stop error propagation in the end-to-end relation extraction literature! In: Proceedings of the 2020 Conference on Empirical Methods in Natural Language Processing (EMNLP 2020), pp. 3689–3701. Association for Computational Linguistics, Online (2020). https://www.aclweb.org/anthology/2020.emnlp-main.301.pdf
30. Tay, Y., et al.: CharFormer: fast character transformers via gradient-based subword tokenization. arXiv preprint arXiv:2106.12672 (2021)
31. Theodoropoulos, C., Henderson, J., Coman, A.C., Moens, M.F.: Imposing relation structure in language-model embeddings using contrastive learning. In: Proceedings of the 25th Conference on Computational Natural Language Learning, pp. 337–348. Association for Computational Linguistics, Online (2021). https://doi.org/10.18653/v1/2021.conll-1.27, https://aclanthology.org/2021.conll-1.27
32. Tiedemann, J., Thottingal, S., et al.: OPUS-MT-building open translation services for the world. In: Proceedings of the 22nd Annual Conference of the European Association for Machine Translation. European Association for Machine Translation (2020). https://aclanthology.org/2020.eamt-1.61
33. Wang, J., Lu, W.: Two are better than one: joint entity and relation extraction with table-sequence encoders. In: Proceedings of the 2020 Conference on Empirical Methods in Natural Language Processing (EMNLP), pp. 1706–1721. Association for Computational Linguistics, Online (2020). https://doi.org/10.18653/v1/2020.emnlp-main.133, https://aclanthology.org/2020.emnlp-main.133
34. Wolf, T., et al.: Transformers: state-of-the-art natural language processing. In: Proceedings of the 2020 Conference on Empirical Methods in Natural Language Processing: System Demonstrations, pp. 38–45. Association for Computational Linguistics, Online (2020). https://doi.org/10.18653/v1/2020.emnlp-demos.6, https://aclanthology.org/2020.emnlp-demos.6
35. Wu, Y., et al.: Google's neural machine translation system: bridging the gap between human and machine translation. arXiv preprint arXiv:1609.08144 (2016)
36. Xue, L., et al.: ByT5: towards a token-free future with pre-trained byte-to-byte models. Trans. Assoc. Comput. Linguist. 10, 291–306 (2022). https://aclanthology.org/2022.tacl-1.17
37. Yan, Z., Zhang, C., Fu, J., Zhang, Q., Wei, Z.: A partition filter network for joint entity and relation extraction. In: Proceedings of the 2021 Conference on Empirical Methods in Natural Language Processing, pp. 185–197. Association for Computational Linguistics, Online and Punta Cana (2021). https://doi.org/10.18653/v1/2021.emnlp-main.17, https://aclanthology.org/2021.emnlp-main.17
38. Zhang, H., Tan, L.: Textual representations for crosslingual information retrieval. In: Proceedings of The 4th Workshop on e-Commerce and NLP, pp. 116–122 (2021). https://aclanthology.org/2021.ecnlp-1.14.pdf
39. Zhao, S., Hu, M., Cai, Z., Liu, F.: Modeling dense cross-modal interactions for joint entity-relation extraction. In: Bessiere, C. (ed.) Proceedings of the Twenty-Ninth International Joint Conference on Artificial Intelligence, IJCAI-20, pp. 4032–4038. International Joint Conferences on Artificial Intelligence Organization, Online (2020). https://doi.org/10.24963/ijcai.2020/558

Early Parkinson's Disease Detection from EEG Traces Using Machine Learning Techniques

Lerina Aversano[1](✉)(iD), Mario Luca Bernardi[1](iD), Marta Cimitile[2](iD),
Martina Iammarino[1](iD), Debora Montano[3](iD), and Chiara Verdone[1](iD)

[1] Department of Engineering, University of Sannio, Benevento, Italy
aversano@unisannio.it
[2] UnitelmaSapienza University, Rome, Italy
[3] Universitas Mercatorum, Rome, Italy

Abstract. Parkinson's disease (PD) affects over 10 million people worldwide. Tremors, stiffness, voice changes, delayed movement, and difficulty walking are typical symptoms of the condition. In the early stage of the disease, these symptoms are difficult to identify and therefore it becomes increasingly important and necessary to be able to predict Parkinson's and diagnose it as soon as possible. In particular, more studies have focused on the differences found in the electroencephalogram (EEG) of patients with PD. The EEG is used to measure the electrical activity of the brain. The detection of unusual signals is indicative of a pathological condition such as Parkinson's. This work proposes a new way of researching the diagnosis and surveillance of PD. The results are satisfactory and better when compared with those of other studies conducted on the same data. This indicates that the proposed method can effectively improve early Parkinson's diagnosis by reducing the time and effort required.

Keywords: Parkinson's Disease · EEG traces · Diagnosis · Health informatics · Machine Learning

1 Introduction

Parkinson's disease is a neurodegenerative disease affecting the central nervous system, characterized by a slow and progressive evolution and mainly related to the degeneration of nerve cells located in a deep area of the brain, which produce dopamine, a neurotransmitter responsible for the activation of circuits that control movements and balance. It is considered a'Movement Disorder' as it is characterized by the appearance of motor symptoms such as bradykinesia, rigidity, and tremor, associated with postural instability. In addition to these typical common symptoms, the condition could also cause specific symptoms in each individual. In any case, the first symptoms of the disease are evident when 60%–80% of these dopamine-producing cells are damaged. The diagnosis of the disease is not easy and is mainly clinical because it is based on the presence of the typical symptoms (confused language, laboured writing, tremor) detectable during a thorough neurological examination. Therefore, early identification of the disease can lead to better therapy and better results in treating the condition, improving patients' quality of life.

In recent years, the combination of Artificial Intelligence and Machine Learning (ML) techniques has proved to be of great help in predicting the diagnosis of multiple pathologies such as heart disease, thyroids, cancer, and not least PD, based both on motor problems and on particular biological conditions [3,6]. The clinical outline is assessed using international rating scales such as the Unified Parkinson's Disease Rating Scale (UPDRS) [12], which analyzes and assigns a score from 0 to 4 to mental state, physical capacity, daily activities, life, and potential motor complications. The sum of the values obtained indicates the current state of the disease. Early-stage disease is often one-sided, maintaining a side prevalence with disease progression, so any asymmetry in symptoms needs to be carefully examined.

Diagnostic tests, such as Electroencephalograms, particularly in the early stages of the disease, can help the doctor make the diagnosis. Therefore, this study focuses on EEG trace analysis to distinguish PD patients from healthy patients. Specifically, the context of the analysis exploits a data-set of traces in which the weak electrical charges generated by the activation of neurons are detected by the electrodes placed on the skull in different strategic positions. These electrical pulses at the micro-volt level are amplified and then recorded by the appropriate equipment.

The main contributions of our work are:

- Our approach allows us to use a few synthetic indices, easy and fast to calculate, able to take into account the entire history of the EEG signal rather than using a long series of measurements ((1;4) vs (60000;140000)).
- Our experiments show that cross-validation is preferable to the hold-out method even in the presence of a small sample.
- Our research highlights the need to find the best hyper-parameters for the algorithms because they return better results. To this end, the use of a function able to find the best set of parameters is the best way because it is extremely easy to use and takes little time to find the best set of parameters.

The document is structured as follows: Sect. 2 offers an overview of the state of the art, while Sect. 3 introduces the ML algorithms chosen for the analysis and briefly describes statistical indices used to summarize the EEG signals. Section 4 describes the data, and the approach employed, while Sect. 5 highlights all the experimental results. Finally, the conclusions and new research possibilities suggested by the approach are illustrated in Sects. 6.

2   Related Work

Several studies have been conducted on the use of ML for the diagnosis of Parkinson's, based on the conditions of motor and non-motor problems but also on clinical and biological conditions [3, 5, 7, 8]. PD affects nearly 3% of people over the age of 65 and age, gender and ethnicity are some intrinsic characteristics that influence the incidence of the disease. It has emerged that before age 50, PD is rare, but between the sixth and ninth decade of life, the frequency increases by five to ten times [15, 16]. Several instrumental procedures can be used to diagnose PD, including high-field nuclear magnetic resonance, SPECT DAT-scan, brain-PET, and cardiac scintigraphy. Among these, EEG is one of the most used tests to support clinical diagnosis. In particular, this test can be used to accurately and cost-effectively discover and analyze bio-markers for the severity of non-motor symptoms. Milan Koch et al. use the EEG time series with deep brain stimulation of 40 candidates [13]. EEG has been performed through the use of 21 electrodes which produced 21 different time series. Data have been recorded with a sampling rate of 500 Hz, a 16-bit analogue-to-digital converter, and a band filter of 0.16–70.0 Hz. During the recording, patients were lying down and staring closed in a state of wakefulness. Five epochs of 8, 192 seconds in total have been selected by the EEG by visual inspection, to ensure that all time series were free of noises caused by movements such as involuntary muscle contractions, blinking, and small movements that affect the EEG by altering it in some places. After that, the TsFresh algorithm has been used with its default settings for the feature extraction phase, extracting a total of 16674 features. In addition to the characteristics extracted from the TsFresh algorithm, the spectral characteristics of the Fast Fourier Transformation (FFT) from the time series have also been taken into consideration For the selection of the characteristics, the Boruta algorithm has been used which builds a model of random forests on real characteristics and the so-called shadow functions that are created by randomly mixing the values of each real characteristic. A real feature is considered for selection if its importance is greater than the maximum importance of all shadow features. Finally, the selected features have been used to train an optimized Random Forest (RF) classifier using the Bayesian Global Efficient Parallel-to-Integer Optimization (MIP-EGO) algorithm. The best performance has been obtained using a space of initial characteristics with self-extracting characteristics and 10 clinical characteristics (Accuracy of 84%), thus concluding also on the basis of the other tests that the addition of unselected clinical characteristics reduces the accuracy of the classifier. M. Isabel Venegas et al. classify PD and monitors patients by analyzing EEG spectra and demonstrate that EEG spectra during visual stimulation improve the accuracy of the classification [17]. The analysis of the EEG revealed substantial differences in the spectral power of the EEG between healthy subjects and patients with PD, more precisely in the theta, alpha, and beta frequencies of the EEG recorded by the electrodes in the central parietal regions. As a first step, they use machine learning to model and identify the most relevant factors from EEG spectra above the visual stimulation range. Using EEG, visually evoked responses during steady state (ssVEP) are measured in a visual suppression paradigm setting, simultaneously recording the control gain and temporal aspects of the optical response. Three learning models were then tested: logistic regression, decision tree, and extra tree. To evaluate the performance of the various classifications, they choose the AUC metric. Finally, the extra tree algorithm shows the best performance. For the treatment of symptoms of both post-encephalitic and symptomatic Parkinsonism, the drug Levodopa is used. It is a precursor to the neurotransmitter dopamine which works by crossing the blood-brain barrier to enter dopaminergic neurons, where it is rapidly converted into dopamine. When EEG is performed during the period of drug administration, it has been shown to reduce that cortical oscillatory synchronization in patients with PD, masking the differences between PD and healthy patients [14].

In our study, we have decided not to take into account the possible influences of the drug Levodopa on the results of patient classification. Specifically, the classification has been performed by combining all EEG of patients with PD to test the classifiers independently of dopaminergic drugs. This aspect is fundamental for the generalizability of the results obtained from the study.

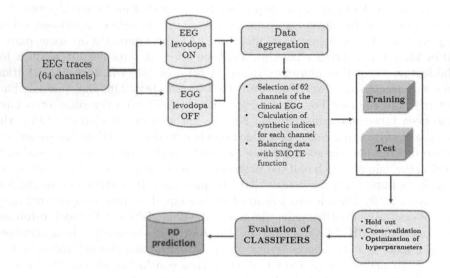

Fig. 1. Outline of the followed approach

3   Background

ML refers to many processes capable of creating systems that learn or improve performance over time based on data use. The characteristics of the data have a significant impact on the performance of ML algorithms because different representations can more or less trap and hide the various explanatory elements of the variation that underlie the data. In recent years, ML algorithms have proved to be particularly effective in the early prediction of multiple pathologies [1, 2, 4]. In particular, in this study, we have used several iterative algorithms based on self-learning (Random Forest and Extra trees), able to progressively adapt the composition of the training set in order to focus attention on incorrectly classified records (Boosting Methods). In particular, we have considered the following algorithms: *Decision Trees* (DT), *Random Forests* (RF) and *Extra Trees* (ET),*eXtreme Gradient Boosting Classifier* (XGBC), *Ada Boost* (AB), *Gradient Boosting* (GB) and *CatBoost* (CB). The high explainability of the approaches based on trees, a vital trait for clinical data and analysis, led to the selection of these specific ML algorithms.

3.1   Statistical Synthetic Index

A synthetic index expresses the synthesis of observations relating to a phenomenon's characteristics or the relationship between several phenomena. These indices have statistical origins and each index takes on a specific denomination about what it represents; in fact, they are divided into position and variability indices. The *position indices* indicate the order of magnitude of the data in our possession, while the *variability indices* help understand the "trend" of the data, i.e. they measure the "difference" help understand a representative centre, giving information about the attitude of a phenomenon to take more or less different measures. In particular, in this work, we use:

– **MEAN:** or arithmetic average, is a single numerical value that succinctly describes a set of data. It is the best-known position index and is calculated by adding all the available values x_i and dividing the result by the total number of data:

$$m = 1/n \sum_{i=1}^{n} x_i. \tag{1}$$

– **VARIANCE:** is the mean of the square of the deviations from the mean. It is always major of 0 and grows as the differences in value between the data increase:

$$var = \frac{\sum_{i=1}^{n}(x_i - \bar{x})^2}{n}. \tag{2}$$

In addition to these two indices, we also calculate the **MINIMUM** and **MAXIMUM** i.e. the minimum and maximum value of the distribution of the signal.

4   Approach

The presented method proposes a binary classification of patients, identifying those without PD from those with PD. The model was trained using synthetic indices of the patients' EEGs described in Subsect. 3.1.

The details of the approach are shown in Fig. 1 where the following steps are illustrated: the ***preliminary study of the data*** to read the raw data and verify the presence of possible inconsistencies; the ***methodology*** used to select EEG channels, calculate synthetic indexes and balance data; the ***machine learning*** phase to classify the data processed using the algorithms illustrated in Sect. 3; and the *evaluation* of all results to highlight the best classifiers for the PD.

In particular, this Section is structured as follows: in Subsect. 4.2 the classification methodology and the optimization process of the hyper-parameters and all the metrics used for the evaluation of classifiers are reported, and Subsect. 4.1 deals with data processing and description.

4.1 Data Description

This research has used the open-source data-set[1] that has been made accessible in the University of Iowa archive. The data collection used for the EEG recording includes 27 PD patients and 27 control patients from the University of New Mexico. Specifically, control participants were demographically matched for age and sex to PD patients. In addition, for the 27 patients with PD, the EEG was performed once during regular Levodopa administration, and a second EEG recording was instead performed after stopping the drug for at least 12 hours to prevent the drug. influence of dopaminergic drugs on the EEG traces.

EEG sessions were recorded with both eyes open and closed, as per standard clinical EEG protocol. A 64-channel Brain-Vision system was used to record EEG from Ag/AgCl electrodes tuned to 0.1-100Hz at a sampling rate of 500 Hz, so we have 64 different time series for each patient. EEG recordings were made during the patients' resting phase and tracking disturbances such as blinks were identified and removed using independent component analysis.

The raw data is then composed of 1728 different EEG traces for each patient group: 1728 control patients, 1728 traces for PD patients under the influence of the drug Levodopa, and 1728 traces for PD patients after stopping Levodopa for 12 hours, for a total of 5184 different tracks.

Since routine clinical EEG requires 62 channels, only the most commonly used in clinical EEG were selected from the raw data, also to ensure comparability of the study. After selecting the channel, all traces were summarized using 4 different synthetic indices: the arithmetic means, variance, minimum and maximum.

Therefore, our final data-set is composed of 250 features divided as follows: 62 features take into account the average over a single channel, 62 features report the variance of the channel, 62 features declare the minimum value of the spectral density of the channel, and 62 features give information on the maximum value of the spectral density of the channel. Finally, the last two features are the 'Levodopa' feature which takes into account drug administration in patients with PD (0 if the administration is interrupted for 12 h, 1 if the drug is administered), and the target variable which is a dichotomous variable which concerns the patient's status, 0 for healthy people and 1 for PD patients.

---

[1] https://narayanan.lab.uiowa.edu.

4.2   Experiment Setting

Table 1. Considered optimization hyper-parameters and relative ranges.

APPROACH	HYPERPARAMETERS	DESCRIPTION	VALUES
TREE-based	max depth	The maximum depth of the tree	[1, 5, 10, 15, 20, 25, 30, 35]
	random state	It controls the randomness of the estimator	[1, 0]
	max features	It is the number of characteristics to consider to obtain the best subdivision	[1, 2, 5]
	criterion	It is the function to measure the quality of a split	['gini', 'entropy']
BOOSTING	number of estimators	The number of boosting stages to perform	[10, 50, 100, 500]
	learning rate	The weight applied to each classifier at each boosting iteration	[0.0001, 0.001, 0.01, 0.1, 0.5, 1.0]
	random state	Controls the random permutation of the features at each split	[1, 0]

The model has been evaluated with two different methods: Hold-out and Cross-Validation. For the Hold-Out method, the 70/30 split ratio has been used, so the model has first been trained on the training set (70% of the data) and subsequently tested on the test set (30% of the data). On the other hand, the cross-validation method has been used considering 10 folds. Finally, all the results obtained have been used to provide both the evaluation of the performance of each classifier and to compare the results of the two methods.

The features model is composed of 250 characteristics: 248 of them report the values of the calculated indices, a feature representing the possible administration of Levodopa, and finally, the variable to be predicted.

Table 2. Results of classification with all synthetic indices

CLASSIFIER	BASELINE ALGORITHM								BEST hyper-parameters							
	Hold Out				10k fold Cross Validation				Hold Out				10k fold Cross Validation			
	A	P	R	F	A	P	R	F	A	P	R	F	A	P	R	F
DT	0,750	0,775	0,750	0,744	0,724	0,806	0,723	0,716	0,600	0,604	0,600	0,596	0,749	0,771	0,742	0,740
RF	0,750	0,775	0,750	0,755	**0,790**	**0,859**	**0,755**	**0,753**	0,750	0,775	0,750	0,744	0,760	0,778	0,745	0,722
ET	0,700	0,708	0,700	0,697	0,771	0,833	0,795	0,732	0,550	0,567	0,550	0,520	0,753	0,784	0,740	0,731
XGBC	**0,800**	**0,800**	**0,800**	**0,800**	0,768	0,836	0,755	0,743	**0,850**	**0,854**	**0,850**	**0,849**	0,743	0,713	0,727	0,696
AB	0,650	0,652	0,650	0,649	0,758	0,778	0,742	0,719	0,750	0,753	0,750	0,749	**0,776**	**0,850**	**0,762**	**0,744**
GB	**0,800**	**0,813**	**0,800**	**0,798**	0,713	0,804	0,718	0,710	0,800	0,800	0,800	0,800	0,714	0,766	0,700	0,688
CB	0,700	0,708	0,700	0,697	0,760	0,787	0,743	0,715	0,750	0,753	0,750	0,749	0,713	0,776	0,700	0,685

CLASSIFICATION ON ALL SYNTHETIC INDICES

Table 3. Results of classification with mean index

CLASSIFIER	CLASSIFICATION ON MEAN INDEX															
	BASELINE ALGORITHM								BEST hyper-parameters							
	Hold Out				10k fold Cross Validation				Hold Out				10k fold Cross Validation			
	A	P	R	F	A	P	R	F	A	P	R	F	A	P	R	F
DT	0,550	0,555	0,550	0,540	0,665	0,771	0,695	0,648	0,600	0,642	0,600	0,596	0,650	0,650	0,648	0,640
RF	0,700	0,700	0,700	0,700	**0,825**	**0,828**	**0,798**	**0,754**	0,700	0,708	0,700	0,697	0,789	0,818	0,780	0,778
ET	**0,750**	**0,753**	**0,750**	**0,749**	0,815	0,864	0,755	0,781	0,700	0,738	0,700	0,688	**0,835**	**0,864**	**0,827**	**0,826**
XGBC	**0,750**	**0,753**	**0,750**	**0,749**	0,794	0,845	0,783	0,769	**0,750**	**0,753**	**0,750**	**0,749**	0,720	0,808	0,703	0,672
AB	**0,750**	**0,753**	**0,750**	**0,749**	0,776	0,841	0,765	0,751	0,700	0,708	0,700	0,697	0,737	0,768	0,722	0,693
GB	0,700	0,708	0,700	0,697	0,776	0,824	0,755	0,753	0,700	0,708	0,700	0,697	0,750	0,808	0,738	0,726
CB	0,700	0,700	0,700	0,700	0,794	0,876	0,780	0,758	0,700	0,700	0,700	0,700	0,708	0,705	0,697	0,657

Table 4. Results of classification with variance index

CLASSIFIER	CLASSIFICATION ON VARIANCE INDEX															
	BASELINE ALGORITHM								BEST hyper-parameters							
	Hold Out				10k fold Cross Validation				Hold Out				10k fold Cross Validation			
	A	P	R	F	A	P	R	F	A	P	R	F	A	P	R	F
DT	**0,900**	**0,900**	**0,900**	**0,900**	0,720	0,781	0,712	0,780	0,650	0,652	0,650	0,649	0,705	0,740	0,692	0,678
RF	0,800	0,813	0,800	0,798	0,741	0,773	0,777	0,732	0,650	0,700	0,650	0,627	0,724	0,714	0,710	0,684
ET	0,550	0,598	0,550	0,487	0,756	0,752	0,690	0,673	0,500	0,500	0,500	0,451	0,692	0,684	0,678	0,638
XGBC	0,600	0,619	0,600	0,583	0,722	0,756	0,710	0,688	0,800	0,813	0,800	0,798	0,747	0,716	0,737	0,704
AB	0,700	0,700	0,700	0,700	0,747	0,824	0,738	0,714	0,750	0,753	0,750	0,749	**0,785**	**0,865**	**0,770**	**0,753**
GB	**0,850**	**0,885**	**0,850**	**0,847**	**0,786**	**0,788**	**0,762**	**0,721**	0,850	0,854	0,850	0,849	0,720	0,734	0,710	0,685
CB	**0,850**	**0,854**	**0,850**	**0,850**	0,755	0,708	0,742	0,688	0,700	0,708	0,700	0,697	0,759	0,786	0,745	0,715

Table 5. Results of classification with minimum and maximum indices

CLASSIFIER	CLASSIFICATION ON MINIMUM AND MAXIMUM INDICES															
	BASELINE ALGORITHM								BEST hyper-parameters							
	Hold Out				10k fold Cross Validation				Hold Out				10k fold Cross Validation			
	A	P	R	F	A	P	R	F	A	P	R	F	A	P	R	F
DT	0,600	0,619	0,600	0,583	0,775	0,782	0,773	0,737	0,700	0,700	0,700	0,700	0,718	0,767	0,708	0,694
RF	0,750	0,753	0,750	0,749	0,806	0,831	0,793	0,795	0,750	0,753	0,750	0,749	0,787	0,818	0,780	0,779
ET	**0,800**	**0,813**	**0,800**	**0,798**	0,795	0,846	0,835	0,782	**0,800**	**0,857**	**0,800**	**0,792**	**0,797**	**0,837**	**0,788**	**0,785**
XGBC	0,750	0,753	0,750	0,749	0,804	0,850	0,795	0,787	0,750	0,753	0,750	0,749	0,728	0,757	0,715	0,695
AB	0,650	0,665	0,650	0,642	0,797	0,841	0,777	0,763	0,700	0,708	0,700	0,697	0,757	0,782	0,747	0,732
GB	0,750	0,775	0,750	0,744	**0,814**	**0,863**	**0,815**	**0,830**	0,750	0,753	0,750	0,749	0,746	0,770	0,742	0,735
CB	0,750	0,753	0,750	0,749	0,794	0,870	0,782	0,759	0,700	0,700	0,700	0,700	0,748	0,785	0,737	0,708

Table 6. Best hyper-parameters configuration for classification with all synthetic indices

CLASSIFIER	criterion	max depth	max features	random state	learning rate	number of estimator
DT	Gini	10	7	1	–	–
RF	Gini	10	2	1	–	–
ET	Entropy	5	10	1	–	–
XGBC	–	–	–	1	1.0	10
AB	–	–	–	1	1.0	20
GB	–	–	–	1	0.5	15
CB	–	–	–	0	0.01	15

Table 7. Best hyper-parameters configuration for classification with mean index

CLASSIFIER	criterion	max depth	max features	random state	learning rate	number of estimator
DT	Entropy	5	7	1	–	–
RF	Gini	10	5	1	–	–
ET	Entropy	15	2	0	–	–
XGBC	–	–	–	1	0.5	20
AB	–	–	–	1	0.5	15
GB	–	–	–	0	0.5	15
CB	–	–	–	1	0.1	15

Table 8. Best hyper-parameters configuration for classification with variance index

CLASSIFIER	criterion	max depth	max features	random state	learning rate	number of estimator
DT	Entropy	10	10	1	–	–
RF	Gini	10	7	1	–	–
ET	Entropy	10	10	1	–	–
XGBC	–	–	–	1	0.5	20
AB	–	–	–	1	0.5	15
GB	–	–	–	1	0.5	15
CB	–	–	–	1	0.5	10

Table 9. Best hyper-parameters configuration for classification with minimum and maximum indices

CLASSIFIER	criterion	max depth	max features	random state	learning rate	number of estimator
DT	Gini	5	auto	0	–	–
RF	Gini	5	auto	0	–	–
ET	Gini	10	5	0	–	–
XGBC	–	–	–	1	0.5	20
AB	–	–	–	1	1	20
GB	–	–	–	1	0.1	20
CB	–	–	–	0	0.1	20

The classifiers have been subjected to hyperparameter optimization to find the configurations that led to the best results. In particular, the *GridSearch* function of the Scikit-learn Python toolkit has been used to find the best configuration. *GridSearch* uses a combination of the supplied hyper-parameters and their values, calculates the performance for each combination, and chooses the optimal value for the hyper-parameters [9]. Then the classifiers have been trained first in their baseline version and then with the use of *GridSearch*, thus obtaining the comparison between the baseline and the best combination of hyper-parameters of the algorithm. Specifically, Table 1 shows the parameters evaluated for the enhancement techniques and those based on the decision tree, respectively. The second column shows the name of the hyperparameter, the third a brief description, and the corresponding ranges of evaluated values in the last column.

In addition, the *SMOTE* function of the Imbalanced Learn Python library has been used to balance the data in the training and test set. This technique randomly oversamples the minority class via [11] replication.

Considering that the traces were summarized using 4 different synthetic indices: the arithmetic means, the variance, the minimum, and the maximum, various analyzes were performed for each index calculated. In detail, the first classification is performed taking into account all the indices together, the subsequent ones taking into account only the average, only the variance, and finally the minimum and maximum jointly to obtain the evaluation on the entire range of EEG variation.

Based on the results of the classification, the confusion matrix is created to validate the proposed models; in fact, from it is possible to calculate several metrics, such as: *Accuracy* (A), *Precision* (P), *Recall* (R) and *F1-Score* (F).

5   Discussion of Results

This Section contains a discussion of our study's findings. In Tables 2, 3, 4, 5 we report the results of the evaluation metrics for all the classification methods used with the methodologies described in Subsect. 4.2.

In particular, Table 2 shows the results of the classification with the use of all the synthetic indexes calculated on the EEG channels, Table 3 shows the results of the classification based on the mean index, Table 4 those of the classification with variance index, and Table 5 the results of the classification with the use of minimum and maximum indexes.

Each table shows the classifier, the results of the classification based on the default configuration of the algorithm (baseline), and the results of the best configuration obtained with the optimization of the hyper-parameters. More in detail, both for the baseline and the best configuration are reported both the results, in terms of Accuracy, Precision, Recall, and F-score obtained with the holdout method and those obtained with the cross-validation method

Furthermore, in Tables 6, 7, 8, 9 details of the best configurations for all classifiers and each methodology are shown. classification used. The first column shows the classifier and the following columns show respectively the function used to measure the quality of the division (*criterion*), the *maximum depth* of the trees, the number of features to be considered in each split *max features*, the parameter that controls the randomness of the permuted features in each split *random state*, the *learning rate* used at each iteration and the number of trees used for the boosting *number of estimators*.

Overall, the results show that using cross-validation versus hold-out leads to improved prediction. In 75% of the classifications carried out, cross-validation improved the metrics by at least 5%. Furthermore, the best results, highlighted in bold, are obtained through boosting methods (accuracy, precision, recall, and f1 ≥ 75% score). The search for the best hyper-parameters shows local improvements, particularly when introducing all indices into the classification. Hence, the results show that this technique brings significant improvements as functionality increases.

Comparing our study with other studies that used the same data, our approach is more efficient, obtaining better results. More specifically, Chaturvedi et al. [10] and Vanneste et al. [18] have reached an accuracy of 72.2%, and Yuvaraj et al. [19] have obtained an accuracy of 59.3%. Instead, our model has achieved an accuracy ranging between 75% and 90%.

6 Conclusion and Future Work

Parkinson's disease is a chronic progressive neurodegenerative disease (death of nerve cells). The main features of the disease are problems with the mobility of the body, which manifest themselves in the form of a slowing of movements, muscle stiffness, and possibly tremors. Very frequently, non-motor symptoms are also observed. EGG is one of the most used methods for diagnosing PD.

Therefore, our approach proposes an overview of the adoption of ML classifiers for early Parkinson's prediction based on EEG traces. This study demonstrates how the use of ML algorithms can predict the onset of Parkinson's disease in an effective and timely manner, in particular through synthetic indices, such as the arithmetic means, variance, minimum and maximum. able to synthesize the size of the EEG without loss of information. Our study shows:

- focusing on classification methodologies, it has been shown that cross-validation improves prediction compared to the hold-out method;
- in most classifications, empowerment methods reveal much more satisfactory results than a weaker student such as decision tree, random forest, and extra trees; a big plus because these algorithms are easier to implement;
- boosting approach does well by diversifying the indices to be classified, demonstrating the strong generalizability of our approach;
- the results indicate that as functionality increases, it is advisable to classify the data using the best hyper-parameters, easily and promptly searchable through the GridSearch function of the Scikit-learn Python toolkit.

In future work, we want to explore new features and increase the existing data-set. We also aim to broaden the data-set to examine more complex approaches such as Deep Learning algorithms.

References

1. Aversano, L., et al.: Using machine learning for classification of cancer cells from raman spectroscopy. In: Proceedings of the 3rd International Conference on Deep Learning Theory and Applications, DeLTA 2022, Lisbon, Portugal, 12–14 July 2022, pp. 15–24. SCITEPRESS (2022)
2. Aversano, L., et al.: Thyroid disease treatment prediction with machine learning approaches. Procedia Comput. Sci. **192**, 1031–1040 (2021)
3. Aversano, L., Bernardi, M.L., Cimitile, M., Iammarino, M., Montano, D., Verdone, C.: A machine learning approach for early detection of Parkinson's disease using acoustic traces. In: 2022 IEEE International Conference on Evolving and Adaptive Intelligent Systems (EAIS), pp. 1–8. IEEE (2022)
4. Aversano, L., Bernardi, M.L., Cimitile, M., Iammarino, M., Montano, D., Verdone, C.: Using machine learning for early prediction of heart disease. In: 2022 IEEE International Conference on Evolving and Adaptive Intelligent Systems (EAIS), pp. 1–8. IEEE (2022)
5. Aversano, L., Bernardi, M.L., Cimitile, M., Iammarino, M., Verdone, C.: Early detection of Parkinson's disease using spiral test and echo state networks. In: 2022 International Joint Conference on Neural Networks (IJCNN), pp. 1–8 (2022)
6. Aversano, L., Bernardi, M.L., Cimitile, M., Iammarino, M., Verdone, C.: An enhanced UNet variant for effective lung cancer detection. In: 2022 International Joint Conference on Neural Networks (IJCNN), pp. 1–8 (2022)
7. Aversano, L., Bernardi, M.L., Cimitile, M., Pecori, R.: Early detection of Parkinson disease using deep neural networks on gait dynamics. In: 2020 International Joint Conference on Neural Networks (IJCNN), pp. 1–8. IEEE (2020)
8. Aversano, L., Bernardi, M.L., Cimitile, M., Pecori, R.: Fuzzy neural networks to detect Parkinson disease. In: 2020 IEEE International Conference on Fuzzy Systems (FUZZ-IEEE), pp. 1–8. IEEE (2020)
9. Brownlee, J.: How to grid search hyperparameters for deep learning models in python with keras. Linea (2016)
10. Chaturvedi, M., et al.: Quantitative EEG (QEEG) measures differentiate Parkinson's disease (PD) patients from healthy controls (HC). Front. Aging Neurosci. **9**, 3 (2017)
11. Chawla, N.V., Bowyer, K.W., Hall, L.O., Kegelmeyer, W.P.: Smote: synthetic minority over-sampling technique. J. Artif. Intell. Res. **16**, 321–357 (2002)
12. Goetz, C.G., et al.: Movement disorder society-sponsored revision of the unified Parkinson's disease rating scale (MDS-UPDRS): scale presentation and clinimetric testing results. Move. Disord.: Off. J. Move. Disord. Soc. **23**(15), 2129–2170 (2008)
13. Koch, M., Geraedts, V., Wang, H., Tannemaat, M., Bäck, T.: Automated machine learning for EEG-based classification of Parkinson's disease patients. In: 2019 IEEE International Conference on Big Data (Big Data), pp. 4845–4852 (2019)
14. Miller, A.M., et al.: Effect of levodopa on electroencephalographic biomarkers of the parkinsonian state. J. Neurophysiol. **122**(1), 290–299 (2019)
15. Twelves, D., Perkins, K.S., Counsell, C.: Systematic review of incidence studies of Parkinson's disease. Move. Disord.: Off. J. Move. Disord. Soc. **18**(1), 19–31 (2003)
16. Van Den Eeden, S.K., et al.: Incidence of Parkinson's disease: variation by age, gender, and race/ethnicity. Am. J. Epidemiol. **157**(11), 1015–1022 (2003)
17. Vanegas, M.I., Ghilardi, M.F., Kelly, S.P., Blangero, A.: Machine learning for EEG-based biomarkers in Parkinson's disease. In: 2018 IEEE International Conference on Bioinformatics and Biomedicine (BIBM), pp. 2661–2665 (2018)

18. Vanneste, S., Song, J.-J., De Ridder, D.: Thalamocortical dysrhythmia detected by machine learning. Nat. Commun. **9**(1), 1–13 (2018)
19. Yuvaraj, R., Rajendra Acharya, U., Hagiwara, Y.: A novel Parkinson's disease diagnosis index using higher-order spectra features in EEG signals. Neural Comput. Appl. **30**(4), 1225–1235 (2018)

Cognitive Assistant for Physical Exercise Monitoring in Hand Rehabilitation

J. A. Rincon[1,2(✉)], C. Marco-Detchart[1], V. Julian[1,2], and C. Carrascosa[1]

[1] Valencian Research Institute for Artificial Intelligence (VRAIN),
Universitat Politècnica de València, Camino de Vera s/n, 46022 Valencia, Spain
{cedmarde,vjulian}@upv.es, {jrincon,carrasco}@dsic.upv.es
[2] Valencian Graduate School and Research Network of Artificial Intelligence,
Universitat Politècnica de València, Camí de Vera s/n, 46022 Valencia, Spain

Abstract. This paper introduces a novel, affordable companion robot that has been designed for rehabilitation purposes among the elderly population. The robot is equipped with a camera that records exercises, and an animation screen that delivers clear and easy-to-follow instructions and feedback. To evaluate the device, a machine learning algorithm was used on a dataset of therapy exercises. The results indicate that the robot effectively recognizes gestures and accurately identifies the exercises being performed. This study presents a groundbreaking and cost-effective solution for elderly rehabilitation and has the potential to revolutionize the industry with its cutting-edge technology.

Keywords: EDGE AI · Assistant Robot · Artificial Vision · Elderly people · Rehabilitation

1 Introduction

Edge computing is a type of approach where devices are located in the user's physical location. Enterprises can take advantage of the flexibility of hybrid cloud computing by allowing the users to get faster and more reliable services. With edge computing, users can use and distribute a standard set of resources across many locations. Size reduction and not needing to be continuously connected has advantages for users, being the cornerstone that faster and more stable services can be obtained at a lower cost. They reflected on users as they got a faster and more consistent experience. At the same time, this closeness of the computer systems translates into low latency and high availability applications with permanent monitoring. Many robotics applications are migrating to edge computing technology, most of which are directly related to the industry. Since industrial robots mainly need to perform different tasks under time constraints, they cannot afford latency when receiving the next command from a central server. To execute a welding task, manipulate an object or classify objects using machine vision, etc., industrial robots need to be able to perform different tasks under time constraints. This is why Edge-Computing technology is vital

S. Massanet et al. (Eds.): EUSFLAT 2023/AGOP 2023, LNCS 14069, pp. 620–629, 2023.
https://doi.org/10.1007/978-3-031-39965-7_51

in robotics. Edge-Computing technology is also widely used in cognitive assistants and wearable device applications. The embedded systems used for these applications are computational units capable of executing tasks such as machine vision [1], machine learning [2], speech recognition [3], navigation [4], etc. The increase in life expectancy and population's ageing are devastatingly affecting public administrations that look after the welfare of this population, mainly due to the lack of healthcare personnel. One of the applications of particular interest, both at the research and commercial level, are cognitive assistants in the shape of companion robots. These companion robots, capable of assisting older adults in their daily tasks [5], keeping them company [6], organising their activities [7] and monitoring their medication [7], and cognitive activities [8], are being widely marketed to individuals or senior centres. However, one of the disadvantages of these robots is their price, which makes them not very accessible to people. However, with the advent of new, smaller, cheaper and more powerful devices, it has been possible to adopt a new type of low-cost assistive robots. These robots can execute object recognition models, analyse signals, recognise people, etc. Thus, the aim of this work is to present a cognitive assistant, specifically a companion robot, in charge of classifying rehabilitation exercises for people with arthritis. The idea is that the robot identifies the exercises indicated by a caregiver to the patient so that it can monitor the execution of the exercises and persuasively encourage the patient to perform the exercises. Two of the main aspects of this robot is its low cost compared to other existing approaches and, on the other hand, the possibility of working in off-line mode without the need to be connected to the Internet to perform the classification processes. The rest of the paper is structured as follows: next section describes different related approaches; then the description of the system is presented both from the point of view of the hardware and the necessary software; Finally, some conclusions are presented.

2   Related Work

Several studies have demonstrated the applicability of assistive robots for elderly care. It is possible to find robot assistants for almost all tasks associated with caregiving. In different studies, robot assistants have played a significant role and obtained good results. An example of the latter is the research in which we can highlight the study, G. Perugia [9] presents a new tool to measure the engagement of people with dementia in playing board games and interacting with the social robot Pleo [10]. At the same time, they are conducting a second study to investigate how people with dementia express their engagement in cognitive games and interactions with social robots. The study by S. Šabanović [11] evaluates the PARO robot seal in a multisensory

behavioural therapy context with older adults. The participants in the study were older adults with different levels of dementia. The study showed that PARO provides indirect benefits to users by increasing their activity in specific modalities of social interaction, including visual, verbal and physical. Many of these robots are used as companion robots; MARIO [12] is an example of a social robot developed with and for people with dementia. MARIO promotes social connectivity and reduces loneliness and isolation by providing access to various applications with which they can interact via voice commands and the touch screen. Another possible application for these robot assistants is assisted therapy. Using artificial vision and ML modelling, they can determine whether the user is performing the exercise or not. The research presented by Michelle J. et al. [13] shows that a stimulus-response model may capture some observed relationships between the patient and the therapist in various tasks of daily life and offers a reasonable model of the interactions between the robot and the patient that can approximate real therapy. As can be seen, there are different robot proposals that try to improve interaction with humans, mainly from the point of view of enhancing the quality of life of the elderly. However, many of these works are either very expensive commercial robots or are not commercially available. In the following section, we present our proposal for a companion robot from a low-cost perspective oriented to facilitate the rehabilitation of elderly people with hand arthritis problems.

3   System Description

This section describes the operation of the companion robot, detailing the different software and hardware tools used to create the assistant. The proposed approach is shown in Fig. 1.

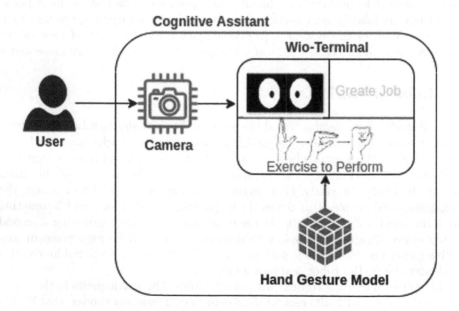

Fig. 1. Architecture of the proposed system.

if the user performs correctly the activity suggested by the caregiver. For the performance of these tasks, the cognitive assistant requires specific hardware and software. This will be described in detail below.

3.1 Hardware Description

The main component of the assistant presented in this paper is the Wio Terminal, a development system from Seeed Studio. The Wio Terminal is based on a SAMD51 microcontroller, and its processing speed is between 120 Mhz and 200 Mhz. The Wio Terminal is equipped with a 2.4" LCD screen, an inertial measurement system (IMU), and a microphone and supports Bluetooth and WiFi (Fig. 2).

Fig. 2. Wio Terminal.

To capture the images, the assistant integrates a camera to capture the respective images. These images will be analysed by the Wio Terminal using the model trained. The model is stored in SD memory to reduce memory usage when integrating firmware. This approach presents two significant advantages; one is that it will not take up segments in the Flash memory, and the second is the ability to update the models for more exercises or other recognised therapies. An eye animation was included to be presented on the screen to make the cognitive assistant more user-friendly. This is intended to reduce frustration or repulsion towards the assistant. The assistant has five different looks that help it interact with the user. Figure 3 shows the cognitive assistant prototype, where it can be seen the camera and the Wio Terminal.

Once the images have been captured, the next step is to check that our device captures the images correctly. To do this, we visualise the image captured by the camera (Fig. 4).

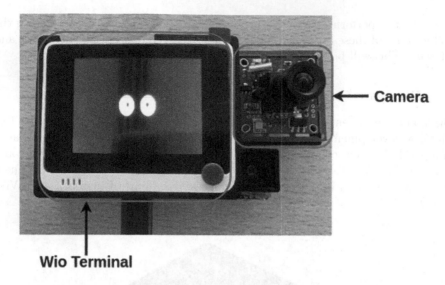

Fig. 3. Prototype Assistance.

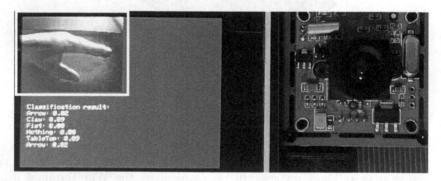

Fig. 4. Using the system.

3.2 Software Description

This section will describe the software tools used to train learning models and assistant programming. It was decided to classify four-hand exercises used for rehabilitating people with arthritis, as can be seen in Fig. 5.

3.3 Image Acquisition

To perform the exercise classification, it is necessary to have a set of images representing the exercises. These images have to be captured from different angles and poses, all this to give the model a better representation of the data to be classified.

We are working with small devices with limited RAM resources and computational capacity. It is necessary to make some small transformations to these

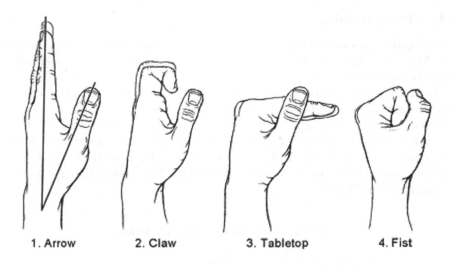

1. Arrow   2. Claw   3. Tabletop   4. Fist

Fig. 5. Hand gesture for basics therapy.

images. Typically, if we use a smartphone camera, the images are huge and with a high resolution, making difficult for the Edge device to analyse them, so they must be resized. After several attempts, it was determined that the optimal image sizes to perform a correct classification on the device used in this project are 32×32 pixels.

There were captured approx. 500 images, 100 per each class of selected exercises, and a class for no activity. These images had an original size of 160×120 and were resized to 32×32 to facilitate their classification.

The model training was performed using the Edge Impulse platform, a powerful tool for creating DL models for Edge devices. On the Edge Impulse website, all the documentation necessary to perform the first training can be found. Figure 6 shows the images resized to 32×32.

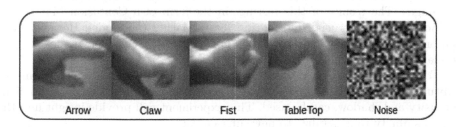

Arrow   Claw   Fist   TableTop   Noise

Fig. 6. The structure of the model.

3.4   Model Training

The training process of the proposed model has been designed to be a straight-forward, visual task. It offers an optimized model for the target device with a quick turnaround time.

A dataset comprised of 258 images per class was created, resulting in a total of 1032 images. This dataset was divided into three subsets, with 80% of the images used for training, 10% for testing, and the remaining 10% for validation. The network architecture utilized for training the model was a Mobilenet V1, with hyperparameters including an Alpha value of 0.5, a Dropout Rate of 0.01, AVG Pooling, weight decay, and a learning rate of 0.001. The model's hyperparameters are presented in Table 1.

Table 1. Model Used in the edge device.

Hyperparameters	Values
No input layers	27.648 features
2D Conv / Pool Layer	32 filters, 3 kernel sisze, 1 layer
2D Conv / Pool Layer	16 filters, 3 kernel sisze, 1 layer
Flatten Layer	
Dropout	rate 0.25
Output Layert	4

It is beyond the scope of this paper to provide an in-depth analysis of the training process or the steps involved in creating a project and uploading images. Information on these topics can be readily obtained from various online resources, including the Edge Impulse website and Google.

Once the model has been validated using a single image, the ability of the model to discriminate between different classes has been demonstrated. The next step in the evaluation process is to test the model using the entire test set of images. The results of this testing, in the form of a Confusion Matrix and F1 Score, provide crucial information for validating the model. However, it is important to note that these results do not necessarily reflect the model's ability to classify data that it has not been trained on.

To further assess the robustness of the model, a validation set of images captured under various environmental conditions, such as variations in light intensity and shadow, can be used. This experiment will provide insight into the model's ability to generalize to new, unseen data.

The confusion matrix is a widely used evaluation tool in the field of machine learning, particularly in the analysis of supervised learning algorithms. The matrix provides a clear and concise representation of the algorithm's perfor-mance, highlighting the ability of the model to correctly classify instances into their corresponding classes. Each column of the matrix represents the number of predictions made by the algorithm for each class, while each row corresponds to the actual class of the instances. This visual representation makes it easy to identify any confusion between classes and to determine areas in which the algorithm may need improvement. The confusion matrix obtained during the classification process is presented in Fig. 7.

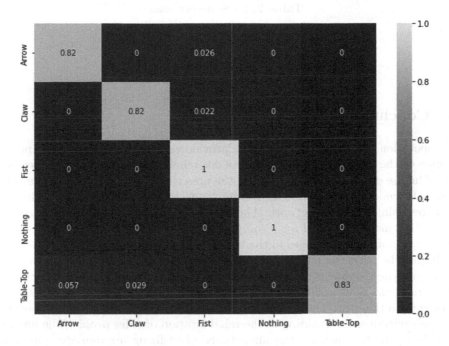

Fig. 7. Confusion Matrix.

The F1-Score, on the other hand, is a measure of the accuracy of the test results. It is calculated as the harmonic mean of precision and recall. Precision is defined as the number of true positive results divided by the total number of positive results identified, including those that were incorrectly identified. Recall, on the other hand, is defined as the number of true positive results divided by the total number of samples that should have been identified as positive. The F1-Score provides a single score that summarizes the precision and recall of the test, making it a useful tool for comparing the performance of different algorithms.

The results of the confusion matrix and F1-Score analysis can be visualized in Fig. 9, which presents the results of the exercise classification experiments. This figure provides a clear representation of the algorithm's performance, allowing for easy comparison of the results with other algorithms or with previous results obtained using the same algorithm. The combination of the confusion matrix and F1-Score provides a comprehensive overview of the accuracy of the algorithm, which is essential in the assessment of the effectiveness of the algorithm for the given task.

Table 2 presents the confusion matrix generated from the classification process, along with the corresponding F1 score. The F1 score provides an estimation of the accuracy of each test, and as can be seen from the results, the performance of the algorithm is quite promising.

Table 2. F1-Score per class

	Arrow	Claw	Fist	Nothing	Table-Rop
F1-Score	0.88	0.89	0.97	1.0	0.91

4   Conclusion

In conclusion, the results of this study provide valuable insights into the performance of the low-cost companion robot for rehabilitation tasks with elder people. The use of a camera for capturing the prescribed exercises and an animation screen for guidance and feedback has proven to be effective in the recognition of gestures using a trained network. The use of a confusion matrix and F1 score as evaluation metrics allowed for a comprehensive assessment of the model's accuracy in classifying the images in the test set. The promising results of this study highlight the potential for further development and optimization of the model.

Future developments of the device will include an increase in the number of therapy exercises and the addition of other sensors to enhance the feedback provided to the user. These improvements are expected to further increase the device's effectiveness in aiding in the rehabilitation of elder people. The findings of this study demonstrate the importance of utilizing appropriate evaluation metrics in the assessment of machine learning algorithms and the potential of low-cost companion robots in the rehabilitation field.

Acknowledgements. This work was partly supported by Universitat Politecnica de Valencia Research Grant PAID-10-19 and PID2021-123673OB-C31 funded by MCIN/AEI/ 10.13039/501100011033 and by "ERDFA way of making Europe", Consellería d'Innovació, Universitats, Ciencia i Societat Digital from Comunitat Valenciana (APOSTD/2021/227) through the European Social Fund (Investing In Your Future) and grant from the Research Services of Universitat Politècnica de València (PAID-PD-22).

References

1. Chen, Y., Wang, C., Lou, S.: Edge artificial intelligence camera network: an efficient object detection and tracking framework. J. Electron. Imaging **31**(3), 033030–033030 (2022)
2. Filho, C.P., et al.: A systematic literature review on distributed machine learning in edge computing. Sensors **22**(7), 2665 (2022)

3. Wei, Y., Gong, Z., Yang, S., Ye, K., Wen, Y.: EdgeCRNN: an edge-computing oriented model of acoustic feature enhancement for keyword spotting. J. Ambient Intell. Humanized Comput. **13**, 1525–1535 (2022)
4. McEnroe, P., Wang, S., Liyanage, M.: A survey on the convergence of edge computing and AI for UAVs: opportunities and challenges. IEEE Internet Things J. **9**, 15435–15459 (2022)
5. Fracasso, F., Buchweitz, L., Theil, A., Cesta, A., Korn, O.: Social robots acceptance and marketability in Italy and Germany: a cross-national study focusing on assisted living for older adults. Int. J. Soc. Robot. **14**(6), 1463–1480 (2022)
6. Stegner, L., Mutlu, B.: Designing for caregiving: Integrating robotic assistance in senior living communities. In: Designing Interactive Systems Conference, pp. 1934–1947 (2022)
7. Fischinger, D., et al.: Hobbit, a care robot supporting independent living at home: first prototype and lessons learned. Robot. Auton. Syst. **75**, 60–78 (2016)
8. Rincon, J.A., Julian, V., Carrascosa, C.: A physical cognitive assistant for monitoring hand gestures exercises. In: Ferrández Vicente, J.M., Álvarez-Sánchez, J.R., de la Paz López, F., Adeli, H. (eds.) IWINAC 2022. LNCS, vol. 13259, pp. 13–43. Springer, Cham (2022). https://doi.org/10.1007/978-3-031-06527-9_2
9. Perugia, G., Doladeras, M.D., Mallofré, A.C., Rauterberg, M., Barakova, E.: Modelling engagement in dementia through behaviour. Contribution for socially interactive robotics. In: 2017 International Conference on Rehabilitation Robotics (ICORR), pp. 1112–1117. IEEE (2017)
10. Moerman, C.J., Jansens, R.M.: Using social robot PLEO to enhance the well-being of hospitalised children. J. Child Health Care **25**(3), 412–426 (2021)
11. Šabanović, S., Bennett, C.C., Chang, W.L., Huber, L.: PARO robot affects diverse interaction modalities in group sensory therapy for older adults with dementia. In: 2013 IEEE 13th International Conference on Rehabilitation Robotics (ICORR), pp. 1–6. IEEE (2013)
12. Mannion, A., et al.: Introducing the social robot MARIO to people living with dementia in long term residential care: reflections. Int. J. Soc. Robot. **12**, 535–547 (2020)
13. Johnson, M.J., Mohan, M., Mendonca, R.: Therapist-patient interactions in task-oriented stroke therapy can guide robot-patient interactions. Int. J. Soc. Robot. **14**(6), 1527–1546 (2022)

Interpretable Neuro-Fuzzy Models for Stress Prediction

Gabriella Casalino⬤, Giovanna Castellano⬤, and Gianluca Zaza⁽✉⁾⬤

Department of Computer Science, University of Bari, Bari, Italy
{gabriella.casalino,giovanna.castellano,gianluca.zaza}@uniba.it

Abstract. Machine learning algorithms are useful in assisting medical judgments, but the resulting models are frequently challenging for doctors to comprehend. Conversely, IF-THEN rules articulated in natural language are successful at describing interpretable models that are returned by Fuzzy Inference Systems. However, the construction of the fuzzy rule basis in conventional fuzzy systems requires human expertise. Neuro-fuzzy systems can infer fuzzy rule-based models from data, saving time by doing away with the need to manually build the rules. Using neuro-fuzzy systems to develop prediction models from data in the form of fuzzy rules that are suitable to enhance decision-making for stress assessment is what we propose in this paper. Our results highlight how well neuro-fuzzy models perform in providing precise predictions while maintaining interpretability.

Keywords: Stress Prediction · Fuzzy Logic · Fuzzy Inference Systems · Neuro-Fuzzy systems · Interpretability

1 Introduction

Stress is a physical and mental condition affecting everyone as a reaction to adverse situations[1]. There are two kinds of stress, namely positive and negative. When negative stress lasts for a long time, that could affect overall well-being [25]. Monitoring stress levels could prevent the onset of more severe pathologies, such as hypertension, stroke, obesity, and diabetes [22]. In the last years, there has been a growing interest in contactless and wearable devices, capable of continuously monitoring vital parameters [11,12,21,27]. The real-time collection of stress data could be used for further automatic analyses to support clinical diagnoses and allow early interventions [29].

Biological signals are commonly used to identify stress levels. Particularly, Photoplethysmographic (PPG) signals, representing fluctuations in blood volume, have been recently proven to be good markers to identify stress levels [26]. Moreover, since PPG is based on light reflectance, it is easy to implement on

---

[1] World Health Organization (WHO) - stress: https://www.who.int/news-room/questions-and-answers/item/stress (last access: February 14, 2023).

© The Author(s), under exclusive license to Springer Nature Switzerland AG 2023
S. Massanet et al. (Eds.): EUSFLAT 2023/AGOP 2023, LNCS 14069, pp. 630–641, 2023.
https://doi.org/10.1007/978-3-031-39965-7_52

smart objects equipped with a light source or a camera (for remote-PGG). Several contactless and wearable devices have been proposed in the literature [24].

Data gathered by these devices need automatic analyses to derive useful insights. To this aim, different machine learning techniques have been used to predict stress levels, such as Support Vector Machine (SVN) [8,13], Random Forest (RF) [1], ensemble methods [23], or Deep Neural Network approaches [28]. However, these algorithms are considered black-box, i.e. they are not able to explain the outcome prediction. Explaining the result is especially important in the medical field because both the clinician and the patient have the right to know the reasons behind a diagnosis when it is provided by an algorithm [14,31]. To make the users easily understand the decision made by a predictive model [5,6,17] XAI (Explainable Artificial Intelligence) algorithms are preferred. Among them, those based on fuzzy logic have proven to be suitable tools for explanations [4]. Particularly, Fuzzy Inference Systems (FISs) can represent uncertain and vague concepts, proper of the medical knowledge, and reason through fuzzy sets, and *IF-THEN* rules, easy to be interpreted by final stakeholders. However, these algorithms require the time-consuming and difficult task of manually defining the knowledge base. In order to avoid this limit, when enough data are available, neuro-fuzzy systems (NFSs) could be used, that combine the interpretability of FISs with the parameter optimization given by the learning of neural networks [19].

One of the limits of NFSs is that their complexity, and thus the number of rules, exponentially grows with the number of fuzzy variables, making their use impractical because too expensive other than no more explainable. In order to overcome this limit, in [10] we proposed a pruning mechanism for NFSs with triangular fuzzy sets, by removing inactive rules from the model. Comparable results, in terms of classification performance, were obtained by NFS models with and without pruning, whilst a high reduction of the number of rules was observed, resulting in models easier to understand. In this paper, we extend our previous work by proposing a first attempt to optimize the number of rules and thus the explainability, other than the computational complexity, of NFS models with Gaussian fuzzy sets.

To evaluate the proposed approach, we consider data acquired through wearable sensors during a pilot study aimed at predicting stress levels [15]. Data refer to 34 subjects, experiencing stressful conditions in a controlled environment. To the best of our knowledge, this is the first time these data are analysed through Machine Learning (ML) and fuzzy methods for stress prediction.

The main findings of this paper are as follows:

1. a quantitative comparison of the NFS model with different ML models on the Stress Predict dataset;
2. a pruning mechanism to reduce the number of rules in NFSs models with Gaussian fuzzy sets;
3. an analysis of the NFS model in terms of explainability.

The article is structured as follows: the Stress Predict dataset is described in Sect. 2.1. The adopted learning models, together with the proposed pruning mechanism, are described in Sect. 2.2. Quantitative and qualitative evaluation of the results are discussed in Sect. 3. Section 4 draws possible future works.

2   Materials and Methods

2.1   Data

The Stress Predict Dataset[2] has been collected during a pilot study to predict the stress level of the subjects involved in [15]. The physiological parameters of each subject were measured through PPG technology embedded in the *Empatica E4 watch*[3]. The dataset is composed of the physiological signals measured in 34 healthy subjects. The volunteers were instructed to do a series of tasks meant to cause stress for a total of 60 min. In detail, pulsed blood volume (BVP), intervals between beats, and Heart Rate (HR) were recorded using the smart device while Respiratory Rate (RR) was derived from the BVP signal. A total of about 3,500 measurements per patient were collected. Raw data representing the signals are publicly available, together with pre-processed data of the HR and RR measurements, of each subject, acquired during the in-vivo experiment. Two classes are reported, namely *stress* and *no stress*. Data are highly imbalanced. In fact, there are 36,815 measures that correspond to the *stress* state, while 75,701 measurements fall under the *no stress* category.

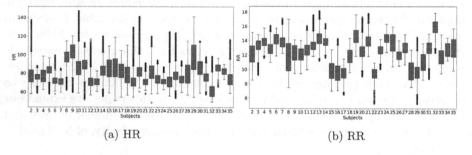

(a) HR   (b) RR

Fig. 1. Box-plots representing data distributions of HR and RR values for each subject.

It is worth noting that stress levels can vary from one patient to another, as stated by the World Health Organization (WHO). Moreover, Fig. 1 shows the data distribution of each subject, considering HR and RR parameters. A high variability, for the two parameters, can be observed in both data belonging to a single subject and within different subjects.

---

[2] Data are publicly available at the following link: https://github.com/italha-d/Stress-Predict-Dataset (last access February 16, 2023).

[3] Empatica E4 watch technical specifications: https://support.empatica.com/hc/en-us/articles/202581999-E4-wristband-technical-specifications (last access February 14, 2023).

2.2   Neuro-Fuzzy System

The objective of this study is to test how effective neuro-fuzzy systems are in the field of medical diagnosis. While accuracy is important in this field, having easily understandable models could lead to greater acceptance from non-technical stakeholders. To achieve this, this study compares neuro-fuzzy models to machine learning models that are not easily explainable. Additionally, a pruning method is applied to remove useless rules and simplify the explanations of the neuro-fuzzy model.

A neuro-fuzzy system has been utilized to create a model for predicting the stress of subjects. This system includes a neural network that incorporates a series of fuzzy rules in an IF-THEN format. Specifically, the study utilizes zero-order Takagi-Sugeno rules, which represent the antecedent using fuzzy sets, and the consequent using fuzzy singletons.

The fuzzy model produces degrees of certainty for each output class through its inference mechanism. The knowledge base contains a set of K rules that are of the type:

IF $(x_1$ is $A_{k1})$ AND $\dots (x_n$ is $A_{kn})$ THEN $(y_1$ is $b_{k1})$ AND $\dots (y_m$ is $b_{km})$

where A_{ki} are fuzzy sets defined over the input variables $x_i (i = 1, ..., n)$ and b_{kj} are fuzzy singletons expressing the certainty degree that the output belongs to one of the m classes $y_j, j = 1...m$.

Fuzzy sets are defined by Gaussian membership functions:

$$u_{ki} = \mu_{ki}(x_i) = \exp\left(\frac{(x_i - c_{ki})^2}{\sigma_{ki}^2} \right) \tag{1}$$

where c_{ki} and σ_{ki} are the centers and the widths of the Gaussian function, respectively. The study utilizes a neuro-fuzzy network that is based on the ANFIS (Adaptive-Network-Based Fuzzy Inference System) architecture [16] to learn the parameters of the fuzzy sets and consequents. The four feed-forward levels of the ANFIS architecture are depicted in Fig. 2. Membership degrees of input values to Fuzzy sets are calculated at layer 1, the activation strength of each fuzzy rule is calculated at layer 2, the normalized activation strengths are calculated at layer 3, and the certainty level for output classes is calculated at layer 4. The backpropagation method, which is based on gradient descent optimization, is

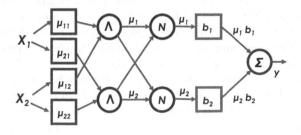

Fig. 2. Architecture of the neuro-fuzzy network.

Algorithm 1. Pruning algorithm

Require: TS, $Rules$, θ
  while $Rules \neq \emptyset$ **do**
    $Avg_{\mu_j} \leftarrow 0$
    while $TS \neq \emptyset$ **do**
      $\mu_j(\mathbf{x}_i) \leftarrow \prod_{i=1}^{n} u_{ji}$
      $Avg_{\mu_j} \leftarrow Avg_{\mu_j} + \mu_j(\mathbf{x}_i)$
    end while
    $Avg_{\mu_j} \leftarrow \frac{Avg_{\mu_j}}{|TS|}$
    if $Avg_{\mu_j} < \theta$ **then** $Rules \leftarrow Rules - R_j$
  end while

---

used to train this network. Certainty degrees values are obtained for each fuzzy term in the consequents, and the class having the highest value is returned.

The complexity of NFS models grows exponentially as the number of input variables increases. Specifically, if n is the number of linguistic variables and m is the number of fuzzy terms for each variable, the total number of rules is m^n. In order to reduce this number, we observe that, because of the Gaussian shape of the membership functions, some fuzzy rules may be fired with a very low, but still not zero, activation value. Thus, we propose the use of a pruning mechanism that cuts off rules whose activation value is below a threshold θ. This removal of useless rules represents a first attempt to improve the explainability of the fuzzy model learned by ANFIS. The steps of the pruning strategy are summarized in Algorithm 1, where TS is the Test Set, $\mathbf{x}_i$ is a sample in TS, $\mu_j(x_i)$ is the activation strength of rule R_j for a given sample $\mathbf{x}_i$, which is computed by means of a t-norm applied to input membership values u_{ji}, and Avg_{μ_j} is the average activation value of rule R_j, over the samples in TS. Despite the simplicity of this method, it is general and can be used to reduce the computational costs required to create the model when many variables are involved. Moreover, it should be noted that this pruning criterium is effective when data is uniformly distributed, as in the Stress Predict Dataset, where data belonging to the two classes, for each subject, has low variance.

3 Results and Discussion

Experiments have the two-fold aim to quantitatively compare the classification performance of the NFS model with black-box models, and to perform an analysis of the explainability of the NFS model. We compared the NFS system with four Machine Learning algorithms, namely Random Forest (RF), Multilayer Perceptron (MLP, Support Vector Machine (SVC), and XGBoost (XGB). These techniques were implemented using the Python Scikit-learn module, and default parameters were utilized[4]. We applied the hold-out method to split the dataset into training (80%) and test (20%) sets. Also, to make the experimentation more robust, we applied the methods of stratification and shuffling in the

---

[4] Scikit-learn library:http://scikit-learn.org/stable/.

dataset splitting phase. In addition, we set the following hyperparameters for the neuro-fuzzy model: *batch size* = 16, *number of epochs* = 100 and *learning rate* = $1e - 2$. Standard classification measures, such as accuracy, precision, recall, and F1-score, were used to quantitatively evaluate the performance of the algorithms.

Table 1 compares the classification performance of the models on the whole data. We can observe that the best results were returned by XGB and RF, with an accuracy of 0.74 each. However, these are ensemble methods, thus while returning more accurate models, they lose in explainability, since they are quite complex due to a combination of different classifiers. In contrast, the NFS model achieved an accuracy of 0.68, which is slightly lower than those of the other models, but it can produce an interpretable model expressed in terms of fuzzy rules, as shown in Table 2.

As previously discussed, different subjects could present different symptoms. Due to the high variability in data, creating a single model for each subject

Table 1. Quantitative evaluation of the NFS model and the black-box models on all the subjects.

	Accuracy	Precision	Recall	F1-score
NFS	0.68	0.64	0.52	0.46
RF	**0.74**	0.71	**0.68**	**0.69**
SVM	0.69	0.68	0.55	0.52
XGB	**0.74**	**0.72**	0.66	0.67
MLP	0.67	0.34	0.50	0.40

Table 2. Fuzzy rules of the neuro-fuzzy model created from all the data of the subjects, before and after pruning.

Before pruning		After pruning	
Premise (IF)	Consequent (THEN)	Premise (IF)	Consequent (THEN)
HR is Low AND RR is Low	Stress		
HR is Low AND RR is Medium	No Stress	HR is Low AND RR is Medium	No Stress
HR is Low AND RR is High	No Stress		
HR is Medium AND RR is Low	No Stress		
HR is Medium AND RR is Medium	Stress	HR is Medium AND RR is Medium	Stress
HR is Medium AND RR is High	Stress		
HR is High AND BR is Low	Stress		
HR is High AND RR is Medium	Stress	HR is High AND RR is Medium	Stress
HR is High AND RR is High	No Stress		

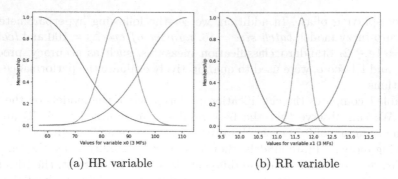

(a) HR variable   (b) RR variable

Fig. 3. Example of membership functions for input variables generated by the NFS, for a single subject.

may result more reliable for stress prediction. Thus, individual models have been created utilizing the considered methods for each of the 34 patients. As an example, Fig. 3 shows an example of the membership functions generated by the NFS model for the fuzzy variables HR and RR, for subject #2. It can be seen that even if the fuzzy sets cover the entire input domain, overlapping in the HR plot confirms the fact that the unbalanced and noisy nature of the data affected the data-driven model. However, these results are not quantitatively comparable because they are generated from different data, so violin plot representation has been used to summarize the classification performance of the considered algorithms over the 34 subjects (Fig. 4). These graphs are an extension of the boxplots, representing both the data distribution (medians and interquartile ranges) and the probability of a given value (the wider the section, the higher the probability). Results on individual models confirm that ensemble methods return the best performance. The median values are close to the maximum value of 1 for all the measures (accuracy, precision, recall, and F1-score). On the contrary, the other methods show higher variability in the results, indicating that they are more dependent on the specific data. MLP gives the worst results, especially in terms of precision and recall, making it unreliable. NFS shows classification performance lower than the ensemble methods, but still good (around 0.8). The variability observed could be justified by the fact that these are data-driven models, and thus, they strictly depend on the data used to train them. But, as shown in Fig. 1, data distribution over subjects is very different, and several outliers have been identified, that could have affected the results of the NFS models.

To increase the readability of the NFS models, we applied the rule pruning phase both on the model generated from the whole data and on individual models generated from data of each subject. We applied a threshold value $\theta = 0.02$ (empirically defined) to delete rules with low strength values. Table 2 shows the fuzzy rules generated from all data, before and after applying the pruning mechanism. As an example of individual models, Table 3 shows an example of fuzzy rules generated from data of subject #2, before and after applying the

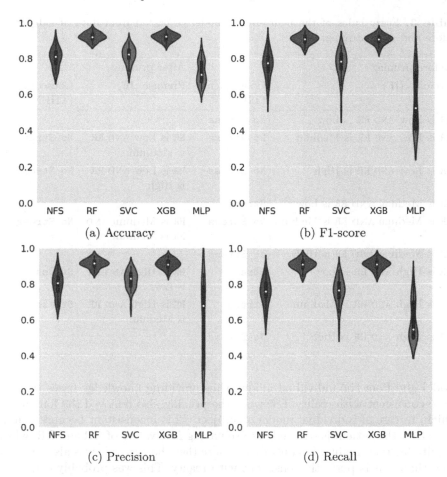

Fig. 4. Violin plot graphs summarizing the classification performance of the NFS and the ML models, for all the subjects, in terms of accuracy (a), F1-score (b), precision (c), and recall (d).

pruning mechanism. In these models, the accuracy was kept almost unchanged after pruning, while improving readability. The values in the consequent parts represent the classes with the highest cetainty degree, for the given rule.

From Table 2 it can be seen that after the pruning phase, only three fuzzy rules are retained out of nine, thus improving the readability of the model while leaving almost unchanged the accuracy of the model that deteriorates of only 5%. From Table 3 it can be seen that after the pruning phase, five fuzzy rules are retained out of nine. We can observe that the rules removed by the pruning phase are in most cases "inconsistent" fuzzy rules. For example, the ninth rule of the model obtained before pruning suggests that a subject with high values of both HR and RR is not stressed. This rule is judged to be inconsistent from a medical point of view. The pruning removed this rule both from the general

Table 3. Fuzzy rules of the neuro-fuzzy model generated from data of subject#2, before and after pruning.

Before pruning		After pruning	
Premise (IF)	Consequent (THEN)	Premise (IF)	Consequent (THEN)
HR is Low AND RR is Low	No Stress		
HR is Low AND RR is Medium	No Stress	HR is Low AND RR is Medium	No Stress
HR is Low AND RR is High	No Stress	HR is Low AND RR is High	No Stress
HR is Medium AND RR is Low	Stress		
HR is Medium AND RR is Medium	No Stress	HR is Medium AND RR is Medium	No Stress
HR is Medium AND RR is High	No Stress		
HR is High AND BR is Low	Stress	HR is High AND RR is Low	Stress
HR is High AND RR is Medium	Stress	HR is High AND RR is Medium	Stress
HR is High AND RR is High	No Stress		

model and from the individual model, thus providing knowledge bases that are more consistent with reality. Likewise, the pruning also removed the fourth rule which, in case of individual model of subject #2 is inconsistent because it indicates that the patient is stressed despite having *Low* values of HR and RR, which is quite far from reality. In contrast, we note that the first rule was also removed even though it is perfectly consistent with reality. This was probably caused by the lack of data samples having low HR and RR values, thus the corresponding rule has a low firing value, leading to its removal. Overall, these preliminary experiments highlight that applying pruning after learning a NFS model can improve the fuzzy rule base by achieving a good balance between simplicity and accuracy. Applying the pruning mechanism, we obtained an average of 5 rules for each examined model. Please note that the pruning mechanism reduces the number of rules, but the number of parameters involved in the model are not changed (e.g. number of fuzzy terms).

4   Conclusions

In this work, we propose the use of Neuro-Fuzzy Systems to support the diagnosis of stress in individuals. These data-driven algorithms are able to learn a fuzzy knowledge base in form of "IF-THEN" rules, whose parameters are optimized through a neural network, thus being interpretable without needing the manual definition of the rules. However, the knowledge base exponentially grows as the number of input variables and fuzzy sets increases, leading to models that are hardly to interpret other than computationally expensive. In this work, we proposed a first attempt to improve the computational complexity and the explainability of these models, through a pruning phase aimed at reducing the number of rules in the fuzzy knowledge base. The Stress Predict Dataset, collecting continuous measurements of vital parameters through a smart watch, has been analysed. This is the first time this dataset is analyzed with machine learning algorithms, thus we compared the NFS model with standard black-box models. Results returned by a quantitative analysis showed that ensemble methods had the best performances despite being not explainable. Whilst, with a negligible reduction in classification performance, NFS returned quite good results other than explanable models. The effectiveness of the pruning phase has been assessed by a semantic analysis of the rules returned by the NFS models. Overall, NFS systems have been proven to be effective for stress assessment, providing a good balance between accuracy and interpretability, two critical requirements in medical applications. Future work will be devoted to improving the pruning mechanism by considering different criteria that do not require the uniform distribution assumption on data. Different datasets will be considered to verify the generality of the proposed method. Also, different types of fuzzy models, such as probabilistic fuzzy models will be considered [7,20]. Moreover, due to the evolving nature of the considered data, evolving and adaptive neuro-fuzzy systems would be suitable for their analysis [9,30]. In addition, we want to investigate the interpretability of the examined models by applying quantitative measures, such as those proposed in [3]. Finally, model explainability will be enhanced through different methodologies [2,18].

Acknowledgment. Gabriella Casalino acknowledges funding from the European Union PON project Ricerca e Innovazione 2014–2020, DM 1062/2021. Gianluca Zaza and Giovanna Castellano acknowledge the support of the PNRR project FAIR - Future AI Research (PE00000013), Spoke 6 - Symbiotic AI (CUP H97G22000210007) under the NRRP MUR program funded by the NextGenerationEU. All authors are members of the INdAM GNCS research group.

References

1. Abouelenien, M., Burzo, M., Mihalcea, R.: Human acute stress detection via integration of physiological signals and thermal imaging. In: Proceedings of the 9th ACM International Conference on PErvasive Technologies Related to Assistive Environments, PETRA 2016. Association for Computing Machinery (2016)
2. Aghaeipoor, F., Sabokrou, M., Fernández, A.: Fuzzy rule-based explainer systems for deep neural networks: From local explainability to global understanding. IEEE Trans. Fuzzy Syst., 1–12 (2023)
3. Alonso, J.M., Castiello, C., Mencar, C.: Interpretability of fuzzy systems: current research trends and prospects. In: Kacprzyk, J., Pedrycz, W. (eds.) Springer Handbook of Computational Intelligence, pp. 219–237. Springer, Heidelberg (2015). https://doi.org/10.1007/978-3-662-43505-2_14
4. Alonso Moral, J.M., Castiello, C., Magdalena, L., Mencar, C.: Toward explainable artificial intelligence through fuzzy systems. In: Explainable Fuzzy Systems.

SCI, vol. 970, pp. 1–23. Springer, Cham (2021). https://doi.org/10.1007/978-3-030-71098-9_1

5. Angelov, P.P., Soares, E.A., Jiang, R., Arnold, N.I., Atkinson, P.M.: Explainable artificial intelligence: an analytical review. Wiley Interdisc. Rev.: Data Min. Knowl. Discov. **11**(5), e1424 (2021)

6. Arrieta, A.B., et al.: Explainable artificial intelligence (XAI): concepts, taxonomies, opportunities and challenges toward responsible AI. Inf. Fusion **58**, 82–115 (2020)

7. van den Berg, J., Kaymak, U., Almeida, R.J.: Conditional density estimation using probabilistic fuzzy systems. IEEE Trans. Fuzzy Syst. **21**(5), 869–882 (2012)

8. Betti, S., et al.: Evaluation of an integrated system of wearable physiological sensors for stress monitoring in working environments by using biological markers. IEEE Trans. Biomed. Eng. **65**, 1748–1758 (2018)

9. de Campos Souza, P.V., Lughofer, E.: An evolving neuro-fuzzy system based on uni-nullneurons with advanced interpretability capabilities. Neurocomputing **451**, 231–251 (2021)

10. Casalino, G., Castellano, G., Kaymak, U., Zaza, G.: Balancing accuracy and interpretability through neuro-fuzzy models for cardiovascular risk assessment. In: 2021 IEEE Symposium Series on Computational Intelligence (SSCI), pp. 1–8. IEEE (2021)

11. Casalino, G., Castellano, G., Nisio, A., Pasquadibisceglie, V., Zaza, G.: A mobile app for contactless measurement of vital signs through remote photoplethysmography. In: 2022 IEEE International Conference on Systems, Man, and Cybernetics (SMC), pp. 2675–2680. IEEE (2022)

12. Coviello, G., Florio, A., Avitabile, G., Talarico, C., Wang-Roveda, J.M.: Distributed full synchronized system for global health monitoring based on FLSA. IEEE Trans. Biomed. Circuits Syst. **16**(4), 600–608 (2022)

13. Ghaderi, A., Frounchi, J., Farnam, A.: Machine learning-based signal processing using physiological signals for stress detection. In: 2015 22nd Iranian Conference on Biomedical Engineering (ICBME) pp. 93–98 (2015)

14. Goodman, B., Flaxman, S.: Eu regulations on algorithmic decision-making and a "right to explanation" (2016). arXiv preprint arXiv:1606.08813 (2016)

15. Iqbal, T., et al.: Stress monitoring using wearable sensors: a pilot study and stress-predict dataset. Sensors **22**(21), 8135 (2022)

16. Jang, J.S., Sun, C.T.: Neuro-fuzzy modeling and control. Proc. IEEE **83**(3), 378–406 (1995)

17. Kaczmarek-Majer, K., et al.: PLENARY: explaining black-box models in natural language through fuzzy linguistic summaries. Inf. Sci. **614**, 374–399 (2022)

18. Kaczmarek-Majer, K., Casalino, G., Castellano, G., Hryniewicz, O., Dominiak, M.: Explaining smartphone-based acoustic data in bipolar disorder: semi-supervised fuzzy clustering and relative linguistic summaries. Inf. Sci. **588**, 174–195 (2022)

19. Karaboga, D., Kaya, E.: Adaptive network based fuzzy inference system (ANFIS) training approaches: a comprehensive survey. Artif. Intell. Rev. **52**, 2263–2293 (2019)

20. Kaymak, U., Van Den Bergh, W.M., van den Berg, J.: A fuzzy additive reasoning scheme for probabilistic Mamdani fuzzy systems. In: 2003 The 12th IEEE International Conference on Fuzzy Systems. FUZZ 2003, vol. 1, pp. 331–336. IEEE (2003)

21. Lofù, D., et al.: MAFUS: a framework to predict mortality risk in MAFLD subjects. arXiv preprint arXiv:2301.06908 (2023)

22. McEwen, B.S.: Protective and damaging effects of stress mediators: central role of the brain. Dialogues Clin. Neurosci. **8**(4), 367–381 (2022)

23. Mozos, O.M., et al.: Stress detection using wearable physiological and sociometric sensors. Int. J. Neural Syst. **27**(02), 1650041 (2017)
24. Namvari, M., et al.: Photoplethysmography enabled wearable devices and stress detection: a scoping review. J. Pers. Med. **12**(11), 1792 (2022)
25. Nath, R.K., Thapliyal, H., Caban-Holt, A., Mohanty, S.P.: Machine learning based solutions for real-time stress monitoring. IEEE Consum. Electron. Mag. **9**(5), 34–41 (2020)
26. Park, J., Kim, J., Kim, S.P.: A study on the development of a day-to-day mental stress monitoring system using personal physiological data. In: 2018 18th International Conference on Control, Automation and Systems (ICCAS), pp. 900–903. IEEE (2018)
27. Pazienza, A., Monte, D.: Introducing the monitoring equipment mask environment. Sensors **22**(17), 6365 (2022)
28. Rachakonda, L., Mohanty, S.P., Kougianos, E., Sundaravadivel, P.: Stress-lysis: a DNN-integrated edge device for stress level detection in the IoMT. IEEE Trans. Consum. Electron. **65**, 474–483 (2019)
29. Samson, C., Koh, A.: Stress monitoring and recent advancements in wearable biosensors. Front. Bioeng. Biotechnol. **8**, 1037 (2020)
30. Škrjanc, I., Iglesias, J.A., Sanchis, A., Leite, D., Lughofer, E., Gomide, F.: Evolving fuzzy and neuro-fuzzy approaches in clustering, regression, identification, and classification: a survey. Inf. Sci. **490**, 344–368 (2019)
31. Tjoa, E., Guan, C.: A survey on explainable artificial intelligence (XAI): toward medical XAI. IEEE Trans. Neural Netw. Learn. Syst. **32**(11), 4793–4813 (2021)

Explainable Deep Ensemble to Diagnose COVID-19 from CT Scans

Lerina Aversano[1], Mario Luca Bernardi[1], Marta Cimitile[2],
Riccardo Pecori[3,4](✉), and Chiara Verdone[1]

[1] Department of Engineering, University of Sannio, 82100 Benevento, Italy
[2] Department of Law and Digital Society, UnitelmaSapienza University,
Rome, Italy
[3] SMARTEST Research Centre, eCampus University, 22060 Novedrate, CO, Italy
riccardo.pecori@uniecampus.it
[4] IMEM-CNR, Parco Area delle Scienze 37/A, 43124 Parma, Italy

Abstract. Research on identification methods for the Coronavirus Disease 2019 (COVID-19) has increased in the last years and the need for automated detection methods has surged as well. Computed Tomography scan images have demonstrated to contain useful and sufficient information to detect COVID-19 by using machine learning and computational intelligence techniques. However, in order to expand their adoption in medical clinics, COVID-19 detection approaches need to drive the experts in the overall comprehension of the classification, to check the validity and meaningfulness of the prediction results. Herein, we propose a deep learning approach based on an ensemble of convolutional neural networks with the aim of detecting, very accurately and in an explainable way, COVID-19 patients by leveraging CT scan images. We also take advantage of transfer learning and apply the aforementioned deep ensemble to a large publicly available dataset, by clustering the images per lung lobe. Our results show good classification performance, good generalization potentials, as well as quite interpretable outcomes.

Keywords: Deep Learning · Coronavirus · CT scans · COVID-19 · Explainable AI

1 Introduction

After COVID-19 spreading worldwide and becoming a devastating pandemic, several methods tried to automate its detection using different Artificial Intelligence (AI) techniques. Even if more than three years have passed since its first surge, COVID-19 is still the focus of several research challenges from both a medical and a technological point of view. Both points of views aim at developing effective and accurate diagnostic and treatment methods [30], exploiting the great quantity of data and information collected during these last three years. Despite the many improvements in the quick identification of COVID-19, the still open challenges regard the necessity to ensure high effectiveness in disease

© The Author(s), under exclusive license to Springer Nature Switzerland AG 2023
S. Massanet et al. (Eds.): EUSFLAT 2023/AGOP 2023, LNCS 14069, pp. 642–654, 2023.
https://doi.org/10.1007/978-3-031-39965-7_53

detection and good capability to drive the experts in the comprehension and checking of the prediction's reasons. Therefore, the usage of AI-based techniques is positively regarded for both the gathering of multiple data types as well as the identification of anomaly patterns caused by COVID-19 [24].

Computed Tomography (CT) scan images are one of the most used diagnosis method, employed also for other diseases [20], because their usage has some relevant advantages [9]. In this context, Deep Learning (DL), especially Convolutional Neural Networks (CNNs), demonstrated to be a valid methodology to identify COVID-19 patients. CT scans provide an internal 3D view of organs, which is exploited by DL models to analyze the effects of the illness on some parts of the lungs. Indeed, some recent researches [2,19] have shown that the sensitivity of CT scans for COVID-19 is greater than that of Reverse Transcriptase-Polymerase Chain Reaction (RT-PCR).

However, a limitation of these studies is the lack of interpretability, which decreases the possibility of using such approaches in real-world practical cases [1,29]. Explainability, interpretability, and causability [17] are very important concepts bound to the implementation of transparency and traceability of statistical black-box machine learning methods, particularly DL. The more the transparency, the more the decisions taken by DL models can be explained, understood, and accepted by doctors in the real daily practice.

In this paper, we propose a deep ensemble, based on different types of convolutional neural networks, capable to identify automatically and accurately COVID-19 by leveraging CT scan images. Three pre-trained convolutional neural networks, whose hyper-parameters have been opportunely optimized, are used to build the deep ensemble classifier. They analyze three different sets of images obtained after the clustering of CT scans, one cluster per lung lobe, a procedure often used in the application of pattern recognition techniques to medical images [6].

To validate this approach, the performed analyses consider a publicly available balanced dataset, made of the integration of other published ones. The dataset is made of the Extensive COVID-19 X-Ray and CT Chest Images Dataset[1] and the Coronavirus (COVID-19) CC-19 dataset[2]. The proposed approach includes a Grad-CAM [25] technique to help transparency and possible human interpretation of the classification results.

The rest of the document has the following structure. Section 2 summarizes the considered convolutional neural networks and the Grad-Cam approach, Sect. 3 discusses some recent related work, making comparisons with respect to the approaches used in this paper, which are described in Sect. 4. Section 5 details the carried out experiments, Sect. 6 reports some discussion thereof, while Section 7 summarizes what has been described in the article and outlines future research directions.

---

[1] https://doi.org/10.17632/8h65ywD2jr.3.
[2] https://github.com/abdkhanstd/COVID-19.

2 Background

In this section, we briefly summarize the considered convolutional neural networks and the used explainable technique, i.e., Grad-CAM.

2.1 Considered Convolutional Neural Networks

VGG-19 [28], i.e., Visual Geometry Group with 16 convolutional layers and 3 fully connected layers, was designed by the University of Oxford for a challenge regarding visual recognition in 2014. In this particular convolutional neural network, the fixed-size RGB image input (224 × 224 pixels), passes into various convolutional layers with 3 × 3 filters and 1-pixel step size. Each of the first two fully connected layers has 4,096 channels, while the third one is endowed with 1,000 channels. The output layer exploits a softmax activation function, whereas the hidden layers take advantage of the RELU function.

ResNet-50 [16] is a residual network, endowed with 50 layers, exploiting the "skip connection" technique to avoid the diminishing gradient issue. This type of convolutional neural network skips some of the stacked levels in the first phases of the training, with the re-use of activation functions of previous levels. This initial procedure compresses the network, making the learning procedure faster. In the following re-training, all the layers are expanded and the remainders investigate better the input image and its feature space.

Xception [7] is a convolutional neural network leveraging on i) "Depth-wise Separable Convolution" and ii) "Shortcuts between Convolutional blocks". Its structure, encompassing both traditional convolutional layers and depth-wise separable convolutional layers, is made of three main parts: Entry Flow, Middle Flow, and Exit Flow. This type of convolutional neural network exploits the "Inception" rationale in an extreme way, i.e., it maps the spatial correlations for each output channel separately and, subsequently, a 1 × 1 depth-wise convolution is performed to catch possible cross-channel correlations.

MobileNet [18] is the first mobile computer vision model based on Tensor-Flow[3] and open-sourced by Google. This model of neural networks is lightweight because it exploits, in order to decrease the number of parameters, depth-wise separable convolutions. Moreover, its speed of training and its power consumption are related to the number of multiply-accumulates, a measure of fused multiplication and addition operations. Thus, this model is capable to get very accurate results also in applications embedded into resource-constrained devices.

2.2 Grad-CAM Technique

Grad-CAM is an evolution of the Class Activation Mapping (CAM) [32], able to generate a class-discriminative localization map for a variety of CNNs. This technique exploits the gradients of the score obtained by the classification model, with respect to the feature maps produced by the final convolutional layer, to

---

[3] https://www.tensorflow.org/.

identify the areas of an input image that most influenced the classification itself. A detailed description and a formalization of Grad-CAM can be found in [25], but we summarize it briefly in the following.

Focusing on the aim of obtaining a localization map $L^c_{Grad-CAM} \in \mathbb{R}^{u \times v}$ of width u and height v for any class c, various steps are performed.

First, given a class c, the gradient of the score y^c (before the softmax) is computed with respect to the activations of the characteristic map A^k of a convolutional layer $(\frac{\delta y^c}{\delta A^k})$. Then, the neuron significance weights α^c_k are computed as follows:

$$\alpha^c_k = \frac{1}{Z} \sum_i \sum_j \frac{\delta y^c}{\delta A^k_{ij}}, \tag{1}$$

where i and j are the indices of width and height on which the back propagated gradients are global-average-pooled. α^c_k encapsulates the relevance of feature map k for a target class c and can be seen as a partial linearization of the network downstream from A.

Finally, when the score for c is calculated, the class-discriminative localization map can be generated. It is obtained as a weighted combination of forward activation maps sent to a ReLU by focusing attention only on the features that positively influence the interest class. The formalization is reported in the following:

$$L^c_{Grad-CAM} = ReLU \left(\sum_k \alpha^c_k A^k \right) \tag{2}$$

3   Related Work

Since 2020, several researches have applied DL for the early detection and diagnosis of COVID-19 [23], initially with no focus on the explainability, but only on the classification performance.

The authors of the contribution in [19] proposed a deep learning framework to automatically identify and classify, in a weakly supervised manner, the infected regions of the lungs of the patients. The proposed solution used retrospective CT images, coming from different sources, and achieved good performance in discriminating various cases of pneumonia and COVID-19. COVNet, a 3D deep learning model, was also proposed in [22], reaching an AUC value equal to 96% for discriminating between ill and healthy patients. In [14], LSTM neural networks and Q-deformed entropy handcrafted features were used to distinguish COVID-19, pneumonia, and healthy cases by using CT scans of the lungs. The best performance topped an accuracy equal to 99.68%. In [3], ten convolutional neural networks were tested, on a specifically built dataset, to identify COVID-19 patients from non-COVID19 ones. The considered neural networks were MobileNet-V2, AlexNet, VGG-19, VGG-16, SqueezeNet, GoogleNet, Xception, ResNet-50, ResNet-101, and ResNet-18. ResNet-101 resulted to be the best one with an AUC equal to 99.40%.

The main drawback of these researches is the small amount of publicly available datasets characterized by high-quality images. As a consequence, in [27] the authors created an integrated dataset of lung CT scans to work on more actual cases, with images coming from various places. However, they also applied data augmentation methods to extend the usable instances.

In the current literature, we can also find ensembles of DL techniques to identify COVID-19 patients from CT scans, solutions that usually have better performance than the single classifiers [33]. An ensemble of LSTM networks is, for example, analyzed in [26], while in [12], an ensemble is employed to decrease the inter-observer variability in the identification of COVID-19 patients.

As regards explainability, it has been tackled only more recently. For example, in [5] the authors apply deep learning and XAI to detect COVID-19, Tuberculosis, and Pneumonia. In this paper, lightweight CNNs were used for the classification, while the explanatory part was in charge of Grad-CAM, SHAP, and LIME. Differently from our study, the considered dataset was composed of CXR images. Zou et al. [34] proposed an XAI ensemble based on SHAP and Grad-CAM++ to detect both Pneumonia and COVID-19, but on a private dataset of CXR images and using Xception and a fully-connected neural network. Differently, the authors of the contribution in [8] apply XAI to predict oxygen requirements and detect 20 abnormal radiographic features by using always CXR images and Grad-CAM in conjunction with deep convolutional neural networks (DenseNet-121). In [11] the authors apply different types of convolutional neural networks, i.e., VGG16, VGG19, EfficientNetB0, ResNet50, and ResNet101, to CT scan images, creating then two ensembles of the best performing networks endowed also with XAI. However, it is no clear which explainable technique has been applied to the considered ensembles. In [15], the authors apply two types of deep convolutional neural networks, namely VGG11 and VGG16, and three explainable techniques, namely Composite Layer-wise Propagation, Single Taylor Decomposition, and Deep Taylor Decomposition, to shed light on the outcomes of the black-box neural network models classifying viral pneumonia, COVID-19, as well as healthy subjects from X-ray images. Finally, in [31], the authors try to apply XAI to CT scans to detect, in an interpretable way, COVID-19 patients. They use, together with a U-Net, an explainable module based on CAM, LIME, and SHAP before the final global average pooling layer, reaching an overall accuracy on the binary classification equal to 89.23%, training on a private Chinese dataset and testing on a publicly available one. However, they do not use an ensemble of neural networks nor the lobes clustering of the lung images.

Differently from the reviewed related papers, we herein apply an ensemble of convolutional neural networks to a novel dataset created through the integration of other publicly available datasets, with no need of data augmentation or synthetic data. This choice allows the improvement of the generalization capabilities of the considered approach, which, moreover, is based on lobe clustering of the CT scan images. This subdivision permits the specialization on a certain lobe because it captures the local distribution of some specific patterns of damages [10]. Moreover, the clustering allows for a better application of XAI and the interpretation of its outcomes on the part of clinicians.

4 Approach

The explainable COVID-19 detection approach proposed in this paper is detailed in Fig. 1. It consists of: i) an ensemble classifier using majority voting, to identify patients suffering from COVID-19 by leveraging CT scan images and ii) a Grad-CAM interpreter, able to identify the areas of the CT scan images more relevant for the prediction.

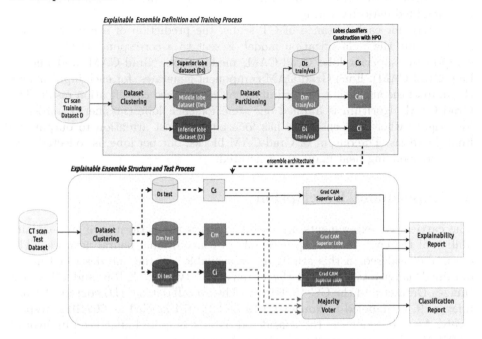

Fig. 1. Considered explainable ensemble of multiple classifiers.

The figure shows, in the upper part, the training process. The initial dataset D was processed using as clustering procedure K-means and as distance metric a variant of the Structural Similarity Index Metric. The suitable number of clusters (i.e., 3) for K-means was found through a silhouette coefficient-based method [4]. As a consequence, three training and validation datasets were generated, perfectly matching the three different segments of a lung (superior lobe, medium lobe, and inferior lobe). According to this, the obtained datasets were named: D_S, D_M, D_I. Consequently, the training process exploited three single neural network classifiers (one for each lobe): C_S, C_M, C_I. In this work, several pre-trained transfer-learning-based CNN classifiers have been tested for the binary classification of CT scan images into two classes, namely Covid and Non-Covid. Overall, the splitting of training, validation, test sets is performed across the images of different patients, not between patients.

The lower part of Fig. 1 describes the ensemble structure when used for the inference of novel, never seen, images. The ensemble is obtained as a combination of C_S, C_M, C_I and uses a majority voting strategy for each instance of CT scan to be classified. The single classifiers produce predictions that are the input of the majority voter component. This component takes all the single classifiers' results and produces the classification report according to the majority of outcomes of the single classifiers. Our approach could be also extended to a multi-classification task (healthy patients and different types or degrees of COVID-19 patients). In this case, when the majority voter cannot find a unique majority, our solution could be easily extended by applying weighted methods, i.e., weighted majority voting.

Finally, for each instance of CT scans, the prediction of every single classifier, within their classification model, is sent to a corresponding Grad-CAM component (superior lobe Grad-CAM, medium lobe Grad-CAM, and inferior lobe Grad-CAM). Each Grad-CAM component generates, for each input image, the map of the areas that better influence the obtained classification result. The Grad-CAM algorithm is applied one time for each lobe classifier, in order to investigate where the ensemble has focused the most attention to output the final diagnosis. The output of Grad-CAM blocks, one per lobe, is collected, and the corresponding heat maps are generated.

5   Experiment Description

The carried out experiments are useful to assess the performance and explainability of the considered deep ensemble of convolutional neural networks. The dataset considered in this study, freely available[4], is the one described in [4], obtained as an integration of the Extensive COVID-19 X-Ray and CT Chest Images Dataset and the CC-19 dataset. The overall dataset (D) contains 23,398 images, 9,324 labeled as Non-COVID19 and 14,074 labeled as COVID19, respectively. As a consequence, the considered dataset is quite imbalanced in favor of COVID19 class according to a ratio of about 60:40.

We evaluated the performance of the proposed approach by considering different pre-trained network models, i.e., VGG, Xception, ResNet, and MobileNet, and various mixes of the following parameters:

- *no. of fully connected layers*: the final fully connected block has a number of fully connected (FC) layers ranging in the [2, 6] interval;
- *scheme of the neurons*: the number of neurons per FC layer varies in the [1, 256] range;
- *dropout probability layout*: varying in the [0.10, 0.25] interval;
- *optimizer*: we have considered SGD with Nesterov's accelerated gradient [13], Nadam, and RMSProp optimization algorithms.

The single deep neural network classifiers have been trained by varying the number of *layers* and the *number of epochs* and using the binary cross-entropy as a loss function. The single neural network classifiers and the deep ensemble have been implemented in Python by leveraging Keras[5] on top of Tensorflow.

---

[4] https://bit.ly/34QJUSd.
[5] https://keras.io/.

Accuracy and *Loss* have been used to validate the training performance. They are inversely proportional: when one is increasing, the other one is decreasing, and vice versa. Moreover, the classification results were evaluated, in the testing phase, by considering the following metrics:

$$\text{Accuracy} = \frac{tp + tn}{tp + tn + fp + fn},$$

$$\text{Precision (P)} = \frac{tp}{tp + fp},$$

$$\text{Recall (R)} = \frac{tp}{tp + fn},$$

$$F1 - score = 2 \times \frac{Precision \times Recall}{Precision + Recall},$$

where *tp* are true positives, *fp* are false positives, *fn* are false negatives, and *tn* are true negatives. We have also considered the ROC Area (Area Under the Curve - AUC), expressing the probability that a randomly selected relevant instance is classified above a not relevant one.

Finally, the carried out experiments also allowed the evaluation of the capability of the deep ensemble to give correct interpretations of the obtained predictions. This evaluation was performed by manually evaluating the correctness of the masks generated by the explainability component with the support of an expert radiologist.

All experiments were carried out by exploiting a machine endowed with an Intel Core i9 7920X (18 cores), with 2 GPUs (NVIDIA RTX 3090 24 GB of RAM) and 64 GB of RAM.

6   Results and Discussion

In this section, we show the main results of the carried out experiments, both in terms of performance and of interpretability.

Table 1 shows, in the first three rows, the best classifier architectures obtained for each lobe (clustered datasets), as well as the relative performance. The last row of the table also reports the overall ensemble performance.

We observe that the best results are obtained by the ensemble and the medium classifiers, which achieve almost the same outcomes in the considered metrics. This suggests that the most interesting images, for the COVID-19 detection goal, are those of the medium lung lobe and are collected in D_m.

In the best cases, highlighted in bold in Table 1, the F1-score, which takes into account the imbalance of the dataset, is equal to 96.9%, so rather high.

Table 1. Best classifiers per lobe, their hyper-parameters, and the final scores of the considered metrics.

Lobe	Base Model	FC Layers	FC Neurons Scheme	FC Dropouts Scheme	Optimizer	P	R	F1
Inferior	VGG19	6	216 -137-124 - 64 - 48 -16	0.15 - 0.15 - 0.15 - 0.10 - 0.12 -0.10	SGD	94.7%	95.1%	94.9%
Medium	RESNET50	5	104 -104 - 50 - 50 - 20	0.25 - 0.10 - 0.14 - 0.13 - N	NADAM	96.7%	**97.1%**	**96.9%**
Superior	VGG19	4	122 - 118 - 64 - 24	0.18 - N - 0.12 -0.10	RMSProp	94.8%	95.1%	95.0%
Ensemble	-	-	-	-	-	**96.8%**	97.0%	**96.9%**

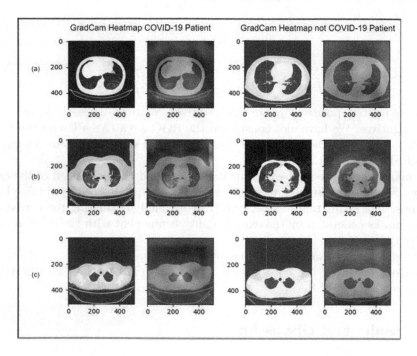

Fig. 2. Examples of the Grad-CAM heatmaps for the inferior lobe (a), the medium lobe (b) and the superior lobe (c) for a sick (left) and a healthy (right) patient.

Considering the point of view of the explainability of the proposed approach, Fig. 2 shows examples of heatmaps generated by using the Grad-CAM components and MobileNet. Indeed, all the neural networks, tested in the classification phase, have been evaluated in terms of explainability, but we chose to show the results of MobileNET since it is a lighter neural network and, by providing comparable explanations, it is much more suitable for being integrated in the context of ready-to-use outpatients and portable devices.

Each row of the figure refers to a specific section of the lung (inferior, medium, and superior). The left side of the figure concerns heatmaps constructed for a COVID-19 patient, while the right part concerns Grad-CAM heatmaps constructed on a healthy control subject.

For each considered patient, we can see a pair of images for each lobe. In particular, the leftmost one is the considered scan of a COVID-19 patient or a healthy control patient, depending on the case, while the rightmost one is the overlapping of the heatmap generated by the Grad-CAM component for the specific scan, superimposed to the scan itself.

Looking at the figures, we observed that the most interesting results are obtained by considering the medium lobe, confirming the previous observation of medium lobe clustering images as the most discriminant ones in terms of performance.

Looking at the medium lobe (b), in the figure, we can observe that in the case of a COVID-19 patient, the heatmap highlights (yellow colored areas) a part of the scan image corresponding to an actual alveolar damage. Indeed, according to the medical literature [21], the highlighted areas can be heavily affected by COVID-19.

Conversely, looking at the healthy patient heatmap for the medium lobe, we observe that in this case, the highlighted yellow area is quite extended and with lower intensity, showing that, when the pathology is missing, the most discriminant classification zones are far less concentrated.

Finally, looking at the other lobes, i.e., superior and inferior, no clear discriminant zones are found in the heatmaps. Only in the case of the superior lobe a tiny yellow area can be detected in the case of COVID-19 patients.

7   Conclusions

In this article, we have applied an explainable deep ensemble approach to identify COVID-19 patients by leveraging CT scan images clustered per lung lobe. Computerized tomography images have been clustered according to the three main parts of a lung (superior, medium, and inferior lobe) and employed to train both single convolutional neural networks and an ensemble of multiple classifiers composed of them. The approach also includes the optimization of the single classifiers and the majority strategy for the final voting procedure in the multiple ensemble classifier. Finally, Grad-CAM components have been included allowing us to obtain the heatmaps that highlight the areas of the CT scan images which influence the most the classifier decision (COVID-19 patient or healthy subject).

The obtained results show good performance of the proposed ensemble classifier in COVID-19 detection (96.9% of F1-score in the best case). While the best result are obtained using the majority voting among all classifiers, the medium lobe seems to be the most discriminating one. This is also confirmed looking at the Grad-CAM heatmaps, which show the best ability to identify widespread alveolar damage exactly in the case of medium lobe.

The main drawback of this study is the limited validation of the proposed approach with respect to its ability to give useful insights to the medical staff. According to this, in our future work, a larger study about the explainable results will be carried out with a larger set of experiments and the participation of a team of medical experts.

Acknowledgments. The authors are grateful to Dr. Gaetana Cremone, Department of Radiology, "G. Fucito" Hospital, Mercato San Severino, SA, Italy, for her contribution in the evaluation of the explainability results. Prof. Riccardo Pecori is a member of the INdAM GNCS research group.

References

1. Explainable AI to improve acceptance of convolutional neural networks for automatic classification of dopamine transporter spect in the diagnosis of clinically uncertain parkinsonian syndromes. Eur. J. Nucl. Med. Mol. Imaging **49**(4), 1176–1186 (2022)
2. Ahuja, S., Panigrahi, B., Dey, N., et al.: Deep transfer learning-based automated detection of COVID-19 from lung CT scan slices. Appl. Intell. **51**, 571–585 (2020)
3. Ardakani, A.A., Kanafi, A.R., Acharya, U.R., Khadem, N., Mohammadi, A.: Application of deep learning technique to manage COVID-19 in routine clinical practice using CT images: results of 10 convolutional neural networks. Comput. Biol. Med. **121**, 103795 (2020)
4. Aversano, L., Bernardi, M.L., Cimitile, M., Pecori, R.: Deep neural networks ensemble to detect COVID-19 from CT scans. Pattern Recognit. **120**, 108135 (2021)
5. Bhandari, M., Shahi, T.B., Siku, B., Neupane, A.: Explanatory classification of CXR images into COVID-19, pneumonia and tuberculosis using deep learning and XAI. Comput. Biol. Med. **150**, 106156 (2022)
6. Bose, A., Mali, K.: Type-reduced vague possibilistic fuzzy clustering for medical images. Pattern Recogn. **112**, 107784 (2021)
7. Chollet, F.: Xception: Deep learning with depthwise separable convolutions. In: 2017 IEEE Conference on Computer Vision and Pattern Recognition (CVPR), pp. 1800–1807 (2017)
8. Chung, J., et al.: Prediction of oxygen requirement in patients with COVID-19 using a pre-trained chest radiograph XAI model: efficient development of auditable risk prediction models via a fine-tuning approach. Sci. Rep. **12**(1), 21164 (2022)
9. Chung, M., et al.: CT imaging features of 2019 novel coronavirus (2019-nCoV). Radiology **295**(1), 202–207 (2020)
10. Colombi, D., et al.: Well-aerated lung on admitting chest CT to predict adverse outcome in COVID-19 pneumonia. Radiology **296**(2), E86–E96 (2020)
11. Dipto, S.M., Afifa, I., Sagor, M.K., Reza, M.T., Alam, M.A.: Interpretable COVID-19 classification leveraging ensemble neural network and XAI. In: Rojas, I., Castillo-Secilla, D., Herrera, L.J., Pomares, H. (eds.) BIOMESIP 2021. LNCS, vol. 12940, pp. 380–391. Springer, Cham (2021). https://doi.org/10.1007/978-3-030-88163-4_33
12. Gifani, P., Shalbaf, A., Vafaeezadeh, M.: Automated detection of COVID-19 using ensemble of transfer learning with deep convolutional neural network based on ct scans. Int. J. Comput. Assist. Radiol. Surg. **16**(1), 115–123 (2021)
13. Gitman, I., Lang, H., Zhang, P., Xiao, L.: Understanding the role of momentum in stochastic gradient methods. In: Wallach, H., Larochelle, H., Beygelzimer, A., d'Alché-Buc, F., Fox, E., Garnett, R. (eds.) Advances in Neural Information Processing Systems, vol. 32. Curran Associates, Inc. (2019)
14. Hasan, A.M., AL-Jawad, M.M., Jalab, H.A., Shaiba, H., Ibrahim, R.W., AL-Shamasneh, A.R.: Classification of COVID-19 coronavirus, pneumonia and healthy

lungs in CT scans using q-deformed entropy and deep learning features. Entropy **22**(5), 517 (2020)

15. Hassan, M.M., AlQahtani, S.A., Alelaiwi, A., Papa, J.P.: Explaining COVID-19 diagnosis with Taylor decompositions. Neural Comput. Appl. (2022). S.I.: Deep Learning in Multimodal Medical Imaging for Cancer Detection

16. He, K., Zhang, X., Ren, S., Sun, J.: Deep residual learning for image recognition. In: 2016 IEEE Conference on Computer Vision and Pattern Recognition (CVPR), pp. 770–778 (2016)

17. Holzinger, A., Langs, G., Denk, H., Zatloukal, K., Müller, H.: Causability and explainability of artificial intelligence in medicine. WIREs Data Min. Knowl. Discov. **9**(4), e1312 (2019)

18. Howard, A.G., et al.: MobileNets: efficient convolutional neural networks for mobile vision applications (2017)

19. Hu, S., et al.: Weakly supervised deep learning for COVID-19 infection detection and classification from CT images. IEEE Access **8**, 118869–118883 (2020)

20. Jeon, B., Jang, Y., Shim, H., Chang, H.J.: Identification of coronary arteries in CT images by Bayesian analysis of geometric relations among anatomical landmarks. Pattern Recogn. **96**, 106958 (2019)

21. Kwee, T.C., Kwee, R.M.: Chest CT in covid-19: what the radiologist needs to know. RadioGraphics **40**(7), 1848–1865 (2020). pMID: 33095680

22. Li, L., et al.: Using artificial intelligence to detect COVID-19 and community-acquired pneumonia based on pulmonary CT: evaluation of the diagnostic accuracy. Radiology **296**(2), E65–E71 (2020)

23. Roy, S., et al.: Deep learning for classification and localization of COVID-19 markers in point-of-care lung ultrasound. IEEE Trans. Med. Imaging **39**(8), 2676–2687 (2020)

24. Santosh, K.C.: AI-driven tools for coronavirus outbreak: need of active learning and cross-population train/test models on multitudinal/multimodal data. J. Med. Syst. **44**(5), 93 (2020)

25. Selvaraju, R., Cogswell, M., Das, A., Vedantam, R., Parikh, D., Batra, D.: Grad-CAM: visual explanations from deep networks via gradient-based localization. arXiv preprint arXiv:1610.02391 (2016)

26. Shastri, S., Singh, K., Kumar, S., Kour, P., Mansotra, V.: Deep-LSTM ensemble framework to forecast COVID-19: an insight to the global pandemic. Int. J. Inf. Technol. **13**, 1291–1301 (2021)

27. Silva, P., et al.: COVID-19 detection in CT images with deep learning: a voting-based scheme and cross-datasets analysis. Inf. Med. Unlock. **20**, 100427 (2020)

28. Simonyan, K., Zisserman, A.: Very deep convolutional networks for large-scale image recognition. In: Bengio, Y., LeCun, Y. (eds.) 3rd International Conference on Learning Representations, ICLR 2015, San Diego, CA, USA, 7–9 May 2015, Conference Track Proceedings (2015)

29. Tamburis, O., Mangia, M., Contenti, M., Mercurio, G., Rossi Mori, A.: The LITIS conceptual framework: measuring eHealth readiness and adoption dynamics across the healthcare organizations. Heal. Technol. **2**(2), 97–112 (2012)

30. Xiaowei, X., et al.: Deep learning system to screen coronavirus disease 2019 pneumoniax (2020)

31. Ye, Q., Xia, J., Yang, G.: Explainable AI for COVID-19 CT classifiers: an initial comparison study. In: 2021 IEEE 34th International Symposium on Computer-Based Medical Systems (CBMS), pp. 521–526 (2021)

32. Zhou, B., Khosla, A., Lapedriza, A., Oliva, A., Torralba, A.: Learning deep features for discriminative localization. In: IEEE Conference on Computer Vision and Pattern Recognition. IEEE Computer Society (2016)
33. Zhou, T., Lu, H., Yang, Z., Qiu, S., Huo, B., Dong, Y.: The ensemble deep learning model for novel COVID-19 on CT images. Appl. Soft Comput. **98**, 106885 (2021)
34. Zou, L., et al.: Ensemble image explainable AI (XAI) algorithm for severe community-acquired pneumonia and COVID-19 respiratory infections. IEEE Trans. Artif. Intell. **4**(2), 242–254 (2023). https://doi.org/10.1109/TAI.2022. 3153754

SPECIAL SESSION 9: Fuzzy Implication Functions

A Study of Monometrics from Fuzzy Logic Connectives

Kavit Nanavati[(✉)][iD], Megha Gupta[iD], and Balasubramaniam Jayaram[iD]

Department of Mathematics, Indian Institute of Technology Hyderabad,
Sangareddy 502284, Telangana, India
{ma20resch01004,ma16m18p100001}@iith.ac.in,
jbala@maths.iith.ac.in

Abstract. Recently, monometrics have attracted interest for their applications in fields such as decision making, penalty-based aggregation, and binary classification. In this work, we investigate various distance functions defined in the literature using fuzzy logic connectives and examine if and when they are monometrics on the unit interval. Further, taking a cue from the construction of distance functions using fuzzy implications, we offer a way to construct distance functions from monotonic fuzzy logic connectives using fuzzy negation and examine the conditions under which they yield a metric and a monometric on a partially ordered set.

Keywords: Fuzzy Logic Connectives · Fuzzy Implication · Distance Function · Monometric

1 Introduction

In the literature, there have been a few works that have dealt with the construction of metrics from fuzzy logic connectives that are commutative, associative, or monotonic on the unit interval [0,1], for instance, t-norms, t-conorms, copulas or quasi-copulas [1–4,7]. Recently [6], Nanavati et *al.* have proposed a construction of a distance function from a fuzzy logic connective that does not satisfy any of the above properties, i.e., from fuzzy implications. Further, the authors have shown the condition under which it is a metric with the help of a transitivity-type functional inequality. Interestingly, this distance function always yields a monometric on the underlying partially ordered set(poset) $(\mathcal{X}, \preceq)$.

1.1 Motivation for and Contributions of This Work

In the recent past, monometrics on a poset, have garnered a lot of attention for their important role in decision-making, penalty-based data aggregation, and binary classification [5,8–10]. One of the major challenges herein is that of obtaining monometrics on a given poset. Our first contribution in this work

---

Supported by SERB under the project MTR/2020/000506.

S. Massanet et al. (Eds.): EUSFLAT 2023/AGOP 2023, LNCS 14069, pp. 657–666, 2023.
https://doi.org/10.1007/978-3-031-39965-7_54

is to show if and when the already proposed distance functions from fuzzy logic connectives yield monometric on [0,1].

Further, taking a cue from the work of Nanavati et al. [6], we see that the property required for a distance function obtained from a fuzzy implication I to be a monometric on [0,1] is essentially the mixed monotonicity of I. Our second contribution is in defining a distance function from any monotonic fuzzy logic connective defined on the unit interval [0,1] using fuzzy negation and showing if and when it is a metric and a monometric on [0,1]. Towards this end, we also show that the monometrics obtained from fuzzy logic connectives, defined on [0,1], can be generalised to a poset $(\mathcal{X}, \preceq)$ through an order-preserving map.

In the quest for defining a distance function using any monotonic fuzzy logic connective, we have also proposed a new class of fuzzy implication using a t-norm T and a fuzzy negation N and have studied its properties in this work.

1.2   Outline of This Work

Firstly, in Sect. 2, we discuss the distance functions that have already been proposed in the literature using various fuzzy logic connectives and show the conditions under which they yield monometrics on [0,1]. Next, in Sect. 3, we show that a distance function defined on [0,1] can be easily lifted to a non-empty set $\mathcal{X}$. In Sect. 4, we propose a construction of a distance function using monotone fuzzy logic connectives on [0,1] and show the conditions under which it is a metric. We also show if and when it yields a monometric on [0,1]. This leads us to propose a new family of fuzzy implications on [0,1], see Sect. 4.1.

2   Distances from FLCs: A Literature Survey

In the literature, several constructions of distance functions from fuzzy logic connectives have been proposed and the conditions under which they yield a metric have been investigated [2,4,6,7]. In this section, we study these distance functions and see if and when these distance functions yield a monometric on [0,1]. We begin by recalling the definition of distance functions and monometrics on the unit interval.

Definition 1. *A symmetric function* $d : \mathcal{X} \times \mathcal{X} \to [0, +\infty)$ *is called a* **distance function** *on* $\mathcal{X}$ *if it satisfies the following property for any* $x, y \in \mathcal{X}$:

$$x = y \implies d(x, y) = 0. \tag{P1}$$

Further, it is called a **metric** *if the converse of* (P1) *holds, and it also satisfies the triangle inequality, i.e., for any* $x, y, z \in \mathcal{X}$,

$$d(x, z) \leq d(x, y) + d(y, z). \tag{P2}$$

Definition 2. *A function* $d : [0,1]^2 \to [0, +\infty)$ *is called a* **monometric** *on* [0,1] *if, for every* $x, y, z \in [0,1]$, (P1) *and its converse holds, and the following mono-compatibility property is satisfied:*

$$x \leq y \leq z \implies \max(d(x, y), d(y, z)) \leq d(x, z). \tag{MC}$$

Below, we examine the existing distances in the literature and investigate when they yield a monometric on [0,1].

2.1   From T-Norms

We begin by discussing the first construction of a distance function using fuzzy logic connectives as proposed by Alsina in [4].

Definition 3 (cf. [4]). *Given a t-norm T, $d_T : [0,1]^2 \to [0,1]$ is defined as:*

$$d_T(x,y) = \begin{cases} 0, & \text{if } x = y, \\ 1 - T(1-x, 1-y) - T(x,y), & \text{otherwise.} \end{cases} \tag{1}$$

Theorem 1 (cf. [4]). *If T is a t-norm and a copula, then d_T is a metric on* [0,1].

However, the converse of the above theorem need not be true, i.e., t-norms that are not copulas can give rise to a metric, for instance, continuous non-strict Archimedean t-norms or nilpotent t-norms (see [7]).

Below, we present examples of t-norms T for which the d_T defined in (1) is a/not a monometric on [0,1].

Example 1 Consider $T(x,y) = \min(x,y)$. Then $d_T(x,y) = |x - y|$ is a monometric on [0,1].

Example 2 Consider $T(x,y) = xy$. Then $d_T(x,y) = x + y - 2xy$ is not a monometric on [0,1], since

$$0.2 \le 0.3 \le 0.4 \text{ but } 0.46 = d_T(0.3, 0.4) > d_T(0.2, 0.4) = 0.44.$$

Below, we characterise t-norms that ensure d_T yields a monometric on [0,1].

Theorem 2 *Let T be a t-norm. d_T is a monometric on* [0,1]*, if and only if for every $x \le y \le z$, $T(1-x, 1-z) + T(x,z) \le T(y,z) + T(1-y, 1-z)$.*

2.2   From T-Norms and T-Conorms

In [2], the authors construct metrics for the more general case of any t-norm and t-conorm, and a characterization of t-norms that define metric is given in case the t-norms have the same zero region as the Łukasiewicz t-norm. We study this distance function in this section.

Definition 4 (cf. [2]). *Given a t-norm T, and a t-conorm S, $d_{T,S} : [0,1]^2 \to$* [0,1] *is defined as:*

$$d_{T,S}(x,y) = \begin{cases} 0, & \text{if } x = y, \\ S(x,y) - T(x,y), & \text{otherwise.} \end{cases} \tag{2}$$

Definition 5. *A function $F : [0,1]^2 \to [0,1]$ satisfies the Lipschitz condition with constant 1 if*

$$|F(x,y) - F(x',y')| \leq |x - x'| + |y - y'|$$

for all $x, x', y, y' \in [0,1]$.

Theorem 3 (cf. [4]). *Let T be a t-norm and S be a t-conorm. If T and S satisfy the Lipschitz condition with constant 1, then $d_{T,S}$ is a metric on $[0,1]$.*

Note that in Sect. 3 of [3], Alsina proposed the same distance function for Quasi-copulas, instead of t-norms, and their dual, not necessarily of the same quasi-copula, for t-conorms, and showed that it always yields a metric. Now, we shall see examples for which $d_{T,S}$ defined in (2) is a/not a monometric on $[0,1]$.

Example 3 Consider $S(x,y) = \max(x,y)$, and $T(x,y) = xy$. Then $d_{T,S}(x,y) = \max(x,y)(1 - \min(x,y))$ is a monometric on $[0,1]$.

Example 4 Consider $S_{\mathbf{LK}}(x,y) = \min(x+y,1)$, and $T(x,y) = \max(x+y-1,0)$. Then

$$d_{T,S}(x,y) = \begin{cases} x + y, & \text{if } x + y < 1, \\ 2 - (x + y), & \text{otherwise.} \end{cases}$$

is not a monometric on $[0,1]$ since

$$0.4 \leq 0.7 \leq 0.8 \text{ but } 0.9 = d_{T,S}(0.4, 0.7) > d_{T,S}(0.4, 0.8) = 0.8.$$

Note that since $T(x,y) = \max(x+y-1,0)$ is a quasi-copula, the distance function given in Sect. 3, [3], also does not always yield a monometric on the unit interval.

Below, we present the conditions that ensure $d_{T,S}$ yields a monometric on $[0,1]$.

Theorem 4 *Let T be a t-norm and S be a t-conorm. $d_{T,S}$ is a monometric on $[0,1]$, if and only if for every $x \leq y \leq z$, $S(x,z) + T(y,z) \geq S(y,z) + T(x,z) \geq S(x,z) + T(x,y) \geq S(x,y) + T(x,z)$.*

2.3   From Quasi-Copulas

In [3], Alsina constructs a distance function using quasi-copulas as defined below and shows that it is always a metric.

Definition 6 (cf. Section 4, [3]). *Given two commutative quasi-copulas Q_1 and Q_2, $d_{Q_1,Q_2} : [0,1]^2 \to [0,1]$ is defined as:*

$$d_{Q_1,Q_2}(x,y) = \begin{cases} 0, & \text{if } x = y, \\ x + y - Q_1(x,y) - Q_2(x,y), & \text{otherwise.} \end{cases} \quad (3)$$

Theorem 5 (cf. Section 4, [3]). *Let Q_1 and Q_2 be quasi-copulas. d_{Q_1,Q_2} is always a metric in $[0,1]$.*

Now, we shall see an example for which d_{Q_1,Q_2} defined in (3) is a monometric on [0,1].

Example 5. If $Q_1(x, y) = \min(x, y)$, an $Q_2(x, y) = xy$, then $d_{Q_1,Q_2}(x, y) = |y - x|$, and it is always a monometric on [0,1].

However, d_{Q_1,Q_2} need not always yield a monometric.

Example 6. Consider $Q_1(x, y) = Q_2(x, y) = xy$. Then $d_{Q_1,Q_2}(x, y) = d_T(x, y)$ in Example 2, which is not a monometric on [0,1].

Below, we present the conditions that ensure d_{Q_1,Q_2} yields a monometric on [0,1].

Theorem 6. *Let Q_1 and Q_2 be quasi-copulas. d_{Q_1,Q_2} is a monometric on [0,1], if and only if for every $x \leq y \leq z$, the following properties hold:*

1. $(Q_1(x, z) - Q_1(x, y)) + (Q_2(x, z) - Q_2(x, y)) \leq z - y$.
2. $(Q_1(x, z) - Q_1(y, z)) + (Q_2(x, z) - Q_2(y, z)) \leq x - y$.

2.4   From Symmetric Differences

In [1], the authors offer a complete characterization of the triple (T, S, N) of t-norm, t-conorm, and fuzzy negation that define symmetric difference functions, which are metrics.

Definition 7. *A symmetric function $\triangle : [0,1]^2 \to [0,1]$ is called a symmetric difference function if for all $a \in [0,1]$,*

$$\triangle(a, a) = 0, \triangle(a, 0) = a, \triangle(a, 1) = N(a),$$

where N is a strong negation.

Definition 8 (cf. [1]). *Given a t-norm T, t-conorm S, and a strong negation N, $d_{T,S,N} : [0,1]^2 \to [0,1]$ is defined as:*

$$d_{T,S,N}(x, y) = S(T(x, N(y)), T(N(x), y)). \tag{4}$$

Theorem 7 (cf. [1]). *Let T be a t-norm, S a t-conorm, and N a strong fuzzy negation. $d_{T,S,N}$ is a symmetric difference function if and only if $T(a, N(a)) = 0$ for all $a \in [0,1]$.*

Theorem 8 (cf. [1]). *Given a triplet (T, S, N), the function $d_{T,S,N}$ defined in (4) is a metric if, and only if, the following conditions hold:*

(i) $T(a, b) = 0$ if, and only if, $b \leq N(a)$.
(ii) *For all $x \in [0,1]$ and any $\epsilon, \delta \in \mathbb{R}$ such that $0 \leq \epsilon \leq 1-x$, $0 \leq \delta \leq 1-N(x)$, the following inequality holds:*

$$T(x + \epsilon, N(x) + \delta) \leq T(x, N(x) + \delta) + T(x + \epsilon, N(x)). \tag{5}$$

Note that $d_{T,S,N}$ need not be always a monometric on the unit interval. Below we present a condition under which it is a monometric on [0,1].

Theorem 9. *Let T be a t-norm, S a t-conorm, and N a strong fuzzy negation. Then the following are equivalent:*

(i) $T(a,b) = 0$ if and only if $b \leq N(a)$, for all $a,b \in [0,1]$.
(ii) $d_{T,S,N}$ is a monometric on [0,1].

Example 7 (cf. [1]). Let T be a nilpotent minimum t-norm and $N(x) = 1 - x$. Then

$$d_{T,S,N}(a,b) = \begin{cases} 0 & \text{if } a = b, \\ b & \text{if } a < b, a + b \leq 1, \\ 1 - a & \text{if } a < b, a + b \geq 1, \\ a & \text{if } a > b, a + b \leq 1, \\ 1 - b & \text{if } a > b, a + b \geq 1. \end{cases}$$

is a monometric on [0,1].

2.5   From Fuzzy Implications

In [6], the authors propose a construction of distance functions from fuzzy implications on [0,1] and show that it is a metric if it satisfies a transitive-type functional equation. They also show that it is always a monometric on [0,1]. Note that throughout the paper, we will only consider fuzzy implications that satisfy the following condition:

$$I(x,y) > 0, \text{whenever } x \leq y, \quad x,y \in [0,1].$$

Definition 9 (cf. [6]). *Given a fuzzy implication I, $d_I : [0,1]^2 \to [0,1]$ is defined as:*

$$d_I(x,y) = \begin{cases} 0, & \text{if } x = y, \\ I(x,y), & \text{if } x < y, \\ I(y,x), & \text{if } y < x. \end{cases} \tag{6}$$

Definition 10. *A function $F : [0,1]^2 \to [0,1]$ is said to satisfy $S_{\mathbf{LK}}$-transitivity if*

$$S_{\mathbf{LK}}(F(x,y), F(y,z)) \geq F(x,z) \text{ for all } x,y,z \in [0,1]. \tag{SFT}$$

Theorem 10 (cf. [6]). *If I satisfies (SFT), then d_I is a metric on [0,1].*

Theorem 11 (cf. [6]). *d_I is always a monometric on [0,1].*

3   Lifting the Distance

We see that the distance functions studied above have all been defined on the unit interval. However, one can easily lift the distance functions d defined on the unit interval to a non-empty set $\mathcal{X}$ as follows.

Remark 1. Let $f : \mathcal{X} \to [0,1]$. Define $d_f^* : \mathcal{X} \times \mathcal{X} \to [0,1]$ as follows: for any $x, y \in \mathcal{X}$,

$$d_f^*(x,y) = d(f(x), f(y)).$$

Note that d_f^* is a metric on $\mathcal{X}$ if d is a metric on the unit interval.

Further, in order to define a monometric on a partially ordered set $(\mathcal{X}, \preceq)$, we need an order-preserving map from $(\mathcal{X}, \preceq)$ to the unit interval. In [6], the authors showed that there always exists an order-preserving map from a partially ordered set to the ordered set of the unit interval.

Theorem 12 (cf. Theorem 5, [6]). *Let $(\mathcal{X}, \preceq)$ be a partially ordered set. Then there always exists a non-constant order-preserving map $f : \mathcal{X} \to [0,1]$, i.e., $x \preceq y$ implies $f(x) \leq f(y)$.*

Using the result given above, one can easily show that given an order-preserving $f : \mathcal{X} \to [0,1]$, d_f^* is a monometric on $(\mathcal{X}, \preceq)$ if d is a monometric on the unit interval.

4   Construction of Monometrics from FLCs

In the previous section, we saw that most of the distance functions defined in the literature using fuzzy logic connectives do not always yield a monometric on $[0,1]$. However, the distance function d_I, obtained using fuzzy implication, always yields a monometric on $[0,1]$. The reason for that is the hybrid monotonicity of fuzzy implications. In this section, taking cue from the construction of d_I, we offer a construction of distance functions using other fuzzy logic connectives. We then explore the conditions under which they yield metrics and monometrics on the unit interval.

Definition 11. *Let F be a monotonic fuzzy logic connective and N be a fuzzy negation. Define $F_N : [0,1]^2 \to [0,1]$ as $F_N(x,y) = F(N(x), y)$. We define $d_{F_N} : [0,1]^2 \to [0,1]$ as:*

$$d_{F_N}(x,y) = \begin{cases} 0, & \text{if } x = y, \\ F_N(x,y), & \text{if } x < y, \\ F_N(y,x), & \text{if } y < x. \end{cases} \tag{7}$$

Theorem 13. *d_{F_N} yields a metric on $[0,1]$ if and only if the following properties are satisfied:*

(i) $F_N(x,y) > 0$ *whenever* $x < y$.
(ii) F_N *satisfies* (SFT).

Theorem 14. *d_{F_N} yields a monometric on $[0,1]$ if and only if $F_N(x,y) > 0$ whenever $x < y$.*

Remark 2. (i) Notice that if F is a fuzzy disjunction, then F_N is a fuzzy implication. Hence, the obtained d_{F_N} would be d_I for a suitable $I = F_N$.
(ii) If F is a positive t-norm, overlap function, or a copula, then d_{F_N} would always yield a monometric for any positive negation N. Further, if F_N satisfies (SFT), d_{F_N} yields a metric.
(iii) When $d_{T,S,N}$ given in Definition 8 is a symmetric difference function, it is of the form d_{T_N}.

The following representation theorem highlights the importance of d_{F_N}.

Theorem 15. *The following statements are equivalent:*

1. *d is a symmetric monometric on $([0,1], \leq)$.*
2. *There exists a monotonic $F : [0,1]^2 \to [0,1]$ and a strong negation N such that $d_{F_N} = d$.*

4.1   Yet Another Class of Fuzzy Implications

We observe that to ensure (MC), we create a function that is decreasing in the first variable by using a fuzzy negation and increasing in the second variable. Our distance function thus satisfies the hybrid monotonicity that a fuzzy implication possesses. If we demand the required boundary conditions, we can construct a fuzzy implication from monotone functions. In the following definition, we propose such a construction.

Definition 12. *Let F be a monotonic fuzzy logic connective and N be a fuzzy negation. Define $F_N : [0,1]^2 \to [0,1]$ as $F_N(x,y) = F(N(x),y)$. We define $I_{F,N} : [0,1]^2 \to [0,1]$ as:*

$$I_{F_N}(x,y) = \begin{cases} 1, & \text{if } x = 0 \text{ or } y = 1, \\ F_N(x,y), & \text{otherwise.} \end{cases} \tag{8}$$

For all monotonic fuzzy logic connectives $F : [0,1]^2 \to [0,1]$, satisfying $F(0,0) = 0$, we have the following theorem.

Theorem 16. *I_{F_N} is a fuzzy implication.*

Remark 3. 1. If F is a t-conorm, we obtain the well-known family of (S,N)-implication.
2. I_{F_N} satisfies the neutrality property if and only if 0 is the left identity of F. Thus for fuzzy logic connectives where 0 is not the left identity, I_{F_N} does not satisfy the neutrality property and is different from the major families of fuzzy implications like (S,N)-, R, and Yager's.

3. If F is a t-norm, we get

$$I_{T_N}(x,y) = \begin{cases} 1, & \text{if } x = 0 \text{ or } y = 1, \\ T_N(x,y), & \text{otherwise.} \end{cases} \tag{9}$$

Notice that I_{T_N} does not satisfy the neutrality property, ordering property, or the identity principle. However, it does satisfy the exchange principle.

5   Concluding Remarks

In this work, we considered the different distance functions that have been defined in the literature using fuzzy logic connectives and explored if and when they yield a monometric on [0,1]. Further, we made use of the construction of distance function from fuzzy implications to offer alternative distance functions using monotonic fuzzy logic connectives. We have also presented the conditions under which they yield a metric and a monometric on [0,1]. Our work, thus expands our armoury of practical distance functions using monotonic fuzzy logic connectives. Finally, we construct a family of fuzzy implications from our distance function, and study its properties. Our work clearly shows that behind every symmetric monometric lurks a fuzzy logic connective.

Acknowledgements. The third author would like to acknowledge the support obtained from SERB under the project MTR/2020/000506 for the work contained in this submission.

References

1. Aguiló, I., Calvo, T., Martín, J., Mayor, G., Suñer, J.: On distances derived from symmetric difference functions. In: 2015 Conference of the International Fuzzy Systems Association and the European Society for Fuzzy Logic and Technology (IFSA-EUSFLAT-15). pp. 632–637. Atlantis Press (2015)
2. Aguiló, I., Martín, J., Mayor, G., Suñer, J.: On distances derived from t-norms. Fuzzy Sets Syst. **278**, 40–47 (2015)
3. Alsina, C.: On quasi-copulas and metrics. In: Cuadras, C.M., Fortiana, J., Rodriguez-Lallena, J.A. (eds.) Distributions With Given Marginals and Statistical Modelling, pp. 1–8. Springer, Dordrecht (2002). https://doi.org/10.1007/978-94-017-0061-0_1
4. Alsina, C.: On some metrics induced by copulas. In: Walter, W. (ed.) General Inequalities 4. International Series of Numerical Mathematics, pp. 397–397. Springer, Basel (1984). https://doi.org/10.1007/978-3-0348-6259-2_38
5. Gupta, M., Jayaram, B.: On the role of monometrics in nearest neighbor classification. (Manuscript under preparation)
6. Nanavati, K., Gupta, M., Jayaram, B.: Pseudo-monometrics from fuzzy implications. Fuzzy Sets Syst. (2022). https://doi.org/10.1016/j.fss.2022.11.001
7. Ouyang, Y.: A note on metrics induced by copulas. Fuzzy Sets Syst. **191**, 122–125 (2012)

8. Pérez-Fernández, R., Baets, B.D.: The role of betweenness relations, monometrics and penalty functions in data aggregation. In: Proceedings of the IFSA-SCIS 2017, pp. 1–6. IEEE (2017)
9. Pérez-Fernández, R., De Baets, B.: On the role of monometrics in penalty-based data aggregation. IEEE Trans. Fuzzy Systems **27**(7), 1456–1468 (2019)
10. Pérez-Fernández, R., Rademaker, M., De Baets, B.: Monometrics and their role in the rationalisation of ranking rules. Inf. Fusion **34**, 16–27 (2017)

Monometrics on Lattice Betweenness Using Fuzzy Implications

Megha Gupta$^{(\boxtimes)}$ (ID), Kavit Nanavati (ID), and Balasubramaniam Jayaram (ID)

Department of Mathematics, Indian Institute of Technology Hyderabad,
Sangareddy 502284, Telangana, India
{ma16m18p100001,ma20resch01004}@iith.ac.in, jbala@maths.iith.ac.in

Abstract. In the recent past, monometrics w.r.t. a ternary relation defined on a set, called the betweenness relation, have garnered a lot of attention for their important role in decision making, penalty-based data aggregation, and binary classification. One of the major challenges herein is that of obtaining monometrics on a given betweenness set $(\mathcal{X}, \mathrm{B})$. In this work, we propose a couple of constructions of monometrics on lattice betweenness, the latter using fuzzy implications. Our work seems to suggest that fuzzy implications are rather a natural choice for constructing monometrics on lattice betweenness. It also justifies the exploration of fuzzy logic connectives on general posets, primarily bounded lattices.

Keywords: Fuzzy Implication · Betweenness Relation · Lattice Betweenness · Monometric

1 Introduction

Betweenness relations were introduced to capture the notion of betweenness amongst a triplet of elements that are either related geometrically or through an order.

The notion of a betweenness relation can be traced back to works done more than a century ago to that of Pasch [15] and Huntington and Kline [11]. It was further studied by Huntington [10], Pitcher and Smiley [21], and Transue [25]. In these works, various types of transitivities of betweenness were proposed and explored. Betweenness relations have traditionally been studied largely theoretically. They have also been explored towards characterizing lattices [3,4,9,22,24], thereby showing their utility in lattice theory.

1.1 Motivation for and Contributions of This Work

Recently, these relations have also been shown to be of use in practical applications, especially in decision-making, penalty-based data aggregation, please see

Supported by SERB under the project MTR/2020/000506.

S. Massanet et al. (Eds.): EUSFLAT 2023/AGOP 2023, LNCS 14069, pp. 667–678, 2023.
https://doi.org/10.1007/978-3-031-39965-7_55

the works of De Baets and his group [16–20], and binary classification [8]. However, one of the major challenges is to define a distance function that captures the underlying betweenness relation(monometric) on a set $\mathcal{X}$. This forms the motivation to carry out our study.

In this work, we show that the distance function defined in [5] is a monometric on the given lattice betweenness relation. Further, we construct a distance function d_I, using a fuzzy implication I, on a given lattice L, and show when it is a monometric on the given lattice betweenness relation, proffering another application of fuzzy implications. Lastly, we examine if and when these distance functions are also metrics.

1.2 Outline of This Work

In the sequel, in Sect. 2, we begin by introducing the betweenness relations and defining one of the three important generalizations of the betweenness relation on a line, namely, lattice betweenness. We then introduce the distance functions compatible over a betweenness relation, known as monometrics, and discuss their existence on lattice betweenness. In Sect. 3, we show a construction of monometrics on the lattice betweenness relation and show the sufficient conditions under which they would be metrics. Finally, we discuss an alternate construction of monometrics on the lattice betweenness relation using fuzzy implications defined on a bounded lattice, highlighting the utility of studying fuzzy logic connectives on bounded lattices.

2   Monometrics on Betweenness Relations

Monometrics play an integral role in applications such as rationalisation of ranking rules, penalty-based aggregation, and binary classification.

In the problem of aggregation of rankings, given a profile of rankings, the aim is to obtain a single ranking that best represents the nature of this given profile. The aggregated rankings can be characterised as minimizing the distance from a consensus state using a distance function. In [20], it was proposed that the distance function should be replaced by a monometric, which essentially preserves the betweenness relation under consideration.

The study of penalty-based aggregation has been mainly confined to the domain of real numbers. In [17], the definition of penalty-based function was extended to accommodate more general structures and expand its scope beyond real numbers by demanding compatibility with a betweenness relation. It was shown that penalty-based functions could be constructed using monometrics on the given betweenness relation.

A distance function appears in almost every Data Analysis or Machine Learning algorithm, either explicitly as a metric or a norm, or implicitly as its dual, similarity measure, for instance, in the form of an inner product. That the general purpose distances may not be appropriate for all situations is well-known, see, for instance, an excellent articulation of the same in [26]. In [8], authors have claimed that the distance functions compatible with the relational structure(monometrics) present in the data are the most appropriate in the problem of binary classification, especially in nearest-neighbor classification.

In this section, we recall the definitions of betweenness relation, lattices, and monometric. We shall employ the definition of the betweenness relation given by Pitcher and Smiley in [21], without demanding the additional conditions concerning transitivity.

Definition 1. *Let* B *be a ternary relation on an* $\mathcal{X} \neq \emptyset$. *Then* B *is said to be a* **betweenness** *relation if* B *satisfies the following for any* $x, y, z \in \mathcal{X}$:

$$(x, y, z) \in \mathrm{B} \iff (z, y, x) \in \mathrm{B}, \tag{BS}$$

$$(x, y, z) \wedge (x, z, y) \in \mathrm{B} \iff y = z. \tag{BU}$$

Remark 1. (i) $(\mathcal{X}, \mathrm{B})$ is known as a Betweenness set or a beset. Also, $(x, y, z) \in \mathrm{B}$ is read as 'y is in between x and z'.

(ii) The minimal betweenneess relation B_0 on $\mathcal{X}$ is defined as follows:

$$\mathrm{B}_0 = \{(x, y, z) \in \mathcal{X}^3 \mid x = y \vee y = z\}.$$

(iii) A betweenness relation B is said to be transitive if for any $o, x, y, z \in \mathcal{X}$:

$$(o, x, y) \in \mathrm{B} \wedge (o, y, z) \in \mathrm{B} \implies (o, x, z) \in \mathrm{B}. \tag{BT}$$

Definition 2. *A* **lattice** *is an algebraic structure* $(L, \vee, \wedge)$, *consisting of a set* L *and two binary, commutative and associative operations* $\vee$ *and* $\wedge$ *on* L *satisfying the following axiomatic identities for all elements* $a, b \in L$ *(sometimes called absorption laws):*

$$a \vee (a \wedge b) = a$$
$$a \wedge (a \vee b) = a$$

Definition 3. *A lattice* $(L, \vee, \wedge)$ *is said to be* **bounded below** *by* $e \in L$, *if* $a \vee e = a$ *and* $a \wedge e = e$ *for every* $a \in L$.

Definition 4. *A lattice* $(L, \vee, \wedge)$ *is said to be a* **modular lattice** *if for any* $a, b \in L$ *such that* $a \vee b = b$ *and* $a \wedge b = a$, *modular law is satisfied for every* $x \in L$, *i.e.,*

$$a \vee (x \wedge b) = (a \vee x) \wedge b.$$

Definition 5 ([23]). **The Lattice Betweenness Relation** - *Let* $(L, \wedge, \vee)$ *be a lattice. Then*

$$\mathrm{B}_L := \{(a, b, c) \in L^3 \mid (a \wedge b) \vee (b \wedge c) = b = (a \vee b) \wedge (b \vee c)\}. \tag{1}$$

Definition 6. *A symmetric function* $d : \mathcal{X} \times \mathcal{X} \to \mathbb{R}_{\geq 0}$ *is called a **metric** on* $\mathcal{X}$ *if it satisfies the following properties for any* $x, y, z \in \mathcal{X}$:

$$x = y \iff d(x, y) = 0. \tag{P1}$$

and

$$d(x, z) \leq d(x, y) + d(y, z). \tag{P2}$$

Definition 7. *Consider a betweenness set* $(\mathcal{X}, \mathrm{B})$. *A function* $d : \mathcal{X} \times \mathcal{X} \to \mathbb{R}_{\geq 0}$ *is said to satisfy **mono-compatibility** (MC) if for every* $(x, y, z) \in \mathrm{B}$, *it holds that:*

$$\max(d(x, y), d(y, z)) \leq d(x, z). \tag{MC}$$

Definition 8 (cf. [17]). *Consider a betweenness set* $(\mathcal{X}, \mathrm{B})$. *A function* $d : \mathcal{X} \times \mathcal{X} \to \mathbb{R}_{\geq 0}$ *satisfying* (P1) *and* (MC) *is called a **monometric**(w.r.t.* $\mathrm{B})$.

In the next section, we present a construction of monometrics on lattice betweenness and show the employability of fuzzy implications for the same.

3 Monometrics on Lattice Betweenness

In [14], the authors define a mono-compatible distance, w.r.t. the betweenness relation $\mathrm{B}_{\preceq}$ obtained from a partially ordered set[1] $(\mathcal{X}, \preceq)$ which is defined as follows:

$$\mathrm{B}_{\preceq} = \mathrm{B}_0 \vee \{(x, y, z) \in \mathcal{X}^3 \mid x \preceq y \preceq z \ \vee \ z \preceq y \preceq x\}. \tag{2}$$

While any lattice $(L, \preceq)$ is a partially ordered set, $\mathrm{B}_{\preceq}$ is not equivalent to B_L, see Example 1. Hence, the problem that we are dealing with - that of obtaining a monometric on a lattice betweenness relation B_L - is different from the problem that has been dealt with in [13,14]. Below we present an example and some results that not only show that $\mathrm{B}_{\preceq}$ is not equivalent to B_L but also show the relation between them.

Example 1. Consider the lattice $(L = \{0, a, b, 1\}, \preceq)$ whose Hasse diagram is given in Fig. 1. Note that $(a, 0, b) \in \mathrm{B}_L$ but $(a, 0, b) \notin \mathrm{B}_{\preceq}$. Hence, $\mathrm{B}_L \neq \mathrm{B}_{\preceq}$.

In the following, we show the relation between the two types of betweenness relations and give the necessary and sufficient conditions for them to coincide.

Lemma 1. *Given a lattice* $(L, \preceq)$, $\mathrm{B}_{\preceq} \subseteq \mathrm{B}_L$.

Corollary 1. *If* d *is a monometric on* (L, B_L), *it is a monometric on* $(L, \mathrm{B}_{\preceq})$.

The following result shows that they actually coincide only when the lattice is of a special type.

Theorem 1. *Let* $(L, \preceq)$ *be a lattice.* $\mathrm{B}_{\preceq} = \mathrm{B}_L$ *if and only if* L *is a chain.*

---

[1] A set equipped with a reflexive, anti-symmetric, and transitive binary relation.

Fig. 1. Hasse diagram of $(L, \preceq)$ given in Example 1.

We now present a couple of constructions of monometrics on lattice betweenness relations and also discuss if and when they will be metrics on the underlying set.

3.1   Monometric on Lattice Betweenness

The construction of metrics on a lattice dates back to 1936 when Glivenko connected the structure of lattice and a metric, see [5,6]. Therein, the author defined a binary function on a lattice and studied when it would yield a metric. In this work, we study the conditions under which Glivenko's distance function yields a monometric with respect to the lattice betweenness relation.

Definition 9 ([5]).   *Let* $(L, \preceq)$ *be a lattice. Define* $d_M : L \times L \to \mathbb{R}_{\geq 0}$ *as*

$$d_M(x, y) = f(x \vee y) - f(x \wedge y) ,$$

where $f : (L, \preceq) \to (\mathbb{R}, \leq)$ *is an order-preserving function.*

Theorem 2.   *The function* d_M *defined on a lattice* L *as in Definition 9, is a monometric on the beset* (L, B_L) *if and only if for any* $x, y \in L$,

$$f(x \vee y) = f(x \wedge y) \iff x = y.$$

Example 2. Consider the lattice given in Example 1. Let us define $f : L \to \mathbb{R}$ as given in Table 1(a). Clearly, d_M, given in Table 1(b), is a monometric on (L, B_L).

Table 1. (a) The mapping f. (b) The pairwise distance matrix on L under d_M.

L	0	x	y	1
f	0	1	1	2

d_M	0	x	y	1
0	0	1	1	2
x	1	0	2	1
y	1	2	0	1
1	2	1	1	0

3.2 Monometric Using Fuzzy Implications

In this section, we utilise fuzzy implications to define a distance function on a given lattice L and show their applicability in obtaining a monometric on the lattice betweenness set (L, B_L). We begin by defining fuzzy implications and providing some examples of the same. We employ the standard definitions of the other fuzzy logic connectives (FLCs) and certain families of fuzzy implications discussed in this work and hence refer the readers to well-known sources in the literature for these definitions [1,12].

Definition 10. *A function* $I : [0, 1]^2 \to [0, 1]$ *is said to be a **fuzzy implication** if it is decreasing in the first variable, increasing in the second variable and satisfies* $I(0, 0) = 1$, $I(1, 1) = 1$ *and* $I(1, 0) = 0$.

We shall denote the set of all fuzzy implications by $\mathbb{FI}$. Table 2 lists a few examples of fuzzy implications. For more examples, see [1].

Table 2. Some examples of fuzzy implications

Name	Formula
Reichenbach	$I_{\mathbf{RC}} = 1 - x + xy$
Weber	$I_{\mathbf{WB}}(x, y) = \begin{cases} 1, & \text{if } x < 1, \\ y, & \text{otherwise.} \end{cases}$

Definition 11. *Let* $I \in \mathbb{FI}$ *and* $(L, \preceq)$ *be a lattice. Define* $d_I : L \times L \to [0, 1]$ *as*

$$d_I(x, y) = \begin{cases} 0, & \text{if } x = y, \\ I(f(x \wedge y), f(x \vee y)), & \text{otherwise.} \end{cases}$$

where $f : (L, \preceq) \to ([0, 1], \leq)$ *is an order-preserving function.*

Note that different fuzzy implications can lead to the same distance function. For instance, every R-implication yields a discrete metric.

Theorem 3. *The function* d_I *defined on a lattice* L *as in Definition 11, is a monometric on the betweenness set* (L, B_L) *if and only if* I *satisfies the following:*

$$I(x, y) > 0, \text{whenever } x \leq y. \tag{3}$$

We shall denote the set of fuzzy implications satisfying the condition (3) by $\mathbb{FI}^+$.

Example 3. Consider the lattice given in Example 1. Let us define $f : L \to \mathbb{R}$ as given in Table 3(a). Consider $I = I_{\mathbf{RC}}$, then d_I, given in Table 3(b), is a monometric on (L, B_L).

Table 3. (a) The mapping f. (b) The pairwise distance matrix on L under d_I.

L	0	x	y	1
f	0.25	0.75	0.75	1

d_I	0	x	y	1
0	0	0.9375	0.9375	1
x	0.9375	0	1	1
y	0.9375	1	0	1
1	1	1	1	0

Remark 2. Since, an order-preserving map $f : (L, \preceq) \rightarrow ([0,1], \leq)$ always exists (see [14], Theorem 5), for every I satisfying the condition in Theorem 3, we can obtain a monometric on $(L, \preceq)$. Thus, fuzzy implications are both a natural choice and a rich source for the construction of monometrics because of their mixed monotonicity.

3.3 Metrics Using Fuzzy Implications

In this section, we study certain conditions on f or I or both, which will ensure that d_I yields a metric.

Theorem 4. *The distance function d_I defined on a lattice L as in Definition 11, is a metric on L if $I \in \mathbb{FI}^+$ and for each $x, y \in L$,*

$$I(f(x), f(x)) + I(f(y), f(y)) \geq I(f(x \wedge y), f(x \vee y)) . \qquad (4)$$

The above result makes it convenient to construct examples of metrics from fuzzy implications, for instance, by allowing us to pick suitable fuzzy implications based on their behaviour on the diagonal. We now show some sufficient conditions on I and f that ensure the satisfaction of (4), and hence lead d_I to become a metric.

Remark 3. (i) A fuzzy implication I satisfying the identity principle, i.e., $I(x,x) = 1$, satisfies (4), and d_I is a discrete metric.
(ii) If $I(x,x) \geq 0.5$ for all $x \in [0,1]$, then it satisfies (4). Note that $I_{\mathbf{RC}}(x,x) \geq 0.5$, and d_I is a non-discrete metric in Example 3.
(iii) Note that not every monometric is a metric. Consider, for instance, the I in Example 2 in [14]. Given the lattice $([0,1], \leq)$, where $\leq$ represents the usual order, with f as the identity map, the same d_I would be obtained. While it is a monometric on $([0,1], B_\leq)$, it is not a metric.

Now, we discuss the sufficient conditions under which some families of fuzzy implications yield metrics.

Corollary 2. *If I is an R-implication then d_I is a discrete metric.*

Theorem 5. *If I is an (S, N)-implication where the pair (S, N) satisfies the law of excluded middle, i.e., $S(N(x), x) = 1$, then d_I is a metric.*

Theorem 6. *If I is an (S, N)-implication where $S \leq S_{\mathbf{LK}}$ then d_I is a metric if any one of the following is true for every $x, y \in L$:*

(i) $N(f(x)) + f(y) \geq N(f(x \wedge y)) + f(x \vee y)$,
(ii) $N(f(x)) + N(f(y)) \geq N(f(x \wedge y)) + f(x \vee y)$,
(iii) $f(x) + N(f(y)) \geq N(f(x \wedge y)) + f(x \vee y)$,
(iv) $f(x) + f(y) \geq N(f(x \wedge y)) + f(x \vee y)$.

4   Betweenness Sets Obtained from a Lattice: A Characterisation

While Theorem 3 depicts the existence of monometrics on betweenness sets obtained from lattices, the existence of a monometric on an arbitrary beset is not clear.

In the following results, by providing a characterisation of betweenness sets obtained from a bounded below modular lattice, we illustrate the scope and applicability of Theorem 3.

Let $(\mathcal{X}, \mathrm{B})$ be a betweenness set such that B satisfies (BT). The relation

$$x \leq_e y \iff (e, x, y) \in \mathrm{B}, \tag{5}$$

always yields a partially ordered set. In the result below, we present the condition that ensures that the obtained relation gives a lattice.

Theorem 7. *Let $\mathcal{X} \neq \emptyset$ and B be a betweenness relation on $\mathcal{X}$ satisfying (BT). Let $e \in \mathcal{X}$ be arbitrary but fixed and define the relation $x \leq_e y$ as in (5). $(\mathcal{X}, \leq_e)$ is a lattice if and only if the following condition is satisfied for any $x, y \in \mathcal{X}$ such that $(e, x, y), (e, y, x) \notin \mathrm{B}$:*

1. *There exists l such that $\{(e, l, x), (e, l, y)\} \subset \mathrm{B}$ and if there exist n such that $\{(e, n, x), (e, n, y)\} \subset \mathrm{B}$ then $(e, n, l) \in \mathrm{B}$.*
2. *There exists m such that $\{(e, x, m), (e, y, m)\} \subset \mathrm{B}$ and if there exist n such that $\{(e, x, n), (e, y, n)\} \subset \mathrm{B}$ then $(e, m, n) \in \mathrm{B}$.*

The above result imposes a condition on the betweenness set B, in relation to the chosen element e, to ensure that the order relation leads not only to a poset but a lattice. In the following theorem, we give the conditions under which we can ascertain if the given betweenness relation is indeed induced from a bounded below modular lattice.

Theorem 8. *Let $(\mathcal{X}, \mathrm{B})$ be a betweenness set satisfying* (BT) *and $(\mathcal{X}, \preceq_e)$ is a lattice such that B satisfies the following property with the special element $e \in \mathcal{X}$: Whenever $x \neq y \neq z \in \mathcal{X}$,*

$$(x,y,z) \in \mathrm{B} \iff \begin{cases} & \{(e,x,y),(e,y,z)\} \subset \mathrm{B} \\ or & \{(e,y,x),(e,z,y)\} \subset \mathrm{B} \\ or & \{(e,y,x),(e,y,z)\} \subset \mathrm{B} \text{ such that} \\ & \exists \text{ no } \ell \in \mathcal{X} \setminus \{x,y,z\} \text{ such that} \\ & \{(e,\ell,x),(e,\ell,z),(x,\ell,z)\} \subset \mathrm{B} \\ or & \{(e,x,y),(e,z,y)\} \subset \mathrm{B} \text{ such that} \\ & \exists \text{ no } \ell \in \mathcal{X} \setminus \{x,y,z\} \text{ such that} \\ & \{(e,x,\ell),(e,z,\ell),(x,\ell,z)\} \subset \mathrm{B} \\ or & (e,x,y) \in \mathrm{B}, \{(e,y,z),(e,x,z)\} \not\subset \mathrm{B} \text{ such that} \\ & \exists \text{ unique } l \text{ such that} \\ & \{(e,l,y),(e,l,z),(x,y,l),(y,l,z)\} \in \mathrm{B} \\ or & (e,y,x) \in \mathrm{B}, \{(e,y,z),(e,x,z)\} \not\subset \mathrm{B} \text{ such that} \\ & \exists \text{ unique } l \text{ such that} \\ & \{(e,y,l),(e,z,l),(y,l,z),(l,y,x)\} \in \mathrm{B} \\ or & (e,z,y) \in \mathrm{B}, \{(e,y,z),(e,z,x)\} \not\subset \mathrm{B} \text{ such that} \\ & \exists \text{ unique } l \text{ such that} \\ & \{(e,l,y),(e,l,x),(z,y,l),(y,l,x)\} \in \mathrm{B} \\ or & (e,y,z) \in \mathrm{B}, \{(e,y,x),(e,z,x)\} \not\subset \mathrm{B} \text{ such that} \\ & \exists \text{ unique } l \text{ such that} \\ & \{(e,y,l),(e,x,l),(y,l,x),(l,y,z)\} \in \mathrm{B} \\ or & \exists \text{ unique } l,m,n,o \in \mathcal{X} \setminus \{e\} \text{ such that} \\ & \{(e,l,x),(e,l,y),(x,l,y),(e,x,m),(e,y,m),(x,m,y), \\ & (e,n,y),(e,n,z),(y,n,z),(e,y,o),(e,z,o),(y,o,z)\} \in \mathrm{B} \ . \end{cases}$$

(6)

Then the following are true:

(i) $L_e = (\mathcal{X}, \preceq_e)$ *is a modular lattice bounded below by e.*

(ii) B_{L_e} *obtained from L_e coincides with B, i.e., $\mathrm{B} = \mathrm{B}_{L_e}$.*

In the following theorem, we characterise the betweenness relations obtained from a bounded below modular lattice.

Theorem 9. *Let $(\mathcal{X}, \mathrm{B})$ be a betweenness set satisfying* (BT). *Then the following are equivalent:*

(i) $L = (\mathcal{X}, \sqsubseteq)$ *is a bounded below modular lattice and $\mathrm{B} = \mathrm{B}_L$.*

(ii) *There exists an $e \in \mathcal{X}$ such that $L_e = (\mathcal{X}, \preceq_e)$ is a lattice, B satisfies (6) with e and $\mathrm{B} = \mathrm{B}_{L_e}$.*

Corollary 3. *Let $(\mathcal{X}, \mathrm{B})$ be a betweenness set satisfying* (BT) *and $(\mathcal{X}, \preceq_e)$ is a lattice such that B satisfies (6) with the special element $e \in \mathcal{X}$. Then there exists a monometric on $(\mathcal{X}, \mathrm{B})$.*

An Alternate Construction: An extension of fuzzy logic, which generalizes the ones considered up to the present, was proposed by Joseph Goguen in 1967, see [7]. In this extension, the membership values are drawn from arbitrary bounded lattices. Since then, various fuzzy logic connectives, including fuzzy implications, see for instance [2], have been extended to the setting of bounded lattices. However, applications of such constructions have not been clearly espoused. Note that if we have an implication defined on a bounded lattice, one can obtain a monometric w.r.t. the lattice betweenness relation by the construction given in the following definition.

Definition 12. *Let $I \in \mathbb{FI}$ and define $d_L : L \times L \to [0,1]$ as*

$$d_L(x,y) = \begin{cases} 0, & \text{if } x = y, \\ f(I(x \wedge y, x \vee y)), & \text{otherwise.} \end{cases}$$

where $f : (L, \preceq) \to ([0,1], \leq)$ is an increasing function.

Theorem 10. *The function d_L defined on a lattice L as in Definition 12, is a monometric on the betweenness set (L, B_L) if and only if*

$$f(x) = 0 \iff x = 0,$$

where 0 is the bottom element of L.

From the above theorem, one can easily construct a monometric on the lattice betweenness set through d_L that highlights the importance of studying fuzzy implications on bounded lattices.

5   Concluding Remarks

In this work, we consider the problem of finding a monometric on a given lattice betweenness relation. We provide two constructions for monometrics. The second construction method utilizes a fuzzy implication, highlighting the applicational value of the fuzzy logic connective. We also examined if and when the distance functions give rise to metrics.

Finally, we emphasize the benefits of studying fuzzy implications on general structures, such as bounded lattices, by providing an alternate construction for monometrics on lattice betweenness. We can then examine if and when d_L leads to a metric, and how properties of d_L vary with the choice of family of fuzzy implications. We intend to undertake such studies in our future works.

Acknowledgements. The third author would like to acknowledge the support obtained from SERB under the project MTR/2020/000506 for the work contained in this submission.

References

1. Baczyński, M., Jayaram, B.: Fuzzy Implications. Studies in Fuzziness and Soft Computing, vol. 231. Springer, Heidelberg (2008). https://doi.org/10.1007/978-3-540-69082-5
2. Bedregal, B., Beliakov, G., Bustince, H., Fernández, J., Pradera, A., Reiser, R.: (S, N)-implications on bounded lattices. In: Baczyński, M., Beliakov, G., Bustince Sola, H., Pradera, A. (eds.) Advances in Fuzzy Implication Functions. Studies in Fuzziness and Soft Computing, vol. 300, pp. 101–124. Springer, Heidelberg (2013). https://doi.org/10.1007/978-3-642-35677-3_5
3. Cibulskis, J.M.: A characterization of the lattice orderings on a set which induce a given betweenness. J. Lond. Math. Soc. 2(1), 480–482 (1969)
4. Düvelmeyer, N., Wenzel, W.: A characterization of ordered sets and lattices via betweenness relations. Results Math. 46, 237–250 (2004)
5. Glivenko, V.: Geometrie des systemes de choses normees. Am. J. Math. 58(4), 799–828 (1936)
6. Glivenko, V.: Contribution á l'Étude des systèmes de choses normées. Am. J. Math. 59(4), 941–956 (1937)
7. Goguen, J.: L-fuzzy sets. J. Math. Anal. Appl. 18(1), 145–174 (1967)
8. Gupta, M., Jayaram, B.: On the role of monodistances in nearest neighbor classification. (Manuscript under preparation)
9. Hedlíková, J., Katriňák, T.: On a characterization of lattices by the betweenness relation—on a problem of M. Kolibiar. Algebra Univ. 28, 389–400 (1991)
10. Huntington, E.V.: A new set of postulates for betweenness, with proof of complete independence. Trans. Am. Math. Soc. 26(2), 257–282 (1924)
11. Huntington, E.V., Kline, J.R.: Sets of independent postulates for betweenness. Trans. Am. Math. Soc. 18(3), 301–325 (1917)
12. Klement, E.P., Mesiar, R., Pap, E.: Triangular Norms, Trends in Logic, vol. 8. Kluwer Academic Publishers, Dordrecht (2000)
13. Nanavati, K., Gupta, M., Jayaram, B.: Monodistances from fuzzy implications. In: Ciucci, D., et al. (eds.) IPMU 2022. CCIS, vol. 1601, pp. 169–181. Springer, Cham (2022). https://doi.org/10.1007/978-3-031-08971-8_15
14. Nanavati, K., Gupta, M., Jayaram, B.: Pseudo-monometrics from fuzzy implications. Fuzzy Sets Syst. 466, 108429 (2022)
15. Pasch, M.: Vorlesungen über neuere Geometrie, vol. 23. Teubner, Leipzig, Berlin (1882)
16. Pérez-Fernández, R., Alonso, P., Díaz, I., Montes, S., De Baets, B.: Monotonicity-based consensus states for the monometric rationalisation of ranking rules and how they are affected by ties. Int. J. Approx. Reason. 91, 131–151 (2017)
17. Pérez-Fernández, R., De Baets, B.: The role of betweenness relations, monometrics and penalty functions in data aggregation. In: 2017 Joint 17th World Congress of International Fuzzy Systems Association and 9th International Conference on Soft Computing and Intelligent Systems (IFSA-SCIS), pp. 1–6. IEEE (2017)
18. Pérez-Fernández, R., De Baets, B.: On the role of monometrics in penalty-based data aggregation. IEEE Trans. Fuzzy Syst. 27(7), 1456–1468 (2019)
19. Pérez-Fernández, R., Díaz, I., Montes, S., De Baets, B.: Monotonicity of a profile of rankings with ties. In: Medina, J., et al. (eds.) IPMU 2018. CCIS, vol. 854, pp. 313–322. Springer, Cham (2018). https://doi.org/10.1007/978-3-319-91476-3_26
20. Pérez-Fernández, R., Rademaker, M., De Baets, B.: Monometrics and their role in the rationalisation of ranking rules. Inf. Fusion 34, 16–27 (2017)

21. Pitcher, E., Smiley, M.F.: Transitivities of betweenness. Trans. Am. Math. Soc. **52**(1), 95–114 (1942)
22. Sholander, M.: Trees, lattices, order, and betweenness. Proc. Am. Math. Soc. **3**(3), 369–381 (1952)
23. Smiley, M.F.: A comparison of algebraic, metric and lattice betweenness. Bull. Am. Math. Soc. **49**, 246–252 (1943)
24. Smiley, M., Transue, W.: Applications of transitivities of betweenness in lattice theory. Bull. Am. Math. Soc. **49**(4), 280–287 (1943)
25. Transue, W.: Remarks on transitivities of betweenness. Bull. Am. Math. Soc. **50**(2), 108–109 (1944)
26. Wang, Z., Bovik, A.C.: Mean squared error: love it or leave it? A new look at signal fidelity measures. IEEE Signal Process. Mag. **26**(1), 98–117 (2009)

Fuzzy Implications Using Bandler-Kohout Subproduct

Katarzyna Miś[1](✉)[iD], Kavit Nanavati[2][iD], and Megha Gupta[2][iD]

[1] University of Silesia in Katowice, Bankowa 14, 40-007 Katowice, Poland
katarzyna.mis@us.edu.pl
[2] Department of Mathematics, Indian Institute of Technology Hyderabad,
Telangana 502284, India
{ma20resch01004,ma16m18p100001}@iith.ac.in

Abstract. Bandler-Kohout subproduct is one of the well-known compositions of fuzzy relations. Recently, it has been shown that this can be used for constructing fuzzy implications. In this contribution, we further investigate this method by composing different fuzzy logic connectives such as conjunctions, t-norms, and t-conorms. We focus on the essential properties of these obtained fuzzy implications and analyse if they fulfill examined properties.

Keywords: Fuzzy Implication · T-norms · T-conorms · Bandler-Kohout subproduct

1 Introduction

In recent years, many different construction methods of fuzzy implications (FIs) have been investigated. This includes various compositions of two fuzzy logic connectives. The most known one is the $\sup -T$ composition, which was introduced in [10], and in general, can be given in the following way [13]:

$$(I \overset{T}{\circ} J)(x,y) = \sup_{z \in [0,1]} T(I(x,z), J(z,y)), \quad x, y \in [0,1], \tag{1}$$

where I, J are FIs and T is a t-norm. Another one is:

$$(I \circledast J)(x,y) = I(x, J(x,y)), \quad x, y \in [0,1],$$

where I, J are given FIs (see [9]). Note that $I \overset{T}{\circ} J$ is a fuzzy implication if and only if $(I \overset{T}{\circ} J)(1,0) = 0$ (see [1, Theorem 6.4.4]). However, $(I \circledast J)$ is always a fuzzy implication. Recently, another composition was considered to construct fuzzy implications, called the Bandler-Kohout subproduct(BKS) [2], given by:

$$(F_1 \overset{I}{\triangleleft} F_2)(x,y) = \inf_{z \in [0,1]} I(F_1(x,z), F_2(z,y)), \quad x, y \in [0,1], \tag{2}$$

S. Massanet et al. (Eds.): EUSFLAT 2023/AGOP 2023, LNCS 14069, pp. 679–688, 2023.
https://doi.org/10.1007/978-3-031-39965-7_56

where I is an FI but F_1, F_2 can be some other fuzzy logic connectives. $F_1 \overset{I}{\vartriangleleft} F_2$ is an FI, if F_1, F_2 are semicopulas or aggregation functions with neutral element 0, and I satisifes the property of the identity principle (see [7]).

In this contribution, we investigate the last mentioned construction type of FIs, focusing on the properties of received FIs. The paper is organised as follows. In Sect. 2, we give some definitions and properties of fuzzy logic connectives used in the sequel. In Sect. 3, we investigate properties of obtained FIs when F_1, and F_2 are t-norms. Section 4 involves the construction of FI when F_1 is a conjunction, and F_2 is an FI. In Sect. 5, we study if and when we obtain FIs using t-conorms. Finally, we give some conclusions and plans for future work.

2   Preliminaries

In this section, we begin by recalling the related definitions that will be useful in the sequel. For basic definitions and examples of fuzzy logic connectives such as t-norm, and t-conorm, we refer the readers to see [1,5,11].

Definition 1. *A function $C : [0,1]^2 \to [0,1]$ is called a **conjunction** if it satisfies the following conditions:*

(i) $C(0,1) = C(1,0) = 0$ and $C(1,1) = 1$,
(ii) C is non-decreasing with respect to each variable.

Definition 2 ([3]). *A function $C: [0,1]^2 \to [0,1]$ is called a **semicopula** if it satisfies the following conditions:*

(i) $C(x,1) = C(1,x) = x, \qquad x \in [0,1]$,
(ii) C is non-decreasing with respect to each variable.

Definition 3 ([1]). *A function $I: [0,1]^2 \to [0,1]$ is called a **fuzzy implication** if it satisfies the following conditions:*

(I1) I is non-increasing with respect to the first variable,
(I2) I is non-decreasing with respect to the second variable,
(I3) $I(0,0) = I(1,1) = 1$ and $I(1,0) = 0$.

The family of fuzzy implications will be denoted by $\mathcal{FI}$.

Definition 4 (see [1]). *We say that a fuzzy implication I satisfies*

*(i) the **identity principle**, if*

$$I(x,x) = 1, \qquad x \in [0,1], \tag{IP}$$

*(ii) the **left neutrality property**, if*

$$I(1,y) = y, \qquad y \in [0,1], \tag{NP}$$

*(iii) the **exchange principle**, if*

$$I(x, I(y, z)) = I(y, I(x, z)), \qquad x, y, z \in [0, 1], \qquad \text{(EP)}$$

*(iv) the **ordering property**, if*

$$I(x, y) = 1 \iff x \leq y, \qquad x, y \in [0, 1]. \qquad \text{(OP)}$$

Definition 5 ([1, **Definition 2.5.1**]). *A function* $I \colon [0, 1]^2 \to [0, 1]$ *is called an R-implication if there exists a t-norm* T *such that*

$$I(x, y) = \sup\{t \in [0, 1] : T(x, t) \leq y\}, \qquad x, y \in [0, 1]. \qquad (3)$$

If I *is generated from a t-norm* T, *then it will be denoted by* I_T.

Note that it is possible to generate an R-implication from just a fuzzy conjunction with specific properties (see [6]). Moreover, we will use the following result for a particular subclass of R-implications.

Theorem 1 ([1, **Proposition 2.5.2**]). *Let* T *be a t-norm. Then the following statements are equivalent:*

(i) T *is left-continuous.*
(ii) A pair (T, I_T) *satisfies the residual principle*

$$T(x, z) \leq y \iff I_T(x, y) \geq z, \qquad x, y, z \in [0, 1]. \qquad \text{(RP)}$$

(iii) The supremum in (3) *is the maximum, i.e.,*

$$I_T(x, y) = \max\{t \in [0, 1] \mid T(x, t) \leq y\}, \qquad x, y \in [0, 1].$$

Definition 6 ([1, **Definition 1.4.15**]). *Let* $I \in \mathcal{FI}$. *The function* $N_I : [0, 1] \to [0, 1]$ *defined as*

$$N_I(x) = I(x, 0), \qquad x \in [0, 1],$$

is called the natural negation of I.

3   Implications Using T-Norms

In [7], the author studied the construction of fuzzy implications using BKS composition of two t-norms. Therein, she observed that if I satisfies (IP) then the BKS composition of any two t-norms(or conjunctions) yields a fuzzy implication. She also studied if and when the obtained fuzzy implications satisfy (NP) and (IP) when I is an R-implication.

In this section, we study the other important properties such as (EP) and (OP) that are satisfied by the fuzzy implications obtained from some specific BKS composition of t-norms.

Proposition 1. *Let T_1, T_2 be t-norms such that $T_1 \leq T_2$ and $I \in \mathcal{FI}$ satisfy* (OP). *Then $T_1 \overset{I}{\vartriangleleft} T_2$ satisfies* (OP).

Proof. Let $J = T_1 \overset{I}{\vartriangleleft} T_2$ and $x, y \in [0, 1]$ such that $x \leq y$. Then, we have $T_1(x, z) \leq T_2(x, z) \leq T_2(y, z)$ for every $z \in [0, 1]$. Thus

$$J(x, y) = \inf_{z \in [0,1]} I(T_1(x, z), T_2(z, y)) = 1 .$$

Now, let us assume that $J(x, y) = 1$, then $I(T_1(x, z), T_2(z, y)) = 1$ for every $z \in [0, 1]$. Since, I satisfies (OP), for all $z \in [0, 1]$, we have $T_1(x, z) \leq T_2(z, y)$. Hence, $T_1(x, 1) \leq T_2(1, y) \implies x \leq y$.

Note that the converse of the above result is also true. In fact, a weaker condition (IP) is sufficient to prove it.

Proposition 2. *Let T_1, T_2 be t-norms and $I \in \mathcal{FI}$ satisfy* (OP). *If $T_1 \overset{I}{\vartriangleleft} T_2$ satisfies* (IP), *then $T_1 \leq T_2$.*

Proof. Since $T_1 \overset{I}{\vartriangleleft} T_2$ satisfies (IP), for all $x \in [0, 1]$, we have

$$\inf_{z \in [0,1]} I(T_1(x, z), T_2(z, x)) = 1 \implies I(T_1(x, z), T_2(z, x)) = 1 \text{ for all } z \in [0, 1],$$

which implies for all $z \in [0, 1]$, $T_1(x, z) \leq T_2(z, x)$, since I satisfies (OP) and hence $T_1 \leq T_2$.

In [7], various properties of $F = T_1 \overset{I_{T_i}}{\vartriangleleft} T_2, i = 1, 2$, were studied and the next result was shown for the case of $T_1 \leq T_2$. But it can be easily proved without this additional condition as shown below.

Proposition 3. *Let T_1, T_2 be t-norms such that T_2 is left-continuous, then* $T_1 \overset{I_{T_2}}{\vartriangleleft} T_2$ *satisfies* (NP).

Proof. Consider

$$(T_1 \overset{I_{T_2}}{\vartriangleleft} T_2)(1, y) = \inf_{z \in [0,1]} I_{T_2}(T_1(1, z), T_2(z, y)) = \inf_{z \in [0,1]} I_{T_2}(z, T_2(z, y)) .$$

Since T_2 is left-continuous, we have $T_2(z, y) \leq T_2(z, y) \iff I_{T_2}(z, T_2(z, y)) \geq y$. Hence, $\inf_{z \in [0,1]} I_{T_2}(z, T_2(z, y)) \geq y$.

Now, for $z = 1$, we have

$$I_{T_2}(1, T_2(1, y)) = I_{T_2}(1, y) = y ,$$

which implies $\inf_{z \in [0,1]} I_{T_2}(z, T_2(z, y)) = y$. Hence, $T_1 \overset{I_{T_2}}{\vartriangleleft} T_2(1, y) = y$.

In the following results, we show the conditions under which the operator $F = T_i \overset{I_{T_m}}{\vartriangleleft} T_j, i, j = 1, 2, m \in \{i, j\}$, satisfies (EP), and (OP).

The results follow from the fact that these operators lead to R-implications I_{T_1} or I_{T_2} as shown in [7, Propositions 3,4] and since R-implications obtained from left-continuous t-norms satisfy (EP), and (OP), the following corollaries hold.

Corollary 1. *Let T_1, T_2 be t-norms such that $T_1 \leq T_2$, and T_1 is left-continuous. Then the following statements hold:*

(i) $T_1 \overset{I_{T_1}}{\vartriangleleft} T_2$ satisfies (EP), and (OP).

(ii) $T_2 \overset{I_{T_1}}{\vartriangleleft} T_1$ satisfies (EP), and (OP).

4 Implications Using a Conjunction and an Implication

We know that the BKS composition of two t-norms yields a fuzzy implication. In this section, we see that if C is a conjunction and J is a fuzzy implication, then $C \overset{I}{\vartriangleleft} J \in \mathcal{FI}$, i.e., the BKS composition of a conjunction and fuzzy implication also yields a fuzzy implication.

Proposition 4. *Let C be a conjunction and $I, J \in \mathcal{FI}$, then $C \overset{I}{\vartriangleleft} J \in \mathcal{FI}$.*

Proof. Let us first verify the boundary conditions.

$$(C \overset{I}{\vartriangleleft} J)(1, 0) = \inf_{z \in [0,1]} I(C(1, z), J(z, 0))$$
$$\leq I(C(1, 1), J(1, 0)) = 0$$

Thus $(C \overset{I}{\vartriangleleft} J)(1, 0) = 0$. Similarly,

$$(C \overset{I}{\vartriangleleft} J)(0, 0) = \inf_{z \in [0,1]} I(C(0, z), J(z, 0))$$
$$= \inf_{z \in [0,1]} I(0, J(z, 0)) = 1$$

Similarly,

$$(C \overset{I}{\vartriangleleft} J)(1, 1) = \inf_{z \in [0,1]} I(C(1, z), J(z, 1))$$
$$= \inf_{z \in [0,1]} I(C(1, z), 1) = 1$$

We now need to check if $C \overset{I}{\vartriangleleft} J$ satisfies mixed monotonicity.

$$x_1 \leq x_2 \implies C(x_1, z) \leq C(x_2, z)$$
$$\implies I(C(x_2, z), J(z, y)) \leq I(C(x_1, z), J(z, y))$$
$$\implies \inf_{z \in [0,1]} I(C(x_2, z), J(z, y)) \leq \inf_{z \in [0,1]} I(C(x_1, z), J(z, y))$$

Thus, $C \overset{I}{\vartriangleleft} J$ is non-increasing in the first variable. Similarly,

$$y_1 \leq y_2 \implies J(z, y_1) \leq J(z, y_2)$$
$$\implies I(C(x, z), J(z, y_1)) \leq I(C(x, z), J(z, y_2))$$
$$\implies \inf_{z \in [0,1]} I(C(x, z), J(z, y_1)) \leq \inf_{z \in [0,1]} I(C(x, z), J(z, y_2))$$

Thus, $C \overset{I}{\vartriangleleft} J$ is non-decreasing in the second variable, and $C \overset{I}{\vartriangleleft} J$ is a fuzzy implication.

Note that, unlike the case of BKS composition of two t-norms(or conjunctions) where the corresponding fuzzy implication has to satisfy (IP), in the above theorem, the fuzzy implication I need not satisfy any further properties to ensure that $C \overset{I}{\vartriangleleft} J$ yields a fuzzy implication.

Since $C \overset{I}{\vartriangleleft} J$ is a fuzzy implication, we can define a finite sequence of the $\overset{I}{\vartriangleleft}$ composition, leading to multiple examples of fuzzy implications.

Proposition 5. *Let $n \in \mathbb{N}$, $C_1, \ldots, C_n$ be conjunctions and let $I_1, \ldots I_{n-1}, I_n, J \in \mathcal{FI}$. Then*

$$C_1 \overset{I_1}{\vartriangleleft} (C_2 \overset{I_2}{\vartriangleleft} (\ldots (C_n \overset{I_n}{\vartriangleleft} J))) \in \mathcal{FI}. \tag{4}$$

In the following theorem, we investigate the construction of the fuzzy implication when the conjunction is a semi-copula.

Proposition 6. *If C is a semi-copula and $I, J \in \mathcal{FI}$, then $(C \overset{I}{\vartriangleleft} J)(x, y) = I(x, J(1, y))$.*

Proof. For all $z \in [0, 1]$, we have $C(x, z) \leq C(x, 1) = x$, and $J(z, y) \geq J(1, y)$. Thus, by mixed-monotonicity of I, we have

$$(C \overset{I}{\vartriangleleft} J)(x, y) = \inf_{z \in [0,1]} I(C(x, z), J(z, y))$$
$$= I(C(x, 1), J(1, y))$$
$$= I(x, J(1, y))$$

Corollary 2. *If C is a semi-copula and $I, J \in \mathcal{FI}$ such that J satisfies (NP), then $C \overset{I}{\vartriangleleft} J = I$.*

Remark 1. (i) From Proposition 6 and its proof, we note that if C is a conjunction which is not a semicopula, we get $(C \overset{I}{\vartriangleleft} J)(x, y) = I(C(x, 1), J(1, y))$.

(ii) If J does not satisfy (NP), we do not recover I. Consider for instance the T-power based implications given in [12]. Any such implication J satisfies $J(1, y) = 0$ for all $y \in [0, 1)$. Thus,

$$(C \overset{I}{\vartriangleleft} J)(x, y) = I(x, J(1, y)) = \begin{cases} N_I(x), & \text{if } y < 1, \\ 1, & \text{otherwise.} \end{cases}$$

(iii) Note that if J is a fuzzy implication satisfying (NP) and C is a semicopula, then $J \overset{I}{\triangleleft} C$ is a conjunction if I satisfies (IP).

(iv) In the above, $J \overset{I}{\triangleleft} C$ need not yield the same conjunction C, unlike the case of BKS composition $C \overset{J}{\triangleleft} I$ (see Corollary 2). For instance, consider

$$I_{\mathbf{GD}}(x,y) = \begin{cases} 1, & x \leq y, \\ y, & x > y. \end{cases}, \quad J(x,y) = 1 - x + xy, \text{ and } C(x,y) = xy \ .$$

Then, we obtain the least conjunction, i.e., $(J \overset{I_{\mathbf{GD}}}{\triangleleft} C)(x,y) = \begin{cases} 1, & x = y = 1, \\ 0, & \text{otherwise.} \end{cases}$

5   Implications Using T-Conorms

In [7], it was shown that one can use aggregation functions with the neutral element 0 to obtain a fuzzy implication from the BKS composition. The following theorem examines the condition under which this composition yields a fuzzy implication.

Proposition 7 (cf. [8, Remark 3.3, Proposition 3.4], [7, Proposition 1]). *Let C_1, C_2 be semicopulas (or aggregation functions with neutral element 0) and $I \in \mathcal{FI}$, then the following statements are equivalent:*

(i) I satisfies (IP).

(ii) $C_1 \overset{I}{\triangleleft} C_2 \in \mathcal{FI}$.

In this section, we shall consider a particular family of fuzzy logic connectives with 0 as the neutral element, t-conorms. Let us start with the basic properties of such a composition.

Proposition 8. *Let S_1, S_2 be t-conorms and $I \in \mathcal{FI}$ satisfy (IP). If $S_1 \leq S_2$, then $S_1 \overset{I}{\triangleleft} S_2$ satisfies (IP).*

Proof. Let us assume $S_1 \leq S_2$, then we have for $x, z \in [0, 1]$,

$$I(S_1(x,z), S_2(z,x)) \geq I(S_2(x,z), S_2(z,x)) = 1.$$

Hence, $\inf_{z \in [0,1]} I(S_1(x,z), S_2(z,x)) = 1$, so $S_1 \overset{I}{\triangleleft} S_2$ satisfies (IP).

Note that the converse of the above result need not be always true. The following result shows the condition under which it will hold. Also, the proof is similar to the proof of Proposition 1.

Proposition 9. *Let S_1, S_2 be t-conorms such that $S_1 \leq S_2$ and $I \in \mathcal{FI}$ satisfy (OP). Then $S_1 \overset{I}{\triangleleft} S_2$ satisfies (OP).*

The proof of the following result is similar to the proof of Proposition 2. In fact, a weaker condition (IP) is sufficient to prove it.

Proposition 10. *Let S_1, S_2 be t-conorms and $I \in \mathcal{FI}$ satisfy (OP). If $S_1 \stackrel{I}{\vartriangleleft} S_2$ satisfies (IP), then $S_1 \leq S_2$.*

Proposition 11. *Let S_1, S_2 be t-conorms and $I \in \mathcal{FI}$ be such that $S_1 \vartriangleleft S_2 \in \mathcal{FI}$. Then the following statements are equivalent:*

(i) I satisfies (NP).

(ii) $S_1 \stackrel{I}{\vartriangleleft} S_2$ satisfies (NP).

Proof. Let $y \in [0,1]$. Then

$$(S_1 \stackrel{I}{\vartriangleleft} S_2)(1,y) = \inf_{z \in [0,1]} I(S_1(1,z), S_2(z,y)) = \inf_{z \in [0,1]} I(1, S_2(z,y))$$
$$= I(1,y).$$

Therefore, $(S_1 \stackrel{I}{\vartriangleleft} S_2)(1,y) = y \iff I$ satisfies (NP).

Now, let us mention Example 5 in [7], where the following fuzzy implication was obtained.

$$(S_{\mathbf{P}} \stackrel{I_{\mathbf{GG}}}{\vartriangleleft} S_{\mathbf{M}})(x,y) = \begin{cases} 1, & x = 0, \\ \frac{y}{x+y-xy}, & x > 0. \end{cases}$$

$$= \begin{cases} 1, & x = 0, \\ I_{\mathbf{GG}}(S_{\mathbf{P}}(x,y), S_{\mathbf{M}}(y,y)), & x > 0. \end{cases}$$

Motivated by this example, we define an operator in a similar way.

Definition 7. *Let $I \in \mathcal{FI}$ and S_1, S_2 be t-conorms such that $S_1 \geq S_2$. Then, an (S_1, S_2)-operator is a function $I_{S_1,S_2} : [0,1]^2 \to [0,1]$ given by*

$$I_{S_1,S_2}(x,y) = \begin{cases} 1, & x = 0, \\ I(S_1(x,y), S_2(y,y)), & x > 0. \end{cases} \tag{5}$$

Remark 2. It is easy to see that the operator given by (5) satisifes (I1) and (I3) from Definition 3. However, (I2) does not have to be satisfied.

Example 1. Let I be the Fodor implication given by

$$I_{\mathbf{FD}}(x,y) = \begin{cases} 1, & x \leq y, \\ \max\{1-x, y\}, & x > y. \end{cases}$$

Also, let us take $S_1 = S_{\mathbf{P}}$ and $S_2 = S_{\mathbf{M}}$. Then

$$I_{S_1,S_2}(x,y) = \begin{cases} 1, & x \leq y, \\ \max\{1-x-y+xy, y\}, & x > y. \end{cases}$$

For $x = 0.5, y_1 = 0.1$, and $y_2 = 0.15$, we have

$$I_{S_1,S_2}(0.5,0.1) = 0.45 > 0.425 = I_{S_1,S_2}(0.5,0.15).$$

Thus, in this example, the condition (I2) from Definition 3 is not satisfied.

Therefore, it is important to find necessary and sufficient conditions for (S_1, S_2)-operator to be a fuzzy implication. One of the sufficient conditions is given below. First, let us recall the notion of special implications.

Definition 8 ([4, **Definition 1.1**]). *A fuzzy implication I is called special if*

$$\forall_{x,y\in[0,1]} \forall_{\varepsilon>0} (x + \varepsilon, y + \varepsilon) \in [0,1] \Rightarrow I(x,y) \leq I(x + \varepsilon, y + \varepsilon)). \tag{SP}$$

Proposition 12. *Let $I \in \mathcal{FI}$ satisfy (SP) and S_1, S_2 be t-conorms such that $S_1 \geq S_2$. If*
$$S_1(x,y_2) - S_1(x,y_1) \leq S_2(y_2,y_2) - S_2(y_1,y_1)$$
for $x, y_1, y_2 \in [0,1]$ such that $y_1 \leq y_2$, then $I_{S_1,S_2} \in \mathcal{FI}$.

Proof. Let $I \in \mathcal{FI}$ satisfy (SP), and $x, y_1, y_2 \in [0,1]$ be such that $y_1 \leq y_2$. Now, let us take $\varepsilon = S_1(x,y_2) - S_1(x,y_1) \geq 0$. Then, we have

$$\begin{aligned}
I(S_1(x,y_1), S_2(y_1,y_1)) &\leq I(S_1(x,y_1) + S_1(x,y_2) - S_1(x,y_1),\\
&\quad S_2(y_1,y_1) + S_1(x,y_2) - S_1(x,y_1))\\
&= I(S_1(x,y_2), S_2(y_1,y_1) + S_1(x,y_2) - S_1(x,y_1))\\
&\leq I(S_1(x,y_2), S_2(y_2,y_2)).
\end{aligned}$$

Therefore, the condition (I2) from Definition 3 is satisfied.

Remark 3. Note that for an I that satisfies (NP), I_{S_1,S_2} satisfies (NP) if and only if $S_2(x,y) = \max(x,y)$. Since most of the major families of fuzzy implications satisfy (NP), I_{S_1,S_2} potentially yields a new family of fuzzy implications.

6 Conclusions

In this paper, we have considered three different cases of constructing fuzzy implications from BKS composition. We have investigated some crucial properties of such FIs. Moreover, we have proposed the definition of (S_1, S_2)-operators. In our future work, we would like to characterize them and investigate when they are FIs. Moreover, we intend to answer whether they must be the operators obtained from the BKS composition. Also, we want to look deeper into the other properties of FIs obtained from BKS composition.

References

1. Baczyński, M., Jayaram, B.: Fuzzy Implications. In: Studies in Fuzziness and Soft Computing, vol. 231, Springer, Heidelberg (2008). https://doi.org/10.1007/978-3-540-69082-5
2. Bandler, W., Kohout, L.J.: Fuzzy relational products as a tool for analysis and synthesis of the behaviour of complex natural and artificial systems. In: Wang, P.P., Chang, S.K. (eds.) Fuzzy Sets: Theory and Applications to Policy Analysis and Information Systems, pp. 341–367. Springer, Boston, MA (1980). https://doi.org/10.1007/978-1-4684-3848-2_26
3. Durante, F., Sempi, C.: Semicopulae. Kybernetika **41**(3), 315–328 (2005)
4. Jayaram, B., Mesiar, R.: On special fuzzy implications. Fuzzy Sets Syst. **160**, 2063–2085 (2009)
5. Klement, E.P., Mesiar, R., Pap, E.: Triangular Norms. Kluwer Academic Publishers, Dordrecht (2000)
6. Król, A.: Dependencies between fuzzy conjunctions and implications. In: Galichet, S., Montero, J., Mauris, G. (eds.) Proceedings of the 7th Conference of the European Society for Fuzzy Logic and Technology (EUSFLAT-2011) and LFA-2011. Advances in Intelligent Systems Research, vol. 1, 230–237. Atlantis Press (2011)
7. Miś, K.: Construction of. In: Ciucci, D., et al. (eds.) IPMU 2022. Communications in Computer and Information Science, vol. 1601, pp. 219–229. Springer, Cham (2022). https://doi.org/10.1007/978-3-031-08971-8_19
8. Miś, K., Baczyński, M.: Different forms of generalized hypothetical syllogism with regard to R-implications. In: Rutkowski, L., Scherer, R., Korytkowski, M., Pedrycz, W., Tadeusiewicz, R., Zurada, J. (eds.) ICAISC 2019. Lecture Notes in Computer Science, vol. 11508. Springer, Cham (2019). https://doi.org/10.1007/978-3-030-20912-4_29
9. Vemuri, N.R., Jayaram, B.: The ⊛-composition of fuzzy implications: closures with respect to properties, powers and families. Fuzzy Sets Syst. **275**, 58–87 (2015)
10. Zadeh, L.A.: Outline of a new approach to the analysis of complex systems and decision processes. IEEE Trans. Syst. Man Cyber. **3**, 28–44 (1973)
11. Klir, G.J., Yuan, B.: Fuzzy Sets and Fuzzy Logic: Theory and Applications. Prentice-Hall Inc, USA (1995)
12. Massanet, S., Recasens, J., Torrens, J.: Some characterizations of T-power based implications. Fuzzy Sets Syst. **359**, 42–62 (2019)
13. Wangming, W.: Fuzzy reasoning and fuzzy relational equations. Fuzzy Sets Syst. **20**, 67–78 (1986)

The Form of Fuzzy Implication Functions Satisfying a Multiplicative Sincov's Equation

Michał Baczyński[1]($\boxtimes$)(iD), Włodzimierz Fechner[2](iD), Mateusz Pieszczek[1](iD), and Sebastia Massanet[3,4](iD)

[1] Faculty of Science and Technology, University of Silesia in Katowice, Bankowa 14, 40-007 Katowice, Poland
{michal.baczynski,mateusz.pieszczek}@us.edu.pl
[2] Institute of Mathematics, Lodz University of Technology, al. Politechniki 8, 93-590 Łódź, Poland
wlodzimierz.fechner@p.lodz.pl
[3] Soft Computing, Image Processing and Aggregation (SCOPIA) research group Department of Mathematics and Computer Science, University of the Balearic Islands, 07122 Palma, Balearic Islands, Spain
s.massanet@uib.es
[4] Health Research Institute of the Balearic Islands (IdISBa), 07122 Palma, Balearic Islands, Spain

Abstract. The analysis of the additional properties of fuzzy implication functions often leads to studying some functional equations. Among them, the solution of a multiplicative Sincov's type equation connected with the characterization of power-based implications was recently published. In this paper, we provide a counterexample of this previous result, and the corrected result is presented, describing all fuzzy implication functions that satisfy the equation. Finally, we illustrate the result with several examples.

Keywords: Fuzzy implication function · Functional equation · Sincov's equation

1 Introduction

In the last decades, one of the leading research lines on the topic of fuzzy implication functions is the study of the additional properties that these operators may fulfil [2]. This research line is boosted by two crucial features of fuzzy implication functions. First of all, the not-so-demanding axioms of their definition allow the existence of a plethora of families of these operators, each of these with their own expression, method of construction, and additional properties. Second, many of these additional properties are not exclusively connected with one of such families, but members of different families can fulfill them. Therefore, in some recent studies, an additional property is fixed, and the corresponding

© The Author(s), under exclusive license to Springer Nature Switzerland AG 2023
S. Massanet et al. (Eds.): EUSFLAT 2023/AGOP 2023, LNCS 14069, pp. 689–697, 2023.
https://doi.org/10.1007/978-3-031-39965-7_57

functional equation is solved, finding all those fuzzy implication functions fulfilling the property. As important examples, we can highlight the law of importation [9], the distributivity properties [5] or the invariance property [6], among many others.

One of the functional equations which has been studied recently is a multiplicative version of Sincov's functional equation given by

$$I(x,y) \cdot I(y,z) = I(x,z), \quad 1 > x > y > z > 0, \tag{1}$$

where I is a fuzzy implication function. The importance of this functional equation is twofold. Namely, it is used in [8] to characterize the family of power based implications, and moreover, the fulfilment of Eq. (1) in the domain $x \leq y \leq z$ is a necessary and sufficient condition for being a unidimensional T'-preorder, with T' the product t-norm (see [4]). In [3], a generalization of this functional equation by understanding the internal product as the product t-norm and changing it to a general arbitrary continuous Archimedean t-norm was deeply analysed. Focusing on the original Eq. (1), due to its importance, in [1], a characterization result of all fuzzy implication functions satisfying Eq. (1) was presented. Unfortunately, as it will be proved later in this paper, that characterization result is not entirely correct, and a revision is needed. This constitutes the main contribution of this paper. First, we will present an example of a fuzzy implication function satisfying Eq. (1) but not being a solution provided by the characterization theorem. After that, a new characterization result that provides the solution to our problem will be proved jointly with several examples that illustrate the result.

The structure of the paper is as follows. After the preliminaries, in Sect. 3, the characterization result given in [1] is recalled, and the counterexample proving that the result needs revision is presented. Then, in Sect. 4, the corrected result is proved along with some illustrative examples. Finally, the paper ends with some concluding remarks.

2   Preliminaries

In this section, we will recall the basic definitions and concepts of fuzzy implication functions that will be used throughout the paper. First, the definition of a fuzzy implication function is provided.

Definition 1 ([2, Definition 1.1.1.]). *A binary operation* $I \colon [0,1]^2 \to [0,1]$ *is said to be a* fuzzy implication function *if it satisfies, for all* $x, y, z \in [0,1]$:

(I1) $I(x,z) \geq I(y,z)$, *when* $x \leq y$,
(I2) $I(x,y) \leq I(x,z)$, *when* $y \leq z$,
(I3) $I(0,0) = I(1,1) = 1$, *and* $I(1,0) = 0$.

From the definition it is clear that $I(0,x) = I(x,1) = 1$ for all $x \in [0,1]$. However, neither $I(x,0)$ nor $I(1,x)$ are determined for all $x \in (0,1)$. This flexibility allows the potential fulfilment of many additional properties from which we recall next to the ordering property, which will be used later.

Definition 2 ([2, **Definition 1.3.1.**]). *We say that a fuzzy implication function I satisfies the* ordering property, *if:*

$$x \le y \quad \Longleftrightarrow \quad I(x, y) = 1, \quad x, y \in [0, 1]. \tag{OP}$$

On the other hand, the monotonicities of the fuzzy implication function imply the following straightforward result.

Lemma 1. *Let* $I \colon [0, 1]^2 \to [0, 1]$ *be a fuzzy implication function. Define*

$$Q_I := \{(x, y) \in [0, 1]^2 : x > y \text{ and } I(x, y) = 1\}.$$

Then it holds that $I(u, v) = 1$ *for each* $(u, v) \in R_I$, *where*

$$R_I := \bigcup\{[0, x] \times [y, 1] : (x, y) \in Q_I\}. \tag{2}$$

3   Previous Characterization Result and Counterexample

In [1], the characterization result that was presented for the fuzzy implication functions satisfying Eq. (1) stated as follows.

Theorem 1 ([1, **Theorem 14**]). *Let* I *be a fuzzy implication function. If* I *solves Eq. (1), then there exist* $y_0 \in [0, 1]$ *and a non-increasing function* $f \colon (y_0, 1) \to (0, +\infty)$ *such that* I *is given by:*

$$I(x, y) = \begin{cases} \frac{f(x)}{f(y)}, & \text{if } y \in (y_0, 1), x \in (y, 1), \\ 0, & \text{if } y \in [0, y_0), x \in (y, 1). \end{cases} \tag{3}$$

Conversely, for every point $y_0 \in [0, 1]$ *and for every function* $f \colon (y_0, 1) \to (0, +\infty)$, *every mapping* $I \colon [0, 1]^2 \to \mathbb{R}$ *which on the set*

$$\{(x, y) \in [0, 1] \mid y \in (y_0, 1), x \in (y, 1) \text{ or } y \in [0, y_0), x \in (y, 1)\}$$

is given by Eq. (3) is a solution to Eq. (1) postulated for all $x, y, z \in [0, 1]$ *such that* $1 > x > y > z > y_0$.

As it has been already aforementioned, this theorem contains an error and not every solution can be described in such way. Indeed, let us define an example of a fuzzy implication function which satisfies Eq. (1) but it is not of the form given by Eq. (3):

Example 1. Let us define the following operator $I \colon [0, 1]^2 \to [0, 1]$ given by:

$$I(x, y) = \begin{cases} 1, & \text{if } (x \le y) \text{ or } (x < \frac{1}{2}) \text{ or } (y > \frac{1}{2}), \\ 0, & \text{otherwise.} \end{cases} \tag{4}$$

Figure 1 gives the structure of I. It is easy to check that such a function is a fuzzy implication function. Now, on the one hand, by a simple computation, it can be proved that this implication fulfils Sincov's equation (1). However, it is clear that this implication cannot be written in the form of Eq. (3). Consequently, this results in a counterexample of Theorem 1, which needs a deep revision.

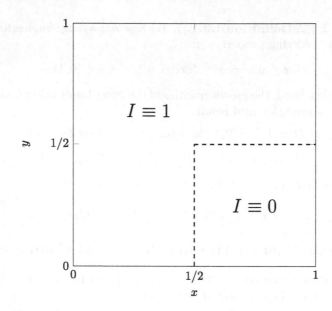

Fig. 1. Plot of the fuzzy implication function used in Example 1.

This example can be easily generalized. Indeed, there is nothing special about point $\frac{1}{2}$ used in the construction, and we can take any $y_0 \in (0,1)$. Moreover, the fuzzy implication function does not need to be constant on the two triangles with vertices:

- $(0,0), (y_0, y_0), (y_0, 0)$,
- $(y_0, y_0), (1, y_0), (1, 1)$.

Example 2. Let us consider $y_0 \in (0,1)$ and the non-increasing functions $f : (y_0, 1) \to (0, +\infty)$ and $g : (0, y_0) \to (0, +\infty)$. Then the binary operator $I : [0,1]^2 \to [0,1]$ given by

$$I(x,y) = \begin{cases} 1, & \text{if } x \le y, \\ \frac{f(x)}{f(y)}, & \text{if } y \in (y_0, 1), x \in (y, 1), \\ \frac{g(x)}{g(y)}, & \text{if } x \in (0, y_0), y \in (0, x), \\ 0, & \text{otherwise,} \end{cases}$$

is a fuzzy implication function which is a solution of Eq. (1). In Fig. 2 the structure of I is depicted. However, again it is easy to check that it cannot be written in the form of Eq. (3).

4   New Characterization Result

The main goal of this section is to present a new characterization result that fixes Theorem 1.

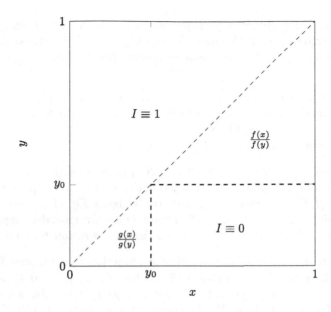

Fig. 2. Plot of the fuzzy implication function used in Example 2.

Assume that J is a nontrivial interval and denote $\Delta_J := \{(s,t) \in J^2 : s \le t\}$. Gergely Kiss and Jens Schwaiger in [7] proved the following result.

Theorem 2 (see [7, **Theorem 3.11**]). *Let $f \colon \Delta_J \to \mathbb{R}$ be a solution of*

$$f(s,t) \cdot f(t,u) = f(s,u), \quad (s,t),(t,u) \in \Delta_J. \tag{5}$$

Then there exists a countable (possibly empty) family $\mathcal{S}$ of pairwise disjoint nontrivial intervals $I \subseteq J$ and a function $d \colon \bigcup_{I \in \mathcal{S}} I \to \mathbb{R}\setminus\{0\}$ such that

$$f(x,y) = \frac{d(y)}{d(x)}, \quad x,y \in I, \ I \in \mathcal{S}, \ x \le y. \tag{6}$$

Moreover, fixed $I \in \mathcal{S}$, $x \in I$ and $y, z \in (J\setminus I)$ such that $z < x < y$, then

$$f(x,y) = f(z,x) = 0.$$

Further,

$$f(x,x) = \begin{cases} 1, & \text{if } x \in \bigcup_{I \in \mathcal{S}} I, \\ 1 \text{ or } 0, & \text{otherwise.} \end{cases}$$

Moreover, as it was observed in the last sentence of the proof of this theorem, it holds also that $f(x,y) = 0$ if $x,y \notin \bigcup_{I \in \mathcal{S}} I$ and $x < y$.

We will apply the above theorem to obtain a new characterization of the family of fuzzy implication functions fulfiling Eq. (1) amending the gap in Theorem 1, our earlier result.

Corollary 1. *Let $I: [0,1]^2 \to [0,1]$ be a fuzzy implication which satisfies Eq. (1). Then, there exists a countable (possibly empty) family S of pairwise disjoint nontrivial intervals $I \subseteq [0,1]$ and a non-increasing function $d: \bigcup_{I \in S} I \to [0, +\infty)$ such that:*

(a) *if $x, y \in I$ with $I \in S$ and $x > y$, then $I(x,y) = d(x)/d(y)$,*
(b) *if $x > y$ and x, y do not belong to the same member of S (or one or both of them are outside the set $\bigcup S$), then $I(x,y) = 0$,*
(c) *if $x < y$ and $x \in \text{int}\bigcup_{I \in S} I$, then $I(x,y) = 1$.*

Conversely, for every countable family S of pairwise disjoint nontrivial intervals $I \subseteq [0,1]$ and every non-increasing function $d: \bigcup_{I \in S} I \to [0, +\infty)$, the map $I: [0,1]^2 \to [0,1]$ described by (a), (b), (c) satisfies Eq. (1). Moreover, if I is mixed monotone (in the sense of Definition 1) on the (possibly empty) set that is not covered by (a), (b), (c), then it is a fuzzy implication function.

Proof. Assume that I is a fuzzy implication function that satisfies Eq. (1). We will follow the idea of [7, Remark 3.15]. Define $f: \Delta_{[0,1]} \to [0,1]$ as $f(x,y) = I(y,x)$ when $x < y$ and $f(x,x) = 1$ for $x \in [0,1]$. One can see that f is a solution of Eq. (5) on $\Delta_{[0,1]}$. By Theorem 2 there exists a family S of disjoint nontrivial intervals $I \subseteq J = [0,1]$ and a function $d: \bigcup_{I \in S} I \to \mathbb{R} \setminus \{0\}$ such that Eq. (6) holds. Further, by the same theorem, $I(x,y) = f(y,x) = 0$ for $x > y$ in the following two cases: $(x, y \notin \bigcup_{I \in S} I)$ or $(x \in I$ with $I \in S$ and $y \notin I)$. Therefore, (b) holds. Since I attains only non-negative values, we can assume that $d: \bigcup_{I \in S} I \to (0, +\infty)$. We thus have

$$I(x,y) = \frac{d(x)}{d(y)}, \quad x, y \in I, \ I \in S, \ x > y. \tag{7}$$

It is important to remember that $I(x,x)$ needs not to be equal to $f(x,x)$, thus we have excluded in Eq. (7) the possibility $x = y$. Thus, (a) holds. Moreover, without loss of generality, thanks to (I3), we may assume that $d(0) = 1$.

At this point, since map d is monotone, has at most countably many points of discontinuity. Moreover, d is bounded on every closed subinterval contained in $\bigcup_{I \in S} I$. Therefore, the value $I(x,y)$ is arbitrarily close to 1 when $x, y \in [x_0, y_0] \subseteq I$ are such that $x > y$ and x approaches to y. Consequently, using Lemma 1, for every $x, y \in [0,1]$ such that $x < y$ and $x \in \text{int}\bigcup_{I \in S} I$ we have $I(x,y) = 1$, thus (c) holds. Further, since I is non-decreasing with respect to the second variable, then the map d is non-increasing on each interval from the family S.

Conversely, any function $I: [0,1]^2 \to [0,1]$ described by (a), (b), (c), for any countable family S of pairwise disjoint nontrivial intervals $I \subseteq [0,1]$ and any non-increasing function $d: \bigcup_{I \in S} I \to [0, +\infty)$, it is easy to check that Eq. (1) holds. We cannot ensure that $\bigcup_{I \in S} I \supseteq [0,1]$ as it can be seen in Fig. 3. Thus we have to assume monotonicity for points $x, y \notin \bigcup_{I \in S} I$, for I to be a fuzzy implication function. □

Note that each fuzzy implication function, continuous or not, such that $I(x,y) = 0$ for $x > y$ trivially solves Eq. (1). In this case the family S is empty.

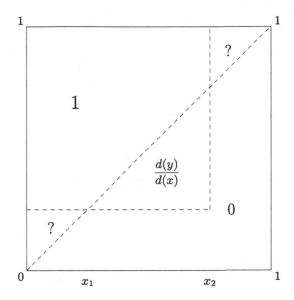

Fig. 3. In the above example $\mathcal{S} = \{(x_1, x_2)\}$, and d is strictly monotone on (x_1, x_2). The set Q_I is empty, I is discontinuous and not determined everywhere on $[0, 1]^2$ and **(OP)** may hold or not.

We can see exemplary application of Corollary 1 in Fig. 4. Such fuzzy implication function can be constant and equal to 1 on some intervals for $x > y$.

Next, we will deal with the continuous case.

Corollary 2. *Assume that $I: [0, 1]^2 \to [0, 1]$ is a continuous fuzzy implication function that satisfies Eq. (1). Then there exists a continuous and non-increasing function $d: [0, 1] \to [0, 1]$ such that $d(1) = 0$, $d(0) = 1$ and $d(x) > 0$ for $x < 1$ and*

$$I(x, y) = \frac{d(x)}{d(y)}, \quad x, y \in [0, 1], \; x > y \tag{8}$$

*with the convention $0/0 = 1$. Moreover, in this case I satisfies **(OP)** if and only if d is decreasing.*

*Conversely, for every continuous and non-increasing function $d: [0, 1] \to [0, 1]$ such that $d(1) = 0$, $d(0) = 1$ and $d(x) > 0$ for $x < 1$, the map $I: [0, 1]^2 \to [0, 1]$ defined by (8) and $I(x, y) = 1$ for $x \leq y$ satisfies Eq. (1) and is a fuzzy implication function. Moreover, it satisfies **(OP)** if and only if d is decreasing.*

Proof. Let us assume that I is a continuous fuzzy implication function that satisfies (1). From Corollary 1, we know that there exist a family $\mathcal{S}$ and a non-increasing function d such that (a), (b) and (c) hold. Continuity of d follows from continuity of I. Moreover, the continuity of I implies that either $\bigcup_{I \in \mathcal{S}} I = \varnothing$ or $\bigcup_{I \in \mathcal{S}} I \supseteq (0, 1)$ since otherwise I would have a $1 - 0$ discontinuity at each point $(x_0, x_0) \in [0, 1]^2$ such that $x_0 \in (0, 1) \backslash \bigcup_{I \in \mathcal{S}} I$.

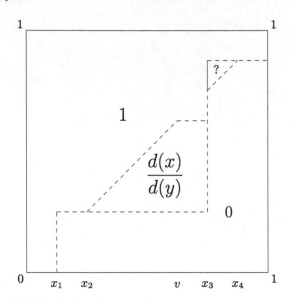

Fig. 4. In the above example $\mathcal{S} = \{(0, x_1), (x_2, x_3), (x_4, 1)\}$, $d(x) = 1$ on $(0, x_1) \cup (x_4, 1)$ and d is arbitrary monotone on (x_2, x_3) and constant on (v, x_3). Moreover, I is discontinuous and not determined everywhere on $[0, 1]^2$ and **(OP)** does not hold.

However, the case $\bigcup_{I \in \mathcal{S}} I = \varnothing$ also leads to a contradiction with continuity. Using (b) we can see that $I(x, y) = 0$ for $x > y$, but from (I3) we also know that $I(1, 1) = 1$. So if we take an arbitrary non-decreasing sequence $(x_n)_\mathbb{N}$, such that $x_n \in [0, 1]$ and $\lim_{n \to +\infty} x_n = 1$, then $\lim_{n \to +\infty} I(1, x_n) = 0 \neq 1 = I(1, 1)$. Thus such solutions do not exist.

Therefore, the only viable case is when $\bigcup_{I \in \mathcal{S}} I \supseteq (0, 1)$. In that case, function d has finite limits at 0 and 1, and thus it can be continuously extended to $[0, 1]$. From the proof of Corollary 1, we know that without loss of generality, $d(0) = 1$. Note that the last part of the condition (I3) implies that $[0, 1] \notin \mathcal{S}$. Therefore, if we want to extend the map d in such a way that it is defined at 1, then necessarily $d(1) = 0$. This, in turn, implies that because of the second part of (I3), one needs to adopt a convention that $0/0 = 1$. After this agreement, Eq. (7) covers the cases $I(1, 1)$ and $I(1, 0)$ as well. As a consequence, Eq. (7) holds for all $x, y \in [0, 1]$ such that $x > y$.

Conversely, if we consider map $I : [0, 1]^2 \to [0, 1]$ defined by Eq. (8) and $I(x, y) = 1$ for $x \leq y$, where $d : [0, 1] \to [0, 1]$ is an arbitrary continuous and non-increasing function such that $d(1) = 0$, $d(0) = 1$ and $d(x) > 0$ for $x < 1$, then it is easy to check that I satisfies Eq. (1) and is a fuzzy implication function.

Regarding **(OP)**, we know that if $\bigcup_{I \in \mathcal{S}} I \supseteq (0, 1)$, then $I(x, x) = 1$ for all $x \in [0, 1]$. From this, it also follows that $I(x, y) = 1$ for all $x, y \in [0, 1]$, such that $x \leq y$. If d is constant on a nontrivial subinterval $[v, u] \subseteq \bigcup_{I \in \mathcal{S}} I$, then by Eq. (7) we get $I(u, v) = 1$. Conversely, if $I(u, v) = 1$ for some $u > v$, then d is constant on $[v, u]$. Thus, I satisfies **(OP)** if and only if d is decreasing.

5   Conclusions

In this paper, we obtained a description of fuzzy implication functions that satisfy the multiplicative Sincov's functional equation described in Eq. (1). With this contribution, we corrected a gap in our earlier work [1], and we supplemented the research with some illustrative examples. The new characterization result is based on a new result of Kiss and Schwaiger, published in [7], that deals with the Sincov's equation. From these papers, this equation shows its importance in information science and economy. We believe further studies on the topic will bring new interesting results and further applications of the equation.

Acknowledgments. S. Massanet acknowledges the support of the R+D+i Project PID2020-113870GB-I00-"Desarrollo de herramientas de Soft Computing para la Ayuda al Diagnóstico Clnico y a la Gestión de Emergencias (HESOCODICE)", funded by MCIN/AEI/10.13039/501100011033

References

1. Baczyński, M., Fechner, W., Massanet, S.: A functional equation stemming from a characterization of power-based implications. In: 2019 IEEE International Conference on Fuzzy Systems (FUZZ-IEEE), pp. 1–6 (2019)
2. Baczyński, M., Jayaram, B.: Fuzzy Implications, Studies in Fuzziness and Soft Computing, vol. 231. Springer, Heidelberg (2008). https://doi.org/10.1007/978-3-540-69082-5
3. Baczyński, M., Fechner, W., Massanet, S.: On a generalization of multiplicative Sincov's equation for fuzzy implication functions. Fuzzy Sets Syst. **451**, 196–205 (2022). Recent Trends in Aggregation - In Honour of Radko Mesiar's 70th Birthday
4. Boixader, D., Recasens, J.: Generation and characterization of fuzzy t-preorders. Appl. Artif. Intell. **29**(5), 514–530 (2015)
5. Dombi, J., Baczyński, M.: General characterization of implication's distributivity properties: the preference implication. IEEE Trans. Fuzzy Syst. **28**(11), 2982–2995 (2020)
6. Fernandez-Peralta, R., Massanet, S., Mir, A.: On strict T-power invariant implications: properties and intersections. Fuzzy Sets Syst. **423**, 1–28 (2021)
7. Kiss, G., Schwaiger, J.: Sincov's and other functional equations and negative interest rates. Aequat. Math. **97**, 629–637 (2023). https://doi.org/10.1007/s00010-022-00936-9. in Press
8. Massanet, S., Recasens, J., Torrens, J.: Some characterizations of T-power based implications. Fuzzy Sets Syst. **359**, 42–62 (2019)
9. Massanet, S., Torrens, J.: Characterization of fuzzy implication functions with a continuous natural negation satisfying the law of importation with a fixed t-norm. IEEE Trans. Fuzzy Syst. **25**(1), 100–113 (2017)

SPECIAL SESSION 10: New Challenges and Ideas in Statistical Inference and Data Analysis

Improved DE-MC Algorithm with Automated Outliers Detection

Kamila M. Rychlik[1] and Maciej Romaniuk[2,3]($\boxtimes$) (iD)

[1] Faculty of Mathematics and Information Science, Warsaw University of Technology, Koszykowa 75, 00-662 Warsaw, Poland
[2] Systems Research Institute PAS, Newelska 6, 01-447 Warsaw, Poland
mroman@ibspan.waw.pl
[3] Warsaw School of Information Technology, Newelska 6, 01-447 Warsaw, Poland

Abstract. The DE-MC algorithm joins two approaches: the differential evolution and the theory of the Markov chains. This population MCMC method aims to improve the numerical effectiveness and the convergence speed of the Metropolis-Hastings algorithm. In this paper, we equip this standard approach with different unsupervised and automated methods for outlier detection and replacement. As our numerical experiments suggest, the obtained DE-MC-out algorithm convergences faster and produces output samples that are closer to the desired target density than the DE-MC method without the increased timing.

Keywords: Statistical simulations · Markov chain · Outliers · Unsupervised learning · Non-parametric model

1 Introduction

The Monte Carlo (MC) and Markov Chain Monte Carlo (MCMC) methods are important simulation tools that are widely used in statistical inference and other real-life applications (see, e.g., [16]). Generation of random variables is also crucial in simulations and resampling of fuzzy numbers (see, e.g., [6–8,17–19]). To generate a sample from the complex, multidimensional distribution, the Metropolis-Hastings (abbreviated further as MH) algorithm equipped with the simple and all-purpose instrumental density can be used. Usually, the normal distribution is applied as such a density. However, its specific form (like its covariance matrix) can have a great impact on the numerical effectiveness of the whole algorithm and its convergence speed.

Therefore, the DE-MC algorithm was proposed in [3] to increase the effectiveness of the MCMC procedures. This approach links the differential evolution (DE) method with the theory of the Markov chains (MC). As it was shown, the DE-MC algorithm significantly improves the quality of the MH method. Further modifications of the standard DE-MC approach were also proposed, e.g. to weak some of its assumptions (see [2]) or to introduce a more complex formula for jumps between the chain states (see [23,24]).

© The Author(s), under exclusive license to Springer Nature Switzerland AG 2023
S. Massanet et al. (Eds.): EUSFLAT 2023/AGOP 2023, LNCS 14069, pp. 701–712, 2023.
https://doi.org/10.1007/978-3-031-39965-7_58

In this paper, we propose another extension of the standard DE-MC algorithm: the DE-MC-out method. Contrary to the above-mentioned approaches, instead of a more complicated and possibly not so numerically efficient algorithm, we combined the DE-MC method with another important statistical tool: the detection and replacement of the outliers (see, e.g., [14]).

Outliers are values that differ significantly from other observations in the same sample. They can be outcomes of some errors (e.g., during the collection of a sample) as well as some important phenomenon (e.g., a heavy-tailed distribution used in the simulations). Therefore, the outlier detection may be also profitable for the DE-MC algorithm.

Our aim is to equip the DE-MC with a method to detect and replace the existing outliers to improve the overall quality of the algorithm without decreasing its numerical effectiveness, keeping in mind its non-parametric approach. Then, three different detection methods, which are based on the unsupervised learning, together with two very intuitive replacing approaches are applied for this purpose. The obtained simulation results for the DE-MC-out algorithm are then compared with the outputs for the standard DE-MC approach. It seems that the proposed method improves the quality of the obtained final sample without increasing the mean timing of the conducted simulations.

The paper is organized as follows. In Sect. 2, some basic facts concerning the DE-MC algorithm are recalled. In Sect. 3, the applied methods for outlier detection and replacing are summarized. The proposed DE-MC-out algorithm is described in Sect. 4, together with the analysis of the numerical simulations. Then, some final remarks are presented in Sect. 5.

2   DE-MC Algorithm

The Markov Chain Monte Carlo (MCMC) methods are widely applied to generate a statistical sample from some (usually a difficult one) target density $f(x)$ using a simpler instrumental density (see, e.g., [16]). However, a selection of this instrumental density, which is used to jump from one state to another state of the Markov chain, may be crucial, e.g., in the MH algorithm to improve its numerical efficiency. A common example of such a density is the multivariate normal random distribution. Then its covariance matrix should be adequately specified so that the chain visits all states often enough.

In [3], an interesting approach was proposed to solve the above-mentioned problem. The Differential Evolution Markov Chain (DE-MC) method is a connection of the differential evolution (DE) algorithm with the Markov chain (MC) theory. The differential evolution is a genetic algorithm used to optimize a target function in real parameters space (see, e.g., [12,13]). In the DE-MC method, n chains are simulated in parallel. A state of the i-th chain is given by a d-dimensional vector $\mathbf{x}_i$. These vectors are members of a population $\mathbf{X}$ and they form an $n \times d$ matrix (i.e. the members are given as its rows), where $n > d$.

Firstly, the primary population is independently drawn from some initial d-dimensional distribution. Then, for each chain, its new state $\mathbf{y}_i$ is proposed using the following formula

$$\mathbf{y}_i = \mathbf{x}_i + F(\mathbf{x}_{r_1} - \mathbf{x}_{r_2}) + \epsilon, \tag{1}$$

where ϵ is drawn from a symmetric distribution with a small variance and unbounded support (e.g., the d-dimensional normal distribution with zeros as the expected value and some small variance b, i.e., $N(0, b \cdot \mathbf{1}^d)$), and $\mathbf{x}_{r_1}, \mathbf{x}_{r_2}$ are randomly selected without replacement from a whole population devoid of $\mathbf{x}_i$. The aim of (1) is to construct the Markov chain for which the whole state space can be reached (contrary to the classical DE scheme, see, e.g., [3]). Then, $\mathbf{y}_i$ is accepted as a new state $\mathbf{x}_i^*$ with the probability

$$p(\mathbf{x}_i, \mathbf{y}_i) = \begin{cases} \min\left\{\frac{f(\mathbf{y}_i)}{f(\mathbf{x}_i)}, 1\right\} & \text{if } f(\mathbf{x}_i) > 0 \\ 1 & \text{if } f(\mathbf{x}_i) = 0 \end{cases}. \tag{2}$$

It leads to the DE-MC version of the classical MH algorithm (see Algorithm 1).

Algorithm 1. DE-MC standard algorithm

Generate initial population $\mathbf{X} = \{\mathbf{x}_1, \mathbf{x}_2, \ldots, \mathbf{x}_n\}$
while stop condition is not fulfilled **do**
    for all $i \in \{1, 2, \ldots, n\}$ **do**
        Select randomly $\mathbf{x}_{r_1}, \mathbf{x}_{r_2}$ from $\mathbf{X}$ without $\mathbf{x}_i$
        Generate $\epsilon \sim N(0, b \cdot \mathbf{1}^d)$
        $\mathbf{y}_i = \mathbf{x}_i + F(\mathbf{x}_{r_1} - \mathbf{x}_{r_2}) + \epsilon$
        Set $\mathbf{x}_i^* = \begin{cases} \mathbf{y}_i & \text{with probability } p(\mathbf{x}_i, \mathbf{y}_i) \\ \mathbf{x}_i & \text{with probability } 1 - p(\mathbf{x}_i, \mathbf{y}_i) \end{cases}$,
    end for
    Set $\mathbf{X} = \{\mathbf{x}_1^*, \mathbf{x}_2^*, \ldots, \mathbf{x}_n^*\}$
end while
return X

The following important theorem was proved in [3] to establish the correctness of the DE-MC algorithm:

Theorem 1. *The DE-MC algorithm yields a Markov chain, with the unique stationary distribution given by $\pi^n(\mathbf{x})$.*

Then, the DE-MC method is also the population MCMC approach, and the individual chains are independent when they are independent of their initial state. In this case, the $\hat{R}$ Gelman-Rubin statistic (see, e.g., [5,22]) can be directly applied to monitor the convergence of the obtained Markov chains. This diagnostic compares the between- and within-variance of the chains and when its value is below some level (usually 1.1 or 1.2, as indicated in the literature), the overall convergence can be stated.

3 Methods for Outliers Detection and Replacement

Outliers in statistics are values that differ significantly (in some sense) from other observations. Detection of the outliers is very important because they can potentially lead to errors in further statistical analysis, uncover such errors made during previous steps, or indicate some important ("positive" or "negative" for us) outcomes. The same applies to simulations, where these "strange values" can be related, e.g., to problems with the numerical convergence of the MCMC estimator or necessary outcomes for a heavy-tailed distribution (see, e.g., [16]). Therefore, the detection of the outliers may be also profitable for the DE-MC algorithm.

Many methods to identify outliers are known in the literature. In our DE-MC-out algorithm, we applied three of them: Local Outlier Factor (abbreviated as LOF, see [4]), Connectivity-Based Outlier Factor (COF, see [21]), and Isolation Forest (iF, see [9]).

In the first method, the measure of "being outlier" is just known as the local outlier factor (LOF) and it is related to the k-distance of the given point to its nearest neighbors. The value of LOF higher than one indicates that such a point can be potentially an outlier. In the second method, the respective connectivity-based outlier factor is calculated using the so-called set-based nearest path. The higher value of COF can be also associated with a possible outlier. And the last algorithm is the unsupervised learning method related to the decision trees. Therefore, it is based on a completely different approach that tries to isolate possible outliers using the so-called anomaly score instead of profiling single points.

When the outliers are identified, they can be either removed or replaced using other values. The first way may be inadvisable, as it decreases the number of observations. Therefore, using some method to replace the outliers can be more useful. In the proposed DE-MC-out algorithm, two such approaches were applied, i.e. the min-max, and weighted quantiles methods.

The first one is a very intuitive idea. The outlier of a low value is replaced with the minimum from $\mathbf{X}_{(-\text{outliers})}$, i.e., the whole sample devoid of the outliers, and the high-value outlier – with the respective maximum, otherwise – the mean is used. In the second case, the special replacement density

$$f_{\text{rep}}(x) = \frac{f(x)}{f(q_{0.25}) + f(q_{0.5}) + f(q_{0.75})} \tag{3}$$

is calculated, where $f(.)$ is our target density in the DE-MC algorithm, and $q_{0.25}, q_{0.5}, q_{0.75}$ are the respective quantiles (the first, second, and third one) from the whole sample $\mathbf{X}$. Then, the new replacing values, which are equal to these three quantiles, are generated using their respective probabilities $f_{\text{rep}}(q_{0.25})$, $f_{\text{rep}}(q_{0.5})$, $f_{\text{rep}}(q_{0.75})$.

4   Modification of the DE-MC Method

As it was previously mentioned, detection and replacement of the outliers are important ideas in statistics. Therefore, we improved the standard DE-MC approach using the methods described in Sect. 3 to obtain the new DE-MC-out algorithm (see Sect. 4.1). Other methods for detecting and replacing the outliers can be also used in this setting. Two numerical examples concerning the comparison between the DE-MC and DE-MC-out algorithms are provided in Sect. 4.2. Other simulation results are available upon request.

4.1   Modified Approach

The proposed DE-MC-out algorithm (see Algorithm 2) has the following modifications if it is compared with the standard approach (see Algorithm 1):

1. The initial population is drawn from the density with either the compact or the unbound support (e.g., $n \times d$ iid samples are generated from the uniform density $U([0,1])$ or $N(0,1)$). As our numerical experiments suggested, the improper selection of this density (e.g., using the one with the infinity support, when it is bounded for $f(.)$) leads to serious problems during the simulations.
2. When the number of the step j is divisible by the input parameter m_{out}, the outliers in the respective population $\mathbf{X}$ are detected using the LOF, COF, or iF method. Two first methods are implemented using *DDoutlier* package (see [10]), and the third one – *solitude* package (see [20]). If the outliers exist, then they are replaced using either the min-max or the weighted quantiles method (see Sect. 3). This procedure is implemented only during the selected steps to increase the numerical effectiveness of the whole algorithm and to ensure convergence of the obtained Markov chain (see [16] for the respective theoretical reasoning in similar situations). Because of the same reasons, after m_{mod} iterations, the DE-MC-out reverts to the DE-MC algorithm.
3. As the stop condition, $\hat{R}$ statistic is used. Its value is calculated only if j is divisible by the input parameter m_R to increase the speed of the whole algorithm. For the one-dimensional $\hat{R}$ statistic, the respective function from *asbio* package is applied (see [1]), and for its multi-dimensional version, our implementation or *coda* package (see [15]) can be used.

4.2   Numerical Analysis

During our numerical analysis, we focused on $\mathbf{X}$, i.e. the output population of the chains, and compared the results for the DE-MC algorithm (denoted further by $\mathbf{X}_0$) and the DE-MC-out method ($\mathbf{X}_{ident\_rep}$, respectively). In this second case, *ident* stands for the identification method (LOF, COF or iF), and *rep* denotes the replacing algorithm (m – the min-max, q – the weighted quantiles method, respectively). In the following graphs, the theoretical target density was drawn with a black, solid line, and the estimated density based on the simulations

---

Algorithm 2. DE-MC-out (modified) algorithm

Generate initial population $\mathbf{X} = \{\mathbf{x}_1, \mathbf{x}_2, \ldots, \mathbf{x}_n\}$
$j = 0$
while stop condition is not fulfilled **do**
    $j = j + 1$
    for all $i \in \{1, 2, \ldots, n\}$ **do**
        Select randomly $\mathbf{x}_{r_1}, \mathbf{x}_{r_2}$ from $\mathbf{X}$ without $\mathbf{x}_i$
        Generate $\epsilon \sim N(0, b \cdot \mathbf{1}^d)$
        $\mathbf{y}_i = \mathbf{x}_i + F(\mathbf{x}_{r_1} - \mathbf{x}_{r_2}) + \epsilon$
        Set $\mathbf{x}_i^* = \begin{cases} \mathbf{y}_i & \text{with probability } p(\mathbf{x}_i, \mathbf{y}_i) \\ \mathbf{x}_i & \text{with probability } 1 - p(\mathbf{x}_i, \mathbf{y}_i) \end{cases}$,
    end for
    Set $\mathbf{X} = \{\mathbf{x}_1^*, \mathbf{x}_2^*, \ldots, \mathbf{x}_n^*\}$
    if j is divisible by m_{out} and $j < m_{\text{mod}}$ **then**
        find outliers in $\mathbf{X}$ using the selected method
        if there are outliers in $\mathbf{X}$ **then**
            replace the outliers using the selected method
        end if
    end if
    if j is divisible by m_R **then**
        calculate the $\hat{R}$ statistic and update the stop condition
    end if
end while
return $\mathbf{X}$

– with a gray, dashed line. To improve readability, we focused on one-dimensional outcomes. The burn-in period was set to 10% of the beginning iterations and $n = 500$ chains were initialized in our experiments.

The heavy-tailed Weibull distribution $\mathcal{W}(\lambda, k)$ with the scale parameter $\lambda = 1$ and the shape parameter $k = 1.5$ was our first target density. When the DE-MC algorithm was used, it converged after 960 iterations for the stop condition $\hat{R} = 1.05$. However, there were outliers in the last population $\mathbf{X}_0$ (see Fig. 1a). They even sometimes did not belong to the target density support, i.e. $[0, \infty)$. Therefore, the standard algorithm did not work correctly. Moreover, it seems that the obtained histogram was not "close enough" to the expected result (see Fig. 1b). The mean calculated for the subsequent iterations behaved sometimes in an unpredictable manner and the obvious problems with its convergence existed (see Fig. 2a).

The DE-MC-out algorithm worked much better. It converged after 220 (for the pairs of methods LOF_q, COF_q, iF_q, iF_m), 280 (for LOF_m) or 320 iterations (for COF_m, respectively) when the same value $\hat{R} = 1.05$ was set. Based on histograms (see Fig. 3 for some examples), the best results were obtained for the LOF and COF coupled with the weighted quantiles method. The mean was close to its true value even after 50 iterations (see Fig. 2a), especially fast in the case of the Isolation Forest. The detailed comparison of the sample means together with their absolute distances related to the expected value of the Weibull distribution (for the same number of iterations as in Fig. 2) can be found in Table 1.

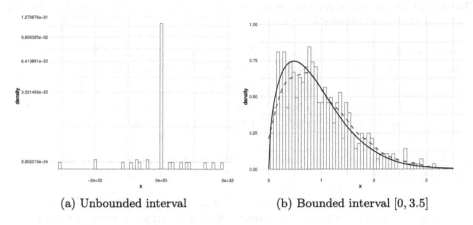

(a) Unbounded interval

(b) Bounded interval $[0, 3.5]$

Fig. 1. Histograms for the DE-MC algorithm and the target density $\mathcal{W}(1, 1.5)$.

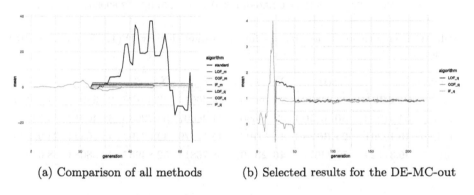

(a) Comparison of all methods

(b) Selected results for the DE-MC-out

Fig. 2. Convergence of the means for the target density $\mathcal{W}(1, 1.5)$.

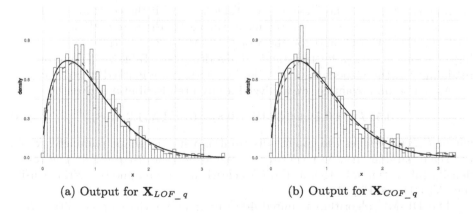

(a) Output for $\mathbf{X}_{LOF\_q}$

(b) Output for $\mathbf{X}_{COF\_q}$

Fig. 3. Histograms for the DE-MC-out algorithm and the target density $\mathcal{W}(1, 1.5)$.

Table 1. Comparison of the sample means and their distances related to the expected value for the target density $\mathcal{W}(1, 1.5)$.

Iteration	$\mathbf{X}_0$	$\mathbf{X}_{LOF\_m}$	$\mathbf{X}_{COF\_m}$	$\mathbf{X}_{iF\_m}$	$\mathbf{X}_{LOF\_q}$	$\mathbf{X}_{COF\_q}$	$\mathbf{X}_{iF\_q}$
65	−31.0765	1.8813	2.0333	**0.9129**	0.8845	0.9134	0.8779
	3542.45%	108.40 %	125.24 %	1.12 %	2.02 %	1.19 %	2.75%
220	1818918.8285	**0.9060**	0.8868	0.9489	0.8859	0.9224	0.8600
	201487389.63%	0.36%	1.77%	5.11%	1.86%	2.17%	4.74%

Table 2. Comparison of the timings for the target density $\mathcal{W}(1, 1.5)$ and the stop condition $\hat{R} = 1.05$

Time	$\mathbf{X}_0$	$\mathbf{X}_{LOF\_m}$	$\mathbf{X}_{COF\_m}$	$\mathbf{X}_{iF\_m}$	$\mathbf{X}_{LOF\_q}$	$\mathbf{X}_{COF\_q}$	$\mathbf{X}_{iF\_q}$
min	7.197741	5.122742	**5.051063**	6.569676	5.136206	5.368514	6.617399
mean	20.750838	7.479085	**5.592550**	7.063164	5.639146	6.222402	6.875949
median	17.167058	5.554406	5.526236	6.791383	**5.208733**	6.136694	6.933876
max	53.070627	16.071382	**6.356860**	8.915157	8.057195	7.699364	7.083551

Table 3. Comparison of the timings for the target density $\mathcal{W}(1, 1.5)$ and $j = 1000$ iterations.

Time	$\mathbf{X}_0$	$\mathbf{X}_{LOF\_m}$	$\mathbf{X}_{COF\_m}$	$\mathbf{X}_{iF\_m}$	$\mathbf{X}_{LOF\_q}$	$\mathbf{X}_{COF\_q}$	$\mathbf{X}_{iF\_q}$
min	**22.17918**	22.84838	23.26643	24.46614	23.45126	23.38978	24.38424
mean	34.51912	**30.49203**	39.29660	41.46607	38.22036	38.40010	33.54266
median	40.19291	**24.66288**	42.43190	45.17979	43.03493	43.76344	24.95335
max	46.37724	50.34671	**46.23601**	58.76814	52.84967	48.68084	58.67952

Then, all approaches were also compared taking into account their numerical effectiveness using *microbenchmark* package (see [11]). When the stop condition was used, the mean timing of the DE-MC-out was even equal to about 25% of the mean time for the DE-MC (see Table 2). And if the constant number of iterations were set to $j = 1000$, the mean timing for the pair LOF_m was lower than for the DE-MC, and for the worst DE-MC-out case (i.e., iF_m) it was bigger about 14% than for the standard algorithm (see Table 3). To improve the readability of the respective tables, the best results are marked in boldface.

As our second example, we analyzed a mixture distribution, given by

$$0.5 \cdot \Gamma(20, 0.1) + 0.3 \cdot \mathcal{W}(4, 0.8) + 0.2 \cdot LN(1.2, 0.08), \tag{4}$$

where $\Gamma(k, \theta)$ denotes the gamma distribution with the shape parameter k and the scale parameter θ, and $LN(\mu, \sigma)$ – the lognormal distribution. The target density (abbreviated further as $GWLN$) clearly did not remind the initial density (i.e. $N(0, 1)$, see Fig. 4).

The DE-MC algorithm required 400 iterations for the stop condition $\hat{R} = 1.05$, while the DE-MC-out converged after 220 steps, regardless of the methods

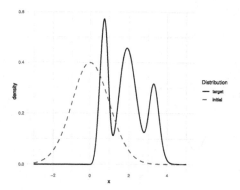

Fig. 4. Comparison of the initial $N(0,1)$ and target density $GWLN$.

applied for the outliers detection/replacement. Moreover, in the case of the DE-MC, many outliers were visible (see Fig. 5a) and the obtained histogram was sometimes "far" from the target density (see Fig. 5b). For the DE-MC-out, there were no outliers and the simulated results resembled the GWLN to a greater extent, especially for the pair m_iF (see Fig. 6 for some examples).

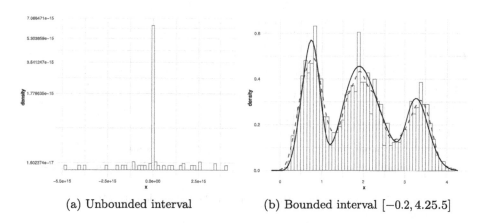

(a) Unbounded interval   (b) Bounded interval $[-0.2, 4.25.5]$

Fig. 5. Histograms for the DE-MC algorithm and the target density $GWLN$.

Because of the existing outliers, the mean for the DE-MC exhibited problems with its behavior and it even moved away from the true theoretical value (see Fig. 7a and Table 4). Meanwhile, the mean for the DE-MC-out converged even after 40 iterations in the case of the weighted quantiles method (see Fig. 7b) and after 75 steps for the min-max approach.

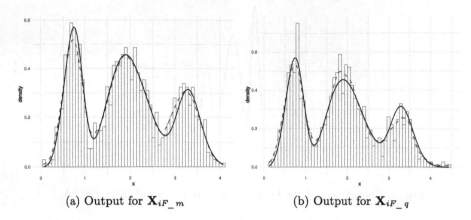

(a) Output for $\mathbf{X}_{iF\_m}$ (b) Output for $\mathbf{X}_{iF\_q}$

Fig. 6. Histograms for the DE-MC-out algorithm and the target density $GWLN$.

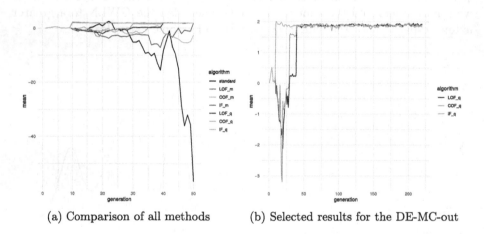

(a) Comparison of all methods   (b) Selected results for the DE-MC-out

Fig. 7. Convergence of the means for the target density $GWLN$.

Table 4. Comparison of the sample means and their distances related to the expected value for the target density $GWLN$.

Iteration	$\mathbf{X}_0$	$\mathbf{X}_{LOF\_m}$	$\mathbf{X}_{COF\_m}$	$\mathbf{X}_{iF\_m}$	$\mathbf{X}_{LOF\_q}$	$\mathbf{X}_{COF\_q}$	$\mathbf{X}_{iF\_q}$
50	−56.521525	1.863561	−2.547404	**1.891953**	1.882735	1.872665	1.845434
	1968.01%	38.41%	184.19%	37.47%	37.78%	38.11%	39.01%
220	−9280625.2049	1.8844	1.8210	1.8940	**1.9135**	1.8859	1.8357
	306721036%	37.72%	39.82%	37.40%	36.76%	37.67%	39.33%

5 Conclusions

Generation of random variables is very important in simulations and resampling of random fuzzy numbers. We extended the standard version of the DE-MC algorithm using three automated unsupervised methods for the detection of the outliers and two intuitive approaches for their replacement. As our preliminary results suggest, the proposed DE-MC-out algorithm converges faster and generates output samples that are closer to the target density than the standard approach. Moreover, its timing is sometimes better than for the DE-MC. Of course, further experiments are necessary, e.g., using other methods for the outlier detection and replacement. Moreover, the application of other useful and important statistical tools, e.g., aimed at modes detection, may be also fruitful.

References

1. Aho, K.: asbio: a collection of statistical tools for biologists (2022). https://CRAN. R-project.org/package=asbio
2. ter Braak, C.J.F., Vrugt, J.A.: Differential evolution Markov chain with snooker updater and fewer chains. Stat. Comput. **18**(4), 435–446 (2008). https://doi.org/ 10.1007/s11222-008-9104-9
3. Braak, C.J.F.T.: A Markov chain Monte Carlo version of the genetic algorithm differential evolution: easy Bayesian computing for real parameter spaces. Stat. Comput. **16**(3), 239–249 (2006). https://doi.org/10.1007/s11222-006-8769-1
4. Breunig, M., Kriegel, H.P., Ng, R., Sander, J.: LOF: identifying density-based local outliers. ACM SIGMOD Rec. **29**(2), 93–104 (2000)
5. Gelman, A., Carlin, J., Stern, H., Dunson, D., Vehtari, A., Rubin, D.: Bayesian Data Analysis. Chapman and Hall/CRC (2013). https://doi.org/10.1201/b16018
6. Grzegorzewski, P., Hryniewicz, O., Romaniuk, M.: Flexible bootstrap for fuzzy data based on the canonical representation. Int. J. Comput. Intell. Syst. **13**(1), 1650–1662 (2020). https://doi.org/10.2991/ijcis.d.201012.003
7. Grzegorzewski, P., Romaniuk, M.: Bootstrap methods for epistemic fuzzy data. Int. J. Appl. Math. Comput. Sci. **32**(2), 285–297 (2022). https://doi.org/10.34768/ amcs-2022-0021
8. Grzegorzewski, P., Romaniuk, M.: Bootstrap methods for fuzzy data. In: Atanassov, K.T., et al. (eds.) IWIFSGN BOS/SOR 2020. LNNS, vol. 338, pp. 28–47. Springer, Cham (2022). https://doi.org/10.1007/978-3-030-95929-6_3
9. Liu, F., Ting, K., Zhou, Z.H.: Isolation forest. In: Giannotti, F., Gunopulos, D., Turini, F., Zaniolo, C., Ramakrishnan, N., Wu, X. (eds.) Proceedings of the Eighth IEEE International Conference on Data Mining, pp. 413–422. IEEE (2008). https://doi.org/10.1109/ICDM.2008.17
10. Madsen, J.H.: DDoutlier: distance & density-based outlier detection (2018). https://CRAN.R-project.org/package=DDoutlier
11. Mersmann, O.: Microbenchmark: accurate timing functions (2021). https://CRAN. R-project.org/package=microbenchmark
12. Opara, K., Arabas, J.: Comparison of mutation strategies in differential evolution - a probabilistic perspective. Swarm Evol. Comput. **39**, 53–69 (2018). https://doi. org/10.1016/j.swevo.2017.12.007

13. Opara, K.R., Arabas, J.: Differential evolution: a survey of theoretical analyses. Swarm Evol. Comput. **44**, 546–558 (2019). https://doi.org/10.1016/j.swevo.2018.06.010

14. Panjei, E., Gruenwald, L., Leal, E., Nguyen, C., Silvia, S.: A survey on outlier explanations. VLDB J. **31**(5), 977–1008 (2022). https://doi.org/10.1007/s00778-021-00721-1

15. Plummer, M., Best, N., Cowles, K., Vines, K.: CODA: convergence diagnosis and output analysis for MCMC. R News **6**(1), 7–11 (2006). https://journal.r-project.org/archive/

16. Robert, C.P., Casella, G.: Monte Carlo Statistical Methods. Springer, Heidelberg (2005). https://doi.org/10.1007/978-1-4757-4145-2

17. Romaniuk, M.: Analysis of the insurance portfolio with an embedded catastrophe bond in a case of uncertain parameter of the insurer's share. Adv. Intell. Syst. Comput. **524**, 33–43 (2017). https://doi.org/10.1007/978-3-319-46592-0_3

18. Romaniuk, M.: On some applications of simulations in estimation of maintenance costs and in statistical tests for fuzzy settings. In: Steland, A., Rafajłowicz, E., Okhrin, O. (eds.) SMSA 2019. SPMS, vol. 294, pp. 437–448. Springer, Cham (2019). https://doi.org/10.1007/978-3-030-28665-1_33

19. Romaniuk, M., Hryniewicz, O.: Discrete and smoothed resampling methods for interval-valued fuzzy numbers. IEEE Trans. Fuzzy Syst. **29**(3), 599–611 (2021). https://doi.org/10.1109/TFUZZ.2019.2957253

20. Srikanth, K.S.: solitude: an implementation of isolation forest (2021). https://CRAN.R-project.org/package=solitude

21. Tang, J., Chen, Z., Fu, A.W., Cheung, D.W.: Enhancing effectiveness of outlier detections for low density patterns. In: Chen, M.-S., Yu, P.S., Liu, B. (eds.) PAKDD 2002. LNCS (LNAI), vol. 2336, pp. 535–548. Springer, Heidelberg (2002). https://doi.org/10.1007/3-540-47887-6_53

22. Vats, D., Knudson, C.: Revisiting the Gelman-Rubin diagnostic (2018). https://doi.org/10.48550/ARXIV.1812.09384, https://arxiv.org/abs/1812.09384

23. Vrugt, J.A., ter Braak, C.F.: DREAM(D): an adaptive Markov Chain Monte Carlo simulation algorithm to solve discrete, noncontinuous, and combinatorial posterior parameter estimation problems. Hydrol. Earth Syst. Sci. **15**(12), 3701–3713 (2011). https://doi.org/10.5194/hess-15-3701-2011

24. Vrugt, J.A., ter Braak, C., Diks, C., Robinson, B.A., Hyman, J.M., Higdon, D.: Accelerating Markov chain Monte Carlo simulation by differential evolution with self-adaptive randomized subspace sampling. Int. J. Nonlinear Sci. Numer. Simul. **10**(3), 273–290 (2009). https://doi.org/10.1515/IJNSNS.2009.10.3.273

A Specialized Xie-Beni Measure
for Clustering with Adaptive Distance

Shidi Deng[1,2], Benoit Albert[2(✉)], Violaine Antoine[2], and Jonas Koko[2]

[1] Technische Universität, Munich, Germany
shidi.deng@tum.de
[2] LIMOS, Université Clermont Auvergne, Clermont-Ferrand, France
{benoit.albert,violaine.antoine,jonas.koko}@uca.fr

Abstract. To certify good data partitioning, it is necessary to use an evaluation measure. This measure must take into account the specificity of the modeled partition. For centroid-based fuzzy partitioning, different measures exist. However, none of them takes into account the adaptive distance that some clustering models use. In our study, we extend the Xie-Beni measure, using both the Mahalanobis distance and the Wasserstein distance. The numerical results show the relevance of our new index.

Keywords: Clustering · Internal measure · Mahalanobis distance · Xie-Beni index

1 Introduction

Clustering is an unsupervised learning method that does not require prior class labels to implement observational learning. Clustering is employed to group collections of physical or abstract objects into multiple classes of similar objects. There are various clustering algorithms such as partition-based clustering, hierarchical clustering, density-based clustering, grid-based clustering, and model-based clustering. These clustering algorithms can also be split following the type of partition generated: a hard partition or a soft partition. A hard partition assigns with total certainty an object to a cluster, whereas a soft partition allows to produce doubt regarding the class membership of an object. Among soft partitions, the probabilistic partition is the most famous one.

Various clustering methods can be applied for a data analysis. Thus, it is important to choose among the algorithms the partition that best fits the data. For this, validity indexes have been proposed. Such indexes attempt to measure the correspondence between a partition and the underlying structure of the data.

The validity indexes can be divided into internal and external indexes. An external index, such as the Normalized Mutual Information (NMI) or the Adjusted Rand Index (ARI) [14], allows to compare two partitions. It is generally used to measure the accuracy of a clustering partition by comparing it with the partition derived from the ground truth. Inversely, an internal index seeks

S. Massanet et al. (Eds.): EUSFLAT 2023/AGOP 2023, LNCS 14069, pp. 713–724, 2023.
https://doi.org/10.1007/978-3-031-39965-7_59

to describe the intrinsic structure of the data without any prior information. It employs the notion of compactness within clusters and/or the notion of separability between clusters. The compactness quantifies how much the members of each cluster are close to each other. The separability, on the other hand, measures the distance between the different clusters. Cluster validity research is a difficult task and lacks a strict theoretical background [2].

In the case of a fuzzy partition-based clustering algorithm, such as Fuzzy C-Means (FCM) [4], there exists some specific and well-known internal indexes: the *Partition Coefficient PC*, the *Partition Entropy PE* [5], and the *Fuzzy Hyper Volume index FHV* [10] are the indexes that measure only compactness. The *Fuzzy Silhouette FS* [9], the *Xie-Beni XB* [21], and the *Partition Coefficient And Exponential Separation PCAES* [20] are measures combining compactness and separability.

However, with the exception of *Fuzzy Hyper Volume index* [10], they are all based on the Euclidean distance. If a clustering algorithm uses Mahalanobis distances, as it is the case for FCM-GK [12] and its extensions [1], these indexes will not take this information into account and it can lead to incorrect quantification of the compactness and separability of the partition. Plus, although the *Fuzzy Hyper Volume index* [10] handles Mahalanobis distances, it only measures the compactness of the partition. It is therefore necessary to describe a new measure adapted to the compactness and separability for clustering algorithms using Mahalanobis distances.

This study aims to propose an extension of the Xie-Beni index to deal with partitions obtained with Mahalanobis distances. The paper is organized as follows: Sect. 2 details the necessary knowledge to introduce the Xie-Beni index in Sect. 3 and its extension in Sect. 4. Numerical experiments are presented in Sect. 5 and a conclusion and perspectives are given in the last section.

2   Background

2.1   The Fuzzy C-Means Algorithm

Let $X = (x_1 \dots x_n)$ be a data set with n objects $x_i \in \mathbb{R}^p$ and p be the number of attributes describing the objects. The objective is to obtain a partition that groups objects into c clusters $2 \leq c < n$. A fuzzy partition $U = (u_{ij})$ is a matrix of membership degrees $(n \times c)$ such that $u_{ij} \in [0,1]$ is the probability that the object x_i belongs to the cluster j. The FCM clustering algorithm and its variants are centroid-based methods, i.e. each cluster is identified by its centroid $V = \{v_1, \dots, v_c\}$, $v_j \in \mathbb{R}^p$. The notion of similarity between an object and a group is then the calculation of the distance d_{ij}^2 between the object i and the center of gravity j:

– Euclidean distance in the FCM model [4,7]

$$d_{ij}^2 = (x_i - v_j)^\top (x_i - v_j). \tag{2.1}$$

– Mahalanobis distance in the FCM-GK model [12]

$$d_{ij}^2 = (\boldsymbol{x}_i - \boldsymbol{v}_j)^\top \boldsymbol{S}_j (\boldsymbol{x}_i - \boldsymbol{v}_j), \tag{2.2}$$

In FCM-GK, there exists a specific Mahalanobis distance for each cluster. These Mahalanobis distances are characterized by symmetric positive definite matrices $\boldsymbol{S} = \{\boldsymbol{S}_1, \dots, \boldsymbol{S}_c\}$ also referred to as variance covariance matrices. Remark that if the variance covariance matrix $\boldsymbol{S}_j$ defined for the cluster j corresponds to the identity, it represents a Euclidean distance.

In FCM-GK, the unknown variables $(\boldsymbol{U}, \boldsymbol{V}, \boldsymbol{S})$ are determined by optimizing the following problem:

$$\min_{(\boldsymbol{U}, \boldsymbol{V}, \boldsymbol{S})} J(\boldsymbol{U}, \boldsymbol{V}, \boldsymbol{S}) = \sum_{i=1}^n \sum_{j=1}^c u_{ij}^m d_{ij}^2, \tag{2.3}$$

with the constraints

$$u_{ij} \geq 0, \quad \forall i, j \in [1, n] \times [1, c] \tag{2.4}$$

$$\sum_{j=1}^c u_{ij} = 1, \quad \forall i \in [1, n] \tag{2.5}$$

$$\sum_{i=1}^n u_{ij} > 0, \quad \forall j \in [1, c] \tag{2.6}$$

$$\det(\boldsymbol{S}_j) = \rho_j, \quad \forall j \in [1, c] \tag{2.7}$$

The volume constraint (2.7) has been added in order to avoid trivial minimization where all $\boldsymbol{S}_j$ matrices are set to zero.

The method used to resolve this constrained problem is the alternating optimization method (AO) [4,7,12]. The resulting minimization steps are described in Algorithm 1. The FCM algorithm is similar except that the co-variance matrices of the set $\boldsymbol{S}$ are not updated and remain identity matrices.

2.2   The Wasserstein Distance

Originating from work on the optimal transport problem, this distance models the difficulty of changing one amount of earth to another, hence its other name Earth Mover's Distance (EMD) [15,19]. Mathematically, it is defined as the measure of the difference between two probability distributions. Let $g_1 = \mathcal{N}_1(\mu_1, \Sigma_1)$ and $g_2 = \mathcal{N}_2(\mu_2, \Sigma_2)$ be two multivariate Gaussians distribution. The 2-Wasserstein distance between the two Gaussians is:

$$W_2(g_1, g_2)^2 = \| \mu_1 - \mu_2 \|_2^2 + tr\left(\Sigma_1 + \Sigma_2 - 2\sqrt{\Sigma_2^{1/2} \Sigma_1 \Sigma_2^{1/2}} \right), \tag{2.8}$$

where $\| \cdot \|_2$ is the Euclidian norm, and $tr(.)$ the trace function. In computer science, this distance is widely used for image comparison, especially in content-based image search [18] and pattern recognition [3].

Algorithm 1. FCM-GK

1: **Intput :** X the data set, c the number of cluster

2: $err = 0, k = 0,$

3: U^0 random initialization.

4: **while** $err > 10^{-3}$ **do**

5:     $k \leftarrow k + 1$

6:     compute $\mathcal{V}^k$: $v_j^{k+1} = \frac{\sum_{i=1}^n u_{ij}^{k+1} x_i}{\sum_{i=1}^n u_{ij}^{k+1}},$

7:     compute $\mathcal{S}^k$:

$$\Sigma_j = \sum_{i=1}^n u_{ij}^{k+1} (x_i - v_j^{k+1})(x_i - v_j^{k+1})^\top$$

$$S_j^{k+1} = \det(\Sigma_j)^{\frac{1}{p}} (\Sigma_j)^{-1}$$

8:     compute U^k: $u_{ij}^{k+1} = \left[\sum_{\ell=1}^c \frac{(x_i - v_j^{k+1})^\top S_j^k (x_i - v_j^{k+1})}{(x_i - v_\ell^{k+1})^\top S_\ell^k (x_i - v_\ell^{k+1})} \right]^{-1}$

9:     $err \leftarrow \| U^k - U^{k-1} \|$

10: **end while**

11: **Output:** $U^k, \mathcal{V}^k, \mathcal{S}^k$

---

3   A Valitidy Measure: The Xie-Beni Index

Xie and Beni proposed a validity measure for fuzzy clustering to evaluate the quality of Fuzzy c-Means (FCM) cluster partitions [21]. This measure takes into account both compactness (intra-cluster gaps) and separability (distances between cluster centers) by computing a ratio between the mean quadratic error and the minimum of the squared distances between the centroids. It is widely used to compare two clustering methods [11,13,16].

3.1   Compactness

The compactness formulation is an extension of the "Partition Coefficient" [6] which measures the degree of overlap between fuzzy clusters. It is a weighted center-based distance, with the use of a Euclidean distance and the fuzzy partition as weights:

$$compactness = \frac{1}{n} \sum_{j=1}^c \sum_{i=1}^n u_{ij}^2 (x_i - v_j)^\top (x_i - v_j). \tag{3.1}$$

Remark that this formulation is very close to the FCM cost-to-minimize function (2.3).

3.2   Separability

In the Xie-Beni index, the separability is defined as the minimum Euclidean distance between two centroids:

$$separability = \min_{j,k \in [1,c], j \neq k} \| v_j - v_k \|_2^2. \tag{3.2}$$

3.3 XB Index

The Xie-Beni index (noted V_{XB}) is the ratio between compactness and separability. A good partitioning must have high compactness and high separability, so XB is an index to be minimized.

$$(\downarrow)V_{XB} = \frac{compactness}{separability} = \frac{\sum_{j=1}^{c}\sum_{i=1}^{n} u_{ij}^2 (\boldsymbol{x}_i - \boldsymbol{v}_j)^\top (\boldsymbol{x}_i - \boldsymbol{v}_j)}{n \min_{j,k\in[1,c],j\neq k} \| \boldsymbol{v}_j - \boldsymbol{v}_k \|_2^2}. \tag{3.3}$$

4 Improvement of V_{XB}

The Xie-Beni index is not appropriate for partitions obtained with clustering algorithms using a specific distance for each cluster, as FCM-GK. The two following examples presents the limits of the Xie-Beni measure and the way to extend the formulas to obtain XBMW, a new Xie-Beni index taking in account Mahalanobis distances.

4.1 Improvement of the Compactness Measure

Let us considerate a 2-dimensional data set with two well-separated classes as shown in the Fig. 1. The first class has a spherical structure whereas the second class is characterized by an ellipsoidal shape. The FCM and FCM-GK algorithms have been applied on the data set and the obtained co-variances matrices are presented Fig. 1. Note that FCM is represented by identity covariance matrices.

For the first cluster ω_1, both methods detect the same structure. Thus, the compactness is the same. For the second cluster ω_2, the FCM-GK method better detects the real shape of the cluster and should have a better compactness than the FCM algorithm. However, since the compactness measured by the Xie-Beni index uses the Euclidean distance, the values are similar.

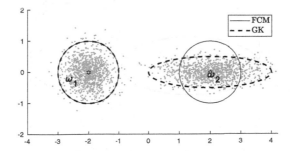

Fig. 1. Data set with two classes. The co-variance matrices obtained by FCM-GK are in dotted lines and in lines for FCM

Therefore, we propose to modify the Euclidean distance by the Mahalanobis distance:

$$compactness_m = \frac{1}{n}\sum_{j=1}^{c}\sum_{i=1}^{n}u_{ij}^2(\boldsymbol{x}_i - \boldsymbol{v}_j)^\top \boldsymbol{S}_j(\boldsymbol{x}_i - \boldsymbol{v}_j). \quad (4.1)$$

When $\boldsymbol{S}_j = I$ for all $j \in [1, c]$ then the new compactness measure is similar to the compactness measure of the Xie-Beni index.

4.2   Improvement of the Separability Measure

In the V_{XB} index, separability is the minimum Euclidean distance between two centroids. Such distance does not take into account the possible difference of importance between attributes that can exists with ellipsoidal shapes. Let us consider an example of three clusters where the second and third cluster have the same centroids but different variance co-variance matrices (cf. Fig. 2). The Euclidean distance $d(\omega_1, \omega_2)$ between the cluster $(\omega_1 : \boldsymbol{v}_1, \boldsymbol{S}_1)$ and the cluster $(\omega_2 : \boldsymbol{v}_2, \boldsymbol{S}_2)$ is the same as the Euclidean distance $d(\omega_1, \omega_3)$ between the cluster $(\omega_1 : \boldsymbol{v}_1, \boldsymbol{S}_1)$ and the cluster $(\omega_3 : \boldsymbol{v}_2, \boldsymbol{S}_3)$.

It can be noticed in this example that cluster 3 gives much more importance to the attributes carried by the ordinate axis, unlike the two other clusters. We propose to use the Wasserstein distance to measure the difference between two clusters, considering that a cluster can be approximated as a distribution characterized by the mean being the centroid ($\mu = \boldsymbol{v}$) and the variance-covariance matrix being the inverse of the distance matrix ($\Sigma = \boldsymbol{S}^{-1}$). The distance between the two clusters is then:

$$W_2(\omega_j, \omega_k)^2 = \|\boldsymbol{v}_j - \boldsymbol{v}_k\|_2^2 + tr\left(\boldsymbol{S}_j^{-1} + \boldsymbol{S}_k^{-1} - 2\sqrt{\boldsymbol{S}_k^{-1/2}\boldsymbol{S}_j^{-1}\boldsymbol{S}_k^{-1/2}}\right). \quad (4.2)$$

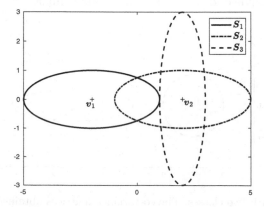

Fig. 2. Figure of two clusters with different shapes

The separability with the Wasserstein distance is

$$separability_w = \min_{j,k \in [1,c], j \neq k} W_2(\omega_j, \omega_k)^2.$$ (4.3)

When the distance matrices are all equal as in FCM where $S_j = I, \forall j \in [1, c]$, then the Wasserstein distance is equal to the Euclidean distance.

4.3   XBMW: A New Xie-Beni Index

Our new index, referred to as V_{XBMW}, is an extension of V_{XB} using the Mahalanobis distance for the compactness and the Wasserstein distance for the separability:

$$(\downarrow)V_{XBMW} = \frac{compactness_m}{separability_w} = \frac{\sum_{j=1}^c \sum_{i=1}^n u_{ij}^2 (x_i - v_j)^\top S_j (x_i - v_j)}{n \min_{j,k \in [1,c], j \neq k} W_2(\omega_j, \omega_k)^2}.$$ (4.4)

5   Numerical Experimentation

5.1   Methodology

In this section, we evaluate the performance of our index. The idea is to show that there exists a better correlation between an external measure and our internal measure than between the same external measure and the Xie-Benie index. The clustering methods used for the experiments are FCM and FCM-GK. Each algorithm is run 10 times with different centroids initializations and only the partition minimizing the cost function (2.3) is kept.

5.2   Datasets

We used 19 datasets, 6 toys datasets, and 9 from the UCI library[1]: Algerian forest (Af), Drybean (Db), Glass, Iris, classes I, J, and L from Letters (IJL) [8], Seeds, WDBC, Wifi, Wine. We also used two synthetic datasets: Asymetric and Skewed [17]. Table 1 references their characteristics, i.e. the number of classes c, the number of objects n, and the number of attributes p. All datasets are normalized, i.e. centered (mean) and reduced (std) for each attribute.

We also have created six toy datasets using a combination of cluster ω. Each cluster corresponds to a specific Gaussian for which 100 points have been generated. The characteristics of each Gaussian is given in the Table 2: mean value v, axis lengths a, b and rotation angle θ. We note $-\omega$, the cluster whose mean is the opposite $-v$. The data set T1 is composed of $(\omega_1, \omega_2, -\omega_1)$, T2: $(\omega_1, \omega_2, \omega_3)$, T3: (ω_4, ω_5), T4: $(\omega_4, \omega_5, \omega_6, -\omega_6, \omega_7, -\omega_7)$, T5: $(\omega_1, \omega_8, \omega_9, \omega_{10}, \omega_{11})$, and T2: $(\omega_{12}, \omega_{13}, -\omega_1)$. Figure 3 shows the obtained datasets.

---

[1] https://archive.ics.uci.edu/ml/datasets.php.

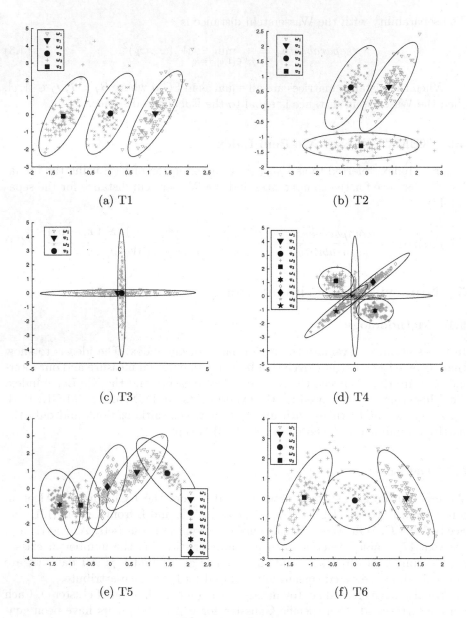

(a) T1

(b) T2

(c) T3

(d) T4

(e) T5

(f) T6

Fig. 3. Toys datasets

Table 1. Characteristics of datasets.

	Af	Db	Glass	Iris	IJL	Seeds	WDBC	Wifi	Wine	Asymetric	Skewed
c	2	7	2	3	3	3	2	4	3	5	6
n	243	13611	214	150	2263	210	569	2000	178	1000	1000
p	10	16	9	4	16	7	30	7	13	2	2

Table 2. Characteristics of Gaussians (i.e. clusters)

	ω_1	ω_2	ω_3	ω_4	ω_5	ω_6	ω_7	ω_8	ω_9	ω_{10}	ω_{11}	ω_{12}	ω_{13}
v	$\begin{pmatrix}\frac{3}{5}\\0\end{pmatrix}$	$\begin{pmatrix}0\\0\end{pmatrix}$	$\begin{pmatrix}\frac{-2}{5}\\0\end{pmatrix}$	$\begin{pmatrix}0\\0\end{pmatrix}$	$\begin{pmatrix}0\\0\end{pmatrix}$	$\begin{pmatrix}-3\\3\end{pmatrix}$	$\begin{pmatrix}3\\3\end{pmatrix}$	$\begin{pmatrix}1.2\\0\end{pmatrix}$	$\begin{pmatrix}\frac{-1}{2}\\\frac{-1}{3}\end{pmatrix}$	$\begin{pmatrix}\frac{-9}{10}\\\frac{-1}{3}\end{pmatrix}$	$\begin{pmatrix}0\\\frac{-1}{6}\end{pmatrix}$	$\begin{pmatrix}\frac{3}{5}\\0\end{pmatrix}$	$\begin{pmatrix}0\\0\end{pmatrix}$
a	$\frac{1}{6}$	$\frac{1}{6}$	$\frac{1}{2}$	2	2	1	2	$\frac{1}{6}$	$\frac{1}{12}$	$\frac{1}{12}$	$\frac{1}{6}$	$\frac{1}{6}$	$\frac{1}{6}$
b	$\frac{1}{18}$	$\frac{1}{18}$	$\frac{1}{18}$	$\frac{1}{10}$	$\frac{1}{10}$	1	$\frac{1}{4}$	$\frac{1}{18}$	$\frac{1}{12}$	$\frac{1}{12}$	$\frac{1}{12}$	$\frac{1}{18}$	$\frac{1}{18}$
θ	30	30	0	0	90	0	45	-30	0	0	45	-30	0

5.3 External Evaluation Measure

We used the Ajusted Rand Index [14], which compares two hard partitions. Since FCM and FCM-GK generates fuzzy partitions, these partitions are transformed into hard partitions by assigning to each object the class with the highest membership. Let π_1 and π_2 be two partitions, a be the number of pairs of objects which are in the same group in π_1 and π_2, b be the number of pairs of objects which are in different groups in π_1 and π_2, c be the number of pairs that are in the same group in π_1 but not in π_2 and d be the number of pairs that are in the same group in π_2 but not in π_1. The ARI is then defined as follows:

$$ARI(\pi_1, \pi_2) = \frac{2(ab - cd)}{(a + d)(d + b) + (a + c)(c + b)}$$

If two partitions are identical then the ARI score is one. The better partitioning will have a higher ARI score and a lower index value.

5.4 Results

A better partitioning is a larger ARI and a smaller index. We use a simple matching coefficient (SMC), between the difference in the ARI score for FCM and GK, and the difference in the index. When ARI increases and the index decreases it is a true positive (TP), but if the index increases then it is a false negative (FN). If ARI decreases and the index decreases it is a false positive (FP) but if the index increases it is a true negative (TN).

$$SMC = \frac{TP + TN}{TP + TN + FP + FN} \tag{5.1}$$

As it can be observed Table 3, there exists a better matching for our new index. Details are given in the Tables 4, 5, and 6. This is especially the case for

Table 3. Matching between XB, XBMW and ARI

	TP	TN	FP	FN	SMC
V_{XB}	2	4	1	10	0.35
V_{XBMW}	11	2	3	1	**0.76**

Table 4. ARI, XB, XBMW for toys datasets

(a) T1

	FCM	GK	
ARI	0.42	1	
V_{XB}	0.18	0.61	FN
V_{XBMW}	0.18	0.21	FN

(b) T2

	FCM	GK	
ARI	0.79	0.97	
V_{XB}	0.18	0.28	FN
V_{XBMW}	0.18	0.13	**TP**

(c) T3

	FCM	GK	
ARI	0.26	0.86	
V_{XB}	0.72	33.3	FN
V_{XBMW}	0.72	0.005	**TP**

(d) T4

	FCM	GK	
ARI	0.61	0.91	
V_{XB}	0.33	13.5	FN
V_{XBMW}	0.33	0.01	**TP**

(e) T5

	FCM	GK	
ARI	0.41	0.93	
V_{XB}	0.33	0.68	FN
V_{XBMW}	0.33	0.31	**TP**

(f) T6

	FCM	GK	
ARI	0.27	0.96	
V_{XB}	0.20	0.53	FN
V_{XBMW}	0.20	0.14	**TP**

Table 5. ARI, XB, XBMW for Synthetic datasets

(a) Asymmetric

	FCM	GK	
ARI	0.89	0.96	
V_{XB}	0.09	0.12	FN
V_{XBMW}	0.09	0.06	**TP**

(b)Skewed

	FCM	GK	
ARI	0.65	0.99	
V_{XB}	0.24	0.66	FN
V_{XBMW}	0.24	0.06	**TP**

Table 6. ARI, XB, XBMW for UCI datasets

(a) Algerian forest

	FCM	GK	
ARI	0.34	0.54	
V_{XB}	0.35	0.38	FN
V_{XBMW}	0.35	0.01	**TP**

(b)Dry bean

	FCM	GK	
ARI	0.68	0.70	
V_{XB}	16.55	0.64	**TP**
V_{XBMW}	16.55	6.10^{-6}	**TP**

(c)Glass

	FCM	GK	
ARI	0.55	0.41	
V_{XB}	1.45	0.84	**TN**
V_{XBMW}	1.45	2.10^{-3}	FP

(d)Iris

	FCM	GK	
ARI	0.63	0.74	
V_{XB}	0.22	0.79	FN
V_{XBMW}	0.22	0.16	**TP**

(e)IJL

	FCM	GK	
ARI	0.04	0.26	
V_{XB}	7.06	1.15	FN
V_{XBMW}	7.06	0.10	**TP**

(f)Seed

	FCM	GK	
ARI	0.77	0.72	
V_{XB}	0.21	0.22	**TN**
V_{XBMW}	0.21	0.01	FP

(g)WDBC

	FCM	GK	
ARI	0.68	0.41	
V_{XB}	0.48	2.16	**TN**
V_{XBMW}	0.48	0.02	FP

(h)Wifi

	FCM	GK	
ARI	0.82	0.41	
V_{XB}	0.34	6.10^4	**TN**
V_{XBMW}	0.34	1.10^4	**TN**

(i)Wine

	FCM	GK	
ARI	0.90	0.33	
V_{XB}	0.47	70.0	**TN**
V_{XBMW}	0.47	4.19	**TN**

the toy sets, which allow us to highlight our index. We observe that for case T1, the limit of the Wasserstein distance is because if the clusters have the same shape then it will be equal to the Euclidean distance. Our new index favors GK (chosen 14 times out of 17) contrary to Xie Beni's index which favors FCM (chosen 14 times out of 6).

Let us also remark that our new index is more sensitive to a high number of attributes, especially for the WDBC dataset.

6 Conclusion

In this study, the interest was to take into account the adaptability of the metrics to measure the quality of the partitioning methods. Indeed, for the internal criteria, it is important to evaluate the compactness and separability according to the particular distances of each cluster. This is why we have extended the Xie-Beni measure with the Mahalanobis distance for the compactness and the Wasserstein distance for the separability. We compared two methods, one based on Euclidean distance (FCM) and its variant based on adaptive distances (FCM-GK). The results are satisfactory as the index allows us to analyze a good fit with an external measure.

This study is encouraging and offers some perspectives. First of all, it would be interesting to compare two clustering methods that are both using Mahalanobis distances. We can also consider selecting another metric for separability. Finally, we focused our study on the Xie-Beni index, but it could be interesting to adapt other internal validation measures to the Mahalanobis distances, in particular to find an optimal number of clusters.

References

1. Antoine, V., Quost, B., Masson, M.H., Denoeux, T.: CECM: constrained evidential c-means algorithm. Comput. Stat. Data Anal. **56**(4), 894–914 (2012)
2. Arbelaitz, O., Gurrutxaga, I., Muguerza, J., Pérez, J.M., Perona, I.: An extensive comparative study of cluster validity indices. Pattern Recogn. **46**(1), 243–256 (2013)
3. Arjovsky, M., Chintala, S., Bottou, L.: Wasserstein generative adversarial networks. In: International Conference on Machine Learning, pp. 214–223. PMLR (2017)
4. Bezdek, J.C.: Fuzzy mathematics in pattern classification. Cornell University (1973)
5. Bezdek, J.C.: Numerical taxonomy with fuzzy sets. J. Math. Biol. **1**(1), 57–71 (1974)
6. Bezdek, J.C.: Objective function clustering. In: Bezdek, J.C. (ed.) Pattern Recognition with Fuzzy Objective Function Algorithms. AAPR, pp. 43–93. Springer, Boston, MA (1981). https://doi.org/10.1007/978-1-4757-0450-1_3
7. Bezdek, J., Dunn, J.: Optimal fuzzy partitions: a heuristic for estimating the parameters in a mixture of normal distributions. IEEE Trans. Comput. **100**(8), 835–838 (1975)

8. Bilenko, M., Basu, S., Mooney, R.J.: Integrating constraints and metric learning in semi-supervised clustering. In: Proceedings of the Twenty-First International Conference on Machine Learning, p. 11 (2004)
9. Fukuyama, Y.: A new method of choosing the number of clusters for the fuzzy c-mean method. In: 1989 Proceedings of the 5th Fuzzy System Symposium, pp. 247–250 (1989)
10. Gath, I., Geva, A.B.: Unsupervised optimal fuzzy clustering. IEEE Trans. Pattern Anal. Mach. Intell. **11**(7), 773–780 (1989)
11. Ghosh, A., Mishra, N.S., Ghosh, S.: Fuzzy clustering algorithms for unsupervised change detection in remote sensing images. Inf. Sci. **181**(4), 699–715 (2011)
12. Gustafson, D., Kessel, W.: Fuzzy clustering with a fuzzy covariance matrix. In: 1978 IEEE Conference on Decision and Control Including the 17th Symposium on Adaptive Processes, pp. 761–766. IEEE (1979)
13. Huang, C., Molisch, A.F., Geng, Y.A., He, R., Ai, B., Zhong, Z.: Trajectory-joint clustering algorithm for time-varying channel modeling. IEEE Trans. Veh. Technol. **69**(1), 1041–1045 (2019)
14. Hubert, L., Arabie, P.: Comparing partitions. J. Classif. **2**(1), 193–218 (1985)
15. Kantorovich, L.V.: Mathematical methods of organizing and planning production. Manage. Sci. **6**(4), 366–422 (1960)
16. Mitra, S., Pedrycz, W., Barman, B.: Shadowed C-means: integrating fuzzy and rough clustering. Pattern Recogn. **43**(4), 1282–1291 (2010)
17. Rezaei, M., Fränti, P.: Can the number of clusters be determined by external indices? IEEE Access **8**, 89239–89257 (2020)
18. Valle, M.E., Francisco, S., Granero, M.A., Velasco-Forero, S.: Measuring the irregularity of vector-valued morphological operators using wasserstein metric. In: Lindblad, J., Malmberg, F., Sladoje, N. (eds.) DGMM 2021. LNCS, vol. 12708, pp. 512–524. Springer, Cham (2021). https://doi.org/10.1007/978-3-030-76657-3_37
19. Vaserstein, L.N.: Markov processes over denumerable products of spaces, describing large systems of automata. Probl. Peredachi Inform. **5**(3), 64–72 (1969)
20. Wu, K.L., Yang, M.S.: A cluster validity index for fuzzy clustering. Pattern Recognit. Lett. **26**(9), 1275–1291 (2005)
21. Xie, X.L., Beni, G.: A validity measure for fuzzy clustering. IEEE Trans. Pattern Anal. Mach. Intell. **13**(08), 841–847 (1991)

Classification Error in Semi-Supervised Fuzzy C-Means

Kamil Kmita[(✉)][iD], Katarzyna Kaczmarek-Majer[iD], and Olgierd Hryniewicz[iD]

Systems Research Institute, Polish Academy of Sciences,
Newelska 6, 01-147 Warsaw, Poland
{kmita,kaczmar,hryniewi}@ibspan.waw.pl

Abstract. Semi-Supervised Fuzzy C-Means (SSFCMeans) model
enables inclusion of additional knowledge about the true class of a part
of the training data. With this partial supervision, there comes a new
possibility to use this model as a classifier. The main goal should be thus
to minimize the classification error, just as in the fully supervised setting. However, the typical problems with minimizing the training error,
test error, and avoiding the phenomenon of overfitting must be carefully
considered with respect to the characteristics of the SSFCMeans model.
In this work, we fill the identified research gap and analyze the way
of handling partial supervision in Semi-Supervised Fuzzy C-Means and
its impact on the aforementioned issues. We investigate this relationship experimentally using artificially simulated data. We show that the
training error for the training phase is directly related to the scaling factor α and is deterministically assured to be equal to 0 in some cases. We
further illustrate our main findings for real-life partially labeled data collected from smartphones of patients with bipolar disorder in a problem
of predicting the phase of the disease.

Keywords: Semi-Supervised Learning · Fuzzy Clustering ·
Semi-Supervised Fuzzy C-Means · Classification · Bipolar Disorder ·
Mental Health Monitoring

1 Introduction

Semi-supervised fuzzy clustering (SSFC) is a class of fuzzy clustering models
that incorporate additional knowledge which is called partial supervision since
it provides labels $y \in \{y^{(1)}, \ldots, y^{(c)}\}$ only for a part of M observations out of
all N available observations, $M < N$. Other forms of supervision are possible as
well (e.g. pairwise constraints), but in this paper, we focus on labels.

SSFC is a multidisciplinary approach involving elements from unsupervised
learning, fuzzy set theory, and supervised learning. Clearly, we are dealing with

Supported by Small Grants Scheme (NOR/SGS/BIPOLAR/0239/2020-00) within the
research project: "Bipolar disorder prediction with sensor-based semi-supervised Learning (BIPOLAR)" http://bipolar.ibspan.waw.pl/.

S. Massanet et al. (Eds.): EUSFLAT 2023/AGOP 2023, LNCS 14069, pp. 725–736, 2023.
https://doi.org/10.1007/978-3-031-39965-7_60

the task of clustering, i.e. grouping observations x_j into c clusters so that observations in the same cluster are similar to each other while being dissimilar to the observations from other clusters. The methods we consider in this paper measure the similarity using a chosen metric. The *fuzzy* character of SSFC relies on the idea of a soft assignment of each observation to each cluster to some degree of membership that has its roots in fuzzy set theory. Such an approach differs from crisp clustering which treats an observation as belonging unambiguously to a single cluster only.

Last but not least, SSFC is categorized into the Semi-Supervised Learning (SSL) setting. Note that SSL is often described as a setting "in the middle", between (completely) unsupervised and (completely) supervised learning (see e.g. [16]), but its goal is the same as in the fully supervised problem. [8, p. 16], the authors of a thorough overview of SSL, clearly state that "The semi-supervised learning problem belongs to the supervised category since the goal is to minimize the classification error (...)". Classifying observations in SSFC relies on a *cluster assumption*: "If points are in the same cluster, they are likely to be of the same class" [8, p. 5]. By arbitrarily establishing a one-to-one mapping between clusters and classes, we introduce partial information into the clustering and push the memberships of supervised observations towards the clusters associated with respective classes during the learning process.

Many works investigate extensions of SSFCMeans and perform simulations or experiments that evaluate clustering quality or classification quality and apply them in various application scenarios [1,4–7,10,11,14,15]. In this paper, we further extend research in this line and investigate the relationship between the key mechanism of handling partial supervision in SSFCMeans and the classification error. Specifically, we focus on the relationship between the training error and the test error and the issue of overfitting. Inducing the classifier $\hat{\pi} : x_j \mapsto y_j$ from the training data $\mathcal{D}$ one may possibly find $\hat{\pi}$ that achieves great performance on $\mathcal{D}$ by fitting too much to the local characteristics of $\mathcal{D}$. The generalization capability of the classifier, associated with its test error (classification performance on independent data $\mathcal{T}$ that did not take part in the learning process), is decreasing in such case.

The main novelty of this paper is showing that a way of handling partial supervision in SSFCMeans based on the hyperparameter α (called a scaling factor) may result in a deterministically over-optimistic training error. In consequence, one cannot analyze overfitting for Semi-Supervised Fuzzy C-Means in the context of its typical meaning described above. We support our findings with simulation results.

The rest of this paper is structured as follows. Section 2 recalls basic definitions and the SSFCMeans algorithm. Section 3 discusses the impact of the scaling factor α on the training error in classification. Section 4 presents the simulation results on artificial datasets. Next, Sect. 5 explains the experimental setup and gathers numerical results for real-life data collected from bipolar disorder patients. Finally, Sect. 6 concludes the paper and outlines the future directions of our research.

2   Semi-Supervised Fuzzy C-Means

Semi-Supervised Fuzzy C-Means model proposed in [16] can be categorized as a distance-based model [15] that incorporates the partial knowledge to modify the distances between jth observation and kth cluster. Having chosen a metric d, the distance d_{jk}^2 is calculated between a vector $x_j \in R^p$ representing jth observation and vector $v_k \in R^p$ representing kth cluster (called a prototype).

An objective function for SSFCMeans based on [16] is

$$J_{\text{SSFCM}}(U, V) = \underbrace{\sum_{j=1}^{N}\sum_{k=1}^{c} u_{jk}^2 d_{jk}^2}_{Q(U,V;X)} + \alpha \underbrace{\sum_{j=1}^{N}\sum_{k=1}^{c} b_j(u_{jk} - f_{jk})^2 d_{jk}^2}_{Q'(U,V;X,F)}. \quad (1)$$

Note that it consists of two components: unsupervised Q and supervised Q'. $U = [u_{jk}]$ is a membership matrix, $V = [v_k]$ is a prototypes matrix, and d_{jk}^2 denotes a Euclidean distance between jth observation and kth prototype. The supervised component Q' introduces matrix $F = [f_{jk}]$ that encodes the one-to-one mapping between clusters and classes. It contains a priori information $f_{jk} \in \{0, 1\}$ such that $f_{jk} = 1$ iff jth observation is known to belong to kth class. Scalar b_j is a binary indicator stating whether jth observation is supervised or not. Finally, the hyperparameter $\alpha \geq 0$ that is called a scaling factor is used to "maintain a balance between the supervised and unsupervised component within the optimization mechanism" [16, p. 789]. The bigger the α, the stronger the influence of the supervised observations on the outcomes of the algorithm.

The task of Semi-Supervised Fuzzy C-Means is formalized as a minimization problem of the J_{SSFCM} function from (1). One wants to find

$$\arg\min_{U,V} J_{\text{SSFCM}}(U, V; X, F, \alpha)$$

$$\text{s.t.} \quad \sum_{k=1}^{c} u_{jk} = 1, \quad 0 < \sum_{j=1}^{N} u_{jk} < N, \quad u_{jk} \in [0, 1]. \quad (2)$$

A commonly used optimization algorithm described in [3] is based on the observation that problem (2) is NP-hard, but there exist analytical solutions to minimizing $J_{\text{SSFCM}}(U)$ and $J_{\text{SSFCM}}(V)$ separately. One thus holds V fixed and finds optimal $\hat{U}$, and then the analogous process is performed to find $\hat{V}$.

The optimal membership $\hat{u}_{jk}$ is found to be

$$\hat{u}_{jk} = \frac{1 + \alpha \cdot \left(1 - b_j \cdot \sum_{s=1}^{c} f_{js}\right)}{1 + \alpha} \cdot \frac{1}{\sum_{s=1}^{c}\left(d_{jk}^2/d_{js}^2\right)} + \frac{\alpha}{1 + \alpha}\left(f_{jk} \cdot b_j\right). \quad (3)$$

Extensions of the classical SSFCMeans were proposed over the years. For example, [7] and [6] adapted it to handle streaming data, as the original model works with batch data only. In the remainder of this paper, we focus on the core SSFCMeans algorithm and investigate in detail the relationship between the scaling factor α, and the training and test classification errors.

3   The Scaling Factor α and Its Relationship with the Training Error

To consider any classification error of the observation - either the training one or the test one - we need to know two components: the true class y and the predicted class $\hat{y}$. Since partial supervision provides labels only for M out of all N available observations, we will use the index $i = 1, \ldots, M$ to denote the supervised observations that constitute the training set $\mathcal{D}$, on which we will calculate the training error. Recall that in SSFCMeans, the true class y_i of ith supervised observation is associated with one of the columns in matrix F. We will use a function $s(i) \in \{1, \ldots, c\}$ to select the correct column associated with y_i, i.e. $s(i)$ is such that $f_{i,s(i)} = 1$.

The outcome of the SSFCMeans model for ith observation is a tuple $\langle \hat{u}_{i1}, \ldots, \hat{u}_{ic} \rangle$. Therefore, to obtain a second component: a predicted class, one needs to perform a *defuzzification*. A simple idea is to predict the class associated with the cluster to which the membership was the highest. A corresponding decision rule π can be formulated as

$$\pi : i \mapsto k = \arg\max_{k} u_{ik}. \tag{4}$$

Let us now consider a test set $\mathcal{T}$ and a boundary $\beta \in (0,1)$. If any given membership $\hat{u}_{ik_0}$ exceeds $\beta_{0.5} = 0.5$, then it is guaranteed that k_0 is the argument maximum because of the constraint $\sum_{k=1}^{c} u_{jk} = 1$ in (2). The reverse does not hold. For example, in a 3-class problem, a possible outcome of the SSFCMeans model may be $\langle 0.33, 0.3, 0.37 \rangle$ and the argument maximum $\hat{u}_{i3}$ does not exceed $\beta_{0.5}$.

The situation is more complex for the training error since there exists a special relationship between the β boundary and the scaling factor α. By (3), the optimal membership $\hat{u}_{i,s(i)}$ is expressed as

$$\hat{u}_{i,s(i)} = \frac{1}{1+\alpha} \cdot \frac{1}{\sum_{s=1}^{c} \left(d_{ik}^2 / d_{is}^2 \right)} + \frac{\alpha}{1+\alpha}. \tag{5}$$

Note that we are guaranteed

$$\hat{u}_{i,s(i)} \geq \frac{\alpha}{1+\alpha}. \tag{6}$$

We call the quantity $\frac{\alpha}{1+\alpha}$ the Absolute Lower Bound to stress its meaning.

For any value of $\alpha \geq 1$, we are guaranteed that the cluster indexed by $s(i)$ will be the argument maximum since the associated membership $\hat{u}_{i,s(i)} \geq \beta_{0.5}$. This leads to a 0% training error regardless of the performance metric used to measure the classification error (e.g. precision, recall, or F1 score). Such situations may disturb the classical overfitting analysis, as the classifier is not even fitting too much to the local characteristics of the training data $\mathcal{D}$, but is deterministically assured to achieve artificially great performance regardless of the data evidence.

We thus suggest considering a *margin of making the training error* $\epsilon \in [0, \beta_{0.5}]$ in a process of selecting the optimal value α with regard to the training and test classification performance. In terms of the scaling factor α, we postulate to consider α such that

$$\frac{\alpha}{1+\alpha} = \beta_{0.5} - \epsilon. \tag{7}$$

Note that applying the margin of making the training error ϵ may still result in 0% training error, but in such a case a classical overfitting analysis can be meaningful because the performance would not be deterministic. It would be rather the high data evidence or excessive adjusting of the SSFCMeans to the characteristics of the training dataset $\mathcal{D}$.

In this paper, we use F1 score (a harmonic mean of precision and recall) to measure both the training and test classification errors. Note that the better the F1 score, the lower the classification error.

4 Experiments on Simulated Data

We perform a simulation experiment to show the potential problems with studying overfitting described in Sect. 3. Two datasets are created: separable and unseparable. In each case, we simulate 200 observations from two classes $y^{(1)}$ and $y^{(2)}$, having 400 observations in total. We then split the data so that 85% observations from each class go to the training dataset $\mathcal{D}$, and the remaining 15% goes to the test dataset $\mathcal{T}$. Next, to mimic the partial supervision, we randomly select 15% observations from $\mathcal{D}$ that will remain supervised (sustaining the class balance), artificially treating the rest of the data from $\mathcal{D}$ as unsupervised.

In the next step, we fit SSFCMeans models for a grid of ϵ values. Specifically, we consider 11 values of ϵ: $\epsilon_g = g \cdot 0.05$, $g = 0, 1, \ldots, 10$. For each SSFCMeans(ϵ_g) model, we calculate the F1 score both on the training set $\mathcal{D}$ and test set $\mathcal{T}$. We use the argument maximum decision rule from (4) when predicting a class of the observation. Table 1 presents a grid of ϵ values used in the experiments, together with corresponding α and Absolute Lower Bound $\frac{\alpha}{1+\alpha}$. Note that $\epsilon = 0.5$ results in excluding partial supervision effect (since the corresponding scaling factor α is equal to 0).

The experimental setting consists of simulating a dataset 15 times, and then randomly selecting the observations that will remain supervised 15 times for each dataset. In total, we have $15 \cdot 15 = 225$ simulation runs. We calculate the median F1 score for both training and test sets on the results of all the simulation runs, and present the overall statistics in Fig. 1c and Fig. 1d. For test F1 score we additionally display the interquartile range IQR by highlighting the respective areas of the plot in grey.

The unseparable dataset was created by sampling observations from each class y from the same $\mathcal{N}_2(\mu, \Sigma)$ distribution, where $\mu = (5, 5)$ and $\Sigma = \text{diag}(0.5, 0.5)$. An example of a single dataset is presented in Fig. 1b. The corresponding simulation results in Fig. 1d prove that even in the case of completely unseparable data, the training error goes to 0% for $\epsilon = 0$. A corresponding test error remains around the level of 0.5, which corresponds to a random prediction of a class: the

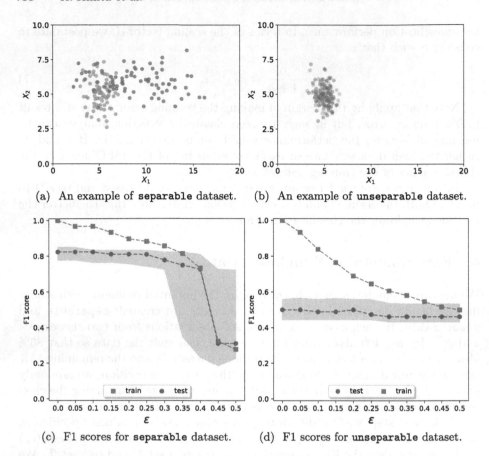

(a) An example of **separable** dataset.   (b) An example of **unseparable** dataset.

(c) F1 scores for **separable** dataset.   (d) F1 scores for **unseparable** dataset.

Fig. 1. Results for 225 simulation runs on training and test sets. Red dots represent corresponding median F1 scores for each ϵ on the test set, and green squares represent median F1 scores on the training set. Areas highlighted in grey represent IQR for test F1 score. (Color figure online)

Table 1. Values of ϵ and the corresponding α values.

g	0	1	2	3	4	5	6	7	8	9	10
ϵ	0.0	0.05	0.1	0.15	0.2	0.25	0.3	0.35	0.4	0.45	0.5
α	1.0	0.82	0.67	0.54	0.43	0.33	0.25	0.18	0.11	0.05	0.0
$\frac{\alpha}{1+\alpha}$	0.5	0.45	0.4	0.35	0.3	0.25	0.2	0.15	0.1	0.05	0.0

only true possible performance in such a case. This example shows a problem with training error being deterministically too optimistic even in extreme cases.

A different situation is examined in **separable** dataset. The data for class $y^{(1)}$ are simulated from $\mathcal{N}_2\big(\mu = (5,5), \Sigma = \mathrm{diag}(1,1)\big)$, but for class $y^{(2)}$ we simulate data from $\mathcal{N}_2\big(\mu = (3,6), \Sigma = \mathrm{diag}(1,1)\big)$ and stretch it by multiplying the resulting features matrix by matrix diag(3, 1). An example of such a dataset is presented in Fig. 1a. This way of simulating allows for partial separation of the classes with a clearly distinguishable area of overlapping.

The simulation results presented in Fig. 1c seemingly present a typical example of overfitting. Starting from $\epsilon = 0.5$, the training and test F1 scores increase. Note the high variability in the test F1 score depicted by wide IQR for $\epsilon \geq 0.3$ and the impact of introducing partial supervision. With no partial supervision ($\epsilon = 0.5$), both F1 scores remain low, as compared to lower values of ϵ that represent a stronger impact of partial supervision. For $\epsilon < 0.3$, as $\epsilon \to 0$, the dynamics change. The training F1 score further increases, but the test F1 score remains roughly the same: around the value of 0.8 with a narrow IQR. We do not observe the phenomenon of overfitting, i.e. that increasing classification results on training dataset $\mathcal{D}$ finally result in decreasing performance on the test set $\mathcal{T}$. The reason for that may be that the true training error is higher, but the deterministic relationship of the values $\alpha \geq 1$ and the predictions based on (4) artificially increase the F1 score. This observation, however, is specific to our simulations and requires further study.

5   Experiments on Real-Life Data

5.1   Application Example in the Smartphone-Based Classification of Bipolar Disorder Patients

Bipolar disorder is a serious mental illness characterized by fluctuations in the mood phases from depressive to manic. Passive observation of the patient by analyzing objectively collected sensor data (e.g. data from patients' smartphones) has the potential to revolutionize the detection of phase changes due to its objectivity and early alert capabilities. Various machine learning algorithms have been proposed in recent years for resolving this health status monitoring problem [2]. However, in the majority of the state-of-the-art solutions, low accuracy is reported due to various forms of uncertainties related to this particularly sensitive mental health application scenario and its related data collection process, such as e.g., the vague nature of data collected from sensors, the subjectivity of data collected from psychiatrists about labels, etc.

In the majority of the state-of-the-art, the episode prediction problem is stated as a supervised learning task. Supervised techniques require a substantial amount of labeled data (results of the psychiatric assessment in this context), and providing these data on a day-to-day basis is almost infeasible in the bipolar disorder monitoring context. On the other hand, unsupervised learning techniques such as clustering algorithms or statistical process control, see e.g., [12], overcome these limitations since they try to find the structure information in unlabeled data to construct a classifier or a control chart. However, due to the absence of labels, purely unsupervised clustering methods may give highly inconsistent data partitions that include instances from different classes. Hopefully, semi-supervised learning algorithms have the potential to improve classification performance by using a combination of both labeled and unlabeled data. To

Table 2. Total number of supervised calls in the `bipolar` dataset by class corresponding to the mental state of the patient.

class	depression	mixed	euthymia	dysfunction	total
# supervised calls	58	55	85	63	261
# unsupervised calls	–				1034

alleviate the problems of uncertainty about patients' state and limited data, [13] showed that an advanced approach to handling uncertainty about psychiatric assessments and feature engineering enables to increase the accuracy of episode prediction. In our previous works, we also applied dynamic incremental fuzzy semi-supervised clustering, see [6,10]. The semi-supervised approach is very promising but it is also observed that the results depend on the randomly selected chunks [11]. Thus, the robustness of the Semi-Supervised Fuzzy C-Means algorithm needs to be further studied.

5.2   About Dataset Used for Experiments

Data for this work were collected from patients diagnosed with bipolar disorder within a prospective observational study[1] carried out by the Institute for Psychiatry and Neurology and Systems Research Institute, Polish Academy of Sciences in Warsaw, Poland in years 2017–2018. For the protocol of this study, we refer the reader to [9]. A dedicated application using an open-source software library *opensmile*[2] was installed on patients' smartphones that transformed patients' speech into a set of acoustic features which are physical descriptors, such as e.g., loudness. Next, the collected frames of each call were preprocessed and summarized with basic statistics, and we applied the feature selection to reduce the dimensionality of this dataset. As a result, five voice characteristics that describe different types of jitter, shimmer, and the spectrum of the signal (spectral flux and spectral centroid) were selected. In addition, psychiatric assessments of patients' health status were collected on a regular basis. Doctors were classifying the mental state into one of the four phases: depression, dysfunction, euthymia, and the mixed state.

In this paper, we use the data from a single patient for the purpose of the experiments. The partial supervision is an effect of the so-called ground truth labeling process: data from phone calls falling into the time window starting from 7 days before the assessment to 2 days after the assessment are treated as supervised, and the rest remains unsupervised. See [14] for the detailed discussion about the ground-truth period approach. Table 2 presents the main characteristics of the `bipolar` dataset used for experiments in the remainder of this Section.

---

[1] The study obtained the consent of the Bioethical Commission at the District Medical Chamber in Warsaw (agreement no. KB/1094/17).

[2] https://www.audeering.com/research/opensmile/.

5.3   Numerical Results

The main purpose of the experiments was to verify how the selection of the margin of making the training error ϵ impacts on the classification performance. We consider the same experimental settings as in the Sect. 4: ϵ values range from Table 1 and F1 score as a performance measure. Since we distinguish four phases of bipolar disorder, we are working with a multi-class prediction problem. We calculate F1 score for each class separately.

Figure 2 presents results from simulations for the `bipolar` dataset. We consider 3 training-test splits: 90/10, 50/50, and 10/90. The first part of each split refers to the percentage of M supervised observations that are included in the training dataset $\mathcal{D}$, and the second part refers to the percentage of M observations that go to the test set $\mathcal{T}$. For each of the 3 above partial supervision scenarios, 30 repetitions of the random training-test split are performed sustaining the class balance in the test set. Each dot on the plots represents the median F1 score for a specific class y calculated on all 30 simulation results.

As observed in Fig. 2, when ϵ is 0, the performance measured with F1 for the training datasets is equal to 1 regardless of the partial supervision scenario. For all classes, the F1 score decreases when ϵ increases. We observe that the dynamic of this decrease slightly differs between partial supervision scenarios. For example, for the observations coming from the mixed state (which is very difficult to classify according to clinical practice), the drop in the F1 score in training sets is more sudden for the scenarios with a lower percentage of partial supervision. In particular, we observe in Fig. 2a that F1 drops below 0.4 for ϵ of 0.3. At the same time, in Fig. 2c and Fig. 2e we see that F1 is below 0.4 for ϵ of 0.2. A similar tendency is observed for other classes.

For the test sets, similarly as for the training sets, we clearly see that the results depend on the rate of labeled observations included in the training, and as could have been expected the absolute results are the highest for the highest percentage of training percentage of supervised observations. Nonetheless, the results are unsatisfactory in terms of the considered performance metric. Also, the decrease of F1 with the increase of ϵ is not so evident for the test sets. These results confirm that especially for the situations when the number of labeled observations is sufficient to train a well-performing model, the selection of ϵ (which translates to the selection of α) influences both the training and test performances.

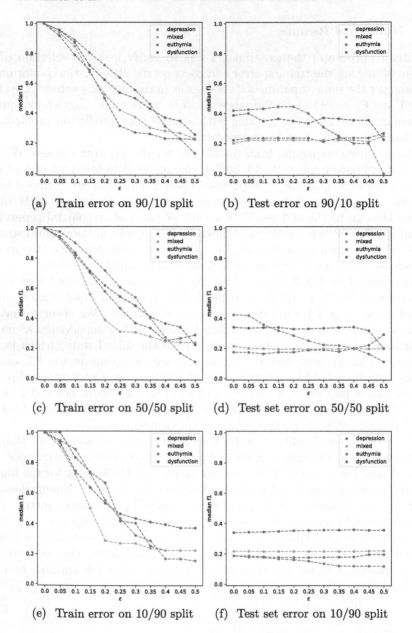

Fig. 2. Results for 30 simulations on `bipolar` dataset. Each a/b train-test split denotes a situation where $a\%$ supervised observations where included in the training set $\mathcal{D}$, and the remaining $b\%$ supervised observations were left out for the test set $\mathcal{T}$. Each dot represent a corresponding median F1 score for a specific class y.

6 Conclusion and Future Work

In this work, we considered the important problem of adequate handling of partial supervision in the Semi-Supervised Fuzzy C-Means algorithm in relation to the training and test classification errors measured by F1 score. We showed with simulations on both artificially generated and real-life data about the medical use case that the SSFCMeans model is highly dependent on its hyperparameter α that needs to be provided prior to the modeling. Last but not least, we established a relationship between α and a deterministically assured 0% training error that may bias the overfitting analysis of the SSFCMeans.

The results presented in this paper can be further extended and shall be generalized to the broader Semi-Supervised Fuzzy Clustering context. Furthermore, we plan to investigate the importance of α in the dynamic environment based on the recently proposed Dynamic Incremental Semi-Supervised Fuzzy C-Means (DISSFCM) [6] which is claimed to handle the evolving structure of data using special splitting mechanisms. Moreover, in certain practical problems, uncertainty may arise if the labels are equally valid. In [14], SSFCMeans is used to build a wrapping Confidence Path Regularization (CPR) algorithm that estimates a so-called adjusted confidence factor which reflects the degree of label validity in a data-driven manner. In further work, we plan to validate the findings presented in this paper with the CPR algorithm.

References

1. Antoine, V., Labroche, N.: Semi-supervised fuzzy c-means variants: a study on noisy label supervision. In: Medina, J., et al. (eds.) IPMU 2018. CCIS, vol. 854, pp. 51–62. Springer, Cham (2018). https://doi.org/10.1007/978-3-319-91476-3_5
2. Antosik-Wójcińska, A.Z., et al.: Smartphone as a monitoring tool for bipolar disorder: a systematic review including data analysis, machine learning algorithms and predictive modelling. Int. J. Med. Inform. **138**, 104131 (2020). https://doi.org/10.1016/j.ijmedinf.2020.104131
3. Bezdek, J.C., Ehrlich, R., Full, W.: FCM: the fuzzy c-means clustering algorithm. Comput. Geosci. **10**(2–3), 191–203 (1984). https://doi.org/10.1016/0098-3004(84)90020-7
4. Bouchachia, A., Pedrycz, W.: A semi-supervised clustering algorithm for data exploration. In: Bilgiç, T., De Baets, B., Kaynak, O. (eds.) IFSA 2003. LNCS, vol. 2715, pp. 328–337. Springer, Heidelberg (2003). https://doi.org/10.1007/3-540-44967-1_39
5. Bouchachia, A., Pedrycz, W.: Enhancement of fuzzy clustering by mechanisms of partial supervision. Fuzzy Sets Syst. **157**(13), 1733–1759 (2006). https://doi.org/10.1016/j.fss.2006.02.015
6. Casalino, G., Castellano, G., Galetta, F., Kaczmarek-Majer, K.: Dynamic incremental semi-supervised fuzzy clustering for bipolar disorder episode prediction. In: Appice, A., Tsoumakas, G., Manolopoulos, Y., Matwin, S. (eds.) DS 2020. LNCS (LNAI), vol. 12323, pp. 79–93. Springer, Cham (2020). https://doi.org/10.1007/978-3-030-61527-7_6

7. Casalino, G., Dominiak, M., Galetta, F., Kaczmarek-Majer, K.: Incremental semi-supervised fuzzy c-means for bipolar disorder episode prediction. In: 2020 IEEE Conference on Evolving and Adaptive Intelligent Systems (EAIS), Bari, Italy, pp. 1–8. IEEE (2020). https://doi.org/10.1109/EAIS48028.2020.9122748
8. Chapelle, O., Schölkopf, B., Zien, A. (eds.): Semi-supervised Learning. Adaptive Computation and Machine Learning. MIT Press, Cambridge (2006)
9. Dominiak, M., et al.: Behavioral and self-reported data collected from smartphones for the assessment of depressive and manic symptoms in patients with bipolar disorder: Prospective observational study. J. Med. Internet Res. **24**, e28647 (2021)
10. Kaczmarek-Majer, K., Casalino, G., Castellano, G., Hryniewicz, O., Dominiak, M.: Explaining smartphone-based acoustic data in bipolar disorder: semi-supervised fuzzy clustering and relative linguistic summaries. Inf. Sci. **588**, 174–195 (2022). https://doi.org/10.1016/j.ins.2021.12.049
11. Kaczmarek-Majer, K., Casalino, G., Castellano, G., Leite, D., Hryniewicz, O.: Fuzzy linguistic summaries for explaining online semi-supervised learning. In: 2022 IEEE 11th International Conference on Intelligent Systems (IS), pp. 1–8 (2022). https://doi.org/10.1109/IS57118.2022.10019636
12. Kaczmarek-Majer, K., et al.: Control charts designed using model averaging approach for phase change detection in bipolar disorder. In: Destercke, S., Denoeux, T., Gil, M.Á., Grzegorzewski, P., Hryniewicz, O. (eds.) SMPS 2018. AISC, vol. 832, pp. 115–123. Springer, Cham (2019). https://doi.org/10.1007/978-3-319-97547-4_16
13. Kamińska, O., et al.: Self-organizing maps using acoustic features for prediction of state change in bipolar disorder. In: Marcos, M., et al. (eds.) KR4HC/TEAAM 2019. LNCS (LNAI), vol. 11979, pp. 148–160. Springer, Cham (2019). https://doi.org/10.1007/978-3-030-37446-4_12
14. Kmita, K., Casalino, G., Castellano, G., Hryniewicz, O., Kaczmarek-Majer, K.: Confidence path regularization for handling label uncertainty in semi-supervised learning: use case in bipolar disorder monitoring. In: 2022 IEEE International Conference on Fuzzy Systems (FUZZ-IEEE), pp. 1–8 (2022). https://doi.org/10.1109/FUZZ-IEEE55066.2022.9882759
15. Lai, D.T.C., Garibaldi, J.M.: A comparison of distance-based semi-supervised fuzzy c-means clustering algorithms. In: 2011 IEEE International Conference on Fuzzy Systems (FUZZ-IEEE 2011), Taipei, Taiwan, pp. 1580–1586. IEEE (2011). https://doi.org/10.1109/FUZZY.2011.6007562
16. Pedrycz, W., Waletzky, J.: Fuzzy clustering with partial supervision. IEEE Trans. Syst. Man Cybern. Part B (Cybern.) **27**(5), 787–795 (1997). https://doi.org/10.1109/3477.623232

A New Two-Sample Location Test for Fuzzy Data

Przemyslaw Grzegorzewski[1,2]([⊠]) [iD] and Milena Zacharczuk[1]

[1] Faculty of Mathematics and Information Science, Warsaw University
of Technology, Koszykowa 75, 00-662 Warsaw, Poland
`pgrzeg@ibspan.waw.pl`
[2] Systems Research Institute, Polish Academy of Sciences, Newelska 6,
01-447 Warsaw, Poland
{`przemyslaw.grzegorzewski,milena.zacharczuk.stud`}`@pw.edu.pl`

Abstract. The two-sample location problem is one of the most important issues in statistics. Unfortunately, its extension for imprecise data encounters considerable difficulties to generalize classical tests into the fuzzy environment in a simple way. However, combining the credibility index with some kind of randomization, we propose a promising generalization of the two-sample Mann-Whitney test for fuzzy data.

Keywords: Fuzzy data · the Mann-Whitney test · Random fuzzy numbers · Credibility

1 Introduction

Two-sample tests for the difference in location belong to the most often used statistical procedures having many applications in various fields. For instance, before a new drug is allowed to be used, a random group of patients suffering from a particular disease is taken and divided into two independent samples: one who will be treated with a new drug (called the treatment group) and the other who will receive a placebo (called the control group). Based on these samples we wish to investigate the presence of a treatment effect. Usually, we verify the null hypothesis of no effect against the alternative hypothesis asserting that measurements from the treatment population tend to be larger (or smaller) than from the control population. Under strict assumptions including the normality of both samples, the well-known t-test can be used there. However, usually, it does not hold so we have to use one of the nonparametric tests like the Wilcoxon rank-sum test [21] or the Mann-Whitney test [17] (which is equivalent to the first one). However, if the available data are also imprecise none of these tests can be used because imprecise measurements are not generally linearly ordered. Furthermore, additional obstacles to the statistical analysis of imprecise data are the absence of suitable models and limit results for the distribution of fuzzy random variables used for describing imprecise data.

S. Massanet et al. (Eds.): EUSFLAT 2023/AGOP 2023, LNCS 14069, pp. 737–748, 2023.
https://doi.org/10.1007/978-3-031-39965-7_61

In this paper, we have used the credibility index [13, 15] to measure the extent of the degree of the dominance relationship for each pair of random variables. In addition, using permutation tests which allow omitting the determination of the exact distribution of the test statistic we have been able to generalize the Mann-Whitney test for fuzzy data.

2 Fuzzy Data

When dealing with imprecise outcomes of experiments fuzzy numbers can be viewed as counterparts of typical results in the form of real numbers. A **fuzzy number** is a mapping $\widetilde{A} : \mathbb{R} \to [0, 1]$, called a membership function, such that its α-cut (α-level sets) defined by

$$\widetilde{A}_\alpha = \begin{cases} \{x \in \mathbb{R} : \widetilde{A}(x) \geqslant \alpha\} & \text{if} \quad \alpha \in (0, 1], \\ cl\{x \in \mathbb{R} : \widetilde{A}(x) > 0\} & \text{if} \quad \alpha = 0, \end{cases} \tag{1}$$

is a nonempty compact interval for each $\alpha \in [0, 1]$, where cl in (1) stands for the closure. The value of the membership function at x indicates to what extent this point belongs to $\widetilde{A}$. On the other hand, the α-cut $\widetilde{A}_\alpha$ is the set of all points $x \in \mathbb{R}$ that belong to A with a degree of at least α. Therefore, each fuzzy number is fully characterized both by its membership function $\widetilde{A}(x)$ and by a family $\{\widetilde{A}_\alpha\}_{\alpha \in [0,1]}$ of all its α-cuts. Further on, a family of all fuzzy numbers will be denoted by $\mathbb{F}(\mathbb{R})$. Two α-cuts play a crucial role in this modeling: $\widetilde{A}_1 = \text{core}(\widetilde{A})$, called the **core**, which contains all $x \in \mathbb{R}$ fully compatible with the concept described by the fuzzy number $\widetilde{A}$, and $\widetilde{A}_0 = \text{supp}(\widetilde{A})$, i.e. the **support**, of those $x \in \mathbb{R}$ which are compatible to some extent with the concept corresponding to $\widetilde{A}$.

Membership functions can take an infinite number of different forms. Therefore, we are most willing to consider such subfamilies of $\mathbb{F}(\mathbb{R})$ that abound in curves of various shapes, and at the same time can be easily parameterized. An example of such a family of fuzzy numbers is the family of so-called **LR-fuzzy numbers** defined as follows

$$\widetilde{A}(x) = \begin{cases} L\left(\frac{x - l_A}{c_A - l_A}\right) & \text{if} \quad l_A \leqslant x \leqslant c_A, \\ R\left(\frac{r_A - x}{r_A - c_A}\right) & \text{if} \quad c_A < x \leqslant r_A, \\ 0 & \text{if} \quad x \in \mathbb{R} \setminus [l_A, r_A], \end{cases} \tag{2}$$

where $L, R : [0, 1] \to [0, 1]$ are continuous and strictly increasing function such that $L(0) = R(0) = 0$ and $L(1) = R(1) = 1$, and $l_A, c_A, r_A \in \mathbb{R}$ such that $l_A \leqslant c_A \leqslant r_A$. The most often used subfamily of the LR-fuzzy numbers are the so-called **triangular fuzzy numbers** with $L(x) = R(x) = 1 - x$ for all $x \in [0, 1]$. If $\widetilde{A}$ is a triangular fuzzy number, its membership function is simply given by

$$\widetilde{A}(x) = \begin{cases} \frac{x - l_A}{c_A - l_A} & \text{if} \quad l_A \leqslant x \leqslant c_A, \\ \frac{r_A - x}{r_A - c_A} & \text{if} \quad c_A < x \leqslant r_A, \\ 0 & \text{if} \quad x \in \mathbb{R} \setminus [l_A, r_A], \end{cases} \tag{3}$$

which means that it is completely described by the triple (l_A, c_A, r_A) and hence is often denoted as $\widetilde{A}(x) = (l_A, c_A, r_A)_T$.

Another subfamily of LR-fuzzy numbers, suitable in an approximation of more complex fuzzy numbers, are the k-**knot piecewise linear fuzzy numbers** [2], with L and R functions that are polygons consisting of $k \in \mathbb{N}$ segments.

α-cuts turn out to be extremely useful for defining basic arithmetic operations on fuzzy numbers. Indeed, the sum of $\widetilde{A} \in \mathbb{F}(\mathbb{R})$ and $\widetilde{B} \in \mathbb{F}(\mathbb{R})$ is given by the Minkowski addition of the corresponding α-cuts, i.e. we have

$$(\widetilde{A} + \widetilde{B})_\alpha = \left[\inf \widetilde{A}_\alpha + \inf \widetilde{B}_\alpha, \sup \widetilde{A}_\alpha + \sup \widetilde{B}_\alpha\right], \text{ for all } \alpha \in [0,1],$$

while the product of a fuzzy number $\widetilde{A} \in \mathbb{F}(\mathbb{R})$ by a scalar $\lambda \in \mathbb{R}$ is defined by the Minkowski scalar product for intervals

$$(\lambda \cdot \widetilde{A})_\alpha = \left[\min\{\lambda \inf \widetilde{A}_\alpha, \lambda \sup \widetilde{A}_\alpha\}, \max\{\lambda \inf \widetilde{A}_\alpha, \lambda \sup \widetilde{A}_\alpha\}\right], \text{ for all } \alpha \in [0,1].$$

Although fuzzy arithmetic seems simple, unfortunately, $(\mathbb{F}(\mathbb{R}), +, \cdot)$ has not linear but a semilinear structure, because in general $\widetilde{A} + (-1 \cdot \widetilde{A}) \neq \mathbb{1}_{\{0\}}$. Consequently, the Minkowski-based difference does not satisfy, in general, the addition/subtraction property, i.e. $(\widetilde{A} + (-1 \cdot \widetilde{B})) + \widetilde{B} \neq \widetilde{A}$. The so-called Hukuhara difference [14] has been proposed to overcome this problem t but the Hukuhara difference does not always exist. And this makes it necessary to develop some special alternative approaches to avoid subtraction problems in statistical reasoning with fuzzy observations, e.g. based on distances (see, [1]).

Although various metrics are defined in $\mathbb{F}(\mathbb{R})$, the most often used in statistical context is is perhaps the distance proposed by Gil et al. [5] and Trutschnig et al. [22], defined for any $\widetilde{A}, \widetilde{B} \in \mathbb{F}(\mathbb{R})$ as follows

$$D_\theta^\nu(\widetilde{A}, \widetilde{B}) = \left(\int_0^1 \left[(\operatorname{mid} \widetilde{A}_\alpha - \operatorname{mid} \widetilde{B}_\alpha)^2 + \theta \cdot (\operatorname{spr} \widetilde{A}_\alpha - \operatorname{spr} \widetilde{B}_\alpha)^2\right] d\nu(\alpha)\right)^{1/2}, \quad (4)$$

where $\operatorname{mid} \widetilde{A}_\alpha = \frac{1}{2}(\inf \widetilde{A}_\alpha + \sup \widetilde{A}_\alpha)$ and $\operatorname{spr} \widetilde{A}_\alpha = \frac{1}{2}(\sup \widetilde{A}_\alpha - \inf \widetilde{A}_\alpha)$ denote the mid-point and the radius of the α-cut $\widetilde{A}_\alpha$, respectively. Moreover, ν stands for a normalized measure associated with a continuous distribution on $[0,1]$ which allows weighting of the α-cut's influence, while θ is a positive constant used to weight the impact of the distance between spreads of the α-cuts and the distance between their mid-points. Usually ν is the Lebesgue measure on $[0,1]$, while the most common choice value of the weight is $\theta = 1$ or $\theta = \frac{1}{3}$.

Statistical inference based on imprecise data requires a model which allows grasping two kinds of uncertainty present in such data: just imprecision and randomness. To handle imprecise data Puri and Ralescu [19] introduced the notion of a **fuzzy random variable**, also known as a **random fuzzy number**. It combines fuzzy set theory used to describe imprecision and probability theory which, as we know, is a proper tool for describing randomness.

Definition 1. *Let $(\Omega, \mathcal{A}, P)$ be a probability space. A mapping $\widetilde{X} : \Omega \to \mathbb{F}(\mathbb{R})$ is a random fuzzy number if for all $\alpha \in [0,1]$ the α-level function is a compact random interval.*

It is not currently our goal to develop the theory of random fuzzy numbers. We just want to mention that it is not easy to transfer well-known facts from classical statistics to a fuzzy environment. Besides problems with subtraction and division of fuzzy numbers mentioned above, fuzzy numbers are not linearly ordered, which makes it impossible to use the rank methods popular in nonparametric statistics. Another difficulty, certainly even more fraught with consequences and limitations in statistical reasoning is the absence of suitable models for the distribution of random fuzzy numbers. And last but not least, it seems that there are not yet satisfying Central Limit Theorems for random fuzzy numbers that can be applied directly in practical applications. It all means that statistical inference and decision-making with fuzzy data requires usually ingenuity and new innovative solutions. For instance, previous experience shows that the use of the bootstrap (cf. [6,16,18]) or permutation tests (cf. [8–12]) might be the recommended solution in hypothesis testing. The latter approach will be used in this contribution.

3   The Two-Sample Location Problem

Suppose, our data consist of two random samples: $\mathbb{X} = (X_1, \ldots, X_n)$ and $\mathbb{Y} = (Y_1, \ldots, Y_m)$ from two populations. We assume that the X's, as well as the Y's, are independent and identically distributed. Moreover, X's and Y's are mutually independent. One can think of it as a sample from the treatment population and a sample coming from the control population, where X's and Y's stand for observations or measurements of a certain feature that characterizes the treatment under study. Our goal is to investigate the presence of a treatment effect that results in a shift in the location.

More formally, let F and G denote distribution functions of the considered feature in the first and the second population, respectively. We assume that both distributions are continuous but at least one of them is unknown. Hence, we wish to verify the null hypothesis of no treatment effect

$$H_0 : F(t) = G(t), \quad \text{for every } t \in \mathbb{R}, \tag{5}$$

against the one-sided alternative that X is stochastically larger than Y (or X is stochastically smaller than Y), i.e. $H_1 : X \overset{st}{>} Y$, (or $H_1 : X \overset{st}{<} Y$). Here, $X \overset{st}{>} Y$ means that $\mathbb{P}(X > t) \geq \mathbb{P}(Y > t)$ for all $t \in \mathbb{R}$ and $\mathbb{P}(X > t) > \mathbb{P}(Y > t)$ for some $t \in \mathbb{R}$ or, equivalently, that $F(t) \leq G(t)$ for all $t \in \mathbb{R}$ and $F(t) < G(t)$ for some $t \in \mathbb{R}$. We may also consider a general two-sided alternative that some effect exists, i.e. $H_1 : F(t) \neq G(t)$, for some $t \in \mathbb{R}$.

Many nonparametric tests have been proposed to solve the aforementioned testing problems. However, the most popular and appreciated are the Wilcoxon rank-sum test [21] and the Mann-Whitney test [17]. It can be shown that although the first one is based on ranks of observations in the combined sample while the second utilizes pairwise comparisons of observations, both tests are statistically equivalent which reflects in the terminology by calling both tests with a single name: the Mann-Whitney-Wilcoxon test. Further on we will discuss our testing problem using the Mann-Whitney settings.

Therefore, to verify the null hypothesis (5) we use a test statistic denoted traditionally by U and defined as the number of times when the X's are greater than the Y's in the sequence of $N = n + m$ observations from the combined samples arranged together in increasing order, i.e.

$$U(\mathbb{X}, \mathbb{Y}) = \sum_{i=1}^{n} \sum_{j=1}^{m} \mathbb{1}(X_i > Y_j), \tag{6}$$

where $\mathbb{1}(.)$ stands for the indicator function. Situations when most of the X's are greater than most of the Y's discredit the null hypothesis of identical distributions. Hence, if U is large enough, we reject H_0 in favor of the alternative hypothesis that X is stochastically larger than Y. Critical values for some small and moderate sample sizes are given in [17]. If sample sizes $n, m \to \infty$, the null distribution of the standardized Mann-Whitney statistic

$$T(\mathbb{X}, \mathbb{Y}) = \frac{U(\mathbb{X}, \mathbb{Y}) - \frac{1}{2}mn}{\sqrt{\frac{1}{12}mn(N+1)}}, \tag{7}$$

approaches the standard normal distribution, which eases decision-making.

4   The Generalized Mann-Whitney Test

A direct generalization of the Mann-Whitney test for fuzzy data is not obvious because, as has been stated above, its test statistic counts the number of pairs (X_i, Y_j), with $X_i \in \mathbb{X}$ and $Y_j \in \mathbb{Y}$, such that $X_i > Y_j$, while this majority relation for fuzzy numbers is not clearly defined since fuzzy numbers are not linearly ordered. In the literature, one can find several attempts to generalize the aforementioned test to the fuzzy domain (see, e.g., [7]) but none of them was satisfactory enough, because in fact, they amounted to a form of defuzzification that allowed unambiguous ranking.

To take a step toward obtaining the desired generalization of the Mann-Whitney test for fuzzy data, we have to start by agreeing on how to compare any two fuzzy numbers. It seems that a promising solution is to look at the problem of ordering from the perspective of possibility theory. There we find well-established possibility and necessity measures [3] for ranking fuzzy numbers $\widetilde{A}$ and $\widetilde{B}$, defined as follows

$$\text{Pos}(\widetilde{A} \succ \widetilde{B}) = \sup_{x>y} \min\{\widetilde{A}(x), \widetilde{B}(y)\}, \tag{8}$$

$$\text{Nes}(\widetilde{A} \succ \widetilde{B}) = 1 - \text{Pos}(\widetilde{A} \preceq \widetilde{B})$$
$$= 1 - \sup_{x \leqslant y} \min\{\widetilde{A}(x), \widetilde{B}(y)\}. \tag{9}$$

Obviously, $\text{Nes}(\widetilde{A} \succ \widetilde{B}) > 0$ implies that $\text{Pos}(\widetilde{A} \succ \widetilde{B}) = 1$.

By taking into account the whole shapes of fuzzy numbers, each of the above indices characterizes a different aspect of the dominance relation. Following the solution proposed by Liu [15] in his credibility theory, we can aggregate both indices by the mapping $\text{Cr} : \mathbb{F}(\mathbb{R}) \times \mathbb{F}(\mathbb{R}) \to [0, 1]$, defined as follows

$$\text{Cr}(\widetilde{A} \succ \widetilde{B}) = \frac{\text{Pos}(\widetilde{A} \succ \widetilde{B}) + \text{Nes}(\widetilde{A} \succ \widetilde{B})}{2}, \tag{10}$$

to obtain the credibility degree that $\widetilde{A}$ is larger than $\widetilde{B}$.

If $\widetilde{A}$ and $\widetilde{B}$ are triangular fuzzy numbers, i.e. $\widetilde{A} = (l_A, c_A, r_A)$ and $\widetilde{B} = (l_B, c_B, r_B)$, it can be shown that (10) takes the following explicit form

$$\text{Cr}(\widetilde{A} \succ \widetilde{B}) = \begin{cases} 0, & \text{if } c_A < c_B \text{ and } r_A \leq l_B, \\ \frac{h(r_A, l_B) - r_A}{2(c_A - r_A)}, & \text{if } c_A < c_B \text{ and } r_A > l_B, \\ \frac{1}{2}, & \text{if } c_A = c_B, \\ 1 - \frac{h(l_A, r_B) - l_A}{2(c_A - l_A)}, & \text{if } c_A > c_B \text{ and } l_A < r_B, \\ 1, & \text{if } c_A > c_B \text{ and } r_B \leq l_A, \end{cases} \tag{11}$$

where

$$h(r_A, l_B) = \frac{r_A c_B - l_B c_A}{c_B - l_B - (c_A - r_A)}, \tag{12}$$

$$h(l_A, r_B) = \frac{l_A c_B - r_B c_A}{c_B - r_B - (c_A - l_A)} \tag{13}$$

denote the abscissa of the intersection between the right arm of $\widetilde{A}$ with the left arm of $\widetilde{B}$ and between the left arm of $\widetilde{A}$ with the right arm of $\widetilde{B}$, respectively.

Now, suppose, we observe two independent fuzzy samples $\widetilde{\mathbb{X}} = (\widetilde{X}_1, \ldots, \widetilde{X}_n)$ and $\widetilde{\mathbb{Y}} = (\widetilde{Y}_1, \ldots, \widetilde{Y}_m)$, each consisting of independent and identically distributed imprecise observations modeled by triangular random fuzzy numbers.

Applying the credibility index (11) we can determine the credibility degree that $\widetilde{X}_i$ is larger than $\widetilde{Y}_j$ for any pair of observations belonging to the samples $\widetilde{\mathbb{X}}$ and $\widetilde{\mathbb{Y}}$, respectively. Consequently, to evaluate how much $\widetilde{X}$'s dominate $\widetilde{Y}$'s, we may compute the following statistic

$$U_{CR}(\widetilde{\mathbb{X}}, \widetilde{\mathbb{Y}}) = \sum_{i=1}^{n} \sum_{j=1}^{m} \text{Cr}(\widetilde{X}_i \succ \widetilde{Y}_j). \tag{14}$$

It is clear that (14) is a natural generalization of the test statistic (6), since if all observations in both samples are no longer fuzzy but crisp, U_{CR} reduces to U.

It is also worth noticing that U_{CR} coincides with the original Mann-Whitney test statistic in the presence of ties. Indeed, keeping in mind the middle case in (11), we obtain one-half which corresponds to the standard treatment of the tied crisp observations when computing U.

Unfortunately, since our data are random samples of fuzzy numbers, we cannot apply the same rejection rule as for the crisp test statistic (6), because we know nothing about the actual distribution function of its generalized version (14) which is our current test statistic of the extended Mann-Whitney test. This problem is crucial, especially for small or moderate sample sizes, when any considerations of using asymptotic distributions are not justified. Fortunately, to determine a rejection rule for our new test we can use a specially adapted randomization technique, as we have done with some permutation tests for fuzzy data discussed in [8–12]. Below we show how to create a permutation test for fuzzy data based on statistic (14).

Let $\widetilde{\mathbb{x}} = (\widetilde{x}_1, \ldots, \widetilde{x}_n)$ and $\widetilde{\mathbb{y}} = (\widetilde{y}_1, \ldots, \widetilde{y}_m)$ denote the experimental realisations of independent random fuzzy samples $\widetilde{\mathbb{X}} = (\widetilde{X}_1, \ldots, \widetilde{X}_n)$ and $\widetilde{\mathbb{Y}} = (\widetilde{Y}_1, \ldots, \widetilde{Y}_m)$, respectively. Firstly, we have to compute a value of our test statistic (14) for given experimental data, i.e.

$$u_0 = U_{CR}(\widetilde{\mathbb{x}}, \widetilde{\mathbb{y}}) = \sum_{i=1}^{n} \sum_{j=1}^{m} Cr(\widetilde{x}_i \succ \widetilde{y}_j). \tag{15}$$

Now, starting from the initial dataset we will design a specific permutation procedure. Let $\widetilde{\mathbb{w}} = \widetilde{\mathbb{x}} \uplus \widetilde{\mathbb{y}}$, where $\uplus$ stands for vector concatenation pooling the two samples into one, i.e. $\widetilde{w}_i = \widetilde{x}_i$ if $1 \leqslant i \leqslant n$ and $\widetilde{w}_i = \widetilde{y}_{i-n}$ if $n+1 \leqslant i \leqslant N$.

Let $\widetilde{\mathbb{w}}^*$ denote a permutation of the initial dataset $\widetilde{\mathbb{w}}$. Suppose, we take the first n elements of $\widetilde{\mathbb{w}}^*$ and assign them to sample $\widetilde{\mathbb{x}}^*$, while the remaining m elements create the second sample $\widetilde{\mathbb{y}}^*$. Thus, it works like a random assignment of $N = n + m$ elements into two samples of the size n and m, respectively. Then, for such constructed samples $\widetilde{\mathbb{x}}^* = (\widetilde{x}_1^*, \ldots, \widetilde{x}_n^*)$ and $\widetilde{\mathbb{y}}^* = (\widetilde{y}_1,^* \ldots, \widetilde{y}_m^*)$ we calculate the corresponding value of the test statistic (14), i.e.

$$U_{CR}(\widetilde{\mathbb{x}}^*, \widetilde{\mathbb{y}}^*) = \sum_{i=1}^{n} \sum_{j=1}^{m} Cr(\widetilde{x}_i^* \succ \widetilde{y}_j^*). \tag{16}$$

We can repeat the whole procedure by considering successive permutations of observations $\widetilde{\mathbb{w}}^*$, dividing them into two samples $\widetilde{\mathbb{x}}^*$ and $\widetilde{\mathbb{y}}^*$, and computing test statistic (16) values. Moreover, if the null hypothesis holds, i.e. all observations are independent and identically distributed, no matter what sample they come from, then all permutations are equally likely and the probability of each randomly selected $\widetilde{\mathbb{w}}^*$ under H_0 is $\mathbb{P}_{H_0}(\widetilde{\mathbb{w}}^* = (\widetilde{w}_1^*, \ldots, \widetilde{w}_N^*)) = \frac{n!m!}{N!}$. This formula might be used for the exact p-value of our test. However, in practice, this can only be computed efficiently for small N. Therefore, according to the common practice for permutation tests, we consider not all but a large number B of permutations (where B about 1000 is a typical number of repetitions).

This way we obtain B test statistic values $U_{CR}(\widetilde{\mathbb{x}}_b^*, \widetilde{\mathbb{y}}_b^*)$, where $b = 1, \ldots, B$, which we will use to determine the approximate p-value of our test given as follows

$$\text{p-value} = \frac{1}{B} \sum_{b=1}^{B} \mathbb{1}(U_{CR}(\widetilde{\mathbb{x}}_b^*, \widetilde{\mathbb{y}}_b^*) \geqslant u_0), \tag{17}$$

where u_0 stands for the test statistic value (15) obtained for the original fuzzy sample. The whole procedure could be succinctly written in Algorithm 1.

Algorithm 1: The generalized Mann-Whitney test for fuzzy data

---

Data: Fuzzy samples $\widetilde{\mathbf{x}} = (\widetilde{x}_1, \ldots, \widetilde{x}_n)$ and $\widetilde{\mathbf{y}} = (\widetilde{y}_1, \ldots, \widetilde{y}_m)$

Result: Test p-value

$u_0 \longleftarrow \sum\limits_{i=1}^{n} \sum\limits_{j=1}^{m} Cr(\widetilde{x}_i \succ \widetilde{y}_j)$;

Pool the data $\widetilde{\mathbf{w}} = \widetilde{\mathbf{x}} \uplus \widetilde{\mathbf{y}}$;

$k \longleftarrow 0$;

for $b = 1$ *to* B **do**

    Take a permutation $\widetilde{\mathbf{w}}^* = (\widetilde{w}_1^*, \ldots, \widetilde{w}_N^*)$ of the pooled data $\widetilde{\mathbf{w}}$;

    $\widetilde{\mathbf{x}}^* = (\widetilde{x}_1^*, \ldots, \widetilde{x}_n^*) \longleftarrow (\widetilde{w}_1^*, \ldots, \widetilde{w}_n^*)$;

    $\widetilde{\mathbf{y}}^* = (\widetilde{y}_1,^* \ldots, \widetilde{y}_m^*) \longleftarrow (\widetilde{w}_{n+1}^*, \ldots, \widetilde{w}_N^*)$;

    $U_{CR} \longleftarrow \sum\limits_{i=1}^{n} \sum\limits_{j=1}^{m} Cr(\widetilde{x}_i^* \succ \widetilde{y}_j^*)$;

    if $U_{CR} \geqslant u_0$ **then**

        | $k := k + 1$

    end

end

p-value $\longleftarrow k/B$

Finally, if we consider the null hypothesis against the one-sided alternative that X is stochastically larger than Y, we reject the null hypothesis H_0 at significance level δ if p-value $\leqslant \delta$.

It should be stressed that the proposed generalized Mann-Whitney test for fuzzy data, as other permutation tests, requires very limited assumptions. Indeed, the only requirement is the so-called *exchangeability* (i.e., under the null hypothesis we can exchange the labels on the observations without affecting the results). If the observations in a sample are independent and identically distributed – as it is in our case – then they are exchangeable.

5   Simulation Study

To examine some properties of the proposed generalized Mann-Whitney test we conducted a simulation study. Although the test itself was designed for arbitrary random fuzzy numbers, in our simulations we will limit ourselves to fuzzy samples whose experimental realizations are triangular fuzzy numbers described by (2). Following the accepted notation each triangular fuzzy number $\widetilde{A}$ can be denoted as a triple $\widetilde{A} = (l_A, c_A, r_A)_T$. Consequently, a random fuzzy number $\widetilde{X}$ can be characterized by the following triple $\widetilde{X} = \langle \xi_X, \eta_X, \zeta_X \rangle$, where ξ_X, η_X, ζ_X are all independent real-valued random variables. We assume that ξ_X and ζ_X are nonnegative. Then, given the particular realization of ξ_X, η_X, ζ_X we obtain the desired realization of a triangular random fuzzy number $\widetilde{x} = (l_X, c_X, r_X)_T$ where

$$l_X = \eta_X - \xi_X, \quad c_X = \eta_X, \quad r_X = \eta_X + \zeta_X. \tag{18}$$

Thus, the considered fuzzy samples $\widetilde{\mathbf{x}} = (\widetilde{x}_1, \ldots, \widetilde{x}_n)$ and $\widetilde{\mathbf{y}} = (\widetilde{y}_1, \ldots, \widetilde{y}_m)$ are constructed by simulating three independent real-valued random variables for each $\widetilde{x}_i = \langle \xi_{Xi}, \eta_{Xi}, \zeta_{Xi} \rangle$ and three for each $\widetilde{y}_j = \langle \xi_{Yj}, \eta_{Yj}, \zeta_{Yj} \rangle$, respectively, with the first and the last random variables in each triple being nonnegative. In particular, we generated random fuzzy numbers using the following real-valued random variables: η_{Xi}, η_{Yj} from the standard normal distribution and $\xi_{Xi}, \xi_{Yj}, \zeta_{Xi}, \zeta_{Yj}$ from the uniform distribution. Then, following (18), we obtain $\widetilde{x}_i = (l_{Xi}, c_{Xi}, r_{Xi})_T$, for $i = 1, \ldots, n$, and $\widetilde{y}_j = (l_{Yj}, c_{Yj}, r_{Yj})_T$, for $j = 1, \ldots, m$.

Figure 1 shows a histogram illustrating the null distribution of the standardized version of the test statistic (15) obtained for fuzzy samples of size $n = m = 10$ generated by independent random variables η_X and η_Y from the standard normal distribution $N(0, 1)$ and ξ_X, ξ_Y and ζ_X, ζ_Y from the uniform distribution $U(0, 0.5)$. In the considered situation we have obtained 0.1697 as a value of the standardized version of our test statistic, marked on the graph by the vertical red line. The p-value $= 0.448$ corresponds to the area of the histogram right to the red line. In our case leads the suggested decision is: do not reject H_0. On the other hand, in Fig. 2 we have a histogram made for the test statistic distribution obtained for two fuzzy samples of identical size $n = m = 10$ but which differ in location. Namely, η_X was generated from the standard normal distribution $N(2, 1)$, but η_Y from $N(0, 1)$, while ξ_X, ξ_Y and ζ_X, ζ_Y were, as before, uniformly distributed from $U(0.0.5)$. In this case, we have obtained 3.5815, illustrated by a vertical red line, and p-value $= 0.0000$. Here it is easily seen that the area of the histogram right to the red line is almost zero, hence the immediate decision is: to reject H_0.

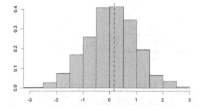

Fig. 1. Empirical null distribution of the new test under H_0.

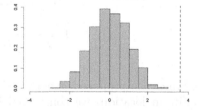

Fig. 2. Empirical null distribution of the new test under H_1.

The aforementioned figures show that our new test works correctly, i.e. behave in an expected and predictable way, in obvious situations. But to be able to somehow assess the quality of this test, we need to examine the stability of its size and its power. Firstly, we examined the proposed generalized

Mann-Whitney test concerning its size (i.e. the supremum of the probability of making a type I error). Thus, 1000 repetitions of the test at 5% significance level performed under H_0 were considered. In each test, $B = 1000$ permutations were drawn. Samples were simulated as in the first experiment considered above. Then empirical percentages of rejections under H_0 were determined. The results both for equal and nonequal sample sizes are gathered in Table 1. It shows that the size of our test is stable at the desired level.

Table 1. Empirical size of the test for various sample sizes.

n	m	empirical size
5	5	0.053
10	10	0.059
20	20	0.06
10	15	0.044
10	20	0.049

Next, we conducted a power study to compare our new test with the goodness-of-fit test introduced by Grzegorzewski in [8] based on the distance between sample averages, i.e.

$$T_G(\widetilde{\mathbb{X}}, \widetilde{\mathbb{Y}}) = D_\theta^\nu \left(\overline{\widetilde{X}}, \overline{\widetilde{Y}} \right)$$

and the goodness-of-fit test based on the energy distance between $\mathbb{X}$ and $\mathbb{Y}$, given by (cf. [4, 20])

$$\mathcal{E}_N(\mathbb{X}, \mathbb{Y}) = \frac{nm}{n+m} \left[\frac{2}{nm} \sum_{i=1}^{n} \sum_{j=1}^{m} D_\theta^\nu(X_i, Y_j) \right.$$
$$\left. - \frac{1}{n^2} \sum_{i=1}^{n} \sum_{j=1}^{n} D_\theta^\nu(X_i, X_j) - \frac{1}{m^2} \sum_{i=1}^{m} \sum_{j=1}^{m} D_\theta^\nu(Y_i, Y_j) \right].$$

Since the proposed generalized Mann-Whitney test is dedicated to detect a shift in location, we considered both samples from the normal distribution, generated as in the size study, but with different means. The power curves for increasing difference in means between $\widetilde{X}$'s and $\widetilde{Y}$'s and three tests based on fuzzy samples of the sizes $n = m = 10$ performed at 5% significance level are shown in Fig. 3.

It is seen that our new generalized Mann-Whitney test dominates both the test by Grzegorzewski [8] and the goodness-of-fit test based on the energy distance, manifesting quite similar power.

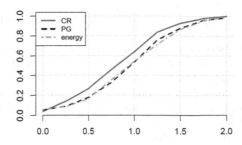

Fig. 3. Power comparison for the increasing difference in location.

6 Conclusions

Hypothesis testing with imprecise data usually cannot be generalized straight forwardly from their original crisp prototypes into a fuzzy environment. This is due to many difficulties that we encounter in statistical reasoning with fuzzy data, such as the lack of linear ordering of fuzzy numbers or the absence of suitable probabilistic models and limit results for the distribution of random fuzzy numbers. By using the credibility measure applied to the dominance relation and combining it with the methodology of permutation tests we have succeeded in generalizing the classical two-sample Mann-Whitney test for location. It is completely distribution-free and the preliminary results of its properties, like the power, are quite promising.

References

1. Blanco-Fernández, A., et al.: A distance-based statistical analysis of fuzzy number-valued data. Int. J. Approximate Reason. **55**(7), 1487–1501 (2014). https://doi.org/10.1016/j.ijar.2013.09.020
2. Coroianu, L., Gagolewski, M., Grzegorzewski, P.: Piecewise linear approximation of fuzzy numbers: algorithms, arithmetic operations and stability of characteristics. Soft. Comput. **23**(19), 9491–9505 (2019). https://doi.org/10.1007/s00500-019-03800-2
3. Dubois, D., Prade, H.: Ranking fuzzy numbers in the setting of possibility theory. Inf. Sci. **30**, 183–224 (1983). https://doi.org/10.1016/0020-0255(83)90025-7
4. Gadomska, O.: Goodness-of-fit test for fuzzy data. Master's thesis, Warsaw University of Technology (2021)
5. Gil, M.A., Lubiano, M., Montenegro, M., López, M.: Least squares fitting of an affine function and strength of association for interval-valued data. Metrika **56**, 97–111 (2002). https://doi.org/10.1007/s001840100160
6. González-Rodríguez, G., Montenegro, M., Colubi, A., Ángeles Gil, M.: Bootstrap techniques and fuzzy random variables: synergy in hypothesis testing with fuzzy data. Fuzzy Sets Syst. **157**(19), 2608–2613 (2006). https://doi.org/10.1016/j.fss.2003.11.021
7. Grzegorzewski, P.: Distribution-free tests for vague data. In: Lopez-Diaz, M., Gil, M., Grzegorzewski, P., Hryniewicz, O., Lawry, J. (eds.) Soft Methodology and

Random Information Systems, pp. 495–502 (2004). https://doi.org/10.1007/978-3-540-44465-7_61

8. Grzegorzewski, P.: Permutation k-sample goodness-of-fit test for fuzzy data. In: 2020 IEEE International Conference on Fuzzy Systems (FUZZ-IEEE), pp. 1–8 (2020). https://doi.org/10.1109/FUZZ48607.2020.9177765

9. Grzegorzewski, P.: Two-sample dispersion problem for fuzzy data. In: Lesot, M.-J., Vieira, S., Reformat, M.Z., Carvalho, J.P., Wilbik, A., Bouchon-Meunier, B., Yager, R.R. (eds.) IPMU 2020. CCIS, vol. 1239, pp. 82–96. Springer, Cham (2020). https://doi.org/10.1007/978-3-030-50153-2_7

10. Grzegorzewski, P.: Two-sample test for comparing ambiguity in fuzzy data. In: 2022 IEEE International Conference on Fuzzy Systems (FUZZ-IEEE), pp. 1–8 (2022). https://doi.org/10.1109/FUZZ-IEEE55066.2022.9882757

11. Grzegorzewski, P.: Paired sample test for fuzzy data. In: García-Escudero, L.A., et al. (eds.) SMPS 2022. Advances in Intelligent Systems and Computing, vol. 1433, pp. 200–207. Springer, Cham (2023). https://doi.org/10.1007/978-3-031-15509-3_27

12. Grzegorzewski, P., Gadomska, O.: Nearest neighbor tests for fuzzy data. In: 2021 IEEE International Conference on Fuzzy Systems (FUZZ-IEEE), pp. 1–6 (2021). https://doi.org/10.1109/FUZZ45933.2021.9494432

13. Hesamian, G., Akbari, M.G., Yaghoobpoor, R.: Quality control process based on fuzzy random variables. IEEE Trans. Fuzzy Syst. **27**(4), 671–685 (2019). https://doi.org/10.1109/TFUZZ.2018.2866811

14. Hukuhara, M.: Integration des applications measurables dont la valeur est un compact convexe. Funkcialaj Ekvacioj **10**, 205–223 (1967)

15. Liu, B.: Uncertainty Theory: An Introduction to its Axiomatic Foundations. Springer, Heidelberg (2004). https://doi.org/10.1007/978-3-540-39987-2

16. Lubiano, M.A., Montenegro, M., Sinova, B., de la Rosa de Sáa, S., Gil, M.N.: Hypothesis testing for means in connection with fuzzy rating scale-based data: algorithms and applications. Eur. J. Oper. Res. **251**(3), 918–929 (2016). https://doi.org/10.1016/j.ejor.2015.11.016

17. Mann, H.B., Whitney, D.R.: On a test whether one of two random variables is stochastically larger than the other. Ann. Math. Stat. **18**, 50–60 (1947)

18. Montenegro, M., Colubi, A., Casals, M., Gil, M.: Asymptotic and bootstrap techniques for testing the expected value of a fuzzy random variable. Metrika **59**(1), 31–49 (2004). https://doi.org/10.1007/s001840300270

19. Puri, M.L., Ralescu, D.A.: Fuzzy random variables. J. Math. Anal. Appl. **114**(2), 409–422 (1986). https://doi.org/10.1016/0022-247X(86)90093-4

20. Székely, G.J., Rizzo, M.L.: Energy statistics: a class of statistics based on distances. J. Stat. Plann. Inference **143**(8), 1249–1272 (2013). https://doi.org/10.1016/j.jspi.2013.03.018

21. Wilcoxon, F.: Individual comparisons by ranking methods. Biometrics **1**, 80–83 (1945)

22. Wolfgang, T., Gil, G.R., Ana, C., María Ángeles, G.: A new family of metrics for compact, convex (fuzzy) sets based on a generalized concept of mid and spread. Inf. Sci. **179**(23), 3964–3972 (2009). https://doi.org/10.1016/j.ins.2009.06.023

Author Index

S. Massanet et al. (Eds.): EUSFLAT 2023/AGOP 2023, LNCS 14069, pp. 749–751, 2023.
https://doi.org/10.1007/978-3-031-39965-7

Printed in the United States
by Baker & Taylor Publisher Services

Printed in the United States
by Baker & Taylor Publisher Services